Status and Conservation of Midwestern Am

STATUS AND CONSERVATION OF midwestern amphibians

EDITED BY MICHAEL J. LANNOO

UNIVERSITY OF IOWA PRESS IOWA CITY

Printed in the United States of America

Design by Karen Copp

http://www.uiowa.edu/~uipress

Printed on acid-free paper

Library of Congress Cataloging-in-Publication Data
Status and conservation of midwestern amphibians / edited by Michael J. Lannoo.
p. cm.
Includes bibliographical references (p.) and index.
ISBN 0-87745-631-3, ISBN 0-87745-632-1 (pbk.)
1. Amphibians—Middle West. 2. Wildlife conservation—Middle West. I. Lannoo, Michael J.
QL653.M53S735 1998
741.9'074'7443—dc21 97-48748

98 99 00 01 02 C 5 4 3 2 1
98 99 00 01 02 P 5 4 3 2 1

We dedicate this book to the people of the Midwest—the folks who funded the many studies reported here. As conservation biologists we are interested in the quality of the world of our children; kids and frogs just go together. We also do this for the amphibians, for they are still able to generate in us the same sense of wonder that they generated as we, in other aspects, were growing up.

Contents

Regional and State Status

Diseases and Toxins

Conservation

Monitoring and Applications

Introduction

Michael J. Lannoo

On 19 and 20 February 1990, an international group of about forty biologists gathered in Irvine, California, to discuss rumored declines in the number of amphibians. This workshop, entitled "Declining Amphibian Populations: A Global Phenomenon?" (Wake and Morowitz 1991), was sponsored by the Board on Biology, United States National Research Council. At this meeting it became apparent that there was good reason for concern: amphibian disappearances biologists had previously thought were simply a local problem were not—the problem was global. What was most disturbing about these discussions was not that amphibians are disappearing in areas disturbed by humans—this was expected—but rather that they are disappearing in regions of the world once thought to be pristine.

In response, the Species Survival Commission, a division of the World Conservation Union, established the Declining Amphibian Populations Task Force (DAPTF). The mission of the DAPTF is: "To determine the nature, extent and causes of declines in amphibians throughout the world, and to promote means by which the declines can be halted or reversed" (Vial and Saylor 1993). Toward these ends three fundamental questions need to be addressed: (1) are amphibians declining; (2) if so, why; and (3) if so, what can be done to halt these losses?

The DAPTF is organized into six regions—Nearctic, Palearctic, Ethiopian, Oriental, Neotropical, and Australian—encompassing the world. The Nearctic Region includes the United States, Canada, and Mexico. The United States is divided into twelve divisions: Pacific Northwest, California/Nevada, Rocky Mountains, Southwest, Northern Plains, Southern Plains, Great Lakes, Central, Mississippi Delta, Northeast, Appalachia, and Southeast. The focus of this book is on the midwestern United States, specifically the DAPTF Central Division, composed of Missouri, Iowa, Illinois, Indiana, and Ohio, and the Great Lakes Division, composed of Minnesota, Wisconsin, and Michigan.

In the Midwest, amphibian numbers have declined with Euro-American settlement and the conversion to an agriculturally dominated landscape. In northwestern Iowa, we estimate that amphibian numbers have declined by about three orders of magnitude since the early 1900s, when commercial harvesters were reported to be sending 20 million northern leopard frogs (*Rana pipiens*) to market annually (Lannoo et al. 1994; Lannoo 1996b). To envision the extent of this loss, imagine a large football stadium at capacity, say 75,000 people. Now imagine it with 75 people. This is the estimated magnitude of our loss. Key questions are whether these initial historical declines in amphibian populations have now ceased and populations have leveled off and whether declines are continuing or accelerating (Fig. I-1). As we will see, these questions must be addressed on a species-by-species basis. For some midwestern amphibian species, severe declines have occurred and are continuing to occur.

The reasons underlying amphibian declines are in some cases thought to be known; in others, the reasons are completely unknown. In the Midwest, there are several suspects but few smoking guns. In other areas of the country, indeed the world, ultraviolet light, acid rain, and pesticide overuse have all been implicated. Ultraviolet light is a mutagen; acidic conditions are not

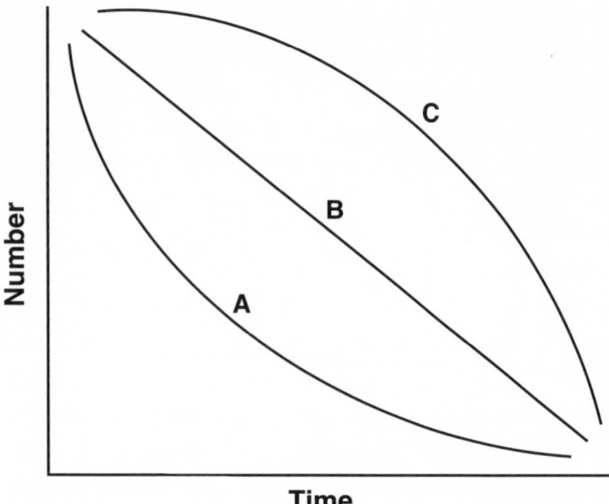

Figure I-1. Potential scenarios for amphibian declines. Lannoo et al. (1994) estimate that leopard frog numbers have declined by between two and three orders of magnitude since 1900. In A, severe amphibian declines occurred early in the century and have since leveled off. In B, amphibian declines have been constant and are still occurring at steady rates. In C, severe amphibian declines have been more recent and catastrophic.

consistent with normal biochemical processes, especially during critical developmental periods; pesticides are biocides. In the Midwest, habitat loss and landscape fragmentation have been major factors. More recently, increasing aquacultural uses of natural wetlands appear to be devastating amphibian numbers. Bullfrog introductions have eliminated populations of native amphibians, and collecting for the biological supply trade has reduced the number of individuals within populations.

The problem with documenting amphibian declines is that in most regions and for most species we have no historical data to compare to data from our current studies. A few reliable scientific studies exist (e.g., Blanchard 1923), but these are for only limited regions and therefore do not allow us to make generalizations. In Indiana, we have a treasure in Sherman Minton. For the past forty-five years, Minton has been following midwestern amphibian and reptile populations and has given us an accurate record of changes through his meticulous field notes (see Minton, Chpt. 24, this volume). The goal of this book is to put between two covers what we know about the current status of midwestern amphibians. By doing this we hope not only to take stock of where we are but to establish a readily accessible historical record for future studies.

The midwestern region is well represented by state field guides, which include: Minton's (1997) *Amphibians and Reptiles of Indiana*, Smith's (1961) "The Amphibians and Reptiles of Illinois," Pfingsten and Downs's (1989) *Salamanders of Ohio*, Walker's (1946) *The Amphibians of Ohio*, Johnson's (1992) *The Amphibians and Reptiles of Missouri*, Christiansen and Bailey's (1991) *The Salamanders and Frogs of Iowa*, Vogt's (1981) *Natural History of Amphibians and Reptiles of Wisconsin*, Casper's (1996) *Geographic Distributions of the Amphibians and Reptiles of Wisconsin*, Harding and Holman's (1992) *Michigan Frogs, Toads, and Salamanders*, Oldfield and Moriarty's (1995) *Amphibians and Reptiles Native to Minnesota*, and Harding's (1997) *Amphibians and Reptiles of the Great Lakes Region*. Other recently published books of interest include Stebbins and Cohen's (1995) *A Natural History of Amphibians* and Levell's (1995) *A Field Guide to Reptiles and the Law*.

In the Midwest, we have seventy-six recognized (species and subspecies) amphibians: forty-five salamanders (order Caudata) and thirty-one frogs (order Anura; Table I-1). The midwestern salamander species represent seven families: Sirenidae (one species), Amphiumidae (one species), Proteidae (one species, two subspecies), Cryptobranchidae (one species, two subspecies), Salamandridae (one species, two subspecies), Ambystomatidae (eleven species, one with two subspecies), and Plethodontidae (twenty-two species, three with two subspecies each). The midwestern frog species represent five families: Pelobatidae (two species), Microhylidae (two species), Bufonidae (four species, two with two subspecies each), Hylidae (ten species, one with two subspecies), and Ranidae (nine species, one with two subspecies).

In this region, salamanders are more diverse than frogs. The 45 salamander taxa comprise almost 60 percent of midwestern amphibians. The 31 frog taxa, however, contain species that are more widespread. The average midwestern state contains about 18 taxa of frogs (58 percent of midwestern frogs) but only about 15.5 salamander taxa (34 percent of midwestern salamanders; Table I-1). Another way to look at this is that a single salamander taxon is found in an average of 2.75 states, while the average frog taxon is found in 4.6 states. Only 2 salamander taxa are found in all eight states; 10 taxa of frogs are found in all eight states (although it appears that Blanchard's cricket frog (*Acris crepitans blanchardi*) may be extirpated from Minnesota; see Moriarty, Chpt. 20, this volume).

The restricted ranges and/or habitat requirements of

salamanders appear to be reflected in their conservation status. Thirteen taxa (30 percent) of midwestern salamanders are listed in at least one state, while eight taxa (26 percent) of midwestern frogs are state listed (Table I-1). Five taxa (11 percent) of salamanders are listed in more than one midwestern state; five taxa of frogs (16 percent) are listed in more than one state.

The foundation for this project was laid in October 1994 at the first meeting of the DAPTF Central Division at Reis Biological Station, operated by St. Mary's University, St. Louis, Missouri. It was here that the idea to assemble this book was formed and agreed upon. Papers given the following year at the second annual Central Division meeting held at Indiana Dunes National Lakeshore in September 1995 establish the basis for the work presented here.

This book is organized as follows. The introductory section is followed by Landscape Patterns and Biogeography, which details the formation of the modern midwestern landscape, the time period when amphibians colonized this newly formed habitat, the modern patterns of amphibian biogeography, and modern amphibian assemblages. The third and fourth sections, Species Status, and Regional and State Status, detail our current knowledge about the distribution and conservation status of midwestern amphibians. Our coverage of species and regions is necessarily uneven, as researchers are limited in where they can sample and states vary both in the amount of funding they are willing to allocate to their natural resources and in the programs they have established for the study of these resources. Therefore, the species accounts given here tend to be geographically incomplete but provide a starting point for future studies.

The fifth section, Diseases and Toxins, describes the infectious diseases of amphibians, the toxicity of amphibians to agricultural and industrial chemicals, and the results of such contaminations. The effect of lampricides on mudpuppy (*Necturus maculosus*) populations is considered, as is an extensive account of the nature of Minnesota northern leopard frog limb and eye malformities. The Conservation section addresses many of the factors thought to be responsible for amphibian declines in the Midwest. Amphibian repatriations, polymorphisms, and the responses of amphibians to drought cycles are considered. Recommendations are given for cooperative efforts among conservation groups and for managing landscapes for amphibians. The seventh section, Monitoring and Applications, describes ongoing approaches for establishing the abundance and distribution of amphibians, gives guidance on how to access historical information on the status of amphibians, provides statistical considerations involved in establishing monitoring studies, and instructs in how to conduct a Geographic Information System (GIS) analysis. The Conclusion summarizes the book's major themes and discoveries.

This book contributes to a growing literature that has arisen since the 1990 meeting. Canadian biologists published *Declines in Canadian Amphibian Populations: Designing a National Monitoring Strategy* (Bishop and Pettit 1992); Kathryn Phillips (1994) published *Tracking the Vanishing Frogs: An Ecological Mystery*; Heyer et al. (1994) published *Measuring and Monitoring Biological Diversity: Standard Methods for Amphibians*, recommending sampling procedures for amphibians; and Canadian biologists have just published their second volume, *Amphibians in Canada: Population Status and Decline* (Green 1997). Additionally, the North American Amphibian Monitoring Program (NAAMP) has been established (North American Amphibian Monitoring Program 1996; Mac 1996), with the idea of using trained volunteers and statistically rigorous sampling protocols to survey amphibian populations.

This book will not present a complete story. It would, of course, be best if we could document the exact range and abundance of each midwestern amphibian species and identify the most immediate threats to its survival. But we cannot yet do this, nor may we ever be able to do this—amphibian numbers fluctuate both within and across years, and the extent of our knowledge about potential threats to amphibians is too primitive. What we hope to do instead is present a snapshot of what we know at this moment in time. As a group, we in the Midwest were scattered, and this effort reflects our first attempt to come together. In the future, our goal will be to expand upon and improve this database. In the process, we hope to be able to continue to publicize the value and vulnerability of amphibians. We will have met our goal if, upon considering this present work, a future generation concludes that the current state of our knowledge is indeed primitive. We will not have met our goal if future biologists are forced to conclude—based on the relative numbers of species and individuals available to them—that these were the good old days.

Acknowledgments

Each of these chapters has been peer reviewed and edited. A majority of the reviews have come from other

Table I-1. Midwestern amphibians and their state status

		Missouri	Iowa
Order Caudata			
Family Sirenidae			
Western lesser siren	*Siren intermedia nettingi*	X	
Family Amphiumidae			
Three-toed amphiuma	*Amphiuma tridactylum*	X	
Family Proteidae			
Red River mudpuppy	*Necturus maculosus louisianensis*	X	Threatened
Mudpuppy	*Necturus maculosus maculosus*	X	Endangered
Family Cryptobranchidae			
Eastern hellbender	*Cryptobranchus alleganiensis alleganiensis*	X	
Ozark hellbender	*Cryptobranchus alleganiensis bishopi*	X	
Family Salamandridae			
Central newt	*Notophthalmus viridescens louisianensis*	X	Endangered
Red-spotted newt	*Notophthalmus viridescens viridescens*		
Family Ambystomatidae			
Ringed salamander	*Ambystoma annulatum*	X	
Streamside salamander	*Ambystoma barbouri*		
Jefferson salamander	*Ambystoma jeffersonianum*		
Blue-spotted salamander	*Ambystoma laterale*		Endangered
Spotted salamander	*Ambystoma maculatum*	X	
Marbled salamander	*Ambystoma opacum*	X	
Silvery salamander	*Ambystoma platineum*		
Mole salamander	*Ambystoma talpoideum*	Rare	
Smallmouth salamander	*Ambystoma texanum*	X	X
Eastern tiger salamander	*Ambystoma tigrinum tigrinum*	X	X
Gray tiger salamander	*Ambystoma tigrinum diaboli*		
Tremblay's salamander	*Ambystoma tremblayi*		
Family Plethodontidae			
Green salamander	*Aneides aeneus*		
Spotted dusky salamander	*Desmognathus conanti*		
Northern dusky salamander	*Desmognathus fuscus*		
Mountain dusky salamander	*Desmognathus ochrophaeus*		
Northern two-lined salamander	*Eurycea bislineata*		
Southern two-lined salamander	*Eurycea cirrigera*		
Longtail salamander	*Eurycea longicauda longicauda*	X	
Dark-sided salamander	*Eurycea longicauda melanopleura*	X	
Cave salamander	*Eurycea lucifuga*	X	
Graybelly salamander	*Eurycea multiplicata griseogaster*	X	
Oklahoma salamander	*Eurycea tynerensis*	X	
Kentucky spring salamander	*Gyrinophilus porphyriticus duryi*		
Northern spring salamander	*Gyrinophilus porphyriticus porphyriticus*		
Four-toed salamander	*Hemidactylium scutatum*	Rare	
Western slimy salamander	*Plethodon albagula*	X	
Redback salamander	*Plethodon cinereus*		
Ozark zigzag salamander	*Plethodon dorsalis angusticlavus*	X	
Eastern zigzag salamander	*Plethodon dorsalis dorsalis*		
Northern slimy salamander	*Plethodon glutinosus*		
Ravine salamander	*Plethodon richmondi*		
Southern redback salamander	*Plethodon serratus*	X	
Wehrle's salamander	*Plethodon wehrlei*		
Midland mud salamander	*Pseudotriton montanus diasticus*		
Northern red salamander	*Pseudotriton ruber ruber*		
Grotto salamander	*Typhlotriton spelaeus*	X	
Total number of salamanders	45	23	6
Listed	13	2	4

Illinois	Indiana	Ohio	Minnesota	Wisconsin	Michigan	Listed/Present
X	X				Extirpated?	0/3
						0/1
						0/1
X	Special Concern	X	X	X	X	2/8
Endangered	Endangered	Endangered				3/4
						0/1
X	X		X	X	X	1/7
	X	X			X	0/3
						0/1
	X	X				0/2
X	X	X			X	0/4
X	Special Concern	Endangered	X	X	X	3/7
X	X	X		X	X	0/6
X	X	X			Threatened	1/5
Endangered		X				1/2
X						1/2
X	X	X			Endangered	1/6
X	X	X	X	X	X	0/8
			X			0/1
		X				0/1
	Endangered	Endangered				2/2
Endangered						1/1
	X	X				0/2
		X				0/1
		X				0/1
X	X	X				0/3
X	X	X				0/4
X						0/2
X	X	Endangered				1/4
						0/1
						0/1
		X				0/1
		X				0/1
Threatened	Endangered	Special Concern	Endangered	Special Concern	Special Concern	7/7
						0/1
X	X	X	X	X	X	0/6
						0/1
X	X					0/2
X	X	X				0/3
	X	X				0/2
						0/1
		X				0/1
		X				0/1
	Endangered	X				1/2
						0/1
21	23	28	7	7	11	
4	6	5	1	1	3	

Table I-1. (cont.)

		Missouri	Iowa
Order Anura			
Family Pelobatidae			
Eastern spadefoot	*Scaphiopus holbrookii holbrookii*	Rare	
Plains spadefoot	*Spea bombifrons*	X	X
Family Microhylidae			
Eastern narrowmouth toad	*Gastrophryne carolinensis*	X	
Great Plains narrowmouth toad	*Gastrophryne olivacea*	X	
Family Bufonide			
American toad	*Bufo americanus americanus*	X	X
Dwarf American toad	*Bufo americanus charlesmithi*	X	
Great Plains toad	*Bufo cognatus*	X	X
Canadian toad	*Bufo hemiophrys*		
Fowler's toad	*Bufo woodhousii fowleri*	X	X
Woodhouse's toad	*Bufo woodhousii woodhousii*	X	X
Family Hylidae			
Blanchard's cricket frog	*Acris crepitans blanchardi*	X	X
Bird-voiced treefrog	*Hyla avivoca*		
Cope's gray treefrog	*Hyla chrysoscelis*	X	X
Green treefrog	*Hyla cinerea*	X	
Eastern gray treefrog	*Hyla versicolor*	X	X
Mountain chorus frog	*Pseudacris brachyphona*		
Northern spring peeper	*Pseudacris crucifer crucifer*	X	X
Illinois chorus frog	*Pseudacris streckeri illinoensis*	Rare	
Upland chorus frog	*Pseudacris feriarum*	X	
Boreal chorus frog	*Pseudacris triseriata maculata*		X
Western chorus frog	*Pseudacris triseriata triseriata*	X	X
Family Ranidae			
Northern crawfish frog	*Rana areolata circulosa*	X	Endangered
Plains leopard frog	*Rana blairi*	X	X
Bullfrog	*Rana catesbeiana*	X	X
Bronze frog	*Rana clamitans clamitans*	X	
Green frog	*Rana clamitans melanota*	X	X
Pickerel frog	*Rana palustris*	X	X
Northern leopard frog	*Rana pipiens*	Rare	X
Mink frog	*Rana septentrionalis*		
Southern leopard frog	*Rana sphenocephala*	X	X
Wood frog	*Rana sylvatica*	Rare	
Total number of frogs	31	26	18
Listed	8	4	1

[1] See Moriarty, Chpt. 20, this volume.
[2] See Hay, Chpt. 11, Casper, Chpt. 22, this volume.
[3] Recommended for threatened listing in Harding (1997).

Illinois	Indiana	Ohio	Minnesota	Wisconsin	Michigan	Listed/Present
X	Special Concern	Endangered				3/4
						0/2
X						0/2
						0/1
X	X	X	X	X	X	0/8
X	X					0/3
			X			0/3
			X			0/1
X	X	X			X	0/6
						0/2
X	X	X	Endangered[1]	Endangered[2]	Protected[3]	3/8
X						0/1
X	X	X	X	X	X	0/8
X						0/2
X	X	X	X	X	X	0/8
		X				0/1
X	X	X	X	X	X	0/8
Threatened						2/2
X	X	?				0/4
			X	X	Special Concern	1/4
X	X	X	X	X	X	0/8
X	Endangered					2/4
X	Special Concern				X	1/5
X	X	X	X	X	X	0/8
X						0/2
X	X	X	X	X	X	0/8
X	X	X	X	X	X	0/8
X	Special Concern	X	X	X	X	2/8
			X	X	X	0/3
X	X	?				0/4
X	X	X	X	X	X	1/7
23	18	14	15	13	15	
1	4	1	1	1	2	

authors in this volume; a few have not. For these we thank Kenneth Dodd, Michael Dorcas, David Pfennig, Raymond Semlitsch, and Michael Sredl. Thanks also to Danette Pratt for using her considerable artistic talents to redraw and standardize the figures.

Support for publication costs has been generously provided by Biological Research Division (U.S. Geological Survey, formerly National Biological Service), Northern Prairie Science Center, Jamestown, North Dakota, through Doug Johnson; Ball State University's Publications and Intellectual Properties Committee, through Ione DeOllos; Illinois Department of Natural Resources Wildlife Preservation Fund, through Todd Strole; Wisconsin Electric Power Company, through Noel Cutright; Wisconsin Department of Natural Resources, through Joanne Kline; Savannah River Ecology Laboratory publication support funds, through Howard Whiteman; Wisconsin Wetlands Asociation; and contributions from members of the U.S. Central Division of the Declining Amphibian Populations Task Force.

A personal thanks to Richard Wassersug, friend and mentor, who set the bar high. Thanks also to Ralph Grundel, Indiana Dunes National Lakeshore, for hosting the 1994 meeting, where a majority of the papers included here were presented. Finally, I thank each of the authors. While the title page of this book bears my name, it is you who have done the real work, and it is you who deserve the credit.

Landscape Patterns and Biogeography

1

Late Quaternary Environmental Changes in the Midwestern United States

Richard G. Baker

Ancestors of modern amphibian populations in the Midwest have been subjected to large changes in climate and vegetation. Herpetofaunas in the northern two tiers of states were displaced numerous times during the last 2.5 million years by advancing glaciers. The long-held concept that North America was subjected to four glacial periods interrupted by three interglacial episodes has been disproven. The number of glacial episodes is uncertain, but at least eight to ten have occurred in western Iowa (Hallberg 1986; Richmond and Fullerton 1986), and paleoclimatic episodes in deep sea cores suggest that there may have been as many as fifteen to twenty (Raymo 1994). Each time climate warmed to conditions similar to the present, the ranges of both plants and animals presumably expanded northward into deglaciated terrains. However, these two extremes, the full glacial and full interglacial condition, represent perhaps only 20 percent of the Quaternary; the rest of the time conditions fluctuated but were generally cooler than the present (Dansgaard et al. 1993; Imbrie et al. 1984). For example, the previous interglacial was an approximately 10,000-year-long interval centering around 125,000 yr B.P. Following that warm period, climate fluctuated greatly between cool and cold intervals, including, perhaps, some glacial advances. The major (Late Wisconsinan) glaciation in the Midwest reached its maximum only about 21,000 to 18,000 yr B.P. in most areas.

It is only the last part of the most recent of these glacial periods, the Late Wisconsinan, that is sufficiently well known to be useful in constructing a synopsis of change for the Midwest and of direct importance to the distribution of plants and animals in the millennia that followed the Wisconsinan ice retreat. The purpose of this chapter is to outline the environmental history of the Midwest in order to provide a conceptual basis for understanding past changes in amphibian distribution. The approach will be to outline the past environments of four intervals: (1) 30,000 to ca. 22,000 yr B.P., when climate began to cool and glaciers advanced; (2) ca. 22,000 to ca. 16,000 yr B.P., when glaciers were at or close to their maximum; (3) ca. 16,000 to 10,000 yr B.P., when glaciers were retreating and rapid warming occurred; and (4) the last 10,000 yr B.P. (the Holocene), when more subtle changes in climate occurred (Figs. 1-1–1-4). The dates are in uncorrected radiocarbon years before present and are rounded off to the nearest 1000 yr B.P. The area covered is from western Ohio to western Iowa. This approach may help us to understand present distribution patterns not only of amphibians but also of other organisms. The source of information for this chapter is the physical record of glacial deposits and the biotic record from pollen and plant macrofossil analyses, paleoentomology, and vertebrate paleontology. Papers in Wright et al. (1993) provide summaries of environmental change and climate models of key intervals for many areas of the world. Two additional sources of biotic data are the databases that have been established for pollen (assembled by Eric Grimm, Illinois State Museum, Springfield, and available free from the North American Pollen Database by ftp at ngdc.noaa.gov) and for vertebrates (FAUNMAP Working Group 1994). Finally, this chapter is intended as a brief summary of recent environmental change; it is not exhaustive but instead is meant to set the tone for the following chapters on amphibian distribution and abundance.

Late Quaternary Environments

Interval 1: 30,000 to ca. 22,000 yr B.P.

The interval from 30,000 to ca. 22,000 yr B.P. is still relatively poorly known, with most of the work having been done in Iowa and Illinois (Fig. 1-1). There is no evidence that glaciers were present in Ohio and Indiana. In Illinois, the loess sequence was thought to be inextricably tied together with the glacial sequence; when there were glaciers present in Illinois, loess (windblown silt) was deposited. Although this link was true for the younger Peoria Loess (see below), it has been questioned for the Roxana Loess. The Roxana Loess has been dated from about 55,000 to slightly younger than 30,000 yr B.P. (Leigh and Knox 1994) and was thought to correspond to the Altonian ice advance. It has become clear that no glaciers were in Illinois during this time (Curry 1989; Johnson and Follmer 1989), and there seems to be no correlative glacial deposits in the state. However, several sites in central Iowa show that glacial till was at times present between over 40,000 and 26,000 yr B.P. Apparently, an ice sheet advanced out of the Hudson Bay region between 55,000 and 26,000 yr B.P., but its extent in both space and time is poorly known; Illinois, and apparently Indiana and Ohio as well, was free of ice during this period.

The few pollen sequences from this time indicate that a spruce-pine forest was present in west-central and north-central Illinois from before 30,000 to about 25,000 yr B.P. (Baker, Sullivan, et al. 1989; Meyers and King 1985). This forest gave way to a spruce-larch forest about 25,000 yr B.P., and pine apparently disappeared from the Midwest as cooler conditions prevailed. These forests have pollen spectra very similar to those in the modern boreal forest (Baker, Van Nest, and Woodworth 1989). By 22,000 yr B.P., these forests became more open and subarctic plants began to appear, suggesting that climate became even colder (Baker, Sullivan, et al. 1989; Baker, Van Nest, and Woodworth 1989). Similar sequences were found by King (1973) in the Missouri Ozarks and by Van Zant et al. (1980) and Mundt and Baker (1979) in eastern Iowa (Fig. 1-1).

In the northeast corner of Kansas, pollen evidence suggests that a boreal spruce-dominated parkland was present at 25,000 yr B.P., but by about 23,000 yr B.P. the vegetation changed to closed spruce forest until after 16,000 yr B.P. (Grüger 1973). Studies of vertebrate fossils from western Iowa suggest that an open, grassy, boreal woodland was present in southwestern Iowa at 23,000 yr B.P. (Rhodes 1984).

I am unaware of any pollen-bearing sites of this age in Indiana or Ohio, but sites in Kentucky and Tennessee indicate that the vegetation there was similar to the present conifer-hardwood forest in the northern Midwest (Delcourt and Delcourt 1987). Climate was cooler than present in these two states and undoubtedly in Ohio and Indiana as well. No records are available from the northern tier of states for this time period. If sites are present in these areas, they lie beneath the Late Wisconsinan till sheets. Mean July temperatures were 14° to 17°C in Ohio, Indiana, and Illinois at this time (versus 21° to 24°C at present), and they suggest that coniferous woodland was present in Ohio and Indiana and that closed spruce forest was present in Illinois (Elias 1994).

Interval 2: ca. 22,000 to ca. 16,000 yr B.P.

Late Wisconsinan glacial ice probably began to advance from Canada about 22,000 yr B.P.; it formed lobes that reached their maximum position from southern Ohio to southern Illinois by about 21,000 yr B.P. (Fig. 1-2; Mickelson et al. 1983). These ice lobes retreated into the Lake Michigan and Erie basins by the end of this interval. In Minnesota, the ice reached a standstill about 20,500 yr B.P. (Wright et al. 1973), and it did not reach its maximum in Iowa until much later (Fig. 1-2). The thick and widespread Peoria Loess was deposited throughout the period of this glacial advance, covering much of the Midwest with a layer of windblown silt. Loess thickness ranges from tens of meters near major meltwater rivers to less than a meter in areas distant from floodplain sources.

At this time climate in the unglaciated parts of the Midwest was apparently at its coldest since the previous Sangamonian interglacial ended ca. 120,000 yr B.P. Although there are few fossil sites in the Midwest that represent this interval, several trends are nonetheless clear. Tundra plants and insects began to appear in western and central Illinois as glaciers began to advance into the Midwest about 21,000 yr B.P. (Baker, Sullivan, et al. 1989; Baker, Van Nest, and Woodworth 1989; Garry et al. 1990; Mickelson et al. 1983; Schwert 1992). Areas in Minnesota free of ice during part of the Late Wisconsinan glacial advance (Fig. 1-2) had a tundralike vegetation with no indication of trees (Birks 1976). In Iowa, the vegetation during this interval was analogous to the arctic tree-limit, with a few scattered spruce trees amid a vegeta-

Figure 1-1. Inferred and generalized vegetation from 30,000 to ca. 22,000 yr B.P. The position of continental glacial boundaries is unknown; there is evidence of glaciation in Iowa at times during this period, but ice probably was not present elsewhere in the Midwest.

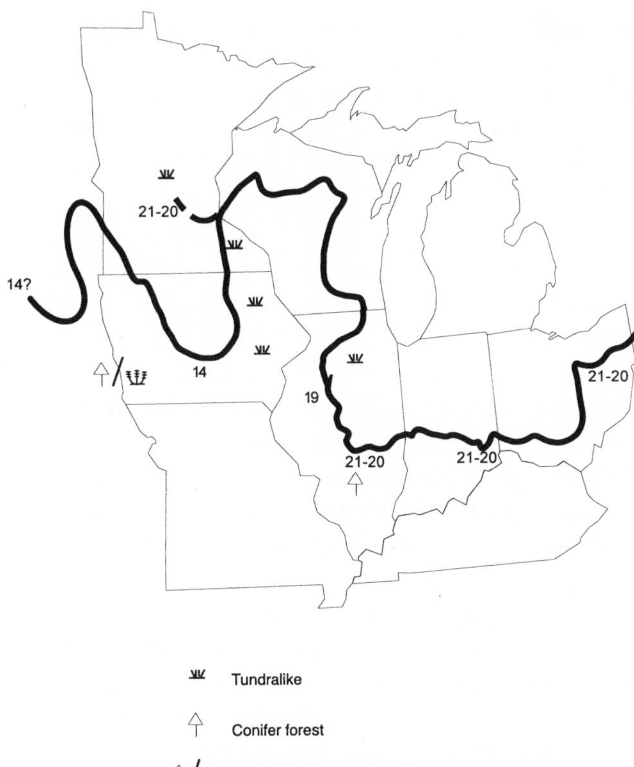

Figure 1-2. Inferred and generalized vegetation from ca. 22,000 to ca.16,000 yr B.P. The maximum extent of the Wisconsinan glacier is shown by the dark line (adapted from Dyke and Prest 1987a and Mickelson et al. 1983); numbers are approximate radiocarbon ages for the maximum extent in thousands of years. The vegetation symbol within the glacial limit in Illinois indicates that site was underneath the till of the last advance. The Minnesota locality may have been free of ice during this period, or the basal date is anomalous.

tion comprised of tundra plants (Baker et al. 1986). Small mammals and insects from several sites in Iowa and Illinois also indicate open and arcticlike conditions, with mean July temperatures of 10° to 12°C (Baker et al. 1986; Foley and Raue 1987; Schwert 1992). In southwest Wisconsin, Foley (1984) interpreted small vertebrates dated at 17,000 yr B.P. as representing a mosaic of marsh, steppe, spruce parkland, and tundralike communities. The vertebrate and insect faunas and the plant macrofossils of most of these full glacial sites are largely sympatric in subarctic to arctic regions.

No pollen sites representing this interval are available from Indiana, Ohio, or Michigan. Sites from Kentucky and Tennessee suggest that a closed boreal forest was present there (Delcourt and Delcourt 1987). It seems likely that open parklands or tundralike areas occupied unglaciated Indiana and Ohio.

Interval 3: ca. 16,000 to 10,000 yr B.P.

Glaciers were generally retreating across the Midwest during the interval from ca. 16,000 to 10,000 yr B.P. (Fig. 1-3). Their retreat was not uniform but rather occurred in pulses interspersed with periods of standstill or readvance of the glacier front, a process that left a series of recessional moraines (Mickelson et al. 1983). Some of these oscillations correlate well with climatic oscillations observed in Greenland ice cores and in oceanic records of paleoclimate and with European pollen records (Stuiver et al. 1995), but others do not. The Younger Dryas cold interval between 11,000 and 10,000 yr B.P., for example, is now recognized as a worldwide event. However, the advance of the Des Moines Lobe in Iowa between ca. 15,000 and 12,000 yr B.P. does not seem to match any cold interval in other paleoclimatic records and may indicate a series of glacial surge events (Kemmis 1991). The James Lobe in southeastern South Dakota apparently had a similar history.

Numerous fossil pollen sites exist for the latter part of this interval, and they indicate that it is a time of great change in climate and habitat (Keltner 1993–1994). I will summarize general trends across the area from review articles, where detailed site reports are mapped and cited (Jacobson et al. 1987; Webb et al. 1983; Webb et al. 1993). Kutzbach et al. (1993) have detailed climatic model reconstructions for North America.

Some fossil pollen sites in Michigan and Minnesota had early stages of tundralike vegetation lasting until between 13,000 and 11,000 yr B.P., depending on the locality. A short interval of shrubby vegetation consisting of subarctic taxa such as shrub birch was a common transition between this tundralike vegetation and the forest. The ensuing late-glacial landscape was dominated by spruce-larch forests with associated poplar and black ash across the entire Midwest (Webb et al. 1983; Webb et al. 1993). In many areas, this forest may have been growing on the glacier itself, or rather on debris that had melted out on the surface of stagnant (no longer flowing) glacial ice.

Between ca. 12,000 yr B.P. in the south and ca. 10,000 yr B.P. in the north, the spruce forest was replaced, in many places rapidly, by a succession of trees now characteristic of the Great Lakes conifer-hardwood forest. These include jack pine, fir, birch, alder, oak, elm, and hornbean/hophornbeam. In a few places in Ohio and Indiana (Shane 1987), a climatic reversal (spruce to hardwoods back to spruce) between 11,000 and 10,000 yr B.P. appears to correlate with the Younger Dryas cold event in Greenland ice cores (Stuiver et al. 1995); most other areas do not show such a reversal. There appears to be no modern analogs for many of the plant communities that were present during this late-glacial time of rapid change.

Fossils from this period indicate that arctic beetle faunas were extirpated south of the glacial front in the Midwest between 16,000 and 15,000 yr B.P., and they were replaced by an assemblage of open-ground species that do not presently co-occur in the taiga and western montane regions; this was clearly a fauna with no modern analog (Schwert 1992). By 14,000 yr B.P. in Illinois and 12,000 yr B.P. in Minnesota, the open-ground forms had largely been replaced by species characteristic of closed spruce forests.

Vertebrate fossils from the late-glacial interval are characterized by higher species diversity than at present and the coexistence of taxa that are now allotopic (Lundelius et al. 1983; Semken 1988). These characteristics have been explained by hypothesizing a more equable climate, where summer and winter temperature extremes were reduced. This reduction allowed animals whose distributions are limited by the extremes to coexist in the Pleistocene, thereby increasing the diversity of these faunas. The other important feature of the vertebrate record is the extinction of many large mammals, which has been attributed either to overkill by Paleoindian hunters (Martin and Klein 1984) or to rapidly changing environmental conditions (Graham and Lundelius 1984).

The Holocene

The Holocene, also referred to as the present interglacial, is a time of continuing change, but the bulk of climatic warming had occurred during the previous late-glacial period. In fact, the maximum summer insolation for the last 18,000 years occurred between 11,000 and 9000 yr B.P. (Kutzbach and Webb 1993). Nevertheless, glaciers were still in the Lake Superior basin 10,000 yr B.P. (Fig. 1-3). Even at 8000 yr B.P., a large ice sheet remained in eastern Canada (Dyke and Prest 1987a,b), which may have had a substantial effect on the biota of the Midwest (Wright 1992). By 7000 yr B.P., the ice was almost completely gone. Temperature fluctuated much less in the Holocene than previously. Perhaps the most dramatic changes in the Holocene biota occurred where moisture deficits were an important factor: at the prairie-forest boundary in the western part of the region.

A large database on pollen sequences is available for the Holocene (Keltner 1993–1994), and several good summaries are available (Davis 1983; Webb et al. 1983; Webb et al. 1993). What follows is a brief synopsis of the main themes (Fig. 1-4).

The early Holocene was a time of continuing adjustment, as species migrated into and out of the Midwest at different rates. In the northern tier of midwestern states, pine became dominant in the early Holocene and remained abundant; jack pine, the earliest migrant, was superseded or partially replaced by white pine between 8000 and 6000 yr B.P. in most areas. Most of the other trees of the present conifer-hardwood forest also arrived early, including fir, birch, oak, elm, maple, basswood, and hornbeam/hophornbeam. Beech and hemlock were slower immigrants, arriving in the middle Holocene in Michigan and in the late Holocene near their western limit in Wisconsin.

Figure 1-3. Inferred and generalized vegetation from ca.16,000 to 10,000 yr B.P. The dark lines show approximate positions of the retreating Wisconsinan glacier in thousands of years (adapted from Dyke and Prest 1987a). Vegetation symbols connected by an arrowhead show changes from one type to another during this period. Question marks indicate that the area was ice free but that the vegetation in the first part of this interval is unknown because sedimentation at the site did not begin until later.

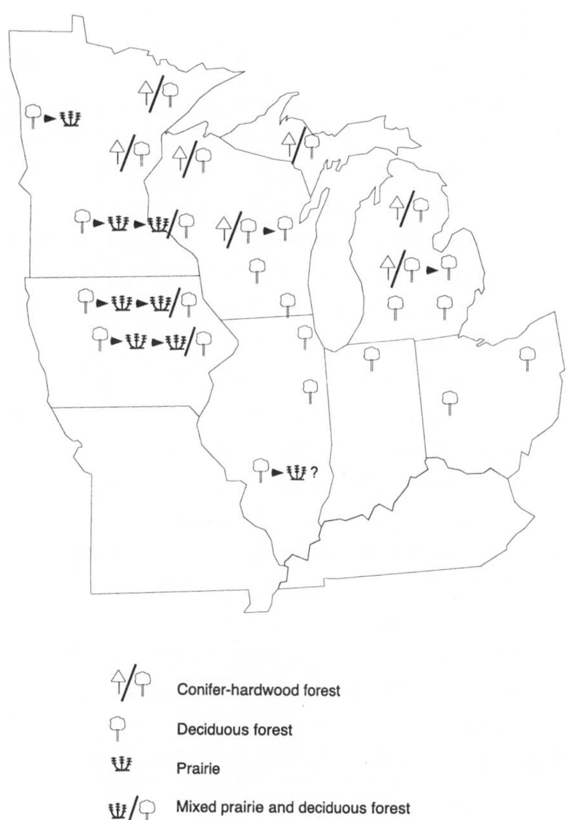

Figure 1-4. Inferred and generalized vegetation from 10,000 yr B.P. to pre-Euro-American settlement time. The glacier had retreated from the Midwest by 10,000 yr B.P., but it was still present in the Hudson Bay region in Canada until about 8000 yr B.P. (Dyke and Prest 1987b). Vegetation symbols connected by an arrowhead show changes that occurred during the last 10,000 years. The question mark in southern Illinois indicates that the dating and interpretation are less certain than at other sites.

From Ohio to eastern Iowa, mesic deciduous forest was the prevalent vegetation throughout the Holocene. Dominant taxa were oak, hickory, elm, hornbeam/hophornbeam, maple, basswood, and, in the late Holocene in the eastern half in the region, beech. Some prairie openings may have formed after about 5500 yr B.P., especially in Illinois and north into southwestern Wisconsin, but there is little evidence that prairie ever was dominant over large areas of the landscape.

In Iowa and Minnesota, the early Holocene was also dominated by conifer-hardwood forests, and these continued to the present in northern Minnesota. In western Minnesota and Iowa, prairie began to encroach by 9000 yr B.P., spreading eastward into the central parts of these states by 8000 to 7000 yr B.P. By 5000 yr B.P., oak began to advance westward from central Minnesota and Iowa, and by 3000 yr B.P., it reached western Iowa, probably in the form of oak groves in protected locations.

Few Holocene vertebrate or insect faunas are available from this prairie-forest transition. Most of the Holocene vertebrate localities are on the Great Plains, but a few in Iowa generally show the gradual encroachment of prairie habitats into deciduous forest from early to middle Holocene time (Semken and Falk 1987). The one Holocene insect fauna that I am aware of is in northeastern Iowa, where little change was observed in the Holocene (Baker et al. 1996).

Conclusions

Prior to the last glacial advance, conditions in the Midwest generally seem to have been similar to those of the modern boreal forest. The border of this forest with the mixed conifer-hardwood forest (similar to the modern forest that lies in the northern Great Lakes region) appears to have extended from southern Ohio to southern Illinois. In western Iowa and Missouri, more open grassland environments prevailed.

The modern arctic provides the closest analog for full-glacial environments in the Midwest. Although there are many physical and climatic differences between modern arctic and midwestern full-glacial conditions (including day length, angle of incident radiation, total precipitation, and seasonality), the plants and animals present during the latter were nearly all tree-line or tundra taxa.

The late-glacial interval is one of rapidly changing environments in which allotopic distributions were common throughout the biota. The retreat of glaciers in a changing climate resulted in major changes in species distribution and created novel communities that no longer persist.

During the early Holocene, conifer-hardwood forests and their mammal and insect assemblages were present over much of the region. Many fossil pollen assemblages do not match any modern site, suggesting that even as late as the early Holocene, many areas had no modern analogs. By the middle to late Holocene (ca. 5000 to 3000 yr B.P.) the biota in the Midwest evolved toward their modern equivalents. Conifer-hardwood forest in the northern Midwest remained in place as its constituents changed, and it became analogous to modern forests there. Similar patterns were present in the deciduous forest to the south and in the prairie along the western edge of the region.

The fossil record of the past 30,000 years demonstrates one thing that has been clear to paleoecologists for several decades: plant and animal communities are not tightly bound assemblages that have evolved together for millennia; rather, they are loose associations of organisms that happen to live together at any given time. Species react individually to change, and the past and present distribution of amphibians should reflect this. Amphibians have been in their present locations for only a few thousand years. They could not have been present much longer, because these areas were covered by Wisconsinan glaciers, which reached their maxima between 21,000 and 18,000 yr B.P. in most areas and still covered much of the northern United States as late as 12,000 to 10,000 yr B.P. Even in areas beyond the glacial margin, conditions were sufficiently cold that many amphibians probably would not have been present. After the glaciers retreated, environments were still changing, substantially in some areas and slightly in others. Past amphibian associations were probably very different from those at present.

Summary

The Midwest has experienced profound and repeated changes in climate and other environmental factors during the Quaternary Epoch. Because events of the last 30,000 years are representative of the range of environmental variation in the entire Quaternary and lead directly up to the present, they are important in understanding modern plant and animal distributions and their communities.

During the interval from 30,000 to ca. 22,000 yr B.P., the Midwest was largely unglaciated and was covered by conifer forests that compare closely with the modern boreal forest. Climate was cool and moist. Glaciers then advanced into the Midwest, reaching their maximum in most areas between 20,000 and 18,000 yr B.P., when climate was coldest and tundra or tree-line conditions were widespread. From ca. 16,000 to 10,000 yr B.P., glaciers retreated in most areas (though they were at their maximum in Iowa between 14,000 and 13,000 yr B.P.), spruce-larch forests were widespread, and the maximum climatic warming was occurring. The effects of changing environmental conditions on amphibians, as on the rest of the biota, were profound. There are no modern analogs for these past communities. During the Holocene, climate and biotic communities continued to change rapidly in the early stages, but by the middle to late Holocene (ca. 5000 to 3000 yr B.P.), they approached their modern counterparts.

Acknowledgments

I thank E. A. Bettis III, Laura Strickland, and Joseph Krieg for critical comments on this chapter.

2

Amphibian Recolonization of Midwestern States in the Postglacial Pleistocene

J. Alan Holman

Until recently, there has been an almost complete lack of Pleistocene records of amphibians from stratigraphically controlled sites in the Midwest. Nevertheless, herpetologists have speculated from time to time about the possible relationships between glacial boundaries and the distribution patterns of modern amphibians. In the Midwest, Smith and Minton (1957) and Minton (1972) pointed out that the Shelbyville moraine in Indiana, which marks the southern limits of the Wisconsinan glaciation, is an important boundary in the distribution of terrestrial amphibians and reptiles. Minton (1972) observed that eighteen herpetological forms currently have most of their range south of the moraine, while nine are confined mostly to the north.

Holman (1992) developed a model suggesting patterns of the postglacial herpetological recolonization of recently glaciated landscapes based on vegetational development and the ecological tolerances of modern amphibians. The data presented here from stratigraphically controlled sites in Michigan, Indiana, and Ohio begin to test this model.

Late Wisconsinan Glaciation

Mickelson et al. (1983) showed that about 20,000 yr B.P. the Late Wisconsinan Laurentide Ice Sheet moved southward to similar latitudes in central Illinois, Indiana, and southern Ohio (Fig. 2-1; see also Baker, Chpt. 1, this volume). This obliterated huge areas of amphibian habitat and restricted amphibian distribution to the southern, unglaciated parts of these states. Other advances occurred about 19,000, 18,000, 17,000, 16,700 and 15,500 yr B.P. (Fig. 2-2).

After 14,800 yr B.P., the ice began its final retreat, reexposing habitat for the reinvasion of amphibian species. The movement of amphibians into these newly exposed

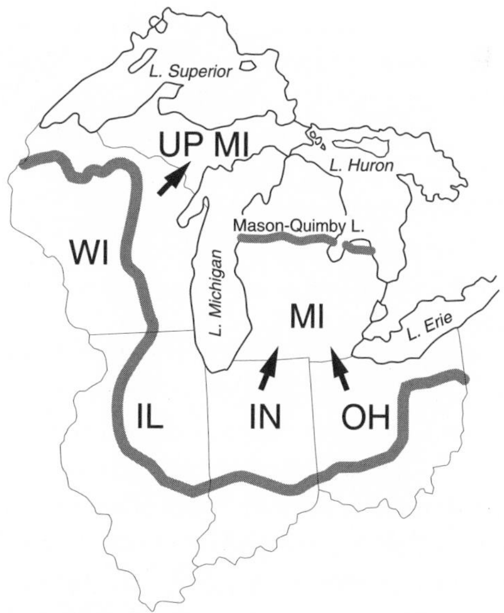

Figure 2-1. Map of the Great Lakes region including: (1) major routes (indicated by arrows) of herpetological recolonization of postglacial Michigan; (2) the Mason-Quimby Line; and (3) the approximate maximum extent of the Laurentide Ice Sheet in Wisconsin, Illinois, Indiana, and Ohio (heavy line in these states); modified from Holman (1992).

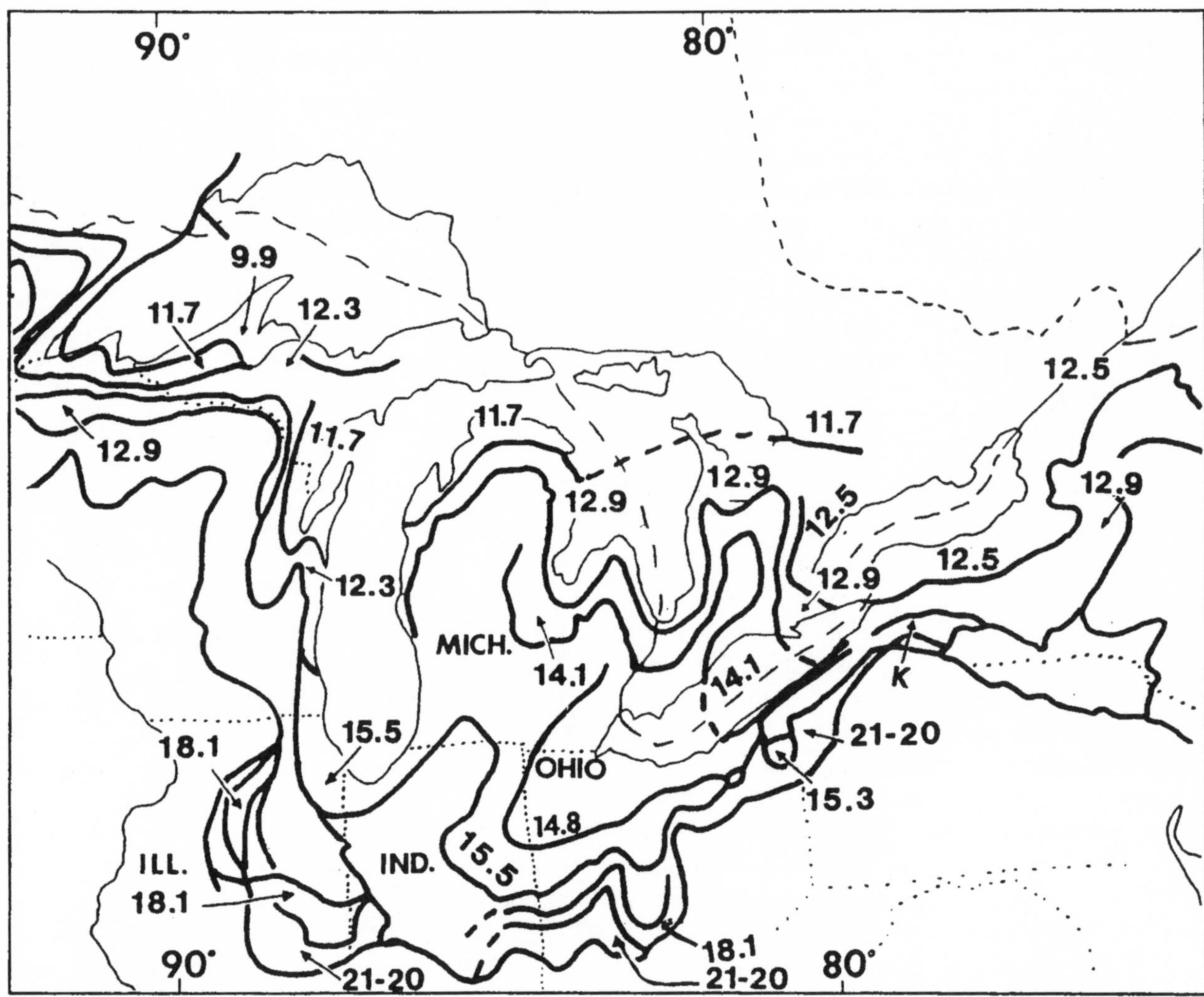

Figure 2-2. Ice margin positions in the Great Lakes region in thousands of years B.P.; modified from Holman (1995).

areas established the modern amphibian fauna of the northeastern Midwest, including the entire state of Michigan and northern Illinois, Indiana, and Ohio.

The timing of the reinvasion of amphibian species into recently deglaciated habitats is of great interest to paleoecologists, as most amphibian species tended to stay put in the nonglaciated regions of North America during the Pleistocene (Holman 1995). Moreover, these Pleistocene patterns might be considered somewhat of an analog to possible forthcoming amphibian recolonizations.

The Michigan Model

The Pleistocene herpetological record is weakly developed in Michigan (Holman 1988). Thus, a model that postulated patterns of the herpetological recolonization of postglacial Michigan was proposed (Holman 1992). This model was based mainly on the present distribution and ecological tolerances of modern amphibians and reptiles correlated with the pollen record of the development of postglacial vegetation. The model assumes that amphibian (and reptile) species of several thousand years ago had essentially the same ecological tolerances and habitat preferences that they do today.

Routes of Entry

Routes of entry for glacially displaced amphibians and reptiles into Michigan (Fig. 2-1) were suggested by Holman (1992). The postglacial amphibian fauna of the Upper Peninsula probably was largely derived from a Wisconsin corridor because of the width and depth of the Straits of Mackinac. This invasion must have occurred sometime after 9900 yr B.P., as at this time the Upper Peninsula had glacial ice along its northern edge (Kapp et al. 1990). The Lower Peninsula probably derived its postglacial amphibian fauna mainly through Indiana and Ohio. The paleobotanical record and the lag time necessary for vegetation to develop suggest that the first herpetological species (possibly the tundra-tolerant species, the wood frog [*Rana sylvatica*]) might have reached southern Michigan by about 13,000 yr B.P.

Categories of Recolonizing Amphibians

The model proposes three categories (Table 2-1) of invading species: (1) primary invaders, whose ecological tolerances included coniferous forest and, in one case (the wood frog), tundra areas; (2) secondary invaders

Table 2-1. Amphibian taxa considered to be primary, secondary, and tertiary invaders of postglacial Michigan (from Holman 1992)

Primary	Secondary	Tertiary*
Blue-spotted salamander *Ambystoma laterale*	Blanchard's cricket frog *Acris crepitans blanchardi*	Marbled salamander *Ambystoma opacum*
Spotted salamander *Ambystoma maculatum*	Fowler's toad *Bufo woodhousii fowleri*	Smallmouth salamander *Ambystoma texanum*
Eastern tiger salamander *Ambystoma tigrinum tigrinum*	Cope's gray treefrog *Hyla chrysoscelis*	Western lesser siren *Siren intermedia nettingi*
Four-toed salamander *Hemidactylium scutatum*		
Mudpuppy *Necturus maculosus maculosus*		
Eastern newt *Notophthalmus viridescens*		
Redback salamander *Plethodon cinereus*		
American toad *Bufo americanus americanus*		
Eastern gray treefrog *Hyla versicolor*		
Northern spring peeper *Pseudacris crucifer crucifer*		
Western chorus frog *Pseudacris triseriata triseriata*		
Bullfrog *Rana catesbeiana*		
Green frog *Rana clamitans melanota*		
Pickerel frog *Rana palustris*		
Northern leopard frog *Rana pipiens*		
Mink frog *Rana septentrionalis*		
Wood frog *Rana sylvatica*		

*All the tertiary invaders occur only in the southern part of the Lower Peninsula of Michigan today and exist in peripheral or isolated populations.

adapted for mixed coniferous-broadleaf forest situations; and (3) tertiary invaders adapted to exist in broadleaf forest areas. It is noteworthy that these tertiary invaders are today all restricted to the southern part of the Lower Peninsula of Michigan and are represented by peripheral or isolated populations (Table 2-1).

The Mason-Quimby Line

The Mason-Quimby Line (Fig. 2-1) is an important physiographic and biotic boundary in Michigan, as it roughly divides the coniferous and mixed coniferous-broadleaf forests of the Upper Peninsula from the broadleaf forests of the Lower Peninsula (Holman 1992). No authentic records of Pleistocene vertebrates are known from north of the Mason-Quimby Line, probably because this preglacial area never developed enough stable Pleistocene interglacial communities to support a sufficient number of vertebrate species to contribute to the fossil record.

Three amphibian species, rare in Michigan today, are restricted to areas south of the Mason-Quimby Line (Table 2-1). These are the marbled salamander (*Ambystoma opacum*), the smallmouth salamander (*Ambystoma texanum*), and the western lesser siren (*Siren intermedia nettingi*). On the other hand, the wood frog is restricted to regions north of the line and occurs only in the Upper Peninsula (Table 2-1).

The Recolonizers

It is suggested that the wood frog, which is able to tolerate tundra conditions today, may have been the first primary species to invade postglacial Michigan as the great mass of sterile, glacially derived mud and sand gave way to tundra vegetation between 14,800 and 13,000 yr B.P. Other primary forms (Table 2-1) probably invaded southern Michigan about 12,500 yr B.P. as the first spruce forests developed and later (ca. 11,800 yr B.P.) as jack and red pine communities began to develop. Primary species probably did not reach the Upper Peninsula until at least 9900 yr B.P. as glacial ice retreated to rim the northern border of the area.

Secondary invaders (Table 2-1) probably began to enter southern Michigan about 10,600 yr B.P. as mixed coniferous-broadleaf forests began to develop in the southern part of the state. The entrance of tertiary invaders (Table 2-1) probably began with the establishment of mixed hardwood forests in southern Michigan about 9900 yr B.P. and persisted through the warming period that lasted until about 2500 yr B.P.

The Fossil Record

Pre-Late Wisconsinan Evidence

Unfortunately, pre-Late Wisconsinan evidence is mainly lacking in the Great Lakes states, making it difficult to set the stage for Late Wisconsinan amphibian interpretations. Nevertheless, the Hopwood Farm locality in Montgomery County in south-central Illinois (King and Saunders 1986) indirectly indicates that the amphibian and reptile fauna of the Sangamonian were probably well developed. The Sangamonian horizon of this locality yielded the remains of a giant land tortoise (*Geochelone crassiscutata*), which strongly suggests that above-freezing temperatures occurred there throughout most of the year (King and Saunders 1986). By additional implication, one would expect a diverse herpetofauna for the area during Sangamonian times (Holman 1992). Certainly, the later advances of the Wisconsinan ice masses must have altered the picture considerably.

Late Wisconsinan Evidence, ca. 14,500 yr B.P.

Prairie Creek D Site, Daviess County, Indiana. At Prairie Creek D (Fig. 2-3; ca. 14,500 yr B.P.), the ice margin may have been as close as the northeastern part of Indiana (Fig. 2-2), yet the herpetofauna was quite diverse (Holman and Richards 1993). Most of the reptiles and some of the amphibians of this fauna must have recolonized southwestern Indiana rather rapidly from more southern areas, for during the 21,000 to 20,000 yr B.P. interval, the ice margin was as near as 95 kilometers from the Prairie Creek D site, south of Indianapolis in northern Morgan and Johnson Counties (Fig. 2-2). One would certainly expect the vegetation at the time of the 21,000 to 20,000 yr B.P. advance, and even as late as the 14,800 yr B.P. advance (Fig. 2-2), to have been boreal forest (Delcourt et al. 1983), an environment that would have been inhabitable by only a few cold-adapted herpetological species.

The Prairie Creek D amphibian fauna consists of one salamander and five anurans, namely *Ambystoma* sp., an otherwise unidentified toad (*Bufo* sp.), the bullfrog (*Rana catesbeiana*), the green frog (*Rana clamitans melanota*), the northern leopard frog (*Rana pipiens*), and the wood frog. All four amphibians identified to the specific level are considered to be primary invaders of postglacial Michigan (Holman 1992) and may be found in areas with substantial coniferous vegetation today.

Figure 2-3. Location of Pleistocene amphibian sites discussed in the text: PC—Prairie Creek D, Daviess County, Indiana (14,500 yr B.P.); CB—Christensen Bog, Hancock County, Indiana (13,000 to 11,700 yr B.P.); SP—Sheriden Pit, Wyandot County, Ohio (11,700 yr B.P.); SM—Shelton Mastodon, Oakland County, Michigan (12,300 to 11,700 yr B.P.); WW—Water Well, St. Clair County, Michigan (ca. 13,000 yr B.P.).

Late Wisconsinan Evidence, 13,000 to 11,700 yr B.P.

Christensen Bog Mastodon Site, Hancock County, Indiana. A limited glimpse of herpetological life in central Indiana ca. 13,000 to 11,700 yr B.P. is provided by the Christensen Bog Mastodon Site Bone Bed Qmp3 Zone, Hancock County, Indiana (Fig. 2-3). This herpetofauna was reported by Graham et al. (1983) and lies just southwest of the Union City Moraine, which is correlated with the 14,800 yr B.P. ice advance. Thus, one would expect that Hancock County, Indiana, would have been tundralike at 14,800 yr B.P. and practically uninhabitable for any herpetological species.

Nevertheless, by Christensen Bog time, when the ice front was probably situated in the northern part of lower Michigan and in southern Ontario (Fig. 2-2), a frog and three species of turtles inhabited the area. The northern leopard frog today occurs northward into areas with significant amounts of coniferous vegetation and was considered to be a primary invader of postglacial Michigan by Holman (1992).

Water Well Site, St. Clair County, Michigan. A record of the American toad (*Bufo americanus americanus*) in St. Clair County, Michigan (Fig. 2-3), from a water well excavation was reported by Holman (1988). This occurrence is of considerable interest if the interpretation of its age is correct. The specimen was found below lake sediments that are thought to represent those of Glacial Lake Whittlesey and thus is probably a little older than 13,000 yr B.P. Considering the ice front advances in Michigan (Fig. 2-2), this specimen could be interpreted as indicating a quite rapid reinvasion of previously ice-covered land by American toads, as well as an occurrence relatively near the ice margin.

Shelton Mastodon Site, Oakland County, Michigan. The Shelton Mastodon site (Fig. 2-3) has been radiocarbon dated as 12,300 to 11,700 yr B.P. and has yielded a frog scapula and an ilium. These bones were reported as an otherwise unidentified frog (*Rana* sp.) by Holman (1988). DeFauw and Shoshani (1991) identified the scapula as from the green frog and the ilium as from the bullfrog. Holman (1992) suggested that the Shelton scapula and ilium both represent the green frog. Ice covered the Shelton site region at the 14,800 yr B.P. interval; as recently as 12,900 yr B.P., the glacier was as close to Oakland County, Michigan, as to Tuscola, Huron, and Sanilac Counties in the "thumb" area of Michigan (Fig. 2-2). The Shelton Mastodon site thus indicates a rather rapid reinvasion of a *Rana* species into a formerly glaciated area.

Sheriden Pit Site, Wyandot County, Ohio. The Sheriden Pit site (Fig. 2-3) in northwestern Ohio (Holman 1995) yielded a fossil herpetofauna that is placed at about 11,700 yr B.P. on the basis of several radiocarbon dates of bone and organic material from a partially stratified cave site. All of the amphibians and reptiles found at the Sheriden Pit site (see below) occur in northern Ohio today. This site has provided by far the largest Pleistocene amphibian fauna in the entire Great Lakes basin and in the midwestern states.

Amphibian species from the Sheriden Pit site include one salamander and at least nine anurans: the blue-spotted salamander (*Ambystoma laterale* complex), the American toad, Fowler's toad (*Bufo woodhousii fowleri*), an unidentified toad, the chorus frog (*Pseudacris triseriata*), the bullfrog, the green frog, the leopard frog, the wood frog, and an unidentified frog (*Rana* sp.). Seven of these amphibians are considered to be primary invaders of postglacial Michigan whose ecological tolerances include coniferous forest and, in one case (the wood frog), tundra areas. Fowler's toad is considered to be a secondary invader adapted for mixed coniferous-broadleaf situations.

At 14,800 yr B.P., ice still covered northwestern Ohio, but by 11,700 yr B.P. the ice margin had moved north to the upper part of the Lower Peninsula of Michigan and southern Ontario (Fig. 2-2). Thus, the reinvasion of this rather large number of amphibian species must have taken place within at least 2,400 years. The amphibian fauna, however, was one that could have tolerated coniferous or mixed coniferous-deciduous forest environments.

Remarks

A model for the postglacial Pleistocene reinvasion of amphibians (and reptiles) in Michigan based mainly on the distribution and ecological tolerances of modern animals correlated with the pollen-documented development of postglacial vegetation is reviewed in the light of this fossil record. Three categories of invading amphibians (and reptiles) were suggested by Holman (1992): (1) primary invaders whose ecological tolerances include coniferous forest and, in one case, tundra areas; (2) secondary invaders adapted for mixed coniferous-broadleaf forest situations; and (3) tertiary invaders adapted to exist in broadleaf forest areas (Table 2-1).

Does the fossil record bear out the model? In Michigan, Ohio, and Indiana, the amphibians that have been identified from postglacial Pleistocene deposits consist entirely of primary invaders, with the exception of the secondary invader, Fowler's toad, which occurs in the Sheriden Pit site fauna in northwestern Ohio. Thus, it would appear that the fossil record in Michigan, Ohio, and Indiana would support at least the primary invader category of the Michigan model.

Are there any aspects of this work that might be used to reflect on movements of modern amphibians in the Midwest? Let us suppose that, for a variety of reasons, future amphibian populations become extirpated from large geographic areas. At what rate might we expect amphibian populations to recolonize such areas? Perhaps a consideration of Pleistocene reinvasion patterns as analogs for such events might be in order. A rather unsophisticated estimate from the midwestern fossil record follows.

Four species of anurans—the bullfrog, green frog, wood frog, and northern leopard frog—co-occur in the Prairie Creek D site (ca. 14,500 yr B.P.) in southwest Indiana (Fig. 2-3) and in the Sheriden Pit site (ca. 11,700 yr B.P.) in northwest Ohio (Fig. 2-3). The latitudinal difference between the two sites is about 280 kilometers. Assuming that these populations represent the earliest amphibian reinvaders in each area, reinvasion movement would be about 0.1 kilometer per year (distance in kilometers divided by difference in number of years [2800]). This would indicate it took an average of about 1,000 years for the four frog species to move 100 kilometers northward during postglacial times. As crude as this estimate may be, it does indicate that it might take *groups* of amphibian species a considerable length of time to recolonize a large area naturally , in fact many human lifetimes.

This slow rate may indirectly argue for modern reintroduction by humans, as no one wishes to wait several generations for animals to find suitable habitats. But it should be pointed out that Pleistocene recolonization may reflect habitat reestablishment time rather than possible rates of amphibian movements. On the other hand, postglacial recolonizations were probably accomplished in uninterrupted habitats rather than in the fragmented landscapes that occur today, and fossil sites in Michigan indicate that rather rapid reinvasions of *individual* species of amphibians (e.g., the American toad and the green frog) might have occurred.

Summary

A model for amphibian recolonization of Michigan in the postglacial Pleistocene is reexamined in the light of fossil evidence in Michigan, Ohio, and Indiana. The three categories of invaders recognized in the model are: (1) primary invaders whose ecological tolerances include tundra and coniferous forest; (2) secondary invaders adapted for mixed coniferous-broadleaf forest situations; and (3) tertiary invaders adapted to exist in broadleaf forest areas. Pleistocene amphibians from sites ranging in age from about 14,500 to about 11,700 yr B.P. in Michigan, Ohio, and Indiana yielded primary invaders with one exception, Fowler's toad (*Bufo woodhousii fowleri*), a secondary invader, from a site in northwestern Ohio. An estimate of recolonization time based on a comparison of radiocarbon-dated sites in southwestern Indiana and northwestern Ohio indicates that four species of ranid frogs moved northward at a rate of about 100 kilometers per 1,000 years in the postglacial Pleistocene. This slow rate may indirectly argue for modern repatriation efforts by humans, although Pleistocene recolonization may reflect habitat reestablishment rather than potential rates of amphibian movement. Postglacial recolonizations were probably accomplished in uninterrupted habitats rather than in the fragmented landscapes that occur today.

3

Amphibian Habitat in the Midwestern United States

Kenneth S. Mierzwa

The five-state region within the Central Division of the Declining Amphibian Population Task Force (Illinois, Indiana, Iowa, Missouri, and Ohio) includes eastern forests, western grasslands, and small areas of southern coastal plain swamps. Because of the resulting habitat diversity, thirty-four species of salamanders (25 percent of the country's total) and twenty-five species of frogs and toads (29 percent of the total) occur within the region.

Most authors writing state-level accounts of midwestern herpetofauna have, at some level, addressed habitat. Smith (1961) included a map of the "herpetofaunal divisions of Illinois" as part of a detailed discussion of factors controlling the distribution of amphibians and reptiles. This discussion was based in part on an earlier article by Smith and Minton (1957), which examined the biogeography of the herpetofauna of Indiana and Illinois. Minton (1972) briefly discussed physiography and other habitat features in the introduction to his first Indiana book. Pfingsten and Downs (1989) included chapters on geology and physiography in their publication on Ohio salamanders.

However, classification of habitat is more problematic. Published articles on amphibian field research often do not identify habitat type(s) or do so only in general terms. Even fewer studies discuss the quality of habitat(s) at the research site. Why is it important to classify and describe habitat accurately? There are a number of reasons.

The type, quality, and amount of habitat exert a profound influence on the richness, composition, diversity, and equitability of amphibians at any given location. An old-growth forest is likely to support more amphibians, both in number of species and number of individuals, than a young successional stand in the same geographic area. Welsh and Lind (1991) documented the numerous habitat variables influencing the distribution of the northern California–Oregon coast range herpetofauna. Many of the same principles apply in the Midwest, although in general they have not been as thoroughly studied.

When the number of species and number of individuals are plotted on the two axes of a rank/abundance graph, a log-normal distribution is thought to characterize a mature and diverse habitat (Magurran 1988). In such a situation, a few species are abundant, most are of intermediate abundance, and some are rare. However, degraded situations such as urban vacant lots often support a skewed distribution, with a few common species and little else. This is perhaps an extreme example of a degraded habitat, but even moderately degraded sites have altered species composition, with resulting changes in predator-prey and competitive interactions. Conducting a study of amphibians in a second-growth forest may provide useful data, but it will not necessarily reflect predisturbance conditions. Studies conducted at high-quality remnants of natural communities, particularly at larger sites, can provide valuable baseline data for studies on declining amphibians. The concept of utilizing undisturbed or least-disturbed sites as a baseline for comparison with other sites is not new. For example, it is a common botanical practice and has been incorporated by ichthyologists into the Index of Biotic Integrity (IBI), a metric used to assess the biological quality of streams and rivers (Karr et al. 1986; Karr 1991).

Of course, pristine habitats are all too rare today. About 60 percent of Illinois was once grassland, but only 0.01 percent of the original prairie remains (Illinois Department of Energy and Natural Resources 1994). Most of the remnants are small and isolated, and there is no place in the state where one can stand within a prairie without seeing the influence of humans. High-quality oak savanna is perhaps among the rarest ecosystems in the world (Botts et al. 1994), although brush-choked or otherwise degraded oak groves are common enough. Other ecosystems have suffered nearly as badly (Whitney 1994). The overwhelming majority of the midwestern landscape consists of second-growth woods, successional fields, farmland, and developed land. Surviving elements of the herpetofauna consist of some portion of the species once present on the pre-Euro-American settlement landscape. Biogeographic patterns are explainable only within the context of the habitat types that once dominated an area. A thorough understanding of habitat and an ability to describe that habitat in a standardized or at least widely understood format are necessary before recovery plans can be written, conservation strategies implemented, and restorations begun. In today's fragmented landscape, restoration may be the key to long-term survival for many species.

I attempt to summarize our current knowledge of amphibian habitat, highlight recent advances in our understanding, and provide an extensive list of literature citations so that a worker in a particular state or region can quickly identify relevant references. Before describing midwestern habitats and methods of classifying them, it is necessary to define a few terms. Ecologists often employ a hierarchical method of describing the world around them (Noss and Cooperrider 1994). Starting with the big picture and moving through a successively finer sequence of subsets, commonly used levels include landscape, ecosystem, community, species, population, individual, and genetic (see also Krzysik, Chpt. 42, this volume). Not everyone agrees on which of these terms should be included within a hierarchy, and not everyone uses the same definition of limits for each term.

For the following discussion, I will define "*landscape*" from a regional perspective as large functional units that share some geological and biological features. Similarly, Forman and Godron (1986) define *landscape* as a "heterogenous land area composed of a cluster of interacting ecosystems that is repeated in similar form throughout" (see also Krzysik, Chpt. 42, this volume).

An *ecosystem* may occur at a variety of scales and typically is based on both biotic and abiotic factors. Processes, such as the flow of energy through the system, are often emphasized at the ecosystem level (Noss and Cooperrider 1994).

Communities consist of discrete assemblages of plants and animals. Communities may be a few square meters or a few hectares in size. Abiotic factors such as substrate type and hydrology may be used to help describe communities, but communities are usually identified by the presence of certain characteristic or dominant plant species. A community may also be defined by the presence of a unique assemblage of animal species. Specific amphibian collecting sites are often described or categorized at the community level.

The concepts of species, populations, and individuals are clear enough. These are the units herpetologists typically study, such as a species of salamander throughout its range or a population or an individual of a particular species of frog.

The following discussion begins with a landscape-level overview, useful for understanding similar study sites over a region including portions of one or more states. This section is intended to help explain why the distributions of some amphibians coincide with regional landscape features. Sources are then provided for standard community classifications, which are often appropriate for use at one or a few specific study sites within a small geographic area. Finally, the implications of understanding habitat for amphibian ecology and conservation are presented.

Landscape

Early attempts to identify landscape-level units typically emphasized physical features. The resulting maps of physiographic provinces identified units such as the Allegheny Plateau, the Interior Lowland, and the Ozark Plateau (Fenneman 1938). More detailed physiographic maps are also available for Illinois (Leighton et al. 1948), Indiana (Malott 1922), Iowa (Prior 1991), Missouri (Collier 1955), and Ohio (Pfingsten and Downs 1989).

A number of attempts have been made to map major vegetation types, sometimes referred to as biomes or ecosystems, on a regional or national level (Braun 1950; Barbour and Billings 1988; Kuchler 1964). All of the national vegetation maps suffer shortcomings related to scale, resolution, and other factors. The Kuchler (1964) map is the most detailed of those cited here. It maps "potential" natural vegetation; in practice, this means the regional climax community that would theoretically develop under optimal conditions. It does not account for the effects of major ecosystem-level forces, such as fire or other natural disturbance, and does not address local complexity induced by variation in abiotic factors, such as topography, slope aspect, substrate depth and type, or microclimate.

Keys et al. (1995), Bailey (1994), Omernik (1987), and Omernik and Gallant (1988) expanded this concept by grouping units of related physiography, climate, vegetation, and animals. The resulting maps of ecoregions are useful tools and are among the few nationwide systems of landscape-level classification based on both biotic and abiotic factors. The ecoregion concept is used by a variety of government agencies, including the U.S. Environmental Protection Agency, the U.S. Forest Service, and the Ohio Environmental Protection Agency. Ecoregions are a useful tool for biologists working across large geographic areas or in more than one state.

Natural divisions are similar to ecoregions but are typically mapped at a statewide level and are considerably more detailed (Iffrig and Bowles 1983). They are a powerful descriptive device when studies are entirely within one state or region. Natural division maps are available for Illinois (Schwegman 1973), Indiana (Homoya et al. 1985), Missouri (Thom and Wilson 1980), Ohio (Anderson 1983), and the Chicago region (twenty-two counties in parts of Illinois, Indiana, Michigan, and Wisconsin [Swink and Wilhelm 1994]).

The following discussion emphasizes major terrestrial features, perhaps best described by Albert et al. (1986) as "Regional Landscape Ecosystems," based on the maps cited above. Wetland, aquatic, and other community types that commonly occur within a given ecosystem are briefly discussed, but additional community types are frequently present. Characteristic amphibian species are given for each ecosystem, but many other species are present as widespread generalists or specialists in particular communities.

Mixed mesophytic forest is a diverse ecosystem with affinities to the prehistoric Arcto-Tertiary forests that covered much of North America in Miocene times. Centered in southeastern Kentucky (Martin 1992) and today best represented in the sheltered coves of the Great Smoky Mountains, this forest type extends west into the unglaciated Allegheny Plateau of Ohio. There is no clear dominant species in the tree canopy, although beech, tulip tree, yellow buckeye, sugar maple, white basswood, red oak, white oak, white ash, red elm, hemlock, and other species are usually present (Martin 1992; Braun 1989). Chestnut was often present before it was nearly exterminated by a bark disease in the 1920s (Gordon 1969). Old-growth stands of mixed mesophytic forest are characterized by high species richness and diversity, an uneven age structure with several size classes of trees present, the presence of large and old trees, numerous snags and downed logs in various stages of decay, and light gaps caused by windthrow (Martin 1992).

Because of the diverse topography of the Allegheny Plateau, there is considerable variation in forest composition. Mixed mesophytic forest occurs in sheltered coves and ravines and on north- and east-facing slopes. Higher elevation slopes often support oak forests, xeric pine stands are sometimes present on exposed ridgetops, and riparian forests follow the high-gradient streams and rivers that are typical of the region. A variety of other plant communities are interspersed within the mesophytic forest and function as part of the overall ecosystem (Whittaker 1956). Although old-growth examples of mixed mesophytic forest are relatively rare, as much as 70 percent of the unglaciated Allegheny Plateau is forested. Numerous mature second-growth forests exist (Martin 1992) and if properly managed will continue to provide amphibian habitat. Red salamanders (*Pseudotriton ruber*), spring salamanders (*Gyrinophilus porphyriticus*), Wehrle's salamanders (*Plethodon wehrlei*), and mountain chorus frogs (*Pseudacris brachyphona*) are characteristic amphibians of this ecosystem.

A slightly less diverse ecosystem referred to as western mesophytic forest extends through parts of southern Indiana and into extreme southeastern Illinois. It supports most of the same characteristic trees, but usually fewer species are present on any single site. Green salamanders (*Aneides aeneus*) and streamside salamanders (*Ambystoma barbouri*) occur within this ecosystem.

Northern hardwood forest, characterized by hemlock, white pine, red maple, yellow birch, and American beech, barely enters the region in northeastern Ohio, although it is widespread in adjacent Pennsylvania (Rooney 1995; Whitney 1990; Braun 1989). Mountain dusky salamanders (*Desmognathus ochrophaeus*) occur in the northern hardwood forest region.

Oak-chestnut forest, also called Appalachian oak forest, covers much of eastern Ohio just south of the northern hardwood forest region. Chestnut is no longer present as a canopy tree, and the ecosystem today is comprised largely of various oak species (Stephenson et al. 1993), especially white oak, chestnut oak, and northern red oak. The amphibian fauna is similar to that of the mixed mesophytic forest region.

Beech-maple forest was once the most widespread of the eastern forest types in the region, covering much of Ohio and Indiana (Parker 1989; Yahner 1995). It was best developed on relatively level mesic soils. Because little light penetrates the tree canopy, old-growth forests dominated by beech and sugar maple have a sparse understory, except for a profusion of early spring wildflowers, which bloom before the tree leaves have fully opened. Although beech-maple forests historically covered a vast area, they were far from homogenous. It has been estimated that in pre-Euro-American settlement times, about 70 percent of the eastern forest consisted of old growth, with the balance in various successional stages (Lorimer and Frelich 1994). Disturbances occurred as large-scale but relatively rare events, such as tornadoes or blowdowns, or more commonly as small gaps created by the death of one or a few large trees (Runkle 1982, 1991). In addition, wetlands occupied poorly drained low areas. These frequently were swamps, but other wetland types were present as well.

Several good examples of old-growth beech-maple forest have been preserved, including Shrader-Weaver Nature Preserve in Fayette County, Indiana. Characteristic amphibians of beech-maple forests include spotted salamanders (*Ambystoma maculatum*), redback salamanders (*Plethodon cinereus*), and wood frogs (*Rana sylvatica*). A sugar maple and basswood variant occurs in northeastern Iowa and extreme northern Illinois but does not always support the characteristic amphibians because of its peripheral location.

Unlike the preceding forest types, which usually were closed canopied or nearly so except for small light gaps, oak-hickory woodland was probably more variable in density and cover. "Woodland" is defined here as including a range of canopy cover, from 30 to 70 percent (Botts et al. 1994). Most oak-dominated woodlands burned occasionally (Ladd 1991), and the frequency of fire influenced both tree density and the shrub layer (Bowles et al. 1994). Ladd (1991) made a compelling case that oak-hickory woodlands were once much more open than they are today. He quoted numerous accounts by early settlers and historians, including Houck (1908), who described the Missouri Ozarks as "open woods and a growth of wild prairie grasses and flowers filling the broad spaces between the trees . . . all the forests were free from undergrowth, and open and park like in appearance."

Within a few decades of Euro-American settlement, fire suppression had allowed the oak-hickory woodlands to grow into dense, closed canopy forests. One of the very few intact examples of the natural condition is on Walpole Island in Lake St. Clair, Ontario, Canada, where Native Americans still burn the woods (G. Wilhelm, personal communication).

Oak-hickory woodlands were once widespread throughout the region. Most extensive in western Indiana, the Shawnee Hills of southern Illinois, and the Missouri Ozarks, they occurred as smaller, community-level entities in all states. In Ohio and Indiana, oak-hickory woodlands were common on well-drained slopes. In Iowa, much of Illinois, and northern Missouri, examples were found along river bluffs. In general, sites in the eastern part of the region are more mesic than those in the west (Shifley and Schlesinger 1994). Characteristic amphibians include eastern tiger salamanders (*Ambystoma tigrinum tigrinum*) and northern and western slimy salamanders (*Plethodon glutinosus* and *Plethodon albagula*, respectively).

Variants referred to as flatwoods occur on postglacial lacustrine beds, where claypan soils support stunted oaks and numerous vernal ponds. In the northern part of the region, blue-spotted salamanders (*Ambystoma laterale*) reach their maximum abundance in flatwoods characterized by swamp white oak. In southwestern Indiana and southern Illinois north of Shawnee Hills, southern flatwoods with pin oak and shingle oak are widespread. Smallmouth salamanders (*Ambystoma texanum*) are common.

Oak-pine woodlands were once widespread on the Ozark Plateau of southern Missouri. Characterized by shortleaf pine and post oak, this fire-maintained community was relatively open, with a grassy understory (Skeen et al. 1993; D. Ladd, personal communication). An excellent example can be seen at Hawn State Park, about 90 kilometers south of St. Louis.

The oak-pine areas are relatively xeric and often occur on poor soil or thin soil over bedrock; as a result, relatively few amphibians occur on uplands. However, this hilly region is cut by numerous high-gradient streams and deep, shaded ravines that support moist forest. These areas support a variety of interesting amphibians, including longtail salamanders (*Eurycea longicauda*), many-ribbed salamanders (*Eurycea multiplicata*), southern redback salamanders (*Plethodon serratus*), and western slimy salamanders. Pond breeders such as ringed salamanders (*Ambystoma annulatum*) also occur here.

Oak savanna has been used to describe a wide range of partially wooded communities; Botts et al. (1994) and Eiten (1986, 1992) discuss this issue at length. In a broad sense, a savanna is "any area where scattered trees and/or shrubs and other large persistent plants occur over a continuous and permanent groundlayer visually dominated by herbs, usually graminoids" (Botts et al. 1994). Here the term is used to distinguish the more open end of the continuum, areas with a tree or shrub canopy cover from 5 to about 30 percent. These are the areas often described by the early surveyors as "scattering timber." Savannas were maintained in an open condition by frequent fire, and good examples of this community are extremely rare today.

Savannas once occurred in all of the states in the region (Nuzzo 1985). Middle Fork Savanna, in Lake Forest, Illinois, is one of the very few intact black-soil savannas surviving today. Restoration efforts are under way on several overgrown savannas (Packard 1993). Good-quality sand savannas are more common, and in Missouri a few savannas persist on thin soils over bedrock.

Because of the rarity of high-quality savannas, little is known about the original amphibian assemblage. Elements of the savanna fauna frequently persist on the periphery of overgrown oak groves and were called forest-edge species by earlier authors. At Middle Fork Savanna, blue-spotted salamanders, tiger salamanders, American toads (*Bufo americanus americanus*), western chorus frogs (*Pseudacris triseriata triseriata*), and northern leopard frogs (*Rana pipiens*) are the most common amphibians. In midwestern sand savannas the eastern tiger salamander is usually the only salamander, although a variety of frogs and toads may be present. Illinois chorus frogs (*Pseudacris streckeri illinoensis*) frequently occur in the sand savannas of west-central Illinois (see Tucker, Chpt. 14; Brandon and Ballard, Chpt. 15; Brown and Cima, Chpt. 30, this volume).

Prairie occurs in all five states within the region, although in Indiana it is mostly limited to the northwestern and west-central parts of the state and in Ohio is present only as isolated openings. These eastern openings are thought to be remnants of a prairie peninsula (Transeau 1935) that extended into and possibly beyond Ohio during the warmer hypsithermal period several thousand years ago.

Mesic prairie is characterized by big bluestem and Indian grass. On drier prairies, including those on sand, little bluestem is usually common. Prairies are fire-adapted communities and burned frequently in pre-Euro-American settlement times (Higgins 1986). Grazing by bison and native ungulates may once have been an important ecological process on western prairies (Ryan 1990).

In northwestern Iowa, prairie was once the dominant ecosystem. In the remainder of Iowa, northern and western Missouri, and much of central and northern Illinois, vast prairies were dotted with scattered oak groves. Marshes and sedge meadows were common, especially in the more northern areas covered by the Wisconsinan glaciation.

Unfortunately, almost all of the prairie fell to the plow during the early days of Euro-American settlement. Most of the remnants are small, although a few larger sites remain in the western part of the region. Cayler Prairie, in Dickinson County, Iowa, includes a variety of glacial landforms, such as eskers, knobs, and kettles, which form prairie pothole wetlands. Hayden Prairie, in Howard County, Iowa, is the largest prairie remnant in the state at just under 100 hectares (Iowa State Preserves Board 1981). Amphibians commonly encountered on prairies include plains leopard frogs (*Rana blairi*), northern leopard frogs, Woodhouse's toads (*Bufo woodhousii woodhousii*), American toads, and chorus frogs. Blanchard's cricket frog (*Acris crepitans blanchardi*) inhabits the banks of prairie streams and permanent ponds.

Wetlands generally occurred as community-level inclusions within the terrestrial ecosystems described here. However, there were at least three exceptions large enough to map at a regional level.

Swamps characterized by American elm, black ash, and red maple once covered a vast area in northwestern Ohio and northeastern Indiana on the bed of former glacial Lake Maumee (Homoya et al. 1985). The amphibian fauna was influenced by the surrounding beech-maple forest.

A large area of marsh once existed in the Kankakee River valley of northwestern Indiana and adjacent Illinois (Meyer 1936). Probably consisting of bulrush, sedges, and a variety of emergent and aquatic plants (Homoya et al. 1985), marshes were utilized by many of the amphibians present on adjacent sand savannas and sand prairies. Degraded remnants have been preserved at Jasper-Pulaski Fish and Wildlife Area, near Medaryville, Indiana (see Brodman and Kilmurry, Chpt. 17, this volume).

Bottomland hardwood forest, also known as southern floodplain forest, is associated with riparian borders of rivers and streams and is subject to occasional frequent flooding (Sharitz and Mitsch 1993). The bottomland hardwood forest ecosystem is characteristic of the southeastern coastal plain and barely enters the southern fringe of the region. Characteristic trees include bald cypress, water tupelo, and a variety of oaks. Within this area, bottomland hardwood forest is most common in the Missouri bootheel and in extreme southern Illinois and extends up the Ohio and Wabash River valleys into extreme southwestern Indiana. Excellent examples can be seen at Big Oak Tree State Park in Mississippi County, Missouri, and at Heron Pond–Little Black Slough near Vienna, Illinois. Several Gulf Coast amphibians, including mole salamanders (*Ambystoma talpoideum*), bird-voiced treefrogs (*Hyla avivoca*), green treefrogs (*Hyla cinerea*), and three-toed amphiumas (*Amphiuma tridactylum*), occur within this area.

Community Classification

Community classifications usually consider vegetation physiognomy or structure (forest, savanna, prairie), dominant or characteristic species of plants, and soil moisture (wet, mesic, dry-mesic). Substrate type is also important. Thus, dry-mesic sand savanna, wet dolomite prairie, and mesic upland forest are all community types (see also Krzysik, Chpt. 42, this volume). Additional information on habitat classification can be obtained from the staff of state natural heritage programs, which are usually part of the state's Department of Natural Resources or Department of Conservation, or from The Nature Conservancy.

National and Regional Community Classification Systems

Various attempts have been made to compile regional, national, and international community classifications. An international classification was published by UNESCO (1973), and Driscoll et al. (1984) compiled a United States classification.

National Wetland Inventory (NWI) maps are another readily available nationwide resource. NWI maps are based on interpretation of aerial photographs (see Krzysik, Chpt. 42, this volume) and are available as overlays on U.S. Geological Survey 7.5' topographic quadrangles. Wetlands are clearly marked and identified to type by a hierarchical system. Unlike most other classifications, the NWI is based primarily on hydrology, and vegetation is considered only at lower hierarchical levels. Because so many amphibians are dependant on wetlands for breeding, NWI maps can be used not only to classify habitat but also to quickly locate potential amphibian localities in unfamiliar regions. As with most systems based on remote sensing, there are limitations to the accuracy of NWI maps. The NWI system is explained in detail by Cowardin et al. (1979).

The Nature Conservancy has provided regional classifications, including one for the Midwest Region (Faber-Langendoen 1993; Ambrose et al. 1994). An example of one community type from Faber-Langendoen (1993) is given below. This classification is hierarchical; the physiognomic category—in this case woodland-grassland, or WG (a descriptive term for oak savanna)—is further subdivided into categories defined by dominant or characteristic vegetation. It is then "crosswalked," or cross-referenced with equivalent designations from state heritage programs:

WG 4 = Bur oak–mixed oak–big bluestem opening)
IA Bur oak–mixed oak opening
IL Dry-mesic savanna
IL Mesic savanna
MO Dry, dry-mesic savanna
OH Oak savanna

State Community Classification Systems

Illinois. The community classification developed for the Illinois Natural Areas Inventory (White and Madany 1978) is the standard system in use statewide. Some workers have modified the system slightly to account for recent advances in the understanding of savanna and woodland communities. Discussions of northeastern Illinois natural communities are included in Swink and Wilhelm (1994).

Indiana. The community classification in general use in Indiana is similar to that used in Illinois (J. Bacone, personal communication) but is available only as an unpublished report (Indiana Heritage Program 1995). Homoya et al. (1985) discussed the characteristics of some community types in the context of natural regions. Wilhelm (1990) mapped and described communities in the Indiana Dunes National Lakeshore of northwestern Indiana. Lindsey (1966) includes a coarse-scale statewide plant community map.

Iowa. The Iowa community classification is also unpublished but is available as a database printout (Iowa Natural Areas Inventory 1995; J. Pearson, personal communication). Iowa communities have been cross-referenced with the hierarchical regional system of Faber-Langendoen (1993). Weller (1969) includes a coarse-scale statewide plant community map.

Missouri. Unlike most other states in the region, a Missouri community classification has been published in book form and is readily available (Nelson 1987). The system is generally compatible with those of Illinois and Indiana but places greater emphasis on the variety of bedrock substrates common in the Ozarks.

Ohio. The current Ohio community classification is available only as an unpublished report (Anderson 1982). An older publication by Gordon (1969) includes detailed descriptions of Ohio community characteristics and has a large foldout map of Ohio pre-Euro-American settlement vegetation.

Trends in Community Classification

Most of the classifications described above were constructed on the basis of best professional judgment. A few recent efforts to classify communities have emphasized quantitative techniques based on intensive field sampling, either to improve levels of documentation for Environmental Impact Assessment (Sawyer and Keeler-Wolf 1995) or to enhance conservation strategies (O'Neil et al. 1995). Quantitative classification is most advanced in the western states, but hierarchical quantitative classifications are likely to become increasingly common. Some quantitative classifications are based on dominant or characteristic vegetation identified in sample plots, which may not consider structural factors of great importance to amphibians and other animals (Welsh and Lind 1991). O'Neil et al. (1995) have addressed this issue by correlating a vegetation-based community classification with wildlife habitat relationship (WHR) models. O'Neil et al. (1995) used breeding occurrences of 420 animal species (including twenty-four types of amphibians) to group 130 vegetation types into thirty distinct habitat units. At appropriate scales (Hamel et al. 1986), such correlations may enhance the power of WHR models to predict amphibian occurrences.

Implications for Future Studies

Many amphibians require more than one habitat type to complete their life cycle successfully. For example, breeding may take place in a vernal pond or marsh, while the remainder of the year is spent in an adjacent oak-hickory woodland.

As noted above, landscapes typically consist of a mosaic of interspersed community types. In addition to this spatial variation, it is important to remember that temporal changes occur as well (Baker, Chpt. 1; Holman, Chpt. 2, this volume). Only 12,000 years ago, the northern part of the Midwest was covered by glacial ice. Considerable climate variation has occurred since the glacial retreat, with plant communities responding to warmer, colder, wetter, or drier conditions. Because plant and animal species respond to these changes at different rates (Delcourt and Delcourt 1991), most of our present ecosystems have existed in their current form for not more than a few thousand years. Even on a shorter time scale, variation in precipitation over a few years or decades influenced fire frequency and the location of the prairie-woodland border. Today, the landscape is changing faster than ever, as human development contributes to the fragmentation of remaining natural areas.

Many amphibians occur in metapopulations, a series of populations connected through occasional immigration and emigration (Gilpin and Hanski 1991; Mierzwa 1994a; Cortwright, Chpt. 9; Lannoo, Chpt. 34, this volume). Even in an undisturbed situation, some of these populations undergo periodic extinctions. For example, a series of dry years may result in the loss of populations inhabiting early drying ponds. Ephemeral ponds may be sink habitat and result in a net reproductive loss to the population. Nearby ponds that reliably hold water may be source habitat, providing excess individuals that recolonize sink sites during good reproductive years (Pulliam 1988). Extinctions may also occur through random demographic processes (Meffe and Carroll 1994). Sjögren Gulve (1994) found that isolated frog populations were more likely to undergo stochastic extinctions than those in close proximity to other populations, presumably because of the difference in immigration and emigration rates. These factors must be considered when allocating resources to preserve or restore amphibian habitat. Some locations or boundary configurations may be better able to support viable amphibian metapopulations than others.

Understanding habitat, it is possible to identify the places where limited resources can best be used to preserve biodiversity. Gap analysis is a concept that uses a computerized Geographic Information System (GIS) to map vegetation, topography, existing preserve boundaries, and the distribution of species of interest (Scott et al. 1993; Krzysik, Chpt. 42, this volume). When layers with this information are overlaid, it is possible to identify plant communities or animal species not protected within existing preserves or otherwise at risk (Meffe and Carroll 1994; Strittholt and Boerner 1995). The same maps can be used to identify potential localities to search for particular amphibian species, assuming that the habitat has been well defined. Scott et al. (1993) describe the application of gap analysis; Strittholt and Boerner (1995) describe the use of gap analysis for preservation planning at the Edge of Appalachia, a regional nature reserve in southern Ohio.

If habitat has been defined, populations located, and life history data collected, it becomes possible to predict the effects of different land-use or management scenarios. Spatially explicit models link population models, including demographic data, with landscape-level habitat information, such as GIS maps (Dunning et al. 1995). The effects of different management strategies can then be modeled and the effect on target species predicted. For example, the effects of various logging rotations on a rare salamander can be predicted using a spatially explicit model if adequate demographic information is available and relevant habitat features are well enough understood to be mapped in a meaningful way.

An understanding of habitat can thus be used to understand the causes of some amphibian declines, to anticipate and prevent others, and, through intelligent restoration, to help some species recover. Only by preserving reasonably large expanses of related habitat types can we hope to ensure the long-term survival of the amphibian fauna. Saving one vernal pond may not be enough. Saving several nearby ponds, and the surrounding forest, greatly increases the probability that future generations will be able to enjoy the sound of calling frogs on rainy spring nights.

Summary

Accurate classification of habitat is essential for understanding amphibian distribution, identifying potential inventory or monitoring sites, evaluating factors influencing abundance and long-term trends of amphibian populations, and designing viable conservation plans. I summarize regional landscape and ecosystem-level habitat features that affect amphibian distribution, identify standard community-level classification methods appropriate for use at amphibian study sites, and discuss methods of using habitat classification to enhance amphibian inventory and monitoring efforts and to improve restoration and recovery efforts.

Acknowledgments

I thank Brian Armitage, John Bacone, Don Faber-Langendoen, Lisa Hemesath, Patricia Jones, Doug Ladd, and John Pearson for providing information on ecosystem and community classification; Ellin Beltz, Sue Crispin, Tom Johnson, Victoria Nuzzo, Steve Packard, Wayne Schennum, Jack White, and Gerould Wilhelm for participating in discussions on amphibian habitat; and TAMS Consultants, Inc., for general encouragement.

4

Biogeography of Midwestern Amphibians

Robert Brodman

Most previous works concerning the distributions of amphibians in the midwestern United States have been descriptive (Walker 1946; Smith 1961; Minton 1972; Pentecost and Vogt 1976; Vogt 1981; Johnson 1987; Pfingsten and Downs 1989; Christiansen and Bailey 1991; Harding and Holman 1992; Oldfield and Moriarty 1994). From these studies and others, soil, vegetation, and climatic conditions have been recognized as important extrinsic factors that affect species distributions (Allee and Schmidt 1951; Smith 1961; Minton 1972). Furthermore, the analysis of the distribution of individuals within a species has shown that along many environmental gradients various species show bell-shaped curves or Poisson distributions (Gauch et al. 1974; Redmond 1991). In fact, Kiester (1971) demonstrates that amphibian abundance in North America conforms to a two-dimensional normal distribution centered in the southern Appalachians.

While the above studies are interesting, they are either qualitative or too coarse to be useful when addressing problems of amphibian declines. The assumptions of normality or randomness in a species distribution allow the use of statistical methods to evaluate the effect of physical environmental parameters on the distribution of species and community assemblages (Udvardy 1969). Examinations of climatic data and county distribution records of amphibians by cluster and principal components analyses have been conducted in Illinois (Bock et al. 1981), Colorado (Lambert and Reid 1981), and Michigan (Brodman 1989). However, correlations between environmental parameters and amphibian biogeography have not been tested with statistical rigor on a larger regional scale.

The purposes of this study are to: (1) define and delineate statistically defensible ecoregions in the Midwest based on amphibian distributions and community assemblages; (2) determine the relationship between amphibian biogeography and environmental factors; and (3) use results from this study to make suggestions for amphibian population monitoring programs conducted in the Midwest.

Methods

Species Distributions

Distributions of sixty-one amphibian species in eight midwestern states (Ohio, Michigan, Indiana, Wisconsin, Illinois, Minnesota, Iowa, and Missouri) were obtained from published distributions (Walker 1946; Smith 1961; Minton 1972; Pentecost and Vogt 1976; Vogt 1981; Minton et al. 1982; Johnson 1987; Camper 1988; Pfingsten and Downs 1989; Christiansen and Bailey 1991; Conant and Collins 1991; Harding and Holman 1992; Oldfield and Moriarty 1994) and new records from reports in *Herpetological Review.* A map of the Midwest was then transected into 400 quadrants of equal size (60 by 60 kilometers) by beginning with the northwesternmost tip of Minnesota and then delineating a section eastward and southward every 60 kilometers. Sections completely within a Great Lake were excluded from analysis. The presence (one) or absence (zero) of each species was noted for each section.

Hybrid populations of the Jefferson salamander–blue-spotted salamander (*Ambystoma jeffersonianum –A. laterale*)–polyploid complex were grouped as a separate and single taxon regardless of chromosomal contributions and hypothesized lineage. Likewise, many of the records of the gray treefrog complex (*Hyla chrysoscelis* and *Hyla versicolor*) cannot be distinguished (Bogart and Jaslow 1979; Conant and Collins 1991), and therefore both species have been combined for the purpose of this study.

Environmental Effects

Environmental effects were evaluated as follows. Average annual temperature and precipitation (National Atlas of the United States of America 1970), as well as vegetation type (Kuchler 1964), physical geology (Hammond 1964), ecoregion (Omernik 1986), and river system (National Atlas of the United States of America 1970), were obtained for each of the 400 quadrants.

Statistical Analysis

Biogeographic relationships of amphibian species across quadrants were determined by a hierarchical cluster analysis on the basis of the coefficient of community (Jacard 1902). The coefficient of community (J) is a similarity index that measures the faunal resemblance as the percentage of species occurring in common between pairwise comparisons of quadrants:

$$J = a \times (a + u)^{-1}$$

where a represents the number of species occurring in both sections being compared and u represents the number of species present in one but not both sections. For example, if two clusters share three of four species, J would equal 75 percent. Negative matches (species not found in both locations) were excluded; otherwise, relatively depauperate sections would be deemed highly similar even when no species co-occurred.

To demonstrate hierarchical relationships among quadrants, the cluster analysis uses root mean squared (RMS) distance coefficients to construct a similarity matrix and dendrogram. The RMS values represent distance among clusters, which is both a function of the coefficient of community (J) and the number of species considered from among the compared clusters (with more species giving a lower RMS value for a given level of J). Geographical relationships among clusters of quadrants with high similarities (low RMSs) were determined by applying an analysis of variance (ANOVA) to the similarity matrices. Clusters that differed significantly at the $p \leq 0.05$ level were considered to delineate primary amphibian faunal regions (PAFRs).

The quadrants were also categorized according to environmental data. Co-phenetic correlation coefficients (CCC) were calculated to determine the relationships between RMS distances and environmental parameters. All statistical tests were performed by using SAS (Statistical Analysis System) software. Statistical significance was established at the $p \leq 0.05$ level.

Results

Species Distributions

Results support the formation of eight distinct clusters (Table 4-1; Fig. 4-1). I will refer to these clusters of similarity as PAFRs 1 through 8.

PAFR 1 is the most species-poor region. Located in western Minnesota, PAFR 1 is characterized by flat and irregular plains with cropland and small sections of bluestem and wheatgrass prairie. Nine species of amphibians are the common inhabitants of this region: American toads (*Bufo americanus americanus*), Canadian toads (*Bufo hemiophrys*), Great Plains toads (*Bufo cognatus*), northern leopard frogs (*Rana pipiens*), wood frogs (*Rana sylvatica*), the gray treefrog complex, mudpup-

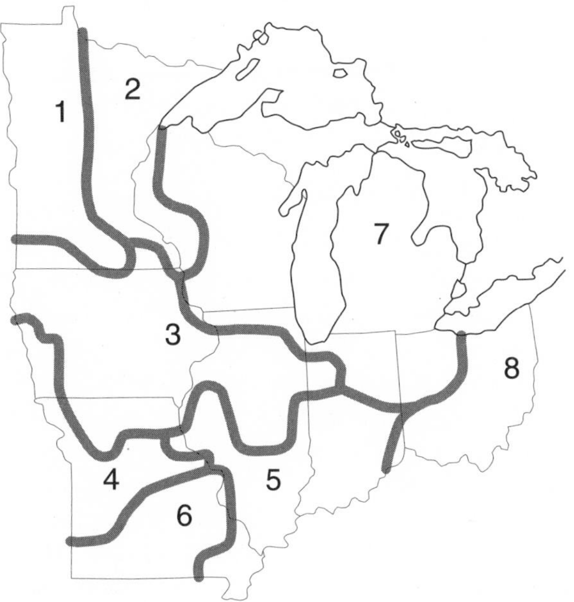

Figure 4-1. Primary amphibian faunal regions (PFARs) in the midwestern United States as defined in the text.

Table 4-1. Hierarchical relationships among PAFRs. Root mean squares (RMS) with significant differences (*) at the $p \leq 0.05$ level

```
                                                          PAFR        Habitat

                 |--------------------------------------   1          Prairie-Plains
            |--  |*
            |    |--------------------------------------   2          Conifer-Plains
      |--   |*
      |     |                    |----------------------   3          Prairie-Plains
      |     |--------------------|*
      |                          |----------------------   4          Prairie-Plains
      |
------|*
      |                       |-------------------------   5          Oak-Hick. Hills–Plains
      |            |----------|*
      |            |          |-------------------------   6          Oak-Hick.-Pine Hills
      |------------|*
                   |             |----------------------   7          N. Hardwood-Plains
                   |-------------|*
                                 |----------------------   8          Mesophytic-Hills

  1.2   1.1    1.0      0.9       0.8      0.7      0.6               RMS
```

pies (*Necturus maculosus*), and eastern tiger salamanders (*Ambystoma tigrinim tigrinum*). Canadian toads are not found in any other PAFR and thus are the indicator species of PFAR 1.

PAFR 2 represents the plains and open hills of eastern Minnesota. This region is vegetated by combinations of cropland, pasture, and northern hardwood forests. Thirteen species typify the amphibian fauna of this region: American toads, the gray treefrog complex, northern spring peepers (*Pseudacris crucifer crucifer*), chorus frogs (*Pseudacris triseriata*), Blanchard's cricket frogs (*Acris crepitans blanchardi*), green frogs (*Rana clamitans melanota*), northern leopard frogs, mink frogs (*Rana septentrionalis*), wood frogs, blue-spotted salamanders, eastern tiger salamanders, and redback salamanders (*Plethodon cinereus*). There are no species unique to this region.

PAFR 3, located in Iowa and central Illinois, is composed of irregular and smooth plains with extensive cropland and natural areas of bluestem prairie, oak-hickory forests, and oak savanna. Sixteen amphibian species are found throughout this area: American toads, Woodhouse's toads (*Bufo woodhousii woodhousii*), spring peeper, chorus frogs, Blanchard's cricket frogs, the gray treefrog complex, green frogs, bullfrogs (*Rana catesbeiana*), northern leopard frogs, pickerel frogs (*Rana palustris*), plains leopard frogs (*Rana blairi*), mudpuppies, eastern newts (*Notophthalmus viridescens*), eastern tiger salamanders, and smallmouth salamanders (*Ambystoma texanum*). All of these species are found in other PAFRs.

PAFR 4 includes the irregular plains of western Iowa and northwestern Missouri. Cropland and pasture intermixed with small sections of bluestem prairie and oak-hickory forests provide habitat for eighteen species of amphibians: plains spadefoot toads (*Spea bombifrons*), Great Plains narrowmouth toads (*Gastrophryne olivacea*), American toads, Woodhouse's toads, Great Plains toads, spring peepers, chorus frogs, Blanchard's cricket frogs, the gray treefrog complex, bullfrogs, plains leopard frogs, northern leopard frogs, southern leopard frogs (*Rana sphenocephala*), crawfish frogs (*Rana areolata*), mudpuppies, eastern tiger salamanders, and smallmouth salamanders. Plains spadefoot toads and narrowmouth toads are endemic indicator species of this region.

PAFR 5 represents southern Indiana and southern Illinois and is characterized by irregular plains, open hills, tablelands, and flat floodplains. Southern (oak-tupelo-cypress) floodplain forest and a mosaic of cropland, pasture, forest, woodland, and swamp provide habitat for at least thirty-four species: eastern spadefoot toads (*Scaphiopus holbrookii*), American toads, Woodhouse's toads, eastern narrowmouth toads (*Gastrophryne carolinensis*), spring peepers, chorus frogs, Illinois chorus frogs (*Pseudacris streckeri illinoensis*), Blanchard's cricket frogs, the gray treefrog complex, green treefrogs (*Hyla cinerea*), bird-voiced treefrogs (*Hyla avivoca*), green frogs, bullfrogs, southern leopard frogs, plains leopard frogs, pickerel frogs, wood frogs, crawfish frogs, western lesser sirens (*Siren intermedia nettingi*), hellbenders (*Cryptobranchus alleganiensis*), mudpuppies, three-toed amphiumas (*Amphiuma tridactylum*), eastern newts, tiger salamanders, smallmouth salamanders, Jefferson salamanders, spotted salamanders (*Ambystoma maculatum*), marbled salamanders (*Ambystoma opacum*), mole salamanders (*Ambystoma talpoidium*), longtail salamanders (*Eurycea longicauda longicauda*), cave salamanders (*Eurycea lucifuga*), redback salamanders (*Plethodon cinereus*), slimy salamanders (*Plethodon glutinosus*), and zigzag salamanders (*Plethodon dorsalis*). Illinois chorus frogs, green treefrogs, bird-voiced treefrogs, three-toed amphiumas, mole salamanders, lesser sirens, and zigzag salamanders are found primarily in this southern region of the Midwest and are indicator species of this region.

PAFR 6 comprises the hills of the Ozarks. Oak-hickory and pine forests along with a mosaic of cropland, pasture, and woodland provide unique habitat for twenty-five amphibian species: eastern narrowmouth toads, American toads, Woodhouse's toads, spring peepers, chorus frogs, Blanchard's cricket frogs, the gray treefrog complex, green frogs, southern leopard frogs, pickerel frogs, hellbenders, mudpuppies, eastern newts, eastern tiger salamanders, ringed salamanders (*Ambystoma annulatum*), spotted salamanders (*Ambystoma maculatum*), marbled salamanders, longtail salamanders, cave salamanders, Oklahoma salamanders (*Eurycea tynerensis*), graybelly salamanders (*Eurycea multiplicata*), grotto salamanders (*Typhlotriton spelaeus*), western slimy salamanders (*Plethodon albagula*), and southern redback salamanders (*Plethodon serratus*). Ringed salamanders, graybelly salamanders, Oklahoma salamanders, grotto salamanders, western slimy salamanders, southern redback salamanders, and the following subspecies—Ozark hellbenders (*Cryptobranchus alleganiensis bishopi*), Red River mudpuppies (*Necturus maculosus louisianensis*), and Ozark zigzag salamanders (*Plethodon dorsalis angusticlavus*)—are endemic to the Ozarks.

The largest in area, PAFR 7 encompasses all of Michigan, most of Wisconsin, and parts of northern Illinois, Indiana, and Ohio. These plains of cropland and pasture interspersed with northern hardwood and spruce-fir forests are typically inhabited by twenty-one species of amphibians: American toads, Fowler's toads (Bufo woodhousii fowleri), chorus frogs, spring peepers, Blanchard's cricket frogs, the gray treefrog complex, green frogs, bullfrogs, pickerel frogs, mink frogs, wood frogs, mudpuppies, eastern newts, *Ambystoma* hybrids, blue-spotted salamanders, smallmouth salamanders, eastern tiger salamanders, marbled salamanders, redback salamanders, and four-toed salamanders (*Hemidactylium scutatum*). There are no species endemic to this region.

PAFR 8, which represents Ohio's hills and irregular plains, consists of mosaics of cropland and pasture and is forested by stands of mixed mesophytic, oak-hickory, beech-maple woodlands. This region is the most species rich of the Midwest, with thirty-eight amphibian species: eastern spadefoot toads, American toads, Fowler's toads, chorus frogs, spring peepers, mountain chorus frogs (*Pseudacris brachyphona*), Blanchard's cricket frogs, the gray treefrog complex, green frogs, bullfrogs, northern leopard frogs, pickerel frogs, wood frogs, hellbenders, mudpuppies, eastern newts, *Ambystoma* hybrids, streamside salamanders (*Ambystoma barbouri*), eastern tiger salamanders, smallmouth salamanders, Jefferson salamanders, spotted salamanders, marbled salamanders, northern dusky salamanders (*Desmognathus fuscus*), mountain dusky salamanders (*Desmognathus ochrophaeus*), red salamanders (*Pseudotriton ruber*), mud salamanders (*Pseudotriton montanus*), spring salamanders (*Gyrinophilus porphriticus*), northern two-lined salamanders (*Eurycea bislineata*), southern two-lined salamanders (*Eurycea cirrigera*), longtail salamanders, green salamanders (*Aneides aeneus*), redback salamanders, slimy salamanders, ravine salamanders (*Plethodon richmondi*), Werhle's salamanders (*Plethodon werhlei*), and four-toed salamanders. Mountain chorus frogs, streamside salamanders, northern dusky salamanders, mountain dusky salamanders, spring salamanders, northern and southern two-lined salamanders, red salamanders, mud salamanders, green salamanders, ravine salamanders, and Werhle's salamanders are endemic indicator species of this region.

PAFRs 1 through 4 and 5 through 8 form two distinctly different megaclusters dividing the amphibian fauna into the relatively depopulated prairie regions (1 through 4) and the highly diverse forest regions (5 through 8). Few species are endemic to PAFRs 1 through

Table 4-2. Amphibian endemism in the PAFRs of the Midwest. Values are number of species in each region (n) and the number of species endemic to each region (e)

PAFR	Anurans		Salamanders		Total	
	n	e	n	e	n	e
1	7	1	2	0	9	1
2	10	0	3	0	13	0
3	12	0	4	0	16	0
4	15	2	3	0	18	2
5	18	3	16	4	34	7
6	11	0	14	6	25	6
7	12	0	9	0	21	0
8	14	1	23	11	37	12
1–4	20	3	6	0	26	3
5–8	22	4	35	21	57	25
Total	26	7	35	21	61	28

4 and PAFR 7, but almost half of the amphibian species found in PAFRs 5, 6, and 8 are endemic (Table 4-2). PAFR 7 appears to be a depopulated version of PAFRs 5 and 8, while sharing two northern species (mink frogs and blue-spotted salamanders) with PAFR 2.

Environmental Effects

Habitat preferences of each amphibian species indicate that prairie specialists, lacustrine-riverine species, and species with broad habitat preferences (e.g., tiger salamanders, green frogs, and American toads) are found about equally distributed among the eight PAFRs (Table 4-3). However, stream, ravine, and woodland species are found almost exclusively in PAFRs 5 through 8 (Table 4-3).

Correlations (CCC) between the coefficient of community (J) and environmental data indicate that ecoregions and physical geology explain most of the variation in amphibian distributions (Table 4-4). Average temperature and river systems explain about half of the variation in amphibian faunas, while vegetation and precipitation contribute the least to changes in the amphibian fauna of the Midwest (Table 4-4).

Discussion

Primary Amphibian Faunal Regions

Statistical rigor can be usefully applied on a regional basis in biogeography (Udvardy 1969). In the present study, cluster analysis was used to distinguish eight significantly different PAFRs. Nearly half (twenty-eight) of the sixty-one species were endemic to one of these PAFRs.

The eight PAFRs differ from provinces based on other faunas. For example, studies on mammals divide Michigan and Wisconsin into northern and southern provinces, and there is no distinction between the mammalian fauna of Ohio (PAFRs 7 and 8) and Iowa (PAFR 3; Hagmeier and Stults 1963; Hagmeier 1966). Although there is agreement that the amphibian fauna of Michigan changes most sharply in the southern third of the Lower Peninsula (Brodman 1989; see also Holman, Chpt. 2, this volume), in the present study all of Michigan is included in PAFR 7.

Biotic provinces of North America defined by Dice (1943) as Illinoian, Canadian, and Carolinian are consistent with the division of PAFRs 1 through 4 from 5 through 8. However, Dice would place PAFR 2 into a cluster with PAFR 7 and divide southern Michigan into two provinces. The division of Illinois into PAFRs 3, 5,

Table 4-3. Numbers of species associated with specific habitat types in each PAFR

Habitat	PAFR								
	n	1	2	3	4	5	6	7	8
Stream-ravine	15	0	0	1	0	4	7	1	11
Woodland terrestrial	8	0	1	0	0	3	2	1	5
Woodland pond-swamp	15	2	4	3	3	9	7	11	12
Aquatic lake-river	8	2	2	4	3	6	3	4	3
Prairie–sandy soil	6	1	0	3	5	4	1	1	2
Variable	9	4	5	5	6	7	5	4	4
Total	61	9	12	16	17	33	25	22	37

and 7 is in partial agreement with previous herpetofauna and biotic provinces (Dice 1943; Bock et al. 1981).

In this analysis I did not use subspecies as taxonomic units. However, suggestions have been made to elevate several subspecies to specific status based on the criteria of allopatric distributions, morphological distinctiveness (Collins 1991), and allozyme frequencies (Gergus 1995). Collins recommended that three salamander subspecies endemic to the Ozarks be elevated to species status (*Cryptobranchus bishopi, Necturus louisianensis, Plethodon angusticlavus*). This lends further support to the separation of PAFR 6 from 5. The allozyme data of Gergus (1995) supporting species status for Fowler's toad (*Bufo fowleri*) are consistent with the separation of PAFRs 3 and 4. The specific/subspecific statuses of most other subspecies present in the Midwest (e.g., eastern newts, spring salamanders, and longtail salamanders) are not currently questioned and are also not cleanly separated by PAFR analysis.

Environmental Effects

Physical geology is a stronger predictor of amphibian distributions in the Midwest than are precipitation and vegetation (but see Krzysik, Chpt. 5, this volume). This may be best explained by the habitat preferences of salamander species that are found in ravines, fast streams, and cool springs and are therefore endemic to PAFRs 5, 6, and 8. Few species are prairie or cold climate specialists, resulting in low levels of endemism in PAFRs 1 through 4 and PAFR 7.

Although amphibian faunal differences were not explained by precipitation or vegetation type, this may be an artifact due to the scale of the analysis. Few amphibian species distributions are affected by small changes in forest association (e.g., beech-maple to oak-hickory forest, northern hardwood to spruce-fir). However, the broad prairie and forest biomes clearly divide the amphibian fauna into two clusters: PAFRs 1 through 4 cluster as a prairie and conifer forest fauna and PAFRs 5 through 8 cluster as a species-rich deciduous forest fauna.

Kiester's (1971) analysis shows an overall east-west trend in amphibian abundance across North America based on rainfall and a north-south trend based on temperature. In the Midwest, the east-west precipitation and north-south temperature gradients do not have as sharp an effect as physical geology, ecoregion, and biome differences but possibly are involved synergistically. The hillier, wetter environments of the southern and eastern portions of the Midwest have the greatest species richness and endemism.

Monitoring Amphibian Populations in the Midwest

The delineation of eight primary amphibian faunal regions can be useful in establishing a systematic study to monitor amphibian populations in the Midwest. Faunal associations, species richness, degrees of endemism, and, undoubtedly, abundance of amphibians vary greatly among PAFRs and must be considered when planning large-scale surveys and population studies. Spacious areas in PAFRs 5 through 8 receive more attention from

Table 4-4. Correlations between coefficient of community (J) comparing grid sections and environmental data

Environmental Parameter	J
Ecoregion	0.60
Physical geology	0.60
Average temperature	0.51
River system	0.48
Vegetation	0.39
Precipitation	0.31

herpetologists, while fluctuations in depauperate communities are less well understood (although see Lannoo, Chpt. 34 , this volume). Projects designed to gather baseline data on populations and communities need to be distributed among all eight PAFRs in the Midwest rather than along political boundaries (e.g., states, counties, or preserves), although I recognize that there are fewer sources of funding for such projects. Data from well-placed, detailed surveys of amphibians under the direction of herpetologists and naturalists augment the volunteer-based projects initiated in several states.

Summary

This study describes the biogeographic patterns of sixty-one amphibian species in the midwestern states of Ohio, Michigan, Indiana, Illinois, Wisconsin, Minnesota, Iowa, and Missouri. Four hundred quadrants were characterized by the presence or absence of amphibian species, as well as by their vegetation, climate, and physical geology. My purpose was to define amphibian faunal regions in the Midwest and their relationship to these environmental variables. Quadrants then served as discrete units in cluster and principal components analyses. Amphibian distributions correlated better with physical geology and temperature than with vegetation or precipitation. Salamander endemism was restricted to species associated with hills, fast streams, springs, and ravines. Applications of these results to amphibian population monitoring programs are discussed.

Acknowledgments

I thank R. Neely and E. Waffle for inspiration, guidance, and encouragement. An earlier version of this manuscript benefited from comments by D. Karns.

5

Amphibians, Ecosystems, and Landscapes

Anthony J. Krzysik

There is growing concern and empirical evidence that amphibians, even species that were considered historically to be abundant, are experiencing global population declines (Barinaga 1990; Blaustein and Wake 1990; Phillips 1990; Wyman 1990; Wake 1991). Phillips (1994) has written a popular book on the subject. Declines have been reported for the western (Hayes and Jennings 1986) and southwestern (Clarkson and Rorabaugh 1989) United States and the Caribbean (Hedges 1993). Lannoo et al. (1994) documented dramatic changes in an Iowa amphibian community between 1920 and the early 1990s.

Although amphibian declines have been discussed as a global phenomenon, there are regions of the globe that have not shown declines—the southeastern United States, Amazon basin, Andean slopes, central Africa, southeast Asia, Borneo, and the Philippines (Hedges 1993). Much of the decline in amphibian populations parallels comparable declines in other taxa and is the direct result of habitat loss, fragmentation, and degradation (including pollution) from anthropogenic activities, especially deforestation (e.g., Lowe 1985; Corn and Bury 1989; Dodd 1991; Hedges 1993). Reported declines have been associated with habitat loss or degradation (pollution), exotic fish or bullfrog introductions, acid deposition, disease, and increased ultraviolet (UV-B) radiation (ozone depletion). The stocking of trout (often by aircraft) in natural fishless alpine lakes of the western United States probably represents important predation on tadpoles. However, some amphibian population declines have occurred in relatively pristine areas that have not been impacted by humans (Heyer et al. 1988; Blaustein and Wake 1990; Czechura and Ingram 1990; Bradford 1991; Wake 1991; Crump et al. 1992; Carey 1993). Many declines remain a mystery, and an overall model including synergistic interactions and cumulative effects has not been proposed. The assessment of cumulative impacts are important for understanding environmental degradation (e.g., Johnston, Detenbeck, and Niemi 1990; Gosselink et al. 1990). Some researchers have urged caution and have noted that certain reports of amphibian declines may be explained as natural stochastic fluctuations (Pechmann et al. 1991).

There are at least four important reasons for considering a comprehensive global-scale amphibian monitoring program:

1. Hypothesis testing—are there declines in amphibian populations on local, regional, national, and global scales? What are the taxonomic and scale issues? What are the causes with respect to taxa, scale, and environmental, ecological, or natural history requirements? Are the declines relevant to order (i.e., only frogs), specific families, genera, species, or populations? To what extent are amphibian declines global, national, regional, or local issues? Is there one cause for the decline, or are there few or many causes? What are the implications for synergisms and cumulative effects?

2. Amphibian species are strongly associated with their habitats (ecosystems), and some species requirements are highly stenotopic (i.e., have narrow environmental requirements). A large majority of amphibians require landscape mosaics of two or more

ecosystems and spatial habitat integrity (i.e., dispersal corridors) to complete life history requirements. This implies sensitivity to habitat fragmentation. Therefore, amphibians represent excellent ecological indicators or barometers of the ecological condition of landscapes. A global monitoring program for amphibian populations and communities in an ecoregional context represents an integral component of spatial and temporal trend analysis and risk assessment in monitoring the ecological integrity of global ecosystems.

3. There are legal mandates under the Federal Endangered Species Act, state legislation, and international statutes and agreements. Many amphibian species are already listed on international, federal, and state levels as threatened, endangered, or sensitive (see Lannoo, Introduction, this volume).

4. There are the conservation implications of taxa that are rare or possess very limited distributions.

The landscape ecology approach and spatial technologies in the framework of Geographic Information Systems (GIS) (e.g., remote sensing and spatial analysis/modeling) represent powerful tools for monitoring and modeling the distribution, density patterns, and metapopulation dynamics of amphibian populations. Additionally, GIS can be instrumental in extending these data into other applications relevant to the conservation biology of amphibians. (See Krzysik [Chpt. 42, this volume] for an introduction to, and examples of, GIS, landscape ecology, and spatial modeling.)

Landscapes and Ecosystem Classification

It is important to distinguish between scale, landscapes, and ecological hierarchies. Scale is defined by spatial extent (see Krzysik, Chpt. 42, this volume, Table 42-2). Landscape can refer to two attributes: spatial scale (which inherently includes pattern) or spatial pattern (at any scale). Landscape scales are on the order of 1 to 10,000 square kilometers, while landscape patterns refer to the spatial context of landscape mosaics and environmental gradients (see Krzysik, Chpt. 42, this volume).

Ecological hierarchies represent the hierarchical organization of biological systems, consisting of genes/populations, communities/ecosystems, ecoregions, and the globe. In this series the higher hierarchy is comprised of elements from the next lower one. Species and subspecies consist of one, few, or many populations defined by genetic structure in a spatial/temporal context. Species are not evenly distributed in the landscape but respond to environmental/ecological mosaics and gradients (i.e., habitat selection). Populations of a species or subspecies on the landscape can be classified on the basis of gene flow as panmictic, metapopulations, or isolated. Panmictic refers to potentially freely and randomly interbreeding individuals in a single gene pool (approximately at one genetic exchange per generation; reviewed in Lande and Barrowclough 1987). A metapopulation represents the situation where, as spatially explicit populations become extinct, colonization occurs from other occupied patches, and a long-term equilibrium is possible (Levins 1969; Gilpin and Hanski 1991). However, a more recent review has challenged some of the assumptions of traditional metapopulation dynamics and stresses the need for a better understanding of the spatial scales and the ecological and genetic processes operating on local populations (Hastings and Harrison 1994). Isolated populations have no genetic exchange, and therefore there is the potential for either genetic divergence or extinction (Franklin 1980; Soulé 1980, 1987).

Communities are species/population assemblages characterized by composition, functions, and interactions (e.g., competition, predation, mutualism, and parasitism). Communities can be defined in a specific spatial/temporal context at any scale. An ecosystem consists of one or more communities within a spatial/temporal context of any scale, characterized by its processes and the flow (transfer) of energy, materials, and organisms into and out of the system. Ecoregions are global-scale (continental) landscapes spatially distinct from one another by their climate, physiography, hydrology, and biota.

Ecologists, geographers, and philosophers will always argue over ecological classifications and boundaries. This is not surprising, because nature abhors classifications and boundaries. Nevertheless, even in the context of the reality of the spatial complexity of biological, physical, and chemical gradients/mosaics and temporal dynamics, in making ecologically responsible land-use and management decisions it is necessary to develop ecosystem classifications and boundaries in order to assess and monitor natural resources and to conserve biodiversity. For more information, see the review by Bailey (1996).

This chapter introduces a systematic hierarchical approach to the classification of ecosystems. Although ecosystems are not spatially static but represent dynamic trajectories, ecosystem classifications portray a convenient spatial and functional reality. Terminology must first be introduced. The environment is the complete spatial and temporal context of biotic and abiotic attributes. Environmental attribute sets (EASs) are eleven sets of environmental attributes that completely and explicitly define the environment at any scale. Environmental attributes are parameter sets that define the environment (e.g., temperature, precipitation, topography, streams, roads, and vertebrates). Environmental parameters (variables) are specific quantifiable variables that define attributes (e.g., maximum or minimum or variance of daily temperature, amount of rainfall per month, elevation, percent slope, number of second-order streams per square kilometer, average instream flow rate, length of secondary roads per square kilometer, number of species of vertebrates, and density of carnivores per square kilometer).

Table 5-1 presents the eleven EASs. Note that this is the baseline of a hierarchy (e.g., the coarsest scale) that characterizes ecosystems and determines their identification (or habitat gestalt), composition, and processes. Note also that the EASs are closely related and interdependent. For the objectives of a given analysis or project, each EAS can consist of a single parameter or multiple parameters, and some EASs are superfluous or may be ignored. The system is valid at any extent (scale) and at any grain (resolution), and the details of hierarchies, EASs, and parameters considered are user relevant. I will briefly discuss the eleven EASs.

Table 5-1. Environmental attribute sets (EASs) for any extent and grain

1. Climate
2. Geomorphology-Geology
3. Hydrology-Hydrography
4. Soils-Substrate Texture
5. Plants
6. Microbes
7. Animals
8. Disturbance Regimes
9. Anthropogenic Disturbance
10. Biogeography
11. Stochasticity

Climate

The climate of a region determines the nature of its landscape and ecosystems. Climate is determined by spatial location on earth relative to the energy flux of the sun (intensity and duration), proximity to large bodies of water (e.g., oceans), topography (e.g., elevation or mountain rain shadow), prevailing winds, and ocean currents. Therefore, the most important parameters include latitude, longitude, and elevation, which in turn determine temperature, precipitation, humidity, and actual and potential evapotranspiration. Temperature extremes (maximum, minimum, or some measure of temperature regimes) and the seasonal distribution (variance and predictability) of rainfall are more important predictors of biotic responses than averages. A single variable representing energy flux—potential evapotranspiration—was successful at predicting 80 to 93 percent of the variability in species richness of amphibians, reptiles, birds, and mammals in North America north of Mexico (Currie 1991; in contrast, see Brodman, Chpt. 4, this volume).

Continental-scale climatic parameters are directly associated with floral and faunal patterns (i.e., ecoregions or biomes). However, microclimates are undoubtedly important for amphibians, invertebrates, and other taxa, especially when considering moisture gradients. The next three EASs that will be discussed directly influence the development of microclimates.

Geomorphology-Geology

Geomorphology, or physiography, defines landform and its geology and is applicable at any scale, from continental-scale physiographic provinces and geological formations to microtopography. The three main physiographic provinces of the Southeast—mountains, piedmont, and coastal plain—exemplify biological differentiation, well illustrated by the regions, herpetofauna, including subspecies. Topography is important for the distribution/abundance patterns of amphibians. Important ecosystem parameters are elevation, topographic complexity, percent slope, slope aspect, depressions for pools of rainwater, and geological outcrops. Important habitat elements for salamanders include flaking sandstone cliffs for the green salamander (*Aneides aeneus*), flaking shale in moist forests for the longtail salamander (*Eurycea longicauda*), and cave sites for the cave salamander (*E. lucifuga*).

Hydrology-Hydrography

Hydrology represents wetland, aquatic, and riparian ecosystems. This is an important EAS not only for amphibians but also for landscape and regional biodiversity. Hydrology readily lends itself to hierarchical classification (e.g., Cowardin et al. 1979). Important hierarchical attributes include:

1. Surface waters
   - a. Lentic—stationary waters: lakes, ponds, sloughs, quiet pools of streams, temporary pools (including floodplains)
   - b. Lotic—running waters: rivers and streams, including springs. Lotic systems are readily classified into stream orders (e.g., Strahler, 1964).
   - a1 or b1. Perennial waters—permanent water
   - a2 or b2. Intermittent waters—predictable seasonal water, present at least several months to most of the year, generally absent in midsummer through fall
   - a3 or b3. Ephemeral waters—unpredictable waters of shorter duration, lasting from several hours—for example, in desert washes—to several weeks and usually less than one or two months. Temporary waters are probably highly significant landscape elements, but their ecology is poorly known (Williams 1987). Vernal pools are important landscape elements, particularly in Mediterranean regions of the world, that are endangered ecosystems (Zedler 1987).
2. Subsurface or subterranean waters—underground ecosystems that are poorly known. The unexpected fauna of the hyporheos is just beginning to be appreciated (reviewed in Ward 1992).

Riparian ecosystems are classified according to their association with perennial, intermittent, or ephemeral waters as hydroriparian, mesoriparian, and xeroriparian, respectively.

Soils-Substrate Texture

Soil classes (reflecting their physical, chemical, and biological properties), texture, organic content, and soil depth are important EASs characterizing ecosystems. Soil types determine moisture capacity, infiltration, erosion potential, suitability for burrowing, and vegetation types. Because the technical definition of soil is rock that is exposed to weathering (Jenny 1980; Huggett 1995), substrate texture is a component of soil classification. Soil texture directly determines flora and fauna species compositions based on the relative distribution of particle sizes: clay, silt, sands, gravels, cobbles, and boulders (Table 5-2 presents a useful classification for soil or substrate texture).

Plants, Microbes, and Animals

Because of their importance, plants, microbes, and animals were classified into three EASs, but they just as effectively could have been considered as three high-

Table 5-2. Soil or substrate texture classification

Texture Class	Particle Size Range (mm)	Coarse Classification*
Clay	0.00025 – < 0.004	
Silt	0.004 – < 0.0625	
Fine sand	0.0625 – < 0.5	Fine
Coarse sand	0.5 – < 4	Sand
Fine gravel	4 – < 15	Fine gravel
Coarse gravel	15 – < 75	Coarse gravel
Cobbles	75 – < 300	
Small boulders	300 – < 600	Rocks
Medium boulders	600 – < 1200	
Large boulders	1200 – < 2400	
Very large boulders	> 2400	Boulders

*A coarse classification may be useful for some applications and with little practice can rapidly be conducted by eye without actual measurements.

order attributes in a single EAS, the biological environment. Plants, microbes, and animals are interdependent and interact among themselves and with other EASs, which are also closely interdependent and which influence one another to a large extent. The biological environment determines the specific structure (including composition), dynamics, and patterns of competition, predation, mutualism, parasitism, and disease/pathogens in an ecosystem classification framework.

Disturbance Regimes

Natural disturbance regimes influence the seven EASs above them in Table 5-1, and both ecosystem processes and the maintenance of biodiversity are dependent on them. Examples of attributes include flood pulses, fire regimes, storms and windthrows, and pest and pathogen outbreaks. These are usually modeled as stochastic processes, and specific estimated parameters (often empirically derived) are used for frequency, extent (spatial), duration (temporal), and intensity. Global events on geological time scales, such as volcanism and asteroids, are not considered in this category.

Anthropogenic Disturbance

Human dominance of landscapes—with its inevitable habitat conversions, destruction, and degradations, from local to global scales—is geologically and evolutionarily a recent phenomenon, but it is already challenging the intensity and scale of the two greatest mass extinctions the planet has faced: those at the Permian-Triassic and Cretaceous-Tertiary boundaries (Ward 1994). Quantitative measures of human presence and disturbance to the landscape are important for amphibian monitoring and include road density (classified by interstates, secondary roads, rural dirt roads, jeep trails, etc.), fractal dimension, contagion, land cover type, ecosystem/habitat areas, fragmentation, connectivity, adjacent ecosystems, and landscape pattern. Langton (1989) discusses the effects of roads on amphibians. Various metrics for quantification are discussed in Krzysik (Chpt. 42, this volume).

Biogeography and Stochasticity

Species distribution and density patterns from local to global scales are primarily dependent on the EASs discussed above. However, several other factors are also responsible and in specific circumstances may be important, but they are difficult to quantify and are included as EASs for completeness. These attributes represent biogeography (spacial, temporal, and historical factors) and stochasticity, which represents random unpredictable events, including catastrophes such as volcanos, earthquakes, meteors/asteroids, and extreme cases of the natural disturbance regimes discussed above.

Amphibians on the Landscape

I constructed a baseline classification of ecosystems relevant to amphibian ecology and natural history requirements. The classification was based mainly on hydrology but also reflected topography (see Table 5-3). It is important to note that there is a substantial ecological difference and implications between riparian zones and the presence of both aquatic and terrestrial habitats. Riparian zones have their own ecological identity based on structure, function, and processes and are characterized by steep moisture, physical, and chemical environmental gradients. The functionality of these ecosystems, as well as the response of biological organisms to them, is unique and cannot be considered as either aquatic or terrestrial habitat or both. Species that are riparian specialists require the environmental, biological, and spatial contexts of this water-land interface. Although riparian systems represent a wide variety and complexity of classes (mainly dependent on region and geomorphology), they remain unique in the landscape and should be classified as such (Gregory et al. 1991; Franklin 1992; Malanson 1993). A federal symposium on the value of riparian habitats was instrumental in initiating a great deal of interest and research in these previously ignored ecosystems (Johnson and Jones 1977). If riparian zones are degraded (by humans or cattle), riparian species are dramatically affected, but species requiring aquatic or both terrestrial and aquatic habitats may not be affected. It is well documented that the ecological integrity of riparian zones directly affects water quality, instream flows, and flooding regimes (Karr and Schlosser 1978; Osborne and Wiley 1988; Johnston, Detenbeck, and Niemi 1990; Schlosser 1991; Becker and Neitzel 1992).

I matched the ecosystem classification of Table 5-3 with all of the amphibian genera in North America north of Mexico (Collins 1990; Table 5-4). Note that three genera in the Midwest fauna (*Desmognathus, Eurycea, Gyrinophilus*) include species outside of the Midwest that have different ecosystem requirements. A subset of these data consisted of genera occurring in the midwestern states included here. Amphibian genera represent major ecological adaptive themes (e.g., Inger 1958) and therefore provide a foundation to characterize and monitor natural history requirements in the

Table 5-3. General ecosystem classes important to amphibians. See text for explanation of terminology.

Terrestrial			
Aquatic	Surface	Lentic	Perennial
			Intermittent
			Ephemeral
		Lotic	Perennial
			Intermittent
			Ephemeral
	Subsurface		
Riparian		Lentic	Perennial
			Intermittent
			Ephemeral
		Lotic	Perennial
			Intermittent
			Ephemeral
Wetlands			Marshes, fens, bogs
			Swamps, floodplains

context of environmental trends and habitat condition, including landscape-scale ecosystem requirements, spatial patterns, and temporal trends. However, the use of subspecies (or metapopulations or gene pools) is the preferred approach, because populations are the inherent units in natural selection and fitness, providing the adaptations for exploiting their spatial environmental resources—ecosystem requirements (specialized ecological adaptations). Additionally, a further hierarchical finer resolution of the ecosystem classification presented here provides a foundation for amphibian conservation. Indeed, analysis at one hierarchical level provides the data for more detailed ecosystem classification.

Figure 5-1 shows that most salamanders are completely terrestrial or aquatic or require the ecotone (interface) between these ecosystems. Most anurans require both terrestrial and aquatic ecosystems in the landscape. There are no anurans in our fauna that are completely aquatic or found in subterranean waters, and only two genera are completely terrestrial. These data suggest that anurans would be more susceptible to landscape fragmentation than are salamanders because they are more dependent on landscape mosaics, the patterns developed by two or more ecosystem types.

Although thirty-one ecosystem combinations are possible in Table 5-3 (sixteen single classes and fifteen when pairing terrestrial with one of the other fifteen classes), only eleven ecosystem classes were required to classify on a baseline scale the ecology and natural history requirements of all amphibian genera (Table 5-5). Figure 5-2 shows the relationships of the United States and Canadian (USC) amphibian fauna to the eight single ecosystem classes, and Figure 5-3 shows the comparable data for the Midwest fauna. Trends in the Midwest fauna are in general comparable to trends in the USC fauna. The major differences are that the Midwest has no completely terrestrial anurans (the two terrestrial genera are tropical-subtropical), has a higher proportion of completely aquatic salamanders, is less represented by subterranean forms, and has a higher proportion of wetland (including riparian-lentic) anurans. Figures 5-4 and 5-5 show comparable data on the respective faunas that require both terrestrial and aquatic ecosystems to complete their life histories. Again, the midwestern fauna reflects the USC fauna, with the main differences being that a higher proportion of USC anurans rely on ephemeral breeding pools than do those in the Midwest (reflecting western adaptations to arid and semi-arid

Table 5-4. Legend

TER	Terrestrial
AQ-LE	Aquatic-Lentic-Perennial Waters; may include marsh habitat
RIP-LE	Riparian-Lentic-Perennial Waters
AQ-LO	Aquatic-Lotic-Perennial Waters
RIP-LO	Riparian-Lotic-Perennial Waters; includes springs
SUB	Subsurface, Subterranean Waters
WET-M	Wetlands-Marshes, Fens, Bogs
WET-S	Wetlands-Swamps, Floodplains
LE-P	Terrestrial and Aquatic Lentic-Perennial Waters
LE-IE	Terrestrial and Aquatic Lentic-Intermittent or Ephemeral Waters; may include floodplain pools
LO-PIE	Terrestrial and Aquatic Lotic-Perennial, Intermittent, or Ephemeral Waters

Table 5-4. The ecosystem classifications of Table 5-3 matched with the amphibian genera in North America north of Mexico

Genus	TER	AQ-LE	RIP-LE	AQ-LO	RIP-LO	SUB	WET-M	WET-S	LE-P	LE-IE
Ambystoma									Mid, C	Mid, C
Amphiuma		Mid		Mid						
Aneides	Mid, C									
Batrachoseps	US, C				US, C					
Cryptobranchus				Mid						
Desmognathus	US		US		Mid, C			US		
Dicamptodon					US, C					
Ensatina	US, C									
Eurycea	Mid			US	Mid, C	US				
Gyrinophilus					Mid, C	US				
Haideotriton						US				
Hemidactylium	Mid, C									
Hydromantes	US				US					
Leurognathus				US						
Necturus		Mid, C		Mid, C						
Notophthalmus									Mid, C	
Phaeognathus	US									
Plethodon	Mid, C									
Pseudobranchus		US		US						
Pseudotriton			Mid		Mid			Mid		
Rhyacotriton					US					
Siren		Mid		Mid						
Stereochilus			US		US			US		
Taricha									US, C	US, C
Typhlomolge						US				
Typhlotriton						Mid				
Acris			Mid, C		Mid, C					
Ascaphus					US, C					
Bufo									Mid, C	Mid, C
Eleutherodactylus	US									
Gastrophryne										Mid
Hyla								Mid, C	Mid, C	Mid, C
Hypopachus										US
Leptodactylus										US
Osteopilus									US	US
Pseudacris								Mid, C	Mid, C	Mid, C
Pternohyla										US
Rana			Mid, C		Mid, C		Mid, C	Mid, C	Mid, C	Mid, C
Rhinophrynus										US
Scaphiopus									Mid	Mid
Smilisca									US	US
Spea										Mid, C

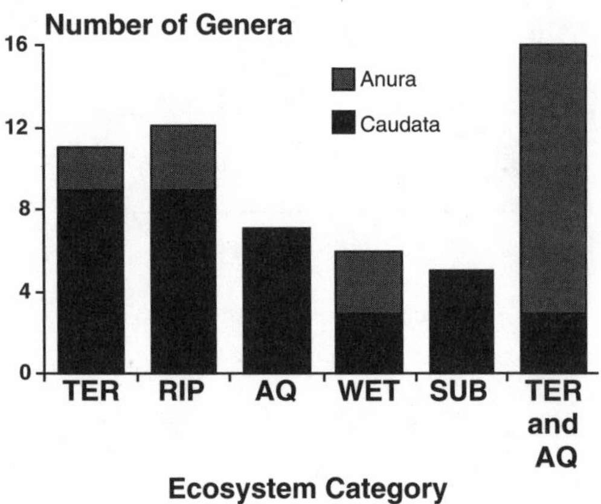

Figure 5-1. Distribution of United States and Canadian amphibian genera in six general ecosystem classes. For explanation of abbreviations, see Table 5-4. Note that the last class is the only one that consists of two ecosystem classes—terrestrial and aquatic.

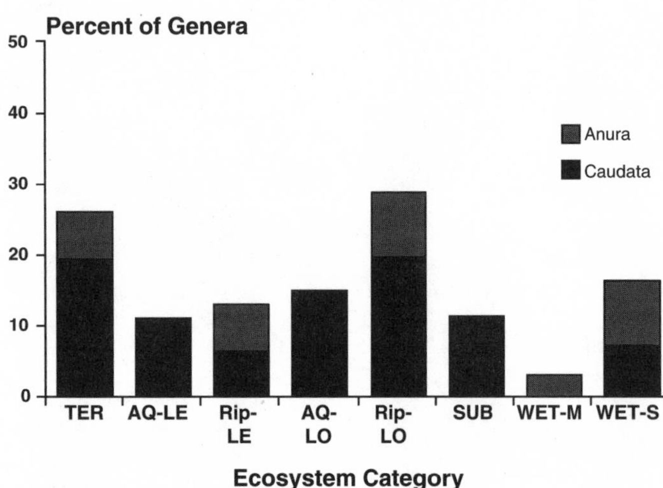

Figure 5-2. Percent of United States and Canadian amphibian genera classified by ecosystem requirements. For explanation of abbreviations and for the specific requirements of each genus, see Table 5-4.

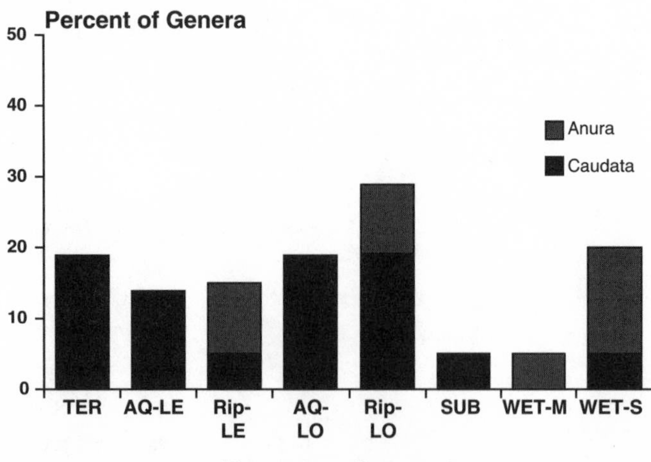

Figure 5-3. Percent of Midwest amphibian genera classified by ecosystem requirements. For explanation of abbreviations and for the specific requirements of each genus, see Table 5-4.

landscapes) and the importance of Pacific coast streams as breeding sites for some *Taricha* species.

The classification of each subspecies based on a finer resolution ecosystem hierarchy, including regional differences, would be most illuminating for designing a national monitoring program. Some genera are species rich. Although some of this diversity represents allopatric geographical divergence, much of it undoubtedly underlies environmental adaptations that would enrich the hierarchical classes of Table 5-5 and provide more detailed environmental requirements and ecosystem relationships. Species-rich genera based on Collins (1990), not including recognized subspecies, are *Plethodon* (forty-two), *Rana* (twenty-four), *Bufo* (eighteen), *Ambystoma* (fourteen), *Pseudacris* (thirteen), *Desmognathus* (twelve), *Eurycea* (twelve), *Hyla* (ten), and *Batrachoseps* (ten). *Batrachoseps* and *Ensatina* (only one species with seven subspecies) are two taxa that are currently being revised, and undoubtedly their richness will increase.

Assessing and Monitoring Amphibian Populations with GIS

Below is an outline of the potentials of GIS for assessing and monitoring amphibian/ecosystem parameters and analyzing and modeling their relationships.

1. Database management
    a. Spatial database needs and analytical requirements
    b. Distribution and abundance data for amphibian populations
    c. Ecosystem attributes (Tables 5-3, 5-4) and hierarchical extensions

Table 5-5. Eleven ecosystem classes important to amphibian ecology and natural history. See text for explanation of terminology.

Terrestrial			
1			
		Lentic	Perennial
2			
Aquatic	Surface		
		Lotic	Perennial
3			
	Subsurface		
4			
		Lentic	Perennial (intermittent)
5			
Riparian			
		Lotic	Perennial (intermittent)
6			
		Marshes, fens, bogs	
7			
Wetlands			
		Swamps, floodplains	
8			
			Perennial
9			
		Lentic	
			Intermittent, ephemeral
10			
Terrestrial and Aquatic			
			Perennial, intermittent
11		Lotic	
			Ephemeral

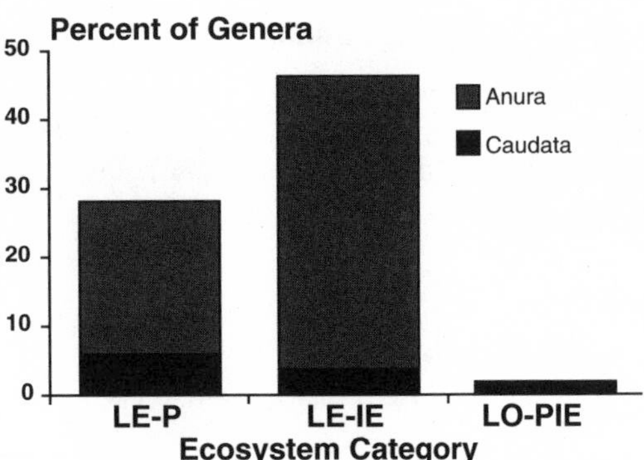

Figure 5-4. Percent of United States and Canadian amphibian genera needing both terrestrial and aquatic ecosystems. For explanation of abbreviations and for the specific requirements of each genus, see Table 5-4.

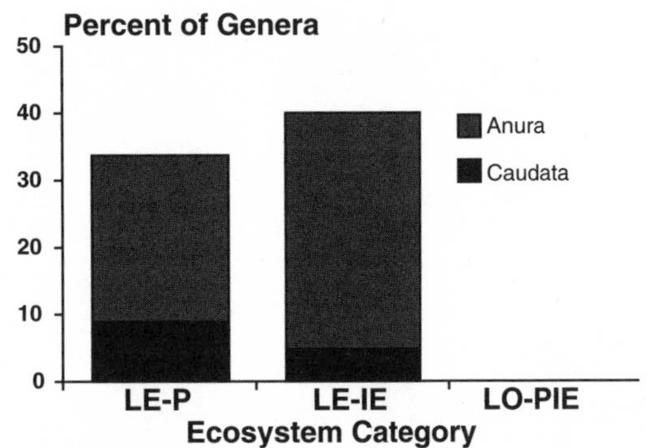

Figure 5-5. Percent of Midwest amphibian genera requiring both terrestrial and aquatic ecosystems. For explanation of abbreviations and for the specific requirements of each genus, see Table 5-4.

2. Coverage manipulations and transformations
   a. Transformations of scale—extent and grain
   b. Changes in cartographic projection
   c. Georeferencing and classification of thematic maps
   d. Merging of thematic maps
3. Identification of specific ecosystems
   a. Selection of specified ecosystems—absolute or probability based
   b. Deletion of specific ecosystems
   c. Ranking of ecosystems
4. Disturbance
   a. Natural regimes
   b. Anthropogenic
5. Spatial contexts of ecosystems
   a. Metrics—size, shape, and condition
   b. Metrics—patterns, mosaics, fragmentation, connectivity, density, association, distance, texture, and similarity indices
   c. Ordinations, classifications—environmental gradients
6. Temporal contexts of ecosystems
   a. Monitoring ecosystem trends
   b. Monitoring spatial contexts
7. Modeling
   a. Species-habitat (environment) relationships
   b. Metapopulation dynamics in spatial and temporal contexts
   c. Natural and anthropogenic disturbances in spatial and temporal contexts
8. Sampling
   a. Develop sampling design
   b. Select specific sampling sites
   c. Model validity, efficiency, and economy
9. Outputs
   a. Visual displays, maps, tabular output, and magnetic/electronic data
   b. Identification of data needs
   c. Protection, conservation, and management needs

Summary

There is growing concern that amphibian populations are declining from local to global scales. A robust hierarchical ecosystem classification system is presented that is applicable at any scale and resolution (more correctly, extent and grain in landscape ecology terminology). From this conception, a baseline ecosystem classification is developed that is relevant to amphibian ecology and conservation. Although there are many ecosystem combinations possible in this classification, including combinations requiring two or more ecosystems, only eleven ecosystem classes were required to classify on a baseline scale the natural history requirements of all the amphibian genera of North America north of Mexico. Amphibian genera represent major ecological adaptive themes and therefore provide a foundation to characterize and monitor natural history requirements in the context of environmental trends and habitat condition. General trends for ecosystem requirements in this fauna are discussed, including a comparison with genera occurring in the Midwest. Trends in the Midwest fauna are in general comparable to the continental fauna. The major differences, based on genera, are that the Midwest: (1) has no completely terrestrial anurans, (2) has a higher proportion of completely aquatic salamanders, (3) is less represented by subterranean forms, and (4) has a higher proportion of wetland (including riparian-lentic) anurans. The continental fauna has a higher proportion of anurans that rely on ephemeral breeding pools, reflecting western adaptations to arid and semi-arid landscapes.

Species Status

6

Distribution, Habitats, and Status of Four-toed Salamanders in Illinois

Thomas G. Anton, David Mauger, Ronald A. Brandon, Scott R. Ballard, and Donald M. Stillwaugh Jr.

The four-toed salamander (*Hemidactylium scutatum*) occurs throughout the northeastern United States and adjacent Canada (Conant and Collins 1991; Neill 1963). To the south and west of its contiguous range, disjunct and apparently post-Pleistocene relict populations are known from Alabama, Arkansas, Florida, Georgia, Illinois, Indiana, Kentucky, Louisiana, and Oklahoma (Conant and Collins 1991). This distributional pattern has been interpreted (Smith 1957) as resulting from the southward movement of a boreal species during Pleistocene glaciation and a subsequent range retraction and fragmentation related to post-Pleistocene climate change and development of the prairie peninsula. At the time of Smith's (1961) report on the herpetofauna of Illinois, only the four northeasternmost populations in the Northeastern Mesic Woodlands Division, east of the Des Plaines River in Cook and Lake Counties, had been discovered. None of the fifteen or so museum specimens had been collected more recently than 1932. It is doubtful that these four populations persist, because habitats at the historic sites have been destroyed. Between 1965 and 1991, seven additional populations were discovered at scattered localities in Illinois, from Ogle County in the north to Lawrence County in the south (Frankland and Vogel 1980; Lynch 1965; Phillips 1991; Schramm and Nordgren 1978; Smith 1974; Thurow 1981; Thurow and Sliwinski 1991). Following a status survey of this species in the state (Brandon and Ballard 1991) submitted to the Division of Natural Heritage, Illinois Department of Conservation (now Department of Natural Resources), the Illinois Endangered Species Protection Board (1994) listed the four-toed salamander as threatened in Illinois. This chapter reviews all previous Illinois reports and voucher specimens, reports the recent discovery of a population in Will County, and summarizes the habitats of Illinois populations.

Materials and Methods

Habitat descriptions are taken from field notes, published and unpublished reports, and personal communications. Museum records were reviewed and summarized, and voucher specimens verified. All but the most northeastern historic sites were examined during fieldwork in 1990 and 1991 (Brandon and Ballard 1991); the Will County site was examined from March to October 1995 by T.G.A., D.M., and D.M.S.

Results

In Illinois, four-toed salamander localities are scattered both east and west of the Grand Prairie, in glaciated country. Physiographic regions (Leighton et al. 1948) and herpetofaunal divisions (Smith 1961) in which populations are known to have occurred are the Chicago Lake Plain (Northeastern Mesic Woodlands), Wheaton Morainal Country (Woodlands of the Grand Prairie Division), Rock River Hill Country (Western Division Woodlands), Bloomington Ridged Plain (Wabash Border Division), Lincoln Hills (Upper Mississippi Border Division), and Mt. Vernon Hill Country (Southern Division Woodlands). The eight extant and four apparently extirpated populations (Fig. 6-1) are summarized alpha-

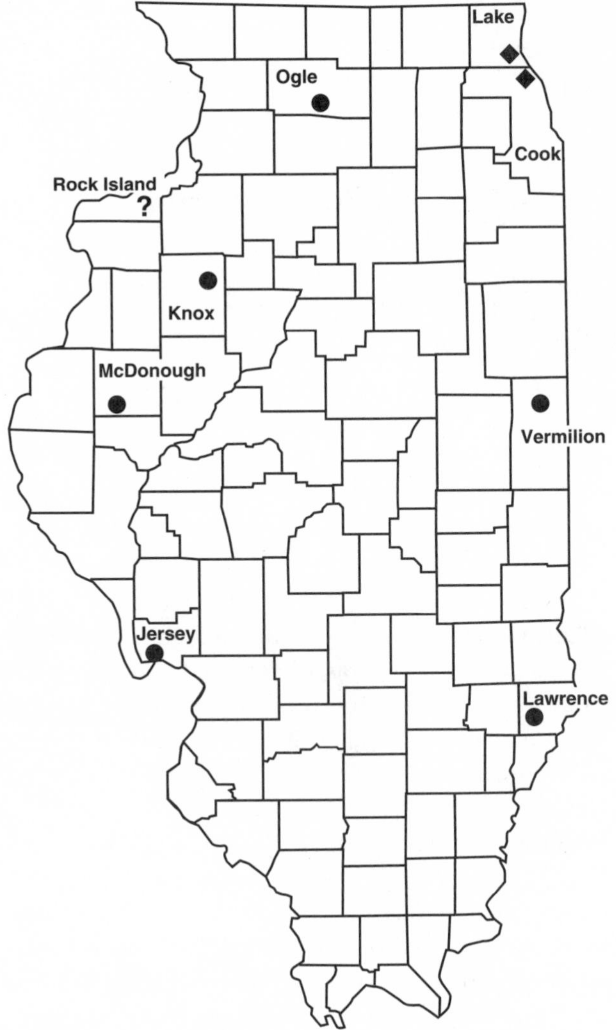

Figure 6-1. Current distribution of the four-toed salamander (*Hemidactylium scutatum*) in Illinois. Solid circles indicate populations discovered between 1965 and 1995; solid diamonds represent populations probably extirpated; the question mark indicates an undocumented locality.

betically by county, documentation, and current status. Available ecological information is reviewed for each.

Cook County

Robert Kennicott collected specimens from Cook County in the 1850s (Chicago Academy of Sciences, CA 262-3, 266). Two additional specimens (CA 264 and CA 265) are misidentified as the four-toed salamander: the first is *Eurycea* sp. in poor condition; the second is a *Gyrinophilus* sp. from Pennsylvania. These errors are probably a result of switched data and/or a specimen. Field Museum of Natural History (FMNH) specimen 2851, from Shermerville, Skokie Marsh, probably collected before 1925, is missing and could not be examined. Skokie Marsh no longer exists; it was drained by the Civilian Conservation Corps in the 1930s. This marsh extended from Dundee Road in the north, southeast to Forestway Drive and Willow Road, and west to the Chicago, Milwaukee, and St. Paul Railroad. The area is currently bisected by U.S. 41 (Interstate 94) and incorporates the villages of Winnetka, Northfield, and Glencoe.

A site owned by the Cook County Forest Preserve District (Deer Grove Forest Preserve) in northwest Cook County appears to contain excellent habitat; a reported sighting of the four-toed salamander in the 1970s could not be verified. The site features sphagnum, swamp white oak, black ash, buttonbush, royal and sensitive ferns, shiny club moss, and spinulose wood fern. These species are associated with moist, boggy woods (Swink and Wilhelm 1994). Smaller fragments of similar habitat in Cook County exist at Busse Woods, located about eleven miles south of Deer Grove. No specimens were found at either site in 1995.

Jersey County

One animal (Southern Illinois University-Edwardsville, SIUE 164) was found on 4 April 1967 on moss about 30 centimeters above water in a concrete spring box at the bottom of a rock creek bed (Smith 1974). On 4 May 1967, Smith found four more animals under rocks in a ravine about 1.7 kilometers away, at the waterline of a 1-by-1.3 meter leaf-filled, spring-fed pool. Three animals (SIUE 165-167) were under the same rock with two clusters of eggs; the fourth was about 30 centimeters away. The surrounding forest, dominated by mature oaks, hickories, and maples, was littered with fallen logs. Similar habitat exists in nearby Pere Marquette State Park, where Brandon and Ballard (1991) found no four-toed salamanders.

Knox County

Schramm and Nordgren (1978) reported a population at the Knox College Green Oaks Biological Field Station, 6.5 kilometers south of Victoria. John Murphy (personal communication) considered this to be one of the best populations in Illinois, but we know of no voucher specimens, and it was not examined by Brandon and Ballard (1991).

Lake County

According to Lynch (1965), P. W. Smith judged two specimens (FMNH 12997–12998) from Deerfield to have been collected between 1912 and 1925. Another specimen (FMNH 17133) was collected 24 April 1932 in Highland Park "under a log in wet, swampy woods," according to the Field Museum catalog (Deerfield on 17 April according to Lynch 1965). Because these localities have been developed, the four-toed salamander may be extirpated here. The species has not been observed in Lake County during the past sixty-three years.

Lawrence County

Thurow (1981) reported a specimen (Western Illinois University, WIU-106) collected at Red Hills State Park on 18 September 1963. On 11 October 1991, two of us (R.A.B. and S.R.B.), along with T. Fink and J. Howard, examined the floors and lower slopes of four seep-fed ravines and found four-toed salamanders to be abundant on well-drained, moist, sandy soil under superficial cover (e.g., logs, branches, and leaves; Brandon and Ballard 1991). In one instance, six individuals were found under the same branch. Apparently, at this location they burrow into damp, sandy soil. Eighteen four-toed salamanders (35 to 42 millimeters snout to vent length) were measured, and four were kept as vouchers (Southern Illinois University-Carbondale, SIUC H-4001–4003, 4005). The ravine floors were covered mostly with touch-me-not, false nettle, poison ivy, grass, sedges, small elms, dogwoods, and sugar maples. Larger trees on the slopes included sycamore, yellow poplar, and white oak. The sandy soil was moist on the ravine floor but drier on the slopes.

McDonough County

Frankland and Vogel (1980) reported collecting two males (Illinois Natural History Survey, INHS 10616) on 4 October 1979 at a site 17.7 kilometers south of Macomb. The site consisted of a small sandstone outcrop along a dry creek bed in a wooded area.

Ogle County

Lynch (1965) collected three four-toed salamanders (University of Illinois Museum of Natural History, UIMNH 56597–56598 and INHS 9700) on 18 October 1964 near Castle Rock, north of Grand Detour. The animals were found beneath logs after a rain at the bottom of a cool, moist, and lush valley "in . . . the black oak stage of the sandstone sere" (Lynch 1965). According to Lynch, the area featured maidenhair ferns, other ferns, black oaks, white oaks, and witch hazel. Brandon and Ballard (1991) examined the habitat, which still seemed suitable for four-toed salamanders, but found none.

Rock Island County

Thurow and Sliwinski (1991) indicated that four-toed salamanders occur in northwestern Rock Island County, but no voucher has been located. Neither ecological information nor a precise locality is available; this locality remains undocumented.

Vermilion County

Phillips (1991) reported one specimen from the Middle Fork State Fish and Wildlife Area (UIMNH 95645) and found another in 1995. The first animal was found under a log, adjacent to an ephemeral pond separated from a large sweetflag marsh by an earthen berm that appeared to be made by humans. The surrounding bottomland forest was dominated by white oak, hickory, and sugar maple. Many of the logs were covered with a moss. In summer, aquatic vegetation in the pond consists of pondweeds, arrowheads, and duckweeds.

Will County

The first four-toed salamander population documented in Will County, and the first in northeastern Illinois since 1932, was discovered in Crete Township on 1 May 1995 by two of us (T.G.A. and D.M.S.). An adult female about 43 millimeters total length was found brooding a clutch of fifteen to twenty embryos that were attached to rootlets running along the underside of a moist, moss-covered log at the edge of a vernal pond. This pond was located in wet mesic upland forest dominated by black ash, green ash, and slippery elm. Prevalent understory vegetation included touch-me-not, skunk cabbage, poison ivy, nannyberry, and swamp white oak. The presence of skunk cabbage indicates groundwater seepage. Plants within the vernal pond included buttonbush, black ash, and duckweeds. The surrounding upland forest consisted of black walnut, red oak, white oak, basswood, black cherry, bitternut hickory, and ironwood.

A juvenile (30 millimeters total length) was found approximately 150 meters away under a log on a forested slope, 1.5 meters from a smaller pond. The female and egg mass were collected, photographed (SIUC H-5048), and returned to the site of capture. On 7 May 1995, an adult male (INHS 12064), 92 millimeters total length, was collected under a log 2 meters from the larger pond. The site is owned by the Forest Preserve District of Will

County and is located about 40 kilometers southwest of Indiana Dunes State Park. At Indiana Dunes, between March and October Alan Resetar (personal communication) collected four-toed salamanders in drift fences at the borders of hydromesophytic forest and mesophytic forest on organic soil over sand. Vegetation at this site included yellow birch, skunk cabbage, cress, marsh marigold, blue beech, cut-leaved grape fern, and papaw. The habitat featured low areas, which fill with rain or meltwater, and raised hummocks.

Discussion

The necessary habitat requirements for the four-toed salamander appear to include mature forest near water for adults and ample damp cover (leaves, mosses, logs, etc.) bordering cold, fishless water for the nests and the approximately two-month larval period (Johnson 1987). Undisturbed or mature forest (deciduous or evergreen) with bogs near woodland pools and seeps containing mosses is preferred habitat in Ohio (Daniel 1989). Minton (1972) described their habitat in northern Indiana as undisturbed swamp forest containing many shallow, shaded pools; he found individuals in moist, rotten logs. Information on the habitat and life history of this species was summarized by Daniel (1989). Adults court on land in late summer and autumn, and in Ohio, females have been found brooding embryos from early April through May. Smith (1974) found females brooding embryos in Jersey County, Illinois, in early May. Nest cavities, sometimes communal, have been found in mosses, the undersides of stumps, grass hummocks, rotten logs, and leaf litter on islets covered by moss within semipermanent bogs or wet areas (Breitenbach 1982).

Bogs are not a habitat component of four-toed salamanders in some disjunct localities; cold spring water surrounded by damp cover seems to suffice. In Jersey County, Illinois, Smith (1974) found two nests under a rock at the edge of a spring pool. Minton (1972) found eggs "in moss at the roots of trees standing in ponds." In Alabama, Mount (1975) found eggs in the cavity of a rotting log that protruded into a shallow woodland pool. In Mammoth Cave National Park, Kentucky, Brandon (1965) found five nests under damp leaves and moss on the bank of a small intermittent stream that probably was spring-fed. In Missouri, individuals have been found in mosses along spring-fed streams and around sinkhole ponds (Johnson 1987).

Four-toed salamanders are now listed as threatened in Illinois, and remaining habitats merit protection. Pentecost and Vogt (1976) considered four-toed salamanders to be a sensitive species, one that disappears with deforestation, urbanization, and intensive agriculture involving pesticide use and perhaps by the reduction of dissolved oxygen in larval habitat. Some of the known populations are currently being protected on public or private lands (Green Oaks Biological Field Station, Red Hills State Park, Castle Rock State Park, Middlefork State Fish and Wildlife Area, and Will County Plum Valley Area 2), but the extreme disjunction of remaining populations and continuing development render the species highly vulnerable to extirpation in Illinois.

Summary

In Illinois, populations of the four-toed salamander (*Hemidactylium scutatum*) are boreal relicts isolated by the postglacial Pleistocene xenothermic period. We summarize the Illinois material and available habitat information for Illinois sites. Populations in two (Cook and Lake) of the nine counties (Jersey, Knox, Lawrence, McDonough, Ogle, Rock Island, and Vermilion) where it is known to have occurred probably have been extirpated. Another population was discovered recently in Will County. In Illinois, habitat requirements include wet mesic forest with mosses, leaf litter, decaying logs, and clean, fishless vernal pools shaded by ample forest canopy cover.

Acknowledgments

This project was supported by the Forest Preserve District of Will County and by a contract from the Illinois Department of Conservation Division of Natural Heritage, which also gave permission to collect a voucher specimen from Will County and vouchers from Lawrence County. Valued field assistance and data were provided by Chris Anchor (Forest Preserve District of Cook County) and Chris Phillips (Illinois Natural History Survey). For database printouts and the receipt of voucher specimens collected during this project: Alan Resetar (Field Museum of Natural History), Mike Redmer (Southern Illinois University-Carbondale), James Whitcomb (University of Illinois-Chicago), and Jeff Dal Ponte (Eastern Illinois University-Charleston).

7

Population Sizes of Two Endangered Ohio Plethodontid Salamanders, Green Salamanders and Cave Salamanders

J. Eric Juterbock

Green salamanders (*Aneides aeneus*) range from the southern portion of the Appalachian Mountains northward to their limits in southern Ohio and southeastern Pennsylvania (Gordon 1967; Juterbock 1989). The habitat of green salamanders is rock outcrops containing fissures, into which the salamanders retreat. Cave salamanders (*Eurycea lucifuga*) are distributed from western Virginia in the east to northeastern Oklahoma in the west and from southern Indiana in the north to northern Alabama in the south. They are primarily associated with caves in limestone areas (Hutchison 1966), and the occasional populations found in other limestone-associated habitats (Merkle and Guttman 1977; Smith 1961) are local exceptions to the species' typical habitat. However, in southwestern Ohio, cave salamanders are associated only with limestone ravines and are found at numerous localities in western Hamilton and southwestern Butler Counties (Guttman 1989).

The state of Ohio lists both cave salamanders and green salamanders as endangered species, due at least in part to their highly restricted ranges and the uncertain knowledge of their ecology in the state. The current state of knowledge of these species is summarized by Guttman (1989) and Juterbock (1989); little previous study of either species has been conducted in Ohio.

I studied various local populations of these species between 1982 and 1987, using mark-release-recapture techniques. One goal was estimations of population sizes. These estimates offer a baseline to which future evaluations of the status of these populations can be compared.

Materials and Methods

The two Adams County green salamander sites are located within 2 kilometers of each other in Green Township at approximately 83° 30' W longitude and 38° 45' N latitude. The salamanders inhabit partially shaded outcrops of Bisher Dolomite, which occasionally extend 10 meters above the ground. The surrounding forest is a diverse, mature, deciduous forest with no strongly dominant tree species. It is generally much drier on top of the outcrops than below them, and the outcrops range from approximately 5 to greater than 25 meters away from small streams.

Site 1 possessed a huge piece of dolomite, which separated from the main outcrop and slid downhill, producing a cool, moist ravine with connections to an underground cave system. Salamanders were found along the 120-meter length of a west-facing wall and along another 10 meters of the east-facing main outcrop. The outcrops at site 2 lie on either side of a stream that flows south through the ravine. Salamanders were taken on both sides, although no individual was found on both, and the two rock faces are considered as separate units. The outcrops extend for approximately 175 meters from where the stream intersects the dolomite bed. All green salamanders were found on the rock faces.

The studied populations of cave salamanders were located in the Hamilton County Park District, Miami-Whitewater Forest (MWF; sites 1 to 3) and in the Clarence Newberry Wildlife Sanctuary (site 4), separated by approximately 12.5 kilometers.

All three sites at MWF are small ravines in deciduous woodlots. Site 1 extends 50 to 55 meters downslope, where it more or less disappears on a bench; site 2, on the opposite side of the same ridge, extends 150 meters downslope, where it empties into a larger ravine; both are smaller and steeper than site 3 and have sinkholes above their heads. Site 3 is larger, with no obvious sinkhole nearby. All three sites have intermittent water flow.

The primary capture points at site 4 were in a muddy seep located on a limestone shelf at the base of a hillside. This seep is located 5 meters from the main stream, which is about 7.5 meters wide and flows through deciduous forest. A couple of captures were made at the edge of a small tributary ravine nearby. The main stream is permanent, but the seep and tributary intermittently have water.

In order to minimize disruption of the habitat, I removed no rocks from the Adams County outcrops and rarely removed the bark of dead trees. All collecting was done at night with the aid of flashlights. Collecting in the Hamilton County ravines after May 1985 was conducted during daylight hours, because nighttime searches on each of the first four visits to one or more of these sites were less successful than daytime searches. All appropriate habitat was searched on each visit. Rocks, logs, and debris piles, from the streambed up to about 1 meter away, were turned with as little disturbance as possible. On several occasions I also searched on the surrounding hillsides, although no cave salamanders were found.

Captured salamanders were placed individually in marked plastic bags and returned to the laboratory. After processing, they were returned to the original capture site as soon as possible (usually during the next day but always within a couple of days). Salamanders were anesthetized in an aqueous solution of benzocaine for processing. While the salamanders were relaxed, the sex, size, and reproductive condition of each individual were recorded; secondary sexual characteristics were used for these determinations as necessary. Mature females possess a wrinkled vent lining and, in those females' yolking follicles, the ova were visible through the abdominal musculature. Females just maturing possessed the wrinkled vents but no yolking follicles. Adult males possess papillose vent linings. Body length (snout to vent length [SVL]) was obtained by placing the relaxed salamander on a ruler and viewing it through a dissecting microscope.

Marking involved photographing the still-relaxed salamanders and later matching the individuals' color patterns from projected slides. The pattern of black melanophore clusters on the orange ground color of cave salamanders, or of green blotches on the black ground color of cave salamanders, acts as a unique "fingerprint" (the process is termed "pattern mapping" by Donnelly et al. 1994). These marks do not appear to change in adults (greater than ca. 55 millimeters SVL in cave salamanders and ca. 45 millimeters SVL in green salamanders) and change only slightly and in recognizable ways in subadults and most juveniles. Only recently transformed cave salamanders that had not yet developed either the orange ground color or well-defined melanophore clusters posed any subsequent recognition problem. Because some of these individuals were recognized later, it did not appear likely that their rate of recapture was much different from the recapture rate for other juveniles. Hatching-sized juvenile red salamanders were captured and photographed too rarely to evaluate, so the ability to recognize recaptured hatchlings in this species is unknown. On a few occasions, salamanders were captured and photographed without any other data being obtained.

Once the number of recaptured individuals was determined, the procedures of Begon (1979) were used for estimating population size. Using this procedure, population size at day i ($\hat{N}_i$) is estimated by considering the total number of marked animals on day i (M_i), the number of individuals in the day i sample (n_i), and the number of marked individuals caught on day i (m_i), using the formula:

$$\hat{N}_i = \frac{\Sigma M_i n_i}{(\Sigma m_i) + 1}$$

This technique has all of the assumptions of a Peterson estimate but uses data accumulated over several days—a considerable advantage for studies with few recaptures (Begon 1979). For statistical comparisons of the two populations, or of the two sexes, I used chi-square analysis of two-by-two or two-by-three contingency tables.

Results

In the two studied green salamander populations, 256 captures were made of 109 individuals. Both the collecting effort and level of salamander activity were sufficient to allow some inferences regarding population size between 1982 and 1984 at site 1 and between 1985 and 1987 at site 2 (Table 7-1). The number of immatures (and thus individuals) varied more between years at site

2 than at site 1. A comparison of the weighted means estimates of population size (Begon 1979) with the actual number of salamanders captured (Table 7-1) indicates that I was apparently capturing well over half of the population.

With the exception of 1986 at site 2, there were more captures of adults than of immatures during any particular year. When all individuals are included, there were no differences between the two parts of site 2 (χ^2 = 0.81, 2 degrees of freedom [d.f.], p = 0.67) or between the two populations (χ^2 = 1.05, 2 d.f., p = 0.59) in proportions of adults and immatures. The overall ratio of males to females (1.45:1) was neither different between sites (χ^2 = 0.51, 1 d.f., p = 0.48) nor significantly different from 1:1 (χ^2 = 1.85, 1 d.f., p = 0.17).

I captured 143 individual cave salamanders 254 times at four sites. I also was apparently capturing at least half of the individuals in these populations (Table 7-2). The most salamanders, 79, were captured at site 1. The number of individual adults caught in any single year at site 1 ranged from 7 to 21; that of immatures, from 9 to 21. At this site, there were more captures of adults (87, equal to 59 percent of total captures) than of immatures (61), although here, too, there were more immature individuals (55 percent of total individuals) than adult individuals caught during the study. At site 2, there were 32 (86 percent) captures of 18 (78 percent) adults. There was little change in either the cumulative number of adults captured (from 15 to 18 over three years) or the estimate of population size after the first year ($\hat{N}$ ranged from 20.1 to 21.2; the $SE_{\hat{N}}$ decreased from ±12.1 to ±5.9). Most of the adults at this site appear to have been captured. Too few immatures were captured to allow an estimate of the number of immatures in the population. Three visits to site 3 yielded only 4 adults, and none were recaptured; it is not clear that these individuals even represent a resident population. At site 4, there were 33 (60 percent) captures of 26 (74 percent) immatures. In the year between September 1984 and September 1985, there were enough captures and recaptures of immatures to estimate their number in the population (Table 7-2).

The 26 males comprise 40 percent of the adults captured at all four sites. Only at site 1 is there any difference in the sex ratio. There, the 11 males and 23 females do not represent a 1:1 ratio (χ^2 = 4.24, p = 0.04). The overall sex ratio of 26 males to 39 females is not significantly different from 1:1 (χ^2 = 2.6, p = 0.11).

Discussion

There is probably no completely accurate way to determine the population size of these species. Censusing is not effective because capture results indicate that most of the population is inaccessible for most of the year. With the possible exception of the capture of cave sala-

Table 7-1. Numbers of individuals captured and estimates ($\hat{N} \pm SE_{\hat{N}}$) of population sizes for two populations of green salamanders in Adams County, Ohio

Year	Group	Actual Number of Individuals	$\hat{N} \pm SE_{\hat{N}}$	Actual Number of Individuals	$\hat{N} \pm SE_{\hat{N}}$
		Site 1			
1982	Adults	10	9.1 ± 3.2		
	Immatures	5	7.0 ± 5.7		
1983	Adults	12	10.5 ± 3.1		
	Immatures	10	10.6 ± 6.1		
1984	Adults	17	22.7 ± 8.6		
	Immatures	8	8.8 ± 4.4		
		Site 2A		Site 2B	
1985*	Adults	9	9.9 ± 4.4	7	7.0 ± 4.8
1986	Adults	5	4.4 ± 1.4	4	
	Immatures	11	13.4 ± 6.0	15	26.0 ± 14.9
1987*	Adults	6	6.3 ± 1.3	7	6.8 ± 4.6

*No immatures were captured at site 2A and only two each year at 2B.

Table 7-2. Numbers of individuals captured and estimates ($\hat{N} \pm SE_{\hat{N}}$) of population size for three populations of cave salamanders in Hamilton County, Ohio

Year	Group	Actual Number of Individuals	$\hat{N} \pm SE_{\hat{N}}$
		Site 1	
1985	Adults*	14	29.0 ± 25.6
	Immatures	21	28.5 ± 9.5
1986	Adults	19	25.4 ± 9.7
	Immatures	9	12.0 ± 10.6
1987	Adults	21	34.6 ± 11.6
	Immatures*	14	10.0 ± 2.0
		Site 2	
1985	Adults	15	21.2 ± 12.1
		Site 4	
1984–1985	Immatures	18	26.7 ± 13.4

*Estimate is based upon a single recapture sample.

manders during four to six weeks in May and June, it seems unlikely that a majority of the individuals in any population were captured. Some individuals disappeared for a year or two at a time. Certain assumptions of population estimation techniques utilizing mark-release-recapture (Begon 1979; Donnelly and Guyer 1994) were violated. Some individuals were caught often (an adult male green salamander was captured twenty-three times between 1982 and 1987), while others were rarely caught. The spatial distribution of green salamanders, at least, makes complete mixing between capture episodes unlikely. There must be mortality from year to year, especially among immature salamanders, and new animals are recruited to the population. These violations of the assumptions tend to inflate the estimates. Failure of the marked animals to distribute themselves randomly among the unmarked population would inflate the estimates if they were less likely to be recaptured or deflate the estimates if they were more likely. Both the seasonal occurrence of distinct portions of the population in cave salamanders and the actual recapture histories (Juterbock, unpublished data) suggest that deflation is more likely for these data.

Still, given the endangered status of these species and the apparent minimal size of the populations, it is useful to establish some reasonable estimate of population size. The estimates presented for these populations are probably minimum estimates, due to the seasonal occurrences and relatively poor mixing of marked and unmarked animals. In spite of all these potential sources of error, I do not believe that the estimates are grossly in error. Several factors support my conclusion. The actual numbers of individuals captured during any estimation period represent a substantial proportion of the estimated population (Tables 7-1, 7-2), implying that the numbers are not inordinately large. Immatures were the least likely to be recaptured. But I captured a greater percentage of immature cave salamanders than did Hutchison (1958; whose highest recapture percentage was 33.3 percent) in his study of four Virginia cave populations. The number of times the populations were sampled (the least-sampled one was sampled ten times in three years) also implies that the number of uncounted animals could not have been too large.

Therefore, reasonable estimates of the minimum number of adult green salamanders seem to have been fifteen to twenty for site 1 and eight to ten each for sites 2A and 2B. The number of immatures fluctuated more widely, but ten to twenty at each site does not seem unreasonable for the better years. Such numbers represent only one or two clutches, and there were known to be several more adult females than this at these sites. The majority of first-year immatures at each site were captured in restricted areas, reinforcing the idea of one or two clutches. The numbers of adults compare favorably to those cited by Gordon (1952) for his North Carolina population. The numbers of immatures in his population were similar to the numbers found in "off" years in the Ohio populations. He observed much larger numbers of recently hatched individuals, but he had also been monitoring nests during his study.

Gordon (1952) reported a ratio of male to female green salamanders of 1.6:1, significantly different from 1:1. This value is similar to the 1.45:1 reported here. He attributed the excess of males to the timing of his collecting activity, when females were brooding. I concur with this reasoning and add that, while the proportion of females recaptured is the same as that of males, females were captured and recaptured fewer times, although the difference was not always significant (Juterbock 1989). All things considered, differential behavior seems the best explanation of the male-biased sex ratio.

A dramatic decline in the number of captures (only three individuals) at site 1 in 1985 is both interesting and unexplainable. A few individuals continued to be caught between 1985 and 1987, so it seems unlikely that the decline was due to any cumulative effects of the capture/processing procedures. Capture effort was only significantly lower at site 1 than at site 2 in 1986 (Juterbock, unpublished data), so this explanation seems unlikely. The sites are so close together that climatic/weather variation also seems unlikely. It is possible that changes in the surface features of the outcrops reduced activity. At site 1, the outcrops appeared to have had more moss and debris on them than previously, which could have affected salamander activity or observability. An alternative explanation may be that the number of animals within populations of terrestrial plethodontid salamanders fluctuates as widely as has been demonstrated for pond-breeding amphibians (Pechmann and Wilbur 1994).

The data on immature cave salamanders at site 1 are best for 1985 (Table 7-2). In the absence of any evidence for fluctuations in population size, I believe these data support an estimate of thirty to thirty-five adults and a similar number of immatures in that population. An estimate of sixty to seventy postmetamorphic salamanders is within the range of estimates for three of the four cave populations evaluated by Hutchison (1958). Because he gave no data on the amount of available habitat, it is impossible to compare densities. In my study, although the site 2 ravine is three times longer than site 1, the number of adults was almost certainly fewer (Table 7-2). A population of twenty to twenty-five adult salamanders seems likely at this site. A possible explanation for the apparent lack of immatures is that the site tends to have surface water much less often (personal observation), and thus the surface is likely to be a less hospitable habitat.

The highest density habitat was the seep at site 4. The number of adults captured (nine) was not large, but twenty-five immatures were captured between September 1984 and August 1986. An estimate of twenty-five to thirty immatures at this site does not seem unreasonable. The maximum extent of the seep is 2 by 10 meters, making it roughly equivalent in extent to a 10-meter segment of ravine. If five to ten adults and twenty-five to thirty immatures inhabited the site, it would have twice the density of site 1 and over five times the density of site 2.

It appears, though I cannot be certain, that the sex ratio data in Hutchison (1958) are based upon captures, not individuals. In any case, his ratio of 1.51 males to each female is different than that of this study. The overall sex ratio among adult cave salamanders in Hamilton County, though biased 1:1.5 against males, is not significantly different from 1:1.

Summary

I studied populations of the green salamander (*Aneides aeneus*) in Adams County and the cave salamander (*Eurycea lucifuga*) in Hamilton County, Ohio, using mark-release-recapture techniques. In two populations of green salamanders, I made 256 captures of 109 individuals. The sex ratio (1.45 males to 1 female) was not significantly different from 1:1; slightly more immatures than adults were captured over the entire course of the study. Minimum population sizes of 25 to 40 individuals seem reasonable at both sites. For cave salamanders, I had 254 captures of 143 individuals. Three sites appear to have had 20 to 25, 30 to 40, and 60 to 70 postmetamorphic salamanders, respectively; this is a density of greater than 1 individual per meter of ravine habitat at two of the sites. The ratio of adult males to adult females was 1:1.5.

Acknowledgments

Special thanks are due D. Burt and D. Imbrogno of the Cincinnati Museum of Natural History (CMNH) for making the study of green salamanders possible by granting permission to work in, and by making available the facilities of, the Edge of Appalachia Preserve. At the preserve, F. and E. Denney, N. Lewis, and P. Mehlhop were especially friendly and helpful. Numerous science camp participants and others associated with CMNH or the Ohio Chapter of The Nature Conservancy assisted with logistics and/or fieldwork. Financial support was received from the Ohio Chapter, The Nature Conservancy; the Divisions of Natural Areas and Preserves and of Wildlife, Ohio Department of Natural Resources (ODNR); and the Research Committee of the Ohio State University at Lima, and was greatly appreciated.

The logistic and financial support of the Hamilton County Park District contributed greatly to the completion of the cave salamander project; I thank J. Klein, S. L. Welsh, and A. Winstel. The cave salamander fieldwork in 1985 and 1986 was also supported by a grant from the Division of Natural Areas and Preserves, ODNR. This support was greatly appreciated.

I thank the Non-game Wildlife Office, Division of Wildlife, ODNR, for granting the required endangered species permits. Permission to conduct this work was granted by the Ohio State University Institutional Laboratory Animal Care and Use Committee. I also thank M. A. Cunningham and several students, including J. Gossard, D. Ulman, N. Griffith, F. Schenk, and D. Baker, who assisted in fieldwork and/or data entry.

8

Discovery of Green Salamanders in Indiana and a Distributional Survey

Robert F. Madej

I discovered a single female green salamander (*Aneides aeneus*) on 24 August 1993 in Crawford County, Indiana, while surveying habitat for eastern woodrats (*Neotoma floridana*; Madej 1994). Green salamanders were not previously known to occur in the state (Minton 1972; Minton et al. 1983). The identification of the specimen was verified by A. R. Resetar of the Chicago Field Museum of Natural History, where the specimen is deposited (FMNH 251486). Identification of green salamanders in the east is not difficult, because it is the only species of *Aneides* east of New Mexico (Juterbock 1989). Specimens are easily distinguished by body coloration and shape. Green, lichenlike blotches on a dark ground color serve as the primary indicator. Green salamanders are the only extensively green salamander in the United States (Conant and Collins 1991; Smith and Barlowe 1978). The body is flattened dorsoventrally, while the eyes are noticeably protuberant (Juterbock 1989).

The initial discovery led me to investigate the status of the population at the collection site and to examine other sites for additional populations. The Indiana Department of Natural Resources Special Projects Program supported this investigation.

Here, I discuss the present status of green salamanders throughout their range, describe life history aspects, and describe my survey results. Specific locations of Indiana sites will not be reported here at the request of the Nongame and Endangered Wildlife Program, Indiana Department of Natural Resources.

Status and Life History

Green salamanders are locally distributed throughout the Allegheny Plateau from Fayette County in southwestern Pennsylvania to northern Alabama and Mississippi (Gordon 1967; Juterbock 1989). Presumably isolated populations exist in the Blue Ridge Mountains of North Carolina, South Carolina, and Georgia (Gordon 1967; Fig. 8-1). Populations in Ohio (Walker and Goodpaster 1941; Gordon 1967; Juterbock 1989, Chpt. 7, this volume), Tennessee (McKinney 1973), and the Indiana locality (Madej 1994) also appear to be disjunct.

Information from state heritage programs within the range of green salamanders indicates there is concern for the continued existence of the species (Table 8-1). The Nature Conservancy ranks overall green salamander status as apparently secure but possibly rare in parts of its range. The Nature Conservancy also suggests that the species is vulnerable because of its restricted range and the local nature of its occurrences. The green salamander is imperiled in eight of thirteen states in which it is known to occur. Snyder (1983, 1991) observed crashes of Blue Ridge populations in the late 1970s. In Alabama, Kentucky, Tennessee, Virginia, and West Virginia, existing populations are considered relatively secure, although no monitoring programs have been established. In fact, to my knowledge no monitoring programs are established in any state within the range of green salamanders. Snyder (1991) suggests that green salamanders may serve as an indicator species.

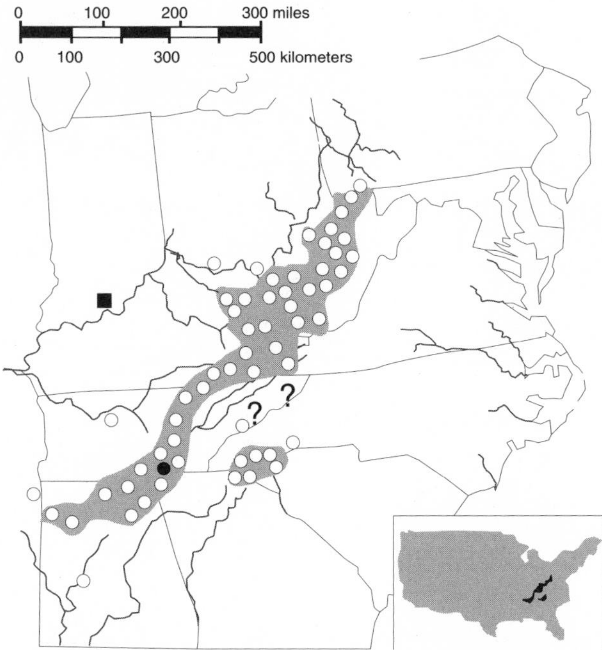

Figure 8-1. Distribution of green salamanders (*Aneides aeneus*), including recent range extensions (modified from Gordon 1967). Closed circle indicates types locality.

Although a popular field guide (Behler and King 1979) describes the habitat of green salamanders as crevices in sandstone outcrops, green salamanders have been reported in a variety of rocky and arboreal habitats. Generally, green salamanders inhabit rock crevices in well-shaded, mixed mesophytic forests (Gordon 1952), although in Ohio, many populations dwell in unshaded limestone cliffs (Juterbock 1989). Dolomite habitats are known from Virginia, while sandstone, granite, and quartzite are also utilized (Gordon and Smith 1949). Green salamanders have been found beneath the loose bark of trees (Gordon and Smith 1949; Gordon 1952; Pope 1928), with some populations distinctly arboreal (Gordon 1952). It appears that rock type or arboreal refuge is less important than the crevice structure, moisture, and exposure (Gordon and Smith 1949).

This habitat specialization and the local nature of suitable habitat result in a localized population structure. Population densities range from 0.1 to 0.25 individual per square meter (Gordon 1952; see also Juterbock, Chpt. 7, this volume). Low density populations are probably due to lack of adequate habitat, but Cupp (1980) showed that male green salamanders exhibit territoriality, which could further limit habitat utilization.

Life history and ecology of the green salamander are described in relatively few studies. Gordon and Smith (1949), Gordon (1952), Woods (1968), Snyder (1971), and Cupp (1991) provided overviews that are the basis of our knowledge. Cupp (1991) summarized annual cycles from different regions (Table 8-2) in four periods. Breeding occurs over much of the spring and summer. Cupp (1991) observed breeding into early November in southeast Kentucky. In the late fall, before hibernating, green salamanders aggregate near crevices that are

Table 8-1. State heritage program rankings of green salamanders (*Aneides aeneus*)

State	Ranking
Alabama	S3, rare or uncommon
Georgia	S2, imperiled because of rarity
Indiana	S1/S2, imperiled because of rarity
Kentucky	S4, apparently secure
Maryland	S2, imperiled because of rarity
Mississippi	S1, critically imperiled because of extreme rarity
North Carolina	S1, critically imperiled because of extreme rarity
Ohio	S2, imperiled because of rarity
Pennsylvania	S1, critically imperiled because of extreme rarity
South Carolina	S1, critically imperiled because of extreme rarity
Tennessee	S?, possibly in peril but status uncertain
Virginia	S3, rare or uncommon
West Virginia	S3, rare or uncommon

Table 8-2. Comparison of the annual cycle of green salamanders (*Aneides aeneus*) at different localities

Period	SE Kentucky (Cupp 1991)	Highlands, N.C. (Gordon 1952)	Toshomingo Co., Miss. (Woods 1968)
Breeding	Late April–early November	Late May–late September	Late March–November
Pairing and mating	Late March–early November	Late May–early June	Late May–June
Egg deposition	25 June–25 July	June	15–20 July
Egg hatching	14 September–6 October	Early September	7–20 October
Brooding of hatchlings	3–5 weeks	4 weeks	—
Prehibernation dispersion and aggregation	Late October–mid-December	Late September–November	October–November
Hibernation	Mid-December–mid-March	November–April	December–March
Posthibernation aggregation and dispersion	Mid-March–late April	Late April–late May	Late March–early April

sufficiently deep to prevent freezing over in winter. The length of time green salamanders are in hibernation depends upon local climate. Following hibernation, green salamanders stay aggregated for a short period and then disperse. Cupp (1991) reported that populations (or at least the ability to observe them) in eastern Kentucky peaked in mid-March to late April (during posthibernation aggregation and dispersal) and again in late October to mid-December. Juterbock (1989, Chpt. 7, this volume) has made similar observations but could not locate individuals after 28 October in southern Ohio.

Movement and activity appear to be limited both temporally and spatially (Gordon 1961; Williams and Gordon 1961). Green salamanders are generally nocturnal but may be active on cloudy and humid or rainy days. Other than during the migration and dispersal periods discussed above, long-distance movement appears to be temporally restricted. Dry periods may also place temporal restrictions on movement by green salamanders. Spatial constraints on movement are apparently imposed by a lack of rock features.

Lee and Norden (1973) found that green salamanders eat a variety of invertebrates. Beetles, ants, and mosquitoes made up the majority of the contents of twenty-five stomachs they analyzed. Other prey were arachnids, wasps, crickets, true bugs, and lacewings. Nonfood items such as moss, leaf fragments, and sand were also found in stomachs.

My observations confirm that the same general behaviors detailed by the authors cited above are observed in the Indiana population.

Methods

I searched for additional green salamanders at the original collection site in Crawford County, Indiana, and then characterized the population. The site was visited on rainy or humid nights during the fall of 1993 and spring and summer of 1994. For each individual encountered in the 1994 field season, the location (crevice), snout-vent length (SVL), and sex were recorded. I determined the sex by the presence or absence of a mental gland, head shape, and visibility of eggs through the abdomen (P. Cupp, personal communication). Individuals were identified by sketching the pattern of markings on their head and neck. Cupp (personal communication) has used this technique to identify individuals. A template and example sketches of two individuals are shown in Figure 8-2.

I searched for other Indiana sites where green salamanders might be present. I selected ten sites with potential to provide habitat for green salamanders by examining topographic maps and by discussing the species' habitat requirements with state and federal property managers. I was also familiar with conditions at several sites from previous visits to those areas. All sites were distributed along the Ohio River in Crawford and Harrison Counties.

Sites were visited during optimal conditions (i.e., night and/or humid or rainy periods) to detect the presence of green salamanders. At each site, the extent of potential habitat was assessed and noted. Suitable crevices were examined with a flashlight, and salamanders, if not immediately identifiable to species, were carefully

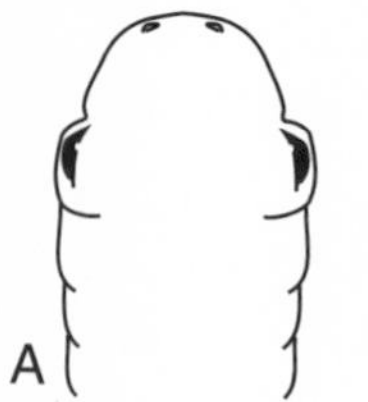

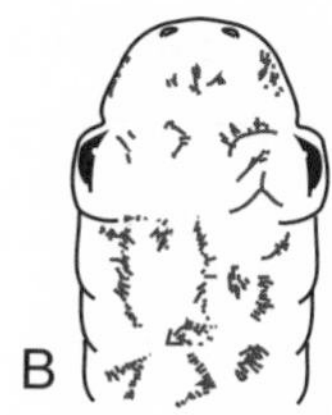

Figure 8-2. (A) Template of green salamander (*Aneides aeneus*) head and neck used to sketch individual marking patterns. (B, C) Head pattern examples of two individuals.

prodded from crevices with a blunt-tipped, sixteen-gauge wire. Green salamanders encountered were photographed and released.

Results

Original Collection Site

The original collection site lies within a deep valley. Although the valley is relatively broad, mature forest provides shade and protection for several tiers of low bluff. Bluff faces at this site are generally 3 meters or less in height and extend for only about 600 linear meters. Both sandstone and limestone occur on the site, with the general condition being a layer of sandstone above a layer of limestone. Often, the interface of these two rock types provided deep, low crevices where green salamanders could be found. Crevices created when horizontal layers of rock broke away from each other were also favored by green salamanders.

Subsequent visits to the original collection site revealed a viable population of green salamanders (Table 8-3). Over the twelve months following collection of the first specimen, I returned to the site fifteen times. On only three occasions was I unable to find green salamanders. I observed a variety of age (size) classes from adults and older juveniles to individuals that had apparently hatched the previous fall (approximately 30 millimeters total length). In fact, juveniles were observed as frequently as adults (Table 8-3), suggesting a stable or growing population.

Green salamanders were individually identified unless prodding the salamander from its crevice risked the crevice's stability. Many crevices in which green salamanders were observed were breakaways that appeared unstable. Information I could gain from identification of all individuals did not justify this potential habitat destruction.

Some individuals were observed in the same crevice they occupied during previous visits, while other individuals moved around (Table 8-3). Crevice 8 was occupied by a female (007), and I assumed it would become a maternity site. No eggs were ever observed in this crevice, however. Crevice 12 was at one time occupied by an adult male and two juveniles. I observed one crevice previously used by green salamanders that was taken over by cave crickets and another that was overrun by ants.

Other Amphibians

Other amphibians observed at this site were northern spring peepers (*Pseudacris crucifer crucifer*), western chorus frogs (*Pseudacris triseriata triseriata*), bullfrogs (*Rana catesbeiana*), wood frogs (*Rana sylvatica*), two-lined salamanders (*Eurycea bislineata*), cave salamanders (*Eurycea lucifuga*), slimy salamanders (*Plethodon glutinosus*), and newts (*Notophthalmus viridescens*). Cave salamanders were the most common amphibian at the site, followed by green salamanders. I observed cave salamanders in crevices that had also been used by green salamanders and in other crevices that appeared to be suitable for green salamanders. These species may compete for limited crevice space.

Other Investigated Sites

Potential sites chosen from topographic maps were field inspected for suitable habitat and for green salamanders (Table 8-4). Four of the ten sites provided suitable habitat, while the others offered limited habitat. None of the other sites visited contained the extent of suitable habitat found at the discovery site. Green salamanders were found at one additional site (site 10). A single specimen (male) was discovered within a crevice on a large sandstone bluff in Crawford County. The site lies within the Hoosier National Forest.

Discussion

My discovery of green salamanders in Indiana has resulted in the species being placed on the state's Endangered Species list. Attempts to locate other populations warrant this action, as the species appears to be extremely rare, even in the vicinity of the discovery site.

Subsequent visits to the discovery site revealed a small but apparently reproductive population. Because I observed, on average, 50 percent juveniles, I infer the population is stable or growing. However, only 500 to 600 meters of linear rock habitat exists on this site, and other areas of extensive habitat are not nearby. Thus, it

Table 8-3. Field observations of green salamanders (*Aneides aeneus*) at the original Crawford County site

Survey Date	Identification	Age Class/ Sex	Crevice Number
24 August 1993	Voucher FMNH 251486	Adult female	—
1 September 1993	—	—	—
3 September 1993	Unidentified	3 adults, 2 juveniles	—
27 September 1993	Unidentified	1 adult	—
9 October 1993	—	—	—
17 October 1993	Unidentified	1 juvenile	—
19 October 1993	Unidentified	1 adult	—
20 October 1993	Unidentified	1 juvenile	—
13 March 1994	—	—	—
21 March 1994	001	Adult female	2
21 March 1994	Unidentified	Juvenile	20
21 April 1994	003	Adult male	4
21 April 1994	004	Adult female	1
21 April 1994	005	Adult female	3
22 April 1994	006	Juvenile	5
22 April 1994	005	Adult female	3
22 April 1994	Unidentified	Adult	6
22 April 1994	003	Adult male	4
28 April 1994	006	Juvenile	5
28 April 1994	Unidentified	Juvenile	near 5
28 April 1994	Unidentified	Juvenile	7
28 April 1994	Unidentified	Juvenile	7
28 April 1994	007	Adult female	8
28 April 1994	Unidentified	Juvenile	9
28 April 1994	005	Adult female	3
28 April 1994	Unidentified	Juvenile	10
28 April 1994	Unidentified	Juvenile	—
28 April 1994	Unidentified	Juvenile	—
28 April 1994	Unidentified	Adult	11
28 April 1994	Unidentified	Juvenile	5
29 April 1994	Unidentified	Juvenile	5
29 April 1994	Unidentified	Juvenile	5
4 June 1994	Unidentified	Juvenile	5
4 June 1994	Unidentified	Adult	12
4 June 1994	Unidentified	Juvenile	12
4 June 1994	Unidentified	Juvenile	12
4 June 1994	008	Adult male	—
4 June 1994	Unidentified	Adult	1
4 June 1994	007	Adult female	8
4 June 1994	Unidentified	Juvenile	—
4 June 1994	Unidentified	Juvenile	near 3
4 June 1994	Unidentified	Juvenile	near 8
3 July 1994	008	Adult male	7
3 July 1994	Unidentified	Juvenile	7
3 July 1994	007	Adult female	8
26 August 1994	Unidentified	Juvenile	7
26 August 1994	008	Adult male	—
26 August 1994	Unidentified	Juvenile	—
26 August 1994	Unidentified	Adult	near 10
26 August 1994	Unidentified	Adult	near 4

Table 8-4. Additional Indiana sites searched for green salamanders (*Aneides aeneus*) and their habitat

Site Number	County/ Topographic Quadrangle	Survey Date(s)	Description of Site Features	Linear Habitat Surveyed (meters)	Suitable Habitat Present?	*Aneides* Observed?
2	Harrison/ Leavenworth	3 October 1993 22 April 1994	Limestone bluff	200	Yes	No
3	Harrison/ New Amsterdam	22 April 1994 4 June 1994	Limestone bluff, sandstone outcrops	400	Limited	No
4	Harrison/ Leavenworth	3 July 1994	Limestone outcrops	250	Limited	No
5	Harrison/ Leavenworth	3 July 1994	Limestone bluff	200	Limited	No
6	Harrison/ Leavenworth	6 August 1994	Limestone bluff and outcrops	350	Limited	No
7	Harrison/ Leavenworth	6 August 1994	Limestone bluff and outcrops	180	Limited	No
8	Harrison/ Leavenworth	6 August 1994	Limestone bluff, sandstone bluff	400	Limited	No
9	Crawford/ Beechwood	6 August 1994 27 August 1994	Limestone bluff	350	Yes	No
10	Crawford/ Alton	27 August 1994	Limestone bluff, sandstone bluff	1,000	Yes	Yes
11	Crawford/ Alton, Beechwood	27 August 1994	Limestone bluff, sandstone bluff	400	Yes	No

appears that limited habitat and barriers to dispersal impose a constraint on population size.

The green salamander discovery site is on private property. The site is a unique Indiana natural feature worthy of protection from development. The U.S. Forest Service (Hoosier National Forest) is attempting to purchase and protect this site.

Habitats similar to the discovery site exist along much of Indiana's Ohio River corridor. In my searches of ten additional sites, however, I did not find the extent of suitable habitat found at the discovery site. As my field searches show, most of these habitats do not appear to be used by green salamanders. Only one of ten sites investigated contained green salamanders. The absence of green salamanders at other sites should not be considered conclusive; finding animals is difficult. Many potential crevices were not accessible, either because they were situated high on vertical rock faces or they were too deep for visual inspection. My opinion is that other populations are likely to exist in suitable habitat along the Ohio River, although documenting their presence will be time consuming. Hopefully, discovery of this species in Indiana will spur increased interest in protecting and monitoring amphibians in Indiana and throughout the Midwest.

Summary

I discovered a population of green salamanders (*Aneides aeneus*) in Crawford County, Indiana, in August 1993. This species was not previously known to occur in Indiana. The Indiana Department of Natural Resources Amphibian and Reptile Technical Advisory Committee recommended that the species be listed as State Endangered in lieu of sufficient population information. Subsequently, the Indiana Department of Natural Resources Special Projects Program supported my survey of ten additional sites for green salamanders.

I discuss the global population status and life history of green salamanders, the variety of habitats the species is reported to use, the population of green salamanders at the discovery site, and the results of surveys at ten sites in Harrison and Crawford Counties, Indiana.

9

Ten- to Eleven-Year Population Trends of Two Pond-Breeding Amphibian Species, Red-spotted Newts and Green Frogs

Spencer A. Cortwright

Reviews of long-term population dynamics typically do not feature studies of amphibian populations (e.g., Blaustein 1994; Connell and Sousa 1983; Schoener 1985; Turchin and Taylor 1992). Connell and Sousa (1983) argue that our best insights on population dynamics will be derived from population studies of much longer than one population turnover. Yet studies of such duration are extremely rare for amphibians (e.g., Berven 1990; Pechmann et al. 1991; Stewart 1995; reviewed in Blaustein 1994). Several studies of roughly one population turnover exist but are of limited use in long-term analysis (e.g., Doty 1978; Husting 1965; Williams 1973).

Obtaining a census of amphibian populations is notoriously difficult, time consuming, and prone to systematic error (Gill 1978a,b, 1985). Yet with concern over the potential widespread decline of amphibans, such data are in critical need (Blaustein and Wake 1995). With few long-term population data sets, it is difficult to determine whether many of these reported declines are actually natural population fluctuations (Blaustein 1994; Pechmann et al. 1991; Pechmann and Wilbur 1994). If amphibian declines are real, there are many reasons to investigate their underlying causes (Blaustein and Wake 1995). One is that amphibians play important roles in nutrient cycling and energy flow in forest ecosystems (Burton and Likens 1975). On a community level, the position of amphibians in the middle of the food web impacts species above and below them. Also, amphibians appear to serve as early bioindicators of environmental changes that may later impact other species, including humans (Blaustein 1994; Blaustein and Wake 1995). For example, many amphibians possess a thin and exposed skin through which gas exchange and intimate contact with soil (resulting in the uptake of water and an assessment of territorial conditions) occur (Jaeger and Gabor 1993; Jaeger et al. 1993; Simons and Felgenhauer 1992; Zug 1993). Many species live in aquatic and terrestrial habitats during their life cycle. Their eggs lack shells, and embryos are often exposed directly to sunlight or shielded only by shallow water, features that cannot be so commonly ascribed to any other group of vertebrates. Therefore, when atmospheric, terrestrial, or aquatic environments are destroyed or degraded, amphibians are the most likely group of vertebrates to experience declines.

Habitat destruction is clearly the largest factor in the decline of amphibian populations (Pechmann and Wilbur 1994) and many other kinds of organisms on earth today (Wilson 1992). For example, it is estimated that at least 87 percent of Indiana's wetlands have been destroyed, and other Great Lakes states feature between 42 and 90 percent destruction (Mitsch and Gosselink 1993; see also Leja, Chpt. 36, this volume). Of those remaining, a significant percentage likely exist in degraded form, with partial filling, residential lawns extending to the wetland's edge, invasion of non-native plants, and artificial explosion of native organisms (e.g., cattails and filamentous algae) as key degrading factors. In addition, habitat destruction and degradation diminish the extent of natural amphibian metapopulations (Pechmann and Wilbur 1994). Local populations tend to be more isolated, which should lead to a greater chance of local extinction. For example, Hanski et al. (1995) document for the Glanville fritillary butterfly that the presence of immigrants from neighboring populations acts to decrease the probability of local population extinction. This same ecological process probably applies to amphibian populations isolated as a result of habitat destruction and degradation, although few supportive data exist (e.g., Mann et al. 1991; Sjögren Gulve 1994).

Reviews of the available data reveal declines of several species in widely separated ecosystems for which determining factors are not clear (Blaustein, Hoffman, et al. 1994; Pechmann and Wilbur 1994). One possible mechanism features partial destruction of the stratospheric ozone layer by human activities on earth. Blaustein, Hoffman, et al. (1994) and Blaustein et al. (1995) present evidence for certain amphibian species in the northwestern United States that increased incidence of ultraviolet B (UV-B) radiation can increase the mortality rate of eggs and early embryos. This is especially true of species that lay eggs in sunny microhabitats near or on the water's surface, a setting in which there occurs little filtering of UV-B radiation by water. Other potential causes for declines include pollution, habitat acidification, disease, increased frequency of extended dry periods, introduction of bullfrogs and fishes, and human hunting for food or the pet trade (Blaustein and Wake 1995; Stewart 1995; Dunson et al. 1992).

This study contributes relatively long-term—ten to eleven years—population data for two pond-breeding amphibians, red-spotted newts (*Notophthalmus viridescens viridescens*) and green frogs (*Rana clamitans melanota*). Both species are widespread and common (Conant and Collins 1991; Minton 1972). However, aspects of their life history (see below) suggest that green frogs should be more vulnerable to elevated UV-B radiation than are newts. Therefore, this study not only presents trends in population dynamics but also some insight into the role of UV-B incidence and other factors on amphibians in the study area. These results are not explicit tests of UV-B incidence and amphibian population dynamics; they merely offer some insight into the ecological conditions under which UV-B incidence may or may not influence amphibian survival.

Study Area

The study area encompasses portions of Yellowwood State Forest and Hoosier National Forest in Brown County of south-central Indiana. The area was left uncovered by the Wisconsinan glaciation and consists of a peneplain of narrow ridgetops and steeply eroded stream valleys. Canopy vegetation consists of mixed hardwoods. Ridgetops feature areas dominated variously by black, white, and chestnut oaks and pignut and shagbark hickories, as well as scattered similar areas with sugar and red maples present. Slopes leading into valleys grade into classic beech-maple forest. Regions of select-cut timber harvest generally maintain their species composition, while small clear-cut regions (ca. 1 to 3 hectares) tend to become dominated by tulip trees.

Most natural wetlands have been destroyed; they were located in wider floodplains, which contained the best soil for agriculture, or were beaver dam ponds. A few natural ponds exist in natural depressions on wider ridgetops, but these are widely scattered. Most breeding ponds currently used by amphibians were made by humans. A few of these are homestead ponds, probably made by horse and plow roughly around 1900. Most are bulldozed wildlife watering ponds created during the mid-1960s. Also present are scattered craters, which are dynamited cisterns, and logging road depressions. The craters and depressions tend to dry each year and hence are not used by either species, both of which require ponds that typically contain water all year. Bulldozed ponds never dry; homestead ponds rarely dry. Bulldozed and homestead ponds are most commonly only 100 to 200 square meters; hence they are small. Most receive only transient amounts of sunlight, which often range from only a few minutes to about two hours per day. A few ponds are more exposed and receive sunlight in patches for six to ten hours per day.

Bulldozed and homestead ponds on average are about 0.5 to 1 kilometer apart. Clearly, amphibians readily disperse among ponds, because within twenty years, and probably considerably sooner, all amphibian species had colonized each of the thirty-nine bulldozed ponds. Habitat between ponds is almost universally acceptable for each species. Only infrequent small clearings are found, and these rapidly become tree covered. Therefore, between most ponds lies a mixture of second-growth forest (ridgetop, slope, and stream valley) and small select- or clear-cut openings. (Wider stream valleys are located nearby but are not part of the study site.) The exceptions to this description are the nine study ponds in Hoosier National Forest, where active timber harvests have not been pursued for several decades.

Natural History

Newts

Newts feature a complex life cycle. Some adult newts

remain in ponds all year; others disperse into ponds during February and March; and many typically leave during July and August. Eggs are laid from May to July. Eggs are typically attached to vegetation (the female may crease the leaf to cover the egg) or leaf litter. Hence the eggs are largely protected from UV-B radiation, both by the physical nature of the vegetation and by the column of water above the eggs. Larvae metamorphose from August to October. No paedomorphic individuals have been detected in this study area. Metamorphosed efts are terrestrial for an unknown period of time, presumably about two to seven years, as has been found in other studies (summarized in Forester and Lykens 1991). The lifespan of adults on the study site is unknown but again should be similar to the one-to-nine-year period indicated in other areas (summarized in Forester and Lykens 1991). Therefore, the range of lifespan for adults is three to sixteen years. Forester and Lykens (1991) found no adults older than nine years in western Maryland in habitats similar to those of Brown County. Thus, it is likely that the ten to eleven years of census reported here effectively cover about one and a fraction population turnovers of newts.

Green Frogs

Some adult green frogs probably overwinter in ponds, whereas most adults and juveniles probably overwinter in streambeds (Martof 1956). The existence of terrestrial overwintering is unknown. Breeding occurs from late May to early August, often, but not always, following periods of rain. Eggs are preferentially laid in sunny areas, although sunny sites are typically limited in these ponds. The eggs form a surface film, and UV-B radiation is filtered only by a thin layer of water. Tadpoles hatch within two to five days, depending on water temperature. Tadpoles always overwinter in these ponds. The overwhelming majority metamorphose about one year after hatching; a few in densely populated ponds will metamorphose early in the summer at an age of nearly two years. Metamorphosed juveniles leave the pond and disperse widely, usually after at least 0.25 centimeter of rainfall. Juveniles and occasionally females are seen near road depressions, near dynamited cisterns, and in stream valleys. To my knowledge, longevity of green frogs is unknown. Martof's (1956) data suggest that population turnover is rapid, perhaps about three to four years. This is especially true for males, because considerable time is spent along the pond's edge, a microhabitat in which northern water snakes (*Nerodia sipedon*) and many other predators readily hunt for green frogs. Few congeneric northern leopard frogs (*Rana pipiens*) live four to five years of age (Leclair and Castanet 1987). Congeneric wood frog (*Rana sylvatica*) females live only a maximum of three years (Berven 1990). Congeneric Asiatic stream frogs (*Rana sakuraii*) are estimated to have a virtually complete population turnover every four years (Kusano et al. 1995). In sum, it is probably safe to estimate that at least two population turnovers of green frogs occurred during the ten-to-eleven-year period of this study.

Materials and Methods

Accurate censusing of newts and green frogs is difficult, laborious, and time consuming. Estimates of population trends, or indications thereof, can be more easily made. The goal of this study is to estimate trends for many local populations, not to render a perfect census for one or a very few local populations. Methods for each species will be presented in sequence.

For newts, one can take advantage of the fact that no dispersal of adults into or out of breeding ponds occurs during April to June, a period during which all sexually mature adults, except for those that have skipped a breeding season, should be in ponds. Censusing during this time gives a reliable indication of adult population density, which can be compared among ponds and across years. For green frogs, censusing adults, especially females, is impractical for many ponds, because females arrive at the pond sporadically throughout an extended breeding period. As an indication of population trends, I chose to census the population of tadpoles in each pond late in their larval period. This census gives an indication of the production of soon-to-be metamorphosed juveniles, a population from which adults must recruit. Metamorphosis occurs during June, so a May or very early June census allows for an estimate of juvenile production from each pond—an estimate that can be compared among ponds and across years.

My census method is to employ a drop box sampler similar to that used by Wilbur (1984) and Harris et al. (1988). The plywood box measures 1 by 0.5 by 1 meter (length, width, height) and is open on its top and bottom. Sheets of aluminum flashing were screwed into the bottom and extend about 4 centimeters beyond the bottom edge of the box. When the box sampler is dropped, the aluminum sheeting cuts through leaf and branch litter and helps embed the box into the pond bottom. Each sample therefore captures 0.5 square meter of pond bottom. Most newts and green frog tadpoles rest on or in the leaf litter; therefore, variation in the volume of water above the 0.5 square meter of pond bottom is of little consequence to estimates of density. The sampling period for each pond in each year ranged from mid-May to early June in order to accomplish the aforementioned ideal census estimate.

Drop sites were chosen in sequence as I maneuvered around the pond. Sufficient space between drops was allowed such that minimal movement of animals would have occurred at the next drop site due to activities at the drop site. Initially, six to eight samples per pond were taken, but as my skill level increased, eight to fourteen samples per pond could be taken, except in the smallest ponds. Each drop was made swiftly with as little disturbance as possible. A net, constructed of steel rebar and mosquito mesh, precisely fit the interior dimensions of the box, so collection of animals could be efficiently made. The box was swept six to twelve times on average and more if needed. Variation in the number of sweeps was required because of variation in the amount and nature of leaf litter and sticks, the topography of the pond bottom, and my ability to drag the net precisely along variable bottom surfaces. Newts were usually collected on the first three sweeps; green frog tadpoles usually required up to six to twelve sweeps. When no amphibians of either species were collected in two consecutive sweeps, or more if some sweeps were of dubious quality, sweeping was terminated. All captured green frog tadpoles and adult newts were recorded for each sample and immediately released.

For some ponds, sample years were 1984 to 1987 and 1990 to 1994. For others, the years were 1985 to 1987 and 1990 to 1994. Data were not collected in 1988 and 1989. In total, thirty-nine ponds were surveyed; however, three ponds have insufficient data to be included in the present analysis.

Analysis

Newts. Because data were not collected in 1988 and 1989, data were grouped according to the years 1984/85 to 1987 and 1990 to 1994. Furthermore, because juvenile newts (efts) probably disperse widely, some into nonnatal ponds (Gill 1978a), ponds were geographically grouped together for this analysis. Groups were delimited by clusters of ponds (hereafter "areas") separated by much greater than average distances. Four areas were identified. Distances between neighboring areas were 1, 1.5, and 5 kilometers; for the closer areas only one pond was located toward the neighboring cluster. By no means does this grouping of ponds precisely delineate a metapopulation, but it does acknowledge that population analysis should be performed on clusters of ponds connected by dispersing efts. Data in support of the metapopulation view are presented in Table 9-1 and in the text that follows. The production of efts clearly varied widely both among ponds and across years. Furthermore, the production of 3,140 efts from LJ in 1985 is greater than that estimated from box sampling of any of thirty-six ponds during 1993 and 1994. Yet qualitative and quantitative sampling of LJ and D13 from 1990 to 1994 emphasized that these two ponds remain, as they were in the 1980s, low in adult newts. Why did neither pond ever show a large increase, unless dispersal of efts is fairly common?

The estimated density of adults in a pond in a given year is simply the mean of the number of adults in each box sample. Data were converted to a per-square-meter basis from the 0.5-square-meter area of each box sam-

Table 9-1. Number of efts and adult newts (*Notophthalmus viridescens*) emigrating from two ponds encircled with drift fences. The ponds are separated by only 100 meters.

	Pond			
	LJ		D13	
Year	Efts	Adults	Efts	Adults
1984	192	—	24	—
1985	3,140	86	63	87
1986	570	60	16	82
1987	—	—	0	30

ple. For each year, density estimates for all ponds in each area were averaged. This mean density gives an indication of metapopulation dynamics throughout each area (i.e., cluster of ponds); such data over time then show trends for the area. Use of mean density across ponds in a year was little confounded by variation in pond size, because the bulldozed ponds are similar in size (average of 147 square meters with a standard deviation of 62 square meters; the number of observations was thirty-six). Population trends across the two time periods for each area were compared by t-tests. If variance was strongly related to the mean, then logarithmic transformations of the data were used.

Green Frogs. The mean density of green frog tadpoles in each pond was calculated as for newts, including the expression of data on a per-square-meter basis. Comparisons were not made by areas; rather, data from each pond were compared by a t-test across the two time periods. Again, if variance was strongly related to the mean, then logarithmic transformations of the data were used. Given the relatively low statistical power of even a ten-to-eleven-year study, data were also analyzed by calculating the binomial probability of mean production of large tadpoles going up or down over the second time period when compared to the first period.

Results

Newts

Figures 9-1–9-4 show the population trends for newts from the four areas. For the Ponds 12-5 area, adult populations fluctuated to a peak in 1987 and then showed a general decline from 1990 to 1994 (Fig. 9-1). Future data can assess whether the declining trend persists. Comparison across time periods (1984 to 1987 and 1990 to 1994) shows overall average densities to be indistinguishable across periods ($t = 0.03$, degrees of freedom [d.f.] = 7). The mean density in 1994 was nearly the same as at the starting mean density in 1984. For the Ponds 6-D area, mean density fluctuated relatively little through time and showed no readily discernible trend (Fig. 9-2). The mean adult densities across the two time periods (1985 to 1987 and 1990 to 1994) were not statistically significant ($t = 0.07$, d.f. = 6).

For the Ponds 15-21 area, mean density during 1984 to 1987 was consistent. During 1990 to 1994, mean adult density started low but then showed a strong upward trend through 1994 (Fig. 9-3). A comparison of mean densities between the two time periods (1984 to 1987 and1990 to 1994) showed a marginal, statistically significant difference ($t = 2.12$, d.f. = 7, $p = 0.07$). Given the low statistical power of these comparisons, the upward trend likely is biologically significant. Determining how long this trend will continue awaits analysis of future data. For the Ponds 24-33 area, population trends were not obvious (Fig. 9-4), but mean population density in the second time period was 26 percent lower than in the first time period ($t = 2.39$, d.f. = 7, $p = 0.05$).

Investigation of the mean density of adult newts across several ponds allows for an interpretation of broad-scale population trends but does not emphasize the high level of variation in estimated adult density and eft production in individual ponds. Variation in adult density is shown for two ponds (Fig. 9-5). Pond 11 contained a low to moderate population density of newts. The standard deviation of $\log_{10}$ population densities (hereafter s.d. $\log_{10}$ N) was 0.25. Pond G contained a typically high density of adult newts; its s.d. $\log_{10}$ N was 0.15. The mean s.d. $\log_{10}$ N for all thirty-six local populations was 0.234, with a range from 0.050 to 0.458.

Box samples taken in August estimate the production of large newt larvae approaching metamorphosis. Production of efts was highly variable among ponds and years (Fig. 9-6). In 1993, only 25 percent of the thirty-six ponds produced an estimated one-half larva or more per square meter (Fig. 9-6a). In 1994, only 31 percent did likewise (Fig. 9-6b).

Green Frogs

Trends in density of large green frog tadpoles (estimate of juvenile production) for each pond over the two time periods are shown in Table 9-2. Only three comparisons between the 1984/85 to 1987 and 1990 to 1994 data sets are statistically significant: one suggesting an upward trend and two suggesting downward trends. Given the large number of comparisons (thirty-six), this number of statistical significances could occur by chance alone. However, there is large variance in tadpole production across years (e.g., Fig. 9-7). For example, the s.d. $\log_{10}$ N across years for Pond 11 was 0.29 and for Pond G was 0.50. The values in Table 9-2 are high for vertebrates (Pimm and Redfearn 1988; Schoener 1985). This variance, combined with few data points (even though this study is longer than virtually all for amphibians), reduces the statistical power of these tests. If we consider just the trends in these data, there were twenty-four estimated declines (two significant, twenty-two not significant; Table 9-2) and twelve increases (one significant, eleven not significant; Table 9-2) from the first time period to the second. Assuming an equal probabil-

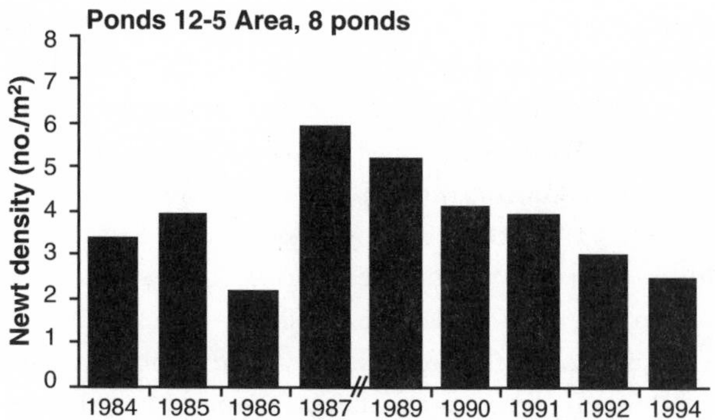

Figure 9-1. Red-spotted newt (*Notophthalmus viridescens viridescens*) population trends expressed in number per meter squared for the ponds 12-5 area. Each bar represents the mean density of eight ponds in the area and is the mean of all the pond means; hence no standard error is given. Compare trends for 1984 to 1987 against 1990 to 1994.

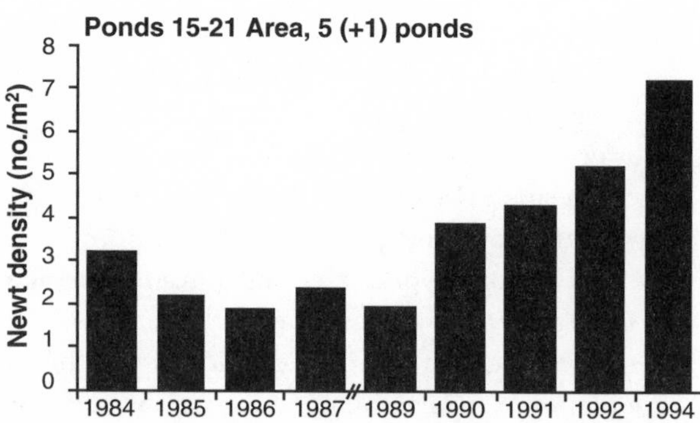

Figure 9-3. Red-spotted newt (*Notophthalmus viridescens viridescens*) population trends expressed in number per meter squared for the ponds 15–21 area. Data as for Figure 9-1 except that the +1 signifies that there is one pond in the area for which insufficient data preclude its inclusion. (Pond 19 does not exist—it was constructed but has never retained water.)

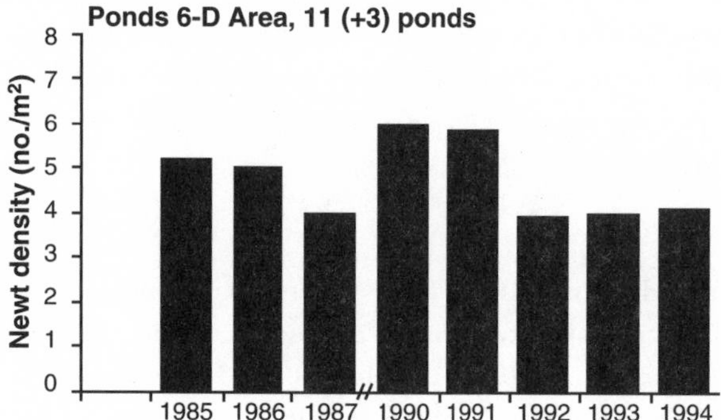

Figure 9-2. Red-spotted newt (*Notophthalmus viridescens viridescens*) population trends expressed in number per meter squared for the ponds 6-D area. Data as for Figure 9-1 except that the first time period is 1985 to 1987 and the +3 signifies that there are three ponds in the area for which insufficient data preclude their inclusion.

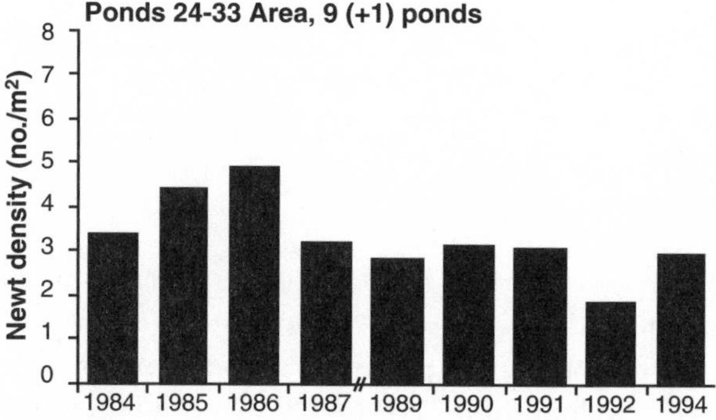

Figure 9-4. Red-spotted newt (*Notophthalmus viridescens viridescens*) population trends expressed in number per meter squared for the ponds 24–33 area. Data as for Figure 9-1 except that the +1 signifies that there is one pond in the area for which insufficient data preclude its inclusion.

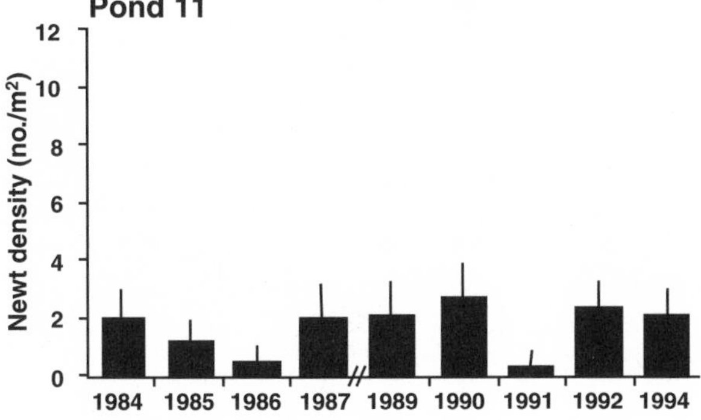

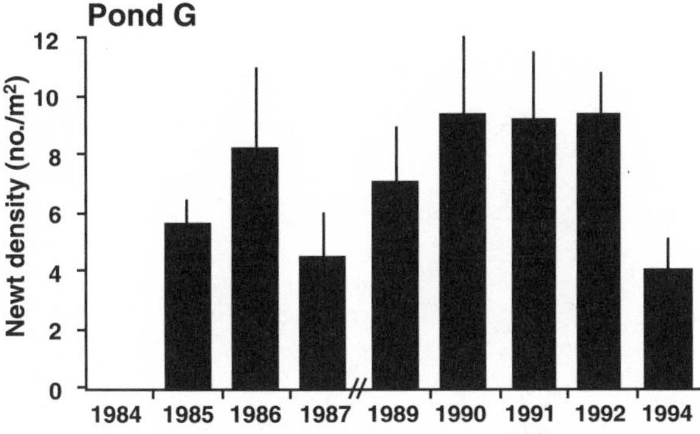

Figure 9-5. Sample trends of adult red-spotted newt (*Notophthalmus viridescens viridescens*) population density expressed in number per meter squared over time for pond 11 (A) and pond G (B). Thin bars represent one standard error (s.e.).

ity of going either direction, the probability of getting twenty-four or more declines is 0.0326. Because no a priori prediction of population trend was made, we should consider the probability of obtaining either extreme: twenty-four or more declines or twenty-four or more increases. This probability is 0.0652, which is marginally statistically significant. Therefore, based on binomial probabilities, there appears to be a trend toward decreased average production of large green frog tadpoles and hence of terrestrial juveniles.

Discussion

No strong trends in population size were detected for either newts or green frogs. Forest succession may play a significant role in future population trends for each species. Past population trends, likely future population trends, and any influence of UV-B radiation will be discussed in the remainder of this section.

Newts

Two areas of ponds show no clear downward or upward trend in average population density of adult newts over a period of ten to eleven years. This should be more than one population turnover, although a few adults could live beyond this time frame. Many cohorts of newts moved into or died out from local populations, thereby giving ample opportunity for population size to change over time. One area shows a barely significant downward trend (26 percent) in population density during the second half of the study period; another area shows a nearly significant upward trend (91 percent) in population density. In sum, these data suggest no clear trend up or down in newt population density over this time span.

Does this mean that newt populations will not change in any directed way in the upcoming decades? No. Newts tend to have their highest populations in sunnier ponds (e.g., pond G). Given that virtually all of the ponds are about thirty years old, forest regrowth around the bulldozed sites should continue. Therefore, even the sunnier ponds will get shadier, and presumably, without forest management, the newt population will decline. Furthermore, the best ponds for the production of efts also tend to be the sunnier ponds. Taken together, without management intervention, adult newt populations and eft production may decline in these ponds in upcoming decades. A similar situation appears to hold for an amphibian community at a site in southeast Michigan over a twenty-five year period (Skelly et al., unpublished manuscript).

For newts, it appears that analysis at the metapopulation level (e.g., Gill 1978a) produces less variable data than does analysis at the population level. Still, local populations feature s.d. $\log_{10}$ N values (average = 0.234 with a range of 0.050 to 0.458) that are similar to numbers available for other vertebrates (Pimm and Redfearn 1988; Schoener 1985). The same values calculated for the four metapopulations give a mean of 0.124 and a range of 0.082 to 0.178. These mean s.d. $\log_{10}$ N values are highly statistically different ($t = 14.83$, d.f. = 38, $p < 0.001$). It is likely, then, that dispersal of efts among local populations plays a major role in reducing variation in metapopulation density of newts. Whether the metapopulation persists in large part due to dispersal of efts cannot be assessed from these data.

Green Frogs

Based on comparisons of changes in mean produc-

Table 9-2. Mean density of large green frog (*Rama clamitans melanota*) tadpoles for each pond in each of two time periods: 1984/85 to 1987 and 1990 to 1994. Abbreviations: s.d. represents the standard deviation of census estimates, which gives an indication of annual variation in juvenile production; s.d. $\log_{10}$ represents the standard deviation of $\log_{10}$ census estimates, a separate indication of annual variation in juvenile production; n represents the number of census estimates; stat. sig. is the statistical significance of a t-test: sig represents statistically significant ($p < 0.05$), and ns represents not statistically significant ($p > 0.05$). Of ns differences, ponds featuring an estimated decline are presented first, those featuring an increase are presented last.

	1984/85 to 1987 Mean Density				1990 to 1994 Mean Density				
Pond	Number per Meter Squared	s.d.	s.d. $\log_{10}$	n	Number per Meter Squared	s.d.	s.d. $\log_{10}$	n	Stat. Sig.
1	6.25	3.66	0.28	4	18.99	6.18	0.18	5	sig
2	26.47	15.74	0.32	4	7.44	4.70	0.31	5	sig
TS	35.58	34.46	0.42	4	8.57	3.01	0.15	5	sig
Trends indicate decrease									
3	8.22	8.85	0.77	4	7.23	5.22	0.42	5	ns
7	7.05	1.47	0.10	3	6.70	5.05	0.31	5	ns
8	10.24	7.74	0.40	3	4.36	4.59	0.42	5	ns
A	33.00	27.51	0.73	3	17.16	9.15	0.25	5	ns
C	34.57	32.74	0.52	3	25.83	9.08	0.15	5	ns
D	53.22	39.19	0.43	3	33.13	15.49	0.23	5	ns
E	15.89	11.70	0.30	3	15.18	10.94	0.41	5	ns
G	42.78	54.26	0.65	3	17.56	15.07	0.44	5	ns
10	18.86	18.22	0.42	3	16.23	9.96	0.46	5	ns
9	19.43	11.96	0.32	3	6.60	6.03	0.37	5	ns
11	22.13	17.94	0.42	4	17.38	7.04	0.20	5	ns
12	6.76	0.14	0.01	2	5.35	3.73	0.47	5	ns
16	26.28	23.43	0.49	4	9.83	8.08	0.38	5	ns
20	20.92	10.77	0.31	4	18.80	12.40	0.29	5	ns
21	32.93	14.40	0.17	4	24.71	16.97	0.34	5	ns
GSP	6.65	5.00	0.38	4	4.40	5.60	0.48	5	ns
24	47.67	58.59	0.45	4	10.93	9.14	0.56	5	ns
25	11.88	14.60	0.46	4	6.88	4.42	0.24	5	ns
27	23.62	23.28	0.46	4	12.73	9.87	0.27	5	ns
28	40.36	71.80	0.84	4	16.94	12.95	0.41	5	ns
30	33.82	19.99	0.30	4	13.20	14.76	0.49	5	ns
33	21.42	7.25	0.15	4	12.72	8.24	0.75	5	ns
Trends indicate increase									
14	11.06	5.02	0.18	3	20.42	14.27	0.33	3	ns
Cl	0.52	0.79	0.12	4	2.77	2.61	0.25	5	ns
5	9.67	7.37	0.33	3	16.51	16.31	0.64	5	ns
B	5.07	4.28	0.34	3	7.62	2.59	0.14	5	ns
H	5.22	6.47	0.57	3	37.27	22.09	0.59	5	ns
15	4.12	3.93	0.53	4	11.73	13.32	0.42	5	ns
18	21.43	16.62	0.49	4	27.23	16.59	0.39	5	ns
26	14.08	10.62	0.42	4	25.09	19.75	0.42	5	ns
29	12.51	9.02	0.35	4	18.26	9.95	0.28	5	ns
31	8.75	6.08	0.30	4	14.11	10.32	0.25	5	ns
32	12.42	16.38	0.61	4	12.98	11.55	0.39	5	ns

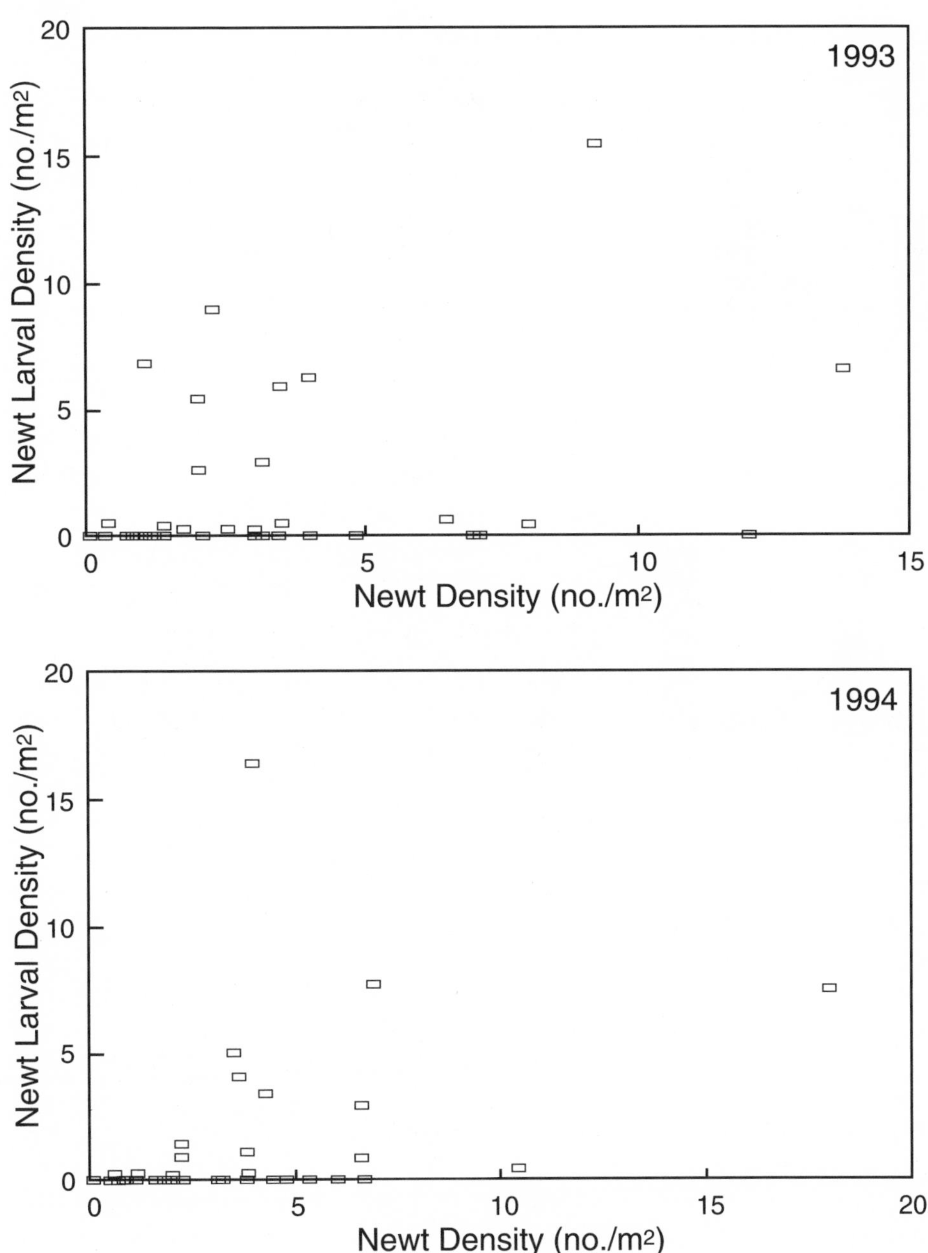

Figure 9-6. Density of late red-spotted newt (*Notophthalmus viridescens viridescens*) larvae expressed in number per meter squared in August in relation to estimated adult density in May for thirty-six ponds in 1993 (A) and 1994 (B).

tion of large tadpoles over the two time periods, there is little evidence that the production of green frog juveniles is declining over a ten-to-eleven-year period. However, the low statistical power of these tests hinders the detection of any real changes, if they exist. Population variability as expressed by s.d. $\log_{10}$ N of large tadpoles is large compared to other vertebrates (Pimm and Redfearn 1988; Schoener 1985). In fact, the data in Table 9-2 most closely resemble data for insects (Pimm and Redfearn 1988). This is not surprising because these data for green frogs focus on the production of juveniles, not adults as is commonly done for vertebrates.

If one assesses simply the direction of population change, a marginally significant trend toward decreased

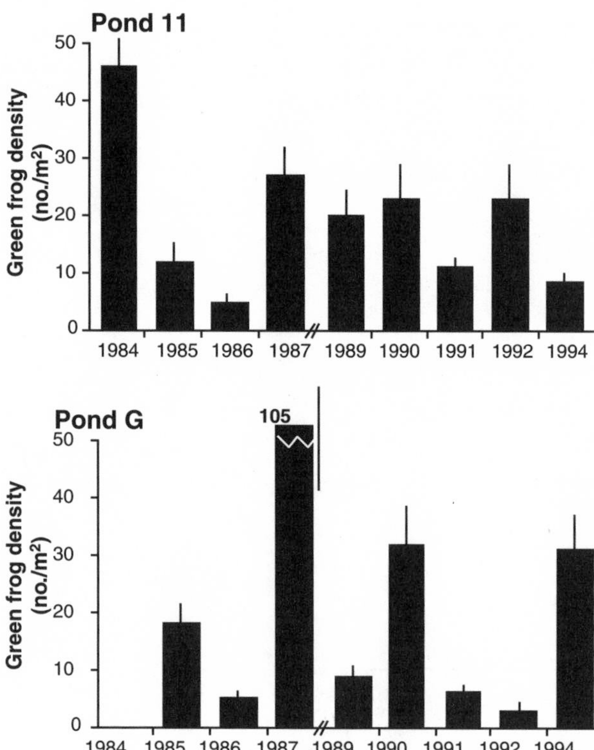

Figure 9-7. Sample trends of density of large green frog (*Rana clamitans melanota*) tadpoles expressed in number per meter squared just prior to metamorphosis across years for pond 11 (A) and pond G (B). Thin bars represent one standard error (s.e.).

production of juvenile green frogs appears. How this change in juvenile production relates to adult population size is unknown, but as yet it may not result in a decline in the adult population size. If real, the decreased production of juveniles is not great. It is possible that less-dense tadpole populations allow for faster growth/development of tadpoles and larger size at metamorphosis (e.g., Wilbur 1987). Although data are not available to test this directly, it was obvious during sampling that green frog tadpoles at low density were large and tadpoles at high density were small. Shorter larval period and larger size at metamorphosis increase survival to maturity and production of eggs (Scott 1994; Smith 1987). Thus, adult populations may not decrease given the trends in juvenile production.

If the decreased production of juvenile green frogs is real, what is causing it? Most likely the answer lies again in forest succession. Green frogs prefer to lay eggs in sunny, warm areas of ponds, which facilitates rapid development. As ponds become shadier, time spent as embryos is extended, offering additional opportunities for predators (e.g., water striders) to consume eggs. Shadier ponds likely will also have a lower net primary productivity, reducing the food available to hatchling and young tadpoles. Reduced food levels should result in slower initial growth and higher initial mortality, again because many predators (e.g., dragonfly larvae, backswimmers, abundant salamander larvae) can take advantage of slower growing tadpoles. The remaining tadpoles, with competition pressure relaxed, could then grow faster, as discussed above. Nonetheless, reduced survival of embryos and young tadpoles should result in reduced production of tapoles as shading increases beyond its present extent. In support of this, my observations strongly suggest that the sunnier ponds on average produce the highest density of tadpoles.

Potential influence of UV-B Radiation

Although no process that directs population change during this time period can be strongly supported by these data, a statement can be made regarding UV-B radiation. If the amount of UV-B radiation hitting south-central Indiana has increased over the ten-to-eleven-year period, which is not known, then it has not impacted newt population density. This is not surprising because the eggs are hidden in the pond bottom and not directly exposed to solar radiation. This supports predictions by Blaustein, Hoffman, et al. (1994) but does so only if incident UV-B has increased over time. Also, newts lay their eggs after new leaf growth on trees has occurred, and most of these small ponds are moderately to heavily shaded.

Can the putative decrease in production of green frog juveniles be due in part to the increased incidence of UV-B radiation? As above, data are not available concerning change in incidence of UV-B radiation impinging on south-central Indiana. Nonetheless, it is unlikely that increased incidence of UV-B radiation has been the primary cause of the decrease in juvenile production. The ponds are becoming shadier, which probably offsets any increase in UV-B. Blaustein, Hoffman, et al. (1994) note adverse impacts of UV-B radiation in species that lay their eggs in highly exposed microhabitats. Green frogs in my study area prefer to lay their eggs in exposed microhabitats, but such microhabitats are not fully exposed because of the ever-increasing shading of these ponds as the disturbed area of the construction site continues to return to full forest. Thus, UV-B radiation should not have a strong influence on species that lay highly exposed eggs in largely shaded environments. This seems obvious, but the data presented here can be used to begin the process of understanding which amphibian species, under which conditions, will decline even in relatively natural environments.

Summary

This study examines relatively long-term population trends for two species of amphibians in south-central Indiana. Red-spotted newts (*Notophthalmus viridescens viridescens*) are widespread and common. Population trends across thirty-six ponds showed no broad upward or downward shifts over a ten-to-eleven-year period. Local populations tended to fluctuate more than did metapopulations, which suggests that a collection of local pond populations connected by the dispersive eft stage is more stable than isolated local populations. Green frogs (*Rana clamitans melanota*) are also widespread and common. The population data suggest some decline in the average production of large tadpoles and hence terrestrial juveniles.

Metapopulation sizes of newts in the future likely will decrease as forest succession around these ponds continues, with the result that the ponds will become cooler and apparently less suitable for adults and for the production of efts. For green frogs, increased shadiness probably increases the duration of the embryonic period and consequently the vulnerability to predators of slow-growing tadpoles. Thus, it is likely that green frogs will also decline to some extent as forest regrowth continues.

Acknowledgments

I thank T. Elison, S. LaBudde, M. Beanan, J. Brown, and W. Kronland for help in and humor during sampling. I thank D. Duncan, L. Eckhart, B. Fisher, and J. Allen for permission to use public forests for research and for many fun conversations. I thank A. Cortwright for help in preparing the figures. The Carpenter family is owed a huge thanks for their hospitality and humorous fellowship over the years. C. Nelson and E. Werner supported my long-term investigations, and for that I am thankful. I am especially appreciative of Dana's and Alexander's support during the many recent trying times. This research was supported by grants from Bart Culver, Sigma Xi, the Indiana Academy of Science, and the Graduate School of Indiana University and from Summer Faculty Fellowships from Indiana University Northwest.

10

Status of Plains Spadefoot Toads in Western Iowa

Eugenia S. Farrar and Jane D. Hey

Plains spadefoot toads (*Spea bombifrons*) are small, toad-like anuran amphibians belonging to the family Pelobatidae. They are characterized by the presence of keratinized spades on their hind feet, which they use for burrowing, and by the presence of vertical, elliptical pupils. They have gray- to green-colored backs that are reticulated with black and brown (Fig. 10-1). Although their skin is relatively smooth, their backs have small protuberances that often are bright yellow or orange. Their bellies are white or sometimes spotted. They are secretive animals and are not often seen in the daytime. They spend most of their time burrowed into the soil and emerge to breed and feed following heavy rains.

Plains spadefoot toads are widely distributed throughout the Great Plains from central Mexico to southern Manitoba. Their distribution in Iowa is thought to be limited to the Missouri River Alluvial Plain and Loess Hills topographic regions of the western tier of counties (Christiansen and Mabry 1985). Bragg (1965) described spadefoot habitat in the Southwest as grasslands with sandy soils. Western Iowa contains xeric habitats similar to those described by Bragg. It is the driest part of Iowa, receiving 60 to 68 centimeters of precipitation per year.

The Missouri River and its alluvial plain form a large portion of the western border of Iowa. The terrain is characterized by stream channels, floodplains, oxbow lakes, terraces, alluvial fans, and sand dunes. Soil types and porosity vary from clayey and silty to sandy (Prior 1991). As the Missouri River was channelized between 1912 and 1960, more of the floodplain was planted in corn and soybeans. Prior to 1912, the river was free to meander across the river valley, and no agricultural land existed within the natural channel.

In western Iowa, the upland Loess Hills mimic the dry conditions of the Great Plains to the west and support a mixed-grass xerophytic prairie flora (Novacek 1985). The hills are composed of wind-deposited silt and form an eastern border to the Missouri River Alluvial Plain throughout its 320-kilometer length, beginning just above the confluence of Iowa with South Dakota and Nebraska and extending southward in Iowa to Missouri. These soils are porous, lightweight, and the most easily erodible soils in the state. The hills are a "crinkled topography of steep slopes featuring narrow ridge crests and branching sidespurs, and are deeply dissected by a dense drainage network" (Prior 1991). Ridgetops support a variety of plant and animal species typically found much farther west. Less steep slopes are terraced and either planted with crops or pastured. Loess hills taper to shallower deposits from west to east and form a more rolling topography where the shallow loess covers older glacial drift plain (Mutel 1989).

The status of spadefoots in western Iowa is of current concern because surveys in the 1980s suggested the species was abundant (Mabry and Christiansen 1982), while recently, volunteers conducting the Iowa Department of Natural Resources' (DNR) frog and toad surveys (Iowa DNR Wildlife Diversity Unit 1995; see also Hemesath, Chpt. 23, this volume) have found very few individuals.

The species was first discovered in 1967 in the southwestern part of the state at DeSoto Bend National Wildlife Refuge in Harrison County by Huggins (Huggins

Figure 10-1. Adult plains spadefoot toad (*Spea bombifrons*) observed in Plymouth County, Iowa, July 1994.

1971). Huggins stated that the nearest population of spadefoots was in Butler County, Nebraska, 80 kilometers southwest of the refuge. The species was placed on the state's threatened animal list. Christiansen and Bailey (1991) extended the range of the species in Iowa to include Mills and Pottawattamie Counties, but the species was still considered to be threatened (Roosa 1977). Roosa recommended that the spadefoot's "population status should be monitored and attempts made to determine its habitat requirements."

The next published account of the spadefoot toad in Iowa occurred in 1978 in a publication listing the endangered and uncommon reptiles and amphibians of Iowa (Christiansen and Burken 1978). The animals were said to occur "almost anyplace within twenty-five miles of the Missouri or Big Sioux Rivers." In 1979, Christiansen and Crawford presented a paper at the Iowa Academy of Sciences meeting in which they stated that the spadefoot toad, "although peripheral to the large population in the western United States, is abundant in the loess hills of western Iowa" (cited in Christiansen 1981). Christiansen (1981) further indicated that spadefoot populations were unchanged from his previous estimates and should not be considered threatened.

In 1985, Christiansen and Mabry (1985) stated that, based on research reported to the Iowa Conservation Commission (now DNR) in 1982, the plains spadefoot is "the only plains species to show a recent increase in abundance." They noted that "it is now one of the most abundant animals" in the Loess Hills and that it "occurs in all western counties except Lyon and Sioux." The 1982 report shows fifty-two locations of spadefoot sightings in the Missouri and Big Sioux River floodplains and in the Loess Hills. In 1988, a list of each state's endangered and threatened species of reptiles and amphibians failed to include plains spadefoot toads on Iowa's list (Allen 1988).

After five years of the Iowa DNR's frog and toad census (Iowa DNR Wildlife Diversity Unit 1995), volunteers have reported spadefoots from only four of the six counties in which they previously have been found: Harrison, Plymouth, Woodbury, and Fremont (L. Hemesath, personal communication). Because of the limited number of sightings, plains spadefoot toads have once again returned to the state's threatened list.

The present status of this species in Iowa needs to be clarified. Either the numbers of spadefoots have declined since 1982 or current censusing methods are failing to find them. Because of the reported global decline in many species of anurans and the need to establish baseline estimates of amphibian numbers to assess future changes (Blaustein, Wake, and Sousa 1994; Pechmann et al. 1991), it is important to determine the status of the plains spadefoot toad in Iowa. Our research, conducted during the summers of 1994 and 1995, begins to address the question of whether spadefoots are declining in western Iowa and to fill the gaps in our knowledge concerning how the natural history of the species may be similar to or different from other spadefoot species living in the Great Plains and in the Southwest.

Methods

The strategies we used to determine whether spadefoots are declining were to re-create surveys done in the past and to survey new areas. Some baseline information is found in the report of their initial discovery in Iowa (Huggins 1971) and in surveys and publications by Christiansen and Mabry (Christiansen 1981; Christiansen and Mabry 1985; Mabry 1984; Mabry and Christiansen 1982, 1991). These surveys used the technique of driving on warm humid nights and after rains, looking for individuals on the roads and listening for calling adults. Survey routes were predominantly in the Loess Hills. These reports document distribution of the species but have little information on numbers of individuals present.

We limited our studies to Harrison, Monona, Woodbury, and Plymouth counties on the western border of Iowa. We drove approximately 3200 kilometers on routes similar to those used by previous researchers and under as similar as possible weather conditions. We recorded topographic and global positioning system (GPS) (the second year) locations of all sites. Relative abundance of individuals heard from the road was estimated using the scale of one (individual call) to three (full chorus). Sex and snout-vent length of individuals found on the road were noted. Site designation was given to a location where an individual was seen on the road or was heard calling from the road or where tadpoles were observed in wetlands near the road.

Because previous studies had mainly surveyed the Loess Hills, we also selected other driving routes that covered the Missouri River floodplain. The first year we drove routes that included all of the major wetlands on the floodplain in the four counties. Also included on the routes were sites where DNR volunteers had reported hearing spadefoots. Routes were driven after rains and on warm humid nights if possible, but surveys were conducted during each of the three periods between 1 April and 10 July, as suggested in the Iowa DNR's frog and toad survey (Iowa DNR Wildlife Diversity Unit 1995). The second year we drove these routes only after heavy rains.

The presence of the Port Neal Field Station, south of Sioux City, Iowa, on the Missouri River floodplain facilitated our study of spadefoot behavior and life cycle. After initial difficulty in pinpointing where spadefoots were breeding, we located tadpoles in flooded farm fields near the lab. We then began monitoring several of these ephemeral wetlands. Information was gathered on breeding times, abundance of calling individuals, tadpole morphology, behavior, and time to metamorphosis. After gaining a better understanding of breeding habitat, we were able to survey other areas for tadpoles by sampling ephemeral ponds with small nets and/or seines.

Results

We found forty plains spadefoot sites during the two-year survey. The locations of these sites are shown in Figure 10-2, along with sites reported by others. Our sites included twenty-one breeding locations where tadpoles were found and nineteen locations where adults were seen on the road or heard calling (Table 10-1). The sites were predominantly in Monona and Woodbury Counties; no new sites were found in Harrison County. All of the breeding sites containing tadpoles were found on the Missouri River floodplain, mainly in the two adjacent townships of Lakeport in Woodbury County and Fairview in Monona County.

Nineteen calling sites were identified. Seven had full choruses, and the remainder had either single individuals or several individuals with nonoverlapping calls. In spite of driving several thousand kilometers at night, we found only eleven individuals on the roads. Snout-vent lengths of these animals ranged from 5.7 to 6.2 centimeters.

Adult males reacted to being handled with loud calls and milky secretions. These secretions can cause allergic reactions (Conant and Collins 1991); we recommend that these animals be handled carefully, and surveyors might consider wearing gloves.

In 1995, spadefoot breeding periods in Monona and Woodbury Counties were clearly linked to rainfall and temperature. Breeding followed locally heavy rains of 5 to 10 centimeters that fell on 27 May and 25 July (Monona County only). Air temperatures were above 21°C. Although heavy rains fell earlier in May when temperatures were lower, no breeding occurred in the ponds we were closely monitoring.

Spadefoot breeding sites on the floodplain can be described as flooded farm fields or ephemeral ponds (Fig. 10-3). The sites we have studied are all located on the western edge of the Missouri River floodplain near the river where the water table is high. Much of this area is planted with corn or soybeans, and some is under irrigation. These ephemeral ponds were associated with clayey-silty soils. Pond depths ranged from 5 to almost 40 centimeters. Little aquatic vegetation was associated with the breeding sites. Some ponds had cattails at the edge and a few had floating algal mats. Tadpoles appeared to favor open, turbid water. We found tadpoles in water temperatures ranging from 20° to 38°C. Ephemeral ponds generally contained water for four to six weeks. For example, in 1995 they filled on 27 May and were dry by 4 July.

We were unable to locate tadpoles in the Loess Hills by the same methods employed on the floodplain. The Loess Hills differ from the floodplain in the types of potential spadefoot breeding habitats. The hills have fewer row crops and are covered by mid-grass prairie or pasture grasses; in addition, the water table is lower than on the floodplain. We assume that spadefoots in the hills are breeding in cattle tanks, terraces, and shallow, fishless waters. These areas are difficult to locate even when precise GPS bearings have been recorded for calling sites. Many of the potential sites are on private land occupied by cattle and are not visible from the road. In the hills, there are fewer flooded farm fields than on the floodplain, and those present are better drained. For

Table 10-1. Numbers of plains spadefoot toad (*Spea bombifrons*) sites found in four counties in western Iowa

County	1994 Tadpole	1994 Adult	1995 Tadpole	1995 Adult	Total Sites*
Harrison	0	0	0	0	0
Monona	2	5	3	11	21
Woodbury	10	1	6	0	17
Plymouth	0	2	0	0	2
Total sites	12	8	9	11	40

*A site is defined as a location where tadpoles have been found or adults have been either seen or heard.

example, we returned the next day to a calling site found one evening in Monona County along the Little Sioux River to look for egg masses, only to discover that the water was mostly gone.

We learned several things about spadefoot tadpoles after monitoring breeding sites. Tadpoles metamorphose in three to four weeks depending on water temperatures. They form feeding aggregations. They occur as two morphological types. One rare type exhibits cannibalistic behavior and has a large, serrated horny beak and enlarged jaw muscles. We found only one pond each summer containing this morph. The more common morph had a smooth beak, had smaller jaw muscles, and was not cannibalistic. Whether intermediate morphs exist has yet to be determined.

Fairy shrimp, from the crustacean order Anostraca, commonly live in the ephemeral ponds in association with the spadefoot tadpoles. We found fairy shrimp in ten out of sixteen tadpole sites in Woodbury County and in one out of five sites in Monona County. A few other fairy shrimp sites did not have spadefoot tadpoles at the time we surveyed them. We have tentatively identified two genera of fairy shrimp, *Thamnocephalus* and *Streptocephalus,* from our study areas, and several other specimens have not yet been identified.

Discussion

There are several problems in assessing the status of plains spadefoot toads in Iowa. Baseline information on their past abundance is minimal. We lack long-term records for this species because it has only been known to occur in Iowa since 1967, and anecdotal data are unavailable for reconstructing its early numbers and distribution. Sampling bias has existed in previous studies of the geographic distribution of the species. Christiansen and Mabry's (1985) surveys were conducted predominantly in the Loess Hills and on the edge of the Missouri River floodplain, so we have no floodplain abundance data to compare with our data. The unique behavior of this burrowing species makes adult censusing especially difficult. Spadefoot toads remain burrowed most of the time and are only seen on warm, humid nights or following heavy rains.

If asked whether spadefoots are declining or threatened in western Iowa, we would have to say it is impossible to answer that question at this time. On one hand we have discovered forty new spadefoot sites in the two-year study, including twenty-one breeding sites. This might suggest that the species is abundant and easy to find. However, we have found only one region where spadefoot toads consistently breed, as evidenced by the presence of tadpoles. The majority of breeding sites were found in two adjacent townships on the Missouri River floodplain. Iowa spadefoot breeding sites and tadpole occurrence have not been previously described or monitored, so again, baseline information on abundance is unavailable.

On the other hand, our driving surveys suggest a decline in spadefoot numbers in the Loess Hills. Our results contrast markedly with the findings of Christiansen and Mabry (1985). They assessed the status of the spadefoot toad by driving roads in the Loess Hills after rains and on warm, humid nights. They collected at least 110 specimens in 1981 and 1982 (J.L. Christiansen, personal communication; Christiansen and Mabry 1985; Mabry

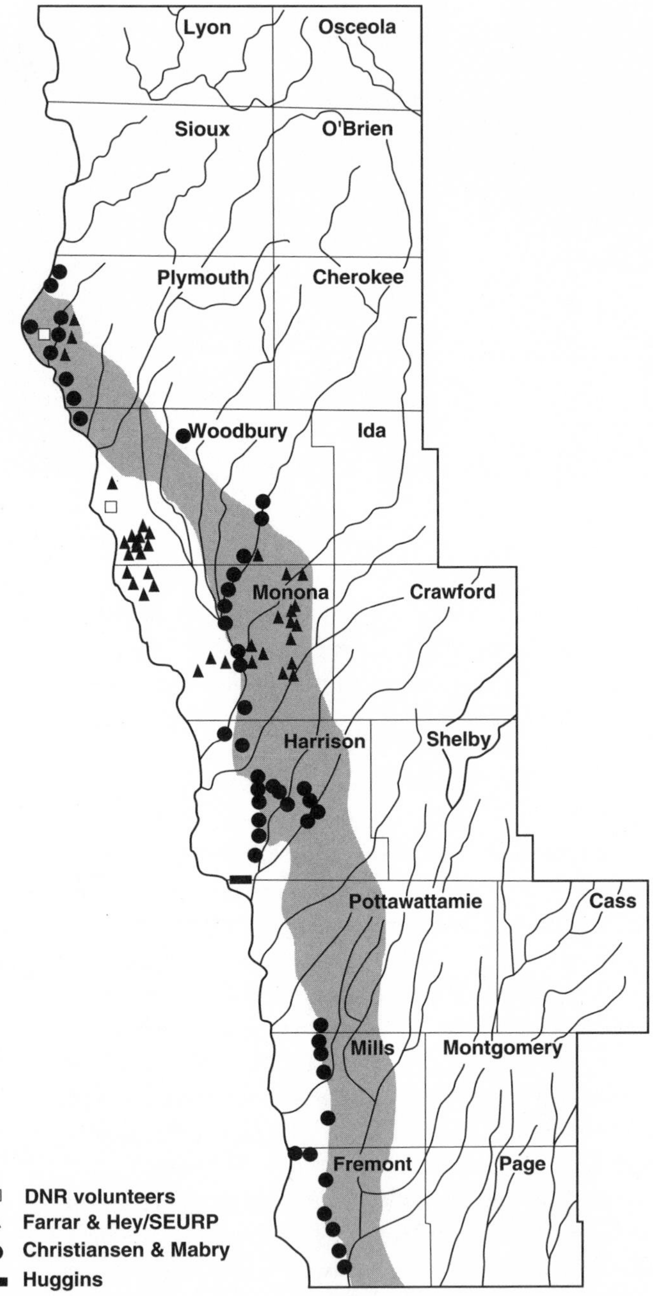

Figure 10-2. Geographic locations of plains spadefoot toad (*Spea bombifrons*) sites found by various researchers in western Iowa. Shaded area corresponds to the Loess Hills topographic region.

and Christiansen 1991). We found only eleven spadefoots when we drove similar routes in four counties during two summers.

Another source of information regarding species abundance is the Iowa DNR's frog and toad survey. This censusing method involves having volunteers monitor several sites of their own choosing for frogs calling during the early, middle, and late portions of the breeding season. Volunteers in western Iowa have seldom reported hearing spadefoot toads. In part this is probably due to the small number of volunteers censusing in western Iowa as compared to other parts of the state. Our results suggest a variety of additional causes for the small number of reports: (1) spadefoot toads may be declining, especially in the Loess Hills, as our driving surveys indicate; (2) volunteers may not be listening on the few evenings, mostly following heavy rains, when spadefoots are breeding; (3) volunteers may ignore flooded farm fields and other ephemeral waters because these habitats may not be considered to be suitable amphibian breeding habitats; (4) volunteers may be discouraged by bad weather, but heavy rains promote spadefoot breeding activity—the census protocol says: "If heavy rains hit during the survey, stop the survey, and repeat it at a later date" (Iowa DNR Wildlife Diversity Unit 1995); (5) volunteers report that spadefoot calls are difficult to discern in a chorus of other frog calls; and (6) the census protocol emphasizes listening at night, whereas spadefoot monitoring may best be achieved by a combination of monitoring methods, including visual sightings of adults and tadpoles.

Uncertainties regarding plains spadefoot distribution in Iowa and factors limiting its distribution pose further challenges in assessing its status in Iowa. The eastern limits of spadefoot distribution in Iowa are currently not known. Chronologically, the species was first found at the western edge of the Missouri floodplain in 1967 and was then found to be abundant in the Loess Hills during the 1970s and 1980s. Christiansen has reasoned that the species could be spreading eastward (Christiansen 1995). Their distribution in Missouri suggests that, given suitable habitats, they can live much farther east, because they are found along the Missouri River floodplain from northwestern Missouri to eastern Missouri (Johnson 1987). An Iowa DNR volunteer frog and toad census taker claims to have found them calling farther to the east of the Loess Hills in Sac County. If the species is expanding eastward, some concern about its possible decline in the Loess Hills would be alleviated.

Factors limiting species distribution could include the presence of suitable breeding habitats and overwintering sites. Christiansen and Mabry (1985) suggest that spadefoot toads are restricted in Iowa to deep loess soils. However, we have found them breeding at the very western edge of the Missouri River floodplain, far from the

Loess Hills and in habitats surrounded by soil types different from loess. This would suggest that species distribution is not limited to deep loess environments. Further research might profitably be directed at describing species distribution and determining factors that limit that distribution, such as overwintering and breeding habitat requirements.

Several aspects of spadefoot toad natural history potentially influence its abundance and distribution. These include specific breeding habitat requirements, maintenance of tadpole polyphenism, and habitat loss. Spadefoot toads frequently breed in the same sites from year to year. Six of our sites were used during both years of the study. Loss of these habitats could negatively impact breeding. We have already witnessed the demise of a particularly interesting site in a sand dune area near the Missouri River after it was quarried. In addition, ephemeral ponds in corn and soybean fields must be influenced by agricultural practices. We need to understand how these practices impact spadefoot toad life history.

Species survival of southern spadefoots (*Spea multiplicatus*) in the desert Southwest may depend on the maintenance of an environmentally induced polyphenism (EIP) based on an association between tadpoles and fairy shrimp (Pomeroy 1981; Pfennig 1992 a,b; see also Whiteman and Howard, Chpt. 32, this volume). Tadpoles exist as two morphs, an omnivore that eats mainly algae and diatoms and a carnivore that develops from the omnivore after feeding on fairy shrimp. The larger carnivorous form survives better in shorter-lived ponds, because it metamorphoses faster and leaves before the pond dries. The omnivore survives better in longer-lived ponds because it accumulates more lipids and has better postmetamorphic success (Pfennig 1992a,b). Carnivorous morphs are induced by ingestion of fairy shrimp, which are more abundant in the most ephemeral ponds.

Plains spadefoot toad tadpoles in Iowa also have this trophic polymorphism. We have found carnivorous and omnivorous morphs resembling those described in southern spadefoots (Pomeroy 1981; Pfennig 1992a,b) and have begun characterizing their anatomical and behavioral differences. The carnivores are rare in our pond system, occurring in only two of the twenty-one sites observed during the two summer field seasons. Finding the polymorphism at all is unexpected in the Midwest (Pfennig 1992b; Whiteman and Howard, Chpt. 32, this volume).

We have observed that plains spadefoot toad tadpoles in our study area often live in association with fairy

Figure 10-3. A plains spadefoot toad (*Spea bombifrons*) breeding site on the Missouri River Alluvial Plain.

shrimp. Eleven of the twenty-one ephemeral ponds had both organisms. Finding fairy shrimp is an unusual event in Iowa, and few, if any, publications concerning their natural history and distribution exist for the state. While it would be tempting to assume that the spadefoot carnivorous morph–fairy shrimp association is similar in these ponds to that observed in desert pools, the cues and triggers for morph induction and differential morph survivorship of Iowa plains spadefoots should be determined experimentally.

Finding polymorphic spadefoot tadpoles in association with fairy shrimp has potentially important implications for interpreting and assessing the status of plains spadefoots in Iowa and across the Great Plains. We need to learn more about the distributions of both the polymorphic tadpoles and fairy shrimp and about the nature of their interrelationships. If plains spadefoot polyphenism is an evolutionarily stable strategy, like that described for southern spadefoot toads (Pfennig 1992b), then species survival of these spadefoots throughout the Great Plains and Midwest could depend on conserving not just the animal but the ecosystem.

Summary

Plains spadefoot toads (*Spea bombifrons*) are widely distributed across the Great Plains, where they spend most of their life burrowed in sandy soils, emerging to breed in ephemeral ponds following hard rains. Their distribution in Iowa is thought to be restricted to the Loess

Hills and the Missouri River Alluvial Plain of the more xeric western counties. They were first discovered near DeSoto Bend National Wildlife Refuge in 1967 and were considered threatened until the early 1980s, when they were found to be common in the Loess Hills. However, recent Iowa Department of Natural Resources volunteer frog and toad censuses report few spadefoot toads. In two seasons of censusing by night driving, we found only eleven adults and seven full choruses. However, we found twenty-one breeding sites that contained tadpoles in flooded farm fields on the Missouri River floodplain. Many of these sites also had fairy shrimp. Tadpoles occurred as carnivorous and omnivorous morphs similar to those found in desert-dwelling spadefoots, where carnivores develop after eating fairy shrimp. Lack of information regarding tadpole morph abundance and distribution, as well as other factors, makes status assessment difficult. Maintenance of the polymorphism could be important for spadefoot toad establishment and persistence in Iowa.

Acknowledgments

Support for this research was provided by Iowa Department of Natural Resources Wildlife Diversity Program and Midwest Power SEURP grants to Morningside College. Thanks to SEURP undergraduate researchers for assistance in surveying and to Tim Orwig for editorial assistance.

11

Blanchard's Cricket Frogs in Wisconsin: A Status Report

Robert Hay

Blanchard's cricket frogs (*Acris crepitans blanchardi*) were historically widespread throughout the southern half of Wisconsin in thirty-one counties (Vogt,1981; see Fig. 11-1; Casper, Chpt. 22, this volume). A retired Wisconsin Department of Natural Resources (WDNR) naturalist stated that these frogs were so abundant in the 1950s that you could seldom walk a warm-water stream or river during the summer in southwestern Wisconsin without seeing and hearing them regularly (G. Knudsen, personal communication). Vogt (1981) reported large populations of Blanchard's cricket frogs along the Wisconsin River bottoms (presumed to be the lower Wisconsin below Prairie du Sac) in the 1960s. Knudsen first noted declines in this species in the late 1950s and 1960s (Les 1979). Vogt (1981) noted rapid declines in the late 1970s. Blanchard's cricket frogs were listed by the WDNR as state endangered in 1982 (WDNR 1989).

Efforts to Document and Monitor Status

Early efforts to determine the status of Blanchard's cricket frogs were nonsystematic but did provide enough evidence to warrant listing of this species. Due in part to the decline of this species, observations of heavy mortality in northern leopard frogs (*Rana pipiens*) in the early to mid-1970s (Hine et al. 1981), and indications that amphibians were in trouble worldwide, the WDNR initiated its annual frog and toad survey based on a censusing method developed by D. K. Jansen and R. K. Anderson (University of Wisconsin-Stevens Point; see Mossman and Hine 1984; Mossman et al., Chpt. 21, this volume). Unfortunately, very few active cricket frog locations fall within the routes established for the survey (five of ninety-seven routes and only 6 of 970 sites in 1994). In addition, the survey is designed to provide general trend data for species and is not designed to quantify numbers of frogs. The Wisconsin Herpetological Atlas Project has added no additional counties to the distribution of this species in ten years (Casper 1996, Chpt. 22, this volume). Specific quantitative surveys have since been conducted for Blanchard's cricket frogs in both 1991 (Jung 1993) and 1994 (Christoffel and Hay 1995).

Summary of 1991 and 1994 Surveys

Jung (1993) conducted a survey of forty historical sites in southwestern Wisconsin in 1991 to quantify calling male Blanchard's cricket frogs, estimate populations, and determine if correlations between presence/absence and habitat, water quality, and surrounding land use existed. Blanchard's cricket frogs were found at only nineteen of forty sites (48 percent), and numbers of calling males at sites ranged from one to approximately twenty frogs. Survey methods were not exhaustive (only calling males were counted [see Perrill and Magier 1988], and only the highest number of calling males for each site was used to make population estimates). Sites were visited an average of 2.6 times. Population estimates are extremely conservative. Assuming a 1:1 sex ratio (Pyburn 1958), Jung estimated the total population of the combined sites to be 250 frogs, with a mean of 14 with a standard deviation of 9.6 frogs per site.

Jung showed that more anuran species were found at

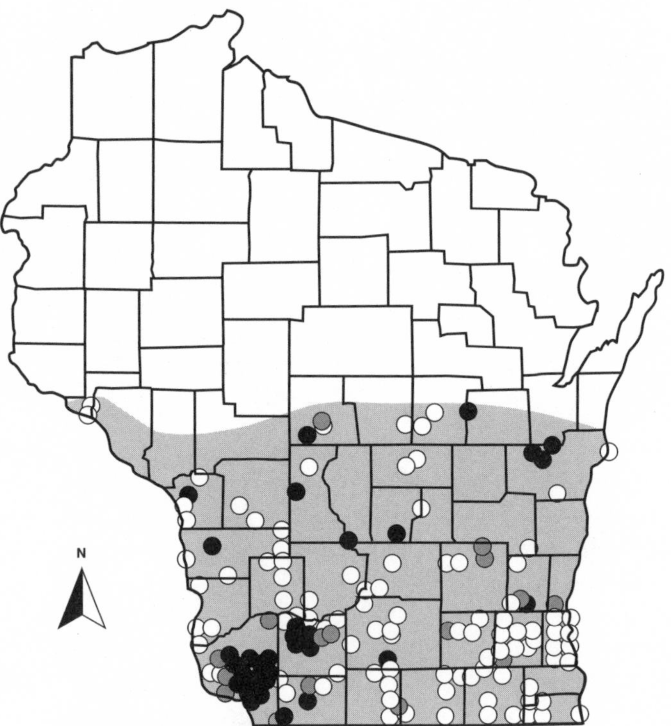

Figure 11-1. Blanchard's cricket frog (*Acris crepitans blanchardi*) occurrences and historical range.

sites without surrounding agricultural fields, and that Blanchard's cricket frogs were present at sites with higher water temperatures. A negative relationship existed between species richness and turbidity. However, there were no significant relationships between cricket frog presence/absence and other habitat characteristics measured.

In 1994, Christoffel conducted a calling male census that included most of the sites Jung found active in 1991, plus many potential sites that had not been previously surveyed (Christoffel and Hay 1995). This survey was prompted by two major flood events in 1993 that occurred during the prime breeding period for Blanchard's cricket frogs. It was suspected that numbers of cricket frogs would be significantly lower due to the flushing of eggs and larvae the previous year (see Burkett 1984 on population dynamics). Streams in southwestern Wisconsin are subject to flash flooding because of steep topography.

Sites were visited several times (average 2.6 times) during the breeding season to ensure sampling during peak breeding activity. In 1994, twenty-four of Jung's forty 1991 sites were resurveyed. Fifty percent (twelve of twenty-four) were active in 1991. Only 21 percent (five of twenty-four) were active in 1994. Several of Jung's other active sites were not revisited due to road construction and time-related constraints. In total, sixty-five sites were visited in 1994. Two sites not surveyed in 1991, but with historical records, yielded cricket frogs in 1994. Four previously unknown cricket frog locations were also discovered, yielding eleven known active sites in 1994. Of these eleven sites, only two were stream/river sites. All four of the newly discovered sites were ponds. Two of the new sites had full choruses of cricket frogs, and numbers of individuals could not be accurately counted. As a result, no overall population estimates were made. The number of calling male cricket frogs at the other nine sites ranged from 1 to 7, and averaged 2.2 per site per visit.

Discussion and Preliminary Conclusions

To date, it is only possible to speculate on the cause(s) of the tremendous decline of Blanchard's cricket frogs, which were once abundant in Wisconsin and elsewhere throughout their upper geographic range (Vogt 1981; Oldham 1992; Mierzwa 1994b). Burkett (1984) describes a life history for Blanchard's cricket frogs that appears to make them vulnerable to stochastic events like flooding and/or severe drought (i.e., life span averaging four months, complete population turnover in sixteen months). While not documented in the field yet demonstrated in the laboratory, drought, especially during the winter, with its corresponding drawdown of permanent water, may contribute significantly to the decline of this species through desiccation and/or freezing (Ralin and Rogers 1972). Burkett (1984) also states that the small surface-to-volume ratio of cricket frogs makes them more susceptible to desiccation than are larger frogs and notes that a high percentage of hibernating cricket frogs are juveniles (99 percent). Bradford (1983) also suggests that winterkill of some species of frogs may be relatively high, especially under certain environmental conditions. All of this suggests that the decline of cricket frogs may very well be related to natural phenomena (i.e., climate), although it certainly does not preclude other factors that may contribute as well (Birge et al. 1980; Hall and Kolbe 1980; Linder et al. 1990). The likelihood that climate is a major contributing factor in the decline of Blanchard's cricket frogs is supported by data showing dramatic declines at the northern fringe of their range, whereas they appear to be stable in the heart of their range.

Habitat changes may figure significantly into the decline of the previously best-known discrete (pond) population of Blanchard's cricket frogs in Wisconsin and may be partially responsible for the declines of other cricket frog pond populations as well. The previously large population occurred in two adjacent farm ponds located slightly up-gradient of a spring-fed sedge meadow and stream. Both of these habitats contained cricket frogs as recently as 1991, and all were heavily utilized by cattle for decades, except for one of the two ponds (which is semipermanent). Cattle activity ceased in 1986. In 1984, Dick Nikolai (WDNR, unpublished data) counted 220 cricket frogs at the two ponds. Since 1984, this population has been monitored using the Wisconsin Frog and Toad Survey method (Mossman and Hine 1984; Mossman et al. Chpt. 21, this volume). The observations of other species were also recorded using this method. Cricket frogs received a call index of three (the highest rating of abundance–full chorus) from 1985 to 1992. Jung (1993) first reported green frogs (*Rana clamitans*) at this site in 1991. Nikolai recorded green frogs in 1992, with a call index of one. This author recorded them with a call index two in 1993 during one visit to the site, and no cricket frogs were heard. In 1994, five visits yielded one calling cricket frog during only one visit. In the same year, Nikolai (personal communication) reported green frogs with a call index of three, and Christoffel (personal communication) noted that "you could walk across the large pond on the backs of the green frogs they were so numerous." No cricket frogs were heard at the down-gradient sedge meadow or stream sites in 1994.

Major habitat changes are the only observable factors accompanying this species shift. The large pond, with its mud banks and low vegetation once trampled and grazed to the soil, appeared to favor Blanchard's cricket frogs (Minton 1972; Burkett 1984). Water quality has shifted from "a turbid, green cow pond" to a clear-water pond with dense submergent vegetation. The lack of grazing and wallowing has allowed the entire bank to revegetate to tall grass. This microhabitat strongly favors green frogs (Vogt 1981; Oldfield and Moriarty 1994). Similar bank revegetation has occurred at the adjacent stream site as well. It is unknown how the lack of grazing relates to cricket frog absence in the sedge meadow.

It is not clear whether or how green frogs compete with Blanchard's cricket frogs. I could find no evidence in the literature of green frog predation on Blanchard's cricket frogs. Understanding the dramatic species shift at the discrete location cited above is further complicated by the observations of Jung (1993) and Christoffel (personal communication), who show green frogs to be the species most commonly associated with cricket frogs. Could it be that this association is partially responsible for cricket frog declines? There are no baseline data on green frog numbers in the 1950s and 1960s, when cricket frogs were still abundant. Could it be that disturbance factors related to grazing and wallowing have historically favored cricket frogs?

Other factors may have also adversly affected cricket frogs. Has habitat fragmentation and isolation coupled with dramatic population declines (possibly attributable to drought or harsh overwintering conditions) prevented cricket frogs from shifting locations (microhabitats) as habitats changed over time? How do changes in shoreline vegetation (from short and/or sparse vegetation to tall and dense vegetation) affect the habitat choice, foraging ability, or susceptibility to predation of Blanchard's cricket frogs? These questions and more need to be answered.

Future experimentation with habitat manipulation is planned at the discrete ponds mentioned above, including the reintroduction of cattle, to determine whether cricket frog populations can be restored at this site. The entire frog community will be monitored throughout this experiment.

Evidence to date indicates that Blanchard's cricket frogs have declined in Wisconsin to the point where recovery looks unlikely. There is still hope that the two new healthy populations with full choruses and other possible unknown populations may buy time for this species in Wisconsin. Factors causing declines must be determined, and appropriate conservation and restoration measures must be determined and applied if we are to save this species from extirpation. Efforts to restore cricket frog habitat are being made under the assumption that climatic factors favor recovery and that other factors contributing to declines can be mitigated.

Summary

Blanchard's cricket frogs (*Acris crepitans blanchardi*) were historically abundant in southern Wisconsin until the 1950s, when declines were first observed. Since then, populations have declined dramatically, and Blanchard's cricket frogs were listed as an endangered species in the state in 1982. Early efforts to monitor cricket frog populations began with the Wisconsin frog and toad survey, and results indicate that this species is facing extirpation in Wisconsin. Only eleven of sixty-five sites contained cricket frogs in a 1994 survey, and only two of these had strong calling choruses. It appears that climate, particularly related to winters, has played a major role in the decline, as this species is disappearing from much of its northern range in the United States and Ontario. In addition to climate, habitat fragmentation and changes in the physical structure of microhabitats (reduced grazing and bank trampling) may figure into these declines. Factors causing cricket frog declines must be determined and mitigated if this species is to remain in Wisconsin.

12

Status and Distribution of Two Uncommon Frogs, Pickerel Frogs and Wood Frogs, in Illinois

Michael Redmer

In Illinois, only one anuran species has official conservation status. Illinois chorus frogs (*Pseudacris streckeri illinoensis*) are considered by the Illinois Department of Natural Resources (IDNR) to be threatened (Herkert 1992). Pickerel frogs (*Rana palustris*) and wood frogs (*Rana sylvatica*) have peripheral ranges in Illinois (Figs. 12-1, 12-2). Since Smith's (1961) comprehensive work on the amphibians and reptiles of Illinois, there have been few references to either species in the state. Although neither has been considered threatened or endangered, the Illinois status of pickerel frogs and wood frogs has been reviewed several times since the early 1970s (Ackerman 1975; Ashton 1976b; Morris 1977; Redmer and Mierzwa 1994). Since first being convened in the mid-1970s, the Illinois Endangered Species Protection Board and some Illinois herpetologists have often discussed the status of pickerel frogs and wood frogs but have recommended no action due to the lack of data.

The objectives of this study were to: (1) review the historical distributions of pickerel frogs and wood frogs in Illinois; (2) search for both species at or near historical Illinois localities and document populations with voucher specimens; and (3) compare the early (records that predate Smith [1961]), recent (records from 1961 to 1987), and current (records from 1987 to 1996) documented distributions in Illinois to determine if either species has declined within its known Illinois range.

Methods

The historical Illinois ranges of pickerel frogs and wood frogs were determined by surveying museum collections for preserved specimens (Table 12-1). Collections from which material was examined include: Burpee Museum of Natural History (BM); California Academy of Sciences (CAS); Chicago Academy of Sciences (CA); Field Museum of Natural History (FMNH); Illinois Natural History Survey (INHS); Illinois State Museum (ISM); Northwestern University (NU, collection housed at CA); Southern Illinois University at Carbondale (SIUC); Southern Illinois University at Edwardsville (SIUE); United States National Museum of Natural History (USNM); University of Illinois Museum of Natural History (UIMNH); and University of Michigan Museum of Zoology (UMMZ).

Collecting permits were obtained from agencies having jurisdiction over natural areas within the Illinois ranges of pickerel frogs and wood frogs. Areas at or near historical localities were visited. Adult or juvenile pickerel frogs or wood frogs were collected as vouchers when encountered. If only egg masses or tadpoles of wood frogs (an "explosive" breeder) were found, a few (fewer than fifty per location) were collected and raised in the lab through metamorphosis, at which time they were preserved as vouchers. Voucher specimens were deposited in the FMNH, INHS, or SIUC herpetology collections (Table 12-2).

When pickerel frogs and wood frogs were encountered, their relative abundance and the condition of their habitat were noted. In-depth studies of a southern Illinois wood frog population have been recently initiated (Redmer, unpublished data).

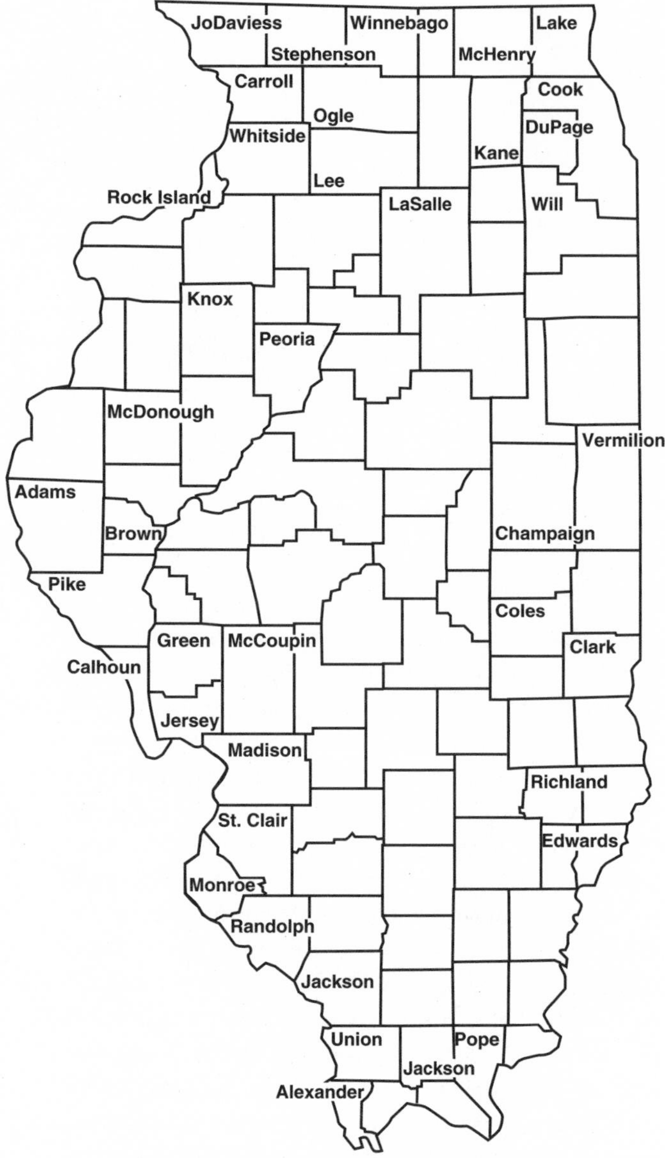

Figure 12-1. Illinois counties where known or reported populations of pickerel frogs (*Rana palustris*) and wood frogs (*Rana sylvatica*) occur.

Results

Surveys for Pickerel Frogs

The historical distribution and current status of pickerel frogs in northern Illinois were reviewed by Redmer and Mierzwa (1994). They found documented pre-1961 records for Carroll, JoDaviess, Kane, McHenry, Ogle, and Stephenson Counties and considered valid a literature record (Olson 1956) for Winnebago County. They reported that pickerel frog populations persisted in Carroll, JoDaviess, Lee, Ogle, and Stephenson Counties. Several undocumented reports (for DuPage, Kane, Lake, LaSalle, Whiteside, and Winnebago Counties) lack voucher specimens or were based on misidentified northern leopard frogs (*Rana pipiens*). Redmer and Mierzwa (1994) found most northern Illinois pickerel frog adults in dense herbaceous vegetation along the margins of cool streams that flowed through or near forest.

In western Illinois, documented pre-1961 records of the pickerel frog are available from Adams, Greene, and Pike Counties (Table 12-1). Specimens (ISM and SIUE collections) from Pike County were collected in the 1960s and 1970s (Table 12-2). In 1994, I collected additional specimens from Adams, Brown, and Pike Counties. At one Pike County locality (ca. 2.5 kilometers southwest of Pearl), pickerel frogs were extremely abundant (from 10 to 200 individuals observed during three visits) in and around a cave. Many of the Pike County museum specimens were also collected at this locality. In Adams and Brown Counties, I observed pickerel frogs in herbaceous vegetation along streams or springs. A specimen (SIUE 1600) collected at Carlinville Lake, Macoupin County, possibly is a released bait animal and may not represent a native population. I visited that locality in April 1995 and found no pickerel frogs and marginal habitat for this species.

In southwestern Illinois, pickerel frogs were first reported from Bluff Lake, St. Clair County (Hurter 1893). That locality was cited by Smith (1961), although he reported no voucher. Specimens collected from 1895 to 1908 were the only St. Clair County vouchers until one was recently collected in a karst area in the western part of the county (Redmer and Ballard 1995). The occurrence of pickerel frogs in Jersey and Madison Counties is documented by specimens collected in the 1960s, 1970s, and more recently (Redmer et al. 1995). Several northern leopard frog specimens from Madison County were found in the SIUE collection of pickerel frogs, with which they apparently were confused (Redmer 1996). Pickerel frogs are well documented from Monroe County by specimens collected before 1961, between 1961 and 1986, and from 1987 to present. Brandon and Ballard (1991) considered this species to be uncommon to common in a floodplain in Randolph and Monroe Counties. A specimen (SIUE 1597) was collected in Randolph County in 1971, and a specimen (SIUC H-4270) collected at the same locality in 1991 was the first reported as a new county record (Redmer and Ballard 1995). An additional Randolph County specimen (SIUC

Table 12-1. Specimens collected before 1986

Pickerel frogs (*Rana palustris*).

Adams Co.: INHS 2659–2660, 2769–2770, 3228–3230; UMMZ 58782. Alexander Co.: FMNH 2162, 2172, 2204; INHS 5317–5318, 6675; SIUC 1276; UIMNH 23894, 26754–26755. Carroll Co.: INHS 3442; UIMNH 4553. Champaign Co.: UIMNH 1801. Jersey Co.: SIUE 1591, 1598, 1601, 1610. JoDaviess Co.: BM 208–210; CA 13159; INHS 4281–4182; UIMNH 3055–3056; UMMZ 67505. Johnson Co.: 1593 (locality suspect). Kane Co.: CA 15350, 15631. Macoupin Co.: SIUE 1600 (locality suspect). Madison Co.: SIUE 1063, 1592. McHenry Co.: INHS 1112–1114. Monroe Co.: BM 212; INHS 3262–3265, 3470–3471, 3509, 4070–4071, 4379–4382 (labels on all four say "Randolph Co.," but distance measurements actually place locality in Monroe Co.), 5838–5841, 7860, 8872; SIUE 1603–1609. Ogle Co.: CA 2157–2158; USNM 167617. Pike Co.: INHS 3374–3377, 3410–3411, 5835–5837, 7099–7102; ISM 621835–621837, 626107–626113, 684465–684466; UIMNH 15795, 16319, 16349, 16559–16561; SIUE 1594–1595, 1599, 1611–1613. Randolph Co.: SIUE 1597. St. Clair Co: CAS 17758; USNM 58003. Stephenson Co: UIMNH 3004–3005; INHS 7286. Union Co.: CA 214–215; UIMNH 1848.

Wood frogs (*Rana sylvatica*).

Champaign Co.: INHS 1147. Clark Co.: INHS 2731, 3730. Coles Co.: INHS 1838–1841, 1892–1897, 1992–1996, 6173, 6890; UIMNH 244–246, 712–715, 73376–73379; UMMZ 151854; USNM 14109. Cook Co: CA 17129, 19446–19447; FMNH 20659, 162067–162069, 162169, 162171–162190; NU 250, 257, 1652–1653. Edwards Co.: INHS 9614. Effingham Co.: INHS 2067. Jackson Co.: FMNH 25938–25939; SIUC H-470–471, 2659. JoDaviess Co.: 6183–6186. Lake Co.: CA 1027–1040, 1926–1928, 17128, 17130–17131, 18723, 19151–19159, 19259–19262, 19478–19490, 19495; FMNH 6745–6746, 11890–11893, 11975–11977, 12994, 31951–31955, 135266, 135274, 155854, 162070–162082, 162088–162090, 162160–162168, 162526–162548, 164594–164607; INHS 6342–6344. Monroe Co.: INHS 3261; SIUC H-2091, H-2321– 2322, H-2656; UMMZ 59754. Richland Co.: UIMNH 16731; USNM 37976, 38428. Rock Island Co.: INHS 3706. Vermilion Co.: INHS 9216, 10198; UIMNH 1805.

H-5071) was collected near Fort Kaskaskia State Park in 1995.

In extreme southern Illinois, pickerel frogs were collected in Union County by Robert Kennicott before 1859. Garman (1890, 1892; cited by Cagle 1942) reported this species from Bluff Lake, but I am not aware of a voucher. Additional Union County specimens were collected at Alto Pass in 1930 and at Ware (SIUC 236; no date, specimen is lost). I collected the only recent Union County specimens in 1988 at Trail of Tears State Forest (specimen is lost) and in 1994 (SIUC H-4780), about 1 kilometer east of Bluff Lake. Both were found close to intermittent streams near the mouths of large valleys. In Alexander County, pickerel frogs are documented by a number of specimens collected in the vicinity of Olive Branch and Horseshoe Lake, the most recent of which was collected in 1952. Despite extensive collecting since the early 1960s (Brandon 1994; L. E. Brown, personal communication), no additional specimens have been found in the Horseshoe Lake area. A specimen (SIUE 1593) collected in 1971 at Burnside is the only one known from Johnson County. In 1995, I visited several localities in the Shawnee National Forest near New Burnside. No pickerel frogs were found, though apparently suitable habitat occurs there. Because no other specimens have been collected in the interior of the Shawnee Hills, I consider this record questionable.

Blanchard and Princen (1976) reported pickerel frogs from the Peoria area in central Illinois but cited no vouchers. This record is well within the interior of Illinois and far from the documented range of pickerel frogs. Of the Blanchard and Princen article, Morris et al. (1983) stated that "some identifications [are] suspect." I do not currently consider this pickerel frog record to be valid.

A literature record (Baker 1922: 116) of pickerel frogs from "the Big Vermilion River Valley," Vermilion County, and a specimen (UIMNH 1801) collected by A. R. Cahn in 1925 at the Urbana Country Club (Champaign County) are the only records of this species from eastern Illinois. Both are questionable. The Champaign-Vermilion County region has been well collected for most of this century. Although Minton (1972) reported pickerel frogs from as near as Warren County, Indiana, and it is possible that this species occurs in the mesic forests of eastern Illinois, I do not consider the Vermilion and Champaign County records to be valid because recent vouchers are not available. A Coles County specimen (FMNH 37860) cataloged as a pickerel frog is the plains leopard frog (*Rana blairi*).

Figure 12-2. Records of pickerel frogs (*Rana palustris*) in Illinois. (A) Pre-1961 records. (B) Records between 1961 and 1986. (C) Records since 1987. Solid circles indicate museum vouchers examined by the author. Solid squares indicate literature reports judged to be valid. Question marks indicate localities represented by vouchers or literature records judged to be invalid. The solid diamond indicates a specimen seen by the author but for which no voucher exists.

Surveys for Wood Frogs

Before the present study, most preserved Illinois wood frog specimens were collected in the northeastern part of the state. These specimens (Table 12-1) document numerous localities in Cook and Lake Counties, and many were reported by early Chicago-area herpetologists (Necker 1939; Pope 1944; Edgren and Stille 1948; Stille and Edgren 1948). Recently, wood frogs have been only infrequently reported from the Illinois part of the Chicago metropolitan area. Pentecost and Vogt (1976) reported wood frogs from Cook and Lake Counties but gave no specific locality. Most recent authors who have reported wood frogs from this region have noted their rarity (Bushey 1979; Murphy 1989; Ludwig et al. 1990, 1992). Since 1987, wood frogs have been reported from a few localities in DuPage (Ludwig et al. 1990, 1992; based on a calling individual that I heard in 1988), Lake, and Cook Counties. In Cook County, I visited a number of historical wood frog localities (in March to June 1995) but found specimens (tadpoles) at only one small pond in the Palos Division Forest Preserve in the southwest part of the county. An additional locality (Deer Grove Forest Preserve) reported to me (C. Anchor and M. Bavetz, personal communication) was documented in 1995 with a voucher specimen (SIUC H-5105), photograph, and audio recording of a small chorus. Deer Grove is several kilometers west of the nearest historical localities in northern Cook County and is reported here as a new locality. I visited only one Lake County locality (Ryerson Woods Nature Preserve) in 1995 and found no wood frogs. Kenneth Mierzwa (personal communication) found wood frogs at this site during a study in the mid-1980s. Several Lake County Forest Preserve staff have indicated to me that wood frogs have since been seen rarely at Ryerson Woods. In 1995, I collected the first wood frog specimens (INHS 12023–12024) from the Lake Michigan drainage of Will County. The mesic forests of that area support an amphibian assemblage found nowhere else in Will County, including several

Table 12-2. Vouchers collected since 1986

Pickerel frogs (*Rana palustris*).
Adams Co.: SIUC H-4723. Brown Co: SIUC H-4718. Calhoun Co.: SIUC H-4738–4739. Carroll Co.: FMNH 250090. Jersey Co.: SIUC H-4740, H-5113–5116. JoDaviess Co.: FMNH 245649–245650, 250080–250081. Lee Co.: FMNH 241348, 250082. Monroe Co.: SIUC H-4315, H-4464. Ogle Co.: FMNH 245648. Pike Co.: SIUC H-4712–4717, H-5072–5076. Randolph Co.: SIUC H-4270, H-5071. St. Clair Co.: SIUC H-4428. Stephenson Co.: FMNH 250092–250094. Union Co.: SIUC H-4780.
Wood frogs (*Rana sylvatica*).
Coles Co.: SIUC H-5069, H-5108. Cook Co.: SIUC H-5070, H-5105. Effingham Co.: SIUC H-5068. Hardin Co.: SIUC H-5117. Jackson Co.: SIUC H-3998, H-4062, H-4156, H-4416, H-4422–4425, H-4426, H-4432, H-4441, H-4477–4479, H-5061–5065. Monroe Co.: SIUC H-4427. Pope Co.: SIUC H-4647–4649, H-5066–5067, H-5118. Saline Co.: SIUC H-5119. Union Co.: SIUC H-4111, H-4695, H-4699, H-5059–5060. Vermilion Co.: SIUC H-4386, H-5106–5107. Will Co.: INHS 12023–12024.

other regionally uncommon species (e.g., spotted salamanders [*Ambystoma maculatum*], four-toed salamanders [*Hemidactylium scutatum*], and northern spring peepers [*Pseudacris crucifer crucifer*]; Anton and Redmer 1995; Anton et al., Chpt. 6, this volume). Two northeastern Illinois records are not plotted on the range maps. Alan Resetar (personal communication) reported that as a youth he captured wood frogs at a Boy Scout camp in extreme southern Cook County, but there is no voucher. The DuPage County locality (Wood Dale Grove Forest Preserve) reported by Ludwig et al. (1990) has been visited numerous times since 1988, but the species has not been encountered, and there is no voucher.

From northwestern Illinois, Smith (1961) reported wood frogs from Rock Island and JoDaviess Counties. JoDaviess County was not covered by the Wisconsinan glaciation, and Smith (1961) noted that the phenotype of these specimens was suggestive of a more northern origin. In particular, several of the specimens collected from JoDaviess County bear a single dorsal stripe, a characteristic unique among Illinois wood frog specimens. Martof and Humphries (1959) mentioned the distinctiveness of these specimens but also noted several other regionally disjunct examples of this phenotype. In Wisconsin, wood frogs have been collected in Grant County (Vogt 1981), which is also driftless, so their presence in JoDaviess County is not unexpected, based on biogeography. Attempts to locate additional specimens in JoDaviess County during 1995 were unsuccessful. The herpetofauna of northwestern Illinois remains poorly known when compared to surrounding regions (Redmer 1991), and additional fieldwork there may produce additional wood frog populations.

In central Illinois, Garman (1890) reported wood frogs from Peoria County, though no voucher is known. Blanchard and Princen (1976) reported a specimen "supposedly caught in Peoria County" but cited no voucher and gave no additional data. Based on these dubious records and on the assumption that wood frogs have been displaced from west-central Illinois by climatic changes, Thurow (1994b) undertook an ill-advised effort to "return" this species to McDonough County (an area where it is not documented to occur otherwise) by introducing animals from a population collected in Brown County, Indiana.

In eastern Illinois, Smith (1947, 1961) reported wood frogs from the mesic forests of Champaign, Vermilion, Coles, Clark, Effingham, and Richland Counties. Morris (1976) later reported an Edwards County record. In March 1995, I visited sites in eastern Illinois and confirmed with voucher specimens that wood frogs persist at localities in Vermilion (e.g., Middle Fork State Fish and Wildlife Area and Kickapoo State Park), Coles (Fox Ridge State Park), and Effingham (Wildcat Hollow State Forest) Counties (Tables 12-1, 12-2). At the Coles and Vermilion County localities, abundant chorusing males were observed and collected in the breeding ponds by day. Elsewhere in Illinois, I have rarely observed daytime breeding choruses.

In extreme southern Illinois (Jackson and Union Counties), Cagle (1942) stated that wood frogs were not common. Since then there have been few additional references to this species in southern Illinois. Smith (1961) plotted only one southern Illinois record (from Jackson County) of this species. Applegate and Zimbleman (1978) reported a single preserved specimen (which I have not examined) from the Dixon Springs Agricultural Center, Pope County. In the SIUC collection, there are few specimens collected before 1991, although this species reportedly is occasionally encountered on Department of Zoology class field trips (R. Brandon and G. Waring, personal communication). Since 1991, I have

Figure 12-3. Records of wood frogs (*Rana sylvatica*) in Illinois. (A) Pre-1961 records. (B) Records between 1961 and 1986. (C) Records since 1987. Circles indicate museum vouchers examined by the author. The solid diamond indicates an introduced population reported in the literature.

collected wood frogs in Hardin (one locality), Jackson (nine localities), northern Pope (six localities), Saline (one locality), and Union (five localities) Counties. Searches for wood frogs at numerous sites in Alexander, Johnson, and southern Pope (especially in the Cretaceous Hills Natural Division) Counties were unsuccessful. At some southern Illinois localities, wood frogs are conspicuous during their short (two to five days; M. Redmer, unpublished data) breeding season. However, this species is rarely encountered during the remainder of the year, and collecting eggs and tadpoles from breeding ponds has been the most reliable method for documenting its presence. Many additional populations likely occur in the Shawnee Hills.

In southwestern Illinois, Smith (1961) reported two wood frog localities from Monroe County. In 1993, the presence of this species was confirmed at a site south of Valmeyer (SIUC H-4427).

Discussion

Between 1961 and 1987 (when this study began), few pickerel frog and wood frog museum specimens had been collected in Illinois (Figs. 12-2B, 12-3B). It is possible this led some herpetologists and resource managers to be concerned for the conservation status of these species during that period.

Since 1987, populations of pickerel frogs have been found in most counties where they were previously documented. Exceptions are the Chicago area (McHenry and Kane Counties), Greene County (which I did not visit), and Madison and Alexander Counties. Several wood frog records from DuPage, Kane, Lake, and McHenry Counties are based on misidentified northern leopard frogs (Redmer and Mierzwa 1994) or on plains leopard frogs (Coles County). Until recently, northern leopard frogs collected in Madison and Sangamon Counties were unreported because they were stored in a jar of pickerel frogs (Redmer 1996). In some parts of Illinois (especially southwestern counties), the common name "pickerel frog" sometimes is applied by local people to all spotted *Rana* (M. Redmer, personal observation), thus leading to additional confusion. Previously unreported or overlooked museum specimens were found for Champaign, Johnson, Macoupin, and Vermilion Counties. All are questionable because the localities lack suitable habitat or because no additional vouchers are available.

In Illinois, pickerel frogs probably have declined in the urbanized Chicago area (where they have not been collected since 1949) and in Alexander County. Redmer and Mierzwa (1994) pointed out that remaining northern Illinois populations of pickerel frogs occur in areas of high natural quality. In the Chicago area, there are few remaining natural areas with suitable habitat. In Alexander County, a number of specimens were collected before 1953, but none have been collected since then. Although Union County in southern Illinois has been one of the most heavily collected counties in the state, there are only six records of pickerel frogs (two since 1988), which apparently infrequently occur there. No specimen has been collected in Madison County (a largely suburban county in the St. Louis metro-east area) since 1967. Other specimens have been collected recently in the less-developed parts of the St. Louis metro-east area (St. Clair and Monroe Counties). This area is rapidly urbanizing, and in the near future some remaining pickerel frog populations will be threatened with extirpation.

Since 1991, wood frogs have been reported or documented from localities (some of which were not previously reported) in ten counties. Throughout most of their Illinois range, wood frogs are rarely encountered after the breeding season, and special efforts (e.g., collection of eggs or tadpoles) are necessary to obtain voucher specimens. In extreme southern Illinois, wood frogs were found to be much more widespread than had been previously known, although large parts of the region still lack records. In eastern Illinois, specimens were collected in several areas of mesic forest habitat. Despite intensive surveys in northern Illinois during 1995, wood frogs were collected at only three localities. Peoria County reports have never been documented, and Thurow's (1994b) introduction of the species in McDonough County succeeded in establishing a nonnative population. The current presence of this species in JoDaviess and Rock Island Counties has not been confirmed; the last records are from 1951 and 1940, respectively.

It is uncertain if wood frogs have recently declined in any Illinois county. However, in several counties (e.g., Cook, Jackson, Pope, Union, Vermilion), wood frogs have been found in numbers, or at new localities, when special searches were made. Habitat loss undoubtedly has contributed to local extinction of some populations in the Chicago area. Preserves in this region contain suitable habitat and breeding ponds, and additional populations may remain to be discovered in northeastern Illinois.

Aspects of the biology of pickerel frogs and wood frogs (e.g., explosive breeding in wood frogs; quiet, inconspicuous breeding vocalizations and habitat specificity in both species) make these frogs difficult to detect consistently by the popular survey method of listening for vocalizing males. Because both are uncommonly encountered in Illinois, future anuran monitoring efforts might profit from using intensive species-specific searches. Additional sampling protocols to quantify population characteristics (e.g., counts of egg masses or tadpoles) should be developed. These methodologies could be used to monitor other anurans that have sporadic activity or are difficult to detect (e.g., eastern spadefoot toads [*Scaphiopus holbrookii*] and eastern narrowmouth toads [*Gastrophryne carolinensis*]) in eastern Illinois and elsewhere.

Summary

Pickerel frogs (*Rana palustris*) and wood frogs (*Rana sylvatica*) have peripheral distributions in Illinois. Both species have been infrequently collected in the state. For the last quarter century, there has been some discussion about the conservation status of these species in Illinois, but neither has been listed as threatened or endangered. Recent surveys for pickerel frogs and wood frogs indicate that, while their ranges are fragmented, populations of both species still occur at or near many historical Illinois localities. Neither species should be listed as threatened or endangered. However, both occur primarily in areas of high natural quality and thus may be sensitive to habitat alteration (especially urbanization). Both are difficult to detect using common sampling techniques. Special efforts to monitor them in Illinois should be implemented.

Acknowledgments

Agencies or individuals who granted permission to conduct fieldwork on land under their control include: Cook County Forest Preserve District; J. Eisbach (Galena, Illinois); Forest Preserve District of DuPage County; Illinois Department of Natural Resources; Lake County Forest Preserves; U.S. Forest Service, Shawnee National Forest; Forest Preserve District of Will County. For assistance with fieldwork, I thank C. Anchor, T. Anton, M. Bavetz, M. Blanford, B. Burke, J. Capps, K. Cook, D. Corgiat, D. Mauger, K. Mierzwa, C. Phillips, K. Tolch, and A. Wilson. Additionally, C. Anchor, S. Ballard, M. Bavetz, and A. Resetar shared with me several unpublished locality records or suggested localities that needed verification. For permission to examine and/or for providing me with loans of specimens under their care, I thank the following: M. Henderson (BM); R. Vasile (CA); J. Vindum (CAS); A. Resetar and H. Voris (FMNH); K. Cummings, L. Page, and C. Phillips (INHS); J. Purdue (ISM); R. Axtell and J. Capps (SIUE); R. Brandon (SIUC); T. Uzzell and J. Werner (UIMNH); A. Kluge and G. Schneider (UMMZ); S. Gotte and R. McDiarmid (USNM). Finally, I thank R. Brandon for helpful advice and for commenting on the manuscript.

13

Status of Northern Leopard Frogs in Northeastern Ohio

Lowell Orr, Jeffrey Neumann, Elke Vogt, and Alexander Collier

The dramatic decline of northern leopard frogs (*Rana pipiens*) in North America has been well described. Some contend that this decline began in the early 1970s and was first noted in the upper Midwest by frog dealers (Koonz 1992) who marketed this economically important species for research and teaching. In Manitoba, the die-off began in 1975 and was nearly complete within one year in areas where leopard frog populations were most dense (Koonz 1992). The decline in Canadian populations of northern leopard frogs was also noted in Saskatchewan (Seburn 1992), British Columbia (Orchard 1992), Alberta (Roberts 1992), and Quebec (Bonin 1992). Rittschof (1975) describes a similar crash that occurred in 1973 in a three-county area in Michigan; he attributed this decline to winterkill. Lannoo et al. (1994) report that northern leopard frogs have declined between two and three orders of magnitude in Dickinson County, Iowa, since 1900. Stebbins and Cohen (1995) provide additional descriptions of declines for this species in Arizona, California, Idaho, Oregon, Washington, and Wyoming.

Because of the suddenness of the decline of northern leopard frogs in the 1970s and the fact that some populations are now recovering (Seburn 1992; Koonz 1992; Stebbins and Cohen 1995), some have speculated that red leg, a common infectious disease of amphibians (see Faeh et al., Chpt. 26, this volume), may have caused the decline. Others propose that the retrogression of the populations may have been caused by competition or predation from introduced fish or bullfrogs (Orchard 1992), airborne or waterborne pollutants (Koonz 1992), overhunting, or changes in agricultural practices (Bonin 1992). The fact that there has never been a consensus among herpetologists as to the cause of the decline in any part of the species' range is troubling; more troubling, however, is the fact that in many parts of its range, the status of the species is unknown.

The purpose of our study is to investigate the status of northern leopard frogs in northeastern Ohio. Although Walker (1946) describes the leopard frog as "one of the most abundant and easily the most familiar of Ohio frogs," a survey of the herptiles of the Cuyahoga Valley National Recreation Area (Orr 1978) in Summit County failed to yield northern leopard frogs. Yearly amphibian collecting trips conducted by Orr with Kent State University students over the past thirty-five years in the vicinity of Kent (Portage County) have also produced few northern leopard frogs.

Methods

Our survey of northern leopard frog populations in northeastern Ohio began in the spring of 1991 and is ongoing. Neumann initiated the survey by attempting to locate historical northern leopard frog populations in northeastern Ohio, which are included in an Ohio Department of Natural Resources database compiled by Douglas Wynn. At that time, the database included records from the Ohio State University Museum, College of Wooster, Bowling Green State University, University of Kansas Museum of Natural History, Cleveland Museum of Natural History, Ohio University Museum of Zoology, Dayton Museum of Natural History, Hefner Zoological Museum at Miami (Ohio) University, National Museum of Natural History, Carnegie Museum, University of Michigan Museum of Zoology, and the private collections of Eric Juterbock and Ralph Pfingsten.

Neumann attempted to locate these populations using the procedure described by Pace (1974). During the breeding season, he drove to the locations at night and located the specific sites by the vocalizations of the northern spring peeper (*Pseudacris crucifer crucifer*). He then listened for the calls of northern leopard frogs with a parabolic microphone. Neumann also requested information about northern leopard frogs in seventy-two letters sent to naturalists at state parks and recreation areas. Finally, he contacted members of the Northern Ohio Association of Herpetologists for information regarding the species. Others in our group searched for populations and contacted environmental consulting firms in northeastern Ohio and the Ohio Department of Transportation for information on northern leopard frog populations.

Results and Discussion

Neumann reexamined sixteen sites listed in the database. Three of these had extant populations of northern leopard frogs, two sites had been destroyed by development, three had been eliminated by high-intensity agriculture, and the remaining eight sites supported other species of frogs but not northern leopard frogs. Other phases of our study yielded twenty-five additional populations of northern leopard frogs in ten counties of northeastern Ohio. All animals we observed appeared to be in good health. Detailed habitat descriptions were obtained for all sites.

The habitats of our twenty-eight populations of northern leopard frogs best fit the description given for this species in the New England states by Whitlock et al. (1994): "pools of standing water surrounded by wet meadow with a broad transition to upland fields or pasture." We would add that, ideally, the pools of water contain no fish. Although our study was not meant to be quantitative, we found that when we correlated the numbers of individuals collected with habitat, a definite pattern emerged: habitats in early stages of succession supported the largest populations. Our largest population was found at a sand and gravel quarry that had undergone one year of succession, included a newly created lake, and was adjacent to a natural wetland. Another large population was found in an area where newly dug ponds were adjacent to an old field, while a third large population was in an area that was mowed and burned periodically.

We propose that in northeastern Ohio, succession is the biggest enemy of northern leopard frogs. Therefore, because most habitats undergo succession, the current status of the species cannot be assessed by determining whether historical populations still exist. Walker's descriptions (1946) of northern leopard frog habitat support our view that they are a colonizing species found primarily in early successional stages. He states that the frogs are "more frequent in open country and occur in numbers in regions of intensive agriculture" and that "permanent water is not required." He later adds that hayfields and grassy ditches may serve as adequate substitutes for the original habitat in Ohio, which he proposed were marshy shores of ponds and streams in the state's primitive forests. We believe this is an astute assessment of the early habitat of northern leopard frogs, because periodic flooding would maintain these habitats in an early successional stage.

Like most colonizing species, or "r strategists," northern leopard frogs disperse widely (Bovbjerg 1965; Dole 1965, 1971), allowing them to move from ecosystems where competition and predation are intensifying. Dole (1971) states that young leopard frogs commonly move more than 800 meters from their place of metamorphosis, a distance greater than that reported for most anurans. Such movements would be adaptive for a species such as the northern leopard frog, which lacks the toxicity of its congener, the pickerel frog (*Rana palustris*), and therefore is more vulnerable to the greater number of aquatic or terrestrial predators in more mature ecosystems. Dunn (1935) notes that garter snakes will not feed on pickerel frogs, while Dole (1965) indicates that the garter snakes are major predators on northern leopard frogs, suggesting that these snakes may have played a major role in leopard frog habitat selection.

Conclusions

Our survey indicated that northeastern Ohio is still supporting many populations of apparently healthy northern leopard frogs. We question if there has been a decline in the species in northeastern Ohio over the past thirty-five years. Earlier failures to observe large numbers of leopard frogs during this time probably is because we had not looked in the right habitats. Our survey was conducted in a national park where environmental disturbances important to northern leopard frogs are minimized; our university field trips when northern leopard frogs were not found were taken to areas where large numbers of amphibian species could be found, not to early successional habitats or disturbed areas. We suggest that northern leopard frog numbers may be underestimated in other parts of its range if investigators attempt to assess its status by determining whether historical populations persist, a method that would be inappropriate for a colonizing species that disperses from habitats undergoing succession. Our richest source of new records for northern leopard frogs has come from dedicated environmental consultants who have shared their population records with us.

The movements of adult northern leopard frogs to breeding habitats during the rains of spring and the extensive dispersal of juveniles from the breeding ponds in July and August make this species vulnerable to highway traffic; as with chorus frogs (*Pseudacris triseriata*) (Walker 1946), its forays into agricultural areas will subject it to herbicides and pesticides. It is important, therefore, that we continue to monitor the status of northern leopard frogs throughout their range and experiment with management practices that will ensure that northern leopard frogs continue to be an important component of our herpetofauna.

Summary

A survey of northern leopard frogs (*Rana pipiens*) populations was initiated in 1991 and continues to determine the status of this species in northeastern Ohio. Only three of sixteen historical populations could be found. However, twenty-five additional extant populations were found in ten counties of northeastern Ohio. The largest populations were found at sites in early stages of succession, such as sand and gravel quarries, new ponds, and mowed fields. We propose that in northeastern Ohio, succession is the biggest enemy of northern leopard frogs. This species disperses widely, allowing it to escape intensifying competition and predation in maturing ecosystems. Because it is a colonizing species, we believe that attempting to assess its status by determining whether historical populations still exist is inappropriate. We find no evidence that northern leopard frogs have declined in northeastern Ohio in the past thirty-five years.

Acknowledgments

We thank A. M. White, R. Pfingsten, T. Matson, D. Wynn, M. Austin, S. Mazzer, and M. Johnson for providing us with numerous records for northern leopard frogs; B. A. Foote and D. W. Waller for valuable suggestions; and D. Benadum for access to private property. The Declining Amphibian Populations Task Force gave us the impetus to conduct the study, and C. F. Walker provided us with a legacy of Ohio herpetological information from which to proceed; hence our gratitude.

14

Status of Illinois Chorus Frogs in Madison County, Illinois

John K. Tucker

Illinois chorus frogs (*Pseudacris streckeri illinoensis*) are restricted to sandy substrates on the floodplains of the Mississippi and Illinois Rivers in Arkansas, Illinois, and Missouri (Conant and Collins 1991). Because these habitats have been converted to agriculture or developed for other human activities, Illinois chorus frogs are now uncommon. They are listed as a threatened species in Illinois (Herkert 1992), as a rare species in Missouri (Anonymous 1992), as a species of special concern in Arkansas (R. Roberg, personal communication), and as a category 2 species by the U.S. Fish and Wildlife Service (Dodd et al. 1985). Several previous publications provide details on the life history of Illinois chorus frogs, including information on underground feeding behavior (Brown 1978), burrowing behavior (Axtell and Haskell 1977; Brown et al. 1972; Tucker 1995; Tucker et al. 1995), chorus sites (Brown and Rose 1988), fecundity (Butterfield et al. 1989; Trauth et al. 1990), postmetamorphic growth (Tucker 1995), and morphological adaptations to fossorial existence (Brown et al. 1972; Brown and Means 1984; Paukstis and Brown 1987, 1991).

In this chapter, I examine the current status of Illinois chorus frogs in Madison County, Illinois. I suggest that the apparently reduced distribution in relation to disturbance of habitats is caused by agricultural impacts interacting with relatively low juvenile and adult survivorship and extensive postmetamorphic dispersal. Although many uncertainties remain due to the difficulty in studying this fossorial frog, the preliminary results suggest that the frog's range in Madison County has been drastically reduced and that preservation of the frog in Madison County and possibly elsewhere depends on protection of tracts of suitable nonbreeding habitat.

Methods

Literature records (Axtell and Haskell 1977; Morris 1991; Taubert et al. 1982) and interviews with George Rose (Illinois Department of Transportation), Scott Ballard (Illinois Department of Natural Resources, Natural Heritage), and Ralph Axtell (Southern Illinois University-Edwardsville) were used to determine the distribution of Illinois chorus frogs in Madison County prior to 1991. The current distribution of these frogs was based on surveys I conducted during 1993 to 1995. Searches were concentrated in locations where choruses had been previously reported, as well as in other areas of the county where sandy soils were present (Goddard and Sabata 1986).

Starting on 19 April 1993 and on 1 March 1994 and 1995, I patrolled roads at night and particularly on nights when rain fell or had fallen in the last twenty-four hours. When an Illinois chorus frog was heard at a particular location, identification was considered tentative if a frog could not be caught and confirmed if a frog was captured. All locations were surveyed two or more times in each year on nights when frogs were actively calling at one or more of the other locations in the county.

Two locations where choruses had previously been reported were also surveyed using drift fences (New Poag Road and Streetcar Road historical sites; Fig. 14-1A and B, respectively). In 1994, drift fences totaling 260 meters in length were constructed of 25-centimeter-tall

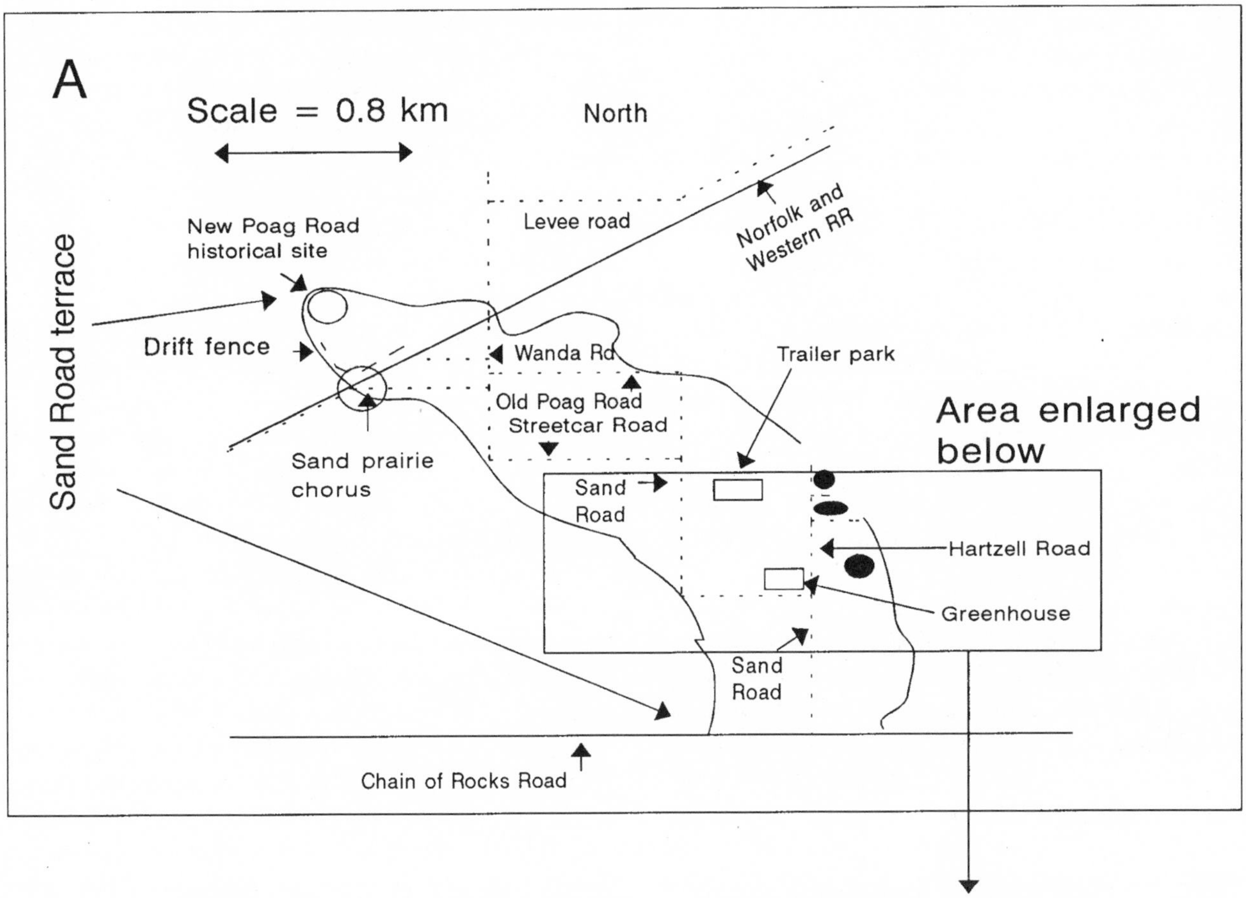

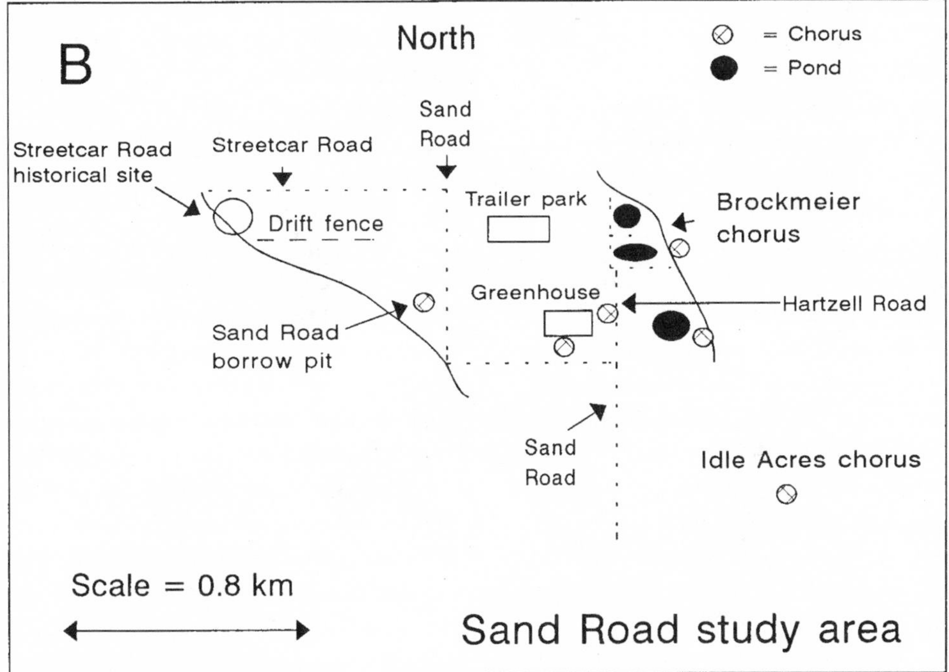

Figure 14-1. (A) The Sand Road terrace showing the relationship of the study area containing the last confirmed choruses of Illinois chorus frogs (*Pseudacris streckeri illinoensis*) in Madison County. (B) The Sand Road study area showing locations of six of the seven chorus sites active between 1993 and 1995.

aluminum flashing. These were placed near the northern edge of the Sand Road terrace between suitable sand habitats and the location of the New Poag Road historical site (Fig. 14-1A). In 1995, a 900-meter drift fence constructed with silt fencing, an impervious material used by construction contractors to prevent siltation, was placed between the location of the New Poag Road historical site and the nearest active chorus (sand prairie chorus, Fig. 14-1A). The bottom of the fence was buried using a backhoe to a depth of 25 centimeters. Once completed, the fence stood 95 centimeters tall throughout its length. Another 300-meter fence of similar construction was placed between the Streetcar Road historical site and the active chorus at the Sand Road borrow pit site (Fig. 14-1B). All fences were monitored daily throughout the time that frogs were calling on the terrace.

Voucher specimens, including a series of thirteen froglets collected in 1993 in the NE1/4 Section 19, T4N, R8W (3.1 kilometers north of the junction of Sand Road and Chain of Rocks Road, Madison County, Illinois; Fig. 14-1B, Brockmeier chorus), were preserved under Illinois Department of Natural Resources permit number 93-8s and deposited in the collections of the Illinois Natural History Survey (INHS 10938–10939; 10946–10956). Twenty-three adult frogs found killed on Sand Road in the N1/2 Section 19, T4N, R8W, in 1994 were also preserved (INHS uncataloged) under Illinois Department of Natural Resources permit A-93.0207.

Estimates of survivorship and straight-line distance from release to recapture points were based on recaptures of a cohort of 722 frogs initially marked by toe clipping as froglets in 1993 (Tucker 1995). Males with darkened vocal pouches and gravid females were considered sexually mature. Nongravid females were considered sexually mature if their snout-vent length (SVL) was within the range observed for gravid females. Females were identified as gravid when eggs could be seen through the thin transparent skin joining the hind legs and abdomen. Nongravid females classified as sexually mature based on their SVL were assumed to have bred prior to capture and were identified as spent.

To determine their direction of travel, in 1994 an intensive survey was undertaken to find as many frogs as possible crossing roads in the Sand Road study area. Between 9 and 30 April, I slowly drove the roads in the Sand Road study site (i.e., Sand Road, Streetcar Road, and Hartzell Road; Fig. 14-1B) three times each night. The first trip began about 2200 hours, the second at about 2400 hours, and the third at about 0200 hours. The distributions of habitats in the study area make it ideal, because the area enclosed by Sand Road and Hartzell Road is completely devoted to lawns or agriculture (i.e., the area surrounding the greenhouse and trailer park; Fig. 14-1B). In contrast, patches of old field habitat bordered the other side of Sand Road.

For each of the forty-three frogs observed on Sand Road, the direction of travel when first observed and the nature of the habitat (i.e., old field, agriculture, or lawn) on each side of Sand Road were recorded. Travel was presumed to be between a particular frog's home range and its breeding site. Although the actual route followed was unknown, it was assumed to be a straight line (Stebbins and Cohen 1995). A particular frog could be moving from its home range to a breeding site or returning from a breeding site to its home range.

For the direction of travel information to be useful, each frog was determined to be either leaving or returning to its home range. Gravid females were presumed to be moving from their home ranges to a breeding site, whereas spent females were presumed to be returning to their home ranges from a breeding site. Distribution of gravid versus nongravid females during the period between 9 and 30 April (Fig. 14-2) was used to arbitrarily divide males into those leaving their home ranges and those returning to their home ranges. Thus, males caught between 9 and 16 April were considered to be leaving their home ranges, whereas those caught after 16 April were considered to be returning to their home ranges.

Results

Choruses of Illinois chorus frogs were found at two locations during 1993. In 1994 and 1995, seven choruses were located (Fig. 14-1). At five of these, I confirmed the identity of the calling frogs by catching one or more individuals (Fig. 14-1B, excluding Idle Acres chorus). Calling frogs were not found in any of the three years at other previously reported locations (Table 14-1).

I also caught no Illinois chorus frogs on the drift fences at two of the historical sites during 1994 and 1995, despite the fact that frogs were caught in each year at other locations. Other anurans (Fowler's toads [*Bufo woodhousii fowleri*], striped chorus frogs [*Pseudacris triseriata*], southern leopard frogs [*Rana sphenocephala*], and bullfrogs [*R. catesbeiana*]) were caught by these fences.

Recaptures of sexually mature frogs marked as froglets yielded a preliminary estimate of survivorship to sexual maturity. In 1994, 20 of the 722 froglets marked in

Table 14-1. Chorus locations for the Illinois chorus frog (*Pseudacris streckeri illinoensis*) in Madison County, Illinois. Bold print denotes choruses active between 1993 and 1995.

Site Name (location)	Source
Granite City (Sec. 8, T3N, R9W)	Axtell and Haskell 1977
Roxana Terrace	
Wagonwheel Road (Sec. 12, T4N, R9W)	Axtell, personal communication
Canal Road (Sec. 7, T4N, R8W)	Rose, personal communication
Levee Road (Sec. 7, T4N, R8W)	Rose, personal communication
Sand Road Terrace	
New Poag Road (Sec. 18, T4N, R8W)	Axtell, personal communication
Poag Road (Sec. 18, T4N, R8W)	Axtell, personal communication
Streetcar Road (Sec. 24, T4N, R9W)	Morris 1992
Pentecostal Church Camp (Sec. 29, T4N, R8W)	Axtell, personal communication
Sand prairie chorus (Sec. 18, T4N, R8W)	
Sand Road borrow pit (Sec. 19, T4N, R8W)	Morris 1992
Brockmeier choruses (Sec. 19, T4N, R8W)	Taubert et al. 1982
Idle Acres Lane chorus (Sec. 29, T4N, R8W)	Ballard, personal communication
Greenhouse choruses (Sec. 19, T4N, R8W)	

1993 were recaptured, resulting in an estimated survivorship to sexual maturity of 2.8 percent. Recaptures consisted of seven females and thirteen males, indicating that males and females may mature after one season of growth. This preliminary result may be low if a significant percentage of froglets did not become sexually mature after a single season of growth.

In 1995, I captured only sixteen adult frogs; six of these were frogs that I had marked in 1993 as froglets. Thus, the preliminary estimate for the number of frogs surviving two years was 0.8 percent. Adult survivorship was estimated to be 30 percent based on these preliminary data. The relatively low juvenile and adult survivorship rates suggest that this frog is not a long-lived species.

Frogs found on Sand Road were not randomly distributed along the road path. Most frogs were caught where the road was bordered by old field habitat on one side. Frogs were not found on sections of the road where agricultural fields or lawns bordered both sides of the road (Fig. 14-3).

The direction of travel (Fig. 14-4) changed abruptly in the study as well. Between 9 and 16 April, seventeen of twenty frogs were found leaving old field habitat. After 16 April, twenty of twenty-three frogs were found crossing Sand Road into old field habitat. The concentration of frog captures at areas of the road where old field habitat occurred, along with the direction of travel, strongly suggest that old field habitats were preferred nonbreeding habitat for these frogs.

Average distance moved between initial capture point to recapture point for the twenty frogs recaptured in 1994 was 0.52 kilometer (range = 0 to 0.9 kilometer, standard deviation = 0.23 kilometer). Females were recaptured an average of 0.59 kilometer from their initial capture point (range of 0.46 to 0.90 kilometer, standard deviation of 0.18 kilometer), whereas males were recaptured an average of 0.49 kilometer (range = 0 to 0.71 kilometer, standard deviation = 0.25 kilometer) from their initial capture point. The distance from point of recapture to the point of initial capture for males and females did not differ statistically (Kruskal-Wallis test, $H = 0.54$, $p = 0.4605$, degrees of freedom = 1).

Not only did frogs move long distances, many did not return to the site where they transformed in 1993 for their 1994 breeding attempt. Three of thirteen males and three of seven females were recaptured at the Sand Road borrow pit chorus. Two males were found at the greenhouse choruses. A single male was recaptured at the site where it transformed in 1993. The remaining eleven frogs were found on Sand Road.

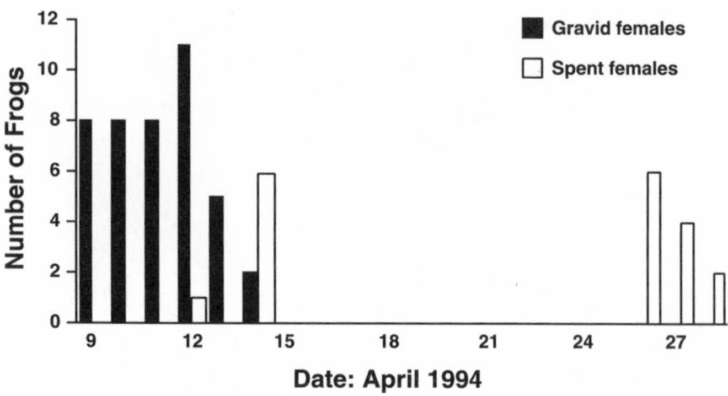

Figure 14-2. Captures of Illinois chorus frog (*Pseudacris streckeri illinoensis*) females by reproductive status, including those caught at choruses and those found killed on Sand Road.

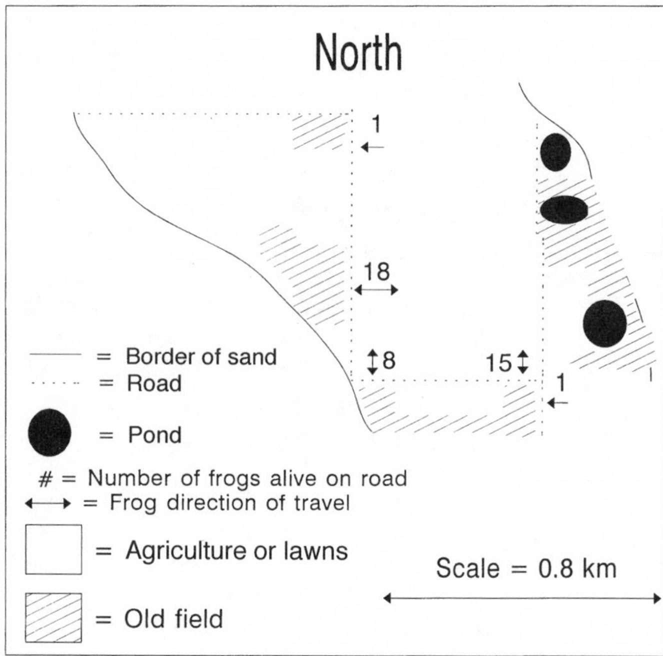

Figure 14-3. Location of Illinois chorus frogs (*Pseudacris streckeri illinoensis*) found alive on Sand Road in relation to old field habitats in April 1994.

Discussion

Axtell and Haskell (1977) reported that Illinois chorus frogs were widely distributed in the "Cahokia crescent." They reported locating five separate populations in a 15-square-kilometer area but did not cite specific localities or collect voucher specimens. Regardless, interviews and unpublished reports (Morris 1991; Taubert et al. 1982) suggest that Illinois chorus frogs were historically more widespread in Madison County than indicated in my 1993 to 1995 survey (Table 14-1).

Similar to the report of Taubert et al. (1982), I did not hear or collect frogs at the Granite City site reported by Axtell and Haskell (1977), even though I searched it in 1994 and 1995 when frogs were calling elsewhere. Likewise, I did not hear or collect frogs at the Roxana terrace sites in any of the three years of the survey (Table 14-1). Extensive drift fencing near two other historical chorus sites also failed to capture frogs. The range of Illinois chorus frogs in Madison County now appears to be restricted to an area of about 100 hectares (Fig. 14-1B) and reduced from a much larger area from the 1970s to 1980s (Axtell and Haskell 1977; Table 14-1).

Extirpation by Attrition

Whatever the cause of the apparent reduction in range of Illinois chorus frogs in Madison County, the reduction suggests a pattern that I term extirpation by attrition. Prior to disturbance (Fig. 14-5A), I assume that the Sand Road sand terrace and other nearby habitats (i.e., Granite City and Roxana terrace) had frogs widely distributed in them, because frogs have been reported from these areas in the past (Table 14-1). Frogs probably bred along the edges of the terrace where soil types allowed water to stand, as well as on the terrace in spots where the water in the sand did not rapidly drain.

The froglets produced likely dispersed widely over the terrace, much as the froglets that I marked in 1993 did on the southern half of the Sand Road terrace. With an average postmetamorphic dispersal distance in excess of 0.5 kilometer, froglets from such choruses could reach most areas of the Sand Road terrace during their postmetamorphic migration from choruses known to be active prior to 1991 (Table 14-1; Fig. 14-1).

I assume that newly matured frogs, similar to the males and females that I recaptured in 1994, move to chorus sites but not necessarily to the ones where they transformed. However, I assume that survivors of this cohort of first-year breeding frogs develop site fidelity (Jameson 1957).

Subsequently, an environmental disturbance, such as the initiation of agricultural practices, makes a portion of the former nonbreeding range unsuitable for froglets (Fig. 14-5B–D). The pattern of movements recorded in 1994 suggests that adult frogs left old field habitats to breed and returned to old field habitats after breeding.

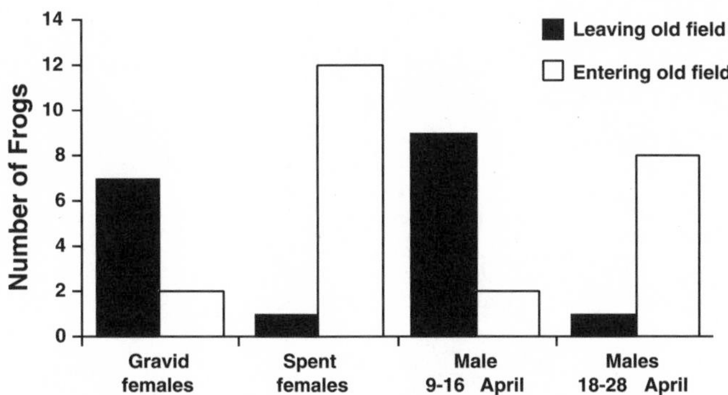

Figure 14-4. Illinois chorus frogs (*Pseudacris streckeri illinoensis*) found entering or leaving old field habitats in relation to reproductive status for females or date of capture for males.

The absence of recaptures along areas of Sand Road where both sides of the road are bordered by agriculture (Fig. 14-3) is consistent with the hypothesis that frogs either do not occupy agricultural fields or cannot survive in them.

Froglets may continue to disperse into disturbed areas after each breeding season (Fig. 14-5B–D). If those settling in such disturbed areas do not live to reproduce, then juvenile recruitment is reduced. Adults whose home ranges did not include the new condition continue to disperse to the breeding chorus where they bred in their first breeding season. However, they are joined only by froglets that did not come to inhabit the unfavorable habitat. Thus, the recruitment into the chorus is reduced.

If the disturbance is not widespread, the chorus will be maintained by the froglets that happen to settle into the remaining suitable habitat and end up at the chorus site on their first breeding trip. Once the disturbance is sufficiently widespread to reduce juvenile survivorship below the rate necessary to replace adults lost each year, the chorus will dwindle and become extinct (Fig. 14-5C, D).

The similarity between the hypothetical scenario and the actual situation in Madison County is striking. The Streetcar Road and New Poag Road historical populations on the Sand Road terrace (Table 14-1; Fig. 14-1) have become extinct. The sand prairie chorus (Fig. 14-1A) may represent a population in the process of extinction. Only choruses at the Sand Road borrow pit and the Brockmeier site appear to be stable.

Another related possibility is that once disturbance has reduced juvenile recruitment into choruses, the frog becomes more vulnerable to extinction due to adverse natural events, such as droughts. Preliminary survivorship data from my study suggest that this frog is not a long-lived species and may be vulnerable to short-term perturbations. The combination of reduced juvenile recruitment due to agricultural and residential development and the associated drainage of wetlands may have led to its restricted distribution in Madison County.

Conservation

The current distribution of Illinois chorus frogs in relation to their likely more widespread distribution in the recent past, a relatively low survivorship, extensive postmetamorphic dispersal, and apparent preference for nonagricultural habitats indicate that preservation of significant tracts of suitable habitat for froglets is critical. Exactly how this habitat should be managed is not clear and cannot be addressed by my study because only highly altered habitats occur in my study area. However, other actions, such as listing the species as threatened or endangered by the various states that have not afforded it any status or by the federal government, will be of little meaning if habitat is not preserved.

Summary

Distribution of Illinois chorus frogs (*Pseudacris streckeri illinoensis*) in Madison County, Illinois, prior to 1991 included choruses located from Granite City to Edwardsville in the Cahokia Crescent. However, surveys conducted from 1993 to 1995 found frogs restricted to a small area of roughly 100 hectares near Edwardsville. These intensive surveys suggest that sexually mature frogs do not use agricultural or residential areas as nonbreeding habitat. Preliminary estimates of survivorship based on recaptures of a cohort of froglets marked in 1993 and recaptured as sexually mature adults in 1994 and 1995 indicate that juvenile survivorship (2.8 percent) and adult survivorship (30 percent) were low. However, froglets dispersed widely, with an average distance between initial capture location and recapture location of 0.52 kilometer (range = 0 to 0.9 kilometer, standard deviation = 0.23 kilometer). A model is proposed to account for the current distribution of these frogs in Madison County. The preservation of these frogs likely depends on protecting tracts of suitable terrestrial sand habitats from disturbance.

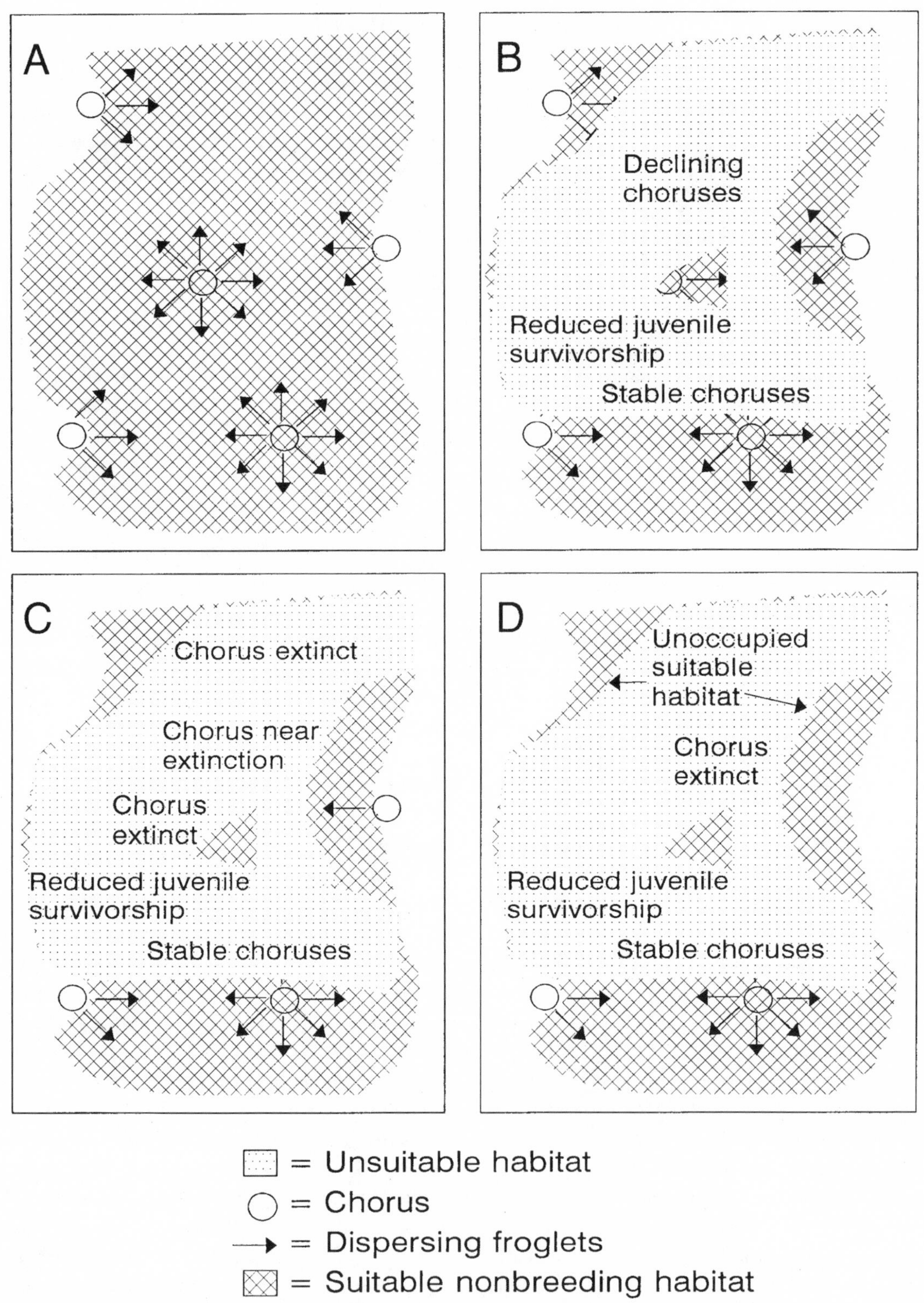

Figure 14-5. Theoretical effects of habitat fragmentation on Illinois chorus frogs (*Pseudacris streckeri illinoensis*). (A) Initial undisturbed habitat. (B) Insertion of an area of disturbed habitat into which froglets continue to disperse but do not survive or have relatively reduced juvenile survivorship. (C) Result at some time after disturbance with three choruses now extinct, one declining, and two stable. (D) After a longer time, only stable choruses remain, leaving seemingly suitable habitat patches unoccupied due to the absence of juvenile recruitment into now-extinct choruses.

Acknowledgments

I thank S. R. Ballard, J. B. Camerer, J. B. Hatcher, G. B. Rose, and M. M. Tucker for field assistance. Lauren E. Brown provided many useful suggestions concerning the biology of the frog and critically read the manuscript. George B. Rose, S. R. Ballard, and R. W. Axtell pointed out the locations of historical records for choruses. Scott R. Ballard located the Idle Acres chorus. Glen E. Kruse provided the permits necessary for this project. Ken Brockmeier, Brockmeier Sod Farms, allowed unrestricted access to his property. The staff at Home Greenhouses allowed unfettered access to their facilities. Marion Odorizzi provided access to property near the sand prairie chorus. Robert Ruder, Baxmeyer Construction, Inc., provided materials, equipment, and crews to construct some of the drift fences used in 1995. In part, this research was supported by Illinois Department of Transportation contracts with the Illinois Natural History Survey, J. K. Tucker and D. P. Philipp coprincipal investigators.

15

Status of Illinois Chorus Frogs in Southern Illinois

Ronald A. Brandon and Scott R. Ballard

Illinois chorus frogs (*Pseudacris streckeri illinoensis*) were described by Smith (1951; type-locality "three miles north of Meredosia, Morgan County, Illinois") from populations in the sand prairies of two counties of the Illinois River valley in west-central Illinois. Additional papers and reports (Beltz 1991, 1993; Brown et al. 1972; Brown and Rose 1988; Paukstis and Brown 1987; Moll 1962; Smith 1961; Taubert et al. 1982) have added to our knowledge of the Illinois River valley populations. Prior to the description of Illinois subspecies, Strecker's chorus frogs (*Pseudacris streckeri*) were thought to occur entirely in Oklahoma and Texas (Bragg and Dundee 1951; Bragg 1950; Wright and Wright 1949). Smith (1966) showed the main range of Strecker's chorus frogs to be in eastern Texas and central Oklahoma, with one population in western Arkansas.

Illinois chorus frogs were not known to occur south of the Illinois River valley until Smith (1955) reported a population in the Missouri bootheel. Subsequently, Holman et al. (1964) discovered calling males 1.5 kilometers west of Horseshoe Lake Conservation Area, 24 kilometers east of the nearest Missouri populations. Nine years later, Brown and Brown (1973) documented four additional localities near Horseshoe Lake: two at or near Miller City and two approximately 3 kilometers northeast of Olive Branch. Taubert et al. (1982) subsequently added two breeding sites about 1 kilometer west of the junction of State Routes 3 and 51. This cluster of populations in Alexander County, 306 kilometers south of those in the Illinois River valley, is in the sandy soils of the Mississippi River valley, which also harbors plains leopard frogs (*Rana blairi*; Brown and Morris 1990; Brown et al. 1993). We now report that Illinois chorus frogs are widespread in the vicinity of Horseshoe Lake Conservation Area, an impounded oxbow channel of the Mississippi River in the Austroriparian portion of Alexander County (Bogner et al. 1985).

Axtell and Haskell (1977) reported a third, geographically intermediate cluster of Illinois populations in the Mississippi River floodplain of Madison County, just east of St. Louis, and a population was discovered farther south, in Monroe County (Gilbert 1986).

To the southwest of Illinois, populations of Illinois chorus frogs are known in extreme southeastern Missouri and from one county in northeastern Arkansas (Butterfield et al. 1989; Johnson 1987; Johnson and Burger 1992). Populations identified as Illinois chorus frogs occur as close as south-central Kansas (Gray and Stegall 1986), west-central Arkansas (Conant and Collins 1991), and northwestern Louisiana (Dundee and Rossman 1989), but a distributional gap remains between *P. s. streckeri* and *P. s. illinoensis.* The geographic separation and degree of genetic divergence have been used by some authors (Collins 1991; Hedges 1986; Morris 1991) as evidence that these two subspecies should be considered separate species.

The entire geographic range of Illinois chorus frogs comprises eight counties in Illinois, seven counties in Missouri (Johnson 1987), and one county in Arkansas (Butterfield et al. 1989). Because of its limited range in Illinois, it is listed as state threatened (Morris and Smith 1981). In Missouri, it is listed as rare (Johnson 1987), and it is listed as a species of special concern in Arkansas (Frank and Ramus 1994). Additionally, Illinois chorus frog is a former category 2 candidate for federal listing as threatened (Dodd et al. 1985).

Despite the remark in an Illinois Department of Conservation publication (Anonymous 1993:12) that "Alexander County's chorus frog population seems to have disappeared and Madison County's appears to be following suit," the frogs remain widely distributed around Horseshoe Lake and persist in Madison County.

We review current information about the distribution of the three clusters of populations (Alexander, Madison, and Monroe Counties) on the Mississippi River floodplain of southwestern Illinois (Fig. 15-1) and summarize the breeding habitats and conservation status of these animals.

Materials and Methods

Published literature on the occurrence of Illinois chorus frogs in Alexander, Madison, and Monroe Counties was reviewed to obtain a preliminary list of sites to examine. Additional sites were discovered during fieldwork on historic localities by identifying and examining likely places indicated on soils maps and by investigating oral reports of calling frogs.

Historic and potential breeding sites were visited at night during appropriate early spring weather, and at least ten minutes were spent listening before moving to the next site. Data recorded where frogs were encountered included air temperature, water temperature, water depth, approximate number of males heard calling, number of males and females actually seen, and other anuran species heard or seen. Tape recordings of calls were made at a few sites. New localities were documented with voucher specimens, which were deposited in the Southern Illinois University at Carbondale Herpetology Collection (SIUC).

Nocturnal surveys in Alexander County were carried out during the years 1992 to 1994. On 3 March 1993, seven people in three vehicles surveyed the floodplain around Horseshoe Lake, listening for Illinois chorus frogs, locating calling males on maps, and estimating numbers of calling males. Soil data for breeding ponds and sites where calling males were heard were taken from Goddard and Sabata (1986; Madison County), Higgins (1987; Monroe County), and Parks and Fehrenbacher (1968; Alexander County). Additional fieldwork during 1993 and 1994 was part of a broader study of animals and plants in the 3,700-hectare Horseshoe Lake Conservation Area (Brandon et al. 1994); thirty-six days (over 235 person-days) were spent in the field during the months of February, March, and April, when breeding male Illinois chorus frogs were calling. Secondary roads throughout the area were driven slowly after dark, during and after rain. At likely locations or where calling males had been heard previously, several minutes were spent listening; the direction of frogs calling in the distance was determined by using a Bionic Ear® (Silver Creek Industries, Manitowoc, Wisconsin). Locations of calling males were marked on 7.5' topographic quadrangle maps, some marked precisely and some only approximately.

Results

Madison County

Fieldwork. John K. Tucker, Illinois Natural History Survey, is monitoring Illinois chorus frog breeding sites in Madison County (see Chpt. 14, this volume). He has been intensively surveying the Poag area, and our data are meant to supplement his more complete study of those localities.

During 1993, one of us (S.R.B.) conducted fieldwork on 10, 16, and 25 March at eight historic sites monitored from 2010 to 0053 hours (Fig. 15-2). These sites included Morris (1991) sites I (divided into north and south), II, III; Axtell sites (from Morris 1991) north and south; the Axtell and Haskell (1977) Granite City site; and a church camp site southeast of Poag (Fig. 15-2). Of the eight sites checked, three yielded Illinois chorus frogs. Productive nights included 10 March (two males heard calling at Morris site I south) and 25 March (ten to fifteen males heard calling, nine males seen at Morris site I south; one male heard calling at Morris site I north; five to ten males heard calling at Morris site II; two males heard calling at church camp site southeast of Poag). Illinois chorus frogs were heard calling at times ranging from 2036 to 2318 hours. Air temperatures on productive nights ranged from 3° to 10°C, mean of 8°C; water temperatures ranged from 5° to 7°C with an average of 6°C; water depth measured at one site was 79 centimeters. One voucher specimen was obtained (SIUC H-4420). Other species encountered during surveys included northern spring peepers (*Pseudacris crucifer crucifer*, 10, 16, and 25 March), chorus frogs (*Pseudacris triseriata*; 16 and 25 March), and southern leopard frogs (*Rana sphenocephala*; 25 March).

During 1994, fieldwork was conducted on 5, 13, and 19 April at five of the eight historic sites, including Morris (1991) sites I (north and south), II, and III and the Axtell and Haskell (1977) Granite City site. Additionally,

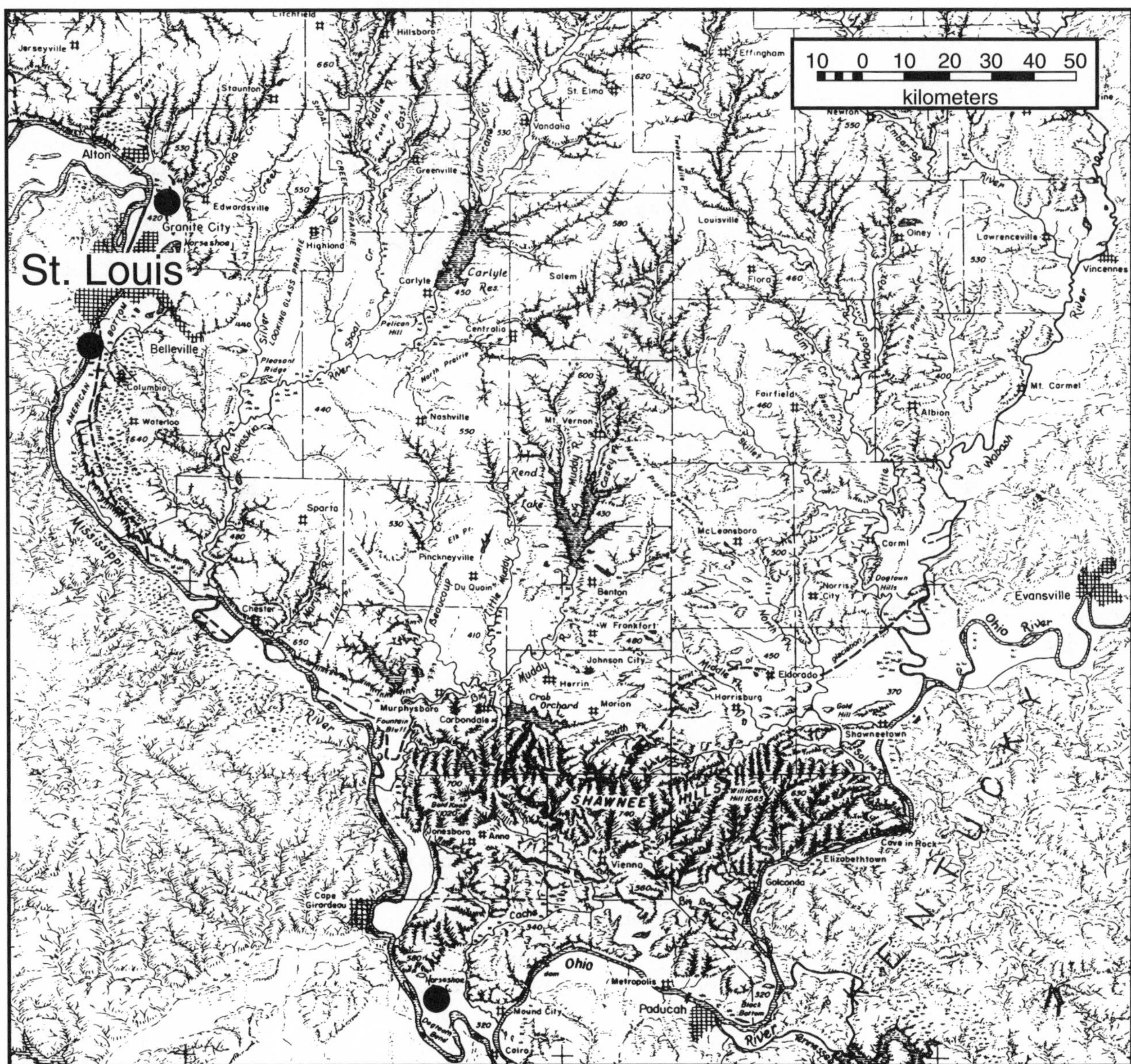

Figure 15-1. Landforms map indicating the known clusters (indicated by solid dots) of Illinois chorus frogs (*Pseudacris streckeri illinoensis*) in southern Illinois.

a site west of a sand prairie in Poag where M. Morris (personal communication) found Illinois chorus frog tadpoles was surveyed. A new site was discovered by one of us (S.R.B.) along Idle Acres Lane, southeast of Poag. Of these seven sites checked, three yielded Illinois chorus frogs. The only productive night was 13 April (two to three males heard calling at Morris site II, three to five males heard calling at Morris site III, ten to fifteen males heard calling at the Idle Acres Lane site). Illinois chorus frogs were heard calling at times ranging from 2320 to 0052 hours. Air temperatures during productive times that night ranged from 11° to 12°C; water temperatures also ranged from 11° to 12°C; water depth at two of the productive sites ranged from 10 to 15 centimeters. Other species encountered during surveys included American toads (*Bufo americanus americanus*; 13 and 19 April), Fowler's toads (*Bufo woodhousii fowleri*; 19 April), the gray treefrog complex (*Hyla versicolor/Hyla chrysoscelis*; 19 April), spring peepers (5, 13, and 19 April), chorus frogs (5, 13, and 19 April), bullfrogs (*Rana catesbeiana*, 19

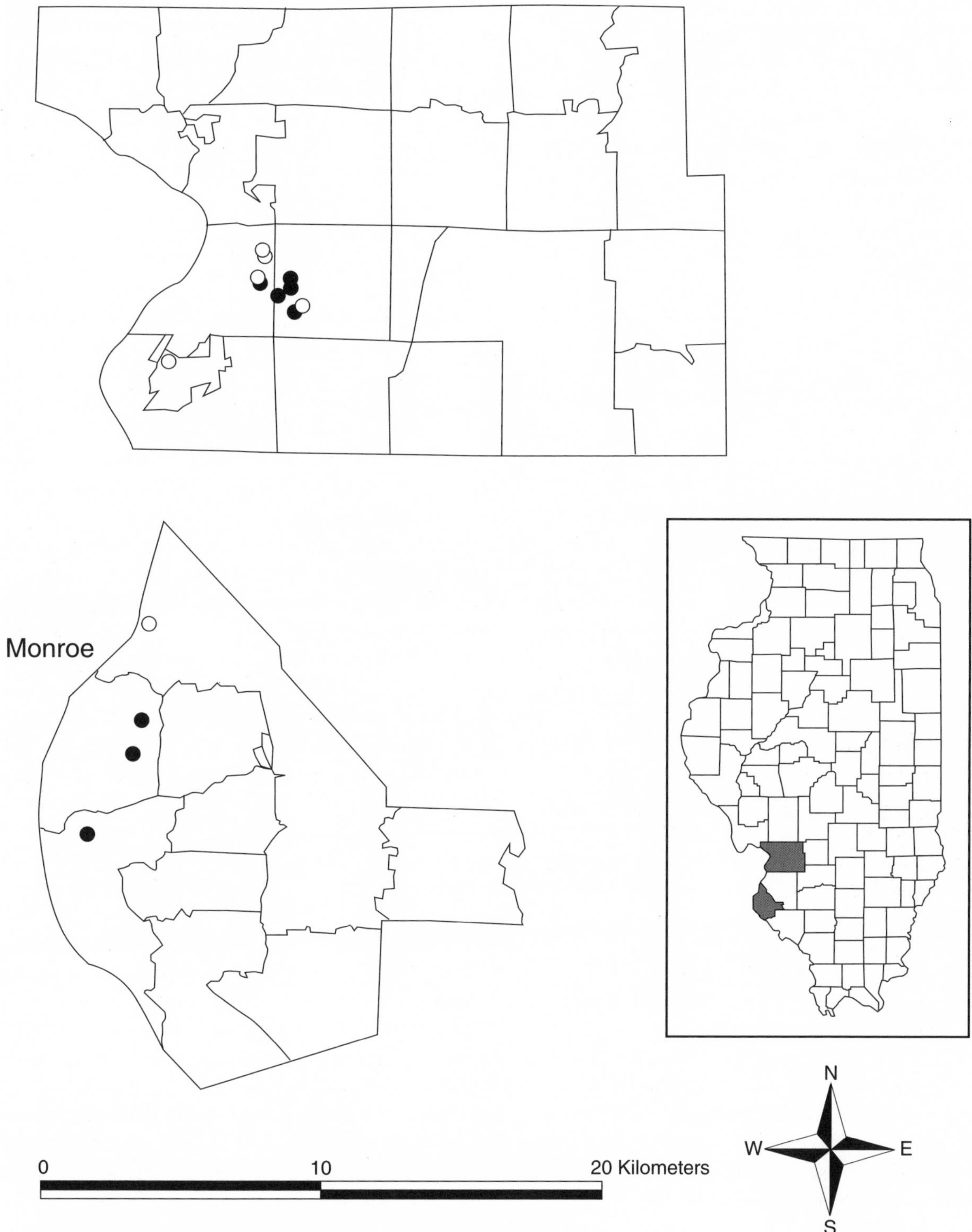

Figure 15-2. Madison and Monroe Counties, Illinois, showing known breeding sites of Illinois chorus frogs (*Pseudacris streckeri illinoensis*). Solid circles indicate 1993 to 1995 breeding activity. Open circles indicate pre-1990 records. Inset map shows locations of Madison and Monroe Counties in Illinois.

April), southern leopard frogs (19 April), and unidentified leopard frogs (13 and 19 April), either plains (*Rana blairi*) or southern.

During 1995, fieldwork was limited to 12 and 14 March. Both nights were productive. On 12 March, males were heard calling from west of the Poag sand prairie site and also from Morris site III, all from 2234 to 2316 hours. On 14 March, one to two males were heard calling from Morris site III, and ten to fifteen males were heard calling (two seen) at Morris site I south, all from 1900 to 2000 hours. One voucher specimen was obtained (SIUC H-5109).

Five productive sites were found in the Poag area during the 1993 to 1995 surveys. The historic Axtell sites north and south (Morris 1991) produced only spring peepers and chorus frogs. The historic Granite City site (Axtell and Haskell 1977) produced only chorus frogs and unidentified leopard frogs (either plains or southern).

Soil Types. The soil types at the breeding ponds of the various sites included Ambraw loam and Orthents, loamy, steep, and undulating at Axtell north and south sites; gravel pits, Beaucoup silty clay loam, and Tice silt loam at Morris sites I and II; and Ambraw loam at Morris site III, the Idle Acres Lane site, and the Poag sand prairie site (Goddard and Sabata 1986). The sandy soils surrounding the breeding ponds were comprised of Bloomfield loamy fine sand, Onarga sandy loam, Ridgeville fine sandy loam, Landes very fine sandy loam, Oakville fine sand, and Landes Variant very fine sandy loam. These sandy soil types fall within the "sand," "loamy sand," or "sandy loam" that was reported for Illinois chorus frogs in the lower Illinois River valley by Brown and Rose (1988).

Alteration of a Breeding Site. Disturbances of even small areas of habitat can have catastrophic consequences and pose serious threats to the species, as the following example in Madison County, where Illinois chorus frogs occur in only one small area (Fig. 15-2), illustrates. A logjam was created during summer 1993 when tenant farmers deposited slash into Cahokia Creek, flooding the main ephemeral breeding pond and introducing predatory fish such as black bullheads (*Ameiurus melas*) and warmouths (*Lepomis gulosus*) into the pond. Although the Army Corps of Engineers issued a Notice of Violation and called for the immediate removal of the slash and the restoration of the area, nothing was done. A ninety-day extension was granted, but, as the slash remained, the Illinois Department of Conservation and the U.S. Fish and Wildlife Service became involved. With a pump obtained from the Kaskaskia State Fish and Wildlife Area, one of us (S.R.B.) and John Tucker attempted to remove water and fish from the pond. Unfortunately, we were unable to remove all of the fish and feared the population of Illinois chorus frogs would be extirpated. According to Tucker (personal communication, Chpt. 14, this volume), the frogs did not use the pond as a breeding site in 1994. They did breed, however, in adjacent shallow water created by flooding. But the survival of this population remains uncertain.

Monroe County

Fieldwork. During 1993, fieldwork was conducted on 16, 23, 24 March and 7 and 9 April. The one historic site and four potential sites were monitored at times ranging from 1835 to 2244 hours. Of the five sites checked, three yielded Illinois chorus frogs (Fig. 15-2). Productive nights included 23 March (four males heard calling south of old Valmeyer), 24 March (five males heard calling, two males seen south of old Valmeyer), 7 April (six to twelve males heard calling south of Fountain), and 9 April (four males heard calling, one male seen south of Fountain, one male heard calling east of Fountain). Illinois chorus frogs were heard calling at times ranging from 1835 to 2207 hours. Air temperatures on productive nights ranged from 6° to 15°C, mean of 10°C; water temperatures ranged from 7° to 15°C with an average of 11°C; water depth ranged from 15 to 56 centimeters. Voucher specimens from two of the three new sites were obtained (SIUC H-4419, SIUC H-4421). Other species encountered during the surveys included American toads (9 April), spring peepers (16 and 24 March, 9 April), chorus frogs (16 and 24 March, 9 April), southern leopard frogs (24 March, 9 April), and eastern spadefoot toads (*Scaphiopus holbrookii*; 9 April). The historic site (Gilbert 1986) may not have been a breeding pond because the specimen was found in November.

On 1 August, the Great Flood of 1993 broke through the Columbia levee at 0830 hours. The floodwaters flowed south throughout the American Bottoms toward the town of Fountain. By 0100 hours on 2 August, the Fountain levee was breached, and the Mississippi River floodwaters reached the town of Valmeyer by 0400 hours. By 3 August, the entire floodplain from Columbia to Prairie du Rocher was under water, with depths of 1.8 to 2.4 meters standing on Bluff Road. By mid-October, floodwaters had receded to the point where Bluff Road could be driven again.

Fieldwork since the flooding of the American Bottoms in Monroe County has revealed no Illinois chorus frogs calling at any of the five previous sites. In 1994, fieldwork was conducted on 5, 13, and 19 April. Monitoring time frames and air temperatures ranged from 1947 to 2120 hours and from 3° to 4°C (5 April), 1938 to 2206 hours and 11° to 15°C (13 April), and 1946 to 2117 hours and 18° to 19°C (19 April). Species encountered were American toads (13 and 19 April), spring peepers (19 April), striped chorus frogs (13 and 19 April), plains leopard frogs (19 April), and unidentified leopard frogs (13 and 19 April). One of us (S.R.B.) found Illinois chorus frogs active in Madison County during this time (13 April), as did John Tucker (9, 14, 15, and 27 April; personal communication, Chpt. 14, this volume).

In 1995, fieldwork was conducted on 27 February, 5 and 19 April, and 10 May. Monitoring time frames and air temperatures ranged from 1954 to 2121 hours and from 3° to 4°C (27 February), 2004 to 2134 hours and 7° to 9°C (5 April), 2032 to 2146 hours and 13° to 14°C (19 April), and 2005 to 2135 hours and 15° to 18°C (10 May). Species encountered were Blanchard's cricket frogs (*Acris crepitans blanchardi*; 10 May), American toads (10 May), Fowler's toads (10 May), spring peepers (27 February, 5 April, 10 May), chorus frogs (5 and 19 April, 10 May), gray treefrogs (10 May), southern leopard frogs (19 April), and unidentified leopard frogs (5 April, 10 May). One of us (S.R.B.) found Illinois chorus frogs active in Madison County during this time (12 and 14 March), as did John Tucker on 11 March and 16 April (personal communication, Chpt. 14, this volume).

Soil Types. The soil types of the breeding ponds of the various sites were loamy Aquents (south of old Valmeyer), Booker clay (south of Fountain), and both Riley loam on 0 to 3 percent slopes and Ambraw silty clay loam (east of Fountain; Higgins 1987). However, all of the sandy soils surrounding the breeding ponds were Landes very fine sandy loam, 1 to 7 percent slopes. The historic site southwest of Columbia was also Landes very fine sandy loam, with the closest potential breeding pond soil type being loamy Aquents. This sandy soil type falls within the "sand," "loamy sand," or "sandy loam" that was reported for Illinois chorus frogs in the lower Illinois River valley by Brown and Rose (1988).

Alexander County

Fieldwork. On 14 February 1992, two to three male Illinois chorus frogs were heard calling near the Holman et al. (1964) site, where one of us (R.A.B.) and Ronn Altig had found a breeding pond in a plowed, sandy field on 10 February 1965 (SIUC H-2209, H-4108); another breeding pond was found in a plowed field near Tankville, 2.8 kilometers northwest of Brown and Brown's (1973) Miller City sites (Fig. 15-3). Here, in water 30 to 40 centimeters deep, we saw eleven calling males and seven noncalling animals, one of them a female that subsequently was amplexed and laid eggs in a plastic bag. The frogs were in and on windblown floating plant debris along one margin of the pond. Three vouchers were collected (SIUC H-4099, H-4100, H-4465). Also vocalizing in the pond were upland chorus frogs (*Pseudacris feriarum*) and southern leopard frogs.

On 22 February 1992, we counted thirty-eight egg masses of Illinois chorus frogs and thirty egg masses of smallmouth salamanders (*Ambystoma texanum*) in the pond, which was greatly reduced from the previous week. No eggs of chorus frogs or upland chorus frogs were observed. Egg masses of these two chorus frog species are loose rather than compact like those of Illinois chorus frogs, and individual eggs are only about half the diameter. The identity of Illinois chorus frog eggs was confirmed by rearing a dozen or so embryos from four masses through metamorphosis in the laboratory and by preserving tadpoles (SIUC H-4108) and one postmetamorphic juvenile (SIUC H-4101) as vouchers. The numbers of gastrula- to neurula-stage embryos counted in single egg masses were 15, 50, 45, 45, 60, 100, and 77. One egg mass of smallmouth salamanders was found in the pond depression, and thirty more, along with six Illinois chorus frog egg masses, were found in a small ditch that had been plowed to drain the pond. In a shallow, weedy roadside ditch along a gravel road, 0.6 kilometer away, several Illinois chorus frog egg masses and one of smallmouth salamanders were found attached to rooted plant stems. Several southern leopard frogs and one spring peeper were calling from the same ditch.

On 6 February 1993, no Illinois chorus frogs were heard in the vicinity of Tankville, although dozens of smallmouth salamander egg masses containing neurula-stage embryos were found in the pond and in a nearby small ditch (water about 20 centimeters deep) running through the same plowed field. During the evening of 3 March 1993, a field crew of eight people in three vehicles recorded male Illinois chorus frogs calling at over twenty locations throughout the region around Horseshoe Lake and Olive Branch, from Tankville to Cache River, and from Willard to Sandusky. Because the goal was to record as many call locations as possible during the short season the frogs were active, in relatively few instances (five) were calling males located and observed. Sound recordings were made at some locations,

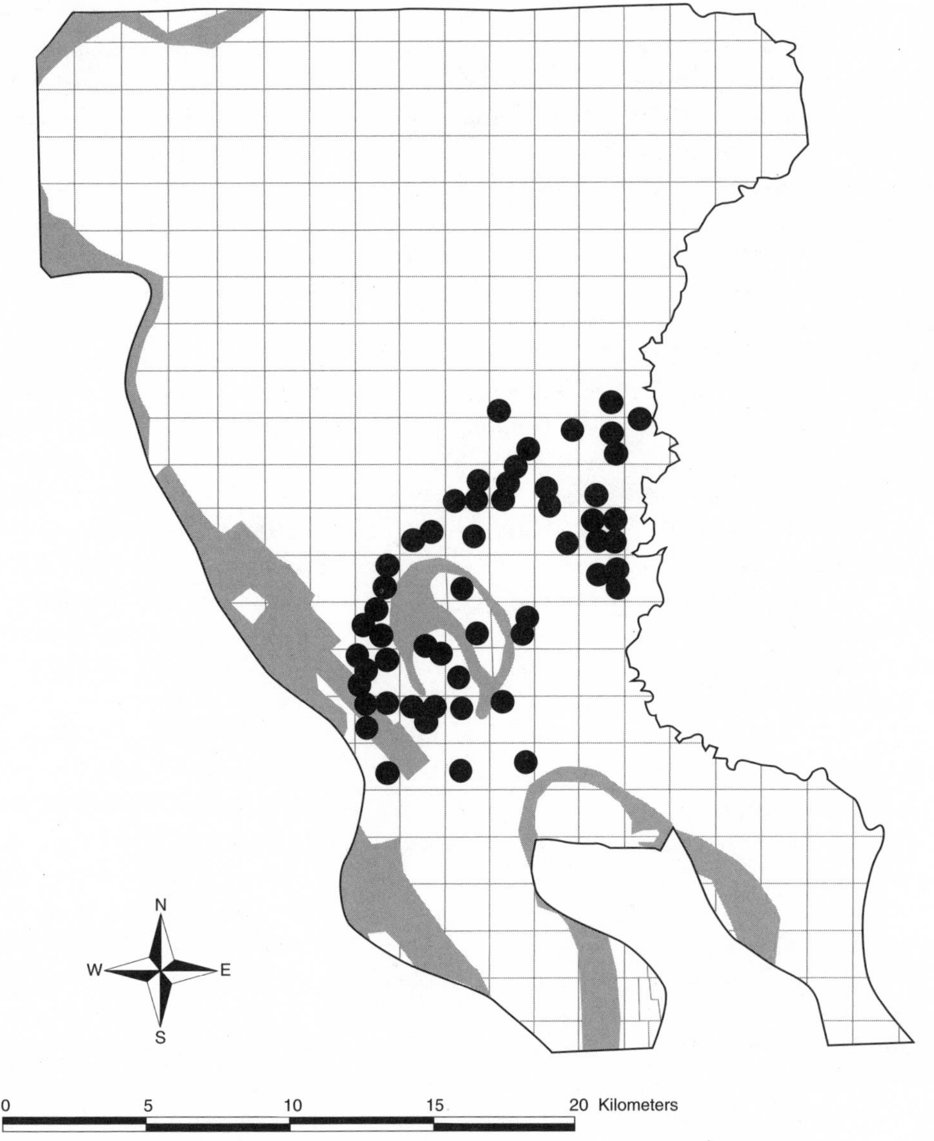

Figure 15-3. Locations of calling male Illinois chorus frogs (*Pseudacris streckeri illinoensis*) in the vicinity of Horseshoe Lake, Alexander County, Illinois, during 1992 to 1994. Dots are scaled more to indicate general distribution than to pinpoint localities. A few overlapping dots were omitted.

and all field crew members could distinguish the sounds made by Illinois chorus frogs from those made by spring peepers. Relatively few males were heard at each station (range of one to five, average of two and one-half). This night and subsequently we observed that within this metapopulation the number of males calling at any one time at most localities was few, commonly only two to three. On 22 March, we recorded eighteen Illinois chorus frogs calling in groups of one to six at eight localities between Sandusky and the south end of Horseshoe Lake; none were heard in the same area on 25 March. Other anurans vocalizing on 22 and 25 March were spring peepers, upland chorus frogs, southern leopard frogs, and American toads; spotted salamanders (*Ambystoma maculatum*), Fowler's toads, and bullfrogs were seen on the wet roads.

During the 1993 to 1994 herpetofaunal survey of Horseshoe Lake Conservation Area, Illinois chorus frogs were observed, or calling males heard, at a dozen locations within the conservation area; at three locations as far south in Dogtooth Bend as Willard; at fourteen sites to the west between the conservation area and the Mississippi River; and at nearly twenty locations as far north of the conservation area as Sandusky (Fig. 15-1). Males were heard calling, usually two to five at a time, on thirteen days between 10 February and 9 April. A few individuals were found on roads near the lake during or after rain on 26 March, 10 April, and 14 July; the animal found in July was a subadult.

Soil Types. Most (81 percent) of the forty-seven calling sites were on alluvial terraces (0 to 4 percent slopes) of fine sandy loam or loamy fine sand or on low silt loam to silty clay loam terraces (0 to 4 percent slopes) intermingled with bottomlands (Parks and Fehrenbacher 1968). Some of these soils are well-drained fine sandy loam terraces suitable for nonbreeding habitat, while other soils are poorly drained and suitable for maintaining vernal breeding ponds. Most of the more northern sites (19 percent) were on poorly drained bottomland soils developed from lake-deposited or slack-water sediments in the Cache River valley (Parks and Fehrenbacher 1968).

Discussion

Additional Localities

Prior to our fieldwork, Illinois chorus frogs were known in Monroe County by only one specimen captured as it crossed a blacktop road on 1 November 1983 (Gilbert 1986) southwest of Columbia. Three new localities up to 21 kilometers farther south were added during this study.

One new locality was added to the eight known previously in Madison County. Since calling males were not heard at three of the historic localities, these populations might be extirpated.

In addition to the seven Alexander County sites previously recorded, Illinois chorus frogs are relatively widespread over much of the Mississippi River/Cache River floodplain around Horseshoe Lake (Bogner et al. 1985). A relatively large area of floodplain, river terraces, and former lake bottoms near the mouth of the pre-Pleistocene Ohio River is occupied by this metapopulation. The area is bounded by the Shawnee Hills on the northwest, the Mississippi River on the west, the Mississippi River and the low-lying Dogtooth Bend on the south, the Cache River on the east, and Sandy Creek on the north. Elevations of calling sites range from approximately 96 to 105 meters above mean sea level and 4.5 to 13.5 meters above mean river level. Apparently suitable habitat lies north of Sandy Creek and east along the lower Cache River, where future fieldwork might find additional populations.

Calling Season and Breeding Habitat

Most of what is known about the habitat of Illinois chorus frogs is based on their breeding habitat when males are calling. Because of the extensive agricultural modification of the Great Plains and midwestern Prairie Peninsula, described breeding habitats probably are relicts persisting in highly disturbed environments: shallow, temporarily flooded low areas in or around pastures and cultivated fields, flooded wheat fields, flooded soybean and cotton fields, heavily vegetated roadside ponds, roadside ditches, standing water in creek arms and river sloughs, borrow ponds, and other temporary bodies of water in and around remnant sand prairies (Burt 1936; Wright and Wright 1949; Bragg 1950; Smith 1951; Brown and Brown 1973; Gray and Stegall 1986; Johnson 1987; Johnson and Burger 1992; Tucker and Philipp 1993). In Illinois, habitats in Madison, Monroe, and Alexander Counties can be characterized the same way.

We made no effort to locate or examine closely all breeding ponds in Alexander County. Many sites from which males called were temporary pools in plowed fields or ditches draining the fields, some of them adjacent to woods. Many were in poorly drained swales between terraced ridges. A few appeared to be borrow ponds or wildlife ponds (this is a major goose and duck overwintering region). Most sites appeared to be ephemeral, a few nearly permanent. Horseshoe Lake itself does not appear to be a required part of the frog's habitat in Alexander County. Management modifications of Horseshoe Lake to maintain a sport fishery, however, have the potential of harming adjacent habitat of Illinois chorus frogs.

The timing and duration of the calling season vary in response to latitude and to annual variation in the transition from winter to spring as reflected in rainfall and rising ground temperature. The boundaries of the calling season in central Illinois (early March to late May) are approximately a month later than in extreme southern Illinois (mid-February to mid-April) and in Missouri and Arkansas (late January to mid-April).

In central Illinois, Smith (1951) reported that breeding activity took place from 6 March through May, while

Taubert et al. (1982) reported choruses from 21 March to 20 May, and Brown and Rose (1988) reported them from 14 March through 1 May with a peak the first week of April. In metro-east Madison County and in Monroe County, males were heard calling from 1 March through 20 May (Axtell and Haskell 1977; Morris 1991; Taubert et al. 1982; Tucker and Philipp 1993). We recorded calls from 10 March through 13 April, and Tucker (1995) reported tadpoles transforming 28 May to 6 June. In Alexander County, calling was recorded earlier, from 27 February through 19 April (Brown and Brown 1973; Holman et al. 1964; Taubert et al. 1982). We observed calling from 10 February through 9 April. In northeastern Arkansas and southeastern Missouri, choruses have been reported from 15 February through 15 April and from late January through early April, respectively (Butterfield 1988; Johnson 1987, 1991; Smith 1955).

Effects of the Floods of 1993 and 1994 on Floodplain Breeding Habitat

Monroe County. The continuing existence of Illinois chorus frog populations in Monroe County will need to be examined closely. Because of its burrowing activities (Axtell and Haskell 1977; Brown et al. 1972; Tucker et al. 1995), the unusual depth and duration of water held on the floodplain during the Great Flood of 1993 could have adversely impacted or eliminated the species there. While flooding used to be a natural event in the floodplain, the speed and intensity of the water flowing across the floodplain from being forced through a levee break were greatly magnified from what would have occurred in a pre-levee flood. The frogs could have been either buried under tons of silt from the floodwaters or swept downstream with the rapidly flowing water. The entire floodplain from Columbia to Prairie du Rocher was under 1.8 meters of water for nearly three months. According to Valmeyer resident R. Bade (personal communication), floods in 1943, 1944, and 1947 reached depths of 0.9 to 1.2 meters and receded more quickly when the valley was protected by only 7.5-meters or less agricultural levees. The more recent 13.5-to-14.5-meter levees protected frog habitat from flooding until 1993.

Alexander County. Horseshoe Lake was formed about 6,000 years ago (Bogner et al. 1985) and at its closest point is no more than 3.3 kilometers from the present Mississippi River. The most distant Illinois chorus frog sites are only 15 kilometers from the Mississippi River but are near the Cache River. Prior to 1927, when a dam and spillway were constructed, the lake had existed as a shallow cypress swamp that mostly dried up during late summer (Bogner et al. 1985). Until 1939, Mississippi River floodwater regularly entered the lake by overland flow through the frog's habitat; Ohio River backwater flooding from the Cache River up and over the spillway also entered the lake. The Fayville levee, completed in 1969, effectively prevented overland flow to the lake and kept the Mississippi River from flooding the surrounding lowlands west and south of the lake until 1993. The levee was breached on 15 July 1993 and again on 13 April 1994, thus keeping much Illinois chorus frog habitat under water for several months during summer and autumn 1993 and spring 1994. The breach sent water across Dogtooth Bend, inundating nearly half of the known Illinois chorus frog sites for several months and reactivating Horseshoe Lake for a few months as a flow channel (Fig. 15-4).

Because Illinois chorus frogs live by burrowing in sandy alluvial deposits (Brown 1978; Brown et al. 1972; Tucker et al. 1995), they probably were able to survive the quickly passing floods of pre-levee days. Their response to much longer periods of inundation, however, is unknown. The 1993 and 1994 floods may have greatly reduced the populations west and south of the lake. Many individuals may have been washed away, drowned, or exposed to predatory birds. Much of their habitat west and south of Horseshoe Lake is greatly modified. New layers of sandy alluvium have been deposited in some places and several meters of older deposits scoured away in others. Systematic, long-term monitoring of Illinois chorus frog calls in this area could be instructive.

Management Guidelines and Buffer Zones for Breeding Sites

Because of the fossorial nature of Illinois chorus frogs, protecting only spring breeding sites is not adequate for this species' long-term survival (see also Tucker, Chpt. 14, this volume). Adjacent nonbreeding habitat must be protected as well. Illinois chorus frogs will move up to 0.9 kilometer (Tucker, Chpt. 14, this volume) from their breeding sites to nonbreeding habitat. In areas of breeding sites for Illinois chorus frogs, a buffer zone of at least 1 kilometer should be set up around the site. This buffer zone, of sandy soils, will be the nonbreeding habitat utilized by Illinois chorus frogs.

The vegetation in the sandy soils buffer area needs to be managed so that thickening or sod formation does not occur (Tucker et al. 1995), as Illinois chorus frog burrows are not found in heavy vegetation. Heavy equipment use in the buffer areas should be avoided at times

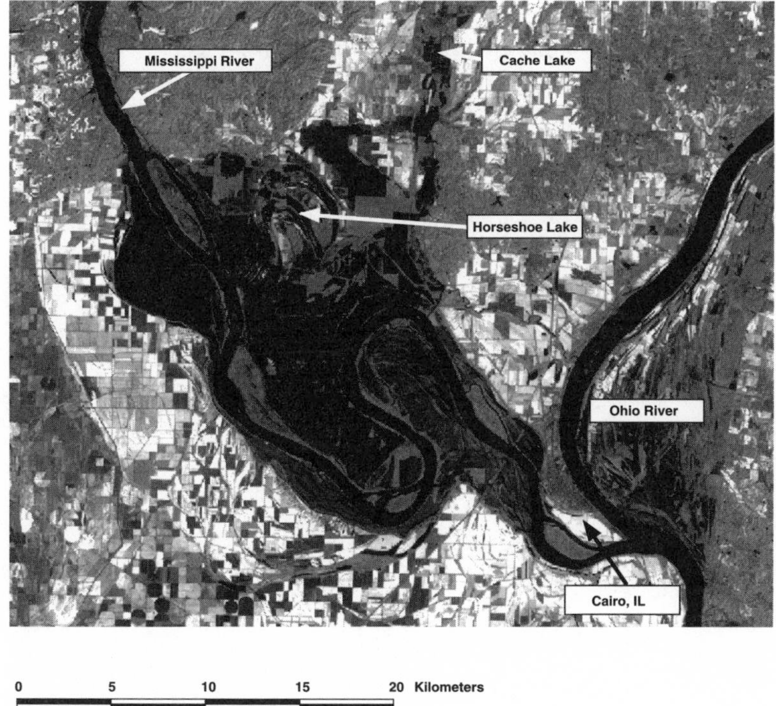

Figure 15-4. Satellite image of Alexander County, Illinois, showing Horseshoe Lake and environs during maximum Mississippi River flooding in 1993.

when the frogs would be in these nonbreeding habitats. Because they are active for only a few weeks early in the spring during breeding season, this would include most of the year. Illinois chorus frogs burrow anywhere from 2 to 23 centimeters deep into the sandy substrate (Axtell and Haskell 1977; Brown et al. 1972; Tucker et al. 1995), and compaction of these soils can be detrimental to the frog. Additionally, Illinois chorus frogs feed underground (Brown 1978).

Because Horseshoe Lake, Alexander County, is nearly surrounded by Illinois chorus frog habitat, management modifications to maintain a sport fishery should be evaluated carefully for their impact on adjacent frog habitat.

Summary

Breeding sites for Illinois chorus frogs (*Pseudacris streckeri illinoensis*) were monitored in Madison, Monroe, and Alexander Counties in southern Illinois. Fieldwork was conducted during the springs of 1993, 1994, and 1995 and, in Alexander County, during the summer of 1993. Extensive distributional data are presented, as are soil types and the other amphibians associated with Illinois chorus frog breeding sites. Effects of the floods of 1993 and 1994 on floodplain breeding habitat in Monroe and Alexander Counties are examined. Management guidelines and buffer zones for breeding sites are recommended.

Acknowledgments

Deanna Glosser (Illinois Department of Conservation [IDOC] Endangered Species Program Manager) permitted us to take one voucher specimen at new localities in Monroe County. Other appropriate permits were provided courtesy of Gretchen Bonfert (Illinois Nature Preserves Commission), William E. McClain ([IDOC] Natural Areas Project Manager), and John Tranquilli ([IDOC] Office of Resource Management). IDOC Office of Law Enforcement Field Sergeant Monty Burnham was helpful in gaining access to flooded areas behind National Guard barricades at Horseshoe Lake. Russell Garrison, Horseshoe Lake Conservation Area Site Superintendent, allowed unrestricted access to the conservation area. The work was partially funded by a contract from the Division of Natural Heritage, Illinois Department of Conservation.

Several people assisted us significantly in fieldwork or provided information on localities: Mark Bavetz, Michael Blanford, Doris Brandon, Beth Burke, Celine D'Onofrio, Terry Esker, Todd Fink, Kelly Hoffmann, Julie Howard, Robert Lindsay, Mark Phipps, Michael Redmer, Jay Rubinoff, Scott Simpson, Todd Strole, and Kirby Tolch.

Todd Fink, IDOC Natural Heritage Biologist, provided detailed information on localities, and he and Bruce McAllister, IDOC Natural Heritage Resident, provided color-coded soils maps of the Horseshoe Lake area. John Tucker, Illinois Natural History Survey, unselfishly shared information with us. The county base maps were provided by D. Kevin Davie, Southern Illinois University-Carbondale Library Affairs.

Regional and State Status

16

Status of Northeastern Illinois Amphibians

Kenneth S. Mierzwa

Northeastern Illinois, including the Chicago region, is located within an ecotone between the once-vast western grasslands and the eastern woodlands and forests. As a result of being covered by glacial ice as recently as 12,000 years ago (Baker, Chpt. 1; Holman, Chpt. 2, this volume), wetlands of various types are common. Although this landscape is young relative to unglaciated regions to the south, a diverse and unique assemblage of amphibians is present because of the convergence of very different ecosystems. Despite the presence of a major city and associated suburbs, extensive areas of open space have been preserved by federal, state, county, and local agencies and by private conservation groups.

Swink and Wilhelm (1994) define the Chicago region as the twenty-two counties in Illinois, Indiana, Michigan, and Wisconsin that are completely or partially within a 120-kilometer radius of downtown Chicago. However, for the present chapter, analysis is restricted to the eleven northeastern Illinois counties within the region, where a considerable amount of information on amphibians has recently been gathered. Figure 16-1 shows the area to be discussed.

The following account summarizes the northeastern Illinois inventory and monitoring efforts to date, briefly discusses the status of the twenty-two species of amphibians native to the Illinois portion of the Chicago region, and presents two case studies illustrating the effects of habitat restoration on local amphibians. I have attempted to show that, despite amphibian declines reported from around the world, it is possible to take actions that benefit at least some salamander and frog species.

Northeastern Illinois Inventory Efforts

The earliest published accounts of northeastern Illinois amphibians are those of Robert Kennicott. Only eighteen years old at the time, Kennicott (1855) listed the species he had noted in Cook County and commented on the relative abundance of each species. Although no precise localities were given in most cases, Kennicott resided near present-day north suburban Glenview, and his family's restored home is preserved as a National Historic Landmark. His correspondence with Spencer Fullerton Baird at the Smithsonian Institution indicates that much early collecting was done within walking or riding distance of Kennicott's home.

Northeastern Illinois was the focus of considerable effort by museum researchers in the 1920s, 1930s, and 1940s. Schmidt and Necker (1935), Necker (1939), Pope (1964), and Stille and Edgren (1948) cataloged the regional herpetofauna and added considerably to our knowledge of species distribution and life history. However, their efforts were generally not quantitative and were characterized by vague locality data.

Subsequent publications on amphibians and reptiles emphasized fieldwork conducted in the less well known downstate portions of Illinois (Smith 1961). By the 1980s, the available information on northeastern Illinois amphibians was largely obsolete, and precise distributional and habitat data were sorely lacking. The area had also changed greatly, with the conversion of agricultural land to sprawling suburbs and population growth to over 7 million people.

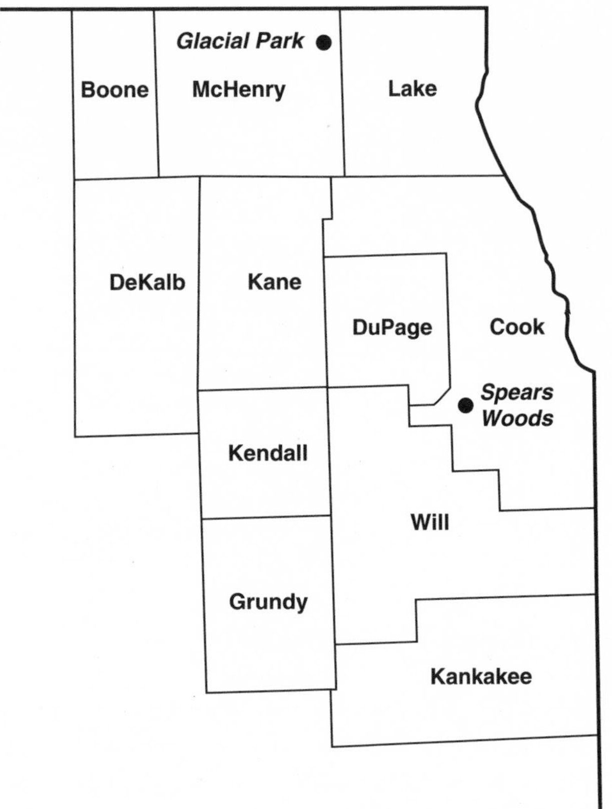

Figure 16-1. Northeastern Illinois counties considered in this chapter.

A few workers were once again actively gathering important data by the 1970s. However, it was not until the natural areas restoration movement blossomed in the 1980s that state, county, and local agencies, as well as private conservation organizations, began to fund herpetofaunal inventories of public lands. Federal regulations have also produced new information. Site investigations have been carried out as part of environmental assessments and environmental impact studies required under the National Environmental Policy Act of 1972 and as part of wetland mitigation proposals mandated by Section 404 of the Clean Water Act.

Two major types of amphibian studies have taken place in recent years. Site inventories have been conducted at numerous locations and typically have resulted in species lists and some information on relative abundance. Inventories often have been intended to determine whether endangered, threatened, or rare species are present or to provide information for the formulation of site management plans. A few studies have been more detailed, including quantitative assessments of habitat utilization or tracking of long-term population trends. Northeastern Illinois studies conducted since 1970 are listed in Table 16-1. The rapidly growing database has made possible an assessment of the current status of the twenty-two species of amphibians native to northeastern Illinois.

Status of Northeastern Illinois Amphibians

Table 16-2 summarizes comments on the relative abundance of northeastern Illinois amphibians over a span of 140 years. The assessments by Kennicott (1855), Schmidt and Necker (1935), and the present author are of necessity subjective and are certainly influenced by differences in geographic coverage, methods of collecting, and perception of each author. Categorizing status is further complicated by the usual problems of describing abundance. Some species may be common and widespread, while others may occur in only a few places but be abundant where they are found.

Kennicott's (1855) observations were made in a setting only a little changed since the first major influx of European settlers twenty years earlier, although fire suppression had probably already allowed the savannas to choke with brush. There is no way to know how many animals Kennicott was referring to when he said a species was "common" or "abundant." Certainly, whatever the numbers, there were many more populations in the days before extensive mechanized agriculture.

By Schmidt and Necker's (1935) time, most of the region was in crops or being grazed, most wetlands had been drained by ditching and tiling, and many streams had been channelized. However, urban development was largely limited to Chicago proper and a scattering of suburbs on major transportation routes. Agricultural use of chemicals was not yet pervasive. The Forest Preserve District of Cook County had been created and had already begun to acquire land.

Schmidt and Necker (1935) mention all of the amphibian species then known from the area but do not give abundance information for several. Cope's gray treefrogs (*Hyla chrysoscelis*) and plains leopard frogs (*Rana blairi*) had not yet been described, and the presence of smallmouth salamanders (*Ambystoma texanum*) in the southern periphery of the region had not yet been discovered.

Today all but the most distant parts of northeastern

Table 16-1. A partial listing of recent northeastern Illinois amphibian studies and their sites

Site	Year(s) of Study	Type*	References
Lake County Forest Preserve District	1975, 1983–1987	Q, I	Bushey 1979; Mierzwa 1986
Tinley Creek Woods	1984 and 1995	Q	Alfaro 1996
Lake Forest Open Lands	1986	I	Mierzwa 1986
Forest Preserve District of Will County	1988	I	Mierzwa 1988
Fermi National Accelerator Laboratory	1989	I	Mierzwa et al. 1990
Forest Preserve District of DuPage County	1988–1990	I	Ludwig et al. 1992
McHenry County Conservation District	1986–1994	Q, I	Mierzwa and Beltz 1994a
Illinois-Indiana Regional Airport Study	1990–1991	I	Mierzwa et al. 1991
Poplar Creek Forest Preserve	1992	I	Sliwinski 1992
Middle Fork Savanna	1994	Q, I	Mierzwa and Beltz 1994b
Joliet Army Ammunition Plant	1993	I	Redmer and Anton 1993
Long Grove Park District	1993–1994	I	Mierzwa et al. 1994
North Branch Prairie Project	1992	I	Anton 1992

*Q = quantitative data; I = inventory data.

Illinois are developing rapidly. Although the rate of population growth has slowed, the area of developed land has increased by 46 percent since 1970 (Northeastern Illinois Planning Commission 1994). Suburban sprawl has aggravated habitat fragmentation, and in the remaining rural areas heavy reliance on agricultural fertilizers and pesticides has degraded ground- and surface-water quality. Tilling too close to streams has resulted in severe siltation in some water bodies. However, forest preserve districts or conservation districts now exist in at least eight of the eleven counties, much open space has been set aside, and restoration techniques are advancing rapidly.

Common and Widespread Species

Five taxa (eastern tiger salamanders [*Ambystoma tigrinum tigrinum*], American toads [*Bufo americanus americanus*], western chorus frogs [*Pseudacris triseriata triseriata*], bullfrogs [*Rana catesbeiana*], and green frogs [*Rana clamitans melanota*]) occur throughout the region and are generally common to abundant. Blue-spotted salamanders (*Ambystoma laterale*) are abundant on the wooded moraines but absent from the more open western and southern parts of the region.

Recent Declines

Two species have declined in recent years. Blanchard's cricket frogs (*Acris crepitans blanchardi*) were once among the most abundant amphibians in the area but disappeared from most of the region during the 1970s. Only a very few populations now survive. Northern leopard frogs (*Rana pipiens*) experienced a die-off in the late 1960s or early 1970s but have since recovered well in counties where extensive wetlands remain. They are now abundant in Lake and McHenry Counties but harder to find in the southern and western parts of the region, where heavy agricultural use has resulted in a loss of most wetlands.

Sporadically Distributed but Locally Common Species

Spotted salamanders (*Ambystoma maculatum*), central newts (*Notophthalmus viridescens louisianensis*), wood frogs (*Rana sylvatica*), and northern spring peepers (*Pseudacris crucifer crucifer*) are forest species more characteristic of areas east and north of this region. In northeastern Illinois, they are essentially restricted to scattered small pockets of mesic forest or woodland. Richard A. Edgren, in a 1940s margin note to his specimen catalog, mentioned observing seventy spotted salamanders in a Lake County breeding pond in one evening. The species is rare at that same location today. While all of the forest species survive in the region, some populations are gone, others are perilously small, and only a few appear to be large and stable.

The gray tree frog complex (*Hyla versicolor* and *Hyla*

Table 16-2. Status of northeastern Illinois amphibians in 1855, 1935 to 1939, and 1995

Species	Kennicott (1855)	Necker (1939)	Modern status (1995)
Mudpuppy (*Necturus maculosus maculosus*)	Listed but no mention of status	Status not given	Uncertain
Central newt (*Notophthalmus viridescens louisianensis*)	"Abundant both in prairie and timber"	Status not given	Uncommon and local
Blue-spotted salamander (*Ambystoma laterale*)	Not mentioned	Status not given	Common
Spotted salamander (*Ambystoma maculatum*)	"Only found . . . in timber"	"Locally abundant"	Uncommon and local
Smallmouth salamander (*Ambystoma texanum*)	Not mentioned	Not mentioned	Peripheral
Eastern tiger salamander (*Ambystoma tigrinum tigrinum*)	"Common . . . breed in great numbers in some of the prairie sloughs"	"Common"	Common and widespread
Southern two-lined salamander (*Eurycea cirrigera*)	Not mentioned	"Two specimens"	Peripheral
Four-toed salamander (*Hemidactylium scutatum*)	"Numerous in particular localities in the timber"	"Extremely rare"	Extremely rare
Redback salamander (*Plethodon cinereus*)	Not mentioned	Status not given	Peripheral
American toad (*Bufo americanus americanus*)	"Common"	Status not given	Abundant and widespread
Fowler's toad (*Bufo woodhousii fowleri*)	Not mentioned	"Limited to sandy areas"	Peripheral
Blanchard's cricket frog (*Acris crepitans blanchardi*)	"Not uncommon"	"Consistently found on the muddy banks of streams"	Nearly extirpated
Northern spring peeper (*Pseudacris crucifer crucifer*)	Not mentioned	Status not given	Sporadically distributed, locally common
Western chorus frog (*Pseudacris triseriata triseriata*)	"Abundant on the prairie"	Status not given	Abundant and widespread
Gray treefrog complex (*Hyla versicolor/chrysoscelis*)	"Common"	Status not given	Uncommon
Plains leopard frog (*Rana blairi*)	Not yet described	Not yet described	Peripheral
Bullfrog (*Rana catesbeiana*)	Not mentioned	"Abundant"	Abundant
Green frog (*Rana clamitans melanota*)	"Abundant"	"Found in practically all permanent water"	Common
Pickerel frog (*Rana palustris*)	Not mentioned	"Absent"	Extremely rare or extirpated
Northern leopard frog (*Rana pipiens*)	"Exceedingly abundant"	"Found throughout the area"	Common
Wood frog (*Rana sylvatica*)	Not mentioned	Status not given	Rare

chrysoscelis) long ago disappeared from some historical localities but is common at others. Cope's gray tree frogs (*Hyla chrysoscelis*) are widespread in the Fox River valley northwest of the city, while most eastern gray tree frog (*Hyla versicolor*) records are in Will and southern Cook Counties.

Rare or Extirpated Species

Four-toed salamanders (*Hemidactylium scutatum*) were once found at several localities in northern Cook and southeastern Lake Counties (Kennicott 1855; Smith 1961; Anton et al., Chpt. 6, this volume). All of the available specimens from those areas were collected before 1932. Dredging of the Skokie Marsh by the Civilian Conservation Corps during the 1930s destroyed most of the remaining habitat, and the species was thought to be extirpated from northeastern Illinois. It was recently discovered at a single Will County locality (Anton et al., Chpt. 6, this volume).

Pickerel frogs (*Rana palustris*) once occurred at a scattering of localities in the Fox River valley, where they were apparently associated with groundwater-fed fens and small streams. Although a number of high-quality fens have been preserved, there have been no valid reports of the species since 1948 (Redmer and Mierzwa 1994; Redmer, Chpt. 12, this volume).

Peripheral Species

Several species barely enter northeastern Illinois. Smallmouth salamanders are known from two specimens collected in Kankakee and Grundy Counties, but the current status is unknown. Several disjunct populations of southern two-lined salamanders (*Eurycea cirrigera*) occur on publicly owned land in Will and Kankakee Counties, and their abundance here has apparently not changed since the early 1930s (Mierzwa 1989). Redback salamanders (*Plethodon cinereus*) were known from a single Cook County locality, where they have apparently been extirpated since 1960. This species is abundant at Indiana Dunes National Lakeshore and other localities not far to the east. In our region, Fowler's toads (*Bufo woodhousii fowleri*) are restricted to sand-areas and still occur near the Kankakee River. Historical populations at Illinois Beach State Park, documented by 1920s and 1930s specimens, are apparently extirpated. Plains leopard frogs (*Rana blairi*) were first described in 1973, so historical information is scarce; a few specimens have been collected in the southern part of the region, and they still occur in Will County in low numbers (Brown and Morris 1990).

Species of Uncertain Status

Mudpuppies (*Necturus maculosus*) are poorly known in northeastern Illinois. The late Michael A. Morris believed that the species may have declined, but difficulties associated with sampling this permanently aquatic species have prevented any detailed assessment. Mud–puppies still occur in Lake Michigan and the Kankakee River and have been taken in the Chain O' Lakes area within the past thirty years.

Case Studies

Spears Woods

Most people associate salamanders with lush, old-growth forests. However, forest was a relatively uncommon habitat type in northeastern Illinois, even at the time of Euro-American settlement. Most of the region was a mosaic of oak savanna, prairie, and wetland, with denser forests largely limited to the eastern, downwind side of major rivers where prairie fires could not reach.

The northeastern Illinois salamander fauna occupies a range of savanna and forest habitat types. Tiger salamanders are most widespread and common in relatively open savannas and woodlands with a dense herbaceous understory. Blue-spotted salamanders are common in a range of woodland and forest types, from 30 percent canopy cover to nearly closed canopy conditions. Spotted salamanders are characteristic of humid, mesic forests and are reported to be adversely affected by any opening in the tree canopy (Vogt 1981).

In the late 1980s, volunteer stewards associated with The Nature Conservancy initiated an aggressive savanna restoration effort within the 5,670-hectare Palos-Sag Valley Forest Preserves of southwestern Cook County, Illinois. In cooperation with the Forest Preserve District of Cook County, an inventory was conducted to identify land that retained native elements and to prioritize restoration efforts (King and Zoars 1991). Spears Woods, a 194-hectare tract with mesic to dry-mesic woodland and savanna, mesic prairie, marsh, and pond communities, was identified as a First Priority Restoration site. The inventory report characterized Spears Woods as follows: "Many of the savanna areas in this site show evidence of wildfires and thus are relatively free of brush. Diverse prairie and savanna grasses and forbs are currently growing in high density. Prairie openings, containing little brush and few weed problems, are nestled between oak savannas. . . .There is good potential habitat for amphibians and reptiles." Indeed, concurrent site inventories by the Chicago Herpetological Society and various individuals documented the presence of at least ten amphibian species at Spears Woods, making it one of the richest amphibian localities in northeastern Illinois.

Management of Spears Woods was intended to restore the savanna community that had once occurred there but had become increasingly rare and to improve the diversity and interspersion of community types. As restoration plans were formulated to clear exotic shrubs, such as buckthorn, from the understory and to design a controlled burn rotation, I submitted a proposal to the Forest Preserve District of Cook County to monitor the effects of habitat restoration on amphibians. A group of about a dozen enthusiastic volunteers, led by Spears Woods steward Steve Bubulka, quickly formed. This group included Tony Dancik, an experienced herpetologist, who educated the volunteers on species identification.

Our hypothesis was simple: spotted salamanders, a characteristic mesic forest species, were expected to decline quickly in response to restoration activities. We anticipated that other species, including tiger salamanders, would eventually benefit from the restoration of the herbaceous understory. The emphasis was on salamanders, but all amphibian species were monitored.

It is important to note that we knew spotted salamanders were common at several nearby sites not scheduled for any intervention or management. Most of these sites were heavily wooded and on north-facing slopes and probably represented original spotted salamander habitat. None of the amphibian species at Spears Woods were rare, and all occurred throughout the Palos-Sag Valley Forest Preserves.

In March 1991, drift fences were installed around a small pond within a diverse oak woodland. Brush clearing and burning were scheduled to begin a few hundred meters north of the pond that same spring, but the canopy opened up more rapidly than expected when a tornado touched down just northwest of the pond a few days after the first salamanders were captured.

Five years of data have now been gathered at the study pond. Nine species of amphibians, including four species of salamanders and five species of frogs, have been captured consistently (Table 16-3). As expected, spotted salamander numbers plummeted in 1992 and have now stabilized at about 23 percent of the total captured in the first year. The decline was probably greatly accelerated by the tornado-related opening of the canopy, because subsequent restoration activities have focused on the shrub and herbaceous layers.

Other species have responded in more complex ways. Blue-spotted salamanders declined in 1993 and 1994, then rebounded in 1995 to nearly initial baseline levels. The decline probably represents normal attrition and lack of recruitment from several relatively dry years (Pechmann et al. 1991). High rainfall and cool summer temperatures in 1993 resulted in high reproductive success, and the resulting cohort of two-year-old males first arrived at the breeding pond in 1995.

Tiger salamander numbers declined in 1993 and then remained stable. Because tiger salamander larvae are the last of the three local *Ambystoma* species to leave the pond, they are most susceptible to drought. Tiger salamanders also reportedly require two to seven years to reach sexual maturity (Pfingsten and Downs 1989; but see Semlitsch et al. 1988), so 1993 recruitment into the population may not be fully measurable until 1997.

Other species were captured in relatively low numbers, so conclusions are less obvious. American toad numbers increased beginning in 1992 and peaked in 1993 and 1994. Spring peeper numbers increased dramatically in 1993 and 1994, then returned to baseline levels. Western chorus frog numbers peaked in 1994. Both of these treefrog species reach sexual maturity in one year (Collins 1975; Duellman and Trueb 1986). Northern leopard frogs have increased from low initial levels and now are consistently captured in moderate numbers. Because this species utilizes herbaceous vegetation for rehydration (Feder and Burggren 1992), it is possible that the increase is attributable to restoration activities. Bullfrogs have been present some years, but these have been transient juveniles dispersing from nearby permanent wetlands, and no breeding has occurred at the study pond.

The Spears Woods study adds further weight to the position of other authors (e.g., Pechmann et al. 1991) that long-term studies are required to distinguish actual population trends from normal cyclical variation related to weather patterns or other factors. The Spears Woods data imply that species respond to environmental factors such as weather and changes in habitat at variable rates because of different life spans and ages at sexual maturity. In this case, it may require ten years or more to identify the actual effects of restoration activities for all species. In the meantime, a tentative statement can be made that stochastic natural disturbance and restoration of oak savanna and woodland at Spears Woods have probably influenced the decline of one forest-associated species (spotted salamanders) and the increase of one species characteristic of wet herbaceous vegetation

Table16-3. Numbers of amphibians captured at Spears Woods, 1991 through 1995

Species	1991	1992	1993	1994	1995
Blue-spotted salamander (*Ambystoma laterale*)	150	145	118	81	130
Spotted salamander (*Ambystoma maculatum*)	62	27	30	15	14
Eastern tiger salamander (*Ambystoma tigrinum tigrinum*)	12	10	3	2	4
Central newt (*Notophthalmus viridescens louisianensis*)	12	13	8	9	7
American toad (*Bufo americanus americanus*)	2	6	9	9	5
Northern spring peeper (*Pseudacris crucifer crucifer*)	4	2	11	15	2
Western chorus frog (*Pseudacris triseriata triseriata*)	5	1	2	16	3
Bullfrog (*Rana catesbeiana*)	0	4	7	0	1
Northern leopard frog (*Rana pipiens*)	1	1	8	6	7

(northern leopard frogs). The effects on the other seven amphibians are less clear and will require additional years of study.

Glacial Park

Glacial Park, a McHenry County Conservation District site located near the Village of Richmond and about 7.5 kilometers from the Illinois-Wisconsin border, covers nearly 1,175 hectares. The site is not only large by Illinois standards, but it is diverse. The most striking features of the landscape are steep-sided delta kames, 30-meter-high gravel and sand hills deposited by meltwater streams flowing on top of stagnating glaciers about 12,000 years ago. Wetlands are present in other parts of the site, mostly on outwash plains and glacial lake beds. Nippersink Creek, a tributary of the Fox River, meanders through the western and northern parts of the site.

Glacial Park is formed around several "core areas" that retain elements of biodiversity despite decades of nearby farming and grazing. The kames, mostly covered by dry-mesic savanna dominated by bur oak, were too steep for most uses other than grazing. The kames and adjacent wetlands, including a kettle marsh and low shrub bog, form the most important core area. Extensive patches of sedge meadow, mesic prairie remnants along an abandoned railroad, and savanna and wetland complexes along Nippersink Creek also supported native species. Most of the land between these cores that was flat enough, dry enough, or could be easily drained had been farmed for many years.

Inventory efforts began in 1986, when McHenry County Conservation District staff began keeping records of animals observed at Glacial Park. My own involvement at Glacial Park began in 1989 with limited drift fencing and extensive random searches and gradually expanded into intensive quantitative monitoring in cooperation with the full-time staff. We documented eighteen species of amphibians and reptiles, the richest herpetofauna in McHenry County. Because of the absence of true forest in this area, only seven amphibian species were present, six of them frogs. An eighth amphibian species, Blanchard's cricket frogs, occurred historically along Nippersink Creek, and this population is represented by several specimens in the collection of the Field Museum of Natural History in Chicago.

Restoration efforts were in early stages when inventory efforts began. Prairies were planted on former cropland as farm leases expired. Savannas were cleared of exotic shrubs, and wetlands were restored by breaking drain tiles and plugging ditches. Parts of the site were burned each spring and fall, with each of eighteen management units on an approximately three-year burn rotation. The fire-adapted prairie and savanna plants responded vigorously. By 1993, Glacial Park once again had the appearance of a largely natural landscape. In 1994, the vast Lost Valley Marsh was restored through construction of a weir. The core areas had once again been linked together.

Early monitoring results were influenced by the drought of 1988 to 1989. Amphibian numbers were presumably lower than normal, and some wetlands required three or four years to fully recharge. When unusually heavy rains arrived in 1993, the first wet year since the restoration began, drift fences were in place.

For most species, numbers of individuals gradually increased from 1987 through 1992, then jumped dramatically in 1993 (Table 16-4). Because the 1993 total includes large numbers of dispersing juveniles, it certainly overestimates long-term abundance. However, such large numbers were captured precisely because habitat once again existed. A few years earlier, most individuals would have probably perished attempting to cross cropland.

Some limited follow-up sampling was conducted in the fall of 1994 but was restricted to sedge meadow and riparian habitats. Because savanna and marsh species were not present at these locations, or were present only as transients, comparisons can be made only for ranid frogs. Results presented in Table 16-5 are based only on drift fence captures and are presented as catch per 1,000 trap nights because of the low sampling effort in 1994 relative to other years.

Conclusions

Of the twenty-two amphibian species documented from northeastern Illinois, only three (smallmouth salamanders [*Ambystoma texanum*], redback salamanders [*Plethodon cinereus*], and pickerel frogs [*Rana palustris*]) have not been collected in recent years. While several types of salamanders and frogs may be less abundant than they once were, declines of two species, Blanchard's cricket frogs and northern leopard frogs, cannot be explained by direct loss or degradation of habitat. Cricket frogs are almost gone from the region, while leopard frogs have recovered at many localities.

One key to maintaining biodiversity of amphibians and of other organisms is the identification, preservation, and enhancement or restoration of regional "hot spots." While there is some controversy over whether preservation sites should be identified on the basis of species richness or the presence of unique species, many locations already in public ownership satisfy both criteria. Because only six amphibian species (27 percent of

Table 16-4. Numbers of amphibians observed at Glacial Park, 1987 through 1993. Data are pooled from all sampling methods and sites.

Species	1987	1989	1991	1992	1993
Eastern tiger salamander (*Ambystoma tigrinum tigrinum*)	3	2	1	12	595
American toad (*Bufo americanus americanus*)	4	10	35	13	1,156
Western chorus frog (*Pseudacris triseriata triseriata*)	1	30	3	64	78
Cope's gray treefrog (*Hyla chrysoscelis*)	3	3	0	0	2
Bullfrog (*Rana catesbeiana*)	0	0	0	1	0
Green frog (*Rana clamitans melanota*)	2	5	18	5	22
Northern leopard frog (*Rana pipiens*)	3	11	14	23	179

Table 16-5. Drift fence captures of ranid frogs at Glacial Park by year. Numbers are standardized and represent captures per 1,000 trap nights.

Year	Green Frogs (*Rana clamitans melanota*)	Northern Leopard Frogs (*Rana pipiens*)
1991	11.0	44.0
1992	0	16.2
1993	7.4	215.5
1994	41.7	114.6

the total) are of fairly general occurrence throughout the region, the wisdom of preserving important community types within each natural division should be clear. Even the best individual sites generally support less than half of the twenty-two amphibian species found within the eleven-county region.

Target sites should be large, should include multiple core areas of moderate to high natural quality, and should incorporate a variety of terrestrial and aquatic habitat types. Restoration of expanses of degraded land separating core areas can allow amphibians to disperse across the landscape, helping historical metapopulation patterns to function once again and decreasing the risk of stochastic extinctions (Meffe and Carroll 1994; Gilpin and Hanski 1991). The value of narrow linear corridors is dubious for most amphibians, with the possible exception of semiaquatic species in riparian buffer strips.

Restoration of habitat requires a clear understanding of the pre-Euro-American settlement condition. While it is usually not possible to identify the precise pre-Euro-American settlement species composition, major community types and landscape patterns can be identified from early survey maps and notes (Bourdo 1956). Where possible, restoration should include both terrestrial and aquatic communities. Managing at the landscape or ecosystem level is generally preferable to single species management, although species can be monitored as one indicator of success. Both spatial and temporal heterogeneity should be encouraged. For example, carefully planned controlled burning in prairie and savanna ecosystems generally benefits amphibians by encouraging the growth of herbaceous vegetation and increasing plant community interspersion. However, regular rotations—that is, always burning the same management unit at the same season and the same interval—should be avoided. Keeping variability in management regimes mimics the stochastic natural disturbances that once operated on a vast scale (Holling and Meffe 1996).

In some areas, it is possible to work with federal agencies to direct wetland mitigation, and the accompanying monitoring requirements, into the most beneficial locations. Volunteers can be of great value in both restoration and monitoring. In general, creative strategies for protection and restoration that represent the best chance of maintaining amphibian biodiversity should be sought.

Summary

The level of northeastern Illinois amphibian inventory and monitoring activity has increased in recent years, largely as a result of natural areas acquisition and restoration. This new information has made possible an assessment of the current status of most northeastern Illinois amphibians, as well as a preliminary analysis of the effects of restoration activities on amphibians. Several amphibian species are probably less common today than they were in the past, a direct result of habitat loss or degradation from agricultural or urban development. Two species, Blanchard's cricket frogs (*Acris crepitans blanchardi*) and northern leopard frogs (*Rana pipiens*), have declined for less obvious reasons, although leopard frogs have partially recovered. Acquisition of natural areas and restoration of upland and wetland habitat on degraded public land have allowed populations of some species to increase in size; this has been especially true on larger sites.

Acknowledgments

I thank J. Ayres, B. Bannon, N. Bent, S. Bubulka, P. Chisholm, E. Collins, T. Dancik, S. Hayden, G. Horn, R. Keller, K. King, L. Meyer, D. Nyberg, J. O'Connor, C. Patrick, D. Petro, G. Precin, R. Reason, W. Schennum, J. Stoddard, B. Woodson, and S. Zoars for their participation in monitoring efforts at Glacial Park and Spears Woods. The Glacial Park effort was funded by the McHenry County Conservation District. The Illinois Department of Natural Resources, Illinois Nature Preserves Commission, Forest Preserve District of Cook County, Lake County Forest Preserve District, Lake Forest Open Lands Association, Nature Conservancy, Volunteer Stewardship Network, and Forest Preserve District of Will County provided permits, funding, information, or field assistance for other studies that contributed to my knowledge of the northeastern Illinois herpetofauna. Many individuals, far too numerous to list, participated in site inventories or discussions that made possible the assessment of northeastern Illinois amphibian status. Special thanks go to S. Barakat, E. Beltz, R. Sliwinski, T. Anton, M. Redmer, D. Mauger, and all of my colleagues at TAMS Consultants.

17

Status of Amphibians in Northwestern Indiana

Robert Brodman and Mary Kilmurry

Reports of amphibian declines have increased the need for the monitoring and management of these nongame species (Freda et al. 1991; Wake 1991; Heyer et al. 1994). Difficulties in documenting current decreases in amphibians and linking these decreases to anthropogenic stresses have been discussed (Pechmann et al. 1991; Pechmann and Wilbur 1994). Despite these problems, aspects of historical accounts of amphibian distribution and abundance can be used quantitatively to determine past trends (Lannoo et al. 1994). However, the amphibian fauna of northwest Indiana has not been well studied, and the necessary baseline data for determining population trends were never collected (Minton 1972).

Prior to the 1970s, surveys of the herpetofauna of the Jasper-Pulaski Fish and Wildlife Area (JPFWA), located on the border of northeastern Jasper and northwestern Pulaski Counties in northwest Indiana, indicated that at least fifteen amphibian species, including four currently state-listed species, inhabited this single area of protected public habitat (Grant 1936; Swanson 1939; Minton 1972; Minton et al. 1982). Collection records from the JPFWA represent some of the southernmost known populations of blue-spotted salamanders (*Ambystoma laterale*) and northern leopard frogs (*Rana pipiens*); some of the northernmost known populations of western lesser sirens (*Siren intermedia nettingi*), smallmouth salamanders (*Ambystoma texanum*), and northern slimy salamanders (*Plethodon glutinosus*); and the easternmost known population of plains leopard frogs (*Rana blairi*) (Minton 1972; Minton et al. 1982; Conant and Collins 1991).

Many of these species accounts are based on notes and voucher specimens and provide little information regarding abundance (Grant 1936; Swanson 1939). Furthermore, there is some indication that early herpetologists may not have sampled during the breeding seasons of each of the species that occur in the area. For example, late-breeding species such as American toads (*Bufo americanus americanus*), bullfrogs (*Rana catesbeiana*), and Blanchard's cricket frogs (*Acris crepitans blanchardi*) are not often represented in the surveys of the 1930s. Additionally, the fauna in the remainder of this agricultural region has largely been ignored. As a result of these problems, past trends in amphibian populations cannot be directly addressed.

Jasper County historically consisted of vast sand and prairie marshes, with patches of oak savanna in the north and prairie grassland to the south (Andreas 1876; Smallwood and Osterholz 1990). By 1917, most wetland habitats had been drained to create farmland. In 1990, farmland covered 86 percent of the county's 1,436 square kilometers (Smallwood and Osterholz 1990). Only the 20 square-kilometer JPFWA contains large tracts of remaining wetlands. Although the amphibian fauna prior to wetland drainage remains unknown, the JPFWA fauna may be considered representative of the pre-Euro-American settlement era.

Here, we report on the first systematic countywide survey of Jasper County. The objectives of this project were to: (1) determine the breeding sites and sequence of each amphibian species, (2) measure the relative abundance and breeding success of each species to determine its current status and therefore to provide baseline data for monitoring future population trends, (3) determine the effect of soil and vegetation types on the distribution and diversity of amphibians, and (4) determine the effect of agriculture on the abundance and diversity of amphibians.

Methods

To determine amphibian breeding phenology, surveys of each township in Jasper County and the JPFWA were conducted by trained students every ten days on fourteen dates from 27 March to 18 August 1994 and on eight dates between 10 March and 8 June 1995. Additionally, two sites were monitored daily between 2030 and 2130 hours from 27 March to 14 May 1994. Water temperature, weather, and habitat type were recorded at each site.

The primary methods used for the assessment of amphibian breeding activity and intensity were directed sampling and opportunistic sampling. Directed sampling consists of intensive sampling in areas that clearly should contain amphibians. This sampling involved auditory frog call surveys and a combination of seine-netting and dip-netting samples during the breeding season. Opportunistic sampling included nighttime road cruising with periodic (every 0.5 kilometer) auditory sampling, visual sweeps through candidate areas to search for terrestrial anurans, and overturning logs near wetland habitats. Breeding success of amphibians was later assessed by seining or by intensive dip netting of larvae in early summer.

Amphibian populations were also assessed by approximately 400 person-hours of nighttime road cruising and by frog breeding call surveys. At least 1.5 kilometers of road along each section was surveyed in every township. Approximately 150 person-hours of dip netting, seine net sampling, and opportunistic sampling were spent in more than 150 vernal and permanent wetlands. Small wetlands were seined thoroughly and systematically. The shallow edges of larger wetlands were randomly sampled at several locations. Egg-mass densities were determined by quadrat sampling (see Brodman 1995). Terrestrial salamanders were monitored by approximately 150 person-hours of daytime hand search-and-seize methods.

Our overall assessment of amphibian population size was based on a combination of parameters measuring breeding success. We estimated population sizes based on the levels of nocturnal breeding calling activity and the density of egg masses or larvae. The scale we used was based on an ordinal breeding chorus intensity index (BI) of 0 to 5, as follows:

0 = no frogs calling; no egg masses or larvae found

1 = single individual calling or a single egg mass or larva found

2 = small chorus (<10 individuals calling) with occasional calling such that individual calls could be counted, or two to ten egg masses or larvae found per person-hour

3 = small chorus; frequent individual calls could be distinguished but with some overlapping of calls, or eleven to thirty egg masses or larvae found per person-hour

4 = large chorus; individual calls could not be distinguished but chorus was not constant or continuous, or thirty-one to sixty egg masses or larvae found per person-hour

5 = very large chorus with constant, continuous, and overlapping calling, or more than sixty-one egg masses or larvae found per person-hour (Karns 1992)

BIs of 1 to 2 represent rare populations that may be at risk of local extirpation. Higher BIs (4 and 5) represent common, abundant, and widespread populations that are more likely to be stable. The BI estimates are subjective in the case of frog calls and may be prone to between-observer error. We believed that our student training was adequate and that the groups of two to three students employed in this study agreed on a more consistent consensus of BI values than researchers working alone. We tested several groups simultaneously on identical road surveys and could detect no variation in species richness or in the location of amphibian breeding sites. Variation in BIs among groups was low (never more than one BI) and therefore considered to be acceptable.

The relationships between the subjective BI values, the objectively measured species richness (S represents the number of species at each site), and the frequency of a given species across sites were determined by calculating the Pearson's Correlation Coefficient (r). Two tests were done. First, to determine the relationship between species richness and breeding intensity, the correlation between S and the mean abundance among species (Σ BI/site) for each breeding site was calculated. If this correlation is strong, the number of breeding individuals of a species at any particular site is proportional to the overall presence of that species across sites. Second, to determine the relationship between breeding intensity within a species and the number of species at a site, the correlation between the frequency across sites and mean BI/site was calculated for each species. Correlations were determined to be significant if $p \leq 0.05$.

To determine the effects of habitat on amphibian abundance and distribution, for each habitat category the following were calculated: the frequency of species present; the abundance (BI/site); the mean species richness (Σ S/site); the mean community abundance (Σ BI/site); and the diversity among sites. Diversity was measured by the equation for the Shannon diversity index (H'):

$$H' = -\Sigma\ (BI/\Sigma\ BI)\ \ln(BI/\Sigma\ BI)$$

A biological interpretation is that H' estimates two components of community structure: the number of species (S) and their relative abundance (BI/Σ BI; Grant et al. 1994). To calculate H', we used BI values from each species at sites within a habitat category.

To determine the effect of habitat on the distribution and diversity of amphibians, each amphibian breeding site was categorized according to its soil association (from Smallwood and Osterholz 1990), vegetation type (farmland, prairie, woodland, floodplain, marsh, swamp, riverine, ditch), and permanence of water in wetlands (vernal, semipermanent, permanent).

Observed abundance (BI/site) of each species and mean abundance (Σ BI/site) were compared to expected values, which were calculated based on the percentage of land area of each soil association, vegetation type, and water permanence. Additionally, the co-occurrence of species at breeding sites was tested against a Poisson distribution. Observed values were compared against expected values using a chi-square analysis. Probability values for determining significant differences were set at 0.01.

Results

Our survey detected 334 breeding sites for 844 amphibian populations (Fig. 17-1). We identified forty-eight megasites (at least four breeding species and Σ BI values of at least ten).

In total, thirteen amphibian species were encountered in Jasper County during the spring and summer of 1994 and 1995. The amphibian fauna was divided into three overlapping breeding groups: (1) an early spring breeding community of blue-spotted salamanders, eastern tiger salamanders (*Ambystoma tigrinum tigrinum*), northern leopard frogs, northern spring peepers (*Pseudacris crucifer crucifer*), and chorus frogs; within this group, blue-spotted and tiger salamanders were never syntopic; (2) a large late spring breeding community of eastern gray treefrogs (*Hyla versicolor*), Cope's gray treefrogs, American toads, Fowler's toads (*Bufo woodhousii fowleri*), western lesser sirens, and central newts (*Notophthalmus viridescens louisianensis*); and (3) a summer breeding community of green frogs (*Rana clamitans melanota*) and bullfrogs (Fig. 17-2).

The relative abundance of the thirteen species encountered was rated based on the breeding call surveys and seine net sampling for aquatic amphibian larvae (Table 17-1). In total, seven of the thirteen species had large populations (BIs of 4 and 5; Table 17-1).

The mean abundance of each species was 2.53. The mean abundance of a species *within* a site was strongly correlated with the frequency of the species' presence *across* breeding sites ($r = 0.96$; $p < 0.05$).

Sites varied from 1 to 8 breeding species, with a mean of 2.72 species. The mean amphibian abundance was 6.83 BI/site. The mean Shannon diversity index value (H') across sites was 1.86. Species richness correlated with the breeding intensity of each species across sites (Σ BI/species/site; Table 17-2).

Species Accounts

Spring peepers, chorus frogs, eastern gray treefrogs, and American toads were the most abundant and widely distributed amphibians. Although less locally abundant, eastern tiger salamanders, green frogs, and Fowler's toads were widespread. American toads and lesser sirens had not been reported in the JPFWA prior to 1972 (Minton 1972; Minton et al. 1982), and a new county record was established for central newts. The newt population in the JPFWA is a range extension, with the nearest known populations more than 50 kilometers away in Marshall and Porter Counties.

Although relatively widespread, northern leopard frogs were one of the least abundant anuran species in Jasper County. Several dead northern leopard frog adults were found following their breeding season in 1994. No dead frogs of any other species were discovered during this survey. Additionally, 18 percent of the active northern leopard frog breeding sites from 1994 had no calling males in 1995.

Blanchard's cricket frogs, plains leopard frogs, northern slimy salamanders, and smallmouth salamanders were not encountered in this survey. Each has historical records in the JPFWA (Grant 1936; Swanson 1939), and

Figure 17-1. Distribution of amphibian breeding sites in Jasper County, Indiana. Large, shaded circles represent megasites with four or more species and $\sum$ BI of at least ten.

Table 17-1. The abundance of amphibians in Jasper County, Indiana. Data are the number of sites, large stable populations (LSP = BI = 4 or 5), abundance (Σ BI), and mean abundance (BI/site) for each species.

Species	Sites*	LSP	Σ BI	BI/Site*
Northern spring peeper (*Pseudacris crucifer crucifer*)	225	71	654	2.91
Western chorus frog (*Pseudacris triseriata triseriata*)	200	39	511	2.56
Eastern gray treefrog (*Hyla versicolor*)	121	31	332	2.74
Green frog (*Rana clamitans melanota*)	61	6	135	2.21
American toad (*Bufo americanus americanus*)	120	10	263	2.19
Fowler's toad (*Bufo woodhousii fowleri*)	42	5	92	2.19
Bullfrog (*Rana catesbeiana*)	22	0	47	2.14
Northern leopard frog (*Rana pipiens*)	22	2	36	1.64
Eastern tiger salamander (*Ambystoma tigrinum tigrinum*)	16	0	29	1.81
Cope's gray treefrog (*Hyla chrysoscelis*)	7	0	11	1.57
Blue-spotted salamander (*Ambystoma laterale*)	6	0	9	1.50
Central newt (*Notophthalmus viridescens louisianensis*)	2	0	4	2.00
Western lesser siren (*Siren intermedia nettingi*)	1	0	2	1.00
Blanchard's cricket frog (*Acris crepitans blanchardi*)	—	—	—	—
Plains leopard frog (*Rana blairi*)	—	—	—	—
Smallmouth salamander (*Ambystoma texanum*)	—	—	—	—
Northern slimy salamander (*Plethodon glutinosus*)	—	—	—	—
Total	845	164	2,125	2.51

*BI/site vs. frequency of sites, $r = 0.96$; $p < 0.05$.

Figure 17-2. Dates of breeding activity levels of Jasper County amphibians. Breeding intensity of BI of 1 to 2 is represented by -; intermediate activity of BI of 3 is represented by *; and intense breeding activity of BI of 4 to 5 is represented by X.

Species	Breeding activity
Eastern tiger salamander (*Ambystoma tigrinum tigrinum*)	-**
Blue-spotted salamander (*Ambystoma laterale*)	**
Northern leopard frog (*Rana pipiens*)	-****———
Northern spring peeper (*Pseudacris crucifer crucifer*)	———*XXXX****—
Western chorus frog (*Pseudacris triseriata triseriata*)	-******XXX*-
Eastern gray treefrog (*Hyla versicolor*)	——****XXXXXXXXXX**************—
Cope's gray treefrog (*Hyla chrysoscelis*)	—————***—————————
Western lesser siren (*Siren intermedia nettingi*)	—***—
American toad (*Bufo americanus americanus*)	—*X******———
Fowler's toad (*Bufo woodhousii fowleri*)	-****X*********———
Central newt (*Notophthalmus viridescens louisianensis*)	—****—
Green frog (*Rana clamitans melanota*)	————********XXX**————
Bullfrog (*Rana catesbeiana*)	———*******X**——
Dates	3/15 4/1 4/15 5/1 5/15 6/1 6/15 7/1 7/15 8/1
Temperature (°C)	5 8 11 15 20 23 25 27 28 28

an additional Jasper County record of cricket frogs comes from outside the JPFWA (Minton 1972).

Habitats

Most species of amphibians were nonrandomly distributed in Jasper County with respect to habitat and cooccurrence with other species. Spring peepers and eastern gray treefrogs were the only species with a nonbiased distribution with respect to all other species. American toads, Fowler's toads, and western chorus frogs were found alone at sites more often than expected ($p < 0.005$). Chorus frogs and Fowler's toads bred in the same wetlands less often than expected ($p < 0.01$). Both species of toads were found in seventeen breeding sites. We did not determine whether they interbred. *Rana* species and salamanders co-occurred more often than expected ($p < 0.001$) and typically inhabited permanent and semipermanent ponds.

The distribution, abundance, and diversity of amphibians were nonrandom with respect to soil, vegetation type, and land use (Table 17-3). The JPFWA had the highest diversity and abundance in the county. Amphibians bred in all but the two largest of the forty-five wetlands in the JPFWA. As many as eight species bred in a single wetland; breeding sites averaged four and one-half species. All thirteen species present in Jasper County were present in the JPFWA. Despite comprising less than 1.5 percent of the land area in the county, the JPFWA contained 13 percent of the breeding sites, 24 percent of the populations, 20 percent of the relative

Table 17-2. Species richness (S) vs. mean abundance per breeding site. The relationship between these variables is significant ($r = 0.95$; $p < 0.05$).

S	Sites	Σ BI/Species/Site
1	74	2.42
2	105	2.45
3	77	2.48
4	34	2.55
5	20	2.51
6	12	2.85
7	9	2.92
8	3	3.09

amphibian abundance (BC), and 54 percent of the megasites. Diversity and species richness values were greater in the JPFWA than in the county as a whole (Table 17-3).

Amphibians were more diverse and abundant than expected in areas with sandy soil associations (Table 17-3). These soil associations range from nearly level, poorly drained sandy and loamy outwash on bottomlands and uplands to strongly sloping, well-drained uplands. These soils also share the characteristic of being poor cropland (Smallwood and Osterholz 1990). The Oakville soil association, characterized by stands of oak on sloping uplands of sandy outwash, had higher relative precentages of breeding amphibian sites, populations, abundance, diversity, and species richness than the bottomland sandy to loamy outwash areas or the level upland silty to loamy soil associations.

Amphibians were also more diverse and abundant than expected in areas with greater than 1 hectare of woodland (Table 17-3). These wooded areas make up less than 15 percent of the land but are near or surrounding the breeding sites of greater than 88 percent of the amphibian populations. Temporary ponds and semipermanent to permanent ponds and swamps are about equally important as breeding habitat for amphibians, with a few of the rarer species preferring permanent ponds. However, amphibians were also significantly less diverse and abundant in areas within riparian zones and their floodplains and in the numerous agricultural ditches (Table 17-3). No terrestrial breeding plethodontid salamanders were found in this survey.

Amphibians were less diverse and abundant than expected in areas with nearly level upland soil associations consisting of silty to loamy soils (Table 17-3). Although comprising two-thirds of the land area in Jasper county, less than a third of the amphibian breeding sites and about a quarter of the populations are located here. These soil associations range from poorly drained to well-drained soils and comprise much of the area considered to be prime cropland (Smallwood and Oster-

Table 17-3. The distribution, abundance, and diversity of amphibians with respect to habitat. Data are land area (% Area), breeding sites (% Sites), populations (% Pop), abundance (% Σ BI), Shannon diversity index (H'), and species richness (S) for each habitat type. Values indicated by (+) are significantly greater than expected based on area; (-) indicates significantly less than expected values based on area at a chi-square value of $p < 0.01$.

Habitat	% Area	% Sites	% Pop	% Σ BI	H'	S
Physiography						
Protected wetland (JPFWA)	1	13(+)	23(+)	26(+)	2.08	13
Bottomland sandy-loamy outwash	20	39(+)	36(+)	36(+)	1.79	10
Level upland silty-loamy soils	67	30(-)	25(-)	23(-)	1.46	8
Land Use						
Agriculture	86	12(-)	9(-)	8(-)	1.45	7
Woodland	14	88(+)	91(+)	92(+)	1.79	13
Wetland Type						
Vernal ponds/wetlands	NA	57	51	41	1.81	9
Permanent ponds/wetlands	1	34(+)	42(+)	54(+)	2.05	13
Riverine/ditch	17	6(-)	6(-)	4(-)	1.28	6

holz 1990). Primary cropland comprises 86 percent of the land use in the county but contains just 12 percent of the amphibian breeding sites.

Amphibian species did not segregate into exclusive habitat types in the county but rather were often associated with certain regions. The most common species were found across habitat types, whereas the rarer species were found primarily in the JPFWA and in the sandy to loamy soil associations (Table 17-4). All thirteen species were found more often than expected in the JPFWA and in breeding sites near woodlands and less often than expected in the level upland silty to loamy soil associations and areas under cultivation.

Salamander and *Rana* species were associated with permanent water more often than were hylids and bufonids (Table 17-4). American toads were more abundant than Fowler's toads throughout the county and in cultivated areas; however, Fowler's toads were more abundant in the JPFWA. Tiger salamanders were the most common and widespread salamander. They were randomly distributed throughout wooded, cultivated, and residential areas but were relatively rare in the JPFWA compared to other species.

Discussion

The breeding phenology (Fig. 17-2) of amphibians is useful in establishing seasonal parameters for surveying. We concur with state-run programs (Mossman et al. 1992; Mossman et al. Chpt. 21; Hemesath, Chpt. 23; Johnson, Chpt. 37, this volume) that three anuran calling surveys conducted in early spring, late spring, and early summer are adequate to determine the presence of each species and its breeding intensity in the upper Midwest.

The amphibian fauna of Jasper County, Indiana, is more similar to the typical fauna of central Illinois and eastern Iowa than to that of southern or northeastern Indiana (Brodman 1997). Although relatively species poor when compared to other regions of Indiana (Minton 1972; Karns 1988), Jasper County has a relatively high density of amphibian breeding sites. The relatively high diversity and evenness values across habitat types suggest good community health.

Relative abundance of amphibian populations has been estimated based on frequency of presence at breeding sites (Lannoo et al. 1994). Species richness (S) and frequency of a species' use of breeding sites ($\sum$ BI/species/site) were good indicators of overall population size in our study.

Species Status

The amphibian distribution and abundance data collected here make it possible to determine the status of each species in Jasper County and in the JPFWA (Table 17-5). Only seven of the seventeen species once thought to inhabit the region are currently common enough to be considered stable. The remaining ten species are rare or absent from Jasper County. Several species (bullfrogs, northern leopard frogs, Cope's gray treefrogs, western lesser sirens, and central newts) are less common in Jasper County than have been reported statewide (Simon et al. 1992). Because within this county blue-spotted salamanders, central newts, and western lesser sirens are found in the JPFWA, they are currently offered some protection. However, their populations are small, and range expansion or immigration is unlikely.

Blue-spotted salamanders were found only in the JPFWA, and only with an intense sampling effort. This species may never have been common. It was considered uncommon in the JPFWA in the 1930s (Grant 1936; Swanson 1939), and Minton collected only one specimen, about 3 kilometers east of Parr in west-central Jasper County, in the 1960s (Minton 1972). Several longtime residents remember seeing small blackish salamanders in the 1970s, but not since. These could have been either blue-spotted or newly metamorphosed eastern tiger salamanders. Intensive surveys in these areas did not uncover additional blue-spotted salamanders. The loss of Jasper County sites outside the JPFWA represents a range reduction of at least 30 kilometers.

Although Blanchard's cricket frogs were present in Jasper County and in adjacent Newton County in the early 1970s (S. Minton, personal communication), cricket frogs appear to have disappeared from Jasper County. They are now also absent from Willow Slough and LaSalle Fish and Wildlife areas in Newton County (personal observations), as well as from Kankakee Marsh and Tippecanoe State Park in northwest Indiana. The decline of cricket frogs in northwest Indiana is likely part of a widespread decrease in the northern range of this species in the Midwest (Faeh et al. 1994; Lannoo et al. 1994; Mierzwa 1994b; Hemesath, Chpt. 23; Casper, Chpt. 22; Hay, Chpt. 11; Lannoo, Chpt. 34; Moriarty, Chpt. 20, this volume). Where present, these frogs are conspicuous on the forest floor near shorelines. Their breeding season is long, and males sing day and night with a distinctive and loud call. Therefore, it is unlikely that the absence of cricket frogs from our survey is due

Table 17-4. The distribution and abundance of amphibian breeding sites in Jasper County, Indiana, by habitat type and by species. Data are the percentage of breeding sites for each species within a given habitat type. Values indicated by (+) are significantly greater than expected based on area; (-) indicates significantly less than expected values based on area at a chi-square value of $p < 0.01$. Species codes: Pc = northern spring peeper (*Pseudacris crucifer crucifer*); Pt = western chorus grog (*Pseudacris triseriata triseriata*); Hv = gray treefrog (*Hyla versicolor*); Ba = American toad (*Bufo americanus americanus*); Rcl = green frog (*Rana clamitans melanota*); Bw = Fowler's toad (*Bufo woodhousii fowleri*); Rct = bullfrog (*Rana catesbeiana*); Rp = northern leopard frog (*Rana pipiens*); Hc = Cope's gray treefrog (*Hyla chrysoscelis*); At = eastern tiger salamander (*Ambystoma tigrinum tigrinum*); Al = blue-spotted salamander (*Ambystoma laterale*); Nv = central newt (*Notophthalmus viridescens louisianensis*); Si = western lesser siren (*Siren itermedia nettingi*).

Habitat	% Area	% Pc	% Pt	% Hv	% Ba	% Rcl	% Bw	% Rct	% Rp	% Hc	% At	% Al	% Nv	% Si
Physiography														
Protected wetland (JPFWA)	1	15 (+)	17 (+)	25 (+)	13 (+)	41 (+)	50 (+)	82 (+)	32 (+)	43 (+)	13 (+)	100 (+)	100 (+)	100 (+)
Sloping upland sandy outwash	20	44 (+)	38 (+)	34 (+)	38 (+)	23	26	5 (-)	27	28	31 (+)	0	0	0
Bottomland sandy-loamy outwash	12	17	16	18 (+)	17	18 (+)	14	9	27 (+)	14	25 (+)	0	0	0
Level upland silty-loamy soils	65	24 (-)	29 (-)	23 (-)	32 (-)	18 (-)	10 (-)	5 (-)	14 (-)	14 (-)	31 (-)	0 (-)	0 (-)	0 (-)
Land use														
Agriculture	86	14 (-)	18 (-)	15 (-)	23 (-)	15 (-)	7 (-)	5 (-)	9 (-)	0 (-)	38 (-)	0 (-)	0 (-)	0 (-)
Woodland	14	75 (+)	89 (+)	87 (+)	88 (+)	90 (+)	95 (+)	82 (+)	91 (+)	100 (+)	62 (+)	100 (+)	100 (+)	100 (+)
Wetland type														
Vernal ponds/wetlands	1	59 (+)	58 (+)	52 (+)	59 (+)	6 (+)	36 (+)	0 (+)	27 (+)	50 (+)	58 (+)	17 (+)	0 (+)	0 (+)
Permanent ponds/wetlands	1	40 (+)	39 (+)	47 (+)	40 (+)	73 (+)	64 (+)	100 (+)	73 (+)	50 (+)	42 (+)	83 (+)	100 (+)	100 (+)
Riverine/floodplain/ditch	17	1 (-)	3 (-)	1 (-)	1 (-)	21	0 (-)	0 (-)	0 (-)	0 (-)	0 (-)	0 (-)	0 (-)	0 (-)
Dry habitat	81	0 (-)	0 (-)	0 (-)	0 (-)	0 (-)	0 (-)	0 (-)	0 (-)	0 (-)	0 (-)	0 (-)	0 (-)	0 (-)

to sampling bias and thus represents a true decline and extirpation within the last twenty-five years.

Range reductions and possible declines were also indicated for plains leopard frogs, northern leopard frogs, northern slimy salamanders, smallmouth salamanders, and blue-spotted salamanders. Plains leopard frogs, northern slimy salamanders, and smallmouth salamanders were not detected by us and have not been encountered in northwest Indiana since the 1930s, when Swanson (1939) collected a single voucher specimen of each species, which were subsequently labeled from "Jasper" (S. Minton, personal communication). The Jasper County records of smallmouth salamanders and northern slimy salamanders would be disjunct populations 50 and 110 kilometers north, respectively, from the nearest confirmed populations. It is possible that northern slimy salamanders and smallmouth salamanders never inhabited Jasper County but instead were misinterpreted from specimens collected in the town of Jasper in southern Indiana, where both species are common (S. Minton, personal communication). However, the plains leopard frog specimen is best interpreted from the JPFWA, and this state-listed species has apparently become extirpated from Jasper County since the 1930s, thereby reducing the known range by at least 70 kilometers.

Table 17-5. Status of amphibians in the Jasper-Pulaski Fish and Wildlife Area (JPFWA) and the remainder of Jasper County, Indiana

Species	JPFWA Status	County Status	State Status*
Salamanders			
Blue-spotted salamander (*Ambystoma laterale*)	Uncommon	Absent	Uncommon**
Eastern tiger salamander (*Ambystoma tigrinum tigrinum*)	Rare	Common	Common
Western lesser siren (*Siren intermedia nettingi*)	Rare	Absent	Uncommon
Central newt (*Notophthalmus viridescens louisianensis*)	Rare	Absent	Uncommon
Smallmouth salamander (*Ambystoma texanum*)	Absent	Absent	Abundant
Northern slimy salamander (*Plethodon glutinosus*)	Absent	Absent	Common
Frogs and Toads			
Northern spring peeper (*Pseudacris crucifer crucifer*)	Abundant	Abundant	Common
Western chorus frog (*Pseudacris triseriata triseriata*)	Common	Abundant	Abundant
Eastern gray treefrog (*Hyla versicolor*)	Abundant	Common	Abundant
American toad (*Bufo americanus americanus*)	Common	Abundant	Common
Green frog (*Rana clamitans melanota*)	Common	Common	Common
Fowler's toad (*Bufo woodhousii fowleri*)	Common	Uncommon	Common
Bullfrog (*Rana catesbeiana*)	Common	Rare	Abundant
Northern leopard frog (*Rana pipiens*)	Uncommon	Rare	Common**
Cope's gray treefrog (*Hyla chrysoscelis*)	Rare	Rare	Abundant
Blanchard's cricket frog (*Acris crepitans blanchardi*)	Absent	Absent	Common**
Plains leopard frog (*Rana blairi*)	Absent	Absent	Rare**

*From Simon et al. 1992.
**State-listed: special concern.

Habitat

By using expected values of amphibian abundance based on land area, we were able to consider some of the effects of agriculture, soil association, and vegetation type on the distribution and diversity of amphibians. The distribution and abundance of each species were nonrandomly distributed in Jasper County, and therefore preferences could be determined. Surprisingly, the best amphibian sites outside of the small protected fish and wildlife area were in the Oakville soil association, which provides habitat for 52 percent of the amphibian breeding sites, 58 percent of the amphibian populations, 57 percent of the amphibian abundance, and 65 percent of the megasites, yet represents only about 20 percent of the Jasper County land surface (Table 17-3).

The direct effect of agriculture on amphibians in this study can only be inferred. However, historical habitat data can be used to estimate the effect of the increasing amount of farmland on the populations of amphibians in northwest Indiana. The pre-Euro-American settlement sandy and prairie marshes, which made up about 40 percent of the land surface, may have been inhabited by a community of amphibians that is still represented in the protected JPFWA. If this assumption is true, then the Oakville soil association may function as a refugium for amphibians from the drained cultivated areas that are currently more depauperate. Habitats in the Oakville soil association now constitute less than 1.5 percent of the land surface. Therefore, the loss of historical amphibian habitat is estimated to be about 94 to 97 percent and should have resulted in a range reduction of at least three to five species. Similar findings have been reported from Iowa (Lannoo et al. 1994).

In the Future

This first systematic, countywide survey of Jasper County, Indiana, met the objectives of determining the breeding sites, sequence of breeding, relative abundance, and habitat preferences of the county's thirteen species of amphibians. The established status of these species will serve as a baseline for monitoring future population trends and as a reference for future studies.

Habitat requirements related to the life history aspects of amphibians must be considered in developing a successful conservation program (McWilliams and Bachmann 1988). If managers and biologists decide further protection efforts are necessary, the primary objective should include preserving ephemeral woodland pond and marsh habitat. This can be best accomplished by protecting existing natural areas and by managing water levels in marshes with wooded shorelines (McWilliams and Bachmann 1988).

We have also shown that undergraduate college students (volunteers) can be effectively trained in a few weeks to collect quantitative data on the status of amphibian populations. We will continue to monitor amphibians in Jasper County to determine ongoing population trends. Clearly, the amphibian fauna has declined during the century, but there are little data to test whether populations continue to decline. Yearly data will be collected on the abundance and distribution of amphibians. Additionally, we will be investigating the effects of water quality on diversity, abundance, and larval survival.

Summary

We present the first countywide survey of amphibians conducted in Jasper County, Indiana. Time-constrained search-and-seize techniques, nighttime road cruising, and breeding call surveys were conducted during the spring and summer of 1994 and 1995 in order to quantify the level of amphibian breeding activity. These data will serve as baseline information for long-term monitoring of amphibian populations. Breeding activity for each of the thirteen species detected was associated with temperature. The locations of 85 percent of the 334 amphibian breeding sites were in wooded areas away from active cultivation and riverine floodplains. Spring peepers (*Pseudacris crucifer crucifer*), western chorus frogs (*Pseudacris triseriata triseriata*), eastern gray treefrogs (*Hyla versicolor*), American toads (*Bufo americanus americanus*), and eastern tiger salamanders (*Ambystoma tigrinum tigrinum*) were the most widely distributed and abundant amphibian species in Jasper County. Two state-listed species, blue-spotted salamanders (*Ambystoma laterale*) and northern leopard frogs (*Rana pipiens*), were rare and restricted primarily to the Jasper-Pulaski Fish and Wildlife Area. Smallmouth salamanders (*Ambystoma texanum*), northern slimy salamanders (*Plethodon glutinosus*), plains leopard frogs (*Rana blairi*), and Blanchard's cricket frogs (*Acris crepitans blanchardi*) were not encountered in this survey and are presumed to be extirpated. A new county record and 50-kilometer range extension were made for the central newt (*Notophthalmus viridescens louisianensis*).

Acknowledgments

We thank the many Saint Joseph's College students for their efforts, especially D. Falk, A. Berry, T. Foldenauer, G. Rottino, J. Ogger, R. Mahns, T. Ziemba, C. McCoy, K. Ruhe, S. Myszak, M. Quasney, B. Rassmusen, S. Ownby, M. Kolaczyk, B. Tobe, and J. Sheerin. We also appreciate the advice and cooperation of S. Minton, S. Cortwright, and A. Resetar.

18

Amphibian Surveys in the Cuyahoga Valley National Recreation Area

Geza Varhegyi, Spiro M. Mavroidis, B. Michael Walton, Cynthia A. Conaway, and A. Ralph Gibson

Urban and suburban environments present difficult challenges to the persistence of amphibian populations. All of the suspected threats influencing amphibian decline may come into play (e.g., habitat degradation and fragmentation, acid precipitation, toxic substances, UV-B radiation, disease) and are likely to be particularly intense and multiple. Further, the potential for recolonization following local extinctions may be low due to isolation by surrounding roads, development, and otherwise unsuitable habitats. It therefore may be surprising that, in pockets of habitat such as parks and undeveloped areas, one still can find amphibians in urban and suburban settings.

Although it may be tempting to write off urban and suburban populations as doomed relicts, amphibian populations increasingly will become confined to these areas as human populations continue to grow, which has already occurred in much of North America. In addition, some effects of urbanization and industrialization are exported via air and water to surrounding, and often quite distant, "natural" areas. For reasons such as these, urban/suburban amphibian populations must not be ignored and indeed may serve as important tools in the development of amphibian conservation strategies. In this context, urban/suburban settings provide valuable research opportunities for investigating the effects of multiple stressors and the resilience of amphibian populations. Finally, most people encounter amphibians in urban/suburban habitats: treefrogs at the porch light or toads at the family picnic can provide a powerful argument for public support of amphibian conservation efforts.

We report here on the initial phases of a long-term amphibian monitoring program in the Cuyahoga Valley National Recreation Area (CVNRA) in northern Ohio. This unit of the National Park Service (NPS) contains 13,360 hectares in a north-to-south corridor along 35 kilometers of the Cuyahoga River and is located between two large urban and industrial centers, Cleveland and Akron (Fig. 18-1). As a National Recreation Area, the CVNRA affords the amphibians some degree of protection. That protection, however, has been in place only since 1974, when the park was established (Cockrell 1992). Further, the park boundaries are close to the two cities (13 kilometers from downtown Cleveland and 10 kilometers from downtown Akron). Residential suburbs, industrial development, heavily trafficked highways and roads, popular recreational/entertainment facilities, railways, and agricultural lands surround and enter the park. At its widest, the CVNRA is only 8.3 kilometers wide east-to-west, but the park is much narrower through much of its extent (as narrow as 0.5 kilometer at one point). The park hosts over a million visitors each year (Cockrell 1992), and use is heaviest in the warmer months during peak periods of amphibian activity. Clearly, there is great potential for multiple anthropogenic challenges to the amphibian populations of the CVNRA, including toxic substances from industrial, residential, or agricultural sources; acid precipitation; salt run-off from roadways; silting of streams due to upstream construction; disruption of migration routes by roads and development; draining of wetlands; clearing of habitat for commercial, residential, or recreational uses; killing by vehicles; and collecting and killing by

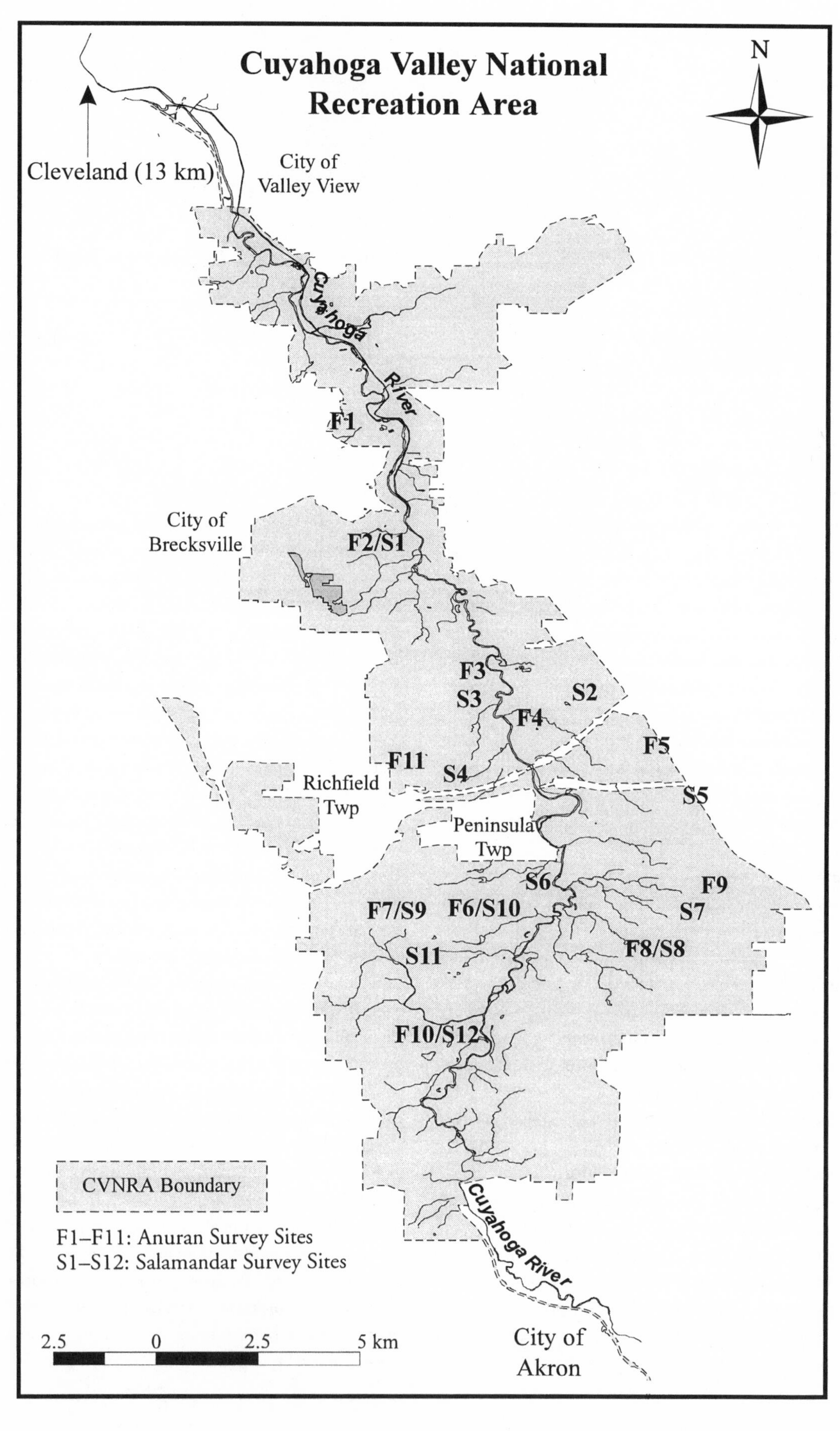
Cuyahoga Valley National
Recreation Area
N
Cleveland (13 km)
City of
Valley View
Cuyahoga
River
F1
City of
Brecksville
F2/S1
F3
S3
S2
F4
F5
F11
S4
Richfield
Twp
S5
Peninsula
Twp
S6
F9
F7/S9
F6/S10
S7
S11
F8/S8
F10/S12
CVNRA Boundary
F1–F11: Anuran Survey Sites
S1–S12: Salamandar Survey Sites
Cuyahoga River
2.5
0
2.5
5 km
City of
Akron

Figure 18-1. Locations surveyed for anurans and salamanders in the CVNRA.

visitors. However, there has been no investigation of the effects of these threats to amphibians in the CVNRA nor of the success of NPS management strategies for mitigating these effects.

The overall goals of this research are: (1) to conduct long-term monitoring of changes in amphibian abundance and species richness; (2) to identify and quantify important threats to amphibian populations; and (3) to investigate the physiological and demographic responses of amphibians in the CVNRA to those threats. We intend for this work to provide useful information for resource management in the park and for amphibian conservation efforts in general. Here, we report data from the first two years of the project, 1994 and 1995. The specific goals of this phase of the research were: (1) to initiate monitoring of abundance and species richness of anurans and of terrestrial and stream-side salamanders; (2) to search for patterns of decline, stasis, or increase through comparisons with historical records; (3) to identify species and/or localities with special problems; and (4) to validate automated call recording techniques for censusing anurans. With regard to the last goal, we present information on the acoustic performance of the automated recording device, the accuracy of the device for measuring population size, and the cost of the technique relative to traditional methods.

Methods and Materials

Performance Evaluation of the Automated Recording Device

Anuran sites were surveyed for calling anurans using two automated call recorders constructed according to the specifications of Peterson and Dorcas (1992, 1994). Peterson and Dorcas (1994) provide a components list and a circuitry schematic for the device. All components of the recording device are housed in a plastic toolbox (36 centimeters by 20 centimeters by 20 centimeters) and are powered by a twelve-volt motorcycle battery. The recorder consists of a timer that activates a tape recorder for a predetermined amount of time at preset intervals. At the onset of an interval, an internal microphone records the time from the voice clock. An external microphone then records sounds from the environment. The box was secured to a tree by a chain and lock and camouflaged by leaves and twigs to avoid vandalism. The external microphone was protected from rain by a camouflaged plastic cowling. A miniature temperature data logger (HOBO XT, Model HTEA-37+46, Onset Computer Corporation) was used to record environmental temperatures (air/water) every five minutes during the operation of the automated recorder.

We tested two aspects of performance of the automated recording device. First, we tested the effects of distance, habitat complexity (e.g., vegetation and topography), and species recorded on the quality of recordings. Second, we tested the utility of the device for estimating abundance of calling males.

Acoustic Performance. An experiment was conducted by placing the automated recording device at its normal recording location at Prucek Pond (F11, Fig. 18-1; Table 18-1) but with a person manually operating the recorder. A second person then played tape-recorded calls of four species (American toads [*Bufo americanus americanus*], eastern gray treefrogs [*Hyla versicolor*], northern spring peepers [*Pseudacris crucifer crucifer*], and western chorus frogs [*Pseudacris triseriata triseriata*]) at a fixed intensity (100 decibels at 1 meter, measured with a Bruel and Kjaer Integrating Sound Level Meter, Type 2225), at 10 meter intervals up to 50 meters from the automated device. This was repeated in four different directions (north, south, east, and west). The person at the recorder scored audibility of the playback from 0 to 4 (with 0 being inaudible and 4 being loud and clear). The same individual then listened to the recorded tape from the automated recorder and again assigned an audibility score. These scores were mapped on a topographical/vegetation map of the site to investigate patterns of audibility associated with habitat features. Variation in sensitivity of the device to calls of the four species was assessed with analysis of variance.

Population Density Estimation. One potentially valuable use of the automated recording device is to estimate population density of calling males. Population density of a species should be estimable by dividing the calling rate produced by a chorus of males by the average calling rate of individual males. Data from the recording device will provide the numerator of this ratio; the denominator, call rates of individuals, can be obtained by focal animal recordings or from the published literature.

One of us (G.V.) is conducting ecological studies of eastern gray treefrogs at Prucek Pond (F11, Fig. 18-1). These studies include nightly censusing of calling males during the breeding season and recording calls of every male in the chorus. Varhegyi has calculated the average

Table 18-1. Anuran survey sites at the CVNRA, brief descriptions of each site, and the species found during four separate surveys. Site identification numbers appear in parentheses following the site names (see Fig. 18-1). Abbreviations: Ba-*Bufo americanus americanus*; Hv-*Hyla versicolor*; Pc-*Pseudacris crucifer crucifer*; Pt-*Pseudacris triseriata triseriata*; Rca-*Rana catesbeiana*; Rcl-*Rana clamitans melanota*; Rp-*Rana palustris*; Rpi-*Rana pipiens*; Rs-*Rana sylvatica*.

		Species Found			
	Description	Walker 1946	Mazzer et al. 1984	Varhegyi et al. 1995	Varhegyi et al., this chapter
Periodically Surveyed Locations					
Fawn Pond (1)	Lowland, shallow pond, surrounded by tall grass	*	*	Ba, Hv, Pc, Rcl, Rp	Ba, Hv, Pc, Rcl
Brecksville (2)	Roadside vernal pools; pine, young birch, and oak trees	*	*	Ba, Hv, Pc, Pt, Rs	Ba, Pc, Pt
Snowville (3)	Some vernal pools, one deep pond, surrounded by tall grass	*	Ba, Hv, Rca, Rcl	Ba, Hv, Pc, Pt, Rca, Rcl, Rp Rpi, Rs	Ba, Hv, Pc, Pt, Rca, Rcl, Rp
Stanford (4)	Shallow pond near youth hostel	Ba**	Rp	Hv, Rp, Rcl	Hv, Pc, Rcl
Pipe Pond (5)	Small deep pond with steep banks, secondary growth forest	**	Rca, Rcl	Rca, Rcl	Rca, Rcl
Valley Picnic Area (6)	Small secluded upland pond, fed by stream, in secondary growth forest	**	Ba, Hv, Pt, Rcl	Pc, Rca, Rcl	Ba, Hv, Pc, Pt, Rca, Rcl
Hickory Pond (7)	Large upland pond, pine forest on one side and young trees and shrubs on other side	**	Ba, Rca	Ba, Pc, Pt, Rca, Rcl, Rs, Rcl, Rp	Ba, Pc, Pt, Rca
Kendall Lake (8)	Large lake (~5 acres), fed by stream, surrounded by secondary growth forest	**	Ba, Hv, Rca, Rcl, Rs	Hv, Pc, Rcl	Ba, Hv, Pc, Pt, Rca, Rcl
Happy Days (9)	Stream in a secondary growth forest near visitors center, deep ravines	Ba, Pc, Rp, Rs**	Rcl, Rp	Hv, Pc, Pt, Rcl, Rs	Ba, Pc
Indigo (10)	~2-acre lake surrounded by tall grass, shrubs, secondary growth forest, fed by stream	Hv, Pc, Pt, Rcl, Rp**	Rcl	Ba, Hv, Pc, Rca, Rcl	Ba, Hv, Pc, Pt, Rca, Rcl
Continuously Monitored Location					
Prucek (11)	Artificial pond, bordering farmland and hickory-maple forest	*	*	Ba, Hv, Pc, Pt, Rca, Rcl, Rp, Rs	Ba, Hv, Pc, Pt, Rca, Rcl, Rp

*Site not surveyed.
**Species found within 1 kilometer of the site.

call rate for males in this population to be eighteen calls per minute (n = 48). This value was used in the following equation to estimate density of calling males:

$$\text{estimated number of calling males} = \frac{\text{call rate of entire chorus (calls per minute)}}{\text{average call rate of individuals (calls per minute)}}$$

This estimate was compared to counts made by direct observation. We tested for correlation of these two population values by Pearson product-moment correlation.

Anuran Survey

Anuran survey sites were chosen to include as many potential breeding sites as possible and to resample previously surveyed locations (Fig. 18-1; Table 18-1). These sites were surveyed for calling anurans using two automated call recorders, previously described. We chose to record for twelve seconds every ten minutes, providing 144 intervals or thirty minutes of recording over a twenty-four-hour period. We found this setting to be efficient for sampling all species, even those that called for short periods. When tapes from the automated call recorder were played back in the laboratory, the time and the species calling were noted for each twelve-second interval. Acoustical evidence of weather conditions (e.g., wind sounds, the sound of rain on the plastic cowling) also was recorded. Temperature data from the data loggers were transferred to a personal computer and merged with the calling records.

The tapes were processed, as described above, by several of the authors (G.V., S.M.M., C.A.C.), by undergraduates doing independent research projects, and by members of the spring 1994 and 1995 undergraduate course in ecology at Cleveland State University. Training of the tape processors included field trips with faculty and/or experienced graduate students to identify calls and listening to recorded calls of known species (e.g., "The Calls of Frogs and Toads: Eastern and Central North America," Lang Elliott NatureSound Studio, Ithaca, New York, 1992). Competence of the tape processors was tested by scoring their ability to recognize species from previously processed tapes. For most cases, two or more people processed a single tape, and an experienced graduate student spot-checked the results. If processors noted ambiguous or unidentified calls, these were checked by experienced graduate students and faculty (e.g., B.M.W. and A.R.G.). All tapes were retained for future reference and verification.

We sought to determine diversity, distribution, and seasonal calling schedules of anurans in the CVNRA. Two sampling methods were used to accomplish these goals simultaneously. To determine diversity and distribution of anurans in the CVNRA, one automated recorder was moved among ten different sites (Fig. 18-1; Table 18-1), returning to the same location approximately every ten days. The second recorder remained at a single location (Prucek Pond, Fig. 18-1; Table 18-1) throughout the breeding season to collect more detailed data on species richness and seasonal variation in calling activity.

Salamander Survey

We surveyed twelve sites within the CVNRA (Fig. 18-1; Table 18-2) that were chosen to sample as many habitat types as possible and to include ten that have been surveyed previously by others (Mazzer et al. 1984; Walker 1946). Surveys were conducted from April through August. Each site was surveyed an average of seven times (minimum = one, maximum = twenty-three).

Surveys were conducted by searching 2-by-25-meter transects. Two observers searched the surface of the transect thoroughly by raking leaves and debris and overturning all rocks and logs. All cover objects were replaced. The general information recorded at the time of each survey included date, beginning and ending time, location, major topographic and vegetative features, weather conditions (e.g., clear, overcast, windy, rain), air, and, if appropriate, water temperature (using an Omega HH23 electronic thermocouple thermometer). We attempted to capture all salamanders within each transect. Data for each animal captured included species, sex, snout-vent length (SVL), distinctive color and pattern characteristics, and other information pertaining to the health and condition of the animal (e.g., gravid, broken tail). All animals were released at the point of capture within one hour of collection.

Results

Performance Evaluation of the Automated Recording Device

Acoustic Performance. Call reception by the automated recording device was as good as that of a trained, experienced listener stationed the same distance from the sound source. The least-squares regression line relating call reception by the recorder to call reception by the observer (the solid diagonal line in Fig. 18-2; $r^2 = 0.77$, $n = 35$) was not significantly different from a hypothetical line of equal performance (the dashed diagonal line in Fig. 18-2; slope of 1, Y-intercept of 0). The slope of the regression line was significantly greater than 0 (0.90 ± 0.08 standard error; $t = 10.79$, $p < 0.001$) but not significantly different from 1 ($t = -1.35$, $p > 0.20$), and the Y-intercept (0.11 ± 0.18 standard error) was not significantly different than 0 ($t = 0.578$, $p > 0.50$).

As is to be expected, quality of the recordings decreased as the distance between the sound source and recorder increased (Figs. 18-3, 18-4; Table 18-3). Recording quality also varied with direction (Figs. 18-3, 18-4; Table 18-3), largely due to variation in topography and vegetation (Fig. 18-3). Calls produced 50 meters away from the device generally were highly audible upon playback when there were no obstructions between the recording device and the sound source (Figs. 18-3, 18-4). In the case of Prucek Pond, recordings of

Table 18-2. Salamander survey sites at the CVNRA, brief descriptions of each site, and the species found during three separate surveys. Site identification numbers appear in parentheses following the site names (see Fig. 1). Abbreviations: Df-*Desmognathus fuscus*; Eb-*Eurycea bislineata*; El-*Eurycea longicauda*; Nv-*Notophthalmus viridescens viridescens*; Pc-*Plethodon cinereus*; Pg-*Plethodon glutinosus*; Pr-*Pseudotriton ruber.*

Location	Description	Mazzer et al. 1984	Species Found Varhegyi et al. 1995	Varhegyi et al., this chapter
Brecksville (1)	Rocky creeks in secondary hickory-maple forest	*	Df, Eb, Pc, Pg	Eb, Df, Nv, Pc
Brandywine Road (2)	Secondary growth forest including sycamore and pine trees, well-shaded ravines	Eb, Nv, Pg	Df, Eb, Pc	Df
Columbia Run (3)	Sandy bottom creek in well-shaded ravines	Eb	*	Df
Blue Hen Falls (4)	Flat shale stone bottom creek at bottom of several hills with secondary growth, including oak and beech trees	Eb, Nv, Pc, Pg	Pc	Df, Eb, Pc
Ledgewood Camp (5)	Well-shaded ravine along hiking/biking trail in secondary growth forest	Df, Eb, El, Pc, Pg, Pr	Df, Eb, Pc, Pg, Pr	Df, Eb, Pc
Deep Lock Quarry (6)	Secondary growth sycamore and oak trees forest, adjacent to farmland	Eb, Pc, Pg	Eb	*
Octagon (7)	Many well-shaded ravines in secondary hickory-maple forest with many sandy and rocky creeks and seeps	Df, Eb, Pc, Pr	Df, Pc, Eb	Df, Eb, Pc
Kendall Lake Area (8)	Large lake (ca. 5 acres), fed by stream, surrounded by secondary growth forest	Eb, Pc, Nv	Df, Eb, Pc	Df, Eb, Pc, Pr
Oak Hill Road (9)	Near road with relatively flat topography, plants include beech, pine, tulip, and sycamore trees	Df, Eb, Pc, Pg	*	Df, Eb, Pc
Valley Picnic Area (10)	Secondary growth with steep ravines, shale stone creeks that often dry in late summer	*	Eb, Pc	Eb, Pc
Furnace Run (11)	Low sloping ravines adjacent to farmland	Df, Eb, Pg	Df, Eb, Pc	Df, Eb, Nv, Pc
Indigo Lake Area (12)	Flat topography with secondary forest adjacent to a major road	Eb	*	Eb, Pc

*Site not surveyed.

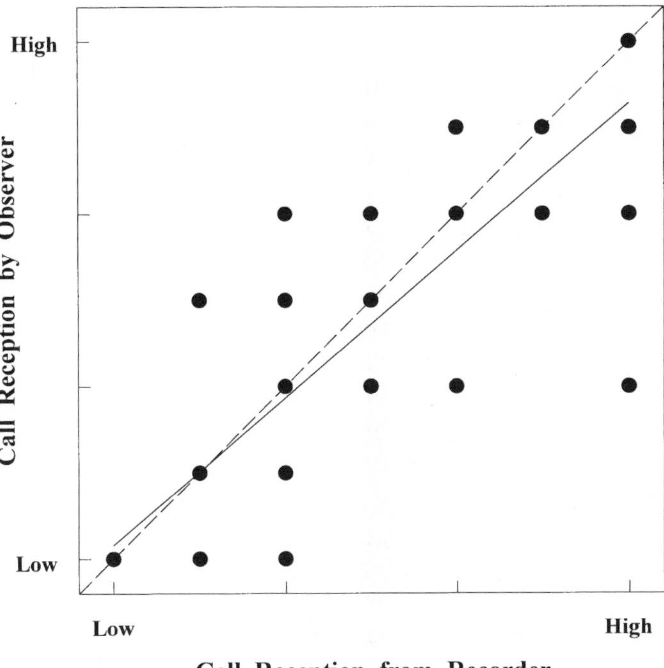

Figure 18-2. Call reception by observer plotted against the call reception from the automated recorder. "Low" indicates no sound reception. The dashed line represents a one-to-one ratio. The solid line is the least-squares regression line through the data points.

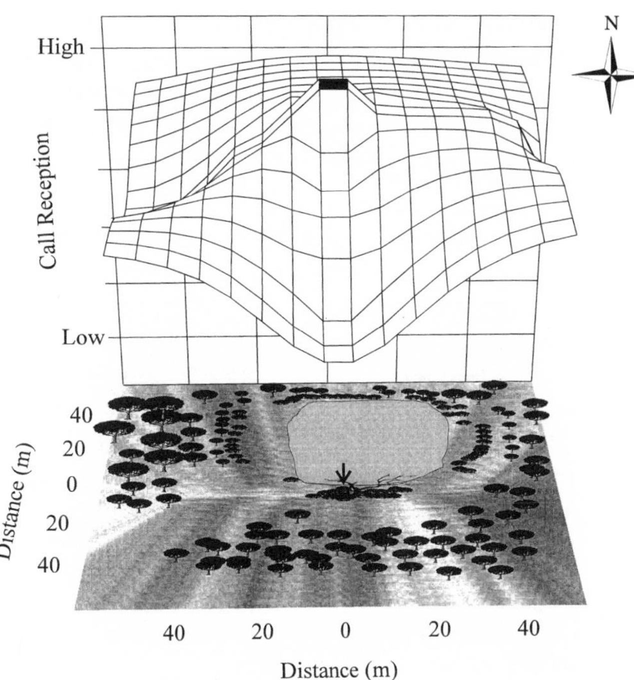

Figure 18-3. Sound reception, assessed subjectively from the automated call recorder, of calls of spring peepers played at a standard intensity at various locations around Prucek Pond (Site F11, Fig. 18-1). The location of the automated recorder (coordinates 0,0) is indicated by the arrow; sound reception of calls played immediately beside the recorder is marked by a rectangle. The plotted three-dimensional mesh surface was fitted using inverse distance weighting (Jandel Scientific).

high quality were obtainable from the entire pond area and from a band approximately 10 to 20 meters away from the pond margins in all directions. This area encompassed the principal calling sites of all species found at Prucek Pond (Table 18-1). Calls were attenuated most severely by dense vegetation, forests, and hillsides to the south and west of the pond (Figs. 18-3, 18-4).

The quality of recordings also differed with the species producing the call, independent of direction or distance (Fig. 18-4; Table 18-3). Recordings of spring peepers were of higher quality generally than were those of the other species tested, regardless of direction or distance (Fig. 18-4). Calls of western chorus frogs attenuated most rapidly with distance (Fig. 18-4).

Population Density Estimates. Population density estimates based on recordings from the automated device were underestimates, but strongly predictive, of the actual number of male gray treefrogs calling at Prucek Pond in 1994. Figure 18-5 illustrates estimated and actual counts of the number of male eastern gray treefrogs calling each night at Prucek Pond for a thirty-one-day period in the summer of 1994 (simultaneous counts and estimates are available for twenty-five of thirty-one days). Direct observational censuses found, on average, 0.48 (± 0.44 standard error) males calling each night. Population estimates obtained with the automated recording device indicated that 2.8 (± 0.26 standard error) males were calling each night. The estimates based on the automated recorder underestimate the actual counts by 38 percent on average. This differential was not constant, however (Fig. 18-5). The slope of the least-squares regression relating estimates to direct counts has a Y-intercept not significantly different than 0 (0.543 ± 0.325 standard error, $t_{Y\text{-}int=0} = 1.67$, $p > 0.10$) and a slope that was significantly greater than 0 (0.503 ± 0.0655 standard error, $t_\beta = -7.68$, $p < 0.001$) but less than 1 ($t_\beta = -7.59$, $p < 0.001$). Hence, the amount by which the automated device underestimated the number of calling males increased as the actual number of calling males increased. Neverthe-

Table 18-3. Analysis of covariance testing for the effects of species (*Bufo americanus americanus, Hyla versicolor, Pseudacris crucifer crucifer,* and *Pseudacris triseriata triseriata*), compass direction (N, S, E, W), and distance from the sound source (10, 20, 30, 40, or 50 m) on quality of recordings obtained by the automatic call recorder

Source of Variation	Degrees of Freedom	Mean Square	*F*-statistic	*P*
Species	3	2.947	15.461	<0.001
Direction	3	7.275	38.167	<0.001
Species x Direction	9	0.086	0.454	0.900
Distance	1	2.219	11.643	0.001
Distance x Species*	1	0.038	0.198	0.658
Distance x Direction†	1	0.633	3.320	0.073
Error	61		0.191	

*Tests for homogeneity of slopes for the relationship between distance and audibility of recordings among species.
†Tests for homogeneity of slopes for the relationship between distance and audibility of recordings among directions.

less, estimates based on the recorder were strongly predictive of the number of calling males actually counted. Night-to-night variation in the direct counts was reflected in variation in the estimates (Fig. 18-5).

Anuran Survey

1994 and 1995 Surveys. Nine species of anurans were identified in the CVNRA through two years of call surveys, comprising over 138 hours of recordings. Total number of species recorded, or species richness, did not differ among the two years of the survey (two-way analysis of variance, $F_{1,10} = 0.204$, $p = 0.661$), although this and subsequent tests that lack replication may only be sensitive to large effects. Sites, however, differed in species richness (two-way analysis of variance, $F_{10,10} = 3.054$, $p = 0.046$). Also, variation in species richness among sites in 1994 was not correlated with species richness in 1995 ($r_p = 0.51$, $n = 11$, $p = 0.11$); the number of species found at a particular site in 1994 was not predictive of the number of species found in 1995. Species richness per site, averaged over both years, was 4.8 species/site (standard error = 0.4, range = 2 to 8 species/site).

Our data are not sufficient yet to establish statistical trends of abundance for individual species. However, these data clearly indicate site-by-site (Fig. 18-6) and yearly variation (Figs. 18-7, 18-8) in the numbers of calling anurans. Year-to-year variation in intensity and duration of calling activity was especially evident at the continuously monitored site, Prucek Pond. We obtained 41.3 hours of recordings in 1994 and 30.2 hours of recordings in 1995 at Prucek Pond (sampling eighty-six and sixty-four days, respectively). The number of calls produced per night and the length of the breeding season were reduced in 1995 in comparison to 1994 (Figs. 18-7, 18-8). All species were affected, but several are particularly noteworthy. Eastern gray treefrogs, for example, were active almost every night from June through early July in 1994 but called only a few nights and in small numbers during the same period in 1995. Similarly, green frogs (*Rana clamitans melanota*] were abundant and active throughout the summer of 1994 but were active at similarly high levels only on a few nights toward the latter part of the season in 1995. Pickerel frogs (*Rana palustris*) were seldom heard in the spring of 1994 and were even less common in 1995.

Comparison to the 1983 Survey. Species richness differed significantly between the study of Mazzer et al. (1984) and the current survey at the same sites in the Cuyahoga Valley (one-way analysis of variance, $F_{2,27} = 3.81$, $p = 0.035$). The average species richness reported in Mazzer et al. (1984) of 2.6 species per site (standard error = 0.53, range = 1–5 species/site) was only about 55 percent of the 1994 (4.9 species per site) and 1995 (4.6 species per site) averages, a significant difference

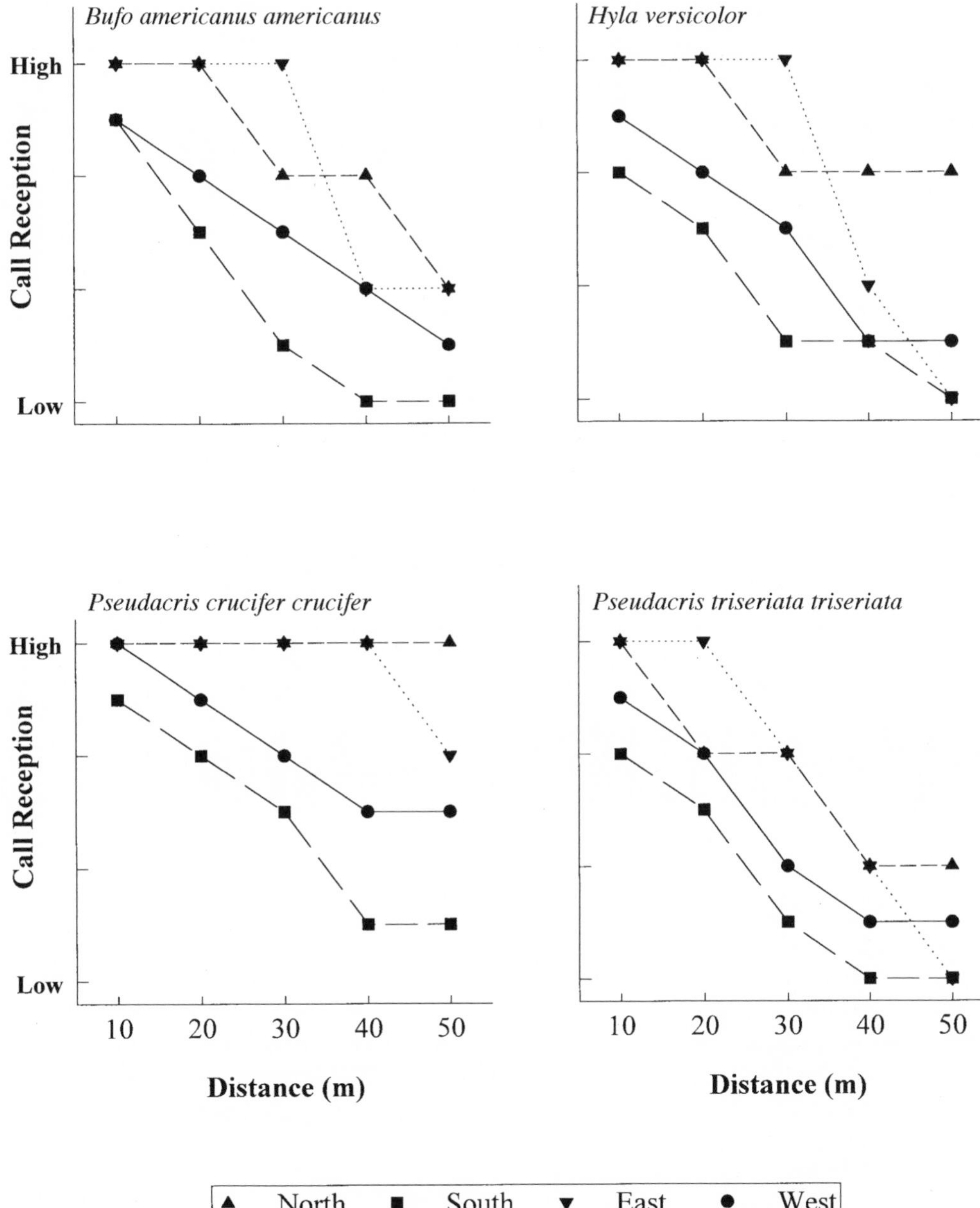

Figure 18-4. Sound reception, assessed subjectively from the automated call recorder, of calls of American toads, gray treefrogs, spring peepers, and chorus frogs played at a standard intensity at various locations and distances around Prucek Pond (F11, Fig. 18-1).

(Student-Newman-Keuls a posteriori multiple range test, $p < 0.05$). Furthermore, variation in species richness among sites in 1983 was not predictive of species richness in 1994 (Spearman rank correlation, $r_S = 0.01$, $n = 8$, $p = 0.99$) or 1995 ($r_S = 0.44$, $n = 8$, $p = 0.28$).

We found all the species reported by Mazzer et al. (1984) and one species, northern leopard frogs (*Rana pipiens*), not found by those workers. Northern leopard frogs were recorded at one site (F3, Snowville) on one evening in 1994. Mazzer et al. (1984) reports only presence/absence of species, data which are not sufficient for more detailed comparisons of species composition and abundance among sites.

Salamander Survey

1994 and 1995 Surveys. Six species of terrestrial and

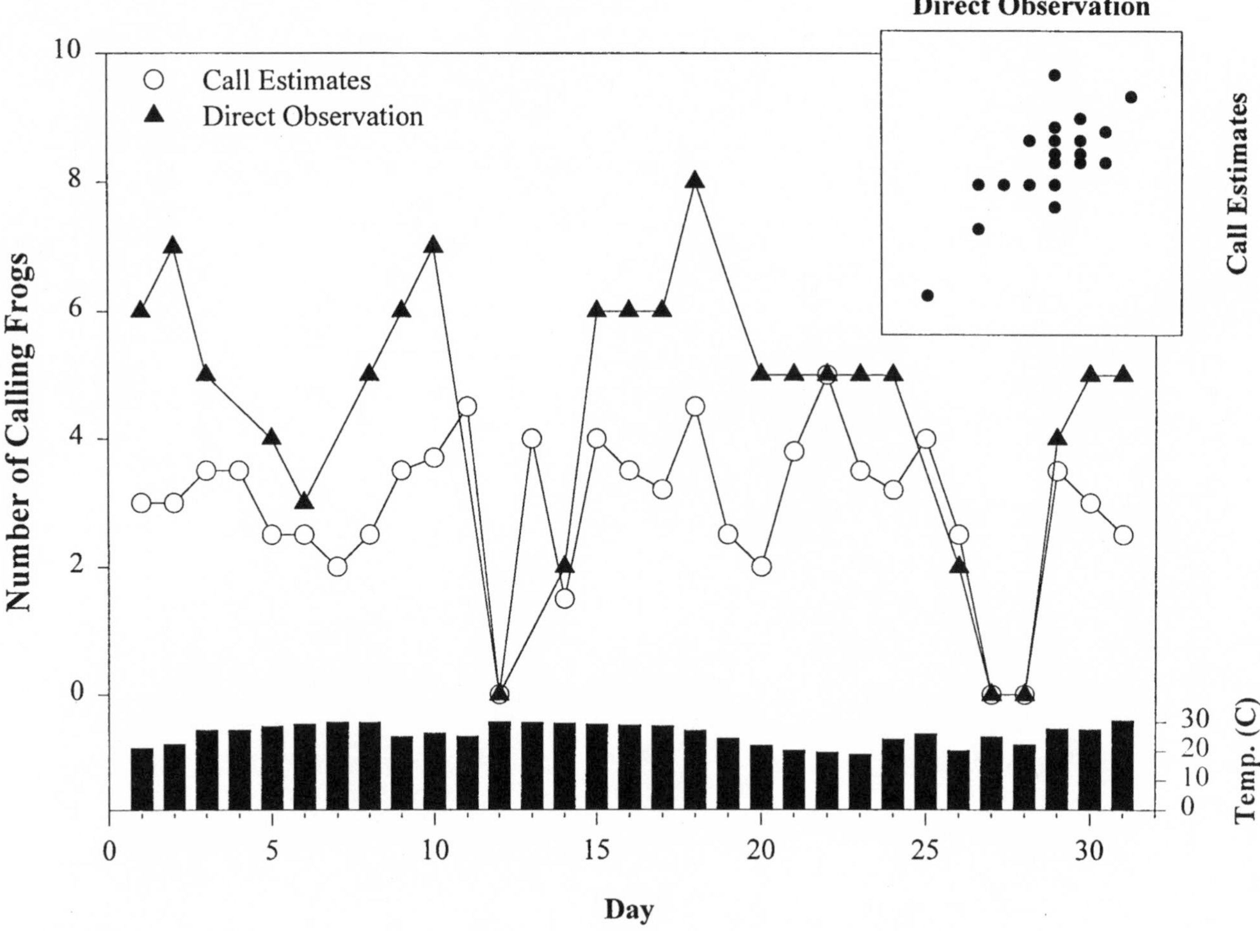

Figure 18-5. The number of calling male eastern gray treefrogs (*Hyla versicolor*) and daily average water temperatures at Prucek Pond plotted across the 1994 breeding season. Triangles are counts of calling males based on direct observation; circles are estimates of the number of calling males based on the automated call recorder (see text). The histogram represents daily average water temperature, and the insert is estimated call totals plotted against the direct counts of calling males.

stream-side salamanders were found in the CVNRA in over 200 person-hours of observation. Species richness did not differ among years (two-way analysis of variance, $F_{1,7} = 0.001$, $p = 1$) or among sites ($F_{11,7} = 1.703$, $p = 0.246$). Species richness at a site in 1994 was not predictive of species richness at that site in 1995 ($r_s = 0.33$, $n = 8$, $p = 0.33$). Mean species richness for 1994 and 1995 combined was 2.8 species/site (standard error = 1.16, range = 1 to 5).

Of the 1,546 individual salamanders found, three species accounted for 99.2 percent of captures: northern dusky salamanders (*Desmognathus fuscus*; 38.2 percent), northern two-lined salamanders (*Eurycea bislineata*; 31.8 percent), and redback salamanders (*Plethodon cinereus*; 29.2 percent). The abundance of these three species varied among sites (Fig. 18-9; chi-square test of association, $\chi^2 = 561.64$, $p < 0.0001$). These species also showed monthly trends of abundance (Fig. 18-10). Northern two-lined salamanders and redback salamanders were most abundant in spring and decreased in our captures in summer. Northern dusky salamanders, in contrast, were scarce in spring and early summer but abundant in late summer.

Comparison to the 1983 Survey. Species richness of terrestrial and stream-side salamanders did not differ between the current and 1983 (Mazzer et al. 1984) surveys (one-way analysis of variance, $F_{2,27} = 0.406$, $p = 0.671$). Species richness in 1983 was not predictive of species richness in 1994 ($r_s = 0.33$, $n = 7$, $p = 0.47$) or 1995 ($r_s =$

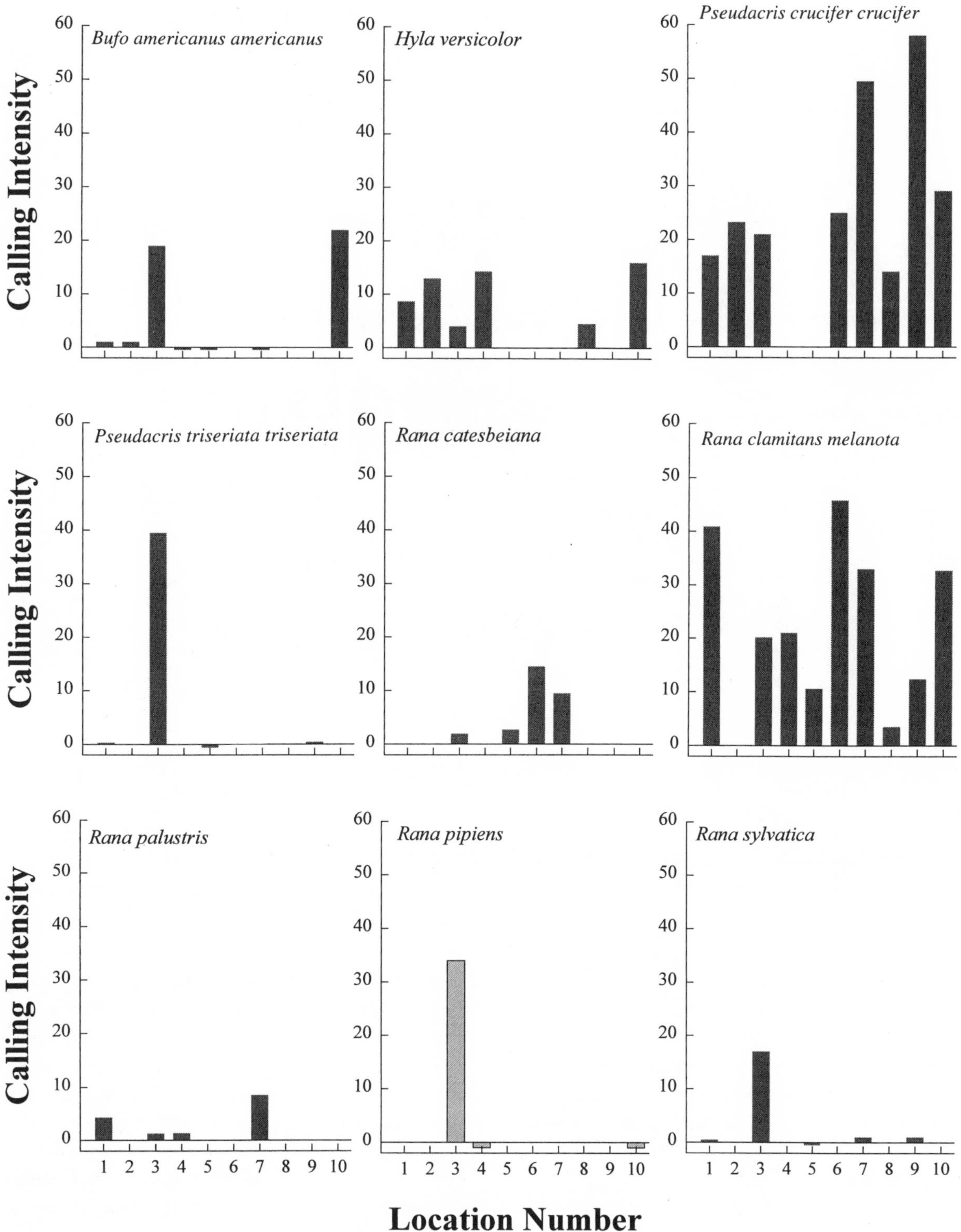

Figure 18-6. An index of calling intensity at each of the periodically surveyed locations in 1994 (Fig. 18-1; Table 18-2) plotted separately for the nine species of anurans recorded from the CVNRA. The calling index is the daily average number of sampling intervals that recorded calls. For each species, calculations were based only on intervals that fell within that species' breeding season. Negative values represent sites not visited during that species' breeding season as defined by the earliest and latest dates of calling. For northern leopard frogs (*Rana pipiens*) which we recorded only on one day, we have assumed a two-week breeding season.

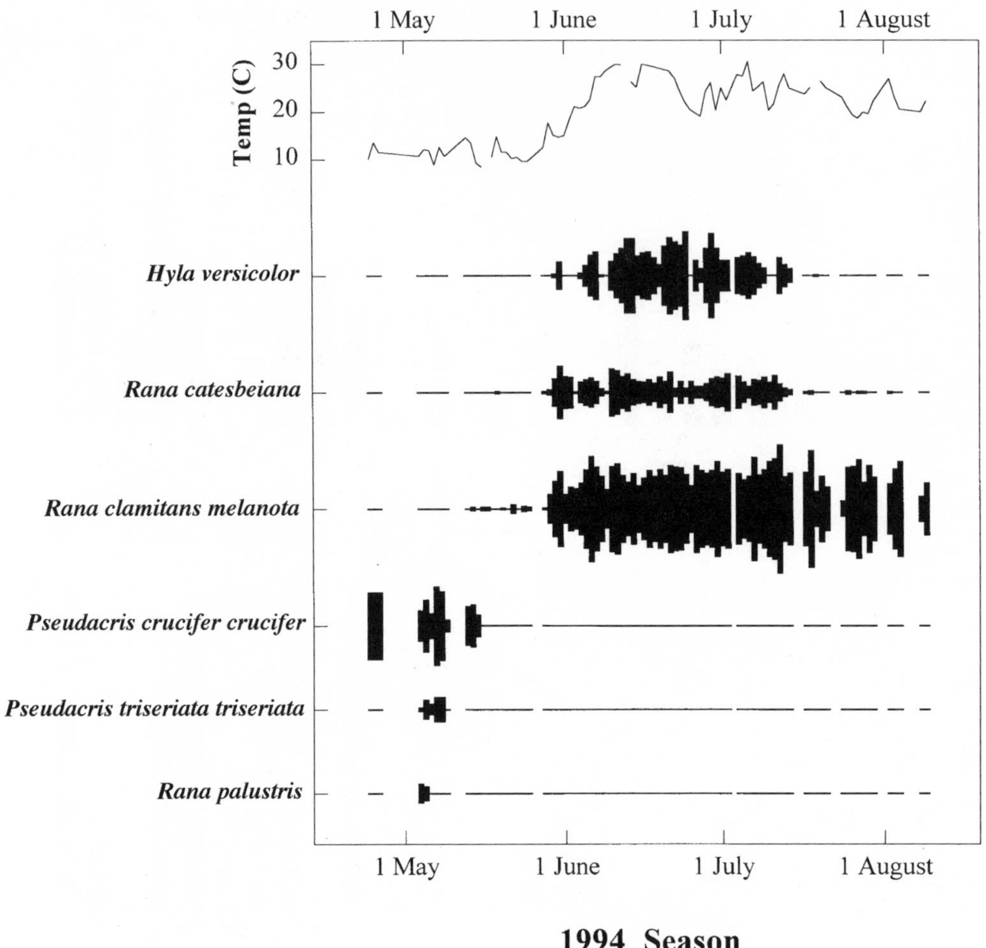

Figure 18-7. Calling activity of six species of anurans and average daily temperature plotted across the 1994 breeding season. The vertical range of each solid bar about the horizontal midline represents the total number of sampling intervals with calls in a twenty-four-hour period.

0.38, n = 9, p = 0.314). Mazzer et al. (1984) found 3.2 (± 0.47 standard error) species per site (range = 1 to 6) in 1983.

We found six of the seven species found in 1983 (Mazzer et al. 1984) but were unable to relocate longtail salamanders (*Eurycea longicauda*), despite repeated searches in 1994 and 1995 of their locality (S5, Ledgewood Camp, Fig. 18-1; Table 18-2).

Discussion

Performance of the Automated Call Recorder

The automated call recorder, often termed a "froglogger," designed by Peterson and Dorcas (1992, 1994) is an effective tool for monitoring calling anurans. The device has many attractive features: (1) an ability to obtain continuous, long-term records of calling activity without relying on human observers; (2) sensitivity of the device to rare species (because of the long records); (3) little or no disturbance of calling anurans, thereby increasing the likelihood of detecting easily disturbed species; (4) sampling of several sites simultaneously (with multiple recorders); (5) ability to correlate environmental conditions with calling activity (if the device is equipped with environmental monitoring devices); and (6) a permanent record that can be used to investigate long-term trends and to verify species identifications (Corn et al. 1995; Dorcas et al. 1995; Varhegyi et al. 1995).

The froglogger, however, is relatively new and has

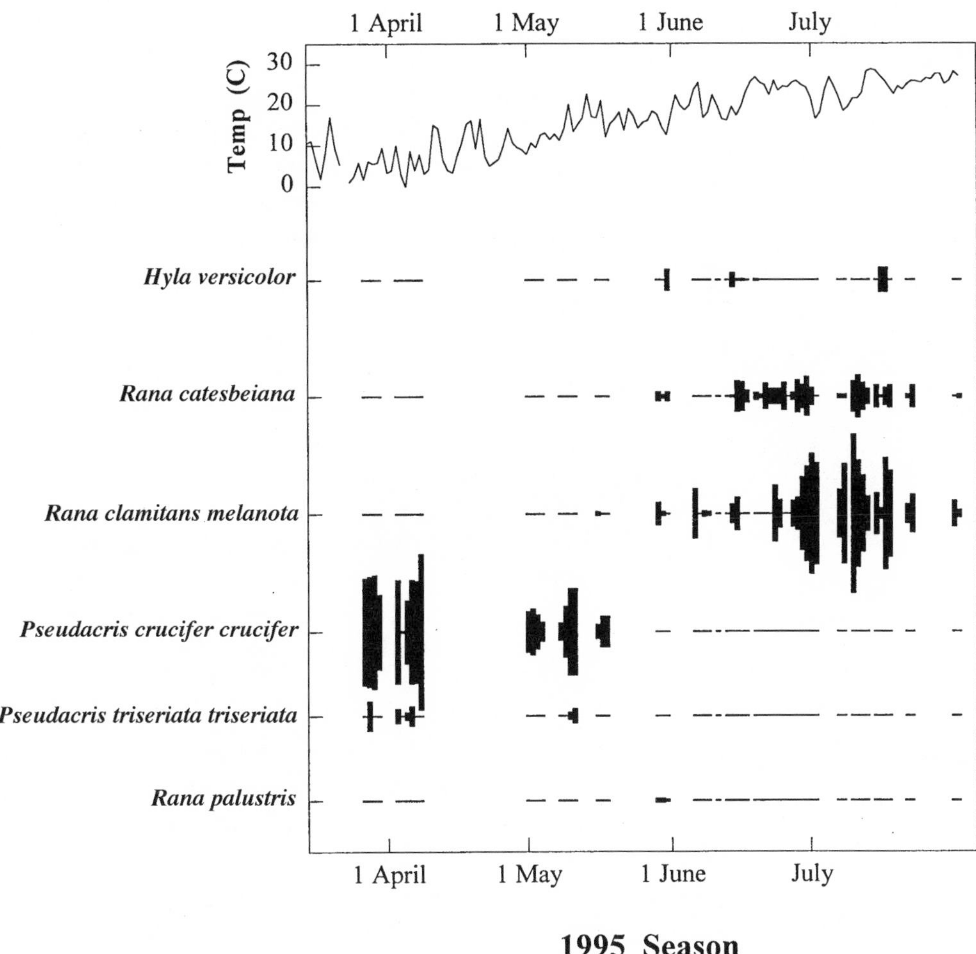

Figure 18-8. Calling activity of six species of anurans and average daily temperature plotted across the 1995 breeding season. The vertical range of each solid bar about the horizontal midline represents the total number of sampling intervals with calls in a twenty-four-hour period.

been used to monitor only a few species in a few habitat types (e.g., Berrill et al. 1992; Dorcas et al. 1994). Before it can be applied generally to anuran population monitoring, it must perform well relative to several criteria. First, it should provide an accurate record of species present at a locality. This means it should sample all species well, regardless of acoustic properties of their calls or length of calling activity (e.g., explosive versus prolonged breeders). Second, it should perform well in all habitats. Third, it should provide data for accurate estimates of population sizes. Finally, it should be cost effective (i.e., low cost per datum). No technique may be expected to satisfy all of these criteria completely. However, the froglogger must perform well according to these criteria in comparison to traditional methods (e.g., roadside surveys and aural transects) if it is to receive broad acceptance. Our goal was to evaluate the device against these criteria.

Overall, the ability of the automated device to record audible calls was as good as the ability of trained, experienced humans to hear those calls, at least within 50 meters of the sound source (Figs. 18-3, 18-4). Previous workers, however, have noted that the froglogger may not obtain audible recordings of all species or individuals present in some habitats (Berrill et al. 1992; Dorcas et al. 1994). Our experiments indicate that variation in acoustic performance with distance, vegetation, and species (Figs. 18-3, 18-4; Table 18-3) may contribute to such underestimates.

Our experiments provide lessons for effective place-

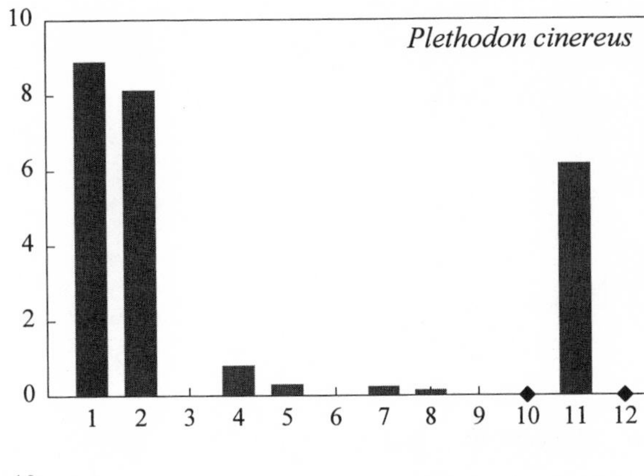

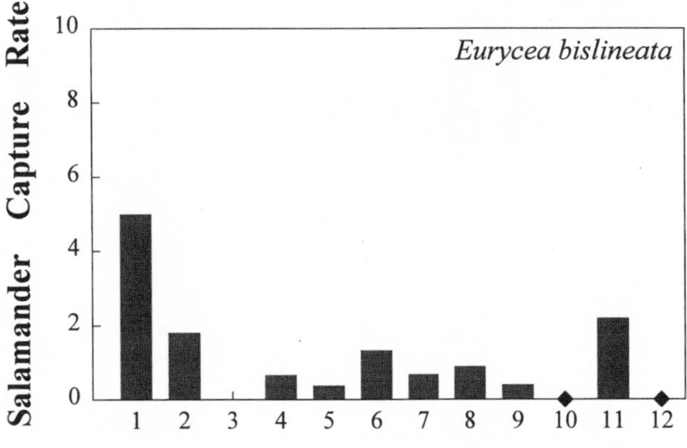

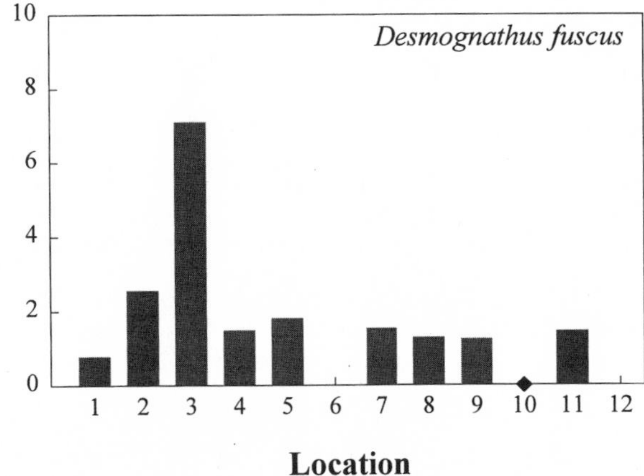

Figure 18-9. An index of salamander abundance at each of the periodically surveyed locations (Fig. 18-1; Table 18-2) plotted separately for the three most abundant species in the CVNRA. The index is the number of salamanders captured per person-hour of search time, combining data for 1994 and 1995. Diamonds represent sites where a species occurred but where data were insufficient for a meaningful index to be calculated. Sites with no bar or diamond represent no capture.

ment of the froglogger. Calls attenuate with distance, and the rate of attenuation varies with the species producing the call (Fig. 18-4; Table 18-3) and with the degree of obstruction by vegetation or topography (Fig. 18-3). As expected, the device functions best when the sound field is free of obstruction. This criterion often is met for species that call from the pond edge or the water but may not be for species that call from under, on, or within vegetation. Further, open areas may be uncommon in wetlands containing dense emergent vegetation (e.g., grassy marshes, bayous). Nevertheless, we obtained audible recordings through 20 meters or more of substantial vegetation (Figs. 18-3, 18-4).

Given these considerations, it may be prudent for investigators using the froglogger to map the sound field of their site in a fashion similar to that depicted in Figure 18-3 and to test the sensitivity of their device to calls of species likely to occur, as shown in Figure 18-4. Although this may take some time, it should reveal the most effective location for placement of the device.

Intensive, continuous monitoring of population sizes (of calling males, at least) and the correlation of population size with environmental parameters promise to be among the most useful applications of the froglogger. In our view, the ability to monitor several sites simultaneously provides an excellent tool for investigating regional variation in population cycles. Population monitoring with this device certainly is much less disruptive and labor intensive than it is with mark-recapture methods.

Although the automated device underestimated the number of calling male gray treefrogs at Prucek Pond by 38 percent on average, population estimates based on the froglogger were strongly correlated with direct counts. We consider this a promising result, indicating that the device is useful for monitoring population size. However, the investigator first must establish the relationship (e.g., through regression analysis) between counts and froglogger-based estimates. Methods for minimizing the discrepancy between counts and froglogger estimates will be helpful.

Difficulty in distinguishing overlapping calls from two or more individuals is the most likely cause for the discrepancy between counts and estimates. Discrimination became especially problematic when population densities were high, as reflected in the increasing differential between estimates and counts as population size increased (Fig. 18-5). Berrill et al. (1992) reported similar difficulties when using the device for monitoring of anuran populations in southern Ontario. However, human

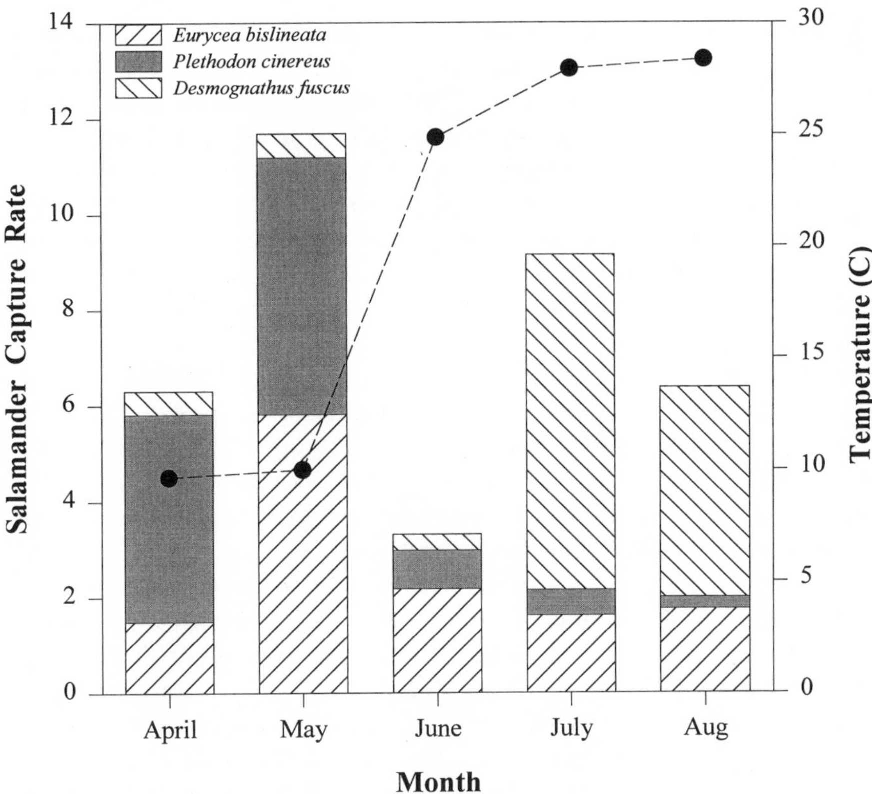

Figure 18-10. Monthly capture rates, an index of abundance, for three species of salamanders and average temperatures. The histogram represents the index, which is the number of salamanders captured per person-hour of search in the CVNRA during 1994 and 1995. Circles represent average monthly temperatures for both years.

listeners stationed at breeding choruses also have difficulty discriminating overlapping calls (Berrill et al. 1992). Because the froglogger tape is a permanent electronic record, it provides some options to minimize this problem that are not available in listener-based techniques. For example, when such conflicts arose in our data, they were addressed by replaying the calls to several trained listeners to obtain independent call counts and/or by inspection of a sonograph of the recording (this was necessary for particularly problematic overlaps of greater than three individuals). In this way, we were able to distinguish individual calls on most recordings. These procedures can be time-consuming, however. Perhaps digital recording systems and pattern recognition software currently in development (Patrick et al. 1995) will address this problem more efficiently.

Temperature variability in calling rates may also have contributed to the discrepancy. Call rates of eastern gray treefrogs generally increase with temperature (Bogart and Jaslow 1979; Gayou 1984), but the call rate used to estimate population size was the average for this population. This may not have been a major difficulty in 1994, because temperatures showed relatively little variation during the eastern gray treefrog breeding season. Nevertheless, we will incorporate temperature-dependence into our estimation algorithm in the future.

Cost is a major factor determining the utility of a monitoring technique. Considering that funding levels for biodiversity work are low and are likely to remain so, no monitoring technique will be accepted widely if it is too expensive, no matter how effective. Unquantified concern that the froglogger is prohibitively expensive for most applications has found its way into the draft "Protocols and Strategies for Monitoring North American Amphibians" (North American Amphibian Monitoring Program 1996; Mac 1996).

Our experience, however, is that the froglogger is much less expensive than is a traditional drive-by survey and indeed is highly cost-effective. We can construct a froglogger for under $300 (less than $200 if we do not equip the devices with temperature data loggers). Costs for gasoline, recording tapes, and replacement parts have averaged less than $250 per year. These costs compare favorably with those for surveys conducted by more traditional methods. For example, the Ontario Task Force on Declining Amphibian Populations has instituted a program of amphibian road call counts (Gartshore et al. 1995). Volunteer participants in this survey drive 7.2-kilometer routes and listen for three minutes each at ten survey points along the route. Each volunteer repeats this route three times during the season for a total of ninety minutes of survey time. In the CVNRA in 1994 and 1995, we surveyed for 8,320 minutes using the automated recorder. A volunteer listener-based survey of the same duration would require ninety-two volunteers, and the cost would be approximately 3.2 times that of the froglogger survey (Table 18-4). Moreover, the froglogger generates permanent audio records that provide easier verification and greater detail than do the corresponding data from drive-by surveys. Corn et al. (1995) conducted a similar cost comparison and found that volunteer-based surveys may cost up to ten times as much as froglogger surveys, per datum.

Drive-by, listener-based surveys in general may yield data that are more expensive, less cost-effective, and less useful than are data from surveys based on automated call recorders. With automated call recorders, the contributions of experienced, motivated volunteers simply may shift from direct data acquisition to servicing the call recorder and processing the data tapes. Frogloggers need to have their batteries recharged and tapes replaced on a routine basis, and in some studies the froglogger itself may need to be rotated around survey sites. Froglogger tapes need to be played back, the recorded calls must be identified accurately, and the data obtained must be transcribed reliably. Obviously, but crucially, all these tasks are best performed by experienced workers who believe in the importance of this program.

Anuran Surveys

Two years is not enough time to establish trends in population change in the amphibians of the CVNRA. The current surveys, however, do establish a basis for subsequent monitoring and provide some useful, albeit preliminary, comparisons to previous surveys.

Perhaps the most remarkable finding was that overall anuran species richness has apparently not changed over at least the past ten years. Our results, in fact, indicate a statistically significant 45 percent average increase in the number of species per site in comparison to 1983. However, we suspect that this increase is attributable more to the intensive sampling made possible by the froglogger than to an actual increase in species numbers. Nevertheless, we were impressed that we found no significant decrease in species richness, despite many human impacts on the CVNRA and the extensive urbanization of surrounding areas. This may be a testament either to the value of habitat protection and sound resource management to amphibian conservation, even in heavily urbanized areas, or to the low power of the

Table 18-4. Approximate cost comparison of two anuran survey methods, based on surveying 8,320 minutes

	Froglogger	Listener-Based Survey
Start-up cost	$200/froglogger x 2 = $400	92 kits[1] x $14/kit[2] = $1288[3]
Topographic map	2 x $9[4] = $18	92 x $9 = $828
Fuel	289 days x $0.45 per day[5] = $130	92 ind. x $0.45/visit x 3 visits = $124
Cassette tapes	289 days x 1 tape/2 days x $1/tape = $145	
Total	$693	$2,240

[1] Survey kits contain instructions, data sheets, training tapes, vehicle signs, etc.
[2] Amy Chabot (personal communication).
[3] These costs will be greater if not all participants return properly completed survey forms. Typical survey response rates may be less than 10 percent (Mahar et al. 1995).
[4] Gartshore et al. 1995.
[5] Value based on $0.10 per mile and a 4.5-mile route.

tests. The CVNRA, however, was established only in 1974. Therefore, the area already was heavily affected prior to implementation of habitat protection. The most serious declines may have occurred during this earlier period. As best as we can tell, this was the time when the once-abundant northern leopard frog underwent its most rapid decreases (discussed below).

We located all nine species of anurans reported to be present historically in or near the CVNRA by Walker (1946). Orr (1978) and Mazzer et al. (1984) provide more recent lists of species within the CVNRA; they located eight of the nine species reported by Walker (1946). The one species lacking from the Orr (1978) and Mazzer et al. (1984) lists was the northern leopard frog, a species in general decline throughout much of its former range (Stebbins and Cohen 1995). Other records indicate that this species was present in the 1970s (MacLaren 1959; Jack McCormick and Associates 1975) in the area that is now the CVNRA, although Mazzer et al. (1984) suspect that these records were misidentified pickerel frogs. Nevertheless, northern leopard frogs were abundant in northeastern Ohio through the mid-1950s (Dexter 1955). We recorded a single northern leopard frog on 18 April 1994 at Snowville Pond. Hence, the species either has persisted essentially undetected for at least twenty years or has reinvaded the area from surrounding areas. Given the extensive development of areas surrounding the CVNRA, we consider the latter possibility unlikely. This recording also attests to the effectiveness of the froglogger for finding rare species.

It is difficult to distinguish trends in other anurans from the available data, but two species merit mention. Bullfrogs (*Rana catesbeiana*) were considered "well established" by Mazzer et al. (1984) but were not found by them in large numbers at any locality in the CVNRA. Our survey, which also found that population sizes at any particular locality are not large, nevertheless documented that bullfrogs have invaded areas in which they were not found in the 1980s (e.g., Valley Picnic Area, F6, Indigo F10), expanding their range to include more southerly areas of the CVNRA. Mazzer et al. (1984) considered wood frogs (*Rana sylvatica*) to be common, even though they located this species only near Kendall Lake. We found wood frogs at sites throughout the CVNRA in 1994, although not at Kendall Lake, but we did not find them at any sites in 1995. We can identify no obvious factor causing the difference for this species between 1994 and 1995. Perhaps this merely reflects the natural potential for dramatic population cycles often characteristic of amphibian species (e.g., Pechmann et al. 1991).

Salamander Surveys

Any statements concerning trends in population sizes or species diversity of salamanders must be considered preliminary. However, the stability of anuran species richness between 1983 and the current survey is mirrored in the terrestrial and stream-side salamanders, suggesting again that habitat protection since 1974 has been beneficial to the amphibians of the CVNRA.

Despite the overall consistency of species richness, our survey indicates possible declines among some salamander species within the CVNRA. Longtail salamanders, for example, have been reported at one location in the CVNRA (Ledgewood Camp, S5) as recently as 1983 (Mazzer et al. 1984; Pfingsten and Downs 1989). However, we were unable to find a single individual, despite repeated visits to this locality over two years, and Sipes (1964) described it as "uncommon" in northeastern Ohio. Similarly, although northern slimy salamanders (*Plethodon glutinosus*) have been considered to be "relatively common" in the park (Mazzer et al. 1984) and "very common" in northeastern Ohio (Sipes 1964), we found a total of six individuals from only two sites in 1994 (fewer than in 1983) and no individuals in 1995. We consider this species now to be uncommon in the CVNRA. Ravine salamanders (*Plethodon richmondi*) are known from the area now occupied by the CVNRA from only a single specimen collected by Walker (1931; Ohio State University Museum 1438). We found none, despite repeated sampling of suitable habitat, the wooded slopes of valleys and ravines (Pfingsten and Downs 1989). Similarly, we found no four-toed salamanders (*Hemidactylium scutatum*), known previously from a single location in the CVNRA (Brecksville, S1; Orr 1978).

Conclusions

Some natural areas in what now is the CVNRA already were protected by state agencies, local parks, and private organizations prior to the establishment of the park (Cockrell 1992). However, the establishment of the CVNRA in 1974 brought greater protection to the area's amphibians and to their habitat. Yet by that time, extensive industrial and residential development had encroached upon the area, bringing multiple threats to amphibians and other natural resources of the CVNRA: acid rain; recycling plants; dumps; landfills; junkyards;

oil and gas drilling; commercial removal of topsoil, limestone, clay, sand, and gravel; pesticides; toxic wastes; illegal or accidental dumping of chemicals and biological wastes into the Cuyahoga River and its tributaries; salt runoff from roads; silting of streams; stream bank destruction; roads and traffic that disrupted migratory movements; introduced exotic species; marijuana cultivation; and numerous other possible threats "constrained only by an individual's imagination" (Cockrell 1992). The NPS and local agencies have taken great strides in mitigating many of these impacts, particularly in the area of water quality. Many of the streams in the park now meet or exceed federal water quality standards (Cockrell 1992). However, many problems still remain from threats both inside and outside the park.

One would hope that the efforts of the NPS and others have resulted in stabilizing local amphibian populations. Unfortunately, there are few data with which to assess this hypothesis. The only reliable data have been collected after the implementation of NPS management (e.g., Mazzer et al. 1984). Comparison of our results with those studies, albeit preliminary, is both encouraging and disturbing. The good news is that numbers of species, in general, have remained stable over the last decade. Several species, however, apparently have experienced reduction or extinction (e.g., northern leopard frogs, longtail salamanders) or currently may be declining (e.g., slimy salamanders). In years to come, we will continue research efforts directed toward verifying these trends and identifying causes of decline.

Summary

We report here on the first two years (1994 and 1995) of a long-term amphibian monitoring program in the Cuyahoga Valley National Recreation Area (CVNRA) in northeast Ohio. Surveys of terrestrial and stream-side salamanders were conducted using transects; surveys of calling anurans were accomplished with an automated call recorder. We identified six salamander species and nine anuran species. These included one anuran, northern leopard frogs (*Rana pipiens*), that has not been found in the area for at least twenty years. Through comparisons with previous surveys conducted at least a decade ago, we identified several species that apparently have undergone decline (e.g., northern slimy salamanders [*Plethodon glutinosus*] and longtail salamanders [*Eurycea longicauda*]) and perhaps local extinction (longtail salamanders). One species (bullfrogs [*Rana catesbeiana*]) may be expanding its distribution in the CVNRA. Despite these changes among a few species, average species richness (number of species/site) has not changed in the last decade. In fact, anuran species richness may have increased somewhat, but we believe this result to be a product of more efficient sampling in the current surveys.

An additional goal of this research was to evaluate the performance of automated call recorders. Overall, we found automated recorders to be an efficient, accurate, and cost-effective method for assessing species richness and population density of calling anurans. However, we also determined that placement, species recorded, and the number of individuals calling may affect their performance. We describe procedures that may mitigate some of these problems.

Acknowledgments

We extend our appreciation to the personnel of the CVNRA for making the study possible and for contributing materially to its success: John Debo and Garee Williamson gave permission to conduct the study, Meg Benke showed us the survey sites, and Anthony Gareau helped us with site coordinates and extended permission to modify a map of the CVNRA for use in the report. Peg Bobel and the Friends of the Cuyahoga Valley Association kindly provided funds for one of the automated call recorders. Charles R. Peterson and Michael Dorcas shared with us the design of the automated call recorder and advised us on its construction and operation. We thank Bruce Stoessner and Mark Pippenger of Cleveland State University and Ned Lagrande III for assembling the automated call recorder and for other technical assistance. Finally, we thank the numerous Cleveland State graduate students and undergraduates who assisted in data collection: Lisa Botic, Ron Canterbury, Barb Catuzza, Jon Cepek, Brenda Cotter, Susanna Dzejachok, Kevin Gajda, Joann Hoty, Janet Kucner, Sheila Lewicki, Lori Mattern, Michele Oblak, Lisa Remly, Ethan Schellenberg, and the members of the 1994 and 1995 undergraduate course in ecology at Cleveland State University.

19

Status of Amphibian Populations in Hamilton County, Ohio

Jeffrey G. Davis, Paul J. Krusling, and John W. Ferner

Located in extreme southwestern Ohio, Hamilton County includes the city of Cincinnati and is home for over 800,000 people. The confluence of the Great Miami and Ohio Rivers occurs at the southwestern limit of Hamilton County, with the Ohio River forming the county's southern boundary. The land area of the county is 1,057 square kilometers. Three major drainages, the Great Miami River on the western end, the Little Miami River along the eastern boundary, and Mill Creek through the middle (Hedeen 1994), drain the county.

Ordovician limestones underlie Hamilton County, while deposits of glacial materials of different ages and thicknesses cover the surface. The deposits of the Illinoisan, Kansan, and Wisconsinan periods have created a diverse topography for the county. Floodplains of ancient rivers, glacial end moraines, and deposits of glacial outwash provide the substrate for a diversity of habitat types, including talus slopes, wooded hillsides, riparian woodlands and floodplains, and their associated microhabitats, such as seeps from glacial end moraines. These habitats, in turn, affect the distribution of amphibians. Southwestern Ohio is characterized by deciduous forest, including mixed mesophytic, oak-hickory, beech-maple, and pin oak communities. One prairie was reported in the 1788 vegetational survey (Bryant 1987), but it is now gone. In some areas of the county, the abundance of ephemeral streams, pools, and ponds provides optimal amphibian breeding sites. Farm ponds occur in rural areas throughout the county. Extensive gravel pits occur in the Great and Little Miami River valleys.

This chapter reviews the status of amphibians in Hamilton County based on recent surveys, museum records, and the historical field notes of local herpetologists. We describe the efforts of the Hamilton County Park District (HCPD) to manage habitats that include amphibians as an important part of the fauna. We also discuss the value of surveys conducted to monitor the status of amphibians on local public lands.

Methods

Museum collections, including the collections of the Cincinnati Museum of Natural History (CMNH), Ohio State University (OSM), Cleveland Museum of Natural History (CMNH), University of Kansas (UK), Miami University (Ohio), and the National Museum of Natural History (USNM), were examined for pertinent records, and literature was reviewed for inclusions of amphibian records. Museum acronyms follow Duellman et al. (1978) and Leviton et al. (1985).

In 1985, the HCPD began offering small grants to researchers for projects of land management value. CMNH herpetology staff and David Rubin of Central State University used a portion of that money to begin a series of complete species inventories that included every parcel of land at that time under the park district's management. Much of what is known about recent trends in Hamilton County's herpetofaunal communities is a result of these surveys. In this program, upon the completion of each field inventory, a report is written to summarize the results and make land management recommendations. Copies are submitted to the County Park District Land Management Department, the Ohio Department of Natural Resources Division of Nongame

Wildlife, the Division of Natural Areas and Preserves, the Ohio Biological Survey, the Cincinnati Museum of Natural History, and the Ohio Natural Heritage Data Base. Recommendations made by the investigators offer ideas to park district personnel that lead to long-term plans for, and immediate adjustments to, land management policies.

Inventory reports written for the HCPD (Table 19-1) were examined for records of all amphibian species from each park. The county park surveys were conducted before the recent attempts to standardize monitoring techniques for amphibians (Heyer et al. 1994; Fellers and Freel 1995; Mac 1996). The fact that a small number of investigators (four) conducted these surveys over a relatively short period of time (six years) in a consistent manner makes these data useful for determining the status of populations. Reports include extensive information on the habitat distribution of species present, numbers found per visit, developmental stages and sex of individuals, and weather conditions. Each individual of each species is also located as a dot on a topographic map.

Status of Hamilton County Amphibians

Museum Records

Museum records do not represent an organized survey of past populations of amphibians; however, they can be used to indicate the occurrence of a species and its habitat preferences (see also Resetar, Chpt. 40, this volume). Records of 327 specimens at six institutions are listed in Table 19-2. An individual longtail salamander (*Eurycea longicauda longicauda*) collected in 1891 is the oldest museum specimen located. The bulk of the specimens collected before World War II were deposited by an active group of young amateur herpetologists in the early 1930s. In the 1950s and 1970s, there were other peaks of collecting activity, but none were part of a systematic survey. The bulk of specimens deposited in museums since 1980 are at the CMNH.

Museum records alone are not sufficient as a means for identifying trends in populations. Uncommon species, such as marbled salamanders (*Ambystoma opacum*) and spring salamanders (*Gyrinophilus porphyriticus*), are generally sought out and are therefore well represented in collections, while abundant species, such as northern spring peepers (*Pseudacris crucifer crucifer*), are poorly represented (Table 19-2). Older collections at the CMNH often contain large series of specimens, such as streamside salamanders (*Ambystoma barbouri*) and northern dusky salamanders (*Desmognathus fuscus*), from a single locality (Table 19-2), while recent collections are more conservative, usually including only a single voucher specimen. An inference for decline or extirpation can be made, however, when there are no recent collections of a species, such as eastern hellbenders (*Cryptobranchus alleganiensis alleganiensis*). When combined with the recent surveys and literature records, a more precise picture of the general population trends can be inferred.

Recent Surveys

Over the last fifteen years, the authors have been working to determine the status of herpetofauna in the Cincinnati region. Twenty-one of the twenty-six amphibian species known to have occurred historically in Hamilton County have been documented within the past three years (Table 19-3). If the five species not found in recent surveys are indeed extirpated from the county, that would represent a 19 percent loss in species richness. Certainly, a great many of the remaining species have been substantially reduced in number as a result of habitat loss associated with urban sprawl. For example, the pin oak swamps once reported for Hamilton County (Braun 1916; Bryant 1987), which provided habitat for spotted salamanders (*Ambystoma maculatum*), marbled salamanders, western chorus frogs (*Pseudacris triseriata triseriata*), and wood frogs (*Rana sylvatica*), are now gone.

Eastern tiger salamanders (*Ambystoma tigrinum tigrinum*) have been removed from the list of species recorded from Hamilton County. Pfingsten and Downs (1989) list two dubious records. The first record, CMNH 42, a donation from the Saint Francis Collection, possibly Saint Francis Seminary, contains no date of collection. Other specimens on the same catalog page were collected between 1890 and 1901, indicating the approximate time of collection. The collector is listed as the Reverend Kroke. The locality information is recorded as "locality uncertain, (Cincinnati?)." Due to the uncertain origin of this specimen, it should be discounted. The second record, two specimens reported from Sharon Woods Park (Collins and McDuffie 1969), should be dismissed as anecdotal. Al Winstel (personal communication), a naturalist for the HCPD, interviewed Warren Wells, the reputed collector, about the origin of the specimens. Winstel concluded that they were most likely brought to Sharon Woods from outside the county, possibly from Warren County, by a visitor seeking their identification. George McDuffie (personal communication) agreed

Table 19-1. Hamilton County, Ohio, parks surveyed for amphibians and reptiles from 1988 through 1993

	Park	Area (hectares)	Source
A	Embshoff Woods and Nature Preserve	126	Krusling (1993); Rubin (1992)
B	Farbach-Werner Nature Preserve	9	Krusling et al. (1991a)
C	Kroger Hill Park, Avoca Park	87	Krusling et al. (1991b)
D	Lake Isabella Park	31	Davis et al. (1991a)
E	Little Miami Golf Center, Bass Island Park	108	Krusling et al. (1991c)
F	Mitchell Memorial Forest	543	Davis and Krusling (1990)
G	Miami-Whitewater Forest, Shaker Trace Wetlands	1,578	Davis et al. (1992); Rubin (1992)
H	Newberry Wildlife Sanctuary	41	Davis et al. (1991b)
I	Richardson Forest Preserve	107	Davis and Krusling (1989)
J	Sharon Woods Park	306	Rubin (1992)
K	Shawnee Lookout Park	415	Rubin (1992); Simon and Krusling (1988)
L	Triple Creek Park	55	Davis and Krusling (1991)
M	Withrow Nature Preserve	109	Krusling et al. (1991d)
N	Woodland Mound Park	377	Rubin (1992)
O	Winton Woods Park, Trillium Trails Preserve	1,032	Rubin (1992)

that they were probably from outside the county. It is possible that an introduced population might become established, because larval tiger salamanders are commonly sold as fish bait and aquarium livestock. Until a breeding population is located, however, any tiger salamander reported from the Cincinnati area is suspect.

Although considered "Victorian science" by some biologists, complete species inventories are imperative for sound habitat management. Data from all HCPD flora and fauna surveys are being compiled into a biodiversity index called the Cincinnati Area Geographical Information System, so that information is easily accessible to wildlife managers and park planners.

Salamander Populations. Table 19-3 summarizes the abundance of salamanders found in the park surveys, with five of the fifteen species previously recorded from the county not being found. Hellbenders have not been collected from Hamilton County since 1961. Hamilton County's hellbender records are primarily from the Ohio and Great Miami and Whitewater River systems. The Ohio River, once complete with riffle zones and water falls, has been impounded by a series of dams stretching from just below its source in Pittsburgh to its mouth at the Mississippi River. Since its impoundment, the Ohio River has become a series of lakes for barge transportation. In addition, agricultural practices have resulted in severe stream siltation. This has greatly reduced and modified hellbender habitat in Ohio (Nickerson and Mays 1973). It is possible that the hellbender persists; anecdotal reports continue to surface from the Great Miami River system, and individuals may wander into the county from the Licking River in northern Kentucky, where hellbenders still occur.

Mudpuppies (*Necturus maculosus*) seem to have followed a decline similar to hellbenders, and for similar reasons, in tributaries of the Ohio River and may now be extirpated from the county. Collins and McDuffie (1969) indicate that hellbenders were often caught by people fishing in the Ohio and Miami Rivers and that mudpuppies were commonly found in the Little Miami River system. We know of no recent reports of their occurrence in these drainages.

While no red-spotted newts (*Notophthalmus viridescens viridescens*) have been reported from Hamilton County for about seventy years, records in nearby counties (Krusling and Ferner 1993) suggest that they may still be present. Spotted salamanders and marbled salamanders are rare, probably as a result of swamp forest habitat loss. Two undated specimens of the northern red salamander (*Pseudotriton ruber ruber*), USNM 8818 and USNM 8841, are recorded from Hamilton County. If these records are valid, they represented a population disjunct from the main body of their distribution in the Allegheny Plateau. The presence of other typically

Table 19-2. Museum records of the twenty-six species of amphibians known from Hamilton County, Ohio

	Pre-1940	1940–1979	1980–1995
Eastern hellbender (*Cryptobranchus alleganiensis alleganiensis*)	7	1	0
Mudpuppy (*Necturus maculosus maculosus*)	0	1	0
Red-spotted newt (*Notophthalmus viridescens viridescens*)	1	0	0
Streamside salamander (*Ambystoma barbouri*)	35	1	12
Jefferson salamander (*Ambystoma jeffersonianum*)	0	3	3
Spotted salamander (*Ambystoma maculatum*)	1	2	1
Marbled salamander (*Ambystoma opacum*)	1	0	3
Northern dusky salamander (*Desmognathus fuscus*)	23	1	1
Southern two-lined salamander (*Eurycea cirrigera*)	8	9	10
Longtail salamander (*Eurycea longicauda longicauda*)	5	9	4
Cave salamander (*Eurycea lucifuga*)	6	3	3
Northern spring salamander (*Gyrinophilus porphyriticus porphyriticus*)	9	14	1
Redback salamander (*Plethodon cinereus*)	16	16	16
Northern slimy salamander (*Plethodon glutinosus*)	1	1	1
Ravine salamander (*Plethodon richmondi*)	2	3	9
Northern red salamander (*Pseudotriton ruber ruber*)	1	0	0
Blanchard's cricket frog (*Acris crepitans blanchardi*)	6	1	4
American toad (*Bufo americanus americanus*)	4	8	5
Fowler's toad (*Bufo woodhousii fowleri*)	4	4	2
Cope's gray treefrog (*Hyla chrysoscelis*)	3	2	4
Northern spring peeper (*Pseudacris crucifer crucifer*)	0	1	0
Western chorus frog (*Pseudacris triseriata triseriata*)	0	0	0
Bullfrog (*Rana catesbeiana*)	1	4	3
Green frog (*Rana clamitans melanota*)	3	5	5

Table 19-2. (cont.)

	Pre-1940	1940–1979	1980–1995
Northern leopard frog (*Rana pipiens*)	7	3	1
Wood frog (*Rana sylvatica*)	0	1	2
Total	144	93	90

Appalachian species such as spring salamanders in Hamilton County and mud salamanders (*Pseudotriton montanus*) in northern Kentucky (Krusling and Ferner 1993) supports the possibility that these records are valid. With no records in decades, the red salamander may have been the first amphibian to be extirpated from Hamilton County.

Northern dusky salamanders (*Desmognathus fuscus*) and slimy salamanders (*Plethodon glutinosus*) have similar distribution patterns in southwestern Ohio. The biogeography of both may have been influenced by prehistoric drainages (see Fenneman 1916; Hedeen 1994) restricting them to the east of the Little Miami River and to the west of the Great Miami River. Habitats where they were found yielded apparently healthy, reproducing populations (Tables 19-3, 19-4).

Seven isolated populations of northern spring salamanders (*Gyrinophilus p. porphyriticus*) are known in Hamilton County (Pfingsten and Downs 1989; Conant and Collins 1991), and at least two of these occur on HCPD property (Krusling and Davis 1992, 1993). The decline of spring salamanders indicated from museum records may be real, as development continues to alter springs and seepage sites in the county.

Frog and Toad Populations. The relative abundance of the frogs and toads found in the HCPD survey is given in Table 19-5. As a result of the three large drainages that cut through the county, floodplain habitats are quite common. Historically these valleys provided optimal and abundant habitat to support a large population of northern leopard frogs (*Rana pipiens*). Written records show that leopard frogs were recognized as being common as early as 1845 (Hedeen 1994). Voucher specimens dating back more than sixty years are at the CMNH. The absence of earlier records might suggest that leopard frogs were so abundant that by oversight they were too common to collect or that no surveys were done before that time. Collins and McDuffie (1970) refer to northern leopard frogs as being "common throughout the Cincinnati area." Herpetology staff from the CMNH have noted a near absence of leopard frogs in collections since the late 1970s. Only one voucher specimen (CMNH 3639, collected on 2 September 1992) has been collected since then despite intensive efforts to find them. What happened to the leopard frog populations?

In northwestern Iowa, Lannoo et al. (1994) reported that the bullfrog (*Rana catesbeiana*) was introduced as an alternate source of frog legs, even though in the early 1900s as many as 20 million northern leopard frogs were harvested from a single county in that area each year. Lannoo et al. (1994) suggested that a competitive edge on the part of bullfrogs may have led to the demise of leopard frogs. Such a competitive edge among frogs may exist in both the adult and larval stages (Moyle 1973). Bullfrogs are aggressive predators of invertebrates, birds, turtles, snakes, small mammals, and other frogs (Ferner et al. 1992; Bruggers 1973). Additional evidence supporting Lannoo et al.'s (1994) perception of bullfrog impact on leopard frogs is the apparent increase in the population of bullfrogs in southwest Ohio (Tables 19-2 and 19-5). As wet meadows and forests have been converted to agricultural- and pastureland, farmers have impounded creeks and created ponds for irrigation and as a water supply for livestock. These ponds have increased the potential habitat for the highly adaptable bullfrogs. One of the authors (J.G.D.) reported bullfrogs from farm ponds, small streams, gravel pits, oxbow lakes, puddles, river shores, reservoirs, fish hatchery ponds, canals, and marshes. During status surveys conducted for eastern massasauga rattlesnakes (*Sistrurus catenatus catenatus*) in Ohio, the same author

Table 19-3. Relative abundance of salamanders in Hamilton County parks. See Table 19-1 for park list key. Abundance abbreviations: A = abundant or too numerous to count; ten or more sighted per visit. C = common; between five and ten individuals per visit. IF = infrequent; less than five but more than one seen per visit. R = rare; only one seen per visit or as few as one for the entire study. EX = extirpated; none located during the current inventories but recorded historically. NR = not recorded in current survey and no previous record from the park. IT = introduced or reestablished population (no numbers monitored).

Parks	A	B	C	D	E	F	G	H	I	J	K	L	M	N	O
Eastern hellbender (*Cryptobranchus alleganiensis alleganiensis*)	NR	NR	NR	NR	NR	NR	EX	NR	NR	NR	EX	NR	NR	NR	NR
Mudpuppy (*Necturus maculosus maculosus*)	NR	NR	NR	NR	NR	NR	NR	NR	NR	NR	NR	NR	NR	NR	NR
Red-spotted newt (*Notophthalmus viridescens viridescens*)	NR	NR	NR	NR	NR	NR	NR	NR	NR	NR	NR	NR	NR	NR	NR
Streamside salamander (*Ambystoma barbouri*)	IT	NR	R	NR	NR	C	C	A	C	C	C	A	C	NR	A
Jefferson salamander (*Ambystoma jeffersonianum*)	IT	NR	C	NR	NR	C	IF	NR	IF	NR	A	A	A	C	NR
Spotted salamander (*Ambystoma maculatum*)	NR	NR	NR	NR	NR	NR	R	NR	NR	NR	NR	NR	NR	NR	NR
Marbled salamander (*Ambystoma opacum*)	NR	NR	NR	NR	NR	NR	R	NR	NR	NR	NR	NR	NR	NR	NR
Northern dusky salamander (*Desmognathus fuscus*)	NR	NR	NR	NR	NR	NR	NR	NR	NR	NR	NR	NR	C	A	?
Southern two-lined salamander (*Eurycea cirrigera*)	NR	NR	A	IF	NR	A	A	A	A	A	A	C	A	A	A
Longtail salamander (*Eurycea longicauda longicauda*)	R	NR	A	IF	NR	NR	R	NR	NR	C	NR	NR	C	C	IF
Cave salamander (*Eurycea lucifuga*)	IF	NR	NR	NR	NR	C	C	A	R	NR	NR	NR	NR	NR	IF
Northern spring salamander (*Gyrinophilus porphyriticus porphyriticus*)	NR	NR	IF	NR	NR	NR	NR	NR	NR	R	NR	NR	NR	NR	NR
Redback salamander (*Plethodon cinereus*)	A	NR	A	A	NR	A	A	A	A	A	NR	A	NR	NR	A
Northern slimy salamander (*Plethodon glutinosus*)	NR	NR	NR	NR	NR	NR	NR	NR	NR	NR	NR	NR	IF	IF	NR
Ravine salamander (*Plethodon richmondi*)	NR	NR	NR	NR	A	R	NR	NR	NR	A	NR	A	A	NR	NR
Northern red salamander (*Pseudotriton ruber ruber*)	NR	NR	NR	NR	NR	NR	NR	NR	NR	NR	NR	NR	NR	NR	NR

Table 19-4. Evidence for reproduction in amphibian populations of Hamilton County parks as listed by park. See Table 19-1 for park list key.

	Eggs, Larvae	Juveniles	Vocalization
Streamside salamander (*Ambystoma barbouri*)	A,C,F,G,H,I,K,O	H	
Jefferson salamander (*Ambystoma jeffersonianum*)	A,C,G,I,K,M	C,F	
Spotted salamander (*Ambystoma maculatum*)	G		
Marbled salamander (*Ambystoma opacum*)	G		
Northern dusky salamander (*Desmognathus fuscus*)	N	M	
Southern two-lined salamander (*Eurycea cirrigera*)	C,D,F,G,H,I,K,M	C,G,H	
Longtail salamander (*Eurycea longicauda longicauda*)		C,M	
Cave salamander (*Eurycea lucifuga*)		F,G,H,O	
Northern spring salamander (*Gyrinophilus porphyriticus porphyriticus*)	C,J	C	
Redback salamander (*Plethodon cinereus*)	F	A,C,D,G,H,I	
Northern slimy salamander (*Plethodon glutinosus*)		M	
Ravine salamander (*Plethodon richmondi*)		F,G,K,M	
Blanchard's cricket frog (*Acris crepitans blanchardi*)	C,G	C,G	C,E,I,K
American toad (*Bufo americanus americanus*)	C,F,I,K,M	C,D,E,F,G,H,I,M	F,C,O
Fowler's toad (*Bufo woodhousii fowleri*)	C,E,F,G,I,K	C,E,F,G,H	C,I
Cope's gray treefrog (*Hyla chrysoscelis*)	F	F,G	C,E,F,H,I,K,M
Northern spring peeper (*Pseudacris crucifer crucifer*)	F,G	G	A,C,G,I
Bullfrog (*Rana catesbeiana*)	C,D,E,I,K	B,C,D,E,F,G,H,I,M	G,H,O
Green frog (*Rana clamitans melanota*)	C,E,G,I,K	C,D,E,F,G,H,I,M	G,I,K,O
Wood frog (*Rana sylvatica*)	C,F,N	C,F	C,N

Table 19-5. Relative abundance of anurans in Hamilton County parks. See Table 19-1 for park list key. Abundance abbreviations: A = abundant or too numerous to count; ten or more sighted per visit. C = common; between five and ten individuals per visit. IF = infrequent; less than five but more than one seen per visit. R = rare; only one seen per visit or as few as one for the entire study. EX = extirpated; none located during the current inventories but recorded historically. NR = not recorded in current survey and no previous record from the park. IT = introduced or reestablished population (no numbers monitored).

Parks	A	B	C	D	E	F	G	H	I	J	K	L	M	N	O
Blanchard's cricket frog (*Acris crepitans blanchardi*)	NR	NR	A	NR	A	A	A	NR	A	NR	A	NR	NR	NR	NR
American toad (*Bufo americanus americanus*)	NR	NR	A	R	IF	A	A	R	A	C	A	C	A	A	C
Fowler's toad (*Bufo woodhousii fowleri*)	NR	NR	A	NR	A	A	A	R	A	NR	A	NR	NR	NR	NR
Cope's gray treefrog (*Hyla chrysoscelis*)	NR	NR	C	NR	NR	A	A	R	A	NR	A	IF	IF	NR	NR
Northern spring peeper (*Pseudacris crucifer crucifer*)	IT	NR	A	NR	NR	A	A	NR	A	NR	A	A	NR	NR	NR
Western chorus frog (*Pseudacris triseriata triseriata*)	NR	NR	NR	NR	NR	NR	NR	NR	NR	NR	NR	NR	NR	NR	NR
Bullfrog (*Rana catesbeiana*)	NR	A	A	A	A	A	A	A	A	IF	A	C	A	C	A
Green frog (*Rana clamitans melanota*)	NR	NR	A	NR	A	A	A	A	A	C	A	C	A	A	R
Northern leopard frog (*Rana pipiens*)	NR	NR	NR	NR	NR	NR	NR	R	R	NR	NR	NR	NR	NR	NR
Wood frog (*Rana sylvatica*)	NR	NR	A	NR	NR	R	NR	NR	NR	NR	NR	NR	R	R	NR

found that leopard frogs were common at most localities where massasaugas were found. The habitat for both species, wet meadows, is not suitable for bullfrogs except where a stream may pass through or a pond might exist. Field notes taken over a two-year period show that few bullfrogs were found at localities where leopard frogs were abundant. In suitable habitat where leopard frogs were absent, bullfrogs were often abundant.

Perhaps the primary cause of Hamilton County's leopard frog population decline is habitat destruction and/or alteration. Hedeen (1994) offers much insight about the decline of the leopard frog population in Mill Creek and its valley. Only 15 percent of the forest cover of Mill Creek Township—essentially all of the city of Cincinnati—remained by 1881. By 1913, industry along Mill Creek included distilleries, stockyards, slaughterhouses, tanneries, soap and wax factories, and mills. These industries contributed the equivalent of one cup of "warm swill" to each gallon of water that flowed through the Mill Creek valley. By 1916, all of the original Mill Creek valley vegetation had been replaced by agriculture or industry. The Cincinnati Chamber of Commerce dismissed the condition of Mill Creek as a "martyr" of the progress of the city. Only eighty years earlier, leopard frogs were considered common in the valley (Hedeen 1994).

What might be the reasons for the loss of northern leopard frogs across the remainder of the county? Recent suggestions imply that acid deposition and/or increased ultraviolet radiation may be responsible in part for declining amphibian populations globally (Blaustein and Wake 1995). Declines are typically not restricted to areas as small as a single county. In Butler County, which borders Hamilton County on the north, the leopard frog still remains abundant. At Butler Metro Park's Gilmore Ponds Interpretive Preserve, a wetland area that comprises the headwaters of Mill Creek, leopard frog populations show limited evidence of decline (although the pending development of a regional airport and a light industry park may alter their breeding habitat). In parts of Warren County, the other bordering county to the north, leopard frogs remain among the most abundant frog species. Krusling and Ferner (1993) found no leopard frogs in the three northern tier counties of Kentucky, which border Hamilton County on the south, and none are known from Dearborn County, Indiana, to the west (Minton 1972; Simon and Krusling 1988; Davis 1994).

No museum records of western chorus frogs from Hamilton County are known. There is a photograph of two individuals from the county taken by Karl Maslowski and Peter Koch included in Walker (1946). Western chorus frogs remain abundant in the pin oak forests in Clermont County, Ohio. George McDuffie (personal communication) confirmed the Walker photographs and has seen chorus frogs in the extreme southeastern portion of Hamilton County.

Due to population declines, Blanchard's cricket frogs (*Acris crepitans blanchardi*) have herpetologists concerned. This species is rapidly becoming less abundant in the northern part of its range, but we have not observed an appreciable decline in Blanchard's cricket frog populations in southwestern Ohio.

Reproduction. Evidence of reproduction was found for twenty species of amphibians in the HCPD survey (Table 19-4). Among salamanders, it is noteworthy that the relatively uncommon species—spotted salamanders, marbled salamanders, northern dusky salamanders, and spring salamanders—all are successfully reproducing in the county. Collins and McDuffie (1968) reported a threatened breeding population of Jefferson salamanders (*Ambystoma jeffersonianum*). Indeed, that population may have been lost. However, our inventories indicate that, with this one exception, the species is doing well in Hamilton County. The only two anurans with no evidence of reproduction were chorus frogs and the northern leopard frogs.

Amphibian Habitat Management Practices in the Hamilton County Park District

The HCPD land management policies are designed for the protection of all wildlife, not just amphibians, but the recent herpetofaunal inventories on lands managed by the park district make the herps better known than any other taxon except birds. Consequently, many land management decisions have been made to protect and promote the well-being of amphibians. In 1996, approximately 5,000 hectares were under park district management. A policy adopted in 1975 declares that "no less than 80 percent of all land under management will remain as undeveloped natural areas." According to HCPD land manager John Klein (personal communication), this stewardship philosophy "will preserve biological communities for future generations of park visitors." The remaining 20 percent is for human recreational facilities, including hiking, bridle and bicycle trails, picnicking, playgrounds, golf, camping, fishing, and motorless boating. Where rare plants and animals exist, land managers make special efforts to protect them.

Copies of herpetological survey reports are distributed to naturalists at each park. The reports become important tools for outdoor education in several regards. In many cases, naturalists are unaware of the herpetofaunal diversity occurring in their park, and the reports serve to educate them about the localities of breeding sites and critical habitat for each species. Information about common species can be included on trail guides and naturalist-guided hikes. Conversely, naturalists can avoid taking park visitors to areas that provide critical habitat for rare or fragile species.

Distributional data from herpetological surveys are added to park district natural features maps to highlight habitat critical to amphibians and reptiles. Unavailable to the public, these maps are used to make land management decisions, and copies are distributed to Operations Department personnel so that the disturbance of populations can be minimized. Trails, roads, buildings, and any other habitat-disturbing structures will not be located near critical habitats marked on these maps. During winter, roads are not treated after snow or ice storms if there is any danger that salt might drain into nearby amphibian breeding streams and/or ponds.

The use of pesticides and fertilizers on park district golf courses, especially those around critical habitats, must be approved by the Land Management Department. Such measures help to protect at least one Hamilton County spring salamander population.

Cave salamanders (*Eurycea lucifuga*) are the only Ohio endangered amphibian documented in any of the Hamilton County parks. Cave salamanders are at the northern edge of their range in southwest Ohio, and Butler County to the north and Adams County in south-central Ohio are the only other counties known in the state with extant populations (Pfingsten and Downs

1989; Pfingsten, Chpt. 25; Juterbock, Chpt. 7, this volume). Most of Ohio's known populations exist on HCPD property (Krusling and Davis 1990; Davis and Krusling 1991, 1993; Rubin 1992; Juterbock 1986). When cave salamanders are discovered in an area that receives moderate to heavy use for hiking and other such activities, the trails are routed around them. Rare species are not pointed out to the public. Instead, the area around their habitat is marked off-limits and left as undisturbed as possible. When endangered species are involved, all departments are willing to cooperate with land managers. Some park district properties are designated as nature preserves, and the entire parcel is off-limits to the public. These measures protect both critical habitats and endangered species.

A herpetological survey of the Shaker Trace Wetlands in the Miami-Whitewater Forest in northwest Hamilton County was conducted in 1992. During the study, a population of marbled salamanders (*Ambystoma opacum*) was discovered in a remnant oak-hickory swamp forest approximately 2 kilometers east of park district property (Davis and McCarty 1993). Only traces of this habitat remain dispersed sporadically among the agricultural fields between the Shaker Trace Wetlands and the remnant swamp forest. Pollen samples taken from the soils in this wetland show that the pre-agricultural vegetation was similar to that where the marbled salamanders were found. Because the 1992 discovery was the first documentation of the species in Hamilton County in over fifty years, plans were made to establish a population at the Shaker Trace Wetlands by relocating larvae into ponds that were specifically excavated for them. Wetland ponds that are large enough to support fish populations are constructed in such a way that they can be drained if fish ever become established and threaten the amphibian larvae. Larvae for reintroduction into the Shaker Trace Wetlands were collected from the newly discovered population. Repatriating amphibians has created controversy and has been debated by several authors (Dodd and Seigel 1991; Burke 1991; Reinert 1991; see also Sexton et al., Chpt. 35, this volume). Careful consideration was given to the collection of animals for repatriation from populations that occurred nearby. This reduced the chance of contamination of the gene pool by distant frogs and salamanders should they move far enough from the Shaker Trace Wetlands to interact with other local populations. The park district is also attempting a similar reintroduction of northern leopard frogs at the Shaker Trace Wetlands using eggs collected from the Gilmore Ponds Interpretive Preserve in neighboring Butler County. Systematic monitoring needs to be continued to determine the success of these repatriations.

The HCPD supports nonconsumptive research to monitor species and encourages the use of its parks as research sites. This philosophy allows the park district to protect a species, such as Blanchard's cricket frogs, before it is in danger of extirpation and to contribute to the protection of the species across its entire range.

Because amphibians serve as good indicator species, investigators have suggested to Land Management Department personnel that the presence or absence of amphibians might be used to gauge the environmental quality of appropriate habitats. These sites should be monitored and maintained. Reasons for the absence of expected species should be investigated. In some cases, new breeding ponds were excavated, and in others, park district environmental specialists conducted water quality monitoring programs to look for answers.

With the completion of the species inventories for amphibians and reptiles, the HCPD now has the opportunity to begin a long-term monitoring program of known populations. Few counties in the Midwest have the historical records, current survey information, and the personnel appropriate to follow up these inventories regarding the biological diversity of amphibians. We recommend that Hamilton County continue to be proactive in amphibian population management.

Summary

The historic status and the recent status of amphibian populations in Hamilton County, Ohio, as determined by surveys conducted by the Hamilton County Park District (HCPD), museum records, and the literature are reviewed. Of the twenty-six-species of amphibians documented from the county over the past century, twenty-one have been recorded since 1980. Recent evidence of successful reproduction exists for twenty of these species. Evidence for population decline of northern leopard frogs (*Rana pipiens*) is discussed in detail. Habitat management and amphibian monitoring policies of the HCPD, including reintroduction strategies, are reviewed.

Acknowledgments

We thank the Hamilton County Parks District for their support of the surveys and J. Klein for providing information on park management. The Cincinnati Museum of Natural History and Thomas More College also provided support for this project. We appreciate the help of J. T. Collins, J. Condit, J. Humphries, T. Matson, S. Menze, S. Moody, and J. Patterson in obtaining museum records. We appreciate a critical reading of the manuscript by W. Bryant.

20

Status of Amphibians in Minnesota

John J. Moriarty

Minnesota currently has twenty species of amphibians, including fourteen anurans and six salamanders. One species, the Blanchard's cricket frog (*Acris crepitans blanchardi*), may be extirpated (Oldfield and Moriarty 1994). Historical information on the abundance and distribution of Minnesota amphibians is limited. Breckenridge (1941, 1944) provided the first reliable information on the distribution of Minnesota amphibians and in doing so provided a baseline for all subsequent studies.

A number of studies were carried out in the 1960s and 1970s on various aspects of anuran natural history. Bellis (1957, 1961) and Fishbeck (1968) studied the ecology and movements of wood frogs (*Rana sylvatica*). Breckenridge and Tester (1961) and Tester and Breckenridge (1964) studied the movements and hibernation of Canadian toads (*Bufo hemiophrys*). Fleming (1976) studied the distribution and ecology of green frogs (*Rana clamitans*). Hedeen (1970, 1971, 1972) examined the ecology and natural history of mink frogs (*Rana septentrionalis*). Merrell (1965, 1970) conducted numerous studies on the ecological genetics of northern leopard frogs (*Rana pipiens*) in Minnesota and wrote "Life History of the Leopard Frog, *Rana pipiens*, in Minnesota" (Merrell 1977). These studies document aspects of the historical abundance and distribution of their respective species. Until recently, there have been no studies designed to monitor these species.

Recent Research

A pilot anuran call survey based on the Wisconsin model (Mossman and Hine 1985; Mossman et al., Chpt. 21, this volume) was started in 1993 (Moriarty 1996). In 1995, his survey consisted of thirty-four routes in twenty-two counties. The Minnesota Department of Natural Resources joined the survey in the spring of 1996 and expanded the number of routes and assisted with the data analysis. The data gathered by the anuran call survey have not indicated any recent major declines during its short history but have expanded the known distribution of wood frogs, bullfrogs (*Rana catesbeiana*), and the gray treefrog complex (*Hyla versicolor/chrysoscelis*).

The Minnesota County Biological Survey (MCBS) has been conducting amphibian surveys since 1988 (Moriarty 1988; Dorff-Hall 1996). The MCBS is not designed for long-term monitoring but rather is intended to conduct a systematic statewide inventory of rare ecosystems and state-listed species. The MCBS has led to a number of important distributional finds, including a discovery of four-toed salamanders (*Hemidactylium scutatum*; Dorff 1995). The MCBS is scheduled to be continued until the year 2008 (Dorff-Hall 1996).

The Minnesota Pollution Control Agency (MPCA) has been involved in the investigation of malformed northern leopard frog populations at three sites in central Minnesota (Helgen 1996; Helgen et al., Chpt. 36, this volume). In the summer of 1995, these populations consisted of a large number of juvenile frogs with multiple or missing appendages. The causes of these malformities are being investigated by the MPCA, the University of Minnesota, and the U.S. Environmental Protection Agency (J. Helgen and R. McKinnell, personal communication).

Recent work on the kandiyohi and burnsi morphs of

the northern leopard frog (Hoppe and McKinnell 1991) has led to an ongoing study examining the decline in numbers of large adult ("lunker") frogs (Hoppe and McKinnell 1996). The decreased abundance of these frogs has raised the concerns of a number of herpetologists.

Current Status

Population information on species other than those listed above is limited. The following comments are summarized from Coffin and Pfannmuller (1988) and Oldfield and Moriarty (1994) unless otherwise cited.

Salamanders

Blue-spotted salamanders (*Ambystoma laterale*) are widespread in northeastern Minnesota, and populations appear stable. The isolated populations in the southern half of the state are restricted to remnant maple-basswood forests and are threatened by additional habitat fragmentation due to urbanization and agriculture.

Eastern tiger salamanders (*Ambystoma tigrinum tigrinum*) are widespread and are the state's most common salamander. Adult and larval tiger salamanders are used by the bait and biological supply trade (Konrad 1996), but there are no data available on the numbers taken. Populations have declined from the past, when people regularly reported finding them in window wells of houses in suburban areas.

Mudpuppies (*Necturus maculosus maculosus*) are found in the larger rivers and associated lakes in Minnesota. They are absent from the Mississippi River drainage north of Saint Anthony Falls (Minneapolis). Their status is unknown, but large quantities are being taken in the Alexandria area for the biological supply trade (Konrad 1996).

Central newts (*Notophthalmus viridescens louisianensis*) are uncommon salamanders in Minnesota. There is no population information on this species. There remains an isolated population in the Twin Cities metropolitan area (Lake Minnetonka), which was recently rediscovered (J. LeClere, personal communication).

Four-toed salamanders have been only recently discovered in Minnesota (Dorff 1995). This salamander is currently only known from several sites in the Chippewa National Forest (J. LeClere, personal communication). Baker (1996) has recommended that it be listed as a special concern species until more can be learned about its Minnesota distribution and habitats.

Redback salamanders (*Plethodon cinereus*) are found in the northeastern portion of Minnesota. They appear to be widespread and stable in that area, but within the state no specific population studies have been performed.

Anurans

American toads (*Bufo americanus americanus*) are found throughout Minnesota and are one of the most common anurans encountered. Populations seem stable. Large choruses are still found in agricultural and suburban areas.

Canadian toads are restricted to the western third of the state and are most common in the northwest region of the state. There have been no data published on this species in the last twenty years, but the sites reported by Breckenridge and Tester (1961) are still extant and should be resurveyed.

Great Plains toads (*Bufo cognatus*) are found in the western counties of Minnesota. There has been little work done on this species in the last twenty years. The status of their populations is unknown.

Blanchard's cricket frogs probably have been extirpated from Minnesota. Recent surveys (Whitford 1991; C. Dorff-Hall, personal communication) have not located calling males. While Baker (1996) has proposed elevating the state status of this species from special concern to endangered, this gesture probably comes too late to save Minnesota populations.

Cope's gray treefrogs (*Hyla chrysoscelis*) are widespread in Minnesota. Their true range is still confused with that of eastern gray treefrogs (*Hyla versicolor*). They are commonly heard during the anuran call surveys.

Eastern gray treefrogs are widespread in Minnesota, although naturally uncommon in the prairie regions of the state. They are common throughout the remainder of the state, and populations appear to be stable.

Northern spring peepers (*Pseudacris crucifer crucifer*) are naturally restricted to the forested regions of the state. Populations in the Twin Cities area have gone through severe declines due to urbanization, but populations appear to be stable in less-affected forested regions.

Minnesota contains both western and boreal chorus frogs (*Pseudacris triseriata triseriata* and *P. t. maculata*, respectively). They remain the most common frog in most areas. Wisconsin's frog and toad survey has shown a long-term decline (M. Mossman, personal communication; Mossman et al. Chpt. 21, this volume).

Bullfrogs have been expanding their range in Minnesota through in-state introductions and range expansions of introduced populations in Iowa and Wisconsin. A proposed change in the state threatened and endangered species list would delist the species (Baker 1996). To date, bullfrogs have not been perceived to be a threat to other anurans, but studies of bullfrog impacts on aquatic ecosystems may change this perspective in the future (Lannoo 1996a).

Green frogs are found throughout the eastern half of Minnesota. There have not been any in-depth surveys in the past twenty years, but green frogs are still found at many sites in the Twin Cities metropolitan region. It appears that populations unaffected by urbanization are stable.

Pickerel frogs (*Rana palustris*) are restricted to the southeastern corner of Minnesota. Recent surveys have discovered a number of new localities (C. Dorff-Hall, personal communication). Pickerel frogs are currently listed as a species of special concern but have been recommended for delisting because populations appear to be stable and more widespread than previously thought (Baker 1996).

Northern leopard frogs are widespread and are the best-known frog in Minnesota. They have been heavily collected for fish bait and for the biological supply trade (Konrad 1996). There is little regulation on the collection of northern leopard frogs in Minnesota. Populations crashed in 1973, which halted the commercial collection for uses other than bait from 1974 until 1987. Recent harvest records report collections of 1,000 to 2,000 pounds per year, compared to reports in the early 1970s that were in the 100,000-pound-per-year range (Tester 1995). Northern leopard frog populations have declined substantially from the past and are currently probably stable or still declining.

Mink frogs are found in northeastern Minnesota. There has been no information collected on the status of this species in the last decade, but populations appear to be stable.

Wood frog populations also appear to be stable. In fact, the range of this species appears to be expanding west into the prairie region (D. Hoppe, personal communication). The biggest threat to this species is forest fragmentation in developing areas.

Future Needs

Current monitoring programs need to be expanded and extended indefinitely. The Minnesota Anuran Call Survey will be increased to 100 routes statewide and modified to adjust for seasonal differences between southern and northern Minnesota.

A state-funded project to develop biological assessment criteria for wetland health was initiated at the University of Minnesota in 1996. This study uses the status of larval amphibian communities as one of the criteria (S. Galatowitsch and J. Tester, personal communication).

Additional surveys and fieldwork will need to be conducted on rare species in Minnesota. The MCBS will be conducting surveys, but its surveys will be restricted to designated counties. The Blanchard's cricket frog localities need to be resurveyed, especially in southwestern Minnesota. The distribution and habitat of the recently discovered four-toed salamander will need to be studied and documented.

Summary

There have been no well-documented studies on population changes in Minnesota's twenty species of amphibians. There have been good ecological studies on some anuran species, but long-term data are lacking. Declines in several species have been noted, including the probable extirpation of Blanchard's cricket frogs (*Acris crepitans blanchardi*). A number of monitoring studies have been initiated to assess the status and changes of Minnesota's amphibian populations.

Acknowledgments

I thank Madeleine Linck and Jo Anne Wetherell-Moriarty for their comments on an earlier version of this chapter.

21

Monitoring Long-term Trends in Wisconsin Frog and Toad Populations

Michael J. Mossman, Lisa M. Hartman, Robert Hay, John R. Sauer, and Brian J. Dhuey

Recent, possibly widespread declines in amphibian populations (Blaustein and Wake 1990) are disturbing because of the important roles of amphibians in many ecosystems. Moreover, their complex life cycles, insectivorous habits, permeable skin, and sensitivity to water chemistry in the egg and larval stages probably make them good bioindicators of environmental stress. There is little geographic or taxonomic pattern to the reported declines, some of which are from sites free from local anthropogenic disturbance. Causative factors are usually unknown and may be various, including habitat destruction, chemical contamination, introduction of predators, global climatic changes, acidic precipitation, or synergistic combinations of these factors (Blaustein and Wake 1990; Phillips 1990; Wyman 1990). Recent discoveries of malformed anurans, including at least seven species in fourteen Wisconsin counties (Dubois 1996), have heightened concern over amphibian populations.

Determining the nature, extent, and causes of amphibian population declines is hampered by a dearth of long-term population data. In fact, many reported declines have been based on local, short-term, or anecdotal evidence and may not reflect important or widespread problems. There is clearly a need for a coordinated system of research and monitoring that will determine and characterize significant population trends and identify causes (Blaustein and Wake 1990; Pechmann et al. 1991). This includes long-term population monitoring for a large number of species over wide areas that will identify changes in geographic ranges and distinguish regional and long-term trends from those that are local or short-term. Such a monitoring system could alert researchers and managers to species and regions in need of attention and suggest patterns or causes of declines. The North American Amphibian Monitoring Program (NAAMP) was initiated in 1994 (Mac 1996; NAAMP 1996) to investigate monitoring needs and methodologies and to suggest standards. For anurans, which advertise their presence during the breeding season with species-specific vocalizations, volunteer-based auditory surveys have been recommended by the NAAMP as the best monitoring method for most of the continent. Suggested standards for these surveys are still being modified, but the basic methodology is based on the long-running Wisconsin Frog and Toad Survey (WFTS).

The WFTS was initiated in 1981 in response to known and suspected declines in several frog species, especially bullfrogs (*Rana catesbeiana*), northern leopard frogs (*Rana pipiens*), pickerel frogs (*Rana palustris*), and Blanchard's cricket frogs (*Acris crepitans blanchardi*). Annual statewide coverage began in 1984. The primary purpose of the WFTS is to determine the status, distribution, and long-term population trends of the state's twelve species. Its secondary purpose is educational. In this chapter, we describe the WFTS and its analytical methods, sample adequacy, and results. We discuss logistical considerations for initiating and maintaining such a program, some of its values and limitations, and possible modifications.

Methods and Study Area

Survey Methodology

The WFTS, begun in 1981 by Ruth Hine of the Wisconsin Department of Natural Resources (WDNR), was based on the initial recommendations and audio instructional tape of Jansen and Anderson (1981). After three years of experimenting and gathering phenological data with the help and comments of several volunteers, Mossman and Hine (1984) standardized the criteria and procedures for the survey. The survey was patterned after the successful North American Breeding Bird Survey (BBS) (Robbins et al. 1986; Peterjohn et al. 1994) and relies on cooperators identifying each of the state's twelve anuran species by their characteristic breeding calls. Cooperators were enlisted through word of mouth, notices in newsletters and magazines, presentations at nature centers and meetings, and contact with reliable observers from other cooperative programs, such as the statewide black tern survey and the natural areas breeding bird survey. In subsequent years, cooperators were added from various sources, and beginning in 1992 WDNR wildlife managers routinely ran surveys or enlisted new cooperators. Initially, routes were established wherever cooperators were available, although poorly sampled areas of the state were increasingly targeted. In the early 1990s, WDNR biologists set a goal with the WFTS of establishing at least two routes in each county. Our current goal is to stratify coverage geographically according to ecoregions and sections established by the U.S. Forest Service (USFS).

By 1995, the survey included approximately 120 permanent roadside routes throughout the state. Each route comprises ten listening stations selected subjectively by a volunteer observer to be within hearing distance of wetlands that represent the range of local anuran breeding habitats, such as ephemeral ponds, lakes, meadows, marshes, and wooded swamps. Stations were located far enough apart that individual frogs could not be heard from more than one station. Depending on the local topography and vegetation characteristics, interstation distances were as close as about 400 meters, but were generally greater, usually on the order of 0.8 to 3 kilometers. Routes were run after sunset under favorable conditions (i.e., relatively warm air temperature, wind less than 13 kilometers, and preferably humid or after recent rains). Most routes were 15 to 40 kilometers long and took two to three hours to complete. At each station the observer listened for five minutes (or up to ten minutes if necessary due to noise interference) and recorded one of the following call index values for each species heard:

1 = individuals can be counted; there is space between calls
2 = calls of individuals are distinguishable, but some calls overlap
3 = full chorus; calls are constant, continuous, and overlapping

Because the annual calling period of each species is usually short and is different from the calling periods of other species, cooperators were asked to run each route a total of three times every year, once each during the following sampling periods:

Early spring = 8–30 April and when pond temperatures have reached 10°C
Late spring = 20 May–5 June and when pond temperatures have reached 15.5°C
Summer = 1–15 July and when pond temperatures have reached 21°C

Water temperatures were recorded where feasible and where they appeared to represent the conditions in which frogs call. Air temperature, wind speed (Beaufort scale), and sky condition were recorded at the beginning and end of each route. Cooperators were asked to comment on such things as changes in wetland conditions and problems with background noise and were encouraged to invite along at least one other reliable observer who could run the survey alone if the primary cooperator was unable to do so at some future time.

To avoid overlap with other routes, when a new route was established we sent the interested cooperator county maps of the area indicating the locations of previously established stations. We suggested that the cooperator run eleven or twelve stations during the first year and then select as permanent stations the ten with the least noise interference or access limitations—problems that were not always initially apparent. The cooperator then returned a county road map with the stations indicated, and we sent back photocopies of the appropriate 7.5' topographic maps on which to mark the exact locations. These photocopies were returned to us along with narrative and legal descriptions of each station location and a general description of nearby wetlands. We checked these for accuracy and clarity and made three clear sets of the route description and of the appropriate topographic and county maps with the station locations marked on them. New cooperators were asked to purchase (at cost) a copy of Jansen and Anderson's (1981) instructional audio cassette tape of anuran breeding calls from the Madison Audubon Society. There were no formal training sessions. People interested in initiating a new route were usually asked first to go along on a previously established route with an experienced cooperator.

Every year in late March we sent each cooperator the appropriate route description and a set of topographic and county route maps, along with standard instructions and information on the natural history, distribution, and identification of each species (including range dot maps from Vogt 1981); two data sheets (Fig. 21-1); a form letter that included news on the survey and other amphibian matters (e.g., discussing a common problem that cooperators had noted or that we had in interpreting data, with recommended solutions); a report on coverage and trends through the previous year (sometimes this was not sent until later in the year); a self-addressed, stamped return envelope; and often photocopies of recent popular or semipopular articles on amphibians. Sometimes we included a personal note or made contact via telephone or e-mail in response to a cooperator's question or problem. The instructional materials, route maps and descriptions, and a completed data sheet were returned to us at the end of the season. A postcard was sent to all cooperators in the fall as a reminder to return data. For a more complete description of the survey methods and sample instructional materials and route description, see Mossman and Hine (1984).

Returned data were checked for accuracy and entered into an SAS computer databank. Records of state-endangered Blanchard's cricket frogs were accepted only with documentation, such as photographs, recordings, or specimens, and documentation was requested for records that were extralimital according to Vogt's (1981) maps. Dubious records or those from far outside the recommended survey periods and temperature ranges were flagged and not used in most analyses; during seasons with a particularly early or late phenology, and based on observer comments, some exceptions were made. In fact, in 1989 we lengthened the first survey period, shifting the starting date from 15 April to 8 April (and allowing even earlier surveys when necessary), because several observers in southern counties believed they were missing wood frogs (*Rana sylvatica*) during years when spring arrived early. For most of the dubious records, we tried to contact the observer to verify that a mistake was not made in entering data onto the data sheet, to ask for verification for that or future records of the same species, or to encourage the cooperator to take special care in recording the species in the future.

All routes are considered permanent. Changes have been allowed only during the first few years of a route's history (in which case the earlier years' data were not used in trend analyses) or on rare occasions when an insurmountable access problem developed or background noise at a particular station increased to the point that results were not comparable with earlier years. These cases were resolved by one of three options: the cooperator replaced the station with another one as similar as possible to the original, the route was abandoned, or the route was changed without regard to similarity to the original and treated as a new route.

During the first few years of the WFTS, we used survey data to examine geographic distributions and to investigate the relationships among call index values, water and air temperatures, and dates. To help with the latter issue, several cooperators conducted surveys at frequent (one-to-ten-day) intervals throughout one or more seasons and years at a single station close to their home. Cooperator Ron Eckstein did this at one site every year during 1983 through 1996. We include his data for 1996 (although we report on trend analysis only through 1995) because phenologically it was instructive as an extremely late year.

Analysis

We used several regression techniques to measure population trends for individual species. Analyses from four techniques are reported here. Three of these techniques were developed recently with the support of the U.S. Geological Survey's Biological Research Division (BRD; formerly known as the National Biological Service), based on their procedures for determining trend "estimating equations" for BBS data (Link and Sauer 1994). In these techniques, a particular route was considered completed for a particular species in a particular year only if it was run during the seasonal sampling period that corresponded to the species' peak calling period (Table 21-1). That is, data from the early spring sampling period were used only for wood frogs, northern spring peepers (*Pseudacris crucifer crucifer*), western and boreal chorus frogs (*Pseudacris triseriata triseriata* and *P. t. maculata*, respectively), leopard frogs, and pickerel frogs. If this was the only period in which a particular route was run during a particular year, then the data were used for computing only these trends. Likewise, data from the late spring period were used to calculate trends for American toads (*Bufo americanus americanus*) and both species of treefrogs (eastern [*Hyla versicolor*] and Cope's [*Hyla chrysoscelis*]), and data from the sum-

WISCONSIN FROG AND TOAD SURVEY -- Field Data Sheet
Bureau of Endangered Resources
Department of Natural Resources
Box 7921, Madison, WI 53707

Observer name(s), RUN 1 ____________
(Add address and phone on back.) RUN 2 ____________
RUN 3 ____________

Route No. ______
Year ______
County ______

INSTRUCTIONS: Use this form for new or established survey routes. Each route consists of 10 listening sites, and is repeated 3 times during the breeding season, according to the minimum water temperatures and approximate range of dates given below for each survey period. Run surveys after dark, when wind velocity is less than 8 mph. Listen 5-10 minutes at each site and record a call index value of 1,2, or 3 (see below) for each species calling. See back of sheet for wind and sky codes and additional comments. Return to above address by 15 August.

FIRST RUN Water 50°F; 15-30 April
BEGIN: Date / Time: / Wind: Sky: / Air temp. (F): END: Time: / Wind: Sky: / Air temp. (F):

SITE NAME	Site Number	Water Temp (F)	Wood frog	Chorus frog	Spring peeper	Leopard frog	Pickerel frog	Am. toad	E. gray tree frog	C. gray tree frog	Cricket frog	Mink frog	Green frog	Bullfrog
1.	1.													
2.	2.													
3.	3.													
4.	4.													
5.	5.													
6.	6.													
7.	7.													
8.	8.													
9.	9.													
10.	10.													
For office use only — Mean														
For office use only — Freq.														

SECOND RUN Water 60°F; 20 May - 5 June
BEGIN: Date / Time: / Wind: Sky: / Air temp. (F): END: Time: / Wind: Sky: / Air temp. (F):

SITE NAME	Site Number	Water Temp (F)	Wood frog	Chorus frog	Spring peeper	Leopard frog	Pickerel frog	Am. toad	E. gray tree frog	C. gray tree frog	Cricket frog	Mink frog	Green frog	Bullfrog
1.	1.													
2.	2.													
3.	3.													
4.	4.													
5.	5.													
6.	6.													
7.	7.													
8.	8.													
9.	9.													
10.	10.													
For office use only — Mean														
For office use only — Freq.														

THIRD RUN Water 70°F; 1-15 July
BEGIN: Date / Time: / Wind: Sky: / Air temp. (F): END: Time: / Wind: Sky: / Air temp. (F):

SITE NAME	Site Number	Water Temp (F)	Wood frog	Chorus frog	Spring peeper	Leopard frog	Pickerel frog	Am. toad	E. gray tree frog	C. gray tree frog	Cricket frog	Mink frog	Green frog	Bullfrog
1.	1.													
2.	2.													
3.	3.													
4.	4.													
5.	5.													
6.	6.													
7.	7.													
8.	8.													
9.	9.													
10.	10.													
For office use only — Mean														
For office use only — Freq.														

*The call index is a rough estimate of the numbers of calling males of a particular species, according to the following index values:

1 Individuals can be counted; there is space between calls.

2 Calls of individuals can be distinguished but there is some overlapping of calls (intermediate between "1," and "3").

3 Full chorus. Calls are constant, continuous and overlapping.

Figure 21-1. Data sheet for Wisconsin Frog and Toad Survey.

Table 21-1. Sampling periods required for each species in Wisconsin Frog and Toad Survey analyses. I = early spring, II = late spring, III = summer.

Species	Trend Analysis Technique Route Regressions (single period)	 Percent Occurrence (combined period)
Wood frog (*Rana sylvatica*)	I	I
Chorus frog (*Pseudacris triseriata*)	I	I and II
Northern spring peeper (*Pseudacris crucifer crucifer*)	I	I and II
Northern leopard frog (*Rana pipiens*)	I	I and II
Pickerel frog (*Rana palustris*)	I	I and II
American toad (*Bufo americanus americanus*)	II	II
Eastern gray treefrog (*Hyla versicolor*)	II	II
Cope's gray treefrog (*Hyla chrysoscelis*)	II	II
Blanchard's cricket frog (*Acris crepitans blanchardi*)	III	II and III
Mink frog (*Rana septentrionalis*)	III	III
Green frog (*Rana clamitans melanota*)	III	III
Bullfrog (*Rana catesbeiana*)	III	III

mer period were used for Blanchard's cricket frogs, mink frogs (*Rana septentrionalis*), green frogs (*Rana clamitans melanota*), and bullfrogs. For each route an index to abundance was computed for each species in each year. In the route frequency regression technique, the number of stations of occurrence was added (range = 0 to 10). The route index regression technique summed the index values from each station (range = 0 to 30). In the route adjusted-index regression technique, we arbitrarily assigned to each call index value a number that we believed better estimated the relative abundance of animals represented by that value (call index 1 equals three calling males, call index 2 equals twenty-five calling males, call index 3 equals fifty calling males); these values were then summed for each route as in the preceding technique (range = 0 to 500).

Trends for each route were then computed by using estimating equations, regressing the appropriate dependent variable (frequency, summed index values, or summed adjusted index values) on year, and these trends were averaged for all routes in each ecoregion, expressed as mean annual percent change for that ecoregion. Before averaging, however, the trend for each species on each route was weighted according to the relative abundance of the species on that route (routes with a high average frequency of occurrence or high mean index value contributed more to the estimated ecoregional trend than did routes in which the species was less common) and an estimate of the variance in the trend estimate (routes in which the trend was precisely estimated contributed more than routes in which the trend was imprecise). The mean trend for each ecoregion was then weighted according to the area of that ecoregion, and these weighted means were averaged to produce a standard trend (Geissler and Sauer 1990).

The fourth technique, percent occurrence, was used early in the WFTS program, and although trends are calculated by a much less sophisticated manner than in the route regression techniques, the data selection procedure was more complicated. Even though each species' calling period usually peaks within one of the three sampling periods, some species are also frequently recorded in another period. Thus, a particular species may be more detectable at individual ponds in either period in a given year; this is presumably because of annual and geographic variations in phenological progression, differences in water temperatures between different ponds (even within a given route), and the effects of different environmental conditions on different survey nights. A species whose main calling period often spans two survey periods is treated as follows for each route in each year: the call index at each of the ten stations is compared between the two periods ("combined period" data, Table 21-1), and the largest value is selected for analysis. Data are not used when only one of the required survey periods was sampled. In other techniques of analysis (not described here), these maximum station-index values were used to calculate trends, but in the percent occurrence technique, these are reduced to presence or absence for each station, and the stations of presence are summed and expressed as a percentage of all stations surveyed statewide that year. These annual percentages are regressed on year, and the slope is compared to zero by using a t-test. Trends are expressed as mean annual change in percent occurrence.

We also ran the three route regression analyses on combined-period data.

A power analysis was used to measure the statistical ability of the WFTS to detect population trends at various levels of certainty over various time periods (Mossman et al. 1996). Power analyses consider variables such as number of routes, counts per route, count variance, duration of monitoring, and interval between monitoring events to evaluate the statistical ability (power) of a monitoring program to detect trends in species abundance, given that a trend actually occurs. A power level of 75 percent, for example, indicates that if a nonzero trend actually exists, the trend analysis is expected to detect this trend in at least 75 percent of cases (i.e., a 25 percent chance of committing a type II error but not rejecting a false null hypothesis). Power depends on the alpha level of the test, which sets the probability of falsely rejecting a null hypothesis. An alpha level of $p < 0.1$ means that when the analysis detects a nonzero trend, it will be associated with true zero trend (type I error) about 10 percent of the time. In our power analyses we used eleven years of data (1984 to 1995) and the statistical methodology described by Sauer (1996). That is, given the variability in the WFTS data set for a particular species, we estimated how many routes would be needed to detect, for example, a mean annual change of 3 percent over a period of ten years or a mean annual change of 1 percent over a twenty-year period. The analysis was run on many combinations of precision parameters, including 1, 2, 3, and 5 percent annual mean changes, ten-year and twenty-year periods, and various levels of power and alpha.

To compare population trends with drought conditions that might affect habitat availability or quality, we used the Palmer Drought Severity Index—a monthly index based on soils and on current and previous precipitation and temperatures (Palmer 1965). Data for the nine Wisconsin climatological regions were acquired from the state climatologist.

In 1987, we mailed cooperators a questionnaire requesting information on occupation, age, experience with amphibians prior to joining the WFTS, how they learned about the WFTS, why they joined the WFTS, what has maintained their interest, and comments on techniques, data forms, instructional materials, reports, coordination, and any other topics.

Ecoregions

We stratified our data and report our results according to the six ecoregional sections found in Wisconsin (McNab and Avers 1994; Keys et al. 1995) and additionally separated the Central Sands from the remainder of southeastern Wisconsin. For brevity, we called these "regions" and have abbreviated their names (Fig. 21-2; Table 21-2).

The Northwest Forest region mostly comprises extinct glacial lake beds with sandy or peaty soils and is dominated by pine and oak barrens and woods, some more mesic forest, and relatively nonintensive agriculture. This region has numerous lakes, streams, marshes, and bogs. The large North-central Forest region is mostly forested with northern hardwoods, although nonintensive agricultural land is scattered and more intensive agriculture dominates some southern parts. Much of this region is on Precambrian shield overlain by morainal deposits and sandy outwash; lakes and bogs are common. The Eastern Forest region was historically dominated by mesic maple, beech, and pine forests, with

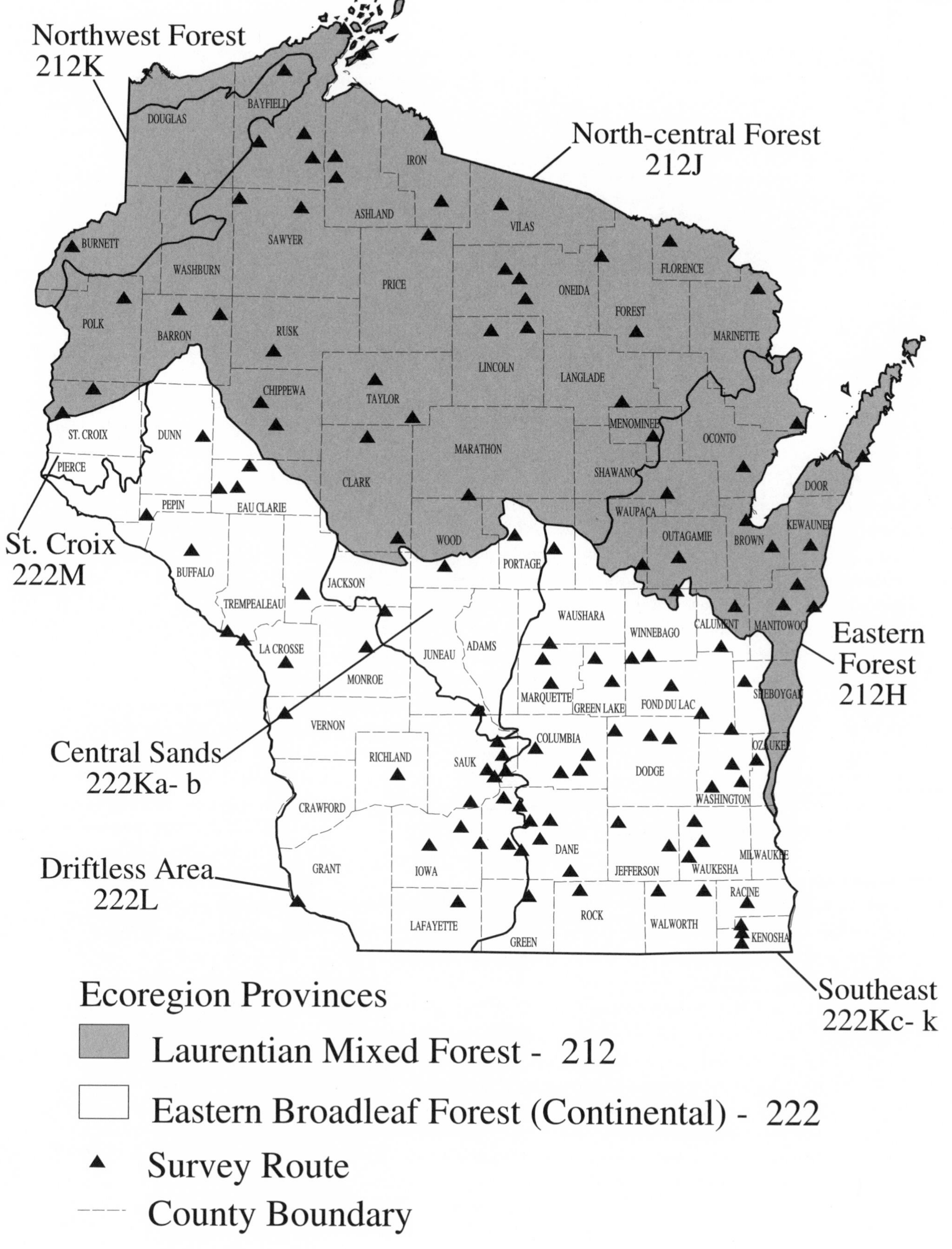

Figure 21-2. Distribution of Wisconsin Frog and Toad Survey routes.

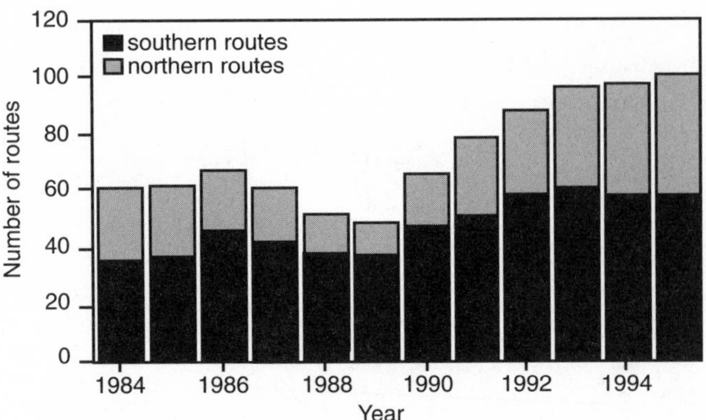

Figure 21-3. Number of Wisconsin Frog and Toad Survey routes run annually, 1984–1995.

substantial cedar swamps. Large marshes were present along the west shore of Green Bay. Forest stands are now concentrated west of Green Bay and are scattered among agricultural fields on the Door County peninsula and southward. Some marshes remain, the largest along the west shore of Green Bay. The area along the Fox River leading into Green Bay is highly industrialized, and the southern lobe of the region is densely populated.

The Central Sands represent the bed of extinct Glacial Lake Wisconsin and its associated uplands. This region includes extensive natural and restored marshes, sedge meadows, lowland hardwoods, and conifer bogs, as well as commercial cranberry operations, irrigated cropland and pasture, and large tracts of pine and oak forest, aspen, and pine plantations. The pre-Euro-American settlement landscape of the Southeast region was primarily oak savanna with some major prairies, oak woodland, and wetland complexes. It is now mostly agricultural with small scattered woodlots and some fairly extensive marshes. Urbanization is spreading from the major metropolitan areas of Milwaukee and Madison.

The hilly Driftless Area, with its characteristic sandstone and dolomite exposures, was missed by the last Pleistocene glaciers. It contains mostly small farms and ridgeside oak and maple woods. Small, wet meadows are occasionally associated with the many spring-fed "coulee" streams. Marshes and lowland hardwoods are concentrated along the Mississippi River floodplain and the several large rivers that feed the Mississippi. Pasture is more common here than elsewhere, especially in stream bottoms and in some of the former prairies and oak savannas south of the Wisconsin River. No routes occurred in the St. Croix region, which is mixed agriculture and woodlots, with scattered ponds and marshes.

Results

Coverage

During the experimental period of 1981 to 1983, 65 routes were run at least once, with five to fifteen stations per route. Most were run multiple years, and 21 of these remained as permanent ten-station routes. Thus, although we consider 1984 as the first year of the survey for data analysis, some routes began as early as 1981. During 1984 to 1995, the annual number of routes surveyed (during at least one of the three periods) ranged from 58 to 100 (Fig. 21-3). Fluctuations in coverage

Table 21-2. Geographic distribution of Wisconsin Frog and Toad Survey routes run at least twice during 1984–1995

Code	Ecoregion Section Description (with abbreviation)	No. Routes	Area (km^2)	Km^2/ Route
212K	West Superior Mixed Forest (Northwest Forest)	3	6,361	2,120
212J	South Superior Mixed Forest (North-central Forest)	37	58,380	1,578
212H	North Great Lakes Mixed Forest (Eastern Forest)	14	13,515	965
222M	Minnesota Morainal Oak Forest (St. Croix)	0	2,039	—
222L	North-central Driftless Broadleaf Forest (Driftless Area)	27	30,427	1,127
222Ka–b	Southwest Great Lakes Broadleaf Forest–Central Wis. Sands (Central Sands)	3	6,941	2,314
222Kc–k	Southwest Great Lakes Broadleaf Forest–Glaciated (Southeast)	38	27,222	716
	Total (or mean)	122	144,885	(1,188)

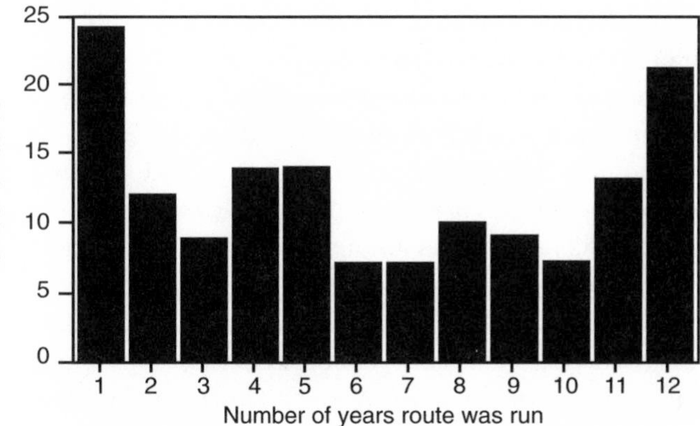

Figure 21-4. Number of years that Wisconsin Frog and Toad Survey routes were run, 1984–1995.

reflect changes in staff effort and agency support, which was greatest during 1981 to 1985, then declined and subsequently recovered as a staff herpetologist (R.H.) was hired, WDNR managers assumed more responsibility for ensuring regional coverage, and a growing concern for declining amphibian populations spurred public interest. One hundred forty-seven routes were run at least once; 122 were run at least twice and thus contributed data to the route regression trend analyses. Sixty-seven routes were surveyed in seven or more years, and 21 were surveyed all twelve years (Fig. 21-4). The geographic distribution of routes run at least twice is summarized in Figure 21-2 and Table 21-2. Routes were not well stratified geographically because volunteers were easiest to enlist around Madison and were especially hard to obtain in the least-populated areas of the state. In particular, the Southeast and Eastern Forest regions were sampled at roughly two to three times the intensity of other regions of the state. Routes in the Driftless Area were concentrated in Dane and Sauk Counties, and large areas of the north were not sampled. New routes were added annually, especially after 1989 in undersampled counties; coverage in the northern half of the state improved from a low of 13 routes in 1989 (26 percent of all routes run that year) to a maximum of 43 (43 percent of the routes) in 1995 (Fig. 21-3). A few routes became inactive when cooperators moved or dropped out of the program and replacements could not be found. Several additional routes—not counted here—were initiated but never completed and provided no data for analysis.

Cooperator Involvement and Comments

Hundreds of people conducted WFTS routes as either primary or secondary observers, several of them for twelve or more years. Thirty-nine cooperators returned questionnaires in 1987. Their occupations ranged widely: professional biologists and naturalists (fourteen), homemakers (six), university professors, a medical doctor, a farmer, an engineer, a librarian, a janitor, a retired accountant, and others. Most (twenty) were between thirty-one and forty years old, with only two younger; three were over age sixty-five. The current age distribution is probably broader, as most of these cooperators are still running surveys and many more have been added. Respondents learned about the WFTS from many sources, including personal contact with WDNR/WFTS staff (sixteen), presentations by WDNR/WFTS staff at professional meetings or naturalist programs (five), other cooperators (three), formal naturalist training programs, other WDNR volunteer surveys, public radio programs, and newsletters and magazines of groups such as the Wisconsin Phenological Society, Wisconsin Wetlands Association, Nature Conservancy, Sierra Club, and WDNR. The range of prior experience with amphibians was wide: most cooperators said they had none, many had minimal experience (e.g., "just my own interest with the frog pond on our land" or "fish bait"), and a few were veterans (e.g., professional field naturalists or "graduate-level herpetology class and collecting experience. Also lots of frogging when I was young.").

Respondent comments on WFTS methodology and logistics conformed to those made over the years in notes, in conversations, and on completed data sheets returned to WFTS staff. The most consistent and important of these were that: (1) materials need to be sent out by mid-March at the latest—well in advance of the breeding season, (2) cooperators need annual reports on findings, and (3) the ranges of acceptable dates and water temperatures, though essential as guidelines, need to be flexible enough to accommodate years with extreme phenologies. As a result of such correspondence and more years' experience with the WFTS, we increased our staffing to provide better reports and more timely mailings to cooperators, extended the beginning date of the first calling period a week, and became slightly less strict about the dates of formal survey periods in unusual years.

Recording water temperatures was time-consuming for some cooperators. These measurements are useful to both the cooperator and WFTS staff in evaluating the count data but need be made only where accessible water appears representative of that in which frogs or toads are breeding.

Our request for verification of extralimital records

met with some resistance and general disregard, because field recordings are bothersome to most volunteers and are often difficult to make with handheld tape recorders and because most of the species' distribution maps provided in the instructional materials were incomplete, resulting in cooperators being asked to document species that may be common in their area. Some cooperators were offended that they were "disbelieved" by WFTS staff, when in fact it was not usually a matter of our belief but one of strengthening the survey's scientific validity. We maintained the requirement that cricket frog records be documented and received some tape recordings.

We did not estimate the frequency of species misidentifications; however, our experience and repeated correspondence with cooperators suggest that they were rare, probably fewer than 2 percent of all accepted records. Early in the WFTS, considerable time was spent corresponding with cooperators to help them with identifications and noting species that merited special attention. It is noteworthy that most of the cooperators who ran surveys during the first year of the survey (1984) already had one to three years' experience from the preceding experimental years. In more recent years, less time was spent with correspondence, but cooperators were still contacted to document unusual or dubious records. In many cases, the observer made no subsequent reports of the species after being contacted by us—we presume this is because of increased attention to species identification rather than simply wanting to avoid the issue of documentation. The most likely species to be mistaken were leopard frogs versus pickerel frogs; eastern gray treefrogs versus Cope's gray treefrogs; Blanchard's cricket frogs versus Virginia rails (all early spring records of Blanchard's cricket frogs were probably the call of this rail). Cooperators also asked for training sessions, especially to help distinguish difficult calls, to help standardize use of the call index, and to meet other cooperators. Some asked for names of cooperators or knowledgeable people in their region to help them verify uncertain calls. We believe that good continuity was maintained over time and between routes by encouraging new volunteers to accompany experienced surveyors prior to becoming primary observers responsible for their own routes and by asking each primary observer to enlist at least one alternate who knows the route and methodology. We and local WDNR wildlife managers helped to enlist alternates in some cases but were unsuccessful in others. Cooperators were generally satisfied with the instructional tape, printed materials, and data form, and most indicated confidence in being able to identify all species in their area.

Several other problems occurred in the WFTS, which anyone initiating such a survey should be prepared to encounter. One involves producing clear and accurate route descriptions and maps. Every new route that was run took considerable staff time and effort to: verify that stations did not overlap others; find, photocopy and send topographic maps; verify that descriptions and maps corresponded; and compose master copies and make three clean copies of each. This often involved additional correspondence with the cooperator. In some cases, adequate descriptions took years to acquire because cooperators were unfamiliar with topographic maps or did not understand the detail necessary to ensure that someone unfamiliar with the route or area could run it correctly, perhaps far in the future, based only on these materials; precise locations are also necessary for our current effort to analyze habitat relationships. Our persistence on these matters probably contributed to at least one cooperator quitting. Another problem occurred when cooperators did not return route descriptions and maps, although this was alleviated somewhat by having multiple central copies (as long as they lasted). Another occurred when, on rare occasions, a cooperator did not visit a station or run the entire route because he or she "knew" that no frogs were calling (e.g., because wetlands had dried up from drought); these negative data would obviously be important. In some cases a cooperator tried to replace a station with one that "has more frogs."

In addition to these experiences were the problems inherent in a program that has generally been understaffed: misplaced materials, inability to respond to all cooperator questions and concerns or to check returned data and route descriptions carefully, and difficulty producing meaningful and timely reports. During 1986 to 1989, staff time was reduced. The remaining time was necessary just to run the program and maintain quality control, nearly to the exclusion of data summary and analysis, or in attempts to enlist new cooperators. The lack of feedback frustrated many cooperators, and although some dropped out temporarily or permanently, most persevered. The program has depended on the patience and perennial communication of both the staff and the cooperators.

Cooperators volunteered for the WFTS for many reasons, the most commonly stated being to contribute to the conservation of amphibians, learn more about frogs and toads, and have a reason to get outside and experience the night. Although some cooperators were apprehensive about being out alone at night, nearly all appeared to enjoy the survey. They said it helped them appreciate not just the anurans they were recording but also the many other night creatures they heard or saw. It helped them enjoy the progression of spring and to learn about the seasonal and longer-term changes in wetlands. For many it was a family event or a chance to expose schoolchildren, Scouts, or friends to nature at night. Some cooperators disseminated instructional materials to schools and elsewhere. Among responses to the questionnaire were:

> With only a dozen calls, listening for frogs and determining species is easily learned. It gives me a good opportunity and impetus to get out and see/listen to familiar wetlands—it's fascinating how they change throughout the season. At times, "curiosity seekers" accompany me—people who are curious to learn and be closer to understanding a little more about the workings of nature. This gives me a good opportunity to share what I know . . . this is a wonderful way to incorporate "laypeople" into DNR work. In addition to monitoring frog species, any observers or interested folk get a better perspective of the variety of life in wetlands. Not to mention they recognize the existence of wetlands "in their own backyard" and the forces that affect them.

> It's a blast: stars overhead, fireflies in the wetlands, and anurans calling everywhere. As a friend put it, "It's an instant institution!"

> If only this type of survey had been conducted fifty years ago in the Green Bay west shore marshes!

> Too many forms. You guys get paid to fill these out. We don't. It is somewhat disconcerting that after six years of describing my survey route, you still haven't figured it out.

Phenology and Call Index Variability

The call phenology—which suggests how we determined which survey periods are required to provide valid data for each—for all species except Blanchard's cricket frogs are illustrated in Figure 21-5. However, daily variation of call index values could be extreme, especially with marked changes in air temperature and wind velocity. This variability is illustrated in Figure 21-6 and emphasizes the desirability of avoiding nights when temperatures have recently dropped.

The broader pattern of call phenology for individual species also varied between wetlands due to differences in water temperature, which may have been affected by factors such as geography, water depth, presence of springs, and wetland size. The earlier calling period of green frogs and gray treefrogs (Fig. 21-7) in a shallow wetland that warmed up relatively quickly in spring (Voss site) is shown in comparison to a deeper, cooler wetland (Rudy site). Daily air temperatures were similar at both sites.

Daily and seasonal patterns of calling sometimes varied markedly from year to year at the same site as a result of annual weather differences, particularly with regard to temperature and precipitation. The difference in the wood frog call phenology at the same site during one of the earliest and latest springs over the 1983 through 1996 period is shown in Figure 21-8. In 1988, wood frogs essentially ceased calling after 13 April, as evening air temperatures dropped from the 3.3° to 10°C range to the -7.7° to 3.3°C range, and water temperatures dropped from the 10° to 11.1°C range to the 2.7° to 3.3°C range; a brief resurgence occurred later in the season as air and water warmed again. In 1996, breeding activity was delayed because of an unusually late spring, although it began when the pond remained half covered with ice. Similar plots for the spring peeper in the same wetland are shown in Figure 21-9 and illustrate the difficulty in establishing fixed sampling periods that are appropriate for the full range of phenologies to be expected over a span of several years.

Species Status, Abundance, and Distribution

WFTS data have contributed to our understanding of species status, abundance, and distribution, as summarized in the species accounts below, where WFTS species distribution maps (Fig. 21-10) are compared with those of Vogt (1981) and the Wisconsin Herpetological Atlas Project (Herp Atlas) (Casper 1996, Chpt. 22, this volume). The Herp Atlas maps incorporate the maps of Vogt (1981); they represent only those records documented by a specimen, photograph, or tape recording; they display distributions only to the county level; and they do not distinguish between recent and historical records. Because of the large number of cooperators running annual WFTS routes (approximately 1,000 listening stations visited one to three times each), it is not surprising that, for many species, the WFTS maps appear more complete than their atlas counterparts. However, except in the case of Blanchard's cricket frogs, most of the WFTS records remain undocumented, and a few may be erroneous. Although we believe that the vast

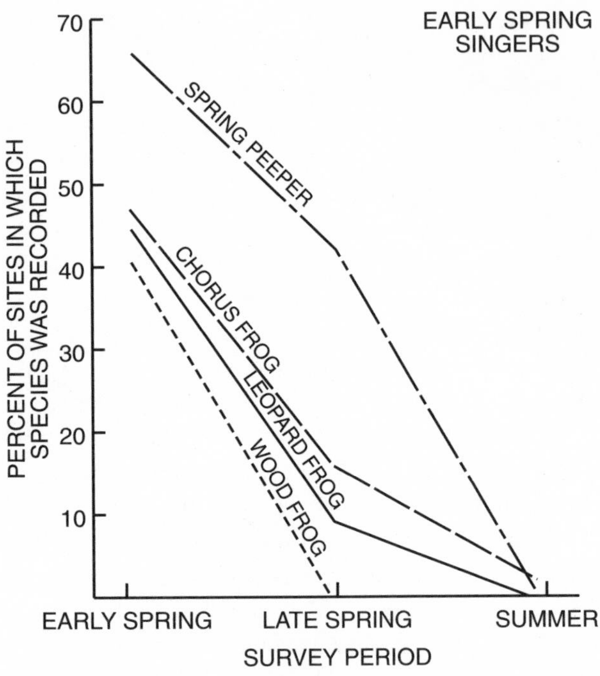

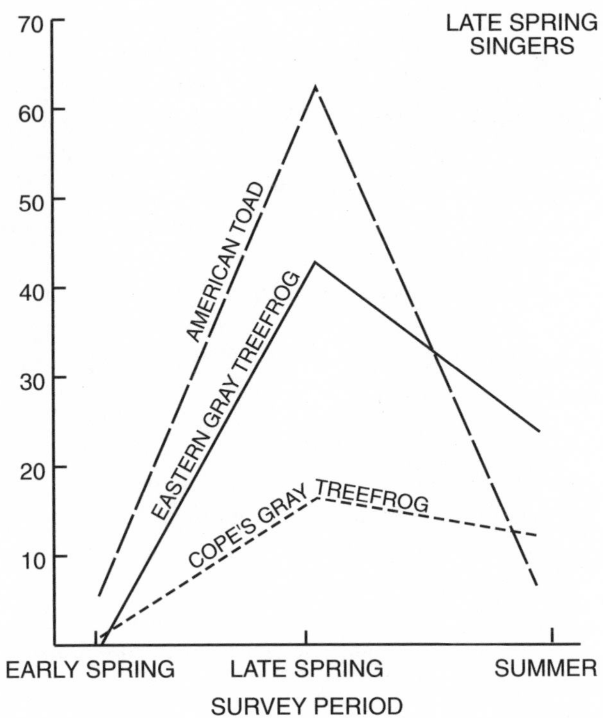

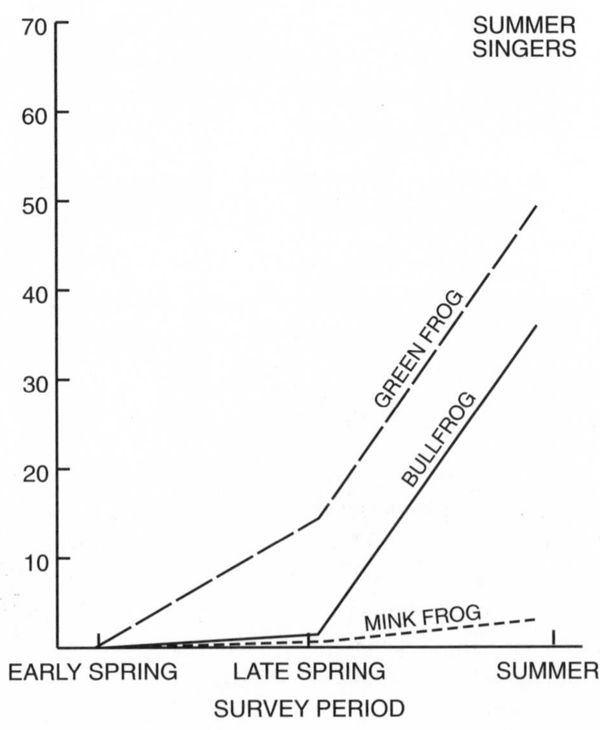

Figure 21-5. General call phenology according to survey period, Wisconsin Frog and Toad Survey, 1981–1983.

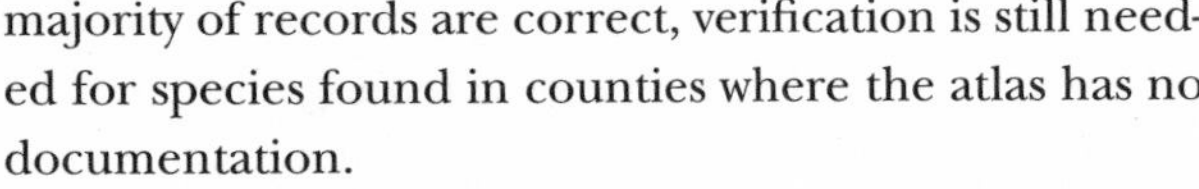

majority of records are correct, verification is still needed for species found in counties where the atlas has no documentation.

The general statewide abundance based on WFTS data and the experience of cooperators and ourselves is summarized in Table 21-3. Mean WFTS occurrence values for each region are also given in this table. These regional values, calculated as part of the route regression analysis, are average percent occurrences, estimated as area weighted averages of route average percent occurrences. Comparisons of abundance between species within the same area must be made cautiously, because species vary in their degree of detectability and because the various habitats may not have been sampled according to their abundance. Moreover, the extent to which these values reflect a given species' comparative abundance in different sections is uncertain, because the routes were chosen subjectively by different observers and because the sample is relatively small and irregularly distributed. However, the more marked discrepancies appear to represent true differences in a species' occurrence across different sections. Strictly speaking, a value in Table 21-3 reflects how widespread a species is in a section, because the value is based on the proportion of stations on which the species was recorded. It

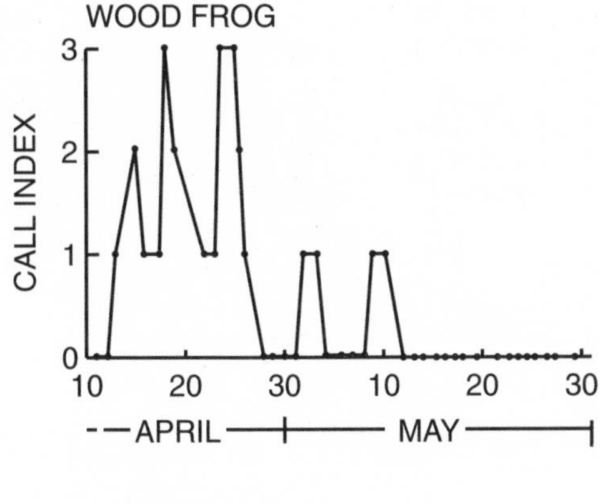

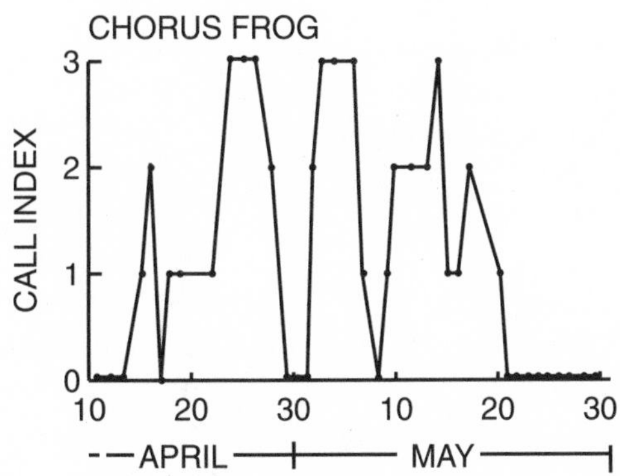

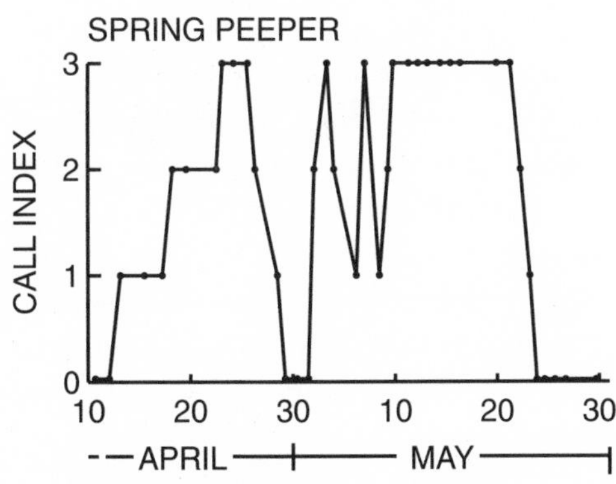

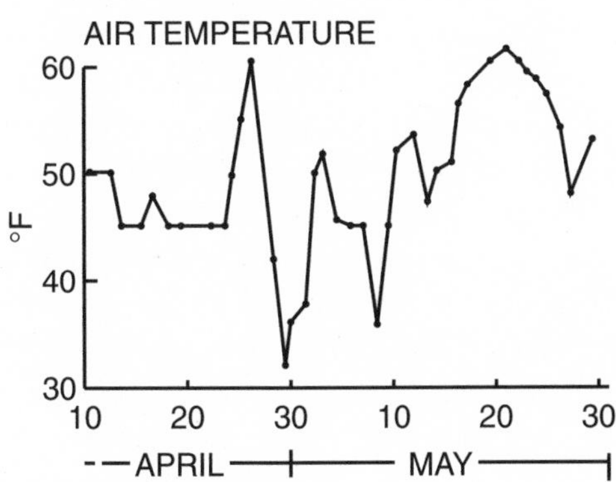

Figure 21-6. Frog call phenology at a bog in Oneida County, Wisconsin, 1984.

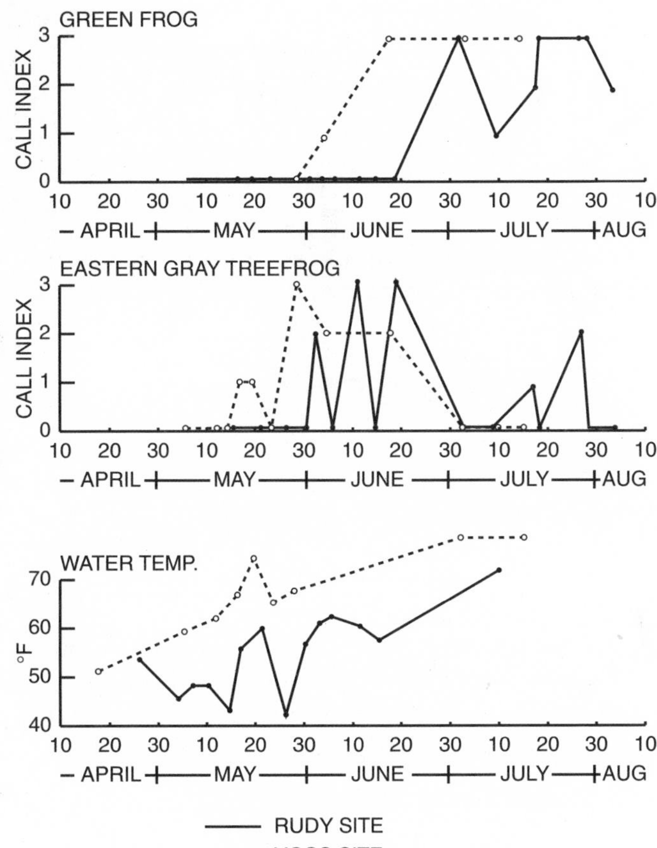

Figure 21-7. Frog call phenology at two Wisconsin wetlands, 1984.

probably also reflects a species' abundance, because a species is presumably easier to detect where it is more abundant, but an analysis of call index data would provide a better insight into the evaluation of abundance. Although most species appear to be fairly widespread across the state on the basis of their occurrence on routes (Fig. 21-10), some species were not recorded on many stations per route, at least in certain parts of the state (Tables 21-3, 21-4).

Several noteworthy patterns are apparent (Table 21-3). The relatively unforested and heavily populated Southeastern region had infrequent occurrences of forest-dwelling species such as wood frogs, spring peepers, and eastern gray treefrogs and frequent records of more open-country frogs such as chorus frogs, northern leopard frogs, and Cope's gray treefrogs. The opposite was true in the North-central Forest region. Both species of gray treefrog were common in the two major sandy sections of the state (Northwest Forest and Central Sands), which are former glacial lake beds. Common,

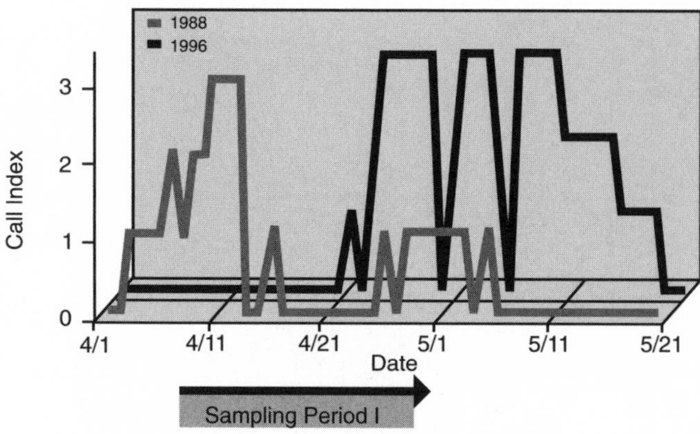

Figure 21-8. Wood frog call phenology at Eckstein North Pond (Oneida County, Wisconsin) in two extreme years, with early spring sampling period.

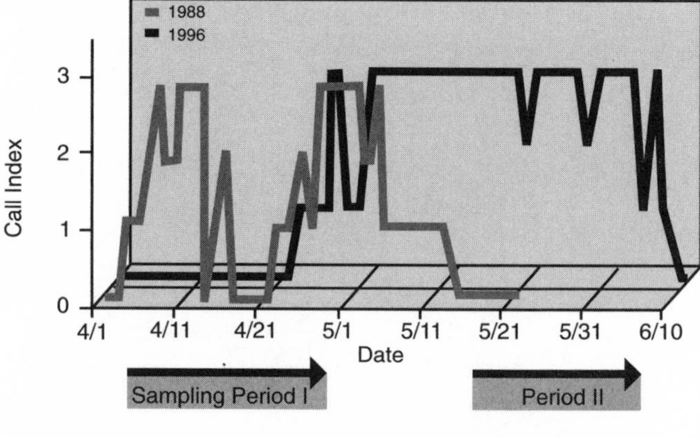

Figure 21-9. Spring peeper call phenology at Eckstein North Pond (Oneida County, Wisconsin) in two extreme years, with spring sampling period.

habitat generalists such as American toads and green frogs showed little geographic pattern, although the infrequent occurrence of green frogs in the Eastern Forest region is conspicuous.

Population Trends

Power analysis of the 1984 to 1994 data indicated that the WFTS sampled seven of the twelve species well enough to detect a 3 percent mean annual change in the frequency of occurrence over a twenty-year period (at $p < 0.10$ and 75 percent power; Table 21-4). The spring peeper is especially well sampled—only four routes of occurrence (with analyzable data) are predicted to be necessary to meet the above adequacy requirement. This is presumably because the species is widespread, detectable, and regular in occurrence; that is, if it is present at a site, it is likely to be heard. Another contributing factor is that the rate and direction of spring peeper population trends apparently do not vary extremely between routes. Cope's gray treefrogs are not quite sampled adequately (they occurred on forty-five routes with analyzable data, whereas forty-seven were required by the above criteria), but their sample is adequate to detect only declines, for which just thirty-four routes are required. We note that in practice at least fourteen routes would be a reasonable minimum sample for any species. With fewer than fourteen samples, it is unlikely that variances can be estimated with sufficient precision to allow statistical tests.

The least well sampled species (followed by the number of routes of occurrence necessary for adequate sampling) were bullfrogs (262), pickerel frogs (150), mink frogs (116), and Blanchard's cricket frogs (too few data to calculate). These species are the least common anurans in the state. They have irregular distributions and typically have low frequencies of occurrence on the routes on which they are found. However, they would be considered adequately sampled if less stringent criteria were used. For example, power analysis estimated that the current set of routes would be adequate to detect a 5 percent mean annual change in populations of pickerel frogs, mink frogs, and bullfrogs over a twenty-year period at $p < 0.2$, and a 50 percent power.

The results of statewide trend analyses are summarized in Table 21-4 and in Figure 21-11. We have selected the route frequency regression as our standard technique because it reduces the results at stations to presence or absence instead of attempting to relate the index values to an actual population size. For example, for a given species the route index regression equates three stations each recording index values of one with a single station recording an index value of three; the route adjusted index regression equates about seventeen stations recording an index value of one with a station recording an index value of three. The two other route regression techniques are useful for comparison. For example, when two or three techniques estimate similar trends for a species, it strengthens the evidence for these trends. Although the percent occurrence technique is simpler than the three route regression techniques and does not control for biases (such as differences in the distribution of routes run annually or oversampling in particular regions), it produces trend graphs similar in most cases to those of the route frequency regression,

Table 21-3. Statewide status and regional occurrence of anurans in Wisconsin

Species	State-wide Status**	Approximate Mean Percent of Stations of Occurrence* Northwest Forest	North-central Forest	Eastern Forest	Driftless Area	Central Sands	Southeast
Wood frog (*Rana sylvatica*)	FC	61	63	59	17	57	21
Chorus frog (*Pseudacris triseriata*)	C	35	35	21	38	48	63
Northern spring peeper (*Pseudacris crucifer crucifer*)	C	93	88	64	74	97	49
Northern leopard frog (*Rana pipiens*)	C	27	19	44	28	40	35
Pickerel frog (*Rana palustris*)	U	2	0	0	10	0	0
American toad (*Bufo americanus americanus*)	A	48	42	44	38	62	37
Eastern gray treefrog (*Hyla versicolor*)	C	70	65	50	50	94	30
Cope's gray treefrog (*Hyla chrysoscelis*)	FC	46	4	1	17	70	21
Blanchard's cricket frog (*Acris crepitans blanchardi*)	R	0	0	0	2	0	0
Mink frog (*Rana septentrionalis*)	U	33	6	0	0	0	0
Green frog (*Rana clamitans melanota*)	A	59	59	26	59	75	54
Bullfrog (*Rana catesbeiana*)	U	0	14	3	1	0	6

*Mean percent of stations on which species occurred each year, for routes run during the appropriate survey period, as approximated in route regression analysis. Data included only for routes that contributed to trend analysis.
**Our assessment. A = abundant, C = common, FC = fairly common, U = uncommon, R = rare.

especially for well-samples species (Fig. 21-11), and provides more comparative information. When the route regression analyses were run on the combined period data (for those species requiring surveys in both the early and late spring periods; Table 21-1), the estimated trends were similar to those computed using data from each species' primary calling period (Table 21-5).

Altogether, these analyses suggest a strong increase for wood frogs, a slow but significant decline for spring peepers, and probable declines for northern leopard frogs, pickerel frogs, and Cope's gray treefrogs. Eastern gray treefrog and American toad populations appear to be stable or increasing. Well-sampled species also showed some significant regional trends (Table 21-6), which are discussed below.

Wisconsin experienced drought conditions during the period 1986-1989, although conditions varied regionally in terms of duration, extent, seasonality, and peak year. This period also included the years of poorest coverage in the WFTS (Fig. 21-3); however, the trend plots for some species (Fig. 21-11) suggest that populations (or at least annual population index) declined temporarily during this period. Trend analyses conducted during those years (e.g., for the period 1984 to 1988) indicated declines for several species and engendered some concern which further monitoring proved to be unwarranted. The trend plot for green frogs—a species that inhabits permanent water bodies statewide—was highly correlated with the July Palmer Drought Index ($r = 0.757$; $p = 0.004$; Fig. 21-12).

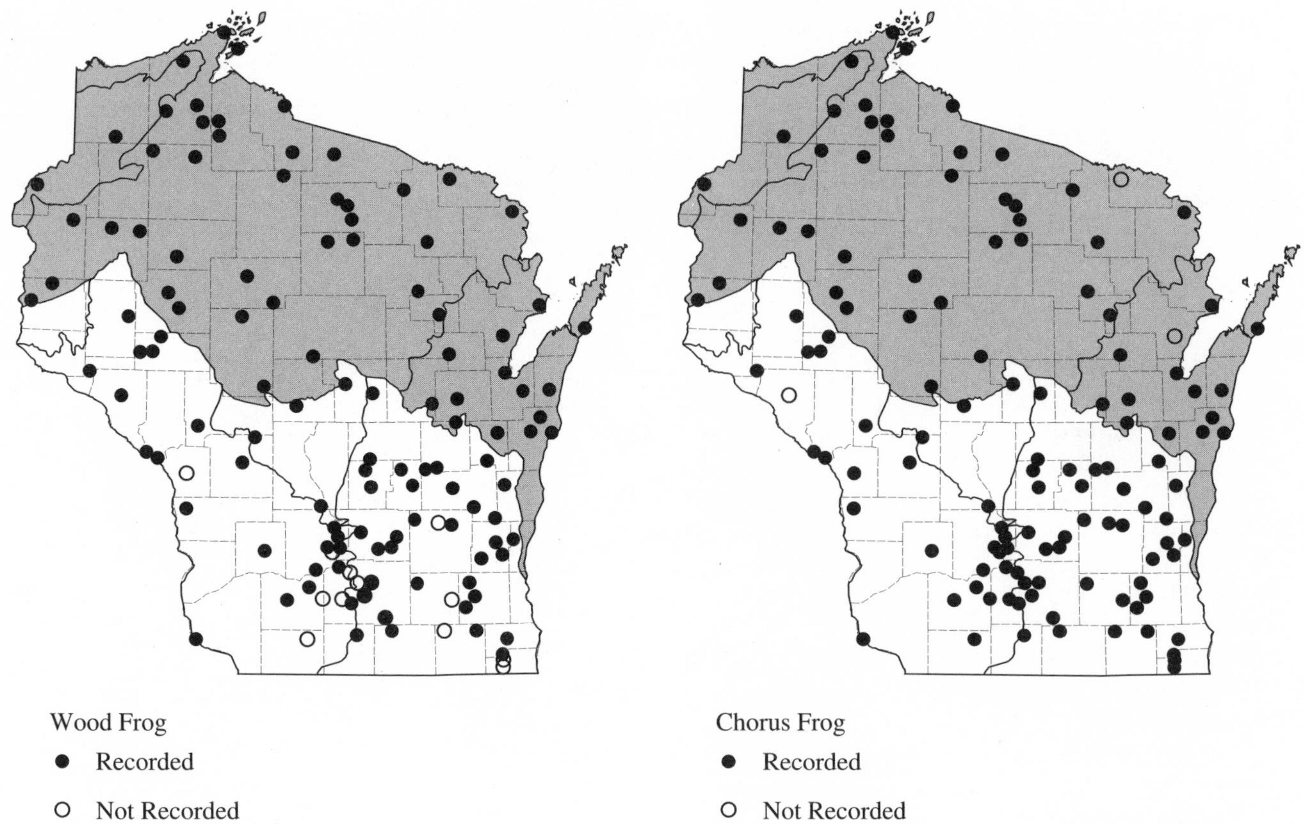

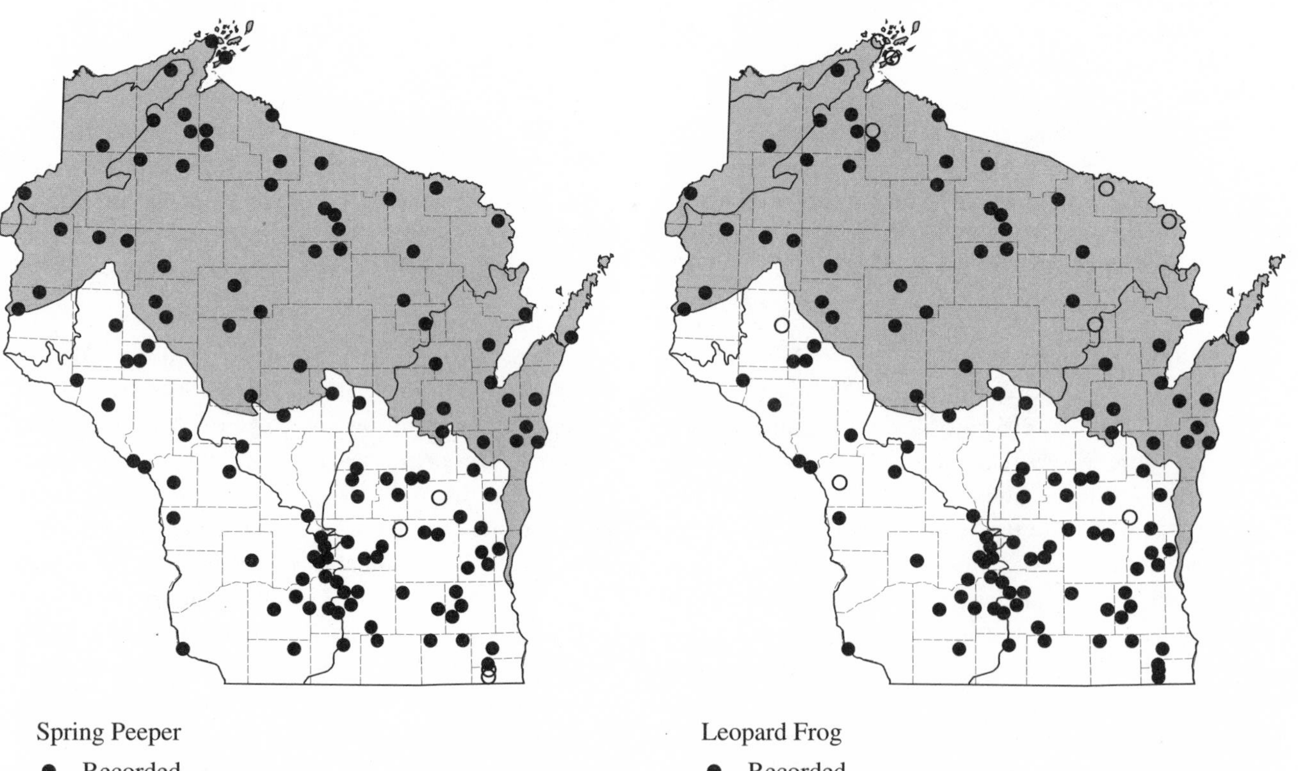

Figure 21-10. Anuran distribution maps based on Wisconsin Frog and Toad Survey data, 1981–1995.

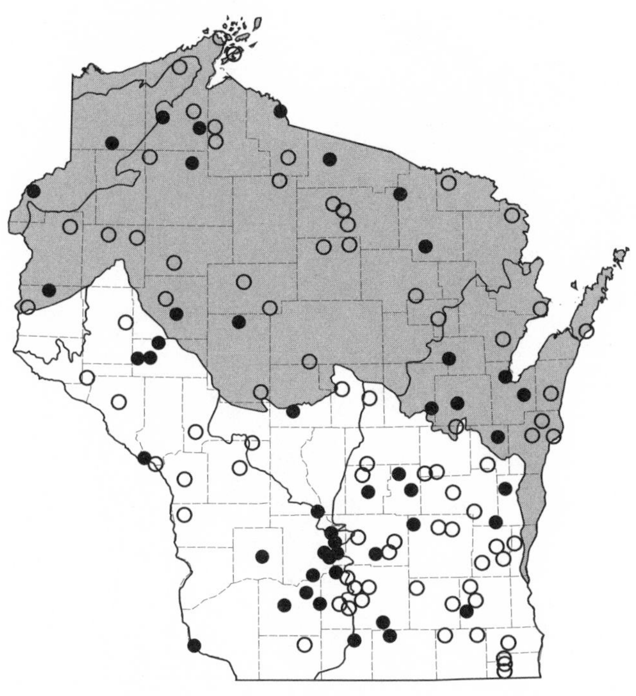

Pickerel Frog
● Recorded
○ Not Recorded

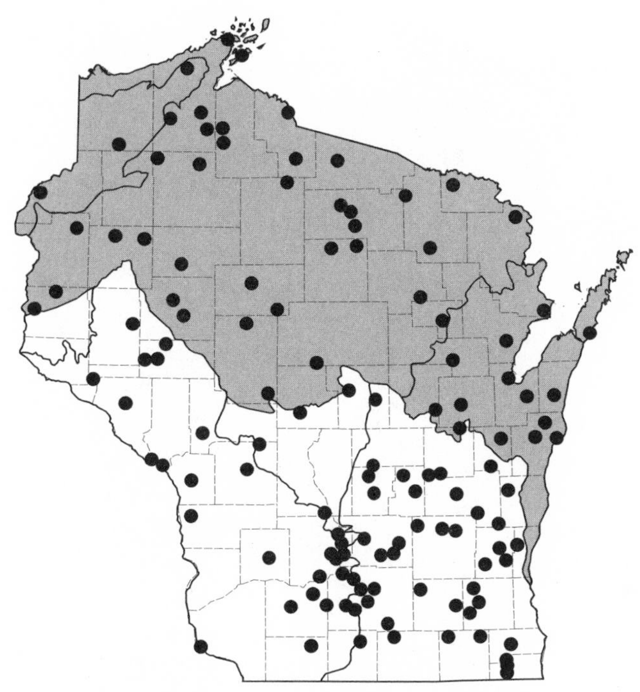

American Toad
● Recorded
○ Not Recorded

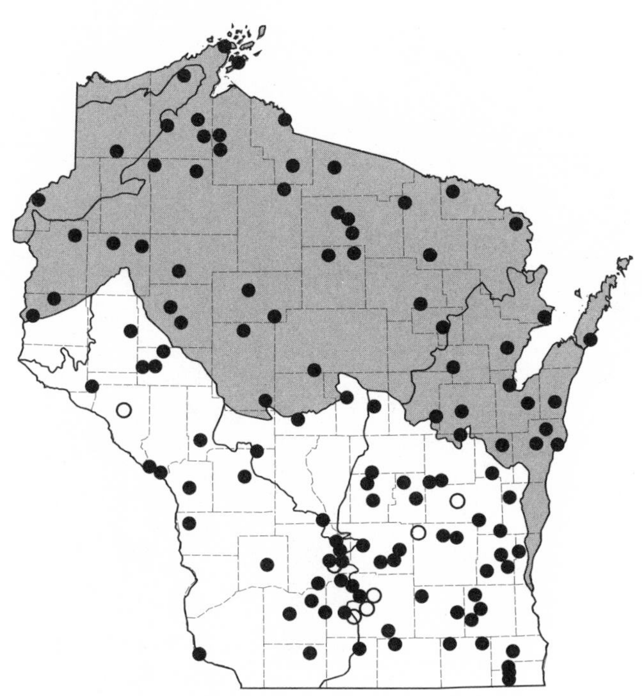

Eastern Gray Treefrog
● Recorded
○ Not Recorded

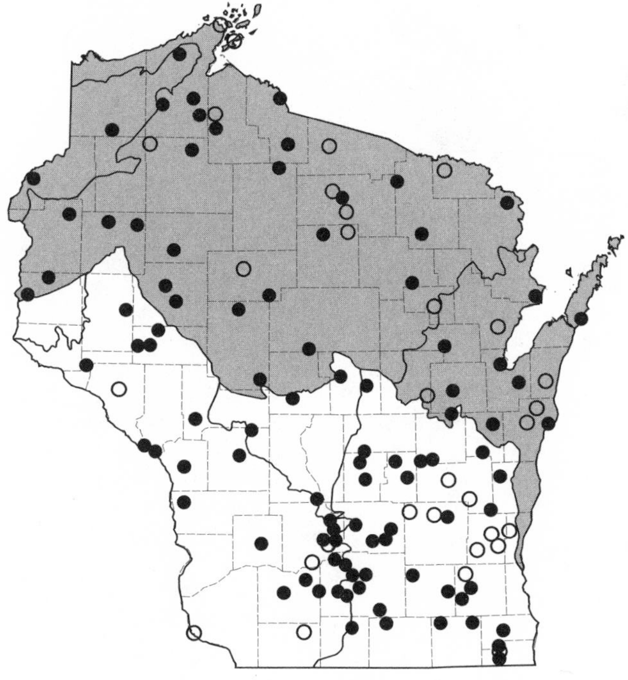

Cope's Gray Treefrog
● Recorded
○ Not Recorded

Figure 21-10. (cont.)

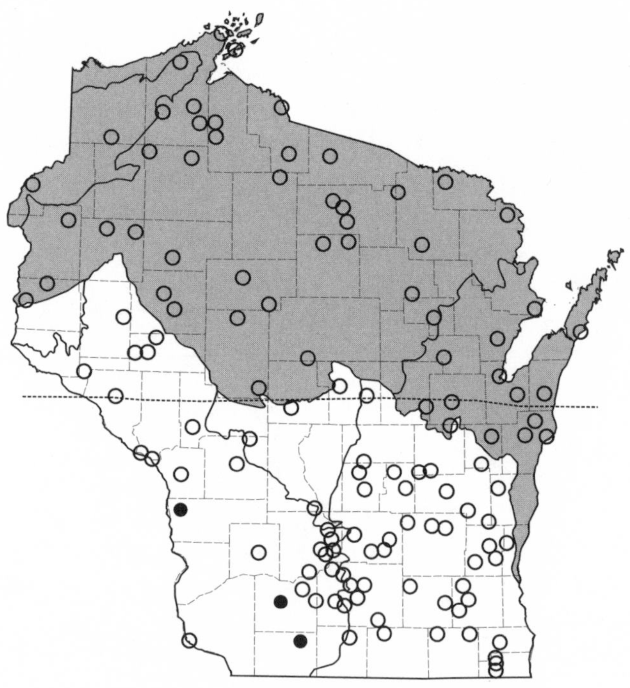

Cricket Frog
● Verified
○ Not Verified
---- Historic Range Limit

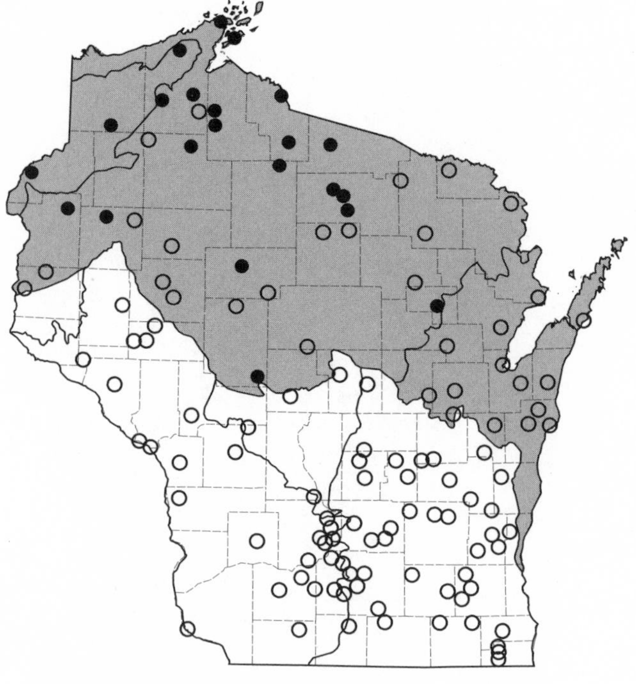

Mink Frog
● Recorded
○ Not Recorded

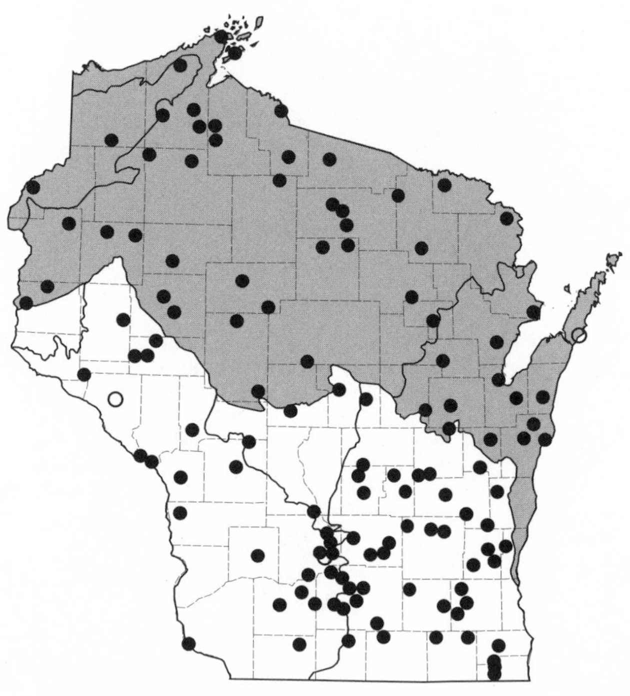

Green Frog
● Recorded
○ Not Recorded

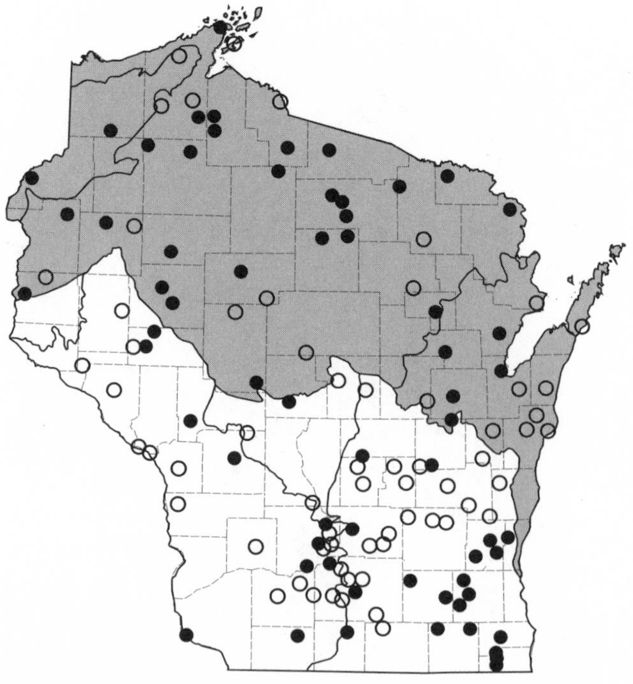

Bullfrog
● Recorded
○ Not Recorded

Figure 21-10. (cont.)

Table 21-4. Relative abundance, sample adequacy, and estimated trends for Wisconsin anurans

	Occurrence		Sample Adequacy[1]					Trend[2]		
Species	Routes[3]	Mean % of Stations[4]	A	B	C	Frequency[5]		Index[6]	Adjusted Index[7]	% Occurrence[8]
Wood frog (*Rana sylvatica*)	90	34	+	+	-	+2.5**	(42)	+4.2***	+5.1**	+0.76
Chorus frog (*Pseudacris triseriata*)	109	49	+	+	+	-1.1	(53)	+0.3	+2.0*	-0.66
Northern spring peeper (*Pseudacris crucifer crucifer*)	109	76	+	+	+	-0.6**	(49)	-1.1***	-1.3***	+0.14
Northern leopard frog (*Rana pipiens*)	91	35	+	+	+	-2.1*	(50)	-1.8	-1.4	-1.19***
Pickerel frog (*Rana palustris*)	19	5	-	-	-	-2.6	(63)	-3.2*	-4.6**	-0.28**
American toad (*Bufo americanus americanus*)	102	44	+	+	-	+1.4	(37)	+1.7	+1.2	+0.42
Eastern gray treefrog (*Hyla versicolor*)	96	53	+	+	+	+0.2	(45)	+0.8	+0.8	+1.06*
Cope's gray treefrog (*Hyla chrysoscelis*)	45	18	-	+	-	-2.4*	(64)	-2.0	-1.3	-0.77**
Blanchard's cricket frog (*Acris crepitans blanchardi*)	2	1	-	-	-	—	—	—	—	—
Mink frog (*Rana septentrionalis*)	12	12	-	-	-	-1.5	(50)	+1.2	+3.2	-0.13
Green frog (*Rana clamitans melanota*)	103	60	+	+	+	-0.4	(58)	+0.6	+2.2**	+0.39
Bullfrog (*Rana catesbeiana*)	36	7	-	-	-	-1.2	(50)	-0.4	+0.0	-0.02

[1] Based on ability of survey to detect given mean annual changes in frequency of station occurrence at $p < 0.10$ and 75 percent power: A = 3%/yr over twenty-year period; B = 3%/yr decline only (1-tailed test) over twenty-year period; C = 3%/yr over ten-year period.

[2] * = $p < 0.10$, ** = $p < 0.05$, *** = $p < 0.01$.

[3] Number of routes for which data were sufficient to contribute to route regression analyses.

[4] Mean percent of stations on which species occurred each year, for routes run during the appropriate survey period.

[5] Route frequency regression technique based on number of stations of occurrence; trend is mean annual percent change (see Methods). Number in parentheses represents percent of routes with estimated declines.

[6] Route index regression technique based on summing call index values for all stations on route; trend is mean annual percent change (see Methods).

[7] Route adjusted-index regression technique based on summing adjusted call index values for all stations on route; trend is mean annual percent change (see Methods).

[8] Percent occurrence technique or regression of pooled, unweighted frequency of station occurrence data for all routes; trend is annual change in percent occurrence (see Methods).

Table 21-5. Comparison of trends from route regression analyses using single-period and combined-period data (see Table 21-1)

Species	Type of Route Regression Analyses					
	Frequency		Index		Adjusted Index	
	Single	Combined	Single	Combined	Single	Combined
Chorus frog (*Pseudacris triseriata*)	-1.1	-1.1	+0.3	-0.3	+2.0*	+0.9
Northern spring peeper (*Pseudacris crucifer crucifer*)	-0.6**	-0.4	-1.1***	-0.6*	-1.3***	-0.8**
Northern leopard frog (*Rana pipiens*)	-2.1*	-1.7	-1.8	-2.0	-1.4	-1.3
Pickerel frog (*Rana palustris*)	-2.6	-2.0	-3.2*	-2.4	-4.6**	-4.0***

*= $p < 0.1$.
**= $p < 0.05$.
***= $p < 0.01$.

Species Accounts

The following accounts are in phenological rather than taxonomic order, according to WFTS data sheets and analyses. Readers should refer to Table 21-3 for statewide status and regional abundance data; to Table 21-4 for statewide abundance, trend, and sample adequacy summaries; to Table 21-6 for significant regional trends; and to Figures 21-10 and 21-11 for distribution maps and trend graphs, respectively. Except where stated otherwise, trend figures refer to percent annual change according to route-frequency regression analysis. For comparison, Herp Atlas maps and narratives are presented in Casper (1996), with an additional narrative in Casper (Chpt. 22, this volume); earlier distribution maps are in Vogt (1981).

Wood Frogs. Wood frogs are the most difficult of the relatively common species to monitor because of their early, short, explosive breeding season. They often begin breeding in vernal ponds while snow is still on the ground and occasionally when ice lingers on some breeding ponds, as early as late March in the southern counties and early April in the north. Although within a particular area they may be found calling over a period of three to four weeks, the peak generally lasts only a week, often less if interrupted by cold weather, and sometimes occurs only on one or two nights (Figs. 21-6, 21-8). The most effective and consistent sampling was done by observers who lived near their route and timed their first run according to the local wood frog activity. Because of these logistical difficulties and annual variations in wood frog breeding activity, year-to-year variation is generally high on individual routes and in regional and statewide data. Several cooperators mentioned that their ability to time the first survey run for wood frogs improved with experience. This factor undoubtedly contributed to the significant annual increases statewide and in the North-central Forest and Central Sands regions, as did the fact that in 1991 we extended the starting date of the early spring sampling period from 15 April to 8 April because several cooperators reported that wood frog activity had waned by 15 April in some years. The trend plot shows a sharp decline indicated during 1984 to 1986 (beginning prior to the onset of drought conditions), followed by a small peak in 1987, then a gradual increase (beginning after the survey period was modified) to a level not quite that of 1984. A more thorough analysis and additional years of data are needed to evaluate the relative effects of bias, drought, and other factors on this trend.

Wood frogs were encountered most frequently in the three northern and eastern forested regions, at about three times its frequency in the Southeast region (where forested habitat is limited) and Driftless Area (where breeding ponds are not common and the species nears its southwestern range limit). WFTS records suggest that the lack of southeastern records in Vogt's (1981) maps represented a relative scarcity rather than absence of the species in those counties. This is also borne out by the recent Herp Atlas data set, which is missing verified records from only eight counties. If populations recorded on the WFTS can be verified, the species will be documented in every county except Lafayette.

Chorus Frogs. Chorus frogs occurred on almost every WFTS route, often in large numbers; however, they were found at low frequencies and call index values in the

Table 21-6. Statistically significant regional trends (1984–1995) for Wisconsin anurans, based on route frequency regression analysis. N is number of routes contributing to trend analysis.

Species	Region	Trend	N
Wood frog	North-central Forest	+2.8*	35
(*Rana sylvatica*)	Central Sands	+6.3*	3
Chorus frog			
(*Pseudacris triseriata*)	Eastern Forest	-16.9**	11
Northern spring peeper	Central Sands	-0.6*	3
(*Pseudacris crucifer crucifer*)	Southeast	-1.5***	31
Northern leopard frog			
(*Rana pipiens*)	North-central Forest	-5.1**	20
American toad			
(*Bufo americanus americanus*)	Driftless Area	+3.3**	22

*= $p < 0.1$.
**= $p < 0.05$.
***= $p < 0.01$.

northeastern counties. The absence of northeastern records in Vogt's (1981) and Conant's (1975) range maps reflects these low densities. The Herp Atlas recently documented records for some of these counties, but WFTS data suggest that more of these counties will be added, as will the western counties of Trempealeau and Jackson. Chorus frog populations apparently rebounded somewhat after a decline in frequency during the drought years. Although the plot suggests an overall decline, statistical tests were equivocal, and the statewide trend is considered stable; however, a significant decline has occurred in the Eastern Forest region.

Northern Spring Peepers. Northern spring peepers were the most frequently encountered anuran in the WFTS, occurring on as many routes as chorus frogs but on more stations per route. To some extent this prevalence is due to the peeper's long calling period and to a call that is loud, persistent, and recognizable. At some stations it may even drown out the calls of chorus frogs and other species. Peepers were usually in full chorus by the middle of the first sampling period statewide, but in the north during the unusually late spring of 1996, they were more detectable during the second period (Fig. 21-9). Peepers evidently occur in every county but are markedly less common in the Southeast region than in other Wisconsin regions. Because of their excellent detectability and consistent calling patterns, they are well sampled by the WFTS, and small population changes can be detected. Almost every type of WFTS analysis since 1987 (except the 1984 through 1996 percent occurrence analysis) has indicated that, though abundant overall, this species has experienced a small but significant decline. The 0.6 percent per year decline in frequency represents a 26 percent loss if extrapolated over a fifty-year period. This is a species for which the survey appears to be well suited to provide early warnings of population declines.

Only 49 percent of spring peeper routes indicated a declining trend, suggesting that declines were more extreme than any increases. The statewide trend resulted mostly from a significant 1.5 percent annual decrease in the rapidly urbanizing Southeast region, where 61 percent of the routes had declining trends. Local peeper populations in this region were known to have disappeared both before and during the time of the WFTS, especially in urban and intensively agricultural regions, where Vogt (1981) noted peepers "do not thrive." Spring peepers warrant concern and further study while populations are still widespread.

Northern Leopard Frogs. Northern leopard frog populations had evidently declined in Wisconsin during decades just prior to monitoring by the WFTS (Vogt 1981). They experienced die-offs from unknown causes associated with red leg infections in the 1970s (Hine et al. 1981) and have been harvested for decades by biological supply companies. According to the WFTS, populations declined from 1984 to 1995. Populations, or at least breeding activity, may also have undergone a temporary

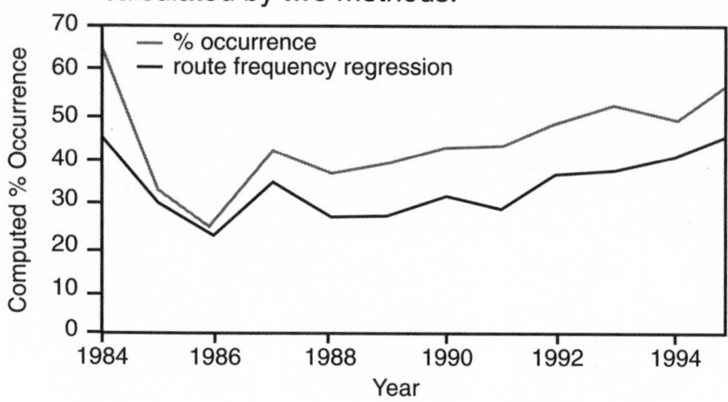

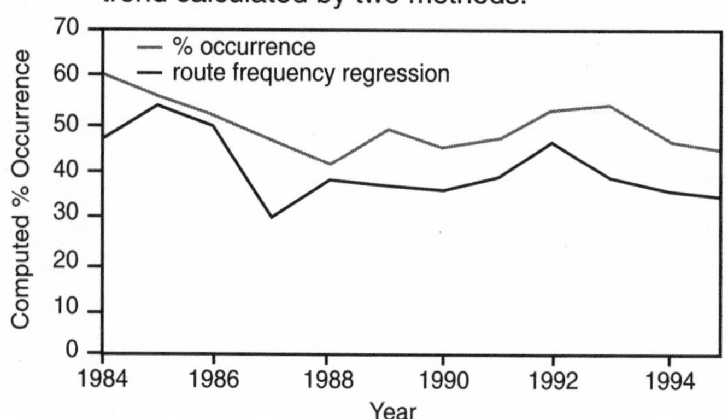

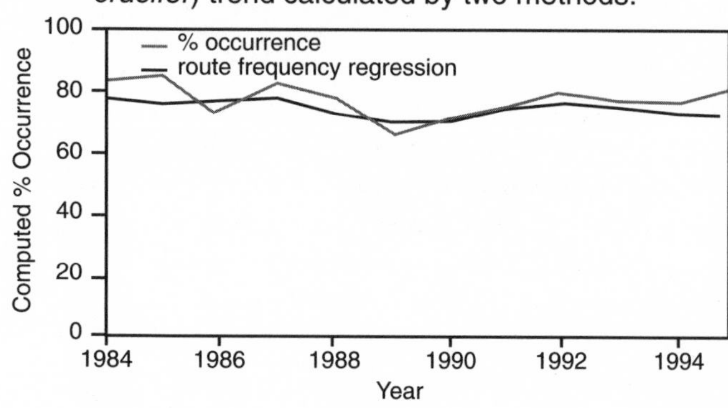

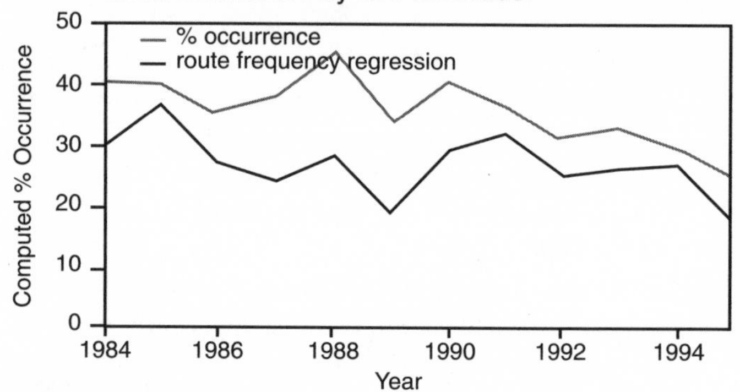

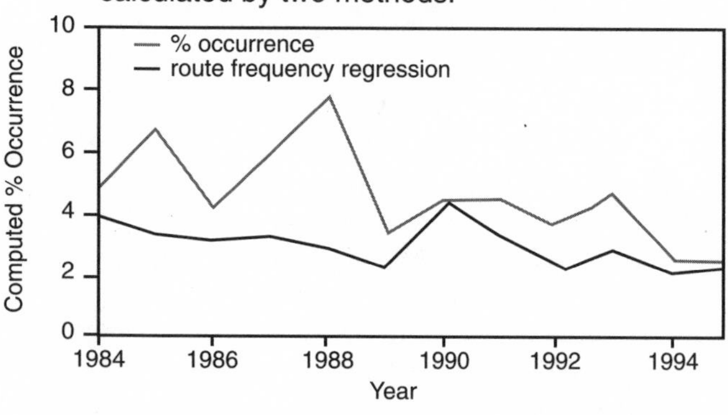

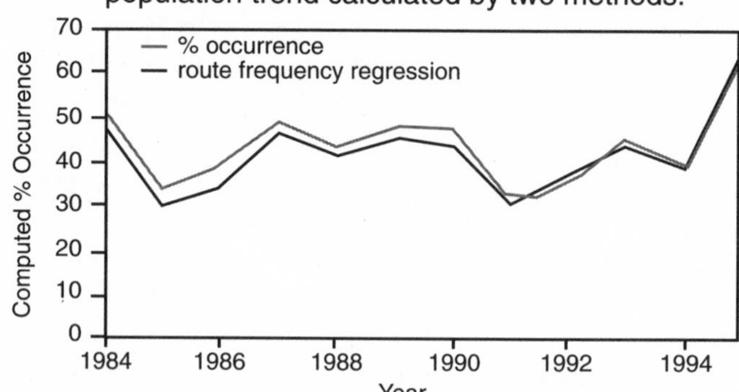

Figure 21-11. Anuran population trend estimates based on percent occurrence and route frequency regression analysis of Wisconsin Frog and Toad Survey data, 1984–1995.

Eastern gray treefrog (*Hyla versicolor*) population trend calculated by two methods.

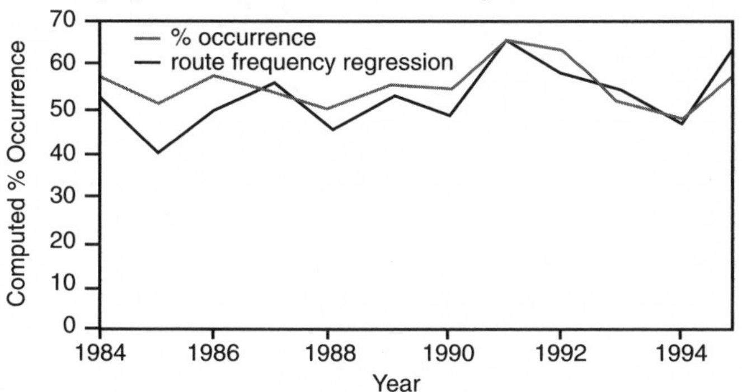

Cope's gray treefrog (*Hyla chrysoscelis*) population trend calculated by two methods.

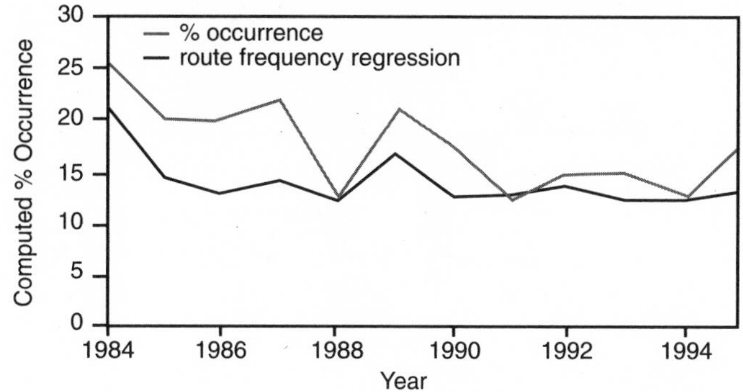

Mink frog (*Rana septentrionalis*) population trend calculated by two methods.

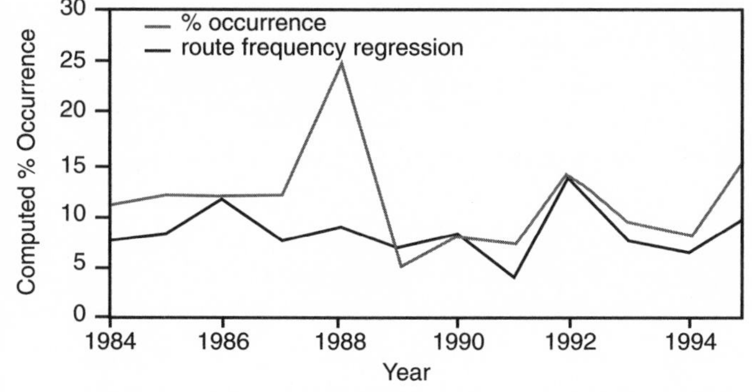

Green frog (*Rana clamitans melanota*) population trend calculated by two methods.

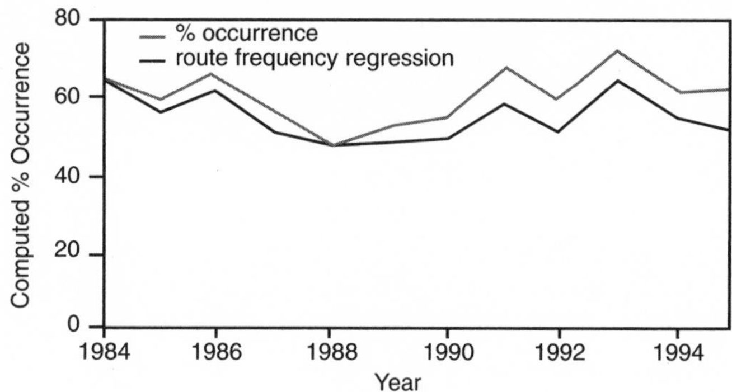

Bullfrog (*Rana catesbeiana*) population trend calculated by two methods.

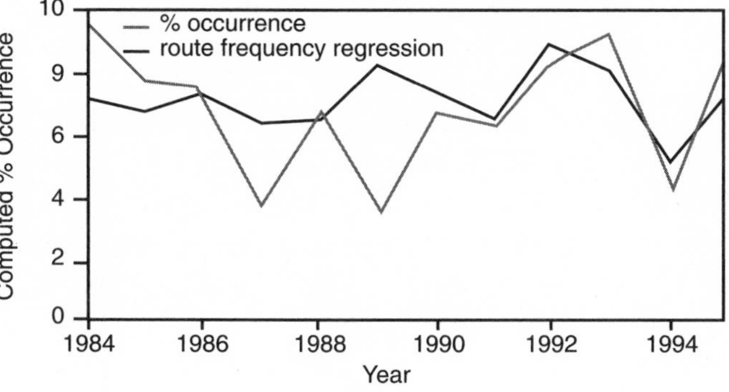

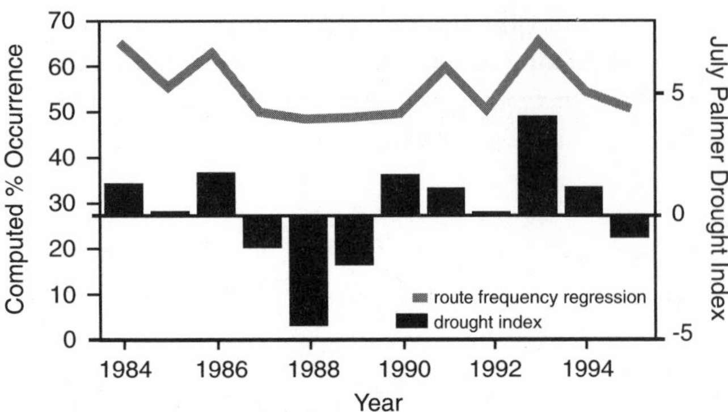

Figure 21-12. The correspondence between green frog (*Rana clamitans melanota*) population trend data and Palmer Drought Index data.

decline during the late 1980s drought. This species will breed in many habitats but is most common in open country. Its distribution is statewide, with frequencies of occurrence being lowest in the most heavily wooded (Northwest and North-central Forest) regions. The North-central Forest region has experienced a significant decline in leopard frog numbers.

Pickerel Frogs. Pickerel frogs were considered threatened in Wisconsin until 1987 but were subsequently downlisted after populations were found to be somewhat widespread. They often breed and overwinter in spring-fed streams and ponds. Although the calls of pickerel and northern leopard frogs can be confused, most cooperators submitting pickerel frog records were certain of them. While WFTS records occur from several counties for which the species has yet to be documented, the distribution of WFTS data resembles that of the Herp Atlas, showing populations concentrated in the Driftless Area and scattered elsewhere. We consider it common (and locally common) in the Driftless Area, rare elsewhere, and uncommon overall. WFTS data suggest that it is second only to Blanchard's cricket frogs in rarity. It was inadequately sampled by the WFTS, although data from nineteen routes suggest a decline that was significant in three of four analyses; 63 percent of these routes had declining trends. Its trend plot resembled that of the closely related leopard frog, which has a similar breeding phenology but occurs in a larger variety of—though generally more open—habitats. Because of its special concern status in the state, a separate monitoring program may be justified.

American Toads. American toads are abundant and breed statewide in a wide range of habitats. American toads occurred on all 122 routes that were run at least twice—about equally in all regions. They have a detectable call, but the calling season can be short during warm springs, when the peak may be missed because it occurs between the early and late spring sampling periods. WFTS data indicate a stable to increasing trend. American toads appeared to increase in abundance during the drought years.

Eastern Gray Treefrogs. Eastern gray treefrogs occur in every county surveyed. The statewide mean frequency of occurrence was second only to spring peepers. Values were highest in the Northwest, North-central, and Central Sands regions and lowest in the Southeast region. WFTS records suggest that this species occurs in several counties, especially in the Southeast, where documentation can be obtained to fill in apparent gaps in the Herp Atlas map. The statewide population trend was stable or increasing, with no apparent response to the drought years.

Cope's Gray Treefrogs. Cope's gray treefrogs are evidently less than half as abundant as the closely related tetraploid eastern gray treefrog (Tables 21-3, 21-4). They were rare in the North-central and Eastern Forest regions and were recorded most frequently in the Northwest Forest and Central Sands regions, areas of predominantly sandy soils dominated by marshes, pine-oak forest, barrens, and conifer bogs. The latter two regions also had high populations of eastern gray treefrogs. Many WFTS records of Cope's gray treefrogs occur in counties for which there are no documented records in the Herp Atlas (Casper 1996). This is especially so in a large area of north-central Wisconsin, where cooperators reported this species from several routes but often from just one or two sites during only one or two years. More documentation is needed because of the difficulty in distinguishing its call from that of the closely related eastern gray treefrog. However, because vocalizations are the most reliable means of detecting and distinguishing between the two gray treefrog species in the field, it is not surprising that a cadre of auditory surveyors would discover populations in areas where no formal documentation existed. We are confident that the species in fact occurs in scattered locations in the north-central counties.

Cope's gray treefrog exhibited a significant 2.4 percent mean annual decline in frequency during 1984 to 1995, with declines noted on 64 percent of the routes on which trends could be computed. Although samples were small in most regions, all but the Eastern Forest region registered declines. Populations deserve continued scrutiny.

Blanchard's Cricket Frogs. Blanchard's cricket frogs, once so common that hundreds were collected from ponds in Madison's Tenney Park (Dernehl 1902) and one of the most common frogs in southern Wisconsin as recently as the 1950s (Hay, Chpt. 11, this volume), are now state endangered. Vogt (1981) noted a precipitous decline in the late 1970s, although the decline had begun previously. Blanchard's cricket frogs, now apparently absent from Madison, were found there as recently as 1972 (Mossman and Hine 1984). On the Lower Wisconsin River, an area of former abundance, cricket frogs had declined substantially by the late 1960s (Vogt 1981; Casper, Chpt. 22, this volume). Extensive daytime and nocturnal surveys along this waterway beginning in 1984 by M.J.M. failed to document a single individual. During 1984 to 1985, M.J.M. conducted five-minute auditory surveys of likely stream and pond habitat at fifty-six sites in the extreme southwestern counties of Grant, Lafayette, and Iowa. These included seven sites where cricket frogs had been found during the previous two years by WFTS cooperators; visual searches were also made at most of these previously reported sites. Cricket frogs were documented at sixteen sites, including six of those previously known. All confirmed sites were in pastured or recently pastured stream bottoms, except for six unpastured sites in Governor Dodge State Park. Some of these confirmed sites were among those checked later, as summarized by Hay (Chpt. 11, this volume). In 1985, M.J.M. also conducted auditory and visual searches at five sites in Kenosha and Washington Counties where cricket frogs had been recently reported, but none were found. Many other sites have been surveyed recently within the cricket frog's historical range in southeastern Wisconsin, but the species was not found (Casper, Chpt. 22, this volume).

Of the approximately seventy WFTS routes run at least once within the historical range of cricket frogs, the species was verified on only three (in Vernon, Iowa, and Lafayette Counties) and was likely on two others (in Iowa and Grant Counties). Two of the three routes with verified records were established specifically to sample potential cricket frog habitat within its current range and included previously identified populations. The third, in Vernon County, reflects one or two individuals tape-recorded in 1991 but not heard subsequently. All other WFTS reports of cricket frogs (including those initially reported by Mossman and Hine 1984) were undocumented and have not been re-reported in recent years; we consider them to be unlikely, although a few might have represented the last individuals of disappearing populations. Most of these apparent errors were made during the early spring sampling period when cricket frogs are not typically calling and at sites in which the species was not found later during the usual summer song period; most or all of these reported cricket frog calls were presumably the similar-sounding "kid-ic" call of the Virginia rail. After being alerted to the similarity and respective phenology of these two species' calls, several observers realized they had made this mistake. Since 1991, cricket frogs have been documented from only two to four stations per year, which is inadequate for monitoring population trends. Therefore, we did not include trend estimates for this species in Table 21-4.

The data from the WFTS, other surveys (Hay, Chpt. 11, this volume), and the Herp Atlas confirm the disappearance of cricket frogs from about 90 percent of their historical range in Wisconsin and their irregular occurrence at isolated sites within their remaining range. Undoubtedly, they now breed on but a fraction of a percent of the sites used as recently as the 1950s. Cricket frogs have also declined—possibly to the point of extirpation—in Ontario (Oldham 1992), Minnesota (Oldfield and Moriarty 1994; Moriarty, Chpt. 20, this volume), and parts of Iowa (Hemesath, Chpt. 23, this volume). The future of this species in Wisconsin may depend on information gathered from research and monitoring in nearby states, where populations are not yet at such critically low levels and where studies on limiting factors may be more fruitful.

Mink Frogs. Mink frogs are uncommon to fairly common in the northern third of the state. The maps of Vogt (1981) and the Herp Atlas (Casper 1996) document their occurrence only as far south as Burnett, Taylor, and Oconto Counties. We and other WFTS cooperators have not found them in apparently suitable boggy marshes in the western part of the Central Sands and adjacent areas; however, they may occur there, as suggested by an undocumented but reliable record from southern Clark County. Mink frogs were most frequently reported in the Northwest Forest region, but the statewide sample is inadequate to monitor trends.

Green Frogs. Green frogs are common to abundant statewide except for the Eastern Forest region, where they were recorded about half as frequently as elsewhere. They were absent from a Door County route that was run for eleven years. The statewide population is apparently stable, although numbers appear to vary according to drought conditions (Fig. 21-12).

Bullfrogs. Bullfrogs are distributed irregularly across Wisconsin, but according to the WFTS and Vogt (1981), they are most common in the North-central Forest region. Numbers were also high, at least during the mid-1980s, along the Mississippi River in Grant County (M.J.M.). Bullfrogs occurred on about half of the routes that were run at least two years. Bullfrogs tend to appear and disappear from individual sites over time, possibly because of introductions (Casper, Chpt. 22, this volume) and harvest (Vogt 1981). Apparently because of their irregular geographic and temporal distributions and relatively small sample, they were inadequately sampled by the WFTS. This species' vocalizations are unmistakable, and WFTS records suggest that many more counties will be added to its documented distribution in the Herp Atlas.

Discussion

The distribution and trend data reported here should be interpreted within the limitations of the survey methodology. The possibility of misidentifications is a qualification common to any study that relies on volunteers, but in this program—despite the lack of any training workshops and formal certification requirements—we consider it minor. Misidentifications are minimized by the quality of instructional materials, by communication between cooperators and staff (e.g., checking with cooperators on unusual records and encouraging new cooperators to accompany experienced ones before starting their own routes), and by the care obviously taken by most cooperators, most of whom have contributed data for several years. Misidentifications are more of a concern for distributional records than for trend calculations. In this regard, it is impractical to expect volunteers to document all potentially disputable records. However, with the help of the Herp Atlas we hope to better target species requiring documentation, which will be secured by the original observer, WFTS staff, or others interested in obtaining distributional records.

A potential problem stems from the qualitative definitions of call index values and the fact that each cooperator does not interpret them identically. Observers in Ontario agreed on presence or absence of species more than 95 percent of the time but agreed on index values of present species only 47 to 83 percent of the time; agreement was greatest among experienced observers (Shirose et al. 1997). Among inexperienced observers in Iowa, agreement was also high for presence or absence but was lower (56 to 83 percent) for call index values (Hemesath, Chpt. 23, this volume). In southeastern Wisconsin, differences in call index values were less between observers than between nights (Kline, Chpt. 38, this volume). Observer bias has not been investigated by the WFTS program, but we consider it to be minimal because: (1) WFTS cooperators are generally experienced (i.e., most have accompanied another observer before being responsible for their own route); (2) most run the same route for many years; (3) changes in personnel on a particular route are usually preceded by the requirement to have the two observers run the route together; and (4) at the beginning of the program most cooperators were already experienced. Further, our analyses thus far have relied primarily on presence or absence data rather than call index data. Nonetheless, it may be worthwhile for us to investigate observer bias and the value of providing training opportunities for observers in order to minimize it.

We have presented limited data here on the effects of date, drought, and air and water temperatures on the frequency and intensity of anuran calling and the sorts of problems these variations can cause for auditory surveys. These factors probably affect precision more than accuracy, and the WFTS has many data that should be used to look more closely at the causes of call variation. We have attempted to minimize these sources of variation by helping cooperators conduct surveys under the most appropriate seasonal and nightly conditions, within the general guidelines of date and water temperature, for each sampling period. We hope to assist cooperators further by enlisting regional contact people who can provide information on current conditions and breeding activity.

Although improvements in the WFTS are always sought, any change must be considered critically in regard to its potential to alter substantially the nature of the data. Thus we try to balance improvements with continuity. In the case of expanding the early spring sampling period in 1991, we opted for a needed improvement but may consequently have biased the wood frog data set, at least in the short term. Overall, we believe that current guidelines, training, and sampling procedures are appropriate; cooperators are in general agreement with this impression.

The most important limitation of the WFTS methodology is the subjective selection of listening stations. Thus, although cooperators established routes to represent the range of available anuran breeding habitat in their area, there is no measure of the actual representation of our sample. Nor have we incorporated a measure of the abundance of these habitats across the state. So, for example, when we find that green frogs have a higher percentage occurrence in the Southeast than in the North-central and Eastern Forest regions, we do not know if this reflects a higher density of green frog populations in the Southeast or simply a more complete sampling of its available habitat there.

The subjective selection of stations makes the interpretation of estimated population trends difficult, because we are not certain just what the sample represents (e.g., Krzysik, Chpt. 41, this volume). Adjustments in the route regression analyses help alleviate some of this uncertainty and potential bias by weighting each route according to the coverage in its region, so that, for instance, a species' calculated statewide trend is not influenced inordinately by its trend in the Southeast, where routes are concentrated. However, routes were not placed evenly across each region, so some landscapes remain sampled more than others. Furthermore, if the suitability of sites naturally fluctuates over time (e.g., decades) according to conditions such as drought, flooding, siltation, and vegetational succession, it is possible that observers tended to choose their stations to be at "good" sites—close to wetlands that were near their maximum suitability at that time. If the suitability of these wetlands subsequently declines while the suitability of unsampled wetlands increases, erroneous population declines might be estimated. To complicate the matter even further, habitat changes that decrease a wetland's suitability for one species may improve it for another. The most obvious bias would occur if new wetlands were actually created or restored where they did not exist at the time the route was established.

These potential biases were recognized early in the WFTS program, and we were among those recommending a more representative selection procedure for the NAAMP protocol (Mossman et al. 1996). However, the problem of identifying potentially suitable habitat is difficult and is still being discussed. The currently recommended NAAMP protocol establishes stratified-random roadside routes along which stations are established at minimum intervals, within hearing distance of wetlands regardless of whether anurans are heard there. However, this protocol also involves a subjective identification of potential habitat, and depending on how well the person establishing the route knows the area and at what time of year it is established, some potential sites (especially ephemeral ones) could be missed The use of wetland maps to help identify potential habitat also has its limitations. For example, these maps often do not include small ponds and wet meadows and rarely include ephemeral ponds, where many species breed free from the pressures of fish predation. The only feasible way to obtain a truly representative sample may be to establish stations regardless of their proximity to wetlands, for example, along sections of BBS routes. Wisconsin has seventy of these roadside routes, each comprising fifty stations located 0.8 kilometer apart and located in a stratified-random pattern across the state. This would require no assumptions about the suitability, potential suitability, or abundance of habitat for various species or the minimum distance to breeding habitat allowed for listening stations to be established. But it leads to a logistical predicament because, for many areas of the continent, very few if any frogs would be heard from most random roadside locations. Sampling intensity would have to be increased considerably, and cooperators might have to be paid (however, randomly chosen sites could also provide much-needed monitoring data for night-calling birds, such as nighthawks, whippoorwills, and owls). Even the recommended NAAMP procedure may reduce encounters and necessitate more routes than what we estimated were required to obtain adequate samples in Wisconsin. However, if the routes are more representative, the data returned should be worth the effort.

One advantage of the subjective selection of stations is that cooperators tend to be dedicated to their routes. Cooperators tend to pay close attention to changes in "their" wetlands and frog populations, and this probably contributes to the long and consistent coverage of so many routes in Wisconsin. Indeed, such a commitment produces cooperator continuity and efficiency and contributes to the educational value of the WFTS. The success of any program with a more objective site selection procedure may depend on the extent that this same sort of commitment can be engendered.

Even considering the above discussion, we are confident that the current WFTS has provided valid results on population trends and general abundance patterns over its relatively short tenure. However, we plan to experiment with NAAMP protocols and perhaps BBS-style survey routes while continuing our established routes. We will do this in order to investigate potential biases, both in our program and in the new sampling systems, and to consider how we might change the WFTS without losing the trend information already present in our current database. We hope that these and other analyses of our dataset will provide information useful to the NAAMP and to other states and provinces (see Moriarty, Chpt. 20; Hemesath, Chpt. 23; and Johnson, Chpt. 37, this volume) in terms of developing methodological protocols, analytical techniques, and background information that will help with data collection and interpretation.

The WFTS has produced a valuable database on Wisconsin anuran distribution and has indicated areas and particular sites where documentation should be sought to fill gaps. The data suggest that two species (mink frogs and Blanchard's cricket frogs) reach their range limits in Wisconsin and are restricted to the northern half and southwestern corner of the state, respectively. American toads are the only species relatively evenly distributed across the state. The remaining nine species are essentially distributed statewide but are either absent from scattered sections of the state (pickerel frogs and perhaps bullfrogs) or are less common in some areas than elsewhere. For some species, these regional patterns of abundance are probably due at least in part to being near range limits (chorus frogs in the northeast, wood frogs in the southwest) or to the limited availability of habitat in certain sections of the state (e.g., for wood frogs, eastern gray treefrogs, and possibly spring peepers in the Southeast region or for northern leopard frogs and Cope's gray treefrogs in the North-central Forest region). In other cases, areas of apparently low abundance are more difficult to explain—for example, green frog and Cope's gray treefrog populations in the Eastern Forest region.

We are now using a Geographic Information System (GIS) to study habitat correlations with anuran abundance at each of a sample of WFTS stations. Hopefully, this will explain some species' patterns of abundance. It should also measure the degree to which the various habitat types are sampled in each region and thus help us better estimate the relative abundance of each species among different regions and the representation of the data used to calculate trends.

We have experimented with several methodologies to calculate population trends, most of them modified from the BBS protocol. An analysis of the 1984 to 1995 data suggests that maintaining a variety of such methods provides useful comparisons and a degree of redundancy that is prudent at this early stage in the development of appropriate analytical techniques. We found route frequency regression to be the most useful technique because it accounted for differences in regional sampling intensity and the fact that most routes are not run every year. However, simple annual percent occurrence approximated the route frequency regression trend plots for most species and were almost identical for a few well-sampled species. Route index regression and route adjusted-index regression results were more difficult to interpret because they incorporated the call index into trend estimates by arbitrarily assigning numbers to each index value; however, they were useful for comparison with the trends estimated from frequency alone. Trends estimated from these four methods agreed fairly well. Route regression trends were also similar when calculated using combined-period data for four typically "early spring" species that are sometimes more detectable during the late spring sampling period. The 1984 to 1995 trend analyses indicate that the added complication of comparing early and late spring data for each of these species at each station and the loss of some early spring data from routes in years when the second period is not sampled do not warrant the use of combined-period data. However, the incorporation of data from 1996—an extremely late year phenologically—may prove otherwise.

Population declines estimated by the WFTS should direct researchers' attention to spring peepers, northern leopard frogs, pickerel frogs, and Cope's gray treefrogs. A closer scrutiny of WFTS data is needed to verify these trends and their geographic and temporal patterns; our current evaluation of WFTS and GIS data may also indicate habitat relationships important to the survival of these species. These evaluations should therefore help identify specific management-related research programs and perhaps highlight additional monitoring needs for these species. A look at species' life histories and known habitat requirements may also suggest common factors that might be involved with declines. For example, the fact that all species with significantly declining trends spend considerable amounts of time in upland habitats, while declines were not detected in the three aquatic ranids (mink frogs, green frogs, and bullfrogs), suggests that upland habitat changes may be worth investigating. Research into the causes of cricket frog declines is desperately needed and should occur across state and provincial boundaries in order to incorporate healthy and declining populations in different parts of its range.

Four species were inadequately sampled by the WFTS. It is probably impractical to establish separate monitoring programs for each of them, but such programs are warranted for endangered cricket frogs and probably for pickerel frogs (state special concern status). More adequate monitoring could be accomplished by the addition of auditory survey routes within a species' range (and run only during its calling period) or by other methods that might include some intensive long-term study areas. Regardless, it is important to continue monitoring these four species with the WFTS, which can still detect more extreme population changes and changes over longer periods of time. Most important, our data can be added to those from other states and provinces to obtain adequate sampling over larger geographic areas.

Developing and maintaining a large volunteer-based survey can be difficult, and the WFTS has required considerable time and energy from many dedicated volunteers, as well as from central program staff who must set and periodically review protocols, solicit cooperators, distribute materials, evaluate survey returns for potential problems, maintain communication with cooperators, analyze data, and interpret results. We have found that in order to maintain quality control, continuity, and an adequately large dataset, the program does not "run itself." However, there is probably no other practical way to monitor these populations over the long term. Plus, such programs have the added advantage of being an effective educational tool.

Conclusions

The WFTS has been an invaluable tool for monitoring trends and distributions of Wisconsin's twelve anuran species. It has also provided useful information on the effects of climate and site factors on anuran breeding-call phenology and breeding activity, which has been essential in interpreting trend estimates; however, in this regard there is much more to be analyzed in the dataset. The survey's fifteen-year history, including the recent development of analytical techniques, demonstrates that the WFTS is an appropriate model for use (with other techniques) in the continent-wide amphibian monitoring program being organized by the NAAMP. The NAAMP's efforts to improve on the subjective placement of listening stations is essential; nonetheless, potential biases in trend and distribution estimates need to be investigated for the WFTS and the NAAMP's stratified-random selection procedures.

Based on several trend analyses conducted on WFTS data, three of the eight adequately sampled species underwent significant population declines during the period 1984 to 1995. Declines had been otherwise suspected for spring peepers and northern leopard frogs—two of the most widespread species in the state—but not for the less common Cope's gray treefrogs. One species (wood frogs) had significantly increasing trend estimates, which may have resulted in part from improvements in observers' abilities to time their surveys for this species' early, explosive breeding season. Three adequately sampled species (American toads, eastern gray treefrogs, and green frogs) exhibited stable to increasing trends. The four inadequately sampled species have limited distributions in the state: bullfrogs and mink frogs showed no indication of decline, but pickerel frogs did. The endangered Blanchard's cricket frog is too poorly sampled for WFTS data to suggest any trends, other than to document its rarity and extreme losses since the 1950s.

Whereas further attention is warranted in Wisconsin to investigate what may be long-term declines in spring peepers, leopard frogs, Cope's gray treefrogs, and possibly pickerel frogs, Blanchard's cricket frogs need to be studied primarily in nearby states where declining populations are larger.

WFTS data have quantified regional distributions of all twelve anuran species and have filled gaps in the known distributions of several species. However, additional documentation is needed for some calling records.

The program has helped educate hundreds of cooperators about the existence, ecology, and conservation of amphibians and the habitats on which they depend, while simultaneously contributing to amphibian conservation. Cooperators have also disseminated to the public information on amphibian population trends and conservation issues, and many have increased the public's involvement in other cooperative projects, such as the Herp Atlas.

Quality control and communication with cooperators are important factors for newly developing volunteer survey programs such as the WFTS, especially during the years before any results from trend analysis become meaningful; these factors have remained essential throughout the tenure of the WFTS. We have modified the program in a number of ways over the years and are now considering minor changes, such as the addition of monitoring night-calling birds, targeting documentation needs, improving the instructional materials, and identifying regional contact people who can help volunteers time their surveys. We will begin establishing some routes using NAAMP standards. These routes will be compared with our traditional routes, and we will be investigating additional uses of the large WFTS dataset, for example, regarding the effects of climatological factors, geography, and habitat on species distributions and trends.

Summary

Suggestions of widespread declines in amphibian populations have encouraged various agencies to initiate long-term monitoring programs, including auditory surveys for anurans based on the Wisconsin Frog and Toad Survey begun in 1984. The Wisconsin survey consists of approximately 120 permanent roadside transects, each comprising ten nocturnal listening stations. Volunteers survey each station in early spring, late spring, and summer, recording an index of abundance for each species based on the general frequency of breeding calls. The survey has been an important educational tool. Results have helped elucidate the breeding phenology, status, distribution, and short-term population fluctuations of Wisconsin's twelve anuran species and suggest that some species are in decline. Most new distributional records need further documentation. Several species apparently suffered short-term declines during the drought years of 1986 to 1989. Spring peepers (*Pseudacris crucifer*), northern leopard frogs (*Rana pipiens*), Cope's gray treefrogs (*Hyla chrysoscelis*), and possibly pickerel frogs (*Rana palustris*) are experiencing more long-term declines. Most species are currently sampled well enough to detect a 3 percent mean annual change over a twenty-year period at $p < 0.10$. Potential biases resulting from the subjective selection of listening stations and the limitations of alternative methods of selection warrant investigation.

Acknowledgments

This survey program would not exist except for the hundreds of cooperators who have volunteered their time, expertise, and travel expenses since its inception. Nor would it have been initiated at such an early date without the foresight of WDNR researcher Ruth Hine and the creative work of Debra K. Jansen and Ray Anderson, then of the University of Wisconsin-Stevens Point. Phenological data were collected and shared by cooperators Ron Eckstein, Karen Voss, Karen Etter Hale, and Carol Rudy. Lisa Dlutkowski, Kelly Kearns, Charlene Gieck, Ricky Lien, and others have helped coordinate the survey or summarize returns. John Huff established the computer database, wrote and modified initial analytical programs, and produced some of the early summaries and analyses. Paul Rasmussen helped with data transfer between the WDNR and the USGS. Janel Pike and Ron Gatti produced the distribution maps. Sam Droege of the USGS helped conduct the power analysis. WDNR supervisors Ruth Hine, Randy Jurewicz, LeRoy Petersen, and Jerry Bartelt helped to ensure the survey's continuation through the lean times.

22

Review of the Status of Wisconsin Amphibians

Gary S. Casper

Wisconsin currently has nineteen recognized amphibian species, seven salamanders and twelve frogs and toads. One species, Blanchard's cricket frogs (*Acris crepitans blanchardi*), is listed as endangered by the Wisconsin Department of Natural Resources (WDNR 1989). No species is currently listed as threatened. Three species are listed as special concern: bullfrogs (*Rana catesbeiana*), pickerel frogs (*Rana palustris*), and four-toed salamanders (*Hemidactylium scutatum*; B. Les, personal communication).

With the exception of data obtained from the Wisconsin Frog and Toad Survey (WFTS), very few quantitative data are available on amphibian status in Wisconsin. The WFTS is addressed in Mossman et al. (1995) and Mossman et al. (Chpt. 21, this volume). Here I give general accounts of known distributions and status of Wisconsin amphibians.

Overview

Two physiographic features influence amphibian distribution in Wisconsin. The Driftless Area is an unglaciated region of southwestern Wisconsin with steep bluffs and valleys characteristic of ancient, highly eroded landscapes unmodified by recent glacial forces. This well-drained topography supports few wetlands (Martin 1965; Fig. 22-1). The Tension Zone is a region of floristic transition, where the northern hardwoods province grades into the prairie forest province. This zone roughly divides the state into northern and southern biomes, with characteristic plant communities (Curtis 1959; Fig. 22-2).

Concern over amphibian declines in Wisconsin began in the 1970s, when field naturalists first noticed that northern leopard frog (*Rana pipiens*) populations were plummeting (Hine et al. 1975). This prompted a study by the WDNR, which indeed revealed a decline in northern leopard frogs (Hine et al. 1981) and ultimately initiated the WFTS. Hine et al. (1981) documented high mortality rates in Wisconsin northern leopard frogs and implicated Atrazine (or other chemical) poisoning and red leg disease. Large-scale commercial collecting by biological supply houses was also suspected as a cause of the decline. A partial rebound of northern leopard frog populations in recent years is suggested from Wisconsin Herpetological Atlas Project (WHAP) data (Milwaukee Public Museum; Casper 1996).

Blanchard's cricket frogs are the only other Wisconsin amphibian for which unequivocal evidence of severe decline is available, and this species is nearing extirpation in the state (see Hay, Chpt. 11; Mossman et al., Chpt. 21, this volume). Cricket frogs were listed as a state endangered species in 1982 (WDNR 1989). Evidence for small but significant declines in several Wisconsin anurans is now becoming available as a result of the accumulating WFTS data, with the most significant declines occurring in spring peepers (*Pseudacris crucifer*), northern leopard frogs, Cope's gray treefrogs (*Hyla chrysoscelis*), and possibly pickerel frogs (Mossman et al., Chpt. 21, this volume). No quantitative data are available on salamander population trends.

Undoubtedly, the most important factors affecting amphibian status in Wisconsin are habitat loss and degradation. The National Biological Service recently sum-

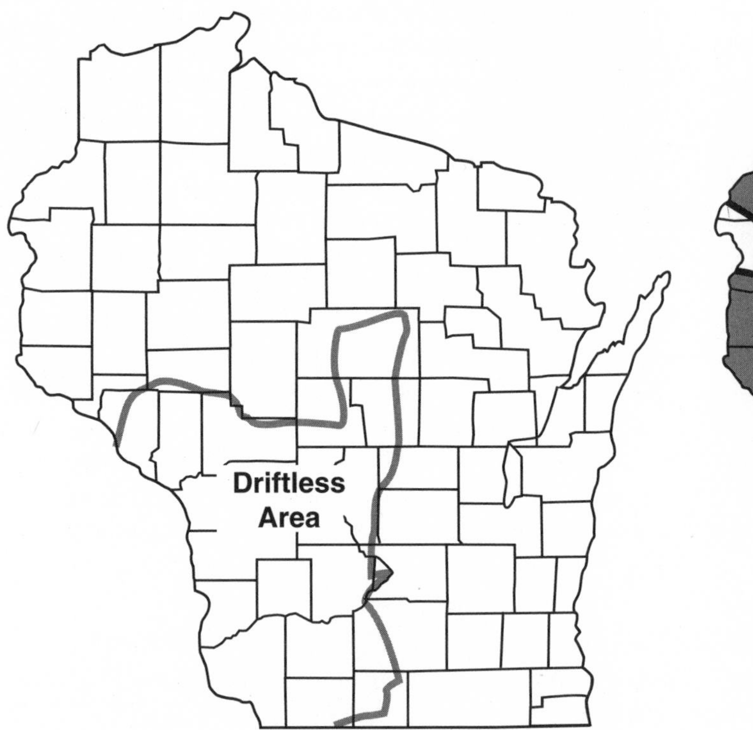

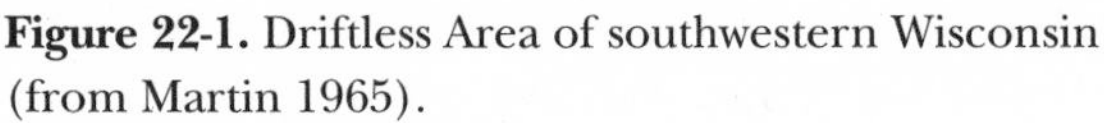
Figure 22-1. Driftless Area of southwestern Wisconsin (from Martin 1965).

Figure 22-2. Tension Zone of floristic transition (from Curtis 1959).

marized habitat losses in the United States (Noss et al. 1995) and offered the following information:

less than 0.004 percent of high-quality savannas in Wisconsin remain;

a 55 percent loss of wetlands in the Great Lakes states;

a 46 percent loss of wetlands in Wisconsin from the 1780s to the 1980s;

a more than 99 percent loss of original sedge meadows in Wisconsin;

oak savannas are considered a critically endangered (more than 98 percent decline) ecosystem in the Midwest;

sedge meadows are considered a critically endangered (more than 98 percent decline) ecosystem in Wisconsin; and

riparian forests are considered a threatened (between 70 and 84 percent decline) ecosystem nationwide.

In addition to outright losses, habitat degradation can have significant impacts on amphibians. Clear-cutting of forests has been demonstrated to affect terrestrial amphibians in Maryland negatively (Blymyer and McGinnes 1977), probably due to changes in soil moisture and acidity. Vogt (1981) believed that forest cutting, urbanization, and agriculture adversely impacted spotted salamanders (*Ambystoma maculatum*) in Wisconsin but that agriculture did not seem to impact eastern tiger salamanders (*Ambystoma tigrinum tigrinum*). Almost no virgin forest remains in Wisconsin. Most managed stands are less than seventy-five years old. Changes in wetland plant communities are also epidemic in Wisconsin, due to the effects of fire suppression and the invasion of exotic species such as purple loosestrife and reed canary grass. Typically, species diversity is compromised when wetlands are invaded by weedy species. Such invasions result in changes in plant species composition, plant density, sedimentation rates and patterns, hydrology, and associated invertebrate communities. Investigation into how these changes impact amphibian communities is sorely needed. Introduced animals, in particular zebra mussels (*Dreissena polymorpha*) and rusty crayfish (*Orconectes rusticus*), are significantly changing the ecology of Wisconsin waters as well. The introduction of fish into fishless ponds can have severe consequences for amphibian populations, compromising egg and larval stages. This practice is common but not quantified in Wisconsin. Vogt (1981) noted the effects of fish predation on central newt (*Notophthalmus viridescens louisianensis*) populations in Wisconsin. Poisoning of "rough fish," usually with rotenone, is another common practice in Wisconsin, with unquantified effects on amphibians.

Environmental contamination often has been suggested as contributing to amphibian declines. Numerous studies have documented a sensitivity to pH in amphibian species, potentially placing them at risk from acid rain (Corn and Vertucci 1992; Freda and Taylor 1992; Frisbie and Wyman 1991, 1992a,b; Harte and Hoffman 1989; Ireland 1991; Karns 1992; Leftwich and Lilly 1992; McCue 1989; Mushinsky and Brodie 1975; Pierce et al. 1984; Pierce et al. 1987; Pierce and Harvey 1987; Pierce and Wooten 1992; Pough 1976; Rowe et al. 1992; Sadinski and Dunson 1992; Wissinger and Whiteman 1992; Wyman 1988; Wyman and Hawksley-Lescault 1987). Studies in Wisconsin investigating the effects of pH on amphibians are scarce. Kutka and Bachmann (1990) concluded that most amphibian species in northern Wisconsin are probably not in immediate danger from acid deposition and that ambystomid salamanders would be the first affected because they use the most sensitive ponds, some of which were found to be within the species' chronically toxic pH range. Most Wisconsin amphibian species have been shown to be sensitive to pH to varying degrees (Kutka and Bachmann 1990). Accumulation of heavy metals in tadpoles has been documented in Wisconsin and may affect survivorship (Hall and Mulhern 1984). Steele et al. (1991) demonstrated a failure of American toad (*Bufo americanus americanus*) tadpoles to avoid lead-enriched water in Ohio, suggesting they may be susceptible to lead poisoning. Matson (1990, Chpt. 28, this volume) demonstrated population declines in mudpuppies (*Necturus maculosus maculosus*) from streams treated with the lampricide TFM (3-triflouromethyl–4-nitrophenol) in Ohio. Numerous investigations have documented chronic toxic effects on ranid frogs from DDT (Weis 1975), copper (Lande and Guttman 1973), lead (Birdsall et al. 1986; Eby 1986; Steele et al. 1989; Strickler-Shaw 1988; Strickler-Shaw and Taylor 1990; Taylor et al. 1990), cadmium (Eby 1986), Atrazine (Hine et al. 1981), the pyrethroid insecticide esfenvalerate (Materna et al. 1995), and sarin (Wilbur 1954). Vogt (1981) suggested that American toads in Wisconsin are negatively impacted by fertilizers and pesticides on agricultural lands.

Wisconsin amphibians are in general decline due to habitat losses and degradation. This decline is most noticeable in the heavily urbanized counties of southeastern Wisconsin, where rampant development is restricting all amphibians to isolated populations, with unknown genetic consequences on long-term viability. Heavily utilized agricultural landscapes, mostly in southern Wisconsin, are also becoming difficult territory for amphibians, as wetlands such as the critically endangered sedge meadow community are destroyed and migration routes are made impassable. In recent years, reports of malformed frogs have been accumulating in Wisconsin. DuBois (1996) collected reports from sixteen sites since 1992. Researchers are actively investigating the causes of these malformities, but it is not known at this time whether malformities are contributing to population declines.

Data accumulating from the WFTS and the WHAP will become increasingly important in monitoring and managing state amphibian populations. The most pressing research need is for investigations into the causes of amphibian declines, followed by basic research on demographics, distribution, and the accuracy and precision of monitoring techniques.

Species Status Review

Salamanders

Blue-spotted Salamanders. Blue-spotted salamanders (*Ambystoma laterale*) are perhaps the most abundant salamander in Wisconsin, with good populations persisting in deciduous and mixed woodland habitat throughout the state. They are uncommon and local where woodland ponds required for breeding are scarce, for example, in the Driftless Area of southwestern Wisconsin and in nonwooded regions of southern Wisconsin. Populations in the urbanized landscapes of southeastern Wisconsin are becoming isolated from each other by development. The formerly recognized Tremblay's salamander is now considered a polyploid hybrid of the *Ambystoma laterale-jeffersonianum* complex (Bogart and Licht 1986; Lowcock et al. 1987) and is included in this discussion. The Wisconsin distribution encompasses fifty-eight of seventy-two counties (Casper 1996; Vogt 1981). No information on status is available, other than continuing and regular occurrence reports to the WHAP. Pentecost and Vogt (1976) rated their status as common throughout the Lake Michigan basin.

Spotted Salamanders. Due to their fossorial nature, spotted salamanders often go undetected in cursory surveys and were listed as a threatened species by the WDNR in 1979. A study in northeastern Wisconsin (Dames and Moore 1981) subsequently documented widespread presence and lent weight to the argument that their apparent rarity was merely a reflection of inadequate survey effort. This resulted in the delisting of the spotted salamander (WDNR 1987). They are still widespread in hardwood and mixed forests north of the Tension Zone, and distribution has been documented in twenty-six of seventy-two counties (Vogt 1981; Casper 1996). Numbers may be reduced by forestry practices, where short stand rotation alters soil moisture and acidity. No quantitative studies on population trends have been conducted in Wisconsin. Their status appears to be precarious in southeastern Wisconsin, where they are limited to local, isolated populations in island habitats of forested moraines with woodland ponds. Populations are still extant in Ozaukee County and possibly in Waukesha County but are threatened by development. Pentecost and Vogt (1976) described their status as common throughout the Lake Michigan basin.

Eastern Tiger Salamanders. Eastern tiger salamanders are common south of the Tension Zone, exclusive of the Driftless Area of southwestern Wisconsin where they are rare to absent. Distributional records are available from thirty-three of seventy-two counties (Casper 1996; Vogt 1981). Knudsen (1989) reported them as common in Dane County in the period 1946 to 1960, and Vogt (1981) reported finding them in great abundance in the metro areas of Madison in 1966. Pentecost and Vogt (1976) considered their status "abundant; common within lower two-thirds of the Lake Michigan basin." I noted good populations in a degraded oak savanna in Walworth County in the 1990s, and they are regularly reported from Washington and Ozaukee Counties (WHAP).

Central Newts. The distribution of central newts in Wisconsin now includes thirty-three counties widely scattered across the state (Casper 1996; Vogt 1981). A need exists for basic survey work on this species, which probably occurs in many more counties than are currently documented. Little information on status is available, but I found them to be common in woodlands of southeastern Wisconsin. I found no evidence of decline. Pentecost and Vogt (1976) described their status as abundant throughout the Lake Michigan basin.

Four-toed Salamanders. Casper (1993a,b) summarized records for four-toed salamanders and discussed distribution, noting that most localities are represented by very few records (one to three). They are now documented from twenty counties widely scattered throughout the state (Casper 1996) and listed as a special concern species by the WDNR (B. Les, personal communication). Efficient and reliable survey methods for these salamanders are lacking. Four-toed salamanders can go undetected for decades; for example, they were first discovered in Minnesota in 1994 (Dorff 1995). Pope (1930) wrote of collecting this species in Vernon County in 1929, stating that "specimens were easily found under both boulders and logs on rather dry hillsides." Spellum reported four-toed salamanders as "common and widely spread over Vernon County" in 1928 (Pope 1930). Pentecost and Vogt (1976) considered their status common throughout the Lake Michigan basin, although rare to absent from agricultural lands. Vogt (1981) considered their Wisconsin distribution to consist of isolated populations. No information on population trends is available. Long-term monitoring at sites where they are known to occur is recommended.

Redback Salamanders. Redback salamanders (*Plethodon cinereus*) are terrestrial salamanders common in forests north of the Tension Zone, but forestry practices may be influencing their distribution and demographics (Wyman 1988). Their Wisconsin distribution now includes thirty-four counties (Vogt 1981; Casper 1996). Pentecost and Vogt (1976) considered their status abundant throughout the Lake Michigan basin.

Mudpuppies. Mudpuppies are distributed statewide in Wisconsin, with records from forty-nine counties (Vogt 1981; Casper 1996). They appear to have disappeared from Sajdak's (1982) study site in Waukesha County. Siltation of streams is a serious problem in agricultural areas of Wisconsin, and the burying of cobble bottoms with fine-grained sediments undoubtedly has compromised mudpuppy populations in many regions. There is no evidence of decline from most waters where they occur, but populations are not being monitored. Mudpuppies are commercially harvested for the biological supply industry. The combination of commercial harvest without population monitoring invites resource exploitation. Very few reports of this species are received by the WHAP, but good numbers were recently reported from a river in northeastern Wisconsin by area fish managers. Pentecost and Vogt (1976) regarded the status of mudpuppies as "common in shallow waters of lakes and streams" throughout the Lake Michigan basin and "rare to absent from heavily polluted waters, marshes, and small creeks."

Frogs and Toads

American Toads. American toads have been documented from all seventy-two counties in Wisconsin (Vogt 1981; Casper 1996). They are one of the most commonly reported amphibians in the state (WHAP) and persist in urban and agricultural landscapes so long as breeding wetlands remain intact. Status information is mostly limited to the WFTS data, which report a slight increasing trend (Mossman et al. 1995; Mossman et al., Chpt. 21, this volume). Knudsen (1989) reported American toads as abundant and widespread in twenty-seven counties during the period 1940 to 1960. Pentecost and Vogt (1976) rated their status as abundant throughout the Lake Michigan basin.

Blanchard's Cricket Frogs. No new counties have been added in recent times to the documented Blanchard's cricket frog distribution in Wisconsin (Casper 1996; Mossman et al., Chpt. 21, this volume). On the contrary, Blanchard's cricket frogs have disappeared from most areas of former occurrence and were listed as an endangered species in Wisconsin in 1982 (WDNR 1989). Remaining populations are restricted to the southwestern portion of the state. Recent reports from southeastern Wisconsin have not been verified. I have never encountered these frogs in ten years of fieldwork in southeastern Wisconsin. Six southeastern Wisconsin sites surveyed in 1990 by Gruenweller (1990) produced negative results. They have been documented on only three of approximately seventy WFTS routes within their former Wisconsin range (Mossman et al., Chapt. 21, this volume). They were absent in 1995 from approximately forty Marsh Monitoring Program routes within their former range in eastern Wisconsin and southern Michigan (Chabot and Helferty 1995). They have suffered significant, possibly irreversible, declines (Hay, Chpt. 11, this volume). They are present on too few WFTS routes to yield significant data (Mossman et al. 1995; Mossman et al., Chpt. 21, this volume). Knudsen (1989) reported a decline along the lower Wisconsin River, with near absence by the mid-1960s. Pope and Dickinson (1928) considered this species common in the 1920s. Pentecost and Vogt (1976) considered their status as "common; locally abundant in the southern one-third of the Lake Michigan basin," while acknowledging that Wisconsin populations were low. Vogt (1981) noted that this species has gone from very common to extremely rare in Wisconsin.

Western Chorus Frogs and Boreal Chorus Frogs. Elevation of the subspecies *Pseudacris triseriata triseriata* and *P. t. maculata* to species status has been proposed (Platz 1989), but they are treated together here. Distributional records now encompass fifty-nine of the seventy-two Wisconsin counties (Vogt 1981; Casper 1996). Chorus frogs remain common in southern Wisconsin but are rare in the northeastern counties, where they reach the northern limit of their Wisconsin range. According to the WFTS, chorus frogs are declining in the eastern and northeastern counties but appear to be stable statewide (Mossman et al., Chpt. 21, this volume). Pentecost and Vogt (1976) deemed their status to be abundant throughout the Lake Michigan basin. Vogt (1981) noted that good populations can be found throughout Wisconsin.

Northern Spring Peepers. Only twelve Wisconsin counties still lack records for spring peepers, mostly in eastern Wisconsin (Vogt 1981; Casper 1996). Mossman and Hine (1984, 1985) reported a decline in this species. Their distribution is patchy in eastern Wisconsin, where they are widely thought to be in decline. I found healthy populations in Forest County in 1994. Quantitative data on status, however, are limited to the WFTS, which shows a significant decline (Mossman et al. 1995; Mossman et al., Chpt. 21, this volume). Knudsen (1989) reported "abundant specimens" and "excellent populations" in thirty-three counties from the period 1935 to 1960. Pentecost and Vogt (1976) appraised its status as abundant throughout the Lake Michigan basin.

Cope's Gray Treefrogs. Cope's gray treefrogs were verified from twenty Wisconsin counties by Vogt (1981), and their Wisconsin distribution is apparently sparse (Casper 1996). Jaslow and Vogt (1977) reported them as uncommon to absent from much of the northern half of the state. However, the WFTS data show them to be more widespread (Mossman et al., Chpt. 21, this volume). I found them to be common in the former savannas of southeastern Wisconsin. Pentecost and Vogt (1976) considered their status as common in the Lake Michigan basin. The WFTS data indicate a significant decline for this species (Mossman et al., Chpt. 21, this volume).

Eastern Gray Treefrogs. Eastern gray treefrogs (*Hyla versicolor*) occur statewide, with the apparent exception of the former savanna and prairie habitats of southeastern Wisconsin, where they are replaced by Cope's gray treefrog. Vogt (1981) verified gray treefrogs from forty-four counties, and seven new counties have been subsequently documented (Casper 1996). The WFTS data show a stable trend for this species (Mossman et al., Chpt. 21, this volume). Knudsen (1989), who did not differentiate between eastern gray treefrogs and Cope's gray treefrogs at the time, reported "abundant specimens" and "excellent to good populations" in seventeen counties from the period 1935 to 1960. Pentecost and Vogt (1976) considered their status as common throughout the Lake Michigan basin. Vogt (1981) considered eastern gray treefrogs to be abundant in southern mesic hardwoods, southern and northern lowland forests, boreal forests, and northern mesic and dry-mesic hardwoods. I noted healthy populations in Forest County in 1994, and a good population in central Ozaukee County persists.

Bullfrogs. Bullfrogs range statewide, with thirty-eight counties of known occurrence (Vogt 1981; Casper 1996). They are listed as a special concern species by the WDNR (B. Les, personal communication). The WFTS indicates greatest abundance in the north-central counties (Mossman et al., Chpt. 21, this volume). Use by the bait industry has led to numerous introductions in the state, and it is now impossible to separate natural from introduced occurrences. The introduction and establishment of bullfrogs into new areas have been linked to declines in other anuran species (Hayes and Jennings 1986; Schwalbe and Rosen 1988), but this phenomenon has not been demonstrated in Wisconsin. Knudsen (1989) reported a "very good population" in Vilas County from the period 1950 to 1960 but considered bullfrogs to be "by far the rarest and most scattered species in Wisconsin" as of 1960. Pope and Dickinson (1928) considered bullfrogs to be in decline in Wisconsin in the 1920s, stating they were "rapidly disappearing from the state" and that "the final passing of the bullfrog from the state was probably imminent." However, Pentecost and Vogt (1976) judged their status as common in the Lake Michigan basin. Vogt (1981) considered bullfrogs to be much more common in northern Wisconsin and mentioned collecting and shoreline degradation as negatively impacting this species. I consider bullfrogs to be uncommon in southeastern Wisconsin. Sampling is inadequate for meaningful data analysis from the WFTS, but data suggest a decline (Mossman et al. 1995; Mossman et al., Chpt. 21, this volume).

Green Frogs. The ubiquitous green frogs (*Rana clamitans melanota*) occur in every Wisconsin county (Casper 1996; Vogt 1981). I consider them to be the most common ranid frog in permanent waters of Wisconsin at this time. The WFTS data show a stable trend (Mossman et al., Chpt. 21, this volume). Knudsen (1989) considered this species as common in thirty-three counties from the period 1935 to 1960. Pentecost and Vogt (1976) considered their status as abundant throughout the Lake Michigan basin. Vogt (1981) considered green frogs as common throughout Wisconsin.

Pickerel Frogs. The Wisconsin distribution of pickerel frogs now encompasses thirty-four counties (Vogt 1981; Casper 1996). Johnson (1984) documented a much more pervasive Wisconsin distribution than was previously known, resulting in the subsequent downlisting of this species from threatened to special concern status (WDNR 1987). The WFTS sample is small but nevertheless shows a downward trend (Mossman et al., Chpt. 21, this volume). Knudsen (1989) reported good populations from Dane and Sauk Counties from the 1950s. Pentecost and Vogt (1976) considered their status as rare in the Lake Michigan basin, and Vogt (1981) reported them as rare in Wisconsin, occurring only in isolated localities. Pickerel frogs are rare in southeastern Wisconsin, and one population in the Southern Kettle Moraine State Forest appears to have disappeared after a shoreline was developed for fishing access.

Northern Leopard Frogs. Northern leopard frogs are known from all seventy-two Wisconsin counties (Vogt 1981). A decline in numbers was widely reported in the 1970s (Hine et al. 1981). WFTS data show a downward trend (Mossman et al., Chpt. 21, this volume), although many field observers have noted a partial rebound since 1985 (WHAP). I noted thousands of newly metamorphosed northern leopard frogs in Winnebago County in 1993 during a summer of record rainfall. Knudsen (1989) considered these frogs to be second only to green frogs in abundance and reported them as abundant in twenty-six counties from the period 1930 to 1960. Pentecost and Vogt (1976) considered their status as abundant throughout the Lake Michigan basin. Vogt (1981) believed northern leopard frogs were once the most common frog in Wisconsin, until the population crash of the 1970s.

Mink Frogs. Mink frogs (*Rana septentrionalis*) are a boreal species restricted to northern Wisconsin (Vogt 1981; Casper 1996). The WFTS does not have adequate sampling of this species for data analysis (Mossman et al. 1995; Mossman et al., Chpt. 21, this volume). They are rarely reported to the WHAP. Pentecost and Vogt (1976) considered their status as common in the northern Lake Michigan basin.

Wood Frogs. Common and widespread in the northern two-thirds of the state, wood frogs (*Rana sylvatica*) are only locally distributed in the southern third of the state, where woodlands with ponds are present. Vogt (1981) mapped wood frogs from forty-six counties, and an additional nineteen counties have since been added (Casper 1996). The WFTS data show an apparent upward trend for this species, although this trend is suspected to be at least partially the result of observer learning bias (Mossman et al., Chpt. 21, this volume). Pentecost and Vogt (1976) considered their status common throughout the Lake Michigan basin. I noted a high abundance in Forest County in 1994 and apparently stable populations in Ozaukee and Washington Counties from 1986 to 1995.

Summary

Wisconsin has nineteen amphibian species, seven salamanders and twelve frogs and toads. One species (Blanchard's cricket frogs [*Acris crepitans blanchardi*]) is listed as state endangered. Three species, bullfrogs (*Rana catesbeiana*), pickerel frogs (*Rana palustris*), and four-toed salamanders (*Hemidactylium scutatum*), are listed as special concern. With the exception of the Wisconsin Frog and Toad Survey, very few quantitative data are available on amphibian status in Wisconsin. Here I give general accounts of known distributions and status of Wisconsin amphibians.

Acknowledgments

I thank Robert Henderson and Michael Mossman for their critical review. Robert Hay and Donald Reed have provided many stimulating accounts of amphibian occurrence over the last decade, for which I am exceedingly grateful. Allen Young has graciously extended institutional support to the Great Lakes Declining Amphibians Task Force. Finally, I thank Jack Puelicher, whose generosity has made the Wisconsin Herpetological Atlas Project a reality.

23

Iowa's Frog and Toad Survey, 1991–1994

Lisa M. Hemesath

Recently, worldwide population declines of amphibians have received much attention in the scientific community (e.g., Barinaga 1990; Blaustein and Wake 1990; Pechmann et al. 1991; Pechmann and Wilbur 1994; Phillips 1990; Wake and Morowitz 1991) and in the popular press. Christiansen (1981) noted declines in Iowa's herptile species over a decade ago, stating that fully 69 percent of Iowa's amphibian and reptile species are believed to be endangered, threatened, or declining. Without a clear-cut reversal in present trends, it is likely that in the next 50 to 100 years less than a third of Iowa's present amphibian and reptile fauna will remain.

In response to these concerns, the Iowa Department of Natural Resources (IDNR) Nongame Program (a.k.a. Wildlife Diversity Program) conducted a one-year auditory survey for calling anurans in 1984 to determine geographic distributions within the state. The survey was reinitiated in 1991 with the intention of establishing an extensive, long-term monitoring program in order to discriminate between short-term population fluctuations and chronic population declines. The goals of the program are to: (1) determine the distributions of Iowa's anuran species, (2) determine population trends for each species, and (3) promote education about aquatic life by using volunteers to conduct the survey. Volunteer-based auditory surveys for frogs and toads are currently being used in the Midwest by Wisconsin (Mossman and Hine 1984; Mossman et al., Chpt. 21, this volume), Minnesota (Moriarty, Chpt. 20, this volume), Missouri (Johnson, Chpt. 37, this volume), and Illinois (S. Ballard, personal communication).

Results of the first four years of data collecting, 1991 through 1994, are presented in this chapter. Information regarding changes in anuran species distributions is emphasized. Advantages and disadvantages of using a volunteer-based survey are discussed, and suggestions are given to improve the accuracy of data collection by volunteers.

Methods

Survey methods used in Iowa are adapted from Wisconsin's annual anuran survey (Mossman and Hine 1984; Mossman et al., Chpt. 21, this volume). Each volunteer receives an informational packet about Iowa's frogs and toads that includes a species identification booklet (Christiansen and Bailey 1991), a tape of anuran calls, a survey route description form, data sheets, and survey instructions. Volunteers are encouraged to familiarize themselves with the calls of fifteen species of anurans and to read the species identification booklet. The volunteer surveyors receive no training beyond the informational packet.

Survey routes typically consist of visits to five wetland sites of the volunteer's choice. Surveyors are encouraged to choose a variety of wetlands. Each wetland site on a route is placed in one of eight categories: ephemeral (e.g., ditches, flooded fields), wet meadow, cattail marsh (temporal or seasonal wetland), open marsh (semipermanent), lakes or farm ponds (permanent), shrub marshes, open riverine (e.g., streams in grassland habitat), and timbered riverine. Locations and descriptions of survey sites are sent to the IDNR along with a route map.

Routes are surveyed three times annually, once during each of three designated time periods: 1–28 April, 7 May–4 June, and 13 June–10 July. The time periods are necessary to ensure that all species are surveyed during their peak calling periods. Survey periods were established based on the known calling phenology of Missouri and Wisconsin anuran species and adapted to fit Iowa's anuran calling phenology (Reeves 1984).

Volunteers are encouraged to run the survey during optimal weather conditions: warm, cloudy evenings with little wind and high humidity. Water temperatures should be at least 10°C during the first survey period, 15°C during the second period, and 21°C during the final period.

Information recorded on the data sheet includes date, starting and ending times, wind velocity, air temperature, and condition of sky (i.e., clear, partly cloudy, overcast, fog, drizzle, rain showers) at the start and end of the survey period. At each survey site, volunteers are encouraged to listen for ten minutes and record the calling index value (a.k.a. relative abundance value) of each species on a scale of one to three: one = individuals can be counted, there is a space between calls; two = calls of individuals can be distinguished but calls overlap; three = full chorus, calls are continuous and overlapping. The general condition of the wetland (wet or dry) and water temperature are also recorded at each survey site.

Similarities in calls between some species caused the IDNR to modify its survey techniques. For example, all three species of leopard frogs in the state, northern leopard frogs (*Rana pipiens*), plains leopard frogs (*Rana blairi*), and southern leopard frogs (*Rana sphenocephala*), were recorded as one species. In addition, because the call of pickerel frogs (*Rana palustris*) is similar to the call of leopard frogs, visual verification of pickerel frogs was encouraged in addition to auditory observation.

To determine the extent of inter-observer variation in the assignment of calling index values, five wetland sites were surveyed by twenty Iowa State University students and staff on one night in June 1994. The twenty surveyors were given the same information to prepare for the survey as typical survey volunteers. To transport the surveyors by vehicle to the survey sites, surveyors were divided into four teams of approximately five people each. The survey began at dark, with the first vehicle leaving for the first survey site. The remaining vehicles were dispersed at ten- to fifteen-minute intervals (i.e., the first group started the census at 9:30 p.m. and the fourth group at 10:05 p.m.). Although wetland sites were surveyed simultaneously by a team, data were collected on an individual basis. Members of a team were instructed not to consult each other on data collection for the duration of the survey. Preliminary results on this aspect of Iowa's frog and toad survey will be covered later in this chapter.

Results and Discussion

Species Distributions and Status

Between 1991 and 1994, 143 routes were established in sixty-eight counties in Iowa (Fig. 23-1). Coverage was poor in some areas of the state, including southern, north-central, and east-central Iowa. Eight hundred and eleven different wetland sites were surveyed from 1991 through 1994. The number of routes run per year and the number of sample sites have varied little since 1992 (Table 23-1). Only 16 of the 143 established routes were run all four years. Just 26 routes were surveyed three out of the four years.

The distributions of Iowa's anuran species as determined by the frog and toad survey closely match known distributions (Figs. 23-2, 23-3; Christiansen and Bailey 1991; Conant and Collins 1991). Most deviations from known distributions are attributed to errors in data collection. When species were detected outside their range, no specimens were taken; thus, verification of range expansion has yet to be undertaken. The low number of survey routes repeated between 1991 and 1994 and inter-observer variation in the assignment of calling index values made it impractical to determine

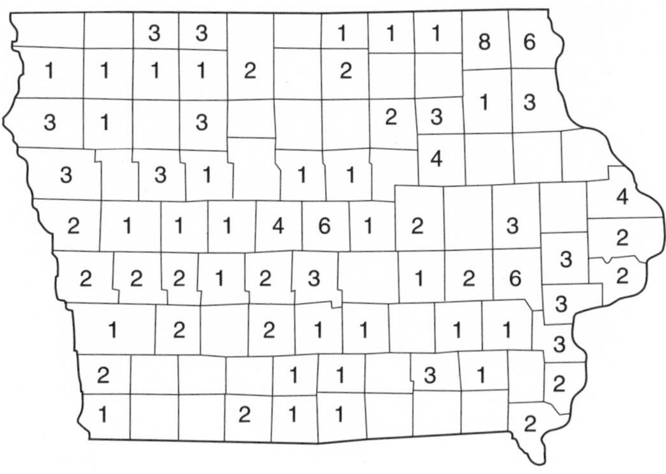

Figure 23-1. The number of frog and toad survey routes established in each county in Iowa, 1991 through 1994.

Table 23-1. Annual number of active routes and number of sites surveyed during Iowa's frog and toad survey, 1991–1994

Year	Number of Routes	Number of New Routes	Number of Previously Established Routes	Number of Sites
1991	46	46	—	249
1992	74	42	32	389
1993	76	27	49	416
1994	75	28	47	401

population trends. Thus, distribution information will be emphasized here. Preliminary results of a study on inter-observer variation will be presented below.

The survey indicated a statewide distribution for the leopard frog complex (sixty-three of sixty-eight counties surveyed; Fig. 23-2), but due to the inability to discriminate species by their calls, individual distributions of northern, plains, and southern leopard frogs could not be determined. According to Christiansen and Bailey (1991) and Conant and Collins (1991), northern leopard frogs are distributed statewide, plains leopard frogs are found in the southern two-thirds of the state, and southern leopard frogs are found only in the extreme southeastern corner of Iowa. The leopard frog complex was detected 701 times at 402 sites across Iowa, making this ranid group the fourth most detected taxa in the state (Table 23-2). However, full choruses were recorded only 38 times between 1991 and 1994 across all sites and survey periods (Table 23-2). Ten of those records came from one county in southeastern Iowa.

The low number of full ranid choruses heard could be an artifact of the species' low-volume call (Bishop et al. 1997) or could reflect a decline in ranid populations such as has been documented in the West (see Hayes and Jennings 1986) and in the North (Wake 1991). Lack of historical information on the abundance of the leopard frog complex in Iowa allows only speculation on its current population status. Lannoo et al. (1994) attributed a decline of northern leopard frogs and other amphibians in Dickinson County, northwestern Iowa, to the local effects of wetland drainage and conversion to row crops, the introduction of bullfrogs, and the use of local natural wetlands for aquaculture. From anecdotal information on the frogging industry (Anonymous 1907; Barrett 1964), Lannoo et al. (1994) have estimated that the number of northern leopard frogs had decreased by two or three orders of magnitude in the county since around 1900. Declines within the last twenty years have been documented elsewhere. In western Canada, northern leopard frogs underwent a drastic population decline in the 1970s, and while some of these populations have recovered and have returned to traditional breeding sites, other areas still contain only low densities of northern leopard frogs or have not been recolonized at all (Koonz 1992; Orchard 1992; Roberts 1992; Seburn 1992). In Wisconsin, northern leopard frogs apparently suffered population declines during the 1970s (Vogt 1981; Casper, Chpt. 22, this volume), and recent frog and toad data (Dhuey et al. 1994; Mossman et al., Chpt. 21, this volume) suggest a continued decline. Contrary to reports in other parts of the United States and Canada, evidence suggests that populations of northern and plains leopard frogs increased during the early 1980s in Iowa (Christiansen 1981). It is probable that the leopard frog complex undergoes periods of population decline and recovery on a local basis, and only the continuation of long-term studies, such as statewide calling surveys, will discriminate between short-term population fluctuations and long-term trends.

Pickerel frogs were recorded in five counties within their known geographic range in eastern Iowa and in three counties outside their known range (Fig. 23-2). These frogs are typically found along cold-water streams feeding into the Mississippi River (Christiansen and Bailey 1991). The paucity of records may reflect my request that volunteers confirm auditory records of this species with visual observation. The difficulty of visually verifying a calling frog in the dark may have encouraged volunteers to record the snore of pickerel frogs as the similar call of the leopard frog complex. While pickerel

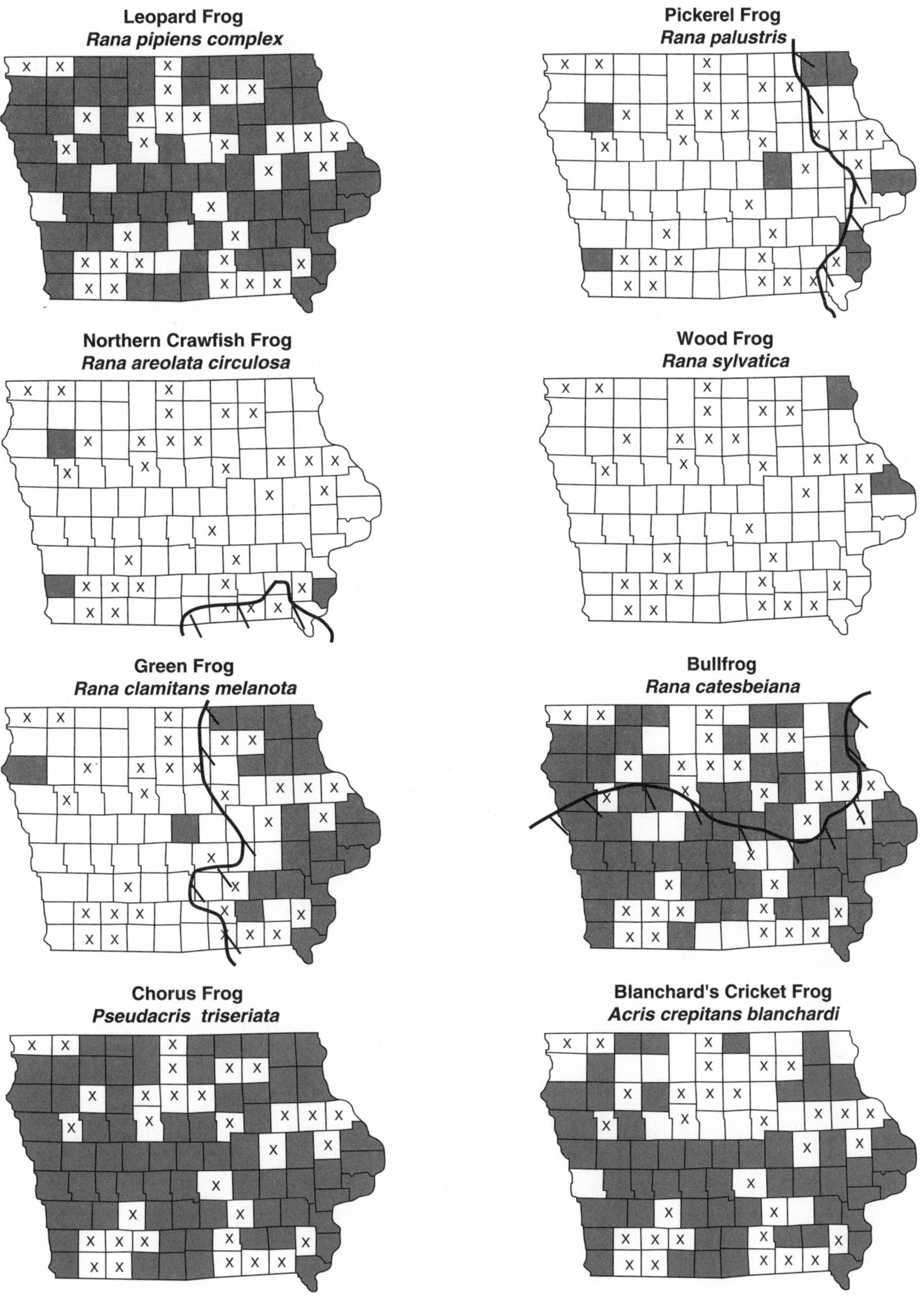

Figure 23-2. The distribution of eight anuran species by county in Iowa according to the frog and toad survey, 1991 through 1994. Gray shading indicates species presence; "x" indicates county was not sampled. Historical range boundaries (lines; after Christiansen and Bailey 1991) are included. With the exception of wood frogs, species showing no range boundaries have a statewide distribution. Wood frogs were not previously known to occur in the state.

Table 23-2. Summary of species detections during Iowa's frog and toad survey, 1991–1994

Species	Number of Times Recorded across All Sites and Survey Periods (n = 3,942)	Number of Times Recorded at Full Chorus across All Sites and Survey Periods (n = 1,761)	Number of Sites Species Was Recorded as Present (n = 811)
Leopard frog complex (*Rana pipiens, R. blairi, R. sphenocephala*)	701	38	402
Pickerel frogs (*Rana palustris*)	26	2	19
Northern crawfish frogs (*Rana areolata circulosa*)	6	0	6
Green frogs (*Rana clamitans melanota*)	6	0	6
Bullfrogs (*Rana catesbeiana*)	576	42	320
Wood frogs (*Rana sylvatica*)	3	0	3
Eastern gray treefrogs (*Hyla versicolor*)	1,173	310	473
Cope's gray treefrogs (*Hyla chrysoscelis*)	273	39	161
Northern spring peepers (*Pseudacris crucifer crucifer*)	455	159	206
Chorus frogs (*Pseudacris triseriata*)	1,424	531	622
Blanchard's cricket frogs (*Acris crepitans blanchardi*)	662	238	320
American toads (*Bufo americanus americanus*)	1,202	379	553
Woodhouse's toads (*Bufo woodhousii*)	99	6	61
Great Plains toads (*Bufo cognatus*)	29	4	21
Plains spadefoot toads (*Spea bombifrons*)	12	2	12

frogs were recorded at nineteen different sites across the state, full choruses were detected only twice (Table 23-2), both times from a county far outside the known distribution range of this species. Extralimital observations may have resulted from either a data-recording error or species misidentification. Also, close proximity of the pickerel frog to the leopard frog complex on the data sheet probably increased the likelihood of recording the data in the wrong column.

Northern crawfish frogs (*Rana areolata circulosa*) are listed as endangered in Iowa, and no observations have been verified since the early 1940s. These frogs were once found in southeastern Iowa and are known to use abandoned crawfish holes as refuges. Crawfish frogs are early breeders and begin calling in mid-April in Iowa (Christiansen and Bailey 1991). They were recorded on the survey in three counties, all outside their known range (Fig. 23-2). Detections in two counties in western Iowa can be attributed to errors in data recording. In both instances, crawfish frogs were recorded during one survey period only in the absence of the leopard frog complex, the latter being detected frequently during other survey periods. Unfortunately, the juxtaposition of the crawfish frog and the leopard frog complex on the data sheet encouraged this type of error. The auditory observation in the southeastern corner of the state was detected in April 1994 in a timbered Mississippi River backwater by county natural resource personnel. In this instance, the volunteer heard the call during the survey and confirmed her observation by listening to the anuran call tape after the survey was completed. She verified the possibility of the frog being present by documenting the presence of crawfish chimneys in the area the next day. Unfortunately, she did not hear the call again and was unable to tape record the call on future visits to the site (S. Kaufman, personal communication).

The presence of wood frogs (*Rana sylvatica*) has never been verified in Iowa, although they are found in southeastern Minnesota, southwestern Wisconsin, and northwestern Illinois (Conant and Collins 1991). Wood frogs are early breeders and begin calling in early spring, often before ice is completely off breeding ponds (Conant and Collins 1991). They were recorded on the Iowa frog and toad survey directly across the Mississippi River from areas that are included in the known range of the species (Fig. 23-2). In Allamakee County, in the extreme northeastern corner of the state, wood frogs were reported calling in 1991 at two different sites at the first calling index level. However, the record is suspect because water temperatures were above 15°C. Farther downriver in Jackson County, the species was reported calling at the first calling index level in 1992. In this case, the record may be credible because it was heard in late April when both air and water temperatures were still near 10°C. In both instances, volunteers insisted that their auditory observations were correct; however, they attempted no verification visually or by tape recording the calls. In neither instance was this species detected again in later years along these routes. It is possible that wood frogs occur in the state, but we are missing their peak calling period by restricting volunteers to wait until water temperatures are at least 10°C. Surveyors on Wisconsin's frog and toad survey have noted that if they wait until water temperatures are above 10°C, they sometimes miss the peak calling period of this species, which is typically brief (Mossman and Hine 1985).

Green frogs (*Rana clamitans melanota*) are found in scattered populations throughout eastern Iowa, becoming more common toward the Mississippi River (Christiansen and Bailey 1991). Except for reports from two counties west of their known geographic range, results of the Iowa frog and toad survey match the known range of green frogs (Fig. 23-2). The lack of green frog reports on the western edge of their range does not suggest a range contraction but is simply due to the absence of survey routes in these areas (Fig. 23-1). The species was recorded at 147 sites, but full choruses were recorded only eleven times during the four years of the survey (Table 23-2).

Historically, bullfrogs (*Rana catesbeiana*) were distributed in the southern two-thirds of the state, with scattered populations elsewhere (Christiansen and Bailey 1991). Due to the introduction of this species into farm ponds and by state fisheries personnel in order to produce frog legs for market, bullfrogs were recorded in fifty-eight counties at 320 sites in this survey and are now considered to have a statewide distribution (Fig. 23-2). Full choruses were recorded forty-two times across all sites and survey periods. The effect of bullfrogs on native amphibians in the northern part of the state has yet to be evaluated. However, the presence of bullfrogs in wetlands in Dickinson County, Iowa, has been associated with the disappearance of northern leopard frogs (Lannoo et al. 1994). The negative effects of bullfrogs on other ranid frog species have been well documented but remain controversial (Hayes and Jennings 1986).

Results of the Iowa frog and toad survey indicate that chorus frogs (*Pseudacris triseriata*) are maintaining a statewide distribution. Recorded in all sixty-eight counties surveyed (Fig. 23-2), chorus frogs were the most frequently recorded species and the most frequently recorded at full chorus (Table 23-2).

Still abundant in many areas of the state, Blanchard's cricket frogs (*Acris crepitans blanchardi*) may be experiencing a range reduction at their northern limits in Iowa (Fig. 23-2). Historically, this species was abundant statewide in Iowa and was absent only from a few centrally located counties along the Iowa-Minnesota border (Christiansen and Bailey 1991; Conant and Collins 1991). Its continuing presence in a few counties in northern Iowa is marginal. With the exception of one county, volunteers reported the presence of cricket frogs at only 10 of approximately 180 wetland sites surveyed in northern Iowa. Out of these 10 sites, only 3 reported full choruses. Data received from the exceptional county are believed to be the result of species misidentification. Statewide, cricket frogs were recorded at 320 sites in fifty-three counties (Table 23-2; Fig. 23-2). This species was the fifth most frequently recorded in the state and also ranked fifth in the number of sites recorded as present. It was the fourth most frequently recorded species at full chorus.

The continual decline of cricket frogs at their northern range limits has been documented since the 1970s. Canada's small population of cricket frogs in southwestern Ontario underwent a dramatic population decline in the 1970s and has not been heard calling since 1987 (Oldham 1992). Once common in southern and central Wisconsin, cricket frogs had almost disappeared from the state by the early 1980s and are now considered a state endangered species (Mossman and Hine 1985; Vogt 1981; Hay, Chpt. 11, this volume). Cricket frogs are a species of special concern in Minnesota (Coffin and Pfannmuller 1988), where a lack of recent records suggests they may already be extirpated (Oldfield and Moriarty 1994; Moriarty, Chpt. 20, this volume). Baker (1996) has proposed elevating the Minnesota status of this species from special concern to endangered. In states south and east of Iowa, the status of cricket frogs varies. In Missouri, cricket frogs underwent a slight decline in numbers coincidental to a two-year drought early in this decade; however, the species showed a remarkable comeback when precipitation increased (T. Johnson, personal communication). Mierzwa and Beltz (1994a) have observed that only a few small populations of cricket frogs remain in northern Illinois, a result of the dramatic population decreases in the mid to late 1970s. Declines in Iowa may have occurred in the 1970s also. In western Iowa, Christiansen and Mabry (1985) found that cricket frogs had disappeared from the eastern and northern sections of the Loess Hills, where populations had once existed prior to 1969. Detailed studies beyond extensive surveys will be needed to determine why cricket frogs are declining at their northern range limits (Hay, Chpt.11; Lannoo, Chpt. 34, this volume).

American toads (*Bufo americanus americanus*) are a species historically distributed statewide and were detected in sixty-four of the sixty-eight counties surveyed (Fig. 23-3) and at 379 sites (Table 23-2). They ranked second among all species in terms of reporting frequency, the number of sites of occurrence, and the frequency at which it was recorded in full chorus (Table 23-2).

There are two subspecies of Woodhouse's toad (*Bufo woodhousii*) in Iowa: Woodhouse's toads (*B. w. woodhousii*) occur in the extreme western portion of the state, while Fowler's toads (*B. w. fowleri*) are found in southeastern Iowa (Christiansen and Bailey 1991). All recent records of this species occurred within its known geographic range (Fig. 23-3). It was recorded from sixty-one different sites but only at full chorus six times (Table 23-2).

Great Plains toads (*Bufo cognatus*) are found in western Iowa and are primarily a toad of the Loess Hills and the Missouri River floodplain (Christiansen and Bailey 1991). With the exception of five sites in a county on their eastern range boundary, all twenty-one sites reporting singing males (Table 23-2) were within the known distribution range of the species (Fig. 23-3). However, information from sources other than the Iowa frog and toad survey indicate that Great Plains toads may be changing their geographic range. Reports from Dickinson County (Lannoo et al. 1994) and Emmet County (Reeves 1984) in northwestern Iowa, outside their known range, may indicate that the species is expanding its range eastward.

Discovered in Iowa in 1959, plains spadefoot toads (*Spea bombifrons*) are considered an abundant anuran of the Loess Hills in western Iowa (Christiansen and Bailey 1991; Christiansen and Mabry 1985). Recent information indicates that this species also breeds in ephemeral pools in floodplain habitat (Farrar and Hey 1994, Chpt. 10, this volume; Johnson 1987). All records of plains spadefoots occur within their known geographic range (Fig. 23-3). Surveyors recorded the presence of this species at only twelve sites (Table 23-2). Plains spadefoots are probably not being sampled effectively by the currently designed frog and toad survey. Farrar and Hey (1994) noted that adults call only during or after heavy rains when the species' ephemeral breeding pools are flooded.

Historically, both gray treefrogs—eastern gray treefrogs (*Hyla versicolor*) and Cope's gray treefrogs (*Hyla chrysoscelis*)—could be found statewide, with the exclusion of the extreme northwestern corner of the state (Christiansen and Bailey 1991). Results of the survey indicate that eastern gray treefrogs were detected three times more frequently than Cope's gray treefrogs. Surveyors reported eastern gray treefrogs at 473 sites in fifty-eight counties, while Cope's gray treefrogs were reported at only 161 sites in thirty-eight counties (Table 23-2; Fig. 23-3). While identification books and tapes describe the call of Cope's gray treefrogs to be of a higher pitch and shorter duration than that of eastern gray treefrogs, the calls of both species vary with temperature, causing the calls to sound similar on successive days (Christiansen and Bailey 1991; Conant and Collins 1991). In other words, the call of Cope's gray treefrogs may sound fast one day but sound like that of eastern gray treefrogs the next day if the temperature decreases. This variability of calls over a wide temperature range may indicate that species differentiation between the two hylids is marginal at best. The resulting distribution maps (Fig. 23-3)

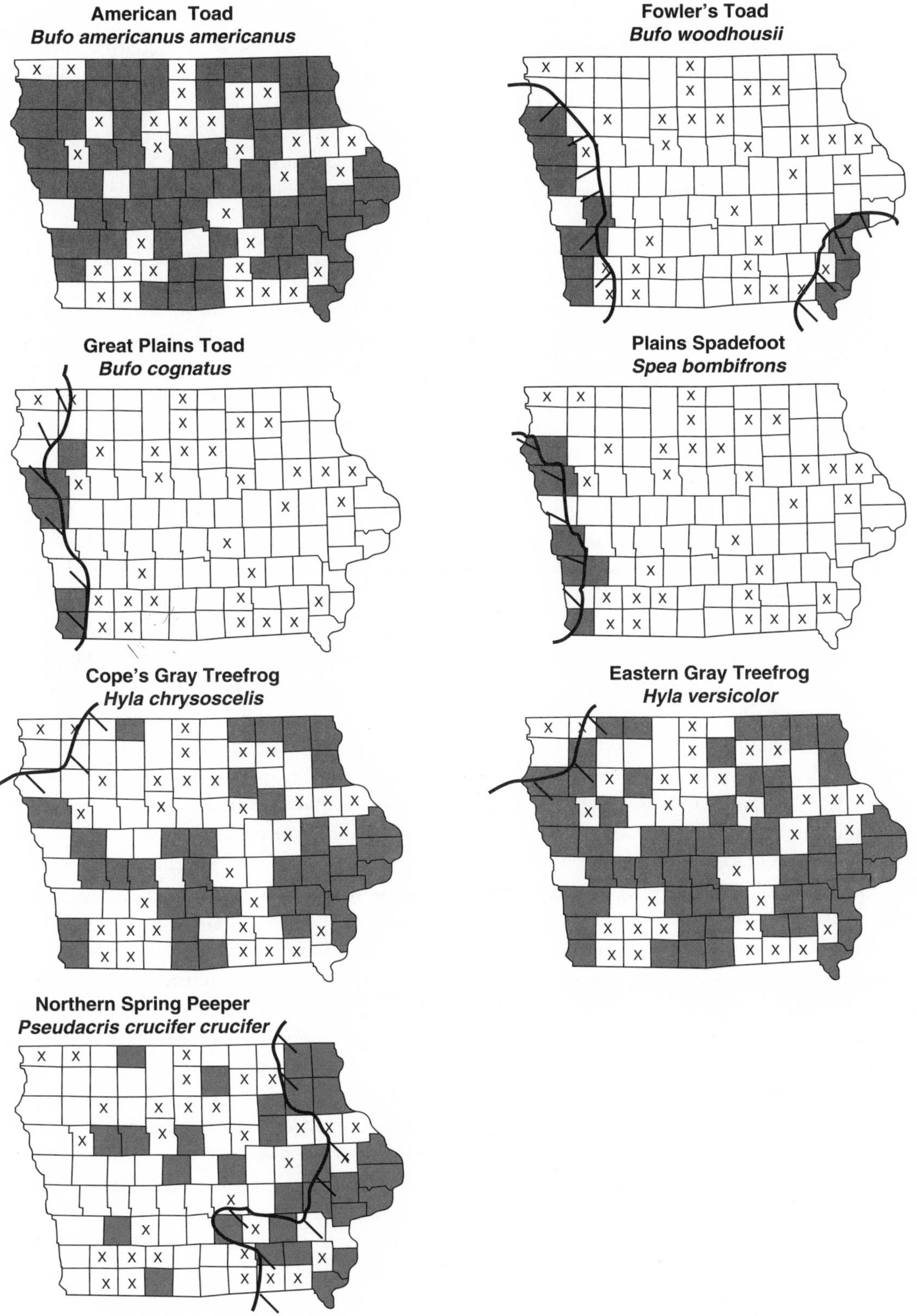

Figure 23-3. The distribution of seven anuran species by county in Iowa according to the frog and toad survey, 1991 through 1994. Gray shading indicates species presence; "x" indicates county was not sampled. Historical range boundaries (lines; after Christiansen and Bailey 1991) are included. Species showing no range boundaries have a statewide distribution.

should be viewed with caution. Both hylids also differed considerably in the number of times they were recorded at full chorus (Table 23-2). Approximately 26 percent of all detections of eastern gray treefrogs were recorded at calling index level three (full chorus) compared to 14 percent for Cope's gray treefrogs. The discrepancy in the assignment of calling index values between species may be due to the difference between the species calls; Cope's gray treefrogs have a faster call that would require a larger chorus in order to be ranked at calling level three. It is also possible that eastern gray treefrogs are naturally more abundant than Cope's gray treefrogs. Finally, it may be possible that Cope's gray treefrogs are declining in numbers. Unlike Cope's gray treefrogs, eastern gray treefrogs seem to be abundant in the state. This species ranks third among all species for frequency of detection, frequency at full chorus, and number of sites of occurrence (Table 23-2).

Northern spring peepers (*Pseudacris crucifer crucifer*) were removed from Iowa's threatened and endangered list in the early 1980s (Reeves 1984). They are now considered common in counties near the Mississippi River (Christiansen and Bailey 1991). This species was recorded in twelve counties outside its known geographic range (Fig. 23-3). Five of the twelve counties were surveyed by professional herpetologists, but specimens were found in only one county (Boone) in the Des Moines River drainage (Van de Walle et al. 1996). Specimens were also found upriver in Webster County, a county that lacked a frog and toad survey route. The westward range of expansion of spring peepers along wooded waterways is consistent with the observations of Mossman and Hine (1984) and Vogt (1981), who noted that the species preferred moist woodlands and avoided intensively farmed areas and urban settings. Van de Walle et al. (1996) speculated that the volunteers in the remaining four counties, where voucher specimens could not be found, may have misidentified spring peepers as chorus frogs due to both species singing simultaneously on the species identification tape. Surveyors who have lost the upper range of their hearing might be unable to hear spring peepers on the tape and might mistakenly associate chorus frog calls with spring peeper calls. While a case of poor hearing explains misidentification of spring peepers in one county in western Iowa, sites surveyed in two other counties still remain as good possibilities for spring peeper habitation. Volunteers in Marshall County, in central Iowa, recorded spring peepers at three sites within a mile of the Iowa River. Calling records of spring peepers in Ringgold County, in southern Iowa, were not near major water courses, but the adjacent county to the east contained spring peeper populations in the 1970s along the Grand River (B. Ehresman, personal communication). Full choruses of spring peepers were heard 159 times at 206 sites during the four-year survey period (Table 23-2), including 21 times in the twelve counties outside their known geographic range.

Advantages of the Survey

An extensive volunteer-based survey has proven useful in determining current distribution ranges of Iowa's common anurans and in alerting the scientific community to possible declines in widespread species, in particular, the range contraction of Blanchard's cricket frogs and the low number of full choruses within the leopard frog complex. These findings should encourage research on these species, which require immediate attention. Additional years of data collecting will make analysis of population trends plausible and help to verify suspected population changes.

This volunteer-based survey has proven to be an excellent means to promote education about wetlands. Students and personnel from several colleges and universities have taken part in the frog and toad survey in conjunction with environmental or ecological classes. Members of the Boy Scouts have participated and may receive merit badges for this activity. Naturalists associated with nature centers or parks have also taken the opportunity to use the survey as an educational tool for teaching about Iowa's wetlands and nocturnal animals. However, most of the survey routes are run by private citizens who seem to be outdoor enthusiasts and simply enjoy learning about Iowa's wildlife and supporting the efforts of the IDNR's Wildlife Diversity Program.

In addition, because money available to conduct surveys and research on nongame animals is usually limited, this volunteer-based survey has proven to be a cost-effective means of collecting data on an extensive scale. Surveyors are recruited effectively by publicizing the need for volunteers in the quarterly *Wildlife Diversity Newsletter*, a publication of the IDNR's Wildlife Diversity Program. This publicity attracts attention from local newspapers and other media and encourages nature enthusiasts statewide to participate in the survey.

Disadvantages of the Survey

The collection of reliable data using volunteers on anuran call surveys can be difficult (see Bishop et al. 1997; Mossman and Hine 1984). New participants in

Iowa's frog and toad survey receive no training beyond what is offered in the informational packet. It is assumed that all surveyors listen to the species identification tape and can correctly identify species by call. This has not always proven to be true. Several participants, for example, have mentioned the difficulty of discriminating between the calls of eastern gray treefrogs and Cope's gray treefrogs. Other states, such as Missouri, have recognized this problem and combine both species on their calling surveys (T. Johnson, personal communication). In addition, individuals who have a partial hearing loss may have difficulty hearing particular species (e.g., spring peepers; Van de Walle et al. 1996). One surveyor wrote on his data sheet, "I use hearing aids, and when my wife went along, I found that I don't hear the chorus frogs unless I'm very close to them." There are also numerous notes on data sheets describing mysterious calls that are not identified and thus never recorded.

While the majority of participants appear to be confident of their species identification, inter-observer variation seems to be high when determining calling index values. Anecdotal information received from some participants who run surveys in pairs suggests that disagreement on call index values is common among co-surveyors. A study conducted in central Iowa with Iowa State University students and staff verified the problem with the calling index. While most surveyors agreed upon the species present at a site, the assignment of the calling index value was subjective. For example, all three index values and two records of absence were recorded for American toads at one wetland site during the same night by twenty observers (Fig. 23-4).

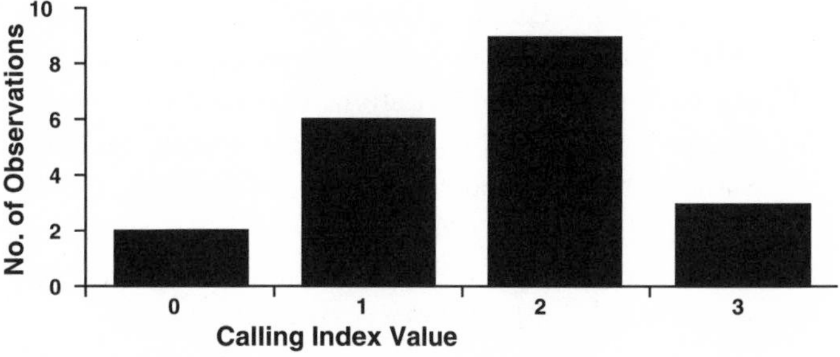

Figure 23-4. The frequency of calling index values assigned to American toads at Kriegley Creek, Ames, Iowa, 13 June 1995.

To analyze further the effect of inter-observer variation, the variance components estimation procedure (PROC VARCOMP; SAS Institute Inc. 1989) was used to estimate the variance of assigned calling index values resulting from differences among sites, teams, individuals in a team, and site times team interactions. Only three species, American toads, Blanchard's cricket frogs, and chorus frogs, were recorded frequently enough to permit this statistical procedure. Results show that variance was high among sites for two species, cricket frogs (variance = 0.642) and chorus frogs (variance = 0.840). There was little between team variation (American toads, variance = -0.022; cricket frogs, variance = -0.038; chorus frogs, variance = 0.019). (Negative estimates are possible with this procedure and indicate variance estimates of zero.) The effects of inter-observer variation within teams across sites were moderate (American toads, variance = 0.479; cricket frogs, variance = 0.159; chorus frogs, variance = 0.217) and seemed to be species specific. The higher variance for American toads may suggest that, for species with long calls, interpretation of the calling index may become more difficult. Variance resulting from the site times team interaction was also low for all species (American toads, variance = -0.034; cricket frogs, variance = 0.007; chorus frogs, variance = -0.028), indicating that teams were consistent in how they assigned calling index values among sites.

Observer variation has also been noted on Ontario's frog and toad survey (Bishop et al. 1997). While co-surveyors were consistent on presence or absence of a species at a site (76 to 92 percent concurrence rate), rates of concurrence on the index values were low (56 to 83 percent).

Correcting inter-observer variation in the assignment of calling index values could occur through the use of species identification tapes that contain examples of all three calling levels for each individual species. Currently, the species identification tape given to volunteers does not provide all three calling index levels. Some species on the tape are recorded at full chorus; other species have only one or two individuals calling at the same time. In 1995 Canada changed its species identification tape to include examples of anuran species at all three call levels. Concurrence among observers on the assignment of a calling index value subsequently improved (C. Bishop, personal communication).

Incomplete data sheets pose another problem when using volunteer-based surveys. Reasons for missing survey periods include illness, time constraints, and weather. When surveys are conducted, time constraints sometimes force surveyors to conduct the survey outside the designated time periods or during marginal weather conditions for calling anurans (i.e., dry, cold, and/or windy). Completing the survey for all time periods during optimal weather conditions is crucial to getting a complete picture of the anuran assemblage at a site. Stressing the importance of co-surveyors or having a secondary surveyor when the primary surveyor is unable to collect data may help increase the chance of collecting quality data during all three survey periods.

Conclusions

Since 1991, Iowa's frog and toad survey has provided important information on the current distributions of Iowa's anurans. Additional surveyors in the southern, east-central, and north-central regions of the state are needed. Species with possible declining populations have been identified (e.g., northern leopard frogs and Blanchard's cricket frogs), and the range expansions of other species have been noted (e.g., chorus frogs and bullfrogs). Research will be directed toward species that may be experiencing population declines. Additional years of data collecting will help show population trends.

Using volunteers has allowed the IDNR to conduct an extensive, cost-effective survey and has provided a means to promote education about wetlands in the state. While problems exist with collecting reliable data, improvement of the informational packet, especially the species identification tape, and increased emphasis in having co-surveyors will help reduce data collection errors, reduce variability in the data, and improve the ability of surveyors to complete their routes.

Summary

The current distributions and relative abundances of Iowa's frog and toad species were determined from auditory surveys from 1991 through 1994. Distribution ranges for some species may have changed compared to historical information. Blanchard's cricket frogs (*Acris crepitans blanchardi*) seem to be undergoing a range reduction in their northern distribution, while chorus frogs (*Pseudacris crucifer*) and bullfrogs (*Rana catesbeiana*) may be expanding their ranges. Other species, such as the leopard frog complex, have undergone no discernible changes in their distributions but are consistently assigned low relative abundance values. Additional years of data collection are needed to determine population trends adequately. Volunteer-based surveys allow for statewide monitoring with minimum cost by state wildlife agencies. Problems encountered with using volunteers include incomplete surveys, surveys conducted under inappropriate weather and time conditions, errors in identification, and inter-observer variability in assigning calling index values. Possible solutions to these problems include the use of co-surveyors and improvements in the species identification tape sent to volunteer surveyors.

Acknowledgments

I thank Bruce Ehresman for coordinating the Iowa frog and toad survey since its initiation, Pat Schlarbaum who created the figures for this chapter, and Anjeanette Perkins and Jim Kienzler for helping in data management and analysis. Thanks to Scott Ballard, Christine Bishop, Jim Christiansen, Bruce Ehresman, Tom Johnson, John Moriarty, Mike Mossman, and Anjeanette Perkins for reviewing this chapter. A huge thanks goes to all the volunteers who contributed time and resources to make this project possible.

24

Observations on Indiana Amphibian Populations: A Forty-five-Year Overview

Sherman A. Minton

A perennial problem in determining the degree of amphibian population declines is a lack of information on populations over long periods. During most of the period from 1948 to 1993, I made field observations of thirty-seven of the thirty-nine amphibian species recorded from Indiana. Although qualitative and anecdotal, at least 540 entries in my notes mention amphibians. Observations were made in all of the state's counties. The record is not uniform or unbroken. Field notes for 1969 to 1972 were lost, although some data were recovered from information accompanying specimens sent to the University of Michigan Museum of Zoology during this period, and I have also relied on my memory. During most of the 1958 to 1962 period, I was not in Indiana. This is also true for most of 1955 and 1980, and there are other gaps that coincide with periods of foreign travel.

Two frogs, northern crawfish frogs (*Rana areolata circulosa*) and northern leopard frogs (*Rana pipiens*), and two large aquatic salamanders, mudpuppies (*Necturus maculosus maculosus*) and hellbenders (*Cryptobranchus alleganiensis alleganiensis*), have declined markedly in numbers throughout their state ranges during the period of these observations. Local and temporal fluctuations in populations of several amphibian species have been observed. Blanchard's cricket frogs (*Acris crepitans blanchardi*) have almost disappeared from the northern quarter of Indiana, and western chorus frog (*Pseudacris triseriata triseriata*) populations in central and southern Indiana showed a marked decrease in numbers between 1975 and 1985 but now seem to be recovering in many places. Bullfrogs (*Rana catesbeiana*) appear to be more plentiful now than when this survey was begun.

In this chapter, eight localities have been selected for detailed discussion (Fig. 24-1). They are: (1) Bacon Swamp, a relict peat bog formerly located in northeast Indianapolis; (2) Renn's Spring on the Knobstone Escarpment near New Albany; (3) Flatrock, a section of Big and Little Flatrock Creeks in northwest Decatur County in the Muscatatuck Flats and Canyons region; (4) Jasper-Pulaski Fish and Wildlife Area, marsh and sand prairie in the Kankakee Sand region; (5) Freeland Park, a part of the Illinois Grand Prairie in western Benton County now heavily cultivated; (6) Muscatatuck Lowland, two sections of swamp forest in the Scottsburg Lowland region; (7) Bear Wallow Pond, an upland pond in the Brown County Hills region; and (8) Springport Pond, a swamp and vernal pond in the Tipton Till Plain of Henry County. These localities represent habitats typical of several of Indiana's natural regions.

Observations of Amphibians at Indiana Sites, 1948 to 1993

Bacon Swamp (Ten Visits, 1948 to 1988). In 1941 Bacon Swamp, a relict peat bog, occupied an area about 1.3 by 0.8 kilometers in northeast Indianapolis. Except for a commercial peat digging operation on 56th Street, it was little disturbed. Mittleman (1947) commented on the impressive frog choruses heard here at that time. During the 1949 to 1954 period, northern leopard frogs were the most frequently observed frog, and eastern

Figure 24-1. Localities mentioned in text: (1) Bacon Swamp; (2) Renn's Spring; (3) Flatrock; (4) Jasper-Pulaski Fish and Wildlife Area; (5) Freeland Park; (6) Muscatatuck Lowland; (7) Bear Wallow Pond; (8) Springport Pond.

gray treefrogs (*Hyla versicolor*) and northern spring peepers (*Pseudacris crucifer crucifer*) were heard in great numbers. Smaller numbers of western chorus frogs, Blanchard's cricket frogs, green frogs (*Rana clamitans melanota*), and bullfrogs were recorded. Smallmouth salamanders (*Ambystoma texanum*) were the only salamander recorded in the 1949 to 1954 period. In 1941 I collected an eft of the eastern newt (*Notophthalmus viridescens*), and about the same time I received several eastern tiger salamanders (*Ambystoma tigrinum tigrinum*) collected by a resident of the area. An interesting reptile record is the spotted turtle (*Clemmys guttata*; Springer 1927). This was the southernmost limit of its occurrence in Indiana. It was rare in 1950 but may have persisted until about 1960. Residential development began encroaching on the swamp in the 1960s and had destroyed it as a natural area by 1980. Today it is a large pond surrounded by apartment buildings and residences. Bullfrogs and cricket frogs still occur.

Renn's Spring (Fifteen Visits, 1948 to 1991). Glades, or balds—steep slopes of exposed siltstone—are characteristic of the southern end of the Knobstone Escarpment and represent a dry, harsh environment. Renn's Spring originally opened onto one of these glades at the crest of the escarpment about 8.1 kilometers north of New Albany. It was enclosed by an old sandstone block springhouse and furnished water and refrigeration for the Renn family. Flow from the spring went down the steep face of the escarpment. The only other permanent water in the immediate vicinity was a small farm pond. Cave salamanders (*Eurycea lucifuga*) were regularly found clinging to the walls of the springhouse. Longtail salamanders (*Eurycea longicauda longicauda*), southern two-lined salamanders (*Eurycea cirrigera*), and pickerel frogs (*Rana palustris*) were present along the spring branch. Until about 1955, zigzag salamanders (*Plethodon dorsalis*) were plentiful under rocks near the springhouse and were often associated with northern slimy salamanders (*Plethodon glutinosus*), but only one redback salamander (*Plethodon cinereus*) was recorded during this period. During the 1970s, suburban homes replaced most of the small farms along the top of the escarpment. The springhouse was destroyed about 1979, and flow from the spring virtually stopped a few years later. About the same time, vegetation began to encroach on the glades, reducing the areas of exposed siltstone. In April 1979 redback salamanders outnumbered zigzag salamanders about five to one, and between 1981 and 1985 the ratio was nearer twelve to one. Few salamanders of any kind have been observed since 1985. Floyd County glades are the only known Indiana localities for two snakes, the scarlet snake (*Cemophora coccinea*) and the southeastern crowned snake (*Tantilla coronata*), and have a relict lizard population, the six-lined racerunner (*Cnemidophorus sexlineatus*). Populations of these reptiles are now believed to be very small.

Flatrock (Forty-one Visits, 1948 to 1993). Flatrock includes areas along Big and Little Flatrock Creeks in northwestern Decatur County. These are medium to large creeks of shallow gradient flowing over limestone slabs and bordered by wooded limestone outcrops in many places. There are numerous springs and a few small caves. The area was originally forested, and some woodland remains. Southern two-lined salamanders, longtail salamanders, and redback salamanders have been consistently plentiful salamanders in this area during forty-five years of observations. American toads (*Bufo americanus americanus*), Blanchard's cricket frogs, and green frogs have been consistently plentiful anurans. Northern dusky salamanders (*Desmognathus fuscus*) were abundant until about 1958 but have become increasingly rare. I last recorded this species in 1979, but it probably still occurs. Fowler's toad (*Bufo woodhousii fowleri*) was found regularly until the 1980s but is now rare. Northern leopard frogs and southern leopard frogs (*Rana sphenocephala*) were recorded a few times prior to 1974 but not recently. Prior to 1958, gray treefrogs and chorus frogs were plentiful but local and have not been recorded since 1964. Ambystomatid salamanders and bullfrogs have not been recorded. Decline of some species may be related to destruction of the few small floodplain ponds that were present in 1948.

Jasper-Pulaski Fish and Wildlife Area (Ten Visits, 1948 to 1993). The Jasper-Pulaski Fish and Wildlife Area is located in the Kankakee Sand region and has been a state game preserve since about 1930. It consists of oak savanna and large marsh created by impoundment. Surrounding it are smaller ponds and ditches. Although the Kankakee Sand region has several reptile species uncommon or absent in other parts of Indiana, the amphibian fauna contains few distinctive species. One is the Austroriparian aquatic salamander the western lesser siren (*Siren intermedia nettingi*), here at the northern limit of its range; another is the blue-spotted salamander (*Ambystoma laterale*), here at the southern limit of its range. The latter species was plentiful in the oak woods during the 1946 to 1971 period but seems to be uncommon today. Blanchard's cricket frogs were reported regularly from 1947 to 1957, but I have not seen them since 1971. Swanson (1939) reported northern slimy salamanders, and there is a voucher specimen in the Carnegie Museum collection. Swanson's collection also contains a plains leopard frog (*Rana blairi*) from Jasper-Pulaski. This frog should be present, but my leopard frog collections contain only northern leopard frogs, which remain plentiful. Recently Brodman et al. (1995; see also Brodman and Kilmurry, Chpt. 17, this volume) added the eastern newt to the fauna.

Freeland Park (Thirteen Visits, 1951 to 1993). The Freeland Park site is within the former Illinois Grand Prairie and lies east of the village of Freeland Park in Benton County. Today it is intensively cultivated, with little habitat for wildlife. In 1951 there were a few apparently natural vernal ponds; there are none today. The only amphibian species that have been found consistently are western chorus frogs and American toads. American toads in this area are large with heavy ventral pigmentation and differ in these features from American toad populations in central and southern Indiana. The only other amphibian species recorded since 1968 are bullfrogs and cricket frogs. Prior to that time, plains leopard frogs were present syntopic with northern leopard frogs. Benton County is the type locality for crawfish frogs and probably afforded suitable habitat in 1878 (Rice and Davis 1878). In 1951 I collected northern crawfish frogs in northern Vermillion County. Characteristic reptiles are plains garter snakes (*Thamnophis radix*), fox snakes (*Elaphe vulpina*), and smooth green snakes (*Opheodrys vernalis*). Blanding's turtles (*Emydoidea blandingi*) were recorded 1952 but apparently do not occur near Freeland Park today.

Muscatatuck Lowland (Thirty-three Visits, 1948 to 1993). The Muscatatuck Lowland consists of two similar areas, one southeast of Seymour on the Muscatatuck National Wildlife Refuge and the other along State Road 256 west of the Scott-Jackson county line. They consist of mixed hardwood forest and swamp, seasonally flooded but retaining areas of permanent water. They still support a rich and fairly diverse amphibian fauna, with southern leopard frogs, bullfrogs, and Blanchard's cricket frogs the most conspicuous species near open water. Jefferson salamanders (*Ambystoma jeffersonianum*), marbled salamanders (*Ambystoma opacum*), redback salamanders, and Cope's gray treefrogs (*Hylas chrysoscelis*) are characteristic of higher patches of woodland. Western chorus frogs were extremely plentiful prior to 1973 but much less so today, particularly in the southern segment. The same is true of smallmouth salamanders, eastern newts, northern dusky salamanders, and wood frogs (*Rana sylvatica*), which were reported regularly in the southern segment prior to 1974 but have not been seen since. There has been some timber cutting in the southern segment but no other obvious habitat disturbance. On the wildlife refuge, there has been modification of the swamp and pond habitat to favor waterfowl, but this does not seem to have greatly affected the amphibians. Redbelly water snakes (*Nerodia erythrogaster*), ribbon snakes (*Thamnophis sauritus*), and Kirtland's snakes (*Clonophis kirtlandi*) are distinctive snakes of this area. All persist in fair numbers.

Bear Wallow Pond (Thirteen Visits, 1953 to 1993). Bear Wallow Pond is a semipermanent, upland, woodland pond of the kind known to early residents of southern Indiana as a bear wallow. It is located a few kilometers east of the west entrance of Brown County State Park. Although in a well-used picnic area, a fairly stable breeding amphibian population has been observed here for forty years. Salamanders include spotted salamanders (*Ambystoma maculatum*), Jefferson's salamanders, marbled salamanders, and eastern newts, while anurans include American toads, spring peepers, Cope's gray treefrogs, bullfrogs, and wood frogs. Northern slimy salamanders, redback salamanders, and zigzag salamanders occur in adjacent woodland. Appreciable mortality was noted in the spring of 1993 among newts and large larvae of the marbled salamander.

Springport Pond (Six Visits, 1969 to 1984). Springport Pond, a semipermanent pond, lies at the base of a low wooded ridge about 2.4 kilometers south of Springport in Henry County. When visited in 1971, it had a remarkable diversity of pond-breeding salamanders, including four-toed salamanders (*Hemidactylium scutatum*), eastern newts, spotted salamanders, smallmouth salamanders, eastern tiger salamanders, and a triploid of the *Ambystoma jeffersonianum* complex. Anuran species included western chorus frogs, spring peepers, Blanchard's cricket frogs, northern leopard frogs, and green frogs. On the ridge was a population of ravine salamanders (*Plethodon richmondi*), here at the northwestern limit of their range. They were syntopic with redback salamanders. The pond and its immediate environs are protected; however, the area is small and entirely surrounded by suburban housing developments. I have no data on the present status of these amphibian populations.

Habitat modification by human agency has occurred in all eight areas during the period of my observations. In five there has been an obvious decrease in the number and diversity of amphibian species. Bacon Swamp has been severely impacted by filling and urban development. The virtual destruction of the spring branch at Renn's Spring has resulted in the decline of several once-common species. Although Jasper-Pulaski has been a state-protected area for more than sixty years, Blanchard's cricket frogs have disappeared and blue-spotted salamanders have greatly decreased in numbers within the last twenty years. The Freeland Park area was intensively cultivated when I began my observations and may never have had a very diverse amphibian fauna. Plains leopard frogs evidently have disappeared, but a few other anuran species survive in this heavily agricultural region. Bear Wallow Pond is the only area where amphibian species diversity has remained the same over the forty years of my observations. It is in Brown County State Park but is surrounded by a heavily used picnic area and is close to a major park road. Most of the amphibian species that use the pond are early spring breeders, and light human use of the park during this season may afford them some protection. Springport Pond about 1970 had a surprisingly diverse (at least thirteen species) amphibian fauna in a very small area. It is now protected, but I have no data on the present status of amphibian populations.

Summary

This summary of field observations on Indiana amphibians during the period 1948 to 1993 chiefly notes qualitative changes in species diversity. Eight localities have been selected for detailed discussion. They represent habitats typical of several of Indiana's natural regions, have been under my observation for at least fifteen years, and have not been intensively studied by other investigators. All have undergone human modification during the observation period, but results have not been wholly predictable.

25

Distribution of Ohio Amphibians

Ralph A. Pfingsten

Recent concerns over reports of amphibian declines (e.g., Wake 1991; Wake and Morowitz 1991; K. Phillips 1994) demand that biologists know the current distributions of species in their region if distributional changes, including range contractions, are to be properly documented. At the conclusion of the first Ohio Declining Amphibian Population Task Force meeting held during the spring of 1994, one fact became clear to me. As a group, we did not have a good grasp of the current distribution of the amphibians in Ohio. Walker's (1946) *The Amphibians of Ohio* was nearly fifty years old, and little work had been done on that group of animals in the intervening years. Pfingsten and Downs's (1989) *Salamanders of Ohio* provided more recent information on this group of animals, but several hundred new locality records and two new species, streamside salamanders *(Ambystoma barbouri)* and southern two-lined salamanders *(Eurycea cirrigera)*, have been described since that work was published.

Over the next year (1994–1995) I produced an updated, informal set of distributional maps to serve as a guide for fieldworkers throughout the state (Figs. 25-1–25-42). Shortly after the maps were released, it was suggested that they be formalized for inclusion in the present work.

Records came from several sources. The largest source was the Herpetological Data Base being compiled by Doug Wynn (1996) for the Ohio Division of Wildlife. While not yet complete, this database contained most of the vouchered and unvouchered records for amphibians and reptiles in Ohio. It included most museum collections that contain Ohio material. Records not yet included in the database were obtained from the literature (e.g., Walker 1946; Wood and Duellman 1947; Duellman 1951; Adler and Dennis 1961; Allen 1963; Ruffner et al. 1969; Blem 1972; Valentine 1974; Ashton 1976a; Pfingsten and Downs 1989) and from recent collections by several herpetologists throughout the state. Most notable of these herpetologists are Tim Matson and myself at the Cleveland Museum, Jeff Davis and Scott Menze at the Cincinnati Museum, and Merrill Tawse of the Richland County Park System.

The format and style of these maps are similar to those used in Pfingsten and Downs (1989). Each map concludes with a list of localities used in preparing or updating the map. County names are abbreviated (following the system provided by the Ohio Department of Transportation) and presented alphabetically. Each symbol on the distribution map represents a township in which at least one locality for that species has been recorded. Circles indicate records prior to 1950; triangles denote records after that time. Overlapping symbols are used when records occur from both areas. A solid symbol shows that a voucher specimen is available, while an open symbol indicates the lack of a voucher specimen. Records that did not identify a specific locality (e.g., bullfrog [*Rana catesbeiana*], Erie County) were not used. Unvouchered records were used only when a vouchered record did not exist. Records are current up to 1 October 1996. Abbreviations are used for the largest museum and private collections of Ohio amphibians. It is my hope that these records will stimulate further interest in Ohio amphibians and encourage workers to undertake the long-term studies needed to provide the information that is necessary to document the changing status of Ohio's native species.

Summary

I present a series of forty-two maps showing the most up-to-date representation of the distribution of Ohio amphibians. These maps have been compiled from Walker (1946), Pfingsten and Downs (1989), and the Ohio Division of Wildlife database (1995).

Ohio County Abbreviations Code

Code	County	Code	County
ADA	Adams	LIC	Licking
ALL	Allen	LOG	Logan
ASH	Ashland	LOR	Lorain
ATB	Ashtabula	LUC	Lucas
ATH	Athens	MAD	Madison
AUG	Auglaize	MAH	Mahoning
BEL	Belmont	MAR	Marion
BRO	Brown	MED	Medina
BUT	Butler	MEG	Meigs
CAR	Carroll	MER	Mercer
CHP	Champaign	MIA	Miami
CLA	Clark	MOE	Monroe
CLE	Clermont	MOT	Montgomery
CLI	Clinton	MRG	Morgan
COL	Columbiana	MRW	Morrow
COS	Coshocton	MUS	Muskingum
CRA	Crawford	NOB	Noble
CUY	Cuyahoga	OTT	Ottawa
DAR	Darke	PAU	Paulding
DEF	Defiance	PER	Perry
DEL	Delaware	PIC	Pickaway
ERI	Erie	PIK	Pike
FAI	Fairfield	POR	Portage
FAY	Fayette	PRE	Preble
FRA	Franklin	PUT	Putnam
FUL	Fulton	RIC	Richland
GAL	Gallia	ROS	Ross
GEA	Geauga	SAN	Sandusky
GRE	Greene	SCI	Scioto
GUE	Guernsey	SEN	Seneca
HAM	Hamilton	SHE	Shelby
HAN	Hancock	STA	Stark
HAR	Hardin	SUM	Summit
HAS	Harrison	TRU	Trumbull
HEN	Henry	TUS	Tuscarawas
HIG	Highland	UNI	Union
HOC	Hocking	VAN	Van Wert
HOL	Holmes	VIN	Vinton
HUR	Huron	WAR	Warren
JAC	Jackson	WAS	Washington
JEF	Jefferson	WAY	Wayne
KNO	Knox	WIL	Williams
LAK	Lake	WOO	Wood
LAW	Lawrence	WYA	Wyandot

Museum/Collections Abbreviations Code

AMNH	American Museum of Natural History
ANSP	Academy of Natural Sciences, Philadelphia
BGSU	Bowling Green State University
CM	Carnegie Museum
CMNH	Cleveland Museum of Natural History
CSNH	Cincinnati Society of Natural History
CU	Cornell University
CW	College of Wooster
DC	Defiance College
DMCP	Dayton-Montgomery County Park District
DMNH	Dayton Museum of Natural History
FMNH	Field Museum of Natural History
FSL	Franz Theodore Stone Laboratory
HC	Heidelberg College
ISU	Indiana State University
JEJ	J. Eric Juterbock
KSU	Kent State University
KU	University of Kansas
LACM	Natural History Museum of Los Angeles County
MC	Marietta College
MCZ	Museum of Comparative Zoology
MU	Miami University
MVZ	University of California at Berkeley
ONU	Ohio Northern University
OSUM	Ohio State University Museum of Zoology
OUVC	Ohio University
OWU	Ohio Wesleyan University
RAP	Ralph A. Pfingsten
ROM	Royal Ontario Museum
TOM	Timothy O. Matson
UF	University of Florida
UIMNH	University of Illinois Museum of Natural History
UMMZ	University of Michigan Museum of Zoology
USNM	National Museum of Natural History

Figure 25-1. Distribution of mudpuppies (*Necturus maculosus maculosus*) in Ohio. Locality records for *N. m. maculosus* that are new since 1988. For a complete list of all records see Pfingsten and Downs (1989). ADA: Meigs Tp. (CMNH). ASH: Jackson Tp. (CW). ATB: Kingsville Tp. (CMNH); Sheffield Tp. (CMNH). ATH: York Tp. (OSUM). COL: Center Tp. (CMNH). DEL: Kingston Tp. (CMNH). ERI: Kelleys Island (KU). FRA: Washington Tp. (OSUM). HOC: Benton Tp. (JEJ); Good Hope Tp. (CMNH). LAK: Kirtland Tp. (KU). LOR: Avon Lake (CMNH). MOE: Perry Tp. (CMNH). MUS: Cass Tp. (CMNH). PIC: Darby Tp. (Nature Conservancy). POR: Windham Tp. (CMNH). SCI: Green Tp. (CMNH); Madison Tp. (CMNH); Nile Tp. (CMNH); Porter Tp. (CMNH). TRU: Mesopotamia Tp. (CMNH). TUS: Warwick Tp. (CMNH).

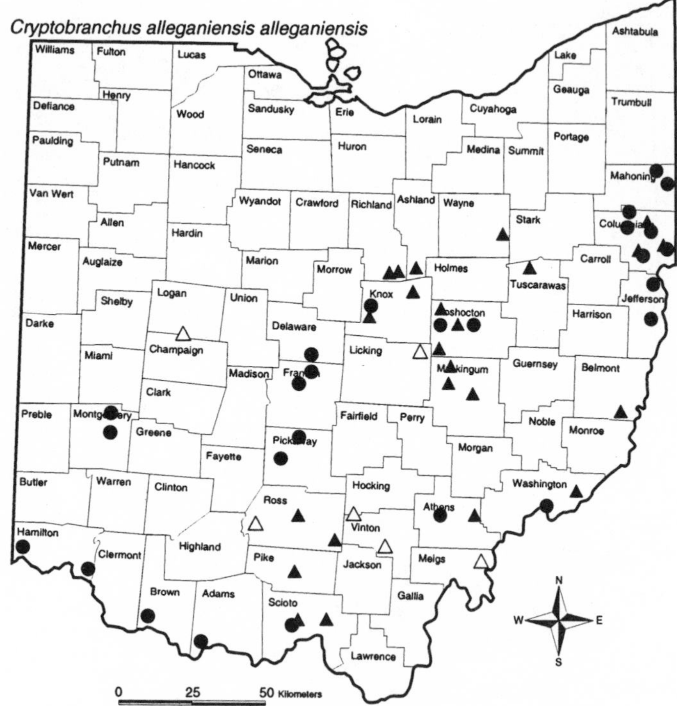

Figure 25-2. Distribution of hellbenders (*Cryptobranchus alleganiensis alleganiensis*) in Ohio. Locality records for *C. a. alleganiensis* that are new since 1988. For a complete list of all records see Pfingsten and Downs (1989). BEL: Washington Tp. (RAP). COL: Elk Run Tp. (RAP); Madison Tp. (RAP); St. Clair Tp. (RAP). COS: Jefferson Tp. (RAP); Newcastle Tp. (RAP). KNO: Howard Tp. (RAP); Morris Tp. (RAP). MUS: Cass Tp. (RAP); Falls Tp. (RAP). RIC: Worthington Tp. (RAP). ROS: Jefferson Tp. (RAP). SCI: Harrison Tp. (RAP); Union Tp. (RAP). TUS: Franklin Tp. (RAP). WAS: Independence Tp. (RAP); Wayne Tp. (TOM).

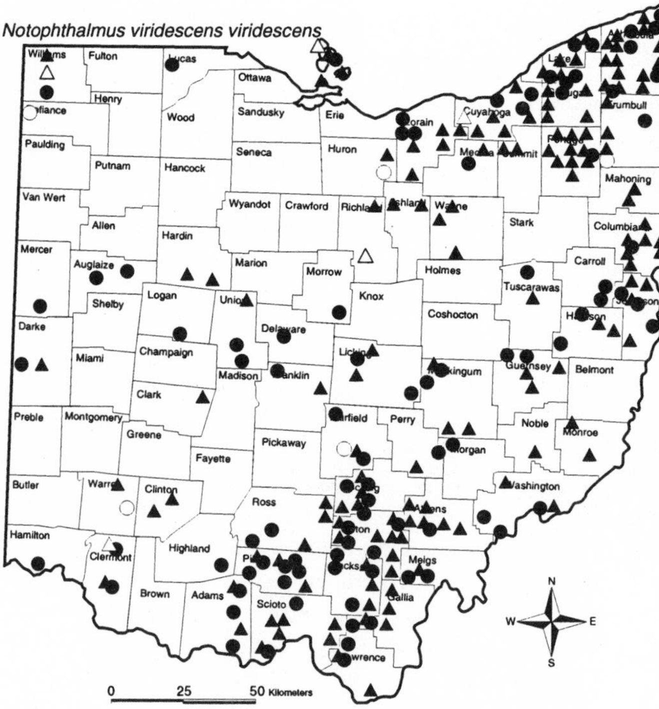

Figure 25-3. Distribution of red-spotted newts (*Notophthalmus viridescens viridescens*) in Ohio. Locality records for *N. v. viridescens* that are new since 1988. For a complete list of all records see Pfingsten and Downs (1989). ADA: Franklin Tp. (UF). ATB: Austinburg Tp. (CMNH); Cherry Valley Tp. (CMNH); Harpersfield Tp. (CMNH); Kingsville Tp. (CMNH); Monroe Tp. (CMNH); Rome Tp. (CSNH). ATH: Canaan Tp. (OUVC). CLA: Pleasant Tp. (Dan Rice). CLE: Batavia Tp. (CSNH). COL: Washington Tp. (CMNH). GAL: Greenfield Tp. (CMNH); Huntington Tp. (CMNH); Perry Tp. (CMNH); Raccoon Tp. (CMNH). HAR: Hale Tp. (Dan Rice). HUR: Clarksfield Tp. (CMNH). JAC: Bloomfield Tp. (CMNH); Madison Tp. (CMNH); Milton Tp. (CMNH). LAK: Leroy Tp. (CMNH). LAW: Elizabeth Tp. (CMNH). LOR: Pittsfield Tp. (CMNH). MAH: Green Tp. (OSUM). MEG: Rutland Tp. (CMNH). MOE: Malaga Tp. (CMNH); Perry Tp. (CMNH). MUS: Blue Rock Tp. (CMNH); Cass Tp. (CMNH). NOB: Enoch Tp. (CMNH). PER: Jackson Tp. (CMNH); Salt Lick Tp. (UMMZ). POR: Charlestown Tp. (CMNH); Freedom Tp. (CMNH); Paris Tp. (CMNH); Windham Tp. (CMNH). SCI: Bloom Tp. (CMNH); Madison Tp. (CMNH); Vernon Tp. (CMNH). TRU: Braceville Tp. (CMNH); Mesopotamia Tp. (CMNH). TUS: Goshen Tp. (CMNH). VIN: Elk Tp. (CMNH); Knox Tp. (CMNH); Madison Tp. (CMNH); Wilkersville Tp. (CMNH). WAS: Newport Tp. (CMNH).

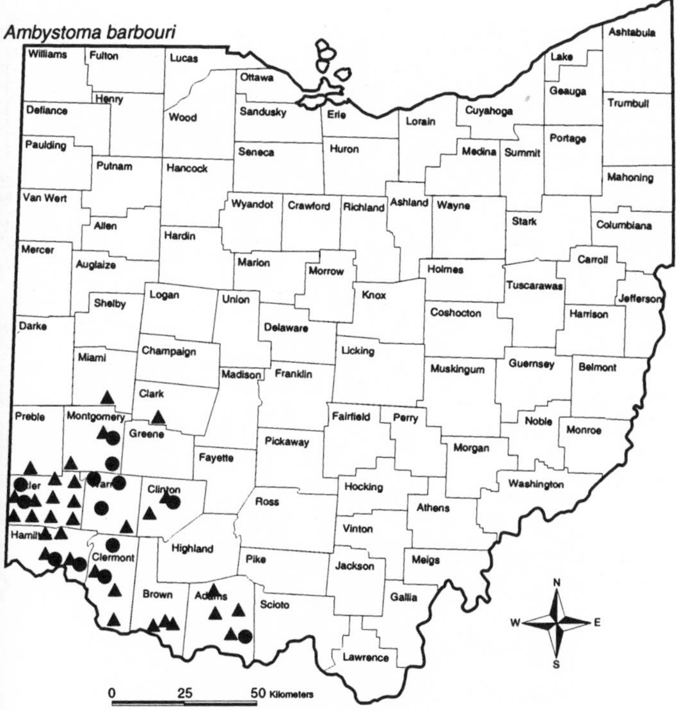

Figure 25-4. Distribution of streamside salamanders (*Ambystoma barbouri*) in Ohio. Locality records for *A. barbouri.* ADA: Brush Creek Tp. (OSUM); Jefferson Tp. (OSUM); Meigs Tp. (OSUM); Oliver Tp. (UMMZ); Scott Tp. (OSUM); Sprigg Tp. (Alan F. Root). BRO: Byrd Tp. (CMNH); Jefferson Tp. (CMNH); Pleasant Tp. (CMNH). BUT: Fairfield Tp. (CSNH, MU); Hanover Tp. (CSNH, MU); Lemon Tp. (CSNH, MU); Liberty Tp. (CMNH, CSNH); Morgan Tp. (CSNH, MU); Oxford Tp. (CM, MU, OSUM); Reily Tp. (CMNH, CSNH, FSL); Ross Tp. (CSNH, DMNH); St. Clair Tp. (MU); Union Tp. (MU); Wayne Tp. (CMNH). CLA: Mad River Tp. (OSUM); Vernon Tp. (CMNH). CLE: Batavia Tp. (CSNH); Franklin Tp. (CMNH); Goshen Tp. (FSL); Union Tp. (CSNH, MU, UMMZ). CLI: Union Tp. (OSUM); Vernon Tp. (CMNH). HAM: Amberly Village (KU, UMMZ); Cincinnati (CM, CSNH); Colerain Tp. (CMNH, CSNH, KU, MU, OSUM); College Hill (OUVC); Columbia Tp. (CMNH, OSUM); French Park (KU, OUVC); Green Tp. (CSNH); Indian Hill (KU); MacFarlane's Woods (CSNH); Mt. Airy Forest (CSNH, FSL, USNM); Springfield Tp. (CSNH); Westwood (CSNH); MIA: Monroe Tp. (DMNH). MOT: Butler Tp. (DMNH); Dayton (CMNH, DMNH, UMMZ); German Tp. (DMCP); Harrison Tp. (DMNH, UMMZ); Mad River Tp. (DMCP); Washington Tp. (UMMZ). WAR: Franklin Tp. (UMMZ); Harlan Tp. (CSNH); Turtle Creek Tp. (OSUM); Wayne Tp. (UMMZ).

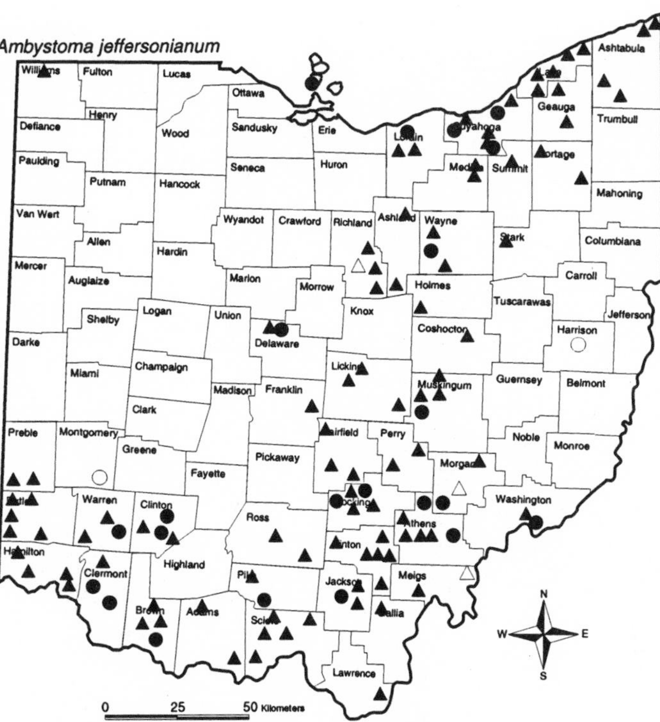

Figure 25-5. Distribution of Jefferson salamanders (*Ambystoma jeffersonianum*) in Ohio. Locality records for *A. jeffersonianum* that are new since 1988. For a complete list of all records see Pfingsten and Downs (1989). ASH: Jackson Tp. (Floyd L. Downs). ATB: Conneaut Tp. (CMNH); Kingsville Tp. (CMNH); Rome Tp. (CSNH); Trumbull Tp. (CMNH). BRO: Jefferson Tp. (OSUM); Washington Tp. (CMNH). BUT: Fairfield Tp. (CSNH); Milford Tp. (MU); Morgan Tp. (CSNH); Reily Tp. (CSNH). CLI: Clark Tp. (OSUM). COS: Keene Tp. (CMNH). GAL: Huntington Tp. (CMNH). HAM: Crosby Tp. (CSNH). JAC: Bloomfield Tp. (CMNH); Milton Tp. (CMNH). LAK: Perry Tp. (CMNH). MED: Hinkley Tp. (CMNH). MEG: Olive Tp. (Leo Schleicher); Rutland Tp. (CMNH). MRG: Bristol Tp. (OSUM). MUS: Licking Tp. (CMNH); Muskingum Tp. (CMNH). PER: Harrison Tp. (CMNH); Jackson Tp. (CMNH). POR: Windham Tp. (CMNH). PRE: Somers Tp. (KU). RIC: Mifflin Tp. (Merrill Tawse); Monroe Tp. (Merrill Tawse); Worthington Tp. (Merrill Tawse). SCI: Madison Tp. (CMNH); Rush Tp. (OSUM). VIN: Madison Tp. (CMNH); Wilkersville Tp. (CMNH). WAR: Deerfield Tp. (CSNH).

Figure 25-6. Distribution of blue-spotted salamanders (*Ambystoma laterale*) in Ohio.

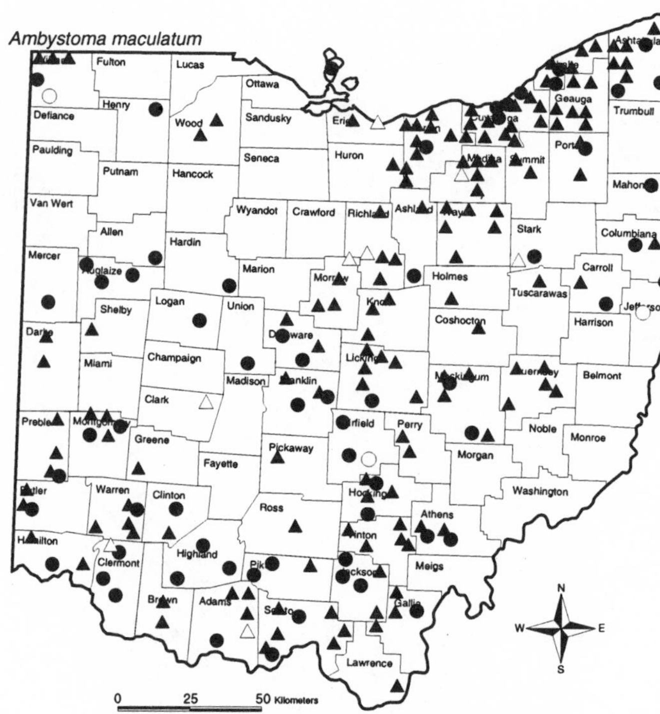

Figure 25-7. Distribution of spotted salamanders (*Ambystoma maculatum*) in Ohio. Locality records for *A. maculatum* that are new since 1988. For a complete list of all records see Pfingsten and Downs (1989). ADA: Bratten Tp. (MU); Franklin Tp. (MU); Meigs Tp. (MU). ATB: Austinburg Tp. (CMNH); Conneaut Tp. (CMNH); Kingsville Tp. (CMNH); Monroe Tp. (CMNH); Rome Tp. (CMNH). BRO: Franklin Tp. (CMNH); Washington Tp. (CMNH). CAR: Monroe Tp. (CMNH). CLA: Pleasant Tp. (Dan Rice). COS: Keene Tp. (CMNH). CUY: Brooklyn (CMNH); Orange Tp. (CMNH). ERI: Perkins Tp. (OSUM). GAL: Greenfield Tp. (CMNH); Huntington Tp. (CMNH); Raccoon Tp. (CMNH). GEA: Russell Tp. (RAP). GUE: Monroe Tp. (CMNH); Westland Tp. (CMNH); Wheeling Tp. (CMNH); Wills Tp. (CMNH). HAM: Crosby Tp. (CSNH). HIG: Concord Tp. (CMNH). HOL: Killbuck Tp. (CMNH). HUR: Clarksfield Tp. (CMNH). JAC: Madison Tp. (CMNH); Milton Tp. (CMNH). LAK: Perry Tp. (CMNH). LOR: Brighton Tp. (MVZ); Pittsfield Tp. (CMNH). MED: Medina Tp. (CMNH). MUS: Blue Rock Tp. (RAP); Cass Tp. (CMNH); Madison Tp. (CMNH); Muskingum Tp. (CMNH). PER: Jackson Tp. (CMNH); Reading Tp. (CMNH). RIC: Butler Tp. (CMNH); Jefferson Tp. (Merrill Tawse); Monroe Tp. (Merrill Tawse); Washington Tp. (Merrill Tawse). SCI: Bloom Tp. (CMNH); Madison Tp. (CMNH); Vernon Tp. (CMNH). VIN: Knox Tp. (CMNH); Madison Tp. (CMNH); Richland Tp. (CSNH). WAR: Deerfield Tp. (CSNH); Harlan Tp. (CMNH); Salem Tp. (CSNH); Washington Tp. (CMNH). WAY: Baughman Tp. (CMNH); Canaan Tp. (CW); Chippewa Tp. (CMNH). WOO: Center Tp. (CMNH).

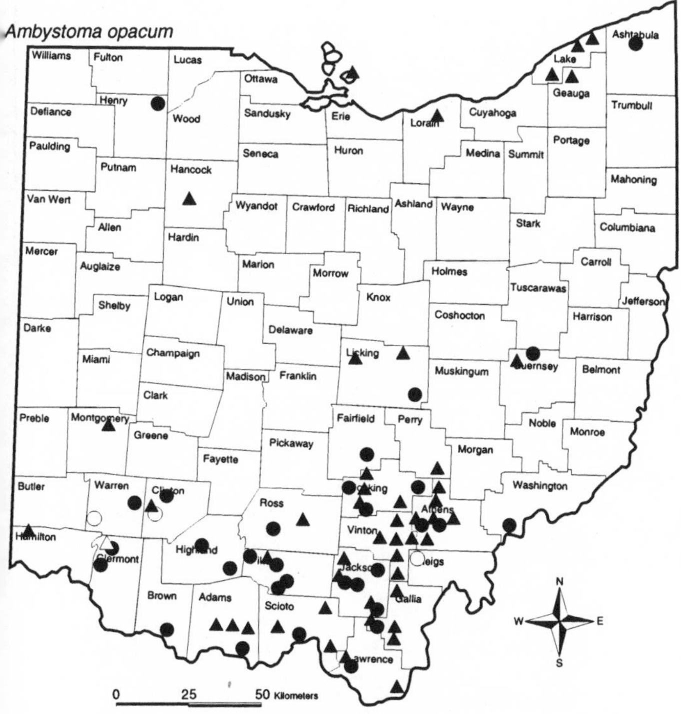

Figure 25-8. Distribution of marbled salamanders (*Ambystoma opacum*) in Ohio. Locality records for *A. opacum* that are new since 1988. For a complete list of all records see Pfingsten and Downs (1989). ADA: Tiffin Tp. (OSUM). ERI: Kelleys Island Tp. (ROM). GAL: Greenfield Tp. (CMNH); Huntington Tp. (CMNH); Perry Tp. (CMNH); Walnut Tp. (CMNH). GEA: Chardon Tp. (Geauga Co. Park Dist.). GUE: Liberty Tp. (CMNH). HAM: Crosby Tp. (CSNH). JAC: Madison Tp. (CMNH). LAK: Perry Tp. (CMNH). LAW: Elizabeth Tp. (CMNH). SCI: Madison Tp. (CMNH); Vernon Tp. (CMNH). VIN: Elk Tp. (CMNH); Knox Tp. (CMNH); Vinton Tp. (CMNH); Wilkersville Tp. (CMNH).

Figure 25-9. Distribution of silvery salamanders (*Ambystoma platineum*) in Ohio. Locality records that are new for *A. platineum* since 1988. For a complete list of all records see Pfingsten and Downs (1989). ATB: Trumbull Tp. (CMNH). LAK: Concord Tp. (CMNH); Madison Tp. (CMNH); Perry Tp. (CMNH).

Figure 25-10. Distribution of large-celled (or small-celled but all female) *Ambystoma* populations not clearly referable to either *Ambystoma tremblayi* (Tremblay's salamander) or *Ambystoma platineum* (silvery salamander) in Ohio. Locality records for unidentifiable *Ambystoma* sp. that are new since 1988. For a complete list of all records see Pfingsten and Downs (1989). HUR: Townsend Tp. (CMNH). LOR: Pittsfield Tp. (CMNH). SEN: Reed Tp. (CMNH); Scipio Tp. (CMNH).

Figure 25-11. Distribution of smallmouth salamanders (*Ambystoma texanum*) in Ohio. Locality records for *A. texanum*. ALL: Auglaize Tp. (OSUM); Bath Tp. (JEJ); Richland Tp. (OSUM). ASH: Clear Creek Tp. (CW); Jackson Tp. (CW); Ruggles Tp. (CW). ATB: Windsor Tp. (CMNH). AUG: Clay Tp. (OSUM); German Tp. (UMMZ); Moulton Tp. (UMMZ); St. Mary's Tp. (UMMZ); Union Tp. (OSUM); Wayne Tp. (OSUM). ATH: Athens Tp. (OSUM). CHP: Adams Tp. (CW); Goshen Tp. (OSUM); Harrison Tp. (OSUM); Rush Tp. (OSUM); Wayne Tp. (OSUM). COS: Tuscarawas Tp. (OSUM). CRA: Chatfield Tp. (CMNH); Whetstone Tp. (CMNH). CUY: Big Creek Reservation (CMNH); Brooklyn (CMNH); Cleveland (CMNH); Lakewood (CMNH); North Olmsted (OSUM); Olmsted Falls (KSU); Richmond Heights (CMNH); Rocky River Reservation (CMNH). DAR: Adams Tp. (OSUM); Brown Tp. (CW); Greenville Tp. (UMMZ). DEF: Defiance Tp. (AMNH). DEL: Delaware Tp. (CMNH); Genoa Tp. (OSUM); Marlboro Tp. (Floyd L. Downs); Orange Tp. (OSUM); Troy Tp. (CMNH). ERI: Groton Tp. (CMNH); Kelleys Island Tp. (CW, ROM); Margaretta Tp. (FSL); Oxford Tp. (CMNH); Perkins Tp. (CMNH). FAI: Lancaster Tp. (E. V. Wilcox); Rush Creek Tp. (Floyd L. Downs); Walnut Tp. (OSUM). FRA: Blendon Tp. (UMMZ); Columbus (ANSP, OSUM, USNM); Jefferson Tp. (CMNH, OSUM); Norwich Tp. (OSUM); Perry Tp. (CMNH); Sharon Tp. (OSUM); Truro Tp. (OSUM); Washington Tp. (Dan Rice). FUL: Franklin Tp. (UMMZ); German Tp. (CMNH, CW). HAN: Eagle Tp. (CU, UMMZ); Marion Tp. (UMMZ); Van Buren Tp. (CMNH). HAR: Blanchard Tp. (OUVC); Dudley Tp.

(Floyd L. Downs); Goshen Tp. (ONU); Hale Tp. (OSUM); Liberty Tp. (ONU, OSUM); Marion Tp. (ONU); McDonald Tp. (ONU); Taylor Creek Tp. (OUVC); Washington Tp. (ONU). HEN: Washington Tp. (AMNH, OSUM). HOC: Goodhope Tp. (OSUM). HUR: Bronson Tp. (Glen Barnhardt); New London (OSUM); Norwalk Tp. (Glen Barnhardt). KNO: Morgan Tp. (OSUM). LAK: Concord Tp. (UMMZ); Kirtland Tp. (CMNH); Painesville Tp. (CMNH); Willoughby Tp. (CMNH). LIC: Burlington Tp. (CW); Liberty Tp. (David M. Dennis); Licking Tp. (CMNH); Lima Tp. (OSUM); St. Albans Tp. (JEJ); Union Tp. (OSUM); Washington Tp. (OSUM). LOG: Richland Tp. (Dan Rice); Stokes Tp. (CMNH); Union Tp. (CMNH). LOR: Avon Tp. (CMNH); Black River Tp. (OC); Brownhelm Tp. (CMNH); Columbia Tp. (CMNH); New Russia Tp. (OC); Oberlin Tp. (OC); Pittsfield Tp. (CMNH); Sheffield Tp. (CMNH, OSUM). LUC: Collins Park (AMNH); Richfield Tp. (UMMZ); Springfield Tp. (UMMZ); Sylvania Tp. (AMNH); Toledo (AMNH, OSUM, UMMZ). MAD: Jefferson Tp. (OSUM). MAR: Big Island Tp. (Floyd L. Downs). MED: Hinckley Tp. (CM); Litchfield Tp. (CMNH). MER: Butler Tp. (Clarence F. Clark); Dublin Tp. (CMNH); Franklin Tp. (FSL); Granville Tp. (OSUM); Jefferson Tp. (Clarence F. Clark). MRW: Harmony Tp. (OSUM); South Bloomfield Tp. (FSL). MUS: Cass Tp. (OSUM). OTT: Danbury Tp. (CW, OSUM); Middle Bass Island (Thomas H. Langlois, UMMZ); South Bass Island (Thomas H. Langlois). PAU: Benton Tp. (OSUM); Brown Tp. (OSUM); Washington Tp. (OSUM). PER: Jackson Tp. (Dan Rice). POR: Aurora Tp. (CMNH). RIC: Butler Tp. (CW). SAN: Reily Tp. (CMNH); Woodville Tp. (OSUM). SEN: Big Spring Tp. (OSUM). SHE: McLean Tp. (CMNH). STA: Sugar Creek Tp. (CM). TRU: Green Tp. (KU); Weathersfield Tp. (CMNH). UNI: Darby Tp. (OSUM); Millcreek Tp. (OSUM); Union Tp. (Floyd L. Downs). WAS: Marietta Tp. (OUVC); Warren Tp. (OUVC). WAY: Baughman Tp. (CW); Canaan Tp. (Floyd L. Downs); Chester Tp. (CW, FSL, UMMZ); Chippewa Tp. (CW, UMMZ); Congress Tp. (BGSU); Franklin Tp. (CM, CW, UMMZ); Plain Tp. (CW); Wooster Tp. (FSL). WIL: Bridgewater Tp. (Floyd L. Downs); Center Tp. (BGSU); Jefferson Tp. (BGSU); Madison Tp. (Floyd L. Downs); Mill Creek Tp. (Floyd L. Downs); Northwest Tp. (Floyd L. Downs); Springfield Tp. (OSUM); Superior Tp. (Floyd L. Downs). WOO: Bowling Green Tp. (OSUM); Freedom Tp. (Floyd L. Downs); Grand Rapids Tp. (BGSU); Liberty Tp. (OSUM); Middletown Tp. (OSUM); Montgomery Tp. (Floyd L. Downs). WYA: Marseilles Tp. (Floyd L. Downs); Pitt Tp. (Floyd L. Downs); Upper Sandusky Tp. (Charles F. Walker).

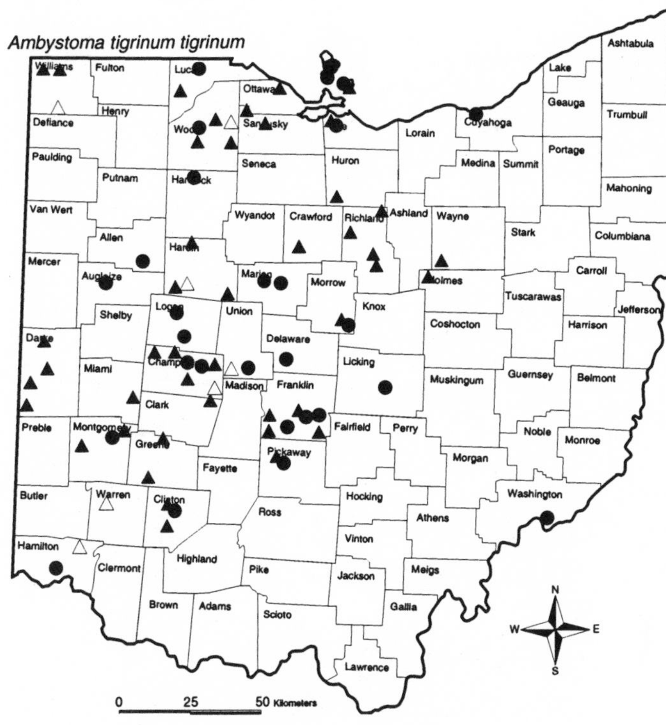

Figure 25-12. Distribution of eastern tiger salamanders (*Ambystoma tigrinum tigrinum*) in Ohio. Locality records for *A. t. tigrinum* that are new since 1988. For a complete list of all records see Pfingsten and Downs (1989). CHP: Goshen Tp. (Dan Rice); Harrison Tp. (Dan Rice). CRA: Bucyrus Tp. (CMNH). DAR: Harrison Tp. (CMNH). GRE: Spring Valley Tp. (CSNH). HAR: Roundhead Tp. (ONU); Washington Tp. (ONU). HUR: Richmond Tp. (CMNH). LUC: Swanton Tp. (Fred Kraus). MIA: Elizabeth Tp. (CSNH). RIC: Sharon Tp. (CMNH). SAN: Woodville Tp. (OSUM). UNI: Union Tp. (Dan Rice). WOO: Center Tp. (CMNH); Freedom Tp. (Dan Rice).

Figure 25-13. Distribution of green salamanders (*Aneides aeneus*) in Ohio. Locality records for *A. aeneus* that are new since 1988. For a complete list of all records see Pfingsten and Downs (1989). ADA: Green Tp. (FMNH); Tiffin Tp. (MU).

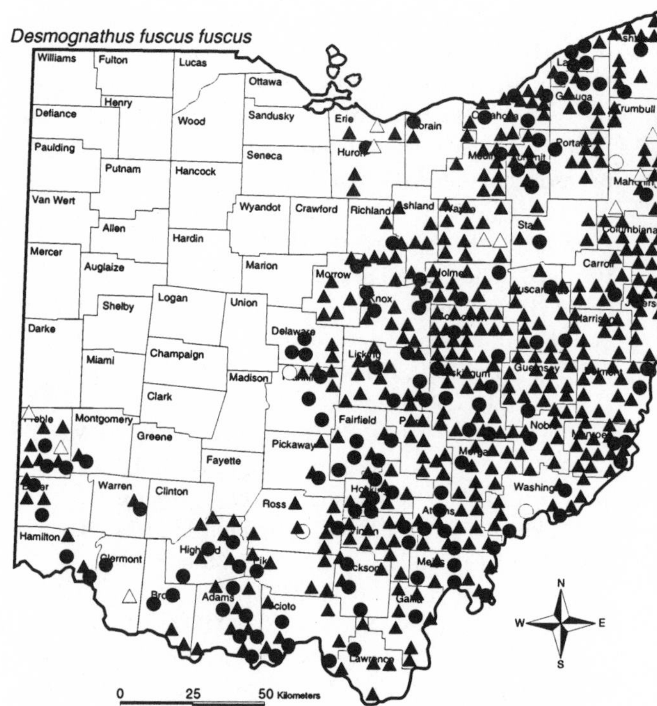

Figure 25-14. Distribution of northern dusky salamanders (*Desmognathus fuscus fuscus*) in Ohio. Locality records for *D. f. fuscus* that are new since 1988. For a complete list of all records see Pfingsten and Downs (1989). ADA: Sprigg Tp. (FMNH). ATB: Monroe Tp. (CMNH); Sheffield Tp. (CMNH). BEL: York Tp. (CMNH). BUT: Oxford Tp. (CSNH); Reily Tp. (CSNH). CAR: Union Tp. (CMNH). COL: Butler Tp. (CMNH); St. Clair Tp. (UP). COS: Adams Tp. (CMNH); Bethlehem Tp. (CMNH); Crawford Tp. (CMNH); Franklin Tp. (CMNH); Keene Tp. (CMNH); Newcastle Tp. (CMNH); Tiverton Tp. (CMNH); Washington Tp. (CMNH). CUY: Orange Tp. (CMNH); Warrensville Tp. (CMNH). FRA: Plain Tp. (CU). GEA: Newbury Tp. (CMNH). HAM: Anderson Tp. (CSNH). HIG: New Market Tp. (CMNH); Penn Tp. (CMNH). HOC: Benton Tp. (MVZ); Good Hope Tp. (CU); Laurel Tp. (MVZ); Salt Creek Tp. (CU). JAC: Milton Tp. (CMNH). LAK: Kirtland Tp. (CMNH). LIC: Granville Tp. (MVZ); Harrison Tp. (MVZ). MEG: Rutland Tp. (CMNH). MOE: Green Tp. (CMNH); Ohio Tp. (CMNH); Summit Tp. (CMNH); Switzerland Tp. (CMNH). MOT: German Tp. (LACM). PER: Bearfield Tp. (CMNH); Monroe Tp. (CMNH); Salt Lick Tp. (CMNH). POR: Charlestown Tp. (CMNH); Freedom Tp. (CMNH); Paris Tp. (CMNH); Windham Tp. (CMNH). ROS: Harrison Tp. (CU); Liberty Tp. (USNM). SCI: Vernon Tp. (CMNH). STA: Washington Tp. (CMNH). SUM: Sagamore Hills Tp. (CMNH). TUS: Clay Tp. (CMNH); Jefferson Tp. (CMNH). VIN: Clinton Tp. (CMNH); Elk Tp. (CMNH); Madison Tp. (CMNH); Wilkersville Tp. (CMNH). WAS: Newport Tp. (CMNH). WAY: Paint Tp. (CMNH).

Figure 25-15. Distribution of mountain dusky salamanders (*Desmognathus ochrophaeus*) in Ohio. Locality records for *D. ochrophaeus* that are new since 1988. For a complete list of all records see Pfingsten and Downs (1989). ATB: Conneaut Tp. (CMNH); Kingsville Tp. (CMNH); Monroe Tp. (CMNH); Plymouth Tp. (CMNH); Sheffield Tp. (CMNH); Wayne Tp. (CMNH). POR: Freedom Tp. (CMNH); Paris Tp. (CMNH); Windham Tp. (CMNH).

Figure 25-16. Distribution of northern two-lined salamanders (*Eurycea bislineata*) in Ohio. Locality records for *E. bislineata.* ASH: Green Tp. (CMNH); Hanover Tp. (CM, CMNH, FSL); Jackson Tp. (CMNH); Lake Tp. (CMNH); Milton Tp. (CMNH); Mohican Tp. (CMNH, OSUM); Montgomery Tp. (CMNH); Orange Tp. (CMNH); Perry Tp. (CMNH); Vermillion Tp. (CMNH). ATB: Colebrook Tp. (CMNH); Conneaut Tp. (KSU); Denmark Tp. (CMNH); Harpersfield Tp. (CMNH); Hartsgrove Tp. (Michael P. Sipes); Jefferson Tp. (OSUM); Kingsville Tp. (CMNH); Lenox Tp. (CMNH); Monroe Tp. (CMNH); Morgan Tp. (CMNH); Pierpont Tp. (CMNH); Plymouth Tp. CMNH); Pymatuning Swamp (AMNH); Sheffield Tp. (CMNH); Wayne Tp. (CMNH); Williamsfield Tp. (KSU); Windsor Tp. (AMNH, CMNH, KSU, OUVC). CAR: Brown Tp. (CMNH); Center Tp. (CMNH); Fox Tp. (CMNH); Harrison Tp. (CMNH); Lee Tp. (CMNH, OSUM); Loudon Tp. (CMNH); Union Tp. (OSUM); Washington Tp. (CMNH). COL: Elk Run Tp. (CMNH); Franklin Tp. (CMNH); Hanover Tp. (CMNH); Knox Tp. (CMNH); Liverpool Tp. (OSUM); Madison Tp. (CMNH); Perry Tp. (CMNH); St. Clair Tp. (KSU, OUVC); Unity Tp. (CMNH); Wayne Tp. (CMNH); West Tp. (CMNH); Yellow Creek Tp. (Michael P. Sipes). COS: Adams Tp. (CMNH); Bedford Tp. (CMNH); Bethlehem Tp. (CMNH); Clark Tp. (CMNH); Crawford Tp. (CMNH); Jackson Tp. (CMNH); Jefferson Tp. (OSUM); Keene Tp. (OSUM); Mill Creek Tp. (CMNH); Monroe Tp. (CMNH); New Castle Tp. (CMNH); Perry Tp. (CMNH); Tiverton Tp. (CMNH); Virginia Tp. (CMNH); Washington Tp. (CMNH); White Eyes Tp. (CMNH). CRA: Bucyrus Tp.

(CMNH); Sandusky Tp. (CMNH). CUY: Bentleyville (CMNH); Brecksville Reservation (CMNH, KSU); Broadview Heights (CMNH); Brookpark (AMNH); Cleveland (CMNH, USNM); East Cleveland (CMNH); Gates Mills (CMNH); Hunting Valley (CMNH); Independence (CMNH); Mayfield (CMNH); North Chagrin Reservation (CMNH); North Royalton (CMNH); Olmsted Falls (CMNH, KSU); Pepper Pike (CMNH); Richmond Heights (CMNH); South Chagrin Reservation (CMNH, KSU, OSUM, OUVC). DEL: Concord Tp. (UL); Delaware Tp. (OSUM); Harlem Tp. (CMNH); Liberty Tp. (OSUM); Orange Tp. (OSUM); Trenton Tp. (CMNH). ERI: Berlin Tp. (BGSU, CMNH); Milan Tp. (CMNH); Oxford Tp. (CMNH, CW). GEA: Chardon Tp. (AMNH, CM, CMNH); Claridon Tp. (CMNH); Hambden Tp. (CMNH); Middlefield Tp. (CMNH); Montville Tp. (CMNH); Newbury Tp. (CMNH); Parkman Tp. (CMNH, OSUM); Thompson Tp. (CMNH). HOL: Berlin Tp. (CMNH); Clark Tp. (CMNH); Hardy Tp. (CMNH); Killbuck Tp. (CMNH, OSUM); Knox Tp. (CMNH); Mechanic Tp. (CMNH); Monroe Tp. (CMNH); Paint Tp. (FSL); Prairie Tp. (CMNH); Richland Tp. (CMNH); Ripley Tp. (CMNH); Salt Creek Tp. (CMNH); Walnut Creek Tp. (CMNH); Washington Tp. (CMNH). HUR: Bronson Tp. (CMNH); Greenfield Tp. (CMNH); Norwalk Tp. (OSUM); Ripley Tp. (CMNH). KNO: Clay Tp. (CMNH); Harrison Tp. (CMNH); Howard Tp. (OSUM); Jefferson Tp. (CMNH, OSUM); Liberty Tp. (CMNH); Middlebury Tp. (OSUM); Monroe Tp. (CMNH); Pleasant Tp. (CMNH); Union Tp. (OSUM); Wayne Tp. (CMNH). LAK: Concord Tp. (CMNH, UMMZ); Kirtland Tp. (CMNH); Leroy Tp. (CMNH); Madison Tp. (CMNH); Perry Tp. (OSUM, UMMZ). LIC: Eden Tp. (OSUM, OUVC); Fallsbury Tp. (OSUM, UMMZ). LOG: Jefferson Tp. (CMNH, OSUM); Lake Tp. (CMNH); Monroe Tp. (CMNH); Perry Tp. (CMNH). LOR: Brownhelm Tp. (CMNH); Columbia Tp. (CMNH); Oberlin Tp. (OC); Sheffield Tp. (OUVC). MAH: Austintown Tp. (Robert B. Howells); Beaver Tp. (CMNH); Berlin Tp. (CMNH); Boardman Tp. (CMNH); Canfield Tp. (CMNH, OUVC); Coitsville Tp. (CMNH); Ellsworth Tp. (CMNH); Goshen Tp. (CMNH); Jackson Tp. (CMNH); Poland Tp. (CM, CMNH); Springfield Tp. (KU); Youngstown Tp. (Michael P. Sipes). MED: Brunswick Hills Tp. (CMNH); Chatham Tp. (CMNH); Granger Tp. (CMNH); Guilford Tp. (CMNH); Harrisville Tp. (CMNH); Hinckley Tp. (CMNH, KU, OSUM); Homer Tp. (CMNH); Lafayette Tp. (CMNH); Liverpool Tp. (CMNH); Medina Tp. (USMN); Montville Tp. (CMNH); Sharon Tp. (CMNH); Wadsworth Tp. (CMNH, OSUM); Westfield Tp. (CMNH). MRW: Franklin Tp. (CMNH); Harmony Tp. (CMNH); Lincoln Tp. (CMNH); Perry Tp. (CMNH); Troy Tp. (CMNH). POR: Charleston Tp. (CMNH); Freedom Tp. (CMNH); Hiram Tp. (KSU); Nelson Tp. (CMNH); Paris Tp. (CMNH); Ravenna Tp. (KSU); Windham Tp. (CMNH). RIC: Butler Tp. (Carl R. Gebhardt); Franklin Tp. (CMNH); Madison Tp. (Merrill Tawse); Mifflin Tp. (CMNH); Monroe Tp. (CMNH); Springfield Tp. (CMNH); Troy Tp. (CMNH); Washington Tp. (Merrill Tawse); Weller Tp. (CMNH); Worthington Tp. (CMNH, OSUM). SHE: Franklin Tp. (CMNH); Orange Tp. (CMNH, OSUM); Perry Tp. (CMNH); Salem Tp. (CMNH). STA: Lexington Tp. (CMNH); Massillon Tp. (FSL); Paris Tp. (CMNH); Tuscarawas Tp. (Michael P. Sipes); Washington Tp. (CMNH). SUM: Bath (OSUM); Boston Tp. (CMNH); Copley Tp. (CMNH); Green Tp. (Michael P. Sipes); Hudson Tp. (CMNH); Northfield Center Tp. (CMNH, OSUM); Northampton Tp. (KSU); Portage Tp. (KSU); Richfield Tp. (CMNH, USNM); Sagamore Hills Tp. (CMNH); Springfield Tp. (CMNH); Twinsburg Tp. (KSU). TRU: Bloomfield Tp. (CMNH); Braceville Tp. (CMNH); Bristol Tp. (CMNH); Brookfield Tp. (CMNH); Farmington Tp. (CMNH); Green Tp. (CMNH); Hartford Tp. (KSU, OSUM, UL); Howland Tp. (Michael P. Sipes); Hubbard Tp. (CMNH); Kinsman Tp. (CMNH); Liberty Tp. (CMNH); Mecca Tp. (CMNH); Mesopotamia Tp. (CMNH); Vernon Tp. (Michael P. Sipes); Vienna Tp. (CMNH). TUS: Auburn Tp. (CMNH); Jefferson Tp. (CMNH); Lawrence Tp. (CMNH); Perry Tp. (CMNH); Union Tp. (CMNH). WAY: Canaan Tp. (CMNH, CW); Chester Tp. (CMNH, CW, UMMZ); Chippewa Tp. (CMNH); Congress Tp. (CMNH, CW); East Union Tp. (OSUM); Franklin Tp. (CW, UMMZ); Green Tp. (CW); Milton Tp. (CM); Paint Tp. (CW); Plain Tp. (CW, KU); Salt Creek Tp. (CW); Sugar Creek Tp. (CW); Wayne Tp. (CW); Wooster Tp. (CMNH, CW, UMMZ).

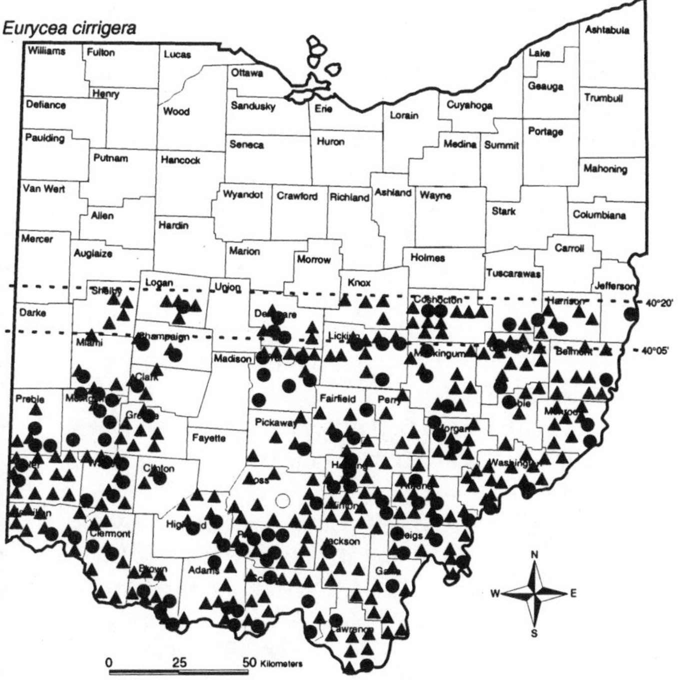

Figure 25-17. Distribution of southern two-lined salamanders (*Eurycea cirrigera*) in Ohio. Locality records for *E. cirrigera.* ADA: Bratton Tp. (OSUM); Brush Creek Tp. (CMNH, OSUM); Franklin Tp. (CMNH); Green Tp. (CMNH, CSNH, OSUM, UMMZ); Jefferson Tp. (CMNH, CSNH, UMMZ); Meigs Tp. (CMNH, CSNH); Sprigg Tp. (CMNH); Tiffin Tp. (CMNH). ATH: Alexander Tp. (OUVC); Ames Tp. (CMNH); Athens Tp. (CMNH, OUVC); Canaan Tp. (OUVC); Carthage Tp. (OUVC); Dover Tp. (OUVC); Lee Tp. (OSUM); Lodi Tp. (OSUM, OUVC); Trimble Tp. (OUVC); Troy Tp. (OSUM, OUVC); Waterloo Tp. (CMNH, OUVC); York Tp. (OUVC). BEL: Colerain Tp. (CMNH); Goshen Tp. (OUVC); Mead Tp. (OSUM); Smith Tp. (CMNH, OUVC); Somerset Tp. (CMNH); Warren Tp. (CMNH); Washington Tp. (CMNH); Wheeling Tp. (CMNH); York Tp. (CMNH). BRO: Byrd Tp. (CMNH); Clark Tp. (CMNH); Franklin Tp. (CMNH); Huntington Tp. (CMNH, KU); Jefferson Tp. (CMNH); Lewis Tp. (CMNH); Pleasant Tp. (CMNH, UMMZ); Scott Tp. (OSUM); Union Tp. (CMNH, OSUM). BUT: Fairfield Tp. (CSNH, MU); Hanover Tp. (CMNH); Liberty Tp. (CMNH, CSNH); Madison Tp. (CMNH); Milford Tp. (MU); Morgan Tp. (CMNH, CSNH); Oxford Tp. (AMNH, CM, CSNH, MU); Reily Tp. (CSNH, OSUM); Ross Tp. (CSNH, MU); St. Clair Tp. (CMNH); Union Tp. (MU); Wayne Tp. (CMNH, CSNH). CHP: Johnson Tp. (CMNH, OSUM); Urbana Tp. (CMNH, OSUM, OUVC, UMMZ). CLA: Bethel Tp. (CMNH, UMMZ); German Tp. (CMNH); Mad River Tp. (DMNH). CLE: Batavia Tp. (CSNH, UMMZ); Goshen Tp. (CMNH); Miami Tp. (CMNH); Ohio Tp. (CMNH); Tate Tp. (CSNH); Union Tp. (CSNH); Washington Tp. (CMNH); Williamsburg Tp. (CMNH). CLI: Adams Tp. (CMNH, OSUM); Union Tp. (OSUM). COS: Adams Tp. (CMNH); Bedford Tp. (CMNH); Bethlehem Tp. (CMNH); Clark Tp. (CMNH); Crawford Tp. (CMNH); Jackson Tp. (CMNH); Jefferson Tp. (OSUM); Keene Tp. (OSUM); Mill Creek Tp. (CMNH); Monroe Tp. (CMNH); New Castle Tp. (CMNH); Perry Tp. (CMNH); Tiverton Tp. (CMNH); Virginia Tp. (CMNH); Washington Tp. (CMNH); White Eyes Tp. (CMNH). DEL: Concord Tp. (UL); Delaware Tp. (OSUM); Harlem Tp. (CMNH); Liberty Tp. (OSUM); Orange Tp. (OSUM); Trenton Tp. (CMNH). FAI: Berne Tp. (OSUM); Bloom Tp. (CMNH); Columbus (AMNH); Hocking Tp. (OSUM); Pleasant Tp. (OSUM); Richland Tp. (OSUM). FRA: Blendon Tp. (OSUM, UMMZ); Jefferson Tp. (OSUM); Norwich Tp. (OSUM); Perry Tp. (OSUM); Plain Tp. (OUVC); Pleasant Tp. (OSUM); Sharon Tp. (CMNH; OSUM); Washington Tp. (CMNH; OSUM). GAL: Addison Tp. (CMNH); Gallipolis Tp. (CMNH); Greenfield Tp. (CMNH; OUVC); Guyan Tp. (CMNH); Harrison Tp. (CMNH); Morgan Tp. (CMNH); Perry Tp. (CMNH); Raccoon Tp. (CMNH, UF); Springfield Tp. (OSUM); Walnut Tp. (CMNH). GRE: Beavercreek Tp. (DMNH); Cedarville Tp. (CMNH); Miami Tp. (AMNH, CMNH, CW, DMNH, MCZ, OSUM, UMMZ); New Jasper Tp. (CMNH); Spring Valley Tp. (CMNH); Sugar Creek Tp. (CMNH); Xenia Tp. (DMNH). GUE: Center Tp. (CMNH); Jackson Tp. (CMNH); Knox Tp. (CMNH); Liberty Tp. (CMNH); Londonderry Tp. (CMNH); Monroe Tp. (CMNH, OSUM); Oxford Tp. (CMNH); Valley Tp. (OSUM); Washington Tp. (CMNH); Wheeling Tp. (AMNH, CMNH); Wills Tp. (CMNH). HAM: Amberly Village (KU); Anderson Tp. (OUVC); Cincinnati (OUVC, USNM); Colerain Tp. (CMNH, KU, OSUM); College Hill (OUVC); Columbia Tp. (CMNH, CSNH); Crosby Tp. (CSNH); French Park (OUVC); Harrison Tp. (CMNH); MacFarlane's Woods Park (CSNH, OSUM); Miami Tp. (CSNH); Mt. Airy Forest (CM, CSNH, UMMZ); Springfield Tp. (CSNH); Symmes Tp. (CSNH, OSUM); Whitewater Tp. (OUVC); Winton Woods Park (OUVC). HAS: Archer Tp. (CMNH); Franklin Tp. (CM); Freeport Tp. (CMNH); German Tp. (CMNH); Green Tp. (CMNH); Nottingham Tp. (KSU, OSUM); Washington Tp. (OSUM). HIG: Brush Creek Tp. (CMNH, DMNH, OSUM, UMMZ); Fairfield Tp. (CMNH); Liberty Tp. (OSUM); Madison Tp. (OSUM); Paint Tp. (CSNH, OSUM, UMMZ); Penn Tp. (CMNH). HOC: Benton Tp. (AMNH, CM, CMNH, OSUM, OUVC, UMMZ, USNM); Falls Tp. (Ronald A. Brandon); Goodhope Tp. (AMNH, CSNH, OSUM, UMMZ); Green Tp. (CMNH); Laurel Tp. (CMNH, OSUM, UMMZ); Marion Tp. (OUVC); Salt Creek Tp. (CMNH, OSUM, UMMZ); Washington Tp. (Ronald A. Brandon). JAC: Bloomfield Tp. (CMNH); Franklin Tp. (OSUM); Hamilton Tp. (OUVC); Liberty

Tp. (AMNH, CMNH, OSUM, OUVC, UMMZ); Scioto Tp. (OSUM). JEF: Steubenville (OSUM). KNO: Howard Tp. (OSUM); Monroe Tp. (CMNH); Union Tp. (OSUM); Wayne Tp. (CMNH). LAW: Aid Tp. (CMNH); Decatur Tp. (OSUM); Elizabeth Tp. (OSUM); Fayette Tp. (OUVC); Lawrence Tp. (OUVC); Mason Tp. (OSUM); Union Tp. (UMMZ); Windsor Tp. (OUVC). LIC: Bowling Green Tp. (OSUM); Eden Tp. (OSUM, OUVC); Fallsbury Tp. (OSUM, UMMZ); Jersey Tp. (David M. Sever); Licking Tp. (OSUM); McKean Tp. (OSUM); Newark Tp. (David M. Sever); Newton Tp. (OSUM); St. Albans Tp. (OSUM). LOG: Jefferson Tp. (CMNH, OSUM); Lake Tp. (CMNH); Monroe Tp. (CMNH); Perry Tp. (CMNH). MEG: Bedford Tp. (OUVC); Chester Tp. (CMNH); Columbia Tp. (USNM); Lebanon Tp. (OSUM); Letart Tp. (CMNH); Olive Tp. (OUVC); Rutland Tp. (CMNH, OUVC); Salem Tp. (OSUM, OUVC); Sutton Tp. (CMNH, OUVC). MIA: Bethel Tp. (CMNH, UMMZ); Union Tp. (DMNH, OSUM, UMMZ); Washington Tp. (CMNH). MOE: Adams Tp. (CM, CMNH, FSL, OUVC); Bethel Tp. (CMNH); Center Tp. (CMNH, OUVC); Lee Tp. (OSUM); Malaga Tp. (OSUM); Perry Tp. (CMNH); Sunsbury Tp. (CMNH); Wayne Tp. (CMNH). MOT: Butler Tp. (CMNH, CSNH, DMNH, OSUM, UMMZ); Dayton Tp. (DMNH); German Tp. (DMNH, LACM); Randolph Tp. (DMNH, UMMZ); Van Buren Tp. (DMNH); Washington Tp. (UMMZ); Wayne Tp. (UMMZ). MRG: Bristol Tp. (OSUM); Deerfield Tp. (OSUM); Malta Tp. (CMNH, OSUM, OUVC, UMMZ); Meigsville Tp. (OSUM); Penn Tp. (OUVC); Union Tp. (OUVC); Windsor Tp. (CMNH); York Tp. (OSUM). MUS: Blue Rock Tp. (CMNH, OSUM); Brush Creek Tp. (OSUM); Cass Tp. (OSUM); Falls Tp. (OSUM); Harrison Tp. (OSUM); Licking Tp. (CMNH); Monroe Tp. (CMNH); Perry Tp. (CMNH); Rich Hill Tp. (OSUM); Salt Creek Tp. (CMNH, UMMZ). NOB: Beaver Tp. (CMNH); Buffalo Tp. (FSL); Center Tp. (UMMZ); Jackson Tp. (CMNH); Wayne Tp. (CMNH). PER: Madison Tp. (CMNH); Monroe Tp. (CMNH); Pleasant Tp. (OSUM); Reading Tp. (CMNH); Salt Lick Tp. (OSUM). PIC: Jackson Tp. (CMNH); Madison Tp. (CMNH); Perry Tp. (CMNH); Washington Tp. (CMNH, OSUM). PIK: Beaver Tp. (OUVC); Benton Tp. (DMNH, OSUM, UMMZ); Camp Creek Tp. (OSUM); Jackson Tp. (CMNH); Mifflin Tp. (DMNH, OSUM); Newton Tp. (OSUM); Pebble Tp. (OSUM); Pee Pee Tp. (OSUM); Scioto Tp. (OSUM); Sunfish Creek Tp. (CMNH); Union Tp. (CMNH). PRE: Gasper Tp. (MU, USNM); Gratis Tp. (MU, USNM); Israel Tp. (CMNH, OSUM); Somers Tp. (AMNH, CM, KU, MU, OSUM); Washington Tp. (CM, KU). ROS: Chilicothe (Max Morse); Colerain Tp. (CM, UMMZ); Concord Tp. (OUVC); Franklin Tp. (CMNH, OSUM); Harrison Tp. (CMNH, OSUM, OUVC, UMMZ); Huntington Tp. (CMNH); Jefferson Tp. (CMNH); Liberty Tp. (CMNH); Paint Tp. (CSNH, OSUM, OUVC); Paxton Tp. (OUVC); Twin Tp. (OUVC); Union Tp. (CMNH). SCI: Bloom Tp. (CMNH); Brush Creek Tp. (OUVC); Green Tp. (AMNH); Harrison Tp. (OSUM); Jefferson Tp. (CMNH); Madison Tp. (OUVC); Morgan Tp. (FSL); Nile Tp. (CMNH, KU, OSUM, OUVC, UMMZ); Rarden Tp. (CMNH); Union Tp. (CMNH); Valley Tp. (CMNH); Vernon Tp. (CMNH); Washington Tp. (OUVC). SHE: Franklin Tp. (CMNH); Orange Tp. (CMNH, OSUM); Perry Tp. (CMNH); Salem Tp. (CMNH). TUS: Auburn Tp. (CMNH); Bucks Tp. (CMNH); Jefferson Tp. (CMNH); Lawrence Tp. (CMNH); Perry Tp. (CMNH); Union Tp. (CMNH); Washington Tp. (OSUM). VIN: Brown Tp. (OSUM, OUVC); Clinton Tp. (CMNH); Eagle Tp. (CMNH, OUVC); Elk Tp. (CMNH); Harrison Tp. (CMNH); Jackson Tp. (OUVC); Knox Tp. (OSUM); Richland Tp. (OUVC); Swan Tp. (CMNH); Vinton Tp. (CMNH). WAR: Clear Creek Tp. (OSUM, UMMZ); Deerfield Tp. (Clarence F. Clark); Franklin Tp. (CMNH); Hamilton Tp. (CMNH); Harlan Tp. (CMNH, CSNH); Salem Tp. (CMNH, UMMZ); Washington Tp. (CMNH, CSNH, OSUM); Wayne Tp. (CSNH, DMNH, UMMZ). WAS: Barlow Tp. (CMNH); Belpre Tp. (OSUM); Dunham Tp. (OUVC); Fairfield Tp. (CMNH, CSNH, OSUM); Grandview Tp. (CMNH); Lawrence Tp. (CMNH); Liberty Tp. (CMNH); Ludlow Tp. (OUVC); Marietta (OSUM, OUVC, USNM); Muskingum Tp. (OUVC, UMMZ); Newport Tp. (CMNH); Palmer Tp. (CMNH); Warren Tp. (OUVC); Watertown Tp. (OUVC); Wesley Tp. (OUVC).

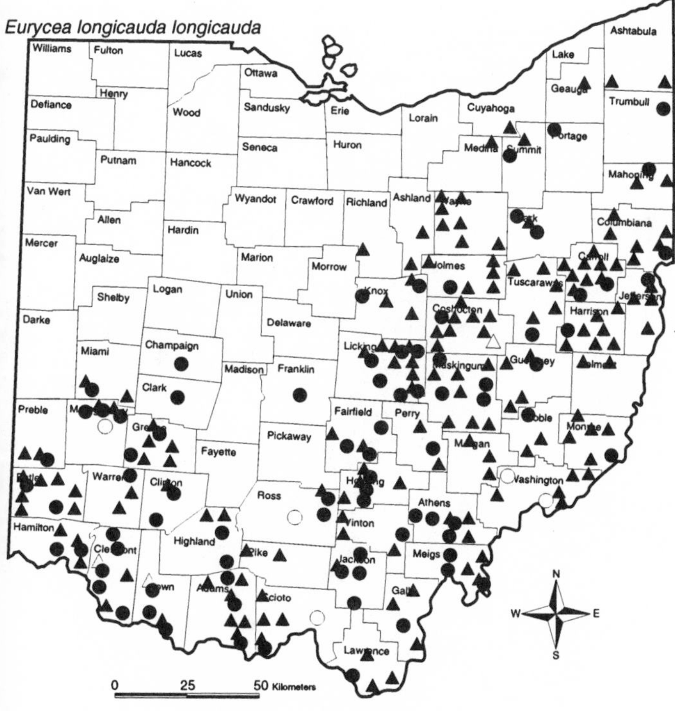

Figure 25-18. Distribution of longtail salamanders (*Eurycea longicauda longicauda*) in Ohio. Locality records for *E. l. longicauda* that are new since 1988. For a complete list of all records see Pfingsten and Downs (1989). ADA: Scott Tp. (MU). BUT: Milford Tp. (CSNH); Reily Tp. (CSNH); Union Tp. (CSNH). CAR: Augusta Tp. (CMNH); Monroe Tp. (CMNH). COL: Washington Tp. (CMNH). COS: Clark Tp. (CMNH); Keene Tp. (BGSU); Pike Tp. (CMNH). CUY: Brecksville (CMNH). GRE: Miami Tp. (FMNH, LACM, MVZ). GUE: Monroe Tp. (CMNH). HAM: Anderson Tp. (CSNH); Columbia Tp. (CSNH); Indian Hill (KU). HOL: Clark Tp. (CMNH); Paint Tp. (CMNH). KNO: Jefferson Tp. (CMNH). LIC: Perry Tp. (CMNH). MUS: Licking Tp. (CMNH); Monroe Tp. (CMNH). PER: Clayton Tp. (CMNH). SCI: Union Tp. (CM). TUS: Clay Tp. (CMNH); Sandy Tp. (CMNH); Wayne Tp. (RAP). VIN: Eagle Tp. (CMNH); Vinton Tp. (CMNH). WAY: Paint Tp. (CMNH).

Figure 25-19. Distribution of cave salamanders (*Eurycea lucifuga*) in Ohio.

Figure 25-20. Distribution of Kentucky spring salamanders (*Gyrinophilus porphyriticus duryi*) in Ohio.

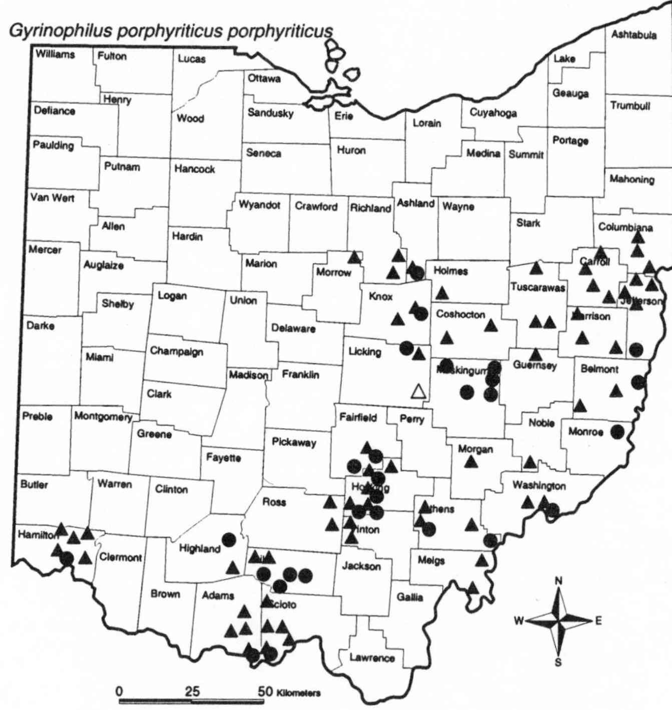

Figure 25-21. Distribution of northern spring salamanders (*Gyrinophilus porphyriticus porphyriticus*) in Ohio. Locality records for *G. p. porphyriticus* that are new since 1988. For a complete list of all records see Pfingsten and Downs (1989). CAR: Augusta Tp. (CMNH); Harrison Tp. (CMNH). GUE: Monroe Tp. (CMNH). HAM: Columbia Tp. (CSNH); Springfield Tp. (KU); Sycamore Tp. (Douglas E. Wynn); Symes Tp. (KU). MEG: Sutton Tp. (CMNH). NOB: Jackson Tp. (CMNH). PIK: Benton Tp. (FMNH). RIC: Monroe Tp. (Merrill Tawse); Worthington Tp. (Merrill Tawse). TUS: Clay Tp. (CMNH); Rush Tp. (CMNH).

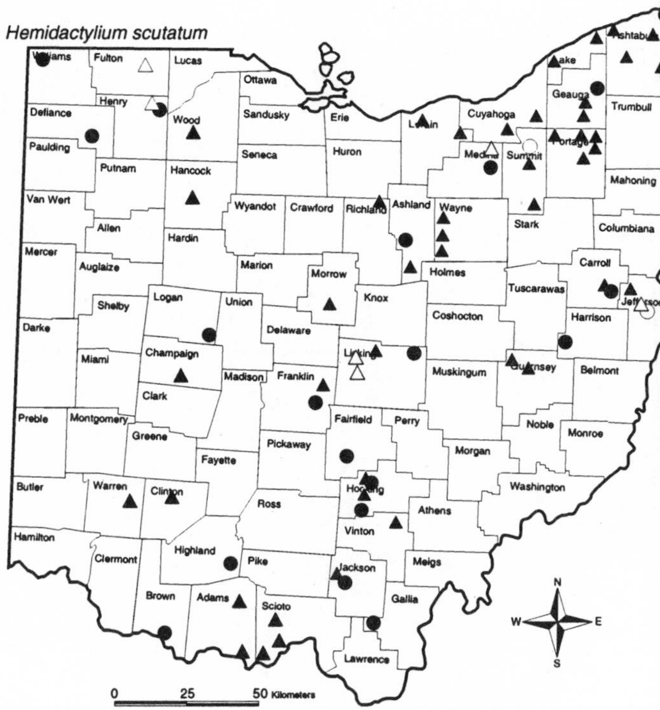

Figure 25-22. Distribution of four-toed salamanders (*Hemidactylium scutatum*) in Ohio. Locality records for *H. scutatum* that are new since 1988. For a complete list of all records see Pfingsten and Downs (1989). ASH: Hanover Tp. (CMNH). POR: Windham Tp. (CMNH). SCI: Nile Tp. (KU).

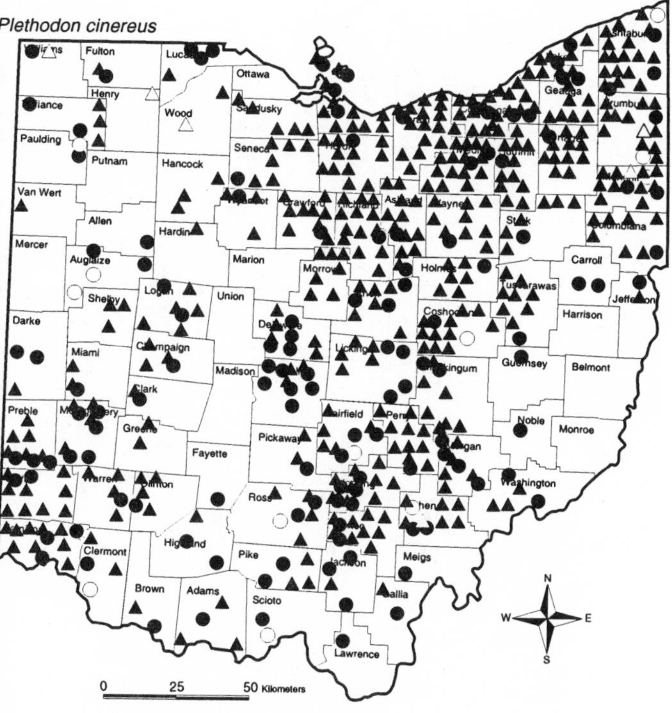

Figure 25-23. Distribution of redback salamanders (*Plethodon cinereus*) in Ohio. Locality records for *P. cinereus* that are new since 1988. For a complete list of all records see Pfingsten and Downs (1989). ADA: Sprigg Tp. (FMNH). ASH: Ruggles Tp. (CMNH); Troy Tp. (CMNH). ATB: Kingsville Tp. (CMNH); Orwell Tp. (CMNH); Rome Tp. (CMNH). BUT: Fairfield Tp. (CSNH); Morgan Tp. (CSNH); Oxford Tp. (CSNH); Reily Tp. (CSNH). CHP: Urbana Tp. (UF). CLE: Miami Tp. (CSNH). CLI: Chester Tp. (CMNH); Washington Tp. (CMNH). COL: Butler Tp. (CMNH); Elk Run Tp. (CMNH); Salem Tp. (CMNH). COS: Adams Tp. (CMNH); Bethlehem Tp. (CMNH); Newcastle Tp. (CMNH). CUY: Brooklyn (CMNH); Lakewood (CMNH). DEF: Richland Tp. (CMNH); Tiffin Tp. (DC). ERI: Perkins Tp. (CMNH). FRA: Perry Tp. (MVZ). GRE: Miami Tp. (FMNH). HAM: Columbia Tp. (CSNH); Crosby Tp. (CSNH); Miami Tp. (CSNH); Mill Creek Tp. (CSNH); Springfield Tp. (CSNH). HOL: Killbuck Tp. (CMNH); Paint Tp. (CMNH). JAC: Scioto Tp. (CMNH). LAK: Leroy Tp. (CMNH). LOR: Wellington Tp. (CMNH). MAH: Beaver Tp. (CMNH); Goshen Tp. (CMNH). MED: Harrisville Tp. (CMNH). MUS: Cass Tp. (CMNH); Licking Tp. (CMNH); Newton Tp. (CMNH). PER: Bearfield Tp. (CMNH); Clayton Tp. (CMNH); Coal Tp. (CMNH); Madison Tp. (CMNH); Monroe Tp. (CMNH); Salt Lick Tp. (CMNH). POR: Freedom Tp. (CMNH); Paris Tp. (CMNH); Windham Tp. (CMNH). PRE: Gasper Tp. (CSNH). SEN: Scipio Tp. (CMNH). STA: Lexington Tp. (CMNH); Marlboro Tp. (CMNH). SUM: Sagamore Hills Tp. (CMNH). TRU: Bristol Tp. (CMNH); Mesopotamia Tp. (CMNH). TUS: Jefferson Tp. (CMNH); Salem Tp. (CMNH). VIN: Clinton Tp. (CMNH); Eagle Tp. (CMNH); Elk Tp. (CMNH); Madison Tp. (CMNH). WAR: Harlan Tp. (CSNH). WAY: Paint Tp. (CMNH); Sugar Creek Tp. (CMNH).

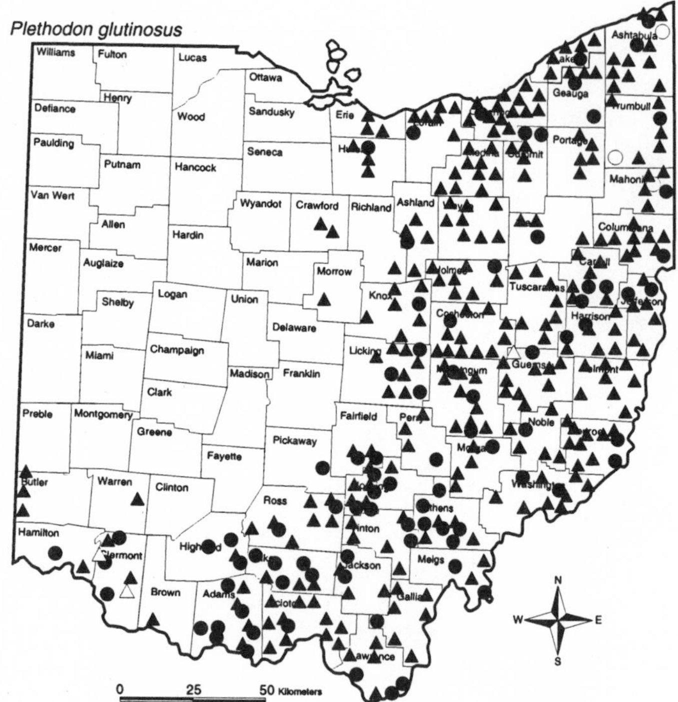

Figure 25-24. Distribution of northern slimy salamanders (*Plethodon glutinosus*) in Ohio. Locality records for *P. glutinosus* that are new since 1988. For a complete list of all records see Pfingsten and Downs (1989). ATB: Denmark Tp. (CMNH); Kingsville Tp. (CMNH). BUT: Morgan Tp. (CMNH); Reily Tp. (CSNH). CAR: Brown Tp. (CMNH). CLE: Miami Tp. (CSNH). COL: Center Tp. (CMNH); Salem Tp. (CMNH). COS: Clark Tp. (CMNH); Washington Tp. (CMNH). CUY: Bedford (CMNH); Bentleyville (CMNH); Garfield Heights (CMNH); Parma (CMNH). ERI: Huron Tp. (UMMZ). HAM: Anderson Tp. (CSNH). JAC: Scioto Tp. (CMNH). LAK: Mentor Tp. (CMNH); Perry Tp. (CMNH). LAW: Elizabeth Tp. (CMNH). LIC: Fallsbury Tp. (MCZ). MAH: Beaver Tp. (CMNH). MOE: Perry Tp. (CMNH); Seneca Tp. (CMNH); Summit Tp. (CMNH). PER: Jackson Tp. (CMNH); Madison Tp. (CMNH); Reading Tp. (CMNH). PIK: Sunfish Creek Tp. (CMNH). POR: Paris Tp. (CMNH); Windham Tp. (CMNH). SCI: Nile Tp. (CMNH). STA: Lawrence Tp. (CMNH). SUM: Sagamore Hills Tp. (CMNH). TRU: Mesopotamia Tp. (CMNH). TUS: Fairfield Tp. (CMNH); Salem Tp. (CMNH); Wayne Tp. (CMNH). WAS: Newport Tp. (CMNH). WAY: Sugar Creek Tp. (CMNH).

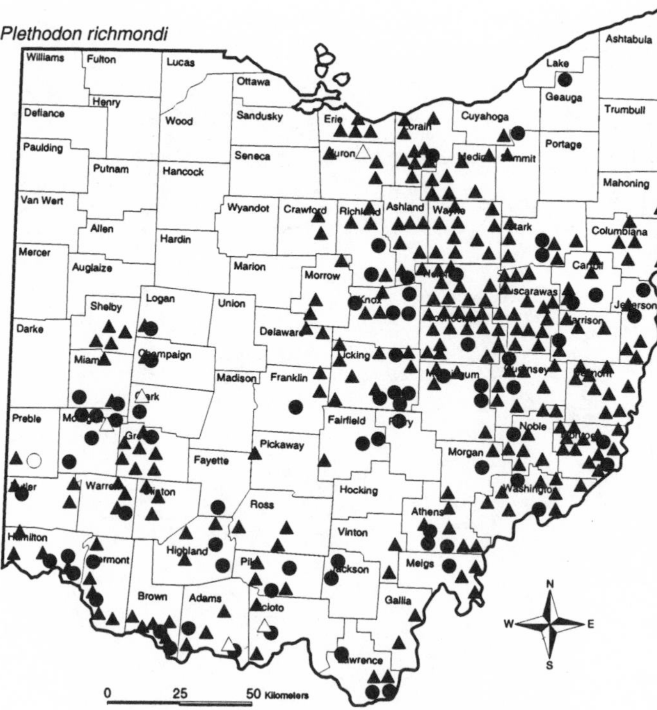

Figure 25-25. Distribution of ravine salamanders (*Plethodon richmondi*) in Ohio. Locality records for *P. richmondi* that are new since 1988. For a complete list of all records see Pfingsten and Downs (1989). BRO: Byrd Tp. (CMNH); Union Tp. (CMNH). BUT: Liberty Tp. (CSNH). CLE: Miami Tp. (CSNH); Pierce Tp. (CSNH). CLI: Chester Tp. (CMNH); Union Tp. (CMNH); Washington Tp. (CMNH). COL: Hanover Tp. (CMNH); Salem Tp. (CMNH). COS: Adams Tp. (CMNH); Bethlehem Tp. (CMNH); Crawford Tp. (CMNH); Keene Tp. (CMNH); Newcastle Tp. (CMNH); Pike Tp. (CMNH). CRA: Jefferson Tp. (CMNH). CUY: Brecksville (CMNH). HAM: Anderson Tp. (CSNH); Crosby Tp. (CSNH); Miami Tp. (CSNH). HIG: New Market Tp. (CMNH); Penn Tp. (CMNH). HOL: Clark Tp. (CMNH). MED: Harrisville Tp. (CMNH); Hinckley Tp. (CMNH). MOE: Malaga Tp. (CMNH); Ohio Tp. (CMNH); Perry Tp. (CMNH); Seneca Tp. (CMNH). MUS: Muskingum Tp. (CMNH). NOB: Jackson Tp. (CMNH). PIK: Sunfish Creek Tp. (CMNH). STA: Lawrence Tp. (CMNH). SUM: Richfield Tp. (CMNH). TUS: Fairfield Tp. (CMNH); Sugar Creek Tp. (CMNH); Warren Tp. (CMNH); Warwick Tp. (CMNH). WAS: Liberty Tp. (CMNH); Newport Tp. (CMNH). WAY: Baughman Tp. (CMNH); Paint Tp. (CMNH).

Figure 25-26. Distribution of Wehrle's salamanders (*Plethodon wehrlei*) in Ohio.

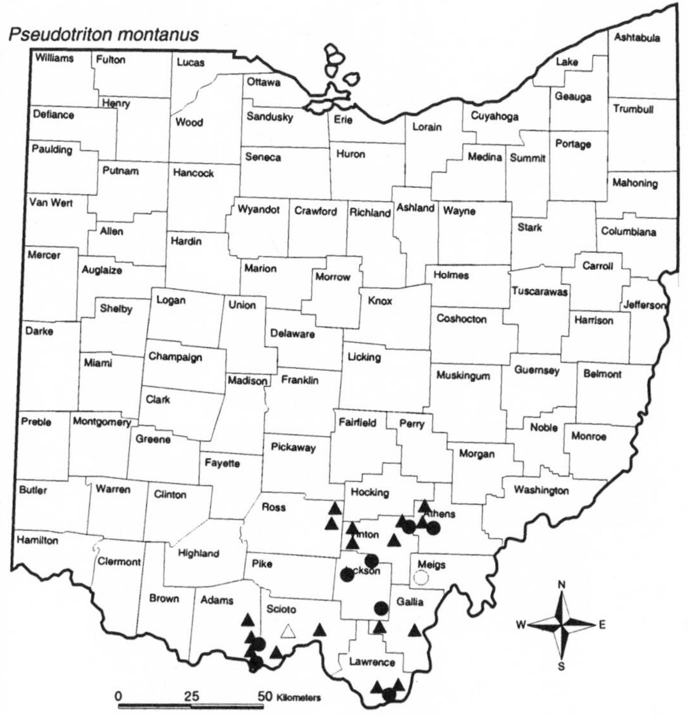

Figure 25-27. Distribution of mud salamanders (*Pseudotriton montanus*) in Ohio.

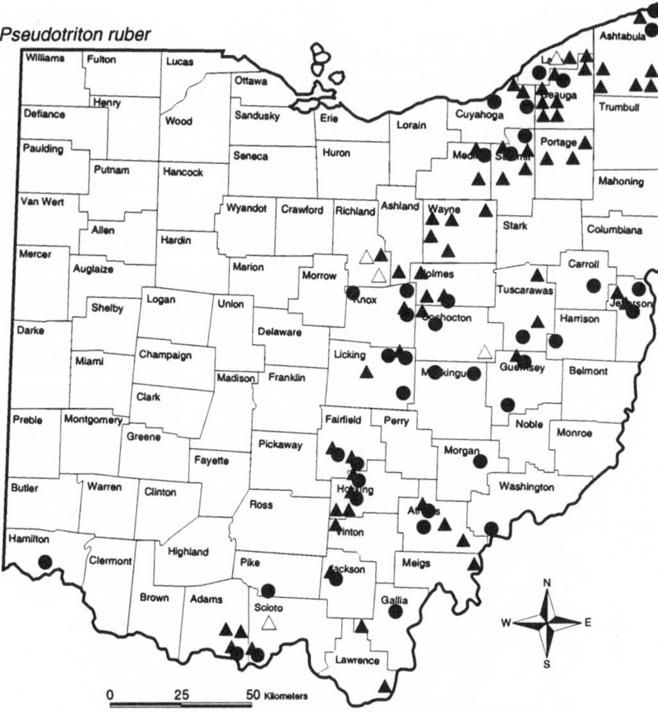

Figure 25-28. Distribution of red salamanders (*Pseudotriton ruber*) in Ohio. Locality records for *P. ruber* that are new since 1988. For a complete list of all records see Pfingsten and Downs (1989). ATB: Kingsville Tp. (CMNH). COS: Tiverton Tp. (CMNH). GAL: Greenfield Tp. (CMNH). GEA: Chester Tp. (CMNH); Newbury Tp. (CMNH); Thompson Tp. (CMNH). GUE: Monroe Tp. (CMNH). JEF: Springfield Tp. (MU). LIC: Granville Tp. (MVZ). POR: Charlestown Tp. (CMNH); Windham Tp. (CMNH). TUS: Rush Tp. (CMNH).

Figure 25-29. Distribution of eastern spadefoot toads (*Scaphiopus holbrookii holbrookii*) in Ohio. Locality records for *S. h. holbrookii*. ATH: Athens Tp. (OUVC, W). LAW: Fayette Tp. (OUVC). PIK: Benton Tp. (OUVC). WAS: Belpre Tp. (OUVC).

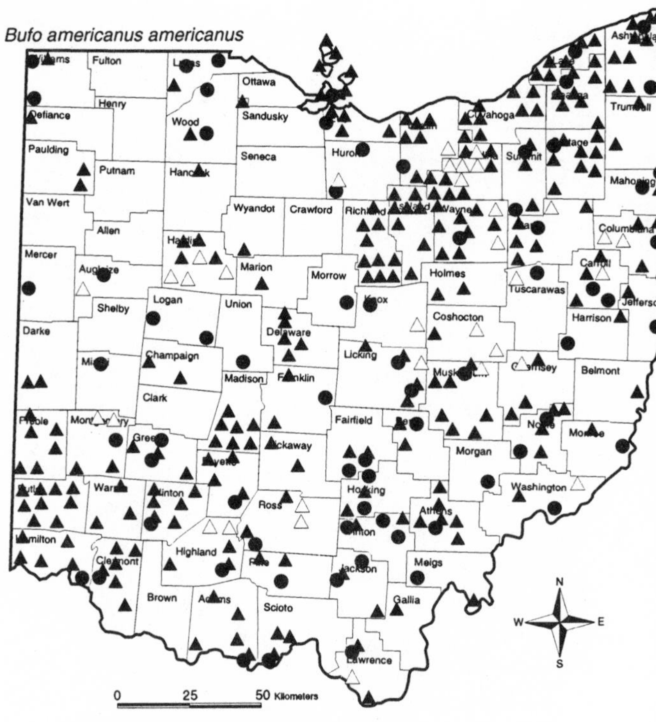

Figure 25-30. Distribution of American toads (*Bufo americanus americanus*) in Ohio. Locality records for *B. a. americanus*. ADA: Brush Creek Tp. (MU); Green Tp. (CMNH, OSUM, W). ASH: Clear Creek Tp. (CSNH); Hanover Tp. (CM, OSUM); Jackson Tp. (CSNH); Milton Tp. (CSNH); Mohican Tp. (OSUM); Orange Tp. (CSNH); Ruggles Tp. (CSNH); Sullivan Tp. (CSNH). ATB: Ashtabula Tp. (CMNH); Conneaut Tp. (CMNH, W); Kingsville Tp. (CMNH, W); Monroe Tp. (CMNH); Morgan Tp. (CMNH); Orwell Tp. (CMNH); Plymouth Tp. (CMNH); Richmond Tp. (CM); Sheffield Tp. (CMNH); Trumbull Tp. (CMNH); Wayne Tp. (W); Windsor Tp. (CMNH). ATH: Athens Tp. (CMNH, W); Canaan Tp. (CMNH, OUVC); Dover Tp. (OSUM); Lodi Tp. (OSUM); Trimble Tp. (OUVC); Waterloo Tp. (CM, CMNH, OUVC). AUG: Moulton Tp. (W); St. Mary's Tp. (TOM). BEL: Pultney Tp. (OSUM). BUT: Fairfield Tp. (CSNH); Hanover Tp. (CSNH); Lemon Tp. (CSNH); Madison Tp. (CSNH); Milford Tp. (CSNH, DMNH); Oxford Tp. (MU); Reily Tp. (CSNH, DMNH, MU); Ross Tp. (CSNH, KU); Wayne Tp. (MU). CAR: Brown Tp. (CMNH); Harrison Tp. (CMNH); Loudon Tp. (W); Orange Tp. (CMNH); Union Tp. (W); Washington Tp. (RAP). CHP: Johnson Tp. (UF); Urbana Tp. (DMNH, W). CLE: Batavia Tp. (CSNH); Goshen Tp. (CSNH); Stonelick Tp. (CSNH); Tate Tp. (CSNH); Union Tp. (KU, W); Wayne Tp. (CMNH). CLI: Adams Tp. (CSNH); Chester Tp. (CSNH); Union Tp. (CSNH); Vernon Tp. (OSUM, W); Washington Tp. (CSNH); Wilson Tp. (CSNH). COL: Elk Run Tp. (W); Fairfield Tp. (CMNH); Hanover Tp. (RAP); Salem Tp. (CMNH);

Washington Tp. (CMNH); West Tp. (RAP). COS: Bethlehem Tp. (OSUM); Jefferson Tp. (W); Keene Tp. (RAP); Linton Tp. (RAP); Newcastle Tp. (CMNH). CUY: East Cleveland (OSUM); Lakewood (CMNH); Mayfield (CMNH); Middleburg Heights (RAP); Olmsted Falls (CMNH); Orange (CMNH); Rocky River (CMNH); Strongsville (CMNH); Warrensville (CMNH). DAR: Liberty Tp. (CSNH); Neave Tp. (CSNH). DEF: Milford Tp. (OSUM); Richland Tp. (DC). DEL: Berlin Tp. (UF); Delaware Tp. (OSUM); Liberty Tp. (OSUM); Marlboro Tp. (OSUM); Orange Tp. (OSUM); Troy Tp. (OSUM). ERI: Florence Tp. (CMNH); Kelleys Island (CMNH); Margaretta Tp. (CMNH, W); Oxford Tp. (CMNH); Perkins Tp. (CMNH). FAI: Berne Tp. (OSUM, W); Hocking Tp. (OSUM); Madison Tp. (W). FAY: Jasper Tp. (CSNH); Jefferson Tp. (CSNH); Paint Tp. (CSNH); Wayne Tp. (CSNH, W). FRA: Perry Tp. (OSUM); Pleasant Tp. (CSNH); Truro Tp. (W). FUL: Franklin Tp. (CMNH). GAL: Raccoon Tp. (OSUM). GEA: Burton Tp. (CMNH); Chardon Tp. (CMNH, W); Chester Tp. (CMNH); Montville Tp. (CMNH); Munson Tp. (CMNH); Newbury Tp. (CMNH); Parkman Tp. (CMNH, OSUM); Thompson Tp. (OSUM). GRE: Beaver Creek Tp. (DMNH); Jefferson Tp. (CSNH); Miami Tp. (W); Xenia Tp. (OSUM, W). GUE: Liberty Tp. (RAP); Monroe Tp. (CMNH); Spencer Tp. (OSUM); Valley Tp. (OSUM). HAM: Anderson Tp. (W); Columbia Tp. (KU); Crosby Tp. (CSNH); Green Tp. (Paul Krusling); Miami Tp. (CSNH); Sycamore Tp. (CSNH, OSUM). HAN: Allen Tp. (BGSU). HAR: Blanchard Tp. (OUVC); Cessna Tp. (OUVC); Dudley Tp. (Charles Blem); Goshen Tp. (OUVC); McDonald Tp. (RAP); Pleasant Tp. (Charles Blem); Roundhead Tp. (Charles Blem); Washington Tp. (OUVC). HAS: German Tp. (MU); Washington Tp. (W). HIG: Brush Creek Tp. (OSUM, W); Fairfield Tp. (Barry Valentine); Madison Tp. (Barry Valentine); Paint Tp. (OSUM); Salem Tp. (CSNH). HOC: Benton Tp. (W); Good Hope Tp. (W); Laurel Tp. (OUVC); Salt Creek Tp. (OSUM). HOL: Hardy Tp. (CMNH); Richland Tp. (OSUM). HUR: Norwalk Tp. (W); Richmond Tp. (RAP, W). JAC: Liberty Tp. (OUVC, W); Madison Tp. (CMNH); Washington Tp. (W). JEF: Springfield Tp. (MU); Steubenville Tp. (W). KNO: Butler Tp. (RAP); Wayne Tp. (W). LAK: Concord Tp. (CMNH); Kirtland Tp. (CMNH); Madison Tp. (CMNH, OSUM); Mentor Tp. (CMNH); Perry Tp. (W); Willoughby Tp. (CMNH). LAW: Decatur Tp. (TOM, W); Fayette Tp. (OSUM); Upper Tp. (RAP). LIC: Bennington Tp. (OSUM); Bowling Green Tp. (OSUM); Eden Tp. (CM, W); Hopewell Tp. (OSUM, W); Perry Tp. (RAP). LOG: Bloomfield Tp. (W); Zane Tp. (W). LOR: Amherst Tp. (CMNH, MVZ); Brownhelm Tp. (CMNH); Brighton Tp. (W); Columbia Tp. (RAP); Grafton Tp. (RAP); Henrietta Tp. (CMNH); Huntington Tp. (CMNH); New Russia Tp. (CMNH). LUC: Springfield Tp. (W); Swanton Tp. (BGSU, CMNH, CSNH); Toledo (W). MAD: Fairfield Tp. (CSNH); Oak Run Tp. (CSNH); Paint Tp. (CSNH); Pleasant Tp. (CSNH); Range Tp. (CSNH); Stokes Tp. (CSNH); Union Tp. (CSNH). MAH: Boardman Tp. (CM); Canfield Tp. (W); Youngstown (W). MAR: Green Camp Tp. (KU); Waldo Tp. (CMNH). MED: Brunswick Tp. (RAP); Chatham Tp. (OSUM); Granger Tp. (RAP); Harrisville Tp. (CMNH); Hinckley Tp. (RAP); Homer Tp. (CMNH); Lafayette Tp. (RAP); Liverpool Tp. (CMNH); Medina Tp. (RAP); Spencer Tp. (CMNH); York Tp. (RAP). MEG: Letart Tp. (OSUM); Salem Tp. (W). MER: Washington Tp. (W). MIA: Washington Tp. (W). MOE: Malaga Tp. (OSUM); Salem Tp. (W). MOT: Butler Tp. (DMNH); German Tp. (DMNH); Mad River Tp. (W); Washington Tp. (CMNH); Wayne Tp. (DMNH). MRG: Windsor Tp. (W). MRW: Chester Tp. (W). MUS: Adams Tp. (RAP); Clay Tp. (OUVC); Harrison Tp. (OUVC); Licking Tp. (CMNH); Madison Tp. (CMNH, W); Muskingum Tp. (CMNH); Newton Tp. (CMNH); Salt Creek Tp. (CMNH). NOB: Beaver Tp. (OSUM); Noble Tp. (CMNH); Olive Tp. (OSUM); Seneca Tp. (CMNH, W); Sharon Tp. (W). OTT: Danbury Tp. (CMNH, OSUM, W); North Bass Island (W); Portage Tp. (W); Put-In-Bay Tp. (OSUM, W); South Bass Island (W). PAU: Brown Tp. (OSUM); Washington Tp. (OSUM). PER: Hopewell Tp. (W); Jackson Tp. (CMNH); Reading Tp. (CM). PIC: Darby Tp. (CSNH); Jackson Tp. (CSNH). PIK: Benton Tp. (DMNH); Newton Tp. (W); Pebble Tp. (CSNH). POR: Charlestown Tp. (CMNH); Franklin Tp. (CMNH); Freedom Tp. (CMNH); Nelson Tp. (CMNH); Paris Tp. (CMNH); Streetsboro Tp. (W); Suffield Tp. (CMNH); Windham Tp. (CMNH). PRE: Israel Tp. (MU); Lanier Tp. (CM, KU); Monroe Tp. (CSNH, KU); Somers Tp. (MU); Twin Tp. (CSNH); Washington Tp. (CSNH). RIC: Butler Tp. (Merrill Tawse); Franklin Tp. (CSNH); Jefferson Tp. (Merrill Tawse); Madison Tp. (CSNH); Monroe Tp. (Merrill Tawse); Perry Tp. (Merrill Tawse); Troy Tp. (Merrill Tawse); Washington Tp. (Merrill Tawse); Weller Tp. (CSNH); Worthington Tp. (OSUM). ROS: Green Tp. (TOM); Paint Tp. (OSUM); Paxton Tp. (W); Springfield Tp. (TOM); Union Tp. (CSNH). SAN: Woodville Tp. (OSUM). SCI: Nile Tp. (CM, KU, OUVC, W); Union Tp. (CM); Washington Tp. (OSUM). STA: Jackson Tp. (W); Lake Tp. (RAP); Lawrence Tp. (CMNH); Lexington Tp. (CMNH); Perry Tp. (CM); Sugar Creek Tp. (CMNH); Tuscarawas Tp. (CMNH). SUM: Boston Tp. (CMNH, W); Franklin Tp. (W); Green Tp. (CM); Northampton Tp. (CMNH); Northfield Tp. (W). TRU: Braceville Tp. (CMNH); Greene Tp. (CM, CMNH). TUS: Lawrence Tp. (W); Wayne Tp. (RAP). UNI: Darby Tp. (CMNH). VIN: Brown Tp. (CM, OSUM); Eagle Tp. (CMNH, W); Madison Tp. (W); Swan Tp. (W). WAR: Deerfield Tp. (CSNH); Washington Tp. (CSNH); Wayne Tp. (CSNH, DMNH). WAS: Ludlow Tp. (RAP); Marietta Tp. (W); Watertown Tp.

(CM). WAY: Baughman Tp. (CW); Chester Tp. (CW); Chippewa Tp. (RAP); Clinton Tp. (UMMZ); Congress Tp. (CW); Franklin Tp. (CW); Milton Tp. (CMNH); Sugar Creek Tp. (RAP); Wayne Tp. (CW); Wooster Tp. (CW, MU, W). WIL: Bridgewater Tp. (CMNH); Northwest Tp. (W); St. Joseph Tp. (W). WOO: Liberty Tp. (BGSU); Perrysburg Tp. (W); Portage Tp. (W). WYA: Marseilles Tp. (OSUM).

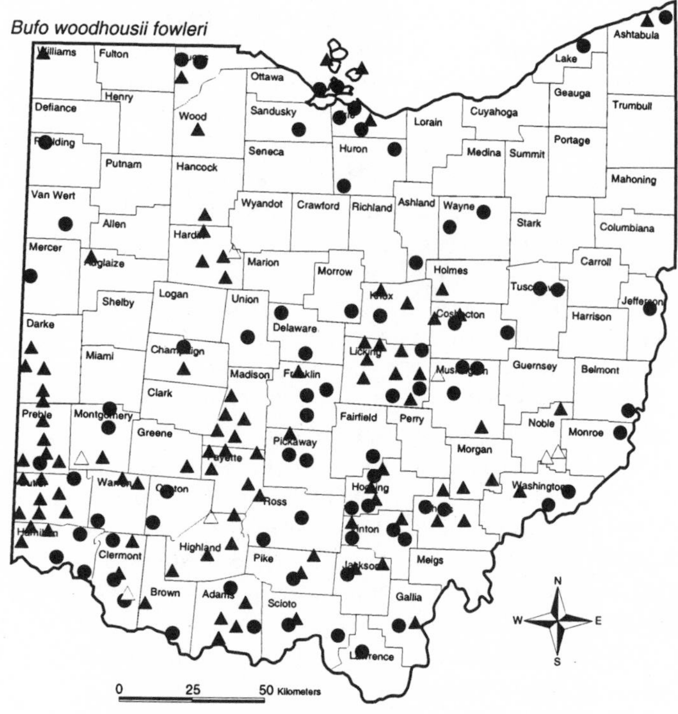

Figure 25-31. Distribution of Fowler's toads (*Bufo woodhousii fowleri*) in Ohio. Locality records for *B. w. fowleri*. ADA: Bratton Tp. (W); Brush Creek Tp. (MU, OSUM); Jefferson Tp. (W); Meigs Tp. (MU); Monroe Tp. (MU); Tiffin Tp. (DMNH, OUVC). ASH: Hanover Tp. (W). ATB: Ashtabula Tp. (CMNH); Conneaut Tp. (W). ATH: Athens Tp. (OSUM); Canaan Tp. (OSUM); Dover Tp. (W); Trimble Tp. (OUVC); York Tp. (W). AUG: Salem Tp. (OSUM). BEL: York Tp. (W). BRO: Clark Tp. (CSNH); Union Tp. (W). BUT: Fairfield Tp. (CSNH); Hanover Tp. (CSNH, MU); Madison Tp. (W); Milford Tp. (CSNH); Morgan Tp. (CSNH, DMNH); Oxford Tp. (MU); Ross Tp. (CSNH, MU); St. Clair Tp. (CSNH). CHP: Salem Tp. (OSUM); Urbana Tp. (DMNH). CLE: Batavia Tp. (CSNH, KU, OSUM, W); Goshen Tp. (W); Tate Tp. (TOM, W); Wayne Tp. (CMNH). CLI: Marion Tp. (W); Union Tp. (W). COS: Jefferson Tp. (OSUM, W); Oxford Tp. (W); Newcastle Tp. (OSUM). DAR: Butler Tp. (CSNH); Liberty Tp. (CSNH); Neave Tp. (CSNH); Washington Tp. (CSNH). DEF: Farmer Tp. (W). DEL: Orange Tp. (W); Radnor Tp. (W). ERI: Kelleys Island (OSUM); Margaretta Tp. (W); Milan Tp. (OSUM, W); Sandusky Tp. (W). FAI: Berne Tp. (W). FAY: Jasper Tp. (CSNH); Jefferson Tp. (CSNH); Madison Tp. (CSNH); Paint Tp. (CSNH); Wayne Tp. (CSNH). FRA: Columbus (W); Hamilton Tp. (W); Sharon Tp. (OSUM); Truro Tp. (W). GAL: Green Tp. (UF); Perry Tp. (W). GRE: Jefferson Tp. (CSNH); Miami Tp. (William Duellman). HAM: Anderson Tp. (W); Cincinnati (W); Colerain Tp. (KU); Crosby Tp. (CSNH); Sycamore Tp. (W); Whitewater Tp. (CSNH). HAR: Blanchard Tp. (OUVC); Buck Tp. (OUVC); Dudley Tp. (OUVC); Goshen Tp. (Charles Blem); Hale Tp. (KU). HIG: Clay Tp. (CSNH); Fairfield Tp. (Barry Valentine); Madison Tp. (OSUM); New Market Tp. (OUVC); Paint Tp. (OSUM). HOC: Benton Tp. (BGSU, W); Good Hope Tp. (CMNH, W); Laurel Tp. (W); Salt Creek Tp. (W). HOL: Richland Tp. (OSUM). HUR: Richmond Tp. (W); Wakeman Tp. (W). JAC: Liberty Tp. (OUVC, W); Milton Tp. (W). JEF: Cross Creek Tp. (W). KNO: Berlin Tp. (OSUM); Clinton Tp. (W); Howard Tp. (OSUM). LAK: Perry Tp. (W). LAW: Decatur Tp. (W). LUC: Spencer Tp. (W); Springfield Tp. (W); Swanton Tp. (CSNH). MAD: Oak Run Tp. (CSNH); Paint Tp. (CSNH); Range Tp. (CSNH); Stokes Tp. (CSNH); Union Tp. (CSNH). MER: Washington Tp. (W). MOE: Salem Tp. (W). MOT: Butler Tp. (DMNH); German Tp. (Bill Dare); Harrison Tp. (DMNH); Miami Tp. (DMNH). MRG: Homer Tp. (OSUM); Windsor Tp. (OSUM). MRW: South Bloomfield Tp. (W). MUS: Adams Tp. (W); Falls Tp. (W); Harrison Tp. (OUVC); Licking Tp. (TOM); Madison Tp. (W). NOB: Beaver Tp. (CMNH); Elk Tp. (TOM); Jefferson Tp. (TOM). OTT: Danbury Tp. (W); Portage Tp. (W); Put-In-Bay Tp. (CW). PER: Pleasant Tp. (W); Salt Lick Tp. (OUVC). PIC: Jackson Tp. (W); Muhlenberg Tp. (W); Scioto Tp. (OSUM). PIK: Newton Tp. (OSUM, W). PRE: Gasper Tp. (DMNH, OSUM); Gratis Tp. (KU); Israel Tp. (CM); Monroe Tp. (KU). ROS: Concord Tp. (CSNH); Paxton Tp. (W); Scioto Tp. (W). SAN: Green Creek Tp. (W). SCI: Bloom Tp. (W); Union Tp. (OUVC, W). SHE: McLean Tp. (W). TUS: Fairfield Tp. (W); Warren Tp. (W). UNI: Paris Tp. (W). VAN: York Tp. (OSUM). VIN: Brown Tp. (OUVC, W); Eagle Tp. (OSUM); Harrison Tp. (W); Knox Tp. (W). WAR: Deerfield Tp. (W); Massie Tp. (OSUM); Wayne Tp. (DMNH). WAS: Lawrence Tp. (W); Marietta Tp. (W); Watertown Tp. (CM). WAY: Green Tp. (W); Plain Tp. (W). WOO: Liberty Tp. (OSUM).

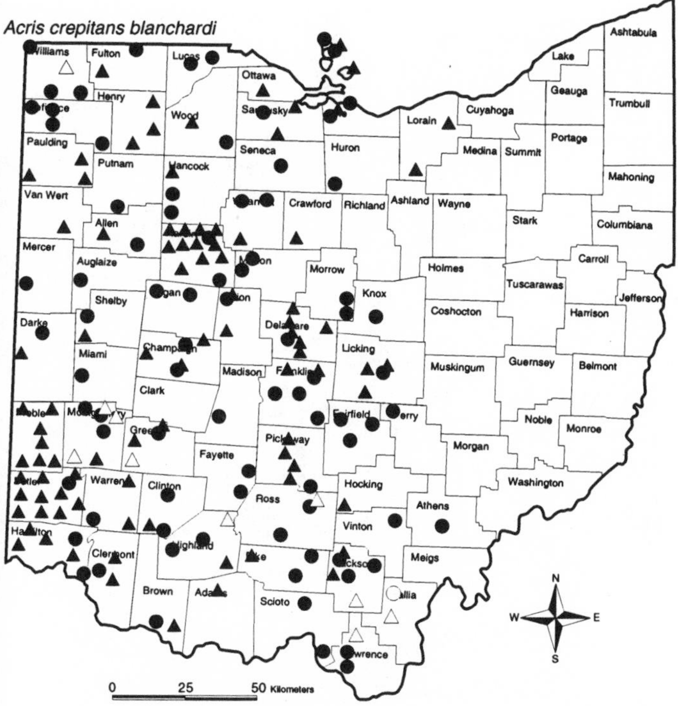

Figure 25-32. Distribution of Blanchard's cricket frogs (*Acris crepitans blanchardi*) in Ohio. Locality records for *A. c. blanchardi.* ADA: Scott Tp. (DMNH). ALL: Amanda Tp. (OSUM); Perry Tp. (W). ATH: Athens Tp. (W). AUG: St. Mary's Tp. (W). BRO: Byrd Tp. (DMNH); Pleasant Tp. (W). BUT: Fairfield Tp. (CSNH, MU); Hanover Tp. (CSNH, MU); Liberty Tp. (MU); Madison Tp. (CSNH, W); Milford Tp. (CSNH, DMNH, MU); Morgan Tp. (CSNH); Oxford Tp. (MU); Reily Tp. (MU); Ross Tp. (CSNH); St. Clair Tp. (CSNH, MU). CHP: Johnson Tp. (UF); Salem Tp. (W); Urbana Tp. (DMNH, W); Wayne Tp. (OSUM). CLE: Batavia Tp. (KU); Stonelick Tp. (OSUM); Union Tp. (W). CLI: Jefferson Tp. (W); Marion Tp. (JEJ); Union Tp. (W). CRA: Dallas Tp. (OSUM). DAR: Brown Tp. (W); Washington Tp. (OSUM). DEF: Defiance Tp. (W); Farmer Tp. (W); Mark Tp. (W); Milford Tp. (W). DEL: Berlin Tp. (OSUM); Delaware Tp. (OSUM, W); Marlboro Tp. (OSUM); Orange Tp. (OSUM); Porter Tp. (OSUM); Troy Tp. (OSUM). ERI: Kelleys Island (CMNH); Margaretta Tp. (CMNH, W); Sandusky (W). FAI: Greenfield Tp. (W); Violet Tp. (W); Walnut Tp. (W). FAY: Marion Tp. (W); Wayne Tp. (W). FRA: Blendon Tp. (OSUM, W); Columbus (W); Madison Tp. (W); Norwich Tp. (W); Perry Tp. (CU). FUL: German Tp. (BGSU); Royalton Tp. (W). GAL: Huntington Tp. (W); Raccoon Tp. (TOM). GRE: Beaver Creek Tp. (DMNH); Miami Tp. (OSUM, OUVC, W); Sugar Creek Tp. (William Duellman). HAM: Anderson Tp. (W); Colerain Tp. (KU); Columbia Tp. (CSNH); Crosby Tp. (CSNH); Sycamore Tp. (W); Whitewater Tp. (CSNH). HAN: Blanchard Tp. (UMMZ); Orange Tp. (W); Union Tp. (W). HAR: Blanchard Tp. (OUVC); Buck Tp. (OUVC); Cessna Tp. (OUVC); Dudley Tp. (OSUM, OUVC); Goshen Tp. (OUVC); Hale Tp. (W); Jackson Tp. (OUVC, W); Liberty Tp. (OUVC); Marion Tp. (OUVC); McDonald Tp. (OUVC); Pleasant Tp. (OUVC); Washington Tp. (OUVC). HEN: Marion Tp. (OSUM); Richfield Tp. (OSUM); Washington Tp. (W). HIG: Brush Creek Tp. (DMNH); Dodson Tp. (W); Liberty Tp. (W); Madison Tp. (Barry Valentine). HOC: Salt Creek Tp. (OSUM). HUR: Richmond Tp. (W). JAC: Jackson Tp. (OUVC, W); Jefferson Tp. (TOM); Liberty Tp. (OUVC); Lick Tp. (W); Milton Tp. (W). KNO: Clinton Tp. (W). LAW: Elizabeth Tp. (W); Decatur Tp. (TOM); Hamilton Tp. (W). LIC: Granville Tp. (MVZ); Newark Tp. (CM, W); Union Tp. (CM, OSUM, OUVC). LOG: Rush Creek Tp. (W); Stokes Tp. (W). LOR: Eaton Tp. (CMNH); Huntington Tp. (OSUM). LUC: Springfield Tp. (W); Toledo (W). MAD: Paint Tp. (W). MAH: Youngstown (W). MAR: Grand Tp. (W); Montgomery Tp. (W). MER: Washington Tp. (W). MIA: Newton Tp. (W). MOT: Butler Tp. (DMNH); German Tp. (DMNH); Harrison Tp. (CMNH); Miami Tp. (DMNH); Randolph Tp. (W); Wayne Tp. (DMNH). MRW: Chester Tp. (W); South Bloomfield Tp. (W). OTT: Harris Tp. (OSUM); Put-In-Bay Tp. (CW, MU, OSUM, UMMZ); Middle Bass Island (W); North Bass Island (W). PAU: Benton Tp. (OSUM); Brown Tp. (OSUM); Washington Tp. (OSUM). PER: Monroe Tp. (KU); Thorn Tp. (W). PIC: Jackson Tp. (CMNH, OSUM); Muhlenberg Tp. (OSUM); Pickaway Tp. (W); Scioto Tp. (OSUM); Wayne Tp. (OSUM). PIK: Newton Tp. (W); Pee Pee Tp. (W); Perry Tp. (DMNH). PRE: Gasper Tp. (CSNH); Gratis Tp. (KU); Harrison Tp. (CM, DMNH, MU); Israel Tp. (CM, KU); Jefferson Tp. (CM, KU); Somers Tp. (KU, MU); Washington Tp. (CM). PUT: Sugar Creek Tp. (W). ROS: Green Tp. (TOM, W); Twin Tp. (W). SAN: Ballville Tp. (CMNH); Riley Tp. (UMMZ); Washington Tp. (W). SCI: Green Tp. (W); Valley Tp. (W). SEN: Clinton Tp. (W). SHE: Loramie Tp. (OSUM); McLean Tp. (W). UNI: Allen Tp. (OSUM); Washington Tp. (OSUM, W). VAN: York Tp. (OSUM). VIN: Brown Tp. (W). WAR: Deerfield Tp. (W); Harlan Tp. (CSNH); Wayne Tp. (DMNH). WIL: Center Tp. (W); Jefferson Tp. (TOM); Northwest Tp. (W); Springfield Tp. (W). WOO: Liberty Tp. (BGSU); Perry Tp. (W). WYA: Crawford Tp. (W); Marseilles Tp. (OSUM); Tymochtee Tp. (W).

Figure 25-33. Distribution of Cope's gray treefrogs (*Hyla chrysoscelis*) in Ohio. Closed symbols have been identified by vocal call analysis and/or erythrocyte examination by Timothy Matson (Cleveland Museum of Natural History). Open circles are from the Ohio Division of Wildlife database (1995) or Walker (1946). Locality records for *H. chrysoscelis.* ADA: Brush Creek Tp. (TOM); Green Tp. (KU); Jefferson Tp. (CMNH). ATH: Athens Tp. (OUVC). BUT: Morgan Tp. (CSNH); Reily Tp. (CSNH, MU); Ross Tp. (MU). CLE: Ohio Tp. (CSNH); Tate Tp. (CMNH); Wayne Tp. (CMNH). FAI: Lancaster Tp. (W); Pleasant Tp. (TOM). GAL: Chesire Tp. (TOM); Huntington Tp. (TOM); Morgan Tp. (TOM); Raccoon Tp. (CMNH); Springfield Tp. (TOM). HOC: Benton Tp. (CMNH); Laurel Tp. (TOM); Perry Tp. (TOM); Salt Creek Tp. (TOM). JAC: Franklin Tp. (TOM); Jefferson Tp. (TOM). LAW: Elizabeth Tp. (CMNH); Decatur Tp. (CMNH); Upper Tp. (KU). MEG: Chester Tp. (TOM); Lebanon Tp. (TOM); Olive Tp. (CMNH); Salem Tp. (TOM); Salisbury Tp. (TOM). MOE: Green Tp. (W). MUS: Blue Rock Tp. (CMNH, W); Salt Creek Tp. (TOM). NOB: Center Tp. (CMNH); Elk Tp. (TOM); Enoch Tp. (CMNH); Jefferson Tp. (TOM); Seneca Tp. (CMNH); Stock Tp. (TOM). ROS: Colerain Tp. (W); Green Tp. (CMNH); Paint Tp. (CMNH); Paxton Tp. (W); Scioto Tp. (W); Springfield Tp. (CMNH); Union Tp. (CMNH). VIN: Eagle Tp. (CMNH); Jackson Tp. (TOM). WAR: Union Tp. (CMNH). WAS: Independence Tp. (RAP).

Figure 25-34. Distribution of eastern gray treefrogs (*Hyla versicolor*) in Ohio. Closed symbols have been identified by vocal call analysis and/or erythrocyte examination by Timothy Matson (Cleveland Museum of Natural History). Open circles are from the Ohio Division of Wildlife database (1995) or Walker (1946). Records near the line could be either eastern gray treefrogs or Cope's gray treefrogs. Locality records for *H. versicolor.* ADA: Green Tp. (OSUM, W); Jefferson Tp. (OSUM); Meigs Tp. (MU, OSUM). ASH: Clear Creek Tp. (CSNH). ATB: Cherry Valley Tp. (TOM); Conneaut Tp. (TOM, W); Harpersfield Tp. (CMNH); Kingsville Tp. (CMNH); Morgan Tp. (CMNH); Plymouth Tp. (CMNH); Trumbull Tp. (CMNH); Williamsfield Tp. (CMNH). ATH: Athens Tp. (OSUM); Dover Tp. (OUVC, W); Trimble Tp. (CMNH); Troy Tp. (OUVC); Waterloo Tp. (OUVC); York Tp. (UMMZ, W). AUG: Salem Tp. (OSUM). CAR: Augusta Tp. (MU); Orange Tp. (RAP). CHP: Salem Tp. (W); Urbana Tp. (W). CLE: Batavia Tp. (W); Monroe Tp. (W); Union Tp. (W); Wayne Tp. (CMNH). CLI: Marion Tp. (W); Union Tp. (W); Urbana Tp. (W). COL: Center Tp. (RAP); Elk Run Tp. (RAP); Hanover Tp. (RAP); West Tp. (RAP). COS: Franklin Tp. (RAP); Newcastle Tp. (RAP); Virginia Tp. (RAP); Washington Tp. (RAP). CRA: Bucyrus Tp. (W); Chatfield Tp. (CMNH); Whetstone Tp. (CMNH). DAR: Greenville Tp. (W); Liberty Tp. (CSNH); Washington Tp. (CSNH). DEF: Noble Tp. (DC); Tiffin Tp. (DC). DEL: Berlin Tp. (UF); Concord Tp. (UMMZ); Delaware Tp. (W); Liberty Tp. (OSUM); Marlboro Tp. (CMNH); Oxford Tp. (CMNH); Troy Tp. (CMNH,

OSUM). ERI: Perkins Tp. (RAP). FAI: Berne Tp. (W); Violet Tp. (W); Walnut Tp. (TOM). FRA: Blendon Tp. (W); Jackson Tp. (W); Madison Tp. (W); Perry Tp. (W); Columbus (W). FUL: Franklin Tp. (TOM); German Tp. (TOM); Gorham Tp. (TOM); Royalton Tp. (W). GAL: Huntington Tp. (W); Perry Tp. (W); Raccoon Tp. (CMNH, OSUM); Springfield Tp. (TOM). GEA: Burton Tp. (CMNH); Parkman Tp. (W); Russell Tp. (CMNH); Troy Tp. (CMNH). GRE: Greene Tp. (W); Miami Tp. (William Duellman). HAM: Anderson Tp. (W); Colerain Tp. (KU); Columbia Tp. (KU). HAR: Dudley Tp. (CMNH); Hale Tp. (W); McDonald Tp. (CMNH). HAS: Monroe Tp. (RAP). HOC: Benton Tp. (W); Good Hope Tp. (W); Laurel Tp. (W). HOL: Killbuck Tp. (RAP); Mechanic Tp. (RAP); Paint Tp. (RAP); Prairie Tp. (RAP); Richland Tp. (OSUM); Washington Tp. (W). HUR: Richmond Tp. (CMNH, W). JAC: Liberty Tp. (W). KNO: Butler Tp. (CM); Harrison Tp. (CM); Howard Tp. (RAP). LAK: Concord Tp. (CMNH); Kirtland Tp. (CMNH); Leroy Tp. (CMNH); Madison Tp. (CMNH). LAW: Upper Tp. (Corsan J. Hirschfeld). LIC: Bennington Tp. (OSUM); Eden Tp. (CM); Fallsbury Tp. (CM, JEJ); Licking Tp. (W); Union Tp. (LACM); Washington Tp. (OSUM). LOG: Union Tp. (W). LOR: Brownhelm Tp. (TOM); Columbia Tp. (CMNH); Huntington Tp. (CMNH). LUC: Spencer Tp. (CMNH); Swanton Tp. (BGSU, CMNH); Sylvania Tp. (TOM); Toledo (W). MAD: Oak Run Tp. (CSNH); Paint Tp. (CSNH); Range Tp. (CSNH); Stokes Tp. (CSNH); Union Tp. (CSNH). MAH: Beaver Tp. (RAP); Boardman Tp. (CMNH); Ellsworth Tp. (W). MED: Brunswick Tp. (RAP); Chatham Tp. (TOM); Granger Tp. (RAP); Harrisville Tp. (RAP); Hinckley Tp. (RAP); Lafayette Tp. (RAP); Liverpool Tp. (RAP); Medina Tp. (RAP); Spencer Tp. (CMNH); Westfield Tp. (RAP). MER: Franklin Tp. (W). MOE: Green Tp. (W). MOT: German Tp. (DMNH). MRW: South Bloomfield Tp. (W). MUS: Blue Rock Tp. (W); Licking Tp. (CMNH); Muskingum Tp. (RAP); Newton Tp. (RAP); Salt Creek Tp. (TOM); Springfield Tp. (W); Washington Tp. (W). NOB: Beaver Tp. (RAP); Center Tp. (TOM); Enoch Tp. (CMNH); Noble Tp. (CMNH); Seneca Tp. (CMNH); Wayne Tp. (CMNH). PAU: Latty Tp. (DMNH). PER: Thorn Tp. (CMNH, W). PIC: Darby Tp. (CSNH, W); Jackson Tp. (CSNH); Muhlenberg Tp. (OSUM). PIK: Newton Tp. (W). POR: Aurora Tp. (CMNH); Charleston Tp. (CMNH); Franklin Tp. (CMNH); Nelson Tp. (CMNH); Paris Tp. (RAP); Windham Tp. (RAP). PRE: Jefferson Tp. (W); Somers Tp. (MU). RIC: Butler Tp. (CMNH); Jefferson Tp. (Merrill Tawse); Monroe Tp. (Merrill Tawse); Perry Tp. (Merrill Tawse); Worthington Tp. (Merrill Tawse). ROS: Colerain Tp. (W); Green Tp. (CMNH); Jefferson Tp. (OSUM); Paxton Tp. (W); Scioto Tp. (W); Twin Tp. (W); Union Tp. (CMNH). SCI: Nile Tp. (CM, W). SEN: Pleasant Tp. (CMNH). SHE: McLean Tp. (W). STA: Lake Tp. (CMNH); Perry Tp. (W); Tuscarawas (RAP). SUM: Bath Tp. (W); Richfield Tp. (CMNH). TRU: Braceville Tp. (RAP). TUS: Franklin Tp. (RAP); Sandy Tp. (RAP); Wayne Tp. (RAP). VAN: York Tp. (OSUM). VIN: Brown Tp. (OUVC); Eagle Tp. (CMNH); Harrison Tp. (W); Knox Tp. (W). WAR: Washington Tp. (DMNH). WAS: Marietta Tp. (MC). WAY: Canaan Tp. (CW); Chester Tp. (CMNH, CW); Franklin Tp. (CW); Paint Tp. (RAP). WIL: Bridgewater Tp. (CMNH); Florence Tp. (W); Jefferson Tp. (UMMZ). WOO: Liberty Tp. (OSUM). WYA: Marseilles Tp. (CMNH).

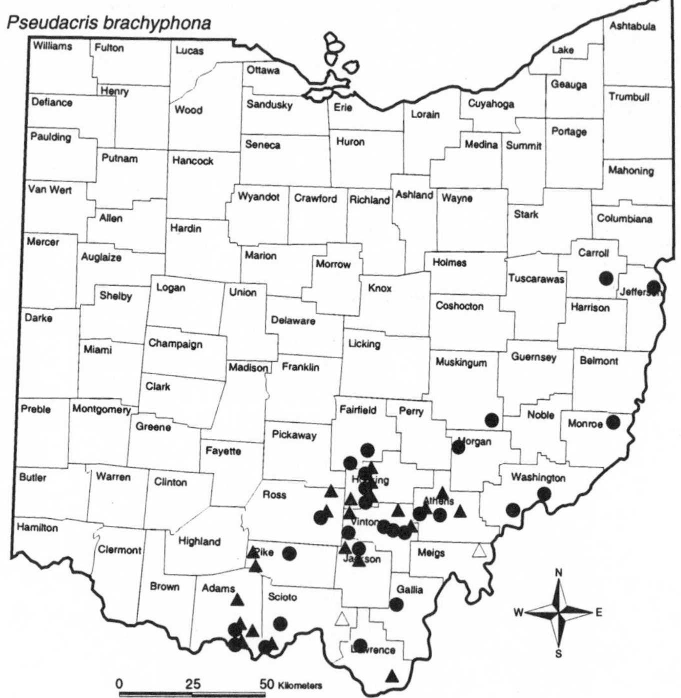

Figure 25-35. Distribution of mountain chorus frogs (*Pseudacris brachyphona*) in Ohio. Locality records for *P. brachyphona*. ADA: Brush Creek Tp. (MU, W); Green Tp. (KU, OSUM, W); Jefferson Tp. (KU); Meigs Tp. (OSUM, UF). ATH: Athens Tp. (W); Canaan Tp. (CM, OUVC); Dover Tp. (OUVC); Waterloo Tp. (CM, CMNH, W). FAI: Berne Tp. (W); Madison Tp. (W). GAL: Raccoon Tp. (W). HOC: Benton Tp. (CM, JEJ, OSUM, UMMZ, W); Good Hope Tp. (CM, CU, JEJ, W); Laurel Tp. (OUVC, W); Salt Creek Tp. (W). JAC: Coal Tp. (OUVC); Jackson Tp. (CM); Washington Tp. (W). JEF: Knox Tp. (W). LAW: Decatur Tp. (W); Windsor Tp. (CMNH). MOE: Green Tp. (W). MRG: Deerfield Tp. (W). MUS: Meigs Tp. (W). PIK: Mifflin Tp. (DMNH); Pebble Tp. (W); Perry Tp. (DMNH). ROS: Colerain Tp. (CM, UMMZ); Harrison Tp. (OSUM, W). SCI: Bloom Tp. (RAP); Nile Tp. (CM, UMMZ, W); Union Tp. (W). VIN: Brown Tp. (OUVC); Eagle Tp. (CMNH, JEJ); Elk Tp. (W); Harrison Tp. (W); Knox Tp. (OSUM, W); Madison Tp. (W). WAS: Dunham Tp. (W); Marietta Tp. (W).

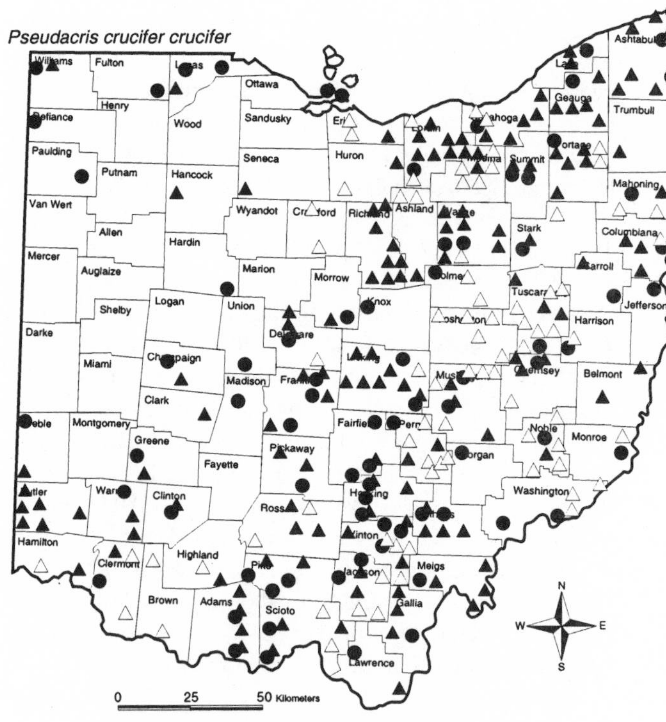

Figure 25-36. Distribution of northern spring peepers (*Pseudacris crucifer crucifer*) in Ohio. Locality records for *P. c. crucifer*. ADA: Franklin Tp. (MU); Green Tp. (CSNH, KU, W); Jefferson Tp. (KU, MU); Meigs Tp. (MU, UF, W). ASH: Hanover Tp. (CMNH); Ruggles Tp. (RAP). ATB: Andover Tp. (W); Conneaut Tp. (W); Kingsville Tp. (CMNH); Monroe Tp. (CMNH, W); Rome Tp. (CMNH); Saybrook Tp. (CMNH); Troy Tp. (RAP); Wayne Tp. (CMNH); Windsor Tp. (CMNH). ATH: Athens Tp. (CM, CMNH, OSUM, OUVC); Canaan Tp. (CMNH); Dover Tp. (W); Waterloo Tp. (CMNH, OUVC); York Tp. (UMMZ, W). BEL: Colerain Tp. (OSUM); Goshen Tp. (OSUM). BRO: Perry Tp. (RAP); Pleasant Tp. (RAP). BUT: Hanover Tp. (CSNH); Liberty Tp. (CSNH); Morgan Tp. (CSNH, MU); Oxford Tp. (MU); Reily Tp. (CSNH, MU); Ross Tp. (CSNH). CAR: Brown Tp. (CMNH); Lee Tp. (W). CHP: Concord Tp. (W); Urbana Tp. (CSNH). CLA: Harmony Tp. (W). CLE: Goshen Tp. (CSNH); Tate Tp. (TOM); Union Tp. (W); Wayne Tp. (TOM). CLI: Union Tp. (OSUM, W). COL: Center Tp. (CMNH); Elk Run Tp. (RAP, W); Hanover Tp. (RAP); Middleton Tp. (CMNH); St. Clair Tp. (W); Washington Tp. (CMNH). COS: Clark Tp. (RAP); Crawford Tp. (RAP); Keene Tp. (RAP); Linton Tp. (RAP). CRA: Chatfield Tp. (RAP); Whetstone Tp. (RAP). DEF: Milford Tp. (W). DEL: Delaware Tp. (CMNH, W); Genoa Tp. (DEW); Marlboro Tp. (KU); Troy Tp. (OSUM). ERI: Florence Tp. (CMNH); Oxford Tp. (RAP); Perkins Tp. (RAP). FAI: Berne Tp. (OSUM, W); Madison Tp. (W); Walnut Tp. (W). FRA: Blendon Tp. (OSUM, USNM, W); Jackson Tp. (W); Jefferson Tp.

(OSUM); Mifflin Tp. (W); Pleasant Tp. (CSNH); Sharon Tp. (OSUM). FUL: Swan Creek Tp. (W). GAL: Green Tp. (W); Huntington Tp. (CMNH); Perry Tp. (CMNH); Raccoon Tp. (CMNH, OSUM). GEA: Burton Tp. (CMNH); Chardon Tp. (W); Montville Tp. (CMNH); Newbury Tp. (OSUM); Parkman Tp. (CMNH); Russell Tp. (CMNH). GRE: Beaver Creek Tp. (W); Spring Valley Tp. (MU). GUE: Liberty Tp. (CMNH); Monroe Tp. (CMNH, W); Westland Tp. (RAP); Wheeling Tp. (CMNH); Wills Tp. (W). HAM: Columbia Tp. (KU); Green Tp. (Paul Krusling). HAN: Blanchard Tp. (UMMZ). HAR: Hale Tp. (W). HIG: Jackson Tp. (OSUM); New Market Tp. (RAP). HOC: Benton Tp. (CMNH, W); Good Hope Tp. (CMNH, CU, JEJ, W); Green Tp. (OUVC); Laurel Tp. (W); Salt Creek Tp. (Douglas E. Wynn). HOL: Mechanic Tp. (RAP); Prairie Tp. (RAP); Washington Tp. (W). HUR: Clarksville Tp. (CMNH); Richmond Tp. (RAP, W). JAC: Coal Tp. (OUVC); Franklin Tp. (CMNH, OSUM); Jefferson Tp. (TOM); Liberty Tp. (W); Madison Tp. (RAP); Milton Tp. (RAP); Washington Tp. (W). JEF: Saline Tp. (W). KNO: Wayne Tp. (W). LAK: Concord Tp. (CMNH, OSUM); Painesville Tp. (CMNH); Perry Tp. (W). LAW: Decatur Tp. (W); Rome Tp. (KU). LIC: Bennington Tp. (OSUM); Burlington Tp. (OSUM); Eden Tp. (W); Granville Tp. (MVZ); Hopewell Tp. (OSUM, W); Jersey Tp. (OSUM); Madison Tp. (CM); Newton Tp. (CM); Perry Tp. (RAP); St. Albans Tp. (JEJ); Union Tp. (OSUM). LOR: Brighton Tp. (W); Brownhelm Tp. (RAP, TOM); Columbia Tp. (CMNH, KU); Eaton Tp. (CMNH); Elyria Tp. (CMNH); Lagrange Tp. (OUVC); New Russia Tp. (CMNH); Pittsfield Tp. (CMNH); Rochester Tp. (RAP). LUC: Springfield Tp. (W); Swanton Tp. (CMNH, DMNH); Toledo (W). MAD: Deer Creek Tp. (W). MAH: Beaver Tp. (RAP); Boardman Tp. (CM); Ellsworth Tp. (W); Goshen Tp. (RAP). MED: Brunswick Tp. (CMNH); Granger Tp. (RAP); Harrisville Tp. (RAP); Hinckley Tp. (RAP); Homer Tp. (RAP); Lafayette Tp. (RAP); Liverpool Tp. (CMNH); Medina Tp. (CM); Montville Tp. (RAP); York Tp. (RAP). MOE: Adams Tp. (RAP); Green Tp. (W). MRG: York Tp. (W). MRW: Bennington Tp. (CMNH); South Bloomfield Tp. (W). MUS: Adams Tp. (RAP); Blue Rock Tp. (CMNH); Falls Tp. (CM, W); Licking Tp. (RAP); Madison Tp. (RAP, W); Monroe Tp. (RAP); Muskingum Tp. (CMNH); Newton Tp. (RAP). NOB: Center Tp. (W); Enoch Tp. (CMNH); Jackson Tp. (RAP); Jefferson Tp. (TOM); Noble Tp. (TOM); Seneca Tp. (TOM); Stock Tp. (RAP). OTT: Catawba Island Tp. (W); Danbury Tp. (W). PAU: Brown Tp. (OSUM). PER: Bearfield Tp. (RAP); Harrison Tp. (CMNH); Jackson Tp. (CMNH); Madison Tp. (RAP); Pike Tp. (RAP); Pleasant Tp. (RAP); Reading Tp. (RAP); Salt Lick Tp. (RAP). PIC: Jackson Tp. (CSNH, OSUM); Muhlenberg Tp. (CSNH); Wayne Tp. (W). PIK: Benton Tp. (DMNH); Camp Creek Tp. (W); Mifflin Tp. (DMNH, W); Newton Tp. (W); Pee Pee Tp. (UMMZ). POR: Aurora Tp. (W); Charlestown Tp. (CMNH); Freedom Tp. (CMNH); Paris Tp. (RAP); Ravenna Tp. (CMNH); Streetsboro Tp. (OSUM); Suffield Tp. (CW); Windham Tp. (RAP). PRE: Israel Tp. (KU); Jefferson Tp. (W). RIC: Blooming Grove Tp. (Merrill Tawse); Butler Tp. (CMNH, CW); Franklin Tp. (Merrill Tawse); Jefferson Tp. (Merrill Tawse); Mifflin Tp. (Merrill Tawse); Monroe Tp. (Merrill Tawse); Perry Tp. (Merrill Tawse); Washington Tp. (Merrill Tawse); Worthington Tp. (Merrill Tawse). ROS: Green Tp. (TOM); Paint Tp. (TOM); Scioto Tp. (OUVC); Springfield Tp. (OUVC); Union Tp. (CSNH). SCI: Bloom Tp. (CMNH); Madison Tp. (RAP); Nile Tp. (KU, OSUM, W); Rush Tp. (OSUM); Union Tp. (W); Vernon Tp. (RAP). SEN: Big Spring Tp. (W). SUM: Bath Tp. (W); Boston Tp. (CMNH, W); Richfield Tp. (TOM). TRU: Braceville Tp. (CMNH). TUS: Auburn Tp. (RAP); Clay Tp. (RAP); Fairfield Tp. (RAP); Goshen Tp. (CMNH); Jefferson Tp. (RAP); Oxford Tp. (RAP); Rush Tp. (RAP); Union Tp. (CMNH); Warren Tp. (RAP); Washington Tp. (W); Wayne Tp. (CMNH). UNI: Darby Tp. (W). WAR: Harlan Tp. (CSNH); Washington Tp. (DMNH, MU); Wayne Tp. (W). WAS: Fairfield Tp. (W); Grandview Tp. (RAP); Lawrence Tp. (RAP); Marietta Tp. (W); Newport Tp. (RAP). WAY: Baughman Tp. (CMNH, CW); Canaan Tp. (CW); Chester Tp. (CW); Clinton Tp. (CW); Congress Tp. (CMNH, CW); Franklin Tp. (CW); Plain Tp. (W); Sugar Creek Tp. (CMNH); Wayne Tp. (CW); Wooster Tp. (W). WIL: Bridgewater Tp. (CW); Northwest Tp. (W).

Figure 25-37. Distribution of western chorus frogs (*Pseudacris triseriata triseriata*) in Ohio. Locality records for *P. t. triseriata*. ADA: Green Tp. (OSUM). ALL: American Tp. (W). ASH: Hanover Tp. (CMNH, W); Ruggles Tp. (RAP); Troy Tp. (RAP). ATB: Andover Tp. (W); Denmark Tp. (CMNH). ATH: Athens Tp. (CMNH, DMNH, OSUM); Dover Tp. (OUVC); York Tp. (W). AUG: St. Mary's Tp. (DMNH, W); Washington Tp. (W). BEL: Kirkwood Tp. (W). BRO: Clark Tp. (CSNH); Perry Tp. (CSNH). CHP: Concord Tp. (W); Urbana Tp. (CSNH, DMNH, MU, OSUM). CLA: Bethel Tp. (DMNH). CLE: Batavia Tp. (CSNH, W); Goshen Tp. (CSNH); Union Tp. (W). CLI: Union Tp. (OSUM, W); Vernon Tp. (OSUM). COS: Keene Tp. (RAP). CRA: Chatfield Tp. (RAP); Cranberry (RAP); Whetstone Tp. (RAP). CUY: Lakewood Tp. (CMNH); Middleburg Heights Tp. (CMNH); North Olmsted Tp. (CMNH); Orange Tp. (OSUM); Parma Tp. (CMNH); Strongsville Tp. (RAP). DAR: Adams Tp. (DMNH); Greenville Tp. (W). DEF: Defiance Tp. (W); Highland Tp. (BGSU); Milford Tp. (W); Noble Tp. (DC). DEL: Berlin Tp. (UMMZ); Delaware Tp. (CMNH, OSUM); Richland Tp. (DC). ERI: Kelleys Island (Corsan J. Hirshfeld); Margaretta Tp. (W); Oxford Tp. (RAP); Perkins Tp. (CMNH); Sandusky (W). FAI: Berne Tp. (OSUM, W); Violet Tp. (W); Walnut Tp. (W). FRA: Clinton Tp. (W); Jackson Tp. (W); Jefferson Tp. (OSUM); Madison Tp. (W); Mifflin Tp. (W); Perry Tp. (CU, OSUM); Sharon Tp. (OSUM, W). FUL: Amboy Tp. (W); Clinton Tp. (W); Swan Creek Tp. (W). GAL: Raccoon Tp. (W). GEA: Chardon Tp. (W); Newberry Tp. (OSUM). GRE: Beaver Creek Tp. (William Duellman); Sugar Creek (DMNH). GUE: Wills Tp. (W). HAM: Anderson Tp. (Corsan J. Hirschfeld). HAN: Eagle Tp. (UMMZ); Van Buren Tp. (UMMZ). HAR: Blanchard Tp. (Charles Blem); Hale Tp. (W); Jackson Tp. (Charles Blem); Taylor Creek Tp. (OUVC). HEN: Richfield Tp. (OSUM); Washington Tp. (OSUM, W). HIG: New Market Tp. (RAP). HOC: Good Hope Tp. (OSUM, W); Green Tp. (CM, OUVC). HOL: Killbuck Tp. (W). HUR: Clarksfield Tp. (CMNH); Richmond Tp. (RAP, W). JAC: Coal Tp. (W); Franklin Tp. (RAP); Jackson Tp. (W); Jefferson Tp. (W); Madison Tp. (CMNH). KNO: Howard Tp. (W). LAK: Mentor Tp. (CMNH). LAW: Washington Tp. (W). LIC: Eden Tp. (W); Granville Tp. (MVZ); Hopewell Tp. (OSUM); Licking Tp. (OSUM); St. Alban's Tp. (JEJ); Union Tp. (JEJ, OSUM). LOG: Richland Tp. (MU, W). LOR: Amherst Tp. (CMNH); Carlisle Tp. (CMNH); Columbia Tp. (CMNH); Eaton Tp. (CMNH); Elyria Tp. (CMNH); Huntington Tp. (RAP); New Russia Tp. (CMNH); Pittsfield Tp. (CMNH); Sheffield Tp. (CMNH). LUC: Richfield Tp. (CW); Spencer Tp. (TOM); Springfield Tp. (W); Sylvania Tp. (W); Toledo Tp. (W). MAD: Paint Tp. (W). MAH: Boardman Tp. (CM); Canfield Tp. (W). MAR: Big Island Tp. (W). MED: Brunswick Tp. (RAP); Granger Tp. (RAP); Harrisville Tp. (CMNH); Hinckley Tp. (RAP); Homer Tp. (RAP); Lafayette Tp. (RAP); Liverpool Tp. (CMNH); Montville Tp. (RAP); Westfield Tp. (CMNH); York Tp. (RAP). MER: Franklin Tp. (W). MIA: Bethel Tp. (DMNH). MOE: Summit Tp. (W). MRG: Malta Tp. (W). MRW: South Bloomfield Tp. (W). MUS: Cass Tp. (RAP); Falls Tp. (CM); Licking Tp. (RAP); Madison Tp. (RAP, W); Monroe Tp. (RAP). NOB: Center Tp. (W); Jackson Tp. (W). OTT: Carroll Tp. (CW); Catawba Island Tp. (W); Danbury Tp. (W). PAU: Brown Tp. (OSUM, W). PER: Jackson Tp. (RAP); Reading Tp. (RAP); Thorn Tp. (W). PIC: Jackson Tp. (CSNH); Muhlenberg Tp. (CMNH, CSNH); Wayne Tp. (OSUM, W). PIK: Mifflin Tp. (W). POR: Aurora Tp. (W); Charlestown Tp. (RAP); Franklin Tp. (W); Freedom Tp. (RAP); Paris Tp. (RAP); Ravenna Tp. (CMNH); Windham Tp. (RAP). PRE: Jefferson Tp. (W). RIC: Butler Tp. (CW); Plymouth Tp. (W); Sharon Tp. (RAP). ROS: Scioto Tp. (OUVC); Union Tp. (W). SEN: Bloom Tp. (RAP); Clinton Tp. (W); Seneca Tp. (RAP). STA: Lake Tp. (RAP); Sugar Creek Tp. (CM). SUM: Bath Tp. (W). TRU: Bloomfield Tp. (Walter Kuhns). TUS: Rush Tp. (CMNH); Union Tp. (CMNH). UNI: Darby Tp. (W); Paris Tp. (W). WAR: Harlan Tp. (CSNH); Washington Tp. (DMNH, W). WAY: Baughman Tp. (CW); Chester Tp. (CW); Chippewa Tp. (CW); Clinton Tp. (W); Congress Tp. (CW, W); Franklin Tp. (CM, CW); Milton Tp. (CMNH); Wayne Tp. (CM, CW); Wooster Tp. (CW). WIL: Bridgewater Tp. (CW); Northwest Tp. (CW); St. Joseph Tp. (W); Springfield Tp. (W); Superior Tp. (CW). WOO: Liberty Tp. (BGSU, OSUM); Perry Tp. (W). WYA: Pitt Tp. (OSUM, W).

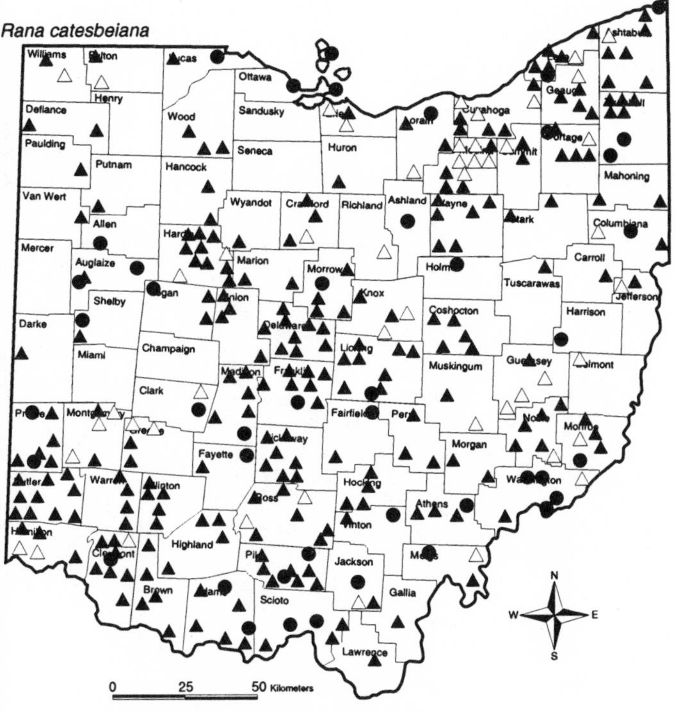

Figure 25-38. Distribution of bullfrogs (*Rana catesbeiana*) in Ohio. Locality records for *R. catesbeiana*. ADA: Bratton Tp. (W); Green Tp. (CSNH, MU); Jefferson Tp. (W); Liberty Tp. (OUVC); Meigs Tp. (MU, OSUM); Monroe Tp. (MU); Winchester Tp. (MU). ALL: Amanda Tp. (OSUM). ASH: Montgomery Tp. (W). ATB: Conneaut Tp. (W); Harpersfield Tp. (TOM); Kingsville Tp. (CMNH); Morgan Tp. (CMNH); Sheffield Tp. (CMNH); Trumbull Tp. (CMNH); Wayne Tp. (CMNH); Windsor Tp. (CMNH). ATH: Athens Tp. (OSUM, OUVC); Berne Tp. (W); Canaan Tp. (CMNH, OUVC); Waterloo Tp. (OUVC). AUG: St. Mary's Tp. (OSUM, W); Union Tp. (W). BRO: Clark Tp. (CSNH); Green Tp. (CSNH); Perry Tp. (CMNH, CSNH); Scott Tp. (OSUM); Union Tp. (MU). BUT: Fairfield Tp. (CSNH); Hanover Tp. (MU); Lemon Tp. (MU); Madison Tp. (CSNH, MU); Morgan Tp. (CSNH, OSUM); Oxford Tp. (CSNH, OSUM); Reily Tp. (CSNH, MU); Ross Tp. (CSNH, MU); Union Tp. (MU); Wayne Tp. (CSNH, MU). CAR: Lee Tp. (CMNH). CLA: Harmony Tp. (W); Pleasant Tp. (Dan Rice). CLE: Batavia Tp. (CSNH, KU); Goshen Tp. (CSNH); Miami Tp. (CSNH); Stonelick Tp. (CSNH, W); Tate Tp. (CSNH); Union Tp. (OSUM); Wayne Tp. (TOM); Williamsburg Tp. (OSUM). CLI: Adams Tp. (CSNH); Chester Tp. (CMNH); Jefferson Tp. (W); Union Tp. (CSNH); Washington Tp. (CSNH). COL: Center Tp. (W); St. Clair Tp. (RAP); West Tp. (RAP). COS: Jefferson Tp. (OSUM); Newcastle Tp. (OSUM); Washington Tp. (OSUM). CRA: Chatfield Tp. (CMNH); Dallas Tp. (OSUM); Liberty Tp. (OSUM); Whetstone Tp. (TOM). CUY: Brecksville (CMNH); Hunting Valley (TOM); Mayfield (CMNH); Middleburg Heights (RAP); North Royalton (CMNH); Olmsted Falls (CMNH); Orange (CMNH); Strongsville (CMNH); West Park (RAP). DAR: Washington Tp. (CSNH). DEF: Hicksville Tp. (OSUM); Richland Tp. (DC). DEL: Berlin Tp. (OSUM); Kingston Tp. (OSUM); Liberty Tp. (OSUM); Marlboro Tp. (KU, OSUM); Orange Tp. (OSUM); Porter Tp. (OSUM); Scioto Tp. (OSUM); Trenton Tp. (CMNH, OSUM, USNM). ERI: Margaretta Tp. (TOM); Oxford Tp. (RAP); Perkins Tp. (CMNH). FAI: Amanda Tp. (OSUM); Walnut Tp. (W). FAY: Jasper Tp. (CSNH, OUVC); Madison Tp. (W). FRA: Blendon Tp. (OSUM); Brown Tp. (OSUM); Clinton Tp. (OSUM); Columbus (W); Mifflin Tp. (OSUM); Plain Tp. (OSUM); Sharon Tp. (CMNH, OSUM); Truro Tp. (OSUM). FUL: German Tp. (TOM); Gorham Tp. (CMNH). GAL: Perry Tp. (CMNH). GEA: Burton Tp. (CMNH); Claridon Tp. (CMNH); Hambden Tp. (RAP); Newbury Tp. (CMNH, OSUM); Parkman Tp. (CMNH). GRE: Bath Tp. (DMCP); Beaver Creek Tp. (DMNH); Miami Tp. (William Duellman); Sugar Creek Tp. (DMNH). GUE: Jefferson Tp. (CMNH); Spencer Tp. (Douglas E. Wynn); Valley Tp. (DC); Wills Tp. (RAP). HAM: Colerain Tp. (KU, OSUM); Columbia Tp. (CSNH); Crosby Tp. (CSNH); Green Tp. (Paul Krusling); Miami Tp. (Douglas E. Wynn). HAN: Delaware Tp. (OSUM); Marion Tp. (OSUM). HAR: Blanchard Tp. (OUVC); Buck Tp. (OUVC); Cessna Tp. (OUVC); Dudley Tp. (OUVC); Goshen Tp. (Charles Blem); Hale Tp. (KU); Jackson Tp. (OUVC); Lynn Tp. (OUVC); McDonald Tp. (RAP); Pleasant Tp. (OUVC); Washington Tp. (OUVC). HAS: Washington Tp. (W). HIG: Clay Tp. (CSNH); Fairfield Tp. (KU); Madison Tp. (OSUM); Paint Tp. (OSUM). HOC: Benton Tp. (BGSU, OUVC); Good Hope Tp. (CMNH); Laurel Tp. (OSUM); Salt Creek Tp. (OSUM). HOL: Prairie Tp. (W). HUR: Richmond Tp. (CMNH). JAC: Franklin Tp. (W); Jefferson Tp. (TOM); Madison Tp. (CMNH). JEF: Ross Tp. (CMNH); Springfield Tp. (RAP). KNO: Butler Tp. (RAP); Harrison Tp. (OSUM); Morgan Tp. (RAP). LAK: Concord Tp. (CMNH); Kirtland Tp. (CMNH, W); Leroy Tp. (TOM); Madison Tp. (CMNH); Willoughby Tp. (CMNH). LAW: Aid Tp. (OSUM). LIC: Bennington (OSUM); Eden Tp. (CM); Etna Tp. (OSUM); Fallsbury Tp. (JEJ); Liberty Tp. (OSUM); Monroe Tp. (OSUM); Newark Tp. (CM, OSUM); Union Tp. (CM, JEJ, OSUM, W). LOG: Bokes Creek Tp. (OSUM); Perry Tp. (OSUM); Stokes Tp. (W). LOR: Columbia Tp. (CMNH); Elyria Tp. (W); Grafton Tp. (CMNH); Henrietta Tp. (CMNH); Huntington Tp. (TOM). LUC: Richfield Tp. (UMMZ); Toledo (W). MAD: Canaan Tp. (OSUM); Fairfield Tp. (CSNH); Jefferson Tp. (OSUM); Monroe Tp. (OSUM); Pike Tp. (OSUM); Pleasant Tp. (W). MAH: Smith Tp. (CMNH); Springfield Tp. (USNM). MAR: Bowling Green Tp. (OSUM); Richland Tp. (W). MED:

Brunswick Tp. (RAP); Chatham Tp. (OSUM); Harrisville Tp. (CMNH, OSUM); Hinckley Tp. (CMNH); Lafayette Tp. (RAP); Liverpool Tp. (RAP); Medina Tp. (RAP); Montville Tp. (RAP); Westfield Tp. (CMNH); York Tp. (RAP). MEG: Lebanon Tp. (OSUM, OUVC); Olive Tp. (TOM); Scipio Tp. (W). MOE: Center Tp. (OSUM); Malaga Tp. (OSUM); Perry Tp. (CMNH); Seneca Tp. (TOM); Washington Tp. (W); Wayne Tp. (RAP). MOT: Butler Tp. (DMNH); German Tp. (DMCP); Harrison Tp. (DMCP); Miami Tp. (DMNH); Wayne Tp. (DMCP). MRG: Union Tp. (CMNH, OSUM); Windsor (OSUM). MRW: Gilead Tp. (W); Lincoln Tp. (OSUM); Perry Tp. (CMNH); Peru Tp. (OSUM); South Bloomfield Tp. (W). MUS: Blue Rock Tp. (TOM); Falls Tp. (CM). NOB: Beaver Tp. (TOM); Jefferson Tp. (TOM); Seneca Tp. (CMNH); Sharon Tp. (OSUM); Wayne Tp. (CMNH). OTT: Danbury Tp. (W); Erie Tp. (W); Put-In-Bay Tp. (OSUM); Middle Bass Island (W). PAU: Brown Tp. (OSUM). PER: Jackson Tp. (CMNH); Madison Tp. (CMNH); Monroe Tp. (KU). PIC: Darby Tp. (OSUM); Deer Creek Tp. (KU); Jackson Tp. (OSUM); Monroe Tp. (OSUM); Muhlenberg Tp. (OSUM); Scioto Tp. (OSUM); Wayne Tp. (OSUM). PIK: Benton Tp. (DMNH, OSUM); Camp Creek Tp. (OSUM); Marion Tp. (OSUM); Newton Tp. (OSUM, W); Pee Pee Tp. (W); Scioto Tp. (OSUM); Seal Tp. (OSUM); Sunfish Tp. (OSUM). POR: Aurora Tp. (CMNH, W); Charlestown Tp. (CMNH); Paris Tp. (CMNH); Ravenna Tp. (CMNH); Windham Tp. (RAP). PRE: Gratis Tp. (KU); Harrison Tp. (DMNH); Israel Tp. (MU); Lanier Tp. (CSNH); Monroe Tp. (W); Somers Tp. (CM, KU, MU, W); Washington Tp. (KU). PUT: Jennings Tp. (OSUM). RIC: Monroe Tp. (RAP). ROS: Concord Tp. (CSNH); Green Tp. (TOM); Jefferson Tp. (OSUM); Liberty Tp. (OSUM); Paint Tp. (TOM); Paxton Tp. (OSUM); Scioto Tp. (OUVC); Union Tp. (CSNH). SCI: Bloom Tp. (CMNH); Harrison Tp. (W); Nile Tp. (OSUM); Rush Tp. (W); Vernon Tp. (CMNH). SHE: Loramie Tp. (OSUM); McLean Tp. (W). STA: Lake Tp. (CMNH); Lawrence Tp. (CMNH). SUM: Boston Tp. (CMNH); Northampton Tp. (CMNH); Richfield Tp. (RAP, TOM). TRU: Bloomfield Tp. (CMNH); Bristol Tp. (CMNH); Farmington Tp. (CMNH); Greene Tp. (CMNH); Mesopotamia Tp. (CMNH); Newton Tp. (W); Warren Tp. (W). TUS: Sandy Tp. (CMNH). UNI: Jerome Tp. (OSUM); Liberty Tp. (OSUM); Washington Tp. (OSUM); York Tp. (OSUM). VAN: Washington Tp. (OSUM). VIN: Brown Tp. (W); Eagle Tp. (CMNH). WAR: Harlan Tp. (CSNH); Massie Tp. (OSUM); Washington Tp. (CSNH, DMNH); Wayne Tp. (DMNH, OSUM). WAS: Adams Tp. (W); Belpre Tp. (OSUM); Grandview Tp. (RAP); Lawrence Tp. (W); Marietta Tp. (W); Salem Tp. (W). WAY: Chester Tp. (CW); Chippewa Tp. (CMNH); Clinton Tp. (CW); Congress Tp. (CMNH); Franklin Tp. (CW); Green Tp. (CW). WIL: Bridgewater Tp. (TOM); Jefferson Tp. (TOM). WOO: Bloom Tp. (BGSU); Liberty Tp. (BGSU); Perry Tp. (BGSU). WYA: Marseilles Tp. (OSUM, OUVC).

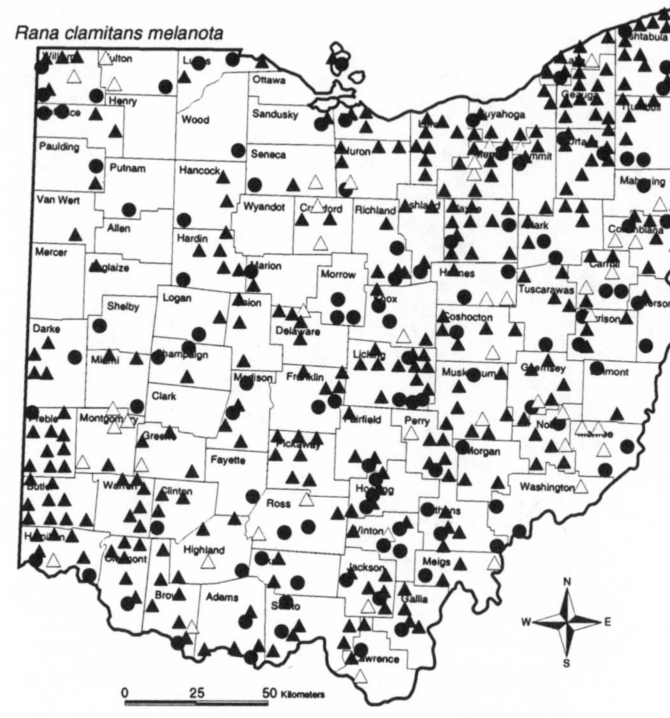

Figure 25-39. Distribution of green frogs (*Rana clamitans melanota*) in Ohio. Locality records for *R. c. melanota.* ADA: Green Tp. (MU, W); Meigs Tp. (MU, W); Monroe Tp. (MU); Sprigg Tp. (DMNH). ASH: Clear Creek Tp. (CW); Hanover Tp. (OSUM, W); Jackson Tp. (CSNH). ATB: Andover Tp. (W); Cherry Valley Tp. (W); Conneaut Tp. (W); Geneva Tp. (W); Harpersfield Tp. (CMNH); Kingsville Tp. (CMNH); Monroe Tp. (CMNH); Morgan Tp. (CMNH); Plymouth Tp. (CMNH); Rome Tp. (CMNH); Saybrook Tp. (CMNH); Sheffield Tp. (CMNH); Trumbull Tp. (CMNH); Wayne Tp. (CMNH, W); Windsor Tp. (CMNH). ATH: Alexander Tp. (OSUM); Athens Tp. (CMNH, W); Canaan Tp. (CMNH, OUVC); Dover Tp. (OUVC); Troy Tp. (W); York Tp. (W). AUG: Salem Tp. (OSUM). BEL: Flushing Tp. (W); Wayne Tp. (OSUM). BRO: Brown Tp. (RAP); Clark Tp. (CSNH); Green Tp. (CSNH); Jefferson Tp. (CMNH); Perry Tp. (CMNH, CSNH); Union Tp. (CMNH, W); Washington Tp. (CMNH). BUT: Fairfield Tp. (CSNH); Hanover Tp. (MU); Liberty Tp. (CSNH); Milford Tp. (CSNH); Morgan Tp. (CSNH); Oxford Tp. (MU); Reily Tp. (CSNH); Ross Tp. (CSNH, MU); St. Clair Tp. (CSNH); Union Tp. (MU). CAR: Augusta Tp. (CMNH); Brown Tp. (CMNH); Lee Tp. (W); Monroe Tp. (RAP); Orange Tp. (CMNH); Union Tp. (W); Washington Tp. (RAP). CHP: Johnson Tp. (W); Salem Tp. (W); Urbana Tp. (DMNH). CLE:

Batavia Tp. (CSNH); Goshen Tp. (CSNH); Miami Tp. (CSNH, KU); Stonelick Tp. (CSNH); Tate Tp. (CSNH, W); Wayne Tp. (CMNH). CLI: Adams Tp. (CSNH); Marion Tp. (W); Union Tp. (CSNH); Vernon Tp. (CSNH). COL: Butler Tp. (CMNH, W); Center Tp. (OSUM); Fairfield Tp. (W); Hanover Tp. (RAP); Middleton Tp. (CMNH); Salem Tp. (CMNH); Washington Tp. (CMNH); West Tp. (RAP). COS: Adams Tp. (OSUM); Bedford Tp. (CM); Franklin Tp. (RAP); Jefferson Tp. (W); Keene Tp. (CMNH); Newcastle Tp. (OSUM); Tiverton Tp. (CMNH). CRA: Chatfield Tp. (TOM); Liberty Tp. (OSUM); Tod Tp. (OSUM); Whetstone Tp. (TOM). CUY: Brecksville (CMNH); Hunting Valley (TOM); Mayfield (CMNH, OSUM); Olmsted Falls (CMNH, W); Orange (CMNH, OSUM); Strongsville (CMNH). DAR: Adams Tp. (W); Brown Tp. (DMNH); Liberty Tp. (CSNH); Neave Tp. (CSNH); Washington Tp. (CSNH). DEF: Farmer Tp. (W); Milford Tp. (W); Richland Tp. (DC); Tiffin Tp. (DC). DEL: Berlin Tp. (OSUM); Marlboro Tp. (TOM); Radnor Tp. (OSUM); Thompson Tp. (OSUM); Troy Tp. (OSUM). ERI: Margaretta Tp. (CMNH, W); Oxford Tp. (CMNH); Perkins Tp. (CMNH). FAI: Berne Tp. (CMNH, OSUM, W); Fayette Tp. (W); Hocking Tp. (W); Violet Tp. (W). FRA: Columbus (W); Jefferson Tp. (OSUM); Mifflin Tp. (OSUM); Perry Tp. (OSUM); Plain Tp. (OSUM); Pleasant Tp. (CSNH, OSUM); Truro Tp. (W). FUL: German Tp. (TOM); Gorham Tp. (TOM); Swan Creek Tp. (W). GAL: Green Tp. (CMNH); Huntington Tp. (OUVC); Perry Tp. (CMNH, W); Raccoon Tp. (OSUM). GEA: Bainbridge Tp. (OSUM); Burton Tp. (CMNH); Chardon Tp. (CMNH); Claridon Tp. (CMNH); Montville Tp. (CMNH); Munson Tp. (CMNH); Newbury Tp. (CMNH); Parkman Tp. (CMNH); Russell Tp. (CMNH); Troy Tp. (CMNH). GRE: Beaver Creek Tp. (DMNH); Jefferson Tp. (CSNH); Miami Tp. (DMNH, OSUM, OUVC); Sugar Creek Tp. (DMCP). GUE: Liberty Tp. (CMNH); Monroe Tp. (CMNH); Richland Tp. (OSUM); Spencer Tp. (Douglas E. Wynn); Valley Tp. (RAP, W); Wills Tp. (CMNH, OSUM). HAM: Anderson Tp. (W); Colerain Tp. (KU); Columbia Tp. (CSNH); Crosby Tp. (CSNH); Green Tp. (Paul Krusling); Miami Tp. (CSNH, W); Springfield Tp. (CSNH). HAN: Amanda Tp. (OSUM); Marion Tp. (OSUM); Orange Tp. (W). HAR: Buck Tp. (OUVC); Cessna Tp. (OUVC); Dudley Tp. (OSUM, OUVC); Jackson Tp. (OUVC); Pleasant Tp. (OUVC); Roundhead Tp. (W). HAS: Franklin Tp. (CM); German Tp. (MU); Monroe Tp. (RAP, W); Washington Tp. (CMNH, W). HIG: Brush Creek Tp. (W); Clay Tp. (CSNH); Madison Tp. (OSUM); New Market Tp. (RAP); Penn Tp. (CMNH). HOC: Benton Tp. (JEJ, W); Good Hope Tp. (JEJ, OSUM, W); Laurel Tp. (OSUM, W); Salt Creek Tp. (Douglas E. Wynn). HOL: Clark Tp. (RAP); Killbuck Tp. (W); Mechanic Tp. (RAP); Paint Tp. (W); Ripley Tp. (CMNH). HUR: Clarksfield Tp. (W); Lyme Tp. (CMNH); Richmond Tp. (TOM); Sherman Tp. (CMNH); Townsend Tp. (CMNH); Wakeman Tp. (CMNH, OSUM). JAC: Bloomfield Tp. (CMNH, W); Franklin Tp. (OSUM); Jefferson Tp. (TOM); Liberty Tp. (OUVC, W); Madison Tp. (CMNH); Milton Tp. (CMNH). JEF: Smithfield Tp. (W); Springfield Tp. (MU, W). KNO: Clinton Tp. (W); Jackson Tp. (OSUM); Middlebury Tp. (OSUM); Morgan Tp. (RAP); Wayne Tp. (W). LAK: Concord Tp. (CMNH); Kirtland Tp. (CMNH, W); Leroy Tp. (TOM); Madison Tp. (CMNH); Mentor Tp. (CMNH); Painesville Tp. (CMNH); Willoughby Tp. (CMNH). LAW: Decatur Tp. (W); Upper Tp. (RAP); Washington Tp. (OUVC). LIC: Bennington Tp. (OSUM); Bowling Green Tp. (W); Eden Tp. (CM, W); Fallsbury Tp. (UMMZ); Hopewell Tp. (OSUM, W); Liberty Tp. (OSUM); Licking Tp. (W); Madison Tp. (CM); Mary Ann Tp. (OSUM); Monroe Tp. (OSUM, W); Newton Tp. (CM); Perry Tp. (CMNH, OSUM); Union Tp. (LACM, OSUM). LOR: Amherst Tp. (CMNH); Camden Tp. (CMNH); Columbia Tp. (CMNH, OUVC); Eaton Tp. (CMNH); Elyria Tp. (OSUM); Huntington Tp. (OSUM); Pittsfield Tp. (CMNH); Russia Tp. (CMNH); Wellington Tp. (CMNH). LUC: Jerusalem Tp. (CMNH); Springfield Tp. (W); Swanton Tp. (UMMZ); Toledo (W). MAD: Monroe Tp. (OSUM); Paint Tp. (CSNH); Range Tp. (CSNH); Union Tp. (CSNH, OSUM). MAH: Beaver Tp. (RAP); Ellsworth Tp. (W); Poland Tp. (W); Springfield Tp. (USNM). MAR: Bowling Green Tp. (OSUM); Montgomery Tp. (W). MED: Brunswick Tp. (RAP); Granger Tp. (RAP); Harrisville Tp. (CMNH, OSUM); Hinckley Tp. (CMNH, W); Lafayette Tp. (RAP); Litchfield Tp. (CMNH); Liverpool Tp. (CMNH); Medina Tp. (CMNH); Montville Tp. (CMNH); Westfield Tp. (CMNH); York Tp. (RAP). MEG: Bedford Tp. (OUVC); Olive Tp. (TOM); Rutland Tp. (CMNH); Salem Tp. (W). MIA: Bethel Tp. (W); Brown Tp. (OSUM); Washington Tp. (W). MOE: Green Tp. (W); Malaga Tp. (TOM); Seneca Tp. (TOM); Washington Tp. (W); Wayne Tp. (RAP). MOT: Butler Tp. (DMCP); German Tp. (DMCP); Harrison Tp. (DMCP); Miami Tp. (DMNH); Wayne Tp. (DMCP). MRG: Union Tp. (OSUM); Windsor Tp. (OSUM); York Tp. (W). MRW: Bennington Tp. (W); Harmony Tp. (W); South Bloomfield Tp. (W). MUS: Blue Rock Tp. (CMNH, OSUM); Falls Tp. (CM); Harrison Tp. (OUVC); Madison Tp. (W); Monroe Tp. (CMNH); Muskingum Tp. (CMNH); Newton Tp. (CMNH); Rich Hill Tp. (OSUM); Salt Creek Tp. (TOM). NOB: Enoch Tp. (CMNH); Jackson Tp. (OSUM); Jefferson Tp. (CMNH); Noble Tp. (CMNH); Seneca Tp. (TOM, W); Stock Tp. (RAP). OTT: Put-In-Bay Tp. (OSUM). PAU: Brown Tp. (W); Washington Tp. (OSUM). PER: Clayton Tp. (CMNH); Harrison Tp. (CMNH); Jackson Tp. (CMNH); Monroe Tp. (OSUM); Perry Tp. (CMNH); Reading Tp. (RAP); Salt Lick Tp. (CMNH, W). PIC: Darby Tp. (CSNH, OSUM); Deer Creek Tp. (OSUM); Harrison Tp.

(OSUM); Jackson Tp. (OSUM); Monroe Tp. (OSUM); Muhlenberg Tp. (CSNH); Salt Creek Tp. (OSUM); Scioto Tp. (OSUM); Wayne Tp. (OSUM). PIK: Benton Tp. (DMNH); Newton Tp. (W); Perry Tp. (W); Sunfish Tp. (OSUM). POR: Aurora Tp. (CMNH, W); Charlestown Tp. (CMNH); Franklin Tp. (CMNH, W); Freedom Tp. (CMNH); Nelson Tp. (CMNH); Paris Tp. (CMNH); Rootstown Tp. (CMNH); Streetsboro Tp. (CMNH); Suffield Tp. (CMNH); Windham Tp. (CMNH, W). PRE: Gasper Tp. (OSUM); Gratis Tp. (CSNH, KU); Harrison Tp. (DMNH); Israel Tp. (MU); Jackson Tp. (KU); Jefferson Tp. (W); Lanier Tp. (KU); Somers Tp. (CM, MU); Twin Tp. (CSNH); Washington Tp. (CSNH). PUT: Sugar Creek Tp. (W). RIC: Jefferson Tp. (Merrill Tawse, W); Mifflin Tp. (W); Perry Tp. (OSUM); Weller Tp. (CSNH); Worthington Tp. (Merrill Tawse). ROS: Green Tp. (TOM); Harrison Tp. (CMNH); Paint Tp. (Barry Valentine, TOM); Scioto Tp. (W); Twin Tp. (W). SAN: Townsend Tp. (OSUM, W). SCI: Bloom Tp. (CMNH); Morgan Tp. (W); Nile Tp. (CM, CMNH); Rush Tp. (OUVC); Union Tp. (W); Valley Tp. (CMNH); Washington Tp. (OSUM). SEN: Big Spring Tp. (W); Bloom Tp. (RAP); Eden Tp. (BGSU). SHE: McLean Tp. (W). STA: Lake Tp. (CMNH); Lawrence Tp. (W); Marlboro Tp. (CMNH); Nimishillen Tp. (CMNH); Perry Tp. (W); Pike Tp. (W); Sugar Creek Tp. (RAP); Tuscarawas Tp. (CMNH). SUM: Bath Tp. (RAP, W); Boston Tp. (CMNH, OSUM); Green Tp. (CM); Richfield Tp. (RAP, TOM); Sagamore Hills Tp. (CMNH). TRU: Bloomfield Tp. (CMNH); Braceville Tp. (CMNH); Farmington Tp. (CMNH); Lordstown Tp. (W); Mesopotamia Tp. (CMNH); Newton Tp. (W). TUS: Goshen Tp. (CMNH); Sandy Tp. (CMNH); Union Tp. (CMNH); Washington Tp. (CMNH, W); Wayne Tp. (CMNH). UNI: Liberty Tp. (OSUM); Union Tp. (OSUM); Washington Tp. (OSUM). VAN: York Tp. (OSUM). VIN: Brown Tp. (BGCU, CMNH, OSUM, OUVC, W); Eagle Tp. (CMNH); Elk Tp. (RAP, W); Madison Tp. (W). WAR: Clear Creek Tp. (OSUM); Harlan Tp. (CSNH); Massie Tp. (OSUM); Salem Tp. (CMNH); Washington Tp. (CMNH); Wayne Tp. (CSNH). WAS: Belpre Tp. (W); Ludlow Tp. (RAP); Wesley Tp. (W). WAY: Baughman (W); Canaan Tp. (CW); Chester Tp. (CW); Chippewa (CMNH, CW); Clinton Tp. (CMNH, CW); Congress Tp. (CW); Franklin Tp. (CMNH, CW, UMMZ); Green Tp. (CW); Paint Tp. (CW); Plain Tp. (OSUM, W); Wayne Tp. (CW). WIL: Bridgewater Tp. (CMNH, CW); Jefferson Tp. (TOM); Madison Tp. (CMNH); Northwest Tp. (CW, W); St. Joseph Tp. (OSUM, W); Springfield Tp. (W). WOO: Perry Tp. (W).

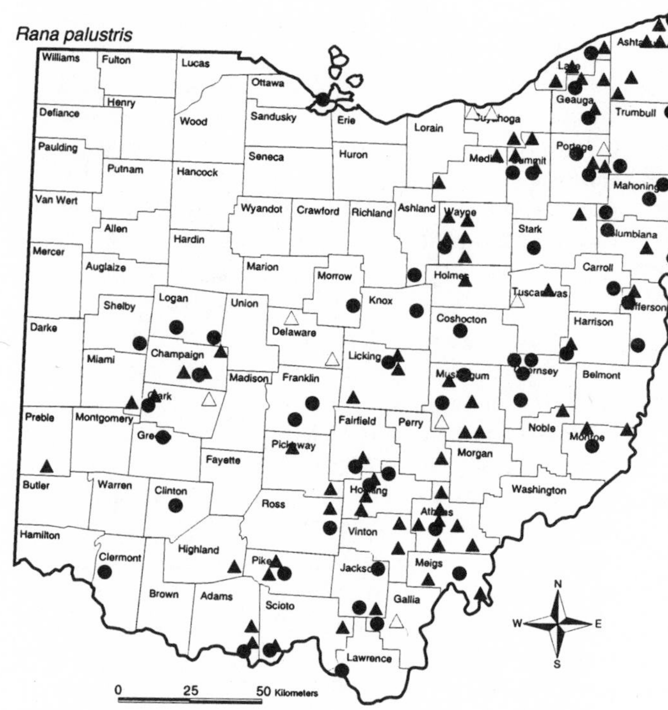

Figure 25-40. Distribution of pickerel frogs (*Rana palustris*) in Ohio. Locality records for *R. palustris*. ADA: Green Tp. (CMNH, KU, W); Jefferson Tp. (CSNH). ASH: Hanover Tp. (W). ATB: Conneaut Tp. (CMNH, W); Kingsville Tp. (CMNH); Plymouth Tp. (CMNH); Rome Tp. (OSUM); Sheffield Tp. (CMNH); Windsor Tp. (CMNH). ATH: Alexander Tp. (CM, OSUM); Athens Tp. (OUVC, W); Canaan Tp. (OUVC); Carthage Tp. (OUVC); Dover Tp. (OUVC); Trimble Tp. (OUVC); Waterloo Tp. (OUVC). CAR: Lee Tp. (W). CHP: Rush Tp. (OSUM); Union Tp. (W); Urbana Tp. (DMNH). CLA: Bethel Tp. (DMNH, W); Pleasant Tp. (Dan Rice). CLE: Union Tp. (W). CLI: Union Tp. (W). COL: Center Tp. (OSUM); Knox Tp. (W); St. Clair Tp. (W). COS: Bethlehem Tp. (W). CUY: Bay Village (RAP); Brecksville (CMNH); Lakewood (RAP). DEL: Harlem Tp. (Dan Rice); Marlboro Tp. (TOM). FAI: Berne Tp. (OSUM, W). FRA: Columbus (W); Jackson Tp. (W). GAL: Greenfield Tp. (W); Perry Tp. (RAP). GEA: Burton Tp. (CMNH, W); Chardon Tp. (CMNH, W); Montville Tp. (CMNH). GRE: Miami Tp. (W). GUE: Jackson Tp. (W); Liberty Tp. (W); Monroe Tp. (W); Wheeling Tp. (W). HAS: Washington Tp. (RAP, W). HIG: Brush Creek Tp. (CMNH). HOC: Benton Tp. (BGSU); Good Hope Tp. (CMNH, JEJ, OUVC, W); Laurel Tp. (OSUM); Marion Tp. (W). HOL: Prairie Tp. (OSUM). JAC: Jefferson Tp. (W); Madison Tp. (CMNH); Milton Tp. (W). JEF: Smithfield Tp. (W); Springfield Tp. (MU, W). KNO: Union Tp. (W); Wayne Tp. (W). LAK: Concord Tp. (CMNH); Kirtland Tp. (CMNH); Madison Tp. (CMNH); Perry Tp. (W). LAW:

Hamilton Tp. (CMNH). LIC: Eden Tp. (CM, W); Harrison Tp. (OSUM); Mary Ann Tp. (OSUM). LOG: Union Tp. (W); Zane Tp. (W). MAH: Canfield Tp. (W); Smith Tp. (W); Youngstown (W). MED: Hinckley Tp. (CMNH); Spencer Tp. (CMNH). MEG: Chester Tp. (W); Lebanon (OUVC); Rutland Tp. (CMNH). MIA: Bethel Tp. (DMNH). MOE: Center Tp. (W); Malaga Tp. (OSUM); Switzerland Tp. (CMNH). MUS: Blue Rock Tp. (CMNH, OSUM); Falls Tp. (W); Harrison Tp. (OUVC); Madison Tp. (W); Muskingum Tp. (CM); Newton Tp. (RAP); Perry Tp. (CMNH). NOB: Beaver Tp. (OSUM); Enoch Tp. (CMNH). OTT: Portage Tp. (W). PER: Bearfield Tp. (CMNH). PIC: Muhlenberg Tp. (OSUM); Salt Creek Tp. (OSUM). PIK: Benton Tp. (CMNH, OUVC); Newton Tp. (W); Sunfish Tp. (OSUM). POR: Charlestown Tp. (CMNH, W); Paris Tp. (CMNH); Shalersville Tp. (W); Windham Tp. (RAP). PRE: Somers Tp. (MU). ROS: Colerain Tp. (UMMZ); Harrison Tp. (W). SCI: Nile Tp. (MU, OUVC, W). SHE: Green Tp. (W). STA: Marlboro Tp. (CMNH); Perry Tp. (W). SUM: Bath Tp. (W); Boston Tp. (CMNH, OSUM, W); Richfield Tp. (W); Sagamore Hills Tp. (CMNH). TRU: Kinsman Tp. (W); Newton Tp. (W). TUS: Auburn Tp. (RAP); Fairfield Tp. (CMNH). VIN: Brown Tp. (OUVC); Eagle Tp. (CMNH); Vinton Tp. (CMNH). WAS: Warren Tp. (OUVC). WAY: Chester Tp. (CW, UMMZ); Franklin Tp. (CW); Plain Tp. (OSUM, W); Wayne Tp. (CW); Wooster Tp. (CW).

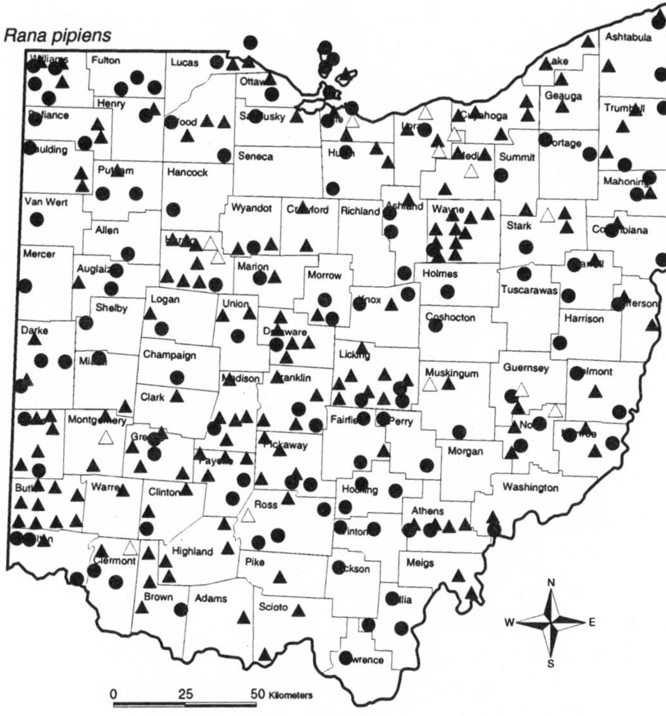

Figure 25-41. Distribution of northern leopard frogs (*Rana pipiens*) in Ohio. Locality records for *R. pipiens*. ADA: Meigs Tp. (W). ALL: Perry Tp. (W). ASH: Clear Creek Tp. (W); Hanover Tp. (W); Milton Tp. (W); Sullivan Tp. (CSNH). ATB: Andover Tp. (W); Conneaut Tp. (CMNH, W); Trumbull Tp. (CMNH). ATH: Athens Tp. (CMNH, OSUM, W); Canaan Tp. (OUVC); Rome Tp. (OUVC); Waterloo Tp. (OUVC, W). BEL: Goshen Tp. (OSUM); Kirkwood Tp. (W). BRO: Clark Tp. (CSNH); Green Tp. (CSNH); Jackson Tp. (W); Perry Tp. (CSNH). BUT: Fairfield Tp. (CSNH); Hanover Tp. (CSNH); Lemon Tp. (CSNH); Milford Tp. (CSNH); Morgan Tp. (CSNH); Reily Tp. (CSNH); Ross Tp. (KU); Union Tp. (CSNH); Wayne Tp. (CSNH). CHP: Urbana Tp. (W). CLA: Moorefield Tp. (DMNH). CLE: Batavia Tp. (W); Miami Tp. (KU); Union Tp. (W); Wayne Tp. (TOM). CLI: Marion Tp. (W); Vernon Tp. (OSUM); Wilson Tp. (CSNH). COL: Butler Tp. (CMNH, W). COS: Jefferson Tp. (W). CRA: Chatfield Tp. (CMNH); Whetstone Tp. (CMNH). CUY: Bay Village (CMNH); Brecksville (CMNH); Lakewood (CMNH); Mayfield (CMNH); Orange (OSUM). DAR: Adams Tp. (W); Brown Tp. (DMNH); Greenville Tp. (W); Liberty Tp. (CSNH); Washington Tp. (CSNH, W). DEF: Defiance Tp. (W); Highland Tp. (Dan Rice); Milford Tp. (W); Richland Tp. (DC); Tiffin Tp. (DC). DEL: Berlin Tp. (OSUM); Delaware Tp. (W); Marlboro Tp. (CW, OSUM, USNM); Orange Tp. (OSUM); Troy Tp. (OSUM, UF). ERI: Kelleys Island (OSUM); Margaretta Tp. (CMNH, W); Oxford Tp. (CMNH); Perkins Tp. (RAP); Sandusky Tp. (W). FAI:

Berne Tp. (W); Rush Creek Tp. (CMNH); Walnut Tp. (W). FAR: Augusta Tp. (MU); Brown Tp. (W); Monroe Tp. (W). FAY: Jasper Tp. (CSNH); Jefferson Tp. (CSNH); Madison Tp. (W); Marion Tp. (W); Paint Tp. (CSNH); Wayne Tp. (W). FRA: Columbus (W); Hamilton Tp. (OSUM); Jefferson Tp. (OSUM); Madison Tp. (W); Perry Tp. (OSUM); Pleasant Tp. (CSNH). FUL: Clinton Tp. (W); Pike Tp. (W); Swan Creek Tp. (W). GAL: Green Tp. (W); Greenfield Tp. (W); Huntington Tp. (W). GEA: Chardon Tp. (CMNH); Newbury Tp. (CMNH). GRE: Beaver Creek Tp. (DMNH); Jefferson Tp. (CSNH); Miami Tp. (William Duellman); Spring Valley Tp. (CSNH); Xenia Tp. (W). GUE: Jackson Tp. (RAP, W); Valley Tp. (OSUM). HAM: Anderson Tp. (W); Colerain Tp. (CSNH, KU); Crosby Tp. (W); Harrison Tp. (W); Madeira Tp. (KU). HAN: Union Tp. (W). HAR: Blanchard Tp. (OUVC); Buck Tp. (OUVC); Goshen Tp. (Charles Blem); Hale Tp. (W); Jackson Tp. (Charles Blem); Liberty Tp. (OUVC); McDonald Tp. (OUVC); Pleasant Tp. (OUVC); Roundhead Tp. (OUVC); Taylor Creek Tp. (OUVC); Washington Tp. (OUVC). HAS: Washington Tp. (W). HEN: Washington Tp. (OSUM, W). HIG: Clay Tp. (CSNH); Madison Tp. (OSUM); Paint Tp. (OSUM); Salem Tp. (CSNH). HOC: Good Hope Tp. (W); Green Tp. (W); Salt Creek Tp. (W). HOL: Killbuck Tp. (W). HUR: Clarksfield Tp. (CMNH); Richmond Tp. (W); Ridgefield Tp. (W); Townsend Tp. (CMNH). JAC: Jackson Tp. (W). JEF: Springfield Tp. (MU, W); Steubenville Tp. (W). KNO: Howard Tp. (OSUM); Jefferson Tp. (W); Wayne Tp. (W). LAK: Madison Tp. (CMNH); Mentor Tp. (CMNH). LAW: Decatur Tp. (W). LIC: Bowling Green Tp. (W); Burlington Tp. (OSUM); Etna Tp. (JEJ); Hopewell Tp. (OSUM, W); Licking Tp. (CM, OSUM); Lima Tp. (OSUM); Madison Tp. (OSUM); St. Albans Tp. (JEJ); Union Tp. (JEJ, OSUM, W). LOG: Pleasant Tp. (OSUM); Union Tp. (W). LOR: Amherst Tp. (CMNH); Columbia Tp. (RAP); Eaton Tp. (CMNH); Elyria Tp. (W); Grafton Tp. (RAP); Sheffield Tp. (CMNH, OSUM). LUC: Jerusalem Tp. (CSNH); Oregon Tp. (OSUM); Toledo Tp. (W); West Sister Island (W). MAD: Fairfield Tp. (CSNH); Oak Run Tp. (CSNH); Paint Tp. (CSNH, W); Pike Tp. (OSUM); Pleasant Tp. (CSNH); Range Tp. (CSNH). MAH: Boardman Tp. (CM); Canfield Tp. (W); Youngstown Tp. (W). MAR: Big Island Tp. (W); Marion Tp. (OSUM). MED: Harrisville Tp. (CMNH); Hinckley Tp. (CMNH); Liverpool Tp. (CMNH); Medina Tp. (RAP). MAR: Big Island Tp. (W); Marion Tp. (OSUM). MER: Washington Tp. (W). MIA: Bethel Tp. (DMNH, OSUM); Washington Tp. (W). MOE: Malaga Tp. (OSUM); Perry Tp. (CMNH); Salem Tp. (W); Summit Tp. (W). MOT: Butler Tp. (DMNH); Harrison Tp. (DMCP); Miami Tp. (DMNH). MRW: Bennington Tp. (CMNH); Harmony Tp. (W); South Bloomfield Tp. (W). MUS: Harrison Tp. (OUVC); Licking Tp. (RAP); Muskingum Tp. (W). NOB: Beaver Tp. (TOM); Noble Tp. (OSUM); Olive Tp. (W); Seneca Tp. (W); Sharon Tp. (UMMZ). OTT: Carroll Tp. (UMMZ); Danbury Tp. (W); Middle Bass Island (W); North Bass Island (W); Put-In-Bay Tp. (OSUM, W); Salem Tp. (W); South Bass Island (W). PAU: Brown Tp. (OSUM); Carry All Tp. (W); Washington Tp. (OSUM). PER: Pleasant Tp. (W); Thorn Tp. (W). PIC: Darby Tp. (CSNH, OSUM); Jackson Tp. (CSNH); Muhlenberg Tp. (CSNH, OSUM); Perry Tp. (CSNH); Pickaway Tp. (W); Wayne Tp. (OSUM, W). PIK: Newton Tp. (OSUM). POR: Aurora Tp. (W); Windham Tp. (W). PRE: Gratis Tp. (KU); Harrison Tp. (KU); Israel Tp. (MU); Jefferson Tp. (W); Monroe Tp. (CM); Somers Tp. (W); Twin Tp. (CSNH). PUT: Ottawa Tp. (W); Palmer Tp. (OSUM); Perry Tp. (W). ROS: Buckskin Tp. (Barry Valentine); Colerain Tp. (W); Paxton Tp. (W); Twin Tp. (W); Union Tp. (CSNH). SAN: Reily Tp. (CMNH); Washington Tp. (W). SCI: Nile Tp. (OSUM); Valley Tp. (W). SHE: McLean Tp. (W). STA: Lake Tp. (RAP); Marlboro Tp. (CMNH); Nimishillin Tp. (CMNH); Perry Tp. (W). SUM: Bath Tp. (W); Green Tp. (CM). TRU: Braceville Tp. (CMNH); Bristol Tp. (CMNH); Greene Tp. (CMNH); Kinsman Tp. (W). TUS: Lawrence Tp. (W). UNI: Leesburg Tp. (OSUM); Liberty Tp. (OSUM); Paris Tp. (W); Pleasant Tp. (W). VAN: Pleasant Tp. (W). VIN: Eagle Tp. (W). WAR: Deerfield Tp. (W); Wayne Tp. (CSNH). WAS: Belpre Tp. (W); Dunham Tp. (OUVC). WAY: Canaan Tp. (CW); Chester Tp. (CW); Chippewa Tp. (CW, UMMZ); Clinton Tp. (CW); Franklin Tp. (CW, UMMZ); Green Tp. (CW); Milton Tp. (CMNH); Plain Tp. (CW, W); Wayne Tp. (CW); Wooster Tp. (CW). WIL: Bridgewater (CMNH, CW, W); Center Tp. (W); Florence Tp. (W); Jefferson Tp. (CW); Northwest Tp. (OSUM, W). WOO: Center Tp. (BGSU); Freedom Tp. (CW); Grand Rapids Tp. (W); Liberty Tp. (BGSU, CW); Perry Tp. (W). WYA: Antrim Tp. (OSUM); Marseilles Tp. (OSUM); Pitt Tp. (W).

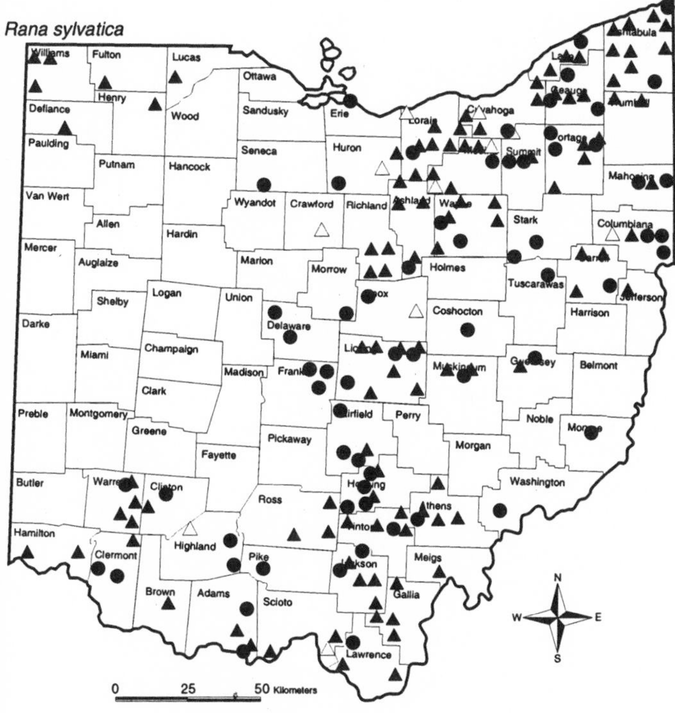

Figure 25-42. Distribution of wood frogs (*Rana sylvatica*) in Ohio. Locality records for *R. sylvatica.* ADA: Brush Creek Tp. (MU); Green Tp. (CSNH, KU, MU, OSUM, W); Meigs Tp. (W). ASH: Clear Creek Tp. (CW); Hanover Tp. (OSUM, W); Jackson Tp. (CMNH, CW); Ruggles Tp. (OSUM). ATB: Conneaut Tp. (W); Geneva Tp. (OSUM); Kingsville Tp. (CMNH); Monroe Tp. (CMNH); Morgan Tp. (CMNH); Richmond Tp. (CM, CMNH); Rome Tp. (CMNH); Saybrook Tp. (CMNH); Sheffield Tp. (CMNH); Trumbull Tp. (CMNH); Wayne Tp. (W); Windsor Tp. (CMNH). ATH: Athens Tp. (OUVC); Canaan Tp. (CM); Trimble Tp. (OUVC); Waterloo Tp. (CMNH, OUVC, W). BRO: Franklin Tp. (CMNH). CAR: Augusta Tp. (CMNH); Brown Tp. (CMNH); Lee Tp. (W); Orange Tp. (CMNH). CLE: Batavia Tp. (W); Union Tp. (W); Wayne Tp. (CMNH). COL: Center Tp. (CMNH); Elk Run Tp. (W); Hanover Tp. (RAP); Middleton Tp. (W); St. Clair Tp. (W). COS: Bethlehem Tp. (W). CRA: Whetstone Tp. (RAP). CUY: Berea (RAP); Brecksville (CMNH); Mayfield (CMNH); North Olmsted (CMNH); Olmsted Falls (CMNH); Orange (CMNH); Strongsville (CMNH). DEF: Delaware Tp. (OSUM). DEL: Delaware Tp. (W); Radnor Tp. (W). ERI: Sandusky (W). FAI: Berne Tp. (OSUM, W); Hocking Tp. (W); Violet Tp. (W). FRA: Blendon Tp. (W); Mifflin Tp. (W); Plain Tp. (W). FUL: German Tp. (CW). GAL: Greenfield Tp. (CMNH); Huntington Tp. (CMNH); Perry Tp. (CMNH); Walnut Tp. (CMNH). GEA: Burton Tp. (CMNH); Chardon Tp. (W); Newbury Tp. (CMNH, OSUM); Parkman Tp. (W); Russell Tp. (CMNH, W). GUE: Liberty Tp. (CMNH); Monroe Tp. (W). HAM: Columbia Tp. (CSNH); Miami Tp. (CSNH). HAN: Van Buren Tp. (UMMZ). HEN: Washington Tp. (UMMZ). HIG: Brush Creek Tp. (W); Paint Tp. (W); Union Tp. (RAP). HOC: Benton Tp. (JEJ, W); Good Hope Tp. (CMNH, JEJ, OSUM, W); Laurel Tp. (W); Salt Creek Tp. (W). HUR: Clarksfield Tp. (CMNH); Fitchville Tp. (Dan Rice); Richmond Tp. (W). JAC: Bloomfield Tp. (CMNH); Franklin Tp. (CMNH); Liberty Tp. (OUVC, W); Madison Tp. (CMNH); Washington Tp. (W). JEF: Springfield Tp. (MU). KNO: Butler Tp. (RAP); Morris Tp. (W). LAK: Concord Tp. (CMNH); Kirtland Tp. (CMNH); Leroy Tp. (OSUM); Perry Tp. (W). LAW: Decatur Tp. (W); Windsor Tp. (CMNH). LIC: Bennington Tp. (OSUM); Burlington Tp. (OSUM); Eden Tp. (CM, W); Fallsbury Tp. (OSUM, W); Hopewell Tp. (OSUM); Lima Tp. (W); Mary Ann Tp. (JEJ). LOR: Brighton Tp. (W); Brownhelm Tp. (RAP); Carlisle Tp. (CMNH); Columbia Tp. (OUVC); Grafton Tp. (CMNH); Huntington Tp. (CMNH); Lagrange Tp. (CMNH); Pittsfield Tp. (CMNH). LUC: Swanton Tp. (UMMZ). MAH: Boardman Tp. (CM); Canfield Tp. (W); Poland Tp. (W). MED: Brunswick Tp. (CMNH); Granger Tp. (W); Harrisville Tp. (CMNH); Hinckley Tp. (RAP); Homer Tp. (RAP); Liverpool Tp. (CMNH); Medina Tp. (CMNH); Spencer Tp. (BGSU). MEG: Rutland Tp. (CMNH). MOE: Center Tp. (W). MRW: South Bloomfield Tp. (W). MUS: Cass Tp. (CMNH); Madison Tp. (CMNH, W). PIK: Mifflin Tp. (W). POR: Aurora Tp. (W); Charlestown Tp. (CMNH); Freedom Tp. (CMNH); Streetsboro Tp. (W); Suffield Tp. (CMNH); Windham Tp. (CMNH, W). RIC: Jefferson Tp. (Merrill Tawse); Monroe Tp. (Merrill Tawse); Washington Tp. (Merrill Tawse); Worthington Tp. (Merrill Tawse). ROS: Colerain Tp. (UMMZ); Huntington Tp. (CSNH); Liberty Tp. (CM). SCI: Green Tp. (RAP); Nile Tp. (OSUM, OUVC); Vernon Tp. (CMNH). SEN: Seneca Tp. (W). STA: Perry Tp. (W); Sugar Creek Tp. (W). SUM: Bath Tp. (W); Boston Tp. (CMNH, OSUM, W). TRU: Greene Tp. (CM); Mesopotamia Tp. (CMNH). TUS: Sandy Tp. (W). VIN: Brown Tp. (OUVC); Eagle Tp. (CMNH); Elk Tp. (CMNH); Knox Tp. (OUVC); Madison Tp. (W). WAR: Harlan Tp. (CSNH); Salem Tp. (CSNH); Washington Tp. (CSNH, DMNH, MU); Wayne Tp. (RAP, W). WAS: Fairfield Tp. (W). WAY: Baughman Tp. (CW); Canaan Tp. (CW); Chester Tp. (CW, W); Chippewa Tp. (CW, UMMZ); Clinton Tp. (CW, UMMZ); Wooster Tp. (W). WIL: Bridgewater Tp. (CW); Florence Tp. (CM); Northwest Tp. (CW).

Diseases and Toxins

26

Infectious Diseases of Amphibians

Sandra A. Faeh, Donald K. Nichols, and Val R. Beasley

This chapter presents summary information on the important infectious diseases of amphibians that have been documented in captivity as well as in the wild. Most of the information available relates to amphibians in captivity; one reason for this is that these animals are closely observed and more likely to be presented for veterinary care. Animals in captivity also may be more likely to be stressed due to confinement and/or overcrowding. In addition, poor hygiene in the captive environment can allow pathogens such as bacteria and parasites to become ubiquitous. Similar circumstances may arise in the wild. Stressful situations occur, such as habitat destruction, untoward weather conditions (e.g., droughts or floods), increased predation, reproduction, and overwintering. In both wild and captive situations, stresses compromise the capacity of the immune system, allowing pathogens the opportunity to multiply. Therefore, many diseases that occur in captivity potentially occur in the wild.

Diagnostic Techniques

In order to determine the causes of a major mortality event, a declining population, or the death of a single amphibian, one must be aware of the techniques necessary to obtain, preserve, and test diagnostic specimens (Speare 1989). Detailed examinations of multiple specimens are generally needed to determine conclusively whether a particular outbreak of illness is due to a given etiologic agent. Because of the small size of many amphibians, specimens obtained may be depleted rapidly, and therefore it may be necessary to collect additional individuals in order to perform all the necessary tests. In any case, provided the animals are present in adequate numbers, sufficient tissue should be obtained to perform assays not recognized as necessary at the outset. Healthy specimens and specimens that appear to be ill but are still alive are the best sources for comparative information. Such animals can be used for serological, parasitological, bacteriological, mycological, histological, and toxicological studies. Although necropsy results from animals that have died are usually difficult to obtain for lesions because of autolytic decomposition and for pathogens because of potential overgrowth with nonpathogens, such decomposing tissues often can be used for many (but not all) types of toxicologic tests (Green 1993).

Eggs, larvae, juveniles, and adults should be obtained from each of the affected species to ensure that the health status of animals during all life stages is documented. When conducting a gross necropsy, an initial examination of the animal's general body condition should be performed. The skin, eyes, and body orifices should be examined for evidence of abnormality resulting from trauma and/or infection, such as abrasions, lacerations, hemorrhages, or exudates. Skin scrapings and wet mounts can be performed to determine if fungi or ectoparasites are present. Subsequently, after disinfection of the skin with iodine or 70 percent alcohol, a ventral midline incision should be made from the mandibular symphysis to the vent. Lesions seen upon examination of the viscera may be aseptically sampled for viral, fungal, and/or bacterial cultures. Any adult or encysted larval parasites should be removed and examined with a light or an electron microscope for identification as to species (or as close as possible). When bacterial septicemia (systemic disease caused by circulating microorganisms in the blood) is suspected and the carcass is fresh, a sample of heart blood should be collected for culture. If heart blood is not obtainable, one may sample a piece of liver for culture (Nichols 1989).

Standard media should be used for the culture of routine anaerobic and aerobic bacteria. It may be useful to incubate replicate cultures at 25°C as well as at 37°C because some bacterial pathogens of ectothermic animals grow better at "body temperature," while others grow better at "room temperature." Specimens for viral, bacterial, and fungal studies should be properly refrigerated if travel time to the laboratory is short (e.g., up to two days) or frozen if travel time is long (e.g., over two days; Nichols 1989).

Once specimens have been cultured, tissue sections (less than 1 centimeter thick) should be fixed in ten times the tissue volume of 10 percent neutral buffered formalin and processed for histopathologic studies. Such tissues routinely should include liver, kidney, lung and/or gill, heart, stomach, intestine, brain, muscle, skin, gonads, and bone. Freezing tissue samples intended for histologic studies is not recommended because it greatly alters cell structure.

Analysis for persistent fat soluble toxicants is generally best performed on males. Females tend to store such compounds in the large egg masses that are shed each year. Therefore, analysis of the female specimen, after the eggs have been laid, may not provide a reliable indication of the overall toxicant exposure of the population. Conversely, ovaries from females may by assayed to determine the concentration present prior to fertilization and development. Specimens for toxicologic assays should be frozen and sent to an appropriate diagnostic laboratory. Selection of tissues for toxicologic studies is described in Diana and Beasley (Chpt. 27, this volume).

Viruses

Polyhedral Cytoplasmic Amphibian Virus

Polyhedral cytoplasmic amphibian viruses (PCAVs) are a group of DNA viruses in the iridovirus family (a family of viruses including the iridescent viruses of insects). PCAVs have been isolated from normal-appearing tissues of northern leopard frogs (*Rana pipiens*), bullfrogs (*Rana catesbeiana*), and eastern newts (*Notophthalmus viridescens*) but have not been identified as a cause of lesions or illness in these species. However, experimental inoculation of Fowler's toads (*Bufo woodhousii fowleri*) resulted in mortality (Clark et al. 1969).

Tadpole Edema Virus

The tadpole edema virus (TEV), actually a group of related iridoviruses, is another PCAV (Marcus 1981) found in American bullfrogs and other anurans. It causes mortality in tadpoles and in newly metamorphosed frogs. Gross and histologic features include subcutaneous edema, petechial hemorrhages, and necrosis in liver, kidney, gastrointestinal tract, and skeletal muscle (Crawshaw 1992; Wolf et al. 1969). Transmission of the virus occurs in the water (Marcus 1981). Adults are rarely affected (Crawshaw 1992). Diagnosis is established by viral culture.

Frog Erythrocytic Virus

Frog erythrocytic virus (FEV) is an iridovirus reported in wild populations of bullfrogs, green frogs (*Rana clamitans melanota*), and mink frogs (*Rana septentrionalis*). A relationship between this virus and the tadpole edema virus has not been established. Red blood cells infected with FEV are usually spheroidal instead of ellipsoidal, have eccentrically displaced nuclei, and contain round to trapezoidal cytoplasmic inclusions (Gruia-Gray and Desser 1992). Although no clinical disease has been proven to be associated with this virus, studies by Gruia-Gray and Desser (1992) suggest that infected juvenile bullfrogs have a decreased survival rate to adulthood. Diagnosis is established by demonstration of typical erythrocyte changes in peripheral blood smears.

Poxvirus

During an investigation of apparently high mortalities in wild populations of European common frogs (*Rana temporaria*) in Great Britain, a poxvirus (a family of large, complex viruses that exhibits an affinity for skin tissue) was associated with the presence of cutaneous lesions (Cunningham et al. 1993). Gross lesions consisted of cutaneous reddening and/or ulceration. Histologically, there was epidermal hyperplasia (increase in volume due to the formation and growth of new cells) with necrosis and ulceration. Viral particles typical of poxviruses were demonstrated by electron microscopic examination of these lesions.

Lucké Renal Adenocarcinoma

Lucké renal adenocarcinoma, an invasive neoplasm (tumor) in the northern leopard frog, was the first tumor to be associated with herpes viruses (Lucké 1934;

Mizell 1969; McKinnell 1984). These tumors are most evident during the winter and spring months when intranuclear inclusions are present (Lucké 1934; Lucké et al. 1953). Transmission is thought to occur in the spring during breeding when adults gather in small ponds and the virus is spread via urine (McKinnell 1984). Transmission may be high in ponds with large numbers of frogs in localized areas (Granoff and Darlington 1969). Maturation of the virus occurs within the host during its hibernation (McKinnell et al. 1972), and release of the herpes virus is dependent on increased environmental temperatures, as occur during the breeding season (Zambernard and Vatter 1966). The infection is usually latent, however, until the frog is two years of age (Marcus 1981).

In normal leopard frogs, the kidney is brick red, dorsoventrally flattened, and elongated, with its long axis parallel to that of the body. A strip of bright yellow adrenal cells, also parallel to the long axis of the body, lies on the ventral aspect of the mesonephros. By contrast, a neoplastic kidney typically has cream-colored nodules, with lumps or bulges, either singly or in multiples, in the matrix or on the surface of the organ, unilaterally or bilaterally (McKinnell 1965). Histologically, the tumor cells appear as a well-differentiated simple epithelium or as an epithelium comprised of several layers of columnar cells (McKinnell 1984). It is thought that the proximal portion of the distal tubules is the site of origin for this tumor. Only after the tumor is palpable for several weeks or months do the frogs show any signs of deteriorating health, such as weight loss (Gibbs et al. 1966; Crawshaw 1992). Once metastasis has begun, signs related to the deterioration of the involved organs develop rapidly (Gibbs et al. 1966).

Bacteria

Due to their ubiquitous presence in the environment, bacteria are a major cause of morbidity (disease) and mortality in amphibians. Many bacteria cause disease primarily in old and/or debilitated animals. In order to establish a diagnosis, isolation of a bacterial pathogen must be coupled with demonstration of appropriate histologic lesions.

Red Leg

Septicemia in amphibians, often called red leg, involves one or a combination of mostly gram-negative, hemolytic (destructive to blood cells) bacteria. These bacteria probably enter the body via wounds or skin abrasions. Lesions usually include capillary dilation of the lower abdomen and inner thighs of the animals, resulting in a red-legged appearance (Canadian Council on Animal Care 1984). As the septicemia progresses, the animals become lethargic and anorexic and have large hemorrhagic areas over the entire body, often with septic thrombi (blood clots that often obstruct vessels) and miliary (small, millet seed–sized) abscesses (Hunsaker and Potter 1960). Death commonly occurs. Lesions at postmortem commonly include cutaneous hemorrhage and edema (an accumulation in tissue of watery fluid). Hepatic and splenic enlargement with hemorrhage and necrosis, or with ulcers and granulomas (nodular inflammatory lesions), are frequently present in the chronic stage of the disease (Crawshaw 1992).

The causative organisms of red leg often result in mass mortality, both in captivity and in the wild. *Aeromonas hydrophila, Aeromonas* spp., *Pseudomonas* spp., *Mima* spp., *Citrobacter* spp., and *Proteus* spp. are a few of the gram-negative bacteria known to cause red leg (Crawshaw 1992).

Aeromonas hydrophila, an ubiquitous and hemolytic organism, was first isolated in 1891 from experimental frogs. At that time, it was given the name *Bacillus hydrophilus fuscus* (Russell 1898). Though it often is considered the causative agent of red leg (Amborski et al. 1977; Temple and Fowler 1984), it has been isolated from healthy frogs as well (Hird et al. 1981). *Aeromonas* is a classic opportunistic pathogen, causing disease in stressed and debilitated animals. It may be transmitted by contact with water, in which the bacteria are ubiquitous. Some of the signs noted with the disease, such as twitching, convulsing, or severe lethargy, do not often occur when the animal is in a terminal state. The cardinal lesion of this type of infection is the presence of petechiae (pinpoint hemorrhages) on the skin, as well as on the mucosal and serosal surfaces (Marcus 1981). The liver appears dark and swollen. Frequently, necrotic areas are present in muscle (Caselitz 1966; Deesi 1949).

Aeromonas can be cultured readily on ordinary media at either 25°C or 37°C. However, it is easily overlooked or mistaken for an enteric bacterium (Shotts and Bullock 1975, 1976). Therefore, culturing *Aeromonas* on a selective medium such as RS is advantageous, because the colonies have a characteristic yellow color (Shotts and Rimler 1973; Rimler et al. 1974).

Gas Bubble Disease and Potential Confusion with Red Leg

Gas bubble disease results when frogs are exposed to water supersaturated with atmospheric gases (Machado et al. 1987). This may occur as a consequence of malfunctions of pumps or when water deep in the ground rapidly escapes at the surface. Small, clear bubbles and a decrease in the mucous coating on the skin usually result within twenty-four to forty-eight hours after exposure. The bubbles initially appear parallel to the digits in the interdigital webbing of the hind legs. Bubbles expand in size and numbers and eventually spread to the forelimbs. The legs become increasingly hyperemic (accumulate blood within vessels), often with petechial and ecchymotic hemorrhages (extravascular blood). Frogs slowly lose the ability to stay submerged in water. Also, affected frogs gradually lose the ability to locate and ingest food, resulting in a progressive anorexic state. Severely affected animals may become infected with *Aeromonas hydrophila,* often leading to a misdiagnosis of red leg, or septicemia (Colt et al. 1984). To determine the underlying cause, lesions should be examined histologically and cultured as soon as possible after the onset of the disease. Tests should be performed at the site to determine if the water is supersaturated with atmospheric gases.

Chlamydiosis

Chlamydia psittaci causes a spectrum of diseases in animals. Infection has been reported in African clawed frogs (*Xenopus laevis*). Affected frogs often become lethargic, develop a state of disequilibrium, and tend to surface more frequently to breathe. Gross lesions resemble those seen in red leg and include subcutaneous edema, coelomic effusion, hepatosplenomegaly (enlarged liver and spleen), and cutaneous petechiation as well as ulceration. Histologically, the liver, spleen, lungs, and heart develop a pyogranulomatous (granular and pus-forming) inflammatory response. Definitive diagnosis is made through culture and/or histologic demonstration of aggregates of chlamydial organisms (which appear as small basophilic granular inclusions) within the cytoplasm of endothelial cells and histiocytes (Newcomer et al. 1982).

Mycobacteriosis

Mycobacteriosis was first reported in amphibians in 1905 when a hepatic infection was reported in a frog (Kuster 1905). Mycobacteriosis of amphibians is caused by various bacteria in the genus *Mycobacterium* (e.g., *M. xenopei, M. ranoe, M. ranicola, M. marinum,* and *M. glae*). The organisms are gram positive and have a wide distribution (Brownstein 1984), occurring in soil, dust, and water. When present in frogs and other vertebrate species, the mycobacteria cause opportunistic infections (Darzins 1952; Runyon et al. 1974; Smith 1972). They undergo optimum growth at temperatures below the body temperatures of birds and mammals, so amphibians are the preferred hosts (Brownstein 1984). Although mycobacterial diseases are recognized most often in captive exhibit and lab animals, they occur in stressed and debilitated wild animals as well.

Mycobacteriosis typically causes chronic illness in amphibians. The hallmark of the disease is granulomatous inflammation with tubercle (a well-circumscribed, spheroidal, and firm lesion) formation (Brownstein 1984; Marcus 1981; Temple and Fowler 1984). In toads (*Bufo* sp.), the lesions appear tumorlike, while in frogs they generally appear more ulcerated (Shively et al. 1981; Machicao and Laplaca 1954).

Most frequently, mycobacteriosis in amphibians is of alimentary origin, with hepatosplenic involvement, as well as clinical signs including chronic anorexia and cachexia (wasting). The liver contains superficial and deep tubercles that appear as multiple, discrete, cream-to-yellow-colored nodules up to 1 centimeter in diameter. The spleen is enlarged and contains lesions similar to those in the liver. Tubercles often are grossly evident on the serosal surface of the intestine and in the mesentery. Brownstein (1984) states that the kidneys, gonads, fat bodies, heart, and mediastinum rarely are affected, while others indicate that the liver, spleen, testes, and kidneys commonly are involved (Temple and Fowler 1984; Reichenbach-Klinke and Elkan 1965). Transmission may be through skin trauma or mucosal lesions in the alimentary tract (Temple and Fowler 1984).

Primary chronic cutaneous mycobacteriosis occurs frequently in anurans. It begins as well-circumscribed dermal indurations (the process of becoming firm or hard), which expand in a manner similar to that of fungal lesions. Infrequently, these lesions become disseminated over the body surface and lead to early death due to loss of cutaneous osmoregulation (Brownstein 1984).

Diagnosis of mycobacteriosis is based, in part, on histopathologic identification of the tubercles with a homogeneous caseous (coagulated necrotic) center that rarely calcifies. In addition, the organism may be cultured on tubed or bottled egg media, such as Lowenstein-Jensen media. A series of cultures of the organism should be sealed and incubated at 24°, 32°, 37°, and 45°C. The mycobacteria may appear as early as one week and as late as six weeks after inoculation (Brownstein 1984).

Fungi

Chromomycosis

Chromomycosis, a fungal disease characterized by ulcerative or granulomatous skin lesions and/or disseminated granulomas on internal organs (Miller et al. 1992; Schmidt 1984), was first reported in 1910 in South American bullfrogs (*Leptodactylus pentadactylus*; Carini 1910). The causative organisms are a group of naturally pigmented, saprophytic fungi that are distributed worldwide, with a greater frequency in tropical or subtropical areas (Emmons et al. 1970). Presenting signs often include papular and ulcerative skin lesions on the ventral surface of the animal. Despite these lesions, the animals initially remain alert and active, with normal appetites (Rush et al. 1974). Internally, the fungi primarily affect the liver, kidneys, and lungs, which appear enlarged and often contain firm gray-black to sometimes yellow-white nodules (Anver 1980; Schmidt and Hartfiel 1977; Rush et al. 1974). Wasting, debilitation, lethargy, and anorexia progress for four to eleven months, often followed by death. Transmission of these fungi most likely occurs via environmental contact, rather than from contact between infected and noninfected frogs (Anver 1980). Toads tend to be more resistant and become infected only if severely debilitated.

Chromomycosis can be diagnosed by histopathologic examination of granulomatous lesions. The organisms are characterized by either brown septate hyphae (branching, tubular cells) or a brown tissue-phase consisting of one to four cells.

Fungi isolated from lesions consistent with chromomycosis include *Fonsecaea* (*Hormiodendrum*) *pedrosoi*, *Hormiscium* (*Fonsecaea*) *dermatitidis*, and *Phialophora* spp. *Cladosporium trichoides* also has been isolated from similar lesions. In addition to the signs characteristic of chromomycosis, *C. trichoides* also may cause central nervous system dysfunction (Anver 1980).

Saprolegniasis

Saprolegniasis is a disease of aquatic amphibians caused by any of a wide range of water-borne fungal organisms. As with most amphibian diseases, the presence of this disease often is secondary to other stressors, such as concurrent bacterial infections or trauma (Crawshaw 1992). It commonly affects toads, fish, turtles, and salamanders and is a frequently encountered problem in the mudpuppy (*Necturus maculosus*; Bragg and Bragg 1958; Conti and Crawley 1939; Tiffney 1939). Gross lesions appear as opaque, cottony growths on the skin and/or gills. The best method of diagnosing this disease is either isolating the organisms from these lesions or demonstrating them in wet mounts. Demonstrating their presence in histologic lesions often is difficult, because the fungi tend to form superficial infections and usually become detached during processing (Nichols 1989).

Phycomycosis

Phycomycosis is caused by saprophytic organisms in the family Zygomycetes, which includes members of the *Absidia*, *Mucor*, *Rhizopus*, and *Basidiobolus* genera. Grossly, lesions resemble those seen with chromomycosis. Histologically, however, the granulomatous lesions contain nonpigmented fungal hyphae. Diagnosis is based on histologic lesions and culture of the organism (Crawshaw 1992).

Parasites

Amphibians, especially if they are wild-caught, are usually hosts for many metazoan and protozoan parasites. Rarely do these parasites cause clinical diseases. However, if the host becomes compromised to such a degree that the natural balance between host and parasite is disturbed, the parasite may become much more abundant and problems may occur, such as damage to, or obstruction of, the particular organ system.

Nematodes

Rhabdias spp., a group of lungworms, infect the respiratory tracts of Ranidae and Bufonidae (Baker 1978). Adults lay their eggs in the lungs, where they are coughed up into the oral cavity and then swallowed. Development continues in the gastrointestinal tract, and embryonated eggs or larvae are passed in the feces. Either infective larvae or free-living male and female lungworms develop. The free-living organisms mate and produce infective larvae. These are swallowed or penetrate the skin to gain access to a definitive host, and they then migrate to the lungs (Brannian 1984). In some animals, they may be found in the coelomic cavity. *Rhabdias* generally is pathogenic only when infections are so heavy that they impair growth (Goater and Ward 1992) or respiration (Crawshaw 1992). Antemortem diagnosis is established when embryonated eggs and/or larvae are found in the respiratory tract. Eggs and larvae also may be seen in the feces of infected animals (Brannian 1984).

Cutaneous infection by *Pseudocapillaroides xenopi* (also known as *Capillaria xenopodis*) is a common problem in captive colonies of African clawed frogs (Cromeens et al. 1987). Grossly, affected frogs have thickened skin with excessive cutaneous mucus secretion. Death may result from loss of the skin's ability to maintain osmotic regulation and/or a secondary bacterial infection. The life cycle of these parasites is assumed to be direct. Diagnosis may be made by finding the worms or their eggs (which have a bioperculate morphology typical of capillarid ova) in skin scrapings. Histologic lesions consist of epidermal thickening and hyperkeratosis with mild to moderate inflammation of the underlying dermis associated with the presence of worms and eggs in the epidermis.

Cestodes

Cestodes located in the intestines may cause gastrointestinal obstructions, while larval forms encysted in muscle and internal organs are usually of little or no significance to the health of the amphibian intermediate host (Crawshaw 1992).

Trematodes

Gyrodactylus spp. are members of a group of trematodes that commonly affect fish, tadpoles, and adult frogs in North America and Europe (Cameron 1956; Hoffman and Putz 1964). The adult parasites are tiny, with a bilobed anterior tip without eye spots or oral suckers (Hoffman 1967; Noble and Noble 1961). The haptor, or posterior attachment point, is outlined by sixteen small hooks, each of which can move independently. These parasites attach to the gills, skin, and fins of tadpoles and to the skin of adults. They ingest blood from superficial capillaries (Cameron 1956; Cheng 1964), and affected areas become covered with a layer of mucus. Large numbers on the gills may lead to death by asphyxiation. Diagnosis is based on demonstration of the organisms in the affected areas (Flynn 1973).

Digenetic trematodes of the Echinostomatidae are widespread parasites of avian and mammalian definitive hosts. Some species utilize amphibians as intermediate hosts, and encysted forms may cause minimal to severe kidney infections in tadpoles and amphibians. Severe infections may be associated with substantial loss of renal tissue (Martin and Conn 1990; Greenwell et al. 1996). Diagnosis is based on histopathologic identification of the encysted trematodes.

Protozoa

Most gastrointestinal and blood parasites are considered nonpathogenic for most species of terrestrial amphibians, but some of these parasites have the capacity to cause disease in salamanders. For instance, *Hexamita* and *Opalina* are associated with gastroenteritis in axolotls but are generally considered nonpathogenic in other amphibians (Crawshaw 1992). The protozoan *Charchesium polysinum* may grow on the skin of tadpoles, and if the gills become heavily infected, death may result (Pollack 1971).

Hemoflagellates, such as trypanosomes, are transmitted to amphibians by invertebrate intermediate hosts and vectors, such as leeches (Marcus 1981). It is thought that tadpoles and salamander larvae are infected by leeches, while adults are infected by mosquitos (Walton 1964). Infected animals develop degenerated erythrocytes, become debilitated and anorexic, and subsequently die. The degree of parasitemia and severity of lesions are related to environmental temperature, with the greatest hazard at 15°C and with a much lower hazard at between 20° and 25°C (Barrow 1958; Nigrelli 1929). The parasites can be visualized easily by mixing a small amount of blood with an equal amount of a citrate-saline solution (0.5 percent sodium citrate, 0.65 percent sodium chloride). Trypanosomes can be recognized easily because of their shape and their rapid, wavy motion (Flynn 1973).

A die-off of captive European toads (*Bufo bufo*) in Great Britain was attributed to infection with the microsporidian *Plistophora myotropica* (Marcus 1981). Affected toads became weak and lost body condition over a period of weeks until death occurred. Grossly, there was pale white streaking of most muscle fibers, which histologically was shown to be caused by the presence of numerous protozoa. The mode of parasite transmission was not determined.

Myxosporidial infections have been reported as incidental findings in the gonads of several species of wild-caught anurans (Reichenbach-Klinke and Elkan 1965). In histologic sections, these protozoa are oval and have polar nuclei.

Conclusions

Outbreaks of infectious diseases of amphibians can sometimes serve as important indicators of stress and environmental mismanagement. As with other species, preservation of suitable habitat and maintenance of a diverse gene pool are of critical importance in limiting the ultimate impact of a range of infectious agents. Additional research is warranted to establish the inherent virulence of infectious agents, as well as the contributions of infective dose and a range of stress factors, in the occurrence of infectious diseases in natural amphibian populations. Improving our understanding of the important risk factors that lead to serious diseases in amphibian populations during and after ecological restoration efforts is an area that will require future study.

Summary

Infectious diseases of amphibians can be important indicators of stress and environmental mismanagement. This chapter reviews the important infectious diseases of amphibians that have been documented both in captivity and in the wild. Diagnostic techniques are first reviewed, followed by a consideration of the viruses, bacteria, fungi, and parasites that are known to affect amphibians. Additional research is warranted to establish the inherent virulence of infectious agents, as well as the role of various stress factors in the occurrence of significant outbreaks of diseases that threaten natural amphibian populations.

27

Amphibian Toxicology

Stephen G. Diana and Val R. Beasley

There can be little doubt that chemical contamination of habitats has played a significant role in amphibian population declines and extinctions on local levels. It would hardly be surprising, for example, if amphibian species that rely on a stream habitat experienced a substantial reduction in population as a consequence of heavy metal contamination from a nearby, improperly managed mineral mine. The role of chemical contamination in declines of amphibian populations on a regional or global scale, however, is far more elusive. Clearly, anthropogenic compounds are present in sites where amphibian population declines are occurring. There is nowhere on the earth, whether in the Arctic, in the Tropics, high in the mountains, or in midocean, where agricultural and industrial chemicals are not detectable. However, definitive links, if any, between pervasive chemical contamination and global amphibian population declines remain to be established.

Toxicants may affect individual animals or populations either directly or indirectly. Direct toxicity relates to the effects of a toxicant on an experimental animal in isolation. Most of the toxicological literature involving amphibians, or any other animal group for that matter, describes direct toxicity, usually with regard to acute lethality. This is not surprising considering that most toxicological research is done in laboratories where experimental conditions can be carefully controlled, replication is relatively easily accomplished, and mortality is the easiest, most incontrovertible endpoint measureable.

Acute, lethal effects of chemicals are commonly reported in terms of LC_{50} and/or LD_{50} values. An aquatic LC_{50} is the concentration of a chemical estimated to be lethal to 50 percent of the animals held in it for a specified period of time. Similarly, an LD_{50} is the dose of a chemical, administered by a specified route, estimated to be lethal to 50 percent of the animals to which it is administered. Detailed lists of acute toxicity values have been compiled by Harfenist et al. (1989) and Devillers and Exbrayat (1992) and will not be reproduced here.

The relevance of information on the lethal effects of chemicals, however, tends to be marginal at best, because acutely lethal concentrations of contaminants are relatively infrequently encountered by vertebrates in the field. Nevertheless, direct lethal toxicity may occur, especially in restricted areas, such as land directly treated with pesticides and sites of inadvertent chemical spills, or when animals (e.g., fish) have been intentionally poisoned. Far more important from an ecological point of view are a toxicant's direct sublethal or chronic effects, such as reproductive impairment, immune suppression, growth inhibition, endocrine abnormalities, and behavioral changes.

Indirect toxicity describes the adverse effects of a toxicant on an animal or population via its impacts on other living organisms in the shared environment. This may be accomplished by damaging a population's food base, removing vegetation that serves as cover, decreasing a population that serves as an alternative food base for a common predator, or other mechanisms. Given the complexity of most ecosystems and the wide variety of biotic components, each with its own toxicant sensitivity, it is likely that most compounds that adversely affect amphibians in their communities do so, at least in part, indirectly.

Relatively few studies describe the indirect effects of toxicants on aquatic organisms, and only a small fraction involve amphibians. Studies for toxicity testing at this level of ecologic organization are far more complex than simple laboratory studies of direct toxicity. They require at least a microcosm level of complexity and commonly involve treatments of mesocosms or entire ponds. Nevertheless, the value of such studies in understanding toxicants in the field cannot be overstated.

Effects of Individual Toxicants

The majority of amphibian toxicology studies involve addition of a compound to the water in which the animals are held. In the reports listed below, if not otherwise stated, the toxicant concentrations given pertain to amounts added to (and/or present in) the water.

Organic Industrial Chemicals

Polychlorinated Biphenyls. Polychlorinated biphenyls (PCBs) were produced as coolant and dielectric fluids for use in electrical capacitors from the 1930s to the 1970s. They also were used in paints, carbon paper, mimeograph ink, and a range of other products. Although they are no longer being produced, their environmental persistence and volatility have caused them to become globally distributed toxicants of current concern. Their effects on wildlife are typically associated with chronic toxicity, attributable in large measure to their tendency to bioaccumulate. At present, particularly active areas of research pertaining to PCBs include their interference with endocrine function, reproduction, and neurologic development. Although many studies have focused on concerns for the health of humans, birds, fish, and other vertebrates, only a few reports have described the effects of PCBs on amphibians.

The acute lethal toxicity of PCBs to American toad (*Bufo americanus americanus*) and Fowler's toad (*Bufo woodhousii fowleri*) embryos was investigated by Birge and Cassidy (1983). In American toads, ninety-six-hour LC_{50}s were 0.007, 0.002, and 0.002 milligram/liter for Aroclors (PCB mixtures) 1016, 1242, and 1254, respectively, while corresponding values in Fowler's toads were 0.02, 0.01, and 0.003 milligram/liter, respectively. The last two digits of the Aroclor designations pertain to the chlorine content (as a percentage), and, in general terms, the more highly chlorinated PCB mixtures, such as 1254, tend to be more persistent in the environment than the lower chlorinated PCBs, such as 1016.

One of the earliest studies of PCBs involving amphibians addressed the metabolism of Aroclor 1254 and 4,4'-dichlorobiphenyl by northern leopard frogs (*Rana pipiens*; Safe et al. 1976). The animals were dosed by intraperitoneal injection, and their water was collected at four and eight days for analysis. Metabolites included the hydroxylated derivatives $C_{12}H_9ClO$, $C_{12}H_8Cl_2O$, and $C_{12}H_7Cl_3O$ for Aroclor 1254, as well as 4,4'-dichloro-3-biphenylol for 4,4'-dichlorobiphenyl. The toxicity of metabolites of PCBs is currently an area of active research, and some hydroxylated products have antithyroid and estrogenic potential (Hansen 1994).

Benzene. Benzene is a volatile hydrocarbon and an important component of fossil fuels, including gasoline. It is also used as an industrial solvent, although less commonly than in the past because of concerns regarding its toxicity to hematopoietic organs and its carcinogenic potential. Pulsatile exposure of crested newt (*Triturus cristatus*) adults to benzene at 250 milligrams/liter in air over a period of forty-three days caused leukocytosis and macrocytic anemia (Garavini and Seren 1978). Forty-eight-hour LC_{50} values for benzene in adult axolotls (*Ambystoma mexicanum*) and African clawed frogs (*Xenopus laevis*) were reported at 370 and 190 milligrams/liter, respectively (Slooff and Baerselman 1980; Slooff et al. 1983). In embryos of leopard frogs exposed to benzene at fertilization, the ninety-six-hour LC_{50} was 3.66 milligrams/liter (Birge and Cassidy 1983).

Phenol. Concentrated phenol is used as a disinfectant, and phenol and related compounds are important constituents of coal tar. Gorge et al. (1987) investigated the distribution and metabolism of radiolabeled phenol, injected at a dose of 3 to 5 milligrams/kilogram, in the European common frog (*Rana temporaria*). Radiolabel accumulated in the kidney reached a maximum at two hours and in the gallbladder reached a maximum at fifteen hours. The major metabolites identified were, in decreasing order, phenol, phenylglucuronide, quinolsulfate, and phenylsulfate. A similar profile of metabolites was observed in African clawed frogs, except that no phenylglucuronide was detected.

Crankcase Oil. Used crankcase oil, at concentrations found in urban runoff, may inhibit amphibian growth. When green treefrog (*Hyla cinerea*) eggs and larvae were incubated in water spiked with crankcase oil at 0, 10, 55, or 100 milligrams/liter, hatching success was not affected. However, growth rates in artificial ponds varied inversely with concentrations of this oil, and none of the larvae at the highest treatment level metamorphosed (Mahaney 1994). At least part of this effect may have been indirect, due to the observed inhibition by the oil of algal growth in the high-dose ponds.

Metals

Mercury. Mercury enters the environment as a consequence of its release through coal burning and its use in gold mining, paints, fungicides, batteries, thermometers, dental amalgams, and a range of other applications. Metallic mercury (Hg^0) is volatile and capable of transport in the atmosphere to areas far removed from its source. In anaerobic layers of aquatic sediments, metallic mercury is readily methylated by microorganisms, to form methyl- or dimethylmercury. These compounds are fat soluble and can bioaccumulate in aquatic organisms and in the terrestrial organisms that feed on them. Methylmercury tends to be a significant hazard to aquatic animals due to its tendency to bioaccumulate in food webs and its affinity for the central nervous system, including that of the developing young. By contrast, most inorganic forms of mercury tend to target the kidney, which serves as the major excretory pathway for the metal.

Although mercury toxicosis has been explored to a significant degree in several warm-blooded species and in fish, only a limited number of studies have involved amphibians. When eggs of African clawed frogs were exposed to methylmercury at concentrations as high as 0.1 milligram/liter, there was a dose-dependent failure to hatch. Although 23 percent of the control eggs successfuly hatched, only 8 percent hatched in the presence of methylmercury at 0.1 milligram/liter (Dumpert and Zietz 1984). When eggs of leopard frogs were exposed to low concentrations (up to 0.03 milligram/liter) of methylmercury for three days, an increased incidence of developmental abnormalities was noted beginning at concentrations of 0.005 to 0.010 milligram/liter (Dial 1976).

Whole body concentrations of mercury ranging from 3.09 to 16.06 milligrams/kilogram were identified in juvenile Blanchard's cricket frogs (*Acris crepitans blanchardi*) inhabiting Illinois ponds. In these ponds, mercury was present in water and sediment only at nondetectable concentrations (detection limits were 0.01 and 0.1 milligram/liter for water and sediment, respectively; V. Beasley, unpublished data). Although the residue concentrations were not correlated with population densities or summer reproductive success, they may still be toxicologically significant. In any case, these findings suggest bioaccumulation, implying that the mercury was most likely in the methylated or dimethylated form.

Punzo (1993a) examined the effects of dissolved mercuric chloride on ovaries and reproductive tracts of adult female river frogs (*Rana heckscheri*). Exposure to mercuric chloride at 0.88 milligram/liter for thirty and sixty days resulted in weight loss, degeneration of ovarian follicles, and decreases in the mass of both ovaries and oviducts. $Mercury^{2+}$, at 0.8 milligram/liter, has also been reported to interfere with development of primordial germ cells in the Asian *Rana nigromaculata* (Hah 1978).

Fertilization of river frog ova in vitro was partially blocked in the presence of mercuric chloride at 1.0 or 2.5 milligrams/liter and completely prevented at 5 milligrams/liter. Larvae allowed to develop for two to three weeks in water containing mercuric chloride at more than 1 milligram/liter were more likely than controls to have developmental abnormalities, such as a lateral kink at the base of the tail and an upward curvature of the tail. LC_{50} values for fertilized eggs (at three hours) and stage twenty seven larvae (at ninety-six hours) were 1.43 and 0.68 milligrams/liter, respectively (Punzo 1993b).

Cadmium. Cadmium is an environmental contaminant that arises from zinc mining and a range of industries, including production of alloys, paints, and batteries. Sewage sludge from communities with industries that use cadmium can be a major source of cadmium in the environment.

Exposure of larval leopard frogs and bullfrogs (*Rana catesbeiana*) to cadmium, at 0.4 and 0.8 milligram/liter for six weeks, was shown to increase B lymphocyte numbers in the liver and mesonephros and to increase serum hemaglutinating antibody titers. Cadmium was concentrated selectively in larval livers and, to a lesser degree, in the mesonephros (Zettergren et al. 1991). A stage-dependent sensitivity to acute (twenty-four hour) cadmium-induced lethality was observed in embryos of the South American toad *Bufo arenarum* (Herkovits and Perez Coll 1993). The stage most sensitive to cadmium was the neural tube stage, in which 100 percent mortality occurred at 0.25 milligram/liter. Least sensitive were embryos of only two blastomeres, followed by late gastrulae, which exhibited 100 percent mortality in the presence of cadmium at 4 and 2 milligrams/liter, respectively.

Lead. Lead contamination of the environment arises through mining, discarding and reckless procedures used in recycling storage batteries, burning of leaded gasoline, and the use of lead-based paints, lead shot, lead sinkers, and other lead-containing materials. Considerable amounts of lead may be found at the edges of roads due to previous burning of gasoline formulated with tetraethyl lead. The weight of this material tends to keep it from moving far from the roadside.

Exposure of fertilized eggs of *Rana nigromaculata* to lead at 70 milligrams/liter was shown to reduce the number of germ cells in the resulting larvae (Hah 1978). Lesions seen in bullfrog larvae following exposure to lead acetate or lead nitrate at 25 milligrams/liter in water included hemolysis as well as necrosis of the liver, spleen, and intestinal mucosa (Barrett 1947).

Hydrogen Ions (Acidification) and Aluminum. Acidification of the environment occurs largely from atmospheric fallout of the products of fossil fuel combustion. Among the more important effects of acidification of the aquatic environment on amphibians is reduced hatching of eggs and reduced rates of growth, setting the stage for increased losses due to predation. Based on a study on the effects of acidification on amphibian development, Gosner and Black (1957) determined that pH values at which 50 percent of embryos of a number of amphibian species were unable to hatch and develop ranged from 4.7 to 3.8. Among the species tested, cricket frogs were most sensitive to acidity, while wood frogs (*Rana sylvatica*) and carpenter frogs (*Rana virgatipes*) were least sensitive.

Similarly, Brodman (1993) raised eggs and larvae of Jefferson salamanders (*Ambystoma jeffersonianum*) and spotted salamanders (*Ambystoma maculatum*) in water acidified with sulfuric acid to pH 4.3, 5.3, 6.3, or 7.0; at pH 4.3, none of the eggs hatched. For Jefferson salamanders, hatching success was uniformly high at pH values above 4.3, whereas with spotted salamanders hatching rates improved with increasing pH. Larvae of both species were more sluggish at pH 5.3 than at pH 7.0, but this effect was more pronounced in spotted salamanders. The growth rate of spotted salamanders was lower at pH 5.3 than at pH 7.0, while that of Jefferson salamanders was not significantly affected by pH. Considering this combination of species-specific effects of pH on activity and growth rate, it was not surprising that, when the two species were raised together, predation on spotted salamanders by Jefferson salamanders was higher at pH 5.3 than at pH 7.0. A similar increase in predation on spotted salamanders by the predaceous diving beetle (*Dytiscus verticalis*) was noted at pHs below 4.8 (Kutka 1994).

By contrast, Rowe et al. (1992) found a greater sensitivity of Jefferson salamanders than spotted salamanders to a low pH. After seven days of exposure, mortality in Jefferson salamanders was greater at pH 4.2 than at pH 4.7 to 5.35. Similarly, after four months of exposure, mortality was greater at pH 4.2 than at pHs above 6.0. The mortality of spotted salamanders and wood frogs was unaffected by pH values within this range. Time required to complete metamorphosis was increased in wood frogs by the four-month exposure to pH 4.2. Effects of interspecific predation were not examined in this study.

Horne and Dunson (1994) reported a preference of metamorphic Jefferson salamanders for artificial terrestrial substrates at higher pH values within the range of 3.5 to 5.0. Furthermore, the natural ponds in Pennsylvania in which this species failed to breed were those with adjacent soil pH values below 3.7.

One complication that amphibians experience as a consequence of living in acidic water is an increased loss of body sodium (Freda and Dunson 1984). Frisbie and Wyman (1992a) observed that adults and efts of eastern newts (*Notophthalmus viridescens*) lost sodium when held in water at pH 3.0 but not at pH 5.0.

A major concern regarding acidification of the environment is the increase in hazards related to aluminum. Aluminum is among the most abundant mineral constituents of natural soils. Although the aluminum concentration of surface waters can be increased by input of the metal, in general the greatest increase in the bioavailability and toxicity of aluminum seems to be related to environmental acidification. Lower water pH, brought about by acid precipitation, can alter the speciation of aluminum, thereby increasing its toxicity (Clark and LaZerte 1985). Especially important is the tendency for acidification to increase the formation of inorganic monomeric aluminum, an extremely toxic form of the metal. For example, Beattie et al. (1992) found that survival rates of *Rana temporaria* embryos were decreased by increasing the concentrations of aluminum and decreasing the pH. Exposures were done during the period of time between the two to four cell and the gill circulation stages. Survival approached 0 percent at aluminum concentrations of 200 to 400 micrograms/liter at pH 4.5. At pH 6, 19 percent of the dissolved aluminum was in the inorganic monomeric form, while at pH 4.5, 88 percent was in this form (Beattie et al. 1992).

In addition to causing direct toxicity and associated mortality, aluminum has been reported to increase susceptibility of anuran larvae to predation. Jung and Jagoe

(1995) reported increased mortality in larval green frogs (*Rana clamitans melanota*) exposed for ninety hours to aluminum at 250 and 400 micrograms/liter at pH 4.5 but not at pH 5.5 and not to aluminum at 150 micrograms/liter at either pH. Tadpole length declined with increasing aluminum concentration at both pHs but more markedly at pH 4.5. Maximum swimming speed of the tadpoles decreased with increasing aluminum concentrations at pH 4.5. Larvae exposed to aluminum at 150 micrograms/liter at pH 4.5 were more heavily preyed upon by larval dragonflies than were those held in aluminum-free water at pH 4.5 or 7.0.

Agricultural Chemicals

The density of farmland in the Midwest results in an enormous intentional release of agricultural chemicals into the environment. Amphibians in this region often live in proximity to and/or in waters draining agricultural lands. The investigation of the ecotoxicologic effects of agricultural chemicals, with emphasis on amphibian populations, should be considered a priority.

Nitrate Fertilizers. The exposure of larval European toad (*Bufo bufo*) and the Australian *Litoria caerulea* to sodium nitrate in distilled water at nitrate ion concentrations of 40 and 100 milligrams/liter significantly increased mortality and decreased the growth rate as compared to exposure to distilled water alone (Baker and Waights 1993, 1994). In the case of *L. caerulea*, metamorphic delay also was noted. By contrast, control treatments involving culture in sodium chloride solutions with concentrations of sodium identical to those of the fertilizers did not negatively impact the larvae (Baker and Waights 1994). When this study was repeated, however, using reconstituted pond water as the culture medium, rather than distilled water, the adverse effects of the nitrate were greatly diminished (J. Baker, personal communication).

When American toad, chorus frog (*Pseudacris triseriata*), leopard frog, and green frog larvae were evaluated, ninety-six-hour LC_{50} values for ammonium nitrate ranged from 13.6 to 39.3 milligrams/liter NO_3-N (which corresponds to nitrate ion concentrations of 60.2 to 174 milligrams/liter) in charcoal-filtered tap water (Hecnar 1995). Clinical signs in the ammonium nitrate–treated animals included weight loss, reduced activity, poor response to prodding, and developmental abnormalities. Significant mortality was associated with exposure of chorus frogs and leopard frogs to ammonium nitrate at an NO_3-N concentration of 10 milligrams/liter (corresponding to a nitrate ion concentration of 44.3 milligrams/liter) for 100 days. Fewer chorus frogs metamorphosed in this treatment group, and at a greater body weight, than in controls.

The possible contribution of nitrate enrichment of water bodies to amphibian population declines in the intensively agricultural midwestern United States has become a topic of considerable concern. The average NO_3-N concentrations in Illinois surface waters from 1973 to 1991 were 3.7 milligrams/liter for streams, with some values as high as 88 milligrams/liter, and 1.06 milligrams/liter for lakes, with some values as high as 39 milligrams/liter (Ramamurthy 1994). A concentration of 1 milligram/liter NO_3-N corresponds to approximately 4.4 milligrams/liter of nitrate ion. Thus, if the laboratory experiments on nitrate toxicity described above are truly representative of the responses of animals in the field, nitrate enrichment of Illinois waters may be exerting significant adverse effects on local amphibian populations through contamination of both otherwise suitable habitat and migration corridors.

Herbicides

Triazine Herbicides and Trichlopyr. Triazine herbicides, such as atrazine and simazine, are used widely in corn production. They exert their phytotoxic effects by inhibiting photosynthesis. Compared to a range of insecticidal compounds, the triazines are of comparatively low acute toxicity. Atrazine, for example, has been shown to be lethal to bullfrog larvae only at concentrations approaching 200 milligrams/liter (Boschulte 1995). Although atrazine is commonly applied to agricultural fields as a solution or suspension of approximately 6,000 milligrams/liter, concentrations found in lakes and rivers are generally in the low microgram per liter range, with occasional reports of low milligram per liter concentrations in waters directly adjacent to treated fields (DeNoyelles et al. 1982; Wauchope 1978). It is unlikely, therefore, that atrazine concentrations capable of causing direct lethality would be encountered commonly by amphibians in the field.

In contrast, the potential for indirect effects of atrazine on amphibian populations is considerable, although only a limited amount of research has focused on this possibility. In experimental pond mesocosms, DeNoyelles et al. (1989) found that atrazine, at concentrations as low as 20 micrograms/liter, the lowest concentration tested, caused a significant reduction in biomass of volunteer bullfrog tadpoles when grass carp (*Ctenopharyngodon idella*) were included in the aquatic community. This effect was considered to be indirect, likely due to loss of aquatic macrophytes (via combined effects of the herbicide and grass carp) that provide refuge from predators and substrates for periphyton growth.

Berrill et al. (1993) examined the direct effects of two herbicides: triclopyr, a picolinic acid derivative, and hexazinone, a triazine. These compounds are commonly used in management of coniferous forests for timber harvest and to control woody plants near roads and railroads. Effects were examined in embryos and tadpoles of leopard frogs, green frogs, and bullfrogs. Exposure of neurula-stage embryos to each compound individually at concentrations up to 8 milligrams/liter and 4.8 milligrams/liter, respectively, resulted in no decrease in hatchability or delay in development. By contrast, newly hatched tadpoles of each species failed to respond to prodding following a forty-eight-hour exposure to triclopyr at 1.2 milligrams/liter. Triclopyr at 2.4 milligrams/liter or greater caused 100 percent mortality of green frog and bullfrog tadpoles. Among leopard frog tadpoles, mortality was low at these concentrations, although response to prodding was absent. Exposure to hexazinone at 100 milligrams/liter for nine days caused no mortality in any of the tested species, although response to prodding was diminished in bullfrogs.

Phenoxy Herbicides. The chlorinated phenoxy herbicides have been used not only in agriculture, including for rice paddies, and lawn care, but also for control of aquatic weeds, including water hyacinth, water milfoil, common coontail, arrowhead, bulrush, cattail, and water lily. The phenoxy compounds often are used in combination with one another or with other herbicidal agents. At sufficient doses, the phenoxy herbicides cause muscle membrane instability in mammals (and presumably other species), resulting in myotonia with potential stiffness and, eventually, profound weakness (Beasley et al. 1991). The most widely used of the phenoxy herbicides is 2,4-dichlorophenoxyacetic acid (2,4-D). Recommended aquatic application rates of 2,4-D have ranged from 1 to 2 milligrams/liter (Hiltibran and Anderson 1990). Exposure of *Rana temporaria* tadpoles to 2,4-D at a concentration of 1 to 2 milligrams/liter has been shown to delay metamorphosis (Buslovich and Borushko 1976).

Dipyridyl Herbicides. Paraquat and diquat are dipyridyl herbicides that, in mammals, exhibit different spectrums of organ system effects. The former tends to accumulate in lungs, resulting in pulmonary toxicity. The latter is somewhat less hazardous but at toxic doses has caused cerebral hemorrhage, lethargy, coma, and kidney damage. Paraquat is used in agriculture as a defoliant and general herbicide, while diquat is primarily used as an aquatic herbicide, applied at a final concentration of 0.5 to 1 milligram/liter (Hiltibran and Anderson 1990), and in sugarcane production. Both paraquat and diquat are inactivated when they come in contact with soil particles, and photodegradation is a major mechanism of environmental detoxification, at least for the former.

Paraquat bioaccumulates in aquatic plants. Dial and Dial (1995) reported final concentrations of paraquat of 1,011 milligrams/kilogram in the milfoil *Myriophyllum* exposed to water containing the herbicide at 1.81 milligram/liter for eight days and 72.6 milligrams/kilogram in *Elodea* exposed to the same concentration for eleven days. These plants were then dried, crushed, and fed ad libitum to twenty-one-day-old Rio Grande leopard frog (*Rana berlandieri*) larvae. Survival among tadpoles fed contaminated *Myriophyllum* was 19.4 percent at fifteen days, while in controls it was 81.1 percent. Abnormalities in tail development and swimming behavior and a decreased rate of growth also were noted in this group. No abnormalities were found among larvae fed contaminated *Elodea*. In a separate study involving northern leopard frog embryos, paraquat resulted in mortality rates of 24.5 percent, 30.9 percent, 94.5 percent, 100 percent, and 100 percent twelve days following the onset of exposure at 0, 0.1, 0.5, 2, and 10 milligrams/liter, respectively (Dial and Bauer 1984).

Exposure of leopard frog gastrulae to diquat at 5 and 10 milligrams/liter resulted in reduced survival at sixteen days (Dial and Dial 1987). In a field study involving diquat application to ponds, a concentration of 1 milligram/liter resulted in initial growth retardation of European toad larvae followed by a growth rebound such that toads from treated ponds were heavier than those from control ponds by thirty-two days posttreatment. It was assumed that the rebound was due to an algal bloom following treatment, in part because the intestines of the tadpoles from the diquat-treated ponds contained more ingesta on days eighteen and thirty-two than those from control ponds (Cooke 1977). Any disturbance that decreases macrophyte density, however, may increase the susceptibility of amphibian larvae to predation and may potentially decrease the acceptability of the area as a site for oviposition.

Glyphosate. Vehicles included in commercial herbicides may play a significant role in the toxicity of the final formulation. This was reflected in the observation that Roundup® (the formulated herbicide) was more toxic to the Australian *Crinia insignifera* and *Litoria moorei* than was technical glyphosate, the generic active ingredient. The ninety-six-hour LC_{50}s (as glyphosate equivalents) for adult *C. insignifera* were 78 and 39.7 milligrams/liter of active ingredient for technical glyphosate and Roundup 360®, while for larval *L. moorei* these values were 110.8 and 7.66 milligrams/liter, respectively (Bidwell and Gorrie 1995). It is possible that detergent components in the vehicle enhanced the toxicity of the glyphosate or, perhaps more likely, that the primary toxic effects of the vehicle simply superceded those of glyphosate.

Insecticides

Most studies of the potential impacts of insecticides on amphibians relate to direct toxicity measurements. Many insecticides formerly applied directly to water are no longer available for this use in the United States, including many of those discussed below. However, runoff from treated fields, lawns, and other areas may still be a problem. Among the most recently developed insecticides, and among those of current importance in application to water for mosquito control, are the insect hormone mimics. Such compounds tend to be of extremely low toxicity to vertebrates. Accordingly, few if any discernable direct toxic effects would be expected in amphibians; however, indirect effects via toxicity in arthropods may pose a much greater concern. Indeed, for insecticides of many different chemical families (old and new), the potential for direct toxicity to organisms that form the food base of amphibians, especially insects, undoubtedly deserves greater study.

Pyrethroids. Pyrethroid insecticides are rapidly becoming more widely used on animals, in homes, and in the outdoors, including for agriculture. These synthesized compounds exert toxic effects similar to those of the natural pyrethrins, which are insecticides produced by certain exotic chrysanthemums. Pyrethrins degrade so rapidly in the environment that their uses in outdoor insect control are minimal. As compared to the pyrethrins, however, the pyrethroids generally are more persistent in the environment. Pyrethrins and all pyrethroids act at sodium channels of neurons, resulting in partial depolarization, while pyrethroids with an α-cyano group also block gamma aminobutyric acid (GABA) channels, such that these compounds may cause more violent neurotoxic effects.

Signs of pyrethroid insecticide toxicosis in amphibians include behavioral and developmental abnormalities. Salibian (1992) studied the acute toxicity of deltamethrin in tadpoles of the South American toad (*Bufo arenarum*). Clinical signs of toxicosis included hyperactivity, spiral swimming, and hyper-responsiveness, followed by inactivity, lateral or dorsal recumbency, lateral curving of the body or tail, and death. Younger larvae (stages twenty-six to twenty-seven), which had a ninety-six-hour LC_{50} of 0.00044 milligram/liter, were more sensitive to the toxicant than were older larvae (stages twenty-eight to thirty). When exposed to esfenvalerate at as low as 0.00013 milligram/liter in well water or 0.00036 milligram/liter in water of pond enclosures, leopard frog larvae (species not reported) displayed decreased activity (Materna et al. 1995). Exposure of green frog larvae to permethrin at as low as 0.1 milligram/liter for ninety-six hours caused developmental abnormalities, reduced avoidance behavior, and transient suppression of growth (Berrill et al. 1993).

Cholinesterase-Inhibiting Insecticides. Carbamate and organophosphorus (OP) insecticides are widely employed to control insect pests in agriculture, in gardens, on animals, and in homes. All members of these insecticide groups are potent inhibitors of the enzyme acetylcholinesterase, which normally cleaves the neurotransmitter acetylcholine and thus is responsible for terminating a range of nervous system, neuromuscular, and neuroglandular impulses. The carbamates function by reversible inhibition of the enzyme, while the effect of the OPs is largely irreversible. In the presence of these inhibitors, the buildup of acetylcholine results in uncontrolled depolarization of cholinergic postsynaptic receptors in the brain and the periphery. In mammals and birds, this often leads to excitation or depression, hypersalivation, diarrhea, bradycardia, seizures, bronchoconstriction, increased bronchial secretion, respiratory paralysis, and death.

Carbamate Insecticides. Carbamates tend to break down in animals and in the environment, such that bioaccumulation is generally not a problem. Thus, the major effect of concern pertains to acute neurotoxicity. Some carbamates also have been shown to affect the developing young. In a study examining the acute and developmental toxicity of primicarb to Old World *Rana perezi* tadpoles, histologic findings included degeneration of gill epithelium covering the basal portion of branchial sheets, retardation of liver parenchymal compaction with a large number of lipid inclusions in hepatocytes, flattening of gallbladder epithelium, weakening of the auricular walls in the heart, and irregular development of the notocord (Honrubia et al. 1993). Abnormalities were seen with exposures via either water or food and at concentrations of 20 and 140 milligrams/liter via each route.

Carbaryl (Sevin®) is one of the most widely used carbamate insecticides. It is employed extensively in gardening and for control of pests on pets. *Rana temporaria* tadpoles exposed to carbaryl for twenty-four hours and ten days at 110 milligrams/liter, respectively, exhibited stunting and permanent tail abnormalities, causing difficulty in swimming, followed by significant mortality (approximately 90 percent) by the end of the ten-day exposure period (Rzehak et al. 1977).

Organophosphorus Insecticides. Hatching and developmental rates of embryonic and larval northern leopard frogs, green frogs, and bullfrogs were unaffected by exposure to fenitrothion at 0.5 to 8.0 milligrams/liter for twenty-four hours. However, northern leopard frogs and green frogs exhibited temporary paralysis at 4.0 and 8.0 milligrams/liter, respectively. Bullfrog larvae were more sensitive, exhibiting unresponsiveness to prodding with fenitrothion at 0.5 and 2 milligrams/liter, as well as paralysis, high mortality, and subsequent stunting in survivors at 4 and 8 milligrams/liter (Berrill et al. 1994). In contrast, no mortality was noted in larval bullfrogs at twenty-four hours following an application of fenitrothion to 20- to 30-centimeter-deep experimental ponds at rates of 0.2 and 0.9 kilogram/hectares (equivalent to an approximate concentration of 0.08 to 0.36 milligram/liter; Mulla et al. 1963).

Exposure of yolk plug-stage embryos of the Asiatic *Microhyla ornata* to fenitrothion for twenty-four, forty-eight, seventy-two, or ninety-six hours resulted in rates of developmental abnormalities of more than 60 percent at 3 milligrams/liter and 100 percent at 7 milligrams/liter (Pawar and Katdare 1983). Effects included growth retardation, behavioral abnormalities, and poor pigmentation, as well as head, trunk, and tail defects. There was an inverse relationship between fenitrothion concentrations in ambient water and hatching success in *M. ornata* (Pawar and Katdare 1984). Exposures of yolk plug-stage embryos for twenty-four hours resulted in decreased hatching rates at or above 3 milligrams per liter, with total failure to hatch at 13 milligrams/liter. Constant exposure of Indian *Rana tigerina* larvae to fenitrothion at 0.1 milligram/liter and 0.2 milligram/liter increased the time required to complete metamorphosis, and at 4 milligrams/liter there was a decrease in the percentage of larvae that successfully metamorphosed (Mohanty-Hejmadi and Dutta 1981).

Fenthion is an OP compound that has been used as a "pour-on" systemic insecticide for cattle and dogs and on perches as an avicide. Sometimes the avicidal products have resulted in relay toxicosis (i.e., poisoning of a scavenger that consumes the lethally affected target animal). Fenthion was shown to reduce the tolerance of larval Pacific treefrogs (*Hyla regilla*) and juvenile western toads (*Bufo boreas*) to high temperatures at concentrations as low as 25 micrograms/liter and 60 micrograms/liter, respectively (Johnson 1980; Johnson and Prine 1976). Larval bullfrogs exposed to fenthion at 5 milligrams/liter for ninety-six hours showed no mortality, but they accumulated enough of the insecticide to cause death in mallard ducklings that subsequently fed upon them (Hall and Kolbe 1980).

Parathion is among the OP insecticides that have been used most heavily in agriculture. No mortality occurred among larval western toads or western spadefoot toads (*Scaphiopus hammondii*) twenty-four hours following an application of parathion at rates of 0.1 or 0.4 kilogram/hectare to 20- to 30-centimeter-deep ponds (equivalent to approximate concentrations of 0.004 or 0.16 milligram/liter; Mulla et al. 1963). Leukopenia, anemia, inactivity, and poor avoidance responses were found in adult leopard frogs exposed to parathion at 5 to 25 milligrams/liter for fifteen days (Kaplan and Glaczenski 1965).

Like parathion, methyl parathion has been used heavily in agriculture. Many agricultural workers have been poisoned by methyl parathion. However, methyl parathion caused no mortality in western toads and eastern spadefoot toads following application to 20- to 30-centimeter-deep experimental ponds at 0.1 or 0.4 kilogram/hectare (equivalent to approximate concentrations of 0.04 or 0.16 milligram/liter; Mulla et al. 1963). Nevertheless, exposure of adult western toads to methyl parathion at 0.025 milligram/liter and of larval Pacific treefrogs at 0.025, 0.05, and 0.1 milligram/liter resulted in reduced thermal tolerance (Johnson and Prine 1976; Johnson 1980). Exposure of *Rana tigerina* to methyl parathion from the egg stage through metamorphosis increased the time required to complete metamorphosis (at 0.1 milligram/liter) and reduced the percentage of larvae that successfully metamorphosed (at 0.2 milligram/liter or greater). When exposure was delayed until after the larvae had begun feeding, the same effects were seen, although at methyl parathion concentrations of 0.1 milligram/liter or greater or 0.4 milligram/liter or greater, respectively (Mohanty-Hejmadi and Dutta 1981). Concentrations of methyl parathion of only 0.04 to 0.23 microgram/liter were found in streams, rivers, and lakes in a survey performed in the early 1970s (U.S. Department of Health and Human Services 1992). However, substantially higher concentrations are likely in waters immediately adjacent to sites at which this compound has been used.

Malathion is used widely in agriculture and gardening and, to a lesser degree, on animals and in household pest control. Although it is not approved for direct application to water, it is approved for control of adult mosquitos, which may result in some spray drift reaching water bodies. The percentage of *Rana tigerina* larvae that successfully metamorphosed was reduced, the time required to complete metamorphosis was increased, and the mean length at metamorphosis was reduced by malathion at concentrations of at least 3 milligrams/liter, 1 milligram/liter, and 7 milligrams/liter, respectively (Mohanty-Hejmadi and Dutta 1981). Also, exposure of leopard frog adults to malathion at 50 to 175 milligrams/liter caused a dose-dependent increase in mortality, anemia, and leukopenia characterized by neutropenia and lymphocytosis (Kaplan and Glaczenski 1965).

Chlorpyrifos is widely used in and around homes for flea and termite control, on lawns, and in agriculture, such as for control of corn rootworms. Chlorpyrifos at 0.0025 to 0.005 milligram/liter lowered the thermal tolerance of tadpoles or adults of Pacific treefrogs and western toads (Harfenist et al. 1989). The LD_{50} for chlorpyrifos to bullfrogs has been calculated to be greater than 400 milligrams/kilogram body weight. Despite the comparatively strong tendency of this compound (as compared to most other OP insecticides) to concentrate in living organisms, its limited solubility in water and its high binding affinity for soil particles probably limit hazards of direct toxicity to amphibians. When applied to soils at rates used in agriculture (i.e., 10 milligrams/kilogram of soil), chlorpyrifos degrades over a period of months to noninsecticidal metabolites, despite its binding to soil. However, when applied at rates used for termite control (i.e., 1,000 milligrams/kilogram of soil), it is far more persistent (Racke et al. 1993).

Organochlorine Insecticides. Organochlorine (OC) insecticides are, for the most part, environmentally persistent compounds that were used in agriculture and for domestic insect control until their withdrawal from the United States market in the 1970s and 1980s. Methoxychlor, which is the least persistent in animal tissues, is still in use in the United States, and several such compounds are still employed in insect control in many developing nations. The environmental persistence of most of the OCs, as well as their atmospheric transport from countries currently using these compounds, causes them to continue to be found not only in areas of previous use but also at sites with no previous history of intentional OC insecticide exposure.

Among the OC insecticides, the diphenylethane derivatives, such as dichlorodiphenyltrichloroethane (DDT), methoxychlor, and related compounds, are believed to exert their neurotoxic effects through partial opening of neuronal sodium channels and interference with the opening of potassium channels. In vertebrates, these mechanisms tend to result in tremors and, much less often, in seizures. By contrast, the cyclodiene OCs antagonize the inhibitory neurotransmitter, gamma aminobutyric acid, and therefore tend to cause profound seizures, at least in mammals and birds. Other OC insecticides include toxaphene (which is actually a mixture of compounds from chlorinated camphene), as well as the environmentally persistent lindane, mirex, and kepone. Several OC compounds exert not only acute neurotoxic effects but also hormonal agonist or antagonist effects.

Signs of acute toxicosis induced by DDT in amphibians typically include hyperactivity, uncoordination, and death (Cooke 1970; Harri et al. 1979). Direct sublethal effects may be particularly important because of alterations in interspecies interactions. For example, when crested newts were given a choice between tadpoles of *Rana temporaria* that were showing signs of acute DDT toxicosis and others with normal behavior, they selectively attacked the former (Cooke 1971).

When bullfrog larvae were held in 20- to 30-centimeter-deep ponds sprayed with DDT at 0.1 or 1 kilogram/hectare (equivalent to approximate concentrations of 0.04 or 0.4 milligram/liter, respectively), death occurred only at the highest dose, with 30 percent of the larvae dying within one day and 80 percent dying within two days (Mulla 1963). Nevertheless, aerial application of DDT for tent caterpillar control in Minnesota caused no observed mortality of wood frogs in contaminated areas when examined at two and thirty-three hours following application. Heavy mortality was observed, however, beginning at two and a half days after application; by ten to twelve days posttreatment, no live frogs were observed (Fashingbauer 1957).

DDT is no longer used legally in the United States. However, due to transport of DDT in the atmosphere and subsequent deposition, the parent compound and especially DDE, its persistent metabolite, are routinely identified in soil and biota, not only at sites of previous use but also in relatively pristine areas. Because of their propensity to bioaccumulate, DDT and DDE concentrations are typically much greater in biota than in water or soil and much greater in animals at higher trophic levels than in those at the base of the food web. Tissue DDT and DDE concentrations of 0.16 and 1 milligram/kilogram, respectively, were identified in 1993 in northern spring peepers (*Pseudacris crucifer crucifer*) inhabiting a Canadian park in which DDT use was discontinued in 1967 (Russell et al. 1995). Tissue *p,p'*-DDE concentrations of 5.8 milligrams/kilogram have been reported in alligator (*Alligator mississippiensis*) eggs collected from heavily contaminated Lake Apopka, Florida (Heinz et al. 1991). Among the reported effects of *p,p'*-DDE is competitive inhibition of androgen activity (Kelce et al. 1995). The anti-androgenic effects of *p,p'*-DDE have resulted in abnormalities in sexual differentiation in alligators inhabiting Lake Apopka (Guillette et al. 1994); however, the effects of this compound on androgen-mediated behaviors and sexual development in amphibians have not yet been evaluated.

Exposure of larval Australian *Limnodynastes tasmaniensis* to the cyclodiene OC insecticide dieldrin at 0.1 milligram/liter for seven days resulted in developmental abnormalities (21 out of 150) including pigmentary and otolith defects, but no significant mortality (Brooks 1981). Northern leopard frogs exposed to dieldrin at 0.05 to 0.1 milligram/liter for thirty days exhibited rigidity, tremors, and disorientation. Mortality occurred only in the 0.1 milligram/liter exposure group, in which 50 percent of the animals died (Kaplan and Overpeck 1964). Application of dieldrin at 0.1 kilogram/hectare to 20- to 30-centimeter-deep ponds (equivalent to an approximate concentration of 0.4 milligram/liter) resulted in 100 percent mortality in larval bullfrogs within twenty-four hours (Mulla 1963).

LC_{50}s for dieldrin have been reported at 0.0055 milligram/liter for African clawed frog tadpoles exposed for four days, 0.0083 milligram/liter for leopard frog tadpoles exposed for twenty-eight days, and 0.00534 milligram/liter for leopard frog adults exposed for twenty-eight days. Spinal malformities in larvae of African clawed frogs were present at as low as 0.0013 milligram/liter following a ten-day exposure and at as low as 0.0254 milligram/liter in leopard frogs following a twenty-one-day exposure (Schuytema et al. 1991).

Dieldrin is the epoxide of aldrin and is the major metabolite of aldrin in many species of animals. In addition, dieldrin is the major product of biological metabolism of aldrin following application of the latter to soil. Aldrin has been used in agriculture to control corn rootworms and for termite control. Application of aldrin to 20- to 30-centimeter-deep ponds at 0.1 kilogram/hectare (equivalent to an approximate concentration of 0.04 milligram/liter) caused 10 percent, 30 percent, and 30 percent mortality in bullfrog tadpoles held within the pond after one, two, and five days, respectively. At a rate of 0.5 kilogram/hectare, mortality rates were 80 percent and 100 percent at one and two days, respectively (Mulla 1963). Northern leopard frogs exposed to aldrin at up to 0.3 milligram/liter for thirty days developed dose-dependent decreases in white blood cell counts. Red blood cell counts also decreased in a dose-dependent manner, except for a slight increase at the lowest treatment concentration (0.15 milligram/liter). Rigidity, tremors, and disorientation were seen in all treatment groups. Mortality was 40 percent at 0.3 milligram/liter (Kaplan and Overpeck 1964).

Cricket frog adults exhibited reduced sensitivity to aldrin, following previous exposure to three OC insecticides (DDT, toxaphene, and endrin), as well as to the OP insecticide methyl parathion. Frogs taken from areas known to be contaminated with these four compounds showed no mortality following a thirty-six-hour topical exposure to filter paper containing 1 milliliter of a solution of aldrin at 30,000 and 50,000 milligrams/liter. However, frogs from relatively uncontaminated areas showed 30 percent and 57 percent mortality at the respective exposure levels (Vinson et al. 1963). While the authors speculated that the apparent resistance was a result of natural selection, it is also likely that induction of metabolic enzyme (liver monooxygenase) activity by DDT, toxaphene, and endrin may have increased the rate at which aldrin, and its metabolite dieldrin, could be metabolized and eliminated by frogs from contaminated sites.

For many years, chlordane, a cyclodiene OC, was the major termiticide used in the United States. When 20- to 30-centimeter-deep experimental ponds containing stocked bullfrog larvae were sprayed with chlordane at 0.1 or 0.5 kilogram/hectare (equivalent to approximate concentrations of 0.04 and 0.2 milligram/liter), no mortality was observed at the low application rate, but at the high rate, mortality was 0 percent, 30 percent, 30 percent, and 30 percent at one, two, five, and six days following application, respectively (Mulla 1963). In another study (Kaplan and Overpeck 1964), red and white blood cell counts were reduced in northern leopard frogs following exposure to chlordane at up to 0.5 milligram/liter for thirty days, and mortality at the high concentration was 40 percent. Signs of toxicosis included tremors and convulsions.

Endrin is among the most highly lethal cyclodiene OC insecticides. It was commonly used for insect control on wheat fields. Also, it was previously used on treated perches to kill unwanted birds. Concentrations of endrin necessary to induce disorientation, erratic swimming, or other neuromuscular deficits within twenty-four hours in 50 percent of animals (EC_{50} values) for larval cricket frogs, spotted salamanders (*Ambystoma maculatum*), marbled salamanders (*Ambystoma opacum*), American toads, bullfrogs, southern leopard frogs (*Rana sphenocephala*), and wood frogs were 0.023, 0.048, 0.018, 0.008, greater than 0.040, 0.013, and less than 0.016 milligram/liter, respectively (Hall and Swineford 1981). Application of endrin, at 0.1 kilogram/hectare (equivalent to approximately 0.04 milligram/liter), to 20- to 30-centimeter-deep experimental ponds containing stocked bullfrog larvae caused 50 percent, 90 percent, and 90 percent mortality at one, two, and five days, respectively. At 0.5 kilogram/hectare (equivalent to approximately 0.2 milligram/liter), the mortality rate was 100 percent at one day following application. Restocking of the high-rate ponds following the first observation resulted in 90 percent and 100 percent mortality at two and five days following application. Thus, as is the case with mammals and birds, endrin appears to be one of the most toxic OC insecticides to amphibians (Mulla 1963). As with several other members of this group, endrin, at concentrations of 0.015 and 0.030 milligram/liter, caused decreased red and white blood cell counts in northern leopard frogs following a thirty-day exposure (Kaplan and Overpeck 1964).

Lindane, the γ-isomer of hexachlorocyclohexane, is an OC insecticide that sometimes has been employed on agricultural fields, as well as for insect and mange mite control on animals. Lindane and other isomers are sometimes present in products identified by the misnomer benzene hexachloride (BHC), the technical grade of which consists primarily of the a-isomer (65 to 70 percent), followed by the γ-isomer (13 percent) and the β- and ∂-isomers (5 to 6 percent each). Despite the name, neither lindane nor BHC should be confused with the fungicide and persistent environmental pollutant hexachlorobenzene. Lindane is a stimulant of the nervous system and may affect hematopoiesis (production of blood).

Exposure of eggs of African clawed frogs to lindane at 2 milligrams/liter decreased hatching success. When the animals were exposed at 0.5 milligram/liter beginning at the egg stage, completion of metamorphosis was delayed by four weeks (Marchal-Segault and Ramade 1981). Similarly, there was a dose-dependent decrease in hatching percentage following exposure of the eggs of the Asian *Microhyla ornata* to lindane at up to 70 milligrams/liter (Pawar and Katdare 1984). At the highest concentration, hatching success was zero. A mortality rate of 10 percent after six days resulted after the application of lindane at 0.5 kilogram/hectare to 20- to 30-centimeter-deep experimental ponds (equivalent to approximately 0.2 milligram/liter) stocked with larval bullfrogs (Mulla 1963).

Toxaphene formerly was used in the United States to treat corn, cotton, soybeans, and peanuts, as well as for cattle dips. When toxaphene was applied at 0.5 kilogram/hectare to 20- to 30-centimeter-deep experimental ponds (equivalent to approximately 0.2 milligram/liter), all of the stocked bullfrog larvae died within twenty-four hours. Moreover, all the tadpoles restocked into the same ponds after the first day also died within twenty-four hours (Mulla 1963). Exposure of adult leopard frogs to toxaphene at 0.6 milligram/liter for thirty days resulted in 25 percent mortality. Although white blood cell counts declined in a dose-dependent manner, red blood cell counts did not (Kaplan and Overpeck 1964). LC_{50}s for toxaphene-induced disorientation, erratic swimming, or other neuromuscular abnormalities in cricket frogs, spotted salamanders, marbled salamanders, bullfrogs, southern leopard frogs, and wood frogs were greater than 1, 0.034, 0.170, 0.312, 0.193, and 0.036 milligram/liter, respectively (Hall and Swineford 1981).

Piscicides

Rotenone is a plant-derived piscicidal and insecticidal compound commonly used in the eradication of undesired fish stock. This compound acts by blocking mitochondrial oxidative phosphorylation. Tissues of rotenone-poisoned animals are unable to use oxygen in cellular respiration, inducing signs of oxygen deficit, even when air or water oxygen concentrations are adequate. Twenty-four-hour LC_{50}s for rotenone ranged from 0.1 to 0.58 milligram/liter for larval amphibians (Chandler and Marking 1982; Hamilton 1941), approximating the lethal doses reported for fish (Fontenot et al. 1994). Treatment of waters for fish eradication, therefore, likely kills larval amphibians as well. Indeed, Stewart (1975) reports apparent eradication of anurans from rotenone-treated ponds encountered in northern New York. She estimated that ten to fifteen years were required for pond recolonization and full recovery of amphibian populations. Adult amphibians appear to be more resistant to the effects of rotenone, perhaps due to their ability to breath air. Reported LC_{50}s for rotenone in adults ranged from 4.8 to 24 milligrams/liter (Farringer 1972).

Ultraviolet Radiation

Blaustein, Huffman et al. (1994) examined the effects of UV-B irradiation on hatching success in eggs of Pacific treefrogs, western toads and Cascades frogs (*Rana cascade*) and correlated species-specific sensitivity with activity in eggs of photolyase, an enzyme involved in repair of UV-B-induced damage to DNA. Photolyase activity was higher in Pacific treefrogs than in western toads and Cascades frogs by approximately fourfold. Placement of UV-B blocking filters over egg masses in high-altitude ponds more than doubled the proportion of larvae surviving until hatching in western toads and Cascades frogs but had no effect on Pacific treefrogs. Local populations of Pacific treefrogs were believed to be vigorous, while those of western toads and Cascades frogs had undergone significant declines. The results of this study suggest that UV-B irradiation may be responsible, at least in part, for the declines of western toads and Cascades frogs in the Pacific Northwest.

Some Areas of Particular Concern for Midwestern Amphibian Populations

The intentional application of chemicals to agricultural lands represents a staggering release of xenobiotics into the environment. The intensity and ubiquity of agriculture in the midwestern United States require that the possible contribution of agricultural chemicals to midwestern amphibian population declines be investigated.

The impact of environmental contaminants on endocrine function has become a subject of considerable concern for scientists, federal and state regulators, and the general public (Colborn et al. 1993). Compounds such as PCBs, halogenated dibenzodioxins and dibenzofurans, OC insecticides, alkylphenols, and some herbicides, and/or metabolites of these compounds, have been shown to interfere with the activity of estrogen (Bergeron et al. 1994; Jansen et al. 1993; Krishnan and Safe 1993; White et al. 1994), androgen (Babic-Gojmerac et al. 1989; Kelce et al. 1995), and thyroxine (Ness et al. 1993). Exposure to such compounds, at sufficient concentrations, could disrupt sexual differentiation, function, and behavior and may delay or prevent metamorphosis.

Habitat fragmentation and destruction have undoubtedly played significant roles in declines of amphibian metapopulations. Clearly, the magnitude of wetland destruction in the Midwest has severely limited the potential for dispersion and recolonization of habitats. Pollution of some of the remaining, otherwise suitable, habitats as well as the corridors between these areas may have a devastating impact on the viability of amphibian metapopulations.

Conclusions

Most studies on amphibian toxicology have dealt only with acute lethality. Acute toxicity studies focused on individual animals in laboratory settings provide vital information. However, many of the subtle effects of toxicoses will go undetected unless subacute and chronic exposure tests are employed and unless populations and communities, rather than individual animals, are considered as experimental units. Most of the studies cited in this chapter, for example, would not recognize the potential for changes in cold tolerance, increased susceptibility to predation, reduced ovulation rates, aberrant sexual behavior, alterred water balance, less effective feeding behavior, and/or decreased resistance to viral, bacterial, or parasitic disease, each of which might exert marked negative effects on amphibian populations.

Although there have been many reports on the effects of toxicants on the dynamics of microcosm, mesocosm, and whole-pond communities, almost none of these have included data on the amphibians in such systems. There is a great need for ecotoxicologic studies involving amphibians in realistic communities (Rowe and Dunson 1994). When carefully conducted, analyzed, and interpreted, such studies have great potential to increase our understanding of the effects of natural and anthropogenic chemicals on the viability of amphibian populations.

Summary

This chapter reviews the current knowledge of the effects of environmental contaminants on amphibian health. Industrial organic compounds, metals, habitat acidification, agricultural pesticides and fertilizers, and UV-B radiation are considered. Areas of particular concern for midwestern amphibian populations are identified, and a case is made for the importance of conducting population- and community-based toxicologic research.

28

Evidence for Home Ranges in Mudpuppies and Implications for Impacts Due to Episodic Applications of the Lampricide TFM

Timothy O. Matson

The utilization of chemicals to control sea lampreys (*Petromyzon marinus*) in the Great Lakes began in 1958 with applications of the lampricide 3-trifluoromethyl-4-nitrophenol (TFM) to tributary streams of Lake Superior (Howell 1966). TFM is now used in tributaries of all the Great Lakes. Ammocoetes burrowed in the substrate become irritated by the lampricide, leave their burrows, and are killed while in the water column through hemorrhage, suffocation, and the uncoupling of oxidative phosporylation. Streams infested with sea lampreys are treated with TFM at three- to five-year intervals. The frequency of application is dependent upon ammocoete numbers and their body sizes relative to transformer size (the size at which transformation to the parasitic stage occurs) and is timed so that all age classes of ammocoetes will be subjected to the lampricide before transformation (National Research Council of Canada [NRCC] 1985). When applied at the minimal concentrations required to kill sea lampreys, TFM is not considered to cause a serious negative impact to most nontargeted aquatic animal populations over the long term. However, diverse macroinvertebrate taxa, such as *Hydra* sp., *Hexagenia* sp., Tubificoidea, Annelida, and Turbellaria (Gilderhus and Johnson 1980; MacMahon et al. 1987; Smith 1967), have shown dramatic reductions in population size during and following TFM application. Knolton et al. (1986) found that populations of *Chimarra* sp. and Tubificoidea had not returned to pretreatment numbers after thirty weeks, and MacMahon et al. (1987) found that abundances of *Dolophilodes* and Tubificoidea were below pretreatment abundances 350 days posttreatment.

The sensitivity of teleost fish to TFM has received considerable attention (Applegate et. al. 1961; Applegate and King 1962; NRCC 1985). Species most sensitive to TFM include rainbow trout (*Salmo gairdneri*), yellow perch (*Perca flavescens*), yellow bullheads (*Ameiurus natalis*), stonecat madtoms (*Noturus flavus*), and white suckers (*Catostomus commersoni*). However, susceptibility of amphibians to the lampricide has received minimal attention (Chandler and Marking 1975; Howell 1966; Kane et al. 1985), despite frequent mention of mortality of frog tadpoles and mudpuppies (*Necturus maculosus maculosus*). Gilderhus and Johnson (1980) note mortality in anuran tadpoles in 16 percent of field treatment summaries; mortality in mudpuppies was noted in about 33 percent of field observations from Lakes Superior and Michigan, and 18 percent of those summaries cited large numbers of mudpuppies killed. In an Ohio population study of mudpuppies, Matson (1990) estimated a minimum decline in population size of 29 percent following TFM application. The purposes of the present study were to obtain site fidelity, movement, and quantitative activity range data that would assist in predicting long-term persistence of mudpuppies in streams subjected to reapplication of lampricide on a three- to five-year schedule.

Materials and Methods

The study site was a 700-meter length of the Grand River located in Madison Township, Lake County, in northeastern Ohio (Thompson, Ohio, USGS 7.5' topographic map 1960, photorevised 1970). Substrate in the river channel consisted of siltstone bedrock from the Chagrin Shale Formation, silt, gravel, cobble, large glacial erratics, and slabs of siltstone. Pool substrates consisted of sand, silt, and large boulders with siltstone slabs, whereas other pools collected detritus and silt to depths of 10 to 15 centimeters. Two meanders, one riffle, two gravel bars, and several pools were prominent channel features (Figs. 28-1–28-3). Water depth ranged from 0.1 meter to approximately 2 meters and was subject to dramatic fluctuations from severe drought in 1991 to spring flooding (see Matson 1990 for additional site description).

Fieldwork extended from late May or early June through August or early September over the period 1989 through 1991. Occasional visits were made to the site during the summers of 1992 to 1995 to search for animals marked during the previous three-year period. Twelve stations were located on the shoreline along the length of the site. The distance between consecutive stations was measured, and an azimuth between consecutive stations was taken to establish their relative spatial configuration. Azimuths from appropriate stations were used to determine coordinates of points along the channel margins in order to generate a map of the site.

Fieldwork was not conducted each week, but the entire length of the site was searched for mudpuppies before starting again from the downstream end. Mudpuppies were captured by manually overturning siltstone slabs and sweeping beneath the rock with the side of the foot toward a 1.8-meter seine. Individuals less than 14 centimeters total length were released immediately at the site of capture, whereas mudpuppies with larger total lengths were measured to the nearest half centimeter and were then marked with a numbered plastic I-tag inserted through the proximal one-third of the tail musculature below the caudal vertebrae. Each marked animal was returned to the point of capture, submersed, and released under or beside the slab from which it had been netted. No mudpuppies were marked after 1991. The intersection of azimuths from two shoreline stations located points of capture for which the coordinates were later used in activity range area calculations.

The area of the triangle or polygon formed by connecting the peripheral capture points of each mudpuppy captured three or more times was calculated to estimate the size of the summer activity range for each animal. Because the number of times animals were recaptured was small, a Kruskal-Wallis one-way nonparametric analysis of variance was used to test the validity of pooling the home range data for all individuals (Sokal and Rohlf 1969). This method of home range estimation was used in preference to other parametric and nonparametric methods to permit direct comparison

Figure 28-2. Part of the mudpuppy (*Necturus maculosus maculosus*) study site in the Grand River, Lake County, Ohio. The photograph was taken in April looking upstream to the northeast from a point with coordinates 200 meters north by 300 meters east on the map in Figure 28-3. Note the shrubless sand point for reference.

Figure 28-1. Part of the mudpuppy (*Necturus maculosus maculosus*) study site in the Grand River, Lake County, Ohio. The photograph was taken in July looking downstream to the southwest from a point with coordinates 275 meters north by 360 meters east on the map in Figure 28-3. Note the vegetated gravel bar near midstream for reference.

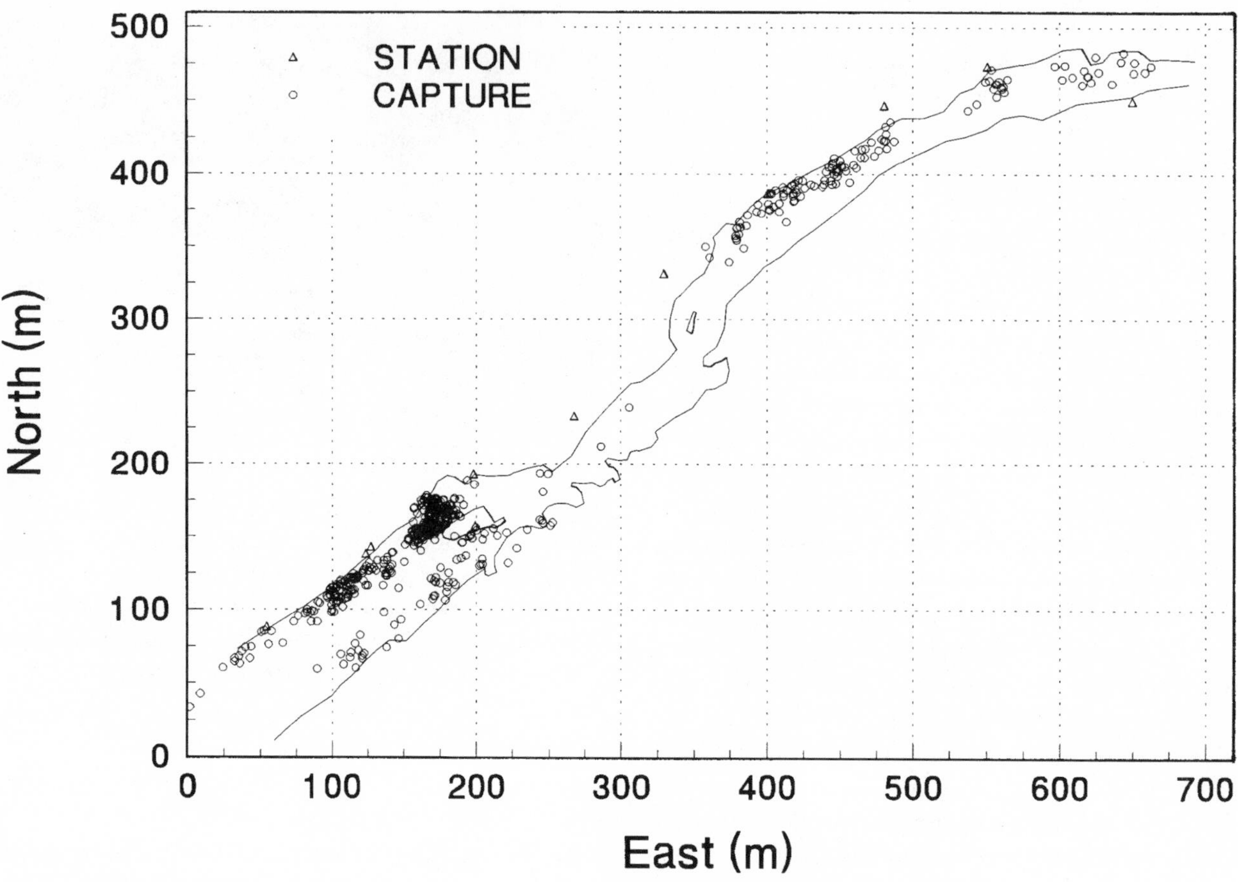

Figure 28-3. Computer-plotted map of the Grand River study site in Lake County, Ohio. Each circle represents 1 of 609 captures of 382 mudpuppies (*Necturus maculosus maculosus*). Two midstream gravel bars are indicated; the first bar has grid coordinates 300 meters north by 350 meters east, the second 150 meters north by 200 meters east. Grid size is 100 meters by 100 meters. Triangles indicate on-shore stations from which azimuths were taken to locate coordinates of captured mudpuppies and shoreline positions for mapping the mudpuppy site.

with the data of Ashton (1985) for the Neuse River waterdog (*Necturus lewisi*).

Results

Six hundred nine captures of 382 mudpuppies were made during the 1989 through 1991 period (Fig. 28-3). Two hundred thirty-eight (62.3 percent) marked individuals were captured only once; the remaining 144 (37.7 percent) mudpuppies were captured from two to six times (Table 28-1; Figs. 28-3–28-5). Of those recaptured, all captures of 137 (35.9 percent) individuals were made during the year in which they were first marked. Seven mudpuppies were recaptured in more than one field year; one (number 128) was caught six times over two consecutive years (Table 28-2; Fig. 28-4); one (number 168) was captured twice over nonconsecutive years (Fig. 28-5); one (number 267) was captured four times over three consecutive years (Fig. 28-5); two (numbers 88 and 152) were captured four times over two consecutive years; and two (numbers 111 and 147) were captured twice, once each in consecutive years.

Mudpuppies captured three or more times were considered residents within the study area, whereas those captured only once or twice were considered transients. The number of times an animal was captured within a segment of stream may be dependent upon numerous factors other than whether the animal is a resident of that stretch of river. Catchability of the animal due to capture technique, individual escape behavior, disturbance of nest slabs resulting in emigration, or marginal accessibility to portions of the site to the researcher (pri-

Table 28-1. Mudpuppies (*Necturus maculosus maculosus*) captured one to six times in the Grand River, Lake County, Ohio, and the percent captures of each category. The data include 609 captures of 382 marked animals.

	Number of Times Captured					
	1	2	3	4	5	6
Number of marked mudpuppies	238	91	31	15	6	1
Percent of total marked mudpuppies	62.3	23.8	8.1	3.9	1.6	0.3

marily due to water depth) may restrict the number of times an animal may be caught; consequently, the assumption that a mudpuppy captured only one or two times is a transient may be incorrect. However, this rationale facilitates comparisons.

The length of time a mudpuppy remained within the site was estimated by determining the number of days between the first and last capture. For example, mudpuppies 88 and 267 were captured in the site over periods of 340 and 764 days, respectively, and were assumed to be in residence for those lengths of time. The mean number of days between recaptures of residents was 29.7 days, whereas that of nonresidents (mudpuppies recaptured once) was 41 days. The samples represent populations having statistically different distributions ($n = 231$, $p = 0.042$, Mann-Whitney U-test). The statistical distributions of linear distance between consecutive capture positions when compared between residents (average = 22.1 meters) and transients (average = 28.0 meters) were from the same population ($n = 231$, $p = 0.425$, Mann-Whitney U-test). These sets of data imply that a portion of the transient population consists of residents, because the distance moved between capture positions by transients was similar to that of residents but the time between captures was greater, or that there is great variability in the rate at which transients move through the site.

Activity ranges varied greatly in size (Table 28-3) between groups with different numbers of captures and within groups having equal number of captures. The Kruskal-Wallis one-way nonparametric analysis of variance for area by number of captures was not significant ($n = 53$, $p = 0.14$), therefore the activity ranges of all animals were lumped and the mean value of 136.1 meters representing all mudpuppies captured three or more times was used as the estimate of the activity range for the population.

Data presented in the next section of this chapter concerning the estimated decline of mudpuppies in the Grand River are from Matson (1990), who used Schnabel's (1938) censuses of toe-clipped mudpuppies of all size and age cohorts to estimate population size both before and after a riverine application of TFM. Two sets of population estimates were made and compared. In the first comparison, population estimates within the March–April time period were made in 1987, in which the application of TFM took place, and 1988. Application of TFM to the river was made 27 April 1987; the pretreatment population estimate of the March–April period in 1987 established the population baseline. In the second comparison, population estimates of March–July were compared between years. Ninety-five percent confidence interval estimates (C.I.E.) were calculated for each population estimate. The rate of population growth reported here was 0.71 and was determined by dividing the upper C.I.E. value for the March–July population estimate for 1988 (397 mudpuppies per kilometer) by the lower C.I.E. value obtained for the corresponding population estimate for 1987 (556 mudpuppies per kilometer). This rate of population growth is crude and assumes negligible recruitment from births or immigration and negligible decreases from emigration; it also assumes that all deaths were attributed to TFM. Under these biased assumptions for mudpuppies, the rate of population growth is equal to the rate of survivorship, and the rate of population decline is equal to the rate of mortality (1-survivorship), or 0.29 (29 percent).

Discussion

Over 86 percent of the mudpuppies marked during this study were captured only one or two times and are considered transients. However, the time and distance

Table 28-2. Marked resident mudpuppies (*Necturus maculosus maculosus*) captured three to six times. Data include the assigned number, total length (TL), number of times captured, number of days between the dates of first and last capture (inclusive), and activity range.

Necturus Number	TL (centimeters)	Number of Times Captured	Number of Days	Activity Range (square meters)
128	3.4	6	370	20.5
100	38.5	5	57	92.5
164	32.5	5	65	121.9
166	32.0	5	90	858.9
228	23.5	5	42	71.8
305	25.5	5	47	104.0
385	27.5	5	71	223.3
71	32.0	4	80	5.0
88	30.5	4	340	555.8
152	32.0	4	319	214.8
191	33.5	4	40	216.6
211	28.5	4	36	6.5
231	24.0	4	42	587.5
243	33.5	4	35	7.9
257	32.5	4	22	174.6
267	32.0	4	764	78.3
303	34.0	4	81	5.6
312	16.5	4	32	11.0
327	34.0	4	78	135.9
334	34.5	4	64	15.4
360	36.0	4	43	378.3
902	26.0	4	42	43.0
4	30.0	3	13	7.5
21	19.5	3	41	6.4
73	38.0	3	61	—
80	29.0	3	15	198.5
105	30.0	3	57	29.1
106	29.0	3	63	42.0
125	32.5	3	20	23.6
142	31.0	3	9	74.6
169	18.0	3	65	2.9
175	37.0	3	33	43.5
176	31.5	3	74	57.3
178	33.0	3	33	6.3
180	22.5	3	39	32.5
185	30.5	3	43	26.5
180	32.0	3	54	131.0
190	23.0	3	31	1,095.5
221	31.5	3	21	135.3
226	34.0	3	31	3.0
236	37.0	3	18	4.9
247	28.5	3	47	324.6
261	—	3	22	120.0
298	28.0	3	12	8.8
306	32.5	3	67	97.5

Table 28-2. cont.

Necturus Number	TL (centimeters)	Number of Times Captured	Number of Days	Activity Range (square meters)
414	17.5	3	31	107.0
325	23.0	3	23	24.4
326	23.0	3	64	107.8
339	30.0	3	64	13.5
377	33.5	3	59	49.0
378	33.0	3	59	495.6
379	22.0	3	57	7.9
386	32.0	3	57	2.1
292	22.5	3	57	5.1

moved between recapture data indicate that this estimate is excessive and that some of these animals probably were residents and remained in a section of the stream. The data presented in table 1 of Shoop and Gunning (1967) are consistent with this hypothesis. They found that forty-six of sixty-nine marked mudpuppies in Big Creek, Louisiana, were captured only once and that six others were captured twice (three mudpuppies were captured three to four times) within a two-year period; therefore, fifty-two of the sixty-nine (75 percent) could be termed transients employing the terminology used in the current study. Their data indicate that an additional fourteen mudpuppies (20.3 percent) captured once during their initial study were not detected a second time until a second sampling period 1,469 to 2,089 days later was conducted. These fourteen mudpuppies would be lumped with nonresidents (n = 66, or 95.6 percent) if the secondary sampling period had not been conducted, but they were either resident within that section of the creek or else represented a transient group that by chance was detected within a section of stream on two occasions as they passed through.

In the present study, several secondary sampling periods during 1992 to 1994 produced few recaptures of marked animals. By the middle of the 1991 field season, it was evident upon close examination that the plastic T-tags used for marking individuals had pulled out, or in a few cases had ripped out, of numerous individuals, thereby resulting in the loss of marks and of many additional capture records. However, "once-marked" animals, those bearing scars or healed wounds where tags would have been placed, when detected early in the field season, indicate that the animals were marked one or more years earlier; consequently, they lend additional support to the hypothesis that mudpuppies exhibit site fidelity across years.

Shoop and Gunning (1967) conducted occasional collecting of mudpuppies and the Gulf Coast waterdog (*Necturus beyeri*) up to 0.8 kilometer both upstream and downstream from their study areas, but they did not capture any marked animals. Similar occasional searches for marked mudpuppies in the Grand River up to 0.5 kilometer both upstream and downstream of the study area did not reveal the presence of marked or "once-marked" animals. Movement beyond 0.5 kilometer upstream or downstream of the site could partially explain the paucity of marked mudpuppies within these areas. However, these observations lend further credence to the hypothesis that the resident proportion of the population is larger than multiple recapture results would indicate. The difficulty in capturing mudpuppies in their aquatic habitat and the habitat disturbance resulting from capture methodologies probably account for reduced recapture success within the study site.

Observations concerning the movements of mudpuppies in streams or lakes have been reported for species of *Necturus* by Ashton (1985), Bishop (1941), Cagle (1954), Gibbons and Nelson (1968), Harris (1959), and Shoop and Gunning (1967). Only Ashton (1985), working with the Neuse River waterdog in the Little River of North Carolina, collected quantitative data on home range and calculated area. Using ^{60}Co wires for tagging, Ashton accumulated numerous relocations on five adult waterdogs. For comparative purposes, I combined and

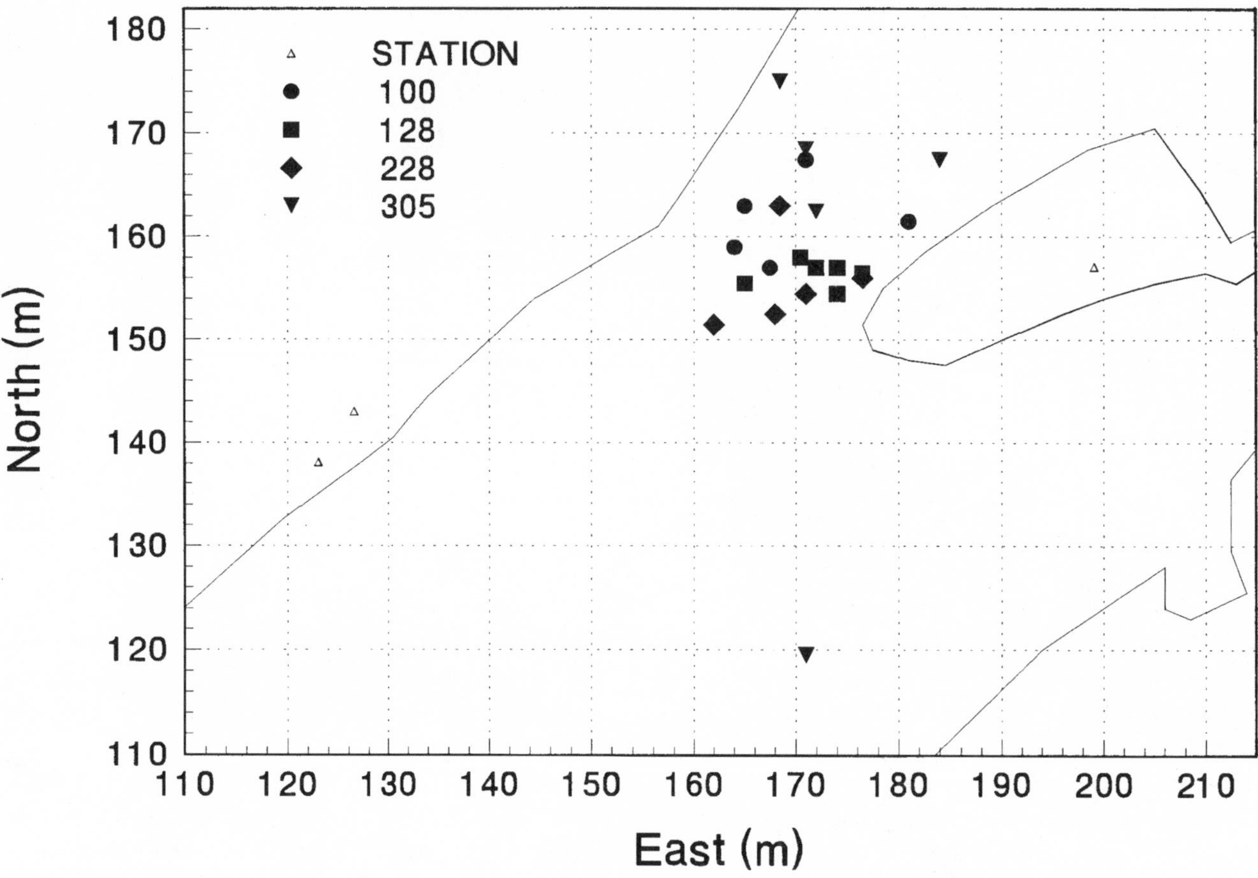

Figure 28-4. Capture positions of four mudpuppies (*Necturus maculosus maculosus*) in the Grand River, Lake County, Ohio. The summer activity range (in square meters) was calculated for each mudpuppy and is presented in Table 28-3. Activity ranges show much overlap among individuals. Part of a midstream gravel bar is located in the upper right corner. Grid size is 10 meters by 10 meters.

averaged the data presented in table 5 of Ashton (1985) for the home range of male and female waterdogs to derive a value (51.7 square meters) for the population. The home range of mudpuppies reported here (136.1 square meters) is much larger than that of the morphometrically smaller species, the Neuse River waterdog. It should be noted that the estimates of home range for this waterdog were derived using different marking and relocation methodologies in geographically distant and distinct habitats and that the area estimates for this waterdog are based upon many more relocations per individual. The activity range of 136.1 square meters for mudpuppies is probably conservative because the number of captures is low and the distribution of capture points of some animals captured three times was nearly linear.

Summer activity ranges (subset of home range) of mudpuppies in the Grand River showed much overlap. Sections of the river providing optimum habitat supported numerous mudpuppies, with portions of the activity range of an individual shared with that of conspecifics. Ashton (1985) also established that home ranges of the Neuse River waterdog overlapped regardless of sex or season. Cagel (1954) reported that one setline hook caught eight Red River mudpuppies (*Necturus maculosus louisianensis*) within forty-one hours over three days in February. The high capture rate suggests that placement of the hook must have been in optimum habitat within the shared home range of numerous individuals or within the route frequently traveled by transients.

Seasonal recapture or relocation data on mudpuppies collected over time within a segment of a stream are implicit evidence supporting the hypothesis that at least

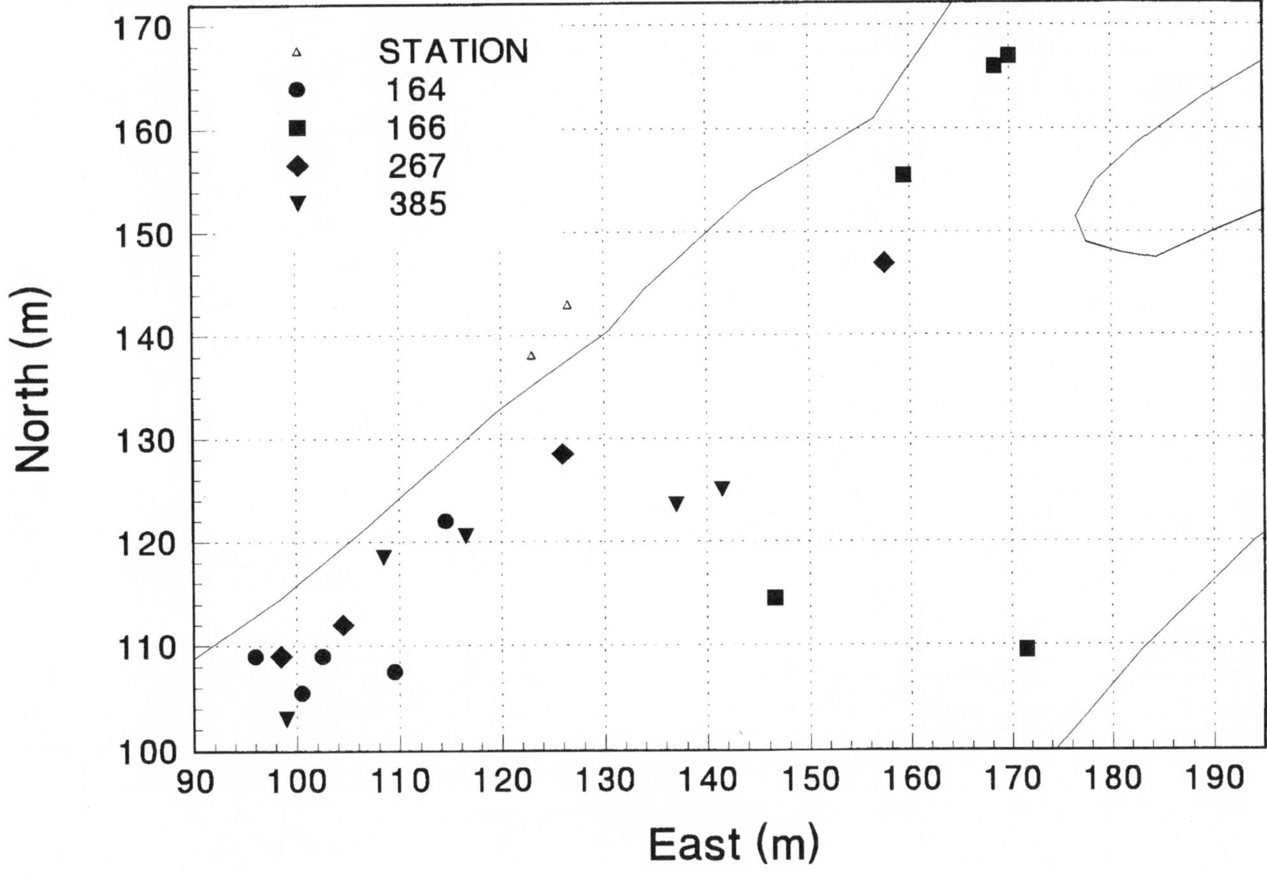

Figure 28-5. Capture positions of four mudpuppies (*Necturus maculosus maculosus*) in the Grand River, Lake County, Ohio. The summer activity range (in square meters) was calculated for each mudpuppy and is presented in Table 28-3. Activity ranges show much overlap among individuals. Part of a midstream gravel bar is located in the upper right corner. Grid size is 10 meters by 10 meters.

some individuals within the population exhibit site fidelity. An alternative hypothesis is that members of the population are transient and that their detection at a later time is a stochastic event. Recapture data presented here support the contention that individuals of the population exhibit site fidelity, establish activity ranges, and remain within the site for times ranging from several months (part of one May-to-September period) to approximately three years. Recapture data presented by Shoop and Gunning (1967) for mudpuppies over several seasons and after two to five years also demonstrate site fidelity to a segment of stream. Furthermore, the Neuse River waterdog exhibits site fidelity over at least the short term since the frequency of relocation within approximately one year permitted Ashton (1985) to quantify home range for individuals in the Little River.

In summary, data presented here supplemented by movement and home range studies of both congeners and conspecifics support the contention that a portion of a mudpuppy population exhibits site fidelity. Some members of the population may remain within a preferred stretch of stream for three to five years, perhaps longer. Long-term studies are required to determine the length of time that mudpuppies may be resident within a stretch of stream. With this information to supplement natural history information, we can examine the persistence of mudpuppy populations subjected to episodic perturbations by lampricides targeted toward the sea lamprey.

Growth and development of mudpuppies in northwestern Pennsylvania and New York state were described in detail by Bishop (1926, 1941). He determined that most mudpuppies reach sexual maturity at six years of age and after attaining a minimum total length of 200

Table 28-3. Mean summer activity range (square meters) for mudpuppies (*Necturus maculosus maculosus*) in the Grand River, Lake County, Ohio. Standard error in parentheses; range in brackets.

	Number of Times Captured			
	3 (n = 31)	4 (n = 15)	5 (n = 6)	6 (n = 1)
Mean activity range	105.9 (38.02) [2.1,1096]	162.5 (51.25) [5.0,587.5]	245.4 (124.6) [71.8,858.9]	20.5
Pooled mean activity range	136.1 (48.19) [2.1,1096]			

millimeters. Although few individuals could be expected to approach the maximum life span of twenty-three years (Nigrelli 1954), the reproductive life of females could potentially extend eighteen years. The mean number of eggs per clutch for mudpuppies in stream habitats was 107 (n = 3, range 87–140) in Pennsylvania and 85 (n = 85, range 48–125) in New York (Bishop 1941). In the Grand River, I found the average clutch size to be 83 (n = 13, range 60–120). Reproduction in mudpuppies has not been investigated in sufficient detail to determine if ovulation and spawning by adult females occurs annually, biennially, or otherwise. Survivorship to sexual maturity has not been studied in mudpuppies; consequently, basic information regarding life history and reproductive potential for a population, which is vital to assessing its potential to recover from perturbations, is not available.

Howell (1966) noted that mudpuppies seemed to be as susceptible to TFM as lampreys were, and Matson (1990) observed a minimum 29 percent decline in population size following application of TFM to the Grand River. Mudpuppies of all sizes and age cohorts are subject to the toxic effects of TFM (Matson 1990; personal observations in other treated streams). TFM administered at three- to five-year intervals indiscriminately removes reproductive adults and young with each successive application; therefore the numbers of young and reproductive residents would be expected to continue to decrease over time. Many hatchlings, resulting from reproduction of adults that either survived a TFM application or immigrated into the area following treatment, and many young in cohorts of ages one to three years would be killed by the next lampricide treatment before reaching sexual maturity. Consequently, the population would not be resilient but would continue to decline if solely dependent upon reproduction from the resident population. If the estimated 29 percent decrease in population size of mudpuppies in the Grand River is reasonable and is indicative of TFM-induced population declines in general, then the population could be reduced by 75 percent if subjected to four applications in twelve to twenty years. This estimate of population decline assumes a constant growth rate ($\lambda = 0.71$) across all treatments of the river with TFM. The calculation equation used was $N_t = N_o \lambda^t$, where N_o equals the population size at time zero before the first treatment, N_t equals the population size at time t, and t = 4, following the fourth application (Caughley 1977). Some streams in the Great Lakes drainage have been repeatedly treated with TFM for thirty or more years.

The transient population may be of utmost importance for long-term persistence of mudpuppies in streams subjected to repeated TFM applications. Transients within a stretch of stream treated with TFM are predicted to suffer mortality at a rate similar to that of residents. However, transient mudpuppies upstream from the initial point source of lampricide introduction may serve as a source of animals to recolonize downstream sections. Similarly, untreated tributary streams supporting mudpuppies may be a source for recolonization in some drainage systems. Bishop (1941) points out that no nests of mudpuppies were found in small tributaries; mudpuppies in those streams spawned near the mouth of the tributary in the higher order stream. In the Grand River, sections of the river upstream from the initial TFM point source harbor large numbers of mudpuppies. The three largest tributary streams downstream from the point source, Mill Creek, Paine Creek, and Big Creek, do not support mudpuppies.

The lake or stream into which a treated stream drains may serve as a source population of mudpuppies that could move upstream and recolonize sections of a stream with low population numbers and open niches. Annual upstream movements from Lake Michigan were noted by Pope (1964). The Grand River flows into Lake Erie, which formerly supported large numbers of mudpuppies (Pearse 1921; Sipes 1964; Pfingsten and White 1989). The recent status of mudpuppies in Lake Erie has not been assessed, but the lake remains a potential source of mudpuppies for recolonization.

Summary

The lampricide TFM (3-trifluoromethyl-4-nitrophenol), used in the control of sea lampreys (*Petromyzon marinus*) in the Great Lakes watershed, is known to induce mortality in mudpuppies (*Necturus maculosus maculosus*). The goal of this project was to supplement existing natural history information, especially on home range and site fidelity, for mudpuppies and to use existing estimates of mortality induced by TFM to predict the impact of episodic application of TFM on the long-term persistence on a local mudpuppy population. Data indicate that part of the population does exhibit site fidelity during the summer and that some individuals inhabit the same segment of the river from one year to the next. Both young and adults suffer mortality from TFM. With minimal immigration from a source population, recruitment into reproductive age classes will decline, and the population will function as a sink. If immigration of transients occurs at higher rates from outside the treated area, the population may persist.

Acknowledgments

I greatly appreciate assistance in the field over the years from Jill Levy, Mike Johnson, Paul Ondreko, Heidi Raynor, and Linda Woods. I am grateful for financial support from the Kirtlandia Society, Adopt-A-Student program, and to the Cleveland Museum of Natural History, Department of Botany, Natural Areas Stewardship Grant Program. My thanks are extended to Gordon McCarty for his help with data analysis and computer mapping and to Ralph Pfingsten for reviewing the manuscript.

29

Investigation of Malformed Northern Leopard Frogs in Minnesota

Judy Helgen, Robert G. McKinnell, and Mark C. Gernes

In August 1995 staff at the Minnesota Pollution Control Agency (MPCA) received a report from a teacher in Le Sueur, Minnesota, that her students had found malformed northern leopard frogs (*Rana pipiens*) around a restored wetland on a farm. The site is located on the bluff above the eastern side of the Minnesota River in Le Sueur County. In the next few weeks, over two hundred malformed frogs were collected from the wetland, and similar frogs were collected from an adjacent farm. Soon, another report came in from the teacher about malformed frogs observed on a farm across the Minnesota River south of Henderson in Sibley County. Collections by MPCA staff confirmed the presence of malformities very similar to those seen in the original Le Sueur County site. It was not just a problem centering around one isolated wetland. Media coverage began locally and expanded widely.

Shortly thereafter, a teacher in Litchfield, Minnesota, read a newspaper story about the Le Sueur County frogs to her science students, and a few days later a boy came into class with a bucket of six malformed leopard frogs. This led MPCA staff and others to collect ninety-one tiny malformed frogs from north of Litchfield at the end of September 1995 from a created pond in the yard of a former farm site, a short distance from the North Fork of the Crow River in Meeker County. The resident told of a man who had seen malformed frogs at another site, a few miles north of her property. Another man described finding malformed frogs in September in an area south of Litchfield, where he had collected small frogs for fishing over the years. Since then, additional reports, which have also not been confirmed with collections, have been made of malformed frogs in at least four other counties in central Minnesota. None of the citizens making these reports could recall seeing malformed frogs before 1995. In 1995 we did not know how widespread the occurrences were, nor if they would recur. In 1996 more than 160 citings of abnormal frogs were reported to the MPCA from fifty-four counties in Minnesota.

In the fall of 1993, after the heavy flooding in the Minnesota River valley in May and June, MPCA staff became involved in an investigation of malformed frogs reported by a local resident near the river south of Granite Falls, Yellow Medicine County, in west-central Minnesota. Collections were made by staff of the Minnesota Department of Natural Resources (MDNR) and MPCA of three malformed young leopard frogs, two with one eye missing and one with a missing rear leg. The collections at least confirmed the landowner's report but did not provide enough tissue for contaminant analysis. The investigation of Granite Falls frogs is discussed in more detail in Helgen (1996).

All of the malformed frogs collected in 1995 have been northern leopard frogs, although MPCA received one report of malformed gray treefrogs (*Hyla versicolor/chrysoscelis*) near the city of Elk River and one report of malformed small toads (*Bufo* sp.) from a suburb in the St. Paul metropolitan area. Neither of these reports has been confirmed. In the Le Sueur County site, an estimate of the proportion of malformed frogs was roughly a third or more of the population observed around the wetland.

The malformities in the Le Sueur County frogs

were largely in the rear limbs. All of the malformed individuals were the young of the year, with an average snout-vent length (SVL) of 37.4 millimeters (standard deviation = 4.63, n = 137). Of these frogs, forty-six had a contorted and incomplete rear leg. Many of these limbs looked normal at the base, but distal growth was disorganized, the outgrowing limb folded back and forth with boney protrusions in any direction (Fig. 29-1). Thirty-eight frogs (Fig. 29-2) had a leg that was emaciated and often also paralyzed, projecting straight out from the side of the body or straight backward. Some of these had malformed, thin, or clublike feet (Fig. 29-3). Twenty-three frogs had cutaneous fusion, or "webbed" skin that pulled across the bend of the rear leg, making it difficult to extend or move the leg (not shown). Twenty frogs had an incomplete limb (Fig. 29-3A, B), twenty had a leg entirely missing (Fig. 29-4A, B), and twenty had a small foot at the base (not shown). Twelve frogs had an extra leg at the rear, most often arising from the base of a more normal rear leg (Fig. 29-5A, B). One frog had a supernumerary, extra limb arising from its ventral surface rostral to the pectoral girdle (Fig. 29-6). The most extremely malformed frog had two thin extra rear legs projecting ventrally (Fig. 29-7). It is difficult to envision how a frog with an extra set of useless legs beneath its abdomen could locomote and feed. Nineteen of the 137 frogs had extra feet or legs branching off from the rear leg (Fig. 29-8).

Figure 29-2. Thirty-eight affected adult northern leopard frogs (*Rana pipiens*) exhibited rear legs that were emaciated and often paralyzed. Some of these frogs, such as the one shown here, exhibited thin or clublike feet.

Figure 29-1. Forty-six affected adult northern leopard frogs (*Rana pipiens*) exhibited contorted rear legs. Many of these limbs looked normal at their proximal end but exhibited abnormal distal growth. All frogs shown here and in the subsequent figures are young of the year and were collected in August 1995 in Le Sueur County, Minnesota.

More than fifty of the Le Sueur County frogs had a "spike" projecting dorsally from the posterior end, probably from the base of the spine where the tail had resorbed, a common malformity that often co-occurred with a limb malformity. Two frogs had the tadpole tail not completely resorbed; one of these had the full tadpole tail as a young frog (Fig. 29- 9). Three frogs were missing one eye (Fig. 29-10).

In spite of these developments, many of the surviving malformed frogs had insects in their stomachs and digested material in their intestines. Although measurements were not made on the apparently normal frogs, the malformed frogs from Le Sueur County did not

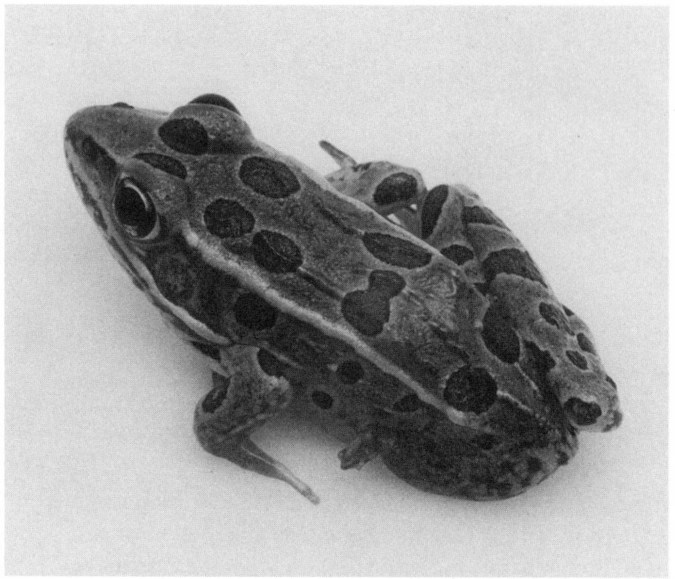

Figure 29-3. Twenty affected adult northern leopard frogs (*Rana pipiens*) exhibited incompletely developed limbs. The animal shown in second photo is a burnsi color pattern morph.

appear to be noticeably smaller.

The malformities seen in the frogs collected from the farm adjacent to the Le Sueur County site were similar to those seen in the Le Sueur County frogs. Missing legs, contorted or shortened legs, double feet, and webbed skin across rear legs were observed in the young frogs collected. In frogs from the site south of the town of Henderson and west of the Minnesota River in Sibley County, similar malformities were seen. There were four frogs with a complete extra leg, two with an extra leg branching off a rear leg, three with a shortened or contorted leg, two with a thin leg, and two with an extra foot.

How extensive the mortality may have been for the malformed frogs is impossible to estimate, retrospectively. There were tracks of raccoons and other animals around the muddy edge of the Le Sueur County wetland. The frogs with a missing rear leg, in attempting to leap, would pitch over, white belly up, undoubtedly making them vulnerable to predation. According to the students who had first discovered the frogs, some of the malformed frogs could not swim straight or well. They were much easier to capture than the normal young frogs.

The malformities in the young frogs in the Meeker County site differed from those seen in Le Sueur County. The malformities in the former were all in the rear limbs, with the exception of one young frog with an unresorbed tail. Out of ninety-three total tiny frogs collected, only two appeared normal. Of the ninety-one malformed frogs, seventy-three had one or both rear legs reduced to stumps. Sixty-nine of these had very tiny "nubs" for legs, sometimes just a thin sticklike projection only 3 to 4 millimeters long, sometimes more fleshy. Twenty of the sixty-nine frogs had tiny stumps at the site of both rear legs. The stumps were mobile; the thin stick could rotate freely when the frog was held in the hand. There were eleven frogs missing one rear leg; at least four of these had just a small nub for the other leg. One frog had no rear legs; it would pull itself along by its front legs.

In the Meeker County site, it was difficult to estimate the percentage of abnormalities in the population of leopard frogs. All of the young frogs were in or at the edge of a pond excavated in a seep area in the owner's yard. About twenty-five of the frogs were collected from the site earlier in the day before we (J.H. and M.C.G.) arrived. Adult frogs found at some distance from the small wetland, near the North Fork of the Crow River, all appeared to be normal. One dead adult was found by the pond.

How the Meeker County frogs were able to survive as long as they had is difficult to imagine. They clearly had not been able to grow; their body mass appeared to be that of a mature tadpole, not what one expects at the end of September. Average SVL of the ninety-one frogs

Figure 29-4. Twenty affected adult northern leopard frogs (*Rana pipiens*) had a leg entirely missing (shown here), had a reduced limb, or grew only a small foot present at the base.

was 31.6 millimeters (standard deviation = 3.2). It seemed as if the Meeker County frogs were either not feeding or not able to feed. In recent preliminary necropsies of these frogs, many had little or no material in the stomach or intestine, but there was evidence some of them had fed. Having been created two years earlier, the pond had almost no vegetation on its dirt banks, and the grass of the yard was mowed right up to the edge of the pond, leaving little habitat for insects.

Preliminary postmortem necropsies by visual inspection of the dissected frogs from Le Sueur County by one of the authors (R.G.M.) showed over a third of thirty-eight males having testes that appeared to be of diminished size and structure. All forty-four females had ovaries that appeared normal. Three of eighty-five frogs had no obvious gonads. Preliminary visual observations of the Meeker County malformed frogs suggest that males and some females have diminished gonads. Any suspected alterations in the gonads will need to be confirmed by histological analysis. Reduced testes size may not relate to reduced sperm production (M. Oeullet, personal communication), and tests of reproductive capacity will be needed.

Most of the Le Sueur County malformed frogs had what appears to be parasitic cysts in the thigh muscles. The frequency of parasitic cysts in normal frogs is unknown because these frogs were released at the site. Two large adults collected from the Le Sueur County site had heavy loads of cysts but appeared normal in external and internal morphology. The Meeker County malformed frogs showed no visible appearance of parasitic cysts in the legs. The parasitic cysts in the Le Sueur County malformed frogs are being identified by a veterinary parasitologist at the University of Minnesota. There is an interest in the possible role of metacercarial cysts of trematodes causing extra limbs in frogs. Researchers have hypothesized that cysts embedded at the base of the developing limbs could have caused supernumerary limbs observed in a population of the Pacific treefrog (*Hyla regilla*; Sessions and Ruth 1990). The authors reported that extra limbs were triggered in 20 percent of experimental frogs when small resin beads were implanted in the legs. However, all the treefrogs collected in the field sites had metacercarial cysts, even the frogs with normal limbs.

A framework for investigating what could have caused the malformities in the northern leopard frogs we observed can be built from the following elements of knowledge: (1) where and when the frogs could have been exposed to a teratogenic agent, (2) which agents could have caused malformities and would likely be present during critical times for exposure, and (3) which of the agents could be shown to have been present at levels or concentrations that could cause malformities during the critical stages of exposure.

The first framework element used during the life cycle

Figure 29-5. Twelve affected adult northern leopard frogs (*Rana pipiens*) had an extra leg, usually at the rear and most often arising from the base of a more normal rear leg.

of the leopard frog encompasses three environments (see Table 29-1): the breeding wetland, the feeding landscape of the frogs, and the overwintering site. Breeding occurs and deposition of eggs takes place in shallow wetlands or ditches that are often seasonal and lack gamefish. Such wetlands often naturally lack oxygen, may be periodically dry in late summer, or may freeze to the bottom in winter, thereby reducing the possibility of fish predation on the tadpoles. Tiles, ditches, and landscape runoff can convey contaminants to the breeding sites, where the embryos and tadpoles could be exposed to water-borne pollutants by direct uptake into the embryo or across the skin. As tadpoles feed, they browse on algae coatings on the surfaces of aquatic vegetation, on algae overlying benthic sediments, and on decomposing vegetation. Any contaminants accumulated in the algae or vegetation would be taken up as the tadpoles feed.

After metamorphosis, the newly transformed frogs feed primarily on insects in the area around the breeding wetland, eventually dispersing from the wetland into the surrounding landscape. Exposure of the young adult frogs to teratogenic agents could come directly, if there were contaminants on the surfaces of moist

Figure 29-6. One northern leopard frog (*Rana pipiens*) exhibited an extra limb arising from its ventral region, rostral to the pectoral girdle.

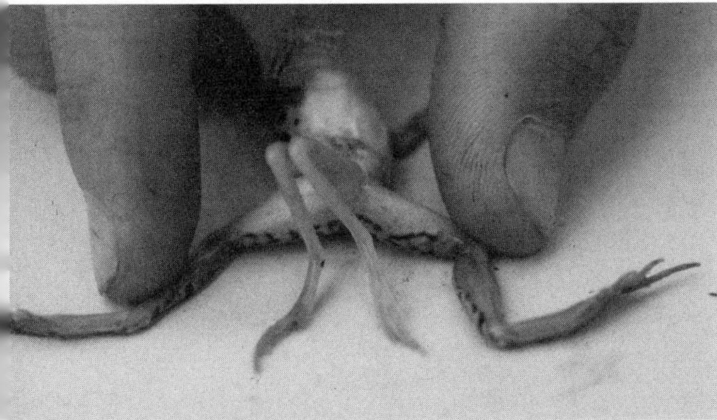

Figure 29-7. The most extreme case of extra limbs involved an adult northern leopard frog (*Rana pipiens*) that had two thin extra rear legs projecting ventrally from its abdomen.

Figure 29-8. Nineteen affected adult northern leopard frogs (*Rana pipiens*) had extra feet or legs branching off from the rear leg.

Figure 29-9. More than fifty of the Le Sueur County northern leopard frogs (*Rana pipiens*) had a "spike" projecting dorsally from the posterior end, probably from the base of the spine where the tail had resorbed. Two frogs had not completely resorbed their tail; one of these had the full tadpole tail (shown here).

Figure 29-10. Three affected adult northern leopard frogs (*Rana pipiens*) were missing one eye.

grasses or other vegetation, and indirectly from contaminants accumulated in the tissues of the insects eaten. Water in ditches and ponds visited by the frogs as they disperse could be another source of contaminant contact. The adult frogs, then, could be accumulating a body burden of pollutants that might affect the developing eggs or sperm. By the fall of their second year, adult females contain the masses of eggs for the reproductive season in the following spring. Therefore, it is possible that malformities observed in young frogs in summer could have been caused by contaminants accumulated from the aquatic and terrestrial landscape by the parent frogs during the year before the eggs were laid and passed into the developing yolky eggs. Sperm may be similarly affected.

The third environment where frogs might be exposed

Table 29-1. Environments, seasons, and life-cycle stages that could expose amphibians to teratogenic agents

Habitat/Environment	Exposure Season	Life Cycle Exposed
Breeding pond or wetland	Mid-April–June	Eggs, sperm, embryos, tadpoles
Terrestrial feeding near wetland	July–August	Froglets, adult frogs
Terrestrial feeding away from wetland	August–October	Adult frogs
Wet areas	August–October	Adult frogs
Overwintering in riverine pond, lake*	Mid-October–April	Adult frogs
Habitats of previous year	Previous year	Eggs and sperm

*Some species of frogs, such as wood frogs, overwinter on land.

to pollutants is from the water of the overwintering site by uptake through the skin. In Minnesota, leopard frogs typically pass the winter in relatively deep, oxygenated ponds, lakes, or rivers (Breckenridge 1944). They sit on the bottom rather than burrow into the sediments. In Le Sueur County, observations by local teachers, schoolchildren, college faculty, college students, and MPCA staff led to finding possible overwintering areas in the floodplain of the Minnesota River, particularly in a shallow floodplain pond containing seepage areas visible around the edges and a flow going through the middle to the mainstem of the river.

The second element of the framework of an investigation into malformities is knowledge about the agents that could possibly cause the kinds of malformities that were observed and the likelihood of these agents being present during the exposure seasons, habitats, and life-cycle stages described above. There is a great need for more research on the causes of teratogenesis and malformities in amphibians in natural populations and for bringing together existing knowledge on contaminants and amphibians. The updating of the toxicological review of the Canadian Wildlife Service (Harfenist et al. 1989) will be very useful in this regard (B. Pauli, personal communication). In conducting this investigation, many ideas about possible causes of malformities have been suggested, such as heritable mutations, both the active and "inert" ingredients of some pesticides, heavy metals, any pollutants that act as endocrine disrupters, and environmental factors like temperature, diet, and parasitic cysts.

For a complete investigation, sediments and site water from both the breeding pond and the overwintering site, frog tissues and eggs, algae or aquatic vegetation, insects eaten by frogs, and possibly even vegetation could be measured for concentrations of heavy metals, pesticides, PCBs and other potential teratogens (see Diana and Beasley, Chpt. 27, this volume). Ideally, normal frogs from the population in question, as well as reference frogs from a population known to be removed from contaminant exposure, are needed as a basis for evaluating tissue chemical data. Analysis of tissue contaminants and water and sediment chemistry is costly.

The same principle holds for the analysis of the potential for parasites as a causal agent in malformities. Surveys need to be done of normal and abnormal animals in the affected area and compared with animals in reference areas to determine the presence and extent of parasitic cysts in limbs and malformities. Ultimately, noninfected, healthy control animals would need to be infected with the parasite to determine directly whether it can cause the observed malformities.

A third element in the investigation framework is to demonstrate that the agents that could cause the malformities were present in the exposure habitats at sensitive life-cycle stages in concentrations high enough to cause malformities. Because this investigation began in August 1995, well after the critical events of amphibian development had occurred, it was not possible to measure contaminant levels or other conditions in the wetlands and landscape during the actual times of potential exposure. The tadpoles had already passed through the metamorphic transition, so there are no data on tadpole malformities or condition, let alone the extent of these in early-stage embryos. Likewise, there are no samples of sediments or water from the critical exposure time of spring or early summer. A retroactive investigation is more limited than a predictive one and makes it more difficult to ascertain cause.

Nonetheless, sampling of the breeding ponds and

potential riverine overwintering sites was done by MPCA staff in the late summer and early fall of 1995 to explore whether there might be high concentrations of undegraded pesticides, heavy metals, or PCBs in the sediments and water. A large number of malformed frogs were collected to permit future analysis of tissues from both the Le Sueur County and Meeker County sites. Chemical analyses were carried out by laboratories cooperating with the MPCA. Analysis of water and sediment samples for insecticides and herbicides was done by the Minnesota Department of Agriculture. None were detected in the wetlands where the malformed frogs were found, but MCPP, 2,4-D, and Dicamba were detected in seepage water in the fall of 1995 in an overwintering site, a shallow riverine pond in the Minnesota River basin. Department of Agriculture staff often find these herbicides in watersheds below urban areas, but they are detected more commonly in spring than in fall.

Analysis of selenium and metals in sediments was done by the Department of Geology, University of Montana. The data suggest background levels of selenium at all sites, including the breeding site where the malformed frogs were found. The overwintering pond had the highest level of selenium in sediment, 1.8 milligrams per kilogram. This value was just below the lower range for expected biological effects from sediments, from 2 to 4 milligrams per kilogram (Skorupa and Ohlendorf 1991; Lemly and Smith 1987). While the levels of selenium were low in sediment and water in the breeding pond, selenium has been shown to bioaccumulate in algae and aquatic plants (J. Moore, personal communication), which could increase the amount ingested by tadpoles.

Plans for continued investigation include an analysis of heavy metals and pesticides in the tissues of the malformed frogs and experiments to determine the quality of the eggs in overwintering females. In the spring, portions of field-collected egg masses of northern leopard frogs will be caged at the site while other portions of the same masses will be reared in the laboratory. Assuming the conditions present in the laboratory prevail in the wetlands, which may not happen, and developmental abnormalities do appear again, this approach is intended to demonstrate whether the water of the breeding pond could cause malformities. Tests for possible effects of diet could be set up in the ponds. One report describes skeletal malformations in tadpoles of Old World *Rana perezi* reared on various diets in tanks (Martinez et al. 1992). Female frogs will be induced to ovulate, and the eggs will be fertilized with sperm from males from control areas and from affected populations. Fertilization percentage and embryo and larval abnormalities will be scored. Histological work on the gonads and on parasitic cysts will be done.

Mutation as a cause of frog abnormalities is not considered to be highly likely because of the sudden, widespread appearance of malformed frog populations in 1995 on both sides of the Minnesota River and in other areas of Minnesota (e.g., Meeker County). If the abnormalities are heritable, this would raise the unlikely possibility of the widespread appearance of some mutagenic agent in central Minnesota in 1994 or 1995. There is one report of a recessive semilethal mutation in African clawed frogs (*Xenopus laevis*) that causes abnormal limb development in laboratory animals (Droin and Fischberg 1980). Classical breeding and cross-breeding experiments with adult frogs from the Le Sueur site will be initiated to determine if there is genetic transmission of the defects.

The genetic material of frog cells will be examined for visible damage to the chromosomes and measurable changes in the genome, that is, the amount of DNA content in each cell. The rationale for the chromosome and DNA content analysis is to see whether a gene-damaging, or genoclastic, agent has been affecting the frogs. We believe such an analysis is crucial because the liver of frogs, like that of humans, has a profound ability to activate many classes of pro-mutagenic chemicals to the final active mutagenic form (Cheh et al. 1980). Frogs are known to be sensitive to gene-altering, or mutagenic, agents, and chromosomal damage occurs in a dose-related manner with leopard frogs (McKinnell et al. 1979) and African clawed frogs (McKinnell et al. 1980). It has been known for many years that chromosomal damage can result in grossly abnormal embryos and larvae in amphibians (Fankhauser and Humphrey 1950). Abnormal chromosomes and irregular DNA content in the cells of malformed frogs indicate an exposure to a potential or active genoclastic agent. If leopard frogs are shown to have normal chromosomes and normal genomic DNA content, their exposure to gene-damaging agents is highly unlikely. In the latter event, teratogenic substances must be sought that do little or no damage to the genome.

Chromosomes of malformed and normal frogs from affected and reference areas will be analyzed for damage that is visible when the chromosomes are most condensed during cell division. Aberrations can result from breakage and additions of parts of chromosomes, resulting in recognizable fragments, rings, and other configurations determined to be abnormal. Flow cytometry has the power to detect subtle quantitative changes in the amount of DNA in cells and therefore provides an indirect method to assess chromosomal damage. In normal frogs, the DNA content, or the genome, should be constant. In flow cytometry, blood cells are stained with propidium iodide, which binds in proportion to the amount of DNA. Cells are then treated with an enzyme to remove their RNA and are examined in the flow cytometer for the amount of fluorescence emitted from the DNA-bound stain.

It has been known that chemicals called osteolathyrogenic agents cause skeletal abnormalities in other animals during development. Such agents include sweet pea seeds, thallium, organic nitriles (cyanides), and semicarbazides (hydrazines) (Riggin and Schultz 1986; Roth 1978, 1988; Schultz et al. 1985). Insecticides, such as certain organophosphates and carbamates (Alvarez et al. 1995; Cooke 1981; Fulton and Chambers 1985; Fikes 1990; Honrubia et al. 1993), and chlorinated hydrocarbons, like dieldrin and DDT (Cooke 1973; Schuytema et al. 1991), have been shown to cause malformities (see also Diana and Beasley, Chpt. 27, this volume). Arsenic (Eisler 1994; Harfenist et al. 1989), cadmium (Harfenist et al. 1989), mercury (Harfenist et al. 1989), and selenium (Eisler 1985; Lemly 1993a,b, 1994) are known to cause developmental malformities (see also Diana and Beasley, Chpt. 27, this volume).

A new and even less researched area for disturbance to amphibian development and reproductive biology is that of endocrine disruption, or hormone mimics (Colborn 1995; Colborn and Clement 1992; Katzenellenbogen 1995; see also Diana and Beasley, Chpt. 27, this volume). This can occur when molecules structurally similar to natural hormones disrupt natural hormonal action. In frogs, thyroid hormone (thyroxin) drives the developmental process (Etkin 1968), especially metamorphic changes. Disruption of hormonal action by such chemicals has been implicated as a potential cause of some abnormalities of sexual development in wildlife (Colborn and Clement 1992; Guillette et al. 1995). The two-ringed iodinated chemical structure of thyroxin is somewhat similar to DDT, some PCBs, and dioxin, so these molecules might act as mimics, thereby disrupting the actions of thyroxin. In addition, in experimental studies thyroid hormone can penetrate through the skin, so similar molecules could also be expected to be permeable from the surrounding water through the skin. Disturbers, or mimics, of molecules that work with thyroxin, such as retinoic acid, may need to be researched (P. Schoff, personal communication).

Of possible interest may be the role of prolactin, which has been used experimentally to prevent resorption of the tadpole tail (Dodd and Dodd 1976). Prolactin acts to maintain the larval condition, while thyroid hormone drives the metamorphic changes (Etkin and Gona 1967). In Minnesota in 1995 at each site there were one or two frogs retaining the full, unresorbed tail. Prolactin is made in the anterior pituitary gland and presumably can be stimulated by estrogen or estrogen-mimicking chemicals.

A collaborative effort will be sought to determine whether the yolk protein, vitellogenin, is induced in the blood of the male frogs from affected and reference areas. This will test for the activity and presence of estrogen-mimicking chemicals (Heppell et al. 1995; Sumpter and Jobling 1995; Korach and McLachlan 1995) in the environment of the frogs. Of interest is the possibility of disturbance to the gonads, both ovaries and testes, caused by estrogenic chemicals (Gray 1992). There may be other pertinent assays for endocrine disruption in amphibians.

Finally, amphibian malformities have raised a great deal of consciousness about the apparent fragility of the environment of amphibians, if not of humans. The schoolchildren and teachers, MPCA staff, and others have been featured in the press, at legislative hearings, and on the internet telling the story. The media have treated this concern sensitively, and there has been very little joking about the frogs. A widespread, expanding, cooperative, and helpful network of scientists, students, teachers, environmental educators, and citizens is emerging, with people offering to help and to share their knowledge and ideas. A global education center is planning a national amphibian watch day for schools, and a "Thousand Friends of Frogs" (Hamline University) project involving youth is beginning.

By fostering a cooperative, rather than competitive, way of doing scientific research, the teachers, students, and researchers are providing a model for environmental science projects in which state agencies, schools, universities, and citizens are all working together to find the answer to a problem. The concern about the damage to the frogs in Minnesota will not go away, not when the damage has been so widespread and so widely publicized. There is no way to know in advance whether the extent of malformities will be seen again in Minnesota, but the preliminary data on the poor egg quality of two overwintering females are suggestive of problems ahead for this population of frogs. This report is being composed during an ongoing investigation. Clarification and changes are expected as the work proceeds.

Summary

This chapter describes the malformities observed in collections of young northern leopard frogs (*Rana pipiens*) from Le Sueur, Sibley, and Meeker Counties in Minnesota, made during August and September 1995 by the Minnesota Pollution Control Agency and Robert McKinnell. The majority of abnormalities were in the rear legs, but other abnormalities were observed. Results of preliminary necropsies are given. A framework for investigating possible causes of malformities in frogs is suggested. Three elements of such an investigation are: (1) where and when exposure to a teratogenic agent could occur, (2) which agents known to cause developmental abnormalities might be present at the critical life stages, and (3) which agents are actually measured at exposure concentrations in frog habitats at critical times. Some of the agents that might cause malformities are described, including the possibility of endocrine disruption of the normal hormonal expression during development. Some of the plans for the research to be conducted are mentioned, including DNA content and chromosome analysis and histopathology. There are now several counties in Minnesota where malformed frogs were reported from 1995, and there is a widespread concern among citizens, media, and researchers as to what could have caused so many malformed frogs.

Acknowledgments

Judy Helgen and Mark Gernes of MPCA acknowledge the contributions of many people in this investigation. Joel Chirhart and Jon Haferman were steadfast assistants. Johnnie Moore and graduate student Yi Chian Zhang of the University of Montana gave their time to analyze metals in sediments; the Minnesota Department of Agriculture gave time to analyze pesticides; David Hoppe gave knowledge of leopard frogs; Joe Magner of MPCA tested porewater. A special acknowledgment goes to Cindy Reinitz, a teacher at the Minnesota New Country Charter School in Le Sueur, for the many ways she created the cooperative nature of this project; Art Straub, an elementary teacher in Henderson, Minnesota, for his deep knowledge of the wildlife of the Minnesota River basin; Gail Thovson, a science teacher in the Litchfield Middle School; the citizens who allowed collections on their property; and news reporters Sarah Malchow of the *Henderson Independent*, Dean Rebuffoni of the *Minneapolis Star Tribune*, and Ken Speaks of television Channel 11 News in St. Paul. MPCA acknowledges Don Ney, landowner and farmer, for allowing numerous visits to his property, for his openness and trust. We thank the students of the Minnesota New Country School, the Litchfield Middle School, and other students who have given MPCA information about frogs. We acknowledge the work of Eric Cole and John Campion from St. Olaf College for performing dives in shallow riverine ponds with fourteen inches of ice to help find overwintering frogs. Finally, we acknowledge with gratitude the lifelong work and steadfast concern for the environment, more recently focused on wetlands and frogs, demonstrated by Minnesota State Representative Willard Munger, age eighty-five.

Conservation

30

Illinois Chorus Frogs and the Sand Lake Dilemma

Lauren E. Brown and John E. Cima

In the past few years there has been a large number of popular newspaper and magazine articles on the decline of amphibians (see bibliography in K. Phillips 1994). These articles frequently contain magnificent color photographs of endangered and threatened species. The use of such illustrations can be justified because they do a good job of generating publicity and probably elicit sympathy from the reader. However, the naive layperson might assume that only beautifully colored amphibians are threatened with extinction. In reality, the majority of endangered and threatened amphibians are cryptically colored and could probably not be considered glamorous. A case in point is the state-threatened Illinois chorus frog (*Pseudacris streckeri illinoensis*) (Smith 1951; Fig. 30-1), which is a pallid, squat animal that might even be considered unattractive. However, the fascinating behavioral traits of this frog make it one of the most unusual amphibians in the United States, if not the world. The objectives of this chapter are to review the highlights of the biology of the Illinois chorus frog that are pertinent to the theme of this book and to examine the involvement of the frog in a major environmental controversy.

Biological Characteristics of Illinois Chorus Frogs

Fossorial Behavior

The most fascinating and unique biological attribute of the Illinois chorus frog is its forward burrowing behavior (Brown et al. 1972). The frog makes exclusive use of its forelimbs for digging in a manner analogous to a human swimmer doing the breaststroke. Progress is rapid, and it often takes less than two minutes for a frog to be completely covered with soil. Almost all other fossorial species of anurans burrow backward with their hind feet. Furthermore, the Illinois chorus frog is one of the few species in the treefrog family Hylidae that is fossorial.

Adult Illinois chorus frogs are highly fossorial in the laboratory, spending most of their time buried well below the substrate surface (Brown 1978; Brown et al. 1972), and this also appears to be true for adults in the field (Axtell and Haskell 1977; Smith 1961; Tucker et al.

Figure 30-1. Illinois chorus frog (*Pseudacris streckeri illinoensis*) photographed 24.1 kilometers east of Havana, Mason County, Illinois, by John C. Murphy.

1995). However, newly metamorphosed froglets dig shallow, open burrows in the field, and many have been found sitting in the mouth of the burrow (Tucker et al. 1995).

Substrate discrimination experiments indicate the frog's strong preference for burrowing in the friable sand characteristic of its habitat and its incapability of digging in more resistant black prairie sod (Brown et al. 1972). Field observations also indicate that burrowing sites are selected in areas devoid of vegetation or in areas lacking heavy vegetation (Axtell and Haskell 1977; Tucker et al. 1995).

Success in capturing subterranean prey can be increased with forward burrowing, and Brown's (1978) experiments indicate that the Illinois chorus frog can indeed feed underground. No other anuran species are known to be subterranean feeders.

Morphological Adaptations for Burrowing

The globose, toadlike bodies of Illinois chorus frogs are similar to those of many other fossorial anurans and quite different from the trim, slender bodies of many members of the treefrog family Hylidae. The Illinois chorus frog's muscular, stocky forelimbs and stout fingers lacking toe pads are highly adapted for digging (Brown et al. 1972) and contrast greatly with the slender, elongated limbs and adhesive toe pads that facilitate arboreal life in the majority of hylids. Furthermore, the Illinois chorus frog has an enlarged palmar tubercle (Brown and Means 1984), and the intercalary cartilage and the alignment of the phalanges in the forelimb digits (Paukstis and Brown 1987, 1991) are highly modified for forward burrowing.

Habitat and Environmental Disturbance

Sand prairie was first identified by Smith (1951, 1966) as the habitat of the Illinois chorus frog. However, most of the original pre-Euro-American settlement vegetation of the pristine sand prairie had probably disappeared long before the frog was described in 1951. More recent studies (Tucker, Chpt. 14; Brandon and Ballard, Chpt. 15, this volume; Brown and Rose 1988; Taubert et al. 1982; Tucker et al. 1995) have more precisely identified the specific sandy soil types utilized by the Illinois chorus frog. Vegetational associations presently inhabited by the frog are variable and almost always disturbed.

The two most profound environmental disturbances within the range of the Illinois chorus frog involve intensive agriculture and disruption of natural wetlands. The former has vastly changed the original sand prairie through tilling the soil, monoculture, movement of heavy equipment over the land, soil compaction, application of toxic agricultural chemicals (herbicides, insecticides, fertilizers), and hog raising. Wetland alteration has involved construction of levees along rivers and streams, channelization, digging many new drainage ditches, and installing underground drainage tiles. These alterations have resulted in the elimination of many wetlands, with such areas now being used for agriculture. Some other areas that probably experienced only seasonal inundation in pre-Euro-American settlement times are now permanently flooded lakes. There are many other localized environmental disturbances (Brown 1996; Brown and Rose 1988; Taubert et al. 1982), but none have altered the landscape as extensively as agriculture and wetland destruction.

Reproduction

A variety of breeding sites are utilized (Brown and Rose 1988; Taubert et al. 1982). Ephemeral sites (e.g., flooded fields, rain pools, ditches) are often used, as are more permanent sites (e.g., small ponds). All sites where breeding was observed were human-created or modified and thus were disturbed environments. There was nothing unique about these sites, and they were also used by other anuran species. Lotic environments and larger floodplain lakes are not used for breeding by Illinois chorus frogs.

The breeding season is most typically in March (Smith 1961), but calling can start as early as late January and extend into May (Butterfield et al. 1989; Taubert et al. 1982). Illinois chorus frogs are often one of the earliest spring breeders among anuran species in the Midwest.

The male mating call is a short whistle that is repeated relatively rapidly (Brown and Rose 1988). Males are able to tolerate cold temperatures and can call even when there are patches of snow on the ground and at an air temperature slightly below freezing (L. E. Brown, personal observations). Fecundity averages 462.3 to 608.2 eggs per female (Butterfield et al. 1989; Tucker, Chpt. 14, this volume), and sexual maturity can be attained in one year (Tucker 1995).

Distribution

The Illinois chorus frog is known from isolated, scattered localities: on the east side of the Illinois River in west-central Illinois (Cass, Mason, Menard, Morgan, Scott, and Tazewell Counties), in southwestern Illinois (Madison and Monroe Counties), in extreme southern Illinois (Alexander County), in southeastern Missouri

(Cape Girardeau, Dunklin, Mississippi, New Madrid, Pemiscot, Scott, and Stoddard Counties), and in northeastern Arkansas (Clay County) (Axtell and Haskell 1977; Beltz 1991; Brandon and Ballard, Chpt. 15, this volume; Brown and Brown 1973; Brown and Rose 1988; Gilbert 1986; Holman et al. 1964; Johnson 1987; Moll 1962; Smith 1951, 1955, 1961, 1966; Taubert et al. 1982). Numerous other areas of seemingly appropriate habitat have been searched to no avail. However, it is possible that additional localities may be discovered, particularly along the Illinois and Mississippi Rivers.

Rarity

Extensive fieldwork by a number of researchers indicates that usually fewer than ten calling males (often only one to three) are heard in typical breeding choruses, and it is unusual to hear choruses with over twenty calling males (Brown and Rose 1988). However, one chorus was estimated by Brown and Rose (1988) as possibly having around 100 calling males. In great contrast, the upland and striped chorus frogs *Pseudacris feriarum* and *Pseudacris triseriata* (both of which breed at the same sites as the Illinois chorus frog) often form choruses of over 100 calling males.

Detailed studies of numbers of Illinois chorus frogs have usually not been undertaken primarily because: (1) of time constraints (e.g., such censuses involve considerable time, and the frog is only available on the surface for a short period during its breeding season); (2) there is no guarantee that all unmarked and marked animals are equally available for capture and recapture, because all males do not call on a given night; (3) marking by toe clipping may adversely affect recapture and/or survival; (4) censusing breeding choruses does not constitute a random method of sampling; (5) it seems likely that there is substantial variation in numbers at a given locality within and between years (L. E. Brown, field observations; Tucker 1995); (6) it is difficult to capture all (or even a substantial portion) of a chorus because the males stop calling and hide themselves when the investigator starts moving around in the water; and (7) of other reasons given by Brown and Moll (1979).

Listing

On 1 October 1977, a group of Illinois herpetologists (R. Axtell, R. Brandon, L. Brown, R. Funk, E. Moll, M. Morris, J. Murphy, A. Resetar, P. Smith, G. Thurow, and H. Walley) participated in the Workshop on Rare and Endangered Amphibians and Reptiles of Illinois sponsored by the Illinois Endangered Species Project and hosted by the Illinois Natural Areas Inventory at the University of Illinois in Urbana. The main outcome of this meeting was an interim list of the state's endangered and threatened species, which included Illinois chorus frogs as threatened because of their rarity and disrupted habitat. Subsequently, this designation was made official by the Illinois Endangered Species Protection Board (Herkert 1992; Illinois Department of Conservation 1978; Morris and Smith 1981). In Missouri, Illinois chorus frogs are now listed as rare, and they are a species of special concern in Arkansas (Ramus 1996). Illinois chorus frogs have also been designated as a category 2 taxon by the U.S. Fish and Wildlife Service (Dodd et al. 1985). This signifies that Illinois chorus frogs may qualify for federal listing as endangered or threatened (under the law as of October 1995), but more information may be needed to determine their status and vulnerability.

The Sand Lake Dilemma

Endangered and threatened species are sometimes associated with environmental problems involving humans. The Sand Lake dilemma is one such problem and involved a natural environmental disaster, humans, and Illinois chorus frogs. This case is instructive because it is probably representative of the types of problems faced by Illinois chorus frogs over a hundred years ago that went unrecorded by humans. Moreover, this type of problem is also being faced today by many species, be they endangered, threatened, or unlisted.

Historical Background

Approximately 135 years ago an African American male operated a small grocery store (where local people also gathered to play cards and drink whiskey) located just south of an ephemeral lake in the sand prairie southeast of Havana, Illinois (Mason County Democrat 1993a; Speckman 1960). The reasons why the man selected this locality are obscure, but there is some indication he was a driver of a circus wagon that mired down in the road going through the wetland. He may have avoided living in Havana (a river town) to escape harassment and prejudice. In former times, some central and southern Illinois towns prohibited African Americans from residing within their borders. Furthermore, in the 1930s any African Americans who entered Pekin, Illinois, only 44.3 kilometers northeast of Havana, were quickly escorted to the edge of the city by the police (A. Harding, personal communication). As the years passed, the wetland came to be known as "Nigger Lake" by most local people, and it is still widely known by this bigoted, offensive name (although one map—USGS Havana Quadrangle, 7.5', 1948—refers to it as Negro Lake). Recently, a long overdue change occurred when the press started to use the name Sand Lake for the wetland.

In many years, Sand Lake is reduced to a small remnant of its maximum size, and sometimes in late summers or in periods of drought (e.g., the late 1980s) the lake is completely dry. When water has been lacking, Sand Lake, or portions of it, has been farmed.

At approximately twenty- to forty-year intervals (1888 [1898?], 1926 to 1927, early 1940s to 1946, 1972 to 1974, 1993 to 1994), Sand Lake has experienced substantial flooding and expansion well beyond its usual size (Environmental Science and Engineering 1993a,b). In the late 1800s, a 61-centimeter diameter tile drain was installed between Sand Lake and a storm sewer in southern Havana. However, a section of this tile was removed in the early 1960s, and thus it is questionable what effect this tile would have had on subsequent flood events. In about 1926 overflow from Sand Lake flooded eastern Havana to a depth of a few meters. The 1972 to 1974 flood resulted in the inundation of Illinois State Highway 97, and the Illinois Department of Transportation raised the level of the road 45.7 centimeters. However, none of the floods prior to 1993 to 1994 were considered severe enough to undertake major plans (other than the installation of the early tile drain) for the drainage of Sand Lake, eastern Havana, or intervening areas (Environmental Science and Engineering 1993b).

The Physical Environment

Sand Lake is located about 1.6 kilometers southeast of Havana in Sections 7, 8, 17, and 18, T21N., R8W., Havana Township, Mason County, Illinois (Fig. 30-2). The Illinois River is a short distance (ca. 3.2 to 4.0 kilometers) to the west. The wetland is above the floodplain on the Manito Terrace (Henry Formation, Mackinaw Member, Woodfordian outwash), which is composed of highly erosional, fine to medium sand and gravel (Labotka and Hester 1971). Soil types include the Dickinson-Onarga-Ade and Pittwood-Milroy associations (U.S. Department of Agriculture, Soil Conservation Service, and Illinois Agricultural Experiment Station 1970). The soils in the area facilitate rapid precipitation recharge of the underlying aquifer (Clark 1995). The landscape is relatively flat, but low-level dunes occur to the northwest and southwest of the wetland. Elevation is 143.3 meters at the edge of the lake (Geological Survey, U.S. Department of the Interior, and Corps of Engineers, U.S. Department of the Army 1948).

The aquifer is made up of Sankoty Sand (Kansan) and overlying outwash of Wisconsinan sand and gravel (Walker et al. 1965). Deposits are 30.5 to over 45.0 meters deep. Wells in the Havana region are often shallow as a consequence of the high water table. The potential yield of the aquifer was estimated at 1,325 million liters per day, and irrigation and other pumpage have not affected the water table in most of the area (Sanderson and Buck 1995; Walker et al. 1965).

The two most obvious human modifications of the physical environment are agriculture and roadways. Portions of the wetland are farmed in row crops (corn and soybeans), but only intermittently due to inundation. Wetland vegetation (e.g., cattails *Typha* sp.) sprouts up vigorously among planted corn, and old corn stubble can be seen through the clear water when the wetland is rejuvenated. Illinois State Highway 97 diagonally crosses the southwestern portion of the wetland. This is a major transportation route serving the Havana area. Roadside ditches serve as drainage channels for Sand Lake in times of flooding (this is the only drainage system for the wetland). Another east-west gravel road across the southern part of the wetland appears to have little effect other than being a repository for litter from travelers. The 1948 USGS Havana Quadrangle 7.5' map shows a railroad line crossing diagonally through the middle of the wetland, but this railroad line is no longer in existence. The railroad grade remains but has been breached at a point in the middle of the wetland. It is possible that soot, cinders, coal, and creosote associated with this former railroad line pollute Sand Lake when it is at flood stage.

The Biotic Environment

We are not aware of any comprehensive, coordinated survey of the biota of Sand Lake. However, numerous professional biologists as well as amateur birders have visited the wetland and recorded their findings. Following are synopses for the best-known groups of organisms.

Frogs and Toads. Eight species of anurans have been encountered at Sand Lake. Illinois chorus frogs were first heard by L. E. Brown and J. Brown at the site on 25 March and subsequently on 3 April 1986 when L. E. Brown was carrying out an endangered species survey for the Illinois Department of Transportation, preliminary to the construction of the Pecan Creek Bridge in

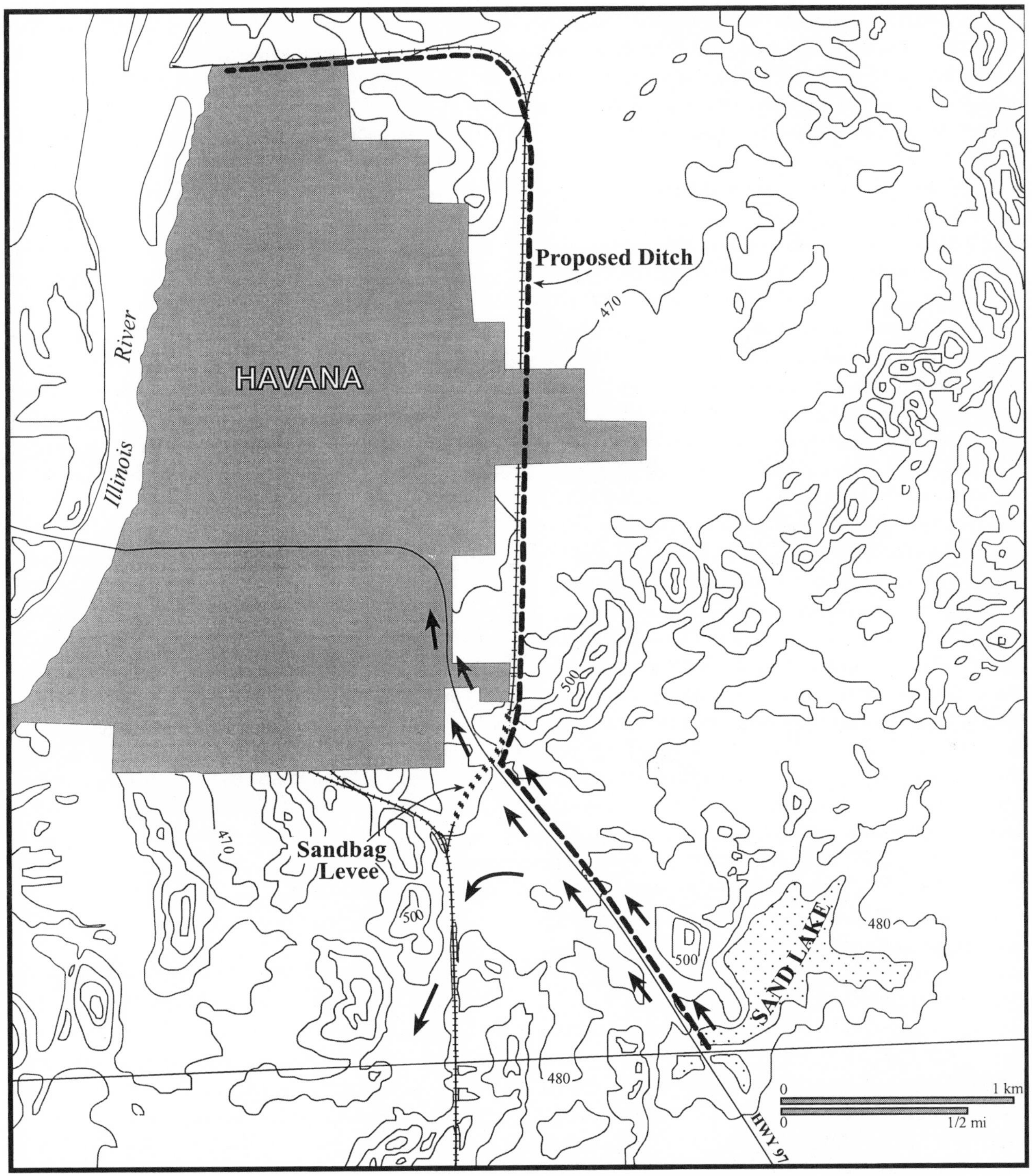

Figure 30-2. Sand Lake and Havana, Mason County, Illinois. Arrows indicate direction of water flow from Sand Lake into east Havana; the short, jagged diagonal line shows location of sandbag levee along railroad tracks to stop water flow into east Havana; the heavy dashed line indicates proposed location of the ditch to drain the wetland. Adapted from maps prepared by Environmental Science & Engineering, Inc., and the USGS Havana Quadrangle, 7.5', 1948, topographic. Cartographer: Jill Freund Thomas.

southern Mason County (Brown 1986). At these times, the number of calling males was estimated at over fifty (which is among the largest of the choruses we have heard). The site was again visited on 25 March 1989, when L. E. Brown led a field trip for the Central Illinois Herpetological Society to listen for the frog. That was during the height of a major drought, and the wetland was completely dry. Consequently, no frogs were heard. On 12 April 1994 L. E. Brown took the students in his Herpetology Seminar to Sand Lake, which had inundated surrounding areas. Again, a large chorus of Illinois chorus frogs was heard. In June 1994 J. E. Cima saw about twenty newly metamorphosed froglets at the site.

Hundreds of striped chorus frogs were heard by L. E. Brown and J. Brown on 25 March and 3 April 1986 and on 12 April 1994. The species was also heard on 11 May 1995 by P. Grap (personal communication).

On 28 June 1995 a chorus of over twenty-five calling male Blanchard's cricket frogs (*Acris crepitans blanchardi*) was heard by L. E. Brown and P. Grap. This is a relatively large number for this species in central Illinois, where chorus sizes of under ten calling males are more typical. The species is in decline in the northern and central Midwest (Greenwell et al. 1996; Vial and Saylor 1993; Lannoo 1996a; Casper, Chpt. 22; Hay, Chpt. 11; Lannoo, Chpt. 34; Moriarty, Chpt. 20, this volume).

A large chorus of eastern gray treefrogs (*Hyla versicolor*) estimated at over sixty calling males was heard by L. E. Brown and P. Grap on 28 June 1995. Tadpoles were identified the previous day.

Exceedingly large numbers of bullfrogs (*Rana catesbeiana*) have been seen on several field trips by L. E. Brown, J. Cima, and P. Grap. Tadpoles, several age classes of juveniles, and calling as well as noncalling adults were found.

On 3 April 1986 L. E. Brown and J. Brown heard a small chorus of plains leopard frogs (*Rana blairi*) at Sand Lake. Only small choruses of this species have been heard elsewhere in Mason County by L. E. Brown.

On 11 May 1995 P. Grap (personal communication) heard a chorus of southern leopard frogs (*Rana sphenocephala*) at Sand Lake.

Large numbers of calling male Fowler's toads (*Bufo woodhousii fowleri*), many tadpoles, thousands of newly metamorphosed toadlets, and numerous road-killed adults were encountered on 27 and 28 June 1995 by L. E. Brown, J. Cima, and P. Grap. Calling males were also heard earlier (11 May 1995) by P. Grap (personal communication).

Two other species—northern spring peepers (*Hyla crucifer crucifer*) and American toads (*Bufo americanus americanus*)—have often been encountered by L. E. Brown and J. Brown in Mason County and may breed at Sand Lake.

Birds. More is known about the birds of Sand Lake than any other group of organisms. This reflects the keen interest of amateur birders and professional ornithologists who have been attracted to the site for many years (L. E. Brown first became familiar with the wetland when he made a brief stop there in the early 1970s with D. Birkenholz to observe shorebirds). Brown and Moorehouse (1996) present a list of ninety-five species of birds that utilize Sand Lake (based on information supplied by several persons, particularly A. Moorehouse, as well as our own observations; this list is not to be considered complete). The site is best known for waterfowl and shorebirds, and many species are exceedingly abundant. The most significant finds include:

- American Bittern (*Botaurus lentiginosus*), state endangered
- Swainson's Hawk (*Buteo swainsoni*), state endangered
- Great Egret (*Casmerodius albus*), state threatened
- Piping Plover (*Charadrius melodus*), federally and state endangered
- Black Tern (*Chlidonias niger*), state endangered
- Little Blue Heron (*Egretta caerulea*), state endangered
- Common Moorhen (*Gallinula chloropus*), state threatened, nesting/young observed
- Bald Eagle (*Haliaeetus leucocephalus*), federally and state endangered
- Loggerhead Shrike (*Lanius ludovicianus*), state threatened
- Black-crowned Night Heron (*Nycticorax nycticorax*), state endangered
- Wilson's Phalarope (*Phalaropus tricolor*), state endangered
- Pied-billed Grebe (*Podilymbus podiceps*), state threatened, nesting/young observed
- King Rail (*Rallus elegans*), state threatened, nesting observed
- Common Tern (*Sterna hirundo*), state endangered
- Yellow-headed Blackbird (*Xanthocephalus xanthocephalus*), state endangered, nesting observed

Herkert (1991, 1992, 1994, 1995) has presented the most recent lists of state endangered and threatened birds (as well as other organisms) for Illinois; federally endangered species are listed in U.S. Fish and Wildlife Service, Division of Endangered Species (1993). Brown and Moorehouse (1996) and Newman (1996) provide additional information on the birds of Sand Lake.

Other Animal Species. Aquatic snails are common at Sand Lake. Dragonflies and damselflies are diverse in species and numerous in individuals. A variety of fishes are present (bluegill [*Lepomis macrochirus*] dead on shore; large school of young catfish [*Ictalurus* sp.]; many other minnows and fry). It is unclear how these fish got into this ephemeral wetland. A vole (*Microtus* sp.) and opossum (*Didelphis virginiana*) were observed near the lake, and several muskrat (*Ondrata zibethicus*) lodges were seen in the lake.

Plants. The wetland vegetation at Sand Lake is diverse in species and numerous in individuals. A list of twenty-seven species found at the site has been complied by W. McClain (personal communication), and we have found two additional species. The most notable species is Hall's bulrush (*Scirpus hallii*), which is state endangered (Herkert 1991). Recently, another state endangered plant, the weak bulrush (*Scirpus purshianus*), was identified at Sand Lake (Schwegman 1996).

Rodgers (1978) completed a detailed study of the pre-Euro-American settlement (ca. 1823) vegetation of Mason County by examining the original land survey records. She found that the area around Sand Lake was prairie.

Wetland Status. The National Wetlands Inventory (1988) officially identified Sand Lake as a palustrine wetland (PEMAf, PEMC, PEMCx, PEMF, P(EM/SS1)F, PSSIC, PUBG). This characterization was based on vegetation, visible hydrology, and geography.

The Great Flood

During the spring and summer of 1993, the upper Mississippi River and its tributaries in the Midwest experienced extensive flooding, which resulted in much human hardship and economic loss. Mason County also suffered severe flooding in 1993, but this was unrelated to high riparian water levels. Events in the summer of 1993 in the Scarborough Estates residential subdivision at the northeast edge of Havana foreshadowed problems of far greater magnitude to the south. A high water table resulting from excess rainfall (55.4 centimeters above normal) in the first nine months of 1993 caused wet basements and failure of septic systems in the subdivision (Environmental Science & Engineering 1993a). Two major rainfalls in the first half of September (9.4 centimeters during 2 to 6 September; 10.9 centimeters during 13 to 14 September) then caused the overflow of Sand Lake (Environmental Science & Engineering 1993a,b). Water flowed northwesterly toward Havana along the drainage ditches bordering Illinois State Highway 97 and through a depression (Walker Forge Pond) west of the roadway (Fig. 30-2). Soon much of southeastern Havana was flooded. Residential basements suffered significant flooding and structural damage from high water pressure. Inoperable furnaces and water heaters in flooded basements made many residences nearly uninhabitable. Also affected were two schools and a number of industrial and commercial businesses.

Agricultural land was significantly impacted, with Sand Lake having expanded to cover about 81 to 121 hectares. Over one-fourth of the farmland in Mason County was flooded (Aldus 1993; Bouyea 1993), and more than 171 groundwater lakes appeared (Clark 1995). Illinois State Highway 97 was inundated with more than 30 centimeters of water, and a number of roads in the Havana area were closed (Environmental Science & Engineering 1993b; Daily Times 1993).

The flooding was caused by prolonged above-average rainfall, which resulted in high groundwater levels and saturated soils. The water table rose above ground level, and because of limited topographic relief and poorly developed natural drainage systems, drainage into streams or rivers was impossible (Environmental Science & Engineering 1993a,b).

The Human Response

As could be expected for a disaster of this type, the human response was confusion. Citizens were frightened, frustrated, and sometimes angry. Numerous meetings were held involving the public and city, county, state, and federal officials (Environmental Science & Engineering 1993a). Many individuals wanted Sand Lake to be drained. Precise information was lacking in regard to elevation, and thus no one could predict how the flooding would progress. The Illinois Department of Transportation again proceeded (as it did in the 1970s) to elevate Highway 97, first by gravel and later by asphalt (Environmental Science & Engineering 1993a,b). To address the flooding problems, the Sand Lake Task Force was created.

Environmental Science & Engineering, Inc., of Peoria, Illinois, was contracted to provide assistance in analyzing the problem and suggesting solutions (Environmental Science & Engineering 1993a,b). The urgency of the problem negated the initiation of any long-term solution through time-consuming construction projects. Thus, three short-term options providing temporary relief were activated: sandbagging, pumping, and ditching. Sandbagging was mainly carried out along Illinois State Highway 97 to protect businesses and residences and along the southeastern edge of Havana on the embankment for the Chicago and Illinois Midland Railroad line, which crosses Highway 97 (Fig. 30-2). When this was completed, water flow into the city was significantly reduced. However, the sandbag levee caused water to be diverted into agricultural lands to the south, which resulted in complaints by farmers as well as litigation (Environmental Science & Engineering 1993a; Williams 1993a).

Pumping was also initiated in eastern Havana by connecting 1,219 meters of 35.6-centimeter-diameter aluminum irrigation pipe to a powerful pump. The pipe was laid over the north-south hill of central Havana and emptied into a storm sewer on the west side (Environmental Science & Engineering 1993a; Mason County Democrat 1993b). A limited amount of ditching was carried out, which probably relieved some areas as water was directed toward the pump. However, as there was no nearby stream or river to receive floodwater, no major ditching efforts were pursued.

Relief was not immediate, but these measures, plus evaporation, eventually eliminated the flooding in east Havana.

The Super Ditch

Environmental Science & Engineering (1993b) identified a number of long-term options that might relieve the flooding problem: constructing a levee around Sand Lake, constructing a flood control device to direct water westward, purchasing flood easements, and constructing various drainage ditches. The most popular option among citizens and local governments was a surface drainage ditch extending from Sand Lake northward along the east side of Havana and then west along the north side of Havana into the Illinois River (Fig. 30-2). This plan was favored because it was perceived not only as a solution for draining Sand Lake but also because it might provide drainage for eastern Havana (W. Ingram, personal communication). The estimated cost for this super ditch was approximately $1.3 million. A request for funding was made to the Infrastructure Subcommittee of the Interagency Mitigation Advisory Group in Springfield, Illinois, with the hope that the application would be forwarded to the Federal Emergency Management Agency (FEMA). However, the pre-application was turned down because various criteria were not satisfied (W. Blessman, personal communication; Mason County Democrat 1994a,b). The U.S. Soil Conservation Service, in cooperation with the Mason County Soil and Water Conservation District, is investigating a long-term solution (Williams 1994), but a plan has not yet been developed. In October 1995 a committee was formed in Havana to study options, apparently as a result of the belief that other initiatives were not progressing satisfactorily (W. Ingram, personal communication).

The Permit Issue

Flood control construction projects involving wetlands are regulated by the Federal Water Pollution Control Act (Section 404—dredge and fill activities), known as the Clean Water Act (Environmental Science & Engineering 1993b, 1994). This act requires an application for a permit from the U.S. Army Corps of Engineers for impacts that are unavoidable. The applicant must demonstrate that other alternatives were considered and that the proposed project has the least environmental impact. Furthermore, endangered and threatened species must be considered, and there must also be mitigation of impacted wetlands. A more detailed field investigation would be a requirement for a permit, and the presence of any toxic waste dumps (e.g., the cinder fill area along the railroad) would further complicate the application process. The permit application is forwarded to a number of governmental agencies for input (e.g., Illinois Department of Transportation, Illinois State Water Survey, Illinois Environmental Protection Agency, Illinois Department of Natural Resources, U.S. Fish and Wildlife Service). If the project is federally funded, the applicant must demonstrate compliance with Executive Order 11990, "Protection of Wetlands," which requires that destruction or degradation of wetlands be minimized. Thus, the process of applying for permission to alter a wetland substantially is lengthy and comprehensive. Moreover, there is ample opportunity for counterchecks if laws and regulations are enforced and if governmental agencies perform the review process in an appropriate manner.

Discussion

There are substantial indications that Sand Lake is a nearly pristine wetland community. First, a large number of endangered and threatened species (fifteen birds, one frog, two plants) utilize the wetland. Second, there is considerable species diversity among the birds found at the site (including a number of rare but unlisted species). Third, the numbers of individual birds and anurans that use the wetland are quite large. Fourth, cattails have not become overdominant. Many wetlands at disturbed sites become dominated by cattails (Odum 1988), which establish dense thickets and reduce species diversity; however, at Sand Lake, cattails do not cover the entire wetland but are dispersed in clumps with other wetland plant species intervening, which is characteristic of a more mature wetland plant community. Fifth, the intermittent farming that does occur appears to be rather nonintrusive. When flooding occurs, the wetland vegetation aggressively rejuvenates from an apparently ample seed bank.

In our many years of fieldwork, we have heretofore never seen a pristine breeding site for Illinois chorus frogs. All sites utilized were modified or created by human activities (primarily through agriculture and manipulation of wetlands). Sand Lake is the least disturbed site we have found, and it may represent one of the original pre-Euro-American settlement types of breeding sites used by Illinois chorus frogs. It seems quite likely that other areas that are presently farmed intensively were utilized as breeding sites by Illinois chorus frogs in the past before the land was tiled and ditched.

The destruction of Sand Lake will not, by itself, result in the extinction of Illinois chorus frogs, as populations are known from other localities. However, such action would result in the elimination of the only known nearly pristine breeding habitat for Illinois chorus frogs. Thus, Sand Lake is important as a model for the restoration of other breeding habitats for this species and other endangered and threatened species known to utilize the habitat at Sand Lake.

Many anuran breeding sites in central Illinois are utilized by a relatively small number of species (often a maximum of three or four). The occurrence of eight chorusing species at Sand Lake is unusual (further fieldwork may even reveal two additional species). The numbers of individuals for five of the species present were also unusually large.

We have never worked at a locality that has as many endangered and threatened species as Sand Lake (eighteen). Fifteen of these are birds, and because of the great enthusiasm of laypersons in promoting the conservation of birds, we might anticipate a rare case where the birds may save the frog.

The present attempt to drain Sand Lake is a classic case of history revisited. Bellrose et al. (1983) indicated: "Early in the 1900's, the bottomland water areas of the Illinois River were almost pristine. . . . Water areas of numerous shapes and sizes were scattered along both sides of the Illinois River. . . . They took the forms of river marshes, long narrow sloughs, oval ponds or small lakes, and lakes of large size that were often ameboid in shape. Those water areas fed by springs or streams maintained continuous outlets to the river." However, things soon changed drastically due to the devastating effects of human environmental modification (Bellrose et al. 1983). These alterations involved the diversion of a large amount of water into the Illinois River from Lake Michigan through the Illinois and Michigan Canal and the Chicago Sanitary and Ship Canal; the construction of five locks and dams; an alarmingly excessive deposition of silt from erosion due to agriculture; the establishment of numerous drainage and levee districts; and urban water pollution from the Chicago area (Bellrose et al. 1983). This resulted in the killing of thousands of hectares of trees from inundation; the destruction of most aquatic bed plants; the elimination of many smaller wetlands and extensive marshes; the merging of some water bodies to form larger lakes; the exposure of large mud flats; increased wave action, which had a detrimental effect on shorelines; a decrease in dissolved oxygen and an increase in turbidity in the Illinois River; and a reduction in lake depths in the Illinois River (due to sedimentation), which curtails the capacity to conduct floodwater and thus enhances the possibility of flooding (Bellrose et al. 1983). Presently, much of the formerly wetland-rich floodplain is devoted to intensive agriculture, made possible by the construction of additional channelized ditches and levees and the laying of underground drainage tiles.

Upland areas, as well, are now dominated by agriculture. By 1883 much of the Illinois prairie had been converted to agricultural use (Ridgway 1889). The detrimental effects of "tiling, ditching, and cultivation of the soil" in central Illinois were commented on as early as the nineteenth century by Garman (1892). Much of the original prairie in Illinois was noted for poor drainage, which resulted in extensive marshes and potholes (White 1978). These areas had to be drained for agriculture to predominate, and this resulted in the destruction of nearly the entire prairie ecosystem in Illinois. Thus, the threat posed to Illinois chorus frogs at Sand Lake is nothing new but is rather a replay of similar types of environmentally degradative attempts that were initiated over a century ago by humans to control water.

There are probably at least seven interrelated reasons why Sand Lake has persisted to the present: (1) it can still be farmed (perhaps two or three years out of every five), and therefore modest economic benefits can accrue in spite of the flooding; (2) there is no nearby stream that can receive floodwaters; (3) construction of a drainage ditch would be quite costly (in terms of cost versus income, it could not be justified because of the relatively low returns from farming); (4) the land has remained in private ownership, so public monies for ditch construction were not provided in the past; (5) property taxes are probably low; (6) Havana is flooded only infrequently (every twenty to forty years); and (7) the wetland has probably been of value for waterfowl hunting (the area along the Illinois River has been of major importance for duck hunting for many years [Parmalee and Loomis 1983]; at the time of this writing there are duck blinds in the wetland).

As might be expected, there have been considerable negative feelings directed toward Sand Lake. Could this, in part, reflect a subconscious prejudice due to the use of the derogatory common name "Nigger Lake"? If true, the future destruction of the wetland could be based partially on racial discrimination. Many local people are convinced that the lake was the cause of the problems, in spite of repeated attempts by Environmental Science & Engineering to enlighten the community (W. Ingram, personal communication). In reality, the wetland is a symptom, not a cause, of the flooding. The cause is a high water table, which reflects soil type, rainfall, topography, subsurface geology, and probably a number of other factors. `W. Ingram, a water resources engineer at Environmental Science & Engineering, pointed out that the drainage ditch would not alleviate, to a substantial degree, flooded basements or any other flooding unrelated to Sand Lake (Williams 1993b). Recall that east Havana was having water problems even before the overflow of Sand Lake. It is questionable if a drainage ditch would provide adequate relief to east Havana. Furthermore, preliminary cost analysis has indicated that identified benefits of the drainage ditch are only about equal to the cost of the project (Environmental Science & Engineering 1993b). Secondary benefits and secondary damages were not included in that analysis.

There would seem to be five major obstacles to ditch construction or other major flood control measures: (1) the high cost of construction; (2) the questionable issue of costs versus benefits; (3) the difficulty in obtaining the necessary permits because of the presence of eighteen endangered and threatened species at the site; (4) the possible destruction or modification of a nationally recognized wetland; and (5) the distinct possibility that the ditch may be ineffective in the control of future water problems. Nonetheless, we feel sympathetic to the plight of the citizens of east Havana and the agricultural community to the south of the city. It would seem likely that, should another flood occur (and that eventuality is only a matter of time), local citizens will exert strong political pressure to initiate some type of relief action.

We offer no solutions to the Sand Lake dilemma but urge that the status quo be maintained in regard to the wetland. Construction of ditches may permanently drain and hence destroy the wetland. Surrounding the wetland with a levee may turn it into a permanent lake (which has happened previously along the Illinois River valley). This would result in a drastic change in the biota, and the site would no longer be used for breeding by Illinois chorus frogs and probably some of the other endangered and threatened species. We do not know whether Illinois chorus frogs would travel uphill over a dike to reach a breeding site.

We urge that a state or federal commission be established to study the Sand Lake dilemma and offer recommendations. Preferably it would include experts from a number of areas (e.g., hydrology, engineering, geology, sociology, conservation, ornithology, herpetology, botany, agriculture) and citizen representatives. Because of the significance of the wetland and its impact, it would seem logical that state or federal funding be made available. Hopefully, a solution to the Sand Lake dilemma would be arrived at which not only saves the wetland but also acknowledges the rights and expectations of the citizens of east Havana and the farm community to the south. The recognition and conservation of Sand Lake as a major, nearly pristine breeding site for the threatened Illinois chorus frog will be a significant step toward enhancing the status of the frog and will provide a model for future conservation efforts.

Summary

Illinois chorus frogs (*Pseudacris streckeri illinoensis*) are state-threatened animals under consideration for federal listing. They have a highly unusual forward burrowing behavior and are one of the few fossorial species in the treefrog family Hylidae. The forelimbs are enlarged and have other morphological adaptations for burrowing. These are the only frogs known to be subterranean feeders. Relictual sand habitats are occupied along the Illinois and Mississippi Rivers in Illinois, Missouri, and Arkansas. Intensive agriculture and wetland disruption are the main types of environmental degradation affecting these frogs.

In 1986 a relatively large chorus of Illinois chorus

frogs was discovered at a nearly pristine ephemeral wetland (Sand Lake) near Havana, Illinois. The wetland has had a long history of flooding (at about twenty- to forty-year intervals), and in 1993 it overflowed into east Havana causing considerable property damage. Efforts to obtain funding to construct a ditch to drain Sand Lake have been unsuccessful. A stalemate exists at present, but citizen concern remains high due to the potential of future flooding.

A large number (eighteen) of endangered and threatened species utilize Sand Lake, and especially large numbers of bird and frog species have been found at the site. The attempt to drain Sand Lake is a classic case of history revisited, as innumerable attempts by humans to control water in central Illinois have been undertaken in the twentieth century. These activities have played a major role in the destruction of the prairie ecosystem in Illinois as well as many wetlands along the Illinois River valley. Sand Lake represents the only known nearly pristine breeding site for Illinois chorus frogs, and the conservation of the wetland would be a significant step toward enhancing the status of these frogs, as well as providing a model for future conservation efforts. We suggest that a commission be formed to study the Sand Lake dilemma and recommend solutions that will save the wetland and also protect the citizens of the Havana area from future flooding.

Acknowledgments

We thank A. Moorehouse for providing extensive information on the birds of Sand Lake; F. Bellrose, D. Birkenholz, R. Bjorklund, H. Gasdorf, D. Glosser, and J. Herkert for providing additional information on birds; W. McClain for providing a list of plants; J. Brown and P. Grap for field assistance; P. Grap for providing information on frog choruses he observed; J. Murphy (photographer), the Chicago Herpetological Society, and C. Warwick (Illinois Natural History Survey) for permission to publish Figure 30-1; J. Thomas for preparing Figure 30-2; A. Capparella, G. Clark, R. Martin, and W. Martin (Mason County Democrat) and A. Moorehouse for providing literature references; R. Anderson, W. Blessman, K. Donoho, A. French, D. Glosser, A. Harding, J. Herkert, W. Ingram, W. Martin, and W. McClain for discussion; C. Giscombe and R. Schmitt for enlightenment; and R. Anderson, R. Brandon, J. Brown, C. Giscombe, W. Ingram, G. Paukstis, and J. Tucker for critically reading the manuscript. The Illinois Department of Transportation provided funding to L. E. Brown in 1986 for an endangered species survey, which incidentally resulted in the discovery of the large chorus of Illinois chorus frogs at Sand Lake.

31

Cooperative Resolution of an Environmental Dilemma: A Case Study

Owen J. Sexton, Christopher A. Phillips, Mathew Parks, John F. Stinn, and Robert E. Preston

Conservation is widely appreciated throughout the United States. Nonacademic supporters include people interested in hunting, fishing, and trapping, as well as bird-watchers, hikers, bikers, shooters, picnickers and campers, rock hounds, flower and insect enthusiasts, general nature lovers, and those who revel in occasional bouts of solitude. Such a broad array of supporters has both positive and negative aspects. A positive one is the political power, engendered by a large body of voters, to influence or even coerce elected and appointed governmental officials to address conservation issues. Failing success at attaining desired goals through more regular political channels, conservation enthusiasts can, at least in certain states, petition and present referenda to be voted on by the citizens directly. For example, when legislators of the State of Missouri would not enact a special sales tax to support conservation, a citizens' group circulated a statewide petition that proposed a one-eighth-cent sales tax to be devoted entirely to conservation. This referendum passed and has resisted further attack by the state legislature. A negative aspect is that this broad spectrum of support inherently encompasses subgroups that may have conflicts of interest. Each side in any conflict can view its opponent in a negative way. In turn, these conflicts can weaken the very stability of the broad political structure needed for political success. In order to maintain political stability, some general forum of internal conflict resolution must be developed.

The conflict presented here represents a unique case, as all cases may well be. It arose not because of deliberate malice or neglect by any party but from a lack of understanding of the biological situation and by construction constraints imposed by a less than well considered plan. The conflict centered around the destruction of an old constructed breeding pond utilized by several species of mole salamanders (*Ambystoma* sp.) in favor of a shooting range. The locale was a state-owned conservation area whose preservation had been demanded by conservationists. Elements needed to resolve the issue included: (1) a survey of relevant scientific information; (2) information on the historical background of the conflict; (3) development of realistic options to reduce or eliminate the conflict; (4) execution of selected options; and (5) follow-up studies of the effectiveness of the execution.

Scientific Background

Although eastern tiger salamanders (*Ambystoma tigrinum tigrinum*) and marbled salamanders (*Ambystoma opacum*) also bred in the destroyed pond (R.P., personal observation), we will concentrate our comments on spotted salamanders (*Ambystoma maculatum*), the most abundant of the three species. Many investigators have described the use of fish-free ponds as breeding sites by this species (Andrews 1897; Smith 1907; Wright 1908; Wright and Allen 1909; Blanchard 1930; Dempster 1930; Finneran 1951; Baldauf 1952; Peckham and Dineen 1954; Husting 1965; Shoop 1965, 1967; Hillis 1977; Stenhouse 1985; Sexton et al. 1986; Phillips 1989). These works include information about time of entry into and exit from the pond, numbers of individuals, sex ratio, body size, and meteorological parameters.

Several studies have revealed that adults leave the breeding ponds at or near their entry point (Shoop

1965, 1968; Douglas and Monroe 1981; Stenhouse 1985; Sexton et al. 1986; Phillips and Sexton 1989) and often utilize corridors between the aquatic and terrestrial habitats (Shoop 1968; Sexton et al. 1986). Some investigators have suggested that postbreeding adults do not disperse far from their pond. Individuals tagged by Douglas and Monroe (1981) dispersed between 6 and 220 meters (average = 150 meters) from the ponds and then occupied subterranean burrows of rodents within a 12- to 14-square-meter area of the forest floor. Whitford and Vinegar (1966) estimated that spotted salamanders could migrate to the breeding ponds from a distance of 213 meters. Sexton et al. (1986) captured very few immigrants at a drift fence located 172 meters from the pond. They also demonstrated that, under unusually favorable conditions, 76 percent and 87 percent of females and males, respectively, of the breeding population arrived at the pond on one night, suggesting that most individuals lived within one night's travel. On the basis of their orientation studies, Whitford and Vinegar (1966) estimated that the mean rate of travel from release sites to the breeding ponds was between 9.1 and 12.2 meters per hour. Stenhouse (1985) has suggested that individual salamanders utilize the same postbreeding retreats yearly.

Several field studies with marked salamanders have disclosed that some individuals return to the same breeding pond in successive years while others return at less regular intervals (Husting 1965; Whitford and Vinegar 1966; Shoop 1968; Stenhouse 1985; Phillips and Sexton 1989). Whitford and Vinegar (1966) made extensive collections at other breeding ponds within an 0.8-kilometer radius of their study pond and encountered none of their marked salamanders. They hypothesized that spotted salamanders bred only in one pond. Shoop (1968) released experimental animals from one pond near a second pond. He also released control animals from the second pond at the same location. None of the experimental and most of the control animals returned to the second pond.

The use of particular ponds for breeding suggests that spotted salamanders are able to orient. Whitford and Vinegar (1966) showed that displaced individual salamanders could orient to their breeding pond from a distance of 128 meters. Shoop (1968) demonstrated that some spotted salamanders could regain their home pond from 500 meters. The potential methods or cues by which salamanders can orient or navigate include random search, rheotaxis, sun, stars, geomagnetism, olfaction, and sound. Finneran (1951) and Whitford and Vinegar (1966) suggested that rheotaxis may be a prime candidate for orienting, but Shoop (1968) did not concur. Ferguson (1971) has offered olfaction as a likely cue for those species of amphibians that migrate on dark, rainy nights when solar and stellar cues would be ineffective. McGregor and Teska (1989) demonstrated experimentally that spotted salamanders can recognize the scent of their home pond. Forester and La Pasha (1982) did not support the roll of frog calls as a likely cue. Studies of other species of amphibians have discussed sun-compass (Landreth and Ferguson 1967) and magnetic (Perry et al. 1985; Phillips 1986) orientation. It must be realized that any one species may rely on more than one cue in orientation and navigation.

The evidence presented above indicates that there is a high degree of pond fidelity (philopatry) in spotted salamanders. Knowledge of salamander philopatry provided the basis for the public outcry about the destruction of a breeding pond on public property. However, C. Phillips (1994) examined mitochondrial DNA variation in 207 individual spotted salamanders from sixteen populations in the Missouri Ozarks. Given the limited dispersal of this species, he expected to find a high degree of genetic partitioning. Instead, he observed a very low level of variation in mitochondrial DNA, which increased slightly from north to south. This pattern was interpreted as evidence for recent and rapid colonization of the northern Ozarks by spotted salamanders following the return of deciduous forest to the area at the end of the hypsithermal interval around 4,000 years B.P. This hypothesis suggests that spotted salamanders have the ability to colonize newly created habitat quickly. This ability is contrary to that predicted on the basis of the pond fidelity and homing experiments discussed above.

Historical Background

In the 1979 to 1982 interval, one of us (R.P.) undertook a full study of the breeding migrations of three species of ambystomatid salamanders. He concentrated on the activities centering around what we term here as Preston Pond, the pond destroyed during the construction of the shooting range. This pond was situated on a hilltop at the border of a sparse deciduous wood and an old field. It was 25 meters in diameter and had a maximal depth of 40 centimeters. Preston constructed a drift fence of window screen, which completely encircled the pond. He placed twenty cans at 4.5-meter intervals adjacent to the outer surface of the fence, with the opening of the cans flush with the ground surface. He operated this system from February to May in 1980 and 1982 to estimate the number of immigrant spotted salamanders. He carried out other less-detailed studies at other nearby ponds. Preston also seined larvae from these ponds and operated the drift fence during several falls. He recorded the presence of all amphibian species observed (Table 31-1). He captured 945 individual spotted salamanders during twenty-four visits between 24 February and 4 April 1980. In 1982 he recorded 429 immigrants during twenty-two visits between 24 February and 3 April. He also noted the presence of immigrating adult marbled salamanders and their terrestrial and transforming young during the fall and spring periods between 1979 and 1982 (Preston and Aldridge 1981). Tiger salamanders were also present at this pond. The report of the presence of these three ambystomatid species at Preston Pond furnished ammunition for the resulting conflict. During the ensuing debate, the number of resident ambystomatid species was elevated to five.

At the time of Preston's study, Forest 44 was privately owned. In the late 1980s it was offered for development. The potential loss of this 358-hectare tract aroused a great deal of concern among local environmental groups for several reasons. First, most of the highly dissected topography was covered with second-growth oak-hickory forest, except for one open portion that was under cultivation. Second, Forest 44 abutted a larger complex of 2,940 hectares comprised of five properties devoted to conservation and education. Forest 44 would expand this complex. Third, Forest 44 provided one side of an Ozark forest edge along a major interstate highway, I-44. Because of the great local public interest in preserving Forest 44, officials of St. Louis County and the Missouri Department of Conservation (MDC) cooperated and conveyed the property to the MDC in 1990 at a cost of $4.5 million.

Table 31-1. Amphibian species observed by R. E. Preston at Preston Pond during 1979 to 1982

American toad (*Bufo americanus americanus*)
Western chorus frog (*Pseudacris triseriata triseriata*)
Northern spring peeper (*Pseudacris crucifer crucifer*)
Eastern gray treefrog (*Hyla versicolor*)
Southern leopard frog (*Rana sphenocephala*
Plains leopard frog (*Rana blairi*)
Central newt (*Notophthalmus viridescens louisianensis*)
Spotted salamander (*Ambystoma maculatum*)
Marbled salamander (*Ambystoma opacum*)
Eastern tiger salamander (*Ambystoma tigrinum tigrinum*)

In December 1993 it became apparent that the MDC planned to build a shooting range at Forest 44, and soon after rumors circulated through the local conservation community that Preston Pond would be eliminated during the construction. One of us (C.A.P.) contacted the MDC office responsible for the management of Forest 44 and inquired about the accuracy of the reports. MDC officials said that destruction of the pond was "very likely at this point." Within a few days, MDC officials wanted to discuss mitigation options concerning pond-breeding amphibians at Forest 44. The MDC had already dug ten to twelve wildlife ponds throughout the property as part of their standard "wildlife habitat improvement" for newly acquired property. They asked if amphibian adults, eggs, and larvae could be moved from Preston Pond into one or more of the newly constructed ponds. A group of volunteers agreed to try, and on 21 March 1993 they moved all egg masses of spotted salamanders and larvae of marbled salamanders that could be seined or dip-netted from Preston Pond to two alternative ponds on the property. East Pond, located north of Preston Pond, existed prior to 1993 and was known to harbor larvae of both spotted and marbled salamanders. It was deepened, and its dam was repaired in December 1993. West Pond, located northwest of Preston Pond, was constructed in December 1993. In addition, the MDC pumped the remaining water from Preston Pond and transported soil and pond debris from it to the two surrogate ponds later in the spring of 1993.

As a consequence of widespread public concern about the loss of the breeding pond, a meeting was held on 31 March 1993, at which representatives of the MDC, the general public, the St. Louis Zoo, and local universities tried to resolve the problem. The result was a list of nine recommendations, two of which had already been carried out, that would mitigate the loss of Preston Pond (Table 31-2).

Test of the Success of the Surrogate Ponds

Among the participants at the 31 March 1993 meeting, there was widespread skepticism about the efficacy of the suggested recommendations in establishing and maintaining viable populations in East and West Ponds, particularly the latter. This skepticism was directed espe-

Table 31-2. Nine recommendations accepted at the 31 March 1993 meeting designed to mitigate the loss of Preston Pond as a breeding locale for ambystomatid salamanders

1. Transfer all of the water from the old salamander pond to both the renovated pond and the new pond.
2. Transfer all of the leaf vegetative substrate possible from the old pond to the new pond. Deposit this substrate along the edge of the new pond. The renovated pond does not need any substrate. This should ensure the pond is inoculated with insect larvae important for the feeding of the salamander larvae.
3. Plant the banks with rye grass to help hold and stabilize the soil. We will plant the grass seed and then mulch using alfalfa. Alfalfa chips are important to reduce the suspended clays in the new pond and make the water clearer.
4. Ensure that no fish become introduced into the new or renovated pond.
5. We do not need to do any tree planting; the renovated pond has adequate tree cover. The new pond is close enough to the edge of the forest that it will receive some shade from existing trees. Planting trees might inhibit tiger salamanders from attempting to use this pond because they prefer more open, field-type conditions.
6. Place a number of large logs in and by the pond. The best method is to place logs perpendicular to the water edge so that the logs are lying both in and out of the water.
7. Install some drift fences in the area of the old pond to possibly capture returning adults next spring, and place them in the new and renovated pond.
8. Attempt to save small waterholes within 100 feet of the old pond from any construction damage. Excavate these waterholes to increase their depth to approximately 3 feet.
9. Our main contact on this project will be C.A.P. However, if anyone else has any suggestions or concerns they can contact J.F.S. or O.S. C.A.P. will act as liaison with the local herpetology community.

cially against the supposition that adult ambystomatids, which had previously bred in Preston Pond, would relocate to the new West Pond. The simplistic hypothesis to be tested was that no adult salamanders (i.e., those too old in 1994 to have been present in West Pond as larvae) would breed there because of their fidelity to their pond of origin.

Field Test, Spring 1994

Procedure. Three separate sections of drift fence were placed parallel to and 2 meters distant from the shore of both East and West Ponds. Drop cans were buried adjacent to the outer side of the fencing at 2-meter intervals; these cans were placed to trap salamanders migrating to the pond. The total length of the three sections of fencing at West Pond was 22 meters, or 27 percent of the total fence perimeter. Similar values for East Pond were 28 meters and 35 percent, respectively. The fences were set up in late February and removed 13 April. The cans were examined on twenty-three occasions over twenty days.

We also examined two (ponds 3 and 4) of the ten newly dug ponds in fall 1993 and early winter 1994. These ponds did not receive the treatments listed in Table 31-1. In each pond we placed ten dowel rods, 1 meter in length and 0.5 centimeter in diameter, in each pond as a site on which female spotted salamanders could deposit eggs. One end of a rod was positioned into the water column. These rods were examined periodically for egg masses. On 28 April 1994 we also seined the ponds for egg masses.

Results. Twenty-five female and thirty-eight male spotted salamanders (2.88 adult salamanders per meter of fence) were obtained at West Pond. The extrapolated numbers of salamanders presumed to have entered the pond along the entire fence perimeter were 93 females and 141 males, or 234 adults. At the reconstituted pond, East Pond, 44 females and 47 males (3.25 adults per meter of fence) were actually captured. No other adult ambystomatids were noted at either pond. No egg masses were ever observed on the ten dowel rods of ponds 3 and 4. Egg masses were seined from each pond on 28 April 1994.

Field Test, Fall 1994

Procedure. Because female marbled salamanders deposit their eggs on land adjacent to ponds which is subject to flooding during the fall rains, we did not use the drift fence technique to record numbers of this species. Around the perimeters of both ponds, we placed a series of 25-by-25-centimeter boards, which served as brooding sites for female marbled salamanders. We also set up a series of transect lines parallel to the pond. At randomly selected points along these transects we examined the adjacent terrain, particularly beneath clumps of grass (Feigel and Semlitsch 1995), for brooding females.

Results. At East Pond we observed only two females

(one brooding approximately 100 eggs) and one male. At West Pond we found only two females brooding eggs.

Conclusions

The data from East and West Ponds provide clear evidence that spotted salamanders responded positively to both as suitable breeding sites. This response is not unexpected for the population of the reconstructed East Pond because those salamanders may have included individuals returning to their home pond. Such is not the case for the new West Pond, and the simplistic hypothesis of obligate philopatry can be rejected. However, there are two explanations to account for the acceptance of this pond. Both assume that the breeders of 1994 were individuals originating from Preston Pond. The first explanation is that those salamanders responded positively to the scent of Preston Pond, which had been transferred to West Pond by transferring water and substrate from the former to the latter. The second explanation is that the salamanders utilized some other unidentified cue or cues to orient to the new pond. That spotted salamanders can do so is indicated by our observations that an unknown number of individuals bred in ponds 3 and 4, ponds that had not received water or substrate from Preston Pond. Phillips (1989) has recorded several other instances where previously unused ponds were invaded by breeding spotted salamanders. The limited data for marbled salamanders are a weak reflection of the situation for spotted salamanders.

Epilogue

What was achieved in the resolution of the conflict between those desiring that a specific part of Forest 44 be used as a shooting range and those who believed that some part should be retained as a breeding pool for salamanders? To perhaps an unequal degree, each side achieved its goals. The shooters clearly obtained a public shooting range. What do the preservationists have? Possibly more than is readily apparent.

Public opinion forced a highly respected state department of conservation to assuage the biological and political damage caused by an unfortunate design decision. That department did so in good grace. Table 31-2 outlines the specific steps designed and executed to ameliorate the earlier design decision. The recommendations were based upon a well-grounded understanding of the biology of spotted salamanders. This prototype should be followed in all cases because of the force of rational arguments. The agency responded to these arguments with a series of specific steps. Furthermore, it constructed a series of ten ponds in addition to the reconstructed one and the surrogate for Preston Pond. Certainly, in the long run, there are more pond resources for salamanders than before. Not listed in Table 31-2 is a further important concession by the department, namely that in the future the local scientific community would be consulted prior to changes in the management of conserved areas that would be detrimental to the biology of resident species. If implemented on a wide scale between contending parties, such a concession would clearly be worth the conflict at Forest 44, because it would reduce or eliminate conflicts within the conservation movement.

Summary

The continued success of the conservation movement is dependent upon a large core of well-informed citizens. Antipathy between otherwise mutually supportive subgroups can greatly reduce the effectiveness of the overall movement. Any agency (private or governmental) faced with conflicting goals of different supportive interest groups must act to resolve disputatious issues in a straightforward manner. Processes used to resolve conflicts include: (1) a survey of relevant scientific information; (2) information on the historical background of the conflict; (3) development of realistic options to reduce or eliminate the conflict; (4) execution of the selected options; and (5) follow-up studies of the effectiveness of the execution. This chapter reviews the history of a specific case that aroused great local concern about the demise of a pond used as a breeding site by spotted salamanders. It also demonstrates that the processes involved in reducing contentious issues may well broaden our scientific understanding of the underlying biological phenomenon.

Acknowledgments

Robert Preston is grateful for the aid of Karen and Ron Goellner during his field studies. Richard Coles hosted the contending parties at the Washington University Tyson Research Center. Gregory Toczylowski, MDC, handled the logistics of our study at Forest 44. Tom R. Johnson reviewed the manuscript. We applaud the steps taken by the MDC to address a contentious issue.

32

Conserving Alternative Amphibian Phenotypes: Is There Anybody Out There?

Howard H. Whiteman and Richard D. Howard

Environmentally induced polymorphisms (EIPs) occur when two or more phenotypes are produced in response to varying environmental conditions (West-Eberhard 1986; Moran 1992), with each alternative's fitness dependent on its match to the prevailing environment (Pfennig 1992a; Whiteman 1994; Kingsolver 1995; Roff, 1996). Among animals, EIPs can be divided into four basic types: color polymorphisms, trophic (feeding) polymorphisms, alternative reproductive morphologies, and alternative life histories. Color polymorphisms occur when alternative color morphs have differential fitness payoffs in different environments. Among some lepidopteran (butterfly) species, wing color polymorphisms appear to influence thermoregulatory mechanisms in seasonal environments (Kingsolver 1995). Trophic polymorphisms occur when different morphs specialize on alternative prey, and morph frequency often depends on the available proportion of each prey type. In many fish species, for example, individuals with alternative trophic morphologies specialize on prey from different parts of the aquatic environment (e.g., benthic versus planktonic; Skúlason and Smith 1995). Alternative reproductive morphologies occur primarily among males and involve differences in morphology and behavior. Among some salmon species, for example, males exhibit either a "hooknose" morphology, with a large, brightly colored body and a toothy, grotesquely hooked jaw, or a "jack" morphology, with a small body and female coloration and morphology. Hooknose salmon are territorial and fight other males for access to mates; jacks use their female resemblance to sneak fertilizations with those females mating with hooknose (Gross 1984, 1991). Finally, alternative life histories include different morphologies related to dispersal or some other aspect of life history, besides those outlined above. For example, insect wing dimorphism often occurs in species living in variable environments. Winged adults can disperse to new habitats, whereas wingless adults must remain in the natal habitat (Harrison 1980; Roff 1986).

In this chapter, we examine two EIPs that occur among amphibians and describe the apparent rarity of such polymorphisms in midwestern amphibians. We then discuss why EIPs are important to amphibian conservation, especially in the Midwest. Finally, we describe future research directions needed to explore midwestern EIPs more thoroughly.

Amphibian Trophic Polymorphisms

Trophic polymorphisms occur in amphibians when environmental conditions create discrete changes in mouth morphology (Fig. 32-1). Morphs either have mouth shapes and prey preferences similar to those of monomorphic populations ("typicals") or have distinctly different mouth morphologies and diet ("alternatives"). Such polymorphisms occur in the larval stages of both spadefoot toads (Fig. 32-2) and salamanders (Fig. 32-3), and resource and competition levels influence morph determination (Collins and Cheek 1983; Pfennig 1990, 1992b; Loeb et al. 1993).

For example, among spadefoot (*Spea* sp.) toad larvae, individuals become either the typical, herbivorous morph, which feeds primarily on algae ("omnivore"),

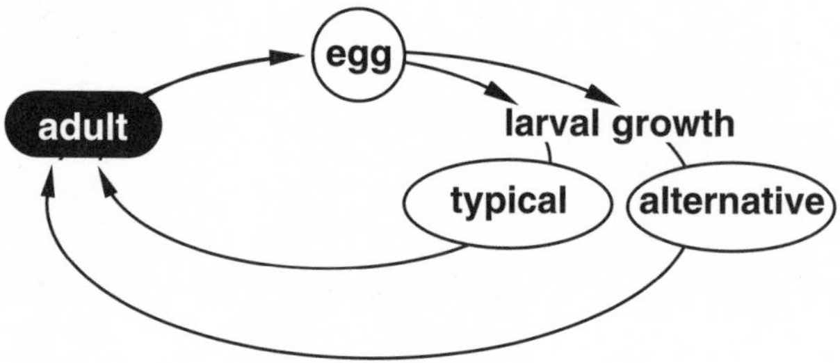

Figure 32-1. Life cycle of amphibian species that exhibit trophic polymorphism. Note that both morphs typically have the same adult morphology (but see Rose and Armentrout 1976).

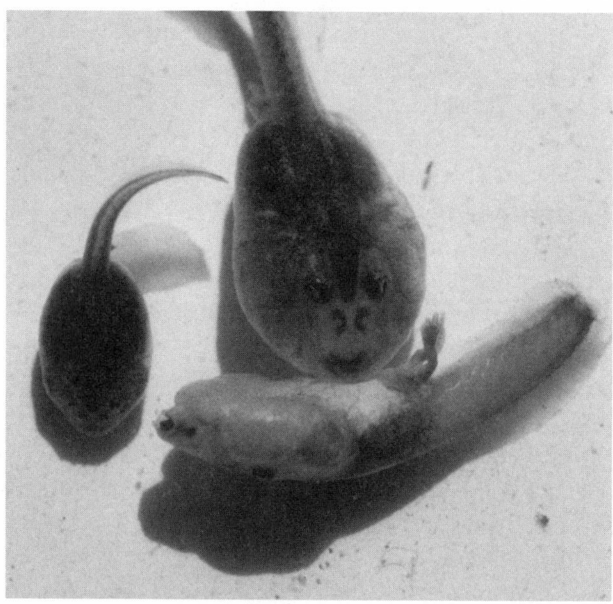

Figure 32-2. Alternative forms of spadefoot toad (*Spea bombifrons*) tadpoles from Arizona. Left: omnivore morph; right: carnivore morph. Note the carnivore is feeding on another carnivore. Photo by David Pfennig.

or a carnivorous morph specializing on zooplankton ("carnivore"; Bragg 1965; Pomeroy 1981; Pfennig 1990). Induction of morphological divergence depends on zooplankton densities and pond ephemerality: when zooplankton densities and pond ephemerality are high, carnivore morphs, which have a wider mouth and more robust jaw muscles than typical tadpoles, can consume fairy shrimp, leading to more rapid development and larger size at metamorphosis (Pfennig 1990, 1992a). Rapid development allows metamorphic animals to escape highly ephemeral ponds before they dry, and larger size at metamorphosis is positively correlated with fitness in many amphibian species (Wilbur 1980; Semlitsch et al. 1988; Scott 1994). In contrast, omnivore morphs accrue advantages in ponds that have lower zooplankton densities and are less ephemeral, because their larger fat reserves increase postmetamorphic survival (Pfennig 1992a). Carnivore morphs are known to occur in at least three of the five species of spadefoot toads: plains spadefoots (*Spea bombifrons*), Great Basin spadefoots (*Spea intermontanus*), and New Mexico spadefoots (*Spea multiplicatus*) (Pomeroy 1981; Pfennig 1990, 1992b).

Cannibalistic morphs in larval salamanders are also environmentally induced; at high conspecific densities, some individuals develop an enlarged gape and impressive vomerine teeth which they use to consume smaller, typical salamander larvae and other large prey (Collins and Cheek 1983; Collins and Holumuzki 1984; Lannoo and Bachmann 1984; Loeb et al. 1993). Because of their diet and ability to consume large prey, cannibal morphs, like larval spadefoot carnivores, develop more quickly and are larger at metamorphosis (Collins and Holumuzki 1984; Lannoo and Bachmann 1984). Cannibal morphs occur in at least three salamander species: tiger salamanders (*Ambystoma tigrinum*) (Powers 1907; Collins and Cheek 1983), long-toed salamanders (*Ambystoma macrodactylum*) (Walls et al. 1993), and the Asiatic *Hynobius retardatus* (Wakahara 1995).

Alternative Life Histories

The major alternative life history polymorphism in amphibians is facultative paedomorphosis, which occurs only among salamanders. Paedomorphosis, in its most general sense, is the retention of juvenile characteristics such as gills and aquatic existence in sexually mature adults (Gould 1977; Alberch et al. 1979; McKinney and McNamara 1991). In some species, paedomorphosis is obligate: all adults remain in a larval (paedomorphic) morphology—for example, hellbenders (*Cryptobranchus alleganiensis*), mudpuppies (*Necturus maculosus*), and lesser sirens (*Siren intermedia*) (Duellman and Trueb 1986). In other species, paedomorphosis is facultative: individuals can either become paedomorphic adults and remain in the aquatic environment or metamorphose into terrestrial adults. This life history "decision" is determined by environmental conditions during the larval stage (Fig. 32-4), available genetic variation, and

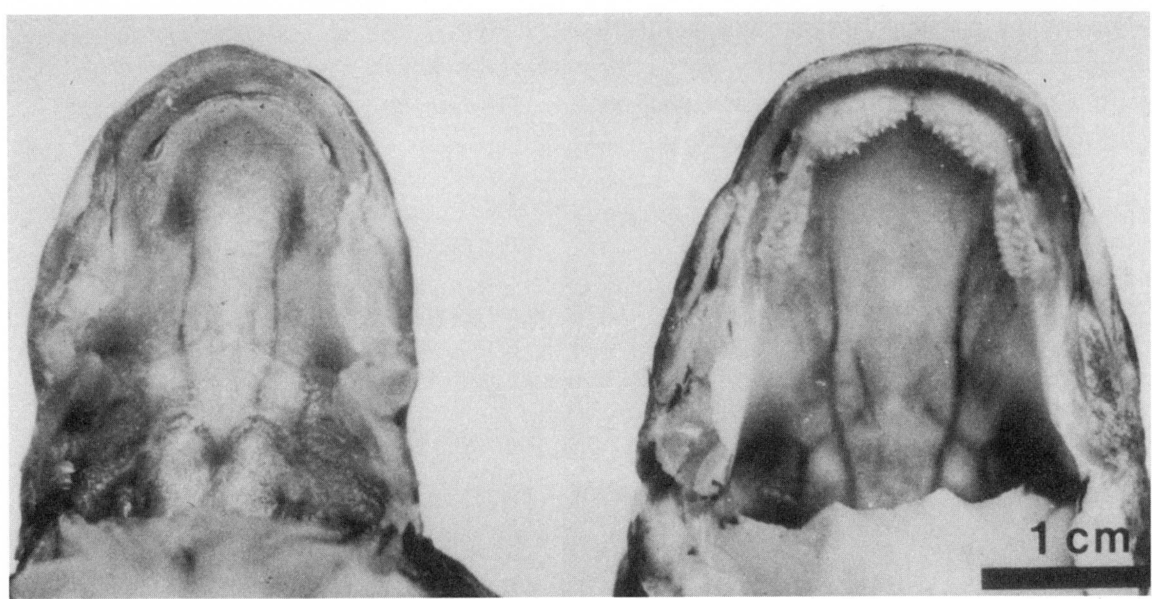

Figure 32-3. Typical and cannibal morph eastern tiger salamander larvae (*Ambystoma tigrinum tigrinum*). Ventral views of the head with the upper jaw exposed. Left: typical larva; right: cannibal morph larva. Note enlarged vomerine ridge in the latter. Photo by Michael J. Lannoo; used with permission of R. P. McIntosh, editor, *American Midland Naturalist.*

subsequent fitness payoffs to each morph (Whiteman 1994). Populations of facultative paedomorphs typically contain both paedomorphic and metamorphic individuals (Whiteman 1994). Facultative paedomorphosis is common in a variety of salamander species, including many species in the genus *Ambystoma*—for example, tiger salamanders (Collins 1981), mole salamanders (*Ambystoma talpoideum*) (Patterson 1978; Semlitsch 1985), and northwestern salamanders (*Ambystoma gracile*) (Eagleson 1976).

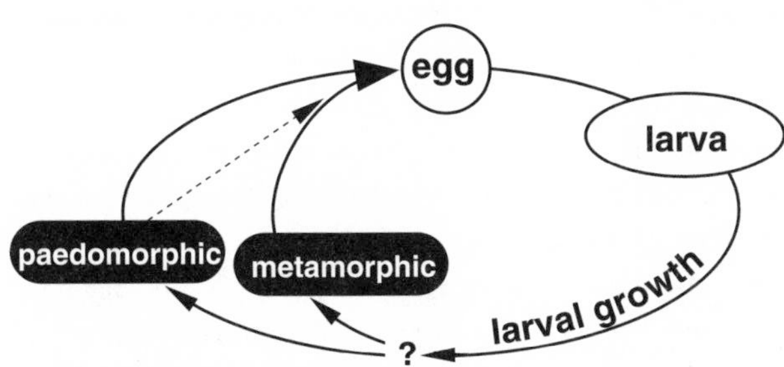

Figure 32-4. Life cycle of facultatively paedomorphic salamanders. The question mark represents the life history "decision" to become paedomorphic versus metamorphic. The dashed line signifies that in at least one species (the mole salamander [*Ambystoma talpoideum*]), paedomorphic animals often metamorphose after reproducing one or more times.

Amphibian EIPS Are Rare in the Midwest

How common are EIPs, particularly in the Midwest? Trophic polymorphisms are common in the southwestern United States, and populations of facultative paedomorphs occur throughout the West, the Southeast, and, to some extent, the Northeast. However, both types of polymorphism have been rarely documented in the Midwest, even though a number of species with the potential for EIPs exist in this region (Tables 32-1, 32-2). For example, trophic polymorphism in midwestern toads has been observed only in plains spadefoot toads from western Iowa (Farrar and Hey, Chpt. 10, this volume). Plains spadefoot toads also inhabit central Missouri (Conant and Collins 1991), but no polymorphic populations have been documented there. In addition, it is unknown whether trophic polymorphisms occur in eastern spadefoot toads (*Scaphiopus holbrookii*), which are distributed throughout the midwestern and eastern United States (Conant and Collins 1991).

Table 32-1. Known amphibian populations exhibiting EIPs in the Midwest

EIP	Locality	Method	Reference
Trophic			
Plains spadefoot toads (*Spea bombifrons*)			
	w IA*	Field	Farrar and Hey, Chpt. 10, this volume
Eastern tiger salamanders (*Ambystoma tigrinum tigrinum*)			
	nw IA	Field	Lannoo and Bachmann 1984
	nw IN	Experiment	Pfennig, personal communication
Life History			
Eastern tiger salamanders (*Ambystoma tigrinum tigrinum*)			
	up MI	Field	Hensley 1966
	n up MI	Field	Hensley 1966
	e MI	Field	Jones et al. 1993
	nw IN	Field	Whiteman, unpublished data
Central newts (*Notophthalmus viridescens louisianensis*)			
	s IL	Field	Brandon and Bremer 1966
			Albert 1967
			Reilly 1986

*States are represented by postal abbreviations; up refers to Upper Peninsula; n, s, e, w refer to compass directions.

Similarly, cannibal morph tiger salamander larvae have rarely been documented in the Midwest. Cannibals have been discovered in northwestern Iowa populations (Lannoo and Bachmann 1984) and experimentally induced in an Indiana population (D. W. Pfennig, personal communication). Although tiger salamanders are ubiquitous throughout the Midwest (Conant and Collins 1991), no other occurrences of cannibal morph larvae have been reported.

Facultatively paedomorphic eastern tiger salamanders (*Ambystoma tigrinum tigrinum*) (Fig. 32-5) have been documented from three sites in Michigan (Hensley 1966; Jones et al. 1993) and one in Indiana (H. Whiteman, unpublished data). Thus, despite the ubiquity of tiger salamanders throughout the Midwest, only a few facultatively paedomorphic populations have been reported. Similarly, paedomorphic central newts (*Notophthalmus viridescens louisianensis*) (Fig. 32-6) have been observed only in southern Illinois populations (Brandon and Bremer 1966; Albert 1967; Reilly 1986), though central or red-spotted (*N. v. viridescens*) newts range throughout much of the Midwest (Conant and Collins 1991).

Why Amphibian EIPS Are Rare in the Midwest

Several amphibian species that could and should exhibit EIPs occur in the Midwest (Table 32-2). Spadefoot toads occur throughout the Midwest, but whether eastern spadefoots exhibit EIPs is currently unknown. Tiger salamanders and eastern newts are common in the Midwest, yet few examples of cannibal morph larvae (tiger salamanders) or paedomorphic adults (both species) have been documented. Thus, EIPs appear to be rare among midwestern amphibians. There are three general explanations for this apparent rarity: EIPs are rare for natural reasons; EIPs are rare for anthropogenic reasons; and populations have not been sampled in a way that would reveal the presence of EIPs. We begin with the last possibility first. Amphibians are often censused using drift fences or through sporadic dip netting. Such censusing methods would be unlikely to reveal paedomorphic salamanders in deep, heavily vegetated ponds and lakes where these animals should be found; these morphs are better collected by seining or using minnow traps. In addition, few researchers have censused spadefoot toad and tiger salamander larvae in the Midwest, and those who have may not have been looking for alternative trophic morphologies, which are sometimes rare even when present in a population (Lannoo and Bach-

Table 32-2. Midwestern amphibians with possible EIPs

	States*
Trophic	
Plains spadefoot toads (*Spea bombifrons*)	IA, MO
Eastern spadefoot toads (*Scaphiopus holbrookii*)	MO, IL, IN, KY, OH
Eastern tiger salamanders (*Ambystoma tigrinum tigrinum*)	Ubiquitous
Life History	
Eastern tiger salamanders (*Ambystoma tigrinum tigrinum*)	Ubiquitous
Central newts (*Notophthalmus viridescens lousianensis*)	Ubiquitous (except OH)
Red spotted newts (*Notophthalmus viridescens viridescens*)	MI, IN, KY, OH

*States are represented by postal abbreviations.

mann 1984; Pfennig et al. 1991; Loeb et al. 1993). Thus, we suggest that basic monitoring is needed to assess the current status of amphibian EIPs in the Midwest.

If EIPs are rare in the Midwest, is their rarity due to natural or anthropogenic causes? A variety of natural factors influence the expression of these polymorphisms, including hydroperiod, competition, predation, and resource distribution (Whiteman 1994; Skúlason and Smith 1995; Roff, 1996). In general, selection from these factors may underlie the observed rarity of alternative morphologies. For example, paedomorphic tiger salamanders might be rare in the Midwest because they share similar habitat requirements (i.e., permanent, fishless wetlands) with bullfrogs (*Rana catesbeiana*), which are voracious predators and have a tremendous colonizing ability (Bury and Weland 1984). Similarly, trophic polymorphisms might be rare in the Midwest because breeding habitats are less temporary than those in the western United States, and thus alternative morphologies do not provide as much of a benefit in terms of escaping a rapidly drying pond.

However, many potential anthropogenic factors could also influence amphibian EIPs in the Midwest. Wetland destruction is probably the most important factor influencing amphibians, because over 50 percent of historic wetlands in the United States have been drained for agricultural and industrial purposes, with values closer to 70 to 80 percent in most midwestern states (Tiner 1984; Russell 1989; Dahl 1991; Leja, Chpt. 36, this volume). Wetland destruction reduces the number of populations available for EIP expression and thus the probability of observing EIPs in the Midwest.

Introduction of fish and bullfrogs into novel habitats may also be important anthropogenic factors influencing EIP distribution. A variety of predacious fish species have been introduced in the Midwest for sport and food (Bowen 1970; Swingle 1970). Although bullfrogs are native to the Midwest, they have also been placed into a number of permanent aquatic habitats and thus must be considered introduced species at these sites (Bury and Weland 1984; Lannoo 1996a). Such introductions might have had the strongest effect on facultatively paedomorphic salamanders, because paedomorphic salamanders are found in fishless, permanent bodies of water, while alternative trophic morphologies are usually found only in species inhabiting temporary ponds (Sprules 1974; Collins and Cheek 1983; Pfennig 1990; Whiteman 1994). Fish introductions appear to have led to the decline of paedomorphic tiger salamander populations in the western United States (Burger 1950; Levi and Levi 1955), and salamander populations in general have been destroyed by fish introductions (Collins et al. 1988; Lannoo 1996; Geraghty and Willey, personal communication). Similarly, bullfrogs have been implicated in the decline of a variety of amphibian species (Moyle 1973; Bury and Luckenbach 1976; Schwalbe and Rosen 1988). By acting as top predators within an aquatic environment, fish and bullfrogs might prey on paedomorphic salamanders as well as outcompete them for food (see Collins et al. 1993).

Agricultural and industrial effluents, common throughout the Midwest, are other potential anthropogenic influences on EIPs. For example, bacterial blooms from cattle waste cause disease and eventual mortality in Arizona tiger salamander larvae (*Ambystoma tigrinum nebulosum*). Cannibal morphs often consume sick larvae

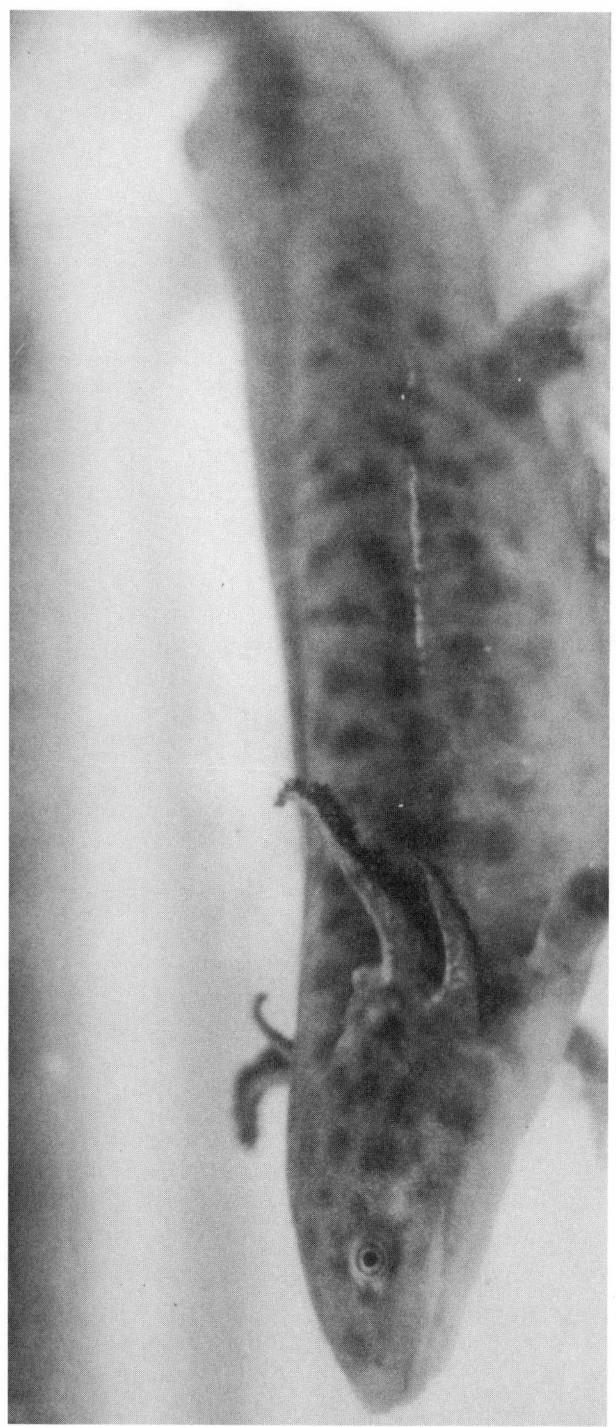

Figure 32-5. Paedomorphic eastern tiger salamander (*Ambystoma tigrinum tigrinum*). Photo by Howard Whiteman.

Figure 32-6. Paedomorphic central newt (*Notophthalmus viridescens louisianensis*). Photo by John Fauth.

and acquire the disease themselves. Such blooms appear to select against cannibalism (Pfennig et al. 1991): cannibal morphs are rare in areas with livestock compared to those without livestock, and experiments reveal that cannibals can be produced from habitats with livestock but at a significantly lower frequency than those populations without livestock. Cannibals might similarly be more likely to pick up industrial effluent present in the tissues of contaminated conspecifics, or such effluent might increase their susceptibility to disease, again selecting against cannibals. Carnivorous spadefoot toad larvae could also be affected by pollutants, because carnivores sometimes prey on conspecifics (Pfennig 1992b; Pfennig et al. 1993). Carnivores might also pick up more pesticide residue, as a result of biomagnification in zooplankton, than typical larvae that are herbivorous (Flint and van den Bosch 1981).

Paedomorphic salamanders should also be influenced by agricultural and industrial pollution. The life history decision to become metamorphic or paedomorphic is thought to depend on the relative quality of the terrestrial versus aquatic environment and on an individual's potential success in each environment (Sprules 1974; Whiteman 1994). Increased pollution in one habitat type should decrease the frequency of the morph specialized for that habitat. Polluted runoff collecting in permanent ponds could select against the maintenance of facultative paedomorphosis because of both direct (i.e., physiological effects) and indirect (i.e., decreased prey abundance, biomagnification of pesticides in prey) effects.

To determine whether natural or anthropogenic factors influence EIPs, we suggest searching historical records, basic monitoring of populations, and experiments. Old records of EIPs might exist in the field notes of early naturalists around the turn of the century, particularly in surveys associated with wetland draining. Localities of potential EIPs could then be found and searched thoroughly with intensive field sampling. Second, basic monitoring is needed to determine the extent to which EIPs presently occur in the Midwest. Patterns of EIP distributions might indicate whether natural or anthropogenic factors are involved. Finally, experiments are needed to determine if genetic variation for EIPs exist and to determine the environmental conditions under which they occur. If such conditions are found in midwestern wetlands but alternative morphs do not occur, then anthropogenic factors would be a likely possibility. For example, density manipulations produced cannibalistic morphs in an Indiana population, although cannibals have never been observed at this site (D. W. Pfennig, personal communication).

EIPs and Amphibian Conservation

Are EIPs important to amphibian conservation, specifically in the Midwest? This question is especially relevant, given that none of the species exhibiting these polymorphisms appear to be threatened in this area (but see Lannoo et al. 1994). There are several pragmatic reasons why biologists and conservationists should be concerned about amphibian EIPs (in addition to moral arguments against the loss of phenotypic and species diversity). Amphibian EIPs may promote genetic diversity because there is genetic variation in the propensity of individuals to become either morph as well as genetic variation for the many trait specializations associated with each morph. Routman (1993) found that facultatively paedomorphic populations of tiger salamanders are more genetically diverse in terms of mitochondrial DNA than completely metamorphic populations, supporting this general idea. Because of habitat fragmentation throughout the Midwest, genetic concerns are now more important to the conservation of midwestern amphibians. In addition, maintenance of increased genetic variation might allow populations to withstand future anthropogenic change (Beardmore 1983; Chesser 1983). Further study in this area is clearly warranted.

Because EIPs are environmentally induced, they are also potential indicators of environmental stress. Anthropogenic stressors could be the reason why midwestern EIPs are currently rare (e.g., cannibalistic morphs in tiger salamander populations near rangeland; Pfennig et al. 1991). Thus, absence or reduced frequency of alternative morphs might indicate environmental degradation. Because other species might also be affected by such degradation, alternative phenotypes could provide an early warning signal for declines in ecosystem health.

EIPs are also important because of their effect on trophic interactions. If these polymorphisms once occurred naturally in the Midwest and have been reduced through anthropogenic causes, then their loss may have cascading food web effects. For example, carnivorous spadefoot toad tadpoles feed heavily on large zooplankton and depress zooplankton densities (Pfennig 1992a). When the carnivore morph is eliminated or reduced in number, large zooplankton species may proliferate, decreasing the abundance of smaller zooplankton species. Alternatively, an abundance of large zooplankton species may alter the prey base in favor of some other vertebrate species.

Finally, studying EIPs can provide further information about differences between midwestern amphibian communities and those in other parts of the continent. By understanding why EIPs are apparently rare in the Midwest, we may gain insight into how other population parameters differ on a regional scale and clarify the current health of amphibian populations in North America.

From a long-term perspective, EIPs are important to amphibian conservation because they promote organic diversity and can lead to speciation events. West-

Eberhard (1989) suggested that selection for alternative phenotypes may buffer a species from extinction as well as promote extreme phenotypic divergence and eventual speciation. EIPs could buffer species from extinction because even under fluctuating environments, one morph can continue to reproduce (when experiencing a good environment) while the other morph is doing poorly. Thus, a species can develop new specializations without abandoning old ones, and new niches can be entered without passing through "maladaptive transitions," which might accompany major adaptive change.

Future Research, Conservation, and Management

Are amphibian EIPs really rare in the Midwest? If so, to what extent are anthropogenic factors responsible for this apparent rarity? And how might this information be used to conserve and manage amphibians with EIPs as well as other amphibian species? Both basic monitoring and experimental analyses are necessary to resolve these questions.

What do we do if anthropogenic effects underlie the rarity of an EIP? The simplest response would be to eliminate the factor negatively influencing the EIP and restore habitat to its original state. Fish could be eradicated from historically fishless ponds and lakes; cattle could be impeded from access to some temporary ponds; use of pesticides and other agrichemicals could be avoided near wetlands. These management practices would obviously benefit other amphibian species as well.

Should we put protective status labels (i.e., endangered, threatened, special concern) on alternative phenotypes? This question is especially important given the controversial status of the Endangered Species Act during the past few years. EIPs are an inherent life history trait of an organism and may influence population viability (see above). Known populations with EIPs found in the Midwest may warrant protective status, at least until we determine whether EIPs are rare in this region.

If future research reveals increased occurrence of EIPs in the Midwest or that their absence is a result of environmental degradation, then more attention needs to be focused on alternative phenotypes in terms of public education. This might lead to more information about where these alternatives occur (with individuals coming forward with information about possible localities) as well as a greater appreciation of such phenotypes, which might encourage citizens to conserve wetland areas or remove bullfrogs and fish from their own wetlands.

Summary

Environmentally induced polymorphisms (EIPs) occur among amphibians in two forms: alternative trophic (feeding) morphologies in spadefoot toads and salamanders and alternative life histories (facultative paedomorphosis) in salamanders. Although common in other regions of North America, EIPs have been rarely documented in the Midwest. The rare occurrence of midwestern EIPs could be a result of biased sampling; few individuals have searched for EIPs, and populations have not been sampled in a way that would reveal the presence of EIPs. However, EIP rarity could also result from natural (habitat quality, predators) or anthropogenic (wetland destruction, agricultural runoff, fish introduction) factors. Searches of historical records, basic monitoring, and experimental manipulations could be used to separate these possibilities. EIPs may have important ecological and evolutionary consequences, may increase population vigor by maintaining high levels of genetic variation, and can act as bioindicators of population and ecosystem health. We suggest that understanding the apparent rarity of EIPs among midwestern amphibians may help future efforts at amphibian and wetland conservation in this region.

Acknowledgments

We thank D. W. Pfennig, D. Larson, N. L. Buschhaus, and J. W. Gibbons for comments on the manuscript. This research was funded in part by an Indiana Academy of Sciences Research Grant and a Purdue Research Foundation Fellowship. Manuscript preparation was supported by Contract DE-AC09-76SROO-819 between the U.S. Department of Energy and the University of Georgia's Savannah River Ecology Laboratory.

33

Tiger Salamander Life History in Relation to Agriculture in the Northern Great Plains: A Hypothesis

Diane L. Larson

Hormones, in concert with the nervous system, are the primary pathways of integration between environmental stimuli and physiological processes; thus they promote homeostasis in vertebrates (Moore and Marler 1987). The endocrine system coordinates development and provides the architecture upon which life history depends (Finch and Rose 1995). Recent studies have focused attention on the potentially disruptive effects of environmental contaminants on the endocrine systems of fish, reptiles, birds, and mammals (Thomas and Colburn 1992; Hontela et al. 1992; Hontela et al. 1995; Bergeron et al. 1994; Fairbrother 1994). The effects of such disruptions are manifested in abnormal stress response (*sensu* Selye 1936) and reproductive disorders.

Ontogenetic changes represent a largely unexplored potential consequence of endocrine disruption. Amphibians are of special interest in this regard: their complex life histories provide ample opportunity to determine if observed endocrine responses translate into developmental abnormalities. Hormonal profiles throughout development are well characterized for many amphibian species (Burggren and Just 1992), so that there exist points of comparison for field and laboratory experiments. The current concern over the conservation status of amphibian populations worldwide suggests the need for a better understanding of the ways in which these animals respond to their environment. This chapter explores the possible endocrine responses to agricultural practices in the northern Great Plains (for a definition of the Great Plains, see Frazier 1989), examines the potential effects on amphibian life history, and suggests questions that need to be answered. Because they are common in wetlands throughout the Great Plains, tiger salamanders (*Ambystoma tigrinum*) were chosen as the model organism.

The Breeding Environment of Tiger Salamanders

Agricultural activities in the Great Plains have resulted in a number of changes to the environment. Wetland drainage has modified salamander breeding habitat at the landscape scale, resulting in fewer wetlands and greater distances separating existing wetlands (Leitch 1989). Irrigation is uncommon in the northern Great Plains. Terrestrial habitat between wetlands may be less hospitable to metamorphosed animals; pathways of dispersal among wetlands may be blocked by acres of plowed fields offering little refuge from heat and predators and often containing residues of pesticides and fertilizers.

Wetlands themselves also have been altered by runoff that contains fertilizers and pesticides from surrounding agricultural land (Grue et al. 1986; Grue et al. 1989; Neely and Baker 1989; Tome et al. 1991). Pesticides alter the habitat by interrupting lower levels of the food chain (Dewey 1986; Kasai and Hanazato 1995) and may directly influence larval growth, development, reproduction, and behavior (Bishop 1992). Fertilizers increase nutrients within wetland basins and may provide rich environments for larval growth. However, high concentrations of ammonia and nitrate are toxic (Hecnar 1995), especially at high pH levels (Boyer and Grue 1995). Because pesticide and fertilizer use may vary from year to year with various crop rotations, habitat quality may be less predictable in an agricultural setting than in non-agricultural areas.

Overlain on these anthropogenic influences is a harsh, variable climate (Borchert 1950) characterized by bitterly cold winters, when wetlands are ice covered and may become depleted of oxygen, and extended drought periods, when very few wetlands hold water. With their well-known plasticity in adult morphology (Rose and Armentrout 1976; Sexton and Bizer 1978; Collins 1981; Collins and Cheek 1983), tiger salamanders would seem to be uniquely suited to exploit this inherent natural variability in the Great Plains: sexually mature tiger salamanders may either retain the brachiate larval (paedomorphic) form or metamorphose into terrestrial adults (Buchli 1969; Rose and Armentrout 1976). Studies in the northern Great Plains indicate that, although overwintering in a neotenic form is not uncommon, the occurrence is variable both among wetlands and within the same wetland from year to year (Buchli 1969; Wiedenheft 1983; Deutschman and Peterka 1988). Its ubiquity in the landscape (Deutschman and Peterka 1988) attests to the tiger salamander's success. The question I pose is whether this phenotypic plasticity in the adult morphology of tiger salamanders is adaptive (Newman 1992) in the agricultural landscape that has emerged in the northern Great Plains over the past century.

Hormonal Control of Tiger Salamander Development: A Thumbnail Sketch

Several hormones are involved in the control of developmental changes associated with metamorphosis in tiger salamanders (Rosenkilde 1985), including thyroid hormones (triiodothyronine [T_3] and thyroxine [T_4]) and prolactin, as well as the adrenal steroids (e.g., corticosterone). Corticosterone, T_3, and T_4 promote metamorphic climax; prolactin, a pituitary hormone that stimulates growth, inhibits metamorphosis.

Corticosteroids increase rapidly in response to any environmental stressor (*sensu* Sutanto and Dekloet 1994; Axelrod and Reisine 1984). Adrenal steroids apparently accelerate metamorphosis only when circulating concentrations of thyroid hormones are high (Burggren and Just 1992; Hayes 1995; Hayes and Wu 1995). Thus, if larvae are physiologically prepared to metamorphose, environmental changes that stimulate increased corticosterone release should hasten metamorphosis (Larras-Regard 1985). Experiments conducted by Denver (1993, 1995) on various anurans suggest that information about environmental conditions is relayed via corticotropin-releasing hormonelike neurotransmitters, which may regulate the thyroid axis during metamorphosis. Increases in corticosterone promote conversion of T_4 to the more potent T_3 in toad (*Bufo* sp.) larvae (Hayes and Wu 1995), which promotes some aspects of metamorphosis but not others.

Environmental influences on thyroid hormones and prolactin are poorly known. Work on facultative metamorphosis of tiger salamanders and axolotls (*Ambystoma mexicanum*) suggests that capture stress and environmental conditions can influence the timing and rate of metamorphosis (Larras-Regard 1985). Typical concentrations of corticosterone, T_3, and T_4 throughout metamorphosis are well known for captive tiger salamanders (Norris et al. 1973; Larras-Regard 1985; Rosenkilde 1985; Carr and Norris 1988; Burggren and Just 1992), but field data are lacking.

Feedback loops exist among the various hormones (Rosenkilde 1985; Burggren and Just 1992), so that each exerts some degree of control over production or binding of one or more of the others. For example, one hypothesis of the regulation of thyroid hormones and corticosterone (Hayes and Wu 1995) suggests that environmental stimulation via corticotropin-releasing factor (CRF) promotes increases in both corticosterone and T_4. Increases in T_4 also promote increased corticosterone, but corticosterone promotes conversion of T_4 to T_3 and feeds back negatively on itself and on CRF. Such feedback loops include many unconfirmed relationships, so although they suggest mechanisms of environmental integration, these hypotheses have not been tested in the field.

Potential Effects of Pesticides

Because agriculture is the primary economic activity in the northern Great Plains (Leitch 1989), I will not discuss the so-called environmental estrogens such as polychlorinated biphenyls (PCBs), which are generally associated with industrial centers. Grue et al. (1986) has provided a list of insecticides and herbicides most frequently used in the Prairie Pothole region of North Dakota, the areal extent of treatment, and relative toxicity to invertebrates, birds, and mammals. Most insecticides used in the northern Great Plains belong to the organophosphate, organochlorine, or carbamate groups. Eighty to 90 percent of planted acres are treated with herbicides; sunflowers are the only common crop heavily treated with insecticides.

The presence of pesticides in wetlands may have direct and/or indirect effects on tiger salamander larval physiology. If the pesticide itself constitutes a stressor, it likely interacts with the adrenal axis, leading to high levels of corticosterone secretion. In larvae too small to metamorphose, the direct effect may be primarily behavioral: pesticide contamination has been found to result in abnormal behavior in larval amphibians (Bishop 1992; Carey and Bryant 1995). Larvae are often lethargic, feeding rates are lower, and responses to stimuli are slowed. Such abnormal activities may make larvae more susceptible to predation or less able to forage.

Another potential consequence of chronically high corticosterone is compromised immunity (Geller and Christian 1982; Auphan et al. 1995). Laboratory evidence suggests that declining immunocompetence during axolotl metamorphosis is induced by thyroid hormones (Phaff and Rosenkilde 1995), although it is not known if this is a general response. If immunity is already naturally lower during metamorphosis, effects of chemical stressors may be accentuated during this period.

Finally, corticosterone can prevent development of the thyroid axis in anuran larvae during early development or at cold temperatures (Hayes and Wu 1995). Although this has not been shown for *Ambystoma*, the implication is that metamorphosis would be blocked. In North Dakota, terrestrial adult tiger salamanders begin breeding in mid-April (Deutschman and Peterka 1988), often before the ice has completely melted from wetlands. Most farmers begin cultivation as soon as fields are dry enough to support equipment, and pre-emergent herbicides are applied as early as mid-April (Grue et al. 1986); the potential for stressors entering the wetland during the early phases of development and under cold temperature conditions is high in the northern Great Plains.

Because corticosterone stimulates conversion of T_4 to T_3, larvae that have reached the minimum size necessary for metamorphosis could metamorphose more rapidly, and at a smaller size, than larvae not subjected to chemical stressors. Metamorphosis at a smaller size likely would put these animals at a disadvantage in the terrestrial environment (Semlitsch et al. 1988).

In summary, pesticides that enter wetlands could result in: (1) decreased survivorship of larvae because of direct toxicity, immunosuppression, or behavioral changes induced by sublethal toxicity; (2) declining rates of metamorphosis because of disruption of the necessary thyroid hormones by induced stress hormones (e.g., corticosterone) in premetamorphic larvae; and (3) a smaller size at metamorphosis and associated reduced survivorship for larvae capable of metamorphosis.

Potential Effects of Fertilizers

Nitrate, nitrite, and ammonia resulting from nitrogen fertilizer runoff into the high-pH wetlands typical of the northern Great Plains would likely produce sublethal effects similar to those discussed above (Hecnar 1995). Fertilizers may also increase nutrient availability in wetlands, resulting in a greater abundance of invertebrate prey. Well-fed larvae that grow rapidly may be less likely to metamorphose (Wilbur and Collins 1973; Sprules 1974), perhaps due to suppression of thyroid function by high levels of prolactin. If metamorphosis is suppressed for a sufficiently long period, cold temperatures will make transformation impossible until the next summer. Having failed to leave the wetland before winter, aquatic forms risk winterkill, as wetlands freeze over and oxygen is depleted (Buchli 1969; Wiedenheft 1983; Deutschman and Peterka 1988; D. Larson, personal observations). Aquatic salamanders that survive the winter may experience the same conditions that delayed metamorphosis in their first year. In addition, the rate of successful metamorphosis may decline in older animals, as Rose and Armentrout (1976) found for tiger salamanders in Texas. Thus, the net result of fertilizers entering wetlands may be decreased survivorship of larvae due to lethal or sublethal toxicity and fewer larvae metamorphosing to the terrestrial form.

Implications for Tiger Salamander Life History

Assuming that each tiger salamander hatches with the potential to mature in either the aquatic or terrestrial form (i.e., there is genetically determined phenotypic plasticity for this trait; Newman 1992; see also Shaffer and Voss 1996; Whiteman and Howard, Chpt. 32, this volume) and that the ability to metamorphose successfully declines with time (Rose and Armentrout 1976), what environmental factors favor maintenance of both phenotypes? Clearly, a population consisting solely of paedomorphic individuals is doomed in the northern Great Plains; virtually no wetland provides suitable habitat indefinitely. Although paedomorphics may be able to metamorphose facultatively in response to drying conditions, anoxia in an ice-covered wetland leaves little opportunity for escape. Given the occurrence of both paedomorphic and metamorphic phenotypes, however, paedomorphics must enjoy an advantage under some circumstances. It can be argued that paedomorphic animals produce more eggs, because fecundity is related to size and paedomorphics tend to be larger than metamorphic animals, at least initially (Buchli 1969; Rose and Armentrout 1976). In addition, paedomorphic animals do not risk leaving a natal wetland that is clearly suitable, assuming it remains so over winter. Thus, during a series of years with adequate precipitation and winter oxygen levels, tiger salamander populations producing mainly paedomorphic animals might leave more offspring than those producing mainly metamorphic animals. During the inevitable winters when the wetland becomes anoxic or when drought causes the wetland to dry before larvae and paedomorphic animals can metamorphose, metamorphic animals from previous years would persist to recolonize.

What influence might agriculture have on this scenario? The answer depends on the degree to which phenotypes are free to vary with environmental factors. If the ratio of paedomorphic to metamorphic animals depends largely on characteristics encountered within the natal wetland—conspecific crowding, dissolved solutes, prey availability, oxygen tension, and water temperature have been linked to the timing of metamorphosis—then this ratio might shift, depending on the presence of pesticides or fertilizers, as discussed above. There is evidence, based first on plasma corticosterone concentrations in free-living larvae and second on days to stage IV for laboratory-reared larvae exposed to atrazine, that larvae in agricultural wetlands may be less likely to metamorphose before their first winter than larvae from otherwise similar nonagricultural wetlands (Larson and Fivizzani, unpublished data).

Whether it follows that these animals become paedomorphic has not been shown. Wiedenheft (1983) reported that young-of-the-year larval-form salamanders captured in September and October in North Dakota wetlands had already developed gonads. Buchli (1969), however, found that paedomorphic animals (of unreported reproductive status) from Devil's Lake, North Dakota, readily metamorphosed in their second year. The possibility exists that some tiger salamanders breed first as paedomorphic animals, then metamorphose into terrestrial adults.

To summarize, tiger salamanders overwintering in the aquatic form are subject to two risks not faced by metamorphosed individuals, both of which could result in catastrophic mortality: winter anoxia and drying of the natal wetland. If agriculture shifts the ratio of paedomorphic to metamorphic individuals toward paedomorphics, a greater percentage of any local population would be subject to these catastrophic events, and fewer individuals would remain to repopulate.

Research Needs

The hypothesis that paedomorphic tiger salamanders will predominate as a response to agricultural activities in the northern Great Plains is just that, a hypothesis. Potential consequences are equally hypothetical. Several questions must be answered, following two general lines of research. The first line of research is physiological. Given that certain hormones are susceptible to perturbation by agricultural pesticides or nutrient enrichment of the environment, how persistent is the perturbation? Does the perturbation translate into ontogenetic changes of ecological significance? Do hormonal changes that might retard metamorphosis persist, even when other environmental cues would hasten metamorphosis? Can paedomorphic salamanders metamorphose with equal success throughout their lifetime?

The second line of necessary research is ecological. Are paedomorphic tiger salamanders more fit than metamorphic individuals? How likely is it that a wetland will become depleted of oxygen over winter? Are there cues that this will occur before cold temperatures and ice block escape? Where do terrestrial tiger salamanders find refuge over winter, and are these refugia affected by agriculture? Answers to these questions will address not only the life history hypothesis proposed here but will also increase our understanding of the mechanisms by which tiger salamanders respond to changing environmental conditions.

Summary

Agriculture has had a profound effect on wetland habitat in the northern Great Plains. The purpose of this chapter is to explore possible tiger salamander (*Ambystoma tigrinum*) endocrine responses to agricultural fertilizers and pesticides and the subsequent effects on salamander life history. Tiger salamanders may mature in either paedomorphic (the retention of juvenile characteristics and therefore aquatic) or metamorphic (terrestrial) form. I argue that effects of pesticides and fertilizers may shift the paedomorphic:metamorphic ratio toward paedomorphics, with the potential result of population extinctions after winter anoxia or severe drought.

Acknowledgments

I thank P. Pietz, B. Smith, M. Sovada, and H. Whiteman for helpful comments made on previous drafts of this chapter. Support for this work was provided by the U.S. National Biological Service, Northern Prairie Science Center, and the U.S. Environmental Protection Agency (Interagency Agreement No. 14-48-0009-92-1929).

34

Amphibian Conservation and Wetland Management in the Upper Midwest: A Catch-22 for the Cricket Frog?

Michael J. Lannoo

Habitat loss is undoubtedly the largest single factor contributing to amphibian declines (Wyman 1990; Wake 1991; Vial and Salor 1993). But habitat loss alone cannot explain all amphibian losses, even in the midwestern United States. For example, in an earlier paper (Lannoo et al. 1994) my colleagues and I estimated about a three-order-of-magnitude decline in northwestern Iowa northern leopard frog (*Rana pipiens*) numbers over the past century. Over this same time period, Iowa has lost somewhere between 90 and 98 percent of its wetlands (Leja, Chpt. 36, this volume), a roughly two-order-of-magnitude drop. Therefore, a full-order-of-magnitude decline in leopard frog numbers in this region remains unexplained. These conclusions are supported by comparing Frank Blanchard's (1923) published descriptions and cataloged field notes with our more recent data. Blanchard reported that leopard frog tadpoles were the "widespread and abundant amphibian of the region" and "at least one specimen [of tiger salamander] was found in nearly every pond seined," while in the early 1990s we found leopard frogs in twenty-four of thirty-four wetlands sampled and tiger salamanders in eighteen of thirty-two wetlands sampled. Blanchard's cricket frog (*Acris crepitans blanchardi*) declines are occurring in the absence of a similar magnitude of wetland loss (and indeed in the absence of similar declines in other amphibian species) in the northern tier of midwestern states. The question that arises is whether the alteration of remaining habitats can explain amphibian declines beyond those predicted by habitat loss.

Wetlands constrain the organisms that inhabit them through hypoxia and desiccation. Animals that have access to the water surface avoid hypoxia by breathing atmospheric oxygen, an option under summer nighttime conditions but not under the ice during northern winters (Manion and Cory 1952; Barica and Mathias 1979; Bradford 1983). Animals avoid desiccation either through aestivation or by seeking alternate habitats. Extreme hypoxia and desiccation generally occur during prolonged (two- to three-year) droughts, which develop in the upper Midwest on a roughly ten-year cycle (Bachmann and Jones 1974; Lannoo 1996a,b).

In the upper Midwest, wetland basins vary in size and depth along a continuum from small, temporary wetlands to large recreational lakes. For the purpose of this discussion, I divide these basins into three types based on oxygen and drying regimes during droughts (Fig. 34-1):

1. Basins that dry—seasonal (e.g., Type III, Stewart and Kantrud 1971; PEMC, National Wetlands Inventory [NWI] classification) and semipermanent wetlands (e.g., Type IV, Stewart and Kantrud 1971; PEMF, NWI classification)
2. Basins that retain water but become hypoxic—permanent wetlands (e.g., Type V, Stewart and Kantrud 1971; PEMH and POWH, NWI classification)
3. Basins that retain water and contain high oxygen levels—lakes (LEM and LOW, NWI classification)

In the Prairie Pothole region of northwestern Iowa (van der Valk 1989), aquatic vertebrates sort themselves out by habitat type. Six or seven native amphibian species, which have lungs as larvae and therefore can breathe atmospheric oxygen, are found in wetlands (Ta-

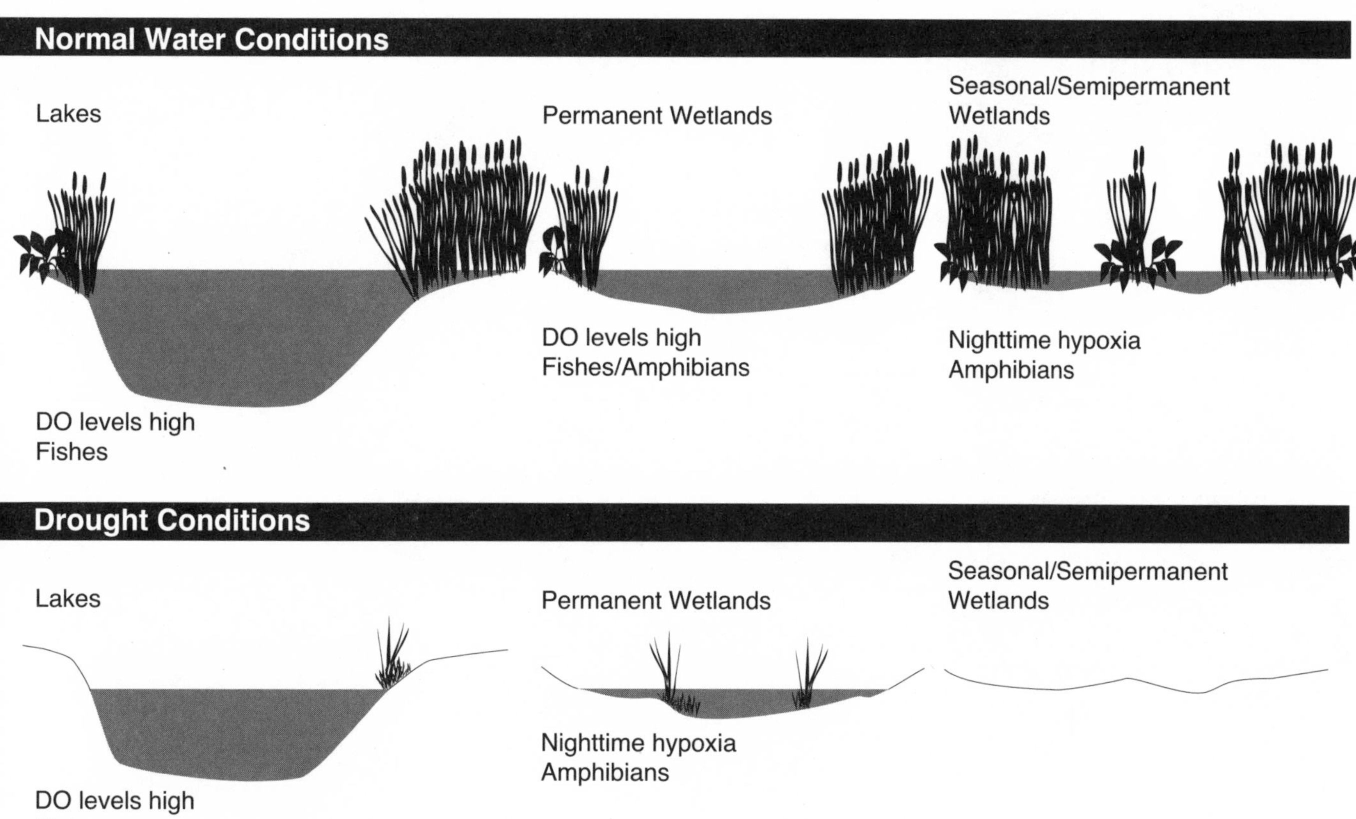

Figure 34-1. Schematic diagrams illustrating interactions between amphibians and wetland types across drought cycles. During average- to high-water years (top), amphibians will successfully reproduce in seasonal and semipermanent wetlands and in the permanent wetlands that do not contain fishes. During droughts (bottom), amphibians will tend to be restricted to breeding in permanent wetlands. These wetlands may lose their fish fauna as they acquire the daily dissolved oxygen (DO) fluctuations characteristic of semipermanent wetlands during average- to high-water years; these wetlands therefore will tend to summerkill and perhaps winterkill.

ble 34-1; Blanchard 1923; Lannoo et al. 1994), while about four dozen fish species are found naturally in lakes (Larrabee 1927a,b; Lannoo 1996a). Habitat separation (allotopy) is nearly complete between these groups; wetland hypoxia and periodic desiccation exclude fishes (Ayles et al. 1976; Barica and Mathias 1979; Peterka 1989), and established predatory fishes in lakes feed upon and eliminate most species of amphibian larvae (Burger 1950; Blair 1951; Levi and Levi 1955; Brandon and Bremer 1967; Efford and Mathias 1969; Pennak 1969; Tanner et al. 1971; McCan 1977; Sexton and Bizer 1978; Petranka 1983; Sexton and Phillips 1986; Semlitsch 1987, 1988; Semlitsch and Gibbons 1988; Figiel and Semlitsch 1990; Bradford 1991; Bristow 1991; Liss and Larson 1991; Holomuzki 1995; but see Taylor 1983; Kats et al. 1988; Lawler 1989; Werner 1991). In the Prairie Pothole region, exceptions to this allotopy include American toad (*Bufo americanus*) tadpoles, which are occasionally found in lakes or river backwaters; Great Plains toad (*Bufo cognatus*) tadpoles, which are reported to occur in rivers (Stebbins 1985); mudpuppies (*Necturus maculosus*), which occur in larger bodies of water (Bishop 1943); and brook sticklebacks (*Culea inconstans*) and minnows in the genus *Pimephales*, which are occasionally found naturally ocurring in pothole wetlands (personal observation; also Peterka 1989).

In the upper Midwest, amphibians successfully reproduce in seasonal and semipermanent wetlands under normal water conditions; they will also successfully reproduce in permanent wetlands if no predatory fishes are present (Petranka 1983; Sexton and Phillips 1986; Bradford 1989, 1991; Bradford et. al. 1993; Fellers and Drost 1993; Brönmark and Edenhamn 1994). Fishes will be found in lakes and in the permanent wetlands that

Table 34-1. The native amphibians of northwestern Iowa, after Lannoo et al. (1994)

Caudata
Ambystomatidae
Eastern tiger salamander (*Ambystoma tigrinum tigrinum*)
Proteidae
Mudpuppy (*Necturus maculosus maculosus*)?
Anura
Bufonidae
American toad (*Bufo americanus*)
Great Plains toad (*Bufo cognatus*)*
Ranidae
Northern leopard frog (*Rana pipiens*)
Hylidae
Gray treefrog complex (*Hyla versicolor/chrysoscelis*)
Western chorus frog (*Pseudacris triseriata triseriata*)
Blanchard's cricket frog (*Acris crepitans blanchardi*)†

*Appears to have naturally immigrated within the past two decades.
†Extirpated.

they have managed to colonize (Fig. 34-1). (For a remarkably similar view of the effects of water permanence on amphibians, with an emphasis on tadpoles, activity levels, and invertebrate predators, see Skelly 1997.) During droughts, amphibians will be excluded from breeding in seasonal and semipermanent wetlands due to dry conditions (Pechmann et al. 1989; Wissinger and Whiteman 1992; Dodd 1993, 1994; Semlitsch et al. 1996) but can breed in permanent wetlands that do not hold fish or once held fish that have since been extirpated through hypoxia (Fig. 34-1). Lakes, of course, hold fish regardless of water regime.

An Empirical Model

Under natural conditions, permanent wetlands will contain a flexible fauna, favoring fishes during high-water years and amphibians during drier years (Fig. 34-2). Permanent wetlands provide reproductive sites for amphibians during prolonged droughts, when seasonal and semipermanent wetlands are unavailable (Dodd 1994). Therefore, the effects of drought on amphibians will depend on the extent that permanent wetlands are anthropogenically impacted, for example, by aquacultural practices (see below; Lannoo 1995, 1996a).

The following specific hypotheses can be derived from the scenario proposed above.

1. Amphibian species with high breeding site fidelity (philopatry) during average- to high-water years will be unlikely to shift breeding sites during droughts from seasonal or semipermanent wetlands to permanent wetlands.

Many studies report either philopatry or small home ranges among amphibian species with a complex life history, including the species and genera represented in the upper Midwest (see Table 34-2; but see also Dodd 1993, 1994). Philopatry is not absolute, however. In several of these species, dispersal has been documented between adjacent populations (Cummings 1912; Semlitsch 1983b; Breden 1987; Caldwell 1987; Sjögren 1991; Sjögren Gulve 1994; Alfaro 1995; Sexton et al., Chpt. 35, this volume). Furthermore, dispersal into new areas occurs. In northwestern Iowa, amphibians naturally recolonize restored wetlands rapidly, in many cases during the first spring following the restoration (Lannoo et al. 1994; Lannoo 1996a,b).

2. The ability of a species to survive a drought will be directly proportional to a species' longevity and/or its tendency to shift breeding sites to permanent wetlands (Dodd 1993).

Many ambystomatid salamanders and bufonid, ranid, and hylid frogs for which there are data (Table 34-3)

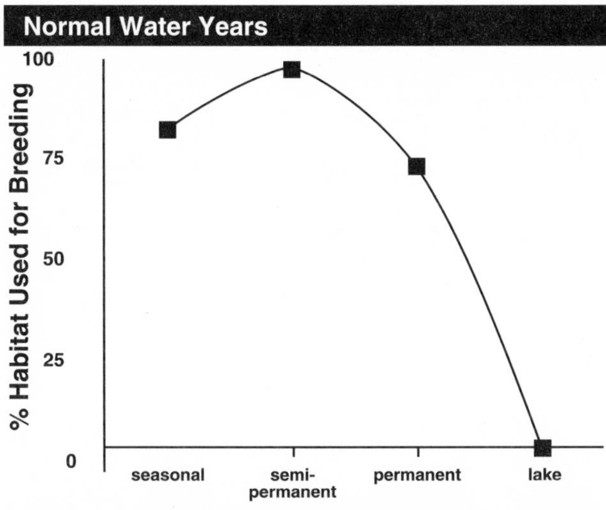

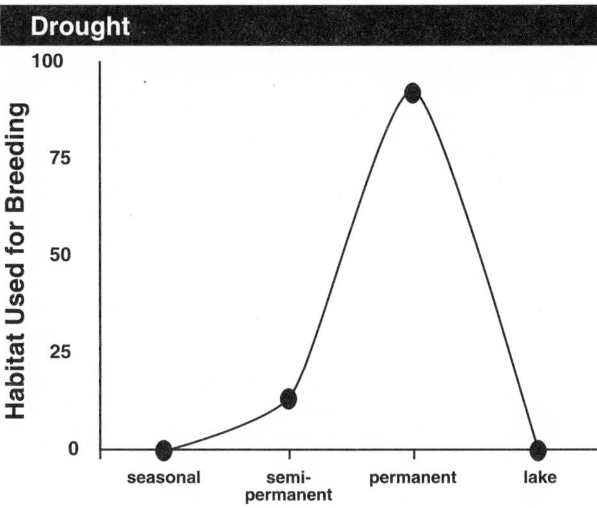

Figure 34-2. The probability that wetlands will support successful reproduction of amphibians varies with water regime. Note that during average- to high-water years, seasonal and semipermanent wetlands support high levels of amphibian breeding (top). During droughts, however, seasonal and semipermanent wetlands dry, and permanent wetlands must support the bulk of amphibian breeding. The probabilities illustrated here assume historical conditions: that virtually all seasonal and semipermanent wetlands support amphibian breeding during average- to high-water years (Blanchard 1923) and that an estimated 75 percent of permanent wetlands are fishless. Again, fishes that managed to colonize permanent wetlands during normal years will likely be extirpated during droughts due to summer and/or winter hypoxic conditions. It follows that anthropogenic alterations of permanent wetlands, which typically make them unsuitable for successful amphibian reproduction, will limit the drought tolerance of amphibian populations.

appear to live long enough to survive two- to three-year droughts. Furthermore, Pechmann et al. (1991) report that tiger salamanders, other *Ambystoma* species, and the ornate chorus frog (*Pseudacris ornata*) can delay reproduction for up to five years under drought conditions. In contrast, Burkett (1984) demonstrates that Kansas populations of Blanchard's cricket frog have a short life span. Average life expectancy is four months; only 5 percent of the population survive the winter; complete population turnover occurs every sixteen months. While cricket frogs in central Indiana do not seem to be affected by a single year of drought (S. Perrill, personal communication), cricket frogs likely cannot postpone breeding past one or two years. Delaying reproduction may prolong the life span of amphibians (Caldwell 1987), but cricket frogs would need to double or triple their life span to survive a prolonged drought. The other option available to them is to shift breeding sites to permanent wetlands (Dodd 1993, 1994; S. Perrill, personal communication).

3. Permanent wetlands will be used as alternative amphibian breeding sites during droughts in proportion to the wetlands' proximity to seasonal and semipermanent wetland breeding sites (see Brown and Dinsmore [1986] for a general discussion and Sjögren [1991] and Sjögren Gulve [1994] for the European *Rana lessonae*).

For many amphibians, wetlands are easier to locate if they are close rather than distant. If distant wetlands are somehow known, migrating to them across a fragmented landscape becomes a greater challenge. Sjögren (1991), Laan and Verboom (1990), and Mann et al. (1991) have found that, in an array of ponds, distance from a source population reduces the probability of the presence of amphibian species.

4. Amphibian species with toxic or distasteful eggs or tadpoles, such as *Bufo* (Licht 1968; Brodie et al. 1978; Kruse and Stone 1984; Brodie and Formanowitz 1987) and bullfrogs (*Rana catesbeiana*) (Kruse and Francis 1977; Formanowitz and Brodie 1982), or with highly efficient antipredator responses to fishes (Brockelman 1969; Beiswenger 1975, 1977; Petranka et al. 1987; Sih et al. 1988; Resitarits and Wilbur 1991; Skelly 1994, 1995; Holomuzki 1995) will be more likely than species without such attributes to be found in permanent wetlands during any phase of the drought cycle (see also Kruse and Francis 1977).

Amphibians that have evolved mechanisms to avoid

Table 34-2. Studies citing philopatry or small home ranges in amphibian genera represented in the upper Midwest

Family Species	Reference
Bufonidae	
American toad (*Bufo americanus americanus*)	Oldham 1966; Dole 1972
Western toad (*Bufo boreas*)	Tracy and Dole 1969
European toad (*Bufo bufo*)	Reading et al. 1991; Schlupp and Podloucky 1994
Marine toad (*Bufo marinus*)	Brattstrom 1962; Carpenter and Gillingham 1987
Fowler's toad (*Bufo woodhousii fowleri*)	Breden 1987
Hylidae	
Pacific treefrog (*Hyla regilla*)	Jameson 1957
Cope's gray treefrog (*Hyla chrysoscelis*)	Ritke et al. 1991
Ornate chorus frog (*Pseudacris ornata*)	Pechmann et al. 1991
Western chorus frog (*Pseudacris triseriata triseriata*)	Smith 1987
Ranidae	
Northern leopard frog (*Rana pipiens*)	Dole 1965
Bullfrog (*Rana catesbeiana*)	McAtee 1921; Raney 1940
Green frog (*Rana clamitans melanota*)	Shirose and Brooks 1995
Mink frog (*Rana septentrionalis*)	Shirose and Brooks 1995
Wood frog (*Rana sylvatica*)	Berven 1990
Ambystomatidae	
Ambystoma	Williams 1973
Jefferson salamander (*Ambystoma jeffersonianum*)	Douglas and Monroe 1981
Spotted salamander (*Ambystoma maculatum*)	Shoop 1965; Whitford and Vinegar 1966; Douglas and Monroe 1981; Stenhouse 1985; Phillips and Sexton 1989
Marbled salamander (*Ambystoma opacum*)	Shoop and Doty 1972; Douglas and Monroe 1981; Stenhouse 1985; Pechmann et al. 1991
Mole salamander (*Ambystoma talpoideum*)	Hardy and Raymond 1980; Semlitsch 1981; Semlitsch et al. 1988; Pechmann et al. 1991
Eastern tiger salamander (*Ambystoma tigrinum tigrinum*)	Semlitsch 1983a; Pechmann et al. 1991

certain predators will always be more successful when exposed to these predators than will other species. Therefore, predator-tolerant species will have a wider variety of breeding habitat options available to them.

5. Amphibians and fishes can co-occur, at least in the short term, if the fishes are nonpredatory.

In northwestern Iowa, examples of nonpredatory fishes that co-occur with amphibian larvae include the brook stickleback and bluntnose and fathead minnows (*Pimephales notatus* and *Pimephales promelas*, respectively) (personal observation; see also Peterka 1989). Interactions between amphibians and these fishes will be based on competitive, rather than predatory, factors. In my experience with *Pimephales* introductions, as the summer progresses competition will eventually favor these fish.

6. Predatory interactions between midwestern fishes and tadpoles will always favor fishes (Bradford 1991; Sjögren 1991; Alfaro 1995), because midwestern tadpoles are herbivorous. Predatory interactions between fishes and tiger salamander larvae will depend more on the size of the interacting individuals than on the fish species involved.

Aquatic vertebrates tend to be "gape-limited" (Zaret 1980). That is, they swallow their prey whole, and therefore the largest prey a predator can ingest depends upon the predator's mouth size, which within a species is typically dependent on body size. The tadpoles of the

Table 34-3. Longevity of amphibian species and genera represented in the Prairie Pothole region of the upper Midwest. Age may vary among populations, particularly along a north-south gradient, so these values should only be used as an estimate of life span in the upper Midwest.

Species	Maximum Age (yrs.)	Technique	Location	Source
American toad				
(*Bufo americanus americanus*)	36 years in captivity			Dickerson 1906
	5*	Osteology	Illinois	Acker et al. 1986
Bullfrog				
(*Rana catesbeiana*)	6+	Osteology	Missouri	Schroeder and Baskett 1968
Northern leopard frog				
(*Rana pipiens*)	4**	Osteology	Quebec	LeClair and Castanet 1987
Asiatic frog				
(*Rana sakuraii*)	5*	Osteology	Japan	Kusano et al. 1995
Blanchard's cricket frog				
(*Acris crepitans blanchardi*)	1.5	Mark-recapture	Missouri	Burkett 1984
Western chorus frog				
(*Pseudacris triseriata triseriata*)	2+	Mark-recapture	Upper Mich.	Smith 1987
Southern chorus frog				
(*Pseudacris nigrita*)	2***	Toe clipping	S. Carolina	Caldwell 1987
Ornate chorus frog				
(*Pseudacris ornata*)	2***	Toe clipping	S. Carolina	Caldwell 1987
Illinois chorus frog				
(*Pseudacris streckeri illinoensis*)	2+	Toe clipping	Cent. Illinois	Tucker, this volume
Ambystoma	25 years in captivity			Duellmann and Trueb 1986
Mole salamander				
(*Ambystoma talpoideum*)	5 females*	Mark-recapture	Louisiana	Raymond and Hardy 1990
	7 males*			

*Reproductive individuals.
**Force (1933) calculates the age of first breeding at three years in populations in the lower peninsula of Michigan.
***Maximum age two years, turnover rate essentially annual.

upper Midwest (with the possible exception of the plains spadefoot toad [*Spea bombifrons*]; see Farrar and Hay, Chpt. 10, this volume) have small mouths specialized for scraping and ingesting algae and periphyton; they are not carnivorous at any stage of their life history. In turn, they are susceptible to fish predation. Salamander larvae are predatory and when large can severely impact larval fish populations (Lannoo 1996a). One form of tiger salamander has uncoupled mouth size from body size. Cannibal morph tiger salamander larvae have proportionately large heads and mouths and hypertrophied vomerine teeth (Powers 1907; Lannoo and Bachmann 1984; Whiteman and Howard, Chpt. 32, this volume) and may have a greater tendency toward piscivory than do typical morph larvae.

7. If prolonged droughts are not adversely affecting amphibian populations, the reappearance of amphibians in rehydrated seasonal and semipermanent wetlands following droughts should closely match the species composition and abundance of the predrought assemblage. Conversely, if droughts are impacting amphibians, recolonization following droughts should be gradual rather than immediate and involve adding species as well as individuals.

In my experience, droughts impact amphibian populations. Postdrought amphibian assemblages are reduced compared to predrought assemblages; over time and with good water levels, numbers increase back to predrought levels (Lannoo et al. 1994). This recruitment can come either from within the population or from adjacent populations. If postdrought reductions do not involve the loss of species, recruitment could come solely from within each population—the offspring of surviving adults. Additional animals could immigrate from neighboring populations. If reductions involve the loss of species, individuals from these species must immigrate from neighboring populations (Corn and Fogleman 1984 for the northern leopard frog). Recolonization rates will be based on regional abundance (Laan and Verboom 1990) and the proximity of breeding adults emerging from overwintering sites to the wetland.

It has become axiomatic in conservation biology that anthropogenic habitat fragmentation poses a major threat to many populations. Fragmentation endangers populations by reducing their size, increasing their isolation, restricting gene flow, reducing habitat quality, reducing habitat area and heterogeneity, and increasing edge effects (Wilcove et al. 1986). Sjögren (1991), Wake (1991), and Wyman (1990) have suggested that habitat fragmentation has played a role in the recent declines and disappearances of amphibian populations. In fact, there are several examples of amphibians disappearing from naturally drought-susceptible habitats where the normal avenues used by recolonizing individuals have been compromised. Corn and Fogleman (1984) have suggested that the local extinctions of northern leopard frogs that they observed might be a common natural occurrence, because small populations in drought-susceptible ponds are separated by dry forests that provide few dispersal routes. Likewise, Bradford (1991) observed that mortality and extinctions in populations of *Rana mucosa* in the Sierra Nevada, California, were probably due to natural causes that occurred irregularly in time and space. The historical persistence of these populations probably depended upon recolonization from other sites following such extinctions, but the widespread introduction of fish to lakes and streams in the Sierra Nevada during this century may now preclude such dispersal. Similarly, Weygolt (1989) feared that forest destruction might prevent the recolonization of hylodine frogs that were probably eliminated by drought from the forests around Santa Theresa, Brazil.

Alternative Interpretations

Several workers have noted an apparent incongruity between the constraint of philopatry and an unpredictable breeding habitat. The usual interpretation is that selection has favored juvenile dispersal (i.e., philopatric associations are determined in juveniles, not in larvae or in metamorphosing animals). For example, Gill (1978a) concluded that, for the newt (*Notophthalmus viridescens*), small pond habitats are population sinks (see below), that homing behavior evolved as a consequence of natural selection within metapopulation centers, and that the eft stage is the mechanism of dispersal to new ponds. Breden (1987) calculated that about 49 percent of juvenile Fowler's toads (*Bufo woodhousii fowleri*) in each generation disperse to adjacent ponds in the Indiana Dunes. Caldwell (1987) suggested that selection has favored juvenile dispersal in *Pseudacris* treefrogs as an alternative to longevity and iteroparity of individual females. But are philopatric adults able to change breeding sites when they discover that their "home" wetland is not suitable for breeding? Brandon and Ballard (Chpt. 15, this volume) and Tucker (Chpt. 14, this volume) demonstrate that, when historic sites are made unsuitable for breeding because of natural fish introductions, Illinois chorus frog (*Pseudacris streckeri illinoensis*) adults migrate to a nearby suitable wetland to breed. A second alternative is for amphibians to remain near the home pond and postpone breeding (Pechmann et al. 1991). But as pointed out above, the success of this behavior is directly related to life span. Therefore, this is not an option for a species with a short life span, such as the cricket frog. Furthermore, what happens when migrating philopatric adults discover a newly established suitable breeding habitat? Some animals must breed in the new basin—restored wetlands are rapidly colonized, even during wet years when natal ponds hold water.

The Metapopulation Concept

The scenario proposed here is consistent with the concept of metapopulations, where the emphasis is placed on the interactions among local populations and the regional metapopulation is treated as the functional unit. In metapopulations, individual populations are generally divided into sources and sinks. Source populations are considered to produce an overabundance of animals, which can then disperse into sink populations. Sink populations lose more individuals than they can gain through reproduction alone (Levin 1976; Pulliam 1988; Hanski and Gilpin 1991; for *Notophthalmus*, see Gill 1978a,b). Typically, our impressions of source and sink populations are tied to habitat quality—source populations inhabit optimal habitats, sink populations occupy suboptimal or marginal habitats—and habitat quality has been assumed to be static over time. Here, I suggest that wetland quality changes for amphibians and that each population can be either a source or a sink depending on habitat type, fish presence, and phase of the drought cycle (Table 34-4). Temporary and semipermanent wetlands should support source populations during average- to high-water years but become sink populations during droughts. Permanent wetlands that contain fish are sinks except during and immediately after droughts, when summer- and/or winterkills reduce or eliminate fishes and provide at least the potential to support source populations. Permanent wetlands that do not hold fish should always support source populations, except perhaps when exposed to heavy predation pressure from invertebrates (Caldwell et al. 1981; Travis et al. 1985).

Management

The question frequently arises: How does one manage for amphibians? The answer in the upper Midwest appears to be to provide a series of fishless wetlands of various types—from seasonal to permanent—placed within the home range of the various native species. These wetlands should be connected by upland migration corridors (or better yet, an undisturbed landscape; see Fahrig and Merriam 1985) and habitat for terrestrial life history stages. If even one of these factors is overlooked—i.e., there are no permanent wetlands, wetlands contain fish, wetlands are too far apart, or there is no adjacent terrestrial habitat—one can reasonably expect that the requirements of amphibians will not be met at some point across the drought cycle and that population sizes and perhaps the number of species will be reduced.

A Case Study: The Cricket Frog

The most intractable mystery involving amphibian declines in the upper Midwest is the disappearance of the cricket frog (Hay, Chpt. 11, this volume). This frog is now extirpated from much of this region, including northwestern Iowa. There, the exact spots where cricket frogs were collected in the early part of the twentieth century have been visited repeatedly (Blanchard 1923; Tweed 1938), and none have been found (Lannoo et al. 1994; Lannoo 1996a,b). Whereas factors such as UV-B radiation and habitat contamination due to agricultural chemicals cannot be ruled out, cricket frog declines may simply be due to a combination of three factors: the cricket frog's short adult life span, prolonged droughts, and anthropogenic alterations of permanent wetlands. In short, the cricket frog's brief life span dictates that this animal must breed annually. If droughts dictate that frogs must breed in permanent wetland, and if permanent wetlands are being rendered unsuitable for successful cricket frog reproduction by anthropogenic factors, then we would expect to find the cricket frog declines that we are now observing. Isolation of habitats due to landscape fragmentation would preclude recolonization and further exacerbate these effects. Ralin and Rogers (1972) demonstrate that cricket frogs are unusually susceptible to drought. Further support for this hypothesis comes from the fact that cricket frogs are declining in the northern portion of their range (dominated by discrete pothole wetlands) but are doing well in the southern portion of their range (dominated by continuous riparian habitats). There may be north-south gradients in UV-B effects and agricultural impacts in the Midwest, but these have not been investigated with reference to amphibian declines. If the scenario described above is true, cricket frogs are faced with a catch-22 situation during prolonged droughts: they may either delay breeding or breed in wetlands that have been co-opted for anthropogenic uses, such as aquaculture. Neither situation will result in reproductive success.

The hypothesis proposed here is not supported by the observation that cricket frog populations inhabiting riparian wetlands are also in decline in the upper Midwest. Drought cycles should have little effect on the reproductive success of riparian populations; in fact, historically in Wisconsin, cricket frog populations were most robust along medium and large rivers, such as the Black, Rock, and Wisconsin Rivers (R. Hay, personal communication). It is true that the seasonal flooding characteristic of these riparian wetlands has been reduced by dams built during the 1930s and 1940s and that in response, populations of paddlefish (*Polyodon spathula*), northern pike (*Esox niger*), and walleye (*Stizostedion vitreum*) have declined (R. Hay, personal communication). The effect of dam building on cricket frogs remains unknown. Wetland cricket frog populations may have declined in response to anthropogenic alterations of permanent wetlands, and riverine populations may have declined in response to dams. It may also be true that wetland and riparian cricket frog populations in the upper Midwest have declined because they have been affected by some common factor as yet unidentified.

General Considerations

For the scenario proposed for cricket frog declines to

Table 34-4. Interactions between amphibians and wetland types across drought cycles (refer to Figs. 34-1 and 34-2) viewed in a metapopulation context

	Wetland Type			
Water Regime	Seasonal	Semipermanent	Permanent	Lake
Normal water levels	Source	Source	Source if fishless	Sink
			Sink if fish present	Sink
Drought	Sink	Sink*	Source	Sink

*Some semipermanent wetlands may hold water long enough to support reproduction in anurans with a brief tadpole stage, such as bufonids.

be realistic, permanent wetlands currently must be undergoing anthropogenic changes on a regional scale. In fact, this may be one of the the strongest components to this argument. I have discussed anthropogenic impacts on permanent wetlands elsewhere (Lannoo 1995, 1996a,b) but will briefly summarize them here: (1) drainage culverts and weirs that connect wetlands to lakes—culverts serve as corridors for fishes to migrate into wetlands; (2) aquacultural practices—the raising of game fish and bait fish has altered many, if not most, of the permanent wetlands of the upper Midwest and involve both publicly and privately owned basins; and (3) bullfrog introductions—because bullfrog tadpoles must overwinter, bullfrogs congregate in and around permanent wetlands. Bullfrogs feed heavily on amphibians (e.g., cricket frogs, Burkett 1984) and other smaller vertebrates to the point of excluding them. In northwestern Iowa, in habitats where introduced bullfrogs occur, native amphibians that were historically present are absent (while native amphibians are present in similar nearby wetlands that do not contain bullfrogs; Lannoo et al. 1994; Lannoo 1996a,b). Introduced bullfrogs spread during high-water years. Bullfrogs introduced into northwestern Iowa have spread into Minnesota (Oldfield and Moriarty 1995).

Finally, it is important to realize that the model proposed here does not address all of the factors involved in the reproductive success of Prairie Pothole amphibians. Other factors that have been shown to influence reproductive success include timing of breeding (Harris 1980; Semlitsch 1983a, 1988; Shirose and Brooks 1995), larval competition (Brockelman 1969; Wilbur 1972; Morin 1983; Alford and Wilbur 1988; Wilbur and Alford 1985), and larval predation (Voris and Bacon 1966; Wilbur 1972; Caldwell et al. 1981; Morin 1983; Semlitsch 1983a; Stenhouse et al. 1983; Wilbur et al. 1983; Lannoo and Bachmann 1984). These factors are important and may be crucial to reproductive success, but each is contingent on animals finding a breeding site across both a naturally changing and an anthropogenically altered landscape.

Summary

While habitat destruction is often implicated as the major factor underlying modern amphibian declines, in the upper Midwest habitat alteration probably plays a larger role. Natural wetlands constrain the organisms that inhabit them through hypoxia and desiccation, conditions contingent on water level. Extreme hypoxia and desiccation generally occur during prolonged droughts, which develop on a roughly ten-year cycle in the upper Midwest. Wetland basins in this region range in size and depth along a continuum from small, temporary wetlands to large recreational lakes. Under normal conditions amphibians here successfully reproduce in seasonal and semipermanent wetlands. Amphibians will also successfully reproduce in permanent wetlands if no predatory fishes are present. During droughts, amphibians will be excluded from successfully reproducing in seasonal and semipermanent wetlands (because they hold little or no water) but can reproduce in permanent wetlands without fish or that once held fish that were extirpated through drought-induced hypoxia. I suggest that, under natural conditions, permanent wetlands contain a flexible fauna, favoring fish during high-water years and amphibians during dry years. Therefore, permanent wetlands provide reproductive sites for amphibians during prolonged droughts, when seasonal and semipermanent wetlands are unavailable. It follows that the effect of droughts on amphibians will depend on the extent that permanent wetlands are impacted by anthropogenic factors, the most serious and widespread probably being aquacultural practices.

While all amphibian species in the upper Midwest have been affected by aquaculture, Blanchard's cricket frogs (*Acris crepitans blanchardi*) may be the hardest hit. These frogs have a life span of only sixteen months and therefore may encounter an ecological situation for which they have no behavioral or life history solution. Faced with drought, modern populations of cricket frogs appear to have two options: postpone reproduction or reproduce in anthropogenically altered permanent wetlands. Neither may ultimately result in successful reproduction; cricket frogs cannot outlive multiyear droughts, and many permanent wetlands are impacted. Cricket frog declines in the northern portion of their range may be at least partially explained by the effects of drought on an anthropogenically altered landscape.

Management for amphibians in the Prairie Pothole region of the upper Midwest should include habitat: (1) that contains relatively closely spaced but isolated, fishless wetlands; (2) that consists of an assortment of wetland types, including temporary and permanent basins; (3) in which wetlands are connected by upland corridors; and (4) that can be used by mammals in their terrestrial life history stages.

Acknowledgments

Thanks to both Steve Perrill and Bob Hay for informative conversations on the biology of cricket frogs and for permission to cite their personal observations. This manuscript has greatly benefited from the comments of the following biologists: Gary Casper, Spencer Courtwright, Ken Dodd, Bob Hay, Susan Lannoo, Diane Larson, Chris Phillips, Ray Semlitsch, Owen Sexton, and Howard Whiteman.

35

Abandon Not Hope: Status of Repatriated Populations of Spotted Salamanders and Wood Frogs at the Tyson Research Center, St. Louis County, Missouri

Owen J. Sexton, Christopher A. Phillips, Thore J. Bergman, Elizabeth B. Wattenberg, and Robert E. Preston

It is widely accepted that long-term studies are essential to evaluate the health of amphibian populations (Vial and Saylor 1993; Heyer et al. 1994; Cortwright, Chpt. 9, this volume). Emphasis to date has been upon the decline of such populations, although it is recognized that the lack of long-term observations confounds the explanation of reported declines as being due to anthropogenic factors (acid rain, habitat fragmentation and destruction, ozone depletion, nonnative predatory amphibians, introduced fish, commercial exploitation, etc.) versus normal population cycles (Pechmann et al. 1991; Corn 1994).

This investigation reports the results of repatriations of two species of amphibians, spotted salamanders (*Ambystoma maculatum*) and wood frogs (*Rana sylvatica*), to a biological preserve in east-central Missouri. The size and dispersal of a breeding population of the first species were followed from 1974 until 1995. The dispersal of wood frogs was followed from 1980 to 1995. Both populations are healthy and exhibit no signs of decline.

Locale

The studies were carried out at the Washington University Tyson Research Center (hereafter, Tyson) and at Forest 44 Conservation Area (hereafter, Forest 44), both located in western St. Louis County, Missouri. The 800-hectare Tyson tract is the central unit of 3,300 hectares of contiguous properties devoted to conservation. The entire tract is situated in the Ozark Border Division (Nigh et al. 1992). This unit is located on the fringe of the Ozark Plateau. The dominant vegetation is oak-hickory forest (Zimmerman and Wagner 1979; Hampe 1984). Washington University obtained Tyson in 1963 as excess federal property. It had been a munitions storage area from World War II until the end of the Korean War and was retained by the federal government until it was acquired by Washington University. In the early 1940s it was surrounded by a 2.4-meter-high chain link fence, which is still intact. Access to Tyson is regulated through a controlled gate so that disturbance from the general public is eliminated. In 1963 to 1965, we located only one small breeding population of spotted salamanders at Tyson. This population produced no more than five egg masses per season. In 1965 we constructed a new pond, Salamander Pond, on a hilltop located within the oak-hickory forest, and in 1966 we introduced egg masses of spotted salamanders into it from a nearby site (Ranken Pond at Forest 44, to be discussed later). During subsequent years, we constructed other potential breeding ponds (Table 35-1) but did not stock them. Historically, wood frogs were known to inhabit St. Louis County (Hurter 1911) but evidently became extinct locally. We repatriated the species at Tyson in 1980 by introducing eleven egg masses from Warren County, Missouri, into four ponds. The source is 50 kilometers from Tyson. Only the Salamander Pond introduction was successful.

Forest 44 is a 358-hectare tract southeast of Tyson and separated from it by a six-lane interstate highway (I-44) with a 30-meter-wide grassy median. Forest 44 is owned and operated by the Missouri Department of Conservation (MDC). The topography and vegetation of Forest 44 are similar to those of Tyson. Ranken Pond is on a

Table 35-1. Actual and potential breeding ponds for spotted salamanders (*Ambystoma maculatum*) and wood frogs (*Rana sylvatica*) at Tyson Research Center and Forest 44, St. Louis County, Missouri. Egg masses of the former species were introduced into Salamander Pond in 1965 and of the latter species in 1980.

Pond	Location	Constructed	Size (meters)	Maximum Depth (meters)
Salamander	Tyson	1965	45 x 5	1.0
Railroad	Tyson	1970	42 x 36	1.0
Pumphouse	Tyson	1979	5 x 3	1.5
New	Tyson	1968	15 diameter	1.0
Lizard Pen	Tyson	1965	12 x 12	1.0
East Twin	Tyson	1965	45 x 25	2.5
Ranken	Forest 44	Pre-1930s	20 x 20	1.0
Preston	Forest 44	Pre-1960s	25 diameter	0.5
East	Forest 44	Pre-1960s	20 x 20	1.5
West	Forest 44	1993	35 x 5	1.0

hilltop and was used as a source of spotted salamander eggs by developmental biologists at Washington University from the 1930s until the 1960s (V. Hamburger, personal communication). One of us (R.P.) carried out a study of three species of mole salamanders (spotted salamanders, eastern tiger salamanders [*Ambystoma tigrinum tigrinum*], and marbled salamanders [*Ambystoma opacum*]) and of the central newt (*Notophthalmus viridescens louisianensis*) at Ranken Pond and two other Forest 44 ponds (Preston and East) from 1979 until 1982. He also recorded the presence of other amphibians that utilized the ponds as breeding sites (Table 35-2). Wood frogs were conspicuously absent. The MDC constructed a fourth pond (West Pond) in 1993. These ponds are described in Table 35-1.

Methods

Spotted Salamanders

During nine breeding seasons between 1974 and 1995 (Table 35-3), we counted the number of spotted salamanders collected in drop cans located at 2-meter intervals along the outer margins of drift fences (Gibbons and Semlitsch 1981) at Salamander Pond. In all years except 1995, the drift fence was made of hardware cloth with a mesh of 0.6 centimeter. In 1995 we substituted aluminum flashing. The cans were at least 15 centimeters in diameter and 17 centimeters deep. Water was provided in the bottom of the cans. The cans were checked prior to the onset of the breeding season and removed after emigrants from the pond were no longer captured in a similar set of cans on the inner side of the

Table 35-2. Amphibians observed by R. E. Preston during 1979 to 1982 at Preston Pond. This pond was located on what is now the Forest 44 Conservation Area.

American toad (*Bufo americanus americanus*)	Bullfrog (*Rana catesbeiana*)
Northern spring peeper (*Pseudacris crucifer crucifer*)	Central newt (*Notophthalmus viridescens louisianensis*)
Western chorus frog (*Pseudacris triseriata triseriata*)	Spotted salamander (*Ambystoma maculatum*)
Eastern gray treefrog (*Hyla versicolor*)	Marbled salamander (*Ambystoma opacum*)
Southern leopard frog (*Rana sphenocephala*)	Eastern tiger salamander (*Ambystoma tigrinum tigrinum*)
Plains leopard frog (*Rana blairi*)	

Table 35-3. Number of breeding adults of spotted salamanders (*Ambystoma maculatum*) and wood frogs (*Rana sylvatica*) captured at drift fences erected around Salamander Pond, Tyson. Captures recorded when fencing was incomplete were extrapolated to complete coverage.

Year	Percent Pond Periphery Fenced	Number of Females	Number of Males	Total Captured	Extrapolated Totals
Spotted Salamanders					
1974	43	128	300	428	995
1975	100	409	592	1,001	1,001
1976	100	340	868	1,208	1,208
1977	100	248	381	629	629
1978	50	136	237	373	776
1986	100	559	773	1,332	1,332
1987	100	665	839	1,504	1,504
1988	100	491	880	1,371	1,371
1995	100	871	1,430	2,301	2,301
Wood Frogs					
1987	100	121	190	311	311
1995	100	111	253	364	364

drift fence. The presence of breeding salamanders at the other Tyson ponds constructed since 1963 was ascertained by the use of drift fences or by the sightings of egg masses.

Wood Frogs

Wood frogs were counted at drift fences at Salamander Pond in 1987 (Guttman et al. 1991) and in 1995. In addition, we assayed the presence of wood frogs at other ponds at both Tyson and Forest 44 by listening for breeding choruses or searching for egg masses or by collections from drift fences similar to the one described above.

Results

Spotted Salamanders

The spotted salamander population in Salamander Pond is healthy and, overall, has increased in size since 1974, in spite of apparent declines in 1977 and 1978 (Table 35-3). Populations have also invaded four new ponds constructed since 1963: Railroad, New, East Twin, and West Twin.

Wood Frogs

The wood frog population is not only maintaining itself at Salamander Pond (Table 35-3) but has also expanded its local range (Table 35-4). Individuals were recorded from drift fences at Railroad Pond each spring from 1993 through 1995. This pond is 2.4 kilometers north-northwest of Salamander Pond. The invasion route from Salamander Pond (elevation, 229 meters) to Railroad Pond (elevation, 133 meters) was probably along a valley connecting them. In 1994 a huge triangular raft of wood frog egg masses (Seale 1982; Waldman 1982), measuring 2 meters along the base and 8 meters to the apex, was observed at Ranken Pond at Forest 44. That pond is east and 0.9 kilometer distant from Salamander Pond. To reach Ranken Pond, dispersing frogs had to descend 34 meters to a valley at 195 meters elevation and cross a major interstate. They then had to ascend 29 meters to Ranken Pond. That same year adult wood frogs were collected in drop cans or eggs were observed at both East and West Ponds, Forest 44. West Pond was constructed in 1993. It is south-southwest of Ranken Pond and 0.76 kilometer distant from it. Frogs dispersing from Ranken Pond to East and West Ponds could move along a ridgetop connecting the three ponds. The distance between maximally separated, invaded ponds—Railroad Pond and West Pond—is 3 kilometers. Clearly, this population is spreading.

Table 35-4. Dispersal distance of wood frogs (*Rana sylvatica*) at Tyson and Forest 44, St. Louis County, Missouri

Source Pond	Elevation (meters)	Target Pond	Elevation (meters)	Map Distance from Source (kilometers)	Dispersal Direction
Salamander	229	Railroad	133	2.4	NNW
Salamander	229	Ranken	224	0.9	NNE
Salamander	229	New	166	1.0	NW
Salamander	229	Pumphouse	154	1.2	NNW
Salamander	229	Lizard Pen	177	0.9	WNW
Salamander	229	East Twin	152	1.1	WSW
Salamander	229	Spring	148	1.4	SW
Ranken	224	East	219	0.7	SSW
Ranken	224	West	223	0.5	SSW

Discussion

The documented success of the repatriations of spotted salamanders and wood frogs at Tyson is the result of a series of fortunate circumstances. The first is that there is historical evidence (Hurter 1911; Johnson 1987) for the presence of both species in the St. Louis area and post-1930s evidence for the presence of spotted salamanders at and near Tyson. Eggs of the spotted salamander used to inoculate Salamander Pond represent a mitochondrial DNA restriction site haplotype widely distributed in the northern Ozark Highlands (C. Phillips 1994).

A second factor is environmental. The Tyson terrain is more than 85 percent covered by oak-hickory forests (Zimmerman and Wagner 1979; Hampe 1984). The leaf litter, fallen timber, and crevices or burrows in the substrate provide suitable habitat for the near fossorial habits of spotted salamanders and refugia for wood frogs. The leaf litter also supports prey of both species. The constructed ponds were designed to attract breeding populations of amphibians. These ponds have never completely dried even during summers of extreme drought (O. Sexton, personal observation). The location of Tyson on the western edge of the greater metropolitan St. Louis area reduces the effect of pollutants from that source because of the prevailing westerly winds. A large electrical power plant west of Tyson does not appear to affect water quality.

Finally, we capitalized on the opportunity to use egg masses as propagules. The ability to transplant populations via egg masses has many advantages: (1) the masses are easy to collect and transport; (2) removal of a modest proportion of egg masses (or just a portion of several masses) need not unduly reduce the size of the residual adult population because of the heavy mortality expected in larval stages; (3) locally gathered egg masses represent genotypes selected for the general area; (4) egg masses from several local sources would increase genetic variability; (5) the transplanted larvae would become imprinted to the location of their new home pond, which would facilitate their return to it at breeding time; (6) dispersal of some eggs from source ponds by human transport would reduce the likelihood that the source pond genotypes could be lost by local extinction.

We recognize that our success may have been due to fortunate stochastic factors. However, similarly favorable conditions undoubtedly occur on a worldwide basis, and procedures equivalent to ours, but adapted or adjusted to local conditions, can lead to success. One criticism that could be raised is that replacement genotypes may not exactly duplicate those that have undergone local extinction. However, it is likely that many pond-breeding amphibian species have evolved under metapopulation (Pulliam 1988) conditions involving high turnover rates locally. Metapopulations consist of source and sink subpopulations. The former are characterized by production of excess young. The latter are maintained by the frequent colonization of the excess of the source subpopulations. Under certain conditions, most individuals of the total metapopulation may be found in the sink component (Pulliam 1988). Under this scenario, genotypes would be continually replaced by similar ones from within the metapopulation. Thus, human intervention, such as the repatriations discussed above, mimic the natural extinction-colonization cycles that may be characteristic of source and sink subpopulations.

Summary

This study demonstrates that not all amphibian populations are at risk. The population size and local dispersal of a salamander and a frog were followed in western St. Louis County, Missouri, between 1974 and 1995. Egg masses of the spotted salamander (*Ambystoma maculatum*) were introduced into the newly constructed Salamander Pond in 1965. Counts of adults immigrating to this pond during the vernal breeding season were made at drift fences. Numbers generally increased from 995 in 1974 to 2,301 in 1995, with a major decline in 1977 to 1978 and a minor decline in 1988. Four other ponds constructed since 1995 have been colonized by this species. Eggs of the wood frog (*Rana sylvatica*) were introduced into Salamander Pond in 1980. In 1987 and 1995 311 and 364 adults, respectively, were captured at drift fences. Wood frogs successfully invaded other ponds, either recently constructed or historically known not to possess them.

Acknowledgments

The Washington University Tyson Research Center and the Missouri Department of Conservation provided access to their properties and financial support. Richard Coles, Washington University, and Steven Spezia, Gregory Toczlowski, and Tom Johnson, all of the Missouri Department of Conservation, aided our study. The Friends of Tyson graciously extended financial support. Numerous undergraduate and graduate student volunteers have assisted over the years. Robert E. Preston acknowledges the help of Karen and Ron Goellner.

36

Aquatic Habitats in the Midwest: Waiting for Amphibian Conservation Initiatives

William T. Leja

Habitat loss or alteration is extensive in the heavily agricultural and industrial Midwest and is undoubtedly the predominant cause of amphibian declines (as has been shown in Europe; Honegger 1981; Kuzmin et al. 1995). Because of this, an analysis of land use in this region may be helpful in suggesting potential conservation projects and conservation research. This chapter focuses primarily on aquatic habitats—essential for the reproduction of many amphibian species—and the changes that have occurred in these habitats over the past two centuries. Because ponds and lakes in particular are often managed for the production of sport fish, there is a strong, but little appreciated, link between fisheries management and amphibian conservation (Lannoo 1996a). The questions arise: which ecosystems can be best managed for sport fisheries, and which can be managed for amphibians and other nongame wildlife? It may be possible through a diversification of aquatic habitats to manage simultaneously for both.

Streams and Lakes

Compared to historic conditions, midwestern streams today have high suspended sediment loads, high nutrient levels, heavy algal growths in shallow areas, and a scarcity of rooted aquatic vegetation. An examination of the conditions of pre-Euro-American settlement streams is instructive and suggests goals for modern restoration efforts. Trautman (1981) describes the history of the Ohio streams back to 1750 and highlights post-Euro-American settlement changes. In 1750, streams tended to be narrower and deeper than today. Trees grew over the streams, their roots extending into the water. In time, with age and weather, the trees fell, producing an abundance of microhabitats for fish and invertebrates. While there was more water on the landscape, it flowed more slowly. Eroded banks with exposed soil were generally absent. Small brooks flowed permanently, and springs abounded. Because erosion was minimal, stream water was clear; stream and even lake bottoms were generally free of inorganic silt and instead were covered by sand, gravel, rock, or muck from the decay of organic matter. The prairie streams, in Trautman's words, "contained a fish fauna dominated by species requiring the clearest of waters." After 1750, agriculture brought changes. Siltation, resulting from agricultural activity, began to affect water quality. Trautman reports that, after the early 1800s, settlers stopped drinking from streams. Today, eroded sediment suspended in streams acts as a carrier for nutrients, pesticides, bacteria, and viruses (U.S. Environmental Protection Agency [U.S. EPA] 1976).

A representative erosion rate for cropland is 200 times that for a forest and 20 times that for a grassland (U.S. EPA 1973). It appears that as much soil loss has occurred in the Midwest since pioneer settlement (200 years) as has occurred between the last glaciation and pioneer settlement (10,000 to 12,000 years).

In Illinois, sedimentation resulting from soil erosion is the leading cause of fish declines (Smith 1971) and of aquatic mollusk extirpations (Cummings 1991). The effects of sediments on a range of aquatic communities are reviewed by Clark et al. (1985). A major effect of sedimentation in rivers is the elimination of macrophytic vegetation. Many streams in this region are devoid of macrophytes, which are replaced by long strings of filamentous algae that grow rapidly during periods of low water. Mats of algae sometimes cover the silt deposits in quiet, shallow areas. Suspended sediment eliminates submersed macrophytes by limiting sunlight penetration into the water column and by covering photosynthetic surfaces. Sediment abrades plant tissues and forms soft, temporary deposits that can be too unstable for plants to take root. Wave action increases after elimination of the submersed plants, destabilizing emergent and floating vegetation. The absence of macrophytes may, in turn, contribute to amphibian declines. In the process of observing European toad (*Bufo bufo*) populations in the Netherlands, van Leeuwen (1979) noted that adult toads and tadpoles disappeared from ditches when grass carp (*Ctenopharyngodon idella*) were introduced to control aquatic vegetation, while toads remained in neighboring carp-free ditches. He believed the cause was disappearance of vegetation, which eliminated sites for courtship and the attachment of eggs, shelter for tadpoles, and periphyton (algae colonizes the surfaces of aquatic plants, a major component of the tadpoles' diet). Indeed, grass carp introductions into a wetland in central Iowa coincided with the elimination of Blanchard's cricket frogs (*Acris crepitans blanchardi*) from this habitat (E. Farrar, personal observation).

Furthermore, rivers in farm and urban areas carry a heavy load of nutrients in dissolved and particulate form. Effects of this nutrient enrichment include heavy algal growths on rocks and stream bottoms and a shift to a benthic invertebrate fauna tolerant of low oxygen levels. Even though high oxygen levels are established in small, nutrient-rich streams by photosynthesis during daylight hours, plant and animal respiration often depletes the available oxygen in small streams during the night (Ball and Bahr 1975; Brooker et al. 1977; Simonsen and Harremoes 1978). Oxygenation is critical to the development of amphibian eggs (Salthe and Meacham 1974). Amphibian reproduction in such streams may be severely limited.

Prairie potholes on the northern Great Plains sometimes become so enriched with nutrients from agricultural runoff that massive blooms and die-offs of algae occur in the spring or summer. The die-offs often result in the complete deoxygenation of the water and a high fish mortality (Barica 1979). Larimore and Smith (1963) observed algal blooms and fish die-offs from anoxia in winter and summer in small streams in east-central Illinois (see also Lannoo 1996a).

Treated effluent from Madison, Wisconsin, rich in phosphorus and nitrogen, caused an extensive algal bloom in a lake along the Yahara River (Mackenthun and Herman 1945). The dying algae later caused downstream anoxia that continued for ten days, resulting in massive fish kills. During this period, samples of river water were reoxygenated and found to remain lethal to fish because of toxins secreted by the algae. Eventually the city solved this problem by rerouting the effluent through a canal around several lakes.

The Illinois River, which drains nearly half of Illinois, has been well studied and is probably representative of the changes that have occurred in most midwestern streams. The river changed drastically in 1900, when engineers from the city of Chicago reversed the flow of the Chicago River, so that it discharged into the Illinois River rather than into Lake Michigan, which supplies Chicago's drinking water (Sparks 1992). The waste discharge from the Chicago River into Lake Michigan was thought to be responsible for the turn-of-the-century cholera and typhus outbreaks. Treatment of waste discharged into the rerouted river did not begin until the 1920s (Starrett 1972). Forbes and Richardson (1913) described the condition of the river at this time 27 kilometers downstream of Morris, 80 kilometers from Chicago: "Its sediments become substantially like the sludge of a septic tank; its color is gray with suspended specks and larger clusters of sewage organisms. . . . On its surface are also floating masses of decaying debris borne up by the gases developing within them, and covered and fringed with the 'sewage fungus' (*Sphaerotilus natans*)." Vascular plants were virtually eliminated from the middle stretch of the river in the period of maximum sewage pollution, 1916 to 1922 (Starrett 1972), but gradually returned as sewage treatment improved.

Sparks (1992) also recounts the slow changes in agriculture in the Illinois Valley that led to gradual increases in soil erosion in this century. Drastic declines in gamefish and duck populations occurred from 1958 to 1961, as the aquatic rooted plants again disappeared. Sparks believes that positive feedback caused the change to occur suddenly. Sediment blocked the light from, and smothered, submerged vegetation. Wave action increased, causing more sediment to become suspended and smothering more vegetation. The problem continues to this day, and a reduction in soil erosion is believed to be the only solution.

This degraded condition has led to a conflict between fisheries and waterfowl managers. Many backwaters have been blocked off from the main channel by levees and are now used to grow aquatic vegetation for waterfowl. Even though the vegetated areas would be useful to gamefish species as nurseries, waterfowl managers are reluctant to open them to the stream water because the turbid river water will smother the vegetation (Sparks 1992). An aerial photograph of a lush, vegetated backwater enclosure on the Illinois River surrounded by turbid, macrophyte-free water appears in Bell (1981).

Since 1985, changes in agricultural practices have begun to reduce soil erosion. Important among these has been the Conservation Reserve Program (CRP), which has removed easily erodible land from production and placed it under ten-year contracts. In the last decade soil erosion has been reduced nationally by one-third (Water Impacts, Michigan State University 1995). Farmers are now required to submit conservation plans in order to maintain eligibility for government subsidies. But many farmers have not renewed their CRP contracts after the initial ten-year period, and the program itself has been in jeopardy.

Vegetated river corridors are being established to control soil erosion and prevent runoffs of fertilizer and pesticides (see below). The American Fisheries Society is attempting to promote the establishment of vegetated corridors by shaping agricultural legislation. In northeast Iowa, river corridor land is being purchased with Sport Fish Restoration funds (generated by taxes on fishing equipment and supplies). Livestock are being excluded from the corridors. As the streams become shaded, summer water temperatures drop, allowing trout to be stocked (Iowa Department of Natural Resources 1994). Such corridors have unquestionable benefits to amphibian species as habitat and dispersal routes.

Macrophytic vegetation has also been disappearing from shallower ponds, lakes, and wetlands in the Midwest. Maltby (1986), studying this problem in Europe, calls the phenomenon "reed-death". The Norfolk Broads northeast of London provide a well-studied example. The Norfolk Broads constitute a series of shallow lakes that, at the start of the twentieth century, harbored a diverse mixture of aquatic plant communities (Harper 1992). Today most of the lakes lack macrophytes, except for slowly receding reed beds near some shores. A few lakes, however, have maintained their original condition, while others are choked with thick beds of aquatic plants. Pollution by nutrients from treated municipal waste and agricultural runoff is clearly related to the observed changes. The lakes with mean total phosphorus levels of less than 50 to 60 micrograms/liter receive little enriched water and remain unaltered (Harper's Phase 1). Those with intermediate phosphorus levels up to 100 to 125 micrograms/liter have thick beds of macrophytes (Harper's Phase 2). At still higher phosphorus concentrations, in lakes where rivers steadily add nutrients, the rooted vegetation has died back and has been replaced with phytoplankton (Harper's Phase 3).

A mechanism to account for macrophyte disappearance in progressively eutrophied lakes, drawing on studies at the Norfolk Broads, was proposed by Phillips et al. (1978). They postulate that high nutrient loadings cause an increased growth of epiphytes and blanketing filamentous algae, leading to the shading of macrophytes and to reduced macrophyte growth. In their weakened condition, the macrophytes decrease their secretion of phytoplankton suppressants, allowing an increase in phytoplankton growth, further shading the macrophytes and causing their eventual extirpation. Later studies (Stansfield et al. 1989) propose that large cladocerans, which grazed on the epiphytes, had been eliminated by earlier toxic levels of organochlorines, allowing the epiphytes to shade and eliminate the macrophytes. Other studies cited by Stansfield et al. (1989) indicate that macrophyte-dominated communities can be stable at high nutrient levels and that an external factor, such as organochlorine contamination, is required before they are replaced by phytoplankton-dominated communities.

Nutrient levels in Illinois aquatic ecosystems appear similar to those involved in the disappearance of rooted vegetation in the Norfolk Broads. Total phosphorus levels are typically 150 to 200 micrograms/liter in Illinois lakes and 400 to 500 micrograms/liter in Illinois rivers (Ramamurthy 1994). Lakes with 35 to 100 micrograms/liter of phosphorus are classified as eutrophic; those with over 100 micrograms/liter are considered hypereutrophic (Harper 1992).

Eutrophication of breeding ponds has been cited as the leading cause of amphibian declines in Denmark (Corbett 1989). Ponds on the Danish island of Bornholm have been restored by the dredging of nutrient-laden sediments (Fog 1988), resulting in most cases in increased breeding success. Eutrophication is a known factor in amphibian declines in European Russia (Kuzmin and Bobrov 1995) and the Caucasus (Tarkhnishvili 1995).

Puckett (1995) presents an overview of nutrient inputs to aquatic environments in the United States. Major nutrient inputs to streams include fertilizer, manure, soil, nitrogen oxides from fossil fuel combustion, treated wastewater, and urban runoff. Since the implementation of the Clean Water Act of 1972, $540 billion has been spent on water pollution abatement. Nearly 90 percent was spent on improved point source control (municipal and industrial waste discharges). Little attempt has been made so far to remove nutrients from point source waste sites. Abatement of nonpoint source nutrient pollution is only beginning.

Restored Stream Corridors

Stream corridors are being restored in order to conserve soil and prevent the runoff of fertilizer and pesticides from farms, as well as to restore damaged riparian and riverine ecosystems. The scientific evidence of the efficacy of the restoration of stream corridors is reviewed by Pajak et al. (1994). The desired width of a riparian buffer strip to protect streams from adverse land management practices is 30 meters (Gore and Bryant 1988). Natural vegetation is reestablished within the buffer strip. In some cases a more natural stream course is reconstructed. The National Academy of Sciences (1992) recommends the restoration of 640,000 kilometers of stream corridors over the next twenty years. The American Fisheries Society is attempting to promote the establishment of revegetated corridors by shaping agricultural legislation (Pajak et al. 1994).

Restored stream corridors could greatly benefit amphibian species by providing habitat and dispersal routes. The remainder of this section explores this supposition and considers the agricultural practices that have resulted in loss of much stream habitat.

In addition to streams, lakes, wetlands, and forests, the rural midwestern landscape consists primarily of crop fields and pastures. Flying over or driving through this landscape one notices that woods generally consist of small lots along stream courses. In a detailed study of a thirteen-county area in west-central Illinois, Iverson and Schwartz (1994) found that 78 percent of the forest land lies within 300 meters of streams, and 22 percent lies within 30 meters. They counted 130,000 wooded parcels smaller than 16 hectares and only 2,000 parcels larger than 16 hectares; 105,000 parcels were smaller than 0.4 hectare. Restoration of stream corridors by linking disjunct wooded parcels is therefore likely to benefit not only the wildlife that inhabits stream corridors but wildlife that depends on forest habitat.

In order to determine the habitat requirements of the amphibians in the states in the Central Division of the Declining Amphibian Populations Task Force (Iowa, Missouri, Illinois, Indiana, and Ohio), a regional field guide (Conant 1975) and four state herpetofaunal works (Black and Sievert 1989; Johnson 1987; Minton 1972; Barbour 1971) were examined for the seventy amphibian taxa that Conant's range maps indicate occur within the five states. Thirty-six of the taxa are found in both stream and forest habitats. Seventeen taxa occur in forest but not stream habitats, while another seventeen occur in stream but not forest habitats. Thus, nearly all amphibians in this region could potentially benefit from stream corridor restoration.

Studies in England and the Netherlands, where crop fields and pasture dominate the rural landscape as they do in the American Midwest, indicate that woodlots and areas of scrub vegetation play an important role as amphibian habitat. Proximity of these habitats to breeding ponds promotes greater amphibian diversity at these ponds (Beebee 1981; Laan and Verboom 1990) and faster colonization of new ponds (Laan and Verboom 1990). Woods or scrub directly in contact with a pond are especially beneficial (Beebee 1977, 1981). Crop fields present less favorable habitat, or a more formidable barrier, to amphibians than does pasture (Cooke and Ferguson 1976; Beebee 1975, 1977). Cooke (1972) suggested that "a change in the nature of the surrounding land from pasture to arable could make a pond unattractive to breeding amphibians by removing the damp cover required during migration to and from the breeding site." The absence of scrub and woods in extensive pasture areas means the virtual absence of amphibians, even when adequate breeding habitat is available (Beebee 1980). However, central European frogs (*Rana ridibunda*), which permanently inhabit aquatic ecosystems, can flourish in pasture areas even in the absence of scrub and woods (Beebee 1980). In summer, when field crops are maturing and pasture grasses are lush, amphibians may be abundant in those habitats if there is sufficient wood and scrub nearby (Strijbosch 1980). Surprisingly, suburban garden ponds now provide a higher density of breeding sites for three of England's native amphibians than do the surrounding agricultural landscapes (Beebee 1981).

Unfortunately, pastureland is disappearing from the Midwest as livestock production shifts increasingly from farms to large feedlots. Pasture is being replaced with large corn- and soybean fields, which now dominate the midwestern landscape and often extend to within less than a meter of streams. To increase acreage available for corn and soybean production, and to improve drainage, many streams have been channelized. In America,

90 percent of the corn crop and over 90 percent of the soybean crop are fed to livestock (Paddock et al. 1986). This new mode of American agriculture—production of livestock feed on farms and production of livestock in feedlots—had its origin in the 1940s, when improvements in crop yields began to outstrip human food requirements. The answer for agriculture was to promote the consumption of animals, particularly beef, which can be raised on the excess crops (Paddock et al. 1986). From that point on, in order to correct the imbalance created by the Green Revolution, meat production has become a cornerstone of American agriculture.

Lappé (1982) reports that 16 kilograms of corn and soybeans are required to produce 1 kilogram of beef, while 6 kilograms are required for 1 kilogram of pork and only 3 kilograms for 1 kilogram of chicken. Lappé's figures suggest that even a small shift in the American diet away from beef can produce a dramatic decrease in the agricultural acreage requirement; a major shift to a vegetarian diet would have serious economic consequences.

The point for amphibian and nongame wildlife conservation is that protection of riparian habitat does not jeopardize agriculture's ability to feed the nation. Rather, it jeopardizes the short-term profitability of an agricultural system that traditionally ignores the cost of soil losses and aquatic ecosystem damage. If these and other less obvious costs of production (Lappé 1982) are recognized, stream restoration would be profitable to agriculturists.

The problem of agricultural overproduction remains unsolved today. When the grain export market disappeared in the early 1980s because of agricultural successes overseas, a partial solution was found in the CRP, which temporarily retired marginal, easily erodible acreage. Hart (1991) suggests even this is not an adequate solution, because fertile land needs to be retired as well. He describes the plight of today's farmers: "The modern farmer is producing too much, and he knows it, but he is not foolish enough to cut back unilaterally when his neighbors are also producing too much. They all depend on exports to an international market that fluctuates unpredictably, and they feel frustrated and helpless when they are battered by its wild gyrations." Hart's interest is in helping the farm community adapt to modern times. He expresses no concern in his book for wildlife conservation.

It is commonly thought that in heavily populated areas, such as the Midwest, there will inevitably be a scarcity of wildlife habitat, but that is not the case. Land-use policy is the true determinant today of wildlife survival. Through the political process, and without jeopardizing food production, Midwest agricultural developments can be guided so that society's broad goals of clean rivers, abundant wildlife, and soil conservation are met. Conservation of soil also will allow future generations to meet their food requirements.

Wetlands

Of the fifty states, the six states with the greatest wetland loss between the 1780s and the mid-1980s (Dahl 1990) have been California (91 percent of wetland acreage lost), Ohio (90 percent of wetland acreage lost), Iowa (89 percent of wetland acreage lost), Indiana (87 percent of wetland acreage lost), Missouri (87 percent of wetland acreage lost), and Illinois (85 percent of wetland acreage lost). Overall wetland loss in the forty-eight conterminous states in the same period was 53 percent. The states in the Central Division of the Declining Amphibian Populations Task Force have lost most of their wetlands. Prior to Euro-American settlement, the percentage of surface covered by wetlands in the Central Division states was 24 percent in Indiana, 23 percent in Illinois, 19 percent in Ohio, 11 percent in Iowa, and 11 percent in Missouri (Dahl 1990). In compiling these numbers, Dahl used the wetland classification developed by the U.S. Fish and Wildlife Service (USFWS; Cowardin et al. 1979).

Most of the wetland loss is due to conversion to agricultural uses. Drainage ditches are dug and porous drain tiles are placed under the soil to promote drainage and lower the water table. A 9.7-hectare cornfield in McHenry County, Illinois, was recently converted back into a wetland. The length of tile removed was 53 kilometers (Swanson 1995). Twenty-seven percent of Illinois is currently underlain by drain tile (U.S. Department of Commerce, cited in Bell 1981). Ninety percent of Champaign County, in the heart of Illinois' largest original wetland region, is now tiled (Bell 1981).

Most of the remaining wetlands in the Central Division states is bottomland forest—forested land along streams that floods in the spring or after heavy rains. If bottomland forest had been excluded from the USFWS wetland classification, calculated wetland losses would be considerably greater.

Although Dahl (1990) reported a wetland loss of 89 percent for Iowa, a loss of 98 percent was calculated from data in Bishop's (1981) Iowa wetlands survey. Bishop reported 10,710 hectares of natural marsh, 4,050 hectares of artificial marsh, and 16,200 hectares of river oxbows and overflow wetlands (a total of 30,950 hectares) in 1981. Dahl's (1990) figure of 1,619,000 hectares of original Iowa wetland was used for the recalculation. Bishop also reported on the amount of natural lakes, artificial lakes and reservoirs, farm ponds, and rivers. Much of these areas would be included as wetlands using the USFWS wetland classification (Cowardin et al. 1979)—both in the numerator and denominator of the calculation. The USFWS wetland classification includes the bottoms of intermittent streams and even the bottoms of permanent streams in areas less than 2 meters deep. Water more than 2 meters deep is classified by the USFWS as deepwater habitat rather than wetland; however, farm ponds are classified as wetlands for convenience, even though much of the pond may be deeper than 2 meters. Precise wetland loss estimates must be interpreted in the context of the wetland classification scheme being used.

Dahl (1990) reports a wetland loss in Illinois of 85 percent and a remaining wetland area of 507,700 hectares. The Illinois Natural History Survey (1991), without specifying its definition, stated that over 95 percent of the state's wetlands had been drained. It further indicated that high-quality wetlands that reflect pre-Euro-American settlement conditions are exceedingly rare today; only about 2,430 hectares remain. Bell (1981), in his table 4, indicates the type of wetland and acreage in each Illinois county for these 2,430 hectares. Most of the high-quality areas were under threat of development. Bell's (1981) table 11 identifies specific threats to each wetland. Only one high-quality wetland was under consideration as a wildlife management area. The Illinois Environmental Protection Agency (EPA) is currently developing agreements with other Illinois agencies, among them the Illinois Department of Natural Resources (Illinois DNR; this agency includes, as of 1995, the former Illinois Department of Conservation). These agreements will "reduce wetland loss by state agencies' actions" (Illinois EPA 1995).

To rely heavily on these few remaining high-quality wetlands for the conservation of amphibians would lead to the isolation and eventual extirpation of these amphibians. Interested parties might wish to encourage landowners and public land managers to manage all aquatic ecosystems, where practical, consistent with amphibian conservation.

In their study of the fishes of Champaign County, Illinois, Larimore and Smith (1963) stated that "no natural lakes, and no permanent swamps and marshes remain in the county." Conversion of wetland to agriculture in the county had been completed by 1920. However, Suloway and Hubbell (1994), following the 1979 USFWS classification (Cowardin et al. 1979), indicated the county has 2,059 hectares of natural wetlands and 340 hectares of artificial wetlands today. Almost all of the wetlands they report is of three types: bottomland forest (1,342 hectares), emergent wetlands (667 hectares), and shallow marsh/meadow (603 hectares). The differences in their findings may rest, at least in part, in the system of wetland classification and in definitions of terms such as "natural."

Ponds

In response to the devastation of the Dust Bowl of the 1930s, the newly created U.S. Soil Conservation Service realized that ponds in low spots in small watersheds would effectively capture eroding soil, and it began a campaign to promote farm and ranch pond construction. In 1934 there were 15,000 artificial ponds nationwide. By 1952 the number had increased to 1,666,000 (Compton 1952). The agency subsidized their construction and worked with fisheries managers to promote designs that were useful secondarily as fish ponds. Modde (1980) indicated that the greatest pond density was in the Southeast and the Great Plains. At that time Missouri had over 150,000 ponds, while Iowa, Illinois, Indiana, and Ohio had between 25,000 and 50,000 ponds each. Flickinger and Bulow (1993) indicated that pond construction was slowing. In 1994 Illinois had 86,000 ponds (Illinois Department of Conservation 1995a) and was adding about 400 ponds per year. About half of these (45,000) are under 0.2 hectare in size and of no use as fish ponds, according to fisheries managers, because they are incapable of producing full-sized gamefish (Lopinot 1973). Bennett (1970) considered ponds under 0.4 hectare useless as fisheries because of the stunting (overpopulation) problem.

Fishing in ponds is a major recreational activity today in the midwestern United States. There are few natural ponds in the southern Midwest, and the rivers—because of high nutrient levels (Becker 1983)—are likely to produce more common carp (*Cyprinus carpio*) than gamefish. Efforts to promote designs of ponds over 0.2 hectare for amphibian conservation are likely to meet with resistance, but nongame wildlife managers may welcome such efforts. Johnson (1979) published a guide to amphibian and reptile conservation for landowners in Missouri that featured an emphasis on pond design.

Wisconsin provides some information on the design of ponds for wildlife use (Wisconsin Department of Natural Resources 1992). More efforts of this sort await programs initiated by wildlife managers, perhaps prompted by the public (Lannoo 1996a).

If a pond is constructed in cropland far from terrestrial habitat such as meadows, woods, or grasslands, it will likely become populated with amphibians that spend their adult lives near water, such as bullfrogs (*Rana catesbeiana*) or green frogs (*Rana clamitans melanota*). This may account for Thurow's (1994a) observation that bullfrogs predominate at farm ponds. Gamefish can radically alter amphibian populations at a pond lacking rooted vegetation (Sexton and Phillips 1986; Fitzpatrick 1993). Gamefish extirpate most amphibian species from macrophyte-free ponds within a few years, but bullfrogs are able to coexist. Hayes and Jennings (1986) described the ability of bullfrogs to survive in permanent waters in the presence of gamefish. Bennett (1970) indicated that weirs can be installed at the outlets of ponds to prevent upstream migration of fish into ponds during floods, although Lannoo (1996a) noted that the smaller individuals of big predatory fish can negotiate weirs.

The gamefish that is usually stocked in midwestern ponds is the largemouth bass (*Micropterus salmoides*). Smaller sunfish in the same family, Centrarchidae, are usually stocked along with the bass to serve as food for the adult bass and as sport for anglers. The smaller centrarchids—for example, the bluegill (*Lepomis macrochirus*)—are referred to as panfish or forage fish. Farther north, in the cooler waters of the Great Lakes basin, state ponds are stocked with trout. In England, surprisingly, the common carp serves as a prized gamefish (Cooper 1987).

Ponds created for fishing purposes must be deeper than wetlands to allow for winter survival of fish (see Lannoo, Chpt. 34, this volume). At least 25 percent of the pond should be over 3 meters deep in northern Illinois (Illinois Department of Conservation 1995a). Steep banks with a near-shore depth of 1 meter are important to discourage growth of macrophytes, which would otherwise shelter panfish and lead to their overpopulation and stunting. Stunting of panfish is a major problem in the Midwest, even in larger ponds. The department recommends that trees and shrubs be kept at least 30 meters from the bank of a fish pond. Sunny banks free of trees and shrubs are important if ponds are to benefit maximally from winter sunlight, which is required for algal production of oxygen under winter ice.

Clearly, wetlands can be lost by conversion to ponds. However, the USFWS considers waters less than 2 meters deep at low water to be wetland, and for practical purposes ponds are classified as wetlands (see above). Whether fishing ponds are considered wetlands thus becomes a matter of wetland classification, not biology. The role fish ponds play in preservation of biodiversity is a separate issue. Gamefish ponds are of little value in amphibian conservation (Lannoo 1996a,b).

Tiner (1987) investigated the causes of wetland loss in the Mid-Atlantic states. He found that in the period 1956 to 1979, wetland conversion to ponds accounted for 38 percent of the loss in Pennsylvania, where it was the leading cause. In the same period in West Virginia, 26 percent of the wetlands were lost by conversion to ponds. Loss of inland wetlands by conversion to ponds (and lakes) in Virginia, Maryland, and Delaware was 7 percent, 27 percent, and 5 percent, respectively. (Tiner did not define the term "pond," but agencies usually define it by size. The Illinois DNR defines ponds as bodies of water under 2.4 hectares.) Loss of coastal wetlands to ponds (and lakes) in these three states was 5 percent, 8 percent, and 6 percent, respectively.

On the basis of the following information, it is unlikely that conversions of wetland to deepwater habitat for fishing or other uses is a significant factor in the Central Division states, at least in Illinois (but see Lannoo, Chpt. 34, this volume). Dahl and Johnson (1991) provided information at the national level on the land areas used for construction of ponds from the mid-1970s to the mid-1980s: 19,900 hectares of marsh, 31,800 hectares of swamp, 91,000 hectares of agricultural land, and 170,000 hectares of "uplands that had not been used for agricultural production." Because nationally less than 10 percent of the ponds are constructed from marsh, it is likely that less than 10 percent of Illinois ponds are converted from marsh. Illinois today has only 6,045 hectares of swamp but 81,600 hectares of marsh (Suloway and Hubbell 1994). The swamp acreage is concentrated at the southern tip of the state, and much of it is protected; new ponds in Illinois, if they result from conversion of wetlands, are likely to arise from conversion of marshes. In the period 1987 to 1994, 1,703 hectares of ponds (3,176 ponds) were constructed in Illinois (Illinois Department of Conservation 1995b). If in this period 10 percent of the pond acreage was formerly marsh, only 170 hectares of marsh out of 81,600 hectares was lost by conversion to ponds. New lakes in the same period totaled 688 hectares.

Fisheries Management

Bennett (1970) summarized the early history of fisheries management and concluded that this profession is rooted in the science of aquaculture rather than ecology. The original name of the American Fisheries Society, a professional organization composed primarily of government fisheries biologists and ichthyologists, was the American Fish Culturist's Association (Neilsen 1993). Its history continues to influence its policies.

The common carp and brown trout (*Salmo trutta*) were introduced during the past 100 years by the U.S. Fish Commission under the guise of improving food resources, but mostly to enhance sport fishing (Courtenay and Moyle 1992). This "improving on nature syndrome" persists today in some circles in fishery management (Courtenay and Moyle 1992). At least seventy exotic fish species have become established in the United States, and at least 158 fish species have been transplanted beyond their ranges (Courtenay and Moyle 1992). The success of sport or forage fish introductions is often judged by short-term angler satisfaction rather than by the effect on the ecosystem. Exotic and transplanted species have contributed to 68 percent of the extinctions of fish over the past 100 years and pose a threat to 44 fish species and populations that are federally listed as endangered or threatened (Wilcove et al. 1992). Pister (1992) believes this problem is traceable to the education received by fishery managers. He notes that their willingness to do what is necessary to fill lakes and streams with gamefish allows them to advance to leadership roles in government agencies. The ethics of introducing exotic or transplanted sport fish was the subject of organized debates in 1994 and 1995 at regional meetings of the American Fisheries Society (Martin 1994; see also Lannoo 1996a,b).

Accidental introduction of the zebra mussel (*Dreissena polymorpha*) prompted Congress to pass the Nonindigenous Aquatic Nuisance and Control Act in 1990. Congress asked the American Fisheries Society to recommend control measures for intentional introductions. Moyle and Li (1994) commented that the final society recommendations "do not go much beyond the status quo; they rely heavily on voluntary compliance by states and individuals; and they do not provide for any new sources of funding to carry out the recommendations." The accelerating pace of invasive species introductions may continue for the foreseeable future.

There are numerous examples in the literature of the introduction of fish to amphibian breeding sites and the subsequent extirpation of the amphibian populations. The Arizona tiger salamander (*Ambystoma tigrinum nebulosum*) has been eliminated by introduced trout from high mountain lakes in Colorado (Burger 1950; Blair 1951). Bradford (1989) examined sixty-seven high mountain lakes in the Sierra Nevada of California and found that the mountain yellow-legged frog (*Rana muscosa*) was absent from every lake that was populated by introduced trout. These High Sierra Nevada lakes were fishless until trout stocking began a century ago. Fellers and Drost (1993) reported the disappearance of the Cascades frog (*Rana cascadae*) from Lassen Volcanic National Park in California, where it was once abundant. They believed that introduced sport fish restricted habitat and limited dispersal of the frogs, contributing to their disappearance. Brönmark and Edenhamn (1994) found that the introduction of fish to formerly fishless ponds in Sweden eliminated populations of European treefrogs (*Hyla arborea*).

Bahls (1992) reviewed the practice of stocking formerly fishless high mountain lakes in the American West. He found "little evidence of concern for the effects of trout stocking on indigenous fauna" and "little understanding of the anglers whom they [state and federal biologists] serve." Fish were often stocked by helicopter in lakes that were rarely or never examined to see if the fish survived, or became stunted from overpopulation, or were actually used by anglers.

Concern over the decline of Wisconsin populations of the northern leopard frog (*Rana pipiens*), which during the 1970s was in wide use for classroom dissection and scientific experimentation, prompted two investigations sponsored by the Wisconsin Department of Natural Resources (Hine et al. 1975; Hine et al. 1981). The reason for the decline was not discovered. Fisheries management activities were not among the factors investigated. Whether leopard frogs serve as food for stocked fish and whether fish toxicants are eliminating frog populations might have been addressed in their reports.

Trout, including the European brown trout, are widely stocked in Wisconsin in lakes, ponds, and streams. The brown trout is known to feed on overwintering European common frogs (*Rana temporaria*) in ponds in Germany (Kabisch and Weiss 1968) and may feed on overwintering leopard frogs in North America. Leopard frogs overwinter underwater (Hine et al. 1981), as do most North American ranids (Pinder et al. 1992). Kabisch and Weiss (1968) found food in the stomachs of twelve of forty-one grass frogs that were collected through the ice in January. They found that the frogs were invariably alert and able to move but were sluggish. They believed predation by trout occurred when the frogs moved in the pursuit of prey. Pinder et al. (1992) indicated similar levels of alertness and movement of North American frogs overwintering underwater.

Streams, ponds, and lakes in Wisconsin and throughout the Midwest are often poisoned with piscicides, usually rotenone, to remove undesired fish species or stunted trout or bass populations (Klingbiel 1975; Lannoo 1996a). Angermeier et al. (1986) noted that there is little documentation in the literature on this practice's impact on nongame species. Winter use of rotenone has been found to be cheaper because less poison is required than during warm weather (Roth and Hacker 1988). Rotenone remains toxic for four months under the ice in Wisconsin lakes. Although rotenone is less toxic to adult frogs than to fish (Hamilton 1939; Fontenot et al. 1994), frogs may not be able to tolerate it for months under ice. There are no published reports on the effect of winter use of rotenone on nontarget animals such as frogs or turtles.

Nongame Wildlife Conservation

In the language of the wildlife management profession, conservation of amphibians is part of nongame wildlife conservation. People who care about amphibians and spend time and effort observing or protecting them are "nonconsumptive wildlife users" or "nongame enthusiasts." "Consumptive users" (hunters and fishers) spend $41 billion annually in the United States in pursuit of their sports (Merwin 1994). Nonconsumptive users are increasing rapidly, and their annual expenditures are increasing correspondingly. Surveys (Mangun et al. 1992) indicate that the number of nonconsumptive users in the United States over the age of sixteen grew from 93 million in 1980 to 135 million in 1985. Their activities include trips to observe, photograph, or identify wildlife. Their annual expenditures were estimated at $10 billion in 1980 and $14 billion in 1985.

In spite of similar game and nongame recreational expenditures by the public, funding for nongame conservation is minimal. This funding disparity has "forced nongame enthusiasts and nonconsumptive users to channel their conservation efforts primarily through private wildlife organizations rather than through government agencies" (Mangun et al. 1992). An important activity for people concerned at this time about the decline of amphibians is to help state and federal agencies in their attempts to develop funding initiatives for nongame wildlife conservation.

Because amphibian declines in the Midwest are clearly related to human activity, it is possible to reverse them. However, political action in shaping agricultural legislation and providing funding for government nongame wildlife management may be essential for success. That will necessarily involve public education, conservation activism, and conservation research.

Summary

Major alterations in natural midwestern streams and wetlands have been brought about by soil erosion and nutrient pollution, which have severely limited the ability of much of these aquatic habitats to support historic levels of amphibians and other nongame wildlife. Restored, revegetated stream corridors protected from livestock use—designed to improve water quality by preventing the loss of soil and reducing agrichemical runoff and to improve fisheries—also have the potential to provide amphibian habitat and dispersal routes. Similarly, hundreds of thousands of artificial ponds have been constructed in the Midwest over the past sixty years. Smaller ponds also prevent regional soil loss, reduce agricultural runoff, and improve water quality. Ponds under 0.2 hectare have been shown to be of no use for sport fishing, but they provide ideal breeding and larval habitat for amphibians. Amphibian conservation initiatives might profit by tying into these more utilitarian functions of created and restored aquatic habitats.

Monitoring and Applications

37

Missouri Toad and Frog Calling Survey: The First Year

Tom R. Johnson

Since its inception, the Missouri Department of Conservation's Natural History Division has conducted numerous surveys, including those for native plants, animals, special features, and natural communities. In 1995 the Missouri toad and frog calling survey was initiated. The survey consists of driving at night along roads near identified breeding habitats and listening for toad and frog breeding calls. This first year's effort was considered a pilot project, because a few midwestern states have had several false starts and wrong turns before their toad and frog breeding surveys were running smoothly. Although I had been considering the planning and design aspects of implementing a Missouri toad and frog calling survey for several years, I had a few misgivings. First, I was reluctant to use volunteers with little or no training or experience in the identification and analysis of toad and frog calls. Second, I had reservations about the usefulness of the data collected by such a workforce.

However, in the early 1990s there was a sudden, unexpected, and in some ways exciting explosion of public interest in amphibians. A media "feeding frenzy" was stimulated by the so-called worldwide decline of amphibian populations. Literally dozens of newspaper, magazine, radio, and television stories declaring a major decline of toads and frogs were seen by millions of people. Articles with such titles as "Where Have All the Froggies Gone" (Barinaga 1990), "Are the Frogs Croaking" (Anonymous 1991), and "The Vanishing Frogs" (Chui 1993) were common. I was as caught up in the declining amphibian issue as anyone. I attended several professional herpetological conferences, and the word was out that we need long-term population studies of our amphibians—especially toads and frogs. My reluctance to form a survey quickly dissolved.

My annual work plan was quickly amended so that a toad and frog calling survey would become a top priority. In early 1994 I began planning such a survey, based on Wisconsin's frog and toad survey (Mossman et al., Chpt. 21; Casper, Chpt. 22, this volume), begun in 1981. Missouri's survey can best be understood by breaking it up into its components: (1) Missouri anurans, (2) the introduction and instruction packet, (3) the recruitment and selection of volunteer surveyors, (4) wetland selection, (5) running a survey route, and (6) the survey computer database.

Missouri Anurans

Missouri's twenty-three species of toads and frogs include three species of true toads, two species of spadefoot toads, eight species of treefrogs, two species of narrowmouth toads, and eight species of true frogs (see Introduction, this volume). Three anurans, the eastern spadefoot toad (*Scaphiopus holbrookii holbrookii*), the Illinois chorus frog (*Pseudacris streckeri illinoensis*), and the wood frog (*Rana sylvatica*), are on the state's rare and endangered species checklist (see Introduction, this volume). A prairie species, the northern crawfish frog (*Rana areolata circulosa*), is a watch-listed species. The survey will not target rare species, but populations of these species will be monitored by the state herpetologist and/or by contracted research projects.

Survey Introduction and Instruction Packet

The survey introduction and instruction packet consists of information on the importance of the survey, its long-term aspects, and the need for volunteers. There is information on how to fill out the field data forms, as well as safety considerations for conducting a nocturnal wildlife survey. There are instructions on scoring (indexing) breeding calls. As with Wisconsin's survey, indexing calls is a matter of giving a numerical value, from one to three, to each species heard at each wetland along a survey route. Unlike in Wisconsin's survey, in Missouri's survey one represents fewer than ten males of a given species calling, two indicates between ten and twenty calling males, and three represents more than twenty calling males (for details of the Wisconsin survey, see Mossman et al., Chpt. 21, this volume).

The packet also contains a small supply of survey informational cards. The cards are designed to be given to people who own the land or live near a wetland that will be surveyed. The cards provide information on why, how, and by whom the survey is being conducted.

The survey volunteer packet includes a cassette tape of the breeding calls of Missouri's toads and frogs. It is assumed that, from this tape, volunteers will be able to identify each species correctly. However, people do not hear frequencies and intensities equally well (see Hemesath, Chpt. 23; Kline, Chpt. 38, this volume). For example, some people can have difficulty distinguishing between the calls of the western chorus frog (*Pseudacris triseriata triseriata*) and the northern spring peeper (*Pseudacris crucifer crucifer*) or between the calls of the pickerel frog (*Rana palustris*) and the southern leopard frog (*Rana sphenocephala*). The only solution to this problem is to have surveyors practice listening to the identification tape and comparing that with what they hear in the field. Determining index values also takes practice and, being more subjective, often comes down to judgment calls. I advise Missouri volunteers to take along a small cassette tape recorder and record any problem calls, then send the tape to me for verification.

Not each of the state's species is easily surveyed. The wood frog, which is rare, breeds so early in the spring and for such a short time period that it is likely to be missed. The two species that compose the gray treefrog complex—the eastern gray treefrog (*Hyla versicolor*) and Cope's gray treefrog (*Hyla chrysoscelis*)—are difficult to discern by their breeding calls; the Missouri survey combines them. The Illinois chorus frog breeds in the winter, is isolated to the former sand prairie areas of the bootheel, and will likely not be surveyed. I will take responsibility for monitoring these species. Fortunately, supplemental materials are available. *The Amphibians and Reptiles of Missouri* (Johnson 1987) has distribution maps of all anuran species, and a pamphlet, *Rare and Endangered Species Checklist of Missouri* (Anonymous 1995), describes many species.

Volunteer Recruitment and Selection

It is difficult to recruit and select volunteers, and I wanted the best possible volunteers. I used our in-house newsletter, "Conservation Currents," to announce the survey and my need for volunteers. During the first year, the survey was conducted by twenty people, all professional biologists, including wildlife and fisheries biologists, conservation agents, Missouri Department of Conservation naturalists, state park naturalists, U.S. Fish and Wildlife Service biologists, and natural history regional biologists. Although some volunteers were clustered into certain regions, a scattering of surveyors over much of the state was achieved. The eventual goal will be to have a total of fifty volunteers distributed across the state. An important part of this project is the long-term involvement of its volunteers, which requires them to stay with their survey route in order to gather many years of data.

Wetland Selection

To make up their survey driving route, all volunteers are required to select up to ten toad and frog breeding sites. The survey seeks to acquire data on as many species as possible from as many habitats as possible. Thus, each survey route should have temporary or ephemeral pools, more permanent marshes or swamps, flooded ditches, fishless ponds, and large ponds or river backwater areas. Volunteers are asked to select as many wetland types as possible in their area. Wetland types are recorded on each survey form.

This format for selecting wetlands is similar to that employed by Wisconsin (Mossman and Hine 1984, 1985; Mossman et al., Chpt. 21, this volume) and other states (e.g., Iowa; Hemesath, Chpt. 23, this volume) but dissimilar to that recommended by the North American Amphibian Monitoring Program (Mac 1996). While the Wisconsin method favors volunteer participation (Hemesath, Chpt. 23, this volume), it unfortunately relies on nonrandom site selection and therefore restricts the generalizability of the data (Mossman et al., Chpt. 21, this volume).

Running a Survey Route

During the breeding season, three trips are made on each survey route. Selecting three trips—one in the spring, one in the late spring, and one in mid-summer—ensures that the majority of calling anurans will be heard. Once a volunteer has selected his or her survey route, favorable breeding nights are chosen during each interval. A favorable breeding night, especially during the spring, is a cloudy, relatively warm (10°C air temperature) night following an afternoon or early evening rain. Volunteers drive from wetland to wetland beginning one hour after sunset. Volunteers spend five to ten minutes at each wetland, during which time toad and frog calls are identified and indexed. A field data form, similar to that used in Wisconsin (see Mossman et al., Chpt. 21, this volume), is filled out for each trip. The completed forms are then sent to my office in Jefferson City, where the database is housed.

Computer Database

The survey computer database has been set up to be simple and easy to access. The database has all the pertinent data fields so that, in time, statistically significant population trends can be followed.

Weather Factors

Surveyors may have a problem selecting the best nights to run their survey route. Local weather reports may make it sound like the perfect night to run a survey, but in rural areas the nearest station may be an hour's drive away. If weather conditions are just a few degrees too cold or too warm, too dry, or too windy, amphibian breeding activity may be reduced. The first year of the survey had various weather-related problems. Several of us were unable to run our routes due to flooding along the Missouri River. The database will note adverse weather-related variables, and analyses of the data will consider these.

Survey Evaluation

The 1995 survey season was the first year of Missouri's toad and frog calling survey. The survey will be continued and expanded to include more volunteers (see above). After the 1995 survey, a few minor changes were made in the survey form, as well as in the instructional material. A review of the returned survey forms from the first year showed no major problems with recording the data (but see Hemesath, Chpt. 23, this volume) or with species identification.

Summary

In 1995 the Missouri frog and toad calling survey was established. This survey is based on the methodology used in the Wisconsin survey, which consists of driving at night along roads near identified breeding habitats and listening for breeding calls. Here I describe the methodology and pitfalls of setting up such a survey, including methods for identifying Missouri's amphibians, compiling a survey and instruction packet, call identification and evaluation techniques, identifying problem species, wetland selection, volunteer recruitment and selection, running a survey route, establishing a computer database, determining optimal weather conditions, and survey evaluation.

38

Monitoring Amphibians in Created and Restored Wetlands

Joanne Kline

The importance of wetland conservation in Wisconsin became apparent in the 1970s, when the economic and environmental impacts of the loss of most of the state's historic wetlands began to be realized. Since then, regulations have been implemented to control further wetland loss, and programs were established to restore wetlands in order to reestablish their beneficial functions.

Many artificial wetlands now reduce flooding and improve water quality by removing pollutants from storm water runoff in urban areas. Artificial wetlands remove nutrients in wastewater from livestock operations and provide compensatory mitigation under the Federal Clean Water Act, which requires that unavoidable wetland loss be mitigated by creating wetland acreage elsewhere. Furthermore, and on a much larger scale, since 1990 private landowners participating in voluntary state and federal wetland restoration programs have been constructing artificial wetlands and restoring drained or degraded wetlands to reduce soil erosion and provide wildlife habitat.

Until recently, most wetland creation and restoration efforts were directed toward developing technically sound design and construction methods for simple systems (Hammer 1992). However, most of these single-purpose artificial wetlands are poor mimics of natural wetlands, whose functions are more varied and complex (Brinson and Lee 1989; Sumner and Preston 1991). Monitoring and assessment of created or restored wetlands are uncommon, and when done are either qualitative or simply quantify the quick and easy-to-measure characters important to achieving a specific project goal. For example, chemical parameters are measured in wetlands created for water quality improvement (Wetland Research, Inc. 1991; Moshiri 1993). The success of mitigation projects is measured by vegetative features (Kentula et al. 1992). Federal programs such as the Natural Resource Conservation Service (NRCS) Wetland Reserve Program, the U.S. Fish and Wildlife Service (USFWS) Partners for Wildlife, and Wetland Restoration Programs determine success by counting wetland acres and/or waterfowl breeding pairs (North American Waterfowl Management Plan [NAWMP] 1986).

Nongame species, secretive organisms, landscape-level effects, and broader ecosystem processes such as food web links and internal nutrient cycling receive little attention when evaluating the success of created wetlands (Galatowitsch and van der Valk 1994; Niswander and Mitsch 1995). Often these "incidental" functions develop in artificial wetlands over time, even when they are not part of the original wetland design (Yencha 1993). Evaluation of created and restored wetlands should focus on the establishment of broad ecosystem processes and use natural wetlands as a basis for comparison. Having clear management goals based on natural wetland processes can enhance the diversity of organisms within artificial wetlands and enhance the success of restoration efforts.

Biotic indicators are well established as a surface water monitoring tool. The occurrence of an organism that exhibits restricted habitat requirements can provide more information about a site than a snapshot physical or chemical measurement. A second advantage is that biotic analyses are less expensive. For wetlands, amphibians are obvious indicator organisms. While not as easily studied as plants or waterfowl, amphibians are indispensable components of most wetland ecosystems, based on such criteria as absolute numbers, total biomass, and their central place in food webs as both predator and prey. Their abundance, physiological features, and short but complex life cycles—which expose most species to both aquatic and terrestrial habitats—make them singularly useful biological indicators of environmental health (Heyer et al. 1994).

Recognizing the importance of amphibians as biomonitors, and recognizing the lack of even baseline population data in Wisconsin, the state's Bureaus of Research and Endangered Resources developed a long-term frog and toad survey to monitor calling amphibian populations in wetlands statewide (Mossman and Hine 1984, 1985; Mossman et al., Chpt. 21, this volume). Until recently, the only information available on occurrence of amphibians in artificial or restored wetlands was through casual observation. Yencha (1993) surveyed fauna in restored wetlands in eastern Wisconsin using calling surveys for amphibians. Richter and Azous (1995) used calling surveys and pitfall trap captures to examine amphibian distribution in ponds associated with urban stormwater in the Pacific Northwest. Leithoff (personal communication) adapted the Wisconsin calling survey method to correlate amphibian species' occurrence with vegetation patterns in artificial and restored wetlands.

Practical considerations of monitoring a large number of varied sites place strict limits on a potential monitoring tool. The ideal monitoring protocol provides an immediate and reliable index, is easy to use, requires no specialized equipment, utilizes minimal time and training, and is available at any time of the year. Of established amphibian survey methods, only calling and larval amphibian surveys have the potential to meet these requirements. Terrestrial surveys are too time intensive and/or habitat destructive to be useful in the uplands surrounding wetlands (Heyer et al. 1994). The Wisconsin frog and toad survey provides the prototype for amphibian calling surveys (Mossman et al., Chpt. 21, this volume). This program has increased greatly the number of people participating in amphibian surveys and the public interest in amphibians. As budget cuts dictate decreases in the professional staff and staff time that can be devoted to monitoring activities, volunteers may provide valuable wetland monitoring information that otherwise would not be available.

This chapter examines calling and larval amphibian surveys as a tool to monitor created and restored wetlands. Before these methods can be used for wetland monitoring, they must be shown to be reliable; that is, they must be reproducible and must reflect the actual amphibian population being sampled. I report on the precision of calling surveys for amphibians using trained volunteers and, by comparison with dip net larval surveys, the accuracy of calling surveys for short-term censusing. I also examine the feasibility of using larval surveys to sample noncalling salamanders and to relate observed species richness to wetland size and landscape setting. This project was planned in part to contribute to the research needs of the North American Amphibian Monitoring Program (Bishop et al. 1994; Mac 1996). Ten species common in southeast Wisconsin were surveyed: western and boreal chorus frogs (*Pseudacris triseriata triseriata* and *P. t. maculata*, respectively), northern spring peepers (*Pseudacris crucifer crucifer*), eastern gray treefrogs (*Hyla versicolor*), Cope's gray treefrogs (*Hyla chrysoscelis*), wood frogs (*Rana sylvatica*), northern leopard frogs (*Rana pipiens*), green frogs (*Rana clamitans melanota*), bullfrogs (*Rana catesbeiana*), American toads (*Bufo americanus americanus*), and eastern tiger salamanders (*Ambystoma tigrinum tigrinum*).

Calling Surveys

Wisconsin's amphibian survey methods are easily adapted to short-term monitoring programs. Calling surveys require little equipment and, beyond getting to the site, take little time. Each of the twelve anurans in Wisconsin has a distinctive call that is easily learned with the help of existing training materials. Disadvantages of calling surveys are that they ignore salamanders, which are noncalling, and that calling typically occurs only during brief, temperature-sensitive breeding periods. Annual fluctuations in weather patterns, such as temperature extremes and prolonged drought or flooding, make the method more reliable for a long-term database than for short-term censusing. Precision and accuracy for short-term censusing are untested, and data from only one or two breeding seasons may not record all species that actually occur. Listening after dark limits surveys either to few sites or to sites with easy road access.

Two types of variation contribute to the precision or repeatability of calling surveys: (1) factors over which the observer has some control, such as observer training and timing the survey to coincide with optimal breeding conditions; and (2) natural variation that results from differences in detectability among species, such as the length of the calling interval and the length of breeding activity. Factors demonstrated to contribute to variation are ambient air temperature (daily variation), antecedent air and water temperatures (variation within the breeding period), and annual weather patterns (long-term variation; Mossman and Hine 1985). Detectability has two aspects: loudness or carrying power of calls (how well they can be heard) and frequency of calling, both daily and within a generalized breeding period. Attempts were made to isolate the effect of natural variation on precision by controlling observer training and weather conditions as much as possible, then asking how consistent are the observations made by different observers on different sampling nights within the same breeding period.

Methods

The precision of calling surveys was examined by using the method developed by Wisconsin's long-term statewide frog and toad survey (Mossman, Chpt. 21; Casper, Chpt. 22, this volume). Using this method, volunteers annually visit sites along established routes on one evening during each of three breeding periods. Observers listen for five to ten minutes at each site and record ambient weather conditions, water temperature, and perceived calling intensity of each species heard—zero for no calls; one for separate, distinct calls; two for overlapping calls; and three for a full chorus.

For this study, eleven sites that form part of a long-term route in Washington County were monitored. The route is coordinated by the environmental educators at Lac Lawrann Conservancy in conjunction with area middle school teachers. Survey sites covered a variety of wetland habitat types, including lake fringes, large riparian corridors, natural ponds, natural marshes, and stormwater ponds. Four calling surveys were conducted during each recommended breeding period by using two different groups of observers on each of two different sampling nights. Volunteers listened for five minutes at each site. Observer differences were controlled by group structure and standardized training and by selecting sampling nights with similar ambient and twenty-four-hour antecedent weather conditions and air and water temperatures. It was assumed that the measured variation for each species in a given wetland was due to detectability differences such as calling frequency within the breeding period and within the same night.

Each group was made up of at least one "experienced listener," one adult/teacher "intraining," and three to five students, grades five through eight. An "experienced listener" was someone who had trained in the monitoring program for at least one breeding season in this area. The second adult in each group led the group in the absence of the "experienced listener" and helped to ensure the continuity of the long-term program.

Training for students consisted of two sessions. The first was a discussion/slide presentation that explained the purpose of the statewide program and provided some basic natural history information on local species. Volunteers were also required to listen to an audiotape with single and multiple calling species (Jansen and Anderson 1981). The second session consisted of a visit to the survey sites during the day to examine specific habitat types and to provide a practice live listening session. The students had no previous survey experience but understood the basic features of amphibian biology and life history. On each sampling night, visits were coordinated so that the second group arrived at each site about one hour after the first group.

For each of the three breeding periods, both sampling nights were run within a five-day interval and with air and water temperatures within the recommended range. Additional limitations on survey times were that there be no major storm event (rainfall over 2.5 centimeters) during the twelve hours prior to each sampling run and that maximum and minimum air temperatures for the day prior to the second sampling night fall within 2°C of that for the first night. Wind speed and cloud cover for each of the sample nights were required to be similar, and the variation in surface water temperature at each site could be no more than 2°C.

Results

Variation between similar sampling nights is generally greater than that between groups of observers (Fig. 38-1). Statistical significance was tested using the Wilcoxon signed-ranks test for two groups arranged as paired observations ($n = 22$; Sokal and Rohlf 1969). The test is meaningful only for species recorded at more than half the total number of sites and here applies to four of the nine calling species that occur.

The difference in the index of calling intensity of chorus frogs, gray treefrogs, and green frogs during the third breeding period both between observer groups and between similar sampling nights was not significantly different from zero (Fig. 38-1). Perceived intensity and occurrence for green frogs were significantly different ($p < 0.01$) between sampling nights, but not between observers, in the second breeding period. Calling intensity and occurrence of American toads varied significantly ($p < 0.01$) between nights, and intensity of toads

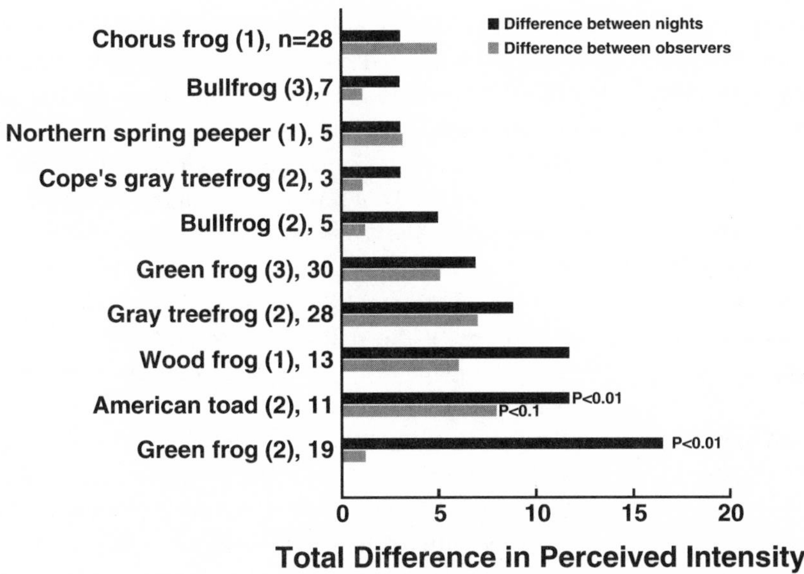

Figure 38-1. Sum of the differences in perceived calling intensity at all sites for each species. Numbers in parentheses refer to standard breeding period.

varied significantly ($p < 0.1$) between observers. Wood frogs appear to vary more between nights than between observers but occurred at too few sites for a meaningful statistical test. Spring peepers, common in previous years at most sites, were rarely heard.

Larval Surveys

Larval amphibian surveys, using dip nets, traps, or seines, are potentially adaptable to routine monitoring. Prior to the recently proposed North American Amphibian Monitoring Program (Mac 1996), no standardized procedure existed for larval surveys, and they were limited to sites where substantial survey time was available or to studies addressing basic research issues in amphibian ecology (e.g., Lannoo et al. 1994). Larval surveys avoid many of the calling survey disadvantages: they can be conducted in the daytime, and larvae are available for sampling over an extended period.

Larval surveys require only waders, buckets, and dip nets. Larval surveys take more time than calling surveys, and the time increases with wetland size and diversity. While larvae are easily observed in the field, identification to species is difficult. Published keys cover large geographic regions and rely on visually small technical characters, such as denticle patterns, that are not easily observed in the field. There is generally a poor relationship between numbers of larvae captured in dip nets and the total population, so netting cannot be used to infer population size (Lannoo and Lang 1995; Reed and Droege 1995). Larval surveys are, however, useful for determining presence/absence, for providing an independent test of calling survey accuracy, and for documenting successful breeding.

Methods

Twenty-one sites in Ozaukee County were chosen from among over 200 wetlands created or restored between 1990 and 1992. All sites are similar to those described in Reinartz and Warne (1993). Created wetlands are constructed in upland soils by altering local hydrology to provide sufficient surface water. Wetlands are constructed by restoring wetland hydrology where it once existed or by excavating existing wetlands that have been filled in with eroded soils. All sites were "prior converted wetlands" (ditched or tiled before 1985), farmed wetlands, or naturally occurring but degraded wetlands. All sites were constructed at the request of landowners by Wisconsin Department of Natural Resources Wildlife Management staff under the USFWS Farm Program, as part of the North American Wildlife Management Plan. Construction techniques involved scraping a basin or creating impoundments by breaking tiles, plugging ditches, or forming embankments according to Natural Resource Conservation Service methods (Soil Conservation Service [SCS] 1992).

Because waterfowl breeding is an important program goal, wetlands are usually designed to provide surface water at least until 4 July in most years. Ephemeral ponds generally have a higher invertebrate density—critical for breeding waterfowl nutrient requirements—than do permanent ponds with a larger fish population. In practice, most landowners have two to six ponds, at least one of which is permanent, to provide a water source in dry years. Whenever possible, pond sites are located adjacent to other existing natural features, such as wood lots, fencerows, or other wetlands, to improve overall wildlife habitat.

Site selection was based on landowner cooperation, successful construction, and location within an 11-kilometer radius to minimize climatic differences, soil type, and travel time. Only wetlands with closed basins were selected in order to avoid sampling larvae that could have immigrated from other breeding sites. Fishes occurred only in the permanent ponds and were limited to small omnivorous forage species such as brook sticklebacks (*Culaea inconstans*) and fathead minnows (*Pimephales promelas*) tolerant of the hypoxic conditions in shallow basins (Peterka 1989; Lannoo 1996a, Chpt. 34, this volume).

Wetlands varied from 0.1 to 2.6 hectares in surface area, with 0.6 to 1.5 meters maximum depth and side slopes typically no steeper than 10 percent to encourage a wide zone of emergent vegetation, such as grasses, sedges, and rushes. Submersed vegetation, typically linear-leaved macrophytes (*Potomogeton foliosus, Potomogeton pectinatus, Ranunculus longirostris,* and *Chara* sp.), covered most wetland beds by late spring. Land use adjacent to the selected wetlands fell naturally into two distinct categories based on vegetation types within 600 meters of the sites: (1) predominant old field or pasture, or (2) a mixture of pasture, wooded wetlands, and herbaceous wetlands.

Calling surveys were conducted at each site throughout the season using the Wisconsin method. Larvae at each site were sampled using National Biological Survey guidelines (D. Larson, personal communication). Surveys were conducted four times from early May through early July, with four permanent stations at each site. Three shallow-water stations were located along the shoreline, either in distinct vegetation zones or equally spaced if the vegetation was homogeneous. The fourth station was the point of maximum water depth. Using a 0.3-meter D-frame dip net with 3.5-millimeter mesh, each station was sampled with 10 sweeps through the water column and into the soft sediment. Early in the season each sweep covered about a 1-meter length. As the season progressed, so did the vegetation density and the size and therefore the speed of the tadpoles, so sweep length was shortened and observed animals were targeted for increased netting efficiency. Larvae from each station were kept separately until the entire pond was sampled. All larvae were identified in the field and returned to the site, except for the voucher specimens, which were occasionally collected. If no larvae were found at any of the stations, up to an additional 100 sweeps were made throughout the site, and occurrences were recorded separately.

Dip nets were used because it was thought that any method useful for a large number of sites needed to be a relatively quick, one-person technique, able to be accomplished with minimal field equipment. Quantitative larval surveys using both small (1 meter by 1 meter) and large (10 meter by 1 meter) seines with 6-millimeter mesh were attempted but were unsuccessful. Early toad (*Bufo* sp.) tadpoles escaped through the mesh, and late season vegetation was too dense to use a moving seine. Using a stationary large seine to isolate portions of the wetland for more complete sampling was too time intensive to use at any but the smallest sites.

Identification training consisted of becoming familiar with published keys (Altig 1970; Vogt 1981), identifying preserved specimens of species likely to be found at the project sites, using a draft key based on field characters (Watermolen and Gilbertson 1996), and occasional professional assistance. Larvae from several sites were collected, reared to adults in aquaria, and returned to their original wetlands. Voucher specimens were collected from several wetlands, preserved in formalin, and identified as soon as possible to support the reliability of field identifications. Voucher specimens have been deposited at the Milwaukee Public Museum.

Results

Larval surveys sampled tiger salamanders, which calling surveys omit. Among anurans, there were significant differences between the calling survey and dip net larval survey results for five species (Table 38-1). Wood frogs and gray treefrogs were recorded calling at sites where we found no larvae. Chorus frog, leopard frog, and American toad larvae were abundant at sites where no adults were heard calling, either during the survey or during incidental site visits. Northern spring peepers, a common species in this area previously, were conspicuously absent using either method.

There was no significant correlation ($r^2 < 0.02$) be-

Table 38-1. Comparison of species occurrence using calling and dip net surveys in artificial and restored wetlands

Site	Size (hectares)	Surface Water	Number of Species	Wood Frog (*Rana sylvatica*)	Chorus Frog (*Pseudacris triseriata*)	Northern Leopard Frog (*Rana pipiens*)	American Toad (*Bufo americanus americanus*)	Gray Treefrog (*Hyla versicolor/ chrysoscelis*)	Green Frog (*Rana clamitans melanota*)	Eastern Tiger Salamander (*Ambystoma tigrinum tigrinum*)
MA-1	0.7	Temporary	5		Dip net only	Dip net only	Dip net only	Call only	Dip net only	
MA-2	0.3	Temporary	3		Dip net only		Dip net only	Call only		
MA-4	0.6	Permanent	6		Dip net only	Dip net only	Dip net only	Call only	Call and dip net	Dip net only
SC-A	0.4	Permanent	1					Call only		
SC-1	0.3	Permanent	4		Call and dip net	Dip net only		Call and dip net		Dip net only
SC-2	0.2	Temporary	3		Call and dip net		Dip net only	Call only		
MC-1	0.2	Temporary	2		Dip net only		Dip net only			
MC-2	0.3	Temporary	2		Dip net only		Dip net only			
MC-3	0.2	Temporary	2		Call only		Dip net only			
MC-4	0.5	Permanent	4		Dip net only	Dip net only	Call and dip net		Call and dip net	
MC-5	0.3	Temporary	0							
MC-B	0.2	Permanent	2				Dip net only		Call and dip net	
DO-A	1.6	Permanent	3	Call only	Call and dip net				Call and dip net	
FE-A	0.6	Permanent	4	Call only	Call and dip net		Call only		Call and dip net	
TE-1	0.1	Temporary	0							
TE-2	0.3	Temporary	2		Call and dip net		Dip net only			
TE-3	0.2	Temporary	0							
TE-4	0.6	Temporary	1				Dip net only			
TE-5	0.2	Temporary	2				Dip net only		Dip net only	
ST-A	2.6	Permanent	1						Call and dip net	
ST-B	1.1	Permanent	5	Call only	Call and dip net	Call and dip net	Dip net only		Call and dip net	

tween species richness and wetland size, but species richness was generally greater at sites that were part of a more varied landscape that included woods, other wetlands, and permanent water (Fig. 38-2). At the two sites located near wooded wetlands (SCA, STA), submerged aquatic macrophytes were sparse, and only one amphibian species was present (Fig. 38-2). All other sites had complete aquatic beds.

Discussion

Precision of Calling Surveys

The results of this study support the use of volunteers in calling survey programs. That there was less variation between observers than between sampling nights supports the reliability of results obtained by trained volunteer observers. For a short-term census, variation might be reduced by increasing the number of observations.

These data are consistent with observations at the study sites at times other than during the calling surveys. Chorus frogs and gray treefrogs were continuous callers for long intervals throughout the breeding period. Wood frogs and toads were much more sporadic callers. Some of the variation in perceived intensity of American toad calls is most likely due to the length of individual calls and observer difference in distinguishing an intensity of two from three. Green frogs were persistent callers late in the season, but early calling was variable and apparently not based on air and water temperatures alone.

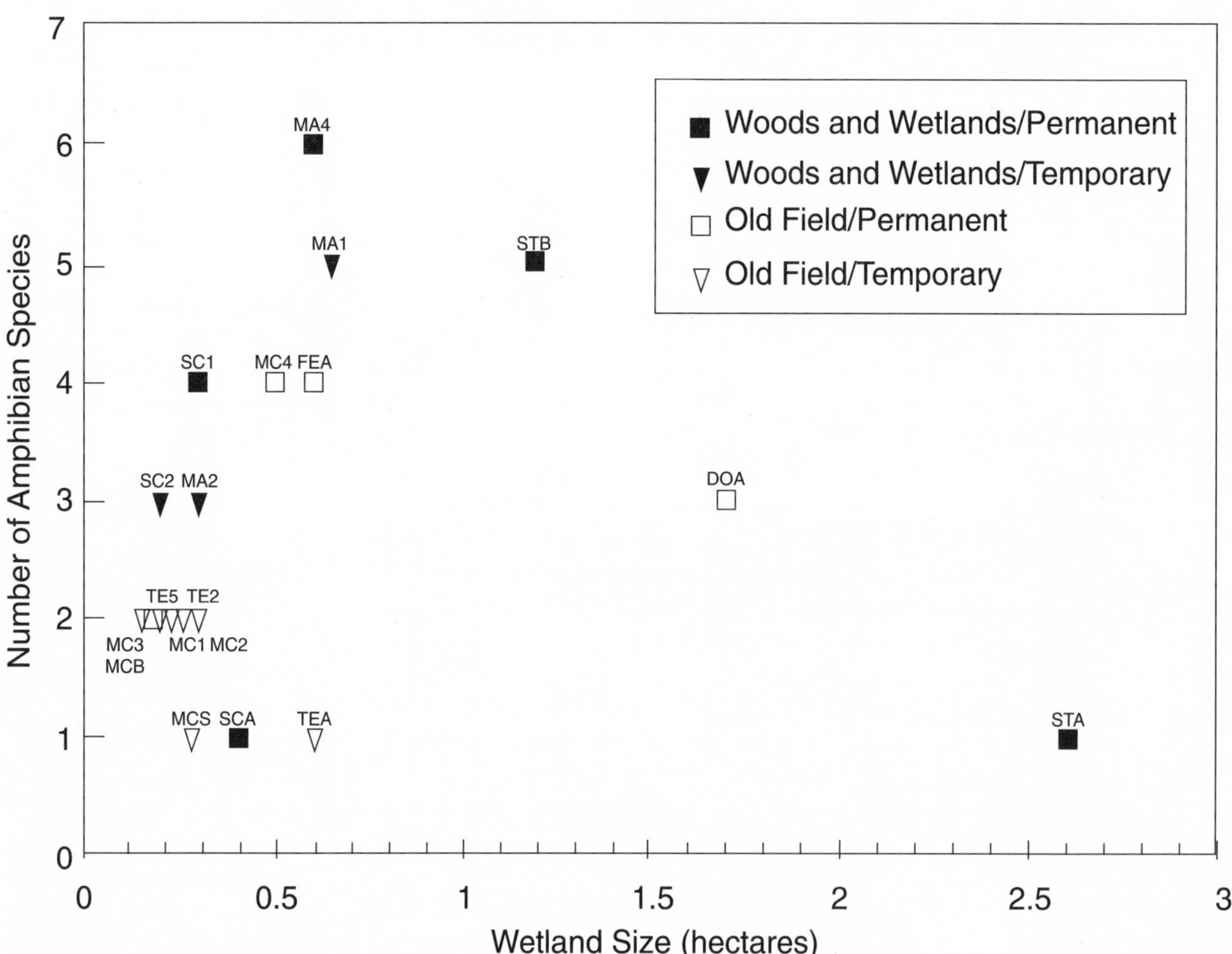

Figure 38-2. Relationship between amphibian species richness and wetland size for different landscape settings.

Accuracy—Comparison of Calling and Larval Surveys

Accuracy of calling surveys when compared to dip net larval surveys and incidental observations was poor. Incidental visits to the natural wetlands recorded leopard frogs, wood frogs, and spring peepers where they were not heard during the survey period. Larval surveys at these wetlands also recorded wood frogs and leopard frogs. Bullfrogs were recorded in an earlier calling survey at one site (MA4; Leithoff personal communication) but were neither heard nor observed in this study. Calling and larval surveys together provide a more accurate record of species occurrence than either method alone. More frequent sampling throughout the breeding season might increase the chance of detecting each species present.

Dip net larval surveys appear to be useful only to determine presence/absence with at best a relative abundance measure (see also Lannoo and Lang 1995; Reed and Droege 1995). Most of the tadpoles, with the exception of chorus frogs, were clumped rather than randomly distributed in each wetland. This, coupled with suspected high mortality rates, appeared to contribute to the decrease in netting efficiency as the tadpoles matured.

Positive identification of larvae is also difficult for some species, especially late in the season. For example, in water stained with humic acids, green frog tadpoles and wood frog tadpoles are difficult to distinguish based on easily observed characteristics. Immediate identification of voucher specimens and the ability to raise tadpoles to adults minimize errors but are not practical for animals collected from a large number of sites.

Factors Affecting Species Richness

Improvements to created wetland habitat require the identification of design features that attract species, followed by an incorporation of these features into wetland restoration plans. Factors that may contribute to amphibian abundance and species richness are wetland size, type and extent of emergent and submerged vegetation, hydroperiod, other fish and wildlife, and proximity to other amphibian habitat (see Lannoo, Chpt. 34, this volume).

No correlation was found between species richness and wetland size, and therefore the results here differ from those reported by Richter and Azous (1995) in their intensive study in the Puget Sound Basin. Amphibian species richness and landscape setting appear to be related at the Wisconsin sites. Incidental observations during this study suggest that waterfowl, shorebirds, and breeding grassland songbirds were also more diverse and abundant at the sites with a more varied landscape. Richter and Azous (1995) did not find a correlation between amphibian species richness and vegetation patterns, or distance to other wetlands, but they noted a decrease in species richness with degree of urbanization. One possible explanation is that the more extensive landscape fragmentation due to development and deforestation in southeastern Wisconsin makes the distance between wetlands more critical than it is in the Pacific Northwest.

Conclusions

This study suggests that: (1) variation in calling survey results among different, minimally trained observers is not significant; (2) variation in calling survey results between different sampling nights within the same breeding period is significant for several species, including green frogs early in their breeding season, American toads throughout their breeding season, and wood frogs; (3) variability is reduced more by increasing the number of observations than it is by increasing observer training; (4) calling amphibian surveys may be used to confirm species presence, but negative calling survey results may not indicate species absence; (5) dip net larval surveys combined with calling surveys provide a more accurate record of species presence than either method alone; and (6) the techniques applied here are sufficiently reliable to provide useful information on colonizing species and their use of created wetlands.

Summary

Monitoring amphibians is a means to extend the evaluation and assessment of constructed wetlands beyond traditional vegetation and waterfowl surveys in order to include a broader range of ecological processes associated with natural wetland communities. The validity of calling amphibian surveys was studied in southeastern Wisconsin by examining their precision and accuracy. The precision of calling surveys was evaluated by using different volunteer observers and different sampling nights at eleven wetlands. The accuracy of calling surveys was tested by comparing results with those of dip net larval surveys at twenty-one created or restored wetlands. Except for green frogs (*Rana clamitans melanota*) and American toads (*Bufo americanus americanus*), there was no significant variation between nights or among observers in the results of calling surveys; i.e., the results were relatively precise. Accuracy of calling surveys was poor, and calling and larval surveys together provided a more accurate estimate of species richness than either method alone. Artificial wetlands, regardless of size, constructed in the vicinity of woods and other wetlands generally supported more diverse amphibian communities.

Acknowledgments

I thank the students and teachers who gave a considerable amount of time to the calling surveys and the landowners who not only restored wetlands but generously allowed us to work on their land. The project is also more successful than it would have been without the help of Gary Casper, Karla Leithoff, Pam Biersach, Armin Schwengel, Diane Larson, Marty Johnson, Tim Kline, and Vic Pappas. Mike Mossman and Jim Reinartz provided thoughtful critiques of an early draft.

39

Anurans as Indicators of Wetland Condition in the Prairie Pothole Region of North Dakota: An Environmental Monitoring and Assessment Program Pilot Project

Dorothy G. Bowers, David E. Andersen, and Ned H. Euliss Jr.

Wetlands across the United States have been drastically altered over the last century as a result of agricultural practices. These alterations include wetland drainage, application of agricultural chemicals, and tillage of uplands and have affected wetland ecosystems by destroying wetlands (Dahl 1990), introducing toxic chemicals (Grue et al. 1986; Hanson 1952; Tome et al. 1991), and increasing turbidity and sedimentation (Dieter 1991). However, a complete understanding of the environmental impacts of these agricultural changes is lacking.

In 1989 the U.S. Environmental Protection Agency (EPA) initiated the Environmental Monitoring and Assessment Program (EMAP) to monitor the status and trends of the nation's ecological resources. EMAP was designed to use resource indicators to quantitatively assess environmental changes. The major objectives of EMAP included: (1) estimate current status, trends, and changes in resource indicators on a regional basis with known confidence; (2) estimate the distribution and extent of the nation's ecological resources; (3) seek associations between selected indicators of natural and anthropogenic stresses and indicators of the condition of ecological resources; and (4) provide annual statistical summaries and periodic assessments of the nation's ecological resources (Stevens 1994). To achieve these goals, the nation's ecological resources were divided into eight resource categories, and a universal sampling framework was created to collect local and regional data (Peterson 1994).

One resource category established by EMAP was EMAP-Wetlands. In 1994 the EMAP-Wetlands resource group began looking for potential resource indicators to evaluate wetland condition. Scientists have postulated that amphibians should be excellent indicators of wetland condition because they depend on both aquatic and terrestrial habitats and possess permeable skin, which may make them susceptible to chemical changes in the environment. Thus, EMAP-Wetlands developed a pilot study in cooperation with the U.S. National Biological Service to determine whether anurans in the Prairie Pothole region (PPR) of North Dakota could be used as potential indicators of wetland condition.

Amphibian monitoring is a relatively new field, and established techniques are limited. Most techniques target one or two species, leaving other species undetected or inadequately sampled. Use of drift fences, pitfall traps, species inventories, visual encounter surveys, area sampling schemes, and larval sampling techniques are limited because they require access to wetlands and can be costly and labor intensive on a regional scale (Heyer et al. 1994). However, methods such as night driving, frog call surveys, and automated recording surveys are suitable for surveying large areas in short time spans and can be conducted on rights-of-way. These methods also eliminate landscape bias that might arise from gaining permission to access more minimally impacted (rather than highly impacted) wetlands. Because these surveys do not require landowner permission, implementation of routine monitoring efforts are logistically feasible and less subject to unfavorable public sentiments. Thus, we concluded that a combination of calling surveys, night driving surveys, and automated recording systems would be suitable for a regional survey effort.

Our goals for the pilot study were to: (1) describe

anuran relative abundance, species composition, and species distribution in selected study sites within the PPR of North Dakota; (2) determine a suitable road survey method(s) for estimating anuran relative abundance and describing anuran distribution; and (3) determine if relationships exist between land-use patterns associated with wetland condition and anuran distribution and relative abundance. We initiated this two-year pilot study in 1995 and will complete surveys in the 1996 field season.

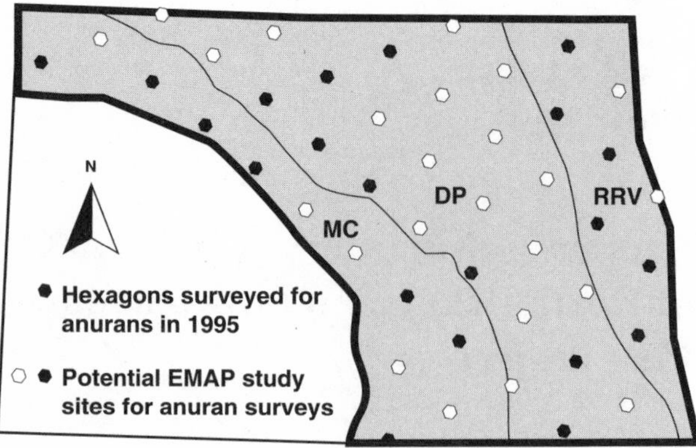

Figure 39-1. Potential EMAP study sites and anuran study sites in the Prairie Pothole region of North Dakota (shaded). MC = Missouri Coteau, DP = Drift Plain, and RRV = Red River Valley.

Study Area

The North Dakota PPR was divided into three ecoregions extending roughly north to south based on physiography (Fig. 39-1). Moving from east to west across the state, these include the Red River Valley, the Drift Plain, and the Missouri Coteau. The Red River Valley is characterized by flat lowlands with fertile soil and is primarily in agricultural tillage. The Drift Plain is at higher elevations. It is composed of terminal moraines with knob and kettle surfaces containing many small lakes, marshes, and boulder fields; ground moraines characterized by smooth rolling till plains, numerous lakes, and marshes; and outwash plains containing gravelly, sandy, and marshy soils (Wheeler and Wheeler 1966). Current agricultural use consists of a combination of pasture and cropland. The Missouri Coteau rises to the west of the Drift Plain and is composed of low hills created from glacial drift. Primary agricultural use is pasture and hayland. Vegetation native to all three ecoregions is tallgrass prairie, except in the northern regions of the Red River Valley and Drift Plain where deciduous forests predominate.

Nine species of anurans inhabit the North Dakota PPR and occur in at least one of the selected study sites. These species include plains spadefoot toads (*Spea bombifrons*), American toads (*Bufo americanus americanus*), Great Plains toads (*Bufo cognatus*), Canadian toads (*Bufo hemiophrys*), Woodhouse's toads (*Bufo woodhousii woodhousii*), boreal chorus frogs (*Pseudacris triseriata maculata*), northern leopard frogs (*Rana pipiens*), and wood frogs (*Rana sylvatica*). In addition, gray treefrogs have been recorded in North Dakota. Eastern gray treefrogs (*Hyla versicolor*) are closely related to Cope's gray treefrogs (*Hyla chrysoscelis*). There are subtle differences in the vocalizations between the two species, which can be distinguished by sonogram analyses of calling patterns (but see Conant and Collins 1991). Cope's gray treefrogs have been recorded in northern Minnesota, eastern gray treefrogs throughout Minnesota, and the two species presumably share the same range (Oldfield and Moriarty 1995). Cope's gray treefrogs are associated with prairie edges, whereas eastern gray treefrogs inhabit deciduous and coniferous woodlands. It is probable that the species in the North Dakota PPR thought to be the eastern gray treefrog is actually the Cope's gray treefrog or that both species are found in the North Dakota PPR. We will hereafter refer to these species as the gray treefrog complex.

Methods

All EMAP resource categories use a triangular point grid sampling framework randomly placed over the conterminous United States. A 40-square-kilometer hexagon surrounds each grid point, creating a network of hexagons that encompasses the nation (and has the potential for global extension). Hexagons selected from this framework constitute primary field sites for collecting resource data. Overton et al. (1990) provide a detailed description of the EMAP sampling design.

Forty-five uniformly distributed hexagons in the North Dakota PPR were selected by the EMAP-Wetlands resource group as potential study sites for the pilot project. From these forty-five hexagons, we selected a minimum of six hexagons/ecoregion as 1995 study sites for anuran surveys (Fig. 39-1). Hexagons were chosen to minimize the range of cropland:grassland ratios between study sites and to contain a sufficient number of wetlands to satisfy survey criteria (see below).

We were unable to measure wetland condition directly, so we used the land-use pattern around individual wetlands and within hexagons as a surrogate for characteristics that might influence anuran occurrence, distribution, and relative abundance. Our assumption is that study sites dominated by agricultural production are most likely to exhibit effects of agricultural practices on anurans and that sites dominated by grasslands are least likely to exhibit these effects. Therefore, we divided land-use into two basic categories: (1) grassland, which included uplands composed of native grasslands or deciduous forests, Conservation Reserve Program lands, hayland, and pastures; and (2) cropland, which included upland crops such as wheat, barley, field corn, soy beans, sunflowers, and sugar beets. Highly modified sites (i.e., agricultural) and relatively unmodified sites were selected to test the response of anuran indicators to extreme conditions. The rationale for this approach was explained by Peterson (1994): if indicators fail to discriminate between extreme conditions, they cannot be expected to differentiate between intermediate conditions.

Within each hexagon, we randomly chose six wetland survey points along rights-of-way within 50 meters of seasonal and semipermanent wetlands. Three of these survey points were located adjacent to wetlands surrounded by cropland, and three were adjacent to wetlands surrounded by grassland. In addition, ten road survey points were selected from an 8-kilometer segment of an established breeding bird survey route so that anuran survey points coincided with breeding bird survey points.

We visited each hexagon three times during the calling season. At each hexagon, four types of surveys were conducted: road calling surveys, wetland calling surveys, night driving surveys, and automated recording surveys (Fig. 39-2). Four technicians performed the surveys in 1995. Two technicians visited one hexagon per night, dividing survey points so that each point was surveyed once by one technician. We did not conduct surveys when wind speeds exceeded 18 kilometers per hour or during heavy precipitation. Minimum air temperatures during surveys were 10°, 15°, and 20°C in the first, second, and third visits, respectively.

Anuran Calling Surveys

Procedures for wetland and road calling surveys were identical, the methods varying only by site selection. We performed ten-minute calling surveys at each survey point between dusk and 0300 the next morning. We identified calling anurans to species and recorded both estimated number of individuals and call index value (CIV). CIVs were adopted from Wisconsin Department of Natural Resources survey procedures (Mossman et al., Chpt. 21, this volume) and ranged from one to three (Scott and Woodward 1994). When observers could not identify anuran calls during a calling survey, calls were tape recorded in the field. In the future we will compare sonograms of these calls with sonograms of known frog calls to determine species' identities. We noted land-use patterns over an estimated 0.4-kilometer radius in each of four quadrants (NW, NE, SE, SW) surrounding wetland and road survey points. In addition, we recorded survey times, air temperature, humidity, precipitation, and wind speed at each survey point.

At randomly chosen survey points, two or more technicians performed simultaneous but independent surveys during the first visit. We determined interobserver variance from these data.

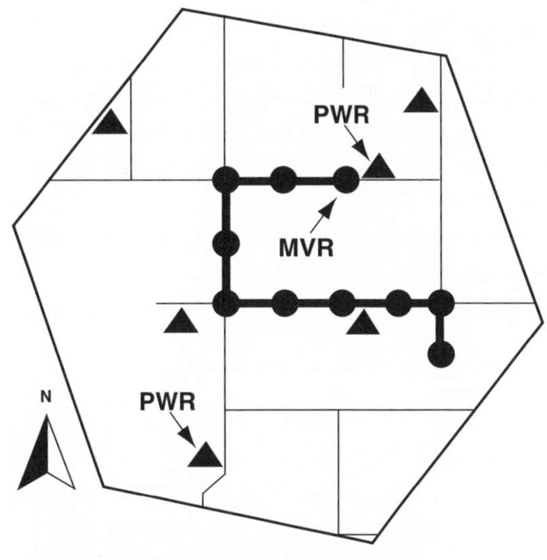

Figure 39-2. Survey sites within a hexagon. Anuran calling surveys were conducted at ten road calling survey points and six wetland calling survey points within each hexagon. Night driving surveys were performed along roads in hexagons. In addition, automated recording systems were utilized within some hexagons to obtain paired wetland recordings and method variance recordings.

Night Driving Surveys

Night driving surveys included recording sightings or aural detections of anurans in the hexagons at times other than during calling surveys. Any anurans that we located but could not identify at night were collected, identified, and released at the collection site within twenty-four hours of capture. We noted collection time, location, land-use pattern, age class, sex, and species.

Automated Recording Systems

We assembled programmable analog recorders with omni-directional microphones using a modification of the Peterson and Dorcas (1994) automated recorder design. Recorders programmed to record at intervals throughout the night were used to satisfy two objectives: (1) compare anuran relative abundance data collected simultaneously in cropland and grassland landscapes; and (2) determine if differences existed between data collected at survey points located adjacent to wetlands and data collected at survey points located along roads.

We used paired wetland recordings (PWR) to satisfy the first objective. We identified thirteen pairs of seasonal wetlands. Each pair was of similar size, with one wetland located in cropland and one located in grassland. We placed recorders programmed to time ten-minute intervals beginning at 2230, 0030, 0230, and 0430 along the roadside adjacent to each wetland.

We used method variance recordings (MVR) to satisfy the second objective. Recorders programmed to record ten-minute intervals beginning at 2230, 0030, 0230 and 0430 were placed midway between road calling survey points and wetland calling survey points in sixteen hexagons. We evaluated estimated number and CIV for each species detected from both the PWR and MVR recordings. All 1995 recordings were analyzed by a single investigator (D.G.B.) to eliminate interobserver variance.

In 1996 we will implement explosive breeder recordings (EBR). EBRs are designed to detect species, such as the plains spadefoot toad, that breed over short time intervals. Recorders will be placed in hexagons at locations identified to be suitable for targeted explosive breeding species and programmed to sample one-minute intervals hourly through several consecutive nights. In addition, we will use recorder data to describe calling activity patterns and to assess the effect of observer presence on calling activity.

Results and Discussion

During the 1995 field season, the first visit extended from 5 May to 1 June, the second visit from 4 June to 22 June, and the final visit from 27 June to 12 July. Due to technical problems with the recording systems, we performed automated recording surveys only during the last visit to hexagons. All thirteen PWR and sixteen MVR sites were sampled. Six MVR locations were located at wetlands surrounded by cropland, ten were surrounded by grassland. Our results at this stage are preliminary and are presented primarily as descriptive summaries. We have not attempted analyses of survey methods and automated recorder data, and only a preliminary test of association between anuran relative abundance and landscape pattern has been completed.

Range Expansions/Contractions

Ranges of the plains spadefoot, northern leopard frog, Canadian toad, and American toad varied from those previously described by Wheeler and Wheeler (1966) and Hoberg and Gause (1992). We located plains spadefoots in hexagons outside the species' previously recorded range. This extension of the range of plains spadefoots could be a result of either range expansion or the lack of previously documented sightings in the new range; it is most likely the result of incomplete records for this species. The ranges of the northern leopard frog, Canadian toad, and American toad were less extensive than previously described. Failure to detect these species in hexagons within their previously described ranges suggests either inadequate sampling techniques or decreased ranges. Data from 1996 surveys should clarify this issue.

Calling Activity

Our results from calling surveys indicate that American toads, Great Plains toads, Woodhouse's toads, the gray treefrog complex, chorus frogs, northern leopard frogs, and wood frogs called between 2130 and 0059, with some species beginning earlier and some continuing later. Mean estimated number of individuals/survey point for all species except Great Plains toads, the gray treefrog complex, and boreal chorus frogs was also highest during this time period (Fig. 39-3). Species such as Great Plains toads, Woodhouse's toads, and the gray treefrog complex that initiate calling late in the season began nightly calling at later hours than species such as

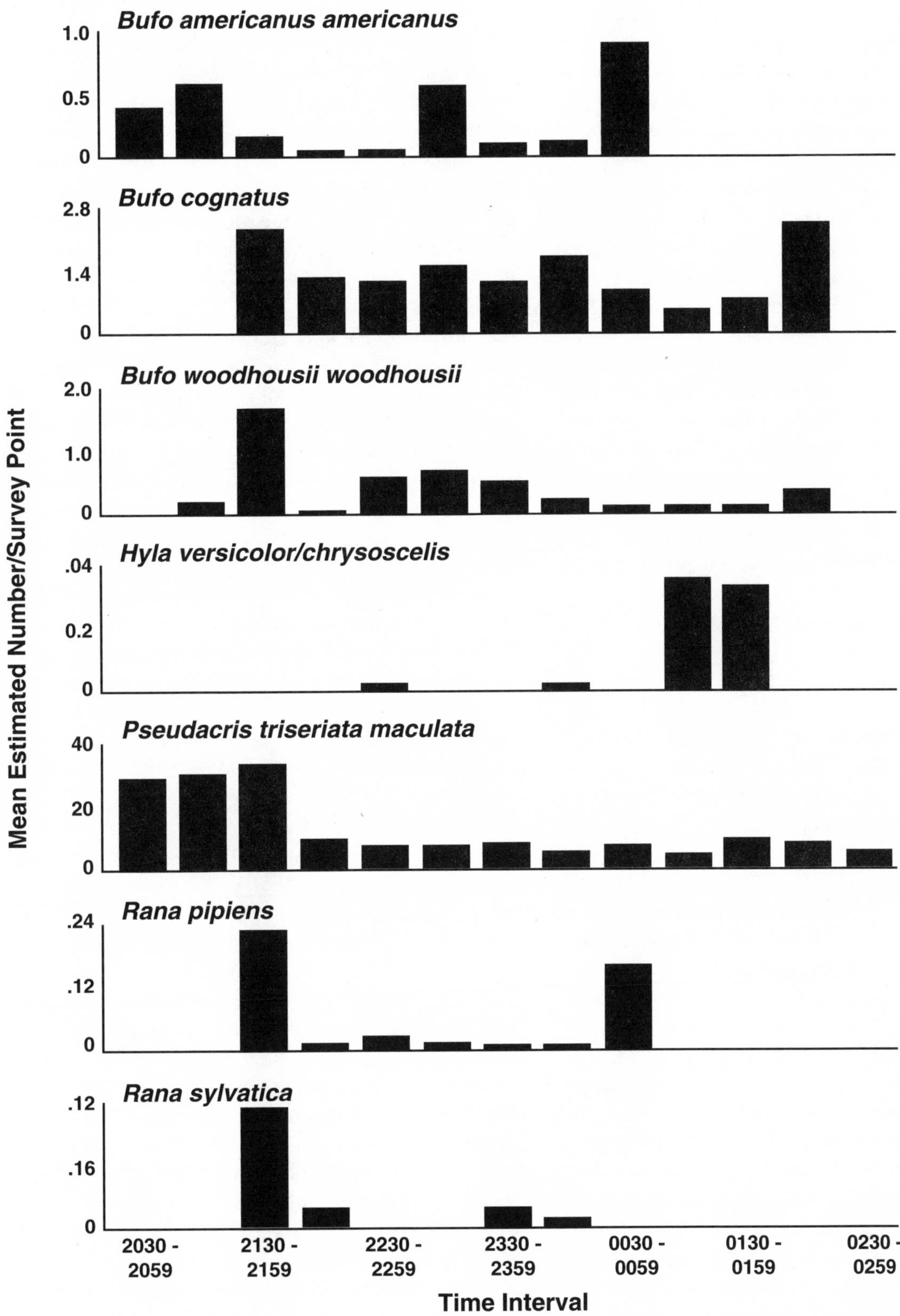

Figure 39-3. Nightly anuran calling activity based on mean estimated number of individuals/survey point from 1995 road and wetland calling surveys. Only survey points where individuals were detected were included in calculations.

American toads and boreal chorus frogs, which initiate calling early in the season.

There is a general correlation between sunset and the onset of nightly calling for toads (*Bufo* species); in particular, the Great Plains toad begins calling almost exactly one half hour after sunset. In the early breeding season when night temperatures fall below 8°C, chorus frogs and northern leopard frogs were also actively calling during the day. This may also be true for other species, such as wood frogs. In 1996 we will program recorders to sample during both day and night to determine when species are calling most actively.

Calling season varied among boreal chorus frogs, northern leopard frogs, wood frogs, American toads, Great Plains toads, Woodhouse's toads, and the gray treefrog complex (Fig. 39-4). Chorus frogs, northern leopard frogs, and wood frogs were all heard calling prior to the first survey. Wood frogs were not heard after the fifth day of the first visit, but both chorus frogs and leopard frogs were heard throughout the survey period. However, peak calling for chorus frogs was completed by mid-June, and northern leopard frogs were only recorded on six nights. The calling season of American toads lasted approximately two weeks, from 10 May to 23 May. Great Plains toad and Woodhouse's toad calling seasons extended from 18 May through 8 July. We first detected the gray treefrog complex in the third week of June and recorded calls through the end of the survey period.

Associations between temperature and humidity and mean estimated number of calling individuals/survey point varied among species (Fig. 39-5). Overall estimated number of calling anurans/survey point was highest between 5° and 25°C, but anurans called when temperatures ranged from less than 5° to more than 25°C. American toads, boreal chorus frogs, northern leopard frogs, and wood frogs called most actively at temperatures less than 10°C, Great Plains toads and Woodhouse's toads at temperatures ranging from 5° to 25°C, and the gray treefrog complex at temperatures between 15° to 25°C. Great Plains toads, Woodhouse's toads, and chorus frogs called actively across the widest range of temperatures. Calling anurans were detected over a humidity range of less than 45 percent to 95 percent. Mean estimated number/survey point of American toads, Woodhouse's toads, and northern leopard frogs was greatest at humidities less than 65 percent. Great Plains toads and chorus frogs were detected across the full range of humidities, the gray treefrog complex from 66 to 85 percent humidity, and wood frogs from 56 to 90 percent humidity.

Influence of Weather on Calling Activity

Our weather criteria for this study were overly conservative in the initial visits, less so in the final visit. Calling activity and call detection were affected more by high winds than by low temperatures (5° to 8°C) and rainfall. We observed several full choruses of boreal chorus frogs and American toads on calm nights when temperatures were below 8°C and choruses of Great Plains toads when temperatures were below 15°C. Thus, early season surveys can be conducted if wind and rainfall do not interfere with audition and if temperatures exceed 5°C.

It is important to complete late season surveys prior to the onset of summer weather conditions. During periods of warm and dry weather, we recorded few calling anurans. Our preliminary analysis indicates that anurans call most actively when temperatures are below 25°C and humidity ranges from less than 45 percent to 85 percent. However, studies of the southwestern toad (*Bufo microscaphus*) in Utah showed that this species calls primarily at humidities between 80 percent and 100 percent (Dorcas and Foltz 1991). During the third visit in 1995, even when humidity fell in these ranges, we recorded few anurans. In the North Dakota PPR, we recommend that calling surveys be completed prior to 30 June, although breeding seasons may extend later depending on annual weather conditions.

Survey Techniques

Our primary survey emphasis was placed on wetland and road calling surveys. We detected seven of nine anuran species present in the PPR of North Dakota from calling surveys. Only plains spadefoot toads and Canadian toads were not recorded using calling surveys. Frogs in the gray treefrog complex were detected; the calls seemed to resemble those of Cope's gray treefrogs rather than eastern gray treefrogs. We have not analyzed sonograms of the recordings of the gray treefrog complex to confirm species identity. We observed all nine species during night driving surveys; however, the frequency of observations during night driving surveys was less than that of calling surveys.

Data gathered in 1995 indicate that a combination of calling surveys and night driving surveys allows a more accurate determination of species composition and distribution within hexagons than either technique used alone. Calling surveys are unreliable for detecting explosive breeding species but provide indications of relative abundance, whereas night driving surveys are

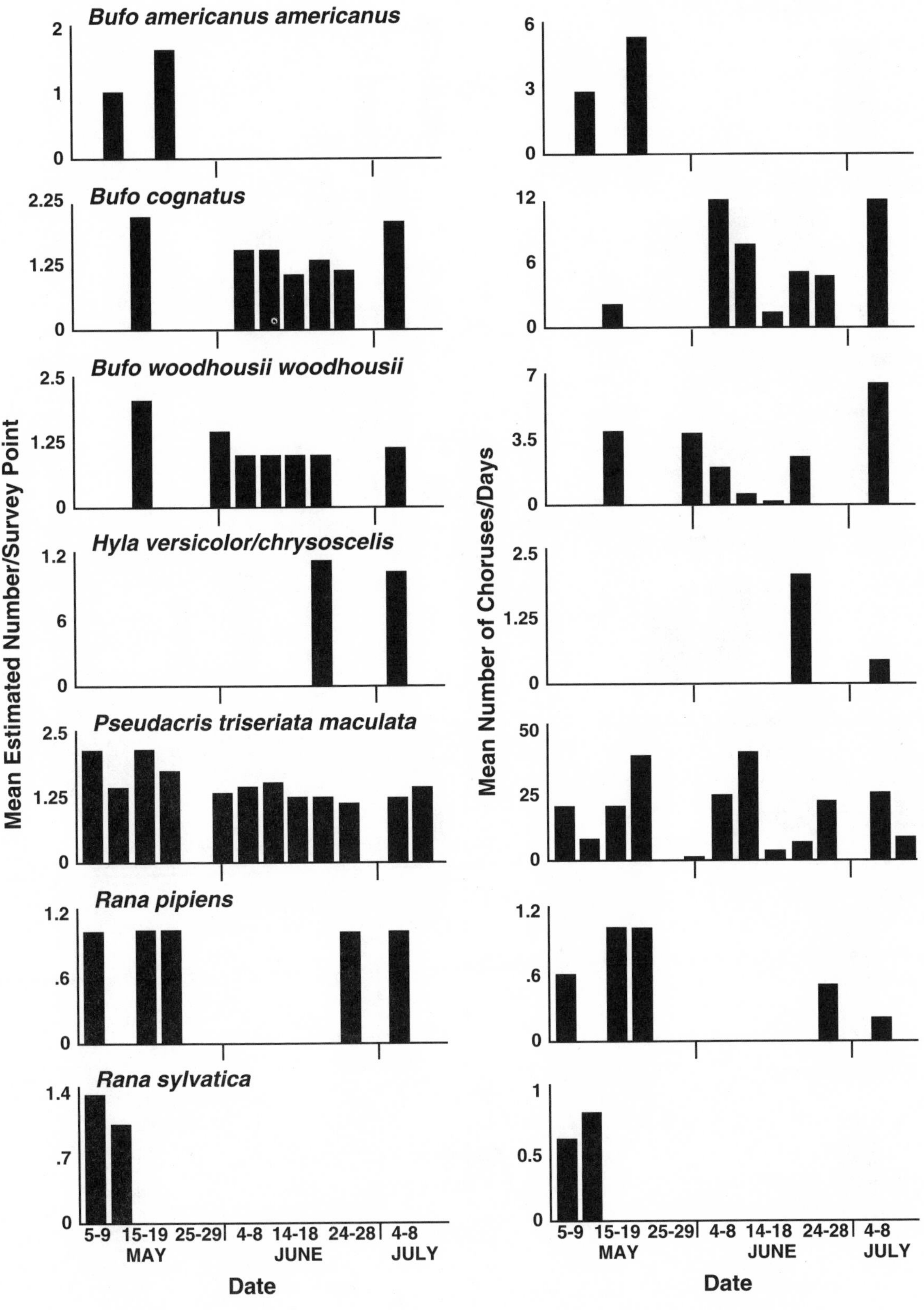

Figure 39-4. Seasonal anuran calling activity based on mean call index value/detection and mean number of choruses/day over five-day intervals. Call index value/detection ranged from one to three and reflected chorus size.

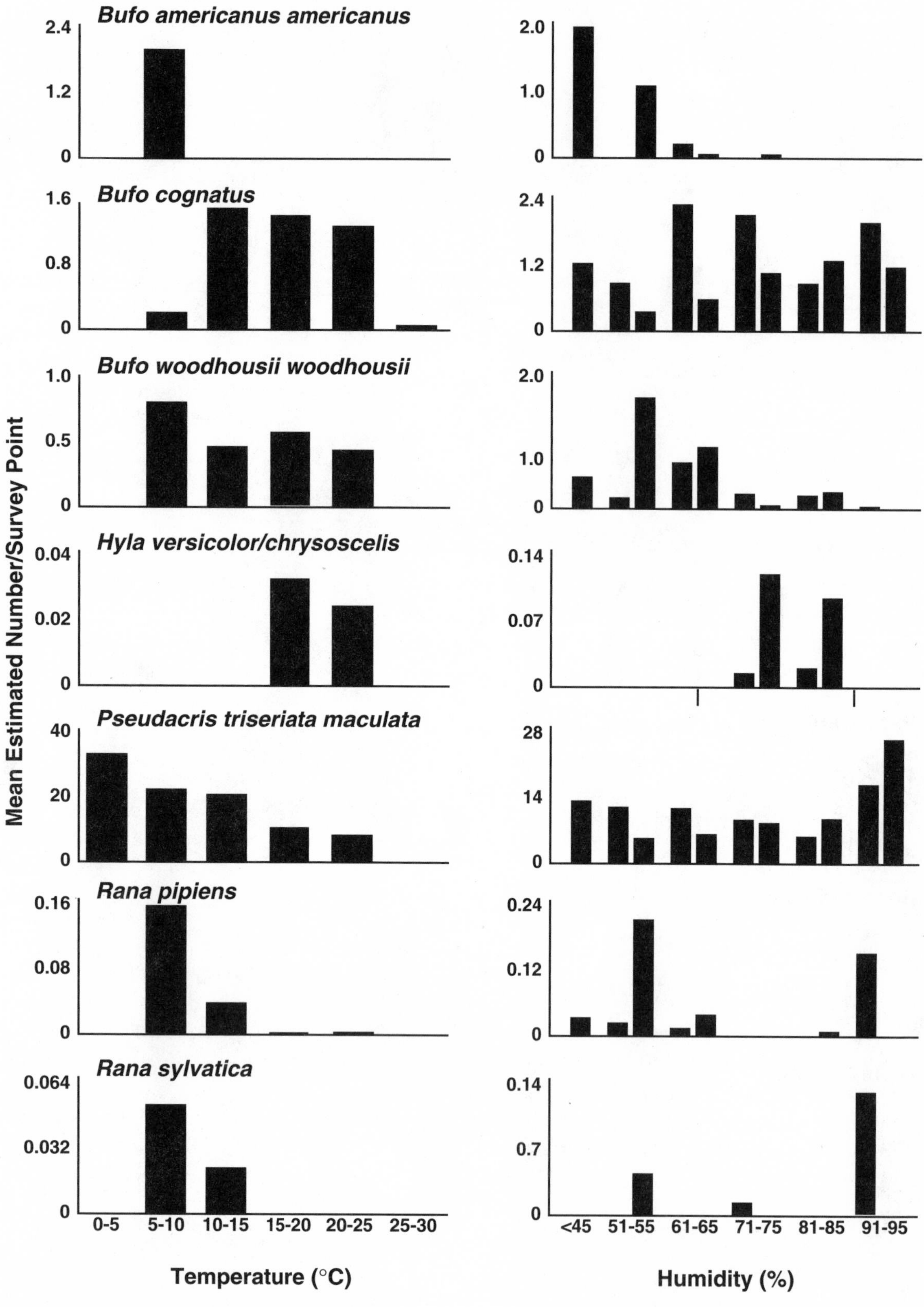

Figure 39-5. Relationship between anuran calling activity and temperature and humidity from 1995 road and wetland calling surveys. Only survey points where individuals were detected were included in calculations.

successful in detecting all species but provide insufficient data on relative abundance.

Road Calling Surveys

Conducting road calling surveys at 0.8-kilometer intervals and recording data for each quadrant worked well in North Dakota where roads follow a north-south, east-west grid system. Roads form convenient boundaries for changes in land use; typically, each quadrant is composed of either cropland or grassland. When this is not the case there is usually a clear, linear division between land-use categories. Assessing land-use pattern is relatively simple in this landscape. However, in many other regions of the United States, roads do not follow grid systems, and more attention is required to classify land use. A similar survey technique used by the Ontario Task Force on Declining Amphibian Populations may be better suited for these areas. This system indicates habitat types and both distance from survey point and location of calling species (Gartshore et al. 1995). However, with this system, and in any area with structures blocking the field of view, detailed habitat data will be difficult to acquire without entering private land.

Automated Recording Surveys

While recording surveys are useful for sampling periodically throughout the night and detecting species that call irregularly, the amount of information that can be obtained from them is limited (see Varhegyi et al., Chpt. 18, this volume). Wind and heavy rainfall decrease recording quality and reduce detection distances. CIV and estimated number of calling anurans are difficult to determine when more than five individuals are calling at one time. In 1996 we will incorporate stereo microphones and digital recorders into recording surveys; this may improve our ability to discriminate individuals. However, for the present, we will use recordings for presence/absence data only. Recorder systems also require large time allocations to evaluate recordings and regular monitoring to replace tapes and recharge batteries. These issues are being addressed by other researchers using automated recording techniques. Ontario Hydro Technologies, the Electric Power Research Institute, Idaho Power, and Southern California Edison are combining efforts to develop an Automated Intelligent Monitoring System (AIMS) that recognizes anuran and bird calls. AIMS is designed to record time and voice- or frequency-activated sounds using either tethered or remote microphones. The most recent prototype monitors four locations simultaneously, and environmental sensors can be added to the system (Patrick et al. 1995).

Ecoregion Species Richness

Overall species richness as measured by calling and night driving surveys ranged from one to six. Species richness ranged from three to six in the Red River Valley ecoregion, from one to five in the Drift Plain ecoregion, and from zero to three in the Missouri Coteau ecoregion. These data indicate that the most agriculturally impacted ecoregion sampled, the Red River Valley, supports the highest species richness of anurans. This may reflect physiographic boundaries, anuran associations with soil type, or climatic conditions. It is also possible that agricultural practices may increase habitat suitability for anurans. Additionally, analyses of relative abundance data are incomplete and ultimately may reveal a different trend.

Potential Indicator Species

Ideally, biological indicators should be sufficiently sensitive to provide an early warning of change, be distributed over a broad geographic area, and provide continuous assessment over a wide range of stresses (Noss 1990). Based on the latter two traits, the chorus frog is the best potential anuran indicator in the North Dakota PPR because it is the most ubiquitous species and its calling activity extends over the longest interval. However, boreal chorus frog distribution does not appear to correlate with land-use pattern. Our preliminary analysis of relative abundance data suggests that, of the seven species detected from calling surveys, three may associate with land-use pattern in the North Dakota PPR: American toads and the gray treefrog complex appear to associate with grassland areas, while Great Plains toads seem to associate with croplands. Chorus frogs, Woodhouse's toads, northern leopard frogs, and wood frogs appear unaffected by upland landscape pattern. The species that may associate with grasslands, American toads and the gray treefrog complex, both have restricted ranges in the North Dakota PPR and short calling seasons and therefore would not be suitable as regional indicators. However, Great Plains toads are widely distributed and have a relatively long calling season and thus may prove to be a suitable indicator of agricultural landscapes.

Future Work

In 1996 we plan to modify our survey procedures to include two complete calling survey visits between 15

April and 15 June, with additional surveys in hexagons within the likely ranges of the gray treefrog complex and plains spadefoots. Surveys will begin in mid-April in 1996 to better sample wood frogs and northern leopard frogs. In addition, we anticipate performing an extensive night driving survey in August when anurans are migrating. Night driving surveys would be conducted over a measured time interval, and number of individuals/species/time would be determined. Age categories (juvenile or adult) would be noted, and indices of breeding success would be derived from juvenile counts. We could then compare these data to calling surveys to determine if effect of land use on intermediate larval stages should be assessed more carefully.

Summary

A two-year Environmental Monitoring and Assessment Program (EMAP) pilot study was initiated to: (1) describe anuran relative abundance, species composition, and species distribution in selected study sites within the Prairie Pothole region (PPR) of North Dakota; (2) determine a suitable road survey method for estimating anuran relative abundance and describing anuran distribution; and (3) determine if relationships exist between anuran distribution and relative abundance and land-use patterns associated with the study site. The first year of the study was completed in 1995, and descriptive summaries of nightly calling intervals, calling seasons, and weather associations are presented. A combination of calling surveys and night driving surveys provided a more complete description of species distributions and species composition in study sites than either method used alone. Additionally, preliminary data suggest that the distribution of American toads (*Bufo americanus americanus*), Great Plains toads (*Bufo cognatus*), and the gray treefrog complex (*Hyla versicolor/chrysoscelis*) may be associated with land-use patterns.

Acknowledgments

We thank D. Anderson, M. Hennecke, and D. Telesco for the late nights and long hours of assistance collecting data; T. Sklebar for generous efforts and extra hours producing maps and wetland data; and D. Plumpton for constructive comments on the manuscript. This research was cosponsored by the U.S. Environmental Protection Agency through Interagency Agreement Reference Number DW14935541-01 and the U.S. National Biological Service (formerly the U.S. Fish and Wildlife Service) Reference Number 14-48-0009-92-1929.

40

Locating Historical Information on Amphibian Populations

Alan R. Resetar

Accurate information on species identification, diversity, and distribution is critical to the assessment of ecological change and species extinction (Systematics Agenda 2000 1994). Specifically related to amphibian populations, Dubois (1990) notes the need for information on changes in abundance. Information is also necessary to apply taxonomic changes to known taxa (Arnold 1991). Preserved collections and the literature contain the historical information that assists in determining trends in populations, communities, and ecosystems (Systematics Agenda 2000 1994). Conservation databases, field notes, and networking supplement the information found in collections and the literature.

In some instances, comparing historical information on amphibian populations with more current information aids in the determination of trends in distribution over time, trends in abundance over time, and trends in species richness over time. In addition, nomenclatural changes made since the time of collection or publication can be assigned if vouchers (specimens or photographs), detailed descriptions, or recorded calls are available (Cagle 1956).

In spite of limitations inherent in the original collection, recording, and reporting of historical data, there are reasons to use them. They are the only baseline data available for some taxa, populations, and localities. Indeed, such data can be quite detailed. When a precise locality is specified by a collector and other details regarding the collection event are recorded, the collection could potentially be duplicated. Preserved specimens function not only as permanent vouchers but as reservoirs of life history information, because they contain food items, parasites, and evidence of reproductive condition (Arnold 1991).

The search for information is time-consuming and may at times yield marginal results. Nevertheless, the search must be exhaustive in order to assure that all relevant sources have been found. This is especially important when determining historical distributions. It is easy to utilize familiar and comfortable sources, such as major topical journals and personal contacts (Council of Biology Editors Style Manual Committee 1983). Unfortunately, such cursory research may miss important information.

The proliferation of biological information sources on the Internet complements more traditional information sources. Internet sites such as the World-Wide Web Virtual Library: Herpetology (Biosciences; see http://xtal200.harvard.edu:8000/herps/), the Biodiversity and Biological Collections Web Server (see http://muse.bio.cornell.edu/), and others are gateways that can be used to find online herpetological databases, bibliographies, and other information resources.

The properly documented, preserved specimen and its data are among the primary baseline sources in assessing historical trends. Preserved material can include adults, juveniles, metamorphic individuals, larvae, and eggs. Major museums and universities are obvious sources of preserved specimens, but small colleges, high schools, private individuals, and federal, state, and local government wildlife or land management agencies may also have preserved collections. Collections may contain auxiliary material that supplements preserved specimens. This material may include sound recordings of individual calls or choruses, collectors' detailed field notes and data, histological preparations of gonads, and photographic images of live animals and collecting localities.

The standard unit of data for a preserved specimen is the specimen record. Each record is divided into data types or fields. The numbers vary, but there are usually fields for the following types of information: specimen catalog number, field number, scientific name (genus, species, subspecies), locality (usually a hierarchical set of geographic divisions), collector, date of collection, number of specimens, sex, fate, condition, type status, donor, and detailed notes. Other taxonomic and geographic fields and files are often relationally linked to the aforementioned fields in data retrieval systems.

An obvious advantage of preserved specimens over other sources of historical data is that actual specimens can be measured and counted (e.g., the snout-vent length, weight, number of specimens collected in one collection event, or the number of eggs per egg mass or female) and identifications verified. In addition, diet analyses can be conducted (prey type, size, and quantity), sex and reproductive condition determined, minimum body size at sexual maturity determined, tissues analyzed for toxin accumulation, parasites identified and counted, predator injuries noted, larval stages or immature individuals correlated with dates of collection, and so on.

A problem with using data from preserved specimens as baseline sources for certain types of trend analyses is that it can be difficult to determine whether taxonomic, geographic, age class, sex, collection technique, or numerical biases by the collector(s) may have affected specific collection events. For example, during specific collecting events, a collector may have only collected one species but ignored others, collected only smaller species or individuals but ignored larger forms or individuals, or collected only a certain number of each species or sex instead of every specimen encountered. Additional problems, such as unusual weather conditions during or preceding the collection event or seasonal factors, may have influenced numbers of individuals or species collected. Geographic biases, such as maximal collecting efforts being directed in certain areas and minimal collecting efforts directed in other areas, can affect the determination of historical distributions. Dodd and Franz (1993) note that an analysis of museum specimens by itself cannot elucidate current distribution and status. The examination of the collectors' original field notes and data or publications on the preserved material may help to determine collector biases or extenuating circumstances at the time of collection.

Care must be exercised when using data from preserved material. Errors in specimen identifications, errors in the original collectors' field notes, museum cataloging errors, and body size changes due to preservation are some of the possible problems. The best way of culling out identification errors is by personal examination of specimens or, if collection policy allows it and staff time and expertise are available, by requesting that the collection staff verify identifications. Errors in data are more difficult to detect. If there appears to be a problem concerning erroneous data, the collection staff should be contacted so that they can investigate the problem.

A further problem is that locality data may be unusable or vague. This happens for many reasons. Boundaries of cities and towns change. For example, a 1920s collection locality west of "Anytown, U.S.A." in 1996 may be inside the town. In some cases, the field collectors may not have known exactly where they were and thus used an approximate locality or approximate distance from a known locality. In other cases, collectors may give nicknames to favorite collecting sites. Fifty years after specimens from these localities are cataloged, the nicknames are meaningless, and the locations of the sites can only be guessed.

There are several useful sources for locating potential depositories of preserved material. Leviton et al. (1985) published a list of major herpetological collections of the world. The Herpetologists Internet Directory (http://crystal.harvard.edu.8000/herps/) is an online source that can be searched for curators of herpetological collections. The directory is searched by using Boolean strategies with words such as "curator" and "museum." The Official Museum Directory lists and indexes museums in the United States and Canada. Various guides or directories to colleges and universities, available in any library, aid in locating addresses of academic institutions that may have small herpetology collections. A comprehensive search for specimens should begin with the large museum or university collections, collections in the geographic area of interest, and collections known to be centers or past centers for the taxon(a) or area(s) being studied. In preparing a checklist of the herpetofauna of the 11,200-square-kilometer Caddo Lake watershed in Texas and Louisiana, Hardy (1995) surveyed sixty-six different collections for specimens from the watershed. Twenty of these collections contained a total of 1,748 specimens. Approximately 95 percent of the specimens located by Hardy were held in institutions in the two states containing the watershed. This does not mean that extralimital collections should not be queried for holdings. Often very important historical collections are deposited outside of the region where the original collections were made. For example, the San Diego (California) Natural History Museum holds Chapman Grant's northwest Indiana collections from the 1930s.

Until online searching of entire museum collection databases is universally available, a letter of inquiry is the initial step in procuring collection-based information. This step is necessary even with collections whose holdings are currently online. At this time, most online collection databases contain only basic holdings information, such as species names, countries of origin, and tallies of numbers of specimens held. If individual specimen records are accessible, institutions may shield some fields or parts of fields. Letters of inquiry should be on official letterhead, if possible. E-mail inquiries may be acceptable, depending on the policy of the particular collection. Inquiries should include a detailed explanation of the project for which the information is needed. For researchers who are not affiliated with an institution or agency and are requesting information on sensitive species, this step is critical. Nonaffiliated individuals, in many cases, have sponsorship or funding from an agency with jurisdiction over the areas or taxa on which research is being conducted. In such cases, an official from the sponsoring or funding agency can write a letter of request on behalf of the individual conducting the study.

Institutions with collections that are not computerized provide data to requestors by copying taxonomically or geographically arranged information from cross-reference files (Simmons 1987) or by a manual compilation of requested information. Institutions with computerized collection databases provide data by printout, disk, or data transmission. The basic levels at which computerized data are typically sorted are taxonomic, geographic, or taxonomic and geographic. For example, a typical database can be queried for all records of Blanchard's cricket frogs (*Acris crepitans blanchardi*), all records for all species from a state or county, or all records of cricket frogs from a state or county. Taxonomic searches can be conducted at the class, order, family, genus, species, and subspecies levels. Geographic searches can be conducted at the regional, continental, country, primary political subdivision (e.g., state or province), or secondary political subdivision (e.g., county or district) levels.

An initial request for information may lead to the need to personally compile data in collections at institutions that for some reason cannot respond to requests for information or to examine specimens or other material held in collections. Visits should be preceded by initial contact with collection staff to alert them of an upcoming visit so that scheduling as well as access to the widest variety of material can be arranged.

Borrowing specimens from collections is possible. Loans are usually made only to established workers and their students. This is due to the storage requirements of preserved material, which necessitate a source of ethyl alcohol or, less often, buffered formalin or isopropyl alcohol, appropriate storage containers, and container closures. Requests by students must be cosigned by an advisor, who will take responsibility for the well-being of the borrowed specimens.

More detailed information on museum specimens or specific collecting events is sometimes available in the form of collectors' field notes and data. Detailed field data are not usually added to specimen records because of the limitations in the hand-cataloging or electronic-cataloging of museum material. Depending on the institution and its staff's ability to provide access, these data, or portion of the data set, may be available to researchers. The best way to determine if these data exist is to query the institution containing the material in question. Field notes and data can include details such as times of capture, weather conditions, collection techniques, size of collecting party, time spent during a particular collecting event, associated species collected, habitat and microhabitat descriptions, measurements including live weight, color notes, preservation techniques, behavior observations, and so on. More advanced data retrieval systems are now capable of linking recorded vocalizations, video footage, and photographic images to specimen records.

The next major sources of historical information are the primary scientific literature and the gray literature. In some cases, papers and monographs in the primary literature may be complemented by preserved material. Papers and monographs may contain lists of specimens, with holding institutions and catalog numbers specified. Because small collections are often acquired by, or deposited in, other collections, determination of the current location of specimens mentioned in the literature may be problematical. Some of the same limitations in using preserved specimens in trend analyses extend to using the literature. An additional problem—the lack of vouchers or detailed physical descriptions—leads to the need to ignore some published information because of the inability to verify taxonomic status (Cagle 1956).

Indexes and specialized bibliographies with online, CD-ROM, and print versions provide access to monographs and journal articles. Monographs should be consulted first because they synthesize earlier literature. Conant and Collins (1991) list regional and state herpetological monographs and guides.

Information in indexes and bibliographies is found by using taxonomic, geographic, author, and subject names. Data on amphibians may be "hidden" in general papers dealing with ecological studies of specific habitats, sites, or geographic areas.

Zoological Record began indexing zoological literature in 1864. Bibliographic records dating back to 1978 are now searchable on Zoological Record Online, which is available through DIALOG Information Retrieval Service. Biological Abstracts is another useful indexing source that is available in print or electronic form. Biological Abstracts began indexing the biological literature in 1926. The online version, available through DIALOG Information Retrieval Services, is called BIOSIS Previews. BIOSIS Previews indexes the biological literature back to 1969. Many academic and some larger public libraries carry the print or CD-ROM versions of these indexes and may have access to the online versions. In some cases, charges for the use of the fee-based online services are covered for patrons, faculty, and students but passed on to requesters who are not affiliated. Stille's (1952) "The Nocturnal Amphibian Fauna of the Southern Lake Michigan Beach" is an example of a paper indexed in these sources.

A valuable source of bibliographic information is the bibliography or literature cited sections of relevant books and papers. One can often be led along a continuum of pertinent sources by simply following bibliographic trails from one source to another. Science Citation Index, which has indexed the literature since 1961, lists citations or references that cite other papers. Thus, if one has a pertinent paper and desires similar papers, Science Citation Index lists later papers that cite it (Bell and Rhodes 1994).

The gray literature includes reports, theses, dissertations, and conference proceedings (Auger 1994). Information in the gray literature is more difficult to locate because it may not be indexed as uniformly or for as long a time as the primary scientific literature. Specialized bibliographies, indexes, and publications such as Wildlife Reviews allow partial access to it.

Technical and research reports sponsored by the United States and foreign governments are indexed in Government Reports Announcements and Index (Auger 1994). An online version of this index is available through the National Technical Information Service (NTIS) database via DIALOG Information Retrieval Service. Publications indexed in this source are available through the NTIS in photocopy or microform formats. Copies of publications for sale through NTIS will soon be available on demand through certain Kinko's copying centers (Kahn 1996). Pentecost and Vogt's (1976) "Amphibians and Reptiles of the Lake Michigan Drainage Basin" is an example of a report available for purchase from NTIS.

The Monthly Catalog of Government Publications is the indexing source for documents issued by various agencies of the federal government. This index, which began in 1895, is now available in electronic and print versions. Copies of federal government publications are available from the government depository library system (contact a local library for locations of depository libraries), issuing agencies, and the U.S. Government Printing Office. If the publication is out of print, photocopies or microform copies are available from the NTIS. Hall's (1994) "Herpetofaunal Diversity of the Four Holes Swamp, South Carolina" is an example of a report found in the Monthly Catalog.

Technical series not indexed in the aforementioned sources, unpublished or in-house reports, and studies of or sponsored by federal, state, county, and local governmental wildlife and land management agencies also exist. Karn's (1986) report to the Indiana Department of Natural Resources is an example of this type of report. These reports may be difficult to locate. Federal agencies issuing reports on amphibians (and reptiles) include the National Biological Service, the Bureau of Land Management, the National Park Service, the Army Corps of Engineers, the Fish and Wildlife Service, and the Forest Service. Many of these agencies issue lists of available reports. The best way to obtain information on the existence of unpublished reports and studies available through these agencies is by contacting them directly. The National Wildlife Federation's annual Conservation Directory lists federal and state wildlife and land management agencies. Most libraries carry this reference. It is also available for purchase from the National Wildlife Federation. The telephone book is another source for tracking down agencies. Local, county, and regional branches of federal and state agencies are listed in a special government section in many telephone books or are listed alphabetically under the city, town, county, or state name in the white pages. Most academic and public libraries will also have current directories of state and federal agencies.

Environmental impact studies can be another potential source of information. One way to learn of the existence of these documents is to contact the government agencies sponsoring or requiring the studies by using the sources mentioned above.

Master's theses and Ph.D. dissertations are indexed by subject by Masters Abstracts (later Masters Abstracts International) and Dissertation Abstracts (later Dissertation Abstracts International). Masters Abstracts and Dissertation Abstracts began indexing in 1962 and 1938, respectively. Most major universities have these sources. The online version of Dissertation Abstracts is called Dissertation Abstracts Online and is available from the DIALOG Information Retrieval Service. Breden's (1982) Ph.D. dissertation is an example of a pertinent dissertation.

Biological Abstracts/RRM and its predecessor, Bioresearch Index, began indexing the conference literature in 1965. These sources include herpetological papers presented at selected meetings and conferences. In some cases, research presented in papers at meetings is never published, and the only bibliographic access to it is through indexes such as these. These sources give the name and date of the conference at which a paper was presented, the title of the paper, the presenter's name, and the presenter's address. A search for the presenter's name in indexing sources for primary scientific literature may turn up published results on the topic of the conference paper. In addition, the researcher may be contacted directly, providing he or she is still active.

Articles in amateur herpetological publications are another source of historical data. While amateur publications are usually not peer-reviewed, they are at least minimally reviewed by an editor. Unfortunately, most amateur publications are not self-indexed or indexed by Biological Abstracts or Zoological Record, making it difficult to find articles on a specific topic. Locating the addresses of the various societies is the first step in finding this literature. The Chicago Herpetological Society Membership Directory, available at a nominal cost, contains the names and addresses of other amateur societies. Some amateur groups may have librarians or other members who may be willing to photocopy tables of contents or articles. Amateur groups often have holdings of each other's journals. Ziomek's (1974) article, "Notes of the Spring Activity of Amphibians in the Palos Hills Area of Swallow Cliff and Crooked Creek Woods, Cook County, Illinois," is an example of an article from an amateur publication.

Complementing the data found in preserved collections, the primary scientific literature, and the gray literature are several other resources. The Association for Biodiversity Information and The Nature Conservancy's Natural Heritage Program and Conservation Data Center Network maintain historical and current data on the distribution of rare and threatened flora, fauna, and communities. The U.S. databases in the network are usually cooperative efforts with state wildlife agencies. Information in these databases is usually accessible by writing to the state heritage programs maintaining the individual databases. The locations of heritage programs for particular states can be obtained by contacting The Nature Conservancy. Researchers approaching state heritage programs for information should follow the same guidelines described previously for approaching museum collections. Because the heritage program databases include literature and museum records, there is likely to be some overlap with information gleaned from other sources.

Field notes and journals of herpetologists are extremely useful. As mentioned previously, some of these sources are found in museums, where they are usually associated with cataloged specimens. Networking with active professionals is a way to determine if there are individuals wishing to share such information. Field notes of local, amateur naturalists can also be useful if these naturalists are familiar with amphibians and reptiles and have rigorously recorded their findings. The location of these naturalists or their field notes can be difficult. Archives at local universities and public libraries may contain collections of older material.

County histories and gazetteers can provide information on past abundances or distributions of more common and/or noteworthy species (Moody, personal communication). In some cases, local naturalists were enlisted to write the natural history sections of these books. Because many of these volumes are old, they are likely to be housed in the local history or special collections sections of libraries.

Networking with local citizens can provide anecdotal information on species occurrences, increases, disappearances, habitat changes, and locations of former or current breeding sites. One way of contacting these citizens is to have a local newspaper profile a project or person studying local amphibians. Such an article could include a request for information on past or current observations. People are surprisingly willing to respond to such requests.

Summary

Preserved specimens, the primary scientific literature, the gray literature, unpublished field notes, conservation databases, and other sources provide historical information on amphibian populations (see also additional sources below). In spite of some limitations in its collection, recording, and reporting, historical information is currently one of the few available sources of baseline data on amphibian populations. In some instances, comparisons of historical information with current information assists in the determination of trends in distribution, abundance, and species richness over time.

Acknowledgments

I thank D. R. R. Resetar, Valparaiso University, and R. F. Inger, Chicago Field Museum of Natural History, for reviewing and commenting on this manuscript. The mention of companies or commercial products is for informational purposes only and does not imply endorsement or approval.

Additional Sources

Cooperrider, A. Y., R. J. Boyd, and H. R. Stuart. 1986. Inventory and Monitoring of Wildlife Habitat. U.S. Department of the Interior, Bureau of Land Management, Service Center, Denver.

Davis, E. B., and D. Schmidt. 1995. Using the Biological Literature. Marcel Dekker, New York.

Declining amphibian populations—a global phenomenon? Workshop sponsored by Board on Biology, National Research Council, 19–20 February 1990, Irvine, California.

DIALOG Database Catalogue. 1993. DIALOG Information Retrieval Services, Palo Alto, California.

Heyer, W. R., M. A. Donnelly, R. W. McDiarmid, L.-A. C. Hayek, and M. S. Foster. 1994. Measuring and Monitoring Biological Diversity, Standard Methods for Amphibians. Smithsonian Institution Press, Washington, D.C.

41

Ecological Design and Analysis: Principles and Issues in Environmental Monitoring

Anthony J. Krzysik

The purpose of this chapter is to identify some important principles and issues in areas that are relevant to field biologists and ecologists and to researchers or environmental managers who are designing and implementing ecological assessment or monitoring programs. It is not meant to provide an introduction, or a comprehensive review, of experimental design or statistical analysis. The principal goal of the chapter is to discuss areas of common pitfalls, confusion, misunderstandings, misapplications, and the typical sources of statistical errors. The intended audience is both the novice and the experienced practitioner. Extensive references to the literature are provided, and these, along with my personal experiences, are synthesized. Although original reference sources are given, the major emphasis has been on identifying practical and useful literature to provide the reader with fundamentals and some examples in the science (some would say art) of experimental design and statistical analysis.

A review of research designs and data analysis, as well as inventory methods relevant to monitoring amphibian populations, is provided by Heyer et al. (1994). Introductory overviews of ecological monitoring are found in Clarke (1986), Goldsmith (1991), and Spellerberg (1991).

Issues in Statistical Analysis

Approaches

Statistical analysis consists of at least six general approaches.

Estimation. A common approach is estimating the mean of a population and, just as important (usually more so), an associated measure of the precision of the estimate. (Population in this chapter will be used in a statistical sense and refers to a collection of observations, measurements, or individuals. In this context it can also refer to a treatment or control group.) The precision in the estimate depends on the inherent variability in the population and the sample size used to estimate the statistic under investigation. Statistical precision is called error and is expressed as standard deviation, standard error, confidence interval, or coefficient of variation.

Inference. Inference, or hypothesis testing, is the most frequently associated and best-known approach for the rationale of statistical analysis. Inference helps the investigator decide if the observed difference in a test statistic (e.g., mean) between two or more populations is due to chance at some a priori set probability. The question is posed as a null hypothesis to falsify (null hypothesis: populations are homogeneous). If there is no difference between two or more populations, what is the probability of selecting samples with differences as large as or larger than those observed? This probability is the familiar p-value, or α. If this probability is small, then one concludes that the differences are unlikely to be due to chance, and there is a statistically significant difference in the populations (null hypothesis rejected) at the p-level. If the probability is large (observed differences may be due to chance alone), then either the populations are homogeneous at the p-level or the statistical power of the test was too low (i.e., some combination of small sample size, high natural variability, or the "difference" selected to assess significance was too small). It is imperative to remember that the null hypothesis can never be proved correct but can only be rejected with a known risk of being wrong.

Exploratory Data Analysis. Exploratory data analysis (EDA) is an important class of statistical analysis that has not been fully appreciated, despite the excellent technical foundation laid by Tukey (1977). EDA has also been called Initial Data Analysis (IDA) by Chatfield (1988), who concludes that the process is indispensable and required by the statistician to get a feeling for the data. EDA is intended to:

1. check the quality of the data, including missing observations, outliers, high variance, or noise
2. compare controls and treatments and to assess the relative magnitude of differences
3. examine patterns in the data
4. calculate and examine descriptive and summary statistics
5. examine and test for suitability of design and analysis assumptions (e.g., parametric, multivariate normality, independence, stratification justification)
6. evaluate the need for data transformations (e.g., to fit parametric assumptions, especially homoscedasticity [homogeneous variances]) or rescaling of data
7. provide an aid for statistical model formulation and for determining or refining final statistical analyses methods

All of these are important to EDA, and their relative merits directly depend on the specific nature of the project or database in question. The routine use of EDA has become a current reality because of the power of modern microcomputers and the availability of interactive graphics and extensive graphics output options in microcomputer statistical software packages (e.g., SAS, S-PLUS, SPSS, SYSTAT). All of these packages are excellent and come with excellent documentation. Comprehensive guides for using S-PLUS (Venables and Ripley 1994) and SYSTAT (Wilkinson et al. 1996) are available. SAS is only available by license, making it accessible to universities but too expensive for individuals and most federal research facilities. While there are other good statistical packages available, I am most familiar with these four.

Interactive graphics enable one to rapidly examine data patterns and trends from scatterplots of raw data, transformed or rescaled data, or residuals; references include Chambers et al. (1983) and Cleveland (1993). An important procedure, available in all four of the above statistical packages, is the scatterplot matrix. If you have ten variables in your study and in your EDA you want to investigate their relationships to each other, the scatterplot matrix routine produces a single plot containing 100 subplots of each combination of the ten variable pairs. The plots above the diagonal are the same as the plots below the diagonal, except that the ordinates and abscissas of all paired variables are interchanged.

The importance of EDA using graphical displays, scatterplots, and visualizing data techniques is exemplified in a most remarkable example discussed by Cleveland (1993). Minnesota agronomists in the early 1930s conducted a field experiment on barley yields at six study plots. The data were subsequently analyzed, reanalyzed, and used as examples, even into the 1960s and 1970s. Sir Ronald Fisher, who developed the foundations of modern statistics, analyzed the data and even used them as an example in his classic book on experimental design (Fisher 1935); Fisher's three seminal books, *Statistical Methods for Research Workers* (1925), *The Design of Experiments* (1935), and *Statistical Methods and Scientific Inference* (1956) were published as a single book, entitled *Statistical Methods, Experimental Design, and Scientific Inference,* in 1990 by Oxford University Press. The statisticians who examined the data consistently concluded that five of the six plots showed a barley yield decrease between 1931 and 1932, while the other plot showed an increase. The use of visualizing data techniques and scatterplots clearly demonstrated that there was a major error in the data set; the study plot with the aberrant trend had its years mistakenly interchanged prior to all subsequent analyses. When this error was corrected, all plots showed remarkable consistency in yield decrease between 1931 and 1932.

In addition to the references noted above, important references on EDA are Ehrenberg (1975), Erickson and Nosanchuk (1977), McNeil (1977), Velleman and Hoaglin (1981), Hoaglin et al. (1983, 1985, 1991), and Chatfield (1985).

Descriptive. The distinction between EDA and descriptive statistics is academic because, for practical purposes, descriptive statistics are an important component of EDA. Descriptive statistics are generally summary statistics for all of the primary parameters or variables in the project, generally stratified by spatial, temporal, or user-defined classes. Summary statistics are provided by all statistical analysis packages. An important part of this category is the art and science of data display and graphics presentations. A foundation for the philosophy and techniques of data display has been the work of Tufte

(1983, 1990). Practical guidance for using graphics effectively can be found in Chambers et al. (1983) and Cleveland (1993). The four statistical packages mentioned earlier also provide advice on producing and displaying graphics. Two high-quality scientific graphics packages that have excellent graphics capabilities and documentation are Axum and SigmaPlot. There is even a book available for providing guidance for using SigmaPlot (Charland 1995).

Modeling. Modeling represents the efforts to verify whether experimentally derived data fit specific mathematical models related to biological, physical, geological, or chemical phenomena or processes. The most common example in statistics is linear regression: do the data fit a straight line? Of course, any kind of polynomial curves in any dimensions can be equivalently modeled, but with much more difficulty. Krzysik (Chpt. 42, this volume) discusses the modeling of "thin-plate spline functions" to interpolate and smooth a surface fit to three-dimensional field data points of estimated population densities.

There are four main strategies in model building: model formulation, model estimation or fitting, sensitivity analysis, and model validation. Model validation includes the familiar:

Experimental data = mathematical model + residuals

For further analysis, the residuals can be subjected to standardization (homogeneous variances), their distribution can be examined by using probability plots, they can be plotted against selected variables, or they can be subjected to additional modeling. The analysis of residuals may provide valuable insight into an important facet or unexpected behavior of the model. More details of statistical modeling are available in Daniel and Wood (1980) and Gilchrist (1984). See also the subsection on Parametric Statistics (below).

Spatial Analysis. Spatial analysis has developed independently from mainstream statistics and has employed its own terminology. Spatial statistics, once the domain of mainframe and minicomputer workstations, is rapidly gaining popularity with the growing use of Geographic Information Systems (GIS; Krzysik, Chpt. 42, this volume) and the availability of high-power microcomputers. Within the next year or two, spatial analysis modules will be available for most popular microcomputer statistics packages. A module for S-PLUS has already been released. Krzysik (Chpt. 42, this volume) presents a summary of interpolation and smoothing methods and a survey of the literature.

Data Analysis

Fundamental Statistical Analysis. For readers not familiar with statistical methods and experienced in the rationale of their use, Motulsky (1995) offers an excellent and basic overview; Chatfield (1988) is advanced but insightful; Abramson (1994), although oriented to epidemiological and clinical studies, presents information for statistical interpretation in an easy-to-read format; and Huff (1954) is mandatory reading for all researchers, managers, and consumers. Good introductory texts in statistics are Campbell (1989), Weinberg and Goldberg (1990), Freund and Wilson (1993), and Zolman (1993). Li (1964) provides an excellent introduction, especially valuable in analysis of variance (ANOVA) fundamentals, but is no longer in print.

The basic fundamental texts for statistical analyses that are used in the classroom as well as by field biologists and ecologists are Box et al. (1978), Steel and Torrie (1980), Zar (1984), Snedecor and Cochran (1989), and Sokal and Rohlf (1994). Arminger et al. (1995) is an advanced text that offers more comprehensive coverage of specialized topics in statistical analysis: missing data, mean- and covariance-structure models, contingency table analysis, latent class models, analysis of qualitative data, analysis of event histories, and random coefficient models. Potvin and Travis (1993) present a summary of references for statistical methods in twelve topic categories: a posteriori testing, density dependence, experimental design, maximum likelihood, multivariate analysis, philosophical issues, ratios, regression analysis, repeated measures analysis, spatial heterogeneity, species associations, and trend analysis.

Parametric Statistics. Parametric statistics represent the well-known statistical methods taught in introductory statistics courses (see references above) and cover the familiar topics of linear regression, ANOVA, and analysis of covariance (ANCOVA). The latter is ANOVA with the addition of a covariate, making it also a linear regression model. A good example of the use of ANCOVA is testing the hypothesis that two salamander populations possess different clutch sizes (an ANOVA model), while simultaneously taking into account that clutch size is a function of body size (a linear regression model). In actuality, linear regression belongs to the family of generalized linear models (GLM), and ANOVA and ANCOVA are special cases of linear regression. Nonlinear, or polynomial, regression and multiple regression (more than one independent or predictor variables) are extensions of the basic model. Fundamentals of GLM and modeling are provided by McCullagh and Nelder (1983), Cullen (1985), Neter et al. (1985), and Dobson (1990). Although regression analysis is well covered in the fundamental texts referenced above, other valuable texts include Draper and Smith (1981), Montgomery and Peck (1982), Neter et al. (1985), and Chatterjee and Price (1991). ANOVA is covered in all basic statistics texts, and an advanced treatise is Searle et al. (1992).

Other regression analyses that have extensive applications in ecology are logistic regression and locally weighed scatterplot smoothing (LOWESS) regression (Trexler and Travis 1993). Logistic regression deals with dichotomous (bivariate) or polychotomous dependent variables and transforms the data to model binomial or multinomial distributions. LOWESS models the relationship between a dependent (response) variable and independent variables under the assumption that neighborhood values of independent variables within a range are good indicators of the dependent variable in that same range.

In traditional least-squares regression, estimators are unbiased (i.e., the expected value is the population parameter). When independent variables are highly correlated (common in ecological data), unbiased estimators produce large variances. Ridge regression has been suggested as a model to obtain biased estimators of regression coefficients and to stabilize variance (Hoerl and Kennard 1970a,b; Montgomery and Peck 1982).

Parametric statistics are based on three important assumptions: (1) population samples or observations are normally distributed; (2) populations (comparisons) possess homogeneous variances (residuals); and (3) observations are independent of one another, that is, that random observations and sampling or experimental errors are independent, therefore avoiding sampling or experimental bias.

These assumptions can be tested formally, but typically they are not. Goodness-of-fit tests and calculations of skewness and kurtosis (available in all basic statistical packages) can test for normality. Bartlett's test assesses homoscedasticity, but its practical value has been questioned (Harris 1975). Sampling independence may be difficult to assess but in some cases can be detected by correlational tests or by the examination of scatterplots of the raw data. In some situations, spatial autocorrelation may present problems for collecting independent samples (see Legendre 1993). Parametric statistical methods are generally considered to be robust with respect to these assumptions when sample sizes are reasonable (e.g., twenty to thirty) and particularly when the raw data have been transformed. A major reliance on robustness is the central limit theorem, which states that the means of variables from nonnormal (e.g., skewed) distributions are themselves normally distributed. Biological data are often log-normally distributed with the mean and variance highly correlated. Biological count data typically form Poisson distributions, where the mean equals the variance. A log transformation for log-normal data and a square-root transformation for data with Poisson distributions are suggested to meet parametric assumptions (Sokal and Rohlf 1994). Additionally, log transformations of the data are effective at stabilizing heterogeneous variances. Therefore, the most critical parametric assumption remains the independence of errors. The violation of this assumption is common and results in a sampling bias.

Milliken and Johnson (1984, 1989) present practical approaches and methods of data analysis for experimental designs and parametric data that are plagued with the well-known problems associated with field data: failures in assumptions, unbalanced designs, lack of replication, repeated measures, multiple comparisons, outliers, and missing data.

Balanced ANOVAs are required to obtain unambiguous interpretations of interaction effects and overall significance. The term "balanced" means that there are equal observations in each experimental treatment. Balanced designs cannot always be used for the practical collection of ecological field data. Shaw and Mitchell-Olds (1993) review ANOVA for unbalanced designs and provide guidelines for the analysis of fixed effects models.

Nonparametric Statistics. Nonparametric statistics (NPS) are also called distribution-free statistics because they make no assumptions about test statistic distribution, variance heterogeneity, and other behaviors. They also respond well to the analysis of ordinal or categorical data. Many researchers believe that nonparametric methods possess low power in contrast to parametric tests. In reality, the difference is not significant (Hollander and Wolfe 1973; Noether 1987). However, what is not always appreciated is that, like parametric tests, nonparametric tests are also subjected to the same two important limitations and violations of statistical analyses: nonindependence of sampling errors (the need for random sampling) and the loss of statistical power when sample sizes are too small (Box et al. 1978; Stewart-Oaten 1995). The chi-square test is the best known, and the most abused, nonparametric test. The fundamental texts for nonparametric analysis are Siegel (1956), Hollander and Wolfe (1973), and Connover (1980).

Potvin and Roff (1993) emphasize the prevalence of nonnormality in environmental data and present the case that distribution-free robust statistical methods should be more extensively used in ecological research and monitoring. Johnson (1995), Smith (1995), and Stewart-Oaten (1995) challenge their conclusion and do not recommend the widespread or routine use of NPS in ecology. Their argument is based on the following issues:

1. NPS should not be a substitute for insufficient sample sizes, poorly conceived experimental or sampling designs, unbalanced data sets, poor field procedures, or just poor data.
2. NPS also require assumptions, which are usually unappreciated, unknown, ignored, or overlooked.
3. It is important that the investigator using the statistical test make an a priori assessment of the relative importance of Type I and Type II errors. See the sections on Statistical Power and Significance Tests (below).
4. Statistical significance is often confused with biological significance or judgment.

Multivariate Statistics. The statistics discussed above deal with data possessing a single dependent (response) variable. Multivariate statistics deal with data that have multiple dependent and independent variables. Suitable introductions are Pielou (1984), Manly (1986), Digby and Kempton (1987), and James and McCulloch (1990). For additional discussion and references, see the review of multivariate methods in Krzysik (1987; Chpt. 42, this volume). Gifi (1990) presents a comprehensive review of multivariate analysis for categorical data and nonlinear models and includes an interesting example of correspondence analysis, where he analyzes and graphically presents the subject material covered in multivariate analysis books (1957–1978). Principal component analysis (PCA) is a powerful procedure for ordination, data reduction, data transformation, and data standardization (Krzysik 1987). PCA produces newly derived variables from linear combinations of the original variables (often highly correlated), such that most of the original variance in the original data is expressed in as few as possible new uncorrelated variables. The use of PCA for ordination has been criticized (e.g., Gauch 1982), but also see the review by Wartenberg et al. (1987).

Nontraditional Statistics. Resampling statistics and permutation/randomization tests represent a rapidly developing field of nontraditional statistics. These are computer intensive procedures that include Monte Carlo methods, the calculation of exact p-values (parametric and nonparametric), jackknifing, bootstrapping (Miller 1974; Efron 1982; Edgington 1987; Noreen 1989; Efron and Tibshirani 1991; Manly 1991; Shao and Tu 1995; Weerahandi 1995), and multiple comparisons (Westfall and Young 1993). These techniques are particularly useful for nonparametric data (appreciable violation of parametric assumptions) and messy data: small samples, unbalanced data (dramatic differences in interpopulation sample sizes), strongly skewed data or residuals, data possessing strange distributions, missing observations, and outliers. Nonparametric tests are desirable because they make no assumptions about the distribution of test statistics. However, like parametric tests, they still rely on asymptotic behavior, which requires reasonable sample sizes and balanced data. Asymptotic theory is not valid for data sets that are small, highly skewed, sparse, or unbalanced. "The difficulty of exact calculations coupled with the availability of normal approximations leads to the almost automatic computation of asymptotic distributions and moments for discrete random variables. . . . How does one justify them? . . . Rigorous answers to [this] question require some of the deepest results in mathematical probability theory" (Bishop et al. 1975). These limitations have been recognized for some time, and Fisher (1935) has suggested the use of permutational p-values for randomized experiments. However, the routine use of permutation methods depends directly on the availability of inexpensive, high-powered computers. Indeed, it is now possible to compute exact permutated p-values for nonparametric tests and thus avoid asymptotic assumptions (Mehta et al. 1988; Agresti et al. 1990; Good 1994).

Jackknifing and bootstrapping are often used to estimate the precision (especially standard error) of descriptive statistics, complicated functions, environmental parameters, and ecological indices. In the jackknife procedure, the original sample data are divided into groups. Usually each group represents a single datum (e.g., a sample with thirty observations would have thirty groups). New samples are generated by deleting each group in turn, one at a time, for the entire original sample. In the above example, there would be thirty new samples, each with twenty-nine observations. The desired statistic (e.g., mean) is calculated from the newly generated samples, and the variability among the samples is used to estimate the standard error of the statistic.

The jackknife procedure reduces bias in the estimated statistic. For a nonnormal distribution, the jackknife is more suitable than the more commonly used F-test (Arvesen and Schmitz 1970).

In the bootstrap, a large number of new sample data sets (usually 1,000 to 50,000) are created from the original data by randomly resampling with replacement from the original data set. For example, let the original data set contain ten observations. Each newly derived data set with its ten observations is generated as follows. The first observation is selected at random from the original data and is "replaced" back into the data set. This process is repeated to select the second observation and is continued until ten observations are obtained. Therefore, for this first resampled data set, a specific observation in the original data may have been selected once, twice, three times, or up to ten times, or it may not be selected at all. This procedure is repeated until the desired number of resampled data sets has been generated. Bootstrapping is a very computer intensive procedure and has only become feasible with the widespread availability of powerful microcomputers. I have run simple algorithms with small data sets (sample sizes ten to thirty) to create 50,000 bootstrapped samples in less than twenty seconds on a 486 PC running at fifty megahertz. Although the bootstrap is much more computer intensive than the jackknife, it is generally considered to be an improvement over the jackknife. Bootstrap and jackknife estimates approach each other asymptotically when sample sizes are large (Efron and Gong 1983).

Reviews of ecological indices are presented in Ludwig and Reynolds (1988), Krebs (1989), and Dixon (1994; see also Krzysik, Chpt. 42, this volume). A practical application of combining several of these techniques for statistical inference in population monitoring can be found in Krzysik (1997).

Analyses of data that are not continuous variables, but represent discrete categories, have become more common with the development of high-power microcomputers and associated statistical software. Important literature in this field includes Cox (1970), Bishop et al. (1975), Everitt (1977), Fienberg (1980), Plackett (1981), Fingleton (1984), Young (1987), Agresti (1990), Gifi (1990), and Nishisato (1994).

Meta-analysis is an important statistical procedure for analyzing as a group the combined results of individual experiments (Cooper and Hedges 1993; Petitti 1994). Its utility is two-fold: (1) none of the individual experiments or studies may have sufficient statistical power to adequately test the significance of the hypothesis posed; and (2) it provides a mechanism to produce generalizable results from possibly very specific experiments. Meta-analysis is a new technique in ecological research (Gurevitch et al. 1992; Gurevitch and Hedges 1993) but has had a strong foundation in medicine and social studies, fields where sample sizes tend to be low, inherent variability tends to be high, manipulative experiments are out of the question or unethical, and data are expensive. Meta-analysis was successfully used by the U.S. Environmental Protection Agency (1990) to assess and verify the risk of lung cancer to women exposed to environmental tobacco smoke. Meta-analysis consists of using the statistical engine to take the data of independent experiments, combine them, and reach valid generalized conclusions.

Another nontraditional approach is Bayesian inference. Although Bayes's theorem was published in 1763, its acceptance and rejection vacillated since that time (Box and Tiao 1973). It is currently increasing in popularity. The strength of the Bayesian approach is that it is based on, and takes full advantage of, incorporating prior information (e.g., previous data or experiments) into a current statistical analysis (Box and Tiao 1973; Lee 1989; Press 1989).

Time series analysis is relevant in many biological, ecological, and environmental applications, representing the measurement and analysis of parameters as a function of continuous or discrete time (Chatfield 1989; Diggle 1990; Brockwell and Davis 1991; Rasmussen et al. 1993).

Data measured as angles, or two- or three-dimensional orientations, are common in the sciences, including biology and in any spatial applications. Important applications in biology would be the design and analysis of experiments in homing; movement of animals from point of release; directional movements of animals in response to external stimuli such as noise, ground vibrations, wind, ocean currents, wildfire, flooding regimes, circadian rhythms, physical or chemical impacts, and habitat manipulations. These data are known as circular, or spherical, data and require specialized statistical analysis with appropriate models (Fisher et al. 1987; Fisher 1993).

Efficient Statistical Inference

Type I (α) and Type II (β) Errors. Every basic text in statistics discusses Type I and Type II errors. A Type I error is the probability of rejecting a true null hypothesis (no significant difference). Selecting a smaller value of α reduces Type I error (e.g., select an α of 0.01 instead of 0.05). α is also known as the p-value and represents the probability of selecting random samples that result in a significant p-value (α) when the difference between group means is Δ.

A Type II error is the probability of failing to reject a false null hypothesis. It is important to note that the correct phrase is "failing to reject" rather than "accepting" a null hypothesis, because a failure to disprove a given null hypothesis does not prove it. Indeed, if I found no "significance difference" and sample sizes were small and/or inherent variability was high, it would be incorrect to state that I "proved" the null hypothesis, when in fact it is more correct to say I failed to reject the null hypothesis, possibly because statistical power was low.

Conservative Analysis. A conservative statistical analysis strategy guards against making a Type I error. A conservative strategy includes the a priori selection of conservative statistical tests or the selection of low α values.

Statistical Power. The power of a statistical test is defined by 1 - β. Therefore, power is the probability of rejecting a false null hypothesis. In other words, high power is directly related to a smaller β (a lower Type II error). β represents the probability of selecting random samples that result in a nonsignificant p-value (α) when the difference between population means is Δ. Both α and Δ must be selected a priori and are independent of statistical intervention. Both are dependent on the technical experience or judgment of the investigator in selecting what the difference between population means should be before it is considered statistically significant under the null hypothesis, with the probability α of making a Type I error. Power represents the probability of obtaining a significant difference when the difference between population means is Δ. The power of an analysis is therefore related to inherent variability, sample size, and the difference between population means (Δ) that I want to call a statistically significant (α) difference.

Statistical power analysis should be conducted as an integral component of the experimental design before a study is implemented and should also be reported in the published results of the study. This applies to both research and environmental management projects. The standard text for power analysis is Cohen (1988), and software to conduct the analysis is available (Borenstein and Cohen 1988).

Statistical results that are reported to have low power, or appear to have low power when no power analysis was reported, should be looked at with skepticism when conclusions are reached that are based on the failure to reject a null hypothesis—the failure to find significance. Peterman (1990a) found that 98 percent of recently surveyed papers in fisheries and aquatic sciences that did not reject a null hypothesis failed to report statistical power or β. Additionally, 52 percent of these papers reached conclusions as if their null hypothesis were true. Peterman (1990a) presents an important fundamental discussion of power analysis in statistical inference and of its implications for researchers, policy makers, and decision makers in environmental management. Peterman (1990b) also draws attention to the absence of power analysis in assessing the effects of acidic deposition on forest declines. These papers should be required reading for researchers and resource managers contemplating the design of any large-scale ecological or environmental monitoring programs. The high inherent variability of natural systems presents a formidable obstacle to designing environmental monitoring programs with sufficient power to detect changes or trends (Pechmann et al. 1991; Osenberg et al. 1994). Additional suggested readings include Tacha et al. (1982), Toft and Shea (1983), de la Mare (1984), Rotenberry and Wiens (1985), Swihart and Slade (1986), Gerrodette (1987), and Green (1989). See also the section on Significance Tests (below).

Increasing Statistical Power. There are several ways to increase statistical power. First, use large or at least appropriate sample sizes, which increases degrees of freedom. Increasing sample size is the most important and usually the most feasible way of increasing power.

Second, design experiments that have small error variance (within population variance) and reduced confounding effects. This produces a smaller denominator in the F-test, and therefore significance can be detected with smaller between treatment variance.

Third, increase the value of α. This is the usual alternative when sample size cannot be increased. Although this increases power and reduces the chances of making a Type II error, it increases the chances of making a Type I error. There is a mutual trade-off when selecting between making a Type I or a Type II error (you cannot have your cake and eat it too).

Fourth, increasing Δ increases power, because at any level of sampling variability, it is more reassuring to attribute significance to larger differences than to smaller differences.

Finally, report a power analysis with your data. Based on your sample size and the inherent variability in your data (error variance), how small a difference could you have detected as significant with the α value that you a priori selected?

Robustness. Large sample sizes create high degrees of freedom. No matter how complicated an ANOVA, the degrees of freedom in the denominator for the F-test are the most important factor for judging significance.

There are two additional important factors to consider. Statistical comparisons (populations compared) should be similar in sample sizes, and two-tailed tests are more robust than one-tailed tests.

Harris (1975) concludes that most data sets in univariate, parametric-based statistical tests are robust to the assumptions of normality and homogeneity of variances, unless sample sizes are small and unequal. Harris (1975) suggests the following guidelines:

$$Var_{max}/Var_{min} < 20 \quad (Var = \text{sample variance})$$

$$N_{max}/N_{min} < 4 \quad (N = \text{sample size})$$

$$\text{Error degrees of freedom} > 10$$

Significance Tests. There is a great deal of empirical evidence (Morrison and Henkel 1970; Roberts 1976; Guttman 1985; Gardner and Altman 1986; Jones and Matloff 1986; Oakes 1986; Perry 1986; Millard 1987; Krebs 1989; Wiens 1989; Yoccoz 1991; McBride et al. 1993; Motulsky 1995) and historical consensus from statisticians (Tukey 1960, 1980, 1991; Wolfowitz 1967; Deming 1975; Pratt 1976; Cox 1977, 1986; Carver 1978) that significance tests have been excessively used and misapplied, particularly in regard to confusion with biological significance or relevance (see also the preceding subsection on Increasing Statistical Power). Statistical practitioners have dismissed the cautions of statisticians for over a half century (Berkson 1942). Salsburg (1985) refers to hypothesis testing as the primary tool in the religion of statistics. There is no empirical or theoretical foundation for selecting $p = 0.05$, as is routinely done in biological data analysis and tests for significance. P-values cannot even be compared among studies, because they are a function of specific project design parameters and sample size (Gibbon and Pratt 1975). In a demonstration of the applicability of significance tests to contrast soil pH among fields and to evaluate United States regulations for groundwater quality, McBride et al. (1993) conclude that significance tests have no practical value or merit and recommend that researchers and environmental managers place more value on statistical power and deciding on "practical differences" when statistical comparisons are being made among means and their variances.

There is an important difference between biological/ecological and statistical significance, although this is often overlooked. Biological/ecological significance represents biological realism and common sense directly relevant to actual ecological systems. Statistical significance is only relevant to sample size in the specific context of the probability of finding an observed difference by chance alone, relative to the inherent variability in the system under investigation. Biological relevance does not enter into the equation. Statistical significance will always be assured as long as sample size is large enough to "statistically detect" even the smallest differences, differences that are undoubtedly irrelevant to the normal course of biological variability. Therefore, a statistical significance is not necessarily of practical or relevant significance. At the other end of the spectrum, sample sizes that are too small relative to the inherent variability of ecological systems (low statistical power) may fail to find biological relevance when it is present. The testing of significance for multiple comparisons is not valid unless equal sample sizes are used.

Although most statisticians and researchers who apply statistics to their experiments do not advocate the abandonment of significance tests, there probably is consensus that more care should be taken in their use. It is more desirable to present means with their standard deviations (standard errors) or confidence intervals and sample sizes (Cochran and Cox 1957; Gardner and Altman 1986; McBride et al. 1993).

Transformations. Probably the most common source of sample heterogeneity in biological data is that the mean and variance are correlated. Data transformation (especially the log transformation)

$$X_T = \ln (x+1)$$

(X_T is the transformed variable x, and ln is the natural logarithm)

removes the functional dependence of the mean and variance. Log transformation is also effective in stabilizing unknown sources of heterogeneity, as long as they are not too extreme. Steel and Torrie (1980) refer to this as irregular error heterogeneity. The source of this heterogeneity could be due to outliers, spatial heterogeneity, or procedural errors. Outliers may represent natural variability (possibly indicating small sample sizes) or important departures from the data, and their removal should be considered cautiously (see Barnett and Lewis [1984] for guidance). Outliers could also be due to procedural errors, which are beyond statistical treatment, and in this case they can be removed. Spatial heterogeneity is best handled by sample stratification, but this is difficult or unmanageable if the spatial pattern is not obvious. Inherent spatial complexity and mosaics, especially at scales much smaller than the sampling area of interest, are best handled by nested sampling designs.

The most commonly used transformations are the log and square root (e.g., Sokal and Rohlf 1994). The log transformation is most frequently used because it possesses many desirable properties, including making variables independent of scale (Jolicoeur 1963a,b; Marriott 1974). Scale independence is a critical consideration, especially in multivariate analysis, otherwise the results of the analysis may depend on the scale of the original measurements (Gower 1967; Orloci 1967; Noy-Meir et al. 1975; Pimentel 1979). The square root transformation is most commonly used in count data, which typically follow a Poisson distribution (mean and variance are equal). Guidance and practical references for data transformations are Elliott (1977), Green (1979), Steel and Torrie (1980), Draper and Smith (1981), Zar (1984), Snedecor and Cochran (1989), Fry (1993), and Sokal and Rohlf (1994).

A broad family of transformations can be derived from modeling power series (Healy and Taylor 1962; Box and Cox 1964; Draper and Smith 1981; McCullagh and Nelder 1983). Southwood (1966) discusses the use of Taylor's power law. Southwood (1966), Poole (1974), Elliott (1977), and Green (1979) discuss the fitting of negative binomial distributions. Williams and Stephenson (1973) discuss cube-root transformations.

Transformations can also include methods that rank, standardize, or statistically manipulate raw data into a "new data set." Green (1979) recommends transforming the raw data to ranks and then using Fisher and Yates tables (a comprehensive set of statistical tables published in 1974) to transform to standardized deviates, making rank values independent of sample size.

An important transformation for multivariate data is the use of principal component analysis (PCA; Krzysik 1987). Significance tests in multivariate analysis, as in parametric analysis, assume independence in independent (predictor) variables. A PCA transformation before multivariate analysis of variance (MANOVA), discriminant analysis, and multiple regression would produce the desired criteria of independence. Green (1979) emphasizes that the assumption of independence is the one most frequently ignored in statistical analysis. Another important advantage of PCA, and using a correlation matrix of original variables as input for the PCA analysis, is that scale magnitude (including logarithmic variables such as pH), and even the mixing of all possible numerical scale variable types (ratio, interval, ordinal or rank, bivariate), is completely and efficiently standardized (mean of zero and unit variance; Krzysik 1987). Nominal scales other than bivariate ones may or may not be combined validly with continuous and rank data. See Hayek (1994) for a description of numerical scales.

Issues in Experimental Design

Experimental Design

The foundations of experimental design were developed by Fisher (1935) for manipulative laboratory (genetic) and agriculture field experiments. Since the classic references in experimental design were first published by Cochran and Cox (1957) and Cox (1958), there was for a time a conspicuous absence of texts in this field. (Both of these texts, Box and Tiao (1973), and others were reprinted in 1992 in the John Wiley and Sons Classics Library Editions.) Treatments of experimental design by standard statistics texts are usually limited to the design of ANOVA comparisons (e.g., factorial, nested, split-plot, Latin square). Lindman (1992) presents a comprehensive treatment of ANOVA in experimental design. With the realization of a vacant niche, a surge of experimental design texts were published in the late 1980s and early 1990s. Selected examples include Kish (1987), Mead (1988), Keppel and Zedeck (1989), Montgomery (1991), Atkinson and Donev (1992), and Manly (1992). In the interim, a Canadian aquatic ecologist published a synthesis of experimental design and data analysis that has been relevant for practicing field biologists and ecologists (Green 1979). Despite its age, the applicability of Green's text remains current, and it is still in print. In this discipline, the publishing date has little bearing on the contemporary applicability. Fisher's (1935) tool box contains the fundamental basics of statistical and design tools, and even at this early stage in the development of experimental design Fisher realized the value of permutation/randomization tests. However, it was only the advent of high-speed microcomputers that made these tests feasible and routine (see the subsection on Nontraditional Statistics, above).

Additional practical discussions of experimental design for field biologists include Milliken and Johnson (1984), Hairston (1989), Skalski and Robson (1992), and Hayek (1994). Two books, Fry (1993) and Scheiner and Gurevitch (1993), address a remarkable range of statistical design and analysis issues in the context of real examples of current research interest and high relevancy to biology and field ecology.

The need for valid experimental designs for environmental monitoring has been emphasized (Leibetrau 1979; Hurlbert 1984; Millard and Lettenmaier 1986; Stewart-Oaten et al. 1986; Legendre et al. 1989; Keith 1990; Eberhardt and Thomas 1991; Rose and Smith 1992; Underwood 1994). Because water quality is of major public concern and represents important issues in environmental policy and politics, experimental designs and sampling protocols for aquatic ecosystems have attracted much more attention than have those for terrestrial landscapes (Montgomery and Hart 1974; Leibetrau 1979; Loftis and Ward 1980; Casey et al. 1983; Hirsch and Slack 1984; Ward and Loftis 1986; Ward et al. 1986, 1990; Perry et al. 1987; Sanders et al. 1987; Hirsch 1988; Taylor and Loftis 1989). Advancements made in the monitoring of water quality include the statistical treatment of data at or below detection limits (Gleit 1985; Porter et al. 1988; Helsel 1990).

Eberhardt (1976), Hurlbert (1984), Eberhardt and Thomas (1991), and Underwood (1991, 1992, 1994) have reviewed the issues and brought renewed attention to the difficulties of achieving true replication in ecological experiments and environmental field settings. The problems encountered in meeting the assumptions and challenges of experimental design principles have been recognized for some time by researchers outside of laboratory settings (Campbell 1957; Stanley 1961; Campbell and Stanley 1963; Cook and Campbell 1979). Campbell and his colleagues refer to environmental and social experiments as quasi-experimental designs. Milliken and Johnson (1989) provide a discussion and practical guidance for the analysis of unreplicated experiments. All the references in this paragraph should be required reading for serious field biologists.

Experimental design has been routinely applied to ecological field studies for both manipulative and mensurative experiments (Hurlbert 1984). Mensurative experiments are defined by Hurlbert (1984) as involving the making of measurements at one or more points in space or time. Space or time is the only experimental treatment. There is no imposition or manipulation of external factors on the experimental units to constitute a treatment. "The defining feature of a manipulative experiment is that the different experimental units receive different treatments and that the assignment of treatments to experimental units is or can be randomized." If true randomization of experimental treatments by manipulative assignment cannot be achieved, then replicates are not independent. Hurlbert called this pseudoreplication, and the testing of treatment effects occurs with an error term inappropriate to the hypothesis being considered. The validity of using unreplicated treatments rests on the tenuous assumption that all experimental units are identical at the start of the experiment or manipulation and that they remain identical (with respect to the treatment) throughout the experiment. Therefore, it follows that the experimenter would not know if the finding or not finding of significance was due to treatment effects or some unknown factor related to the experimental plots not being identical. Hairston (1989) also reviews and discusses issues of ecological field experiments and the potential problems involved.

Pseudoreplication. Pseudoreplication can arise in a variety of ways (Hurlbert 1984), and it is worthwhile for field biologists to review the concept.

1. Replicates are not independent
    a. treatments are spatially or temporally segregated
    b. treatments are correlated, interconnected, or somehow related
    c. "replicates" are samples from a single experimental unit (i.e., subsamples)
2. Nonindependent (nonrandom) assignment of treatments
3. Lack of interspersion
4. Sequential samples for each experimental unit are taken over each of several days
5. Dates are considered replicates of treatments
6. True replicates are pooled prior to analysis
    a. an unfortunate loss of information on the variance among treatment replicates
    b. reduces degrees of freedom and power of analysis
7. Combining variance *among* replicates with variance *within* replicates (subsamples) produces confounding and unknown effects

Components of an Experimental Design. There are four considerations in an experimental design: controls/treatments, randomization, replication, and interspersion.

The terminology of controls can be used in a variety of ways. A control is any treatment against which one or more treatments is compared (Hurlbert 1984).

1. Receives no treatment. This is the familiar identification of a "control."

2. A before-treatment control can also be used as the experimental unit before a treatment is imposed.

3. Regulation of experimental conditions. Controls may refer to the establishment of homogeneous experimental units, the precision of treatment procedures, or the regulation of the physical or chemical environment.

4. A procedural effect control is used to evaluate the effects of a procedure that accompanies a treatment but whose effects are not under investigation or to eliminate confounding effects. Needle injection and the psychological control of placebos are common examples.

5. Temporal change controls are used to monitor potential temporal changes to experimental units.

6. Experimental design features can be used as controls to minimize the effects of sources of confusion in experiments and include randomization, replication, and interspersion (Hurlbert 1984).

Randomization ensures that errors are independent and normally distributed. This guards against experimenter bias and systematic and correlated errors and ensures knowledge of α (the p-value that is necessary for determining significance).

Replication controls for stochastic factors (random error) that are introduced by experimenter-generated variability, inherent or initial variability among experimental units, or chance events affecting an experiment in progress.

Interspersion controls for known or unknown spatial variation due to spatial heterogeneity or environmental gradients for either initial conditions or chance events affecting an experiment in progress. Interspersion also controls for experimenter bias and assures statistical independence.

BA/CI Experimental Designs

Before and after/control and impact (BA/CI) experimental designs address the pseudoreplication issue in environmental or ecological field experiments and were originally discussed by Green (1979). BA/CI designs involve taking samples before the impact (e.g., effluent discharge) begins and after it takes place at both control and impact sites. Sampling is replicated in time. In 1979 I designed a study to test habitat selection parameters in neotropical migrant birds in southern Illinois oak-hickory upland forests. The design was to test the null hypothesis that subcanopy or small understory trees do not affect nest site selection in these species. The study was to take place on lands purchased or leased by a coal company for strip-mining. Six large similar tracts of forest lands were available. Four 20-hectare study plots were placed in the central portion of four forest tracts (randomly determined). The four plots were randomly assigned as two control and two treatment plots. The treatment consisted of the removal of subcanopy trees. The study was designed such that birds would be surveyed for two breeding seasons in all four plots before treatment. The trees would be cut in the two treatment plots in the fall following the second survey season. The breeding bird surveys would continue for two more years in all four plots. Differences between control and treatment could be compared as variance components with time as a "replicate." Funding cuts, however, prevented the implementation of the project.

Stewart-Oaten et al. (1986) designed a similar study to assess experimentally the effects of point source effluent discharge into aquatic ecosystems, but their design had only one control-treatment contrast. The authors review the concept and applicability of BA/CI and provide a rich source of references. A similar BA/CI design was used to assess the effects of nuclear reactor coolant effluent on kelp forests off the coast of southern California (Schroeter et al. 1993). Osenberg et al. (1994) and Thrush et al. (1994) further discuss the BA/CI concept in environmental monitoring.

Underwood (1994) has reviewed and rejected the BA/CI design whenever it has a single control location and therefore no spatial assessment of variance components. Underwood (1994) recommends asymmetrical designs where several control locations are used to assess a given treatment effect. In this way, not only can environmental impacts or changes be assessed in the traditional fashion (e.g., trends in mean population density) but, additionally, impacts that alter temporal variance can be detected, because temporal interaction terms can be statistically tested.

Sampling Design

Technical guidance for sampling is available (Cochran 1977; Elliott 1977; Williams 1978; Desu and Raghavarao 1990; Thompson 1992). An excellent introduction that should be read by all field biologists is Stuart (1984). Nested quadrat designs are typically used to determine the most efficient size of the primary sample unit (Greig-Smith 1964; Kent and Coker 1992). Sample unit size makes no difference in the case of randomly distributed organisms, while with clumped organisms, smaller sample unit size results in estimates with increased precision.

The importance of large sample sizes is that statistical analyses are robust to violations of assumptions when they are based on a large number of error degrees of freedom. There are two reasons for this. Sample means from even nonnormal and heavily skewed distributions approach normal distributions as sample size increases, a consequence of the central limit theorem. The F-statistic, which determines statistical significance, increases as error degrees of freedom increase, and as a result significance can be determined with smaller differences between (among) population means. For all practical purposes, sample size and not the fraction of the population sampled determines the precision of an estimate. In a well-designed sampling and statistical design, three replicates per treatment combination are generally sufficient. An easily derived expression for estimating required sample size is found in (Eckblad 1991):

$$\text{Sample size} \sim (t_{\alpha})(\text{var})/(\text{acc x mean})^2$$

where t = t-value from t-table at the desired α level, var = sample variance, acc = accuracy as desired proportion from the true mean, and mean = sample mean.

King (1980, 1981) provides a good introduction and practical guidance for sampling strategies based on statistical distributions and probability charts. The statistical distributions covered are uniform, normal, lognormal, binomial, chi-square, Weibull, gamma, extreme value, logarithmic extreme value, reciprocal functions, and hazard rate functions.

Ecological Design

The statistical rigor of Hurlbert's (1984) conclusions are undeniable. However, in practical field evaluations of treatment-control effects and using common sense, it is routinely observed that treatment-effect differences are much greater than potential effects relevant to inherent differences in experimental plots.

The term "ecological design" is more appropriate and is recommended as a less ambiguous replacement for the following terminology—experimental design, quasi-experimental design, sampling design, or research design—when used in the context of ecological field experiments or ecological/environmental assessment and monitoring protocols. Ecological design would include field designs that are "true" manipulative experimental designs, unreplicated experiments, sampling protocols, and the field design issues addressed by Eberhardt and Thomas (1991).

Basic Principles of Ecological Design and Analysis

Green (1979) introduces ten principles of research design and analysis that merit discussion.

1. Clearly and completely communicate to your audience or readers the objectives of your study, the statement of your hypothesis, and the formulation of your ecological design, sampling strategy, field methods, and statistical analyses procedures. These concepts must be tightly integrated throughout the entire project. For example, it is invalid to change objectives or hypotheses partway into a project, because the experimental or sampling design may no longer be applicable. Despite the logic, intuition, and necessity of this approach, these fundamentals are commonly violated (Rose and Smith 1992). Once the objectives and approach of your study have been determined, it is advised to seek peer review or design/analysis expertise.

2. Sample replication is required for each combination of treatment-control comparisons or any other controlled variable. Differences between spatial and/or temporal comparisons (and their interactions) can only be determined by comparisons of variability between treatments and controls to variability within treatments and controls. This is the basis of the F-statistic (in ANOVA) or some multivariate analog of it.

3. An equal number of random replicate samples should be taken for each combination of controlled variables (treatments-control). Sampling in "convenient," "representative," or "typical" locations is not random sampling. Random sampling ensures independence of sampling errors, an important assumption of statistical inference. Glass et al. (1972) demonstrate that correlated errors represent the most serious violation to the validity of significance tests.

Most statistical analyses can be conducted with unequal sample sizes, and typical examples include one-way ANOVA and linear regression. Complex ANOVA designs without equal sample sizes can also be easily analyzed with modern computer statistical packages because the complex algorithms and calculations required remain transparent to the user. However, in complex ANOVA, especially factorial designs, equal sample sizes are required for unambiguous interpretation of interaction components of variance and overall effects.

4. To test if a condition or treatment has an effect, sampling must be conducted where the condition is present and where the condition is absent, while everything else is the same. An effect or treatment can only be demonstrated by statistical comparison with a control.

Although this principle is obvious in theory and forms the basis of experimental design, it is controversial in applications of typical field studies (e.g., see Hurlbert 1984).

5. A pilot study is well worth the time and resources invested. Preliminary sampling provides a basis for evaluating sample sizes, statistical power, parameters of sampling design, statistical analysis options, and the logistics and fine-tuning of field methods.

6. Verify if sampling design has adequate and equal efficiency over the entire range of sampling conditions encountered. If there is a variation or bias in the spatial, temporal, or population representativeness you are sampling, treatment comparisons are biased and invalid. For example, suppose you are interested in comparing acorn production by white oaks as a function of canopy closure. Because open forest canopies possess denser ground cover vegetation, one has to ensure that the sampling efficiency of acorns on the ground is independent of ground cover. A temporal example would be an interest in seeing if fish abundance and diversity changed with time in a specific stretch of stream. If a different mesh size in the seine was used on two different occasions, the temporal comparisons are invalid. Similarly, if electroshocking was used on two different occasions when the conductivity of the water was different, temporal comparisons are biased. Animals that become "trap-happy" or "trap-shy" alter the representation of the population being sampled.

7. Stratify sampling in heterogeneous environments. This is also known as blocking in an experimental design. Spatial heterogeneity is typical in all field situations involving ecological experiments, and the experimental design should accommodate this reality (see Dutilleul 1993; Thrush et al. 1994). If a given area to be sampled has a large-scale environmental pattern, the area should be classified into subareas or plots (stratas) that form more homogeneous units. Strata should be constructed such that within-strata variances are minimized while between-strata variances are maximized. The sampling effort should be allocated in proportion to the area of each of the identified plots. The main purpose of stratifying is to increase statistical power by controlling for variance between subplots—reducing within-plot variance and therefore the denominator in the F-statistic.

When it is suspected that sources of variation are hierarchical or on very small scales, nested or subsampling designs are most appropriate.

8. Verify that the size of the sample unit is appropriate to the size, density, and spatial distribution of the organism that is being sampled. Estimate the number of replicates required to obtain a desired level of precision. An important fact of reality is that logistic and economic considerations often determine the size and number of sampling units. As a general rule, fewer large samples are cheaper and/or easier to collect than many small ones. However, from the perspective of sampling theory, many small samples are usually statistically more valid than a few large ones. An important consideration is that results of statistical analyses should be independent of sample size.

9. Test data for adherence to statistical assumptions. Data should be tested to determine if error variation is normally distributed, homogeneous, and independent of the mean. In the case of most field data, these assumptions do not hold, but for practical purposes parametric inference is robust (see subsection on Robustness, above). A number of options are available to the investigator: appropriate data transformation, use nonparametric statistics, use resampling statistics, use an appropriate sequential sampling design, and test against simulated null hypothesis data.

Testing serious deviations from assumptions belongs in the realm of exploratory data analysis. Scatterplots or histograms of raw data, error terms (residuals), and sample variances and covariances provide the best insight into variance heterogeneity. Bartlett's test may be too sensitive to be of practical value (Harris 1975). Sokal and Rohlf (1994) recommend treating the ratio of the largest to the smallest sample variance as an F-statistic and an alternative to Bartlett's test.

Heterogeneity of error variances decreases the power of the analysis, resulting in a higher probability of a Type II error (Cochran 1947). When groups with the larger variances have larger sample sizes, the statistical test employed is more conservative (i.e., the p-value, or α, is in reality smaller than believed; Glass et al. 1972). On the other hand, when groups with the larger variances have smaller sample sizes, the test is more liberal (p-value, or α, is effectively larger).

10. Having chosen the best statistical methods to test your hypothesis, stick with the results of your analyses. It is incorrect and not statistical inference to select a posteriori statistical methods or significance levels to "statistically verify" what you wish your data to demonstrate.

Common Problems in Ecological Design and Analysis

The following is summarized from experience and the references used in this chapter. Green (1979) and Fowler (1990) also provide reviews of the common problems encountered in statistical analyses.

1. Procedural errors almost always have more detrimental effects to the valid outcome of a project than experimental or statistical (sampling, measurement) errors (Lessler and Kalsbeek 1992). This is why a good, efficient sampling design is usually more effective than excessive sample sizes and even 100 percent sampling. Sampling intensity generally increases the occurrence of procedural errors. Procedural errors are those caused by carelessness, sloppy or inappropriate field methods, poor or inappropriate sampling design, lack of a quality assurance and control program, inexperience, fatigue, and mistakes in data collection or recording. Statistical analysis usually cannot control, or make adjustments for, procedural errors.

2. Assumption of independence among independent (predictor) variables. This is especially violated in multivariate statistics where there are many independent variables and several to many dependent variables. Environmental variables by their very nature and the interdependencies of ecological systems are usually (often very strongly) correlated.

3. Hypotheses and p-values (α) must be defined a priori. The null hypothesis can never be proved.

4. Random sampling is absolutely necessary to avoid the serious pitfall of biased sampling. If error terms are not independent, systematic or correlated errors may result, and significance tests are invalid. The nonindependence of error terms precludes us from knowing α.

5. A valid experimental design requires replication of all combinations of treatments and controls. This is usually only feasible and practical in laboratory and agricultural settings. True replication in most environmental field studies is difficult or impossible to realize. This problem has been thoroughly reviewed by Eberhardt (1976), Hurlbert (1984), and Eberhardt and Thomas (1991), but see Hawkins (1986). The case for pseudoreplication has probably been overstated on practical grounds, because field experiments to evaluate "effects" are usually designed such that the differences between treatments and controls typically far exceed the inherent or background environmental differences among experimental units and overshadow the "supposed" confounding effects of using pseudoreplicates instead of "true" replicates.

6. When obvious large-scale spatial variability is present, samples should be stratified. When small-scale heterogeneity is known or suspected, a nested sampling design should be used. In both cases the strategy is to reduce within-sample variance components. This reduces the error term in the F-statistic or its multivariate equivalent, effectively increasing the power of the analysis. This increases the validity of significance testing.

7. Avoid doing many separate t-tests. When you analyze all possible pairs of comparisons, you do not know the true value of α. Your alternatives are to use a priori orthogonal contrasts (Sokal and Rohlf 1994) or design a balanced multifactorial ANOVA. The latter design, with as low as three replicates per treatment combination, represents a powerful analysis because error term degrees of freedom are reasonably high and treatment interactions are tested. A less desirable alternative is to decrease the α-value (i.e., force the significance to be more conservative). This entails adjusting α by the Bonferroni procedure (Day and Quinn 1989; Zolman 1993) or the Dunn-Sidák procedure (Sokal and Rohlf 1994). The same problems arise when doing multiple comparisons of linear regressions. Fry (1993) recommends Bonferroni adjustments to calculate confidence intervals for predictions from regression equations.

8. When you have failed to reject your null hypothesis, calculate the power of your statistical design. Actually, a power test should have been conducted a priori as part of your overall experimental/sampling design. The failure to conduct a test for statistical power is potentially a serious concern in studies relevant to conservation biology and endangered species because a statistical assessment or monitoring program with low statistical power could fail to detect population trends or other experimental parameters of interest.

9. A posteriori multiple comparison tests (MCT) should be used with caution (Perry 1986; Tukey 1991). Adjusting α is also important. Follow the advice of Day and Quinn (1989) and Westfall and Young (1993). MCT are also discussed in Fry (1993), Zolman (1993), and Sokal and Rohlf (1994). A major problem with MCT is the use and determination of significance (adjustments to α). MCT should not be conducted when the main effect in an ANOVA is not significant. A priori orthogonal contrasts (Sokal and Rohlf 1994) and two-way ANOVA with interaction term are preferred alternatives to MCT.

10. Repeated measures or observations of the same individual or population are not independent events. Neither are field experiments where observations or data are spatially or otherwise correlated or collected from the same plot. Nonindependence of measures strongly violates parametric assumptions and requires special analysis (Gurevitch and Chester 1986; Crowder and Hand 1990; Roberts 1992).

11. When using statistical tests, particularly multivariate but also parametric ones, be aware of the assumptions the tests make, and test your data to evaluate them. Check raw data for homogeneity of sample variances. Check residuals for normality and independence of errors. The treatment of categorically dependent variables as continuous variables in an analysis is usually not recommended and should be approached with caution.

12. Interpret interaction effects in multiway ANOVAs correctly (Steel and Torrie, 1980; Fry 1993; Sokal and Rohlf 1994). The area times time interaction term in an ANOVA represents pseudoreplication (Hurlbert 1984).

13. Do not pool populations or plots without justification. Although Sokal and Rohlf (1994) provide guidance about when to pool data, it is not a generally recommended practice. Pooling results in the loss of variance estimates and reduces the degrees of freedom for the error term. Pooling also compounds treatment and population (plot) effects.

14. Avoid step-wise techniques (e.g., step-wise regression, step-wise discriminant analysis). Because environmental variables are usually highly correlated, the use of step-wise techniques to extract a ranking of predictor variables may produce spurious results that would not be relevant to any underlying environmental reality.

15. Be aware of confounding effects in your experimental design. Confounding effects of environmental variables are always present because of their high natural intercorrelations, including spatial and temporal relationships. This is the main reason that step-wise techniques should be avoided (Green 1979).

16. Qualitative data or bivariate data may often be equal to, or superior to, quantitative data and much more efficient and economical to collect. Ranked data may be more efficient (economical) to collect and may be superior to continuous data.

17. Do not conduct statistics on ratios. Ratios follow the Cauchy distribution, possess larger variance than either original variable, represent a biased estimate of the mean, and increase size-dependence when attempting to adjust for scale (summarized in Green 1979). Fleiss (1981) is the standard reference for statistical treatment of ratios.

18. The use, and more important the ease of use, of multivariate statistics has dramatically increased with the availability of modern, high-speed microcomputers and user-friendly software packages. The user is often conducting multivariate procedures without any idea of the fundamental mechanics of the analyses, much less the analyses assumptions and applicabilities. Multivariate techniques may be very sensitive (some more than others) to assumptions of multivariate normality, equivalent dispersion of covariance matrices (comparable to univariate homoscedasticity), and intercorrelation of predictor variables. The need for large sample sizes is the rule and rarely the exception, even with careful ecological designs and high-quality data sets. Discriminant analyses in particular are susceptible to widespread abuse and misunderstanding. See James and McCulloch (1990) for an overview of multivariate analysis and the reviews by Williams (1983) and Williams and Titus (1988) for discriminant analysis.

Designing an Ecological Monitoring Program

The design of any ecological or environmental monitoring program, including the monitoring of ecological indicators, specific taxa (e.g., amphibians), or populations (e.g., endangered species), requires a relatively rigid approach or protocol. This is especially important because costs are high, ecological risk may be at stake (e.g., extinction of a species or population), and temporal considerations are important (i.e., an invalid design or field methods or the collection of inappropriate data parameters relative to stated objectives is discovered several years into the program). The following protocol is recommended. The process will be discussed as an ecological or biological project, but the principles apply to any study. A complete protocol will be described, but the details would depend directly on specific objectives and the magnitude of the project. Obviously a global or detailed regional program would be several orders of magnitude more complex and expensive than a local, focused effort.

Scoping. The scoping process entails the gathering of the major players involved in the project, including sponsors, administrators, environmental managers, field biologists, statisticians (design and analysis), computer specialists (database management, programming requirements, GIS requirements), and those with other specialized expertise (e.g., legal, if legal isuues cannot be avoided). This stage also includes the delegation of specific duties whenever partnerships are involved, and Memorandums of Understanding (MOUs) are required. Regional studies are becoming increasingly common for a number of reasons: economics, avoidance of duplication, sharing of expertise and data, magnitude of project, higher chance of success, leveraging of funding opportunities, balancing of environmental-economic-social conflicts, and the need to share responsibilities and legal mandates. Regional approaches would typically include federal, state, and possibly local agencies; private parties, including property owners and conservation groups; and whatever additional technical and legal experts are required (e.g., consultants and academics). The scoping process assists in generating consensus, project purposes and goals, and individual responsibilities and sets the stage for project objectives.

Objectives. Project objectives are arguably the most important component of a monitoring program. It has been my experience that the failure to develop or follow explicit project objectives is the most common reason for the failure of both large- and small-scale monitoring projects. Objectives must be explicitly stated in a written form and are closely associated with the scoping process. Objectives determine project priorities, focus, and specifics.

Scale and Resolution. Scale and resolution are more specifically defined in landscape ecology terminology as extent and grain (see Krzysik, Chpt. 42, this volume). Extent is the largest spatial unit of the project (e.g., the state of Illinois, the Midwest region, or conterminous United States). Grain is the smallest resolvable unit for analysis (e.g., 1 square kilometer in an Advanced Very High Resolution Radiometer [see Krzysik, Chpt. 42, this volume] remotely sensed satellite image or sampling 1-square-meter quadrats for herbaceous plants).

Accuracy and Precision. The cost of a project is directly related to the accuracy and precision (repeatability) desired. High accuracy requires high precision, while measurements that are highly precise and possess low variance (sampling error) may not be accurate. Accuracy requires that the experimentally derived statistic is close to the "actual value." Accuracy and precision are mainly dependent on the phenomena under investigation. But also important is the experimental or sampling design and sample size. In other words, a poor design may be overcome with high sample sizes, or even better, fewer samples are usually required by a superior sampling design.

An important component of any project is the reporting of sampling or measurement error. A number of terms can be used, and the appropriate one is usually dictated by the project objectives and other specifics. Common statistics include variance, standard deviation, standard error, confidence interval, and coefficient of variation. It is important to report sample size, and sample size is required to convert between values of standard deviation and standard error.

Conceptualization. Project conceptualization means explorations or discussions of ideas with peers or expert consultants and a thorough literature review. The literature review should not be limited only to the subject material directly related to the project, but other potentially relevant literature sources in other disciplines should be searched. Experience and peer consultation are important at this stage.

Design. The design phase is highly project specific and directly dependent on objectives, scale and resolution, and accuracy and precision. The design phase may include experimental design, ecological design, and sampling design.

Field Methods. Field methods, or the implementation of the design, are directly dependent on objectives, scale and resolution, and accuracy and precision desired. They may also depend on the design. A frequent mistake is the confusion of using common methods and collecting common parameters. For example, say that you want to monitor changes in vegetation structure (physiognomy) throughout the United States in all representative plant communities. Canopy cover is an important environmental parameter in this context in any ecosystem. However, it is erroneously believed that only one method should be used throughout the sampling universe to measure this parameter. In reality, the parameter canopy cover should be measured in all ecosystems, but the method used depends upon the magnitude of canopy cover (e.g., 5 or 95 percent), its spatial variance and patchiness, its height, and plant form. We need different methods in different ecosystems because we want to optimize sampling efficiency, accuracy, and precision within each of the unique spatial contexts presented in each ecosystem. The consistent and accurate estimation of parameters with known sampling error is the important factor, not consistent methods. Another important consideration, not often recognized, is that individual field personnel may prefer or be experienced with specific techniques, and therefore sampling efficiency is improved.

Professional Review. At this stage it may be desirable to obtain a peer or expert review from one or more specialists who have had previous experience in similar projects before additional expenses are incurred or an invalid approach is implemented. These reviewers should have expertise in field ecology (including geographical and local habitats), expertise in statistical design/analysis, relevant taxonomy expertise, and project-specific specialties.

Economic and QAC Analyses. The economic and Quality Assurance and Control (QAC) analyses component is critical to the overall success of the project yet is usually overlooked or disregarded as being unimportant. A thorough economic analysis of the complete cost of the project is essential. If the project is allowed to proceed without adequate budget commitments, one or more of the following will of necessity be compromised (often severely): objectives, scale/resolution, accuracy or precision, design, field methods. A QAC analysis is necessary for minimizing procedural error. Procedural error refers to poor, sloppy, or inconsistent field techniques, calibrations, recording of data, and field notes; excessive fatigue; or just plain mistakes regarding data quality. For example, I have heard of a field crew that used machetes to get through the dense brush in placing permanent transects for monitoring vegetation, while a second crew was responsible for estimating habitat parameters along the same transects. Procedural errors usually produce greater errors than sampling (measurement) errors, and 100 percent surveys are often less accurate than well-designed sampling schemes because more effort may increase procedural error. Furthermore, procedural errors cannot be assessed with statistics, which deal only with sampling errors.

Reality Adjustments. Continuing a project while violating economic reality almost always means project failure or at best an exceedingly poor cost-benefit return. At this stage only three alternatives are possible: change objectives and/or scale/resolution and/or accuracy/precision, which usually requires changing the design and/or field methods; get more money; or quit.

It is inappropriate and invalid to make a project more economical by changing the design or field methods while maintaining original objectives, scale/resolution, and accuracy/precision, because by definition the original design and field methods were optimized to provide ecological validity, statistical sufficiency, and sampling economy, while meeting specified project objectives.

Professional Review. A peer or expert review is critical at this stage because the project is ready for implementation with economic and QAC analysis available.

Pilot Study. If the project is of such magnitude and scope that it represents a significant or exceptional commitment of resources in terms of dollars and personnel, then a pilot study is highly recommended to evaluate the design, field methods, logistics, and economics. A pilot study is important for at least six reasons: it is usually needed to obtain design parameters and identify details in field methods; it assesses project feasibility; it assesses economics and QAC; it identifies problem areas, unforeseen circumstances, or the unpredictable logistics of field projects; it provides data to assess or model project feasibility, realities of objectives, design parameters, and field methods; and it provides the foundations for database management.

Professional Review. A peer or expert review is desirable at this stage to assess the success and problem components of the pilot study, including an independent assessment of the success of the design and field methods to meet desired objectives and design parameters.

Implementation: Stage I. Stage I implementation represents a full-scale demonstration project and is used as a final test of project feasibility and economics. It also represents the final fine-tuning of the design and field methods, with lessons learned from the pilot study.

Professional Review. As in reviewing the pilot study results, it is important to receive an independent review of the demonstration project.

Implementation: Stage II. Stage II implementation represents the final and complete monitoring program. Care must be taken to adhere to final decided objectives and all lessons learned from the peer or expert reviewed pilot and demonstration projects. The continuation of QAC in both fieldwork and database management is important.

Analysis, Modeling, or Hypothesis Testing. The analysis, modeling, or hypothesis-testing phases of the project follow directly from the conceptualization and design phases and are directly related to project objectives.

Interpretation. Interpretation logically follows analysis, modeling, or hypothesis testing relative to the stated objectives of the project. It is dependent on the training, experience, knowledge base, and familiarity with the literature by the principal investigators and consultants working on the project.

Literature Search. The results of the analysis, modeling, or hypothesis testing and subsequent interpretation develop new knowledge and new questions. In this new light, an additional literature search is required.

Synthesis. The interpretation and additional information gained from the literature leads to the next logical step—the synthesis of all relevant information, both new and old, to fulfill or complete the objectives and goals of the project.

Preparation and Presentation of Results, Professional Meetings, Symposiums, Seminars, and Workshops. The synthesis is not the final step in the project but leads to the presentation of project findings and results at professional society meetings, symposia, seminars, or workshops. This is also the time for the preparation of technical reports, professional manuscripts, or books. The exact nature is completely dependent on project specifics.

Peer Review. Peer review follows the preparation of manuscripts, book chapters, and presentations.

Publications and Presentations. The relative technical merits or scientific relevance of the project may vary enormously, depending on which of the phases discussed above were most worthy. It may be that the sampling design, the development of new field methods, a novel modeling technique, or new methods of database management were the most relevant.

Conclusions and General Recommendations

1. Use common sense and clearly explain the hows and whys of your experiment: ecological design, statistical analyses, assumptions and how they were evaluated (tested) and met or compromised, spatial and temporal arrangements and details, sample sizes, degrees of freedom, statistical power, and treatment replicates.

2. State objectives clearly and stick to them. Probably the most common violation in monitoring programs is the poor, vague, unfocused, unrealistic, too general, or catch-all formulation of objectives. Sometimes projects will proceed without sponsor, peer group, and investigator's consensus. Sometimes objectives will be changed after the project design and implementation. All of these factors jeopardize the applicability of the original project design and analysis criteria. Therefore, the validity of project findings are tenuous. Clear statements of objectives are important for your audience, including reviewers and editors.

3. In the design and analysis of projects of any scope and magnitude, think a priori. On the contrary, data analyses procedures in most studies are determined a posteriori.

4. Take advantage of your expertise. You know the most about your project and the specific spatial, temporal, and taxa issues involved. It has been my experience that an experienced field biologist with some fundamental knowledge of good sampling design designs better and more practical field studies than a professional statistician with no field experience in the specific study being addressed. Particular field knowledge that is important in study design includes spatial heterogeneity and patterns, organism distribution patterns, sampling intensity requirements, execution or procedural error potential, and field logistics and techniques required.

5. Learn the fundamentals of experimental and sampling design.

6. Systematic (bias) and procedural errors are important in the execution of field sampling. These errors not only extend beyond statistical analysis but are usually difficult to recognize, especially by readers, reviewers, and editors.

7. Do a pilot study. This is a critical step in any project and could save a great deal of time and money. The pilot study generates estimates of design and analysis parameters (e.g., required sample sizes, sample stratification and efficiency, appropriateness of statistical methods) and identifies implementation problems (e.g., quality assurance and control, field logistics, methods).

8. Own more than one statistics book and be familiar with contemporary design and analysis issues, such as where there is consensus and where there is controversy.

9. Learn where and how to find and use information. Libraries provide books, journals, reports, and computer search services. Government agency reports are valuable sources of information and actual data and may provide especially detailed descriptions of experimental and sampling designs, analysis methods and justifications, and field methods. The Internet and its World Wide Web are exponentially becoming a source of information and data but need a great deal of refinement to increase their efficiency at locating specific data requirements.

10. Become familiar with experiments, sampling designs, and statistical methods in other disciplines. Today is the realm of the specialist. However, if you broaden your horizons, you can apply developments in other fields to advance your own discipline. The model used for producing a landscape surface of the distribution and density patterns of desert tortoise (*Gopherus agassizii*) populations (see Krzysik, Chpt. 42, this volume) was originally developed for hydrological modeling of soil erosion and sediment yields. Field ecology is particularly closely related to many disciplines, including geography, geology, hydrology, soil sciences, paleontology,

meteorology/climatology, and many areas of chemistry and physics.

11. Do not believe everything you read. Use common sense and think critically. Just because a journal article is peer reviewed does not guarantee its conclusions, or even that there is universal consensus in the research or resource management community. Due to today's high degree of specialization, it is not uncommon for cliques of reviewers to review each other's manuscripts. Peer-reviewed literature is not all good, and gray literature is not all bad (see Resetar, Chpt. 40, this volume). Agency and consultant reports are considered gray literature because in the majority of cases they receive little or no formal review.

12. Do not overdo statistics. In trying to influence and convince your audience, simplicity and directness are best, especially with administrators, policy makers, and decision makers. It is easy to lose the crowd in even simple statistical demonstrations and the subtleness of Type I and Type II errors and statistical significance, much less the intricacies of complex factorial designs and multivariate statistics. When the differences between population means greatly exceed standard deviations, graphical displays and not statistical inference are in order. Graphical displays should always be used for communicating statistical results and summaries, while tables should rarely be used (tables belong in an appendix for casual or intimate personal perusal). Typically the mean and its standard deviation (or confidence interval) and sample size are the desired statistics. The sample size must always be included so the reader can calculate standard errors, confidence intervals, and degrees of freedom.

13. In statistical analysis, there has been too much emphasis on inference and not enough attention paid to exploratory or descriptive statistics. Significance tests and p-values have been overused. Although this paradigm represents mainstream statistical analysis and all practitioners are guilty as charged, statisticians have been warning of the pitfalls for over a half century. There has been a mind-set that has pervaded ecology (possibly physics envy) that inference and hypothesis testing are the real science in ecology, while exploratory, descriptive, or graphical statistics are not. Data testing and the clear communication of data, interpretations, trends, and relevant summaries to policy makers and decision makers are equally important.

14. There is an important difference between biological or ecological significance and statistical significance, although this is often overlooked. Biological or ecological significance represents biological realism and common sense directly relevant to actual ecological systems. Statistical significance is only relevant to sample size in the specific context of the probability of finding an observed difference by chance alone relative to the inherent variability in the system under investigation.

Summary

This chapter identifies some important principles and issues in experimental design and statistical analysis relevant to field biologists and ecologists, researchers, and environmental managers designing and implementing ecological assessment or monitoring programs. The emphasis is on areas of common pitfalls, confusion, and misapplications. A rich and diverse source of literature is provided. Topics covered include issues and approaches to statistical analyses, efficient statistical inference, statistical power, the abuse of statistical significance tests, issues in experimental design, pseudoreplication, sampling design, basic principles of ecological design and analysis, common problems in ecological design and analysis, and general recommendations. General principles are developed for designing and implementing an ecological or environmental monitoring program. The term "ecological design," when used in the context of ecological field experiments or ecological and environmental assessment and monitoring protocols, is recommended as a less ambiguous replacement for the following terminology: experimental design, quasi-experimental design, sampling design, or research design.

42

Geographic Information Systems, Landscape Ecology, and Spatial Modeling

Anthony J. Krzysik

The objective of this chapter is to introduce the technologies and applications of Geographic Information Systems (GIS), landscape ecology, and spatial modeling to field biologists and herpetologists. The approach is to provide fundamental concepts, examples of applications, and a great deal of selected references for both concepts and examples. A detailed example is presented for spatial modeling of the distribution/density patterns of a vertebrate population on landscape scales by using an interpolation-smoothing algorithm originally developed for hydrological and sediment-yield modeling.

Field herpetologists best know their populations, communities, and specific nuances of habitat. The motivation for this chapter was that the information presented would enable them to reflect on their research design problems and needs and ask more interdisciplinary questions; dig deeper into the literature in unfamiliar books, reports, and journals; and acquire new technologies for their toolbox. In the spatial-temporal context provided by these technologies, important strategies, analyses, and methods could be developed, including identification of appropriate (or inappropriate) habitat features (parameters, elements, patterns), sampling design and site selection, predictive capabilities for taxa distribution, assessment and monitoring of populations, and visual interpretations and demonstrations.

Cartography, or mapping, has played an important role in understanding the ecology and classification of natural systems (Tosi 1964; Wikin and Ironside 1977; Brown et al. 1979, 1980; Bailey 1980, 1983, 1987, 1988, 1996; Rowe and Sheard 1981; Driscoll et al. 1984; Kuchler and Zonneveld 1988). A good introduction for field ecologists and biologists for land surveying and using a compass is Sipe (1979), and a review of methods for mapping and surveying is provided by Ritchie et al. (1988).

Excellent introductions to GIS, the technologies involved, and GIS applications are available (Burrough 1986; Star and Estes 1990; Tomlin 1990; Antenucci et al. 1991; Aronoff 1991; Maguire 1991; Bernhardsen 1992; Johnson et al. 1992; Laurini and Thompson 1992; Berry 1993; Environmental Systems Research Institute [ESRI] 1993; McLaren and Braun 1993; Haines-Young et al. 1993; Korte 1994). Another excellent, but expensive, advanced comprehensive review and encyclopedic treatment is Maguire et al. (1991a,b). There are even books available to assist project managers and administrators in GIS-related issues (Aronoff 1991; Cassettari 1993; Obermeyer and Pinto 1994; Polaris Conferences 1994; Huxhold and Levinson 1995). Maguire et al. (1991c) provide a summary of available textbooks and professional journals that are devoted to GIS.

The integration of GIS with knowledge-based systems (Coulson et al. 1987; Coulson et al. 1991; Smith and Jiang 1991) or with a suite of remote sensing, statistical analysis, ecological modeling, and traditional software (e.g., word processing, spreadsheet, database management) modules (Skole et al. 1993) has a great deal of potential for natural resources management. A comprehensive survey of GIS applications in environmental modeling is presented in Goodchild et al. (1993, 1996).

What Are GIS?

GIS are computer systems consisting of hardware and software for the purpose of inputting, storing, manipulating, classifying, transforming, analyzing, modeling, summarizing, and displaying spatially referenced data and information. Information systems can be defined as a collection of data and tools (e.g., hardware and software) for the purpose of deriving "information" that is not readily apparent from the individual data elements in the database (Laurini and Thompson 1992). Typical and powerful platforms for GIS are minicomputers, a popular one being the Sun-SPARC workstation. GIS are also available for PC and Macintosh microcomputers, including versions of minicomputer-based systems. Microcomputers have reached the speeds, memory, and hard drive capabilities of former minicomputer workstations, and the trend continues. Widespread and routine applications of GIS by nonspecialists may depend on these microcomputer platforms.

GIS are information systems that include quantitative spatial data (parameters for location, position, topological connections, and spatial relationships) and qualitative descriptive data for attributes (information about the spatial parameters). GIS deal with spatially explicit data in a digitized format and combine and/or transform existing variables into new variables. GIS can theoretically be applied to any spatial scale, from solar, global, continental, and national to molecular-level topology, and everything in between. However, the problem with these extreme examples of scale is the acquisition, storage, and registration of accurate and relevant spatial data. Traditional uses for GIS are geographical applications at landscape and regional scales, but the use of GIS at continental and global scales is rapidly increasing as data sets become available and the storage of data at terrabyte capacity becomes more economical. A functional feature of GIS is to convert data among different map scales, cartographic projections, and geographic coordinate systems.

Maps and Scales

All maps must include a scale legend. Bar scales provide the exact linear relationship between distances on the map to actual distances on the earth's surface. An areal scale represents area and is therefore represented by squares or circles. A map scale of "2.64 inches equals 1 mile" means that a 1-inch distance between two points on the map indicates that the two points are in reality separated by 0.38 of a mile on the earth's surface. The scale in this particular example is referred to as 1:24,000 or 1/24,000 = 2.64 inches per mile/(12 inches per foot times 5,280 feet per mile). A map that was 80 centimeters by 80 centimeters at this scale would cover a total area of 364 kilometers. Table 42-1 shows common map scales, their linear equivalents, and typical applications. Table 42-2 defines spatial scales relevant to geographical ecology; see also Delcourt and Delcourt (1988) and Delcourt and Delcourt (1992). Fundamental introductions to using maps include American Society of Civil Engineers (1983), Thompson (1987), Monmonier (1991), Muehrcke and Muehrcke (1992), and Wood (1992). Aerial mapping is reviewed by Falkner (1994).

Global Reference System

Latitude and longitude can be used to locate exact positions on the earth's surface. Latitude circles are called parallels, and longitude circles are called meridians. Parallels and meridians form a gridded network called a graticule. Approaching the poles, circles of parallels become smaller and converge to form a point, and meridians become more closely spaced and similarly converge to a point. In reference to the earth's axis passing through the poles, the origin of the latitude-longitude coordinate system (0, 0) is the intersection of the equator and the prime meridian. The most commonly used reference for the prime meridian is the Greenwich Prime Meridian, which passes through Greenwich, England. Latitude and longitude are traditionally measured in degrees, minutes, and seconds. For latitude, 0° is at the equator, 90° is at the North Pole, and -90° is at the South Pole. For longitude, the 0° meridian begins at the North Pole, passes through Greenwich, and ends at the South Pole. Longitude is measured positively up to 180° east of Greenwich and negatively up to 180° west of Greenwich. Some countries may use different prime meridians.

Longitude and latitude cannot be used to measure distances on the earth's surface. In this spherical coordinate system, positions are related to angles from the earth's center, while accurate distance metrics require a planar coordinate system. Only along the equator does the distance associated with one degree of longitude approximate the distance associated with one degree of latitude, because the equator is the only parallel whose radius equals that of meridians. This Global Reference System is not a map projection (discussed in a later section) but serves as reference positions on the earth's surface for all available map projections.

Table 42-1. Common map scales, map to landscape relationships, and typical map uses. Data from Ruiz and Messersmith (1990).

Map Scale	Cm/Km[1]	Inches/Mile	Typical Map Uses
1:1,200	83.35	52.80	Master planning
1:4,800	20.84	13.20	Master planning
1:15,840	6.314	4.000	Foresters and SCS[2]
1:20,000	5.001	3.168	SCS soil maps
1:24,000	4.168	2.640	USGS[3] 7.5' maps
1:25,000	4.000	2.534	DMA[4] special maps
1:50,000	2.000	1.267	DMA special maps
1:62,500	1.601	1.014	USGS, 15' maps
1:100,000	0.999	0.633	USGS, 30' x 1°
1:250,000	0.399	0.253	USGS, 1° x 2°
1:1,000,000	0.0995	0.063	USGS, 4° x 6°
1:2,000,000	0.0505	0.032	USGS, National Atlas

[1] Data calculated from inches/mile column.
[2] SCS = Soil Conservation Service.
[3] USGS = U.S. Geological Survey.
[4] DMA = Defense Mapping Agency, Hydrographic/Topographic Center.

Cartographic Projections

Cartographic projection is a transformation process that produces a systematic arrangement of the earth's spherical or geographic coordinate system onto a plane (Dent 1990). In essence, a projection is the mathematical transformation or modeling of a three-dimensional surface (the earth) and representing it in two dimensions (a map). For spatial scales on the order of a few square kilometers, projection is unimportant, because the curvature of the earth is negligible for small areas. For spatial scales ranging from 1,000 to 100,000 square kilometers, map projection becomes necessary.

The interest in map projections coincided with the transition between the Middle Ages and the Renaissance (mid-1400s to mid-1600). Lambert developed at least seven map projections in 1772. The history of cartographic projection is extensively summarized in Snyder (1993).

The earth is usually depicted as a smooth sphere, where planar intersections produce circles. In reality, the surface of the earth is highly irregular because of variations in gravity, crust thickness, rock or mineral density, and topography. Additionally, rotational centrifugal forces make the earth bulge at the equator and flatten at the poles. For small-scale maps, the representation of the earth as a sphere is adequate, but for large-scale maps (i.e., 1:1,000,000 or more) the earth must be represented as a spheroid (ellipsoid) with major and minor axes of different diameters (semimajor and semiminor refer to radii) and where planar intersections produce ellipses. The most commonly used parameters for spheroid representation of the earth were surveyed by Clarke in 1866 and are known as the North American Datum 1927 (NAD27). Recently, satellite-measured spheroids are starting to replace ground-based measurements. The ARC/INFO GIS support twenty-six reference spheroids.

Cartographic projection distorts one or more of the properties of shape, area, distance, or direction. Maps can be made using specific projections that preserve desired properties. Conformal maps preserve shape at local scales (no map projection can preserve shapes at large scales), equal-area maps maintain areas at the same map scale, equidistant maps preserve distances between specified points, and true-direction or azimuthal projections give the correct directions or azimuths of all points on the map with respect to its center. The map legend should provide the name of the projection used, along with relevant parameters. The ARC/INFO GIS support over forty-six projections.

Map projections are classified by the projection surface used. Conic, cylindrical, and planar are surfaces

Table 42-2. Definition of scale and associated terminology

Scale	Terminology	Spatial Extent (km^2)	Map Scale	Environmental Features
Micro	Habitat	< 1	< 1:1000	Microhabitats
Meso	Landscape	$1–10^4$	1:1000–1:100,000	Pattern-mosaics, environmental gradients
Macro	Regional	$10^4–10^6$	1:100,000–1:1,000,000	Physiography, elevation
Mega	Global	$> 10^6$	> 1:1,000,000	Ecoregions

Notes: Scale terminology from Delcourt and Delcourt (1988). Local scales refer to the smaller range of landscape scales. Map scale based on the entire spatial extent occupying a 1-by-1-meter map.

most commonly used because they can be flattened without surface distortion, but other classes of projections for specific applications are also possible. Another consideration is the nature of the contact of the projection surface with the sphere (earth). For example, imagine placing a tennis ball (representing the earth) on a large ice-cream cone whose opening is the same size as the tennis ball. This represents a conic projection tangent at the equator (or any latitude could be used, comparable to using a smaller cone), and the tangential circular line is called the standard parallel. Parallel lines of latitude are projected onto the cone as rings, while meridians (longitude) are projected that converge at the apex. The cone can be cut at any desired meridian to produce the final conic projection. The meridian opposite the cut becomes the central meridian. Because distortion increases north and south of the tangency parallel, this projection would be more useful for midlatitude zones. A more complex conic projection, a secant conic projection, could intersect the globe at two locations and would be defined by two standard parallels. Imagine the ice-cream cone centered on a holographic image of a tennis ball. A still more complex conic projection, an oblique conic projection, would be produced when the cone axis does not line up with the global polar axis. An equidistant conic projection would have evenly spaced parallels and would represent equal distances in the north-south directions, but the projection would not be conformal or equal-area. In the Lambert Conic Conformal projection, the central parallels are spaced closer than those at the border, preserving small geographic shapes. The Albers Equal-Area Conic projection spaces northern and southern parallels closer than the central parallels and displays equivalent areas.

Cylindrical projections (a cylinder replaces the cone) can also have a tangency line or two secancy lines around the globe. Two commonly used cylindrical projections are the Mercator and Transverse Mercator. In Mercator projections, the equator represents the line of tangency (cylinder parallel to polar axis), and the meridians are equally spaced (true east and west scales). In Transverse Mercator projections, meridians are used as the lines of tangency (cylinder perpendicular to polar axis), and parallels remain equally spaced (true north and south scales). Secant intersections and oblique cylinder projections are also possible, as in conic projections.

Planar projections (azimuthal) represent a plane touching the globe (tangent point) with polar, equatorial, or oblique aspects. The polar planar projection is commonly used in polar regions. Secant projections are not commonly used and represent the intersection of the plane and globe. The perspective from which spherical data are projected onto a flat surface determines spatial distortion. There are three perspectives used in planar projections: gnomonic projection—center of the earth; stereographic projection—the surface point directly opposite the tangential point (i.e., the South Pole if the planar contact was the North Pole); or orthographic projection—"infinity," a point external from the globe such as a planet or satellite.

For larger scales, such as those on the order of 1:500,000 or 1:1,000,000 or more, projections such as the Albers Equal-Area Conic or Lambert Azimuthal Equal-Area are used to minimize distortion in topological features (Star and Estes 1990).

For additional details and information concerning cartographic projections see American Cartographic

Association (1986, 1988), Snyder (1987, 1993), Dent (1990), Muehrcke and Muehrcke (1992), and ESRI (1994).

Geographic Coordinate Systems

Spatial analysis of GIS data requires that all map layers or themes must be registered to a common coordinate system. Registration represents the association of all parameters with a defined coordinate system or to a reference point, object, or grid that is registered to a coordinate system. The essence of GIS is that all input data are referenced to a two- or three-dimensional coordinate grid, and in all subsequent analyses or modeling, all data parameter sets are registered to identical reference coordinates, spatial scales, and cartographic projections to guarantee that output data are spatially accurate. There are four commonly used geographic coordinate systems.

Cartesian coordinate geometry is a system of intersecting perpendicular lines in plane space and the precise specification of location (Dent 1990). The Cartesian system is applicable in two or three dimensions with location points or raster cell (two-dimensional) data specified by x-y-z coordinates. Cartesian coordinates are useful for finding the relative distance and direction between two or more map features, but features cannot be directly related to specific features on the earth's surface unless the Cartesian system is itself geo-referenced. A common usage of Cartesian coordinates is with raw satellite imagery raster data (e.g., 20-meter, 80-meter, 1-kilometer cells), which eventually must be registered to specific earth features.

The Geographic or Latitude-Longitude coordinate system consists of parallels (latitude) and meridians (longitude), and coordinates are measured in degrees, minutes, and seconds. Any projection can be used for this grid, but in the Geographic Resources Analysis Support System (GRASS; see below), the Plate-Carree projection—where the equator is the standard parallel, the meridians are spaced the same distance as the parallels, and the origin is the intersection of the equator and the prime meridian (generally Greenwich, but prime meridians vary with countries)—is used. The projected grid consists of square cells, north-south coordinates range from 0° to 90°, and east-west coordinates range from 0° to 180°. For analysis and modeling applications, it is convenient to express values in decimal degrees, decimal minutes, or decimal seconds: 54° 20' 15" is equivalent to 54.334 degrees, 3260.25 minutes, or 195,615 seconds.

The State Plane coordinate system (SPCS) is a rectangular system of x-y coordinates defined by the U.S. Geological Survey (USGS) and is unique to each state. In order to minimize projection distortion, each state was divided into two to eight zones (Muehrcke and Muehrcke 1992). Each zone has its own central meridian, and the meridian's (false) origin is established in the southwest of the zone, usually 2 million feet (610 kilometers) west of the central meridian. States whose longest axis runs east-west (e.g., Iowa) use the Lambert Conformal Conic projection for a basis, while states whose longest axis runs north-south (e.g., Illinois) use the Transverse Mercator projection. Coordinates are measured in feet. On newer USGS 7.5' topo maps, SPCS tick marks are shown at 10,000-foot intervals.

The Universal Transverse Mercator (UTM) coordinate system is used for military maps, for spatial modeling, and commonly for maps representing scales of 1:1,000 to 1:250,000. The UTM system divides the earth into sixty longitudinal zones, each being 6° (360 divided by 60) of longitude in width and extending from 84° north to 80° south. The zones are numbered one to sixty eastward from the 180° meridian (e.g., 0° being the Greenwich meridian). Ten zones (numbers ten through nineteen) are represented in the United States, zone ten beginning at 126° longitude and zone nineteen ending at 66° longitude (Muehrcke and Muehrcke 1992). To minimize distortion, each zone is developed from a section of the ellipsoidal Transverse Mercator projection, known as the UTM projection. UTM coordinates are in meters and are referred to as easting and northing. The central meridian of each zone has an easting value of 500,000. Easting values greater than 500,000 lie east of the central meridian, while values less than 500,000 lie west of the central meridian. In the northern hemisphere, northing is expressed as the distance from the equator in meters. A UTM coordinate is identified by four values: easting, northing, zone, and hemisphere (e.g., 563,022E 3,777,019N 11N). The example used locates within 1 meter a Weber grill in the backyard of 61737 Apt. B, Desert Air Road, Joshua Tree, California, in the southern Mojave Desert. The coordinates were determined by a GPS (Global Positioning System), Rockwell International PLGR (Precision Lightweight GPS Receiver, AN/PSN-11). The accuracy is stated at ± 15 meters, but in calibration tests, consistent precision of 1 to 5 meters was achieved. UTM tick marks or grid lines are found on newer USGS 7.5' topo maps at 1,000-meter intervals.

Four other coordinate systems may have important specific applications: Local or Alphanumeric Grid,

Universal Polar Stereographic (UPS), U.S. Army Military Grid Reference System (based on UTM and UPS), and World Geographical Reference System (GEOREF; Muehrcke and Muehrcke 1992).

Thematic Maps

GIS link map layers or themes of data/information. Each map layer is called a data layer, coverage, or thematic map. Thematic maps may represent vegetation or soil classifications, elevation, topographical features (slope, aspect), geological features, hydrology, species distributions, roads or utility lines, land use or ownership, political boundaries, or climatic parameters (Fig. 42-1). Thematic maps can represent choropleth or isopleth maps. Choropleths consist of polygons representing equal-valued parameters defined by sharp boundaries (e.g., counties or states) or at least the appearance of boundaries at the scale of coverage (e.g., plant communities or land-cover classes). Isopleths (isolines) display parameters by lines connecting points of equal value. Common geographical isopleths include topographic contours (elevation), temperature (annual mean, maximum, minimum), average degree days, number of annual frost-free days, mean annual precipitation, and annual potential or actual evapotranspiration. Thematic maps, therefore, consist of topologically linked geographic features and their descriptive data (attributes).

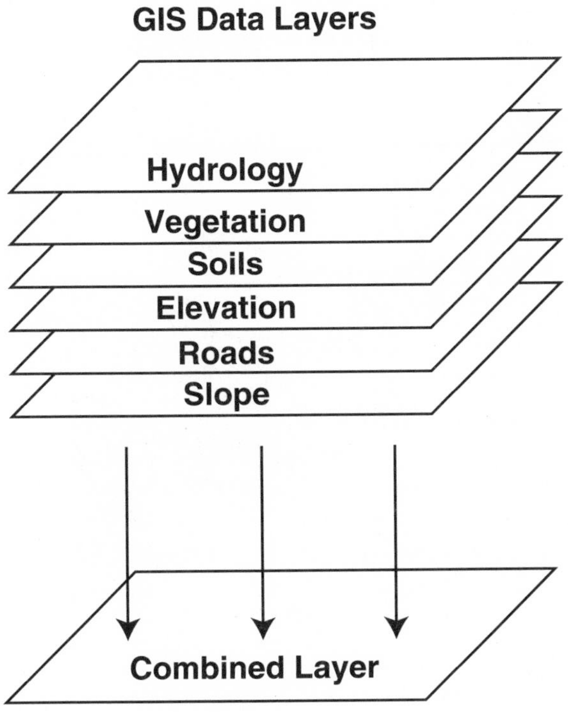

Figure 42-1. An illustration of GIS data layers, coverages, or thematic maps.

Vector and Raster GIS

GIS data can be inputted, stored, manipulated, and outputted in two fundamentally different ways, which are specific to the type of GIS used—raster or vector (McMaster and Shea 1992). In a raster-based system, each data point is represented by a cell located on a coordinate grid, and each cell has an attribute value. These grid cells are also known as pixels. Pixels, or picture elements, represent the smallest unit of information in a grid cell map or scanned image (Burrough 1986). In a vector-based system, data are stored in an x-y (and z for three-dimensional themes) coordinate system represented by the topological entities of points, arcs (lines), and polygons (areas). Each of these entities can possess attribute values. Modern GIS platforms have the capability to readily transform data between raster and vector modes using accessory modules, transforming codes, or proprietary software. Analyses and modeling in GIS projects routinely make use of both modes, because each has its respective strengths and weaknesses. Outputs and displays can be independent of mode of storage or manipulation of data.

Vector Data

Vector data themes are easy to illustrate because they directly relate to map features (Fig. 42-2). A map represents a set of points, lines, and areas that are defined by their spatial location with reference to a coordinate system and by their nonspatial or descriptor attributes (Burrough 1986). The map legend links these nonspatial attributes to spatial data. A region is a set of areas or map loci that are referenced to a single legend in a classification scheme.

Points are represented by single x-y coordinates and can represent springs, wells, mines, waterfalls, sampling stations, and museum specimen records.

Arcs, or lines, are defined as strings of x-y coordinates (vertices) that begin at one location and end at another, and connecting vertices create a line (ESRI 1993). Vertices define shape, and *nodes* define ends. Arcs are spatially defined by connectivity "to a node" (start) and "from a node" (finish) and by contiguity, possessing direction and left-right sides. Nodes are usually grouped into a list describing common attributes. Common ex-

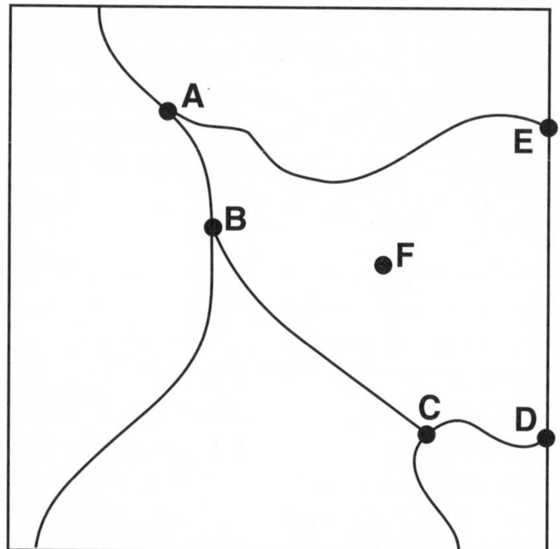

Figure 42-2. An illustration of vector-mode GIS.

amples of arcs include streams, roads, pipelines, power lines, and topographic contours of elevation.

Polygons are features defining a spatial area with coordinates forming an enclosed boundary. Polygons represent x-y line segments connected at nodes. Examples include states and counties, land use and ownership, bodies of water, toxic contaminated sites, and geographic ranges of species.

Topology is the spatial relationship between connecting or adjacent map features. It represents the essence of GIS function and commonly includes changing scales, combining adjacent polygons by decision rules, overlaying geographical and topological features, and modeling of paths through the landscape.

The modeling of paths through the landscape represents an important application of GIS, and some examples of path modeling will be discussed. The shortest route of least resistance, or more typically the path of fastest time or least cost (cost being defined by an explicit function related to landscape features), or even possible route between two points on a landscape is rarely a straight line. Considerations include pattern of roads and trails, topography (e.g., mountains, canyons), water, land use, and land ownership. Travel routes for deer or mountain lions may be dependent on riparian corridors or wooded steep ridges lacking housing developments. Dispersal of smoke plumes or aerosols will be dependent upon winds, thermal updrafts, and topography. Migration routes of anadromous fish will depend on dams, water quality, and instream flows. The successful migration of waterfowl and shore and wading birds through desert regions depends on the availability of wetlands and springs for feeding and resting.

Although arcs, nodes, polygons, and points are the main features of a coverage, six other features are used to completely define a coverage (ESRI 1993). Tics, or control points, represent geographic registration for a coordinate system. Annotations are the feature labels, such as the names of streams and roads. Links are rubber sheeting and adjustment for edge-mapping map sheets and other data adjustments. Routes are linear features composed of one or more arcs or portions of arcs. A section is an arc or portion of an arc to define a route.

Coverage extent defines the map boundary.

Raster Data

Raster data themes or layers represent information in a grid or cell structure (Fig. 42-3). The coordinate grid consists of square cells for spatial uniformity and simplicity in data handling. Actual raster cell sizes are user, project, or objective specific, but data availability, data storage capabilities, economics, time schedules, and practical considerations generally dictate raster resolu-

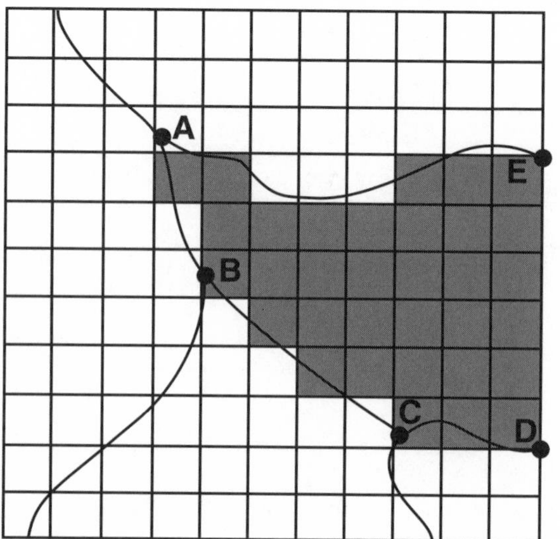

Figure 42-3. An illustration of raster-mode GIS.

tion. Remotely sensed satellite data, commonly used as themes in GIS analyses or modeling, use raster cell sizes that directly reflect the resolution (pixel sizes) of satellite multispectral data (Table 42-3).

Themes for raster cell data include qualitative/quantitative attribute classifications and satellite multispectral data. Raster cell data include soils, geology, vegetation classes (plant communities—series or associations), land cover (e.g., urban, agricultural, natural), and land ownership (e.g., federal, state, private). Each cell can possess a qualitative hierarchical attribute classification that includes an associated quantitative value for its specific classification. For example, in a raster thematic map representing Midwest vegetation, raster cells could be classified as:

1. forest or nonforest, at the coarsest hierarchy
2. forest, savanna, prairie, marshes, pasture, agriculture

At increasing hierarchies, forests could be further classified:

3. forest: deciduous, conifer, mixed
4. forest, deciduous: upland, bottomland
5. forest, deciduous, upland: oak-hickory, maple-beech, maple-basswood
6. further classifications based on subdominant tree species, understory characteristics, forest maturity, disturbance parameters

Additionally, within each of these qualitative classifications further quantitative classifications must be made for the raster cells:

1. bivariate—presence or absence (absence being defined by absolute absence or less than some threshold value)
2. ordinal—ranked value scales for presence or abundance
3. metric—actual or estimated metric values for density, cover, volume, frequency, dominance, importance values; in absolute or relative/percent metrics
4. probabilistic—some measure of the probability of occurrence above some threshold value

Table 42-4 contrasts vector and raster modes of GIS, giving the advantages and disadvantages of each.

GRASS, ARC/INFO, and ERDAS

The two most popular and largest GIS platforms are the raster-based GRASS, developed by the U.S. Army Corps of Engineers, Construction Engineering Research Laboratories (USACERL), Champaign, Illinois; and the vector-based ARC/INFO, commercially developed and marketed by ESRI, Redlands, California.

GRASS (USACERL 1993) conducts analyses in raster format, contains vector and point data programs, and possesses image-processing capabilities. ARC/INFO (ESRI 1993) conducts analyses in vector format and uses a GRID module based on GRASS code for raster capabilities. The analyses of enormous quantities of spatial data in multiple coverages are usually easier, more powerful, more efficient, and faster in raster modes. However, the recent advances in computer processing speeds and data storage capacities have shortened the "advantage gap" of raster systems. ARC/INFO has its own database module (INFO), while GRASS does not. GRASS was originally linked with RIM, which is outdated. ARC/INFO is closely tied with modern powerful database management systems such as Oracle and Informix, which greatly extend its capability to store and retrieve attribute databases rapidly and efficiently. Programs have been written in GRASS to access Informix databases. ARC/INFO is often used in conjunction with ERDAS (Earth Resources Data Analysis System, ERDAS, Inc., Atlanta, Georgia) to take advantage of ERDAS's raster analysis and image processing. Because satellite multispectral data are pixel-based, ERDAS's image-processing capabilities represent a powerful toolbox for inputting, analyzing, modeling, and outputting satellite imagery. A software product from ERDAS, IMAGINE, is marketed as a complete production and applications environment for simultaneous display and analyses of raster and vector databases—including satellite images, aerial photographs, thematic layers, vectors, and annotation—with subsequent map output (ERDAS 1993).

GRASS has traditionally been much easier to learn, understand, and use than ARC/INFO. However, with continuing developments at ESRI, this gap is narrowing. Table 42-5 presents the typical user manuals required for the two GIS.

GUIs (Graphical User Interfaces) are available for both systems. GUIs are user-friendly software programs with pull-down menus and point-and-click capabilities (e.g., Microsoft Windows®) that access and interface complex software systems that possess an extensive command language (e.g., GIS). The GIS GUIs are called XGRASS, GRASSLAND, and ARCVIEW and provide display and output capabilities of GIS formats. Although analyses and modeling capabilities are highly restricted, requiring the direct use of the parent systems, developments are continually progressing to extend GUI power and capabilities.

Table 42-3. Characteristics of four commonly used remote sensing multispectral satellite platforms. Data from Davis and Simonett (1991), Barrett and Curtis (1992), and Rock et al. (1993).

Satellite Sensor	Number of Bands	Spatial Resolution	Repeat Cycle	Spectra (μm)
SPOT	1	10 m (panchromatic)	2.5 days	0.51–0.73
(French)	3	20 m	2.5 days	0.50–0.89
Landsat-TM	6	30 m	16 days	0.45–2.35
(Thematic Mapper) (USA)	1	120 m (thermal)	16 days	10.4–11.7
Landsat-MSS (Multispectral Scanner) (USA)	4	80 m	16 days	0.50–1.1
NOAA-AVHRR (Advanced Very High Resolution Radiometer) (USA)	6	1.1 km	12 hours	0.60–1.1 and thermal

There are a large number of other GIS systems that are much less powerful (for typical applications) in analysis capabilities than GRASS and ARC/INFO. However, these other systems may be more economical, easier to use, or even better suited for specific applications. For example, there are many GIS platforms available for both PC and Macintosh environments that are much more economical but have limited capabilities. Examples for microcomputers include MAPINFO, MAPTITUDE, and PCARC/INFO. Software programs exist to enable both GRASS and ARC/INFO to function in the PC and Macintosh environments, but computer processor speed, memory requirements, and data storage capabilities typically necessitate the use of minicomputer workstations in these systems.

Because the GRASS GIS were developed by a federal agency, all software and associated source codes are in the public domain (free), and documentation is published at cost. However, the cost of computer hardware, operators, maintenance, training, and technical support can be substantial. Because ARC/INFO is a commercial platform, the cost of software, upgrades, and associated documentation is high, and the source code is not available for modification in user-specific applications. Nevertheless, the main costs typically associated with GIS projects are the acquisition of the appropriate or required data. The availability of data that are free or of low cost dramatically increases the economics of GIS.

GIS Input Data

Typical data for GIS are geographical, and therefore most GIS data layers represent the same information as that found in maps. However, maps represent analog data while GIS require digital data (McMaster and Shea 1992; Arlinghaus 1994). Analog data represent gradations such as signal strength and in maps or figures are represented as line thickness, shading, colors, etc. Digital data are the representation of numbers in the binary system, where any number or letter of the alphabet can be expressed in combinations of ones and zeros and therefore directly usable in modern computer systems. The digital format of GIS integrates geographic, cartographic, visual, and multispectral data with mathematical and statistical functionality. For example, the topographical surface of landscape patches can be defined by mathematical expressions. The first derivative of this surface map produces a slope map showing changes in elevation. The second derivative of the surface map produces a roughness map indicating changes in slope, which is directly analogous to an equation for distance traveled as a function of spatial geometry. The first de-

Table 42-4. Advantages and disadvantages of Vector and Raster GIS

Vector Mode GIS
Advantages
Compact data structure
Good representation of many kinds of data
Point attributes
Hydrography
Roads
Boundaries
Networks—utility lines, railroads
Topology completely described with network nodes and linkages
Necessary for network analyses
Accurate graphics and high-quality line drawings
Flexibility and generality in data retrieval, updating, and manipulations of graphics and attributes (may also apply to raster data)
Disadvantages
Complex data structures
Overlays of multiple vector polygon maps or polygon and raster maps may pose difficulties
Modeling is complex, topological units vary
Spatial analysis and filtering within polygons are impossible
Poor flexibility and limitations for custom applications—no access to source codes for proprietary software (e.g., ESRI, ARC/INFO)
Output display and plotting can be expensive, particularly if high resolution, color, and cross-hatching are desired (may also apply to raster data)
Expensive software, especially if all software modules, raster capabilities, and remote-sensed image processing are desired (may also apply to raster data)

Raster Mode GIS
Advantages
Simple data structures and inputs
More power, efficiency, and speed for huge spatial databases and multiple coverages
Directly compatible with remote sensed imagery, whose data are in pixels
Applicable to spatial analysis
Applicable to spatial and topological modeling
Inexpensive and quick overlays of map layer combinations
Used in Cellular automata
Spatial units same size and shape
Access to source codes for customizing user-specific applications if software is in the public domain (e.g., GRASS)
Economical (GRASS software is in the public domain)
Disadvantages
High storage capabilities required for graphic data
Reduction in storage capacity results in loss of resolution (information)
Output maps in raster format are crude in appearance (but depends on resolution)
Difficulties with network linkages
Time-consuming projection transformations (but depends on specific projects)
Need for specialized algorithms or hardware
Software modules required for handling points and arcs

Table 42-5. User's guides and reference manuals recommended by the developer for using GRASS (USACERL) and ARC/INFO (ESRI) GIS software

Recommended User Manual for GRASS GIS (available from U.S. Army Construction Engineering Research Laboratories, Champaign, Illinois)
- GRASS Version 4.1 Geographic Resources Analysis Support System User's Reference Manual

Recommended User Manuals for ARC/INFO GIS (available from Environmental Systems Research Institute, Inc., Redlands, California)
- Getting Started
- What's New at ARC/INFO Version 7?
- ARC/INFO Data Management
- Map Projections: Georeferencing Spatial Data
- ArcScan and Image Integration
- Editing Coverages and Tables with ARCEDIT
- COGO
- ARCEDIT Commands
- Map Display, Query and Output
- ARCPLOT Commands
- ArcStorm and Map Libraries
- Managing Tabular Data
- Data Conversions and Regions
- GRID Commands
- Cell Based Modeling with GRID
- INFO
- Network Analysis
- ARC Commands
- ArcTools
- AML and FormEdit
- AML Commands
- System Administrator's Guide
- License Manager's Guide
- Supported Graphics Devices
- Graphics Device Interface

rivative gives velocity, while the second gives acceleration, both as functions of spatial positions in a reference coordinate system. Although topography is an important coverage in GIS, other data are also relevant. Map information requires a two- or three-dimensional coordinate system where the following data may be represented.

Boundaries—political, land ownership, land use, geology, soil classifications, vegetation cover or classifications, water and wetlands, habitat disturbance, successional stages, species distributions.

Digital Line Graphs (DLGs)—one-dimensional lines in the landscape representing streams, rivers, fluvial channels, roads, utility corridors, and railroads. Although these attributes are in reality two-dimensional, their use is at a higher scale, and for practical considerations they are represented as lines.

Digital Elevation Models (DEMs)—are the digital representation of topographic maps. DEMs represent the three-dimensional topological surface or geomorphology of the landscape (see Table 42-6 for typical applications of DEMs).

Point attributes—represent specific user requirements, and as in DLGs, map scale is large compared to their surface area. Examples include springs or seeps, caves, mines, historical sites, and grave sites.

Important data layers or thematic maps in GIS include:

Existing maps—may represent from few to many coverages: political boundaries, land use, land ownership,

Table 42-6. Examples of applications of Digital Elevation Models (DEMs)

Topographic Contour Maps
Theme maps: elevation, slope, aspect, convexity, concavity
Shaded relief maps
Line of sight maps—cross-country visibility
Block: diagrams, profiles, horizons
Drainage networks
Drainage basin delineation—watersheds
Volume estimation
Model or estimate: runoff, erosion, and sediment yield or deposition
Civil engineering (e.g., road design, location of dams, hydrology)
Landscape architecture and regional planning (e.g., planning and design of landscapes, including urban)
Military applications (e.g., infantry, armor, and pilot training; weapon guidance systems)
Data for landscape and processes modeling
Data for geomorphology research
Data for integration with other thematic maps to produce desired products (e.g., LANDSAT TM, MSS, or AVHRR imagery to produce vegetation or land cover maps)
Attribute modeling (by designating elevation as a user-chosen continuous attribute variable, the DEM surface can represent a variety of features: travel time, cost or effort indices, weather phenomena, visual aesthetics, air pollution or temperature inversions, groundwater, landscape processes, etc.)

natural resources classifications, and management practices

Specialized GIS data—DEMs, DLGs

Digital photography—especially aerial

Remote sensed multispectral digital data—usually from satellite sensors but also from sensors mounted on or in aircraft

Collected field data—spatially referenced, usually with a GPS

Existing maps or photographs must be in a digital format for use in GIS. There are two ways to accomplish this, hand digitizing and electronic scanning. In digitizing, a map is laid perfectly flat on a large digitizing table expressly designed for this purpose, and a digitizing puck is manually used to trace boundaries of areas, elevation, or other contours, lines, and points of interest on the map. In scanning, a map, photograph, painting, figure, graph, or even text is put through a scanner, which transforms all visual information into digital format for magnetic storage on computer systems. Scanning technologies were not practical before modern, "reasonably priced" gigabyte and even terrabyte ultra high capacity storage devices became available, because even relatively simple pictures translate into an enormous amount of digital data.

Data input into modern GIS platforms include available magnetic media (usually tapes)—DEMs, DLGs, boundaries in digital format, satellite imagery; text files; data from digitizers; data from scanners; and interactive data input from keyboard or terminal.

GIS, DC, and CAD

Digital cartography (DC) is the storage of maps and their associated data in a digital format. GIS and DC have a number of features in common: both systems allow input and output editing; in both systems, attributes can be spatially associated; and both systems allow scale and projection changes.

Many map analysis features are not unique to GIS, but when processing time, commitment of resources, or very large scales are considered, GIS represent the only practical and economical alternative. Therefore, modern cartographic analysis and modeling are conducted in a GIS environment (Tomlin 1990).

Traditionally, Computer Aided Design (CAD) systems have been computerized drawing tools used in architecture and have not been used for analyses and modeling of attribute relationships that are spatially registered and referenced. However, modern CAD programs are incorporating GIS capabilities and vice versa (e.g., ARC/CAD).

Cowen (1988) and Parker (1988) provide additional discussions of GIS characteristics and compare GIS with other software systems.

Cartographic analysis and modeling commonly conducted in the GIS environment include:

1. overlays of two or more map layers to merge features spatially
2. updating of data
3. vector-raster transformations
4. buffering—to determine spatial proximity
5. masking—excluding areas from analysis, modeling, or outputs
6. averaging—any desired parameters and attributes
7. extraction of features
8. reclassification of map categories or polygons
    a. calculating areas
    b. averaging areas
    c. ranking, weighing schemes
    d. value, position, size attributes
    e. continuity, fragmentation measures
    f. shape—integrity; convexity, edge, ratio of perimeter to area; intrusion (nature of edges)
    g. pattern—mosaics.

A large number and variety of metrics and indices have been used to quantify landscape pattern and mosaics (See the section on Landscape Ecology [below] for a summary).

Important characteristics of GIS environments include:

1. multiple attribute associations with entities
2. manipulation, transformation, classification, storage, and output of relationships among entities
3. modeling and analyses among ecological elements or parameters and attributes (for a review of quantitative ecology see Legendre and Legendre 1983, 1987; Pielou 1984; Ludwig and Reynolds 1988; Krebs 1989; and Jongman et al. 1995)
4. optimization of spatially explicit metrics and measures
    a. distance
    b. ecological distance metrics or similarity indices (see Ludwig and Reynolds 1988; Krebs 1989)
    c. multivariate metrics (see Pimentel 1979; Dillon and Goldstein 1984; Pielou 1984)
    d. weighed statistical
    e. connectivity
    f. relationships
    g. cartographic neighborhood characterization
    h. spatial algorithms

GIS Capabilities

Important functions of GIS include location, spatial context, spatial pattern, attribute associations, temporal trends, and modeling and simulation. The following examples assume that the required databases, as well as the spatial analytical capabilities and associated algorithms, are available in the GIS platform. The examples used were made up to be illustrative but reflect and are comparable to realistic natural resources management or conservation biology research scenarios.

Location simply refers to the GIS database finding and displaying a desired attribute. Examples include: locate all the mines and springs in Vermillion County, Indiana, and locate the longest river confined to the state of Illinois.

Spatial context refers to location with conditional attribute features. Examples include: locate all lakes and reservoirs greater than 10 hectares in area that are between 10 and 100 kilometers from cities with populations greater than 100,000; locate all second-order stream segments that are downstream from urban developments with populations between 5,000 and 100,000; and locate all forest lands on north aspect 10 to 50 percent slopes that form riparian corridors that are greater than 100 meters in width on both sides of second- and third-order streams and are continuous for at least 2 kilometers.

Spatial pattern refers to the analytical quantification of size, shape, edges, fragmentation, distance, or pattern. Examples include: calculate the mean perimeter/area ratio of all forest patches in each 250-kilometer cell for the Midwest ecoregion grid; calculate the mean and standard error for the distance between forest patches for each county in Wisconsin; and calculate the fractal dimension and contagion for each cell in a specified gridded landscape.

There is a great deal of empirical evidence that the fractal dimension of landscape pattern decreases with increased anthropogenic activities, which can be attributed to landscape patterns becoming simpler and edges becoming straighter. Contagion is a measure of pattern in the landscape based on the probability of finding similar adjacent habitat patches from the pool of all possible habitat types in the landscape. In other words, do similar habitat patches have a tendency to clump, disperse, or occur at random? See the section on Landscape Ecology (below) for a list of potential metrics to quantify landscape pattern-mosaics. The list of potential quantifiable spatial parameters and patterns is limited only by the imagination of the investigator and the time or money to develop the necessary algorithms to carry out the calculations.

Attribute associations refer to combining location, spatial context, and/or spatial pattern to achieve a desired attribute. Recall that attributes are a parameter database associated with a spatial context. For example, from creel census data, what is the harvest rate (catch/person-hour) of smallmouth bass on second-order streams within 40 kilometers of cities with populations of less than 50,000 with respect to parameter RX (a designed analytical index to quantify the ecological condition of riparian habitats)?

Temporal trends refer to the monitoring of desired attributes. For example, what is the rate of deforestation (forest loss/year) in the tropics of Brazil per decade? The routine use of GIS for environmental time-series applications will continue to expand. Potential applications include: decreases/increases in habitats and ecosystems, habitat fragmentation and connectivity, changes in land use, monitoring restoration projects, dynamics of wildlife or biodiversity corridors, and monitoring ecosystem processes or degradation. John Anderson, U.S. Army Corps of Engineers, Topographic Engineering Center, Fort Belvoire, Virginia, is using aerial spectral photography (three bands) to successfully monitor the ecological condition of wetlands contaminated by organic pollutants or heavy metals (J. Anderson, personal communication).

Modeling and Simulation fundamentally refer to conducting "what if" scenarios in the context of geospatial relations, as discussed above, with specific attribute and/or spatially explicit models. For an extensive survey of environmental modeling applications, refer to the conference proceedings of "International Conference/Workshop on Integrating Geographic Information Systems and Environmental Modeling." The first conference, held in Boulder, Colorado, in 1991, established the foundation for Goodchild et al. (1993). The second conference was held at Breckenridge, Colorado, in 1993 (Goodchild et al. 1996). The third conference was held in Sante Fe, New Mexico, in 1996 (conference proceedings to be published).

Applications and Limitations of GIS

GIS are useful for any spatial data that require transforming, analysis, modeling, combining map layers, summarizing, or displaying. Therefore, GIS have potential applications in any technical field for diverse purposes. The theoretical potentials of GIS are virtually unlimited. However, the technical, practical, logistical, or economic constraints may often be formidable. Important uses of GIS and progress in their development have occurred in the following disciplines: the military; natural, earth, economic, social, and political sciences; and engineering. Activities for which GIS analysis and modeling are used include: management, planning, policy setting, decision making, research, and military activities. Typical applications of GIS have been with federal and state agencies and large consulting firms, where they have been used as important tools in managing natural resources (especially forestry), geological and soil resources, national parks and designated wilderness areas, urban and infrastructure development, and military training and testing lands. The potentials for the use of GIS in comprehensive regional planning are just being appreciated. The use of GIS in research has been limited. Possible reasons include high costs (hardware, software, personnel, data) and resource investments, highly specialized and dedicated operator skills, large data requirements, large-scale generalized databases, and unfamiliarity of traditional research disciplines with GIS technologies and platforms.

Although the use of GIS in the natural sciences has dramatically increased in the last few years, most technical papers in the natural sciences that deal with GIS are still found in specialized GIS or highly applied management journals. An examination of herpetology, ichthyology, avian, mammal, wildlife management, conservation biology, and ecology journals over the last five years discloses that only a few studies have used GIS technologies.

It is easy to become overly optimistic about the capabilities of GIS. However, GIS present serious concerns in many potential applications. The enthusiasm generated by vibrant and colorful large-scale maps and the desire for "quick fix" assessments or solutions to environmental and social issues on regional and global scales have facilitated the zealous "oversell" of GIS capabilities and economics (Aangeenbrug 1991). GIS applications and programs are associated with high investment costs: enormous database requirements for acquisition, input, and storage of data; hardware, software, and their maintenance; and the need for highly specialized, dedicated operators commanding a high salary in the current computer age. All of these factors have limited the routine use of GIS. The analysis and modeling of these enormous databases—including quality assurance in checking the validity and accuracy of input data, data transformations, use of accessory software, and obtaining the desired displays and hard copy outputs—are technically formidable, time-consuming, and expensive. Errors of accuracy, precision, and omission are common in spatial data sets (Crapper 1980; Goodchild and Gopal 1989; Chrisman 1991). The additive effects of errors at each thematic layer may drastically limit the accuracy, interpretation, or usefulness of the final product (Burrough 1989). The large number of colors or shadings necessary to represent the complex features and patterns in real-world landscapes has surpassed practical limitations for visual interpretation and additionally presents problems for copy reproductions.

GIS technologies are application tools that cannot replace field investigations, observations, and experiments, despite the claims of some enthusiastic proponents and administrators. Indeed, the success of GIS in any application is strongly and directly dependent on high-quality field data. Just as in statistical analysis, GIS cannot perform magic with poorly designed or carelessly executed inventories, assessment/monitoring programs, or field research. A commonly used metaphor in statistics is equally applicable to GIS: garbage in—garbage out.

Examples of GIS Applications

Remote Sensing

GIS and remote sensing technologies are commonly confused, and sometimes the two terms are used interchangeably. The two terms are not interchangeable. GIS are a separate and independent technology, often used without remotely sensed data. Although remote sensing preceded GIS, the primary current means of inputting, manipulating, analyzing, classifying, and outputting multispectral, remotely sensed data is integrating image-processing systems with raster mode GIS (Curran 1985; Ehlers et al. 1989; Ehlers et al. 1991; Davis et al. 1991; Davis and Simonett 1991; Faust et al. 1991). The value, utility, and interpretation of remotely sensed multispectral imagery are usually dependent on the use of ancillary GIS databases: DEMs, geology, soils, vegetation classifications, and ground field verifications. The classification of remotely sensed imagery into polygons or even into land cover without field verification is termed "unsupervised." Although this is often done, it is strongly discouraged. Satellite imagery may perform poorly for land cover classifications in situations where vegetation cover is sparse (e.g., arid landscapes), and even where vegetation is abundant the imagery may not be able to distinguish between vegetation types. In arid regions, geology profoundly affects spectral images, usually in complex, synergistic, and unpredictable ways. Even small amounts of some minerals or elements (e.g., iron) may affect imagery interpretation dramatically. Important considerations in classification include field verifications and analytical corrections applied to the imagery for atmospheric conditions, light reflectance and scatter, and topographic shadows. Field verification, especially in an iterative mode where repeated fieldwork keeps improving polygon classifications, is the recommended procedure and is termed "supervised" classification.

Remote sensing is usually associated with multispectral data obtained by satellite sensors (U.S. Army Topographic Engineering Center 1995). Table 42-3 summarizes the characteristics of four commonly used remote sensing satellite platforms. Remote sensing also includes aerial photography (color, black-and-white, and infrared), and specialized multispectral sensors can be mounted on aircraft or occasionally on air balloons. Scanners mounted on aircraft can achieve resolutions of 0.5 to 1 meter on the ground. The advantage of satellite sensors is their potential for addressing environmental issues at landscape, regional, continental, and global scales (Table 42-3). Excellent introductions and reviews of remote sensing technologies, capabilities, applications, and interpretations are provided by Campbell (1987), Mather (1987), Sabins (1987), Cracknell and Hayes (1991), Howard (1991), Quattrochi and Pelletier (1991), Barrett and Curtis (1992), Foody and Curran (1994), Lillesand and Kiefer (1994), USATEC (1995), and Verbyla (1995). Remote sensing has provided us with large-scale images of land use, vegetation coverages, land degradation, plant productivity, ecosystem properties, and landscape spatial and temporal patterns of patch mosaics and their boundaries.

Satellite sensors have been important in ecological assessment and monitoring: global ecosystem functions and processes (Hobbs and Mooney 1990), land cover on global scales (Tucker et al. 1986; Townshend and Justice 1988), tropical deforestation (Tucker et al. 1984; Woodwell et al. 1986; Nelson et al. 1987; Malingreau and Tucker 1988; Houghton et al. 1991), and forest declines in the northeastern United States (Vogelmann 1988, 1990; Vogelmann and Rock 1988; Rock et al. 1993) and Germany (Herrmann et al. 1988; Peterson et al. 1988). Remote sensing has also been extensively applied to the earth sciences, including global climatology, geology, hydrology, and oceanography (reviewed in Barrett and Curtis 1992).

An important application of remote sensing has been the capability for spatially and temporally monitoring primary productivity as a function of seasonality and land use using the NDVI (Normalized Difference Vegetation Index) calculated from AVHRR data (Jackson and Huete 1991).

$$NDVI = (B2 - B1) / (B2 + B1)$$

where B1 is the visible red band (580–680 nanometers) and B2 is the near infrared (725–1100 nanometers).

This index has been directly related to:

1. photosynthetic activity of vegetation and the leaf area index (Asrar et al. 1984; Tucker and Sellers 1986; Choudhury 1987)
2. vegetation biomass (Huete and Jackson 1987)
3. vegetation type (Tucker et al. 1985)
4. seasonality of global vegetation (Justice et al. 1985) and crops (Bartholome 1988)
5. grassland productivity and monitoring (Justice 1986)
6. vegetation patterns and biome comparisons between North and South America (Goward et al. 1985; Goward et al. 1987)
7. forest evapotranspiration patterns (Running and Nemani 1988; Nemani and Running 1989)
8. the ecology and epidemiology of the tsetse fly (Rogers and Randolph 1991; Rogers and Williams 1994)

Landscapes: Assessment, Monitoring, and Management

GIS have proved to be valuable tools in assessing and monitoring trends in landscape changes and their patterns from human activities (Iverson and Risser 1987; Iverson 1988), including regional effects of agriculture on water quality (Osborne and Wiley 1988; Johnston, Detenbeck, Bond, and Niemi 1990).

It is not appreciated that animals also represent major players in geomorphic (Butler 1995) and hydrologic (Johnston and Naiman 1987; Johnston 1994) changes in the landscape. Recent increases in beaver population growth has created new ponds at the rate of 0.0042 percent of the landscape per year, which is comparable to rates of anthropogenic changes in the landscape (Johnston 1994). The analysis and modeling of beaver-induced landscape changes by Johnston and her colleagues (Johnston and Naiman 1990a,b,c) represent a classic example of the utility of applying GIS technologies when studying large-scale landscape patterns, disturbance regimes, and ecosystem processes (Naiman et al. 1986; Naiman et al. 1988; Remillard et al. 1987).

It is becoming evident that natural resources need to be managed on larger scales, and the management of entire watersheds is such an approach (Naiman 1992; Satterlund and Adams 1992; Doppelt et al. 1993). GIS provide the capabilities for watershed delineations and monitoring a wide variety of ecosystem attributes and parameters as discussed above.

GIS have provided the foundations for analysis, visual display media, and map outputs for the U.S. Fish and Wildlife Service's National Wetlands Inventory Program.

GIS have probably been applied more to forest management than to any other natural resources discipline. An extensive review is presented by Sample (1994), who stresses the integration of GIS and remote sensing.

GIS technologies were the most important tools used for implementing the U.S. Environmental Protection Agency's Environmental Monitoring and Assessment Program (EMAP; Messer et al. 1991; White et al. 1992; O'Neill et al. 1994; see also Bowers et al., Chpt. 39, this volume). The stated goals of the program were to:

1. estimate the current status, trends, and changes in selected indicators of the condition of the nation's ecological resources on a regional basis with known confidence
2. estimate the geographic coverage and extent of the nation's ecological resources with known confidence
3. seek associations between selected indicators of natural and human stressors and indicators of the condition of ecological resources
4. provide annual statistical summaries and periodic assessments of the nation's ecological resources

Funding cuts have jeopardized the continuation of EMAP. A scientific review of the program is provided in National Research Council (1995).

Conservation Biology

The classic example of using GIS for conservation

planning and setting management priorities is the U.S. Fish and Wildlife Service's GAP Analysis Program (GAP; Scott et al. 1993). To summarize briefly, the GAP GIS database is constructed from three primary coverages or thematic maps at the state level: (1) type of vegetation cover, (2) predicted animal distributions, and (3) land ownership. Data quality and resolution depend a great deal on the current status of state-specific databases, because no new field data are generated. Map layer one is primarily generated from Landsat TM imagery combined with DEMs and existing data on the state distribution of plant communities and their environmental preferences (e.g., elevation). Map layer two comes from the state natural heritage programs and consists of the distributional records of vertebrate species (Vertebrate Characterization Abstracts [VCA]), federal and state threatened/endangered (T/E [or listed]) species, and sometimes butterfly and T/E vascular plant species. Simple wildlife-vegetation models are usually applied to extrapolate to areas where distributional data are lacking. Map layer three represents a gradient in the level of habitat protection. National park and wilderness designations offer the highest levels of protection for resident habitats and biodiversity, while private lands offer the least. Multiple-use federal and state lands offer intermediate protection, which depends directly on site-specific management goals and objectives. These three coverages are used to construct a fourth layer, which geographically identifies "gaps" where listed species, rare species or ecosystems, species with small and limited geographical distributions, or specific species assemblages (communities) are not protected or only have limited protection. These data motivate land acquisition or nature reserve design based on corridor connectivity.

There is a fundamental problem with state natural heritage databases that is not generally appreciated or understood. This problem is independent of accuracy (taxa or location data) or quality assurance in database management. These databases are typically based on collections and not on samples. There is a profound difference between collections and samples based on statistical validity. Collection records are based on museum specimens, university collections or studies, and possibly data from state parks or nature preserves. These collections possess a strong bias for assessing actual spatial distributions (see also Resetar, Chpt. 40, this volume). For example, university field trips, research studies, or collecting trips are strongly dependent on convenience of distance traveled, location accessibility, familiarity with the region, and very importantly, success experienced in previous fieldwork. Museum collections have the same bias, particularly the latter, because a collector in a new region, in order to ensure success at obtaining desired specimens, may select collection sites based on the known success of previous collectors. It would be interesting to verify if biodiversity hot spots were located within 75 kilometers or so of universities. Additionally, because museum (and to some extent state) biologists desire county records, collection sites may be conveniently located near the intersections of several counties, irrespective and independent of the landscape spatial relationships between political and ecological boundaries. Samples, on the other hand, are based on a sampling design or experimental design for the specific purpose of avoiding bias and optimizing representation.

Satellite Telemetry

The integration of GIS and satellite telemetry receivers has enabled wildlife managers to assess and monitor home ranges and dispersal parameters of large vertebrates (Craighead et al. 1971; Amlaner and MacDonald 1980; Timko and Kolz 1982; Fancy et al. 1988; Fancy et al. 1989; Marsh and Rathbun 1990; Keating et al. 1991). GIS have also been used for database management, analyses, and presentation outputs of traditional radiotelemetry studies.

Economic

A traditional use for GIS has been in urban and regional planning (Maguire et al. 1991b). GIS have been used in a wide range of economic applications, from market analysis (Beaumont 1991) to predicting mineral deposits (Bonham-Carter et al. 1990; Bonham-Carter 1991).

Landscape Ecology

Landscape ecology is the study of ecological patterns in a geographic or spatial context and represents an interdisciplinary approach. Although in theory landscape ecology can be applied at any scale, traditional "landscape approaches" have been at meso scales, 1 to 10,000 square kilometers (Table 42-2). From my perspective, landscape ecology is synonymous with geographical ecology, but its interdisciplinary nature has polarized specific disciplines into each of these constructs. A great deal of the patterns that we see on the landscape are due to the activities of humans, resulting in habitat elimination, disturbance, degradation, and successional seres. Landscape ecology deals heavily with anthropogenic patterns, and therefore the disciplines of geography, landscape architecture, planning, engineering, and GIS computer technology are strongly represented. Geographical ecology is dominated by ecologists and other biologists (e.g., systematists) stressing the patterns or processes of ecological systems or taxonomic entities also in a geographic and spatial context.

Landscape ecology had its origins with German geographers in the 1950s and 1960s (Forman and Godron 1986) and is often closely integrated with GIS (Haines-Young et al. 1993). However, it has only recently received a great deal of attention and made appreciable advancements. This can be attributed to advances in GIS and the widespread availability of powerful minicomputer workstations. Another important motivation has been to comprehend and predict the accelerating degradation of natural systems and their patterns by anthropogenic stressors, particularly habitat loss and fragmentation. Landscape ecology is the discipline that deals with ecological phenomena at landscape or larger scales. These phenomena include all ecological attributes that are recognized at local scales: structure (including composition), function, processes, and interactions; these phenomena additionally encompass pattern and emphasize the context of space and time so relevant to large scales. Landscape ecology is more interdisciplinary than traditional ecology because of its natural association with geography, hydrology, geology, soils, climates, and especially GIS and their associated computer-intensive technologies, such as knowledge-based systems. As landscape ecology grades into regional scales, social and economic issues emerge, complicating science with policy and politically driven motivations.

The landscape ecology approach for natural resources research, monitoring, and management is essential for the successful persistence of populations, species, and communities and the ecosystem processes they depend on, including natural disturbance regimes. Excellent foundations and discussions of landscape ecology can be found in Forman and Godron (1986), Turner (1987, 1989), Zonneveld and Forman (1990), Kolasa and Pickett (1991), Turner and Gardner (1991a), Vos and Opdam (1993), and Forman (1995). Forman (1995) represents a current synthesis, containing 1,961 worldwide references. The ecology and physical geography of landscape boundaries and ecotones are important issues in current research (Holland et al. 1991; Furley et al. 1992; Hansen and di Castri 1992).

Landscapes consist primarily of three elements and the dynamics of their resulting patterns: patches, matrices, and corridors. The visual reality of boundaries or ecotones associated with these elements gives rise to the concept of mosaics. The interconnecting pattern of corridors are termed networks. Networks are characterized by linkages, nodes, intersections, and hierarchies (Forman 1995). Hierarchies are an important landscape feature and represent, for example, the dendritic pattern of stream orders. Landscape ecology is the study of the spatial and temporal structure and dynamics of pattern-mosaics and their boundaries, scale dependencies, and how these relate to the flow or movement (or cycling) of organisms, matter, energy, disturbance regimes, and anthropogenic stressors. A great deal of landscape ecology is devoted to quantifying and classifying all possible aspects of patches, matrices, corridors, and their resulting patterns and mosaics and will be discussed in the next section. GIS database development, modeling, and analysis have been instrumental in this research. The concepts of habitat patches, fragmentation, and their dynamics have a good ecological foundation (Burgess and Sharpe 1981; Harris 1984; Pickett and White 1985; Noss 1987; Shafer 1990; Shorrocks and Swingland 1990) and have their origins in island biogeography theory (MacArthur and Wilson 1967; Simberloff and Abele 1976).

Parks are patches of vegetation in a matrix of housing and infrastructure in an urban landscape. In the rural countryside of the Midwest, forest woodlots are patches in a matrix of row crops or pasture. The remaining old-growth forests of the Pacific Northwest are patches in a matrix of early succession forest, and in the southern Rocky Mountains of New Mexico roadless designated wilderness areas are patches in a matrix of multiple-use forestry covered with a dense network of roads.

Corridors are landscape elements that run through the matrix and connect patches. Important corridors are rivers and streams, with their riparian vegetation, or the ridges of mountain ranges. In human-dominated landscapes, fencerows, hedges, and shelterbelts are common features of the landscape. Corridors represent the most important movement, dispersal, and recolonization routes for vertebrates, invertebrates, plants, and undoubtedly microbes. Although corridors are typically ribbonlike in feature (Johnson 1989), corridors can represent the restoration of large areas to permit an ecologically functional link between large, fragmented ecosystem patches (Noss 1992; Noss and Cooperrider 1994).

Corridors are appreciated by professional wildlife managers and the public for their role in linking natural areas and providing habitat routes through urban areas or disturbed habitats, and the concept has been well discussed (Harris 1984; Adams and Dove 1989; Shafer 1990; Noss and Cooperrider 1994; Forman 1995). The benefits of corridors have been well articulated in reference to their use in core reserve design and in conjunction with buffers, multiple-use lands, and urbanization. Corridors are important for population dispersal, recolonization after local extinctions due to environmental catastrophes or deleterious demographic or genetic stochastic events, maintaining metapopulations, and providing valuable habitats (e.g., riparian ecosystems). In a general sense, corridors do not have to be linear but could effectively function where habitat patches form stepping stones for movements of organisms. For example, city parks in urban settings (e.g., Central Park in New York City) may represent valuable resting and feeding places for migratory birds.

Conceptually, landscape corridors have received strong support from land managers and conservation biologists. However, there have been a few skeptics. Simberloff (e.g., Simberloff et al. 1992) has criticized corridors on the following grounds: there is little empirical data or evidence to substantiate specific desired values; corridors could spread disease or disturbance regimes, for example, fire; corridors could disperse predators or act as ambush zones; corridors could provide habitat for weedy species and exotics; and corridors can be expensive to construct and maintain, and precious conservation dollars may be more cost-effectively used for other projects.

Grain is the finest level of spatial resolution in a given data set and represents pixel size for raster or multispectral satellite imagery. Extent is the largest spatial scale for consideration in the data set and usually represents the study area under investigation or duration of the time under consideration. Grain, extent, and other landscape ecology terminologies are discussed in an introductory framework by Turner and Gardner (1991b).

Quantifying Landscapes

Natural systems at all levels of ecological hierarchies (genes/populations, communities/ecosystems, ecoregions or biomes, and the biosphere) form complex and heterogeneous patterns on the landscape. These patterns are of two fundamental types, and both are strongly scale dependent—gradients and mosaics. Gradients represent gradual and more-or-less continuous spatial changes in landscape attributes; climate, soil moisture, general classes of soil types, general classes of vegetation, and species distributions are major examples. Mosaics represent abrupt changes in the landscape with discernable (visual or otherwise) boundaries. Important examples are vegetation, soils, some geological formations, aquatic-terrestrial edges, and riparian zones in arid regions. It should be obvious that any of the landscape attributes listed above can represent either gradients or mosaics or both, depending primarily on scale but also on site-specific conditions. Two important examples are microclimates, which can possess very sharp boundaries, and wetlands, which generally represent a complex of spatial and temporal mosaics and gradients of aquatic and terrestrial habitats instead of either a clear, discernable boundary or an obvious gradient, but either condition is also possible.

Environmental gradients have typically been analyzed and modeled by community ecologists, generally through ordination techniques (Whittaker 1982; Kershaw and Looney 1985; Digby and Kempton 1987; Feoli and Orlóci 1991; Kent and Coker 1992). The most fundamental analytical expression of an environmental gradient is a principal component solution (Krzysik 1987). The most useful techniques for environmental gradient analysis are: Principal Component Analysis (PCA; Pielou 1984; Digby and Kempton 1987), Correspondence Analysis (CA) or Reciprocal Averaging (RA; Hill 1973; Gauch et al. 1977; Greenacre 1984), Detrended Correspondence Analysis (DCA; Hill 1974; Hill and Gauch 1980; Gauch 1982), Canonical Correspondence Analysis (CCA; Ter Braak 1986, 1987; Jongman et al. 1995), and Nonmetric Multidimensional Scaling (NMDS; Kenkel and Orlóci 1986; Faith et al. 1987; Wartenberg et al. 1987; Young 1987). PCA and NMDS often produce comparable results. Pielou (1984) and Digby and Kempton (1987) provide lucid and fundamental introductions into PCA and CA for nonspecialists. All texts in multivariate statistics discuss PCA. Manly (1986) and James and McCulloch (1990) are excellent introductions to this field. PCA remains among the best ordination techniques and method to interpret environmental gradients, despite the new techniques and criticisms in the literature (e.g., Gauch 1982). Analytically, it is a direct and heuristically simple means for tracking and interpreting data variance patterns. DCA, on the other hand, relies on mathematical ad hoc "tweaking and adjustments" to produce "clearer" visual outputs, but possibly at a loss of realism and interpretation. Kenkel and Orlóci (1986) and Wartenberg et al. (1987) discuss shortcomings and interpretation problems with DCA.

The modeling and analysis of mosaics belong to the

discipline of landscape ecology. A number of metrics have been suggested to quantify mosaic patterns. Forman (1995) provides a comprehensive review of analytical functions.

Patch Shape based on:

A. lengths of axes—(1) form, (2) elongation, (3) circularity

B. perimeter and area—(4) compactness, (5) circularity, (6) shoreline development (Patton's diversity)

C. area—(7) circularity, (8) circularity ratio

D. radii—(9) mean radius

E. area and length—(10) form ratio, (11) ellipticity index

F. perimeter—(12) shape factor

G. perimeter and length—(13) grain shape index

Mosaic metrics:

H. diversity measures—(14) relative richness, (15) relative evenness, (16) diversity, (17) dominance

I. boundary or edge measures—(18) edge number, (19) fractal dimension, (20) relative patchiness, (21) boundary length, (22) boundary density

J. patch-centered measures—(23) isolation of a patch, (24) accessibility of a patch

K. all-patch pattern measures—(25) dispersion of patches (aggregation), (26) isolation of patches (standard distance index), (27) nearest neighbor probabilities, (28) contagion, (29) patch density, (30) contiguity

Network metrics:

L. connectivity—(31) gamma index for network connectivity

M. circuitry—(32) alpha index for circuitry

Turner et al. (1991) reviewed analytical methods and statistical procedures for landscape-scale patterns and divided the technologies into two classes: those addressing patterns repeated in the landscape and those with patterns that vary in an irregular manner.

Landscape pattern quantifications have also been subjected to a large variety of texture measures (Musick and Grover 1991). Textures measures are particularly applicable to image processing of remote-sensed multispectral data.

Spatial Modeling

Spatial modeling represents a broad diversity of environmental and ecological applications (Turner 1992; Goodchild et al. 1993; Goodchild et al. 1996; Bonham-Carter 1994; Fotheringham and Rogerson 1994). This discussion will be limited to the interpolation and smoothing of geographic data for prediction, visual interpretations, and demonstrations. A common problem in spatial modeling is to construct a distribution and density surface for some parameter of interest where data are collected from spatially explicit sampling points. The parameters may be biological, geological, or geomorphic. Biological parameters include genetic structure, populations or metapopulations, species, or species assemblages (communities). Geological parameters include soils, substrate textures, and economic deposits of minerals and ores. Geomorphic surfaces are necessary for hydrological, erosional, and sediment transport modeling.

The simplest example of parameter fitting is the well-known two-dimensional least-squares fitting for producing a linear model (equation) from a scatter of data points (linear regression). Nonlinear trends can similarly be modeled with curves or splines derived from polynomial equations, although things become more complicated because one has to decide on the form of the model. Extensions to three (or more) dimensions, although directly comparable to the simple case, become much more complicated.

Surface modeling of geographical spatial data belongs in the realm of spatial statistics, or geostatistics, which has followed a course independent from traditional statistics, including the use of terminology. An important problem in spatial statistics is as follows. We have established a systematic sampling grid on a given region of the landscape and at each sampling point, transect, or quadrat we obtain a series of z values for the parameter of interest (e.g., density of frogs) over the entire region, each associated with grid coordinates x, y (i.e., easting and northing, respectively, in UTM coordinates). How do we interpolate to find the z values between our sampling stations and produce a smooth distribution/density surface that represents the closest unbiased fit to the actual data we collected? A common and practical example is the use of a DEM (Digital Elevation Model), where in this case x, y values represent isolines (contours) for constant values of z (elevation). After interpolation and smoothing, the resulting surface represents a realistic topology of the landscape and is useful to model precipitation runoff and sediment transport.

There are numerous benefits to such a spatial model.

The model visually summarizes data over a much larger scale than sampling alone would permit, economizes sampling effort, assesses spatial and temporal trends (when sampling is repeated), and makes predictions where there are no data. There are four major techniques for spatial interpolation and smoothing: trend surface analysis, moving averages analysis, kriging, and spline methods.

Trend surface analysis (Ripley 1981; Burrough 1986; Haining 1990; Turner et al. 1991; Jongman et al. 1995) is the extension of least-squares curve fitting to produce three-dimensional or any dimensional surfaces. This method is useful for showing broad, large-scale features of the data and emphasizes regional trends. Local trends are obscured. Trend surface analysis can also be used in preliminary analysis to remove "generalized features" from a data set, and then residuals can be analyzed using other multivariate methods. Residuals represent nonsystematic local variation. Trend surface analysis is restricted by the same assumptions as regression methods. Samples must be chosen at random, and the dependent variable (z) is assumed to be normally distributed with its variance independent of spatial context. These are restricted assumptions for geospatial data.

Moving averages analysis (Ripley 1981; Burrough 1986; Isaaks and Srivastava 1989; Haining 1990) is easy to visualize in the following example. Suppose we have sample values of parameter z that we collected along a transect at equidistant sampling points (x_i) and we want to estimate (predict) an unknown z value along the transect that lies between two sampled points. If parameter z represents a complex gradient along the transect, a simple average between the two adjacent known values would possess error. A better strategy would be to select a "window" that includes more than just the adjacent values and calculate the mean weighed by the distances to the known sampling points. The extension of this analogy to the two-dimensional plane is direct and intuitive, replacing x_i with the coordinate vector (x_i, y_i). Points characterized by many variables can be measured by Euclidean, Mahalanobis, Minkowski, Manhatten, etc. distance metrics (Pimentel 1979; Dillon and Goldstein 1984; Pielou 1984). Possibly, a wide range of similarity measures or distance coefficients may be applicable and innovative. Ludwig and Reynolds (1988) and Krebs (1989) provide a good discussion of these coefficients.

Estimates by moving averages are susceptible to clustered data points, but corrections can be made with distance-weighed least-squares methods (Ripley 1981). Of course, there are the problems associated with determining domain or window size, spacing, shape, and orientation, which influence analysis results, including whether local or large-scale variations or trends are emphasized. Because local maxima and minima of the interpolated smoothed surface are only associated with data points, various algorithms have been used to enhance the fit of data points to the surface using second derivatives or Hermitian polynomials (Burrough 1986).

Kriging (Ripley 1981; Burrough 1986; Isaaks and Srivastava 1989; Haining 1990; Webster and Oliver 1990; Cressie 1991) was named after a mining geologist who perfected a method to optimize gold ore extraction in South Africa (Krige 1966). Technically, the method is called the Wiener-Kolmogorov Prediction (Ripley 1981). It has been extensively applied in mining, geological explorations, and soil and groundwater mapping. Kriging is also known as optimal interpolation using spatial autocovariance, because it has its basis in regionalized variable theory. Kriging consists of a variety of methods and is the most widely known and applied geostatistical spatial interpolation technique. The theory assumes that spatial variation of a parameter is a mathematical function (model) of three components: a structural component with its associated constant mean value or a constant trend, a random spatially correlated component, and a random error component (noise). The result is a strong emphasis on spatial dependence between samples as measured by semivariance. Semivariance is a measure of the variance (variability) between sampling points as a function of distance between them and is estimated from the experimental data. The plot of semivariance versus sample spacing produces the semivariogram. The semivariogram is used to determine the weighing coefficients for local interpolation in a procedure similar to moving averages, except that the weights do not come from spatial distances but more appropriately from a statistical foundation (the geostatistical analysis) based on spatial variability (the sample semivariogram).

The advantages of kriging are significant. Kriging represents exact interpolation, because interpolation function values coincide with data point values. The use of spatial dependence in formulation dramatically improves local interpolation and therefore predictive capabilities. Probably of most significance is that kriging yields estimates of errors in interpolation and is the only method discussed that has this capability. The mapping of error terms gives valuable insight about the reliability of the interpolated values over the investigated region.

Kriging strongly depends on the fact that the calculated semivariogram is a true estimator of spatial covariation in an area. The presence of outliers in field data can overly influence the semivariogram and reduce the effectiveness of kriging. An important problem experienced by kriging is the violation of the intrinsic hypothesis (homogeneity of first differences). In other words, these are complex trends in the structure component and heterogeneity in spatial variability.

Spline methods (Ripley 1981; Burrough 1986; Wahba 1990; Cressie 1991) are also known as tessellations and triangulations. A draftsperson is intimately and empirically familiar with spline techniques using flexible rulers (splines) and eyeballing to produce smooth curves through scattered data points. In practice, small segments of curves are fit exactly with cubic spline functions, and in a similar fashion segments are fused to become continuous. The resulting curve with fitted equation parameters represents a continuous cubic polynomial that possesses continuous first and second derivatives. This detail is not possible with trend surface equations. Splines can be used for exact interpolation where the derived function passes through all data points, more typically for smoothing where it is desired to produce a trend curve (or surface), and for circumventing random error in the actual data points. The term "bicubic splines" is given to the three-dimensional case where surfaces instead of lines are interpolated and smoothed to fit data points. However, this surface cannot typically be defined by a single analytic function but can be represented as a mosaic of surface patches (plates) constructed from "spline curve segments." Spline methods are computer intensive, and their widespread use has been closely related to the availability of inexpensive high-speed minicomputers and, more recently, to current high-powered microcomputers.

The advantage of spline methods is that they retain local or small-scale features, in contrast to trend surface and moving averages analyses. Compared to moving averages, spline-fitted surfaces do not require additional adjustments in the vicinity of data points because the interpolated surface can lie on either side of the actual data points. They are also aesthetically pleasing and depict a good overview of data trends. Their main disadvantage is that there is no direct estimate of error terms in the interpolation. However, Dubrule (1984) has estimated error terms by jackknifing (a computer-intensive Monte Carlo resampling strategy for estimating statistical parameters from the original data; see Krzysik, Chpt. 41, this volume). There is also the problem of patch definition and how patches are "sewn" together without introducing extraneous anomalies. Another problem is deciding whether the interpolated surface should coincide with the data points or be interleaved. Each gives different results.

Kriging and spline methods are formally related, because all commonly used spline-based functions are generalized covariances (reviewed in Cressie 1991). These methods are also closely linked through Bayesian analysis (Kimeldorf and Wahba 1970).

Few published studies have compared the suitability of the various methods to the same data set. When splines and kriging were compared by Dubrule (1983, 1984), he concluded that splines produced more attractive maps, while kriging produced better quantitative results but was much more demanding of computer time. Burrough's (1986) table 8.3 provides a concise comparative summary of interpolation methods.

Example of a Landscape-Scale Spatial Model

Researchers at the U.S. Army–Construction Engineering Research Laboratories (USACERL) have been developing a novel technology to interpolate, smooth, and model geographical spatial data. The technique is Smoothing Thin-Plate Splines with Tension (TPS). Preliminary modeling results at USACERL and at Purdue University have shown advantages of TPS over other methods, including kriging. TPS possesses a number of robust properties: it is independent of the spatial distribution of input data, it uses a standard GIS grid structure for topographic analysis, it maintains the quality of contours, and it has consistently demonstrated flexibility and accuracy in model development. TPS is based on a minimization of interpolation-smoothing functions that possess global derivatives of all orders and include a tension parameter for controlling (smoothing) function fit to the geometric scatter of data points. A large tension parameter produces an interpolated surface with sharper points but a closer fit to actual field data. Because field data are associated with random error, this may not be desirable. A smaller tension parameter increases the smoothness of the interpolated surface. TPS is related to kriging (Wahba 1990). TPS algorithms have been developed for hydrological modeling (Mitásová and Hofierka 1993; Mitásová and Mitás 1993; Mitásová et al. 1996), and these are the ones used in this analysis. TPS may have promising applications for ecology and conservation biology in modeling the distribution and density patterns of populations or genetic structure and species-habitat relationships on landscape scales, and research along these lines is continuing.

TPS was used to model the changes in the distribution and density patterns of desert tortoise (*Gopherus agassizii*) populations after six years of landscape-scale military training activities in the central Mojave Desert (Krzysik, 1996). The research was conducted at Fort Irwin, California, the army's national training center, in 1983 and 1989. The study site was 2,600 square kilometers in size. Local patches of tortoise densities were estimated at sample quadrats of 0.64 square kilometer by sampling tortoise burrows and scats along 2.4 kilometers-by-9.1-meter triangular transects and calibrating to Bureau of Land Management permanent study plots of known tortoise densities. Transects were approximately evenly dispersed in potential habitat at the rate of one transect per 3 square kilometers of landscape. Details of field methods and background information are available in Krzysik and Woodman (1991), and statistical analysis of population trends are presented in Krzysik (1996).

Figure 42-4 is a map of Fort Irwin showing the Goldstone Deep Space Communications Complex, closed to army training and off-road vehicles (ORVs), and five impact zones. Although the impact zones are used for live-fire practice, the actual target sites are small, and most of the areas represent extensive buffer zones with high-quality habitats. Figure 42-5 shows Fort Irwin with an overlay of mountain ranges (cross-hatched pattern) and the 1989 distribution of desert tortoise populations (shaded). Compare Figure 42-5 with Figure 42-4 and note that three impact zones lie just south of the Granite Mountains and that there is an impact zone in the southeast corner of the installation.

Figure 42-6 represents the TPS surface model of the 1983 Fort Irwin tortoise population landscape, with the amplitude of the peaks representing tortoise density. Note that the orientation is southward (looking from the northern portion of the installation). This is necessary because of the high tortoise density along the southern boundary. From the northwest to the southeast, note that the locations of Gary Owen, Nelson, Lucky Fuse, and Langford impact zones are masked, because these areas in 1983 contained live, unexploded ordnance and were off-limits to tactical vehicles and tortoise surveyors. The TSP model clearly shows the high tortoise densities along the installation's southern boundary and at Goldstone, visible in the right center of the figure. Importantly, note the tortoise population along the southern bajada (ancient coalesced alluvial fans) of the Granite Mountains, including the large density peak in Granite Pass, between Lucky Fuse and Nelson (fur-

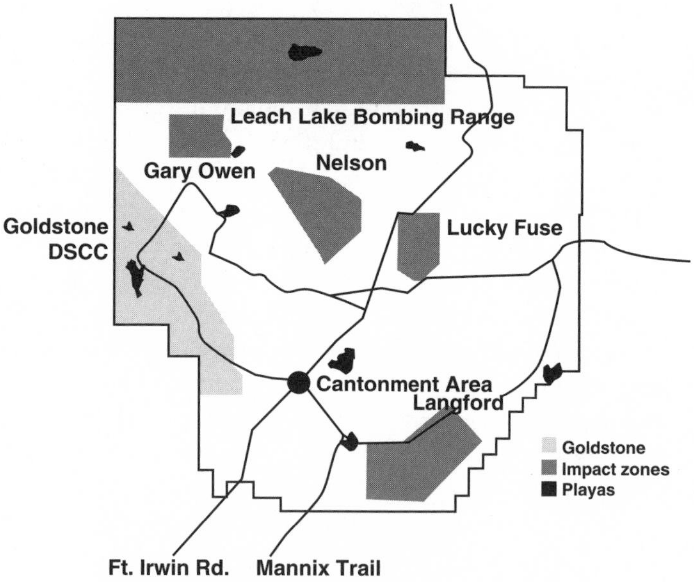

Figure 42-4. Map of Fort Irwin, California, illustrating its three management units: Leach Lake Bombing Range, Goldstone Deep Space Communications Complex, and National Training Center (rest of installation); live-fire impact zones; playas; cantonment area (housing and infrastructure); and major roads.

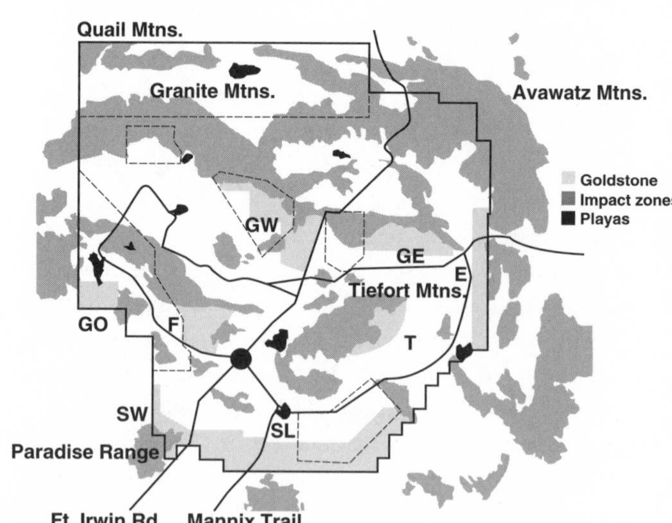

Figure 42-5. Map of Fort Irwin, California. This map is similar to Figure 42-4, with the addition of mountain ranges and the eight desert tortoise populations identified in the 1989 survey.

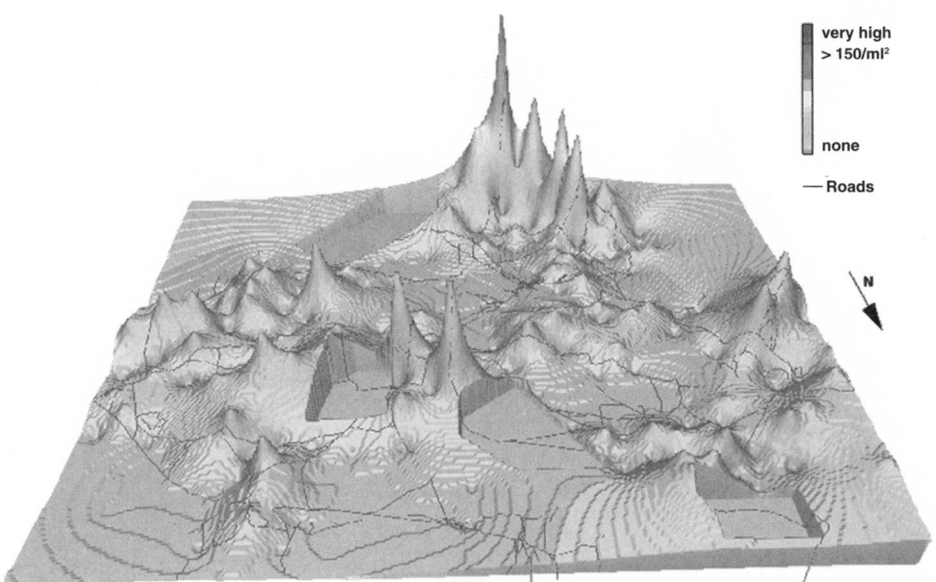

Figure 42-6. Thin-plate splines modeling tortoise density surface at Fort Irwin, California, in 1983. The orientation is toward the south. Compare with Figures 42-4 and 42-5 for pertinent landscape features. Peak amplitudes are proportional to estimated tortoise densities. Note that the impact zones are masked out because these were not cleared of hazardous ordnance until 1984 to 1985.

ther note that density peaks lie on either side of the road through this pass). Tortoises were also found in the northwest corner of the installation between Gary Owen and Goldstone and throughout the east-central valleys.

Figure 42-7 represents the TPS of the 1989 Fort Irwin tortoise populations landscape. The four impact zones were cleared of hazardous ordnance in 1984 to 1985. Note that tortoise populations along installation boundaries and at Goldstone remain viable. The population along the southern boundary extends into the former unsurveyed Langford impact zone, clearly showing a strong density peak in the extreme southeastern corner of the installation. This portion of the installation has been relatively free from tactical vehicles and represents very high quality habitat. The increased sampling effort in 1989 "exposed" the tortoise population in the Multi-Purpose Range Complex (F in Fig. 42-5), which is off-limits to tactical vehicles. The clearing of hazardous ordnance from the impact zones has enabled tactical vehicles to sweep across the landscape in the southern bajada of the Granite Mountains. Note that the former population in Granite Pass is no longer present, and the once continuous population along the southern bajada of the Granites has been fragmented into two smaller populations, GE and GW (Fig. 42-5), which have retreated higher into the bajada. A comparison of the TPS figures demonstrates the loss of tortoises in the northwestern portion and in the east-central valleys of the installation. TPS tortoise density modeling paralleled the results of the statistical analysis.

Summary

This chapter introduces the technologies and applications of Geographic Information Systems (GIS), cartography (maps), landscape ecology, and spatial modeling to field biologists and herpetologists and includes selected references on these topics. The motivation has been to inspire field herpetologists interested in assessing and monitoring amphibian populations to reflect on their research designs and needs in the context of the information presented and to acquire new interdisciplinary approaches and technologies. Concepts discussed in cartography include map scales, map projections, geographic coordinate systems, and thematic maps. Principles of GIS are developed, stressing capabilities and ap-

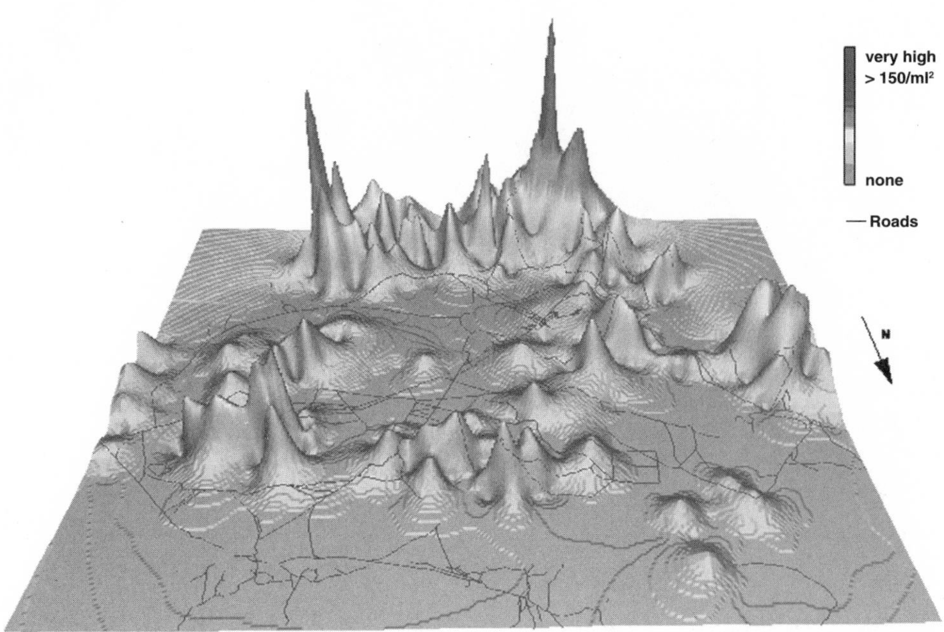

Figure 42-7. Thin-plate splines modeling tortoise density surface at Fort Irwin, California, in 1989. Note the presence of tortoises in the Langford and Nelson impact zones.

plications, nature of input data and analysis, and the relative merits of vector and raster GIS modes. GIS applications in remote sensing, landscape management and assessment/monitoring, conservation biology, and satellite telemetry are reviewed. Fundamental concepts and terminology of landscape ecology are presented, stressing quantitative aspects of landscape patterns, including issues of scale. A major discipline of spatial modeling is reviewed—interpolation and smoothing of geographic field data. An example is demonstrated using thin-plate splines for producing a landscape-scale distribution and density surface of fragmented desert tortoise populations.

Acknowledgments

Helena Mitásová, Jocelyn Aycrigg, and Kevin Seel were instrumental in the science and art of thin-plate splines. The GIS expertise of Diane Szafoni and Jocelyn Aycrigg was important to the readability and organization of this chapter.

Conclusion

Michael J. Lannoo

In this book we have presented an extensive and unprecedented overview of the conservation status of midwestern amphibians. There are several conclusions to be drawn.

The first is that while an enormous amount of information is presented here, we still do not have a complete picture of the status of midwestern amphibians. In essence, by defining what we know we have also defined what we do not know, and it is this lack of information that should now draw our attention.

It is instructive to compare the number of species considered in detail here with the species list presented in the Introduction. Only twelve out of a possible seventy-six midwestern amphibian taxa are considered in any detail, and even for the species considered, there are holes. In many cases, more appears to be known about a species' distribution than other aspects of its biology, such as its life history, home-range sizes, and migration patterns. For instance, while we now know a great deal about the distribution of four-toed salamanders (*Hemidactylium scutatum*) in Illinois, what can we say about their longevity, survival rates through metamorphosis, patterns of adult recruitment, and the minimum area of suitable habitat that can support a viable population? Furthermore, do these aspects vary across populations, for example, with latitude?

Even the distributions listed here—tending to reflect funding sources and therefore limited by political boundaries—represent a subset of the species' entire distribution. We treat in detail mudpuppies (*Necturus maculosus maculosus*) in northeastern Ohio but not throughout the Midwest; a population of cave salamanders (*Eurycea lucifuga*) in Ohio but not populations throughout the rest of Ohio nor throughout the Midwest; two populations of green salamanders (*Aneides aeneus*), one in Ohio, one in Indiana, but not throughout the Appalachians; northern leopard frogs (*Rana pipiens*) in northwestern Ohio but not across North America; and green frogs (*Rana clamitans melanota*) and pickerel frogs (*Rana palustris*) in Illinois, but not throughout eastern North America. This criticism, of course, is in no way meant to belittle the already enormous efforts of particular researchers. These results simply reflect funding sources and the amount of time and energy available for a project. As individuals, we can do no more.

Species that are rare or of concern are relatively better represented than those that do not have these attributes. I find it odd that our most abundant amphibians—northern leopard frogs, bullfrogs (*Rana catesbeiana*), American toads (*Bufo americanus americanus*), chorus frogs (*Pseudacris triseriata*), eastern and Cope's gray treefrogs (*Hyla versicolor* and *Hyla chrysoscelis*, respectively), eastern tiger salamanders (*Ambystoma tigrinum tigrinum*), and eastern newts (*Notophthalmus viridescens*)—are relatively underrepresented in this volume. And, I am deeply concerned that, as a group, our large-water salamanders—mudpuppies and hellbenders (*Cryptobranchus alleghaniensis*)—may be in severe decline and that no efforts are being made, or have even been proposed, to monitor their populations. Likewise, our regional accounts of species assemblages cover only a handful of scattered areas—generally those around major population centers, large parks, field stations, or otherwise convenient or of interest to individual herpetologists.

There is ample opportunity for new research and for graduate students and local researchers (e.g., regional conservation officers, high school teachers, environmental groups) to make large contributions to our base of knowledge.

The second conclusion is that amphibians appear to be responding variously to the environmental pressures presented by current land management practices and by compromises in air and water quality. Blanchard's cricket frogs (*Acris crepitans blanchardi*) are the species of most concern in the Midwest. Extirpated across much of the upper Midwest and apparently still declining at the northern margins of their current distribution, we have not been able to establish a cause-and-effect relationship between any environmental factor and cricket frog declines. In contrast, northern leopard frogs appear to have rebounded from the mysterious declines they experienced during the early 1970s. Likewise, several chapters here report species range expansions—undoubtedly due to an increased effort to find animals rather than true range expansions—but nevertheless good news. Most species tend to be maintaining their numbers at least to the point that, if declines are occurring, these are slow and, using statistical methods, will take years of monitoring to prove.

The third conclusion is that we now have enough information on many midwestern amphibian species to begin to make informed decisions about their management. Managing for amphibians will involve two different efforts. The first is to reverse management decisions negatively affecting amphibians. This effort includes extirpating introduced fish and bullfrog populations and once again isolating wetlands through the installation of standpipes on drainage culverts and the elimination of fish weirs. Amphibians rapidly recolonize such improved habitats. The second effort will involve actively managing habitats for amphibians. Such management activities could include ensuring that good-quality upland habitat is contiguous with good-quality wetland habitat, creating a variety of wetland types when restoring an area, and planting vegetated corridors. Management efforts could further include restoring oxbow and backwater habitats when rehabilitating streams and rivers. In forested regions undergoing harvest, simply leaving slash could benefit amphibians. Wetlands created in forests attract amphibians.

A fourth conclusion is that in assessing amphibian declines we must distinguish between rare for natural reasons and declines for unnatural reasons—state status does not necessarily equate with conservation status. Some species appear to be naturally rare in the Midwest. For example, four-toed salamanders are rare as a result of their post-Pleistocene relictual distribution. This species is, as it deserves to be, listed in each of the states where it occurs. It is important to realize that it would probably be listed independent of any declines it has already experienced. In contrast, Blanchard's cricket frogs are being extirpated in the northern portion of their range. Cricket frogs were naturally abundant throughout much of the Midwest; in some areas they were the most abundant frog, and now most northern populations have disappeared. In states where this extirpation has already occurred—Minnesota, Wisconsin, Michigan—the cricket frog is listed. States where the extirpation is occurring—Iowa, Illinois, Indiana—are responding in different ways. States with a progressive natural resources perspective are recognizing the problem, while more conservative states appear to be content with currently healthy southern populations. Thus the scenario arises that rare but stable four-toed salamander populations are listed, while declining but still regionally numerous cricket frogs are not. It may be that currently rare four-toed salamander populations will persist long after currently healthy cricket frog populations have been extirpated.

A fifth conclusion derives from the fourth, that current abundance does not equate with future conservation status. The most famous illustration of this conclusion is the passenger pigeon (*Ectopistes migratorius*). Stories of the abundance of passenger pigeons are common natural history lore (Erhlich et al. 1988), yet it only took a few decades for this species to become extinct. The midwestern amphibian equivalent to the passenger pigeon is, once again, the Blanchard's cricket frog. The fact that cricket frogs were once the most abundant frog in Illinois has been of no benefit at all to now-extirpated northern Illinois populations. Likewise, leopard frogs were the most abundant midwestern frog, collected at a commercial level, prior to their dramatic declines in the 1970s. Leopard frog numbers have since rebounded (in truth, the reasons for the rebound are as mysterious as the causes of the original declines), and populations currently appear to be stable. The lesson here is that we should not be attempting to predict the future conservation status of a species based on its current abundance.

Finally, for perspective, it is important to realize that, while amphibian declines are currently receiving a great degree of publicity, declines are co-occurring in many nongame groups. Species, or species groups, depend on ecosystems; they do not exist in isolation, nor are they alone likely to be affected by detrimental environmental factors. For instance, declines in amphibians will be mirrored in groups that feed on amphibians, such as reptiles and wading birds. Declines in amphibians due to habitat loss or alteration will be paralleled by declines in other species that use these same habitats. Declines in amphibians due to degradation in water or air quality will be commensurate with declines in other species also affected by poor environmental quality. It follows therefore that attempts to manage for amphibians will benefit many nongame species. The reverse is also true: attempts to manage ecosystems for biodiversity will in turn benefit amphibians.

Perhaps the largest benefit of the news surrounding amphibian declines is the awareness of this problem both among professionals and laypersons. I would like to think that this has translated into an increasing vigilance, reflected in the abundance of recent data accumulated here. If this is true, I would think that, should the declines in northern leopard frogs that occurred in the 1970s be repeated, they would be detected early and that, unlike in the 1970s, a cause could be determined. Countering this optimism, however, and continuing a theme that has run throughout this text is the fact that cricket frog declines continue and continue to be unexplained.

References

Aangeenbrug, R. T. 1991. A critique of GIS. Pp. 101–107. *In* Maguire, D. J., M. F. Goodchild, and D. W. Rhind (Eds.), Geographical Information Systems, Volume I, Principles. John Wiley and Sons, New York.

Abramson, J. H. 1994. Making Sense of Data. Oxford University Press, New York.

Acker, P. M., K. C. Kruse, and E. B. Krehbiel. 1986. Aging *Bufo americanus* by skeletochronology. Journal of Herpetology 20:570–574.

Ackerman, K. 1975. Rare and endangered vertebrates of Illinois. Unpublished report to the Illinois Department of Transportation, Bureau of Environmental Science, Springfield.

Adams, L. W., and L. E. Dove. 1989. Wildlife Reserves and Corridors in the Urban Environment: A Guide to Ecological Landscape Planning and Resource Conservation. National Institute for Urban Wildlife, Columbia, Missouri.

Adler, K. I., and D. M. Dennis. 1961. New herpetological records from Ohio, II. Journal of the Ohio Herpetological Society 3:17–22.

Agresti, A. 1990. Categorical Data Analysis. John Wiley and Sons, New York.

Agresti, A., C. R. Mehta, and N. R. Patel. 1990. Exact inference for contingency tables with ordered categories. Journal of the American Statistical Association 85:453–458.

Alberch, P., S. J. Gould, G. F. Oster, and D. B. Wake. 1979. Size and shape in ontogeny and phylogeny. Paleobiology 5:296–317.

Albert, D. A., S. R. Denton, and B. V. Barnes. 1986. Regional Landscape Ecosystems of Michigan. University of Michigan School of Natural Resources, Ann Arbor.

Albert, E. H. 1967. Life history of neotenic newts *Notopthalmus viridescens louisianensis* (Wolterstorff) in southern Illinois. M.S. thesis, Southern Illinois University, Carbondale.

Aldus, T. L. 1993. Rising waters a county crisis. Daily Times, 16 September, Pekin, Illinois.

Alfaro, S. 1995. Long-term changes in abundance and diversity of amphibians in isolated wetland fragments (Chicago). American Society of Zoologists, Abstract 369.

Alfaro, S. 1996. Long-term changes in amphibian diversity and abundance in the Forest Preserve District of Cook County. Unpublished report to the Forest Preserve District of Cook County, River Forest, Illinois.

Alford, R. A., and H. M. Wilbur. 1985. Priority effects in experimental pond communities: competition between *Bufo* and *Rana*. Ecology 66:1097–1105.

Allee, W. C., and K. P. Schmidt. 1951. Ecological Animal Geography. John Wiley and Sons, New York.

Allen, A. C. 1963. The Amphibia of Wayne County, Ohio. Journal of the Ohio Herpetological Society 4:22–30.

Allen, W. B. 1988. State lists of endangered and threatened species of reptiles and amphibians and laws and regulations covering collecting of reptiles and amphibians in each state. P. 28. *In* Bachmann, M. D., and B. W. Menzel (Eds.), Laboratory Manual for Herpetology. Iowa State University, Ames.

Altig, R. 1970. A key to the tadpoles of the continental

United States and Canada. Herpetologica 26:180–207.

Alvarez, R., M. P. Honrubia, and M. P. Herraez. 1995. Skeletal malformations induced by the insecticides ZZ-Aphox and Folidol during larval development of *Rana perezi*. Archives of Environmental Contamination and Toxicology 28:349–356.

Amborski, R. L., A. H. Carr, and G. F. Amborski. 1977. Microbiological studies on septicemic bullfrogs hemolysin production by gram negative isolates. P. 25. *In* Slepecky, R., and R. A. Finkelstein (Eds.), Abstracts of the Annual Meeting of the American Society for Microbiology, Washington, D.C.

Ambrose, D. M., J. F. Drake, and D. Faber-Langendoen. 1994. Rare plant communities of the conterminous United States: midwestern region. Pp. 211–304. *In* Grossman, D. H., K. L. Goodin, and C. Reuss (Eds.), Rare Plant Communities of the United States: An Initial Survey. The Nature Conservancy, Arlington, Virginia.

American Cartographic Association. 1986. Which map is best?: projections for world maps. American Congress on Surveying and Mapping, Falls Church, Virginia.

American Cartographic Association. 1988. Choosing a world map: attributes, distortions, classes, aspects. American Congress on Surveying and Mapping, Falls Church, Virginia.

American Society of Civil Engineers. 1983. Map Uses, Scales and Accuracies for Engineering and Associated Purposes. American Society of Civil Engineers, New York.

Amlaner, C. J., Jr., and D. W. MacDonald. 1980. A Handbook on Biotelemetry and Radio Tracking. Pergamon Press, Oxford, England.

Anderson, D. M. 1982. Plant communities of Ohio: a preliminary classification and description. Unpublished report to the Ohio Department of Natural Resources, Division of Natural Areas and Preserves, Columbus.

Anderson, D. M. 1983. The natural divisions of Ohio. Natural Areas Journal 3:23–33.

Andreas, A. T. 1876. Illustrated Historical Atlas of the State of Indiana. Baskin, Foster, Chicago.

Andrews, E. A. 1897. Breeding habits of the spotted salamander. American Naturalist 31:635–637.

Angermeier, P. L., R. J. Neves, and J. R. Karr. 1986. Nongame perspectives in aquatic resource management. Pp. 43–57. *In* Hale, J. B., L. B. Best, and R. L. Clawson (Eds.), Management of Nongame Wildlife in the Midwest: A Developing Art. BookCrafters, Chelsea, Missouri.

Anonymous. 1907. Frogs. Okoboji Protective Association Bulletin 3:5.

Anonymous. 1991. It's spring but . . . are the frogs croaking? Wild Flyer, Oregon Fish and Wildlife Publication 2:1–3.

Anonymous. 1992. Rare and Endangered Species of Missouri Checklist. Missouri Department of Conservation, Jefferson City.

Anonymous. 1993. Surveys will document location and status of non-game species. Outdoor Highlights 21:12.

Anonymous. 1995. Rare and Endangered Species Checklist of Missouri. Missouri Department of Conservation, Jefferson City.

Antenucci, J. C., K. Brown, P. L. Croswell, M. J. Kevany, and H. Archer. 1991. Geographic Information Systems: A Guide to the Technology. Van Nostrand Reinhold, New York.

Anton, T. G. 1992. Checklist and map guide to the herpetofauna of the North Branch/Des Plaines River region, 1980–1992. Unpublished report to The Nature Conservancy, Chicago.

Anton, T. G., and M. Redmer. 1995. A herpetological survey of the lower Plum Valley and Spring Valley Preserves, Will County, Illinois. Unpublished report to the Forest Preserve District of Will County, Joliet, Illinois.

Anver, M. R. 1980. Diagnostic exercise. Laboratory Animal Science 30:165–166.

Applegate, R. D., and C. W. Zimbleman. 1978. Herpetofauna of the Dixon Springs Agricultural Center and vicinity, Pope County, Illinois. Bulletin of the Chicago Herpetological Society 13:72–74.

Applegate, V. C., J. H. Howell, H. J. W. Moffe, B. G. H. Johnson, and M. A. Smith. 1961. Use of 3-trifluoromethyl-4-nitrophenol as a selective sea lamprey larvicide. Great Lakes Fisheries Committee, Technical Report 1:1–35.

Applegate, V. C., and E. L. King Jr. 1962. Comparative toxicity of 3-trifluoromethyl-4-nitrophenol (TFM) to larval lampreys and eleven species of fish. Transactions of the American Fisheries Society 91:342–345.

Arlinghaus, S. L. 1994. Practical Handbook of Digital Mapping: Terms and Concepts. CRC Press, Boca Raton, Florida.

Arminger, G., C. C. Clogg, and M. E. Sobel. 1995. Handbook of Statistical Modeling for the Social and Behavioral Sciences. Plenum, New York.

Arnold, N. 1991. Biological messages in a bottle. New Scientist 131:25–27.

Aronoff, S. 1991. Geographic Information Systems: A Management Perspective. WDL Publications, GIS World Books, Fort Collins, Colorado.

Arvesen, J. N., and T. H. Schmitz. 1970. Robust procedures for variance component problems using the jackknife. Biometrics 26:677–686.

Ashton, R. E. 1976a. The herpetofauna of Preble County, Ohio. Ohio Journal of Science 76:33–38.

Ashton, R. E. 1976b. Endangered and threatened amphibians and reptiles in the United States. Herpetological Circular Number 5. Society for the Study of Amphibians and Reptiles, St. Louis.

Ashton, R. E., Jr. 1985. Field and laboratory observations on microhabitat selection, movements, and home range of *Necturus lewisi* (Brimley). Brimleyana 10:83–106.

Asrar, G., M. Fuchs, E. T. Kanemasu, and J. L. Hatfield. 1984. Estimating absorbed photosynthetic radiation and leaf area index from spectral reflectance in wheat. Agronomy Journal 76:300–306.

Atkinson, A. C., and A. N. Donev. 1992. Optimum Experimental Designs. Oxford University Press, New York.

Auger, C. P. 1994. Information Sources in Grey Literature. Bowker, Saur, London.

Auphan, N., J. A. Didonato, C. Rosette, A. Helmberg, and M. Karin. 1995. Immunosuppression by glucocorticoids: inhibition of NF-kappa B activity through induction of I kappa B synthesis. Science 270:286–290.

Axelrod, J., and T. D. Reisine. 1984. Stress hormones: their interaction and regulation. Science 224:452–459.

Axtell, R. W., and N. Haskell. 1977. An interhiatal population of *Pseudacris streckeri* from Illinois, with an assessment of its postglacial history. Chicago Academy of Science, Natural History Miscellanea 202:1–8.

Ayles, G. B., J. G. Lark, J. Barica, and H. Kling. 1976. Seasonal mortality of rainbow trout (*Salmo gairdneri*) planted in small eutrophic lakes of central Canada. Journal of the Fisheries Research Board of Canada 33:647–655.

Babic-Gojmerac, T., Z. Kniewald, and J. Kniewald. 1989. Testosterone metabolism in neuroendocrine organs in male rats under atrazine and deethylatrazine influence. Journal of Steroid Biochemistry 33:141–146.

Bachmann, R. W., and J. R. Jones. 1974. Water quality in the Iowa Great Lakes: a report to the Iowa Great Lakes Water Quality Control Plan. Project Number 1779 of the Iowa State Agriculture and Home Economics Experimental Station, Ames.

Bahls, P. 1992. The status of fish populations and management of high mountain lakes in the western United States. Northwest Science 66:183–193.

Bailey, R. G. 1980. Description of the ecoregions of the United States. U.S. Forest Service, Miscellaneous Publication Number 1391, Washington, D.C.

Bailey, R. G. 1983. Delineation of ecosystem regions. Environmental Management 7:365–373.

Bailey, R. G. 1987. Suggested hierarchy of criteria for multi-scale ecosystem mapping. Landscape and Urban Planning 14:313–319.

Bailey, R. G. 1988. Ecogeographic analysis: a guide to the ecological division of land for resource management. U.S. Forest Service, Miscellaneous Publication Number 1465, Washington, D.C.

Bailey, R. G. 1994. Description of the ecoregions of the United States. U.S. Forest Service, Miscellaneous Publication 1391, Washington, D.C.

Bailey, R. G. 1996. Ecosystem Geography. Springer-Verlag, New York.

Baker, F. C. 1922. The molluscan fauna of the Big Vermilion River, Illinois, with special reference to its modification as the result of pollution by sewage and manufacturing wastes. Illinois Biological Monogaphs 72:105–224.

Baker, J. M. R., and V. Waights. 1993. The effects of sodium nitrate on the growth and survival of toad tadpoles (*Bufo bufo*) in the laboratory. Herpetological Journal 3:147–148.

Baker, J. M. R., and V. Waights. 1994. The effects of nitrate on tadpoles of the tree frog (*Litoria caerulea*). Herpetological Journal 4:106–108.

Baker, M. R. 1978. Morphology and taxonomy of *Rhabdias* spp. (Nematoda: Rhabdiasidae) from reptiles and amphibians of southern Ontario. Canadian Journal of Zoology 56:2127–2141.

Baker, R. G. 1996. Revising Minnesota's list of endangered and threatened species: amphibians and reptiles. Pp. 8–11. *In* Moriarty, J. J., and D. Jones (Eds.), Minnesota's Amphibians and Reptiles: Conservation and Status, Proceedings of Symposium. Serpent's Tale Press, Excelsior, Minnesota.

Baker, R. G., E. A. Bettis III, D. P. Schwert, D. G. Horton, C. A. Chumbley, L. A. Gonzalez, and M. K. Reagan. 1996. Holocene paleoenvironments of northeast Iowa. Ecological Monographs 66:203–234.

Baker, R. G., R. S. Rhodes II, D. P. Schwert, A. C. Ashworth, T. J. Frest, G. R. Hallberg, and J. A. Janssens. 1986. A full-glacial biota from southeastern Iowa,

USA. Journal of Quaternary Science 1:91–107.

Baker, R. G., A. E. Sullivan, G. R. Hallberg, and D. G. Horton. 1989. Vegetational changes in western Illinois during the onset of late Wisconsinan glaciation. Ecology 70:1363–1376.

Baker, R. G., J. Van Nest, and G. Woodworth. 1989. Dissimilarity coefficients for fossil pollen spectra from Iowa and western Illinois during the last 30,000 years. Palynology 13:63–78.

Baldauf, R. J. 1952. Climatic factors influencing the breeding migration of the spotted salamander, *Ambystoma maculatum* (Shaw). Copeia 1952:178–181.

Ball, R. C., and T. G. Bahr. 1975. Intensive survey: Red River, Michigan. Pp. 431–459. *In* Whitton, B. A. (Ed.), River Ecology. Blackwell Scientific Publications, Oxford.

Barbour, M. G., and W. D. Billings. 1988. North American Terrestrial Vegetation. Cambridge University Press, Cambridge.

Barbour, R. W. 1971. Amphibians and Reptiles of Kentucky. University Press of Kentucky, Lexington.

Barica, J. 1979. Massive fish mortalities caused by algal blooms in eutrophic ecosystems. Symposia Biologica Hungarica 19:121–124.

Barica, J., and J. A. Mathias. 1979. Oxygen depletion and winterkill risk in small prairie lakes under extended ice cover. Journal of the Fisheries Research Board of Canada 36:980–986.

Barinaga, M. 1990. Where have all the froggies gone? Science 247:1033–1034.

Barnett, V., and T. Lewis. 1984. Outliers in Statistical Data. John Wiley and Sons, New York.

Barrett, E. C., and L. F. Curtis. 1992. Introduction to Environmental Remote Sensing. Chapman and Hall, New York.

Barrett, W. 1964. Frogging in Iowa. Annals of Iowa 37:362–365.

Barrett, W. C. 1947. The effects of lead salts on the hemopoietic and histiocytic systems of the larval frog. American Journal of Anatomy 81:117–136.

Barrow, J. H., Jr. 1958. The biology of *Trypanosoma diemyctyli*, Tobey: III. Factors influencing the cycle of *Trypanosoma diemyctyli* in the vertebrate host *Triturus v. viridescens*. Journal of Protozoology 5:161–170.

Bartholome, E. 1988. Radiometric measurement and crop yield forecasting: some observations over millet and sorghum experimental plots in Mali. International Journal of Remote Sensing 9:1539–1552.

Beardmore, J. A. 1983. Extinction, survival and genetic variation. Pp. 125–151. *In* Shonewald-Cox, C. M., S. M. Chambers, B. MacBryde, and L. Thomas (Eds.), Genetics and Conservation: A Reference for Managing Wild Animal and Plant Populations. Benjamin-Cummings, Menlo Park, California.

Beasley, V. R., E. K. Arnold, R. A. Lovell, and A. J. Parker. 1991. 2,4-D toxicosis I: a pilot study of 2,4-dichlorophenoxyacetic acid- and dicamba-induced myotonia in experimental dogs. Veterinary and Human Toxicology 33:435–440.

Beattie, R. C., R. Tyler-Jones, and M. J. Baxter. 1992. The effects of pH, aluminum concentration and temperature on the embryonic development of the European common frog, *Rana temporaria*. Journal of Zoology, London 228:557–570.

Beaumont, J. R. 1991. GIS and market analysis. Pp. 139–151. *In* Maguire, D. J., M. F. Goodchild, and D. W. Rhind (Eds.), Geographical Information Systems, Volume II, Applications. John Wiley and Sons, New York.

Becker, C. D., and D. A. Neitzel. 1992. Water Quality in North American River Systems. Battelle Press, Columbus, Ohio.

Becker, G. C. 1983. Fishes of Wisconsin. University of Wisconsin Press, Madison.

Beebee, T. J. C. 1975. Changes in status of the great crested newt *Triturus cristatus* in the British Isles. British Journal of Herpetology 5:481–490.

Beebee, T. J. C. 1977. Habitat of the British amphibians (1): chalk uplands. Biological Conservation 12:279–293.

Beebee, T. J. C. 1980. Habitat of the British amphibians (3): river valley marshes. Biological Conservation 18:281–287.

Beebee, T. J. C. 1981. Habitat of the British amphibians (4): agricultural lowlands and a general discussion of requirements. Biological Conservation 21:127–139.

Begon, M. 1979. Investigating Animal Abundance. University Park Press, Baltimore.

Behler, J. L., and F. W. King. 1979. The Audubon Society Field Guide to North American Reptiles and Amphibians. Alfred A. Knopf, New York.

Beiswenger, R. E. 1975. Structure and function in aggregations of tadpoles of the American toad, *Bufo americanus*. Herpetologica 31:222–233.

Beiswenger, R. E. 1977. Diel patterns of aggregative behavior in tadpoles of *Bufo americanus* in relation to light and temperature. Ecology 58:98–108.

Bell, G. H., and D. B. Rhodes. 1994. A Guide to the Zoological Literature: The Animal Kingdom. Libraries Unlimited, Englewood, Colorado.

Bell, H. E., III. 1981. Illinois wetlands: their value and management. Document Number 81/33, Illinois Institute of Natural Resources, Chicago.

Bellis, E. D. 1957. An ecological study of the wood frog, *Rana sylvatica* LeConte. Ph.D. dissertation, University of Minnesota, Minneapolis.

Bellis, E. D. 1961. Growth of the wood frog, *Rana sylvatica*. Copeia 1961:74–77.

Bellrose, F. C., S. P. Havera, F. L. Paveglio Jr., and D. W. Steffeck. 1983. The fate of lakes in the Illinois River valley. Illinois Natural History Survey Biological Notes 119:1–27.

Beltz, E. 1991. Illinois chorus frog, *Pseudacris streckeri illinoensis*, 1991 survey of Cass, Menard, Morgan and Scott Counties, Illinois. Unpublished report to the Illinois Department of Conservation, Division of Natural Heritage, Springfield.

Beltz, E. 1993. Distribution and status of the Illinois chorus frog, *Pseudacris streckeri illinoensis*, in Cass, Menard, Morgan, and Scott Counties of west-central Illinois. Unpublished report to the Illinois Department of Conservation, Division of Natural Heritage, Springfield.

Bennett, G. W. 1970. Management of Lakes and Ponds. Van Nostrand Reinhold, New York.

Bergeron, J. M., D. Crews, and J. A. McLachlan. 1994. PCBs as environmental estrogens: turtle sex determination as a biomarker of environmental contamination. Environmental Health Perspectives 102:780–781.

Berkson, J. 1942. Tests of significance considered as evidence. Journal of the American Statistical Association 37:325–335.

Bernhardsen, T. 1992. Geographic Information Systems. VIAK IT A/S, Norway. GIS World Books, Fort Collins, Colorado.

Berrill, M., S. Bertram, D. Brigham, and V. Campbell. 1992. A comparison of three methods of monitoring frog populations. Pp. 87–93. *In* Bishop, C. A., and K. E. Pettit (Eds.), Declines in Canadian Amphibian Populations: Designing a National Monitoring Strategy. Occasional Paper Number 76, Canadian Wildlife Service, Ottawa, Ontario.

Berrill, M., S. Bertram, L. McGillivray, M. Kolohon, and B. Pauli. 1994. Effects of low concentrations of forest-use pesticides on frog embryos and tadpoles. Environmental Toxicology and Chemistry 13:657–664.

Berrill, M., S. Bertram, A. Wilson, S. Louis, D. Brigham, and C. Stromberg. 1993. Lethal and sublethal impacts of pyrethroid insecticides on amphibian embryos and tadpoles. Environmental Toxicology and Chemistry 12:525–539.

Berry, J. K. 1993. Beyond Mapping: Concepts, Algorithms, and Issues in GIS. GIS World Books, Fort Collins, Colorado.

Berven, K. A. 1990. Factors affecting population fluctuations in larval and adult stages of the wood frog (*Rana sylvatica*). Ecology 71:1599–1608.

Bidwell, J. R., and J. R. Gorrie. 1995. Acute toxicity of a herbicide to selected frog species. Final report to the Western Australia Department of Environmental Protection, Perth, Australia.

Birdsall, C. W., C. E. Grue, and A. Anderson. 1986. Lead concentrations in bullfrog *Rana catesbeiana* and green frog *R. clamitans* tadpoles inhabiting highway drainages. Environmental Pollution, Series A 40:233–247.

Birge, W. J., J. A. Black, and R. A. Kuehne. 1980. Effects of organic compounds on amphibian reproduction. University of Kentucky, Water Resources Research Institute, Research Report 121, Lexington.

Birge, W. J., J. A. Black, and G. A. Westerman. 1979. Evaluation of aquatic pollutants using fish and amphibian eggs as bioassay organisms. Pp. 108–118. *In* Neilsen, S. W., G. Migaki, and D. G. Scarpelli (Eds.), Animals as Monitors of Environmental Pollutants. National Academy of Science, Washington, D.C.

Birge, W. J., and R. A. Cassidy. 1983. Structure-activity relationships in aquatic toxicology. Fundamental and Applied Toxicology 3:359–368.

Birks, H. J. B. 1976. Late-Wisconsinan vegetational history at Wolf Creek, central Minnesota. Ecological Monographs 46:395–429.

Bishop, C. A. 1992. The effects of pesticides on amphibians and the implications for determining causes of declines in amphibian populations. Pp. 67–70. *In* Bishop, C. A., and K. E. Pettit (Eds.), Declines in Canadian Amphibian Populations: Designing a National Monitoring Strategy. Occasional Paper Number 76, Canadian Wildlife Service, Ottawa, Ontario.

Bishop, C. A., D. Bradford, G. Casper, S. Corn, S. Droege, G. Fellers, P. Geissler, D. M. Green, R. Heyer, D. Johnson, M. Lannoo, D. Larson, R. McDiarmid, J. Sauer, B. Shaffer, H. Whiteman, and H. Wilbur. 1994. A Proposed North American Amphibian Monitoring Program. Conference Proceedings, First General Meeting, September 1994, Indiana Dunes National Lakeshore, National Biological Service, Laurel, Maryland.

Bishop, C. A., and K. E. Pettit, eds. 1992. Declines in Canadian Amphibian Populations: Designing a

National Monitoring Strategy. Occasional Paper Number 76, Canadian Wildlife Service, Ottawa, Ontario.

Bishop, C. A., K. E. Pettit, M. E. Gartshore, and D. A. McLeod. 1997. Extensive monitoring of anuran populations using call counts and road transects in Ontario, Canada (1992–1993). Pp. 149–160. *In* Green, D. M. (Ed.), Amphibians in Decline. Report from the Canadian Declining Amphibian Task Force, Herpetological Conservation Volume 1. Society for the Study of Amphibians and Reptiles, Canadian Association of Herpetologists, Montreal.

Bishop, R. A. 1981. Iowa's wetlands. Proceedings of the Iowa Academy of Science 88:11–16.

Bishop, S. C. 1926. Notes on the habits and development of the mudpuppy *Necturus maculosus* (Rafinesque). New York State Museum Bulletin 268:1–60.

Bishop, S. C. 1941. The salamanders of New York. New York State Museum Bulletin 324:1–365.

Bishop, S. C. 1943. Handbook of Salamanders. Comstock Publishing, Ithaca, New York.

Bishop, Y. M. M., S. E. Fienberg, and P. W. Holland. 1975. Discrete Multivariate Analysis: Theory and Practice. MIT Press, Cambridge.

Black, J. E., and G. Sievert. 1989. A Field Guide to the Amphibians of Oklahoma. Oklahoma Department of Wildlife Conservation, Oklahoma City.

Blair, A. P. 1951. Note on the herpetology of the Elk Mountains, Colorado. Copeia 1951:239–240.

Blanchard, F. N. 1923. The amphibians and reptiles of Dickinson County, Iowa. University of Iowa Studies in Natural History, Lakeside Laboratory Studies 10:19–26.

Blanchard, F. N. 1930. The stimulus to the breeding migration of the spotted salamander, *Ambystoma maculatum*. American Naturalist 64:154–167.

Blanchard, S. E., and L. H. Princen. 1976. Survey on the occurrence of reptiles and amphibians in central Illinois. Proceedings of the Peoria Academy of Science 9:29–35.

Blaustein, A. R. 1994. Chicken Little or Nero's fiddle? a perspective on declining amphibian populations. Herpetologica 50:85–97.

Blaustein, A. R., B. Edmond, J. M. Kiesecker, J. J. Beatty, and D. G. Hokit. 1995. Ambient ultraviolet radiation causes mortality in salamander eggs. Ecological Applications 5:740–743.

Blaustein, A. R., P. D. Hoffman, D. G. Hokit, J. M. Kiesecker, S. C. Walls, and J. B. Hays. 1994. UV repair and resistance to solar UV-B in amphibian eggs: a link to population declines? Proceedings of the National Academy of Science 91:1791–1795.

Blaustein, A. R., and D. B. Wake. 1990. Declining amphibian populations: a new global phenomenon? Trends in Ecology and Evolution 5:203–204.

Blaustein, A. R., and D. B. Wake. 1995. The puzzle of declining amphibian populations. Scientific American 272:52–57.

Blaustein, A. R., D. B. Wake, and W. P. Sousa. 1994. Amphibian declines: judging stability, persistence, and susceptibility of populations to local and global extinctions. Conservation Biology 8:60–71.

Blem, C. R. 1972. An annotated list of the amphibians and reptiles of Hardin County. Ohio Journal of Science 72:91–96.

Blymyer, M. J., and B. S. McGinnes. 1977. Observations on possible detrimental effects of clearcutting on terrestrial amphibians. Bulletin of the Maryland Herpetological Society 13:79–83.

Bock, J. H., C. E. Bock, and R. J. Fritz. 1981. Biogeography of Illinois reptiles and amphibians. American Midland Naturalist 106:258–270.

Bogart, J. P., and A. P. Jaslow. 1979. Distribution and call parameters of *Hyla chrysoscelis* and *Hyla versicolor* in Michigan. Life Science Contributions, Royal Ontario Museum 117:1–13.

Bogart, J. P., and L. E. Licht. 1986. Reproduction and the origin of polyploids in hybrid salamanders of the genus *Ambystoma*. Canadian Journal of Genetics and Cytology 28:605–617.

Bogner, W. C., W. P. Fitzpatrick, and D. S. Blakley. 1985. Sedimentation rates in Horseshoe Lake, Alexander County, Illinois. Illinois State Water Survey Contract Report 364, Champaign.

Bonham-Carter, G. F. 1991. Integration of geoscientific data using GIS. Pp. 171–184. *In* Maguire, D. J., M. F. Goodchild, and D. W. Rhind (Eds.), Geographical Information Systems, Volume II, Applications. John Wiley and Sons, New York.

Bonham-Carter, G. F. 1994. Geographic Information Systems for Geoscientists: Modeling with GIS. Pergamon, Elsevier Science, Tarrytown, New York.

Bonham-Carter, G. F., F. P. Agterberg, and D. F. Wright. 1990. Weights of evidence modelling: a new approach to mapping mineral potential. Geological Survey of Canada Paper 89–90:171–183.

Bonin, J. 1992. Status of amphibians in Quebec. Pp. 23–25. *In* Bishop, C. A., and K. E. Pettit (Eds.), Declines in Canadian Amphibian Populations: Designing a

National Monitoring Strategy. Occasional Paper Number 76, Canadian Wildlife Service, Ottawa, Ontario.

Borchert, J. R. 1950. The climate of the central North American grassland. Annals of the Association of American Geographers 40:1–39.

Borenstein, M., and J. Cohen. 1988. Statistical Power Analysis: A Computer Program. Lawrence Erlbaum Associates, Hillsdale, New Jersey.

Boschulte, D. S. 1995. Toxicity of six commonly used herbicides on larval bullfrogs (*Rana catesbeiana*). Beacon 5:7–10.

Botts, P., A. Haney, K. Holland, and S. Packard. 1994. Midwest oak ecosystems recovery plan. Unpublished report to the U.S. Environmental Protection Agency, Region V, Chicago.

Bourdo, E. A., Jr. 1956. A review of the General Land Office survey and of its use in quantitative studies of former forests. Ecology 37:754–768.

Bouyea, B. 1993. Farms flooded, but the river isn't to blame. Overflowing aquifer has flooded one-fourth of farmland in Mason. Journal Star, 24 August, Peoria, Illinois.

Bovbjerg, R. V. 1965. Experimental studies on the dispersal of the frog, *Rana pipiens*. Proceedings of the Iowa Academy of Science 72:412–418.

Bowen, J. T. 1970. A history of fish culture as related to the development of fishery programs. Pp. 71–93. *In* Benson, N. G. (Ed.), A Century of Fisheries in North America. American Fisheries Society, Washington, D.C.

Bowles, M., M. D. Hutchison, and J. L. McBride. 1994. Landscape pattern and structure of oak savanna, woodland, and barrens in northeastern Illinois at the time of European settlement. Pp. 65–73. *In* Fralish, J. S., R. C. Anderson, J. E. Ebinger, and R. Szafoni (Eds.), Proceedings of the North American Conference on Savannas and Barrens. Illinois State University, Normal.

Box, G. E. P., and D. R. Cox. 1964. An analysis of transformations. Journal of the Royal Statistical Society Bulletin 26:211–252.

Box, G. E. P., W. G. Hunter, and J. S. Hunter. 1978. Statistics for Experimenters: An Introduction to Design, Data Analysis, and Model Building. John Wiley and Sons, New York.

Box, G. E. P., and G. C. Tiao. 1973. Bayesian Inference in Statistical Analysis. Wiley Classics Library Edition 1992, John Wiley and Sons, New York.

Boyer, R., and C. E. Grue. 1995. The need for water quality criteria for frogs. Environmental Health Perspectives 103:352–357.

Bradford, D. F. 1983. Winterkill, oxygen relations and energy metabolism of a submerged dormant amphibian, *Rana muscosa*. Ecology 64:1171–1183.

Bradford, D. F. 1989. Allopatric distribution of native frogs and introduced fishes in high Sierra Nevada lakes of California: implication of the negative effect of fish introductions. Copeia 1989:775–778.

Bradford, D. F. 1991. Mass mortality and extinction in a high elevation population of *Rana muscosa*. Journal of Herpetology 25:174–177.

Bradford, D. F., D. M. Graber, and F. Tabatabai. 1993. Isolation of remaining populations of the native frog, *Rana muscosa*, by introduced fishes in Sequoia and Kings Canyon National Parks, California. Conservation Biology 7:882–885.

Bragg, A. N. 1950. Salientian range extensions in Oklahoma and a new state record. Pp. 34–44. *In* Bragg, A. N., A. O. Weese, H. A. Dundee, H. T. Fisher, A. Richards, and C. B. Clark (Eds.), Researches on the Amphibia of Oklahoma. University of Oklahoma Press, Norman.

Bragg, A. N. 1965. Gnomes of the Night: The Spadefoot Toads. University of Pennsylvania Press, Philadelphia.

Bragg, A. N., and W. N. Bragg. 1958. Parasitism of spadefoot tadpoles by *Saprolegnia*. Herpetologica 14:34.

Bragg, A. N., and H. A. Dundee. 1951. Salientian additions to county lists in Oklahoma. Proceedings of the Oklahoma Academy of Science 30:19–20.

Brandon, R. A. 1965. A second record of *Hemidactylium scutatum*, the four-toed salamander, in Kentucky. Transactions of the Illinois State Academy of Science 58:149–150.

Brandon, R. A. 1994. Herpetofauna of Horseshoe Lake Conservation Area. Pp. 5.1–5.43. *In* Brandon, R. A., B. M. Burr, G. A. Feldhamer, R. J. Gates, and R. C. Heidinger, Potential effects of increased water levels on flora and fauna at Horseshoe Lake, Alexander County, Illinois. Unpublished report to the Illinois Department of Conservation, Division of Natural Heritage, Springfield.

Brandon, R. A., and S. R. Ballard. 1991. Herpetological survey of Fults Hill Prairie Nature Preserve, Kidd Lake Marsh Natural Area, Prairie du Rocher Herpetological Area, and Renault Herpetological Area. Pp. 1–61. *In* Brandon, R. A., and S. R. Ballard. Inventories of amphibians and reptiles in Illinois. Unpublished report to the Illinois Department of Conservation, Division of Natural Heritage, Springfield.

Brandon, R. A., and D. J. Bremer. 1966. Neotenic newts, *Notophthalmus viridescens louisianensis*, in southern Illinois. Herpetologica 22:213–217.

Brandon, R. A., and D. J. Bremer. 1967. Overwintering of larval tiger salamanders in southern Illinois. Herpetologica 23:67–68.

Brandon, R. A., B. M. Burr, G. A. Feldhamer, R. J. Gates, and R. C. Heidinger. 1994. Potential effects of increased water levels on flora and fauna at Horseshoe Lake, Alexander County, Illinois. Unpublished report to the Illinois Department of Conservation, Division of Natural Heritage, Springfield.

Brannian, R. E. 1984. Lungworms. Pp. 213–217. *In* Hoff, G. L., F. L. Frye, and E. R. Jacobson (Eds.), Diseases of Amphibians and Reptiles. Plenum Press, New York.

Brattstrom, B. H. 1962. Homing in the giant toad, *Bufo marinus*. Herpetologica 18:176–180.

Braun, E. L. 1916. The physiographic ecology of the Cincinnati region. Ohio Biological Survey Bulletin Number 2.

Braun, E. L. 1950. Deciduous Forest of Eastern North America. Hafner, New York.

Braun, E. L. 1989. The Woody Plants of Ohio. Ohio State University Press, Columbus.

Breckenridge, W. J. 1941. The amphibians and reptiles of Minnesota with special reference to the black-banded skink, *Eumeces septentrionalis* (Baird). Ph.D. dissertation, University of Minnesota, Minneapolis.

Breckenridge, W. J. 1944. The Amphibians and Reptiles of Minnesota. University of Minnesota Press, Minneapolis.

Breckenridge, W. J., and J. R. Tester. 1961. Growth, local movements and hibernation of the Manitoba toad, *Bufo hemiophrys*. Ecology 42:637–646.

Breden, F. 1982. Population structure and ecology of the Fowler's toad, *Bufo woodhousei fowleri*, in Indiana Dunes National Lakeshore. Ph.D. dissertation, University of Chicago, Chicago.

Breden, F. 1987. The effect of post-metamorphic dispersal on the population genetic structure of Fowler's toad, *Bufo woodhousei fowleri*. Copeia 1987:386–395.

Breitenbach, G. L. 1982. The frequency of communal nesting and solitary brooding in the salamander, *Hemidactylium scutatum*. Journal of Herpetology 16:341–346.

Brinson, M. M., and L. C. Lee. 1989. In-kind mitigation for wetland loss: statement of ecological issues and evaluation of examples. Pp. 1069–1085. *In* Sharitz, R. R., and J. W. Gibbons (Eds.), Freshwater Wetlands and Wildlife. DOE Symposium Series Number 61, U.S. Department of Energy, Office of Scientific and Technical Information, Oak Ridge, Tennessee.

Bristow, C. E. 1991. Interactions between phylogenetically distant predators: *Notophthalmus viridescens* and *Enneacanthus obesus*. Copeia 1991:1–8.

Brockelman, W. Y. 1969. An analysis of density affects and predation in *Bufo americanus* tadpoles. Ecology 50:632–644.

Brockwell, P. J., and R. A. Davis. 1991. Time Series: Theory and Methods. Springer-Verlag, New York.

Brodie, E. D., Jr., and D. R. Formanowitz Jr. 1987. Antipredator mechanisms of larval anurans: protection of palatable individuals. Herpetologica 43:369–373.

Brodie, E. D., Jr., D. R. Formanowitz Jr., and E. D. Brodie III. 1978. The development of noxiousness of *Bufo americanus* tadpoles to aquatic insect predators. Herpetologica 34:302–306.

Brodman, R. 1989. A statistical analysis of amphibian and reptile distribution in Michigan. M.S. thesis, Eastern Michigan University, Ypsilanti.

Brodman, R. 1993. The effect of acidity on interactions of *Ambystoma* salamander larvae. Journal of Freshwater Ecology 8:209–214.

Brodman, R. 1995. Annual variation in breeding success of two syntopic species of *Ambystoma* salamanders. Journal of Herpetology 29:111–113.

Brodman, R., S. Cortwright, and A. Resetar. 1995. Reptile and amphibian surveys of northwest Indiana fish and wildlife properties. Joint meeting of the American Society of Ichthyologists and Herpetologists and the Herpetologist's League, Edmonton, Alberta. Unpublished abstract.

Brönmark, C., and P. Edenhamn. 1994. Does the presence of fish affect the distribution of tree frogs (*Hyla arborea*)? Conservation Biology 8:841–845.

Brooker, M. P., D. L. Morris, and R. J. Hemsworth. 1977. Mass mortalities of adult salmon, *Salmo salar*, in the River Wye, 1976. Journal of Applied Ecology 14:409–417.

Brooks, J. A. 1981. Otolith abnormalities in *Limnodynastes tasmaniensis* tadpoles after embryonic exposure to the pesticide dieldrin. Environmental Pollution, Series A 25:19–25.

Brown, D. E., C. H. Lowe, and C. P. Pase. 1979. A digitized classification system for the biotic communities of North America, with community (series) and association examples for the Southwest. Journal of the Arizona-Nevada Academy of Science 14:1–16.

Brown, D. E., C. H. Lowe, and C. P. Pase. 1980. A digitized systematic classification for ecosystems with an illustrated summary of the natural vegetation of North America. U.S. Forest Service, General Technical Report RM–73, Washington, D.C.

Brown, L. E. 1978. Subterranean feeding by the chorus frog *Pseudacris streckeri* (Anura: Hylidae). Herpetologica 34:212–216.

Brown, L. E. 1986. Field survey for the Illinois chorus frog in the study area for the IL 97/Pecan Creek Bridge (FAP 34), Mason County, Illinois. Unpublished report to the Illinois Department of Transportation, Normal.

Brown, L. E. 1996. Trend toward extinction of the unusual forward burrowing Illinois chorus frog. Reptile and Amphibian Magazine 43 (November/December):70–73.

Brown, L. E., and J. R. Brown. 1973. Notes on breeding choruses of two anurans (*Scaphiopus holbrookii, Pseudacris streckeri*) in southern Illinois. Chicago Academy of Sciences, Natural History Miscellanea 192:1–3.

Brown, L. E., H. O. Jackson, and J. R. Brown. 1972. Burrowing behavior of the chorus frog, *Pseudacris streckeri.* Herpetologica 28:325–328.

Brown, L. E., and D. B. Means. 1984. Fossorial behavior and ecology of the chorus frog *Pseudacris ornata.* Amphibia-Reptilia 5:261–273.

Brown, L. E., and D. Moll. 1979. The status of the nearly extinct Illinois mud turtle (*Kinosternon flavescens spooneri* Smith 1951) with recommendations for its conservation. Milwaukee Public Museum, Contributions in Biology and Geology, Number 3.

Brown, L. E., and A. K. Moorehouse. 1996. The endangered, threatened, and rare birds of Sand Lake, an unusual ephemeral wetland in west-central Illinois. Meadowlark 5:88–92.

Brown, L. E., and M. A. Morris. 1990. Distribution, habitat, and zoogeography of the plains leopard frog (*Rana blairi*) in Illinois. Illinois Natural History Survey Biological Notes 136:1–6.

Brown, L. E., M. A. Morris, and T. R. Johnson. 1993. Zoogeography of the plains leopard frog (*Rana blairi*). Bulletin of the Chicago Academy of Sciences 15:1–13.

Brown, L. E., and G. B. Rose. 1988. Distribution, habitat, and calling season of the Illinois chorus frog (*Pseudacris streckeri illinoensis*) along the lower Illinois River. Illinois Natural History Survey Biology Notes 132:1–13.

Brown, M., and J. J. Dinsmore. 1986. Implications of marsh size and isolation for marsh management. Journal of Wildlife Management 50:392–397.

Brownstein, D. G. 1984. Mycobacteriosis. Pp. 1–23. *In* Hoff, G. L., F. L. Frye, and E. R. Jacobson (Eds.), Diseases of Amphibians and Reptiles. Plenum Press, New York.

Bruggers, R. C. 1973. Food habits of bullfrogs in northwest Ohio. Ohio Journal of Science 73:185–188.

Bryant, W. S. 1987. Structure and composition of the old-growth forests of Hamilton County, Ohio, and environs. Pp. 317–324. *In* Hay, R. L., F. W. Woods, and H. DeSelm (Eds.), Proceedings of the Central Hardwood Forest Conference VI, Knoxville, Tennessee.

Buchli, G. L. 1969. Distribution, food, and life history of tiger salamanders in Devils Lake, North Dakota. M.S. thesis, University of North Dakota, Grand Forks.

Burger, W. L. 1950. Novel aspects of the life history of two *Ambystomas*. Journal of the Tennessee Academy of Science 25:252–257.

Burgess, R. L., and D. M. Sharpe. 1981. Forest Island Dynamics in Man-Dominated Landscapes. Springer-Verlag, New York.

Burggren, W. W., and J. J. Just. 1992. Developmental changes in physiological systems. Pp. 467–530. *In* Feder, M. E., and W. W. Burggren (Eds.), Environmental Physiology of Amphibians. University of Chicago Press, Chicago.

Burke, R. L. 1991. Relocations, repatriations, and translocations of amphibians and reptiles: taking a broader view. Herpetologica 47:350–357.

Burkett, R. D. 1984. An ecological study of the cricket frog, *Acris crepitans.* Pp. 89–103. *In* Seigel, R. A., L. E. Hunt, J. L. Knight, L. Maleret, and N. L. Zuschlag (Eds.), Vertebrate Ecology and Systematics: A Tribute to Henry S. Fitch. University of Kansas Museum of Natural History, Lawrence.

Burrough, P. A. 1986. Principles of Geographical Information Systems for Land Resources Assessment. Clarendon Press, Oxford.

Burrough, P. A. 1989. Matching spatial databases and quantitative models in land resource management. Soil Use and Management 5:3–8.

Burt, C. E. 1936. Contributions to the herpetology of Texas. 1. Frogs of the genus *Pseudacris.* American Midland Naturalist 17:770–775.

Burton, T. M., and G. E. Likens. 1975. Energy flow and nutrient cycling in salamander populations in the Hubbard Brook Experimental Forest, New Hampshire. Ecology 56:1068–1080.

Bury, R. B., and R. A. Luckenbach. 1976. Introduced amphibians and reptiles in California. Biological Conservation 10:1–14.

Bury, R. B., and J. A. Weland. 1984. Ecology and management of the bullfrog. U.S. Fish and Wildlife Service,

Resource Publication Number 155, Washington, D.C.

Bushey, C. L. 1979. A survey of the herpetofauna of the upper Des Plaines River valley, Lake County, Illinois. Transactions of the Illinois Academy of Science 72:22–28.

Buslovich, S. Y., and N. V. Boruchko. 1976. Chloroderivatives of phenoxyacetic acid as antagonists of thyroid hormones. Farmakologiya I Toksikologiya 39:481–483.

Butler, D. R. 1995. Zoogeomorphology: Animals as Geomorphic Agents. Cambridge University Press, New York.

Butterfield, B. P. 1988. Age structure and reproductive biology of the Illinois chorus frog (*Pseudacris streckeri illinoensis*) from northeastern Arkansas. M.S. thesis, Arkansas State University, Jonesboro.

Butterfield, B. P., W. E. Meshaka, and S. E. Trauth. 1989. Fecundity and egg mass size of the Illinois chorus frog, *Pseudacris streckeri illinoensis* (Hylidae), from northeastern Arkansas. Southwestern Naturalist 34:556–557.

Cagle, F. R. 1942. Herpetological fauna of Jackson and Union Counties, Illinois. American Midland Naturalist 28:164–200.

Cagle, F. R. 1954. Observations on the life history of the salamander *Necturus maculosus louisianensis*. Copeia 1954:257–260.

Cagle, F. R. 1956. An outline for the study of an amphibian life history. Tulane Studies in Zoology 4:79–110.

Caldwell, J. P. 1987. Demography and life history of two species of chorus frogs (Anura: Hylidae) in South Carolina. Copeia 1987:114–127.

Caldwell, J. P., J. H. Thorp, and T. O. Jervey. 1981. Predator prey relationships among larval dragonflies, salamanders, and anurans. Oecologia 46:285–289.

Cameron, T. W. M. 1956. Parasites and Parasitism. John Wiley and Sons, New York.

Campbell, D. T. 1957. Factors relevant to the validity of experiments in social settings. Psychological Bulletin 54:297–312.

Campbell, D. T., and J. C. Stanley. 1963. Experimental and Quasi–Experimental Designs for Research. Houghton Mifflin, Boston.

Campbell, J. B. 1987. Introduction to Remote Sensing. Guilford Press, New York.

Campbell, R. C. 1989. Statistics for Biologists. Cambridge University Press, New York.

Camper, J. D. 1988. The status of three uncommon salamanders in Iowa. Journal of the Iowa Academy of Science 95:127–130.

Canadian Council on Animal Care. 1980. Guide to the care and use of experimental animals. Canadian Council on Animal Care 2:27.

Carey, C. 1993. Hypothesis concerning the causes of the disappearance of boreal toads from the mountains of Colorado. Conservation Biology 7:355–362.

Carey, C., and C. J. Bryant. 1995. Possible interrelations among environmental toxicants, amphibian development, and decline of amphibian populations. Environmental Health Perspectives 103:13–17.

Carini, A. 1910. Sur une muisissure qui cause un maladie spontanee du *Leptodactylus pentadactylus*. Annales de l'Institut Pasteur 24:157–162.

Carpenter, C. C., and J. C. Gillingham. 1987. Water hole fidelity in the marine toad, *Bufo marinus*. Journal of Herpetology 21:158–161.

Carr, J. A., and D. O. Norris. 1988. Interrenal activity during metamorphosis of the tiger salamander, *Ambystoma tigrinum*. General and Comparative Endocrinology 71:63–69.

Carver, R. P. 1978. The case against statistical testing. Harvard Educational Review 48:378–399.

Caselitz, R. H. 1966. *Pseudomonas-Aeromonas* und ihre humanmedizinische Bedeutung. Veb Gustav Fisher Verlag, Jona.

Casey, D., P. N. Nemetz, and D. H. Uyeno. 1983. Sampling frequency for water quality monitoring: measures of effectiveness. Water Resources Research 19:1107–1110.

Casper, G. S. 1993a. A preliminary summary of available records for the four-toed salamander, *Hemidactylium scutatum*, in Wisconsin. Bulletin of the Chicago Herpetological Society 28:1-3.

Casper, G. S. 1993b. The reptiles and amphibians of the Baraboo Hills, Sauk County, Wisconsin: historical review, inventory and management recommendations. Unpublished report to The Nature Conservancy, Wisconsin Chapter, Madison.

Casper, G. S. 1996. Geographic Distributions of the Amphibians and Reptiles of Wisconsin. Milwaukee Public Museum, Milwaukee.

Cassettari, S. 1993. Introduction to Integrated Geo-Information Management. Chapman and Hall, New York.

Caughley, G. 1977. Analysis of Vertebrate Populations. John Wiley and Sons, New York.

Chabot, A., and N. Helferty. 1995. Distribution of frog and toad species in 1995. P. 5. *In* Marsh Monitoring Program Newsletter, Number 2, Long Point Bird Observatory, Port Rowan, Ontario.

Chambers, J. M., W. S. Cleveland, B. Kleiner, and P. A. Tukey. 1983. Graphical Methods for Data Analysis. Duxbury Press, Boston.

Chandler, J. T., and L. L. Marking. 1975. Toxicity of the lampricide 3-trifluoromethyl-4-nitrophenol (TFM) to selected aquatic invertebrates and frog larvae. U.S. Fish and Wildlife Service, Investigations in Fish Control 62, Washington, D.C.

Chandler, J. T., and L. L. Marking. 1982. Toxicity of rotenone to selected aquatic invertebrates and frog larvae. Progressive Fish Culture 44:78–80.

Charland, M. B. 1995. Sigma Plot for Scientists. William C. Brown, Chicago.

Chatfield, C. 1985. The initial examination of data (with discussion). Journal of the Royal Statistical Society, Series A 148:214–253.

Chatfield, C. 1988. Problem Solving: A Statistician's Guide. Chapman and Hall, New York.

Chatfield, C. 1989. The Analysis of Time Series: An Introduction. Chapman and Hall, New York.

Chatterjee, S., and B. Price. 1991. Regression Analysis by Example. John Wiley and Sons, New York.

Cheh, A. M., A. B. Hooper, J. Skochdopole, C. A. Henke, and R. G. McKinnell. 1980. A comparison of the ability of frog and rat S-9 to activate promutagens in the Ames test. Environmental Mutagenesis 2:487–508.

Cheng, T. C. 1964. The Biology of Animal Parasites. W. B. Saunders, Philadelphia.

Chesser, R. K. 1983. Isolation by distance: relationship to the management of genetic resources. Pp. 66–77. *In* Shonewald-Cox, C. M., S. M. Chambers, B. MacBryde, and L. Thomas (Eds.), Genetics and Conservation: A Reference for Managing Wild Animal and Plant Populations. Benjamin-Cummings, Menlo Park, California.

Choudhury, B. J. 1987. Relationships between vegetation indices, radiation absorption, and net photosynthesis evaluated by a sensitivity analysis. Remote Sensing of Environment 22:209–233.

Chrisman, N. R. 1991. The error component in spatial data. Pp. 165–174. *In* Maguire, D. J., M. F. Goodchild, and D. W. Rhind (Eds.), Geographical Information Systems, Volume I, Principles. John Wiley and Sons, New York.

Christiansen, J. L. 1981. Population trends among Iowa's amphibians and reptiles. Proceedings of the Iowa Academy of Science 88:24–27.

Christiansen, J. L. 1995. Changes in anuran distribution in Iowa, preliminary observations. Abstract 196. Annual meeting of the Society for the Study of Amphibians and Reptiles, Boone, North Carolina.

Christiansen, J. L., and R. M. Bailey. 1991. The Salamanders and Frogs of Iowa. Iowa Department of Natural Resources, Nongame Technical Series Number 3, Des Moines.

Christiansen, J. L., and R. R. Burken. 1978. The endangered and uncommon reptiles and amphibians of Iowa. Iowa Science Teachers Journal Special Issue, University of Northern Iowa, Cedar Falls.

Christiansen, J. L., and C. M. Mabry. 1985. The amphibians and reptiles of Iowa's Loess Hills. Proceedings of the Iowa Academy of Science 92:159–163.

Christoffel, R. A., and R. W. Hay. 1995. 1994 census of Blanchard's cricket frog (*Acris crepitans blanchardi*) in southwestern Wisconsin. Unpublished report to the Wisconsin Department of Natural Resources, Bureau of Endangered Resources, Madison.

Chui, G. 1993. The vanishing frogs. San Jose Mercury News, 13 July.

Clark, E. H., II, J. A. Haverkamp, and W. Chapman. 1985. Eroding Soils: The Off-Farm Impacts. Conservation Foundation, Washington, D.C.

Clark, G. R. 1995. Mouth of the Mahomet regional groundwater model, Imperial Valley region of Mason, Tazewell and Logan Counties, Illinois. Illinois Department of Transportation, Division of Water Resources, Springfield.

Clark, H. F., C. Gray, F. Fabian, R. Zeigel, and D. T. Karzon. 1969. Comparative studies of amphibian cytoplasmic virus strains isolated from the leopard frog, bullfrog and newt. Pp. 310–326. *In* Mizell, M. (Ed.), Biology of Amphibian Tumors. Springer-Verlag, New York.

Clark, K. L., and B. D. LaZerte. 1985. A laboratory study of the effects of aluminum and pH on amphibian eggs and tadpoles. Canadian Journal of Fisheries and Aquatic Sciences 42:1544–1551.

Clarke, R. 1986. The Handbook of Ecological Monitoring. Oxford University Press, New York.

Clarkson, R., and J. C. Rorabaugh. 1989. Status of leopard frogs (*Rana pipiens* complex: Ranidae) in Arizona and southeastern California. Southwestern Naturalist 34:531–538.

Cleveland, W. S. 1993. Visualizing Data. AT&T Bell Laboratories. Hobart Press, Summit, New Jersey.

Cochran, W. G. 1947. Some consequences when the assumptions for the analysis of variance are not satisfied. Biometrics 3:22–38.

Cochran, W. G. 1977. Sampling Techniques. Wiley Classics Library Edition 1992, John Wiley and Sons, New York.

Cochran, W. G., and G. M. Cox. 1957. Experimental Designs. John Wiley and Sons, New York.

Cockrell, R. 1992. A Green Shrouded Miracle: The Administrative History of Cuyahoga Valley National Recreation Area, Ohio. U.S. Department of the Interior, Office of Planning and Resource Preservation, Cultural Resources Management, Omaha, Nebraska.

Coffin, B., and L. Pfannmuller. 1988. Minnesota's Endangered Flora and Fauna. University of Minnesota Press, Minneapolis.

Cohen, J. 1988. Statistical Power Analysis for the Behavioral Sciences. Lawrence Erlbaum Associates, Hillsdale, New Jersey.

Colborn, T. 1995. Environmental estrogens: health implication for humans and wildlife. Environmental Health Perspectives 103:135–136.

Colborn, T., and C. Clement. 1992. Chemically-Induced Alterations in Sexual and Functional Development: The Wildlife/Human Connection. Advances in Modern Environmental Toxicology, Volume XXI. Princeton Scientific Publications, Princeton, New Jersey.

Colborn, T., F. S. vom Saal, and A. M. Soto. 1993. Developmental effects of endocrine-disrupting chemicals in wildlife and humans. Environmental Health Perspectives 101:378–384.

Collier, J. E. 1955. Geographic regions of Missouri. Annals of the Association of American Geographers 45:368–392.

Collins, J. P. 1975. A comparative study of the life history strategies in a community of frogs. Ph.D. dissertation, University of Michigan, Ann Arbor.

Collins, J. P. 1981. Distribution, habitats and life history variation in the tiger salamander, *Ambystoma tigrinum*, in east-central and southeast Arizona. Copeia 1981:666–675.

Collins, J. P., and J. E. Cheek. 1983. Effect of food and density on development of typical and cannibalistic salamander larvae in *Ambystoma tigrinum nebulosum*. American Zoologist 23:77–84.

Collins, J. P., and J. R. Holumuzki. 1984. Intraspecific variation in diet within and between trophic morphs in larval tiger salamanders (*Ambystoma tigrinum nebulosum*). Canadian Journal of Zoology 62:168–174.

Collins, J. P., T. R. Jones, and H. J. Berna. 1988. Conserving genetically distinctive populations: the case of the Huachuca tiger salamander (*Ambystoma tigrinum stebbinsi* Lowe). Pp. 45–53. *In* Szaro, R. C., K. E. Severson, and D. R. Patton (Eds.), Management of Amphibians, Reptiles, and Small Mammals in North America. U.S. Forest Service, General Technical Report RM-166, Fort Collins, Colorado.

Collins, J. P., K. E. Zerba, and M. J. Sredl. 1993. Shaping intraspecific variation: development, ecology, and the evolution of morphology and life history variation in tiger salamanders. Genetica 89:167–183.

Collins, J. T. 1990. Standard common and current scientific names for North American amphibians and reptiles. Herpetological Circular Number 19. Society for the Study of Amphibians and Reptiles, St. Louis.

Collins, J. T. 1991. Viewpoint: a new taxonomic arrangement for some North American amphibians and reptiles. Herpetological Review 22:42–43.

Collins, J. T., and G. T. McDuffie. 1968. Project salamander. Explorer 10:11–14.

Collins, J. T., and G. T. McDuffie. 1969. Salamanders of the Cincinnati region. Explorer 11:21–24.

Collins, J. T., and G. T. McDuffie. 1970. Frogs and toads of the Cincinnati region. Explorer 12:12–15.

Colt, J., K. Orwicz, and D. Brooks. 1984. "Gas bubble disease" in the African clawed frog, *Xenopus laevis*. Journal of Herpetology 18:131–137.

Compton, L. V. 1952. Farm and ranch ponds. Journal of Wildlife Management 16:238–242.

Conant, R. 1975. A Field Guide to Reptiles and Amphibians of Eastern and Central North America. 2d ed. Houghton Mifflin, Boston.

Conant, R., and J. T. Collins. 1991. Reptiles and Amphibians: Eastern/Central North America. Houghton Mifflin, Boston.

Connell, J. H., and W. P. Sousa. 1983. On the evidence needed to judge ecological stability or persistence. American Naturalist 121:789–824.

Connover, W. J. 1980. Practical Nonparametric Statistics. John Wiley and Sons, New York.

Conti, L. F., and J. H. Crowley. 1939. A new bacterial species, isolated from the chuckwalla (*Sauromalus varius*). Journal of Bacteriology 37:647–653.

Cook, T. D., and D. T. Campbell. 1979. Quasi-Experimentation Design and Analysis Issues for Field Settings. Houghton Mifflin, Boston.

Cooke, A. S. 1970. The effects of p,p'-DDT on tadpoles of the common frog (*Rana temporaria*). Environmental Pollution 1:57–71.

Cooke, A. S. 1971. Selective predation by newts of frog tadpoles treated with DDT. Nature 229:275–276.

Cooke, A. S. 1972. Indications of recent changes in status in the British Isles of the frog (*Rana temporaria*) and the toad (*Bufo bufo*). Journal of Zoology, London 167:161–178.

Cooke, A. S. 1973. The effects of DDT, when used as

a mosquito larvicide, on tadpoles of the frog *Rana temporaria.* Environmental Pollution 5:259–273.

Cooke, A. S. 1977. Effects of field applications of the herbicides diquat and dichlobenil on amphibians. Environmental Pollution 12:43–50.

Cooke, A. S. 1981. Tadpoles as indicators of harmful levels of pollution in the field. Environmental Pollution, Series A 25:123–133.

Cooke, A. S., and P. F. Ferguson. 1976. Changes in status in the British Isles of the frog (*Rana temporaria*) and the toad (*Bufo bufo*) on part of the East Anglican fenland in Britain. Biological Conservation 9:191–198.

Cooper, E. L. 1987. Carp in North America. American Fisheries Society, Bethesda, Maryland.

Cooper, H. M., and L. V. Hedges. 1993. Handbook of Research Synthesis. Russell Sage Foundation, New York.

Cooperrider, A. Y., R. J. Boyd, and H. R. Stuart. 1986. Inventory and Monitoring of Wildlife Habitat. U.S. Department of the Interior, Bureau of Land Management, Service Center, Denver.

Corbett, K. 1989. Conservation of European Reptiles and Amphibians. Christopher Helm Publishers, London.

Corn, P. S. 1994. What we know and don't know about amphibian declines in the West. Pp. 59–67. *In* Covington, W. W., and L. F. De Bano (Eds.), Sustainable Ecological Systems: Implementing an Ecological Approach to Land Management. U.S. Forest Service, Technical Report RM-247, Fort Collins, Colorado.

Corn, P. S., and R. B. Bury. 1989. Logging in western Oregon: responses of headwater habitats and stream amphibians. Forest Ecology and Management 29:39–57.

Corn, P. S., and J. C. Fogleman. 1984. Extinction of montane populations of the northern leopard frog (*Rana pipiens*) in Colorado. Journal of Herpetology 18:147–152.

Corn, P. S., E. Muths, and W. M. Iko. 1995. A comparison of three methods for monitoring breeding amphibians. North American Amphibian Monitoring Program, Burlington, Ontario. Unpublished abstract.

Corn, P. S., and F. A. Vertucci. 1992. Descriptive risk assessment of the effects of acidic deposition on Rocky Mountain amphibians. Journal of Herpetology 26:361–369.

Coulson, R. N., L. J. Folse, and D. K. Loh. 1987. Artificial intelligence and natural resources management. Science 237:262–267.

Coulson, R. N., C. N. Lovelady, R. O. Flamm, S. L. Spradling, and M. C. Saunders. 1991. Intelligent geographic information systems for natural resource management. Pp. 153–172. *In* Turner, M. G., and R. H. Gardner (Eds.), Quantitative Methods in Landscape Ecology. Springer-Verlag, New York.

Council of Biology Editors (CBE) Style Manual Committee. 1983. CBE Style Manual. Council of Biology Editors, Bethesda, Maryland.

Courtenay, W. R., Jr., and P. B. Moyle. 1992. Crimes against biodiversity: the lasting legacy of fish introductions. Transactions of the North American Wildlife and Natural Resources Conference 57:365–371.

Cowardin, L. M., V. Carter, F. C. Golet, and E. T. LaRoe. 1979. Classification of wetlands and deepwater habitats of the United States. U.S. Fish and Wildlife Service, FWS/OBS/-79/31, Washington, D.C.

Cowen, D. J. 1988. GIS versus CAD versus DBMS: what are the differences? Photogrammetric Engineering and Remote Sensing 27:125–131.

Cox, D. R. 1958. Planning of Experiments. Wiley Classics Library Edition 1992, John Wiley and Sons, New York.

Cox, D. R. 1970. Analysis of Binary Data. Chapman and Hall, New York.

Cox, D. R. 1977. The role of significance tests. Scandinavian Journal of Statistics 4:49–70.

Cox, D. R. 1986. Some general aspects of the theory of statistics. International Statistical Review 54:117–126.

Cracknell, A. P., and L. W. B. Hayes. 1991. Introduction to Remote Sensing. Taylor and Francis, Bristol, Pennsylvania.

Craighead, J. J., F. C. Craighead Jr., J. R. Varney, and C. E. Cote. 1971. Satellite monitoring of black bear. Bioscience 21:1206–1211.

Crapper, P. F. 1980. Errors incurred in estimating an area of uniform land cover using Landsat. Photogrammetric Engineering and Remote Sensing 10:1295–1301.

Crawshaw, G. J. 1992. SCAW/LSUSVM Conference on the Care and Use of Amphibians, Reptiles, and Fish in Research. Unpublished abstract.

Cressie, N. 1991. Statistics for Spatial Data. John Wiley and Sons, New York.

Cromeens, D. M., V. W. Robbins, and L. C. Stephens. 1987. Diagnostic exercise: cutaneous lesions in frogs. Laboratory Animal Science 37:58–59.

Crowder, M. J., and D. J. Hand. 1990. Analysis of Repeated Measures. Chapman and Hall, New York.

Crump, M. L., F. R. Hensley, and K. L. Clark. 1992. Apparent decline of the golden toad: underground or extinct? Copeia 1992:413–420.

Cullen, M. R. 1985. Linear Models in Biology. Ellis Horwood, Chichester, England.

Cummings, B. F. 1912. Distant orientation in amphibia. Proceedings of the Zoological Society of London 1912:8–19.

Cummings, K. S. 1991. The aquatic mollusca of Illinois. Illinois Natural History Survey Bulletin 34:428–438.

Cunningham, A. A., T. E. S. Langton, P. M. Bennett, S. E. N. Drury, R. E. Gough, and J. K. Kirkwood. 1993. Unusual mortality associated with poxvirus-like particles in frogs (*Rana temporaria*). Veterinary Record 133:141–142.

Cupp, P. V., Jr. 1980. Territoriality in the green salamander, *Aneides aeneus*. Copeia 1980:463–468.

Cupp, P. V., Jr. 1991. Aspects of the life history and ecology of the green salamander, *Aneides aeneus*, in Kentucky. Journal of the Tennessee Academy of Science 66:171–174.

Curran, P. J. 1985. Principles of Remote Sensing. Longman, London.

Currie, D. J. 1991. Energy and large-scale patterns of animal- and plant-species. American Naturalist 137:27–49.

Curry, B. B. 1989. Absence of Altonian glaciation in Illinois. Quaternary Research 31:1–13.

Curtis, J. T. 1959. The Vegetation of Wisconsin. University of Wisconsin Press, Madison.

Czechura, G., and G. J. Ingram. 1990. *Taudactylus diurnus* and the case of the disappearing frogs. Memoirs of Queensland Museum 29:361–365.

Dahl, T. E. 1990. Wetlands losses in the United States 1780's to 1980's. U.S. Fish and Wildlife Service, Washington, D.C.

Dahl, T. E. 1991. Wetlands, status and trends in the conterminous United States, mid-1970s to mid-1980s. U.S. Fish and Wildlife Service, Washington, D.C.

Dahl, T. E., and C. E. Johnson. 1991. Status and trends of wetlands in the conterminous United States, mid-1970's to mid-1980's. U.S. Fish and Wildlife Service, Washington, D.C.

Daily Times. 1993. A massive underground reservoir—the Sankoty sand aquifer. 16 September, Pekin, Illinois.

Dames and Moore, Inc. 1981. A survey of the distribution and abundance of spotted salamanders in a portion of northern Wisconsin. Unpublished report to the Exxon Minerals Company, Crandon Project, Rhinelander, Wisconsin.

Daniel, C., and F. S. Wood. 1980. Fitting Equations to Data. John Wiley and Sons, New York.

Daniel, P. M. 1989. *Hemidactylium scutatum*. Pp. 223–228. *In* Pfingsten, R. A., and F. L. Downs (Eds.), Salamanders of Ohio. Ohio Biological Survey Bulletin, New Series, Volume 7, Number 2.

Dansgaard, W., S. J. Johnsen, H. B. Clausen, D. Dahl-Jensen, N. S. Gundestrup, C. U. Hammer, C. S. Hvidberg, J. P. Steffensen, A. E. Sveinbjornsdottir, J. Jouzel, and G. Bond. 1993. Evidence for general instability of past climate from a 250-kyr ice-core record. Nature 364:218–220.

Darzins, E. 1952. The epizootic of tuberculosis among the *Gias bahia*. Acta Tuberculosea Scandinavica 26:170–174.

Davis, E. B., and D. Schmidt. 1995. Using the Biological Literature. Marcel Dekker, New York.

Davis, F. W., D. A. Quattrochi, M. K. Ridd, N. S. N. Lam, S. J. Walsh, J. C. Michaelsen, J. Franklin, D. A. Stow, C. Johannsen, and C. A. Johnston. 1991. Environmental analysis using integrated GIS and remotely sensed data: some research needs and priorities. Photogrammetric Engineering and Remote Sensing 57:689–697.

Davis, F. W., and D. S. Simonett. 1991. GIS and remote sensing. Pp. 191–213. *In* Maguire, D. J., M. F. Goodchild, and D. W. Rhind (Eds.), Geographical Information Systems, Volume I, Principles. John Wiley and Sons, New York.

Davis, J. G. 1994. Vertebrate animals of the Oxbow and Great Miami River bottomlands in Dearborn County, Indiana. Pp. 1–22. *In* Environmental Review of Oxbow, Inc.: Properties and Surrounding Areas. Environmental Assessment Services, Middletown, Ohio.

Davis, J. G., and P. J. Krusling. 1989. Report on the reptile and amphibian survey of Richardson Forest Preserve, Hamilton County Park District. Unpublished report to the Hamilton County Park District, Cincinnati.

Davis, J. G., and P. J. Krusling. 1990. Report on the reptile and amphibian survey of Mitchell Memorial Forest, Hamilton County Park District. Unpublished report to the Hamilton County Park District, Cincinnati.

Davis, J. G., and P. J. Krusling. 1991. Report on the amphibian and reptile survey of Triple Creek Park, Hamilton County Park District. Unpublished report to the Hamilton County Park District, Cincinnati.

Davis, J. G., and P. J. Krusling. 1993. Additional records for the cave salamander (*Eurycea lucifuga*) in the Hamilton County Park District. Unpublished report to the Hamilton County Park District, Cincinnati.

Davis, J. G., P. J. Krusling, and W. R. Wauligman. 1991a. Report on the amphibian and reptile survey of Lake Isabella, Hamilton County Park District. Unpublished report to the Hamilton County Park District, Cincinnati.

Davis, J. G., P. J. Krusling, and W. R. Wauligman. 1991b. Report on the reptile and amphibian survey at Newberry Wildlife Sanctuary. Unpublished report to the Hamilton County Park District, Cincinnati.

Davis, J. G., P. J. Krusling, and W. R. Wauligman. 1992. Final report on the herpetological survey of the Shaker Trace Wetlands: Miami Whitewater Forest, Hamilton County Park District. Unpublished report to the Hamilton County Park District, Cincinnati.

Davis, J. G., and C. T. McCarty. 1993. Geographic distribution. *Ambystoma opacum*. Herpetological Review 24:63.

Davis, M. B. 1983. Holocene vegetational history of the eastern United States. Pp. 166–181. *In* Wright, H. E., Jr. (Ed.), Late Quaternary Environments of the United States, Volume 2: The Holocene. University of Minnesota Press, Minneapolis.

Day, R. W., and G. P. Quinn. 1989. Comparisons of treatments after an analysis of variance in ecology. Ecological Monographs 59:433–463.

Deesi, J. L. 1949. The natural occurrence of "red leg" *Pseudomonas hydrophila* in a population of American toads, *Bufo americanus*. Ohio Journal of Science 49:70–71.

DeFauw, S. L., and J. Shoshani. 1991. *Rana catesbeiana* and *Rana clamitans* from the late Pleistocene of Michigan. Journal of Herpetology 25:95–99.

de la Mare, W. K. 1984. On the power of catch per unit effort series to detect declines in whale stocks. Reports of the International Whaling Commission 34:655–662.

Delcourt, H. R., and P. A. Delcourt. 1988. Quaternary landscape ecology: relevant scales in space and time. Landscape Ecology 2:23–44.

Delcourt, H. R., and P. A. Delcourt. 1991. Quaternary Ecology: A Paleoecological Perspective. Chapman and Hall, New York.

Delcourt, H. R., P. A. Delcourt, and T. Webb III. 1983. Dynamic plant ecology: the spectrum of vegetational change in space and time. Quaternary Science Reviews 1:153–175.

Delcourt, P. A., and H. R. Delcourt. 1987. Long-term Forest Dynamics of the Temperate Zone, Ecological Studies 63. Springer-Verlag, New York.

Delcourt, P. A., and H. R. Delcourt. 1992. Ecotone dynamics in space and time. Pp. 19–54. *In* Hansen, A. J., and F. di Castri (Eds.), Landscape Boundaries: Consequences for Biotic Diversity and Ecological Flows. Springer-Verlag, New York.

Deming, W. E. 1975. On probability as a basis for action. American Statistician 29:146–152.

Dempster, W. T. 1930. The growth of larvae of *Ambystoma maculatum* under natural conditions. Biological Bulletin 58:182–192.

DeNoyelles, F., W. D. Kettle, C. H. Fromm, M. F. Moffett, and S. L. Dewey. 1989. Use of experimental ponds to assess the effects of a pesticide on the aquatic environment. Pp. 41–56. *In* Voshell, J. R. (Ed.), Using Mesocosms to Assess the Aquatic Ecological Risk of Pesticides: Theory and Practice. Entomological Society of America, Lanham, Maryland.

DeNoyelles, F., W. D. Kettle, and D. E. Sinn. 1982. The responses of plankton communities in experimental ponds to atrazine, the most heavily used pesticide in the United States. Ecology 63:1285–1293.

Dent, B. D. 1990. Cartography: Thematic Map Design. W. C. Brown, Dubuque, Iowa.

Denver, R. J. 1993. Acceleration of anuran amphibian metamorphosis by corticotropin-releasing hormone-like peptides. General and Comparative Endocrinology 91:38–51.

Denver, R. J. 1995. Environment-neuroendocrine interactions in the control of amphibian metamorphosis. Netherlands Journal of Zoology 45:195–200.

Dernehl, P. H. 1902. Place-modes of *Acris gryllus* for Madison, Wisconsin. Bulletin Wisconsin Natural History Society 2:75–83.

Desu, M. M., and D. Raghavarao. 1990. Sample Size Methodology. Academic Press, New York.

Deutschman, M. R., and J. J. Peterka. 1988. Secondary production of tiger salamanders (*Ambystoma tigrinum*) in three North Dakota prairie lakes. Canadian Journal of Fisheries and Aquatic Sciences 45:691–697.

Devillers, J., and J. M. Exbrayat. 1992. Ecotoxicology of Chemicals to Amphibians. Gordon and Breach, Philadelphia.

Dewey, S. L. 1986. Effects of the herbicide atrazine on aquatic insect community structure and emergence. Ecology 67:148–162.

Dexter, R. W. 1955. The vertebrate fauna on the campus of Kent State University. Biologist 37:84–88.

Dhuey, B., G. Hay, and M. Mossman. 1994. Frog and toad survey 1994. Wisconsin Wildlife Surveys 5:108–113.

Dial, N. A. 1976. Methylmercury: teratogenic and lethal

effects in frog embryos. Teratology 13:327–334.

Dial, N. A., and C. A. Bauer. 1984. Teratogenic and lethal effects of paraquat on developing frog embryos (*Rana pipiens*). Bulletin of Environmental Contamination and Toxicology 33:592–597.

Dial, N. A., and C. A. B. Dial. 1987. Lethal effects of diquat and paraquat on developing frog embryos and fifteen-day-old tadpoles, *Rana pipiens*. Bulletin of Environmental Contamination and Toxicology 38:1006–1011.

Dial, N. A., and C. A. B. Dial. 1995. Lethal effects of the consumption of field levels of paraquat-contaminated plants on frog tadpoles. Bulletin of Environmental Contamination and Toxicology 55:870–877.

Dialog Database Catalogue. 1993. Dialog Information Services, Palo Alto, California.

Dice, L. R. 1943. The Biotic Provinces of North America. University of Michigan Press, Ann Arbor.

Dickerson, M. C. 1906. The Frog Book. Doubleday, Page, New York.

Dieter, C. D. 1991. Water turbidity in tilled and untilled prairie wetlands. Journal of Freshwater Ecology 6:185–189.

Digby, P. G. N., and R. A. Kempton. 1987. Multivariate Analysis of Ecological Communities. Chapman and Hall, New York.

Diggle, P. J. 1990. Time Series: A Biostatistical Introduction. Oxford University Press, New York.

Dillon, W. R., and M. Goldstein. 1984. Multivariate Analysis Methods and Applications. John Wiley and Sons, New York.

Dixon, P. M. 1994. The bootstrap and the jackknife: describing the precision of ecological indices. Pp. 290–318. *In* Scheiner, S. M., and J. Gurevitch (Eds.), Design and Analysis of Ecological Experiments. Chapman and Hall, New York.

Dobson, A. J. 1990. An Introduction to Generalized Linear Models. Chapman and Hall, New York.

Dodd, C. K., Jr. 1991. The status of the Red Hills salamander *Phaeognathus hubrichti*, Alabama, U.S.A., 1976–1988. Biological Conservation 55:57–75.

Dodd, C. K., Jr. 1993. Cost of living in an unpredictable environment: the ecology of striped newts, *Notophthalmus perstriatus*, during a prolonged drought. Copeia 1993:605–614.

Dodd, C. K., Jr. 1994. The effects of drought on population structure, activity, and orientation of toads (*Bufo quercus* and *B. terrestris*) at a temporary pond. Ethology, Ecology, and Evolution 6:331–349.

Dodd, C. K., Jr., G. E. Drewry, R. M. Nowak, J. M. Sheppard, and J. D. Williams. 1985. Endangered and threatened wildlife and plants; review of vertebrate wildlife; notice of review. Part III, 50 CFR Part 17, U.S. Fish and Wildlife Service, Federal Registry 50:37958–37967, Washington, D.C.

Dodd, C. K., Jr., and R. Franz. 1993. The need for status information on common herpetofaunal species. Herpetological Review 24:47–50.

Dodd, C. K., Jr., and R. A. Seigel. 1991. Relocation, repatriation, and translocation of amphibians and reptiles: are they conservation strategies that work? Herpetologica 47:336–350.

Dodd, M. H. I., and J. M. Dodd. 1976. The Biology of Metamorphosis. Pp. 467–579. *In* Lofts, B. (Ed.), The Physiology of the Amphibia, Volume III. Academic Press, New York.

Dole, J. W. 1965. Summer movements of adult leopard frogs, *Rana pipiens* Schreber, in northern Michigan. Ecology 46:236–255.

Dole, J. W. 1971. Dispersal of recently metamorphosed leopard frogs, *Rana pipiens*. Copeia 1971: 221–228.

Dole, J. W. 1972. Homing and orientation of displaced toads, *Bufo americanus*, to their home sites. Copeia 1972:151–158.

Donnelly, M. A., and C. Guyer. 1994. Mark-recapture. Pp. 183–200. *In* Heyer, W. R., M. A. Donnelly, R. W. McDiarmid, L.-A. C. Hayek, and M. S. Foster (Eds.), Measuring and Monitoring Biological Diversity: Standard Methods for Amphibians. Smithsonian Institution Press, Washington, D.C.

Donnelly, M. A., C. Guyer, J. E. Juterbock, and R. A. Alford. 1994. Techniques for marking amphibians. Appendix 2, Pp. 277–284. *In* Heyer, W. R., M. A. Donnelly, R. W. McDiarmid, L.-A. C. Hayek, and M. S. Foster (Eds.), Measuring and Monitoring Biological Diversity: Standard Methods for Amphibians. Smithsonian Institution Press, Washington, D.C.

Doppelt, B., M. Scurlock, C. Frissell, and J. Karr. 1993. Entering the Watershed: A New Approach to Save America's River Ecosystems. Island Press, Washington, D.C.

Dorcas, M. E., and K. D. Foltz. 1991. Environmental effects on anuran advertisement calling. American Zoologist 31:111A.

Dorcas, M. E., C. R. Peterson, J. D. Congdon, and J. W. Gibbons. 1995. Monitoring anuran populations on the Savannah River site using automated recording systems. North American Amphibian Monitoring Program, Burlington, Ontario. Unpublished abstract.

Dorcas, M. E., C. R. Peterson, R. Nagle, T. Tuberville, T.

Lynch, J. D. Congdon, and J. W. Gibbons. 1994. Monitoring anuran vocalizations at the Savannah River site using automated recording systems. Joint meeting of the Herpetologist's League and the Society for the Study of Amphibians and Reptiles, University of Georgia, Athens. Unpublished abstract.

Dorff, C. 1995. Geographic distribution. Caudata. *Hemidactylium scutatum* . Herpetological Review 26:150.

Dorff-Hall, C. 1996. Minnesota county biological survey—amphibian and reptile results, 1988–1994. Pp. 58–63. *In* Moriarty, J. J., and D. Jones (Eds.), Minnesota's Amphibians and Reptiles: Conservation and Status, Proceedings of Symposium. Serpent's Tale Press, Excelsior, Minnesota.

Doty, T. L. 1978. A study of larval amphibian population dynamics in a Rhode Island vernal pond. Ph.D. dissertation, University of Rhode Island, Kingston.

Douglas, M. E., and B. L. Monroe Jr. 1981. A comparative study of topographical orientation in *Ambystoma* (Amphibia: Caudata). Copeia 1981:460–463.

Draper, N. R., and H. Smith. 1981. Applied Regression Analysis. John Wiley and Sons, New York.

Driscoll, R. S., D. L. Merkel, D. L. Radloff, D. E. Snyder, and J. S. Hagihara. 1984. An ecological land classification framework for the United States. U.S. Forest Service, Miscellaneous Publication Number 1439, Washington, D.C.

Droin, A., and M. Fischberg. 1980. Abnormal limbs (abl), a recessive mutation affecting the tadpoles of *Xenopus l. laevis.* Experientia 36:1286–1288.

Dubois, A. 1990. Some preliminary comments. Pp. 1–7. *In* Declining amphibian populations—a global phenomenon. Workshop sponsored by Board on Biology, National Research Council, Irvine, California.

DuBois, R. 1996. Recent observations of deformed anurans in Wisconsin. *In* Third Annual Meeting of the North American Amphibian Monitoring Program. http://www.im.nbs.gov/naamp3/papers/57df.html.

Dubrule, O. 1983. Two methods with different objectives: splines and kriging. Mathematical Geology 15:245–255.

Dubrule, O. 1984. Comparing splines and kriging. Computational Geosciences 101:327–328.

Duellman, W. E. 1951. Notes on the reptiles and amphibians of Greene County, Ohio. Ohio Journal of Science 51:335–341.

Duellman, W. E., T. Fritts, and A. E. Leviton. 1978. Museum acronyms. Herpetological Review 9:5–9.

Duellman, W. E., and L. Trueb. 1986. Biology of Amphibians. McGraw-Hill, New York.

Dumpert, K., and E. Zietz. 1984. Platanna (*Xenopus laevis*) as a test organism for determining the embryotoxic effects of environmental chemicals. Ecotoxicology and Environmental Safety 8:55–74.

Dundee, H. A., and D. A. Rossman. 1989. The Amphibians and Reptiles of Louisiana. Louisiana State University Press, Baton Rouge.

Dunn, E. R. 1935. The survival value of specific characters. Copeia 1935:85–98.

Dunning, J. B., Jr., D. J. Stewart, B. J. Danielson, B. R. Noon, T. L. Root, R. H. Lamberson, and E. E. Stevens. 1995. Spatially explicit models: current forms and future uses. Ecological Applications 5:3–11.

Dunson, W. A., R.L. Wyman, and E. S. Corbett. 1992. A symposium on amphibian declines and habitat acidification. Journal of Herpetology 26: 349–442.

Dutilleul, P. 1993. Spatial heterogeneity and the design of ecological field experiments. Ecology 74:1646–1658.

Dyke, A. S., and V. K. Prest. 1987a. Late Wisconsinan and Holocene retreat of the Laurentide Ice Sheet. Geological Survey of Canada, Map 1702A.

Dyke, A. S., and V. K. Prest. 1987b. Paleogeography of northern North America, 18,000–5000 years ago. Geological Survey of Canada, Map 1703A.

Eagleson, G. W. 1976. A comparison of the life histories and growth patterns of the salamander *Ambystoma gracile* (Baird) from permanent low-altitude and montane lakes. Canadian Journal of Zoology 54:2098–2111.

Earth Resources Data Analysis System. 1993. Monitor, Volume 5, IMAGINE Information Bulletin. ERDAS Inc., Atlanta.

Eberhardt, L. L. 1976. Quantitative ecology and impact assessment. Journal of Environmental Management 42:1–31.

Eberhardt, L. L., and J. M. Thomas. 1991. Designing environmental field studies. Ecological Monographs 61:53–73.

Eby, J. 1986. Sublethal concentrations of cadmium and lead affect acquisition of discriminate avoidance learning in green frog (*Rana clamitans*) tadpoles. M.S. thesis, Miami University, Oxford, Ohio.

Eckblad, J. W. 1991. How many samples should be taken? BioScience 41:346–348.

Edgington, E. S. 1987. Randomization Tests. Marcel Dekker, New York.

Edgren, R. A., and W. T. Stille. 1948. Checklist of Chicago area amphibians and reptiles. Chicago Academy of

Sciences, Natural History Miscellanea 26.

Efford, I. E., and J. A. Mathias. 1969. A comparison of two salamander populations in Marion Lake, British Columbia. Copeia 1969:723–736.

Efron, B. 1982. The Jackknife, the Bootstrap and Other Resampling Plans. Society for Industrial and Applied Mathematics, Philadelphia.

Efron, B., and G. Gong. 1983. A leisurely look at the bootstrap, the jackknife, and cross-validation. American Statistician 37:36–48.

Efron, B., and R. Tibshirani. 1991. Statistical analysis in the computer age. Science 253:390–395.

Ehlers, M., G. Edwards, and Y. Bedard. 1989. Integration of remote sensing with geographic information systems: a necessary evolution. Photogrammetric Engineering and Remote Sensing 55:1619–1627.

Ehlers, M., D. Greenlee, T. Smith, and J. Star. 1991. Integration of remote sensing and GIS: data and data access. Photogrammetric Engineering and Remote Sensing 57:669–676.

Ehrlich, P. R., D. S. Dobkin, and D. Wheye. 1988. The Birder's Handbook: A Field Guide to the Natural History of North American Birds. Simon and Schuster, New York.

Ehrenberg, A. S. C. 1975. Data Reduction: Analyzing and Interpreting Statistical Data. John Wiley and Sons, New York.

Eisler, R. 1985. Selenium hazards to fish, wildlife, and invertebrates: a synoptic review. U.S. Fish and Wildlife Service, Biological Report Number 85 (1.5), Washington, D.C.

Eisler, R. 1994. A review of arsenic hazards to plants and animals with emphasis on fishery and wildlife resources. Pp. 186–259. *In* Nriagu, J. O. (Ed.), Arsenic in the Environment. Part II: Human Health and Ecosystem Effects. John Wiley and Sons, New York.

Eiten, G. 1986. The use of the term "savanna." Tropical Ecology 27:10–23.

Eiten, G. 1992. How names are used for vegetation. Journal of Vegetation Science 3:419–424.

Elias, S. A. 1994. Quaternary Insects and Their Environments. Smithsonian Institution Press, Washington, D.C.

Elliott, J. M. 1977. Some methods for the statistical analysis of samples of benthic invertebrates. 2d ed. Freshwater Biological Association Science Publication Number 25. Ambleside, England.

Emmons, C. W., C. H. Binford, and J. P. Utz. 1970. Medical Mycology. Lea and Febiger, Philadelphia.

Environmental Science & Engineering, Inc. 1993a. Mason County/City of Havana flood control report 1993. Unpublished report to the Mason County Board of County Commissioners and City of Havana, Peoria, Illinois.

Environmental Science & Engineering, Inc. 1993b. Sand Lake watershed flood control feasibility study. Unpublished report to the Mason County Board of County Commissioners and City of Havana, Peoria, Illinois.

Environmental Science & Engineering, Inc. 1994. Preliminary scope of work—Sand Lake wetland investigation. Unsubmitted contract proposal, St. Louis.

Environmental Systems Research Institute, Inc. 1993. Understanding GIS: The ARC/INFO Method. Environmental Systems Research Institute, Inc., Redlands, California. John Wiley and Sons, New York.

Environmental Systems Research Institute, Inc. 1994. Map Projections: Georeferencing Spatial Data. Environmental Systems Research Institute, Inc., Redlands, California.

Erickson, B. H., and T. A. Nosanchuk. 1977. Understanding Data. McGraw-Hill, New York.

Etkin, W. 1968. Hormonal control of amphibian metamorphosis. Pp. 313–348. *In* Etkin, W., and L. I. Gilbert (Eds.), Metamorphosis: A Problem in Developmental Biology. Appleton-Century-Crofts, New York.

Etkin, W., and A. G. Gona. 1967. Antagonism between prolactin and thyroid hormone in amphibian development. Journal of Experimental Zoology 165:249–258.

Everitt, B. S. 1977. Analysis of Contingency Tables. Chapman and Hall, New York.

Faber-Langendoen, D. 1993. Midwest regional community classification. Unpublished report to The Nature Conservancy, Midwest Heritage Task Force, Minneapolis.

Faeh, S., L. Brown, D. Nicols, M. Greenwell, and V. Beasley. 1994. Assessment of the health status of cricket frogs (*Acris crepitans*) and environmental quality in areas of abundant and reduced populations. Meeting of the Central Division of the Declining Amphibian Population Task Force, Indiana Dunes National Lakeshore. Unpublished abstract.

Fahrig, L., and G. Merriam. 1985. Habitat patch connectivity and population survival. Ecology 66:1762–1768.

Fairbrother, A. 1994. Clinical biochemistry. Pp. 63–89. *In* Fossi, M. C., and C. Leonzio (Eds.), Nondestructive Biomarkers in Vertebrates. Lewis Publishers, Boca Raton, Florida.

Faith, D. P., P. R. Minchin, and L. Belbin. 1987. Compositional dissimilarity as a robust measure of ecological distance. Vegetatio 69:57–68.

Falkner, E. 1994. Aerial Mapping: Methods and Applications. CRC Press, Boca Raton, Florida.

Fancy, S. G., L. F. Pank, D. C. Douglas, C. H. Curby, G. W. Garner, S. C. Amstrup, and W. L. Regelin. 1988. Satellite telemetry: a new tool for wildlife research and management. U.S. Fish and Wildlife Service, Resource Publication Number 172, Washington, D.C.

Fancy, S. G., L. F. Pank, K. R. Whitten, and W. L. Regelin. 1989. Seasonal movements of caribou in Arctic Alaska as determined by satellite telemetry. Canadian Journal of Zoology 67:644–650.

Fankhauser, G., and R. R. Humphrey. 1950. Chromosome number and development of progenies of triploid and axolotl females mated with diploid males. Journal of Experimental Zoology 115:207–250.

Farrar, E., and J. Hey. 1994. Plains spadefoot (*Scaphiopus bombifrons*) distribution, breeding habitat characterization, and natural history studies in four counties of western Iowa. Unpublished report to the Iowa Department of Natural Resources, Des Moines.

Farringer, J. E. 1972. Determination of the acute toxicity of rotenone and bayer 73 to selected aquatic organisms. M.S. thesis, University of Wisconsin, La Crosse.

Fashingbauer, B. A. 1957. The effects of aerial spraying with DDT on wood frogs. Flicker 29:160.

FAUNMAP Working Group. 1994. FAUNMAP, a database documenting Late Quaternary distributions of mammal species in the United States. Illinois State Museum Scientific Papers XXV, Numbers 1 and 2.

Faust, N. L., W. H. Anderson, and J. L. Star. 1991. Geographic information systems and remote sensing future computing environment. Photogrammetric Engineering and Remote Sensing 57:655–668.

Feder, M. E., and W. W. Burggren. 1992. Environmental Physiology of Amphibians. University of Chicago Press, Chicago.

Feigel, C. R., Jr., and R. D. Semlitsch. 1995. Experimental determination of oviposition site in the marbled salamander, *Ambystoma opacum*. Journal of Herpetology 29:452–454.

Fellers, G. M., and C. A. Drost. 1993. Disappearance of the Cascades frog *Rana cascadae* at the southern end of its range, California, USA. Biological Conservation 65:177–181.

Fellers, G. M., and K. L. Freel. 1995. A standardized protocol for surveying aquatic amphibians. U.S. Department of the Interior, Technical Report NPS/WRUC/NRTR-95-01, Washington, D.C.

Fenneman, N. M. 1916. Geology of Cincinnati and vicinity. Geological Survey of Ohio, Fourth Series, Bulletin 19.

Fenneman, N. M. 1938. Physiography of the Eastern United States. McGraw-Hill, New York.

Feoli, E., and L. Orlóci. 1991. Computer Assisted Vegetation Analysis. Kluwer Academic, Boston.

Ferguson, D. E. 1971. The sensory basis of orientation in amphibians. Annals of the New York Academy of Science 188:30–36.

Ferner, J. W., T. Rice, and K. S. Neltner. 1992. Predation on birds, at a birdfeeder by bullfrogs, *Rana catesbeiana* Shaw. Greater Cincinnati Herpetological Society Contributions in Herpetology 1:61–62.

Fienberg, S. E. 1980. The Analysis of Cross-Classified Categorical Data. MIT Press, Cambridge.

Figiel, C. R., and R. D. Semlitsch. 1990. Population variation in survival and metamorphosis of larval salamanders (*Ambystoma maculatum*) in the presence and absence of fish predation. Copeia 1990:818–826.

Fikes, J. D. 1990. Organophosphorus and carbamate insecticides. Veterinary Clinics of North America: Small Animal Practice 20:353–367.

Finch, C. E., and M. R. Rose. 1995. Hormones and the physiological architecture of life history evolution. Quarterly Review of Biology 70:1–52.

Fingleton, B. 1984. Models of Category Counts. Cambridge University Press, New York.

Finneran, L. C. 1951. Migration to the breeding pond by the spotted salamander. Copeia 1951:81.

Fishbeck, D. W. 1968. A study of some phases in the ecology of *Rana sylvatica* LeConte. Ph.D. dissertation, University of Minnesota, Minneapolis.

Fisher, N. I. 1993. Statistical Analysis of Circular Data. Cambridge University Press, New York.

Fisher, N. I., T. Lewis, and B. J. J. Embleton. 1987. Statistical Analysis of Spherical Data. Cambridge University Press, New York.

Fisher, R. A. 1935. The Design of Experiments. Oliver and Boyd, Edinburgh.

Fitzpatrick, T. 1993. Signals from the Heartland. Walker and Company, New York.

Fleiss, J. L. 1981. Statistical Methods for Rates and Proportions. John Wiley and Sons, New York.

Fleming, P. L. 1976. A study of the distribution and ecology of *Rana clamitans* Latreille. Ph.D. dissertation, University of Minnesota, Minneapolis.

Flickinger, S. A., and F. J. Bulow. 1993. Small impoundments. Pp.181–203. *In* Kohler, C. C., and W. A. Hubert (Eds.), Inland Fisheries Management in North America. American Fisheries Society, Bethesda, Maryland.

Flint, M. L., and R. van den Bosch. 1981. Introduction to Integrated Pest Management. Plenum Press, New York.

Flynn, R. J. 1973. Parasites of laboratory reptiles and amphibians. Pp. 507–641. *In* Flynn, R. (Ed.), Parasites of Laboratory Animals. Iowa State University Press, Ames.

Fog, K. 1988. Pond restorations on Bornholm. Memoranda Societatis Fauna et Flora Fennica 64:143–145.

Foley, R. L. 1984. Late Pleistocene (Woodfordian) vertebrates from the Driftless Area of southwestern Wisconsin, the Moscow Fissure local fauna. Illinois State Museum Reports of Investigations 39:1–50.

Foley, R. L., and L. E. Raue. 1987. *Lemmus sibiricus* from the Late Quaternary of the midwestern United States. Current Research in the Pleistocene 4:105–107.

Fontenot, L. W., G. P. Noblet, and S. G. Platt. 1994. Rotenone hazards to amphibians and reptiles. Herpetological Review 25:150–156.

Foody, G., and P. Curran. 1994. Environmental Remote Sensing from Regional to Global Scales. John Wiley and Sons, New York.

Forbes, S. A., and R. E. Richardson. 1913. Studies on the biology of the upper Illinois River. Illinois Laboratory of Natural History Bulletin 9:481–574.

Force, E. R. 1933. The age of attainment of sexual maturity of the leopard frog, *Rana pipiens* (Schreber), in northern Michigan. Copeia 1933:128–131.

Forester, D. C., and D. La Pasha. 1982. Failure of orientation to frog calls by migrating spotted salamanders. Bulletin of the Maryland Herpetological Society 18:143–151.

Forester, D. C., and D. V. Lykens. 1991. Age structure in a population of red-spotted newts from the Allegheny Plateau of Maryland. Journal of Herpetology 25:373–376.

Forman, R. T. T. 1995. Land Mosaics: The Ecology of Landscapes and Regions. Cambridge University Press, New York.

Forman, R. T. T., and M. Godron. 1986. Landscape Ecology. John Wiley and Sons, New York.

Formanowitz, D. R., Jr., and E. D. Brodie Jr. 1982. Relative palatabilities of members of a larval amphibian community. Copeia 1982:91–97.

Fotheringham, S., and P. Rogerson. 1994. Spatial Analysis and GIS. Taylor and Francis, Bristol, Pennsylvania.

Fowler, N. 1990. The ten most common statistical errors. Bulletin of the Ecological Society of America 71:161–164.

Frank, N., and E. Ramus. 1994. State, Federal, and C.I.T.E.S. Regulations for Herpetologists. NG Publishing, Pottsville, Pennsylvania.

Frankland, L., and R. Vogel. 1980. Geographic distribution. *Hemidactylium scutatum.* Herpetological Review 11:13.

Franklin, I. R. 1980. Evolutionary change in small populations. Pp. 135–149. *In* Soulé, M. E., and B. A. Wilcox (Eds.), Conservation Biology: An Evolutionary-Ecological Perspective. Sinauer Associates, Sunderland, Massachusetts.

Franklin, J. F. 1992. Scientific basis for new perspectives in forests and streams. Pp. 25–72. *In* Naiman, R. J. (Ed.), Watershed Management: Balancing Sustainability and Environmental Change. Springer-Verlag, New York.

Frazier, I. 1989. Great Plains. Penguin Books, New York.

Freda, J., and W. A. Dunson. 1984. Sodium balance of amphibian larvae exposed to low environmental pH. Physiological Zoology 57:435–444.

Freda J., W. J. Sadinski, and W. A. Dunson. 1991. Long-term monitoring of amphibian populations with respect to the effects of acidic deposition. Water Air Soil Pollution 55:445–462.

Freda, J., and D. H. Taylor. 1992. Behavioral responses of amphibian larvae to acidic water. Journal of Herpetology 26:429–433.

Freund, R. J., and W. J. Wilson. 1993. Statistical Methods. Academic Press, New York.

Frisbie, M. P., and R. L. Wyman. 1991. The effect of soil pH on sodium balance in the red-backed salamander, *Plethodon cinereus*, and three other terrestrial salamanders. Physiological Zoology 64:1050–1068.

Frisbie, M. P., and R. L. Wyman. 1992a. The effect of environmental pH on sodium balance in the red-spotted newt, *Notophthalmus viridescens.* Archives of Environmental Contamination and Toxicology 23:64–68.

Frisbie, M. P., and R. L. Wyman. 1992b. The effect of soil chemistry on sodium balance in the red-backed salamander: a comparison of two forest types. Journal of Herpetology 26:434–442.

Fry, J. C. 1993. Biological Data Analysis: A Practical Approach. Oxford University Press, New York.

Fulton, M. H., and J. E. Chambers. 1985. The toxic and teratogenic effects of selected organophosphorus compounds on the embryos of three species of amphibians. Toxicology Letters 26:175–180.

Furley, P. A., J. Proctor, and J. A. Ratter. 1992. Nature and Dynamics of Forest-Savanna Boundaries. Chapman and Hall, New York.

Galatowitsch, S. M., and A. G. van der Valk. 1994. Restoring Prairie Wetlands: An Ecological Approach. Iowa State University Press, Ames.

Garavini, C., and P. Seren. 1978. Hematologic and hemopoietic alterations following experimental benzene exposure in newts (*Triturus cristatus*). Biochemistry and Experimental Biology 14:247–255.

Gardner, M. J., and D. G. Altman. 1986. Confidence intervals rather than P-values: estimation rather than hypothesis testing. British Medical Journal 292:746–750.

Garman, H. 1890. Notes on Illinois reptiles and amphibians, including several species not before recorded from the northern states. Illinois State Laboratory of Natural History Bulletin 3:185–190.

Garman, H. 1892. A synopsis of the reptiles and amphibians of Illinois. Illinois State Laboratory of Natural History Bulletin 3:215–388.

Garry, C. E., D. P. Schwert, R. G. Baker, T. J. Kemmis, D. G. Horton, and A. E. Sullivan. 1990. Plant and insect remains from the Wisconsinan interstadial/stadial transition at Wedron, north-central Illinois. Quaternary Research 33:387–399.

Gartshore, M. E., M. J. Oldham, R. van der Ham, F. W. Scheuler, C. A. Bishop, and G. C. Barrett. 1995. Amphibian road call counts participants manual. Ontario Task Force on Declining Amphibian Populations, Burlington, Ontario. Unpublished abstract.

Gauch, H. G., Jr. 1982. Multivariate Analysis in Community Ecology. Cambridge University Press, New York.

Gauch, H. G., G. B. Chase, and R. H. Whittaker. 1974. Ordination of vegetation samples by Gaussian species distributions. Ecology 55:1382–1390.

Gauch, H. G., R. H. Whittaker, and T. R. Wentworth. 1977. A comparative study of reciprocal averaging and other ordination techniques. Journal of Ecology 65:157–174.

Gayou, D. C. 1984. Effects of temperature on the mating call of *Hyla versicolor*. Copeia 1984:733–738.

Geissler, P. H., and J. R. Sauer. 1990. Topics in route-regression analysis. Pp. 54–57. *In* Sauer, J. R., and S. Droege (Eds.), Survey designs and statistical methods for estimation of avian population trends. U.S. Fish and Wildlife Service, Biological Report 90(1), Washington, D.C.

Geller, M. D., and J. J. Christian. 1982. Population dynamics, adrenocortical function, and pathology in *Microtus pennsylvanicus*. Journal of Mammology 63:85–95.

Geological Survey, U.S. Department of the Interior, and Corps of Engineers, U.S. Department of the Army. 1948. Havana Quadrangle, Illinois, 7.5 minute series (topographic), N4015–W9000 (map).

Gergus, E. 1995. Systematics of the *Bufo americanus* species group: allozyme evidence. Joint meeting of the American Society of Ichthyologists and Herpetologists and the Herpetologist's League, Edmonton, Alberta. Unpublished abstract.

Gerrodette, T. 1987. A power analysis for detecting trends. Ecology 68:1364–1372.

Gibbon, J. D., and J. W. Pratt. 1975. P-values: interpretation and methodology. American Statistician 29:20–25.

Gibbons, J. W., and S. Nelson Jr. 1968. Observations on the mudpuppy, *Necturus maculosus,* in a Michigan lake. American Midland Naturalist 80:562–564.

Gibbons, J. W., and R. D. Semlitsch. 1981. Terrestrial drift fences with pitfall traps: an effective technique for quantitative sampling of animal populations. Brimleyana 7:1–16.

Gibbs, E. L., T. J. Gibbs, and P. C. Van Dyck. 1966. *Rana pipiens*: health and disease. Laboratory Animal Care 16:142–160.

Gibbs, J. P. 1995. Monitor: software for estimating the power of population monitoring to detect trends in plant and animal abundance. Available at ftp://ftp.im.nbs.gov/pub/software/monitor.

Gifi, A. 1990. Nonlinear Multivariate Analysis. John Wiley and Sons, New York.

Gilbert, H. R. 1986. Geographic distribution: *Pseudacris streckeri illinoensis*. Herpetological Review 17:65.

Gilchrist, W. 1984. Statistical Modelling. John Wiley and Sons, New York.

Gilderhus, P. H., and B. G. Johnson. 1980. Effects of sea lamprey (*Petromyzon marinus*) control in the Great Lakes on aquatic plants, invertebrates and amphibians. Canadian Journal of Fisheries and Aquatic Sciences 37:1895–1905.

Gill, D. E. 1978a. The metapopulation ecology of the red-spotted newt, *Notophthalmus viridescens* (Rafinesque). Ecological Monographs 48:145–166.

Gill, D. E. 1978b. Effective population size and interdemic migration rates in a metapopulation of the red-spotted newt, *Notophthalmus viridescens* (Rafinesque). Evolution 32:839–849.

Gill, D. E. 1985. Interpreting breeding patterns from census data: a solution to the Husting dilemma. Ecology 66:344–354.

Gilpin, M., and I. Hanski. 1991. Metapopulation Dynamics: Empirical and Theoretical Investigations.

Academic Press, New York.

Glass, G. V., P. D. Peckham, and J. R. Sanders. 1972. Consequences of failure to meet assumptions underlying the fixed effects analyses of variance and covariance. Review of Education Research 42:237–288.

Gleit, A. 1985. Estimation for small normal data sets with detection limits. Environmental Science and Technology 19:1201–1206.

Goater, C. P., and P. I. Ward. 1992. Negative effects of *Rhabdias bufonis* (Nematoda) on the growth and survival of toads (*Bufo bufo*). Oecologia 89:161–165.

Goddard, T. M., and L. R. Sabata. 1986. Soil survey of Madison County, Illinois. U.S. Soil Conservation Service, Washington, D.C.

Goldsmith, F. B. 1991. Monitoring for Conservation and Ecology. Chapman and Hall, New York.

Good, P. 1994. Permutation Tests—A Practical Guide to Resampling Methods for Testing Hypotheses. Springer-Verlag, New York.

Goodchild, M. F., and S. Gopal. 1989. Accuracy of Spatial Databases. Taylor and Francis, Bristol, Pennsylvania.

Goodchild, M. F., B. O. Parks, and L. T. Steyaert. 1993. Environmental Modeling with GIS. Oxford University Press, New York.

Goodchild, M. F., L. T. Steyaert, B. O. Parks, C. Johnston, D. Maidment, M. Crane, and S. Glendinning. 1996. GIS and Environmental Modeling: Progress and Research Issues. GIS World Books, Fort Collins, Colorado.

Gordon, R. B. 1969. The natural vegetation of Ohio in pioneer days. Ohio Biological Survey Bulletin, New Series 3:1–113.

Gordon, R. E. 1952. A contribution to the life history and ecology of the plethodontid salamander *Aneides aeneus* (Cope and Packard). American Midland Naturalist 47:666–701.

Gordon, R. E. 1961. The movement of displaced green salamanders. Ecology 42:200–202.

Gordon, R. E. 1967. *Aneides aeneus* (Cope and Packard) green salamander. Catalogue of American Amphibians and Reptiles 30.1–30.2.

Gordon, R. E., and R. L. Smith. 1949. Notes on the life history of the salamander *Aneides aeneus*. Copeia 1949:173–175.

Gore, J. A., and F. I. Bryant. 1988. River and stream restoration. Pp. 23–38. *In* Cairns, J. (Ed.), Rehabilitating Damaged Ecosystems, Volume 1. CRC Press, Boca Raton, Florida.

Gorge, G., J. Beyer, and K. Urich. 1987. Excretion and metabolism of phenol 4 nitrophenol and 2 methylphenol by the frogs *Rana temporaria* and *Xenopus laevis*. Xenobiotica 17:1293–1298.

Gosner, K. L., and I. H. Black. 1957. The effects of acidity on the development and hatching of New Jersey frogs. Ecology 38:256–262.

Gosselink, J. G., G. P. Shaffer, L. C. Lee, D. M. Burdick, D. L. Childers, N. C. Leibowitz, S. C. Hamilton, R. Boumans, D. Cushman, S. Fields, M. Koch, and J. M. Visser. 1990. Landscape conservation in a forested wetland watershed. BioScience 40:588–600.

Gould, S. J. 1977. Ontogeny and Phylogeny. Harvard University Press, Cambridge.

Goward, S. N., D. Dye, A. Kerber, and V. Kalb. 1987. Comparison of North and South American biomes from AVHRR observations. Geocartography International 1:27–39.

Goward, S. N., C. J. Tucker, and D. Dye. 1985. North American vegetation patterns observed with the NOAA-7 advanced very high resolution radiometer. Vegetatio 64:3–14.

Gower, J. C. 1967. Multivariate analysis and multidimensional geometry. Statistician 17:13–28.

Graham, R. W., J. A. Holman, and P. W. Parmalee. 1983. Taphonomy and paleoecology of the Christensen Bog mastodon bone bed, Hancock County, Indiana. Illinois State Museum Reports of Investigation 38:1–29.

Graham, R. W., and E. L. Lundelius Jr. 1984. Coevolutionary disequilibrium and Pleistocene extinctions. Pp. 223–249. *In* Martin, P. S., and R. G. Klein (Eds.), Quaternary Extinctions: A Prehistoric Revolution. University of Arizona Press, Tucson.

Granoff, A., and R. W. Darlington. 1969. Viruses and renal carcinoma of *Rana pipiens*. VIII. Electron microscopic evidence for the presence of herpes virus in the urine of a Lucké tumor-bearing frog. Journal of Virology 38:197–200.

Grant, B. W., K. L. Brown, G. W. Ferguson, and J. W. Gibbons. 1994. Changes in amphibian biodiversity associated with twenty-five years of pine forest regeneration. Pp. 354–366. *In* Majumdar, S. K., F. J. Brenner, J. E. Lovich, J. F. Schalles, and E. W. Miller (Eds.), Biological Diversity: Problems and Challenges. Pennsylvania Academy of Science, Easton.

Grant, C. 1936. Herpetological notes from northern Indiana. Proceedings of the Indiana Academy of Science 44:244–246.

Gray, L. E. 1992. Chemical-induced alterations of sexual differentiation: a review of effects in humans and rodents. Pp. 203–230. *In* Colborn, T., and C. Clement

(Eds.), Chemically-Induced Alterations in Sexual and Functional Development: The Wildlife/Human Connection. Advances in Modern Environmental Toxicology, Volume XXI. Princeton Scientific Publications, Princeton, New Jersey.

Gray, P., and E. Stegall. 1986. Distribution and status of Strecker's chorus frog (*Pseudacris streckeri streckeri*) in Kansas. Transactions of the Kansas Academy of Science 89:81–85.

Green, D. M. (ed.). 1997. Amphibians in Decline: Canadian Studies of a Global Problem. Herpetological Conservation, Volume 1. Society for the Study of Amphibians and Reptiles, St. Louis.

Green, E. D. 1993. Diagnostics, death, and declines. Froglog.

Green, R. H. 1979. Sampling Design and Statistical Methods for Environmental Biologists. John Wiley and Sons, New York.

Green, R. H. 1989. Statistical and nonstatistical considerations for environmental monitoring studies. Environmental Monitoring and Assessment 4:293–301.

Greenacre, M. J. 1984. Theory and Applications of Correspondence Analysis. Academic Press, New York.

Greenwell, N., V. Beasley, and L. E. Brown. 1996. The mysterious decline of the cricket frog. Aquatics: Journal of the Shedd Aquarium 26:1:48–54.

Gregory, S. V., F. J. Swanson, W. A. McKee, and K. W. Cummins. 1991. An ecosystem perspective of riparian zones. BioScience 41:540–551.

Greig-Smith, P. 1964. Quantitative Plant Ecology. Butterworths, London.

Gross, M. R. 1984. Sunfish, salmon, and the evolution of alternative reproductive strategies and tactics in fishes. Pp. 55–75. *In* Potts, G., and R. Wootton (Eds.), Fish Reproduction: Strategies and Tactics. Academic Press, London.

Gross, M. R. 1991. Salmon breeding behavior and life history evolution in changing environments. Ecology 72:1180–1186.

Grue, C. E., L. R. DeWeese, P. Mineau, G. A. Swanson, J. R. Foster, P. M. Arnold, J. N. Huckins, P. J. Sheehan, W. K. Marshall, and A. P. Ludden. 1986. Potential impacts of agricultural chemicals on waterfowl and other wildlife inhabiting prairie wetlands: an evaluation of research needs and approaches. Transactions of the North American Wildlife and Natural Resources Conference 51:357–383.

Grue, C. E., M. W. Tome, T. A. Messmer, D. B. Henry, G. A. Swanson, and L. R. DeWeese. 1989. Agricultural chemicals and prairie pothole wetlands: meeting the needs of the resource and the farmer—U.S. perspective. Transactions of the North American Wildlife and Natural Resources Conference 54:43–58.

Gruenweller, D. 1990. A general herpe [*sic*] survey focusing on *Acris crepitans blanchardi*. Unpublished undergraduate study, University of Wisconsin-Milwaukee.

Grüger, J. 1973. Studies on the Late Quaternary vegetation history of northeastern Kansas. Geological Society of America Bulletin 84:239–250.

Gruia-Gray, J., and S. S. Desser. 1992. Cytopathological observations and epizootiology of frog erythrocytic virus in bullfrogs (*Rana catesbeiana*). Journal of Wildlife Diseases 28:34–41.

Guillette, L. J., D. A. Crain, A. A. Rooney, and D. B. Pickford. 1995. Organization versus activation: the role of endocrine-disrupting contaminants (EDCs) during embryonic development in wildlife. Environmental Health Perspectives 103 (Supplement 7):157–164.

Guillette, L. J., T. S. Gross, G. R. Masson, J. M. Matter, H. F. Percival, and A. R. Woodward. 1994. Developmental abnormalities of the gonad and abnormal sex hormone concentrations in juvenile alligators from contaminated and control lakes in Florida. Environmental Health Perspectives 102:680–688.

Gurevitch, J., and S. T. Chester Jr. 1986. Analysis of repeated measures experiments. Ecology 67:251–255.

Gurevitch, J., and L. V. Hedges. 1993. Meta-analysis: combining the results of independent experiments. Pp. 378–398. *In* Scheiner, S. M., and J. Gurevitch (Eds.), Design and Analysis of Ecological Experiments. Chapman and Hall, New York.

Gurevitch, J., L. L. Morrow, A. Wallace, and J. S. Walsh. 1992. A meta-analysis of field experiments on competition. American Naturalist 140:539–572.

Guttman, D., J. E. Bramble, and O. J. Sexton. 1991. Brief notes on the breeding migration of the wood frog, *Rana sylvatica*, in east-central Missouri. American Midland Naturalist 125:269–274.

Guttman, L. 1985. The illogic of statistical inference for cumulative science. Applied Stochastic Models and Data Analysis 1:3–9.

Guttman, S. I. 1989. *Eurycea lucifuga*. Pp. 210–213. *In* Pfingsten, R. A., and F. L. Downs (Eds.), Salamanders of Ohio. Ohio Biological Survey Bulletin, New Series, Volume 7, Number 2.

Hagmeier, E. M. 1966. A numerical analysis of distributional patterns of North American mammals II. Systematic Zoology 15:279–299.

Hagmeier, E. M., and C. D. Stults. 1963. A numerical

analysis of distributional patterns of North American mammals. Systematic Zoology 13:125–155.

Hah, J. C. 1978. Effects of the heavy metal pollution of the primordial germ cells of developing amphibia. Korean Journal of Zoology 21:43–58.

Haines-Young, R., D. R. Green, and S. H. Cousins. 1993. Landscape Ecology and Geographic Information Systems. Taylor and Francis, Philadelphia.

Haining, R. 1990. Spatial Data Analysis in the Social and Environmental Sciences. Cambridge University Press, New York.

Hairston, N. G. 1989. Ecological Experiments: Purpose, Design, and Execution. Cambridge University Press, New York.

Hall, R. J. 1994. Herpetofaunal Diversity of the Four Holes Swamp, South Carolina. U.S. Department of the Interior, National Biological Survey, Washington, D.C.

Hall, R. J., and E. Kolbe. 1980. Bioconcentration of organophosphorus pesticides to hazardous levels by amphibians. Journal of Toxicology and Environmental Health 6:853–860.

Hall, R. J., and B. M. Mulhern. 1984. Are anuran amphibians heavy metal accumulators? Pp. 123–133. *In* Seigel, R. A., L. E. Hunt, J. L. Knight, L. Maleret, and N. L. Zuschlag (Eds.), Vertebrate Ecology and Systematics: A Tribute to Henry S. Fitch. University of Kansas Museum of Natural History, Lawrence.

Hall, R. J., and D. M. Swineford. 1981. Acute toxicities of toxaphene and endrin to larvae of seven species of amphibians. Toxicological Letters 8:331–336.

Hallberg, G. R. 1986. Pre-Wisconsin glacial stratigraphy of the Central Plains region in Iowa, Nebraska, Kansas, and Missouri. Pp. 11–15. *In* Sibrava, V., D. Q. Bowen, and G. M. Richmond (Eds.), Quaternary Glaciations in the Northern Hemisphere. Pergamon Press, Oxford.

Hamel, P. B., N. D. Cost, and R. M. Sheffield. 1986. The consistent characteristics of habitats: a question of scale. Pp. 121–128. *In* Verner, J., M. L. Morrison, and C. J. Ralph (Eds.), Wildlife 2000: Modeling Habitat Relationships for Terrestrial Vertebrates. University of Wisconsin Press, Madison.

Hamilton, H. L. 1941. The biological action of rotenone on freshwater animals. Journal of the Iowa Academy of Science 48:467–479.

Hammer, D. A. 1992. Creating Freshwater Wetlands. Lewis Publishers, Ann Arbor, Michigan.

Hammond, E. H. 1964. Classes of land surface form in the forty-eight states, U.S.A. Annals of the Association of American Geographers, Volume 54, Number 1.

Hampe, C. L. 1984. A description of species composition, population structures and spatial patterns in a Missouri oak-hickory forest. M.A. thesis, University of Missouri-St. Louis.

Hansen, A. J., and F. di Castri. 1992. Landscape Boundaries: Consequences for Biotic Diversity and Ecological Flows. Springer-Verlag, New York.

Hansen, L. G. 1994. Halogenated aromatic compounds. Pp. 199–230. *In* Cockerham, L. G., and B. S. Shane (Eds.), Basic Environmental Toxicology. CRC Press, Boca Raton, Florida.

Hanski, I., and M. Gilpin. 1991. Metapopulation dynamics: brief history and conceptual domain. Biological Journal of the Linnean Society 42:3–16.

Hanski, I., J. Poyry, T. Pakkala, and M. Kuussari. 1995. Multiple equilibria in metapopulation dynamics. Nature 377:618–621.

Hanson, W. R. 1952. Effects of some herbicides and insecticides on biota of North Dakota marshes. Journal of Wildlife Management 16:299–308.

Harding, J. H. 1997. Amphibians and Reptiles of the Great Lakes Region. Michigan State University Museum, East Lansing.

Harding, J. H., and J. A. Holman. 1992. Michigan Frogs, Toads, and Salamanders. Michigan State University Museum, East Lansing.

Hardy, L. M. 1995. Checklist of the amphibians and reptiles of the Caddo Lake watershed in Texas and Louisiana. Bulletin Museum Life Sciences 10:1–31.

Hardy, L. M., and L. R. Raymond. 1980. The breeding migration of the mole salamander, *Ambystoma talpoideum*, in Louisiana. Journal of Herpetology 14:327–335.

Harfenist, A., T. Power, K. L. Clark, and D. B. Peakall. 1989. A review and evaluation of the amphibian toxicological literature. Technical Report, Series Number 61, Canadian Wildlife Service, Ottawa, Ontario.

Harper, D. 1992. Eutrophication of Fresh Waters. Chapman and Hall, London.

Harri, M. N. E., J. Laitinen, and E. L. Valkama. 1979. Toxicity and retention of DDT in adult frogs *Rana temporaria* L. Environmental Pollution 19:45–55.

Harris, J. P. 1959. The natural history of *Necturus*: I. Habitats and habits. Field and Laboratory 27:11–20.

Harris, L. D. 1984. The Fragmented Forest: Island Biogeography Theory and the Preservation of Biotic Diversity. University of Chicago Press, Chicago.

Harris, R. J. 1975. A Primer of Multivariate Statistics. Academic Press, New York.

Harris, R. N. 1980. The consequences of within-year timing of breeding in *Ambystoma maculatum.* Copeia 1980:719–722.

Harris, R. N., R. A. Alford, and H. M. Wilbur. 1988. Density and phenology of *Notophtalmus viridescens dorsalis* in a natural pond. Herpetologica 44:234–242.

Harrison, R. G. 1980. Dispersal polymorphism in insects. Annual Review of Ecology and Systematics 11:95–118.

Hart, J. F. 1991. The Land That Feeds Us. W. W. Norton, New York.

Harte, J., and E. Hoffman. 1989. Possible effects of acidic deposition on a Rocky Mountain population of the tiger salamander *Ambystoma tigrinum.* Conservation Biology 3:149–158.

Hastings, A., and S. Harrison. 1994. Metapopulation dynamics and genetics. Annual Review of Ecology and Systematics 25:167–188.

Hawkins, C. P. 1986. Pseudo-understanding of pseudoreplication: a cautionary note. Bulletin of the Ecological Society of America 67:184–185.

Hayek, L.-A. C. 1994. Research design for quantitative amphibian studies. Pp. 21–39. *In* Heyer, W. R., M. A. Donnelly, R. W. McDiarmid, L.-A. C. Hayek, and M. S. Foster (Eds.), Measuring and Monitoring Biological Diversity: Standard Methods for Amphibians. Smithsonian Institution Press, Washington, D.C.

Hayes, M. P., and M. R. Jennings. 1986. Decline of the ranid frog species in western North America: are bullfrogs (*Rana catesbeiana*) responsible? Journal of Herpetology 20:490–509.

Hayes, T. B. 1995. Interdependence of corticosterone and thyroid hormones in larval toads (*Bufo boreas*). 1. Thyroid hormone-dependent and independent effects of corticosterone on growth and development. Journal of Experimental Zoology 271:95–102.

Hayes, T. B., and T. H. Wu. 1995. Interdependence of corticosterone and thyroid hormones in toad larvae (*Bufo boreas*). 2. Regulation of corticosterone and thyroid hormones. Journal of Experimental Zoology 271:103–111.

Healey, M. J. R., and L. R. Taylor. 1962. Tables for power-law transformations. Biometrika 49:557–559.

Hecnar, S. J. 1995. Acute and chronic toxicity of ammonium nitrate fertilizer to amphibians from southern Ontario. Environmental Toxicology and Chemistry 14:2131–2137.

Hedeen, S. E. 1970. The ecology and life history of the mink frog, *Rana septentrionalis* Baird. Ph.D. dissertation, University of Minnesota, Minneapolis.

Hedeen, S. E. 1971. Growth of the tadpoles of the mink frog, *Rana septentrionalis* Baird. Journal of Herpetology 5:211–212.

Hedeen, S. E. 1972. Escape behavior and cause of death of the mink frog, *Rana septentrionalis.* Herpetologica 28:261–262.

Hedeen, S. E. 1994. The Mill Creek: An Unnatural History of an Urban Stream. Blue Heron Press, Cincinnati.

Hedges, S. B. 1986. An electrophoretic analysis of Holarctic hylid frog evolution. Systematic Zoology 35:1–21.

Hedges, S. B. 1993. Global amphibian declines: a perspective from the Caribbean. Biodiversity and Conservation 2:290–303.

Heinz, G. H., H. F. Percival, and M. L. Jennings. 1991. Contaminants in American alligator eggs from lakes Apopka, Griffin and Okeechobee, Florida. Environmental Monitoring and Assessment 16:277–285.

Helgen, J. C. 1996. The frogs of Granite Falls. Pp. 55–57. *In* Moriarty, J. J., and D. Jones (Eds.), Minnesota's Amphibians and Reptiles: Conservation and Status, Proceedings of Symposium. Serpent's Tale Press, Excelsior, Minnesota.

Helsel, D. R. 1990. Less than obvious: statistical treatment of data below the detection limit. Environmental Science and Technology 24:1766–1774.

Hensley, M. 1966. The tiger salamander in northern Michigan. Herpetologica 20:203–204.

Heppell, S. A., N. D. Denslow, L. C. Folmar, and C. V. Sullivan. 1995. Universal assay of vitellogenin as a biomarker for environmental estrogens. Environmental Health Perspectives 103:9–15.

Herkert, J. R. 1991. Endangered and Threatened species of Illinois: Status and Distribution, Volume 1—Plants. Illinois Endangered Species Protection Board, Springfield.

Herkert, J. R. 1992. Endangered and Threatened Species of Illinois: Status and Distribution, Volume 2—Animals. Illinois Endangered Species Protection Board, Springfield.

Herkert, J. R. 1994. Endangered and Threatened Species of Illinois: Status and Distribution, Volume 3—1994 Changes to the Illinois List of Endangered and Threatened Species. Illinois Endangered Species Protection Board, Springfield.

Herkert, J. R. 1995. Endangered and threatened birds of Illinois: an overview of the species and their habitats. Meadowlark 4:42–47.

Herkovits, J., and C. S. Perez Coll. 1993. Stage-dependent susceptibility of *Bufo arenarum* embryos to cadmium. Bulletin of Environmental Contamination and Toxicology 50:608–611.

Herrmann, K., B. N. Rock, U. Ammer, and H. N. Paley. 1988. Preliminary assessment of airborne imaging spectrometer and airborne thematic mapper data acquired for forest decline areas in the Federal Republic of Germany. Remote Sensing of Environment 24:129–149.

Heyer, W. R., M. A. Donnelly, R. W. McDiarmid, L.-A. C. Hayek, and M. S. Foster. 1994. Measuring and Monitoring Biological Diversity: Standard Methods for Amphibians. Smithsonian Institution Press, Washington, D.C.

Heyer, W. R., A. S. Rand, C. A. G. Da Cruz, and O. L. Peixoto. 1988. Decimations, extinctions, and colonizations of frog populations in southeastern Brazil and their evolutionary implications. Biotropica 20:230–235.

Higgins, K. F. 1986. Interpretation and compendium of historical fire accounts in the northern Great Plains. U.S. Fish and Wildlife Service, Resource Publication Number 161, Washington, D.C.

Higgins, S. K. 1987. Soil survey of Monroe County, Illinois. Illinois Agricultural Experiment Station Soil Report, Number 126, Springfield.

Hill, M. O. 1973. Reciprocal averaging: an eigenvector method of ordination. Journal of Ecology 61:237–249.

Hill, M. O. 1974. Correspondence analysis: a neglected multivariate method. Journal of the Royal Statistical Society, Series C 23:340–354.

Hill, M. O., and H. G. Gauch. 1980. Detrended correspondence analysis, an improved ordination technique. Vegetatio 42:47–58.

Hillis, D. M. 1977. Sex ratio, mortality rate, and breeding stimuli in a Maryland population of *Ambystoma maculatum*. Bulletin of the Maryland Herpetological Society 13:84–91.

Hiltibran, R., and D. Anderson. 1990. Chemical control of some aquatic plants. Pp. 222–228. *In* Illinois Pest Control Handbook. Cooperative Extension Service, University of Illinois, and Illinois Natural History Survey, Urbana.

Hine, R. L., B. L. Les, and B. F. Hellmich. 1981. Leopard frog populations and mortality in Wisconsin, 1974–1976. Technical Bulletin Number 122, Wisconsin Department of Natural Resources, Madison.

Hine, R. L., B. L. Les, B. F. Hellmich, and R. C. Vogt. 1975. Preliminary report on leopard frog (*Rana pipiens*) populations in Wisconsin. Research Report Number 81, Department of Natural Resources, Madison.

Hird, D. W., S. L. Diesch, R. G. McKinnell, E. Gorham, F. B. Martin, S. W. Kurtz, and C. Dubrovolny. 1981. *Aeromonas hydrophila* in wild-caught frogs and tadpoles (*Rana pipiens*) in Minnesota. Laboratory Animal Science 31:166–169.

Hirsh, R. M. 1988. Statistical methods and sampling design for estimating step trends in surface-water quality. Water Resources Bulletin 24:493–504.

Hirsh, R. M., and J. R. Slack. 1984. A nonparametric trend test for seasonal data with serial dependence. Water Resources Research 20:727–732.

Hoaglin, D. C., F. Mosteller, and J. W. Tukey. 1983. Understanding Robust and Exploratory Data Analysis. John Wiley and Sons, New York.

Hoaglin, D. C., F. Mosteller, and J. W. Tukey. 1985. Exploring Data Tables, Trends, and Shapes. John Wiley and Sons, New York.

Hoaglin, D. C., F. Mosteller, and J. W. Tukey. 1991. Fundamentals of Exploratory Analysis of Variance. John Wiley and Sons, New York.

Hobbs, R. J., and H. A. Mooney. 1990. Remote Sensing of Biosphere Functioning. Springer-Verlag, New York.

Hoberg, T., and C. Gause. 1992. Reptiles and amphibians of North Dakota. North Dakota Outdoors 55:7–18.

Hoerl, A. E., and R. W. Kennard. 1970a. Ridge regression: biased estimation of nonorthogonal problems. Technometrics 12:55–67.

Hoerl, A. E., and R. W. Kennard. 1970b. Ridge regression: applications to nonorthogonal problems. Technometrics 12:69–82.

Hoffman, G. L. 1967. Parasites of North American Fishes. University of California Press, Berkeley.

Hoffman, G. L., and R. E. Putz. 1964. Studies on *Gyrodactylus macrochiri* n. sp. (Trematoda: Monogegea) from *Lepomis macrochirus*. Proceedings of the Helminthological Society 31:76–82.

Holland, M. M., P. G. Risser, and R. J. Naiman. 1991. Ecotones: The Role of Landscape Boundaries in the Management and Restoration of Changing Environments. Chapman and Hall, New York.

Hollander, M., and D. A. Wolfe. 1973. Nonparametric Statistical Methods. John Wiley and Sons, New York.

Holling, C. S., and G. K. Meffe. 1996. Command and control and the pathology of natural reserve management. Conservation Biology 10:328–337.

Holman, J. A. 1988. The status of Michigan's Pleistocene herpetofauna. Michigan Academician 20:125–132.

Holman, J. A. 1992. Patterns of herpetological reoccupation of post-glacial Michigan: amphibians and reptiles come home. Michigan Academician 24:453–466.

Holman, J. A. 1995. Pleistocene Amphibians and Reptiles in North America. Oxford University Press, New York.

Holman, J. A., H. O. Jackson, and W. H. Hill. 1964. *Pseudacris streckeri illinoensis* Smith from extreme southern Illinois. Herpetologica 20:205.

Holman, J. A., and R. L. Richards. 1993. Herpetofauna of the Prairie Creek site, Daviess County, Indiana. Proceedings of the Indiana Academy of Science 102:115–131.

Holomuzki, J. R. 1995. Oviposition sites and fish-deterrent mechanisms of two stream salamanders. Copeia 1995:607–613.

Homoya, M. A., D. B. Abrell, J. R. Aldrich, and T. W. Post. 1985. The natural regions of Indiana. Proceedings of the Indiana Academy of Science 94:245–268.

Honegger, R. E. 1981. Threatened Amphibians and Reptiles in Europe. Akademische Verlagsgesellschaft, Wiesbaden, Germany.

Honrubia, M. P., M. P. Herraez, and R. Alvarez. 1993. The carbamate insecticide ZZ-aphox induced structural changes of gills, liver, gall bladder, heart, and notochord of *Rana perezi* tadpoles. Archives of Environmental Contamination and Toxicology 25:184–191.

Hontela, A., P. Dumont, D. Duclos, and R. Fortin. 1995. Endocrine and metabolic dysfunction in yellow perch, *Perca flavescens,* exposed to organic contaminants and heavy metals in the St. Lawrence River. Environmental Toxicology and Chemistry 14:725–731.

Hontela, A., J. B. Rasmussen, C. Audet, and G. Chevalier. 1992. Impaired cortisol stress response in fish from environments polluted by PAHs, PCBs, and mercury. Archives of Environmental Contamination and Toxicology 22:278–283.

Hoppe, D., and R. McKinnell. 1991. Minnesota's mutant leopard frogs. Minnesota Volunteer 54:56–63.

Hoppe, D., and R. McKinnell. 1996. Observations of the status of Minnesota leopard frog populations. Pp. 37–41. *In* Moriarty, J. J., and D. Jones (Eds.), Minnesota's Amphibians and Reptiles: Conservation and Status, Proceedings of Symposium. Serpent's Tale Press, Excelsior, Minnesota.

Horne, M. T., and W. A. Dunson. 1994. Behavioral and physiological responses of the terrestrial life stages of the jefferson salamander, *Ambystoma jeffersonianum,* to low soil pH. Archives of Environmental Contamination and Toxicology 27:232–238.

Houck, L. 1908. History of Missouri. Lakeside Press, Chicago.

Houghton, R. A., D. S. Leftkowitz, and D. L. Skole. 1991. Changes in the landscape of Latin America between 1850 and 1985. I. Progressive loss of forest. Forest Ecology and Management 38:143–172.

Howard, J. A. 1991. Remote Sensing of Forest Resources: Theory and Application. Chapman and Hall, New York.

Howell, J. H. 1966. The life cycle of the sea lamprey and a toxicological approach to its control. Pp. 263–270. *In* Smith, R. T., P. A. Miescher, and R. A. Good (Eds.), Phylogeny of Immunity. University Press of Florida, Gainesville.

Huete, A. R., and R. D. Jackson. 1987. Suitability of spectral indices for evaluating vegetation characteristics on arid rangelands. Remote Sensing of Environment 23:213–232.

Huff, D. 1954. How to Lie with Statistics. W. W. Norton, New York.

Huggett, R. J. 1995. Geoecology: An Evolutionary Approach. Routledge, New York.

Huggins, D. G. 1971. *Scaphiopus bombifrons* Cope, a species new to Iowa. Journal of Herpetology 5:216.

Hunsaker, D., and F. E. Potter. 1960. "Red leg" in a natural population of amphibians. Herpetologica 16:285–286.

Hurlbert, S. H. 1984. Pseudoreplication and the design of ecological field experiments. Ecological Monographs 54:187–211.

Hurter, J. 1893. Catalogue of reptiles and batrachians found in the vicinity of St. Louis, Mo. Transactions of the Academy of Science, St. Louis 6:251–261.

Hurter, J. 1911. Herpetology of Missouri. Transactions of the Academy of Science, St. Louis 20:59–274.

Husting, E. L. 1965. Survival and breeding structure in a population of *Ambystoma maculatum.* Copeia 1965:352–362.

Hutchison, V. H. 1958. The distribution and ecology of the cave salamander, *Eurycea lucifuga.* Ecological Monographs 28:1–20.

Hutchison, V. H. 1966. *Eurycea lucifuga.* Catalogue of American Amphibians and Reptiles 24.1–24.2.

Huxhold, W. E., and A. G. Levinson. 1995. Managing Geographic Information System Projects. Oxford University Press, New York.

Iffrig, G. F., and M. Bowles. 1983. A compendium of ecological and natural subdivisions of the United States.

Natural Areas Journal 3:3–11.

Illinois Department of Conservation. 1978. Administrative Order, Article CXXXVIII—Illinois list of endangered and threatened vertebrate species issued in accordance with provisions of Section 337 of the Illinois Endangered Species Protection Act.

Illinois Department of Conservation. 1995a. Management of small lakes and ponds in Illinois. Illinois Department of Conservation, Division of Fisheries, Springfield.

Illinois Department of Conservation. 1995b. Ponds and lakes constructed during 1994. Illinois Department of Conservation, Division of Fisheries, Springfield.

Illinois Department of Energy and Natural Resources. 1994. The changing Illinois environment: critical trends. Technical report of the Critical Trends Assessment Project. Volume 3, Ecological Resources. ILENR/RE-EA-94/05(3). Illinois Department of Energy and Natural Resources, Springfield.

Illinois Endangered Species Protection Board. 1994. Checklist of endangered and threatened animals and plants of Illinois. Illinois Deptartment of Conservation, Springfield.

Illinois Environmental Protection Agency. 1995. The condition of Illinois water resources 1972–1994. IEPA/WPC/95-016. Illinois Environmental Protection Agency, Bureau of Water, Springfield.

Illinois Natural History Survey. 1991. Session three: wetlands. Illinois Natural History Survey Bulletin 34:400.

Imbrie, J., J. D. Hays, D. G. Martinson, A. McIntyre, A. C. Mix, J. J. Morley, N. G. Pisias, W. L. Prell, and N. J. Shackleton. 1984. The orbital theory of Pleistocene climate: support from a revised chronology of the marine ^{18}O record. Pp. 269–305. *In* Berger, A., J. Imbrie, J. Hays, G. Kukla, and B. Saltzman (Eds.), Milankovitch and Climate. NATO ASI Series, Series C, Mathematical and Physical Sciences Number 126.

Indiana Heritage Program. 1995. Community classification. Unpublished database, Indiana Department of Natural Resources, Division of Nature Preserves, Indianapolis.

Inger, R. 1958. Comments on the definition of genera. Evolution 12:370–384.

Iowa Department of Natural Resources. 1994. Iowa trout fishing guide. Iowa Department of Natural Resources, Des Moines.

Iowa Department of Natural Resources Wildlife Diversity Unit. 1995. Iowa frog and toad census protocol. Iowa Department of Natural Resources, Des Moines.

Iowa Natural Areas Inventory. 1995. Iowa community classification. Unpublished database, Iowa Department of Natural Resources, Bureau of Preserves and Ecological Services, Des Moines.

Iowa State Preserves Board. 1981. A directory of Iowa nature preserves. Iowa State Preserves Board, Des Moines.

Ireland, P. H. 1991. Separate effects of acid-derived anions and cations on growth of larval salamanders of *Ambystoma maculatum.* Copeia 1991:132–137.

Isaaks, E. H., and R. M. Srivastava. 1989. An Introduction to Applied Geostatistics. Oxford University Press, New York.

Iverson, L. R. 1988. Land-use changes in Illinois, USA: the influence of landscape attributes on current and historic land use. Landscape Ecology 2:45–61.

Iverson, L. R., and P. G. Risser. 1987. Analyzing long-term changes in vegetation with geographic information system and remotely sensed data. Advanced Space Research 7:183–194.

Iverson, L. R., and M. W. Schwartz. 1994. Forests. Pp. 33–66. *In* The Changing Illinois Environment: Critical Trends. Volume 3: Ecological Resources. ILENR/RE-EA-94/05(3), Illinois Department of Energy and Natural Resources, Springfield.

Jacard, P. 1902. Lois de distribution florale daus la zone alpine. Bulletin of the Society Vaudoise Science Naturelles 38:69–130.

Jack McCormick and Associates. 1975. Wildlife of the Cuyahoga Valley project region. Unpublished report to the Ohio Department of Natural Resources, Columbus.

Jackson, R. D., and A. R. Huete. 1991. Interpreting vegetation indices. Preventive Veterinary Medicine 2:167–183.

Jacobson, G. L., Jr., T. Webb III, and E. C. Grimm. 1987. Patterns and rates of vegetation change during the deglaciation of eastern North America. Pp. 277–288. *In* Ruddiman, W. F., and H. E. Wright Jr. (Eds.), Geology of North America, Volume K-3, North America and Adjacent Oceans during the Last Deglaciation. Geological Society of America, Boulder, Colorado.

Jaeger, R. G., D. Fortune, G. Hill, A. Palen, and G. Risher. 1993. Salamander homing behavior and territorial pheromones: alternative hypotheses. Journal of Herpetology 27:236–239.

Jaeger, R. G., and C. R. Gabor. 1993. Intraspecific chemical communication by a territorial salamander via the postcloacal gland. Copeia 1993:1171–1174.

James, F. C., and C. E. McCulloch. 1990. Multivariate analysis in ecology and systematics: panacea or Pandora's box? Annual Review of Ecology and Systematics 21:129–166.

Jameson, D. L. 1957. Population structure and homing response in the Pacific tree frog. Copeia 1957:221–228.

Jansen, D. K., and R. K. Anderson. 1981. Audio tape of calling Wisconsin amphibians. Created as a component of M.S. thesis, University of Wisconsin-Stevens Point.

Jansen, H. T., P. S. Cooke, J. Porcelli, T. C. Liu, and L. G. Hansen. 1993. Estrogenic and antiestrogenic actions of PCBs in the female rat: in vitro and in vivo studies. Reproductive Toxicology 7:237–248.

Jaslow, A. P., and R. C. Vogt. 1977. Identification and distribution of *Hyla versicolor* and *Hyla chrysoscelis* in Wisconsin. Herpetologica 33:201–205.

Jenny, H. 1980. The Soil Resource: Origin and Behavior. Springer-Verlag, New York.

Johnson, A. I., C. B. Pettersson, and J. L. Fulton. 1992. Geographic Information Systems (GIS) and Mapping: Practices and Standards. American Society of Testing and Materials (ASTM), Philadelphia.

Johnson, A. S. 1989. The thin green line: riparian corridors and endangered species in Arizona and New Mexico. Pp. 35–46. *In* Mackintosh, G. (Ed.), Preserving Communities and Corridors. Defenders of Wildlife, Washington, D.C.

Johnson, C. R. 1980. The effects of five organophosphorus insecticides on thermal stress in tadpoles of the Pacific tree frog, *Hyla regilla*. Zoological Journal of the Linnean Society 69:143–147.

Johnson, C. R., and J. E. Prine. 1976. The effects of sublethal concentrations of organophosphorus insecticides and an insect growth regulator on temperature tolerance in hydrated and dehydrated juvenile western toads *Bufo boreas*. Comparative Biochemistry and Physiology 53A:147–149.

Johnson, D. H. 1995. Statistical sirens: the allure of nonparametrics. Ecology 76:1998–2000.

Johnson, M. J. 1984. The distribution and habitat of the pickerel frog in Wisconsin. M.S. thesis, University of Wisconsin - Stevens Point.

Johnson, R. R., and D. A. Jones. 1977. Importance, preservation and management of riparian habitat: a symposium. U.S. Forest Service, General Technical Report RM-43, Fort Collins, Colorado.

Johnson, T. R. 1979. A guide to amphibian and reptile conservation. Missouri Department of Conservation, Jefferson City.

Johnson, T. R. 1991. Sand prairie singer. Missouri Conservationist 52:30.

Johnson, T. R. 1992. The Amphibians and Reptiles of Missouri. Missouri Department of Conservation, Jefferson City.

Johnson, T. R., and L. Burger. 1992. The distribution and status of the Illinois chorus frog, *Pseudacris streckeri illinoensis*, in Missouri and Arkansas. Unpublished report to the U.S. Fish and Wildlife Service, Washington, D.C.

Johnson, W. H., and L. R. Follmer. 1989. Source and origin of Roxana silt and Middle Wisconsinan midcontinent glacial activity. Quaternary Research 31:319–331.

Johnston, C. A. 1994. Ecological engineering of wetlands by beavers. Pp. 379–384. *In* Mitsch, J. W. (Ed.), Global Wetlands: Old World and New. Elsevier, New York.

Johnston, C. A., N. E. Detenbeck, J. P. Bond, and G. J. Niemi. 1990. Geographic information systems for cumulative impact assessment. Photogrammetric Engineering and Remote Sensing 54:1609–1615.

Johnston, C. A., N. E. Detenbeck, and G. J. Niemi. 1990. The cumulative effect of wetlands on stream water quality and quantity. A landscape approach. Biogeochemistry 10:105–141.

Johnston, C. A., and R. J. Naiman. 1987. Boundary dynamics at the aquatic-terrestrial interface: the influence of beaver and geomorphology. Landscape Ecology 1:47–57.

Johnston, C. A., and R. J. Naiman. 1990a. Browse selection by beaver: effects on riparian forest composition. Canadian Journal of Forest Resources 20:1036–1043.

Johnston, C. A., and R. J. Naiman. 1990b. The use of geographical information systems to analyze long-term landscape alteration by beaver. Landscape Ecology 4:5–19.

Johnston, C. A., and R. J. Naiman. 1990c. Aquatic patch creation in relation to beaver population trends. Ecology 71:1617–1621.

Jolicoeur, P. 1963a. Bilateral symmetry and asymmetry in limb bones of *Martes americana* and man. Review of Canadian Biology 22:409–432.

Jolicoeur, P. 1963b. The degree of generality of robustness in *Martes americana*. Growth 27:1–27.

Jones, D., and N. Matloff. 1986. Statistical hypothesis testing in biology: a contradiction in terms. Journal of Economic Entomology 79:1156–1160.

Jones, T. R., D. K. Skelly, and E. E. Werner. 1993. *Ambystoma tigrinum tigrinum* (eastern tiger salamander) developmental polymorphism. Herpetological Review 24:147–148.

Jongman, R. H. G., C. J. F. Ter Braak, and O. F. R. Van Tongeren. 1995. Data Analysis in Community and Landscape Ecology. Cambridge University Press, New York.

Jung, R. E. 1993. Blanchard's cricket frogs (*Acris crepitans blanchardi*) in southwest Wisconsin. Transactions of the Wisconsin Academy of Science, Arts and Letters 1:79–87.

Jung, R. E., and C. H. Jagoe. 1995. Effects of low pH and aluminum on body size, swimming performance, and susceptibility to predation of green tree frog (*Hyla cinerea*) tadpoles. Canadian Journal of Zoology 12:2171–2183.

Justice, C. O. 1986. Monitoring the grasslands of semi-arid Africa using NOAA-AVHRR data. International Journal of Remote Sensing 7:1383–1622.

Justice, C. O., J. R. G. Townshend, B. N. Holden, and C. J. Tucker. 1985. Analysis of the phenology of global vegetation using meteorological satellite data. International Journal of Remote Sensing 6:1271–1318.

Juterbock, J. E. 1986. The ecology of cave salamanders (*Eurycea lucifuga*) in Hamilton County, Ohio. Unpublished report to the Ohio Department of Natural Areas and Preserves, Columbus.

Juterbock, J. E. 1989. *Aneides aeneus* (Cope and Packard) green salamander. Pp. 190–196. *In* Pfingsten, R. A., and F. L. Downs (Eds.), Salamanders of Ohio. Ohio Biological Survey Bulletin, New Series Volume 7, Number 2.

Kabisch, K., and J. Weiss. 1968. *Rana temporaria* L. als Winternahrung von *Salmo trutta fario* (L.). Zoologische Abhandlungen 29:289–291.

Kahn, D. 1996 [8 March]. STS legislative committee monthly summary. Science and Technology Section, Association of College and Research Libraries List [online]. Available through e-mail: STS-L@UTKVM1.BITNET.

Kane, A. S., T. M. Stockdale, and D. L. Johnson. 1985. 3-trifluoromethyl-4-nitrophenol (TFM) control of tadpoles in culture ponds. Progressive Fish-Culturist 47:231–237.

Kaplan, H. M., and S. S. Glaczenski. 1965. Hematological effects of organophosphate insecticides in the frog (*Rana pipiens*). Life Sciences 4:1213–1219.

Kaplan, H. M., and J. G. Overpeck. 1964. Toxicity of halogenated hydrocarbon insecticides for the frog, *Rana pipiens*. Herpetologica 20:163–169.

Kapp, R. O., S. G. Beld, and J. A. Holman. 1990. Paleontological resources in Michigan: an overview. Pp. 14–34. *In* Stoffle, R. W. (Ed.), Cultural and Paleontological Effects in Siting a Low Level Radioactive Waste Storage Facility in Michigan. Institute of Social Research Publication, University of Michigan, Ann Arbor.

Karns, D. R. 1986. Amphibians and reptiles of Jefferson County: analysis of a herpetological community in southeastern Indiana. Unpublished report to the Indiana Nongame and Endangered Wildlife Program, Bloomington.

Karns, D. R. 1988. The herpetofauna of Jefferson County: analysis of an amphibian and reptile community in southeastern Indiana. Proceedings of the Indiana Academy of Science 98:535–552.

Karns, D. R. 1992. Effects of acidic bog habitats on amphibian reproduction in a northern Minnesota peatland. Journal of Herpetology 26:401–412.

Karr, J. R. 1991. Biological integrity: a long-neglected aspect of water resource management. Ecological Applications 1:66–84.

Karr, J. R., K. D. Fausch, P. L. Angermeier, P. R. Yant, and I. J. Schlosser. 1986. Assessing biological integrity in running waters: a method and its rationale. Illinois Natural History Survey Special Publication Number 5, Springfield.

Karr, J. R., and I. J. Schlosser. 1978. Water resources and the land-water interface. Science 201:229–234.

Kasai, F., and T. Hanazato. 1995. Effects of the triazine herbicide, simetryn, on freshwater plankton communities in experimental ponds. Environmental Pollution 89:197–202.

Kats, L. B., J. W. Petranka, and A. Sih. 1988. Antipredator defenses and the persistence of amphibian larvae with fishes. Ecology 69:1865–1870.

Katzenellenbogen, J. A. 1995. The structural pervasiveness of estrogenic activity. Environmental Health Perspectives 103:99–101.

Keating, K. A., W. G. Brewster, and C. H. Key. 1991. Satellite telemetry: performance of animal tracking systems. Journal of Wildlife Management 55:160–171.

Keith, L. H. 1990. Environmental sampling: a summary. Environmental Science and Technology 24:610–617.

Kelce, W. R., C. R. Stone, S. C. Laws, L. E. Gray, J. A. Kemppainen, and E. M. Wilson. 1995. Persistent DDT metabolite *p, p'*-DDE is a potent androgen receptor antagonist. Nature 375:581–585.

Keltner, J. 1993–1994. Siteseer, version 1.1 for Windows [a computer program resulting from the North American Pollen Database]. Illinois State Museum, Springfield.

Kemmis, T. J. 1991. Glacial landforms, sedimentology,

and depositional environments of the Des Moines Lobe, northern Iowa. Ph.D. dissertation, University of Iowa, Iowa City.

Kenkel, N. C., and L. Orlóci. 1986. Applying metric and nonmetric multidimensional scaling to ecological studies: some new results. Ecology 67:919–928.

Kennicott, R. 1855. Catalogue of animals observed in Cook County, Illinois. Transactions of the Illinois State Agricultural Society 1:591–593.

Kent, M., and P. Coker. 1992. Vegetation Description and Analysis: A Practical Approach. CRC Press, Boca Raton, Florida.

Kentula, M. E., R. P. Brooks, S. E. Gwin, C. C. Holland, A. D. Sherman, and J. C. Sifneos. 1992. Wetlands: An Approach to Improving Decision Making in Wetland Restoration and Creation. Island Press, Washington, D.C.

Keppel, G., and S. Zedeck. 1989. Data Analysis for Research Designs. W. H. Freeman, New York.

Kershaw, K. A., and J. H. H. Looney. 1985. Quantitative and Dynamic Plant Ecology. Edward Arnold, Baltimore.

Keys, J., Jr., C. Carpenter, S. Hooks, F. Koenig, W. H. McNab, W. E. Russell, and M. L. Smith. 1995. Ecological units of the eastern United States. First approximation. U.S. Forest Service, Atlanta.

Kiester, A. R. 1971. Species density of North American amphibians and reptiles. Systematic Zoology 20:127–137.

Kimeldorf, G., and G. Wahba. 1970. A correspondence between Bayesian estimation of stochastic processes and smoothing by splines. Annals of Mathematical Statistics 41:495–502.

King, J. E. 1973. Late Pleistocene palynology and biogeography of the western Missouri Ozarks. Ecological Monographs 43:539–565.

King, J. E., and J. J. Saunders. 1986. *Geochelone* in Illinois and the Illinoian-Sangamonian vegetation type of the region. Quaternary Research 25:89–99.

King, J. R. 1980. Frugal Sampling Schemes. Technical and Engineering Aids for Management (TEAM), Tamworth, New Hampshire.

King, J. R. 1981. Probability Charts for Decision Making. Technical and Engineering Aids for Management (TEAM), Tamworth, New Hampshire.

King, K. S., and S. L. Zoars. 1991. Natural areas inventory and management recommendations: Palos and Sag Valley Divisions and portions of the Tinley Creek Division. Forest Preserve District of Cook County, River Forest, Illinois.

Kingsolver, J. G. 1995. Viability selection on seasonally polyphenic traits: wing melanin pattern in western white butterflies. Evolution 49:932–941.

Kish, L. 1987. Statistical Design for Research. John Wiley and Sons, New York.

Klingbiel, J. H. 1975. Use of fish toxicants in Wisconsin, 1941–1973. Pp. 54–58. *In* Eschmeyer, P. H. (Ed.), Rehabilitation of fish populations with toxicants. SpecialPublication Number 4, North Central Division, American Fisheries Society, Bethesda, Maryland.

Knolton, R. J., P. D. MacMahon, K. A. Jeffrey, and F. W. H. Beamish. 1986. Effects of the lampricide 3-trifluoromethyl-4-nitrophenol (TFM) on the macroinvertebrates of a hardwater river. Hydrobiologia 139:251–267.

Knudsen, G. 1989. Unpublished field notes. Milwaukee Public Museum, Milwaukee.

Kolasa, J., and S. T. A. Pickett. 1991. Ecological Heterogeneity. Springer-Verlag, New York.

Konrad, J. 1996. Commercial trade in Minnesota's amphibians and reptiles. Pp. 1–2. *In* Moriarty, J. J., and D. Jones (Eds.), Minnesota's Amphibians and Reptiles: Conservation and Status, Proceedings of Symposium. Serpent's Tale Press, Excelsior, Minnesota.

Koonz, W. 1992. Amphibians in Manitoba. Pp. 19–20. *In* Bishop, C. A., and K. E. Pettit (Eds.), Declines in Canadian Amphibian Populations: Designing a National Monitoring Strategy. Occasional Paper Number 76, Canadian Wildlife Service, Ottawa, Ontario.

Korach, K. S., and J. A. McLachlan. 1995. Techniques for detection of estrogenicity. Environmental Health Perspectives 103:5–8.

Korte, G. B. 1994. The GIS Book. OnWord Press, High Mountain Publishers, Sante Fe, New Mexico.

Krebs, C. J. 1989. Ecological Methodology. Harper Row, New York.

Krige, D. G. 1966. Two dimensional weighted moving average trend surfaces for ore observation. Journal of the South African Institute of Mining and Metallurgy 66:13–38.

Krishnan, V., and S. Safe. 1993. Polychlorinated biphenyls (PCBs), dibenzo-p-dioxins (PCDDs), and dibenzofurans (PCDFs) as antiestrogens in MCF-7 human breast cancer cells: quantitative structure-activity relationships. Toxicology and Applied Pharmacology 120:55–61.

Kruse, K. C., and M. G. Francis. 1977. A predation deterrent in the larvae of the bullfrog, *Rana catesbeiana.* Transactions of the American Fisheries Society 106:248–252.

Kruse, K. C., and B. M. Stone. 1984. Largemouth bass (*Micropterus salmoides*) learn to avoid feeding on toad (*Bufo*) tadpoles. Animal Behaviour 32:1035–1039.

Krusling, P. J. 1993. Report on the reptile and amphibian survey of recently acquired land in Embshoff Woods and Nature Preserve. Unpublished report to the Hamilton County Park District, Cincinnati.

Krusling, P. J., and J. G. Davis. 1990. Report on the reptile and amphibian survey at Mitchell Memorial Forest. Unpublished report to the Hamilton County Park District, Cincinnati.

Krusling, P. J., and J. G. Davis. 1992. An additional record of the spring salamander (*Gyrinophilus porphyriticus*) in the Hamilton County Park District. Unpublished report to the Hamilton County Park District, Cincinnati.

Krusling, P. J., and J. G. Davis. 1993. Report on the status of the spring salamander (*Gyrinophilus porphyriticus*) in the Hamilton County Park District. Unpublished report to the Hamilton County Park District, Cincinnati.

Krusling, P. J., J. G. Davis, and W. R. Wauligman. 1991a. Report on the amphibian and reptile survey of Farbach Werner Nature Preserve. Unpublished report to the Hamilton County Park District, Cincinnati.

Krusling, P. J., J. G. Davis, and W. R. Wauligman. 1991b. Report on the reptile and amphibian survey of Kroger Hill Park and Avoca Park, Hamilton County Park District. Unpublished report to the Hamilton County Park District, Cincinnati.

Krusling, P. J., J. G. Davis, and W. R. Wauligman. 1991c. Report on the amphibian and reptile survey of Little Miami Golf Center and Bass Island Park. Unpublished report to the Hamilton County Park District, Cincinnati.

Krusling, P. J., J. G. Davis, and W. R. Wauligman. 1991d. Report on the reptile and amphibian survey of Withrow Nature Preserve, Hamilton County Park District. Unpublished report to the Hamilton County Park District, Cincinnati.

Krusling, P. J., and J. W. Ferner. 1993. Distribution and status of amphibians in the northern tier counties of Kentucky. Unpublished report to the Cincinnati Gas and Electric Company, Cincinnati.

Krzysik, A. J. 1987. Environmental gradient analysis, ordination, and classification in environmental impact assessments. USACERL Technical Report N-87/19. U.S. Army Corps of Engineers, Construction Engineering Research Laboratories, Champaign, Illinois.

Krzysik, A. J. 1997. Desert tortoise populations in the Mojave Desert and a half-century of military training activities. Pp. 61–73. *In* Van Abbema, J. (Ed.), Conservation, Restoration, and Management of Tortoises and Turtles—An International Conference. American Museum of Natural History, New York.

Krzysik, A. J., and A. P. Woodman. 1991. Six years of army training activities and the desert tortoise. Desert Tortoise Council Symposium 1987–1991:337–368.

Kuchler, A. W. 1964. Potential natural vegetation of the conterminous United States. American Geographic Society Special Publications Number 36, New York.

Kuchler, A. W., and I. S. Zonneveld. 1988. Vegetation Mapping. Kluwer Academic, Dordrecht, Netherlands.

Kusano, T., K. Fukuyama, and N. Miyashita. 1995. Age determination of the stream frog, *Rana sakuraii*, by skeletochronology. Journal of Herpetology 29:625–628.

Kuster, E. 1905. Über kaltblutertuberculose. Muchener Medizinische Wochenschrift 52:57–59.

Kutka, F. J. 1994. Low pH effects on swimming activity of *Ambystoma* salamander larvae. Environmental Toxicology and Chemistry 13:1821–1824.

Kutka, F. J., and M. D. Bachmann. 1990. Acid sensitivity and water chemistry correlates of amphibian breeding ponds in northern Wisconsin, USA. Hydrobiologia 208:153–160.

Kutzbach, J. E., P. J. Guetter, P. J. Behling, and R. Selin. 1993. Simulated climatic changes: results of the COHMAP climate-model experiments. Pp. 24–93. *In* Wright, H. E., Jr., J. E. Kutzbach, T. Webb III, W. F. Ruddiman, F. A. Street-Perrott, and P. J. Bartlein (Eds.), Global Climates Since the Last Glacial Maximum. University of Minnesota Press, Minneapolis.

Kutzbach, J. E., and T. Webb III. 1993. Conceptual basis for understanding Late-Quaternary climates. Pp. 5–11. *In* Wright, H. E., Jr., J. E. Kutzbach, T. Webb III, W. F. Ruddiman, F. A. Street-Perrott, and P. J. Bartlein (Eds.), Global Climates Since the Last Glacial Maximum. University of Minnesota Press, Minneapolis.

Kuzmin, S. L., and V. V. Bobrov. 1995. The status of amphibian populations in European Russia. Pp. 49–53. *In* Kuzmin, S. L., C. K. Dodd Jr., and M. M. Pikulik (Eds.), Amphibian Populations in the Commonwealth of Independent States: Current Status and Declines. Pensoft Publishers, Moscow.

Kuzmin, S. L., C. K. Dodd Jr., and M. M. Pikulik. 1995. Amphibian Populations in the Commonwealth of Independent States: Current Status and Declines. Pensoft Publishers, Moscow.

Laan, R., and B. Verboom. 1990. Effects of pool size and

isolation on amphibian communities. Biological Conservation 54:251–262.

Labotka, T. C., and N. C. Hester. 1971. Sand and gravel resources of Mason County, Illinois. Circular 464, State Geological Survey, Illinois Department of Registration and Education, Urbana.

Ladd, D. 1991. Reexamination of the role of fire in Missouri oak woodlands. Pp. 67–80. *In* Ebinger, J. E., and G. S. Wilhelm (Eds.), Proceedings of the Oak Woods Management Workshop, Eastern Illinois University, Charleston.

Lambert, S., and W. H. Reid. 1981. Biogeography of the Colorado herpetofauna. American Midland Naturalist 105:145–156.

Lande, R., and G. F. Barrowclough. 1987. Effective population size, genetic variation, and their use in population management. Pp. 87–123. *In* Soulé, M. E. (Ed.), Viable Populations for Conservation. Cambridge University Press, New York.

Lande, S. P., and S. I. Guttman. 1973. The effects of copper sulfate on the growth and mortality rate of *Rana pipiens* tadpoles. Herpetologica 29:22–27.

Landreth, H. F., and D. E. Ferguson. 1967. Newts: sun-compass orientation. Science 158:1459–1461.

Langton, T. E. S. 1989. Amphibians and Roads. ACO Polymer Products, Bedfordshire, England.

Lannoo, M. J. 1994. Using species reintroductions to assist in determining whether amphibian declines are the result of current or historical factors. Meeting of the Central Division of the Declining Amphibian Populations Task Force, Indiana Dunes National Lakeshore. Unpublished abstract.

Lannoo, M. J. 1995. Review of "Amphibians and Reptiles Native to Minnesota," by Barney Oldfield and John J. Moriarty. Prairie Naturalist 27:182–184.

Lannoo, M. J. 1996a. Okoboji Wetlands: A Lesson in Natural History. University of Iowa Press, Iowa City.

Lannoo, M. J. 1996b. A fish fry: the role of exotic species and aquacultural practices in producing amphibian declines in the upper Midwest. Pp. 25–27. *In* Moriarty, J. J., and D. Jones (Eds.), Minnesota's Amphibians and Reptiles: Conservation and Status, Proceedings of Symposium. Serpent's Tale Press, Excelsior, Minnesota.

Lannoo, M. J., and M. D. Bachmann. 1984. Aspects of cannibalistic morphs in a population of *Ambystoma t. tigrinum* larvae. American Midland Naturalist 112:103–109.

Lannoo, M. J., and K. Lang. 1995. Attempt to validate the North American Amphibian Monitoring Program's proposed larval amphibian protocol in the prairie pothole region of the upper Midwest. North American Amphibian Monitoring Program, Burlington, Ontario. Unpublished abstract.

Lannoo, M. J., K. Lang, T. Waltz, and G. S. Phillips. 1994. An altered amphibian assemblage: Dickinson Co., Iowa, seventy years after Frank Blanchard's survey. American Midland Naturalist 131:311–319.

Lappé, F. M. 1982. Diet for a Small Planet. Ballantine Books, New York.

Larimore, R. W., and P. W. Smith. 1963. The fishes of Champaign County, Illinois, as affected by sixty years of stream changes. Illinois Natural History Survey Bulletin 28:296–382.

Larrabee, A. L. 1927a. The fishes of the Okoboji lakes. Okoboji Protective Association Bulletin 23:112–123.

Larrabee, A. L. 1927b. An ecological study of the fishes of the Lake Okoboji region. University of Iowa Studies in Natural History 11:1–35.

Larras-Regard, E. 1985. Hormonal determination of neoteny in facultative neotenic urodeles. Pp. 294–312. *In* Balls, M., and M. Bownes (Eds.), Metamorphosis. Clarendon Press, Oxford.

Laurini, R., and D. Thompson. 1992. Fundamentals of Spatial Information Systems. Academic Press, New York.

Lawler, S. P. 1989. Behavioural responses to predators and predation risk in four species of larval anurans. Animal Behaviour 38:1039–1047.

Leclair, R., Jr., and J. Castanet. 1987. A skeletochronological assessment of age and growth in the frog *Rana pipiens* Schreber (Amphibia, Anura) from southeastern Quebec. Copeia 1987:361–369.

Lee, D. S., and A. W. Norden. 1973. A food study of the green salamander, *Aneides aeneus*. Journal of Herpetology 7:53–54.

Lee, P. M. 1989. Bayesian Statistics: An Introduction. John Wiley and Sons, New York.

Leftwich, K. N., and P. D. Lilly. 1992. The effects of duration of exposure to acidic conditions on survival of *Bufo americanus* embryos. Journal of Herpetology 26:70–71.

Legendre, L., and P. Legendre. 1983. Numerical Ecology. Elsevier, New York.

Legendre, P. 1993. Spatial autocorrelation: trouble or a new paradigm. Ecology 74:1659–1673.

Legendre, P., and L. Legendre. 1987. Developments in Numerical Ecology. Springer-Verlag, New York.

Legendre, P., M. Troussellier, V. Jarry, and M. J. Fortin. 1989. Design for simultaneous sampling of ecological variables: from concepts to numerical solutions. Oikos 55:30–42.

Leibetrau, A. M. 1979. Water quality sampling: some statistical considerations. Water Resources Research 15:1717–1725.

Leigh, D. S., and J. C. Knox. 1994. Loess of the upper Mississippi Valley Driftless Area. Quaternary Research 42:30–40.

Leighton, M. M., G. E. Ekblaw, and L. Horberg. 1948. Physiographic divisions of Illinois. Geology 56:16–33.

Leitch, J. A. 1989. Politicoeconomic overview of prairie potholes. Pp. 2–14. *In* van der Valk, A. (Ed.), Northern Prairie Wetlands. Iowa State University Press, Ames.

Lemly, A. D. 1993a. Teratogenic effects of selenium in natural populations of freshwater fish. Ecotoxicology and Environmental Safety 26:181–204.

Lemly, A. D. 1993b. Guidelines for evaluating selenium data from aquatic monitoring and assessment studies. Environmental Monitoring and Assessment 28:83–100.

Lemly, A. D. 1994. Irrigated agriculture and freshwater wetlands: a struggle for coexistence in the western United States. Wetlands Ecology and Management. 3:3–15.

Lemly, A. D., and G. J. Smith. 1987. Aquatic cycling of selenium: implications for fish and wildlife. U.S. Fish and Wildlife Service, Fish and Wildlife Leaflet Number 12, Washington, D.C.

Les, B. L. 1979. The Vanishing Wild. Wisconsin Department of Natural Resources, Madison.

Lessler, J. T., and W. D. Kalsbeek. 1992. Nonsampling Error in Surveys. John Wiley and Sons, New York.

Levell, J. P. 1995. A Field Guide to Reptiles and the Law. Serpent's Tale Press, Excelsior, Minnesota.

Levi, H. W., and L. R. Levi. 1955. Neotenic salamanders, *Ambystoma tigrinum*, in the Elk Mountains of Colorado. Copeia 1955:309.

Levin, S. A. 1976. Population dynamic models in heterogenous environments. Annual Review of Ecology and Systematics 7:287–310.

Levins, R. 1969. Some demographic and genetic consequences of environmental heterogeneity for biological control. Bulletin of the Entomological Society of America 15:237–240.

Leviton, A. E., R. H. Gibbs Jr., E. Heal, and C. E. Dawson. 1985. Standards in herpetology and ichthyology: Part I. Standard symbolic codes for institutional resource collections in herpetology and ichthyology. Copeia 1985:802–832.

Li, C. C. 1964. Introduction to Experimental Statistics. McGraw-Hill, New York.

Licht, L. E. 1968. Unpalatability and toxicity of toad eggs. Herpetologica 24:93–98.

Lillesand, T. M., and R. W. Kiefer. 1994. Remote Sensing and Image Interpretation. John Wiley and Sons, New York.

Linder, G., L. Barbitta, and T. Kwaiser. 1990. Short-term amphibian toxicity tests and paraquat toxicity assessment. Pp. 89–198. *In* Landis, W. G., and W. H. van der Schalie (Eds.), Aquatic Toxicology and Risk Assessment, Volume 13. American Society for Testing and Materials, Philadelphia.

Lindman, H. R. 1992. Analysis of Variance in Experimental Design. Springer-Verlag, New York.

Lindsey, A. A. 1966. Natural Features of Indiana. Indiana Academy of Science, Indianapolis.

Link, W. A., and J. R. Sauer. 1994. Estimating equation estimates of trends. Bird Populations 2:23–32.

Liss, W. J., and G. L. Larson. 1991. Ecological effects of stocked trout on North Cascades naturally fishless lakes. Park Science 11:22–23.

Loeb, M. L. G., J. P. Collins, and T. J. Maret. 1993. The role of prey in controlling expression of a trophic polymorphism in *Ambystoma tigrinum nebulosum*. Functional Ecology 8:151–158.

Loftis, J. C., and R. C. Ward. 1980. Water quality monitoring—some practical sampling frequency considerations. Environmental Management 4:521–526.

Lopinot, A. C. 1973. Use of private ponds by Illinois anglers. Special Fisheries Report No. 44. Illinois Department of Conservation, Division of Fisheries, Springfield.

Lorimer, C. G., and L. E. Frelich. 1994. Natural disturbance regimes in old-growth northern hardwoods: implications for forestry efforts. Journal of Forestry 92:33–38.

Lowcock, L. A., L. E. Licht, and J. P. Bogart. 1987. Nomenclature in hybrid complexes of *Ambystoma* (Urodela: Ambystomatidae): no case for the erection of hybrid "species." Systematic Zoology 36:328–336.

Lowe, C. H. 1985. Amphibians and reptiles in southwest riparian ecosystems. Pp. 339–341. *In* Johnson, R. R., C. D. Zeibell, D. R. Patton, P. F. Ffolliot, and R. H. Hamre (Eds.), Riparian Ecosystems and Their Management: Reconciling Conflicting Uses. U.S. Forest Service, General Technical Report RM-120, Fort Collins, Colorado.

Lucké, B. 1934. A neoplastic disease of the frog, *Rana pipiens*. American Journal of Cancer 20:352–379.

Lucké, B., L. Berwick, and P. Nowell. 1953. The effect of temperature on the growth of virus-induced frog carcinoma. Journal of Experimental Medicine 97:505–509.

Ludwig, D. R., M. Redmer, R. Domazlicky, S. N. Kobal, and B. Conklin. 1990. A survey of amphibians and reptiles within the Forest Preserve District of DuPage County (1988–1990). Unpublished report to the Forest Preserve District of DuPage County, Wheaton, Illinois.

Ludwig, D. R., M. Redmer, R. Domazlicky, S. N. Kobal, and B. Conklin. 1992. Current status of amphibians and reptiles within the Forest Preserve District of DuPage County. Transactions of the Illinois State Academy of Science 85:187–199.

Ludwig, J. A., and J. F. Reynolds. 1988. Statistical Ecology: A Primer on Methods and Computing. John Wiley and Sons, New York.

Lundelius, E. L., Jr., R. W. Graham, E. Anderson, J. E. Guilday, J. A. Holman, D. Steadman, and S. D. Webb. 1983. Terrestrial vertebrate faunas. Pp. 311–353. *In* Wright, H. E., Jr., and S. C. Porter (Eds.), Late-Quaternary Environments of the United States. University of Minnesota Press, Minneapolis.

Lynch, J. D. 1965. Rediscovery of the four-toed salamander, *Hemidactylium scutatum*, in Illinois: a relict population. Herpetologica 21:151–153.

Mabry, C. M. 1984. The distribution and reproduction of the plains spadefoot toad, *Scaphiopus bombifrons*, in Iowa. M.A. thesis, Drake University, Des Moines, Iowa.

Mabry, C. M., and J. L. Christiansen. 1982. Survey of amphibians and reptiles of the Loess Hills. Natural Areas Inventory. Phase II report to the Iowa Conservation Commission, Des Moines.

Mabry, C. M., and J. L. Christiansen. 1991. The activity and breeding cycle of *Scaphiopus bombifrons* in Iowa. Journal of Herpetology 25:116–119.

Mac, M. 1996. Protocols and Strategies for Monitoring North American Amphibians. Internet document available through frog@nbs.gov.

MacArthur, R. H., and E. O. Wilson. 1967. The Theory of Island Biogeography. Princeton University Press, Princeton, New Jersey.

Machado, J. P., D. L. Garling Jr., N. R. Kevern, A. L. Trapp, and T. G. Bell. 1987. Histopathology and the pathogenesis of embolism (gas bubble disease) in rainbow trout (*Salmo gairdneri*). Canadian Journal of Fisheries and Aquatic Sciences 44:1985–1994.

Machicao, N., and E. Laplaca. 1954. Lepralike granulomas in frogs. Laboratory Investigations 3:219–227.

Mackenthun, K. M., and E. F. Herman. 1945. A heavy mortality of fishes resulting from the decomposition of algae in the Yahara River, Wisconsin. Transactions of the American Fisheries Society 75:175–180.

MacLaren, D. B. 1959. Amphibians and reptiles of Virginia Kendall Park. Western Reserve Academy, Natural History Museum Publication 2:35–36.

MacMahon, P. D., K. A. Jeffrey, F. W. H. Beamish, S. C. Ferguson, and R. J. Kalton. 1987. Effects of the lampricide 3-trifluoromethyl-4-nitrophenol (TFM) on the macroinvertebrates of Wilmot Creek. Hydrobiologia 148:25–34.

Madej, R. F. 1994. *Aneides aeneus* (green salamander). Herpetological Review 25:31.

Maguire, D. J. 1991. An overview and definition of GIS. Pp. 9–20. *In* Maguire, D. J., M. F. Goodchild, and D. W. Rhind (Eds.), Geographical Information Systems, Volume I, Principles. John Wiley and Sons, New York.

Maguire, D. J., M. F. Goodchild, and D. W. Rhind. 1991a. Geographical Information Systems, Volume I, Principles. John Wiley and Sons, New York.

Maguire, D. J., M. F. Goodchild, and D. W. Rhind. 1991b. Geographical Information Systems, Volume II, Applications. John Wiley and Sons, New York.

Maguire, D. J., M. F. Goodchild, and D. W. Rhind. 1991c. Introduction. Pp. 3–7. *In* Maguire, D. J., M. F. Goodchild, and D. W. Rhind (Eds.), Geographical Information Systems, Volume I, Principles. John Wiley and Sons, New York.

Magurran, A. E. 1988. Ecological Diversity and Its Measurement. Princeton University Press, Princeton, New Jersey.

Mahaney, P. A. 1994. Effects of freshwater petroleum contamination on amphibian hatching and metamorphosis. Environmental Toxicology and Chemistry 13:259–265.

Mahar, R. D., P. L. Stewart, S. Browne, and P. Kendrick. 1995. Frogwatch '95: approach, volunteer profile and results of Nova Scotia's spring peeper and habitat survey. North American Amphibian Monitoring Program, Burlington, Ontario.Unpublished abstract.

Malanson, G. P. 1993. Riparian Landscapes. Cambridge University Press, New York.

Malingreau, J. P., and C. J. Tucker. 1988. Large-scale deforestation in the southeastern Amazon basin of Brazil. Ambio 17:49–55.

Malott, C. A. 1922. The physiography of Indiana. Pp. 59–256. *In* Logan, W. N., E. R. Cummings, C. A. Malott, S. S. Visher, W. M. Tucker, and J. R. Reeves (Eds.), Handbook of Indiana Geology. Indiana Department of

Conservation Publication 21, Part 2, Indianapolis.

Maltby, E. 1986. Waterlogged Wealth. International Institute for Environment and Development, London.

Mangun, J. C., J. T. O'Leary, and W. R. Mangun. 1992. Nonconsumptive wildlife-associated recreation in the United States: identity and dimension. Pp. 175–200. *In* Mangun, W. R. (Ed.), American Fish and Wildlife Policy: The Human Dimension. Southern Illinois University Press, Carbondale.

Manion, J. J., and L. Cory. 1952. Winter kill of *Rana pipiens* in shallow ponds. Herpetologica 8:32.

Manly, B. F. J. 1986. Multivariate Statistical Methods: A Primer. Chapman and Hall, New York.

Manly, B. F. J. 1991. Randomization and Monte Carlo Methods in Biology. Chapman and Hall, New York.

Manly, B. F. J. 1992. The Design and Analysis of Research Studies. Cambridge University Press, New York.

Mann, W., P. Dorn, and R. Brandl. 1991. Local distribution of amphibians: the importance of habitat fragmentation. Global Ecology and Biogeography Letters 1:36–41.

Marchal-Segault, D., and F. Ramade. 1981. The effects of lindane, an insecticide, on hatching and postembryonic development of *Xenopus laevis* (Daudin) anuran amphibian. Environmental Research 24:250–258.

Marcus, L. C. 1981. Veterinary Biology and Medicine of Captive Amphibians and Reptiles. Lea and Febiger, Philadelphia.

Marian, M. P., V. Arul, and T. J. Pandian. 1983. Acute and chronic effects of carbaryl on survival, growth and metamorphosis in the bullfrog (*Rana tigerina*). Archives of Environmental Contamination and Toxicology 12:271–275.

Marriott, F. H. C. 1974. The Interpretation of Multiple Observations. Academic Press, New York.

Marsh, H., and G. Rathbun. 1990. Development and application of conventional and satellite radio tracking techniques for studying dugong movements and habitat use. Australian Wildlife Research 17:83–100.

Martin, J. 1994. Ecosystem integrity versus fisheries management: 1994–1995 point-counterpoint debates. Fisheries 19:28.

Martin, L. 1965. The Physical Geology of Wisconsin. University of Wisconsin Press, Madison.

Martin, P. S., and R. G. Klein. 1984. Quaternary Extinctions: A Prehistoric Revolution. University of Arizona Press, Tucson.

Martin, T. R., and D. B. Conn. 1990. The pathogenicity, localization, and cyst structure of echinostomatid metacercariae (trematoda) infecting the kidneys of the frogs *Rana clamitans* and *Rana pipiens*. Journal of Parasitology 76:414–419.

Martin, W. H. 1992. Characteristics of old-growth mixed mesophytic forests. Natural Areas Journal 12:127–135.

Martinez, I., R. Alvarez, I. Herraez, and P. Herraez. 1992. Skeletal malformations in hatchery reared *Rana perezi* tadpoles. Anatomical Record 233:314–320.

Martof, B., 1956. Factors influencing size and composition of populations of *Rana clamitans*. American Midland Naturalist 56:224–245.

Martof, B. and R. L. Humphries. 1959. Geographic variation in the wood frog *Rana sylvatica*. American Midland Naturalist 61:351–389.

Mason County Democrat. 1993a. Old stories talk about Negro Lake. 15 September, Havana, Illinois.

Mason County Democrat. 1993b. Monday rains spawn Tuesday flood crisis. 22 September, Havana, Illinois.

Mason County Democrat. 1994a. Doesn't make the first cut. $1.3 M ditch doesn't meet funding criteria. 16 February, Havana, Illinois.

Mason County Democrat. 1994b. County agrees to pursue $2 million for "channel." 15 June, Havana, Illinois.

Materna, E. J., C. F. Rabeni, and T. W. LaPoint. 1995. Effects of the synthetic pyrethroid insecticide, esfenvalerate, on larval leopard frogs (*Rana* spp.). Environmental Toxicology and Chemistry 14:613–622.

Mather, P. M. 1987. Computer Processing of Remotely-Sensed Images: An Introduction. John Wiley and Sons, New York.

Matson, T. O. 1990. Estimation of numbers for a riverine *Necturus* population before and after TFM lampricide exposure. Kirtlandia 45:33–38.

Mazzer, S. J., L. P. Orr, and D. W. Waller. 1984. Wildlife survey of the Cuyahoga Valley National Recreation Area. Department of Biological Sciences, Kent State University. Unpublished report to the National Park Service, Washington, D.C.

McAtee, W. L. 1921. Homing and other habits of the bullfrog. Copeia 1921:39–40.

McBride, G. B., J. C. Loftis, and N. C. Adkins. 1993. What do significance tests really tell us about the environment? Environment Management 17:423–432.

McCan, T. 1977. The influence of predation on the composition of freshwater amphibian communities. Biological Review 52:45–70.

McCue, R. W. 1989. Simulated nitric and sulfuric acid precipitation: the effects on the development of *Rana pipiens*. Transactions of the Kansas Academy of

Science 92:12–17.

McCullagh, P., and J. A. Nelder. 1983. Generalized Linear Models. Chapman and Hall, New York.

McGregor, J. H., and W. R. Teska. 1989. Olfaction as an orientation mechanism in migrating *Ambystoma maculatum*. Copeia 1989:779–781.

McKinnell, R. G. 1965. Incidence and histology of renal tumors of leopard frogs from the north central states. Annals of the New York Academy of Science 126:85–98.

McKinnell, R. G. 1984. Lucké tumor of frogs. Pp. 581–605. *In* Hoff, G. L., F. L. Frye, and E. R. Jacobson (Eds.), Diseases of Amphibians and Reptiles. Plenum Press, New York.

McKinnell, R. G., V. L. Ellis, D. C. Dapkus, and L. M. Steven Jr. 1972. Early replication of herpesviruses in naturally occurring frog tumors. Cancer Research 32:1729–1732.

McKinnell, R. G., B. T. Kren, R. Bergad, M. Schultheis, T. Byrne, and J. W. Schaad IV. 1980. Dominant lethality in *Xenopus laevis* induced with triethylenemelamine. Teratogenesis, Carcinogenesis, Mutagenesis 1:283–294.

McKinnell, R. G., D. J. Picciano, and J. W. Schaad IV. 1979. Dominant lethality in frog embryos after paternal treatment with triethylenemelamine. Environmental Mutagenesis 1:221–231.

McKinney, L. E. 1973. *Aneides aeneus* (green salamander). Herpetological Information Search Systems News Journal 1:152.

McKinney, M. L., and K. J. McNamara. 1991. Heterochrony. Plenum Press, New York.

McLaren, S. B., and J. K. Braun. 1993. GIS applications in mammalogy. Special Publication of the Carnegie Museum of Natural History, Pittsburgh, and the Oklahoma Museum of Natural History, Norman.

McMaster, R. B., and K. S. Shea. 1992. Generalization in Digital Cartography. GIS World Books, Fort Collins, Colorado.

McNab, W. H., and P. E. Avers. 1994. Ecological subregions of the United States: section descriptions. U.S. Forest Service, Publication WO-WSA-5, Washington, D.C.

McNeil, D. R. 1977. Interactive Data Analysis. John Wiley and Sons, New York.

McWilliams, S. R., and M. D. Bachmann. 1988. Using life history and ecology as tools to manage a threatened salamander species. Journal of the Iowa Academy of Science 95:66–71.

Mead, R. 1988. The Design of Experiments: Statistical Principles for Practical Application. Cambridge University Press, New York.

Meffe, G. K., and C. R. Carroll. 1994. Principles of Conservation Biology. Sinauer Associates, Sunderland, Massachusetts.

Mehta, C. R., N. R. Patel, and L. J. Wei. 1988. Computing exact significance tests with restricted randomization rules. Biometrika 75:295–302.

Merkle, D. A., and S. I. Guttman. 1977. Geographic variation in the cave salamander *Eurycea lucifuga*. Herpetologica 33:313–321.

Merrell, D. J. 1965. The distribution of the dominant burnsi gene in the leopard frog. Evolution 19:69–85.

Merrell, D. J. 1970. Migration and gene dispersal in *Rana pipiens*. American Zoologist 10:47–52.

Merrell, D. J. 1977. Life history of the leopard frog, *Rana pipiens*, in Minnesota. Bell Museum of Natural History, Occasional Paper Number 15, Minneapolis.

Merwin, J. 1994. The astonishing power of the sportsman's dollar. Field and Stream February:56–57.

Messer, J. J., R. A. Linthurst, and W. S. Overton. 1991. An EPA program for monitoring ecological status and trends. Environmental Monitoring and Assessment 17:67–78.

Meyer, A. H. 1936. The Kankakee "marsh" of northern Indiana and Illinois. Papers of the Michigan Academy of Science, Arts and Letters 21:359–395.

Meyers, R. L., and J. E. King. 1985. Wisconsinan interstadial vegetation of northern Illinois. *In* Illinoian and Wisconsinan stratigraphy and environments in northern Illinois: the Altonian revised. Illinois State Geological Survey Guidebook 19:75–86.

Mickelson, D. M., L. Clayton, D. S. Fullerton, and H. W. Borns Jr. 1983. The Late Wisconsin glacial record of the Laurentide Ice Sheet in the United States. Pp. 3–37. *In* Wright, H. E., Jr., and S. C. Porter (Eds.), Late-Quaternary Environments of the United States. University of Minnesota Press, Minneapolis.

Mierzwa, K. S. 1986. A survey of amphibians, reptiles, and small mammals at Shaw Prairie, McLaughlin Meadow, and Haffner Meadows. Unpublished report to the Lake Forest Open Lands Association, Lake Forest, Illinois.

Mierzwa, K. S. 1988. Amphibians and reptiles of Will County, Illinois. Unpublished report to the Forest Preserve District of Will County, Joliet, Illinois.

Mierzwa, K. S. 1989. Distribution and habitat of the two-lined salamander, *Eurycea cirrigera*, in Illinois and Indiana. Bulletin of the Chicago Herpetological Society 24:61–69.

Mierzwa, K. S. 1994a. Patch dynamics of amphibians and reptiles in northeastern Illinois savanna landscapes. Pp. 161–165. *In* Fralish, J. S., R. C. Anderson, J. E. Ebinger, and R. Szafoni (Eds.), Proceedings of the North American Conference on Savannas and Barrens. Illinois State University, Normal.

Mierzwa, K. S. 1994b. Report on a cricket frog translocation effort in northwest Illinois. Meeting of the Central Division of the Declining Amphibian Populations Task Force, Indiana Dunes National Lakeshore. Unpublished abstract.

Mierzwa, K. S., and E. Beltz. 1994a. Amphibians and reptiles of Glacial Park, McHenry County, Illinois: a report on monitoring of habitat use in a restored landscape, and on the reintroduction of an extirpated species. Unpublished report to the McHenry County Conservation District, Ringwood, Illinois.

Mierzwa, K. S., and E. Beltz. 1994b. Habitat associations and distribution of amphibians and reptiles at Middle Fork Savanna, Lake County, Illinois. Unpublished report to the Lake Forest Open Lands Association, Lake Forest, Illinois.

Mierzwa, K. S., E. Beltz, and R. P. Sliwinski. 1994. A preliminary inventory of amphibians and reptiles at Reed-Turner Woodland. Unpublished report to the Long Grove Park District, Long Grove, Illinois.

Mierzwa, K. S., S. D. Culberson, K. S. King, and C. Ross. 1991. Illinois-Indiana Regional Airport site selection study: biotic communities. TAMS Consultants, Chicago.

Mierzwa, K. S., D. Mauger, and D. Stillwaugh. 1990. A baseline survey of amphibians and reptiles at Fermilab. Unpublished report to the Fermi National Accelerator Laboratory, Batavia, Illinois.

Millard, S. P. 1987. Environmental monitoring, statistics, and the law: room for improvement. American Statistician 41:249–253.

Millard, S. P., and D. P. Lettenmaier. 1986. Optimal design of biological sampling programs using the analysis of variance. Estuarine Coastal and Shelf Science 22:637–656.

Miller, E. A., R. J. Montali, E. C. Ramsay, and B. A. Rideout. 1992. Chromoblastomycosis in a colony of ornate-horned frogs (*Ceratophrys ornata*). Journal of Zoo and Wildlife Medicine 23:433–438.

Miller, R. G. 1974. The jackknife—a review. Biometrika 61:1–15.

Milliken, G. A., and D. E. Johnson. 1984. Analysis of Messy Data, Volume I: Designed Experiments. Wadsworth, Belmont, California.

Milliken, G. A., and D. E. Johnson. 1989. Analysis of Messy Data, Volume II: Nonreplicated Experiments. Van Nostrand Reinhold, New York.

Minton, S. A., Jr. 1972. Amphibians and Reptiles of Indiana. Indiana Academy of Science Monograph Number 3, Indianapolis.

Minton, S. A., Jr. 1997. Amphibians and Reptiles of Indiana. 2d ed. Proceedings of the Indiana Academy of Science, Indianapolis.

Minton, S. A., Jr., J. C. List, and M. J. Lodato. 1982. Recent records and status of amphibians and reptiles in Indiana. Proceedings of the Indiana Academy of Science 92:489–498.

Mitásová, H., and J. Hofierka. 1993. Interpolation by regularized spline with tension: II. Application to terrain modeling and surface geometry analysis. Mathematical Geology 25:657–669.

Mitásová, H., and L. Mitás. 1993. Interpolation by regularized spline with tension: I. Theory and implementation. Mathematical Geology 25:641–655.

Mitásová, H., L. Mitás, W. M. Brown, D. P. Gerdes, I. Kosinovsky, and T. Baker. 1996. Modeling spatial and temporal distributed phenomena: new methods and tools for open GIS. Pp. 345–351. *In* Goodchild, M. F., L. T. Steyaert, B. O. Parks, C. Johnston, D. Maidment, M. Crane, and S. Glendinning (Eds.), GIS and Environmental Modeling: Progress and Research Issues. GIS World Books, Fort Collins, Colorado.

Mitsch, W. J., and J. G. Gosselink. 1993. Wetlands. Van Nostrand Reinhold, New York.

Mittleman, M. B. 1947. Miscellaneous notes on Indiana amphibians and reptiles. American Midland Naturalist 38:466–484.

Mizell, M. 1969. State of the art: Lucké renal adenocarcinoma. Pp. 1–25. *In* Mizell, M. (Ed.), Biology of Amphibian Tumors. Springer-Verlag, New York.

Modde, T. 1980. State stocking policies for small warmwater impoundments. Fisheries 5:13–17.

Mohanty-Hejmadi, P., and S. K. Dutta. 1981. Effects of some pesticides on the development of the Indian bull frog *Rana tigerina*. Enviromental Pollution, Series A 24:145–161.

Moll, E. O. 1962. Recent herpetological records for Illinois. Herpetologica 18:207–209.

Monmonier, M. 1991. How to Lie with Maps. University of Chicago Press, Chicago.

Montgomery, D. C. 1991. Design and Analysis of Experiments. John Wiley and Sons, New York.

Montgomery, D. C., and E. A. Peck. 1982. Introduction to Linear Regression Analysis. John Wiley and Sons,

New York.

Montgomery, H. A. C., and I. C. Hart. 1974. The design of sampling programmes for rivers and effluents. Water Pollution Control 33:77–101.

Moore, M. C., and C. A. Marler. 1987. Hormones, behavior, and the environment: an evolutionary perspective. Pp. 71–83. *In* Stetson, M. H. (Ed.), Processing of Environmental Information in Vertebrates. Springer-Verlag, New York.

Moran, N. A. 1992. The evolutionary maintenance of alternative phenotypes. American Naturalist 139:971–989.

Moriarty, J. J. 1988. Minnesota County Biological Survey: 1988 Herpetological Surveys. Minnesota Department of Natural Resources Biological Report, Series Number 9, St. Paul.

Moriarty, J. J. 1996. Minnesota's frog and toad survey: results of a pilot program. Pp. 69–74. *In* Moriarty, J. J., and D. Jones (Eds.), Minnesota's Amphibians and Reptiles: Conservation and Status, Proceedings of Symposium. Serpent's Tale Press, Excelsior, Minnesota.

Morin, P. J. 1983. Competitive and predatory interactions in natural and experimental populations of *Notophthalmus viridescens dorsalis* and *Ambystoma tigrinum.* Copeia 1983:628–639.

Morris, M. A. 1976. New herpetofaunal records for Illinois. Herpetological Review 7:126–127.

Morris, M. A. 1977. *Rana palustris* and *Rana sylvatica.* Unpublished report to the Illinois Nature Preserves Commission, Rockford.

Morris, M. A. 1991. Status of 1991 Illinois chorus frog (*Pseudacris illinoensis*) populations in Madison County, Illinois. Unpublished report to the Illinois Department of Transportation, Springfield.

Morris, M. A., R. S. Funk, and P. W. Smith. 1983. An annotated bibliography of the Illinois herpetological literature 1960–1980, and an updated checklist of species in the state. Illinois Natural History Survey Bulletin 33:123–138.

Morris, M. A., and P. W. Smith. 1981. Endangered and threatened amphibians and reptiles. Pp. 21–33. *In* Bowles, M. L., V. E. Diersing, J. E. Ebinger, and H. C. Schultz (Eds.), Endangered and Threatened Vertebrate Animals and Vascular Plants of Illinois. Natural Land Institute, Illinois Department of Conservation, Springfield.

Morrison, D. E., and R. E. Henkel. 1970. The Significance Test Controversy. Aldin, Chicago.

Moshiri, G. A. 1993. Constructed Wetlands for Water Quality Improvement. Lewis Publishers, Ann Arbor, Michigan.

Mossman, M. J., and R. L. Hine. 1984. The Wisconsin frog and toad survey: establishing a long-term monitoring program. Endangered Resources Report Number 9, Wisconsin Department of Natural Resources, Madison.

Mossman, M. J., and R. L. Hine. 1985. The Wisconsin frog and toad survey, 1984. Endangered Resources Report Number 16, Wisconsin Department of Natural Resources, Madison.

Mossman, M. J., J. J. Huff, and R. M. Hine. 1992. Monitoring long-term trends in Wisconsin frog and toad populations. Unpublished report to the Bureau of Research, Wisconsin Department of Natural Resources, Madison.

Mossman, M., P. Rasmussen, J. Sauer, S. Droege, and L. Hartman. 1995. Wisconsin frog survey analysis: sample size estimation for amphibian calling surveys and some surprising trends from an eleven-year analysis of Wisconsin frog and toad survey data. Meeting of the North American Amphibian Monitoring Program, Burlington, Ontario. Unpublished abstract.

Motulsky, H. 1995. Intuitive Biostatistics. Oxford University Press, New York.

Mount, R. H. 1975. The reptiles and amphibians of Alabama. Auburn University Agricultural Experiment Station, Auburn, Alabama.

Moyle, P. B. 1973. Effects of introduced bullfrogs, *Rana catesbeiana,* on the native frogs of the San Joaquin Valley, California. Copeia 1973:18–22.

Moyle, P. B., and H. W. Li. 1994. Good report but it should go much farther. Fisheries 19:22–23.

Muehrcke, P. C., and J. O. Muehrcke. 1992. Map Use. JP Publications, Madison, Wisconsin.

Mulla, M. S. 1963. Toxicity of organochlorine insecticides to mosquito fish *Gambusia affinis* and the bullfrog *Rana catesbeiana.* Mosquito News 23:299–303.

Mulla, M. S., L. W. Issak, and H. Axelrod. 1963. Field studies on the effects of insecticides on some aquatic wildlife species. Journal of Economic Entomology 56:184–188.

Mundt, S., and R. G. Baker. 1979. A mid-Wisconsinan pollen diagram from Black Hawk County, Iowa. Proceedings of the Iowa Academy of Science 86:23–24.

Murphy, J. C. 1989. Musical amphibians of Chicagoland. Field Museum of Natural History Bulletin 60:18–27.

Mushinsky, H. R., and E. D. Brodie. 1975. Selection of substrate pH by salamanders. American Midland Naturalist 93:440–443.

Musick, H. B., and H. D. Grover. 1991. Image textural measures as indices of landscape pattern. Pp. 77–103. *In* Turner, M. G., and R. H. Gardner (Eds.), Quantitative Methods in Landscape Ecology. Springer-Verlag, New York.

Mutel, C. F. 1989. Fragile Giants: A Natural History of the Loess Hills. University of Iowa Press, Iowa City.

Naiman, R. J. 1992. Watershed Management: Balancing Sustainability and Environmental Change. Springer-Verlag, New York.

Naiman, R. J., C. A. Johnston, and J. C. Kelley. 1988. Alteration of North American streams by beaver. Bioscience 38:753–762.

Naiman, R. J., J. M. Melilo, and J. E. Hobble. 1986. Ecosystem alteration of boreal forest streams by beaver (*Castor canadensis*). Ecology 67:1254–1269.

National Academy of Sciences. 1992. Restoration of Aquatic Ecosystems. National Academy Press, Washington, D.C.

National Atlas of the United States of America. 1970. U.S. Geological Survey, Washington, D.C.

National Research Council. 1995. Review of EPA's Environmental Monitoring and Assessment Program. National Academy Press, Washington, D.C.

National Research Council of Canada. 1985. TFM and Bayer 73 lampricides in the aquatic environment. Publication Number NRCC22488, Ottawa, Ontario.

National Wetlands Inventory. 1988. National Wetlands Inventory (maps). U.S. Fish and Wildlife Service, Washington, D.C.

Necker, W. L. 1939. Records of amphibians and reptiles of the Chicago region, 1935–1938. Bulletin of the Chicago Academy of Science 6:1–10.

Neely, R. K., and J. L. Baker. 1989. Nitrogen and phosphorus dynamics and the fate of agricultural runoff. Pp. 92–131. *In* van der Valk, A. (Ed.), Northern Prairie Wetlands. Iowa State University Press, Ames.

Neill, W. T. 1963. *Hemidactylium scutatum.* P. 2. *In* Reimer, W. J. (Ed.), Catalogue of American Amphibians and Reptiles. American Society of Ichthyologists and Herpetologists, Gainesville, Florida.

Neilsen, L. A. 1993. History of inland fisheries management in North America. Pp. 3–31. *In* Kohler, C. C., and W. A. Hubert (Eds.), Inland Fisheries Management in North America. American Fisheries Society, Bethesda, Maryland.

Nelson, P. W. 1987. The Terrestrial Natural Communities of Missouri. Missouri Department of Natural Resources and Missouri Department of Conservation, Jefferson City.

Nelson, R., N. Horning, and T. A. Stone. 1987. Determining the rate of forest conversion in Mato Brosso, Brazil, using Landsat MSS and AVHRR data. International Journal of Remote Sensing 8:1767–1784.

Nemani, R. R., and S. W. Running. 1989. Estimation of regional surface resistance to evapotranspiration from NDVI and thermal-IR AVHRR data. Journal of Applied Meteorology 28:276–284.

Ness, D. K., S. L. Schantz, J. Moshtaghian, and L. G. Hansen. 1993. Effects of perinatal exposure to specific PCB congeners on thyroid hormone concentrations and thyroid histology in the rat. Toxicology Letters 68:311–323.

Neter, J., W. Wasserman, and M. H. Kutner. 1985. Applied Linear Statistical Models: Regression, Analysis of Variance and Experimental Design. Richard D. Irwin, Homewood, Illinois.

Newcomer, C. E., M. R. Anver, J. L. Simmons, and B. W. Wilcke. 1982. Spontaneous and experimental infection of *Xenopus laevis* with *Chlamydia psittaci.* Laboratory Animal Science 32:680–686.

Newman, D. S. 1996. The Sand Lake story. Illinois Audubon 255:4–6.

Newman, R. A. 1992. Adaptive plasticity in amphibian metamorphosis. BioScience 42:671–678.

Nichols, D. K. 1989. Diseases of amphibians. Workshop on the Medicine and Management of Amphibians. Annual Meeting of Zoo Veterinarians, Greensboro, North Carolina. Unpublished abstract.

Nickerson, M. A., and C. E. Mays. 1973. The hellbenders: North American "giant salamanders." Milwaukee Public Museum, Contributions in Biology and Geology, Number 1.

Nigh, T. A., W. L. Pflieger, P. L. Redfearn Jr., W. A. Schroeder, A. R. Templeton, and F. R. Thompson III. 1992. The Biodiversity of Missouri. Missouri Department of Conservation, Jefferson City.

Nigrelli, R. F. 1929. Atypical erythrocytes and erythroplastics in the blood of *Triturus viridescens.* Anatomical Record 43:257–270.

Nigrelli, R. F. 1954. Some longevity records of vertebrates. Transactions of the New York Academy of Sciences, Series II 16:296–299.

Nishihara, A. 1996. Effects of density on growth of head size in larvae of the salamander *Hynobius retardus.* Copeia 1996:478–483.

Nishisato, S. 1994. Elements of Dual Scaling: An Introduction to Practical Data Analysis. Lawrence Erlbaum Associates, Hillsdale, New Jersey.

Niswander, S. F., and W. H. Mitsch. 1995. Functional

analysis of a two-year-old created in-stream wetland: hydrology, phosphorous retention, and vegetation survival and growth. Wetlands 15:212–225.

Noble, E. R., and G. A. Noble. 1961. Parasitology: The Biology of Animal Parasites. Lea and Febiger, Philadelphia.

Noether, G. E. 1987. Sample size determination for some common nonparametric tests. Journal of the American Statistical Association 82:645–647.

Noreen, E. W. 1989. Computer Intensive Methods for Testing Hypotheses: An Introduction. John Wiley and Sons, New York.

Norris, D. O., R. E. Jones, and B. B. Criley. 1973. Pituitary prolactin levels in larval, neotenic and metamorphosed salamanders (*Ambystoma tigrinum*). General and Comparative Endocrinology 20:437–442.

North American Amphibian Monitoring Program. 1996. Accessed at http://www.im.nbs.gov/amphib/naampintro.html or at ftp://ftp.im.nbs.gov.pub/naamp/.

North American Waterfowl Management Plan: A Strategy for Cooperation. 1986. Canada Fish and Wildlife Service, Ottawa, Ontario, and U.S. Fish and Wildlife Service, Washington, D.C.

Northeastern Illinois Planning Commission. 1994. Regional Greenways Plan. Northeastern Illinois Planning Commission and Openlands Project, Chicago.

Noss, R. F. 1987. Protecting natural areas in fragmented landscapes. Natural Areas Journal 7:2–13.

Noss, R. F. 1990. Indicators for monitoring biodiversity: a hierarchical approach. Conservation Biology 4:355–364.

Noss, R. F. 1992. The Wildlands Project: land conservation strategy. Wild Earth 1992:10–25.

Noss, R. F., and A. Y. Cooperrider. 1994. Saving Nature's Legacy: Protecting and Restoring Biodiversity. Island Press, Covelo, California.

Noss, R. F., E. T. LaRoe III, and J. M. Scott. 1995. Endangered ecosystems of the United States: a preliminary assessment of loss and degradation. Biological Report Number 28. U.S. Department of the Interior, National Biological Service, Washington, D.C.

Novacek, J. M. 1985. The Loess Hills of western Iowa: a problem in phytogeography. Proceedings of the Iowa Academy of Science 92:213–218.

Noy-Meir, I., D. Walker, and W. T. Williams. 1975. Data transformations in ecological ordination. II. On the meaning of data standardization. Journal of Ecology 63:778–800.

Nuzzo, V. A. 1985. Extent and status of Midwest oak savanna: presettlement and 1985. Natural Areas Journal 6:6–36.

Oakes, M. 1986. Statistical Significance: A Commentary for the Social and Behavioral Sciences. John Wiley and Sons, New York.

Obermeyer, N. J., and J. K. Pinto. 1994. Managing Geographic Information Systems. Guilford Press, New York.

Odum, W. E. 1988. Predicting ecosystem development following creation and restoration of wetlands. Pp. 67–70. *In* Zelazny, J., and J. S. Feierabend (Eds.), Increasing Our Wetland Resources. Proceedings of a conference, Corporate Conservation Council, National Wildlife Federation, Washington, D.C.

Ohio Division of Wildlife. 1995. State Faunal Database. Columbus, Ohio.

Oldfield, B., and J. J. Moriarty. 1995. Amphibians and Reptiles Native to Minnesota. University of Minnesota Press, Minneapolis.

Oldham, M. J. 1992. Declines in Blanchard's cricket frog in Ontario. Pp. 30–31. *In* Bishop, C. A., and K. E. Pettit (Eds.), Declines in Canadian Amphibian Populations: Designing a National Monitoring Strategy. Occasional Paper Number 76, Canadian Wildlife Service, Ottawa, Ontario.

Oldham, R. S. 1966. Spring movements in the American toad, *Bufo americanus*. Canadian Journal of Zoology 44:63–100.

Olson, R. E. 1956. The amphibians and reptiles of Winnebago County, Illinois. Copeia 1956:188–191.

Omernik, J. M. 1986. Ecoregions of the United States. U.S. Environmental Protection Agency, Environmental Research Laboratory, Corvallis, Oregon.

Omernik, J. M. 1987. Ecoregions of the conterminous United States. Annals of the Association of American Geographers 77:118–125.

Omernik, J. M., and A. L. Gallant. 1988. Ecoregions of the upper Midwest states. U.S. Environmental Protection Agency, Environmental Research Laboratory, EPA-600-3-88-037, Corvallis, Oregon.

O'Neil, T. A., R. J. Steidl, W. D. Edge, and B. Csuti. 1995. Using wildlife communities to improve vegetation classification for conserving biodiversity. Conservation Biology 9:1482–1491.

O'Neill, R. V., K. B. Jones, K. H. Ritters, J. D. Wickham, and I. A. Goodman. 1994. Landscape monitoring and assessment research plan—1994. Report EPA 620/R-94-009. U.S. Environmental Protection Agency, Environmental Monitoring Systems Laboratory, Las Vegas.

Orchard, S. A. 1992. Amphibian population declines in British Columbia. Pp. 10–13. *In* Bishop, C. A., and K. E. Pettit (Eds.), Declines in Canadian Amphibian Populations: Designing a National Monitoring Strategy. Occasional Paper Number 76, Canadian Wildlife Service, Ottawa, Ontario.

Orloci, L. 1967. Data centering: a review and evaluation with reference to component analysis. Systematic Zoology 16:208–212.

Orr, L. P. 1978. A survey of the amphibians and reptiles of the Cuyahoga Valley National Recreation Area. Department of Biological Sciences, Kent State University. Unpublished report to the National Park Service, Washington, D.C.

Osborne, L. L., and M. J. Wiley. 1988. Empirical relationships between landuse/cover patterns and stream water quality in an agricultural watershed. Journal of Environmental Management 26:9–27.

Osenberg, C. W., R. J. Schmitt, S. J. Holbrook, K. E. Abu-Saba, and A. R. Flegal. 1994. Detection of environmental impacts: natural variability, effect size, and power analysis. Ecological Applications 4:16–30.

Overton, W. S., D. White, and D. L. Stevens Jr. 1990. Design report for EMAP. U.S. Environmental Protection Agency, Environmental Monitoring and Assessment Program, EPA-600-3-91-053, Washington, D.C.

Pace, A. E. 1974. Systematic and Biological Studies of the Leopard Frogs (*Rana pipiens* complex) of the United States. Publication Number 148, Museum of Zoology, University of Michigan, Ann Arbor.

Packard, S. 1993. Restoring oak ecosystems. Restoration and Management Notes 11:5–16.

Paddock, J., N. Paddock, and C. Bly. 1986. Soil and Survival. Sierra Club Books, San Francisco.

Pajak, P., R. E. Wehnes, L. Gates, G. Siegwarth, J. Lyons, J. M. Pitlo, R. S. Holland, D. P. Roseboom, L. Zuckerman, and the Rivers and Streams Technical Committee. 1994. Agricultural land use and reauthorization of the 1990 farm bill. Fisheries 19:22–27.

Palmer, W. C. 1965. Meteorological drought. U.S. Department of Commerce Weather Research Paper 45, Washington, D.C.

Parker, G. R. 1989. Old-growth forests of the Central Hardwood Region. Natural Areas Journal 9:5–11.

Parker, H. D. 1988. The unique qualities of a geographic information system: a commentary. Photogrammetric Engineering and Remote Sensing 54:1547–1549.

Parkhurst, D. F. 1985. Interpreting failure to reject a null hypothesis. Bulletin of the Ecological Society of America 66:301–302.

Parks, W. D., and J. B. Fehrenbacher. 1968. Soil survey of Pulaski and Alexander Counties, Illinois. U.S. Soil Conservation Service, Washington, D.C.

Parmalee, P. W., and F. D. Loomis. 1983. Decoys and Decoy Carvers of Illinois. Northern Illinois University Press, DeKalb.

Patrick, P. H., N. Ramani, D. Wilkes, J. Liska, B. Mills, and R. W. Sheehan. 1995. Anuran monitoring using an Automated Intelligent Monitoring System (AIMS). North American Amphibian Monitoring Program, Burlington, Ontario. Unpublished abstract.

Patterson, K. K. 1978. Life history aspects of paedogenic populations of the mole salamander, *Ambystoma talpoideum*. Copeia 1978:649–655.

Paukstis, G. L., and L. E. Brown. 1987. Evolution of the intercalary cartilage in chorus frogs, genus *Pseudacris* (Salientia: Hylidae). Brimleyana 13:55–61.

Paukstis, G. L., and L. E. Brown. 1991. Evolutionary trends in the morphology of the intercalary phalanx of anuran amphibians. Canadian Journal of Zoology 69:1297–1301.

Pawar, K. R., and M. Katdare. 1983. Effect of the insecticide sumithion fenitrothion on embryonic development in a frog *Microhyla ornata*. Experientia 39:297–298.

Pawar, K. R., and M. Katdare. 1984. Toxic and teratogenic effects of fenitrothion, BHC and carbofuran on embryonic development of the frog *Microhyla ornata*. Toxicology Letters 22:7–14.

Pearse, A. S. 1921. Habits of the mud-puppy *Necturus*, an enemy of food fishes. U.S. Bureau of Fisheries. Economic Circular Number 49, Washington, D.C.

Pechmann, J. H. K., D. E. Scott, J. W. Gibbons, and R. D. Semlitsch. 1989. Influence of wetland hydroperiod on diversity and abundance of metamorphosing juvenile amphibians. Wetland Ecology and Management 1:1–19.

Pechmann, J. H. K., D. E. Scott, R. D. Semlitsch, J. P. Caldwell, L. J. Vitt, and J. W. Gibbons. 1991. Declining amphibian populations: the problem of separating human impacts from natural fluctuations. Science 253:892–895.

Pechmann, J. H. K., and H. M. Wilbur. 1994. Putting declining amphibian populations in perspective: natural fluctuations and human impacts. Herpetologica 50:65–84.

Peckham, R. S., and C. F. Dineen. 1954. Spring migration of salamanders. Proceedings of the Indiana Academy of Science 64:278–280.

Pennak, R. W. 1969. Colorado semidrainage mountain

lakes. Oceanography and Limnology 14:720–725.

Pentecost, E. D., and R. C. Vogt. 1976. Amphibians and reptiles of the Lake Michigan drainage basin. *In* Environmental Status of the Lake Michigan Region, Volume 16. Argonne National Laboratory, Argonne, Illinois.

Perrill, S. A., and M. Magier. 1988. Male mating behavior in *Acris crepitans*. Copeia 1988:245–248.

Perry, A., G. B. Bauer, and A. E. Dixon. 1985. Magnetoreception and biomineralization of magnetite in amphibians and reptiles. Topics in Geobiology 5:439–453.

Perry, J. A., D. J. Schaeffer, and E. E. Herricks. 1987. Innovative designs for water quality monitoring: are we asking the questions before the data are collected? Pp. 28–39. *In* Boyle, T. P. (Ed.), New Approaches to Monitoring Aquatic Ecosystems, ASTM STP 940. American Society for Testing and Materials, Philadelphia.

Perry, J. N. 1986. Multiple–comparison procedures: a dissenting view. Journal of Economic Entomology 79:1149–1155.

Peterjohn, B.G., J. R. Sauer, and W. A. Link. 1994. The 1993 summary of the North American Breeding Bird Survey. Bird Populations 2:46–51.

Peterka, J. J. 1989. Fishes in northern prairie wetlands. Pp. 302–316. *In* van der Valk, A. (Ed.), Northern Prairie Wetlands. Iowa State University Press, Ames.

Peterman, R. M. 1990a. Statistical power analysis can improve fisheries research and management. Canadian Journal of Fisheries and Aquatic Sciences 47:2–15.

Peterman, R. M. 1990b. The importance of reporting statistical power: the forest decline and acidic deposition example. Ecology 71:2024–2027.

Peterson, C. R., and M. E. Dorcas. 1992. The use of automated data-acquisition techniques in monitoring amphibian and reptile populations. Pp. 369–378. *In* McCullough, D. R., and R. H. Barrett (Eds.), Wildlife 2001: Populations. Elsevier Science Publishers, Essex, England.

Peterson, C. R., and M. E. Dorcas. 1994. Automated data acquisition. Pp. 47–57. *In* Heyer, W. R., M. A. Donnelly, R. W. McDiarmid, L.–A. C. Hayek, and M. S. Foster (Eds.), Measuring and Monitoring Biological Diversity: Standard Methods for Amphibians. Smithsonian Institution Press, Washington, D.C.

Peterson, D. L., J. D. Aber, P. A. Matson, D. H. Card, N. Swanberg, C. Wessman, and M. Spanner. 1988. Remote sensing of forest canopy and leaf biochemical contents. Remote Sensing of Environment 24:85–108.

Peterson, S. A. 1994. The Environmental Monitoring and Assessment Program (EMAP): its objectives, approach and status relative to wetlands. Pp. 181–195. *In* Aubrecht, G., G. Dick, and C. Prentice (Eds.), Monitoring of Ecological Change in Wetlands of Middle Europe. Proceedings of an international workshop, 1993, Stapfia 31, Linz, Austria, and IWRB Publication Number 30, Slimbridge, United Kingdom.

Petitti, D. B. 1994. Meta-Analysis, Decision Analysis, and Cost-Effectiveness Analysis: Methods for Quantitative Synthesis in Medicine. Oxford University Press, New York.

Petranka, J. W. 1983. Fish predation: a factor affecting the spatial distribution of a stream breeding salamander. Copeia 1983:624–628.

Petranka, J. W., L. B. Kats, and A. Sih. 1987. Predator-prey interactions among fish and larval amphibians: use of chemical cues to detect predatory fish. Animal Behaviour 35:420–425.

Pfennig, D. W. 1990. The adaptive significance of an environmentally-cued developmental switch in an anuran tadpole. Oecologia 85:101–107.

Pfennig, D. W. 1992a. Polyphenism in spadefoot toad tadpoles as a locally-adjusted evolutionarily stable strategy. Evolution 46:1408–1420.

Pfennig, D. W. 1992b. Proximate and functional causes of polyphenism in an anuran tadpole. Functional Ecology 6:167–174.

Pfennig, D. W., M. L. G. Loeb, and J. P. Collins. 1991. Pathogens as a factor limiting the spread of cannibalism in tiger salamanders. Oecologia 88:161–166.

Pfennig, D. W., H. K. Reeve, and P. W. Sherman. 1993. Kin recognition and cannibalism in spadefoot toad tadpoles. Animal Behaviour 46:87–94.

Pfingsten, R. A., and F. L. Downs. 1989. Salamanders of Ohio. Ohio Biological Survey Bulletin, New Series, Volume 7, Number 2.

Pfingsten, R. A., and A. M. White. 1989. *Necturus maculosus* (Rafinesque), mudpuppy. Pp. 72–78. *In* Pfingsten, R. A., and F. L. Downs (Eds.), Salamanders of Ohio. Ohio Biological Survey Bulletin, New Series, Volume 7, Number 2.

Phaff, A., and P. Rosenkilde. 1995. Effect of induced metamorphosis on the immune system of the axolotl, *Ambystoma mexicanum*. General and Comparative Endocrinology 97:308–319.

Phillips, C. A. 1989. Breeding pond fidelity, population structure and the phylogeography of the spotted salamander *Ambystoma maculatum*. Ph.D. dissertation, Washington University, St. Louis.

Phillips, C. A. 1991. Geographic distribution. *Hemidactylium scutatum.* Herpetological Review 22:133.

Phillips, C. A. 1994. Geographic distribution of mitochondrial DNA variants and the historical biogeography of the spotted salamander, *Ambystoma maculatum.* Evolution 48:597–607.

Phillips, C. A., and O. J. Sexton. 1989. Orientation and sexual differences during breeding migrations of the spotted salamander, *Ambystoma maculatum.* Copeia 1989:17–22.

Phillips, G. L., D. Eminson, and B. Moss. 1978. A mechanism to account for macrophyte decline in progressively eutrophicated freshwaters. Aquatic Botany 4:103–126.

Phillips, J. B. 1986. Two magnetoreception pathways in a migratory salamander. Science 233:765–767.

Phillips, K. 1990. Where have all the frogs and toads gone? BioScience 40:422–424.

Phillips, K. 1994. Tracking the Vanishing Frogs—An Ecological Mystery. St. Martin's Press, New York.

Pickett, S. T. A., and P. S. White. 1985. The Ecology of Natural Disturbance and Patch Dynamics. Academic Press, New York.

Pielou, E. C. 1984. The Interpretation of Ecological Data: A Primer on Classification and Ordination. John Wiley and Sons, New York.

Pierce, B. A., and J. M. Harvey. 1987. Geographic variation in acid tolerance of Connecticut wood frogs. Copeia 1987:94–103.

Pierce, B. A., J. B. Hoskins, and E. Epstein. 1984. Acid tolerance in Connecticut wood frogs. Journal of Herpetology 18:159–167.

Pierce, B. A., M. A. Margolis, and L. J. Nirtaut. 1987. The relationship between egg size and acid tolerance in *Rana sylvatica.* Journal of Herpetology 21:178–184.

Pierce, B. A., and D. K. Wooten. 1992. Genetic variation in tolerance of amphibians to low pH. Journal of Herpetology 26:422–429.

Pimentel, R. A. 1979. Morphometrics: The Multivariate Analysis of Biological Data. Kendall/Hunt, Dubuque, Iowa.

Pimm, S. L., and A. Redfearn. 1988. The variability of population densities. Nature 334:613–614.

Pinder, A. W., K. B. Storey, and G. R. Ultsch. 1992. Estivation and hibernation. Pp. 250–274. *In* Feder, M. E., and W. W. Burggren (Eds.), Environmental Physiology of Amphibians. University of Chicago Press, Chicago.

Pister, E. P. 1992. Ethical considerations in conservation of biodiversity. Transactions of the North American Wildlife and Natural Resources Conference 57:355–363.

Plackett, R. L. 1981. The Analysis of Categorical Data. Griffin, London.

Platz, J. E. 1989. Speciation within the chorus frog *Pseudacris triseriata*: morphometric and mating call analyses of the boreal and western subspecies. Copeia 1989:704-712.

Polaris Conferences. 1994. So—Now What? Decision Making with GIS—The Fourth Dimension, Volumes 1 and 2. GIS World Books, Fort Collins, Colorado.

Pollack, E. D. 1971. A simple method for the removal of protozoan parasites from *Rana pipiens* larvae. Copeia 1971:557.

Pomeroy, L. V. 1981. Developmental polymorphism in the tadpoles of the spadefoot toad, *Scaphiopus multiplicatus.* Ph.D. dissertation, University of California, Riverside.

Poole, R. W. 1974. An Introduction to Quantitative Ecology. McGraw-Hill, New York.

Pope, C. H. 1928. Some plethodontid salamanders from North Carolina and Kentucky, with description of a new race of *Leurognathus.* American Museum Novitates 306:1–19.

Pope, C. H. 1944. The Amphibians and Reptiles of the Chicago Region. Chicago Natural History Museum Press, Chicago.

Pope, C. H. 1964. Amphibians and Reptiles of the Chicago Area. Chicago Natural History Museum Press, Chicago.

Pope, T. E. B., 1930. Wisconsin herpetology notes. Transactions of the Wisconsin Academy of Sciences, Arts and Letters 25:273-284.

Pope, T. E. B., and W. E. Dickinson. 1928. The amphibians and reptiles of Wisconsin. Bulletin of the Milwaukee Public Museum 8:1-138.

Porter, P. S., R. C. Ward, and H. F. Bell. 1988. The detection limit. Environmental Science and Technology 22:856–861.

Potvin, C., and D. A. Roff. 1993. Distribution-free and robust statistical methods: viable alternatives to parametric statistics. Ecology 74:1617–1628.

Potvin, C., and J. Travis. 1993. Concluding remarks: a drop in the ocean. Ecology 74:1674–1676.

Pough, F. H. 1976. Acid precipitation and embryonic mortality of spotted salamanders, *Ambystoma maculatum.* Science 192:68–70.

Powers, J. H. 1907. Morphological variation and its causes in *Ambystoma tigrinum.* Studies of the University of Nebraska 7:197–270.

Pratt, J. W. 1976. A discussion of the question: for what use are tests of hypotheses and tests of significance? Communications in Statistics, Series A 5:779–787.

Press, S. J. 1989. Bayesian Statistics: Principles, Models, and Applications. John Wiley and Sons, New York.

Preston, R. E., and R. D. Aldridge. 1981. Migration and reproductive biology of *Ambystoma opacum* in St. Louis County, Missouri. Transactions of the Missouri Academy of Science 15:247.

Prior, J. C. 1991. Landforms of Iowa. University of Iowa Press, Iowa City.

Puckett, L. J. 1995. Identifying the major sources of nutrient water pollution. Environmental Science and Technology 29:408A–414A.

Pulliam, H. R. 1988. Sources, sinks, and population regulation. American Naturalist 132:652–661.

Punzo, F. 1993a. Ovarian effects of a sublethal concentration of mercuric chloride in the river frog, *Rana heckscheri* (Anura: Ranidae). Bulletin of Environmental Contaminants and Toxicology 50:385–391.

Punzo, F. 1993b. Effect of mercuric chloride on fertilization and larval development in the river frog, *Rana heckscheri* (Wright) (Anura: Ranidae). Bulletin of Environmental Contaminants and Toxicology 51:575–581.

Pyburn, W. F. 1958. Size and movements of a local population of cricket frogs, *Acris crepitans*. Texas Journal of Science 10:325–342.

Quattrochi, D. A., and R. E. Pelletier. 1991. Remote sensing for analysis of landscapes: an introduction. Pp. 51–76. *In* Turner, M. G., and R. H. Gardner (Eds.), Quantitative Methods in Landscape Ecology. Springer-Verlag, New York.

Racke, K. D., R. N. Lubinski, D. D. Fontaine, J. R. Miller, P. J. McCall, and G. R. Oliver. 1993. Comparative fate of chlorpyrifos insecticide in urban and agricultural environments. Pp. 70–85. *In* Racke, K. D., and A. R. Leslie (Eds.), Pesticides in Urban Environments: Fate and Significance. American Chemical Society, Washington, D.C.

Ralin, D. B., and J. S. Rogers. 1972. Aspects of tolerance to desiccation in *Acris crepitans* and *Pseudacris streckeri*. Copeia 1972:519–524.

Ramamurthy, G. S. 1994. Chemical surface water quality: ambient water quality trends in streams and lakes. Pp. 13–32. *In* The Changing Illinois Environment: Critical Trends. Volume 2: Water Resources. Technical report of the Critical Trends Assessment Project, Report Number ILENR/RE-EA-94/05. Illinois Department of Energy and Natural Resources, Springfield.

Ramus, E. 1996. 1996–1997 directory—the herpetology sourcebook. Reptile and Amphibian Magazine, Pottsville, Pennsylvania.

Raney, E. C. 1940. Summer movements of the bullfrog, *Rana catesbeiana*, Shaw, as determined by the jaw-tag method. American Midland Naturalist 23:733–745.

Rasmussen, P. W., D. M. Heisey, E. V. Nordheim, and T. M. Frost. 1993. Time-series intervention analysis: unreplicated large-scale experiments. Pp. 138–158. *In* Scheiner, S. M., and J. Gurevitch (Eds.), Design and Analysis of Ecological Experiments. Chapman and Hall, New York.

Raymo, M. E. 1994. The initiation of northern hemisphere glaciation. Annual Review of Earth and Planetary Sciences 22:353–383.

Raymond, L. R., and L. M. Hardy. 1990. Demography of a population of *Ambystoma talpoideum* (Caudata: Ambystomatidae) in northwestern Louisiana. Herpetologica 46:371–382.

Reading, C. J., J. Loman, and T. Madsen. 1991. Breeding pond fidelity in the common toad, *Bufo bufo*. Journal of Zoology, London 225:201–221.

Redmer, M. 1991. A preliminary report on the amphibians and reptiles of five state parks in northwestern Illinois. Pp. 118–140. *In* Brandon, R. A., and S. R. Ballard (Eds.), Inventories of amphibians and reptiles in Illinois. Unpublished report to the Illinois Department of Conservation, Division of Natural Heritage, Springfield.

Redmer, M. 1996. Locality records of the northern leopard frog, *Rana pipiens*, in central and southwestern Illinois. Transactions of the Illinois State Academy of Science 89:215–219.

Redmer, M., and T. G. Anton. 1993. Surveys of the Joliet Training Area and Joliet Army Ammunition Plant for endangered, threatened, and watchlist reptiles. Unpublished report to the Illinois Department of Conservation, Division of Natural Heritage, Springfield.

Redmer, M., and S. R. Ballard. 1995. Recent distribution records for amphibians and reptiles in Illinois. Herpetological Review 26:49–53.

Redmer, M., J. B. Camerer, J. K. Tucker, and J. Capps. 1995. Geographic distribution: *Rana palustris* (pickerel frog), Illinois. Herpetological Review 26:42.

Redmer, M., and K. S. Mierzwa. 1994. A review of the distribution and zoogeography of the pickerel frog, *Rana palustris*, in northern Illinois. Bulletin of the Chicago Herpetological Society 29:21–30.

Redmond, W. H. 1991. Biogeography of amphibians in Tennessee. Journal of the Tennessee Academy of

Science 66:153–160.

Reed, A., and S. Droege. 1995. Validation of sweep net samples for tadpoles. North American Amphibian Monitoring Program, Burlington, Ontario. Unpublished abstract.

Reeves, D. A. 1984. Iowa frog and toad survey. Unpublished report to the Iowa Conservation Commission, Des Moines.

Reichenbach-Klinke, H. H., and E. Elkan. 1965. The Principal Diseases of Lower Vertebrates. Academic Press, New York.

Reilly, S. M. 1986. Ontogeny of cranial ossification in the eastern newt, *Notophthalmus viridescens*, and its relationship to metamorphosis and neoteny. Journal of Morphology 188:315–326.

Reinartz, J. A., and E. L. Warne. 1993. Development of vegetation in small created wetlands in southeastern Wisconsin. Wetlands 13:153–164.

Reinert, H. K. 1991. Translocation as a conservation strategy for amphibians and reptiles: some comments, concerns, and observations. Herpetologica 47:357–363.

Remillard, M. M., G. K. Gruendling, and D. J. Bogucki. 1987. Disturbance by beaver (*Castor canadensis* Kuhl) and increased landscape heterogeneity. Pp. 103–122. *In* Turner, M. G. (Ed.), Landscape Heterogeneity and Disturbance. Springer-Verlag, New York.

Resitarits, W. J., Jr., and H. M. Wilbur. 1991. Calling site choice of *Hyla chrysoscelis*: effect of predators, competitors, and oviposition sites. Ecology 72:778–786.

Rhodes, R. S. 1984. Paleoecology and regional paleoclimatic implications of the Farmdalian Craigmile and Woodfordian Waubonsie mammalian local faunas, southwestern Iowa. Illinois State Museum Reports of Investigation Number 40.

Rice, F. L., and N. S. Davis. 1878. *Rana circulosa.* P. 355. *In* Jordan, D. S. (Ed.), Manual of the Vertebrates of the Northern United States. Jansen and McClurg, Chicago.

Richmond, G. R., and D. S. Fullerton. 1986. Summation of Quaternary glaciations in the United States of America. Pp. 183–196. *In* Sibrava, V., D. Q. Bowen, and G. M. Richmond (Eds.), Quaternary Glaciations in the Northern Hemisphere. Pergamon Press, Oxford.

Richter, K. O., and A. L. Azous. 1995. Amphibian occurrence and wetland characteristics in the Puget Sound Basin. Wetlands 15:305–312.

Ridgway, R. 1889. The ornithology of Illinois—descriptive catalogue. Volume 1. 1913 reprint. Natural History Survey of Illinois, State Laboratory of Natural History, Pantagraph Printing and Stationery Company, Bloomington, Illinois.

Riggin, G. W., and T. W. Schultz. 1986. Teratogenic effects of benzoyl hydrazine on frog embryos. Transactions of the American Microscopical Society 105:197–210.

Rimler, R. B., E. B. Shotts, and P. Ghittino. 1974. Infectious a *Aeromonas hydrophila* chez les poissons, diagnostic rapide a ll'aide du milieu. Les Cahiers de Medicine Veterinaire 43:47–52.

Ripley, B. D. 1981. Spatial Statistics. John Wiley and Sons, New York.

Ritchie, W., M. Wood, R. Wright, and D. Tait. 1988. Surveying and Mapping for Field Scientists. John Wiley and Sons, New York.

Ritke, M. E., J. G. Babb, and M. K. Ritke. 1991. Breeding-site specificity in the gray treefrog (*Hyla chrysoscelis*). Journal of Herpetology 25:123–125.

Rittschof, D. 1975. Some aspects of the natural history and ecology of the leopard frog, *Rana pipiens.* Ph.D. dissertation, University of Michigan, Ann Arbor.

Robbins, C. S., D. Bystrak, and P. Geissler. 1986. The Breeding Bird Survey: its first fifteen years, 1965–1979. U.S. Fish and Wildlife Service, Resource Publication 157, Washington D.C.

Roberts, E. A. 1992. Sequential Data in Biological Experiments. Chapman and Hall, New York.

Roberts, H. V. 1976. For what use are tests of hypotheses and tests of significance? Communications in Statistics, Series A 5:753–761.

Roberts, W. 1992. Declines in amphibian populations in Alberta. Pp. 14–16. *In* Bishop, C. A., and K. E. Pettit (Eds.), Declines in Canadian Amphibian Populations: Designing a National Monitoring Strategy. Occasional Paper Number 76, Canadian Wildlife Service, Ottawa, Ontario.

Rock, B. N., D. L. Skole, and B. J. Choudhury. 1993. Monitoring vegetation change using satellite data. Pp. 153–167. *In* Solomon, A. M., and H. H. Shugart (Eds.), Vegetation Dynamics and Global Change. Chapman and Hall, New York.

Rodgers, C. S. 1978. The presettlement vegetation of McLean and Mason Counties, Illinois. M.S. thesis, Illinois State University, Normal.

Roff, D. A. 1986. The evolution of wing dimorphism in insects. Evolution 40:1009–1020.

Roff, D. A. 1996. The evolution of threshold traits in animals. Quarterly Review of Biology 71:3–35.

Rogers, D. J., and S. E. Randolph. 1991. Mortality rates

and population density of tsetse flies correlated with satellite imagery. Nature 351:739–741.

Rogers, D. J., and B. G. Williams. 1994. Tsetse distribution in Africa: seeing the wood and the trees. Pp. 247–271. *In* Edwards, P. J., R. M. May, and N. R. Webb (Eds.), Large-Scale Ecology and Conservation Biology. Blackwell Scientific, Boston.

Rooney, T. P. 1995. Restoring landscape diversity and old growth to Pennsylvania's northern hardwood forests. Natural Areas Journal 15:274–278.

Roosa, D. 1977. Endangered Iowa Amphibians and Reptiles. Special Report of the Preserves Board, Number 3, Iowa Conservation Commission, Des Moines.

Rose, F. L., and D. Armentrout. 1976. Adaptive strategies of *Ambystoma tigrinum* Green inhabiting the Llano Estacado of west Texas. Journal of Animal Ecology 45:713–729.

Rose, K. A., and E. P. Smith. 1992. Experimental design: the neglected aspect of environmental monitoring. Environmental Management 16:691–700.

Rosenkilde, P. 1985. The role of hormones in the regulation of amphibian metamorphosis. Pp. 221–259. *In* Balls, M., and M. Bownes (Eds.), Metamorphosis. Clarendon Press, Oxford.

Rotenberry, J. T., and J. A. Wiens. 1985. Statistical power analysis and community-wide patterns. American Naturalist 125:164–168.

Roth, J., and V. Hacker. 1988. Fall use of rotenone at low concentrations to eradicate fish populations. Research Management Findings Number 9, Wisconsin Department of Natural Resources, Madison.

Roth, M. 1978. Experimental skeletal teratogenesis in the frog tadpole. Anatomischer Anzeiger 143:296–300.

Roth, M. 1988. The two-stage neuroskeletal pathomechanism of developmental deformities of the limb skeleton. Anatomischer Anzeiger Jena 167:271–279.

Routman, E. 1993. Population structure and genetic diversity of metamorphic and paedomorphic populations of the tiger salamander, *Ambystoma tigrinum*. Journal of Evolutionary Biology 6:329–357.

Rowe, C. L., and W. A. Dunson. 1994. The value of simulated pond communities in mesocosms for studies of amphibian ecology and ecotoxicology. Journal of Herpetology 28:346–356.

Rowe, C. L., W. J. Sadinski, and W. A. Dunson. 1992. Effects of acute and chronic acidification on three larval amphibians that breed in temporary ponds. Archives of Environmental Contamination and Toxicology 23:339–350.

Rowe, J. S., and J. W. Sheard. 1981. Ecological land classification: a survey approach. Environmental Management 5:451–464.

Rubin, D. 1992. Herpetological survey of selected Hamilton County parks, 1990–91. Unpublished report to the Hamilton County Park District, Cincinnati.

Ruffner, D. G., D. Leonard, and G. Scherger. 1969. Checklist of amphibians, reptiles, and mammals of the Tree Farm Natural Area, Defiance County, Ohio. Ohio Journal of Science 68:312–315.

Ruiz, M. S., and J. M. Messersmith. 1990. Cartographic issues in the development of a digital GRASS database. USACERL Special Report N–90/16. U.S. Army Corps of Engineers, Construction Engineering Research Laboratories, Champaign, Illinois.

Runkle, J. R. 1982. Patterns of disturbance in some old growth mesic forests of eastern North America. Ecology 63:1533–1546.

Runkle, J. R. 1991. Gap dynamics of old growth eastern forests: management implications. Natural Areas Journal 11:19–25.

Running, S. W., and R. R. Nemani. 1988. Relating seasonal patterns of the AVHRR vegetation index to simulated photosynthesis and transpiration of forests in different climates. Remote Sensing of Environment 24:347–367.

Runyon, E. H., A. G. Karlson, G. P. Kubica, and L. G. Wayne. 1974. *Mycobacterium*. Pp. 148–174. *In* Lennette, E. H., S. Truant, and J. P. Truant (Eds.), Manual of Clinical Microbiology. American Society of Microbiology, Washington, D.C.

Rush, H. G., M. R. Anver, and E. S. Beneke. 1974. Systemic chromomycosis in *Rana pipiens*. Laboratory Animal Science 24:646–655.

Russell, F. H. 1898. An epidemic septicemic disease among frogs due to the *Bacillus hydrophilus fuscus*. Journal of the American Medical Association 30:1442–1449.

Russell, M. 1989. Keeping promises: EPA and the protection of wetlands. Pp. 711–717. *In* Sharitz, R. R., and J. W. Gibbons (Eds.), Freshwater Wetlands and Wildlife. Symposium Series Number 61, U.S. Department of Energy, Office of Scientific and Technical Information, Oak Ridge, Tennessee.

Russell, R. W., S. J. Hecnar, and G. D. Haffner. 1995. Organochlorine pesticide residues in southern Ontario spring peepers. Environmental Toxicology and Chemistry 14:815–817.

Ryan, M. R. 1990. A dynamic approach to the conservation of the prairie ecosystem in the Midwest. Pp. 93–106. *In* Sweeny, J. M. (Ed.), Management of dynamic ecosystems: proceedings of a symposium held at the 51st Midwest Fish and Wildlife Conference. North Central Section of the Wildlife Society, Springfield, Illinois.

Rzehak, K., A. Maryanska-Nadachowska, and M. Jordan. 1977. The effect of Karbatox 75, a carbaryl insecticide, upon the development of tadpoles of *Rana temporaria* and *Xenopus laevis*. Folia Biologica 25:391–399.

Sabins, F. F., Jr. 1987. Remote Sensing: Principles and Interpretation. W. H. Freeman, New York.

Sadinski, W. J., and W. A. Dunson. 1992. A multilevel study of effects of low pH on amphibians of temporary ponds. Journal of Herpetology 26:413–422.

Safe, S., D. Jones, J. Kohli, L. O. Ruzo, O. Hutzinger, and G. Sundstrom. 1976. The metabolism of chlorinated aromatic pollutants by the frog. Canadian Journal of Zoology 54:1818–1823.

Sajdak, R. 1982. Seasonal activity patterns, habitat selection and population structure of the mudpuppy, *Necturus maculosus*, in a Wisconsin stream. M.S. thesis, University of Wisconsin-Milwaukee.

Salibian, A. 1992. Effects of deltamethrin on the South American toad, *Bufo arenarum*, tadpoles. Bulletin of Environmental Contamination and Toxicology 48:616–621.

Salsburg, D. S. 1985. The religion of statistics as practiced in medical journals. American Statistician 39:220–223.

Salthe, S. N., and J. S. Meacham. 1974. Reproductive and courtship patterns. Pp. 309–521. *In* Lofts, B. (Ed.), Physiology of the Amphibia, Volume II. Academic Press, New York.

Sample, V. A. 1994. Remote Sensing and GIS in Ecosystem Management. Island Press, Washington, D.C.

Sanders, T. G., R. C. Ward, J. C. Loftis, T. D. Steele, D. D. Adrian, and V. Yevjevich. 1987. Design of Networks for Monitoring Water Quality. Water Resources Publications, Littleton, Colorado.

Sanderson, E. W., and A. G. Buck. 1995. Reconnaissance study of ground-water levels in the Havana lowlands area. Office of Ground-Water Resources Evaluation and Management, Hydrology Division, Illinois State Water Survey, Champaign.

SAS Institute Inc. 1989. SAS/STAT User's Guide, Version 6, Volume 2. SAS Institute Inc., Cary, North Carolina.

Satterlund, D. R., and P. W. Adams. 1992. Wildland Watershed Management. John Wiley and Sons, New York.

Sauer, J. R. 1996. Estimation from population indices: validation and efficiency. North American Amphibian Monitoring Program, Burlington, Ontario. Unpublished abstract.

Sawyer, J. O., and T. Keeler-Wolf. 1995. A Manual of California Vegetation. California Native Plant Society, Sacramento.

Scheiner, S. M., and J. Gurevitch. 1993. Design and Analysis of Ecological Experiments. Chapman and Hall, New York.

Schlosser, I. J. 1991. Stream fish ecology: a landscape perspective. BioScience 41:704–712.

Schlupp, I., and R. Podloucky. 1994. Changes in breeding site fidelity: a combined study of conservation and behaviour in the common toad *Bufo bufo*. Biological Conservation 69:285–291.

Schmidt, K. P., and W. L. Necker. 1935. Amphibians and reptiles of the Chicago region. Chicago Academy of Science Bulletin 5:57–76.

Schmidt, R. E. 1984. Amphibian chromomycosis. Pp. 169–181. *In* Hoff, G. L., F. L. Frye, and E. R. Jacobson (Eds.), Diseases of Amphibians and Reptiles. Plenum Press, New York.

Schmidt, R. E., and D. A. Hartfiel. 1977. Chromomycosis in amphibians: review and case report. Journal of Zoo and Wildlife Medicine 8:26–28.

Schnabel, Z. E. 1938. The estimation of the total fish population of a lake. American Mathematical Monthly 45:348–352.

Schoener, T. W. 1985. Are lizard population sizes unusually constant through time? American Naturalist 126:633–641.

Schramm, P., and R. M. Nordgren. 1978. Recent herpetological records for western Illinois including a relic population of the four–toed salamander, *Hemidactylium scutatum*. Transactions of the Illinois State Academy of Science 60:243.

Schroeder, E. E., and T. S. Baskett. 1968. Age estimation, growth rates, and population structure in Missouri bullfrogs. Copeia 1968:583–592.

Schroeter, S. C., J. D. Dixon, J. Kastendiek, R. O. Smith, and J. R. Bence. 1993. Detecting the ecological effects of environmental impacts: a case study of kelp forest invertebrates. Ecological Applications 3:331–350.

Schultz, T. W., J. N. Dumont, and R. G. Epler. 1985. The embryotoxic and osteolathyrogenic effects of semicarbazide. Toxicology 36:183–198.

Schuytema, G. S., A. V. Nebeker, W. L. Griffis, and K. N. Wilson. 1991. Teratogenesis, toxicity and bioconcentration in frogs exposed to dieldrin. Archives of

Environmental Contamination and Toxicology 21:332–350.

Schwalbe, C. R., and P. C. Rosen. 1988. Preliminary report on effect of bullfrogs on wetland herpetofaunas in southeastern Arizona. Pp. 166–173. *In* Szaro, R. C., K. E. Severson, and D. R. Patton (Eds.), Management of Amphibians, Reptiles, and Small Mammals in North America. U.S. Forest Service, General Technical Report RM-166, Fort Collins, Colorado.

Schwegman, J. E. 1973. The Natural Divisions of Illinois. Illinois Nature Preserves Commission, Springfield.

Schwegman, J. E. 1996. Species news. Illinoensis: Newsletter of the Illinois Native Plant Conservation Program 12(1). Illinois Department of Natural Resources, Springfield.

Schwert, D. P. 1992. Faunal transitions in response to an Ice Age: the Late Wisconsinan record of Coleoptera in the north-central United States. Colepterists Bulletin 46:68–94.

Scott, D. E. 1994. The effect of larval density on adult demographic traits in *Ambystoma opacum*. Ecology 75:1383–1396.

Scott, J. M., B. Csuti, R. F. Noss, B. Butterfield, C. Groves, H. Anderson, S. Caicco, F. D'Erchia, T. C. Edwards Jr., J. Ullman, and G. Wright. 1993. Gap analysis: a geographic approach to protection of biological diversity. Wildlife Monographs 123:1–41.

Scott, N. J., Jr., and B. D. Woodward. 1994. Surveys at breeding sites. Pp. 118–125. *In* Heyer, W. R., M. A. Donnelly, R. W. McDiarmid, L.-A. C. Hayek, and M. S. Foster (Eds.), Measuring and Monitoring Biological Diversity, Standard Methods for Amphibians. Smithsonian Institution Press, Washington, D.C.

Seale, D. 1982. Physical factors influencing oviposition by the wood frog, *Rana sylvatica*, in Pennsylvania. Copeia 1982:627–635.

Searle, S. R., G. Casella, and C. E. McCulloch. 1992. Variance Components. John Wiley and Sons, New York.

Seburn, C. N. L. 1992. The status of amphibian populations in Saskatchewan. Pp. 17–18. *In* Bishop, C. A., and K. E. Pettit (Eds.), Declines in Canadian Amphibian Populations: Designing a National Monitoring Strategy. Occasional Paper Number 76, Canadian Wildlife Service, Ottawa, Ontario.

Selye, H. 1936. A syndrome produced by diverse nocuous agents. Nature 138:32.

Semken, H. A., Jr. 1988. Environmental interpretations of the "disharmonius" late Wisconsinan biome of southeastern North America. Pp. 185–194. *In* Laub, R. S., N. G. Miller, and D. W. Steadman (Eds.), Late Pleistocene and Early Holocene Paleoecology and Archaeology of the Eastern Great Lakes Region. Bulletin of the Buffalo Society of Natural Sciences 33.

Semken, H. A., Jr., and C. R. Falk. 1987. Late Pleistocene/Holocene mammalian faunas and environmental changes on the northern plains of the United States. Pp. 176–313. *In* Graham, R. W., H. A. Semken Jr., and M. A. Graham (Eds.), Late Quaternary Mammalian Biogeography and Environments of the Great Plains and Prairies. Illinois State Museum Scientific Papers XXII.

Semlitsch, R. D. 1981. Terrestrial activity and summer home range of the mole salamander (*Ambystoma talpoideum*). Canadian Journal of Zoology 59:315–322.

Semlitsch, R. D. 1983a. Structure and dynamics of two breeding populations of the eastern tiger salamander, *Ambystoma tigrinum*. Copeia 1983:608–616.

Semlitsch, R. D. 1983b. Terrestrial movements of an eastern tiger salamander, *Ambystoma tigrinum*. Herpetological Review 14:112–113.

Semlitsch, R. D. 1985. Reproductive strategy of a facultatively paedomorphic salamander *Ambystoma talpoideum*. Oecologia 65:305–313.

Semlitsch, R. D. 1987. Interactions between fish and salamander larvae. Oecologia 72:481–486.

Semlitsch, R. D. 1988. Allopatric distribution of two salamanders: effects of fish predation and competitive interactions. Copeia 1988:290–298.

Semlitsch, R. D., and J. W. Gibbons. 1988. Fish predation in size structured populations of treefrog tadpoles. Oecologia 75:321–326.

Semlitsch, R. D., D. E. Scott, and J. H. K. Pechmann. 1988. Time and size at metamorphosis related to adult fitness in *Ambystoma talpoideum*. Ecology 69:184–192.

Semlitsch, R. D., D. E. Scott, J. H. K. Pechmann, and J. W. Gibbons. 1996. Structure and dynamics of an amphibian community: evidence from a sixteen-year study of a natural pond. Pp. 217–248. *In* Cody, M. L., and J. Smallwood (Eds.), Long-Term Studies of Vertebrate Communities. Academic Press, New York.

Sessions, S. K., and S. B. Ruth. 1990. Explanation for naturally occurring supernumerary limbs in amphibians. Journal of Experimental Zoology 254:38–47.

Sexton, O. J., and J. R. Bizer. 1978. Life history patterns of *Ambystoma tigrinum* in montane Colorado. American Midland Naturalist 99:101–118.

Sexton, O. J., J. Bizer, D. C. Gayou, P. Freiling, and M. Moutseous. 1986. Field studies of breeding spotted salamanders, *Ambystoma maculatum*, in eastern Missouri, U.S.A. Milwaukee Public Museum, Contributions in Biology and Geology 67:1–19.

Sexton, O. J., and C. Phillips. 1986. A qualitative study of the fish–amphibian interactions in three Missouri ponds. Transactions of the Missouri Academy of Science 20:25–35.

Shafer, C. L. 1990. Nature Reserves: Island Theory and Conservation Practice. Smithsonian Institution Press, Washington, D.C.

Shaffer, H. B., and S. R. Voss. 1996. Phylogenetic and mechanistic analysis of a developmentally integrated character complex: alternate life history modes in ambystomatid salamanders. American Zoologist 36:24–35.

Shane, L. C. K. 1987. Late-glacial vegetational and climatic history of the Allegheny Plateau and the till plains of Ohio and Indiana, U.S.A. Boreas 16:1–20.

Shao, J., and D. Tu. 1995. The Jacknife and Bootstrap. Springer-Verlag, New York.

Sharitz, R. R., and W. J. Mitsch. 1993. Southern floodplain forests. Pp. 311–372. *In* Martin, W. M., S. G. Boyce, and A. C. Echternact (Eds.), Biodiversity of the United States: Lowland Terrestrial Communities. John Wiley and Sons, New York.

Shaw, R. G., and T. Mitchell-Olds. 1993. ANOVA for unbalanced data: an overview. Ecology 74:1638–1645.

Shifley, S. R., and R. C. Schlesinger. 1994. Sampling guidelines for old-growth forests in the Midwest, USA. Natural Areas Journal 14:258–267.

Shirose, L. J., and R. J. Brooks. 1995. Growth rate and age at maturity in syntopic populations of *Rana clamitans* and *Rana septentrionalis* in central Ontario. Canadian Journal of Zoology 73:1468–1473.

Shirose, L. J., C. A. Bishop, D. M. Green, C. J. MacDonald, R. J. Brooks, and N. J. Helferty. 1997. Validation tests of an amphibian call count survey technique in Ontario, Canada. Herpetologica (in press).

Shively, J. N., J. G. Songer, S. Prchal, M. S. Keasey III, and C. O. Thoen. 1981. *Mycobacterium marinum* infection in Bufonidae. Journal of Wildlife Diseases 17:3–7.

Shoop, C. R. 1965. Orientation of *Ambystoma maculatum*: movements to and from breeding ponds. Science 149:558–559.

Shoop, C. R. 1967. Relation of migration and breeding activities to time of ovulation in *Ambystoma maculatum*. Herpetologica 23:319–321.

Shoop, C. R. 1968. Migratory orientation of *Ambystoma maculatum* movements near breeding ponds and displacement of migrating individuals. Ecology 55:440–444.

Shoop, C. R., and T. L. Doty. 1972. Migratory orientation by marbled salamanders (*Ambystoma opacum*) near a breeding area. Behavioral Biology 7:131–136.

Shoop, C. R., and G. E. Gunning. 1967. Seasonal activity and movements of *Necturus* in Louisiana. Copeia 1969:732–737.

Shorrocks, B., and I. R. Swingland. 1990. Living in a Patchy Environment. Oxford University Press, New York.

Shotts, E. B., and G. L. Bullock. 1975. Bacterial diseases of fish: diagnostic procedures for gram-negative pathogens. Journal of the Fisheries Research Board of Canada 32:1243–1247.

Shotts, E. B., and G. L. Bullock. 1976. Rapid diagnostic approaches in the identification of gram-negative bacterial diseases of fish. Fish Pathology 10:187–190.

Shotts, E. B., and R. B. Rimler. 1973. Medium for isolation of *Aeromonas hydrophila*. Applied Microbiology 26:550–553.

Siegel, S. 1956. Nonparametric Statistics for the Behavioral Sciences. McGraw-Hill, New York.

Sih, A., J. W. Petranka, and L. B. Kats. 1988. The dynamics of prey refuge use: a model and tests with sunfish and salamander larvae. American Naturalist 132:463–483.

Simberloff, D. S., and L. G. Abele. 1976. Island biogeography theory and conservation practice. Science 191:285–286.

Simberloff, D. S., J. A. Farr, J. Cox, and D. W. Mehlman. 1992. Movement corridors: conservation bargains or poor investments? Conservation Biology 6:493–504.

Simmons, J. E. 1987. Herpetological Collecting and Collections Management. Society for the Study of Amphibians and Reptiles, Department of Zoology, Miami University, Oxford, Ohio.

Simon, S. M., and P. J. Krusling. 1988. Report of the reptile and amphibian survey of the bottomlands of Shawnee Lookout Park. Unpublished report to the Hamilton County Park District, Cincinnati.

Simon, T. P., J. O. Whitaker Jr., J. S. Castrale, and S. A. Minton Jr. 1992. Checklist of the vertebrates of Indiana. Proceedings of the Indiana Academy of Science 101:95–126.

Simons, R. R., and B. E. Felgenhauer. 1992. Identifying areas of chemical signal production in the red-backed salamander, *Plethodon cinereus*. Copeia 1992:776–781.

Simonsen, J. F., and P. Harremoes. 1978. Oxygen and pH fluctuations in rivers. Water Research 12:477–489.

Sipe, F. H. 1979. Compass Land Surveying. McClain Printing, Parsons, West Virginia.

Sipes, M. P. 1964. A distributional survey of salamanders

inhabiting northeastern Ohio. M.S. thesis, Kent State University, Kent, Ohio.

Sjögren, P. 1991. Extinction and isolation gradients in metapopulations: the case of the pool frog (*Rana lessonae*). Biological Journal of the Linnean Society 42:135–147.

Sjögren Gulve, P. 1994. Distribution and extinction patterns within a northern metapopulation of the pool frog, *Rana lessonae*. Ecology 75:1357–1367.

Skalski, J. R., and D. S. Robson. 1992. Techniques for Wildlife Investigations: Design and Analysis of Capture Data. Academic Press, New York.

Skeen, J. N., P. D. Doerr, and D. H. Van Lear. 1993. Oak-hickory-pine forests. Pp. 1–33. *In* Martin, W. M., S. G. Boyce, and A. C. Echternact (Eds.), Biodiversity of the United States: Upland Terrestrial Communities. John Wiley and Sons, New York.

Skelly, D. K. 1994. Activity level and the susceptibility of anuran larvae to predation. Animal Behaviour 47:465–468.

Skelly, D. K. 1995. A behavioral trade-off and its consequences for the distribution of *Pseudacris* treefrog larvae. Ecology 76:150–164.

Skelly, D. K. 1996. Pond drying, predators and the distribution of *Pseudacris* tadpoles Copeia 1996:599–605.

Skelly, D. K. 1997. Tadpole communities: pond permanence and predation are powerful forces shaping the structure of tadpole communities. American Scientist 85:36–45.

Skelly, D. K., and E. E. Werner. 1990. Behavioral and life historical responses of larval American toads to an odonate predator. Ecology 71:2313–2322.

Skole, D. L., B. Moore III, and W. H. Chomentowski. 1993. Global geographic information systems and databases for vegetation change studies. Pp. 168–189. *In* Solomon, A. H., and H. H. Shugart (Eds.), Vegetation Dynamics and Global Change. Chapman and Hall, New York.

Skorupa, J. P., and Ohlendorf, H. M. 1991. Contaminants in drainage water and avian risk thresholds. Pp. 345–368. *In* Dinar A., and D. Zilberman (Eds.), The Economics and Management of Water and Drainage in Agriculture. Kluwer Academic Publishers, Dordrecht and Boston.

Skúlason, S., and T. B. Smith. 1995. Resource polymorphism in vertebrates. Trends in Ecology and Evolution 9:366–370.

Sliwinski, R. P. 1992. Herpetological inventory of the Poplar Creek Forest Preserve. Unpublished report to The Nature Conservancy, Chicago.

Slooff, W., and R. Baerselman. 1980. Comparison of the usefulness of the Mexican axolotl (*Ambystoma mexicanum*) and the clawed toad (*Xenopus laevis*) in toxicological bioassays. Bulletin of Environmental Contaminants and Toxicology 24:439–443.

Slooff, W., J. H. Canton, and J. L. M. Hermens. 1983. Comparison of the susceptibility of twenty-two freshwater species to fifteen chemical compounds: 1. Subacute toxicity tests. Aquatic Toxicology 4:113–128.

Smallwood, B. F., and L. C. Osterholz. 1990. Soil survey of Jasper County, Indiana. U.S. Soil Conservation Service, Washington, D.C.

Smith, A. J. 1967. The effects of the lamprey larvicide, 3-trifluoromethyl-4-nitrophenol, on selected aquatic invertebrates. Transactions of the American Fisheries Society 96:410–413.

Smith, B. G. 1907. The breeding habits of *Ambystoma punctatum*. American Naturalist 41:381–390.

Smith, D. C. 1987. Adult recruitment in chorus frogs: effects of size and date at metamorphosis. Ecology 68:344–350.

Smith, D. T. 1972. Other species of mycobacteria. Pp. 471–486. *In* Jolik, W. K., and D. T. Smith (Eds.), Zinsser Microbiology. Meredith, New York.

Smith, H. M., and S. Barlowe. 1978. Amphibians of North America. Golden Press, New York.

Smith, P. W. 1947. The reptiles and amphibians of eastern central Illinois. Bulletin of the Chicago Academy of Sciences 8:21–40.

Smith, P. W. 1951. A new frog and a new turtle from the western Illinois sand prairies. Bulletin of the Chicago Academy of Sciences 9:189–199.

Smith, P. W. 1955. *Pseudacris streckeri illinoensis* in Missouri. Transactions of the Kansas Academy of Science 58:411.

Smith, P. W. 1957. An analysis of post-Wisconsin biogeography of the prairie peninsula region based on distributional phenomena among terrestrial vertebrate populations. Ecology 38:205–218.

Smith, P. W. 1961. The amphibians and reptiles of Illinois. Illinois Natural History Survey Bulletin 28:1–298.

Smith, P. W. 1966. *Pseudacris streckeri*. Catalogue of American Amphibians and Reptiles 27.1–27.2.

Smith, P. W. 1971. Illinois streams: a classification based on their fishes and an analysis of factors responsible for disappearance of native species. Illinois Natural History Survey Biological Notes Number 76, Urbana.

Smith, P. W., and S. A. Minton Jr. 1957. A distributional summary of the herpetofauna of Indiana and Illinois.

American Midland Naturalist 58:341–351.

Smith, S. L. 1974. A relict population of the four-toed salamander *Hemidactylium scutatum* (Schlegel) in Jersey County, Illinois. Transactions of the Illinois State Academy of Sciences 67:163–164.

Smith, S. M. 1995. Distribution-free and robust statistical methods: viable alternatives to parametric statistics? Ecology 76:1997–1998.

Smith, T. R., and Y. Jiang. 1991. Knowledge-based approaches in GIS. Pp. 413–425. *In* Maguire, D. J., M. F. Goodchild, and D. W. Rhind (Eds.), Geographical Information Systems, Volume I, Principles. John Wiley and Sons, New York.

Snedecor, G. W., and W. G. Cochran. 1989. Statistical Methods. Iowa State University Press, Ames.

Snyder, D. H. 1971. The function of brooding behavior in the plethodontid salamander, *Aneides aeneus*: a field study. Ph.D. dissertation, University of Notre Dame, South Bend, Indiana.

Snyder, D. H. 1983. The apparent crash and possible extinction of the green salamander, *Aneides aeneus*, in the Carolinas. Association of Southeastern Biologists Bulletin 30:82.

Snyder, D. H. 1991. The green salamander (*Aneides aeneus*) in Tennessee and Kentucky, with comments on the Carolinas' Blue Ridge populations. Journal of the Tennessee Academy of Science 66:165–169.

Snyder, J. P. 1987. Map projections—a working manual. U.S. Geological Survey Professional Paper 1395, Washington, D.C.

Snyder, J. P. 1993. Flattening the Earth: Two Thousand Years of Map Projections. University of Chicago Press, Chicago.

Soil Conservation Service. 1992. Wetland restoration, enhancement, or creation. *In* Engineering Field Handbook. U.S. Soil Conservation Service, Washington, D.C.

Sokal, R. R., and F. J. Rohlf. 1969. Biometry. W. H. Freeman, San Francisco.

Sokal, R. R., and F. J. Rohlf. 1994. Biometry: The Principles and Practice of Statistics in Biological Research. W. H. Freeman, New York.

Soulé, M. E. 1980. Thresholds for survival: maintaining fitness and evolutionary potential. Pp. 151–169. *In* Soulé, M. E., and B. A. Wilcox (Eds.), Conservation Biology: An Evolutionary-Ecological Perspective. Sinauer Associates, Sunderland, Massachusetts.

Soulé, M. E. 1987. Viable Populations for Conservation. Cambridge University Press, New York.

Southwood, T. R. E. 1966. Ecological Methods. Methuen, London.

Sparks, R. E. 1992. The Illinois River–floodplain ecosystem. Pp. 412–432. *In* Restoration of Aquatic Ecosystems. National Research Council, National Academy Press, Washington, D.C.

Speare, R. 1989. Clinical assessment and diagnosis of disease in anurans. Workshop on the Medicine and Management of Amphibians. Annual Meeting of Zoo Veterinarians, Greensboro, North Carolina. Unpublished abstract.

Speckman, F. C. 1960. Facts about "Nigger" Lake. Mason County Democrat, 3 March, Havana, Illinois.

Spellerberg, I. F. 1991. Monitoring Ecological Change. Cambridge University Press, New York.

Springer, S. 1927. A list of amphibians and reptiles taken in Marion County, Indiana, 1924–1927. Proceedings of the Indiana Academy of Science 37:491–492.

Sprules, W. G. 1974. The adaptive significance of paedogenesis in North American species of *Ambystoma* (Amphibia: Caudata): an hypothesis. Canadian Journal of Zoology 52:393–400.

Stanley, J. C. 1961. Analysis of unreplicated three-way classifications, with applications to rater bias and trait independence. Psychometrika 26:205–220.

Stansfield, J., B. Moss, and K. Irvine. 1989. The loss of submerged plants with eutrophication III. Potential role of organochlorine pesticides: a paleoecological study. Freshwater Biology 22:109–132.

Star, J. L., and J. E. Estes. 1990. Geographical Information Systems: An Introduction. Prentice Hall, Englewood Cliffs, New Jersey.

Starrett, W. C. 1972. Man and the Illinois River. Pp.131–169. *In* Oglesby, R. T., C. A. Carlson, and J. A. McCann (Eds.), River Ecology and Man. Academic Press, New York.

Stebbins, R. C. 1985. Western Reptiles and Amphibians. Peterson Field Guides. Houghton Mifflin, Boston.

Stebbins, R. C., and N. W. Cohen. 1995. A Natural History of Amphibians. Princeton University Press, Princeton, New Jersey.

Steel, R. G. D., and J. H. Torrie. 1980. Principles and Procedures of Statistics: A Biometrical Approach. McGraw-Hill, New York.

Steele, C. W., S. Strickler-Shaw, and D. H. Taylor. 1989. Behavior of tadpoles of the bullfrog, *Rana catesbeiana*, in response to sublethal lead exposure. Aquatic Toxicology 14:331–344.

Steele, C. W., S. Strickler-Shaw, and D. H. Taylor. 1991. Failure of *Bufo americanus* tadpoles to avoid lead-enriched water. Journal of Herpetology 25:241–243.

Stenhouse, S. L. 1985. Migratory orientation and homing in *Ambystoma maculatum* and *Ambystoma opacum*. Copeia 1985:631–637.

Stenhouse, S. L., N. G. Hairston, and A. E. Cory. 1983. Predation and competition in *Ambystoma* larvae: field and laboratory experiments. Journal of Herpetology 17:210–220.

Stephenson, S. L., A. N. Ash, and D. F. Stauffer. 1993. Appalachian oak forests. Pp. 255–303. *In* Martin, W. M., S. G. Boyce, and A. C. Echternact (Eds.), Biodiversity of the United States: Upland Terrestrial Communities. John Wiley and Sons, New York.

Stevens, D. L. 1994. Implementation of a national monitoring program. Journal of Environmental Management 42:1–29.

Stewart, M. M. 1975. Habitat management in the Adirondack Park. New York Environmental News 2:1–3.

Stewart, M. M. 1995. Climate driven population fluctuations in rain forest frogs. Journal of Herpetology 29:437–446.

Stewart, R. E., and H. A. Kantrud. 1971. Classification of natural ponds and lakes in the glaciated prairie region. U.S. Fish and Wildlife Service, Resource Publication Number 92, Washington, D.C.

Stewart-Oaten, A. 1995. Rules and judgements in statistics: three examples. Ecology 76:2001–2009.

Stewart-Oaten, A., W. W. Murdoch, and K. R. Parker. 1986. Environmental impact assessment: "pseudoreplication" in time? Ecology 67:929–940.

Stille, W. T. 1952. The nocturnal amphibian fauna of the southern Lake Michigan beach. Ecology 33:149–162.

Stille, W. T., and R. A. Edgren Jr. 1948. New records for amphibians and reptiles in the Chicago area, 1939–1947. Chicago Academy of Science Bulletin 8:195–202.

Strahler, A. N. 1964. Geology. Part II. Quantitative geomorphology of drainage basins and channel networks. Pp. 4-39–4-76. *In* Chow, V. T. (Ed.), Handbook of Applied Hydrology. McGraw-Hill, New York.

Strickler-Shaw, S. 1988. The effects of low-lead concentrations on acquisition and retention of avoidance learning in tadpoles of the bullfrog, *Rana catesbeiana*. M.S. thesis, Miami University, Oxford, Ohio.

Strickler-Shaw, S., and D. H. Taylor. 1990. Sublethal exposure to lead inhibits acquisition and retention of discriminate avoidance learning in green frog (*Rana clamitans*) tadpoles. Environmental Toxicology and Chemistry 9:47–52.

Strijbosch, H. 1980. Habitat selection by amphibians during their terrestrial phase. British Journal of Herpetology 6:93–98.

Strittholt, J. R., and R. E. J. Boerner. 1995. Applying biodiversity gap analysis in a regional nature reserve design for the Edge of Appalachia, Ohio (U.S.A.). Conservation Biology 9:1492–1505.

Stuart, A. 1984. The Ideas of Sampling. Macmillan, New York.

Stuiver, M., P. M. Grootes, and T. F. Braziunas. 1995. The GISP2 d-^{18}O climate record of the past 16,500 years and the role of the sun, ocean, and volcanoes. Quaternary Research 44:341–354.

Suloway, L., and M. Hubbell. 1994. Wetland resources of Illinois: an analysis and atlas. Illinois Natural History Survey Special Publication Number 15, Springfield.

Sumner, R., and E. M. Preston, 1991. Wetlands Research Update. U.S. Environmental Protection Agency, Wetlands Research Program, Corvallis, Oregon.

Sumpter, J. P., and S. Jobling. 1995. Vitellogenesis as a biomarker for estrogenic contamination of the aquatic environment. Environmental Health Perspectives 103:173–178.

Sutanto, W., and E. R. Dekloet. 1994. The use of various animal models in the study of stress and stress-related phenomena. Laboratory Animals 28:293–306.

Swanson, P. L. 1939. Herpetological notes from Indiana. American Midland Naturalist 22:684–695.

Swanson, S. 1995. Unearthing the prairie past. Chicago Tribune, 19 November.

Swihart, R. K., and N. A. Slade. 1986. The importance of statistical power when testing for independence in animal movements. Ecology 67:255–258.

Swingle, H. S. 1970. History of warmwater pond culture in the United States. Pp. 95–105. *In* Benson, N. G. (Ed.), A Century of Fisheries in North America. American Fisheries Society, Washington, D.C.

Swink, F., and G. Wilhelm. 1994. Plants of the Chicago Region. Indiana Academy of Science, Indianapolis.

Systematics Agenda 2000. 1994. Systematics Agenda 2000: Charting the Biosphere: Technical Report. Department of Ornithology, American Museum of Natural History, New York.

Tacha, T. C., W. D. Warde, and K. P. Burnham. 1982. Use and interpretation of statistics in wildlife journals. Wildlife Society Bulletin 10:355–362.

Tanner, W. W., O. L. Fisher, and T. J. Willis. 1971. Notes on the life history of *Ambystoma tigrinum nebulosum* Hallowell in Utah. Great Basin Naturalist 31:213–222.

Tarkhnishvili, D. N. 1995. Amphibians of the Caucasus: status of natural populations and perspectives on conservation. Pp. 106–124. *In* Kuzmin, S. L., C. K. Dodd

Jr., and M. M. Pikulik (Eds.), Amphibian Populations in the Commonwealth of Independent States: Current Status and Declines. Pensoft Publishers, Moscow.

Taubert, B. D., P. W. Shetley, D. P. Phillip, and T. Harrison. 1982. Breeding biology and distribution of the Illinois chorus frog (*Pseudacris streckeri illinoensis*) in Illinois. Unpublished report to the Illinois Department of Conservation, Springfield.

Tayler, J. 1983. Orientation and flight behavior of a neotenic salamander (*Ambystoma gracile*) in Oregon. American Midland Naturalist 109:40–49.

Taylor, C. H., and J. C. Loftis. 1989. Testing for trends in lake and groundwater quality time series. Water Resources Bulletin 25:715–726.

Taylor, D. H., C. W. Steele, and S. Strickler-Shaw. 1990. Responses of green frog (*Rana clamitans*) tadpoles to lead polluted water. Environmental Toxicology and Chemistry 9:87–93.

Temple, R., and M. E. Fowler. 1984. Amphibians. Pp. 81–88. *In* M. E. Fowler (Ed.), Zoo and Wild Animal Medicine. W. B. Saunders, Philadelphia.

Ter Braak, C. J. F. 1986. Canonical correspondence analysis: a new eigenvector technique for multivariate direct gradient analysis. Ecology 67:1167–1179.

Ter Braak, C. J. F. 1987. The analysis of vegetation-environment relationships by canonical correspondence analysis. Vegetatio 69:69–77.

Tester, J. R. 1995. Minnesota's Natural Heritage: An Ecological Perspective. University of Minnesota Press, Minneapolis.

Tester, J. R., and W. J. Breckenridge. 1964. Winter behavior patterns of the Manitoba toad, *Bufo hemiophrys*, in northwestern Minnesota. Annales Academiae Scientiarum Fennicae Series. A. IV Biology 71:423–431.

Thom, R. H., and J. H. Wilson. 1980. The natural divisions of Missouri. Transactions of the Missouri Academy of Science 14:9–23.

Thomas, K. B., and T. Colburn. 1992. Organochlorine endocrine disruptors in human tissue. Pp. 365–394. *In* Colborn, T., and C. Clement (Eds.), Chemically-Induced Alterations in Sexual and Functional Development: The Wildlife/Human Connection. Advances in Modern Environmental Toxicology, Volume XXI. Princeton Scientific Publications, Princeton, New Jersey.

Thompson, M. M. 1987. Maps for America. U.S. Geological Survey, National Center, Reston, Virginia.

Thompson, S. K. 1992. Sampling. John Wiley and Sons, New York.

Thrush, S. F., R. D. Pridmore, and J. E. Hewitt. 1994. Impacts on soft-sediment macrofauna: the effects of spatial variation on temporal trends. Ecological Applications 4:31–41.

Thurow, G. R. 1981. Geographic distribution. *Hemidactylium scutatum* (four-toed salamander). Herpetological Review 12:64.

Thurow, G. R. 1994a. Suggested interim responses to the amphibian decline problem. Bulletin of the Chicago Herpetological Society 29:265–268.

Thurow, G. R. 1994b. Experimental return of wood frogs to west-central Illinois. Transactions of the Illinois State Academy of Sciences 87:83–97.

Thurow, G. R., and R. P. Sliwinski. 1991. Herpetological distribution records from Illinois. Bulletin of the Chicago Herpetological Society 26:129–132.

Tiffney, W. N. 1939. The identity of certain species of the Saprolegnaceae parasitic to fish. Journal of the Elisha Mitchell Scientific Society 55:134–151.

Timko, R. E., and A. L. Kolz. 1982. Satellite sea turtle tracking. Marine Fisheries Review 44:19–24.

Tiner, R. W., Jr. 1984. Wetlands of the United States: Current Status and Recent Trends. U.S. Fish and Wildlife Service, National Wetlands Inventory, Washington, D.C.

Tiner, R. W., Jr. 1987. Mid-Atlantic Wetlands: A Disappearing Natural Treasure. U.S. Fish and Wildlife Service, National Wetlands Inventory Project, Newton Corner, Massachusetts.

Toft, C. A., and P. J. Shea. 1983. Detecting community-wide patterns: estimating power strengthens statistical inference. American Naturalist 122:618–625.

Tome, M. W., C. E. Grue, and L. R. DeWeese. 1991. Ethyl parathion in wetlands following aerial application to sunflowers in North Dakota. Wildlife Society Bulletin 19:450–457.

Tomlin, C. D. 1990. Geographical Information Systems and Cartographic Modeling. Prentice Hall, Englewood Cliffs, New Jersey.

Tosi, J. A., Jr. 1964. Climatic control of terrestrial ecosystems: a report on the Holdridge model. Economic Geography 40:173–181.

Townshend, J. R. G., and C. O Justice. 1988. Selecting the spatial resolution of satellite sensors required for global monitoring of land transformations. International Journal of Remote Sensing 9:187–236.

Tracy, C. R., and J. W. Dole. 1969. Orientation of displaced California toads, *Bufo boreas*, to their breeding sites. Copeia 1969:693–700.

Transeau, E. N. 1935. The prairie peninsula. Ecology 16:423–437.

Trauth, S. E., R. L. Cox, B. P. Butterfield, D. A. Saugey, and W. A. Meshaka. 1990. Reproductive phenophases and clutch characteristics of selected Arkansas amphibians. Proceedings of the Arkansas Academy of Science 44:107–113.

Trautman, M. 1981. Fishes of Ohio. Ohio State University Press, Columbus.

Travis, J., W. H. Keen, and J. Juliana. 1985. The role of relative body size in a predator-prey relationship between dragonfly naiads and larval anurans. Oikos 45:59–65.

Trexler, J. C., and J. Travis. 1993. Nontraditional regression analysis. Ecology 74:1629–1637.

Tucker, C. J., B. N. Holden, and T. E. Goff. 1984. Intensive forest clearings in Rondonia, Brazil, as detected by satellite remote sensing. Remote Sensing of Environment 15:255–261.

Tucker, C. J., and P. J. Sellers. 1986. Satellite remote sensing of primary production. International Journal of Remote Sensing 7:1395–1416.

Tucker, C. J., J. R. G. Townshend, and T. E. Goff. 1985. African land-cover classification using satellite data. Science 227:369–375.

Tucker, C. J., J. R. G. Townshend, T. E. Goff, and B. N. Holden. 1986. Continental and global scale remote sensing of land cover. Pp. 221–241. *In* Trabalka, J. R., and D. E. Reichle (Eds.), The Changing Carbon Cycle: A Global Analysis. Springer-Verlag, New York.

Tucker, J. K. 1995. Early post-transformational growth in the Illinois chorus frog (*Pseudacris streckeri illinoensis*). Journal of Herpetology 29:314–316.

Tucker, J. K., J. B. Camerer, and J. B. Hatcher. 1995. Natural history note: *Pseudacris streckeri illinoensis* (Illinois chorus frog) burrows. Herpetological Review 26:32–33.

Tucker, J. K., and D. P. Philipp. 1993. Population status of the Illinois chorus frog (*Pseudacris streckeri illinoensis*) in Madison County, Illinois, with emphasis on the new Poag Road/FAP 413 interchange and FAP 413 wetland mitigation site. Illinois Natural History Survey Aquatic Ecology Technical Report 93/17, Springfield.

Tufte, E. R. 1983. The Visual Display of Quantitative Information. Graphics Press, Cheshire, Connecticut.

Tufte, E. R. 1990. Envisioning Information. Graphics Press, Cheshire, Connecticut.

Tukey, J. W. 1960. Conclusions vs. decisions. Technometrics 2:423–433.

Tukey, J. W. 1977. Exploratory Data Analysis. Addison-Wesley, New York.

Tukey, J. W. 1980. We need both exploratory and confirmatory. American Statistician 34:23–25.

Tukey, J. W. 1991. The philosophy of multiple comparisons. Statistical Science 6:100–116.

Turchin, P., and A. D. Taylor. 1992. Complex dynamics in ecological time series. Ecology 73:289–305.

Turner, A. K. 1992. Three-Dimensional Modeling with Geoscientific Information Systems. Kluwer Academic, Dordrecht, Netherlands.

Turner, M. G. 1987. Landscape Heterogeneity and Disturbance. Springer-Verlag, New York.

Turner, M. G. 1989. Landscape ecology: the effect of pattern on process. Annual Review of Ecology and Systematics 20:171–197.

Turner, M. G., and R. H. Gardner. 1991a. Quantitative Methods in Landscape Ecology. Springer-Verlag, New York.

Turner, M. G., and R. H. Gardner. 1991b. Quantitative methods in landscape ecology: an introduction. Pp. 3–14. *In* Turner, M. G., and R. H. Gardner (Eds.), Quantitative Methods in Landscape Ecology. Springer-Verlag, New York.

Turner, S. J., R. V. O'Neill, W. Conley, M. R. Conley, and H. C. Humphries. 1991. Pattern and scale: statistics for landscape ecology. Pp. 17–49. *In* Turner, M. G., and R. H. Gardner (Eds.), Quantitative Methods in Landscape Ecology. Springer-Verlag, New York.

Tweed, S. T. 1938. Metamorphic changes in the *Acris gryllus* frog. Unpublished research project, Iowa Lakeside Laboratory, University of Iowa, Iowa City.

Udvardy, M. D. F. 1969. Dynamic Zoogeography. Van Nostrand Reinhold, New York.

Underwood, A. J. 1991. Beyond BACI: experimental designs for detecting human environmental impacts on temporal variations in natural populations. Australian Journal of Marine and Freshwater Research 42:569–587.

Underwood, A. J. 1992. Beyond BACI: the detection of environmental impacts on populations in the real, but variable, world. Experimental Marine Biology and Ecology 161:145–178.

Underwood, A. J. 1994. On beyond BACI: sampling designs that might reliably detect environmental disturbances. Ecological Applications 4:3–15.

United Nations Education, Scientific, and Cultural Organization (UNESCO). 1973. International Classification and Mapping of Vegetation, Series 6. Ecology and Conservation. United Nations Education, Scientific, and Cultural Organization, Paris.

U.S. Army Construction Engineering Research Laboratories. 1993. GRASS Version 4.1 Geographic Resources Analysis Support System User's Reference Manual. U.S. Army Corps of Engineers, Construction Engineering Research Laboratories, Champaign, Illinois.

U.S. Army Topographic Engineering Center. 1995. Multispectral Users Guide. Available from U.S. Army Topographic Engineering Center, Fort Belvoire, Virginia.

U.S. Department of Agriculture, Soil Conservation Service, and Illinois Agricultural Experiment Station. 1970. General soil map of Mason County, Illinois. Mason County Soil and Water Conservation District, Havana, Illinois.

U.S. Department of Health and Human Services. 1992. Toxicological profile for methyl parathion. ATSDR/TP-91/21, Atlanta.

U.S. Environmental Protection Agency. 1973. Methods for identifying and evaluating the nature and extent of nonpoint sources of pollutants. EPA-430/9-73-014, Washington, D.C.

U.S. Environmental Protection Agency. 1976. Erosion and sediment control, surface mining in the eastern U.S., planning. Volume 1. EPA-625/3-76-006, Washington, D.C.

U.S. Environmental Protection Agency. 1990. Health effects of passive smoking. EPA-600-90-006A, Washington, D.C.

U.S. Fish and Wildlife Service, Division of Endangered Species. 1993. Endangered and threatened wildlife and plants. 50 CFR Part 17, 17.11, and 17.12. U.S. Fish and Wildlife Service, Federal Registry, Washington, D.C.

Valentine, B. D. 1974. Herpetological investigations of the Paint Creek Impoundment Area, Ohio. Pp. 278–297. *In* Paint Creek Lake Environmental Analysis Final Report. Volume 1. Submitted to the Department of the Army Huntington District, Corps of Engineers, Huntington, West Virginia, by Ohio State University, College of Biological Sciences, Center for Lake Erie Area Research, and Museum of Zoology, Columbus.

van der Valk, A. 1989. Northern Prairie Wetlands. Iowa State University Press, Ames.

Van de Walle, T. J., K. K. Sutton, and J. L. Christiansen. 1996. Additions to the range of *Pseudacris crucifer* in Iowa, with comments on the Iowa Department of Natural Resources frog and toad survey. Herpetological Review 27:183–185.

van Leeuwen, B. H. 1979. Grass carp: a threat to our amphibia? Environmental Conservation 6:264.

Van Zant, K. L., G. R. Hallberg, and R. G. Baker. 1980. A Farmdalian pollen diagram from east-central Iowa. Proceedings of the Iowa Academy of Science 87:52–55.

Varhegyi, G. G., B. M. Walton, A. R. Gibson, S. M. Mavroidis, C. A. Conaway, J. Hoty, and M. Oblak. 1995. Amphibian population survey of the Cuyahoga Valley National Recreation Area (CVNRA). North American Amphibian Monitoring Program, Burlington, Ontario. Unpublished abstract.

Velleman, P. F., and D. C. Hoaglin. 1981. Applications, Basics, and Computing of Exploratory Data Analysis. Duxbury Press, Boston.

Venables, W. N., and B. D. Ripley. 1994. Modern Applied Statistics with S-Plus. Springer-Verlag, New York.

Verbyla, D. L. 1995. Satellite Remote Sensing of Natural Resources. CRC Press, Boca Raton, Florida.

Vial, J. L., and L. Saylor. 1993. Declining Amphibian Populations Task Force. Working Document Number 1. The Status of Amphibian Populations. A Compilation and Analysis. World Conservation Union (IUCN), Species Survival Commission, Milton Keynes, United Kingdom.

Vinson, S. B., C. E. Boyd, and D. F. Ferguson. 1963. Aldrin toxicity and possible cross-resistance in cricket frogs. Herpetologica 19:77–80.

Vogelmann, J. E. 1988. Detection of forest change in the Green Mountains of Vermont using Multispectral Scanner data. International Journal of Remote Sensing 9:1187–1200.

Vogelmann, J. E. 1990. Comparison between two vegetation indices for measuring different types of forest damage in the northeastern United States. International Journal of Remote Sensing 11/12:2281–2297.

Vogelmann, J. E., and B. N. Rock. 1988. Assessing forest damage in high elevation coniferous forests in Vermont and New Hampshire using Thematic Mapper data. Remote Sensing of Environment 24:227–246.

Vogt, R. C. 1981. Natural History of Amphibians and Reptiles of Wisconsin. Milwaukee Public Museum, Milwaukee.

Voris, H. K., and J. P. Bacon Jr. 1966. Differential predation on tadpoles. Copeia 1966:594–598.

Vos, C. C., and P. Opdam. 1993. Landscape Ecology of a Stressed Environment. Chapman and Hall, New York.

Wahba, G. 1990. Spline Models for Observational Data. Society for Industrial and Applied Mathematics, Philadelphia.

Wakahara, M. 1995. Cannibalism and the resulting dimorphism in larvae of a salamander *Hynobius retarda-*

tus, inhabited in Hokkaido, Japan. Zoological Science 12:467–473.

Wake, D. B. 1991. Declining amphibian populations. Science 253:860.

Wake, D. B., and H. J. Morowitz. 1991. Declining amphibian populations—a global phenomenon? Findings and recommendations. Report to Board on Biology, National Research Council, Workshop on Declining Amphibian Populations, Irvine, California. Reprinted in Alytes 9:33–42.

Waldman, B. 1982. Adaptive significance of communal oviposition in wood frogs (*Rana sylvatica*). Behavioral Ecology and Sociobiology 10:169–174.

Walker, C. F. 1931. The amphibians of Ohio. M.S. thesis, Ohio State University, Columbus.

Walker, C. F. 1946. The Amphibians of Ohio. Part I. Frogs and Toads. Ohio State Museum of Science Bulletin, Volume 1, Number 3.

Walker, C. R., and W. Goodpaster. 1941. The green salamander, *Aneides aeneus*, in Ohio. Copeia 1941:178.

Walker, W. H., R. E. Bergstrom, and W. C. Walton. 1965. Preliminary report on the ground-water resources of the Havana region in west-central Illinois. Cooperative Ground-Water Report 3, State Water Survey and State Geological Survey, Illinois Department of Registration and Education, Urbana.

Walls, S. C., J. J. Beatty, B. N. Tissot, D. G. Hokit, and A. R. Blaustein. 1993. Morphological variation and cannibalism in a larval salamander (*Ambystoma macrodactylum columbianum*). Canadian Journal of Zoology 71:1543–1551.

Walton, A. C. 1964. The parasites of amphibia. Wildlife Diseases 40.

Ward, J. V. 1992. Aquatic Insect Ecology: 1. Biology and Habitat. John Wiley and Sons, New York.

Ward, P. 1994. The End of Evolution: A Journey in Search of Clues to the Third Mass Extinction Facing Planet Earth. Bantam Books, New York.

Ward, R. C., and J. C. Loftis. 1986. Establishing statistical design criteria for water quality monitoring systems: review and synthesis. Water Resources Bulletin 22:759–769.

Ward, R. C., J. C. Loftis, and G. B. McBride. 1986. The "data-rich but information-poor" syndrome in water quality monitoring. Environmental Management 10:291–297.

Ward, R. C., J. C. Loftis, and G. B. McBride. 1990. Design of Water Quality Monitoring Systems. Van Nostrand Reinhold, New York.

Wartenberg, D., S. Ferson, and F. J. Rohlf. 1987. Putting things in order: a critique of detrended correspondence analysis. American Naturalist 129:434–448.

Water Impacts, Michigan State University. 1995. Soil erosion rates decline by one-third, says SCS. Fisheries 20:45.

Watermolen, D. J., and H. Gilbertson. 1996. A key for the identification of Wisconsin's larval amphibians. Wisconsin Endangered Species Report Number 109, Wisconsin Department of Natural Resources, Madison.

Wauchope, R. D. 1978. The pesticide content of surface water draining from agricultural fields—a review. Journal of Environmental Quality 7:459–472.

Webb, T., III, P. J. Bartlein, S. P. Harrison, and K. H. Anderson. 1993. Vegetation, lake levels, and climate in eastern North America for the past 18,000 years. Pp. 415–467. *In* Wright, H. E., Jr., J. E. Kutzbach, T. Webb III, W. F. Ruddiman, F. A. Street-Perrott, and P. J. Bartlein (Eds.), Global Climates Since the Last Glacial Maximum. University of Minnesota Press, Minneapolis.

Webb, T., III, E. J. Cushing, and H. E. Wright Jr. 1983. Holocene changes in the vegetation of the Midwest. Pp. 142–165. *In* Wright, H. E., Jr. (Ed.), Late Quaternary Environments of the United States, Volume 2: The Holocene. University of Minnesota Press, Minneapolis.

Webster, R., and M. A Oliver. 1990. Statistical Methods in Soil and Land Resource Survey. Oxford University Press, New York.

Weerahandi, S. 1995. Exact Statistical Methods for Data Analysis. Springer-Verlag, New York.

Weinberg, S., and K. Goldberg. 1990. Statistics for the Behavioral Sciences. Cambridge University Press, New York.

Weis, J. S. 1975. The effect of DDT on tail regeneration in *Rana pipiens* and *R. catesbeiana* tadpoles. Copeia 1975:765–767.

Weller, M. W. 1969. Distribution of the yellow-headed blackbird in Iowa. Iowa State Agricultural and Home Economics Experimental Station, Journal Paper J-6108.

Welsh, H. H., Jr., and A. J. Lind. 1991. The structure of the herpetofaunal assemblage in the Douglas-fir/ hardwood forests of northwestern California and southwestern Oregon. Pp. 394–413. *In* Ruggiero, L. F., K. B. Aubry, A. B. Carey, and M. H. Huff (Tech. Coords.), Wildlife and Vegetation of Unmanaged Douglas-fir Forests. U.S. Forest Service, General Technical Report PNW–GTR–285, Washington, D.C.

Werner, E. E. 1991. Nonlethal effects of a predator on competitive interactions between two anuran larvae. Ecology 72:1709–1720.

West-Eberhard, M. J. 1986. Alternative adaptations, speciation, and phylogeny (a review). Proceedings of the National Academy of Science USA 83:1388–1392.

West-Eberhard, M. J. 1989. Phenotypic plasticity and the evolution of diversity. Annual Review of Ecology and Systematics 20:249–278.

Westfall, P. H., and S. S. Young. 1993. Resampling-Based Multiple Testing. John Wiley and Sons, New York.

Wetland Research, Inc. 1991. Hydrologic monitoring, 1991, in the Des Plaines River Wetlands Demonstration Project. Progress report to the U.S. Environmental Protection Agency, Grant CR–817120–01–0.1192.

Weygolt, P. 1989. Changes in the composition of mountain stream frog communities in the Atlantic Mountains of Brazil: frogs as indicators of environmental deteriorations? Studies on Neotropical Fauna and Environment 243:249–255.

Wheeler, G. C., and J. Wheeler. 1966. The Amphibians and Reptiles of North Dakota. University of North Dakota Press, Grand Forks.

White, D., A. J. Kimerling, and W. S. Overton. 1992. Cartographic and geometric components of a global sampling design for environmental monitoring. Cartography and Geographic Information Systems 19:5–22.

White, J. 1978. Illinois natural areas inventory technical report—Volume I, survey methods and results. Illinois Natural Areas Inventory, Urbana.

White, J., and M. H. Madany. 1978. Classification of natural communities in Illinois. Pp. 309–405. *In* White, J. (Ed.), Illinois Natural Areas Inventory Technical Report. Illinois Natural Areas Inventory, Urbana.

White, R., S. Jobling, S. A. Hoare, J. P. Sumpter, and M. G. Parker. 1994. Environmentally persistent alkylphenolic compounds are estrogenic. Endocrinology 135:175–182.

Whiteman, H. H. 1994. Evolution of facultative paedomorphosis in salamanders. Quarterly Review of Biology 69:205–221.

Whitford, P. C. 1991. Final report on Blanchard's cricket frog survey of southeastern Minnesota—1990/1991. Unpublished report to the Nongame Wildlife Program, St. Paul, Minnesota.

Whitford, W. G., and A. Vinegar. 1966. Homing, survivorship, and overwintering of larvae in spotted salamanders, *Ambystoma maculatum*. Copeia 1966:515–519.

Whitlock, A. L., N. M. Jarman, and J. S. Larson. 1994. WETthings: Wetland Habitat Indicators for Non-Game Species. Environmental Institute, University of Massachusetts, Amherst.

Whitney, G. G. 1990. The history and status of the hemlock-hardwood forests of the Allegheny Plateau. Journal of Ecology 78:443–458.

Whitney, G. G. 1994. From Coastal Wilderness to Fruited Plain: A History of Environmental Change in Temperate North America from 1500 to the Present. Cambridge University Press, Cambridge.

Whittaker, R. H. 1956. Vegetation of the Great Smoky Mountains. Ecological Monographs 26:1–80.

Whittaker, R. H. 1982. Ordination of Plant Communities. W. Junk, Boston.

Wiedenheft, W. D. 1983. Life history and secondary production of tiger salamanders (*Ambystoma tigrinum*) in prairie pothole lakes. M.S. thesis, North Dakota State University, Fargo.

Wiens, J. A. 1989. The Ecology of Bird Communities. Cambridge University Press, New York.

Wikin, E. B., and G. Ironside. 1977. The development of ecological (biophysical) land classification in Canada. Landscape Planning 4:273–275.

Wilbur, C. G. 1954. Toxicity of sarin in bullfrogs. Science 120:22.

Wilbur, H. M. 1972. Competition, predation, and the structure of the *Ambystoma–Rana sylvatica* community. Ecology 53:3–21.

Wilbur, H. M. 1980. Complex life cycles. Annual Review of Ecology and Systematics 11:67–93.

Wilbur, H. M. 1984. Complex life cycles and community organization in amphibians. Pp. 195–224. *In* Price, P. W., C. N. Slobodchikoff, and W. S. Gaud (Eds.), A New Ecology. John Wiley and Sons, New York.

Wilbur, H. M. 1987. Regulation of structure in complex systems: experimental temporary pond communities. Ecology 68:1437–1452.

Wilbur, H. M., and R. A. Alford. 1985. Priority effects in experimental pond communities: responses of *Hyla* to *Bufo* and *Rana*. Ecology 66:1106–1114.

Wilbur, H. M., and J. P. Collins. 1973. Ecological aspects of amphibian metamorphosis. Science 182:1305–1314.

Wilbur, H. M., P. J. Morin, and R. N. Harris. 1983. Salamander predation and the structure of experimental communities: anuran responses. Ecology 64:1423–1429.

Wilcove, D., M. Bean, and P. C. Lee. 1992. Fisheries management and biological diversity: problems and opportunities. Transactions of the North American Wildlife and Natural Resources Conference 57:373–383.

Wilcove, D. S., C. H. McLellan, and A. P. Dobson. 1986. Habitat fragmentation in the temperate zone. Pp. 237–256. *In* Soulé, M. E. (Ed.), Conservation Biology: The Science of Scarcity and Diversity. Sinauer Associates, Sunderland, Massachusetts.

Wilhelm, G. 1990. Special vegetation of the Indiana Dunes National Lakeshore. Indiana Dunes National Lakeshore Research Program Report Number 90-02.

Wilkinson, L., G. Blank, and C. Gruber. 1996. Desktop Data Analysis with SYSTAT. Prentice Hall, Upper Saddle River, New Jersey.

Williams, B. 1978. A Sampler on Sampling. John Wiley and Sons, New York.

Williams, B. 1983. Some observations on the use of discriminant analysis in ecology. Ecology 64:1283–1291.

Williams, B. K., and K. Titus. 1988. Assessment of sampling stability in ecological applications of discriminant analysis. Ecology 69:1275–1285.

Williams, D. 1993a. Farmer sues Mason County over dam that flooded his land. Journal Star, 15 December, Peoria, Illinois.

Williams, D. 1993b. Ditch proposed to slow flooding. Firm suggests that county drain Sand Lake into Illinois River. Journal Star, 2 December, Peoria, Illinois.

Williams, D. 1994. Agency to examine Havana flooding. Conservation service seeks long-term solution to Mason County floods. Journal Star, 27 January, Peoria, Illinois.

Williams, D. D. 1987. The Ecology of Temporary Waters. Timber Press, Portland, Oregon.

Williams, K. L., and R. E. Gordon. 1961. Natural dispersal of the salamander *Aneides aeneus*. Copeia 1961:353.

Williams, P. K. 1973. Seasonal movements and population dynamics of four sympatric mole salamanders, genus *Ambystoma*. Ph.D. dissertation, Indiana University, Bloomington.

Williams, W. T., and W. Stephenson. 1973. The analysis of three-dimensional data (sites x species x times) in marine ecology. Journal of Experimental Marine Biology and Ecology 11:207–227.

Wilson, E. O. 1992. The Diversity of Life. W. W. Norton, New York.

Wisconsin Department of Natural Resources. 1987. Wisconsin natural heritage inventory rare species working list. Wisconsin Department of Natural Resources, Madison.

Wisconsin Department of Natural Resources. 1989. Endangered and threatened species list. Publication ER–527, Wisconsin Department of Natural Resources, Madison.

Wisconsin Department of Natural Resources. 1992. Pond planner. Publication WZ 012-92, Wisconsin Department of Natural Resources, Madison.

Wissinger, S. A., and H. H. Whiteman. 1992. Fluctuation in a Rocky Mountain population of salamanders: anthropogenic acidification or natural variation? Journal of Herpetology 26:377–391.

Wolf, K., G. L. Bullock, C. E. Dunbar, and M. C. Quimby. 1969. Tadpole edema virus: pathogenesis and growth studies and additional sites of virus infected bullfrog tadpoles. Pp. 327–336. *In* Mizell, M. (Ed.), Biology of Amphibian Tumors. Springer-Verlag, New York.

Wolfowitz, J. 1967. Remarks on the theory of testing hypotheses. New York Statistician 18:439–441.

Wood, D. 1992. The Power of Maps. Guilford Press, New York.

Wood, J. T., and W. E. Duellman. 1947. Preliminary herpetological survey of Montgomery County, Ohio. Herpetologica 4:3–6.

Woods, J. E. 1968. The ecology and natural history of Mississippi populations of *Aneides aeneus* and associated salamanders. Ph.D. dissertation, University of Southern Mississippi, Hattiesburg.

Woodwell, G. M., R. A. Houghton, T. A. Stone, and A. B. Park. 1986. Changes in the area of forests in Rondonia, Amazon Basin, measured by satellite imagery. Pp. 242–257. *In* Trabalk, J. R., and D. E. Reichle (Eds.), The Changing Carbon Cycle: A Global Analysis. Springer-Verlag, New York.

Wright, A. H. 1908. Notes on the breeding habits of *Ambystoma punctatum*. Biological Bulletin 14:284–289.

Wright, A. H., and A. A. Allen. 1909. The early breeding habits of *Ambystoma punctatum*. American Naturalist 43:687–692.

Wright, A. H., and A. A. Wright. 1949. Handbook of Frogs and Toads. Comstock Publishing, Ithaca, New York.

Wright, H. E., Jr. 1992. Patterns of Holocene climatic change in the midwestern United States. Quaternary Research 38:129–134.

Wright, H. E., Jr., J. E. Kutzbach, T. Webb III, W. F. Ruddiman, F. A. Street-Perrott, and P. J. Bartlein. 1993. Global Climates Since the Last Glacial Maximum. University of Minnesota Press, Minneapolis.

Wright, H. E., Jr., C. L. Matsch, and E. J. Cushing. 1973. Superior and Des Moines Lobes. Pp. 153–185. *In* Black, R. F., R. P. Goldthwait, and H. B. Willman

(Eds.), The Wisconsinan Stage. Geological Society of America Memoir Number 136.

Wyman, R. L. 1988. Soil acidity and moisture and the distribution of amphibians in five forests of southcentral New York. Copeia 1988:394–399.

Wyman, R. L. 1990. What's happening to the amphibians? Conservation Biology 4:350–352.

Wyman, R. L., and D. S. Hawksley-Lescault. 1987. Soil acidity affects distribution, behavior, and physiology of the salamander *Plethodon cinereus.* Ecology 68:1819–1827.

Wynn, D. E. 1996. Data base of amphibian and reptile locality records. Unpublished report to the Ohio Division of Wildlife, Columbus.

Yahner, R. H. 1995. Eastern Deciduous Forest. University of Minnesota Press, Minneapolis.

Yencha, A. D. 1993. Fauna and vegetation of restored wetlands in eastern Wisconsin. M.S. thesis, University of Wisconsin-Green Bay.

Yoccoz, N. G. 1991. Use, overuse, and misuse of significance tests in evolutionary biology and ecology. Bulletin of the Ecological Society of America 72:106–111.

Young, F. W. 1987. Multidimensional Scaling: History, Theory, and Applications. Lawrence Erlbaum Associates, Hillsdale, New Jersey.

Zambernard, J., and A. E. Vatter. 1966. The effect of temperature change upon inclusion-containing renal tumors of leopard frogs. Cancer Research 26:2148–2153.

Zar, J. H. 1984. Biostatistical Analysis. Prentice-Hall, Englewood Cliffs, New Jersey.

Zaret, T. 1980. Predation in Freshwater Communities. Yale University Press, New Haven.

Zedler, P. H. 1987. The ecology of southern California vernal pools: a community profile. U.S. Fish and Wildlife Service, Biological Report 85 (7.11), Washington, D.C.

Zettergren, L. D., B. W. Boldt, D. H. Petering, M. S. Goodrich, D. N. Weber, and J. G. Zettergren. 1991. Effects of prolonged low-level cadmium exposure on the tadpole immune system. Toxicology Letters 55:11–19.

Zimmerman, M., and W. L. Wagner. 1979. A description of the woody vegetation of oak-hickory forest in the Northern Ozark Highlands. Bulletin of the Torrey Botanical Club 106:117–122.

Ziomek, J. J. 1974. Notes on the spring activity of amphibians in the Palos Hills area of Swallow Cliff and Crooked Creek Woods, Cook County, Illinois. Bulletin of the Chicago Herpetological Society 9:10–11.

Zolman, J. F. 1993. Biostatistics: Experimental Design and Statistical Inference. Oxford University Press, New York.

Zonneveld, I. S., and R. T. T. Forman. 1990. Changing Landscapes: An Ecological Perspective. Springer-Verlag, New York.

Zug, G. R. 1993. Herpetology: An Introductory Biology of Amphibians and Reptiles. Academic Press, San Diego.

Contributors

David E. Andersen, Minnesota Cooperative Fish and Wildlife Research Unit, Department of Fisheries and Wildlife, University of Minnesota, St. Paul, Minnesota

Thomas G. Anton, Winnetka, Illinois

Richard G. Baker, Department of Geology, University of Iowa, Iowa City, Iowa

Scott R. Ballard, District 23 Natural Heritage Biologist, Illinois Department of Natural Resources, Marion, Illinois

Val R. Beasley, Department of Veterinary Biosciences, University of Illinois at Urbana-Champaign, Urbana, Illinois

Thore J. Bergman, Department of Biology, Washington University, St. Louis, Missouri

Dorothy G. Bowers, Department of Fisheries and Wildlife, University of Minnesota, St. Paul, Minnesota

Ronald A. Brandon, Department of Zoology, Southern Illinois University at Carbondale, Carbondale, Illinois

Robert Brodman, Biology Department, Saint Joseph's College, Rensselaer, Indiana

Lauren E. Brown, Department of Biological Sciences, Illinois State University, Normal, Illinois

Gary S. Casper, Section of Vertebrate Zoology, Milwaukee Public Museum, Milwaukee, Wisconsin

John E. Cima, QST Environmental, Inc., Peoria, Illinois

Alexander Collier, Department of Biological Sciences, Kent State University, Kent, Ohio

Cynthia A. Conaway, Department of Biology, Cleveland State University, Cleveland, Ohio

Spencer A. Cortwright, Department of Biology, Indiana University Northwest, Gary, Indiana

Jeffrey G. Davis, Cincinnati Museum of Natural History, Cincinnati, Ohio

Brian J. Dhuey, Bureau of Integrated Science Services, Wisconsin Department of Natural Resources, Monroe, Wisconsin

Stephen G. Diana, Department of Veterinary Biosciences, University of Illinois at Urbana-Champaign, Urbana, Illinois

Ned H. Euliss Jr., Biological Resources Division (U.S. Geological Survey, formerly National Biological Service), Northern Prairie Science Center, Jamestown, North Dakota

Sandra A. Faeh, Department of Veterinary Biosciences, University of Illinois at Urbana-Champaign, Urbana, Illinois

Eugenia S. Farrar, Zoology and Genetics Department, Iowa State University, Ames, Iowa

John W. Ferner, Cincinnati Museum of Natural History, Cincinnati, Ohio, and Department of Biology, Thomas More College, Crestview Hills, Kentucky

Mark C. Gernes, Minnesota Pollution Control Agency, Water Quality Division, St. Paul, Minnesota

A. Ralph Gibson, Department of Biology, Cleveland State University, Cleveland, Ohio

Lisa M. Hartman, Bureau of Integrated Science Services, Wisconsin Department of Natural Resources, Monona, Wisconsin

Robert Hay, Wisconsin Department of Natural Resources, Bureau of Endangered Resources, Madison, Wisconsin

Judy Helgen, Minnesota Pollution Control Agency, Water Quality Division, St. Paul, Minnesota

Lisa M. Hemesath, Wildlife Research Station, Iowa Department of Natural Resources, Boone, Iowa

Jane D. Hey, Department of Biology, Morningside College, Sioux City, Iowa

J. Alan Holman, Michigan State University Museum, East Lansing, Michigan

Richard D. Howard, Department of Biological Sciences, Purdue University, West Lafayette, Indiana

Tom R. Johnson, Herpetologist, Missouri Department of Conservation, Jefferson City, Missouri

J. Eric Juterbock, Department of Zoology, Ohio State University, Lima, Ohio

Mary Kilmurry, Biology Department, Saint Joseph's College, Rensselaer, Indiana

Joanne Kline, Water Regulation and Zoning, Wisconsin Department of Natural Resources, Milwaukee, Wisconsin

Paul J. Krusling, Cincinnati Museum of Natural History, Cincinnati, Ohio

Anthony J. Krzysik, U.S. Army–Construction Engineering Research Laboratories (USACERL), Champaign, Illinois

Michael J. Lannoo, Muncie Center for Medical Education, Indiana University School of Medicine, Ball State University, Muncie, Indiana

Diane L. Larson, Biological Resources Division (U.S. Geological Survey, formerly National Biological Service), Northern Prairie Science Center, Jamestown, North Dakota

William T. Leja, Aquatic Wildlife Issues Coordinator, Illinois Chapter, Sierra Club, Chicago, Illinois

Robert F. Madej, 3D/Environmental, Cincinnati, Ohio; current address: R. D. Zande and Associates, Inc., Columbus, Ohio

Timothy O. Matson, Department of Vertebrate Zoology, Cleveland Museum of Natural History, Cleveland, Ohio

David Mauger, Forest Preserve District of Will County, Joliet, Illinois

Spiro M. Mavroidis, Department of Biology, Cleveland State University, Cleveland, Ohio

Robert G. McKinnell, Department of Genetics and Cell Biology, University of Minnesota, St. Paul, Minnesota

Kenneth S. Mierzwa, TAMS Consultants, Inc., Chicago, Illinois

Sherman A. Minton, Indiana University School of Medicine, Indianapolis, Indiana

John J. Moriarty, Hennepin Parks, Maple Plain, Minnesota

Michael J. Mossman, Bureau of Integrated Science Services, Wisconsin Department of Natural Resources, Monona, Wisconsin

Jeffrey Neumann, Department of Biological Sciences, Kent State University, Kent, Ohio

Donald K. Nichols, Department of Pathology, National Zoological Park, Washington, D.C.

Lowell Orr, Department of Biological Sciences, Kent State University, Kent, Ohio

Mathew Parks, Department of Biology, Washington University, St. Louis, Missouri

Ralph A. Pfingsten, Berea, Ohio

Christopher A. Phillips, Center for Biodiversity, Illinois Natural History Survey, Champaign, Illinois

Robert E. Preston, Department of Biology, Alpena Community College, Alpena, Michigan

Michael Redmer, Department of Zoology, Southern Illinois University at Carbondale, Carbondale, Illinois

Alan R. Resetar, Division of Amphibians and Reptiles, Field Museum of Natural History, Chicago, Illinois

John R. Sauer, Biological Resources Division (U.S. Geological Survey, formerly National Biological Service), Laurel, Maryland

Owen J. Sexton, Department of Biology, Washington University, St. Louis, Missouri

Donald M. Stillwaugh Jr., Prospect Heights, Illinois

John F. Stinn, Department of Biology, Washington University, St. Louis, Missouri

John K. Tucker, Illinois Natural History Survey, Alton, Illinois

Geza Varhegyi, Department of Biology, Cleveland State University, Cleveland, Ohio

Elke Vogt, Department of Biological Sciences, Kent State University, Kent, Ohio

B. Michael Walton, Department of Biology, Cleveland State University, Cleveland, Ohio

Elizabeth B. Wattenberg, Department of Biology, Washington University, St. Louis, Missouri

Howard H. Whiteman, Savannah River Ecology Laboratory, Aiken, South Carolina; current address: Department of Biological Sciences, Murray State University, Murray, Kentucky

Index